HOLT
PEOPLE, PLACES, AND CHANGE

An Introduction to World Studies

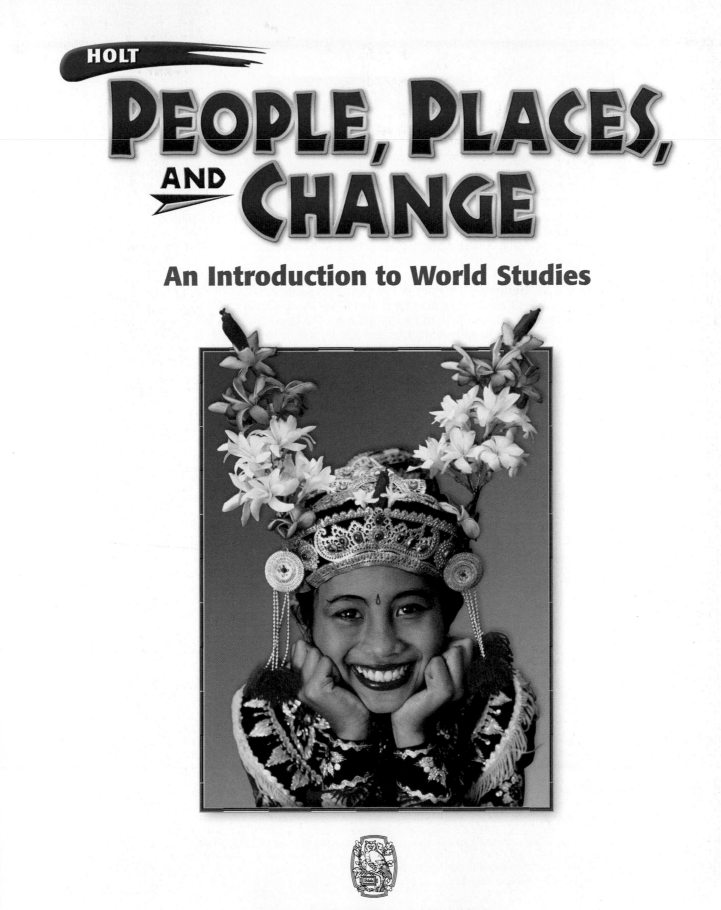

HOLT, RINEHART AND WINSTON

A Harcourt Education Company

Austin • Orlando • Chicago • New York • Toronto • London • San Diego

THE AUTHORS

Prof. Robert J. Sager is Chair of Earth Sciences at Pierce College in Lakewood, Washington. Prof. Sager received his B.S. in geology and geography and M.S. in geography from the University of Wisconsin and holds a J.D. in international law from Western State University College of Law. He is the coauthor of several geography and earth science textbooks and has written many articles and educational media programs on the geography of the Pacific. Prof. Sager has received several National Science Foundation study grants and has twice been a recipient of the University of Texas NISOD National Teaching Excellence Award. He is a founding member of the Southern California Geographic Alliance and former president of the Association of Washington Geographers.

Prof. David M. Helgren is Director of the Center for Geographic Education at San Jose State University in California, where he is also Chair of the Department of Geography. Prof. Helgren received his Ph.D. in geography from the University of Chicago. He is the coauthor of several geography textbooks and has written many articles on the geography of Africa. Awards from the National Geographic Society, the National Science Foundation, and the L. S. B. Leakey Foundation have supported his many field research projects. Prof. Helgren is a former president of the California Geographical Society and a founder of the Northern California Geographic Alliance.

Prof. Alison S. Brooks is Professor of Anthropology at George Washington University and a Research Associate in Anthropology at the Smithsonian Institution. She received her A.B., M.A., and Ph.D. in Anthropology from Harvard University. Since 1964, she has carried out ethnological and archaeological research in Africa, Europe, and Asia and is the author of more than 300 scholarly and popular publications. She has served as a consultant to Smithsonian exhibits and to National Geographic, Public Broadcasting, the Discovery Channel, and other public media. In addition, she is a founder and editor of *Anthro Notes: The National Museum of Natural History Bulletin for Teachers* and has received numerous grants and awards to develop and lead in-service training institutes for teachers in grades 5–12. She served as the American Anthropological Association's representative to the NCSS task force on developing Scope and Sequence guidelines for Social Studies Education in grade K–12.

CONTENT REVIEWERS

Robin Datel
Instructor in Geography
California State University,
Sacramento

David Dickason
Professor of Geography
Western Michigan University

Dennis Dingemans
Professor of Geography
University of California, Davis

Robert Gabler
Professor of Geography
Western Illinois University

Jeffrey Gritzner
Professor of Geography
University of Montana

W. A. Douglas Jackson
Professor of Geography, Emeritus
University of Washington

Robert B. Kent
Professor of Geography
and Planning
University of Akron

Kwadwo Konadu-Agyemang
Professor of Geography
and Planning
University of Akron

Nancy Lewis
Professor of Geography
University of Hawaii

Bill Takizawa
Professor of Geography
San Jose State University

EDUCATIONAL REVIEWERS

Patricia Britt
Durant Middle School
Durant, Oklahoma

Marcia Caldwell
Lamar Middle School
Austin, Texas

Marcia Clevenger
Roosevelt Junior High School
Charleston, West Virginia

James Corley
Durant Middle School
Durant, Oklahoma

Maureen Dempsey
Spring Creek Middle School
Spring Creek, Nevada

Jean Eldredge
Teague Middle School
Altamonte, Florida

Cindy Herring
Old Town Elementary School
Round Rock, Texas

Lois Jordan
Pearl/Cohn Comprehensive
High School
Nashville, Tennessee

Kay A. Knowles
Montross Middle School
Montross, Virginia

Wendy Mason
Corbett Junior High School
Schertz, Texas

Rebecca Minnear
Burkholder Middle School
Las Vegas, Nevada

Jane Palmer
District Supervisor for
Social Studies
Sanford, Florida

Sandra Rojas
Adams City Middle School
Commerce City, Colorado

JoAnn Sadler
Curriculum Supervisor
Buffalo City Schools
Buffalo, New York

Celeste Smith
Crockett High School
Austin, Texas

Frank Thomas
Crockett High School
Austin, Texas

Susan Walker
Beaufort County School District
Beaufort, South Carolina

Field Test Teachers
Ricky A. Blackman
Rawlinson Road Middle School
Rock Hill, South Carolina

Lisa Klien
Daniels Middle School
Raleigh, North Carolina

Deborah D. Larry
Garland V. Stewart Middle School
Tampa, Florida

Linda P. Moore
Cramerton Middle School
Cramerton, North Carolina

Earl F. Sease
Portage Area School District
Portage, Pennsylvania

Christi Sherrill
Grier Middle School
Gastonia, North Carolina

John W. Watkins, Jr.
Clark Middle School
East St. Louis, Illinois

Editorial
Sue Miller, *Director*
Robert Wehnke, *Managing Editor*
Diana Holman Walker, *Senior Editor*
Holly Norman, *Project Editor*
Daniel M. Quinn, *Senior Editor*
Sue Minkler, *Assistant Editorial*
Coordinator
Gina Rogers, *Administrative Assistant*

Pupil's Edition
Andrew Miles, *Editor*

Teacher's Edition
Lissa B. Anderson, *Editor*
Suzanne Hurley, *Senior Editor*

Technology Resources
Annette Saunders, *Editor*

Fact Checking
Bob Fullilove, *Editor*

Copy Editing
Julie Beckman, *Senior Copy Editor*

Text Permissions
Ann B. Farrar,
Senior Permissions Editor

Art, Design and Photo
Book Design
Diane Motz, *Senior Design Director*
Candace Moore, *Senior Designer*
Mercedes Newman, *Designer*

Image Acquisitions
Joe London, *Director*
Tim Taylor,
Photo Research Supervisor
Stephanie Morris,
Photo Researcher
Michelle Rumpf,
Art Buyer Supervisor
Coco Weir, *Art Buyer*
Julie Kelly, *Art Buyer*

Design New Media
Susan Michael, *Design Director*
Kimberly Cammaerata, *Design*
Manager
Grant Davidson, *Designer*

Media Design
Curtis Riker, *Design Director*

Cover Design
Jason Wilson, *Designer*

Pre-press and
Manufacturing
Gene Rumann,
Production Manager
Nancy Hargis,
Production Supervisor
Vivian Hess,
Administrative Assistant
Clary Knapp,
Production Coordinator
Rhonda Farris, *Inventory Planner*
Kim Harrison, *Manufacturing*
Coordinator, Media

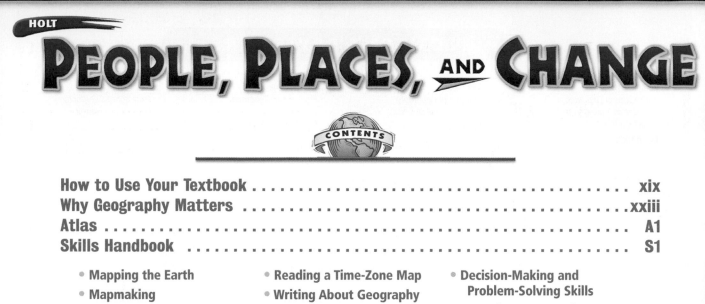

HOLT
PEOPLE, PLACES, AND CHANGE

CONTENTS

UNIT 1 Exploring Our World 1
Notes from the Field

UNIT 2 United States and Canada 96

UNIT 4

Europe 248

Notes from the Field

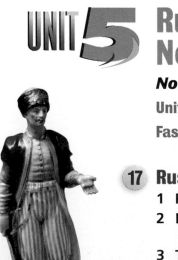

UNIT 5 Russia and Northern Eurasia 340

Notes from the Field

UNIT 6 Southwest Asia 404

Notes from the Field

UNIT 7 Africa 456

Notes from the Field

UNIT 8 East and Southeast Asia 562

Notes from the Field

UNIT 9

South Asia 640

Notes from the Field

FEATURES

FEATURES

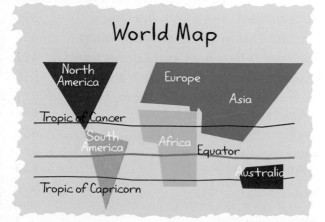

FEATURES

DIAGRAMS, CHARTS, and TABLES

FEATURES

DIAGRAMS, CHARTS, and TABLES *continued*

How To Use Your Textbook

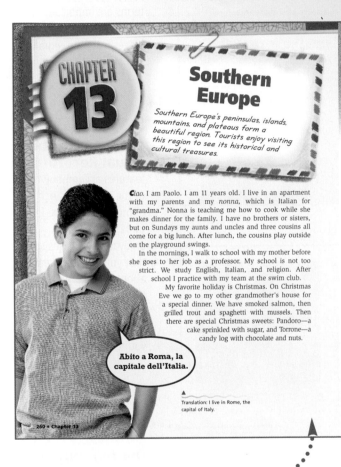

CHAPTER 13

Southern Europe

Southern Europe's peninsulas, islands, mountains, and plateaus form a beautiful region. Tourists enjoy visiting this region to see its historical and cultural treasures.

Ciao. I am Paolo. I am 11 years old. I live in an apartment with my parents and my *nonna*, which is Italian for "grandma." Nonna is teaching me how to cook while she makes dinner for the family. I have no brothers or sisters, but on Sundays my aunts and uncles and three cousins all come for a big lunch. After lunch, the cousins play outside on the playground swings.

In the mornings, I walk to school with my mother before she goes to her job as a professor. My school is not too strict. We study English, Italian, and religion. After school I practice with my team at the swim club.

My favorite holiday is Christmas. On Christmas Eve we go to my other grandmother's house for a special dinner. We have smoked salmon, then grilled trout and spaghetti with mussels. Then there are special Christmas sweets: Pandoro—a cake sprinkled with sugar, and Torrone—a candy log with chocolate and nuts.

Abito a Roma, la capitale dell'Italia.

Translation: I live in Rome, the capital of Italy.

260 • Chapter 13

Section 1

Physical Geography

Read to Discover
1. What are the major land-forms and rivers of southern Europe?
2. What are the major climate types and resources of this region?

Define
mainland
sirocco

Locate
Mediterranean Sea
Strait of Gibraltar

Iberian Peninsula
Cantabrian Mountains
Pyrenees Mountains
Alps
Apennines
Aegean Sea
Peloponnesus

Ebro River
Douro River
Tagus River
Guadalquivir River
Po River
Tiber River

WHY IT MATTERS

Southern Europe's location on peninsulas encouraged its cultures to become great seafarers. Use **CNNfyi.com** or other current events sources to find examples of trade on the region's oceans today. Record your findings in your journal.

Cave painting from 12,000 B.C.

Southern Europe: Physical-Political

Southern Europe • 261

An interview with a student begins each regional chapter. These interviews give you a glimpse of what life is like for some people in the region you are about to study.

Chapter Map The map at the beginning of Section 1 in regional chapters shows you the countries you will read about. You can use this map to identify country names and capitals and to locate physical features. These chapter maps will also help you create sketch maps in section reviews.

Use these built-in tools to read for understanding.

Read to Discover questions begin each section of *Holt People, Places, and Change.* These questions serve as your guide as you read through the section. Keep them in mind as you explore the section content.

Why It Matters is an exciting way for you to make connections between what you are reading in your geography textbook and the world around you. Explore a topic that is relevant to our lives today by using CNNfyi.com.

Define and Locate terms are introduced at the beginning of each section. The Define terms include terms important to the study of geography and to the region you are studying. The Locate terms are important physical features or places from the region you are studying.

Interpreting the Visual Record features accompany many of the textbook's rich photographs. These features invite you to analyze the images so that you can learn more about their content and their links to what you are studying in the section. Other captions ask you to interpret maps, graphs, and charts.

Our Amazing Planet features provide interesting facts about the region you are studying. Here you will learn about the origins of place-names and fascinating tidbits like the size of South America's rain forests.

Reading Check questions appear often throughout the textbook to allow you to check your comprehension. As you read, pause for a moment to consider each Reading Check. If you have trouble answering the question, review the material that you just read.

Use these tools to pull together all of the information you have learned.

Critical Thinking activities in section and chapter reviews allow you to explore a topic in greater depth and to build your skills.

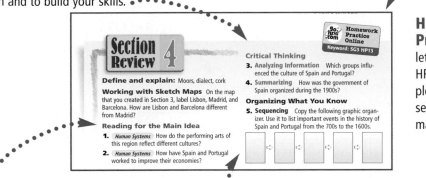

Homework Practice Online lets you log on to the HRW Go site to complete an interactive self-check of the material covered.

Reading for the Main Idea questions help review the main points you have studied in the section.

Graphic Organizers will help you pull together important information from the section.

Building Social Studies Skills activities help you develop the mapping and writing skills you need to study geography.

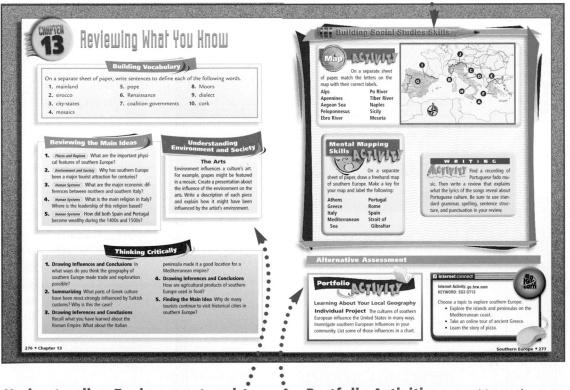

Understanding Environment and Society activities ask you to research and create a presentation expanding on an issue you have read about in the chapter.

Portfolio Activities are exciting and creative ways to explore your local geography and to make connections to the region you are studying.

Use these online tools to review and complete online activities.

go.hrw.com
Homework Practice Online
Keyword: SG3 HP13

Homework Practice Online lets you log on for review anytime. You will find interactive activities for each section of the text.

Internet Connect activities are just a part of the world of online learning experiences that await you on the HRW Go site. By exploring these online activities, you will take a journey through some of the richest world geography materials available on the World Wide Web. You can then use these resources to create real-world projects, such as brochures, databases, newspapers, reports, and even your own Web site!

Why Geography Matters

Have you ever wondered...

why some places are deserts while other places get so much rain? What makes certain times of the year cooler than others? Why do some rivers run dry?

Maybe you live near mountains and wonder what processes created them. Do you know why the loss of huge forest areas in one part of the world can affect areas far away? Why does the United States have many different kinds of churches and other places of worship? Perhaps you are curious why Americans and people from other countries have such different points of view on many issues. The key to understanding questions and issues like these lies in the study of geography.

Geography and Your World

All you need to do is watch or read the news to see the importance of geography. You have probably seen news stories about the effects of floods, volcanic eruptions, and other natural events on people and places. You likely have also seen how conflict and cooperation shape the relations between peoples and countries around the world. The Why It Matters feature beginning every section of *Holt People, Places, and Change* uses the vast resources of **CNNfyi**.com or other current events sources to examine the importance of geography. Through this feature you will be able to draw connections between what you are studying in your geography textbook and events and conditions found around the world today.

The CNNfyi.com Web site

My fall semester project, growing a garden

Geography and Making Connections

When you think of the word *geography*, what comes to mind? Perhaps you simply picture people memorizing names of countries and capitals. Maybe you think of people studying maps to identify features like deserts, mountains, oceans, and rivers. These things are important, but the study of geography includes much more. Geography involves asking questions and solving problems. It focuses on looking at people and their ways of life as well as studying physical features like mountains, oceans, and rivers. Studying geography also means looking at why things are where they

are and at the relationships between human and physical features of Earth.

The study of geography helps us make connections between what was, what is, and what may be. It helps us understand the processes that have shaped the features we observe around us today, as well as the ways those features may be different tomorrow. In short, geography helps us understand the processes that have created a world that is home to more than 6 billion people and countless billions of other creatures.

Geography and You

Anyone can influence the geography of our world. For example, the actions of individuals affect local environments. Some individual actions might pollute the environment. Other actions might contribute to efforts to keep the environment clean and healthy. Various other things also influence geography. For example, governments create political divisions, such as countries and states. The borders between these divisions influence the human geography of regions by separating peoples, legal systems, and human activities.

Governments and businesses also plan and build structures like dams, railroads, and airports, which change the physical characteristics of places. As you might expect, some actions influence Earth's geography in negative ways, others in positive ways. Understanding geography helps us evaluate the consequences of our actions.

ATLAS

CONTENTS

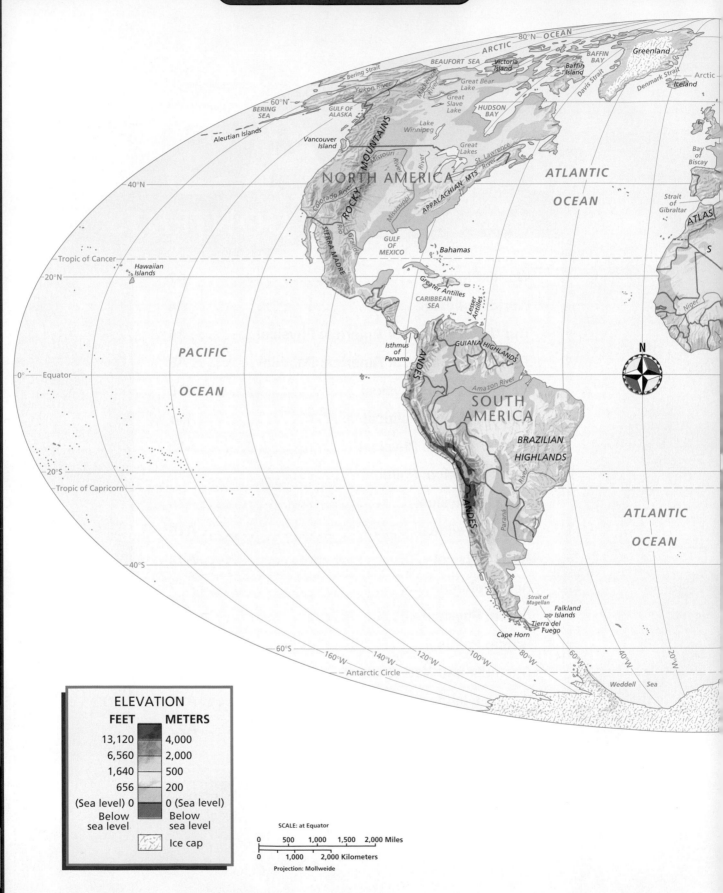

ARCTIC OCEAN
80°N
BEAUFORT SEA
BERING SEA
Bering Strait
Yukon River
Mackenzie River
Great Bear Lake
Great Slave Lake
Victoria Island
BAFFIN BAY
Baffin Island
Davis Strait
Greenland
Denmark Strait
Iceland
Arctic
60°N
GULF OF ALASKA
Aleutian Islands
Vancouver Island
ROCKY MOUNTAINS
Lake Winnipeg
HUDSON BAY
Great Lakes
St. Lawrence River
ATLANTIC OCEAN
Bay of Biscay
40°N
NORTH AMERICA
Missouri River
Mississippi
APPALACHIAN MTS.
Colorado River
Strait of Gibraltar
ATLAS
S
Tropic of Cancer
Hawaiian Islands
SIERRA MADRE
Rio Grande
GULF OF MEXICO
Bahamas
20°N
Greater Antilles
Niger
PACIFIC OCEAN
Isthmus of Panama
CARIBBEAN SEA
Lesser Antilles
ANDES
GUIANA HIGHLANDS
Amazon River
N
0° Equator
SOUTH AMERICA
BRAZILIAN HIGHLANDS
OCEAN
20°S
ANDES
River
Tropic of Capricorn
Paraná
ATLANTIC OCEAN
40°S
Strait of Magellan
Falkland Islands
Tierra del Fuego
Cape Horn
60°S
160°W 140°W 120°W 100°W 80°W 60°W 40°W 20°W
Antarctic Circle
Weddell Sea

ELEVATION

FEET		METERS
13,120		4,000
6,560		2,000
1,640		500
656		200
(Sea level) 0		0 (Sea level)
Below sea level		Below sea level
	Ice cap	

SCALE: at Equator

0   500   1,000   1,500   2,000 Miles

0   1,000   2,000 Kilometers

Projection: Mollweide

ARCTIC 80°N OCEAN
North BARENTS KARA EAST SIBERIAN
Cape SEA SEA LAPTEV SEA SEA
KARA
SEA
Kolyma River
Yenisey Lena River
BALTIC Ob River River 60°N KAMCHATKA
SEA River SEA OF PENINSULA
EUROPE OKHOTSK
URAL MOUNTAINS Lake Amur River Sakhalin
Baikal Island
Volga River ALTAY SHAN
ALPS Balkhash
ARAL Lake Hokkaido
MTS. CASPIAN SEA SEA GOBI SEA 40°N
BLACK SEA ASIA OF
Huang River JAPAN Honshu
MEDITERRANEAN SEA ASIA
HIMALAYAS Chang River Shikoku
Euphrates River Tigris River Indus River EAST Kyushu
SAHARA ARABIAN THAR CHINA
Nile RED SEA PENINSULA DESERT Ganges River Mekong River SEA Taiwan Tropic of Cancer
River Persian Gulf 20°N
AFRICA ARABIAN Bay of SOUTH Philippine PACIFIC
SEA Bengal CHINA Islands
Gulf Sri SEA OCEAN
of Congo River Lanka Strait of MALAY
Guinea Malacca PENINSULA
Lake Borneo
Tanganyika Lake Sumatra Celebes New Equator 0°
Victoria Java Guinea Solomon
Islands
INDIAN OCEAN
Madagascar CORAL Fiji
SEA New Islands
KALAHARI GREAT Hebrides
DESERT Mozambique Channel SANDY New
DESERT AUSTRALIA Caledonia 20°S
GREAT GREAT DIVIDING RANGE Tropic of Capricorn
VICTORIA
DESERT Darling River North
Cape of Island
Good Hope TASMAN NEW
SEA ZEALAND
Tasmania South
Island
20°E 40°E 60°E 80°E 100°E 120°E 140°E 160°E 60°S

ANTARCTICA

Denmark Strait KJÖLEN MTS. North Cape BARENTS KARA
Iceland 10°W 20°E 40°E SEA SEA
0 250 500 750 Miles
N 0 250 500 750 Kilometers URAL MTS.
60°N Projection: Mollweide
NORTH BALTIC Volga
SEA SEA River
British
Isles Rhine River
50°N Danube River
ATLANTIC ALPS
OCEAN Bay
of BLACK
Biscay SEA
40°N
MEDITERRANEAN SEA Tigris R.
Strait of
Gibraltar Crete

Atlas • A3

WORLD: POLITICAL

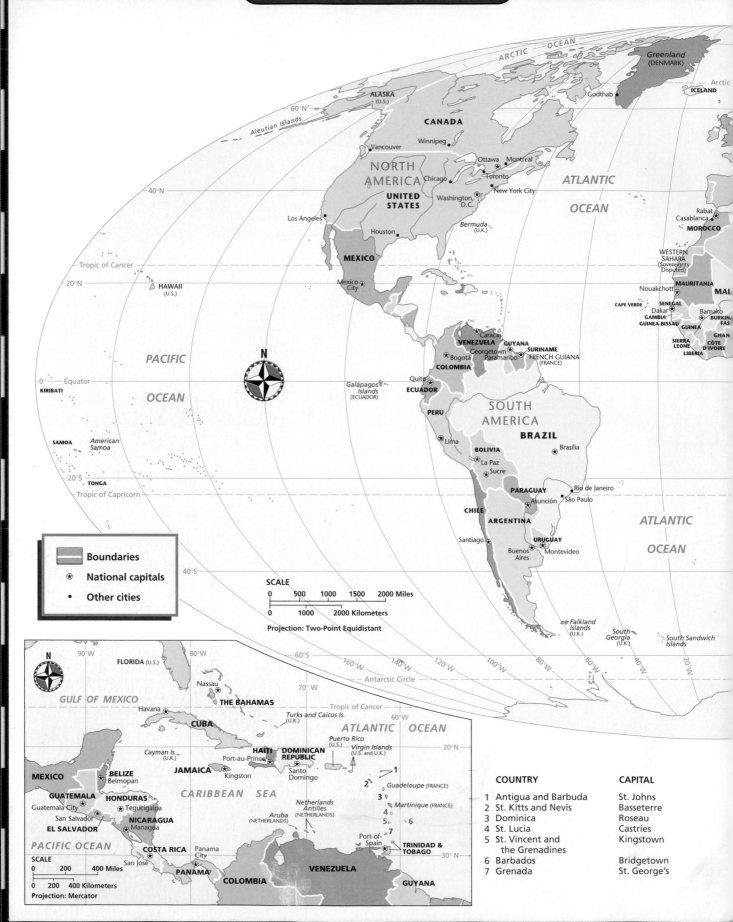

ARCTIC OCEAN

Greenland (DENMARK)

Arctic

ICELAND

ALASKA (U.S.)

Godthab

CANADA

Aleutian Islands

60°N

Winnipeg

Vancouver

Ottawa Montreal

NORTH AMERICA

Chicago Toronto

ATLANTIC

UNITED STATES

Washington, D.C.

New York City

OCEAN

40°N

Rabat
Casablanca

MOROCCO

Los Angeles

Bermuda (U.K.)

Houston

MEXICO

WESTERN SAHARA (Sovereignty Disputed)

Tropic of Cancer

20°N

Mexico City

Nouakchott

MAURITANIA

MAL

HAWAII (U.S.)

CAPE VERDE

Dakar

SENEGAL

Bamako

BURKIN

GAMBIA

FAS

Caracas

GUINEA-BISSAU

GUINEA

VENEZUELA

GUYANA

Georgetown

SURINAME

GHAN

Bogotá

Paramaribo

FRENCH GUIANA (FRANCE)

SIERRA LEONE

CÔTE D'IVOIRE

COLOMBIA

LIBERIA

PACIFIC

Quito

ECUADOR

Galápagos Islands (ECUADOR)

0° Equator

KIRIBATI

OCEAN

SOUTH AMERICA

PERU

BRAZIL

SAMOA

American Samoa

Lima

BOLIVIA

Brasília

La Paz

Sucre

20°S

TONGA

PARAGUAY

Rio de Janeiro

Asunción

São Paulo

Tropic of Capricorn

CHILE

ARGENTINA

URUGUAY

ATLANTIC

Santiago

Buenos Aires

Montevideo

OCEAN

Boundaries
⊛ National capitals
• Other cities

40°S

SCALE

0   500 1000 1500 2000 Miles

0   1000   2000 Kilometers

Projection: Two-Point Equidistant

Falkland Islands (U.K.)

South Georgia (U.K.)

South Sandwich Islands

60°S

140°W

120°W

100°W

80°W

60°W

40°W

20°W

160°W

Antarctic Circle

N

90°W

80°W

FLORIDA (U.S.)

70°W

60°W

20°N

GULF OF MEXICO

Nassau

Tropic of Cancer

Havana

THE BAHAMAS

Turks and Caicos Is. (U.K.)

ATLANTIC OCEAN

CUBA

Puerto Rico (U.S.)

Cayman Is. (U.K.)

Port-au-Prince

HAITI

DOMINICAN REPUBLIC

Virgin Islands (U.S. and U.K.)

1

MEXICO

BELIZE

Belmopan

JAMAICA

Kingston

Santo Domingo

2

Guadeloupe (FRANCE)

GUATEMALA

HONDURAS

CARIBBEAN SEA

3

Martinique (FRANCE)

Guatemala City

Tegucigalpa

Netherlands Antilles (NETHERLANDS)

4

San Salvador

NICARAGUA

Aruba (NETHERLANDS)

5   6

EL SALVADOR

Managua

7

PACIFIC OCEAN

COSTA RICA

San José

Panama City

Port-of-Spain

TRINIDAD & TOBAGO

30°N

SCALE

0   200   400 Miles

PANAMA

COLOMBIA

VENEZUELA

GUYANA

0   200   400 Kilometers

Projection: Mercator

COUNTRY	CAPITAL
1 Antigua and Barbuda	St. Johns
2 St. Kitts and Nevis	Basseterre
3 Dominica	Roseau
4 St. Lucia	Castries
5 St. Vincent and the Grenadines	Kingstown
6 Barbados	Bridgetown
7 Grenada	St. George's

COUNTRY — **CAPITAL**

1 Czech Republic — Prague
2 Slovakia — Bratislava
3 Slovenia — Ljubljana
4 Croatia — Zagreb
5 Bosnia and Herzegovina — Sarajevo
6 Macedonia — Skopje
7 Yugoslavia (Serbia and Montenegro) — Belgrade
8 Lithuania — Vilnius
9 Latvia — Riga
10 Estonia — Tallinn

SCALE

0   250   500   750 Miles

0   250   500   750 Kilometers

Projection: Mollweide

To understand the relative locations of Alaska and Hawaii, as well as the vast distances separating them from the rest of the United States, see the world map.

Projection: Albers Equal Area

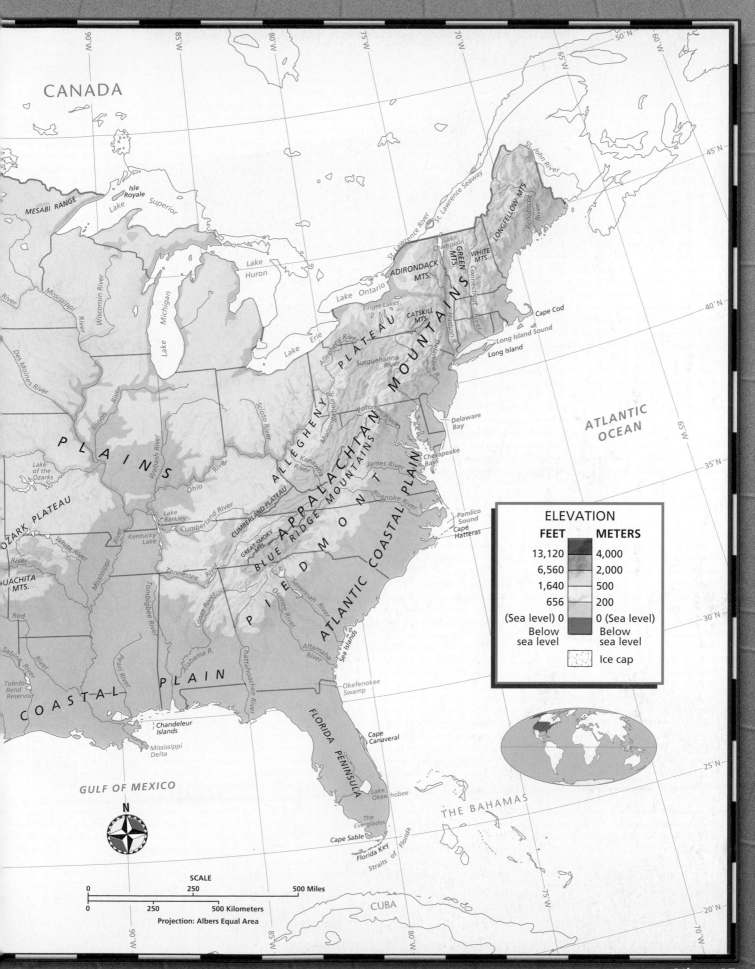

CANADA

MESABI RANGE
Isle Royale
Lake Superior
Lake Michigan
Lake Huron
Lake Ontario
Lake Erie

PLAINS

Mississippi River
Des Moines River
Illinois River
Wisconsin River
Wabash River
Scioto River
Ohio River
Kentucky Lake
Lake Barkley
Cumberland River
Tennessee River
Kentucky River
White River
Red River
Mississippi River
Tombigbee River
Pearl River
Alabama R.
Chattahoochee River

OZARK PLATEAU
Lake of the Ozarks
OUACHITA MTS.

Toledo Bend Reservoir
Sabine River

COASTAL PLAIN

GULF OF MEXICO

Chandeleur Islands
Mississippi Delta

N

ADIRONDACK MTS.
Finger Lakes
CATSKILL MTS.
Allegheny River
Susquehanna River
PLATEAU
APPALACHIAN MOUNTAINS
ALLEGHENY
Monongahela R.
Kanawha River
Potomac River
James River
Roanoke River
CUMBERLAND PLATEAU
GREAT SMOKY MTS.
BLUE RIDGE MOUNTAINS
Cumberland River
Coosa River
Savannah River
Oconee River
Altamaha River
PIEDMONT
ATLANTIC COASTAL PLAIN
Sea Islands

St. Lawrence River
St. Lawrence Seaway
Lake Champlain
GREEN MTS.
WHITE MTS.
LONGFELLOW MTS.
St. John River
Penobscot River
Connecticut River
Hudson R.
Delaware R.
Cape Cod
Long Island Sound
Long Island
Delaware Bay
Chesapeake Bay
Pamlico Sound
Cape Hatteras

ATLANTIC OCEAN

FLORIDA PENINSULA
Okefenokee Swamp
Cape Canaveral
Lake Okeechobee
The Everglades
Cape Sable
Florida Key
Straits of Florida

THE BAHAMAS

CUBA

ELEVATION

FEET	METERS
13,120	4,000
6,560	2,000
1,640	500
656	200
(Sea level) 0	0 (Sea level)
Below sea level	Below sea level
	Ice cap

SCALE
0   250   500 Miles
0   250   500 Kilometers
Projection: Albers Equal Area

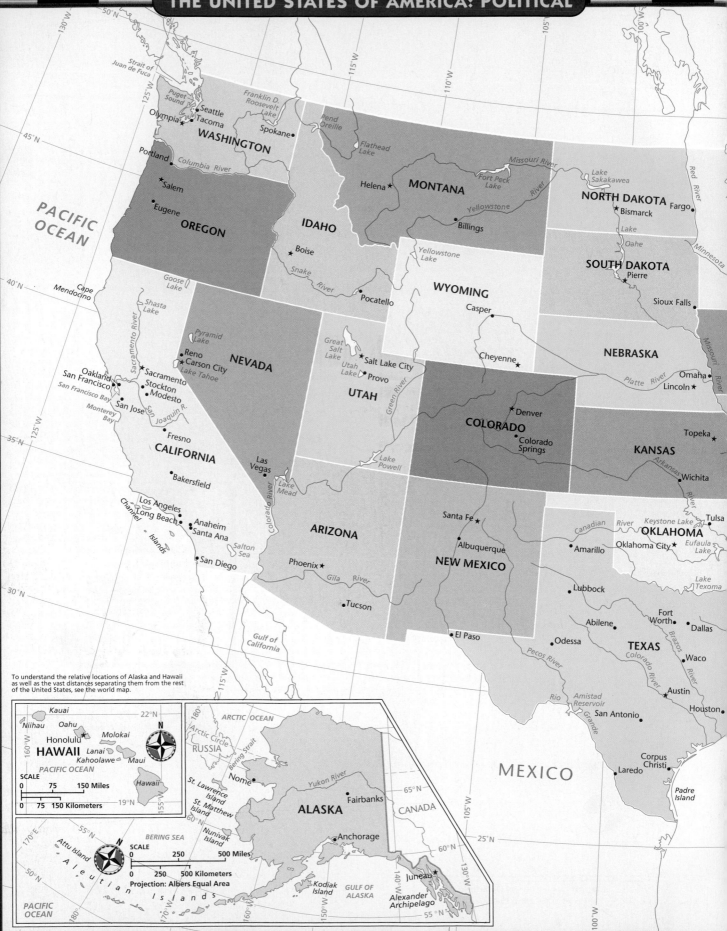

PACIFIC OCEAN

Strait of Juan de Fuca

Puget Sound

Seattle
Tacoma
Olympia ★
Spokane ●

WASHINGTON

Franklin D. Roosevelt Lake

Pend Oreille

Portland ●
Columbia River

Salem ★
Eugene ●
OREGON

Flathead Lake

Helena ★
MONTANA

Fort Peck Lake

Missouri River

Yellowstone River

Lake Sakakawea

NORTH DAKOTA
Bismarck ★
Fargo ●

Red River

IDAHO

Boise ★

Snake River

Billings ●

Yellowstone Lake

WYOMING

Lake Oahe

SOUTH DAKOTA
Pierre ★

Minnesota

Cape Mendocino

Goose Lake

Shasta Lake

Sacramento River

Pyramid Lake

Reno ●
Carson City ★
Lake Tahoe

NEVADA

Great Salt Lake

Salt Lake City ★

Utah Lake
Provo ●

UTAH

Green River

Casper ●

Cheyenne ★

NEBRASKA

Platte River

Missouri River

Omaha ●
Lincoln ★

Oakland ●
San Francisco ●
San Francisco Bay

Sacramento ★
Stockton ●
Modesto ●

San Jose ●
San Joaquin R.

Monterey Bay

Fresno ●

CALIFORNIA

Bakersfield ●

Denver ★

COLORADO

Colorado Springs ●

Topeka ★

KANSAS

Arkansas River

Wichita ●

Las Vegas ●

Lake Powell

Lake Mead

Colorado River

Santa Fe ★

Albuquerque ●

Canadian River

Keystone Lake

OKLAHOMA

Tulsa ●

Los Angeles ●
Long Beach ●
Channel Islands

Anaheim ●
Santa Ana ●

Salton Sea

San Diego ●

ARIZONA

Phoenix ★

Gila River

Tucson ●

NEW MEXICO

Amarillo ●

Oklahoma City ★

Eufaula Lake

Lubbock ●

Lake Texoma

Gulf of California

El Paso ●

Pecos River

Odessa ●

Abilene ●

Fort Worth ●
Dallas ●

TEXAS

Colorado River

Waco ●

Brazos River

Austin ●

Rio Grande

Amistad Reservoir

San Antonio ●

Houston ●

MEXICO

Corpus Christi ●

Laredo ●

Padre Island

To understand the relative locations of Alaska and Hawaii as well as the vast distances separating them from the rest of the United States, see the world map.

Kauai
Niihau
Oahu
Honolulu
HAWAII
Lanai
Molokai
Maui
Kahoolawe
Hawaii

N

PACIFIC OCEAN

SCALE
0   75   150 Miles
0   75   150 Kilometers

ARCTIC OCEAN
Arctic Circle
RUSSIA
Bering Strait
Nome ●
St. Lawrence Island
St. Matthew Island
Nunivak Island
Yukon River
Fairbanks ●
ALASKA
Anchorage ●
CANADA

N

SCALE
0   250   500 Miles
0   250   500 Kilometers
Projection: Albers Equal Area

BERING SEA
Attu Island
Aleutian Islands

Kodiak Island
GULF OF ALASKA

Juneau ★
Alexander Archipelago

PACIFIC OCEAN

CANADA

MINNESOTA
Duluth

Lake Superior

Minneapolis
St. Paul

WISCONSIN

Madison
Milwaukee

IOWA

Cedar Rapids
Rockford

Davenport
Des Moines

MICHIGAN

Grand Rapids
Flint
Lansing
Detroit
Ann Arbor

Lake Michigan

Lake Huron

Chicago
Gary
South Bend
Fort Wayne

Peoria

Springfield

ILLINOIS

INDIANA

Indianapolis

OHIO

Columbus

Dayton
Cincinnati

Toledo
Cleveland
Akron
Youngstown

Lake Erie

PENNSYLVANIA

Pittsburgh

Harrisburg

Lake Ontario

Buffalo
Rochester
Syracuse

NEW YORK

Albany

Susquehanna River

Allentown

St. Lawrence River

Lake Champlain

VT.
Montpelier

N.H.
Concord

MAINE
Augusta

MASS.
Springfield
Boston
Worcester
Hartford
CONN.
Providence
R.I.
New Haven
Bridgeport
Cape Cod

Hudson R.

Newark
New York City
Jersey City
Trenton
Long Island Sound
Long Island

N.J.
Philadelphia

ATLANTIC OCEAN

nsas ty

Kansas City

St. Louis

Lake of the Ozarks

Jefferson City

MISSOURI

Springfield

Fayetteville

ARKANSAS

Little Rock

Illinois River

Wabash River

Louisville

Frankfort
Lexington

Evansville

Ohio River

KENTUCKY

Lake Barkley

Kentucky Lake

Nashville

Memphis

TENNESSEE

Chattanooga

Mississippi River

Huntsville

WEST VIRGINIA

Charleston

Arlington
Alexandria
Washington, D.C.

Baltimore
MD.
Annapolis

DELAWARE
Dover

Delaware Bay

VIRGINIA

Richmond

Roanoke
Newport News
Portsmouth

Chesapeake Bay

Norfolk

Cape Hatteras

Greensboro
Durham
Raleigh

Winston-Salem

Knoxville

NORTH CAROLINA

Charlotte

SOUTH CAROLINA

Columbia

Savannah River

MISSISSIPPI

ALABAMA

Birmingham

Atlanta

GEORGIA

Macon

Columbus

Montgomery

Jackson

Red River

Sabine River

Wedo Bend Res.

LOUISIANA

Shreveport

Beaumont

Baton Rouge

New Orleans

Chandeleur Islands

Mobile

Chattahoochee River

Tallahassee

Savannah

Sea Islands

Jacksonville

FLORIDA

Orlando

Cape Canaveral

Tampa
St. Petersburg

Lake Okeechobee

GULF OF MEXICO

N

Fort Lauderdale
Miami

Cape Sable

Florida Keys

Straits of Florida

THE BAHAMAS

CUBA

	Boundaries
(*)	National capitals
★	State capitals
•	Other cities

SCALE
0   250   500 Miles
0   500   500 Kilometers

Projection: Albers Equal Area

NORTH AMERICA: PHYSICAL

ASIA

EUROPE

North Pole

ARCTIC OCEAN
POLAR ICE PACK

BEAUFORT SEA

St. Lawrence Island
BERING SEA
Nunivak Island

BROOKS RANGE

Mt. McKinley 20,320 ft. (6,194 m)
ALASKA RANGE
Yukon River

Queen Elizabeth Islands
Ellesmere Island

Greenland

Banks Island

Victoria Island

Baffin Bay

Baffin Island

Davis Strait

Denmark Strait

Cape Farewell

GULF OF ALASKA
Kodiak Island
Alexander Archipelago

YUKON PLATEAU

Mackenzie River

Great Bear Lake

Great Slave Lake

Southampton Island

Hudson Strait

LABRADOR SEA

PACIFIC OCEAN

Queen Charlotte Islands
Vancouver Island

Peace River

Lake Athabasca

Athabasca River

CANADIAN

Coats Island
Mansel Island
Hudson Bay

Anticosti Island

Newfoundland

Cape Mendocino

Mount Rainier 14,410 ft. (4,392 m)

COAST RANGE

Fraser River

Columbia River

Snake River

SIERRA NEVADA
CENTRAL VALLEY
COAST RANGES

GREAT BASIN
DEATH VALLEY
Mount Whitney 14,494 ft. (4,419 m)

Saskatchewan River

Nelson River

Lake Winnipeg

SHIELD

GREAT

PLAINS

BLACK HILLS

Missouri River

Great Salt Lake

COLORADO PLATEAU

Colorado River

Platte River

INTERIOR PLAINS

OZARK PLATEAU

Lake Superior

Lake Michigan

Lake Huron

Lake Ontario

Lake Erie

St. Lawrence River
GULF OF ST. LAWRENCE
Prince Edward Island
Cape Breton Island

Cape Cod
Long Island

ATLANTIC OCEAN

Bermuda

Guadalupe Island

BAJA CALIFORNIA

GULF OF CALIFORNIA

SIERRA MADRE OCCIDENTAL

Rio Grande

Arkansas River

Red River

Brazos River

Mississippi River

Ohio River

Cumberland R.

Tennessee River

APPALACHIAN MOUNTAINS

PIEDMONT

ATLANTIC COASTAL PLAIN

Cape Hatteras

SIERRA MADRE ORIENTAL

GULF COASTAL PLAIN

GULF OF MEXICO

Popocatépetl 17,887 ft. (5,452 m)

YUCATÁN PENINSULA

FLORIDA PENINSULA

Cape Canaveral

Florida Keys
Straits of Florida

Bahamas

Cuba

Greater Antilles

Jamaica

Hispaniola

Puerto Rico

Lesser Antilles

Tropic of Cancer

SIERRA MADRE DEL SUR

CENTRAL AMERICA

Lake Nicaragua

CARIBBEAN SEA

ISTHMUS OF PANAMA

Trinidad

SOUTH AMERICA

Equator 0°

ELEVATION

FEET	METERS
13,120	4,000
6,560	2,000
1,640	500
656	200
(Sea level) 0	0 (Sea level)
Below sea level	Below sea level

Ice cap

N

SCALE

0   250   500   750   1,000 Miles

0   250 500 750 1,000 Kilometers

Projection: Azimuthal Equal Area

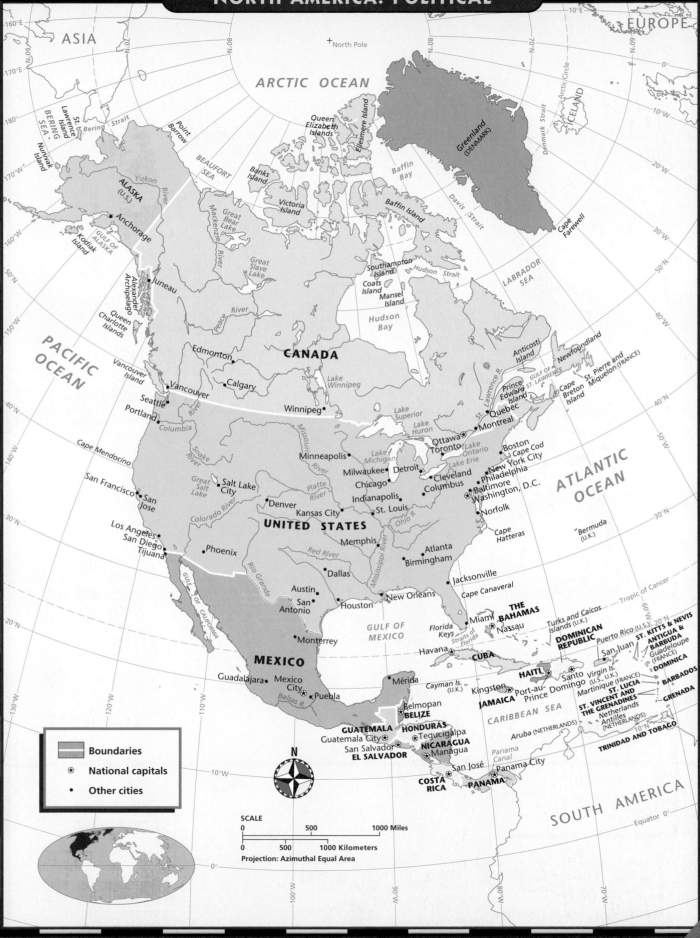

NORTH AMERICA: POLITICAL

Legend:
- Boundaries
- ⊛ National capitals
- • Other cities

SCALE
0 — 500 — 1000 Miles
0 — 500 — 1000 Kilometers
Projection: Azimuthal Equal Area

N

CENTRAL AMERICA

CARIBBEAN SEA

Panama Canal

GULF OF PANAMA

Malpelo Island

Margarita Island

Tobago
Trinidad

Lake Maracaibo

Orinoco River

Orinoco River Delta

LLANOS

Meta River

Cauca River

Magdalena River

▲ Mount Tolima
18,425 ft. (5,616 m)

Angel Falls

GUIANA

HIGHLANDS

Devil's Island
Cape Orange

ATLANTIC OCEAN

N

Caquetá River

Orinoco River

Rio Negro

Japurá River

AMAZON

Amazon River Delta

Galápagos Islands

Equator

▲ Mount Chimborazo
20,561 ft. (6,267 m)

GULF OF GUAYAQUIL

ANDES

Marañón River

Amazon River

BASIN

Amazon River

Equator

Juruá River

Purus River

Ucayali River

Madeira River

Tapajós River

Xingu River

Tocantins River

BRAZILIAN

HIGHLANDS

PACIFIC OCEAN

▲ Mount Huascarán
22,205 ft. (6,768 m)

Lake Titicaca

Beni River

Mamoré River

Araguaia River

São Francisco River

Parnaíba River

▲ Ancohuma Peak
20,958 ft. (6,388 m)

MATO GROSSO
PLATEAU

Lake Poopó

Pilcomayo River

ATACAMA DESERT

ANDES

CHACO

Paraguay River

BRAZILIAN
PLATEAU

Tropic of Capricorn

San Ambrosio Island

San Félix Island

Salado River

Paraná River

Uruguay River

Tropic of Capricorn

Juan Fernández Islands

▲ Mount Aconcagua
22,834 ft. (6,960 m)

PAMPAS

Rio de la Plata

ATLANTIC OCEAN

Salado River

Colorado River

GULF OF SAN MATÍAS

Chiloé Island

PATAGONIA

CHONOS ARCHIPELAGO

GULF OF SAN JORGE

Cape Tres Puntas

Bahía Grande

Strait of Magellan

Falkland Islands

South Georgia Islands

TIERRA DEL FUEGO

CAPE HORN

ELEVATION

FEET		METERS
13,120		4,000
6,560		2,000
1,640		500
656		200
(Sea level) 0		0 (Sea level)
Below sea level		Below sea level

SCALE

0   250   500   750   1,000 Miles

0   250 500 750 1,000 Kilometers

Projection: Azimuthal Equal Area

CENTRAL AMERICA

CARIBBEAN SEA

N

ATLANTIC OCEAN

Barranquilla
Cartagena
Caracas
VENEZUELA
Georgetown
Paramaribo
GUYANA
Cayenne
Medellín
SURINAME
FRENCH GUIANA (FRANCE)
Lake Maracaibo
Orinoco River
Bogotá
COLOMBIA
Cali
Malpelo Island (COLOMBIA)
Rio Negro
Amazon River
Quito
ECUADOR
Guayaquil
Belém
Galápagos Islands (ECUADOR)
Equator 0°
Amazon River
Marañón River
BRAZIL
PERU
Trujillo
Ucayali River
Recife
Callao
Lima
São Francisco River
10°S
Salvador
PACIFIC OCEAN
Arequipa
Lake Titicaca
BOLIVIA
La Paz
Brasília
Lake Poopó
Sucre
Belo Horizonte
20°S
PARAGUAY
Campinas
São Paulo
Rio de Janeiro
Tropic of Capricorn
San Ambrosio Island (CHILE)
Asunción
Curitiba
San Félix Island (CHILE)
Paraguay River
CHILE
Paraná River
Uruguay River
Pôrto Alegre
Juan Fernández Islands (CHILE)
Córdoba
30°S
Valparaíso
Santiago
Rosario
URUGUAY
ATLANTIC OCEAN
Buenos Aires
Montevideo
Río de la Plata
ARGENTINA

Boundaries
⊛ National capitals
• Other cities

SCALE
0   250   500   750   1000 Miles
0   250   500   250   1000 Kilometers
Projection: Azimuthal Equal Area

Strait of Magellan
Falkland Islands (U.K.)
Tierra del Fuego
South Georgia Island (U.K.)

ASIA

URAL MOUNTAINS

CASPIAN SEA

Mt. Elbrus (5,642 m)
18,510 ft.

CAUCASUS MTS.

Ural River

Kama River

Pechora River

BARENTS SEA

KOLA PENINSULA

White Sea

Lake Onega

Lake Ladoga

Volga

Don River

Rybinsk Reservoir

Dnieper

SEA OF AZOV

CRIMEAN PENINSULA

BLACK SEA

SOUTHWEST ASIA

NORTHERN EUROPEAN PLAIN

BALTIC PLAINS

North Dvina River

Duina River

Dzvina R.

GULF OF FINLAND

BALTIC SEA

Vistula River

Oder River

Dnestr River

Nistru River

CARPATHIAN MTS.

TRANSYLVANIAN ALPS

Danube

DINARIC ALPS

BALKAN PENINSULA

SEA OF MARMARA

AEGEAN SEA

Rhodes

Crete

KJØLEN MOUNTAINS

Lake Vättern

Lake Vänern

Kattegat

Skagerrak

Elbe River

Rhine River

Danube River

ALPS

Po River

Tiber River

APENNINES

ADRIATIC SEA

TYRRHENIAN SEA

Sicily

Malta

SEA

North Cape

ARCTIC OCEAN

NORWEGIAN SEA

NORTH SEA

Orkney Islands

Shetland Islands

Faeroe Islands

PENNINES

Thames River

English Channel

British Isles

IRISH SEA

Hebrides

Iceland

Mont Blanc (4,810 m)
15,781 ft.

Lake Geneva

Rhône River

Seine River

Loire River

Garonne River

PYRENEES

Ebro River

Bay of Biscay

Corsica

Sardinia

Balearic Islands

MEDITERRANEAN SEA

AFRICA

IBERIAN PENINSULA

Douro River

Tagus River

Guadiana River

Guadalquivir

Strait of Gibraltar

Cape Finisterre

ATLANTIC OCEAN

Arctic Circle

ELEVATION

FEET	METERS
13,120	4,000
6,560	2,000
1,640	500
656	200
(Sea level) 0	0 (Sea level)
Below sea level	Below sea level

Ice cap

SCALE

0   250   500 Miles

0   500   500 Kilometers

Projection: Azimuthal Equal Area

EUROPE: POLITICAL

ASIA

URAL MOUNTAINS

RUSSIA

ARCTIC OCEAN

BARENTS SEA

WHITE SEA

CASPIAN SEA

Ural River

Volga River

Nizhniy Novgorod

Moscow ✥

Don River

St. Petersburg ●

GULF OF BOTHNIA

FINLAND

Helsinki ✥

Tallinn ✥

ESTONIA

LATVIA

Riga ✥

LITHUANIA

Vilnius ✥

RUSSIA

Minsk ✥

BELARUS

Dnieper River

Kiev ✥

UKRAINE

MOLDOVA

Chişinău ✥

BLACK SEA

SOUTHWEST ASIA

ROMANIA

Bucharest ✥

Danube River

BULGARIA

Sofia ✥

Rhodes

AEGEAN SEA

Crete

NORWAY

SWEDEN

Stockholm ✥

Göteborg ●

Oslo ✥

Bergen ●

North Cape

Warsaw ✥

POLAND

Krakow ●

Belgrade ✥

SERBIA

YUGOSLAVIA

Skopje ✥

MACEDONIA

Tirane ✥

ALBANIA

GREECE

Athens ✥

BALTIC SEA

DENMARK

Copenhagen ✥

Hamburg ●

Elbe River

Berlin ✥

Dresden ●

Prague ✥

CZECH REPUBLIC

SLOVAKIA

Bratislava ✥

Vienna ✥

Budapest ✥

HUNGARY

AUSTRIA

Zagreb ✥

CROATIA

SLOVENIA

Ljubljana ✥

BOSNIA & HERZEGOVINA

Sarajevo ✥

MONTENEGRO

ADRIATIC SEA

SEA

MALTA

Valletta ✥

NORTH SEA

GERMANY

Cologne ●

Bonn ●

Amsterdam ✥

THE NETHERLANDS

The Hague ●

Brussels ✥

BELGIUM

LUXEMBOURG

Luxembourg ✥

Munich ●

Danube River

Rhine River

LIECHTENSTEIN

Vaduz ✥

SWITZERLAND

Bern ✥

Lake Geneva

A L P S

Milan ●

Po River

Rome ✥

VATICAN CITY

ITALY

SAN MARINO

San Marino ✥

MONACO

Monaco ✥

Naples ●

Sicily

Sardinia (ITALY)

Corsica (FRANCE)

ICELAND

Reykjavik ✥

Faeroe Islands (DENMARK)

Shetland Islands

Arctic Circle

SCOTLAND

Edinburgh ✥

UNITED KINGDOM

NORTHERN IRELAND

Belfast ✥

Liverpool ●

ENGLAND

London ✥

WALES

Thames R.

English Channel

Channel Islands (U.K.)

British Isles

IRELAND

Dublin ✥

Paris ✥

FRANCE

Seine River

Loire River

Lyons ●

Rhône River

Marseille ●

SWITZERLAND

Bay of Biscay

PYRENEES

ANDORRA

Andorra la Vella ✥

Barcelona ●

Balearic Islands (SPAIN)

MEDITERRANEAN SEA

AFRICA

ATLANTIC OCEAN

PORTUGAL

Lisbon ✥

Tagus River

SPAIN

Madrid ✥

Seville ●

Valencia ●

Gibraltar (U.K.)

Strait of Gibraltar

N

SCALE

0 | 250 | 500 Miles

0 | 250 | 500 Kilometers

Projection: Azimuthal Equal Area

Boundaries

✥ National capitals

● Other cities

ELEVATION

FEET	METERS
13,120	4,000
6,560	2,000
1,640	500
656	200
0 (Sea level)	0 (Sea level)
Below sea level	Below sea level

Ice cap

NORTH AMERICA

EUROPE

AFRICA

AUSTRALIA

PACIFIC OCEAN

INDIAN OCEAN

SIBERIA

CENTRAL RANGE

KAMCHATKA PENINSULA

SEA OF OKHOTSK

KOLYMA MTS.

CHERSKIY RANGE

VERKHOYANSKY RANGE

STANOVOY MOUNTAINS

YABLONOVY RANGE

Aldan River

Lena River

Amur River

Lake Baikal

SAYAN MOUNTAINS

ALTAY SHAN

MONGOLIAN PLATEAU

GREATER KHINGAN RANGE

NORTH CHINA PLAIN

GREAT WALL

Huang

GOBI

CENTRAL SIBERIAN PLATEAU

Lower Tunguska River

Angara River

Yenisey River

Ob River

WEST SIBERIAN PLAIN

Irtysh River

KAZAKH UPLANDS

Lake Balkhash

TIAN SHAN

TARIM BASIN

TAKLIMAKAN DESERT

KUNLUN MOUNTAINS

PLATEAU OF TIBET

Mount Everest 29,035 ft. (8,850 m.)

HIMALAYAS

Brahmaputra River

Ganges River

QIN LING

Chang

Xi River

NORTH LAND

TAYMYR PENINSULA

URAL MOUNTAINS

USTYURT PLATEAU

KYZYL KUM

URAL LOWLAND

KARAKUM

Syr Darya

Amu Darya

HINDU KUSH

Indus River

Sutlej

THAR DESERT

INDO-GANGETIC PLAIN

DECCAN PLATEAU

Godavari River

EASTERN GHATS

WESTERN GHATS

Bay of Bengal

Sri Lanka

Maldives

Lakshadweep Islands

Andaman Islands

Nicobar Islands

Mentawai Islands

Sumatra

MALAY PENINSULA

Strait of Malacca

GULF OF THAILAND

Chao Phraya River

INDOCHINA PENINSULA

Mekong River

GULF OF TONKIN

Hainan

SOUTH CHINA SEA

Borneo

Bangka

JAVA SEA

Java

CELEBES SEA

Celebes

BANDA SEA

ARAFURA SEA

Moluccas

MAOKE MOUNTAINS

New Guinea

Philippines

Mindanao

Luzon

Luzon Strait

Taiwan

EAST CHINA SEA

Ryukyu Islands

Okinawa

Korea Strait

SEA OF JAPAN

Kyushu

Shikoku

Honshu

Hokkaido

Kuril Islands

Sakhalin Island

JAPAN

BOHAI

HILLS

YELLOW SEA

GULF OF

SHILKA RING

Aleutian Islands

Wrangel Island

New Siberian Islands

BERING SEA

Franz Josef Land

Novaya Zemlya

KARA SEA

BARENTS SEA

Arctic Circle

Ob River

Ural River

CASPIAN SEA

SEA OF AZOV

BLACK SEA

Bosporus

CAUCASUS MTS.

Mount Ararat 16,945 ft. (5,165 m.)

ANATOLIAN PLATEAU

Cyprus

MEDITERRANEAN SEA

SINAI PENINSULA

RED SEA

SYRIAN DESERT

AN-NAFUD

Euphrates River

Tigris River

ZAGROS MTS.

GREAT SALT DESERT

PERSIAN GULF

GULF OF OMAN

Strait of Hormuz

ARABIAN SEA

RUB' AL-KHALI

GULF OF ADEN

Socotra Island

N

SCALE

0   500   1,000 Miles

0   500   1,000 Kilometers

Projection: Modified Oblique Conic

170°W

180°

170°E

160°E

150°E

140°E

130°E

120°E

110°E

100°E

90°E

80°E

70°E

60°E

50°E

40°E

30°E

20°E

10°E

0°

140°E

130°E

120°E

110°E

100°E

90°E

80°E

70°E

Equator

Tropic of Cancer

10°N

20°N

30°N

40°N

50°N

60°N

70°N

80°N

Equator 0°

10°S

Boundaries
⊛ National capitals
• Other cities

ASIA: POLITICAL

PACIFIC OCEAN

IRIAN JAYA

AUSTRALIA

EAST TIMOR (U.N.-administered)

ARAFURA SEA

CELEBES SEA

JAVA SEA Ujung Pandang

INDONESIA

Semarang
Surabaya
Jakarta
Bandung

Medan

BRUNEI
Bandar Seri Begawan

MALAYSIA
Kuala Lumpur
SINGAPORE
Singapore

PHILIPPINES
Manila

Ryukyu Islands (JAPAN)
Luzon Strait

TAIWAN
Taipei

Hong Kong
Macao
Hainan (CHINA)

SOUTH CHINA SEA

VIETNAM
Hanoi
Ho Chi Minh City

CAMBODIA
Phnom Penh

THAILAND
Bangkok

LAOS
Vientiane

GULF OF THAILAND

ANDAMAN SEA

MYANMAR (BURMA)
Yangon (Rangoon)
Mandalay

Andaman Islands (INDIA)
Nicobar Islands (INDIA)

EAST CHINA SEA

JAPAN
Tokyo
Yokohama
Osaka Nagoya
Kyoto
Hiroshima
Nagasaki
Sapporo
Sakhalin Island
Kuril Islands (RUSSIA)

SEA OF JAPAN

Vladivostok

NORTH KOREA
Pyongyang
SOUTH KOREA
Seoul
Pusan
Dalian

Shanghai
Nanjing
Qingdao
Qingdaose

Harbin
Changchun
Fushun
Beijing

CHINA

Wuhan
Chongqing
Guangzhou
Xi'an
Chengdu

Huang River
Chang River
Great Wall of China

MONGOLIA
Ulaanbaatar

Irkutsk
Lake Baykal

RUSSIA

Lena River
Yakutsk

BERING SEA

SEA OF OKHOTSK

Aleutian Islands

Amur River

Novosibirsk
Omsk
Astana

KAZAKHSTAN

Lake Balkhash

Almaty
Bishkek
KYRGYZSTAN
Tashkent
UZBEKISTAN

TAJIKISTAN
Dushanbe

Aral Sea

Ob River

Yekaterinburg
Chelyabinsk

URAL MOUNTAINS

Moscow

EUROPE

ARCTIC Circle

BARENTS SEA

KARA SEA

LAPTEV SEA

BLACK SEA

Istanbul
Izmir
TURKEY
Ankara

GEORGIA
T'bilisi
ARMENIA
Yerevan
AZERBAIJAN
Baku

CASPIAN SEA

TURKMENISTAN
Ashgabat

Mashhad
Tehran
IRAN
Isfahan
Shiraz
Tabriz

AFGHANISTAN
Kabul

PAKISTAN
Islamabad
Lahore
Faisalabad
Karachi

Indus River

NEPAL
Kathmandu

BHUTAN
Thimphu

BANGLADESH
Dhaka
Chittagong

Delhi
New Delhi
Jaipur

INDIA

Ahmadabad
Bhopal
Nagpur
Hyderabad

Kolkata (Calcutta)

Mumbai (Bombay)

Bangalore
Chennai (Madras)

Ganges River
Brahmaputra River

Bay of Bengal

SRI LANKA
Colombo

MALDIVES
Male

Lakshadweep Islands (INDIA)

ARABIAN SEA

INDIAN OCEAN

Mosul
Baghdad
Basra
IRAQ

SYRIA
Aleppo
Damascus

CYPRUS
Nicosia
LEBANON
Beirut
ISRAEL
Tel Aviv
Jerusalem
JORDAN
Amman

Tigris River
Euphrates River

KUWAIT
Kuwait City

BAHRAIN
Manama
QATAR
Doha

UNITED ARAB EMIRATES
Abu Dhabi

OMAN
Masqat (Muscat)

PERSIAN GULF

SAUDI ARABIA
Riyadh
Mecca
Jidda

YEMEN
Sanaa

Socotra (YEMEN)

GULF OF ADEN

RED SEA

MEDITERRANEAN SEA

AFRICA

RUSSIA

N

SCALE
0   500   1000 Miles
0   500   1000 Kilometers

Projection: Two-Point Equidistant

EUROPE

CENTRAL ASIA

SOUTHWEST ASIA

MEDITERRANEAN SEA

Strait of Gibraltar

GULF OF SIDRA

Suez Canal

PERSIAN GULF

QATTARA DEPRESSION

Azores

Madeira Islands

Canary Islands

ATLAS MOUNTAINS

40°N
30°N
Tropic of Cancer
20°N
10°N
0° Equator

Cape Blanc

Cape Verde Islands

Cape Verde

FOUTA DJALLON

Senegal R.

Niger River

White Volta R.

Black Volta R.

Lake Volta

Cape Palmas

GULF OF GUINEA

EL DJOUF

S A H A R A

AHAGGAR MOUNTAINS

AIR MTS.

TIBESTI MOUNTAINS

LIBYAN DESERT

S A H E L

S U D A N

CHAD BASIN

Lake Chad

Benue River

ADAMAWA MTS.

Nile River

Lake Nasser

NUBIAN DESERT

RED SEA

Blue Nile

White Nile

SUDAN BASIN

Lake Tana

ETHIOPIAN HIGHLANDS

GULF OF ADEN

HORN OF AFRICA

SOMALI PENINSULA

Ubangi River

Congo River

CONGO BASIN

Kasai River

Cape Lopez

N

ATLANTIC OCEAN

Ascension

Cuanza River

Lake Albert

Lake Edward

Lake Kivu

MITUMBA MOUNTAINS

WESTERN RIFT VALLEY

Lake Tanganyika

Lake Mweru

Lake Turkana

RIFT VALLEY

EASTERN RIFT VALLEY

Mount Kenya 17,058 ft. (5,199 m)

Lake Victoria

SERENGETI PLAIN

MASAI STEPPE

Mount Kilimanjaro 19,340 ft. (5,895 m)

Zanzibar

Lake Rukwa

INDIAN OCEAN

Seychelles

Lake Malawi (Nyasa)

Cape Delgado

Comoro Islands

Lake Kariba

Zambezi River

Victoria Falls

Okavango Delta

KALAHARI BASIN

NAMIB DESERT

KALAHARI DESERT

Limpopo River

Mozambique Channel

Madagascar

Mauritius

Réunion

Vaal River

Orange River

DRAKENSBERG MOUNTAINS

GREAT KARROO

Cape of Good Hope

Tropic of Cancer
20°N
10°N
Equator 0°
10°S
Tropic of Capricorn
30°S
40°S

ELEVATION

FEET		METERS
13,120		4,000
6,560		2,000
1,640		500
656		200
(Sea level) 0		0 (Sea level)
Below sea level		Below sea level

SCALE

| 0 | 500 | 1,000 Miles |

| 0 | 500 | 1,000 Kilometers |

Projection: Azimuthal Equal Area

AFRICA: POLITICAL

EUROPE

CENTRAL ASIA

SOUTHWEST ASIA

Azores (PORTUGAL)

Madeira (PORTUGAL)

Strait of Gibraltar
Algiers ⊛ ⊛ Tunis
Casablanca ● ⊛ Rabat

MEDITERRANEAN SEA

TUNISIA
● Tripoli

Alexandria ●

MOROCCO
Canary Islands (SPAIN)
El Aaiún ⊛
WESTERN SAHARA (Claimed by Morocco)
Tropic of Cancer

Giza ●⊛ Cairo
Suez Canal

ALGERIA

LIBYA

EGYPT
Nile River
Lake Nasser
Tropic of Cancer

RED SEA

MAURITANIA
Nouakchott ⊛

MALI

NIGER

CHAD

Khartoum ●

ERITREA
Asmara ●

GULF OF ADEN

CAPE VERDE
Praia ⊛
Dakar ⊛ **SENEGAL**
Banjul ⊛ **GAMBIA**
Bissau ⊛ **GUINEA-BISSAU**
Conakry ⊛ **GUINEA**
Freetown ⊛
SIERRA LEONE
Monrovia ⊛
LIBERIA

Niger River
Bamako ⊛
BURKINA FASO
Ouagadougou ⊛
Niamey ⊛

NIGERIA
⊛ Abuja

Lake Chad
N'Djamena ●

SUDAN
White Nile
Blue Nile

DJIBOUTI
Djibouti ⊛

ETHIOPIA
Addis Ababa ●

CÔTE D'IVOIRE
Yamoussoukro ⊛
Abidjan ● **GHANA**
Accra ⊛
TOGO
BENIN
Lomé ⊛
Porto-Novo ⊛
Lagos ●
Malabo ⊛
CAMEROON

CENTRAL AFRICAN REPUBLIC
Bangui ⊛

UGANDA
Kampala ⊛

KENYA
Nairobi ●

SOMALIA
Mogadishu ●

EQUATORIAL GUINEA
SÃO TOMÉ AND PRÍNCIPE
São Tomé ⊛

Yaoundé ⊛
Libreville ⊛
GABON
REPUBLIC OF THE CONGO
Congo River
Kisangani ●

DEMOCRATIC REPUBLIC OF THE CONGO
Brazzaville ⊛
Kinshasa ⊛

RWANDA
Kigali ⊛
Bujumbura ⊛
BURUNDI
Lake Victoria

TANZANIA
Dodoma ⊛
Lake Tanganyika
Dar es Salaam ●
Mombasa ●
Pemba
Zanzibar

Victoria ⊛
SEYCHELLES

INDIAN OCEAN

N

Equator

ATLANTIC OCEAN

Luanda ⊛

ANGOLA

CABINDA (ANGOLA)

Lubumbashi ●
Lake Malawi (Nyasa)

COMOROS
Moroni ●

ZAMBIA
Lusaka ⊛
Zambezi River

MALAWI
Lilongwe ⊛

MOZAMBIQUE

St. Helena (U.K.)

Harare ⊛
ZIMBABWE
Bulawayo ●

Antananarivo ⊛
MAURITIUS
Port Louis ⊛
Réunion (FRANCE)

NAMIBIA
Windhoek ⊛

BOTSWANA
Gaborone ⊛

MADAGASCAR
Tropic of Capricorn

Johannesburg ●
Pretoria ⊛
Maputo ⊛
Mbabane ⊛
SWAZILAND

Orange River
Maseru ⊛
LESOTHO

SOUTH AFRICA

Cape Town ●

Legend

▨	Boundaries
⊛	National capitals
●	Other cities

SCALE

0 — 500 — 1000 Miles

0 — 500 — 1000 Kilometers

Projection: Azimuthal Equal Area

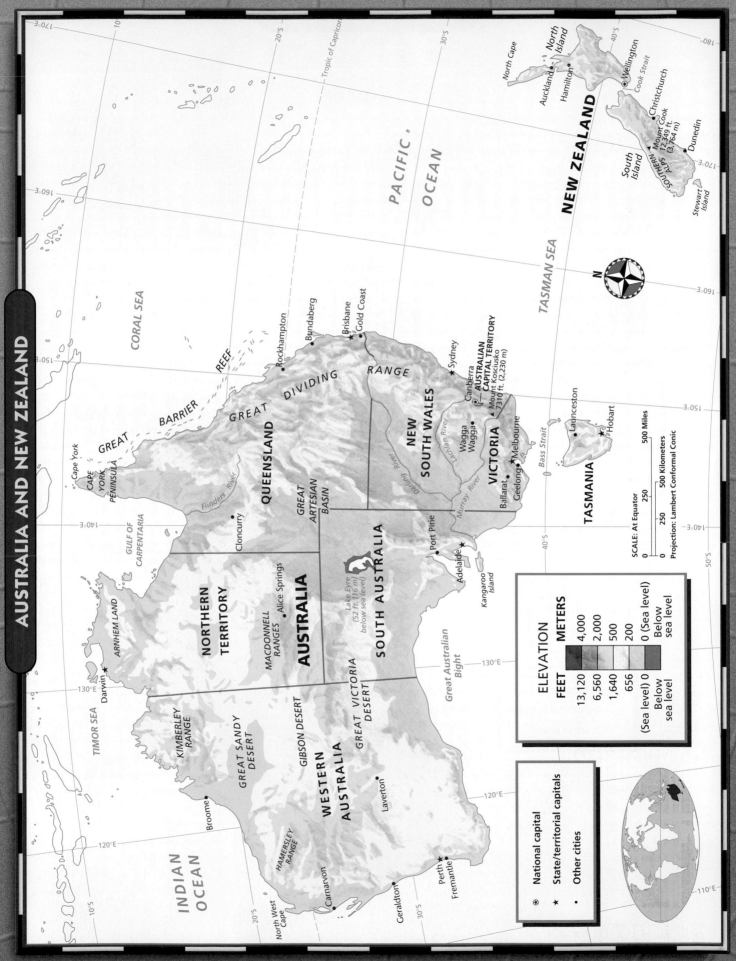

AUSTRALIA AND NEW ZEALAND

NEW ZEALAND

North Cape
North Island
Auckland • Hamilton
Wellington
Cook Strait
Christchurch
Mount Cook 12,349 ft (3,764 m)
SOUTHERN ALPS
South Island
Dunedin
Stewart Island

PACIFIC OCEAN

TASMAN SEA

N

CORAL SEA

GREAT BARRIER REEF

GREAT DIVIDING RANGE

Cape York
CAPE YORK PENINSULA

GULF OF CARPENTARIA

Rockhampton
Bundaberg
Brisbane
Gold Coast

QUEENSLAND

GREAT ARTESIAN BASIN

Flinders River

Cloncurry

Sydney
NEW SOUTH WALES
Canberra
AUSTRALIAN CAPITAL TERRITORY
Mount Kosciusko 7,310 ft (2,230 m)

Lachlan River
Darling River
Wagga Wagga
Murrumbidgee River
VICTORIA
Melbourne
Ballarat
Geelong
Murray River

Bass Strait
Launceston
Hobart
TASMANIA

NORTHERN TERRITORY

MACDONNELL RANGES
Alice Springs

AUSTRALIA

Lake Eyre (52 ft [16 m] below sea level)

SOUTH AUSTRALIA

Port Pirie
Adelaide
Kangaroo Island

Great Australian Bight

TIMOR SEA
Darwin
ARNHEM LAND

KIMBERLEY RANGE

GREAT SANDY DESERT
GIBSON DESERT
GREAT VICTORIA DESERT

WESTERN AUSTRALIA

Laverton

INDIAN OCEAN

Broome

HAMERSLEY RANGE

North West Cape
Carnarvon
Geraldton
Perth
Fremantle

SCALE: At Equator
0 250 500 Miles
0 250 500 Kilometers
Projection: Lambert Conformal Conic

ELEVATION
FEET	METERS
13,120	4,000
6,560	2,000
1,640	500
656	200
(Sea level) 0	0 (Sea level)
Below sea level	Below sea level

⊛ National capital
★ State/territorial capitals
• Other cities

PACIFIC ISLANDS

ASIA

JAPAN

NORTH AMERICA

NORTH PACIFIC OCEAN

SOUTH PACIFIC OCEAN

Tropic of Cancer

Equator

Tropic of Cancer

International Date Line

SOUTH CHINA SEA

PHILIPPINE SEA

Bonin Islands (JAPAN)

Volcano Islands (JAPAN)

Northern Marianas (U.S.)

Guam (U.S.) • Agana

PALAU ⊛ Koror

FEDERATED STATES OF MICRONESIA

Truk Is.

⊛ Palikir

MICRONESIA

Wake Island (U.S.)

Eniwetok I.

MARSHALL ISLANDS

Kwajalein Island

⊛ Majuro

Gilbert Islands • Tarawa

Yaren ⊛ **NAURU**

Midway Island (U.S.)

Johnston Island (U.S.)

Hawaiian Islands

Hawaii (U.S.)

Kingman Reef (U.S.)

Washington Island

Palmyra Island (U.S.)

Fanning Island

Howland I. (U.S.)

Baker I. (U.S.)

Jarvis I. (U.S.)

McKean I.

Gardner

Phoenix Islands

KIRIBATI

Starbuck Island

Tokelau (N.Z.)

Manihiki Island

Cook Islands (NEW ZEALAND)

Rarotonga Island

Marquesas Islands (FRANCE)

Tuamotu Archipelago (FRANCE)

French Polynesia

Society Islands (FRANCE)

Tahiti (FRANCE)

Papeete

Tubuai Islands (FRANCE)

Rapa Island (FRANCE)

P O L Y N E S I A

SAMOA

American Samoa

Pago Pago

Apia

Niue (N.Z.)

Nuku'alofa

TONGA

Wallis & Futuna (FRANCE)

TUVALU

Funafuti

FIJI

Suva

SOLOMON ISLANDS

Honiara ⊛

Guadalcanal I.

Espiritu Santo I.

VANUATU

Port-Vila

Malekula I.

New Caledonia (FRANCE)

Loyalty Islands (FRANCE)

Noumea

Norfolk Island (AUSTRALIA)

Kermadec Islands (NEW ZEALAND)

Chatham Islands (N.Z.)

Bounty Islands (N.Z.)

Auckland Islands (NEW ZEALAND)

NEW ZEALAND

TASMAN SEA

M E L A N E S I A

CORAL SEA

PAPUA NEW GUINEA

Port Moresby ⊛

New Guinea

Bismarck Archipelago

ARAFURA SEA

TIMOR SEA

Christmas Island (AUSTRALIA)

AUSTRALIA

INDIAN OCEAN

Pitcairn (U.K.)

Pitcairn Island

Ducie Island

Easter Island (CHILE)

N

Boundaries

⊛ National capitals

• Other cities

SCALE

1000 Miles

1000 Kilometers

500

500

0

0

Projection: Mercator

30°N, 15°N, Equator 0°, 15°S, 30°S, 45°S

120°W, 135°W, 150°W, 165°W, 180°, 165°E, 150°E, 135°E, 120°E

NORTH POLE map labels:
EUROPE
BARENTS SEA
KARA SEA
ASIA
LAPTEV SEA
NORWEGIAN SEA
GREENLAND SEA
Iceland
ATLANTIC OCEAN
ARCTIC OCEAN
NORTH POLE
Arctic Circle
International Date Line
PACK ICE
Greenland (DENMARK)
Queen Elizabeth Islands
Baffin Bay
NORTH MAGNETIC POLE
Baffin Island
BERING SEA
BEAUFORT SEA
NORTH AMERICA
PACIFIC OCEAN

150°E, 90°E, 30°E, 30°W, 60°W, 90°W, 120°W, 150°W, 180
80°N, 70°N, 60°N, 50°N, 60°N

SCALE
0 250 500 750 Miles
0 250 500 750 Kilometers
Projection: Polar Azimuthal Equidistant

SOUTH POLE map labels:
PACIFIC OCEAN
SOUTH AMERICA
AMUNDSEN SEA
PACK ICE
BELLINGSHAUSEN SEA
ROSS SEA
MARIE BYRD LAND
ANTARCTIC PENINSULA
ELLSWORTH LAND
Vinson Massif 16,066 ft. (4,897 m)
International Date Line
ROSS ICE SHELF
RONNE ICE SHELF
PACK ICE
WEDDELL SEA
EDITH RONNE LAND
QUEEN MAUD MOUNTAINS
Mount Markham over 14,275 ft. (over 4,351 m)
POLAR
SOUTH POLE
PLATEAU
FILCHNER ICE SHELF
COATS LAND
ATLANTIC OCEAN
SOUTH MAGNETIC POLE
ADELIE LAND
WILKES LAND
ANTARCTICA
ICE CAP
QUEEN MAUD LAND
INDIAN OCEAN
SHACKLETON ICE SHELF
AMERICAN HIGHLAND
ENDERBY LAND
Antarctic Circle

180°, 150°W, 120°W, 90°W, 60°W, 30°W, 30°E, 60°E, 90°E, 120°E, 150°E
70°S, 60°S, 50°S

SCALE
0 250 500 750 Miles
0 250 500 750 Kilometers
Projection: Polar Azimuthal Equidistant

SKILLS HANDBOOK

CONTENTS

Studying geography requires the ability to understand and use various tools. This Skills Handbook explains how to use maps, charts, and other graphics to help you learn about geography and the various regions of the world. Throughout this textbook, you will have the opportunity to improve these skills and build upon them.

GEOGRAPHIC

Dictionary

- globe
- grid
- latitude
- equator
- parallels
- degrees
- minutes
- longitude
- prime meridian
- meridians
- hemispheres
- continents
- islands
- ocean
- map
- map projections
- compass rose
- scale
- legend

MAPPING
THE EARTH

The Globe
A **globe** is a scale model of Earth. It is useful for looking at the entire Earth or at large areas of Earth's surface.

The pattern of lines that circle the globe in east-west and north-south directions is called a **grid**. The intersection of these imaginary lines helps us find places on Earth.

The east-west lines in the grid are lines of **latitude**. These imaginary lines measure distance north and south of the **equator**. The equator is an imaginary line that circles the globe halfway between the North and South Poles. Lines of latitude are called **parallels** because they are always parallel to the equator. Parallels measure distance from the equator in **degrees**. The symbol for degrees is °. Degrees are further divided into **minutes**. The symbol for minutes is ´. There are 60 minutes in a degree. Parallels north of the equator are labeled with an *N*. Those south of the equator are labeled with an *S*.

The north-south lines are lines of **longitude**. These imaginary lines pass through the Poles. They measure distance east and west of the **prime meridian**. The prime meridian is an imaginary line that runs through Greenwich, England. It represents 0° longitude. Lines of longitude are called **meridians**.

Lines of latitude range from 0°, for locations on the equator, to 90°N or 90°S, for locations at the Poles. See **Figure 1**. Lines of longitude range from 0° on the prime meridian to 180° on a meridian in the mid-Pacific Ocean. Meridians west of the prime meridian to 180° are labeled with a *W*. Those east of the prime meridian to 180° are labeled with an *E*. See **Figure 2**.

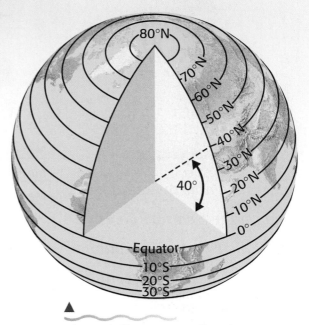

Figure 1: The east-west lines in the grid are lines of latitude.

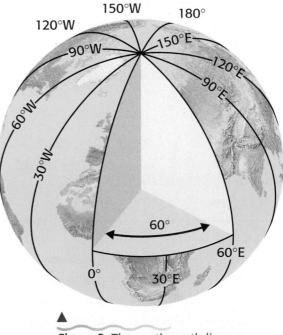

Figure 2: The north-south lines are lines of longitude.

NORTHERN HEMISPHERE

INDIAN OCEAN
ASIA
EUROPE
AFRICA
ARCTIC OCEAN
+ North Pole
PACIFIC OCEAN
ATLANTIC OCEAN
Equator
NORTH AMERICA

SOUTHERN HEMISPHERE

SOUTH AMERICA
Equator
PACIFIC OCEAN
ATLANTIC OCEAN
+ South Pole
ANTARCTICA
AFRICA
AUSTRALIA
INDIAN OCEAN

▶
Figure 3: The hemispheres

EASTERN HEMISPHERE

North Pole
EUROPE
ASIA
AFRICA
Equator
ATLANTIC OCEAN
INDIAN OCEAN
AUSTRALIA
Prime Meridian
ANTARCTICA
South Pole

The equator divides the globe into two halves, called **hemispheres**. See **Figure 3**. The half north of the equator is the Northern Hemisphere. The southern half is the Southern Hemisphere. The prime meridian and the 180° meridian divide the world into the Eastern Hemisphere and the Western Hemisphere. The prime meridian separates parts of Europe and Africa into two different hemispheres. To prevent this, some mapmakers divide the Eastern and Western hemispheres at 20° W. This places all of Europe and Africa in the Eastern Hemisphere.

Our planet's land surface is organized into seven large landmasses, called **continents**. They are identified in **Figure 3**. Landmasses smaller than continents and completely surrounded by water are called **islands**. Geographers also organize Earth's water surface into parts. The largest is the world **ocean**. Geographers divide the world ocean into the Pacific Ocean, the Atlantic Ocean, the Indian Ocean, and the Arctic Ocean. Lakes and seas are smaller bodies of water.

WESTERN HEMISPHERE

North Pole
NORTH AMERICA
ATLANTIC OCEAN
180°
Equator
PACIFIC OCEAN
SOUTH AMERICA
ANTARCTICA
South Pole

YOUR TURN

1. Look at the Student Atlas map on page A4. What islands are located near the intersection of latitude 20° N and longitude 160° W?

2. Name the four hemispheres. In which hemispheres is the United States located?

3. Name the continents of the world.

4. Name the oceans of the world.

MAPMAKING

A **map** is a flat diagram of all or part of Earth's surface. Mapmakers have different ways of showing our round Earth on flat maps. These different ways are called **map projections**. Because our planet is round, all flat maps lose some accuracy. Mapmakers must choose the type of map projection that is best for their purposes. Many map projections are one of three kinds: cylindrical, conic, or flat-plane.

◄ **Figure 4:** If you remove the peel from the orange and flatten the peel, it will stretch and tear. The larger the piece of peel, the more its shape is distorted as it is flattened. Also distorted are the distances between points on the peel.

▲ **Figure 5A:** Paper cylinder

Cylindrical projections are designed from a cylinder wrapped around the globe. See **Figure 5A**. The cylinder touches the globe only at the equator. The meridians are pulled apart and are parallel to each other instead of meeting at the Poles. This causes landmasses near the Poles to appear larger than they really are. **Figure 5B** is a Mercator projection, one type of cylindrical projection. The Mercator projection is useful for navigators because it shows true direction and shape. The Mercator projection for world maps, however, emphasizes the Northern Hemisphere. Africa and South America appear smaller than they really are.

◄

Figure 5B: A Mercator projection, although accurate near the equator, distorts distances between regions of land. This projection also distorts the sizes of areas near the poles.

Conic projections are designed from a cone placed over the globe. See **Figure 6A**. A conic projection is most accurate along the lines of latitude where it touches the globe. It retains almost true shape and size. Conic projections are most useful for areas that have long east-west dimensions, such as the United States. See the map in **Figure 6B**.

Figure 6A: Paper cone

Figure 6B: Conic projection

Flat-plane projections are designed from a plane touching the globe at one point, such as at the North Pole or South Pole. See **Figures 7A** and **7B**. A flat-plane projection is useful for showing true direction for airplane pilots and ship navigators. It also shows true area. However, it distorts true shape.

Figure 7A: Flat plane

Figure 7B: Flat-plane projection

The Robinson projection is a compromise between size and shape distortions. It often is used for world maps, such as the map on page 76. The minor distortions in size at high latitudes on Robinson projections are balanced by realistic shapes at the middle and low latitudes.

YOUR TURN

1. What are three major kinds of map projections?
2. Why is a Robinson projection often used for world maps?
3. What kind of projection is a Mercator map?
4. When would a mapmaker choose to use a conic projection?

MAP ESSENTIALS

In some ways, maps are like messages sent out in code. Mapmakers provide certain elements that help us translate these codes. These elements help us understand the message they are presenting about a particular part of the world. Of these elements, almost all maps have directional indicators, scales, and legends, or keys. **Figure 8**, a map of East Asia, has all three elements.

A directional indicator shows which directions are north, south, east, and west. Some mapmakers use a "north arrow," which points toward the North Pole. Remember, "north" is not always at the top of a map. The way a map is drawn and the location of directions on that map depend on the perspective of the mapmaker. Maps in this textbook indicate direction by using a **compass rose ①**. A compass rose has arrows that point to all four principal directions, as shown in **Figure 8**.

▲
Figure 8: East and Southeast Asia—Physical

Mapmakers use scales to represent distances between points on a map. Scales may appear on maps in several different forms. The maps in this textbook provide a line **scale ②**. Scales give distances in miles and kilometers (km).

To find the distance between two points on the map in **Figure 8**, place a piece of paper so that the edge connects the two points. Mark the location of each point on the paper with a line or dot. Then, compare the distance between the two dots with the map's line scale. The number on the top of the scale gives the distance in miles. The number on the bottom gives the distance in kilometers. Because the distances are given in intervals, you will have to approximate the actual distance on the scale.

ELEVATION

FEET		METERS
13,120		4,000
6,560		2,000
1,640		500
656		200
(Sea level) 0		0 (Sea level)
Below sea level		Below sea level

The **legend** ③, or key, explains what the symbols on the map represent. Point symbols are used to specify the location of things, such as cities, that do not take up much space on a large-scale map. Some legends, such as the one in **Figure 8**, show which colors represent certain elevations. Other maps might have legends with symbols or colors that represent things such as roads. Legends can also show economic resources, land use, population density, and climate.

Size comparison of Canada to the contiguous United States

Physical maps at the beginning of each unit have size comparison maps ④. An outline of the mainland United States (not including Alaska and Hawaii) is compared to the area under study in that chapter. These size comparison maps help you understand the size of the areas you are studying in relation to the size of the United States.

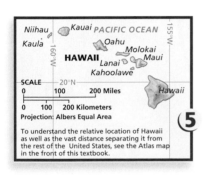

Niihau • Kauai PACIFIC OCEAN
Kaula
Oahu
HAWAII Molokai
Lanai Maui
Kahoolawe

Hawaii

SCALE — 20°N
0   100   200 Miles

0   100   200 Kilometers
Projection: Albers Equal Area

To understand the relative location of Hawaii as well as the vast distance separating it from the rest of the United States, see the Atlas map in the front of this textbook.

Inset maps are sometimes used to show a small part of a larger map. Mapmakers also use inset maps to show areas that are far away from the areas shown on the main map. Maps of the United States, for example, often include inset maps of Alaska and Hawaii ⑤. Those two states are too far from the other 48 states to accurately represent the true distance on the main map. Subject areas in inset maps can be drawn to a scale different from the scale used on the main map.

YOUR TURN

Look at the Student Atlas map on pages A4 and A5.

1. Locate the compass rose. What country is directly west of Madagascar in Africa?

2. What island country is located southeast of India?

3. Locate the distance scale. Using the inset map, find the approximate distance in miles and kilometers from Oslo, Norway, to Stockholm, Sweden.

4. What is the capital of Brazil? What other cities are shown in Brazil?

WORKING
WITH MAPS

The Atlas at the front of this textbook includes two kinds of maps: physical and political. At the beginning of most units in this textbook, you will find five kinds of maps. These physical, political, climate, population, and land use and resources maps provide different kinds of information about the region you will study in that unit. These maps are accompanied by questions. Some questions ask you to show how the information on each of the maps might be related.

Mapmakers often combine physical and political features into one map. Physical maps, such as the one in **Figure 8** on page S6, show important physical features in a region, including major mountains and mountain ranges, rivers, oceans and other bodies of water, deserts, and plains. Physical-political maps also show important political features, such as national borders, state and provincial boundaries, and capitals and other important cities. You will find a physical-political map at the beginning of most chapters.

▲

Figure 9: East and Southeast Asia—Climate

Mapmakers use climate maps to show the most important weather patterns in certain areas. Climate maps throughout this textbook use color to show the various climate regions of the world. See **Figure 9**. Colors that identify climate types are found in a legend with each map. Boundaries between climate regions do not indicate an immediate change in the main weather conditions between two climate regions. Instead, boundaries show the general areas of gradual change between climate regions.

Figure 10: East and Southeast Asia—Population

Population maps show where people live in a particular region. They also show how crowded, or densely populated, regions are. Population maps throughout this textbook use color to show population density. See **Figure 10**. Each color represents a certain number of people living within a square mile or square kilometer. Population maps also use symbols to show metropolitan areas with populations of a particular size. These symbols and colors are shown in a legend.

Land Use and Resources maps show the important resources of a region. See **Figure 11**. Symbols and colors are used to show information about economic development, such as where industry is located or where farming is most common. The meanings of each symbol and color are shown in a legend.

Figure 11: East and Southeast Asia—Land Use and Resources

YOUR TURN

1. What is the purpose of a climate map?

2. Look at the population map. What is the population density of the area around Qingdao in northern China?

3. What energy resource is found near Ho Chi Minh City?

USING

GRAPHS, DIAGRAMS, CHARTS, AND TABLES

Bar graphs are a visual way to present information. The bar graph in **Figure 12** shows the imports and exports of the countries of southern Europe. The amount of imports and exports in billions of dollars is listed on the left side of the graph. Along the bottom of the graph are the names of the countries of southern Europe. Above each country or group of countries is a vertical bar. The top of the bar corresponds to a number along the left side of the graph. For example, Italy imports $200 billion worth of goods.

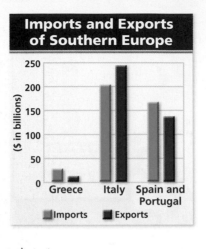

Figure 12: Reading a bar graph

Often, line graphs are used to show such things as trends, comparisons, and size. The line graph in **Figure 13** shows the population growth of the world over time. The information on the left shows the number of people in billions. The years being studied are listed along the bottom. Lines connect points that show the population in billions at each year under study. This line graph projects population growth into the future.

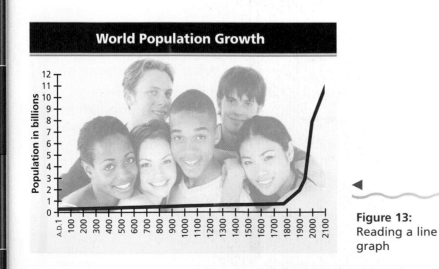

Figure 13: Reading a line graph

A pie graph shows how a whole is divided into parts. In this kind of graph, a circle represents the whole. The wedges represent the parts. Bigger wedges represent larger parts of the whole. The pie graph in **Figure 14** shows the percentages of the world's coffee beans produced by various groups of countries. Brazil is the largest grower. It grows 25 percent of the world's coffee beans.

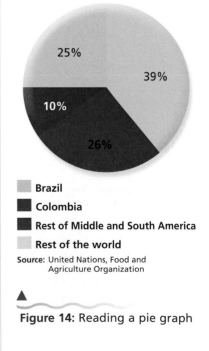

Major Producers of Coffee

- Brazil
- Colombia
- Rest of Middle and South America
- Rest of the world

Source: United Nations, Food and Agriculture Organization

Figure 14: Reading a pie graph

Age structure diagrams show the number of males and females by age group. These diagrams are split into two sides, one for male and one for female. Along the bottom are numbers that show the number of males or females in the age groups. The age groups are listed on the side of the diagram. The wider the base of a country's diagram, the younger the population of that country. The wider the top of a country's diagram, the older the population.

Some countries have so many younger people that their age structure diagrams are shaped like pyramids. For this reason, these diagrams are sometimes called population pyramids. However, in some countries the population is more evenly distributed by age group. For example, see the age structure diagram for Germany in **Figure 15**. Germany's population is older. It is not growing as fast as countries with younger populations.

Germany's Population, 1997

Source: U.S. Census Bureau

Figure 15: Reading an age structure diagram

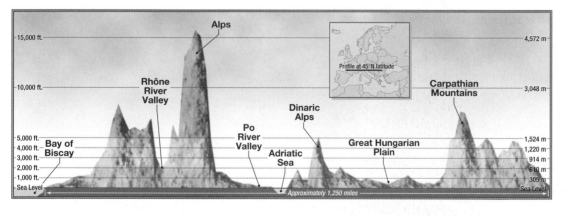

Figure 16: Reading an elevation profile

Each unit atlas includes an elevation profile. See **Figure 16**. It is a side view, or profile, of a region along a line drawn between two points.

Vertical and horizontal distances are figured differently on elevation profiles. The vertical distance (the height of a mountain, for example) is exaggerated when compared to the horizontal distance between the two points. This technique is called vertical exaggeration. If the vertical scale were not exaggerated, even tall mountains would appear as small bumps on an elevation profile.

In each unit and chapter on the various regions of the world, you will find tables that provide basic information about the countries under study.

The countries of Spain and Portugal are listed on the left in the table in **Figure 17**. You can match statistical information on the right with the name of each country listed on the left. The categories of information are listed across the top of the table.

Graphic organizers can help you understand certain ideas and concepts. For example, the diagram in **Figure 18** helps you think about the uses of water. In this diagram, one water use goes in each oval. Graphic organizers can help you focus on key facts in your study of geography.

Time lines provide highlights of important events over a period of time. The time line in **Figure 19** begins at the left with 5000 B.C., when rice was first cultivated in present-day China. The time line highlights important events that have shaped the human and political geography of China.

Spain and Portugal

COUNTRY	POPULATION/ GROWTH RATE	LIFE EXPECTANCY	LITERACY RATE	PER CAPITA GDP
Portugal	10,066,253 0.2%	72, male 80, female	87%	$15,800
Spain	40,037,995 0.1%	75, male 83, female	97%	$18,000
United States	281,421,906 0.9%	74, male 80, female	97%	$36,200

Sources: Central Intelligence Agency, *The World Factbook 2001;* U.S. Census Bureau

Figure 17: Reading a table

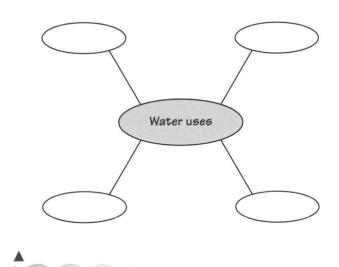

Water uses

Figure 18: Graphic organizer

Historical China: A Time Line

Qin becomes China's first emperor
200s B.C.

Rise of Ming dynasty
1368

Cultural Revolution
1966—1976

| 5000 B.C. | A.D. 1 | 1000 | 1200 | 1400 | 1600 | 1800 | 2000 |

3000 B.C.
First rice farmers cultivate the area near the Chang River

206 B.C. —A.D. 220
Han dynasty dominates China

1200s
Mongols invade China

1912
Republic established with the overthrow of the Manchu dynasty

1989
Government troops crush protesters in Tiananmen Square

Figure 19: Reading a time line

Corn: From Field to Consumer

A Corn can be processed in a variety of ways. Some corn is cooked and then canned.

B Corn is ground and used for livestock feed.

C Corn also might be wet-milled or dry-milled. Then grain parts are used to make different products.

D Corn by-products, such as cornstarch and corn syrup, are used to make breads, breakfast cereals, puddings, and snack foods. Corn oil is used for cooking.

Figure 20: Reading a flowchart

Flowcharts are visual guides that explain different processes. They lead the reader from one step to the next, sometimes providing both illustrations and text. The flowchart in **Figure 20** shows the different steps involved in harvesting corn and preparing it for use by consumers. The flowchart takes you through the steps of harvesting and processing corn. Captions guide you through flowcharts.

YOUR TURN

1. Look at the statistical table for Spain and Portugal in Figure 17. Which countries have the highest literacy rate?

2. Look at the China time line in Figure 19. Name two important events in China's history between 1200 and 1400.

3. Look at Figure 20. What are three corn products?

READING

A TIME-ZONE MAP

The sun is not directly overhead everywhere on Earth at the same time. Clocks are set to reflect the difference in the sun's position. Our planet rotates on its axis once every 24 hours. In other words, in one hour, it makes one twenty-fourth of a complete revolution. Since there are 360 degrees in a circle, we know that the planet turns 15 degrees of longitude each hour. (360° ÷ 24 = 15°) We also know that the planet turns in a west-to-east direction. Therefore, if a place on Earth has the sun directly overhead at this moment (noon), then a place 15 degrees to the west will have the sun directly overhead one hour from now. During that hour the planet will have rotated 15 degrees. As a result, Earth is divided into 24 time zones. Thus, time is an hour earlier for each 15 degrees you move westward on Earth. Time is an hour later for each 15 degrees you move eastward on Earth.

By international agreement, longitude is measured from the prime meridian. This meridian passes through the Royal Observatory in Greenwich, England. Time also is measured from Greenwich and is called Greenwich mean time (GMT). For each time zone east of the prime meridian, clocks must be set one hour ahead of GMT. For each time zone west of Greenwich, clocks are set back one hour from GMT. When it is noon in London, it is 1:00 P.M. in Oslo, Norway, one time zone east. However, it is 7 A.M. in New York City, five time zones west.

WORLD TIME ZONES

As you can see by looking at the map below, time zones do not follow meridians exactly. Political boundaries are often used to draw time-zone lines. In Europe and Africa, for example, time zones follow national boundaries. The mainland United States, meanwhile, is divided into four major time zones: Eastern, Central, Mountain, and Pacific. Alaska and Hawaii are in separate time zones to the west of the mainland.

Some countries have made changes in their time zones. For example, most of the United States has daylight savings time in the summer in order to have more evening hours of daylight.

The international date line is a north-south line that runs through the Pacific Ocean. It is located at 180°, although it sometimes varies from that meridian to avoid dividing countries.

At 180°, the time is 12 hours from Greenwich time. There is a time difference of 24 hours between the two sides of the 180° meridian. The 180° meridian is called the international date line because when you cross it, the date and day change. As you cross the date line from the west to the east, you gain a day. If you travel from east to west, you lose a day.

YOUR TURN

1. In which time zone do you live? Check your time now. What time is it in New York?

2. How many hours behind New York is Anchorage, Alaska?

3. How many time zones are there in Africa?

4. If it is 9 A.M. in the middle of Greenland, what time is it in São Paulo?

WRITING
ABOUT GEOGRAPHY

Writers have many different reasons for writing. In your study of geography, you might write to accomplish many different tasks. You might write a paragraph or short paper to express your own personal feelings or thoughts about a topic or event. You might also write a paper to tell your class about an event, person, place, or thing. Sometimes you may want to write in order to persuade or convince readers to agree with a certain statement or to act in a particular way.

You will find different kinds of questions at the end of each section, chapter, and unit throughout this textbook. Some questions will require in-depth answers. The following guidelines for writing will help you structure your answers so that they clearly express your thoughts.

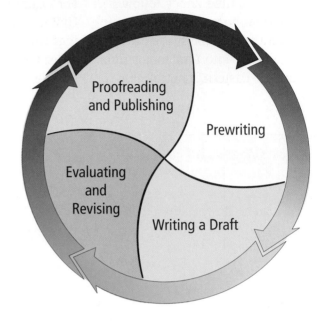

The Writing Process

Proofreading and Publishing

Prewriting

Evaluating and Revising

Writing a Draft

Prewriting Prewriting is the process of thinking about and planning what to write. It includes gathering and organizing information into a clear plan. Writers use the prewriting stage to identify their audience and purpose for what is to be written.

Often, writers do research to get the information they need. Research can include finding primary and secondary sources. You will read about primary and secondary sources later in this handbook.

Writing a Draft After you have gathered and arranged your information, you are ready to begin writing. Many paragraphs are structured in the following way:

- **Topic Sentence:** The topic sentence states the main idea of the paragraph. Putting the main idea into the form of a topic sentence helps keep the paragraph focused.

- **Body:** The body of a paragraph develops and supports the main idea. Writers use a variety of information, including facts, opinions, and examples, to support the main idea.

- **Conclusion:** The conclusion summarizes the writer's main points or restates the main idea.

Evaluating and Revising Read over your paragraphs and make sure you have clearly expressed what you wanted to say. Sometimes it helps to read your paragraphs aloud or to ask someone else to read them. Such methods help you identify rough or unclear sentences and passages. Revise the parts of your paragraph that are not clear or that stray from your main idea. You might want to add, cut, reorder, or replace sentences to make your paragraph as clear as possible.

Proofreading and Publishing Before you write your final draft, read over your paragraphs and correct any errors in grammar, spelling, sentence structure, or punctuation. Common mistakes include misspelled place-names, incomplete sentences, and improper use of punctuation, such as commas. You should use a dictionary and standard grammar guides to help you proofread your work.

After you have revised and corrected your draft, neatly rewrite your paper. Make sure your final version is clean and free of mistakes. The appearance of your final version can affect how your audience perceives and understands your writing.

Practicing the Skill

1. What are the steps in the writing process?
2. How are most paragraphs formed?
3. Write a paragraph or short paper about your community for a visitor. When you have finished your draft, review it and then mark and correct any errors in grammar, spelling, sentence structure, or punctuation. At the bottom of your draft, list key resources—such as a dictionary—that you used to check and correct your work. Then write your final draft. When you are finished with your work, use pencils or pens of different colors to underline and identify the topic sentence, body, and conclusion of your paragraph.

DOING
RESEARCH

Research is at the heart of geographic inquiry. To complete a research project, you may need to use resources other than this textbook. For example, you may want to research specific places or issues not discussed in this textbook. You may also want to learn more about a certain topic that you have studied in a chapter. Following the guidelines below will help you plan and complete research projects for your class.

Planning The first step in approaching a research project is planning. Planning involves deciding on a topic and finding information about that topic.

- **Decide on a Topic.** Before starting any research project, you should decide on one topic. If you are working with a group, all group members should participate in choosing a topic. Sometimes a topic will be assigned to you, but at other times you may have to choose your own. Once you have settled on a topic, make sure you can find resources to help you research it.

- **Find Information.** In order to find a particular book, you need to know how libraries organize their materials. Libraries classify their books by assigning each book a call number that tells you its location. To find the call number, look in the library's card catalog. The card catalog lists books by author, by title, and by subject. Many libraries today have computerized card catalogs. Libraries often provide instructions on how to use their computerized card catalogs. If no instructions are available, ask a library staff member for help.

Most libraries have encyclopedias, gazetteers, atlases, almanacs, and periodical indexes. Encyclopedias contain geographic, economic, and political data on individual countries, states, and cities. They also include discussions of historical events, religion, social and cultural issues, and much more. A gazetteer is a geographical dictionary that lists significant natural physical features and other places. An atlas contains maps and visual representations of geographic data. To find up-to-date facts, you can use almanacs, yearbooks, and periodical indexes.

References like *The World Almanac and Book of Facts* include historical information and a variety of statistics. Periodical indexes, particularly *The Reader's Guide to Periodical Literature*, can help you locate informative articles published in magazines. *The New York Times Index* catalogs the newspaper articles published in the *New York Times*.

You may also want to find information on the World Wide Web. The World Wide Web is the part of the Internet where people put files called Web sites for other people to access. To search the World Wide Web, you must use a search engine. A search engine will provide you with a list of Web sites that contain keywords relating to your topic. Search engines also provide Web directories, which allow you to browse Web sites by subject.

Organizing Organization is key to completing research projects of any size. If you are working with a group, every group member should have an assigned task in researching, writing, and completing your project. You and all the group members should keep track of the materials that you used to conduct your research. Then compile those sources into a bibliography and turn it in with your research project.

In addition, information collected during research should be organized in an efficient way. A common method of organizing research information is to use index cards. If you have used an outline to organize your research, you can code each index card with the appropriate main idea number and supporting detail letter from the outline. Then write the relevant information on that card. You might also use computer files in the same way. These methods will help you keep track of what information you have collected and what information you still need to gather.

Some projects will require you to conduct original research. This original research might require you to interview people, conduct surveys, collect unpublished information about your community, or draw a map of a local place. Before you do your original research, make sure you have all the necessary background information. Also, create a pre-research plan so that you can make sure all the necessary tools, such as research sources, are available.

Completing and Presenting Your Project Once you have completed your research project, you will need to present the information you have gathered in some fashion. Many times, you or your group will simply need to write a paper about your research. Research can also be presented in many other ways, however. For example, you could make an audiotape, a drawing, a poster board, a video, or a Web page to explain your research.

Practicing the Skill

1. What kinds of references would you need to research specific current events around the world?
2. Work with a group of four other students to plan, organize, and complete a research project on a topic of interest in your local community. For example, you might want to learn more about a particular individual or event that influenced your community's history. Other topics might include the economic features, physical features, and political features of your community.

ANALYZING

When conducting research, it is important to use a variety of primary and secondary sources of information. There are many sources of first-hand geographical information, including diaries, letters, editorials, and legal documents such as land titles. All of these are primary sources. Newspaper articles are also considered primary sources, although they generally are written after the fact. Other primary sources include personal memoirs and autobiographies, which people usually write late in life. Paintings and photographs of particular events, persons, places, or things make up a visual record and are also considered primary sources. Because

they allow us to take a close-up look at a topic, primary sources are valuable geographic tools.

Secondary sources are descriptions or interpretations of events written after the events have occurred by persons who did not participate in the events they describe. Geography textbooks such as this one, as well as biographies, encyclopedias, and other reference works, are examples of secondary sources. Writers of secondary sources have the advantage of seeing what happened beyond the moment or place that is being studied. They can provide a perspective wider than that available to one person at a specific time.

How to Study Primary and Secondary Sources

1. **Study the Material Carefully.** Consider the nature of the material. Is it verbal or visual? Is it based on firsthand information or on the accounts of others? Note the major ideas and supporting details.

2. **Consider the Audience.** Ask yourself, "For whom was this message originally meant?" Whether a message was intended for the general public or for a specific private audience may have shaped its style or content.

3. **Check for Bias.** Watch for words or phrases that present a one-sided view of a person or situation.

4. **Compare Sources.** Study more than one source on a topic. Comparing sources gives you a more complete and balanced account of geographical events and their relationships to one another.

Practicing the Skill

1. What distinguishes secondary sources from primary sources?
2. What advantages do secondary sources have over primary sources?
3. Why should you consider the intended audience of a source?
4. Of the following, identify which are primary sources and which are secondary sources: a newspaper, a private journal, a biography, an editorial cartoon, a deed to property, a snapshot of a family vacation, a magazine article about the history of Thailand, an autobiography. How might some of these sources prove to be both primary and secondary sources?

CRITICAL
THINKING

The study of geography requires more than analyzing and understanding tools like graphs and maps. Throughout Holt People, Places, and Change, *you are asked to think critically about some of the information you are studying. Critical thinking is the reasoned judgment of information and ideas. The development of critical thinking skills is essential to learning more about the world around you. Helping you develop critical thinking skills is an important goal of* Holt People, Places, and Change. *The following critical thinking skills appear in the section reviews and chapter reviews of the textbook.*

Summarizing involves briefly restating information gathered from a larger body of information. Much of the writing in this textbook is summarizing. The geographical data in this textbook has been collected from many sources. Summarizing all the qualities of a region or country involves studying a large body of cultural, economic, geological, and historical information.

Finding the main idea is the ability to identify the main point in a set of information. This textbook is designed to help you focus on the main ideas in geography. The Read to Discover questions in each chapter help you identify the main ideas in each section. To find the main idea in any piece of writing, first read the title and introduction. These two elements may point to the main ideas covered in the text.

Also, write down questions about the subject that you think might be answered in the text. Having such questions in mind will focus your reading. Pay attention to any headings or subheadings, which may provide a basic outline of the major ideas. Finally, as you read, note sentences that provide additional details from the general statements that those details support. For example, a trail of facts may lead to a conclusion that expresses the main idea.

Comparing and contrasting

involve examining events, points of view, situations, or styles to identify their similarities and differences. Comparing focuses on both the similarities and the differences. Contrasting focuses only on the differences. Studying similarities and differences between people and things can give you clues about the human and physical geography of a region.

Buddhist shrine, Myanmar   *Stave church, Norway*

Supporting a point of view

involves identifying an issue, deciding what you think about it, and persuasively expressing your position. Your stand should be based on specific information. When taking a stand, state your position clearly and give reasons that support it.

Identifying points of view

involves noting the factors that influence the opinions of an individual or group. A person's point of view includes beliefs and attitudes that are shaped by factors such as age, gender, race, and economic status. Identifying points of view helps us examine why people see things as they do. It also reinforces the realization that people's views may change over time or with a change in circumstances.

Identifying bias

is an important critical thinking skill in the study of any subject. When a point of view is highly personal or based on unreasoned judgment, it is considered biased. Sometimes, a person's actions reflect bias. At its most extreme, bias can be expressed in violent actions against members of a particular culture or group. A less obvious form of bias is a stereotype, or a generalization about a group of people. Stereotypes tend to ignore differences within groups.

Political protest, India

Probably the hardest form of cultural bias to detect has to do with perspective, or point of view. When we use our own culture and experiences as a point of reference from which to make statements about other cultures, we are showing a form of bias called ethnocentrism.

Analyzing

is the process of breaking something down into parts and examining the relationships between those parts. For example, to understand the processes behind forest loss, you might study issues involving economic development, the overuse of resources, and pollution.

Evaluating

involves assessing the significance or overall importance of something. For example, you might evaluate the success of certain environmental protection laws or the effect of foreign trade on a society. You should base your evaluation on standards that others will understand and are likely to consider valid. For example, an evaluation of international relations after World War II might look at the political and economic tensions between the United States and the Soviet Union. Such an evaluation would also consider the ways those tensions affected other countries around the world.

Identifying cause and effect is part of interpreting the relationships between geographical events. A cause is any action that leads to an event; the outcome of that action is an effect. To explain geographical developments, geographers may point out multiple causes and effects. For example, geographers studying pollution in a region might note a number of causes.

Ecuador rain forest

Cleared forest, Kenya

Drawing inferences and drawing conclusions are two methods of critical thinking that require you to use evidence to explain events or information in a logical way. Inferences and conclusions are opinions, but these opinions are based on facts and reasonable deductions.

For example, suppose you know that people are moving in greater and greater numbers to cities in a particular country. You also know that poor weather has hurt farming in rural areas while industry has been expanding in cities. You might be able to understand from this information some of the reasons for the increased migration to cities. You could conclude that poor harvests have pushed people to leave rural areas. You might also conclude that the possibility of finding work in new industries may be pulling people to cities.

Drought in West Texas   *Dallas, Texas*

Making generalizations and making predictions are two critical thinking skills that require you to form specific ideas from a large body of information. When you are asked to generalize, you must take into account many different pieces of information. You then form a main concept that can be applied to all of the pieces of information. Many times making generalizations can help you see trends. Looking at trends can help you form a prediction. Making a prediction involves looking at trends in the past and present and making an educated guess about how these trends will affect the future.

Communications technology, rural Brazil

SKILLS

Like you, many people around the world have faced difficult problems and decisions. By using appropriate skills such as problem solving and decision making, you will be better able to choose a solution or make a decision on important issues. The following activities will help you develop and practice these skills.

Decision Making

Decision making involves choosing between two or more options. Listed below are guidelines to help you with making decisions.

1. **Identify a situation that requires a decision.** Think about your current situation. What issue are you faced with that requires you to take some sort of action?

2. **Gather information.** Think about the issue. Examine the causes of the issue or problem and consider how it affects you and others.

3. **Identify your options.** Consider the actions that you could take to address the issue. List these options so that you can compare them.

4. **Make predictions about consequences.** Predict the consequences of taking the actions listed for each of your options. Compare these possible consequences. Be sure the option you choose produces the results you want.

5. **Take action to implement a decision.** Choose a course of action from your available options, and put it into effect.

Problem Solving

Problem solving involves many of the steps of decision making. Listed below are guidelines to help you solve problems.

1. **Identify the problem.** Identify just what the problem or difficulty is that you are facing. Sometimes you face a difficult situation made up of several different problems. Each problem may require its own solution.

2. **Gather information.** Conduct research on any important issues related to the problem. Try to find the answers to questions like the following: What caused this problem? Who or what does it affect? When did it start?

3. **List and consider options.** Look at the problem and the answers to the questions you asked in Step 2. List and then think about all the possible ways in which the problem could be solved. These are your options—possible solutions to the problem.

4. **Examine advantages and disadvantages.** Consider the advantages and disadvantages of all the options that you have listed. Make sure that you consider the possible long-term effects of each possible solution. You should also determine what steps you will need to take to achieve each possible solution. Some suggestions may sound good at first but may turn out to be impractical or hard to achieve.

5. **Choose and implement a solution.** Select the best solution from your list and take the steps to achieve it.

6. **Evaluate the effectiveness of the solution.** When you have completed the steps needed to put your plan into action, evaluate its effectiveness. Is the problem solved? Were the results worth the effort required? Has the solution itself created any other problems?

Practicing the Skill

1. Chapter 24, Section 2: East Africa's History and Culture, describes the challenges of religious and ethnic conflict occurring in the region. Imagine that you are an ambassador to Rwanda. Use the decision-making guidelines to help you come up with a plan to help resolve the problems there. Be prepared to defend your decision.

2. Identify a similar problem discussed in another chapter and apply the problem-solving process to come up with a solution.

Becoming a Strategic Reader

by Dr. Judith Irvin

Everywhere you look, print is all around us. In fact, you would have a hard time stopping yourself from reading. In a normal day, you might read cereal boxes, movie posters, notes from friends, T-shirts, instructions for video games, song lyrics, catalogs, billboards, information on the Internet, magazines, the newspaper, and much, much more. Each form of print is read differently depending on your purpose for reading. You read a menu differently from poetry, and a motorcycle magazine is read differently than a letter from a friend. Good readers switch easily from one type of text to another. In fact, they probably do not even think about it, they just do it.

When you read, it is helpful to use a strategy to remember the most important ideas. You can use a strategy before you read to help connect information you already know to the new information you will encounter. Before you read, you can also predict what a text will be about by using a previewing strategy. During the reading you can use a strategy to help you focus on main ideas, and after reading you can use a strategy to help you organize what you learned so that you can remember it later. *Holt People, Places, and Change* was designed to help you more easily understand the ideas you read. Important reading strategies employed in *Holt People, Places, and Change* include:

A Tools to help you **preview and predict** what the text will be about

B Ways to help you **use and analyze visual information**

C Ideas to help you **organize the information** you have learned

A. Previewing and Predicting

How can I figure out what the text is about before I even start reading a section?

Previewing and **predicting** are good methods to help you understand the text. If you take the time to preview and predict before you read, the text will make more sense to you during your reading.

1 Usually, your teacher will set the purpose for reading. After reading some new information, you may be asked to write a summary, take a test, or complete some other type of activity.

"After reading about Spain and Portugal, you will work with a partner to present a history of the countries to a travel group..."

Previewing and Predicting

step 1 Identify your purpose for reading. Ask yourself what you will do with this information once you have finished reading.

▼

step 2 Ask yourself what is the main idea of the text and what are the key vocabulary words you need to know.

▼

step 3 Use signal words to help identify the structure of the text.

▼

step 4 Connect the information to what you already know.

2 As you preview the text, use **graphic signals** such as headings, subheadings, and boldface type to help you determine what is important in the text. Each section of *Holt People, Places, and Change* opens by giving you important clues to help you preview the material.

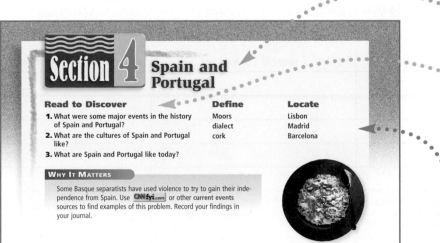

Section 4 Spain and Portugal

Read to Discover
1. What were some major events in the history of Spain and Portugal?
2. What are the cultures of Spain and Portugal like?
3. What are Spain and Portugal like today?

Define
Moors
dialect
cork

Locate
Lisbon
Madrid
Barcelona

WHY IT MATTERS

Some Basque separatists have used violence to try to gain their independence from Spain. Use **CNNfyi.com** or other current events sources to find examples of this problem. Record your findings in your journal.

Paella, a popular dish in Spain

Looking at the section's **main heading** and subheadings can give you an idea of what is to come.

Read to Discover questions give you clues as to the section's main ideas.

Define and **Locate** terms let you know the key vocabulary and places you will encounter in the section.

3 Other tools that can help you in previewing are **signal words**. These words prepare you to think in a certain way. For example, when you see words such as *similar to, same as,* or *different from,* you know that the text will probably compare and contrast two or more ideas. Signal words indicate how the ideas in the text relate to each other. Look at the list below for some of the most common signal words grouped by the type of text structures they include.

SIGNAL WORDS

Cause and Effect	Compare and Contrast	Description	Problem and Solution	Sequence or Chronological Order
because	different from	for instance	the question is	not long after
since	same as	for example	a solution	next
consequently	similar to	such as	one answer is	then
this led to...so	as opposed to	to illustrate		initially
if...then	instead of	in addition		before
nevertheless	although	most importantly		after
accordingly	however	another		finally
because of	compared with	furthermore		preceding
as a result of	as well as	first, second ...		following
in order to	either...or			on (date)
may be due to	but			over the years
for this reason	on the other hand			today
not only...but	unless			when

4 Learning something new requires that you connect it in some way with something you already know. This means you have to think before you read and while you read. You may want to use a chart like this one to remind yourself of the information already familiar to you and to come up with questions you want answered in your reading. The chart will also help you organize your ideas after you have finished reading.

What I know	What I want to know	What I learned

B. Use and Analyze Visual Information

How can all the pictures, maps, graphs, and time lines with the text help me be a stronger reader?

Using visual information can help you understand and remember the information presented in *Holt People, Places, and Change*. Good readers make a picture in their mind when they read. The pictures, charts, graphs, and diagrams that occur throughout *Holt People, Places, and Change* are placed strategically to increase your understanding.

1 You might ask yourself questions like these:

Why did the writer include this image with the text? What details about this image are mentioned in the text?

Analyzing Visual Information

step 1 As you preview the text, ask yourself how the visual information relates to the text.

▼

step 2 Generate questions based on the visual information.

▼

step 3 After reading the text, go back and review the visual information again.

▼

step 4 Connect the information to what you already know.

2 After you have read the text, see if you can answer your own questions.

→ Why are windmills important?

→ What technology do windmills use to pump water?

→ How might environment affect the use of windmills?

2 Maps, graphs, and charts help you organize information about a place. You might ask questions like these:

How does this map support what I have read in the text?

What does the information in this bar graph add to the text discussion?

→ *What is the purpose of this map?*

→ *What special features does the map show?*

→ *What do the colors, lines, and symbols on the map represent?*

Land Use and Resources

→ *What information is the writer trying to present with this graph?*

→ *Why did the writer use a bar graph to organize this information?*

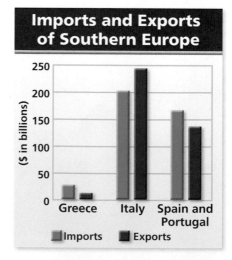

Imports and Exports of Southern Europe

3 After reading the text, go back and review the visual information again.

4 Connect the information to what you already know.

C. Organize Information

Once I learn new information, how do I keep it all straight so that I will remember it?

To help you remember what you have read, you need to find a way of **organizing information**. Two good ways of doing this are by using graphic organizers and concept maps. **Graphic organizers** help you understand important relationships—such as cause and effect, compare/contrast, sequence of events, and problem/solution—within the text. **Concept maps** provide a useful tool to help you focus on the text's main ideas and organize supporting details.

Identifying Relationships

Using graphic organizers will help you recall important ideas from the section and give you a study tool you can use to prepare for a quiz or test or to help with a writing assignment. Some of the most common types of graphic organizers are shown below.

❱ Cause and Effect

Events in history cause people to react in a certain way. Cause-and-effect patterns show the relationship between results and the ideas or events that made the results occur. You may want to represent cause-and-effect relationships as one cause leading to multiple effects,

or as a chain of cause-and-effect relationships.

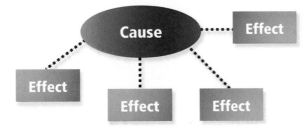

Constructing Graphic Organizers

step 1 Preview the text, looking for signal words and the main idea.

▼

step 2 Form a hypothesis as to which type of graphic organizer would work best to display the information presented.

▼

step 3 Work individually or with your classmates to create a visual representation of what you read.

▶ **Comparing and Contrasting**

Graphic organizers are often useful when you are comparing or contrasting information. Compare-and-contrast diagrams point out similarities and differences between two concepts or ideas.

▶ **Sequencing**

Keeping track of dates and the order in which events took place is essential to understanding the history and geography of a place. Sequence or chronological-order diagrams show events or ideas in the order in which they happened.

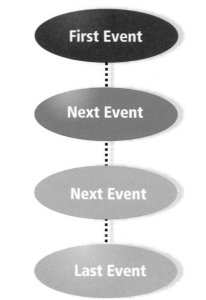

▶ **Problem and Solution**

Problem-solution patterns identify at least one problem, offer one or more solutions to the problem, and explain or predict outcomes of the solutions.

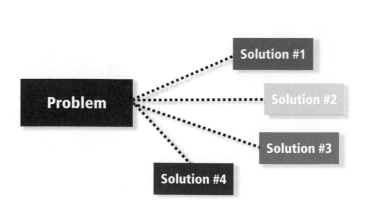

Identifying Main Ideas and Supporting Details

One special type of graphic organizer is the concept map. A concept map allows you to zero in on the most important points of the text. The map is made up of lines, boxes, circles, and/or arrows. It can be as simple or as complex as you need it to be to accurately represent the text. Here are a few examples of concept maps you might use.

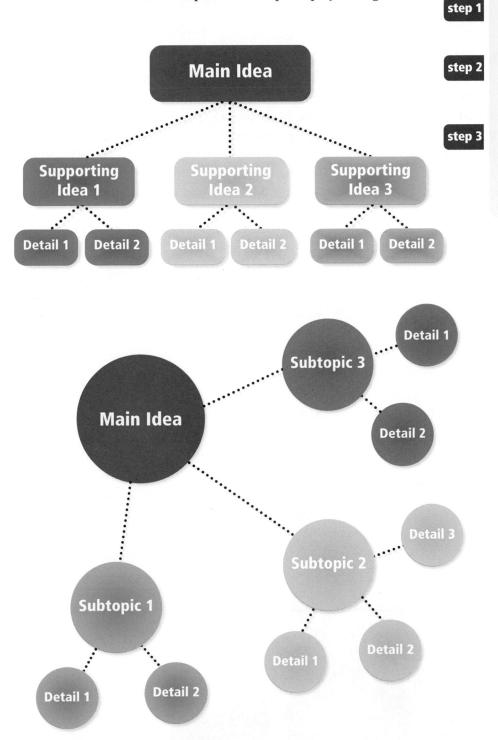

Constructing Concept Maps

step 1 Preview the text, looking for what type of structure might be appropriate to display as a concept map.

▼

step 2 Taking note of the headings, boldface type, and text structure, sketch a concept map you think could best illustrate the text.

▼

step 3 Using boxes, lines, arrows, circles, or any shapes you like, display the ideas of the text in the concept map.

Standardized Test-Taking Strategies

A number of times throughout your school career, you may be asked to take standardized tests. These tests are designed to demonstrate the content and skills you have learned. It is important to keep in mind that in most cases the best way to prepare for these tests is to pay close attention in class and take every opportunity to improve your general social studies, reading, writing, and mathematical skills.

Tips for Taking the Test

1. Be sure that you are well rested.
2. Be on time, and be sure that you have the necessary materials.
3. Listen to the teacher's instructions.
4. Read directions and questions carefully.
5. **DON'T STRESS!** Just remember what you have learned in class, and you should do well.

Practice the strategies at go.hrw.com

Tackling Social Studies

The social studies portions of many standardized tests are designed to test your knowledge of the content and skills that you have been studying in one or more of your social studies classes. Specific objectives for the test vary, but some of the most common include the following:

1. Demonstrate an understanding of issues and events in history.
2. Demonstrate an understanding of geographic influences on historical issues and events.
3. Demonstrate an understanding of economic and social influences on historical issues and events.
4. Demonstrate an understanding of political influences on historical issues and events.
5. Use critical thinking skills to analyze social studies information.

Standardized tests usually contain multiple-choice and, sometimes, open-ended questions. The multiple-choice items will often be based on maps, tables, charts, graphs, pictures, cartoons, and/or reading passages and documents.

Tips for Answering Multiple-Choice Questions

1. If there is a written or visual piece accompanying the multiple-choice question, pay careful attention to the title, author, and date.

2. Then read through or glance over the content of the written or visual piece accompanying the question to familiarize yourself with it.

3. Next, read the multiple-choice question first for its general intent. Then reread it carefully, looking for words that give clues or can limit possible answers to the question. For example, words such as *most* or *best* tell you that there may be several correct answers to a question, but you should look for the most appropriate answer.

4. Read through the answer choices. Always read all of the possible answer choices even if the first one seems like the correct answer. There may be a better choice farther down in the list.

5. Reread the accompanying information (if any is included) carefully to determine the answer to the question. Again, note the title, author, and date of primary-source selections. The answer will rarely be stated exactly as it appears in the primary source, so you will need to use your critical thinking skills to read between the lines.

6. Think of what you already know about the time in history or person involved and use that to help limit the answer choices.

7. Finally, reread the question and selected answer to be sure that you made the best choice and that you marked it correctly on the answer sheet.

Strategies for Success

There are a variety of strategies you can prepare ahead of time to help you feel more confident about answering questions on social studies standardized tests. Here are a few suggestions:

1. Adopt an acronym—a word formed from the first letters of other words—that you will use for analyzing a document or visual piece that accompanies a question.

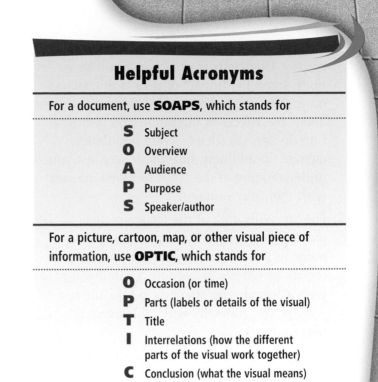

Helpful Acronyms

For a document, use **SOAPS**, which stands for

S Subject
O Overview
A Audience
P Purpose
S Speaker/author

For a picture, cartoon, map, or other visual piece of information, use **OPTIC**, which stands for

O Occasion (or time)
P Parts (labels or details of the visual)
T Title
I Interrelations (how the different parts of the visual work together)
C Conclusion (what the visual means)

2. Form visual images of maps and try to draw them from memory. Standardized tests will most likely include maps showing many features, such as states, countries, continents, and oceans. Those maps may also show patterns in settlement and the size and distribution of cities. For example, in studying the United States, be able to see in your mind's eye such things as where the states and major cities are located. Know major physical features, such as the Mississippi River, the Appalachian and Rocky Mountains, the Great Plains, and the various regions of the United States, and be able to place them on a map. Such features may help you understand patterns in the distribution of population and the size of settlements.

3. When you have finished studying a geographic region or period in history, try to think of who or what might be important enough for a standardized test. You may want to keep your ideas in a notebook to refer to when it is almost time for the test.

4. Standardized tests will likely test your understanding of the political, economic, and social processes that

shape a region's history, culture, and geography. Questions may also ask you to understand the impact of geographic factors on major events. For example, some may ask about the effects of migration and immigration on various societies and population change. In addition, questions may test your understanding of the ways humans interact with their environment.

5. For the skills area of the tests, practice putting major events and personalities in order in your mind. Sequencing people and events by dates can become a game you play with a friend who also has to take the test. Always ask yourself "why" this event is important.

6. Follow the tips under "Ready for Reading" below when you encounter a reading passage in social studies, but remember that what you have learned about history can help you in answering reading-comprehension questions.

Ready for Reading

The main goal of the reading sections of most standardized tests is to determine your understanding of different aspects of a piece of writing. Basically, if you can grasp the main idea and the writer's purpose and then pay attention to the details and vocabulary so that you are able to draw inferences and conclusions, you will do well on the test.

Tips for Answering Multiple-Choice Questions

1. Read the passage as if you were not taking a test.

2. Look at the big picture. Ask yourself questions like, "What is the title?", "What do the illustrations or pictures tell me?", and "What is the writer's purpose?"

3. Read the questions. This will help you know what information to look for.

4. Reread the passage, underlining information related to the questions.

Types of Multiple-Choice Questions

1. **Main Idea** This is the most important point of the passage. After reading the passage, locate and underline the main idea.

2. **Significant Details** You will often be asked to recall details from the passage. Read the question and underline the details as you read, but remember that the correct answers do not always match the wording of the passage precisely.

3. **Vocabulary** You will often need to define a word within the context of the passage. Read the answer choices and plug them into the sentence to see what fits best.

4. **Conclusion and Inference** There are often important ideas in the passage that the writer does not state directly. Sometimes you must consider multiple parts of the passage to answer the question. If answers refer to only one or two sentences or details in the passage, they are probably incorrect.

5. Go back to the questions and try to answer each one in your mind before looking at the answers.

6. Read all the answer choices and eliminate the ones that are obviously incorrect.

Tips for Answering Short-Answer Questions

1. Read the passage in its entirety, paying close attention to the main events and characters. Jot down information you think is important.

2. If you cannot answer a question, skip it and come back later.

3. Words such as *compare, contrast, interpret, discuss,* and *summarize* appear often in short-answer questions. Be sure you have a complete understanding of each of these words.

4. To help support your answer, return to the passage and skim the parts you underlined.

5. Organize your thoughts on a separate sheet of paper. Write a general statement with which to begin. This will be your topic statement.

6. When writing your answer, be precise but brief. Be sure to refer to details in the passage in your answer.

Targeting Writing

On many standardized tests, you will occasionally be asked to write an essay. In order to write a concise essay, you must learn to organize your thoughts before you begin writing the actual piece. This keeps you from straying too far from the essay's topic.

Tips for Answering Composition Questions

1. Read the question carefully.

2. Decide what kind of essay you are being asked to write. Essays usually fall into one of the following types: persuasive, classificatory, compare/contrast, or "how to." To determine the type of essay, ask yourself questions like, "Am I trying to persuade my audience?", "Am I comparing or contrasting ideas?", or "Am I trying to show the reader how to do something?"

3. Pay attention to key words, such as *compare, contrast, describe, advantages, disadvantages, classify,* or *speculate.* They will give you clues as to the structure that your essay should follow.

4. Organize your thoughts on a sheet of paper. You will want to come up with a general topic sentence that expresses your main idea. Make sure this sentence addresses the question. You should then create an outline or some type of graphic organizer to help you organize the points that support your topic sentence.

5. Write your composition using complete sentences. Also, be sure to use correct grammar, spelling, punctuation, and sentence structure.

6. Be sure to proofread your essay once you have finished writing.

Gearing Up for Math

On most standardized tests you will be asked to solve a variety of mathematical problems that draw on the skills and information you have learned in class. If math problems sometimes give you difficulty, have a look at the tips below to help you work through the problems.

Tips for Solving Math Problems

1. Decide what is the goal of the question. Read or study the problem carefully and determine what information must be found.

2. Locate the factual information. Decide what information represents key facts—the ones you must have to solve the problem. You may also find facts you do not need to reach your solution. In some cases, you may determine that more information is needed to solve the problem. If so, ask yourself, "What assumptions can I make about this problem?" or "Do I need a formula to help solve this problem?"

3. Decide what strategies you might use to solve the problem, how you might use them, and what form your solution will be in. For example, will you need to create a graph or chart? Will you need to solve an equation? Will your answer be in words or numbers? By knowing what type of solution you should reach, you may be able to eliminate some of the choices.

4. Apply your strategy to solve the problem and compare your answer to the choices.

5. If the answer is still not clear, read the problem again. If you had to make calculations to reach your answer, use estimation to see if your answer makes sense.

UNIT 1

Exploring Our World

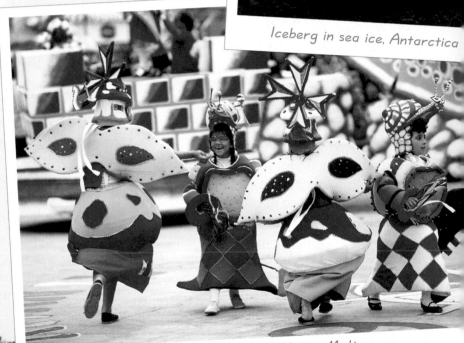

Iceberg in sea ice, Antarctica

Carnival parade in Valletta, Malta

A Physical Geographer in Mountain Environments

Professor Francisco Pérez studies tropical mountain environments. He is interested in the natural processes, plants, and environments of mountains. **WHAT DO YOU THINK?** *What faraway places would you like to study?*

I became attracted to mountains when I was a child. While crossing the Atlantic Ocean in a ship, I saw snow-capped Teide Peak in the Canary Islands rising from the water. It was an amazing sight.

As a physical geographer, I am interested in the unique environments of high mountain areas. This includes geological history, climate, and soils. The unusual conditions of high mountain environments have influenced plant evolution. Plants and animals that live on separate mountains sometimes end up looking similar. This happens because they react to their environments in similar ways. For example, several types of tall, weird-looking plants called giant rosettes grow in the Andes, Hawaii, East Africa, and the Canary Islands. Giant rosettes look like the top of a pineapple at the end of a tall stem.

I have found other strange plants, such as rolling mosses. Mosses normally grow on rocks. However, if a moss plant falls to the ground, ice crystals on the soil surface lift the moss. This allows it to "roll" downhill while it continues to grow in a ball shape!

I like doing research in mountains. They are some of the least explored regions of our planet. Like most geographers, I cannot resist the attraction of strange landscapes in remote places.

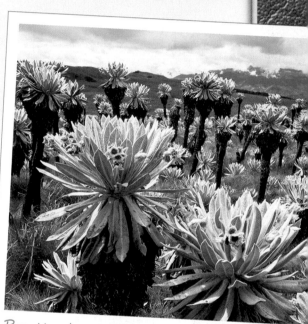

Rosette plants, Ecuador

La Digue Island, Seychelles

Understanding Primary Sources

1. What are three parts of the environment that Francisco Pérez studies?

2. Why do some plants that live on separate mountains look similar?

Sturgeonfish

CHAPTER 1

A Geographer's World

Hand-held compass

Chart of the Mediterranean and Europe, 1559

GPS (global positioning satellite) receiver

Section 1 Developing a Geographic Eye

Read to Discover

1. What role does perspective play in the study of geography?
2. What are some issues or topics that geographers study?
3. At what three levels can geographers view the world?

Define

perspective
spatial perspective
geography
urban
rural

WHY IT MATTERS

What factors would you consider if you were moving to a new town or city? You would probably want to know about its geography. Use CNNfyi.com or other **current events** sources to investigate a place you might like to live. Record your findings in your journal.

World map, 1598

Perspectives

People look at the world in different ways. Their experiences shape the way they understand the world. This personal understanding is called **perspective**. Your perspective is your point of view. A geographer's point of view looks at where something is and why it is there. This point of view is known as **spatial perspective**. Geographers apply this perspective when they study the arrangement of towns in a state. They might also use this perspective to examine the movement of cars and trucks on busy roads.

Geographers also work to understand how things are connected. Some connections are easy to see, like highways that link cities. Other connections are harder to see. For example, a dry winter in Colorado could mean that farms as far away as northern Mexico will not have enough water.

Geography is a science. It describes the physical and cultural features of Earth. Studying geography is important. Geographically informed people can see meaning in the arrangement of things on Earth. They know how people and places are related. Above all, they can apply a spatial perspective to real life. In other words, people familiar with geography can understand the world around them.

This fish-eye view of a large city shows highway patterns.

▼

✓ **READING CHECK:** *The World in Spatial Terms* What role does perspective play in the study of geography?

The movement of people is one issue that geographers study. For example, political and economic troubles led many Albanians to leave their country in 1991. Many packed onto freighters like this one for the trip. Geographers want to know how this movement affects the environment and other people.
Interpreting the Visual Record How do you think Albania has been affected by so many people leaving the country?

Geographic Issues

Issues geographers study include Earth's processes and their impact on people. Geographers study the relationship between people and environment in different places. For example, geographers study tornadoes to find ways to reduce loss of life and property damage. They ask how people prepare for tornadoes. Do they prepare differently in different places? When a tornado strikes, how do people react?

Geographers also study how governments change and how those changes affect people. Czechoslovakia, for example, split into Slovakia and the Czech Republic in 1993. These types of political events affect geographic boundaries. People react differently to these changes. Some people are forced to move. Others welcome the change.

Other issues geographers study include religions, diet (or food), **urban** areas, and **rural** areas. Urban areas contain cities. Rural areas contain open land that is often used for farming.

✓ **READING CHECK:** *The Uses of Geography* What issues or topics do geographers study?

Local, Regional, and Global Geographic Studies

With any topic, geographers must decide how large an area to study. They can focus their study at a local, regional, or global level.

Local Studying your community at the local, or close-up, level will help you learn geography. You know where homes and stores are located. You know how to find parks, ball fields, and other fun places. Over time, you see your community change. New buildings are constructed. People move in and out of your neighborhood. New stores open their doors, and others go out of business.

internet connect

GO TO: go.hrw.com
KEYWORD: SG3 CH1
FOR: Web sites about the geographer's world

The southwest is a region within the United States. One well-known place that characterizes the landscape of the southwest is the Grand Canyon. The Grand Canyon is shown in the photo at left and in the satellite image at right.

Regional Regional geographers organize the world into convenient parts for study. For example, this book separates the world into big areas like Africa and Europe. Regional studies cover larger areas than local studies. Some regional studies might look at connections like highways and rivers. Others might examine the regional customs.

Global Geographers also work to understand global issues and the connections between events. For example, many countries depend on oil from Southwest Asia. If those oil supplies are threatened, some countries might rush to secure oil from other areas. Oil all over the world could then become much more expensive.

✓ **READING CHECK:** *The World in Spatial Terms* What levels do geographers use to focus their study of an issue or topic?

Section Review 1

Define and explain: perspective, spatial perspective, geography, urban, rural

Reading for the Main Idea

1. *The Uses of Geography* How can a spatial perspective be used to study the world?

2. *The Uses of Geography* Why is it important to study geography?

Critical Thinking

3. **Drawing Inferences and Conclusions** How do threatening weather patterns affect people, and why do geographers study these patterns?

4. **Drawing Inferences and Conclusions** Why is it important to view geography on a global level?

Organizing What You Know

5. **Finding the Main Idea** Copy the following graphic organizer. Use it to examine the issues geographers study. Write a paragraph on one of these issues.

Issues geographers study

A Geographer's World • 5

Section 2 Themes and Essential Elements

Read to Discover

1. What tools do geographers use to study the world?
2. What shapes Earth's features?
3. How do humans shape the world?
4. How does studying geography help us understand the world?

Define

absolute location
relative location
subregions
diffusion
levees

Tombs carved out of a mountain in Turkey

WHY IT MATTERS

Geographers often study the effect that new people have on a place. Use **CNNfyi.com** or other **current events** sources to find out how the arrival of new people has changed the United States or another country. Record your findings in your journal.

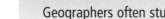

The location of a place can be described in many ways.

Interpreting the Visual Record Looking at the photo of this hotel in Giza, Egypt, and at the map, how would you describe Giza's location?

Themes

The study of geography has long been organized according to five important themes, or topics of study. One theme, *location*, deals with the exact or relative spot of something on Earth. *Place* includes the physical and human features of a location. *Human-environment interaction* covers the ways people and environments affect each other. *Movement* involves how people change locations and how goods are traded, as well as the effects of these movements. *Region* organizes Earth into geographic areas with one or more shared characteristics.

✓ **READING CHECK:** *The Uses of Geography* What are the five themes of geography?

Six Essential Elements

Another way to look at geography is to study its essential elements, or most important parts. The six essential elements used to study geography are The World in Spatial Terms, Places and Regions, Physical Systems, Human Systems, Environment and Society, and The Uses of Geography. These six essential elements will be used throughout this textbook. They share many properties with the five themes of geography.

Location
Every place on Earth has a location. Location is defined by absolute and relative location.

Absolute Location: the exact spot on Earth where something is found

Example: Niamey, the capital of Niger, is located at 13°31' north latitude and 2°07' east longitude.

Relative Location: the position of a place in relation to other places

Example: Yosemite National Park is north of Los Angeles, California, and east of San Francisco, California.

You Be the Geographer
1. Use an atlas to find the absolute location of your city or town.
2. Write a sentence describing the relative location of your home.

The World in Spatial Terms This element focuses on geography's spatial perspective. As you learned in Section 1, geographers apply spatial perspective when they look at the location of something and why it is there. The term *location* can be used in two ways. **Absolute location** defines an exact spot on Earth. For example, the address of the Smithsonian American Art Museum is an absolute location. The address is at 8th and G Streets, N.W., in Washington, D.C. City streets often form a grid. This system tells anyone looking for an address where to go. The grid formed by latitude and longitude lines also pinpoints absolute location. Suppose you asked a pilot to take you to 52° north latitude by 175° west longitude. You would land at a location on Alaska's Aleutian Islands.

Relative location describes the position of a place in relation to another place. Measurements of direction, distance, or time can define relative location. For example, the following sentences give relative location. "The hospital is one mile north of our school." "Canada's border is about an hour's drive from Great Falls, Montana."

A geographer must be able to use maps and other geographic tools and technologies to determine spatial perspective. A geographer must

▲
Places can be described by what they do not have. This photo shows the result of a long period without rain.

also know how to organize and analyze information about people, places, and environments using geographic tools.

Places and Regions Our world has a vast number of unique places and regions. Places can be described both by their physical location and by their physical and human features. Physical features include coastlines and landforms. They can also include lakes, rivers, or soil types. For example, Colorado is flat in the east but mountainous in the west. This is an example of a landform description of place. A place can also be described by its climate. For example, Greenland has long, cold winters. Florida has mild winters and hot, humid summers. Regions are areas of Earth's surface with one or more shared characteristics. To study a region more closely, geographers often divide it into smaller areas called **subregions**. Many of the characteristics that describe places can also be used to describe regions or subregions.

The Places and Regions element also deals with the human features of places and regions. Geographers want to know how people have created regions based on Earth's features and how culture and other factors affect how we see places and regions on Earth.

Physical Systems Physical systems shape Earth's features. Geographers study earthquakes, mountains, rivers, volcanoes, weather patterns, and similar topics and how these physical systems have affected Earth's characteristics. For example, geographers might study how volcanic eruptions in the Hawaiian Islands spread lava, causing landforms to change. They might note that southern California's shoreline changes yearly, as winter and summer waves move beach sand.

Geographers also study how plants and animals relate to these nonliving physical systems. For example, deserts are places with cactus and other plants, as well as rattlesnakes and other reptiles, that can

People travel from place to place on miles of new roadway.
Interpreting the Visual Record What other forms of human systems are studied by geographers?

▼

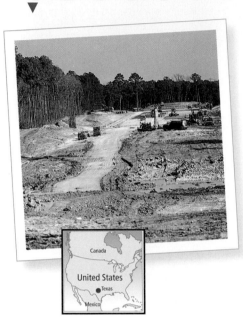

Men in rural Egypt wear a long shirt called a *galabia*. This loose-fitting garment is ideal for people living in Egypt's hot desert climate. In addition, the galabia is made from cotton, an important agricultural product of Egypt.
Interpreting the Visual Record How does the *galabia* show how people have adapted to their environment?

▶

A satellite dish brings different images and ideas to people in a remote area of Brazil.

Interpreting the Visual Record **How might resources have affected the use of technology here?**

live in very dry conditions. Geographers also study how different types of plants, animals, and physical systems are distributed on Earth.

Human Systems People are central to geography. Our activities, movements, and settlements shape Earth's surface. Geographers study peoples' customs, history, languages, and religions. They study how people migrate, or move, and how ideas are communicated. When people move, they may go to live in other countries or move within a country. Geographers want to know how and why people move from place to place.

People move for many reasons. Some move to start a new job. Some move to attend special schools. Others might move to be closer to family. People move either when they are pushed out of a place or when they are pulled toward another place. In the Dust Bowl, for example, crop failures pushed people out of Oklahoma in the 1930s. Many were pulled to California by their belief that they would find work there. Geographers also want to know how ideas or behaviors move from one region to another. The movement of ideas occurs through communication. There are many ways to communicate. People visit with each other in person or on the phone. New technology allows people to communicate by e-mail. Ideas are also spread through films, magazines, newspapers, radio, and television. The movement of ideas or behaviors from one region to another is known as **diffusion**.

The things we produce and trade are also part of the study of human systems. Geographers study trading patterns and how countries depend on each other for certain goods. In addition, geographers look at the causes and results of conflicts between peoples. The study of governments we set up and the features of cities and other settlements we live in are also part of this study.

Environment and Society Geographers study how people and their surroundings affect each other. Their relationship can be examined in three ways. First, geographers study how humans depend on

This woman at a railway station in Russian Siberia sells some goods that were once unavailable in her country.

Interpreting the Visual Record **Which essential element is illustrated in this photo?**

their physical environment to survive. Human life requires certain living and non-living resources, such as freshwater and fertile soil for farming.

Geographers also study how humans change their behavior to be better suited to an environment. These changes or adaptations include the kinds of clothing, food, and shelter that people create. These changes help people live in harsh climates.

Finally, humans change the environment. For example, farmers who irrigate their fields can grow fruit in Arizona's dry climate. People in Louisiana have built **levees**, or large walls, to protect themselves when the Mississippi River floods.

The Uses of Geography Geography helps us understand the relationships among people, places, and the environment over time. Understanding how a relationship has developed can help in making plans for the future. For example, geographers can study how human use of the soil in a farming region has affected that region over time. Such knowledge can help them determine what changes have been made to the soil and whether any corrective measures need to be taken.

Open-air markets like this one in Mali provide opportunities for farmers to sell their goods.

✓ **READING CHECK:** *The Uses of Geography* What are the six essential elements in studying geography?

Section Review 2

Define and explain: absolute location, relative location, subregions, diffusion, levees

Reading for the Main Idea

1. (*The World in Spatial Terms*) How do geographers study the world?

2. (*Physical Systems*) What shapes Earth's features? Give examples.

Critical Thinking

3. **Finding the Main Idea**   How do humans shape the world in which they live?

4. **Analyzing Information**   What benefits can studying geography provide?

Organizing What You Know

5. **Summarizing**   Copy the following graphic organizer. Use it to identify and describe all aspects of each of the six essential elements.

Element	Description

go.hrw.com **Homework Practice Online**
Keyword: SG3 HP1

Section 3 The Branches of Geography

Read to Discover

1. What is included in the study of human geography?
2. What is included in the study of physical geography?
3. What types of work do geographers do?

Define

human geography
physical geography
cartography
meteorology
climatology

WHY IT MATTERS

Nearly every year, hurricanes hit the Atlantic or Gulf coasts of the United States. Predicting weather is one of the special fields of geography. Use CNNfyi.com or other **current events** sources to find out about hurricanes. Record your findings in your journal.

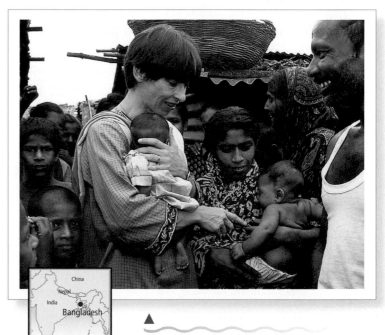

Map of an ancient fortress

Human Geography

The study of people, past or present, is the focus of **human geography**. People's location and distribution over Earth, their activities, and their differences are studied. For example, people living in different countries create different kinds of governments. Political geographers study those differences. Economic geographers study the exchange of goods and services across Earth. Cultural geography, population geography, and urban geography are some other examples of human geography. A professional geographer might specialize in any of these branches.

✓ **READING CHECK:** *Human Systems* How is human geography defined?

A volunteer visits a poor area of Bangladesh. Geographers study economic conditions in regions to help them understand human geography.

Physical Geography

The study of Earth's natural landscapes and physical systems, including the atmosphere, is the focus of **physical geography**. The world is full of different landforms such as deserts, mountains, and plains. Climates affect these landscapes. Knowledge of physical systems helps geographers understand how a landscape developed and how it might change.

CONNECTING TO *Technology*

A mapmaker creates a digital map.

Computer Mapping

Maps are tools that can display a wide range of information. Traditionally, maps were drawn on paper and could not be changed to suit the user. However, computers have revolutionized the art of mapmaking.

Today, mapmakers use computers to create and modify maps for different uses. They do this by using a geographic information system, or GIS. A GIS is a computer system that combines maps and satellite photographs with other kinds of spatial data—information about places on the planet. This information might include soil types, population figures, or voting patterns.

Using a GIS, mapmakers can create maps that show geographic features and relationships. For example, a map showing rainfall patterns in a particular region might be combined with data on soil types or human settlement to show areas of possible soil erosion.

The flexibility of a GIS allows people to seek answers to specific questions. Where should a new road be built to ease traffic congestion? How are changes in natural habitat affecting wildlife? These and many other questions can be answered with the help of computer mapping.

Understanding What You Read
1. How could a GIS help people change their environment?
2. What social, environmental, or economic consequences might future advances in GIS technology have?

Knowledge of physical and human geography will help you understand the world's different regions and peoples. In your study of the major world regions, you will see how physical and human geography connect to each other.

✔ **READING CHECK:** *Physical Systems* What is included in the study of physical geography?

Working as a Geographer

Geography plays a role in almost every occupation. Wherever you live and work, you should know local geography. School board members know where children live. Taxi drivers are familiar with city streets. Grocery store managers know which foods sell well in certain areas.

They also know where they can obtain these products throughout the year. Local newspaper reporters are familiar with town meetings and local politicians. Reporters also know how faraway places can affect their communities. Doctors must know if their towns have poisonous snakes or plants. City managers know whether nearby rivers might flood. Emergency workers in mountain towns check snow depth so they can give avalanche warnings. Local weather forecasters watch for powerful storms and track their routes on special maps.

Some specially trained geographers practice in the field of **cartography**. Cartography is the art and science of mapmaking. Today, most mapmakers do their work on computers. Geographers also work as weather forecasters. The field of forecasting and reporting rainfall, temperature, and other atmospheric conditions is called **meteorology**. A related field is **climatology**. These geographers, known as climatologists, track Earth's larger atmospheric systems. Climatologists want to know how these systems change over long periods of time. They also study how people might be affected by changes in climate.

Governments and a variety of organizations hire geographers to study the environment. These geographers might explore such topics as pollution, endangered plants and animals, or rain forests. Some geographers who are interested in education become teachers and writers. They help people of all ages learn more about the world. Modern technology allows people all over the world to communicate instantly. Therefore, it is more important than ever to be familiar with the geographer's world.

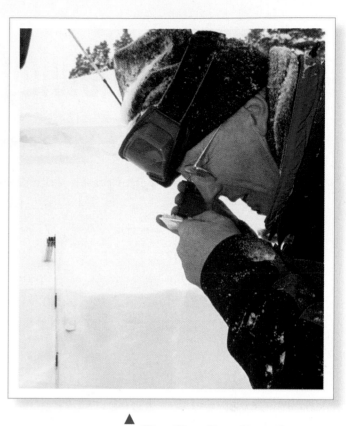

▲

Experts examine snow to help forecast avalanches. They study the type of snow, weather conditions, and landforms. For example, wet snow avalanches can occur because of the formation of a particular type of ice crystal, called depth hoar, near the ground.

✓ **READING CHECK:** (*The Uses of Geography*) What types of work do geographers perform?

go.hrw.com — **Homework Practice Online** — Keyword: SG3 HP1

Define and explain: human geography, physical geography, cartography, meteorology, climatology

Reading for the Main Idea

1. (*Human Systems*) What topics are included in the study of human geography?

2. (*The Uses of Geography*) How do people who study the weather use geography?

Critical Thinking

3. **Finding the Main Idea** Why is it important to study physical geography?

4. **Making Generalizations and Predictions** How might future discoveries in the field of geography affect societies, world economies, or the environment?

Organizing What You Know

5. **Categorizing** Copy the following graphic organizer. Use it to list geographers' professions and their job responsibilities.

Cartographer		
—makes maps		
—studies maps		

Reviewing What You Know

Building Vocabulary

On a separate sheet of paper, write sentences to define each of the following words.

1. perspective
2. spatial perspective
3. geography
4. urban
5. rural
6. absolute location
7. relative location
8. levees
9. diffusion
10. subregions
11. human geography
12. physical geography
13. cartography
14. meteorology
15. climatology

Reviewing the Main Ideas

1. (The World in Spatial Terms) What are three ways to view geography? Give an example of when each type could be used.

2. (The World in Spatial Terms) What kind of directions would you give to indicate a place's absolute location? Its relative location?

3. (Human Systems) What is diffusion, and why is it important?

4. (Places and Regions) Why do geographers create subregions?

5. (The World in Spatial Terms) Why is cartography important? What types of jobs do geographers do?

Understanding Environment and Society

Land Use

You are on a committee that will decide whether to close a park near your school. One proposed use for the land is a building where after-school activities could be held. However, the park is the habitat of an endangered bird. Write a report describing consequences of the park closing. Then organize information from your report to create a proposal on what decision should be made.

Thinking Critically

1. **Analyzing Information** How can a geographer use spatial perspective to explain how things in our world are connected?

2. **Drawing Inferences and Conclusions** When and how do humans relate to the environment? Provide some examples of this relationship.

3. **Summarizing** How are patterns created by the movement of goods, ideas, and people?

4. **Finding the Main Idea** How are places and regions defined?

5. **Finding the Main Idea** How does studying geography help us understand the world?

Map ACTIVITY

On a separate sheet of paper, match the letters on the map with their correct labels.

Africa	Europe
Antarctica	North America
Asia	South America
Australia	

Mental Mapping Skills ACTIVITY

To help you understand the relationships between places, create a seating chart of your classroom. Then draw a sketch of the floor plan of your school. Discuss why certain areas are located in particular parts of the campus.

WRITING ACTIVITY

Write a letter persuading another student to enroll in a geography class. Include examples of professions that use geography and relate that information to the everyday life of a student. Be sure to use standard grammar, spelling, sentence structure, and punctuation.

Alternative Assessment

Portfolio ACTIVITY

Learning About Your Local Geography

Individual Project How do you define your community geographically? Is your community the area around your home or school? Write two or three sentences defining your community to share with the class.

internet connect

Internet Activity: go.hrw.com
KEYWORD: SG3 GT1

Choose a topic to explore online:
- Learn to use online maps.
- Be a virtual geographer for a day.
- Compare regions around the world.

CHAPTER 2

Planet Earth

Erupting volcano

Earth as seen from space

Fossilized shell

Galileo's telescope

Space observatory, Mauna Kea, Hawaii

Section 1 — The Sun, Earth, and Moon

Read to Discover

1. What objects make up the solar system?
2. What causes the seasons?
3. What are the four parts of the Earth system?

Define

solar system
orbit
satellite
axis
rotation

revolution
Arctic Circle
Antarctic Circle
solstice
Tropic of Cancer

Tropic of Capricorn
equinoxes
atmosphere
ozone

WHY IT MATTERS

In 2001 scientists labeled a rocky object beyond Pluto as the new largest minor planet. Use **CNNfyi.com** or other **current events** sources to discover more about this huge frozen rock, called 2001 KX76. Record your findings in your journal.

Mechanical model of the solar system

The Solar System

The **solar system** consists of the Sun and the objects that move around it. The most important of those objects are the planets, their moons, and relatively small rocky bodies called asteroids. Our Sun is a star at the center of our solar system. Every object in the system travels around the Sun in an **orbit**, or path. These orbits are usually elliptical, or oval shaped.

The Solar System

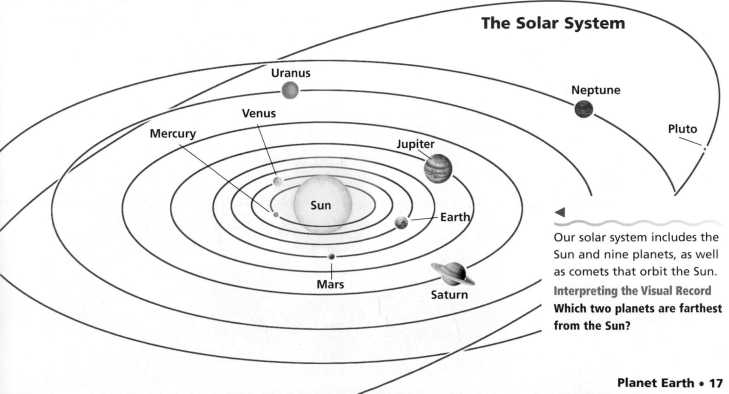

Our solar system includes the Sun and nine planets, as well as comets that orbit the Sun.

Interpreting the Visual Record
Which two planets are farthest from the Sun?

Tides are higher than normal when the gravitational pull of the Moon and the Sun combine. These tides, called spring tides, occur twice a month. Tides are lower than normal during neap tides, when the Sun and the Moon are at right angles.

The planet nearest the Sun is Mercury, followed by Venus, Earth, and Mars. Located beyond the orbit of Mars is a belt of asteroids. Beyond this asteroid belt are the planets Jupiter and Saturn. Even farther from the Sun are the planets Uranus, Neptune, and Pluto.

The Moon Some of the planets in the solar system have more than one moon. Saturn, for example, has 18. Other planets have none. A moon is a **satellite**—a body that orbits a larger body. Earth has one moon, which is about one fourth the size of Earth. Our planet is also circled by artificial satellites that transmit signals for television, telephone, and computer communications. The Moon takes about 29½ days—roughly a month—to orbit Earth.

The Moon and Sun influence physical processes on Earth. This is because any two objects in space are affected by gravitational forces pulling them together. The gravitational effects of the Sun and the Moon cause tides in the oceans here on Earth.

The Sun Compared to some other stars, our Sun is small. It is huge, however, when compared to Earth. Its diameter is about 100 times the diameter of our planet. The Sun appears larger to us than other stars. This is because it is much closer to us than other stars. The Sun is about 93 million miles (150 million km) from Earth. The next nearest star is about 25 trillion miles (40 trillion km) away.

Scientists are trying to learn if other planets in our solar system could support life. Mars seems to offer the best possibility. It is not clear, however, if life can, or ever did, exist on Mars.

✔ **READING CHECK:** (*Physical Systems*) What are the main objects that make up the solar system?

Effects of the Moon and Sun on Tides

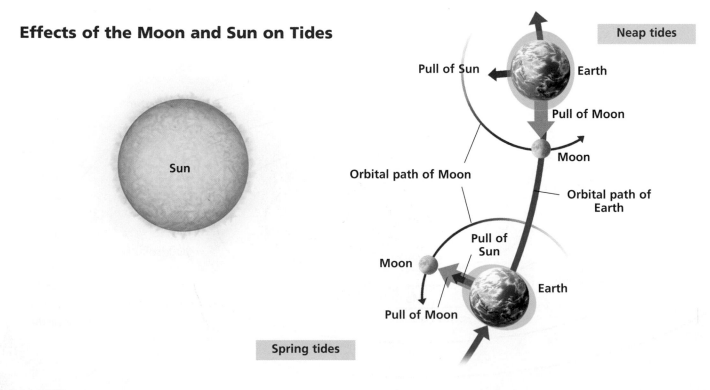

Earth

Geographers are interested in how different places on Earth receive different amounts of energy from the Sun. Differences in solar energy help explain why the tropics are warm, why the Arctic region is cold, and why day is warmer than night. To understand these differences, geographers study Earth's rotation, revolution, and the tilt of its **axis**. The axis is an imaginary line that runs from the North Pole through Earth's center to the South Pole. Rotation, revolution, and tilt control the amount of solar energy reaching Earth.

Rotation One complete spin of Earth on its axis is called a **rotation**. Each rotation takes 24 hours, or one day. Earth turns on its axis, but to us it appears that the Sun is moving. The Sun seems to "rise" in the east and "set" in the west. Before scientists learned that Earth revolves around the Sun, people thought that the Sun revolved around Earth. They thought Earth was at the center of the heavens.

Revolution It takes a year for Earth to orbit the Sun, or to complete one **revolution**. More precisely, it takes 365¼ days. To allow for this fraction of a day and keep the calendar accurate, every fourth year becomes a leap year. An extra day—February 29—is added to the calendar.

Tilt The amount of the Sun's energy reaching different parts of Earth varies. This is because Earth's axis is not straight up and down. It is actually tilted, or slanted, at an angle of 23.5° from vertical to the plane of Earth's orbit. Because of Earth's tilt, the angle at which the Sun's rays strike the planet is constantly changing as Earth revolves around the Sun. For this reason, the point where the vertical rays of

Photographs taken from space can tell us about Earth.

Interpreting the Visual Record Where can you see the presence of water in this view of Earth?

internet connect

GO TO: go.hrw.com
KEYWORD: SG3 CH2
FOR: Web sites about planet Earth

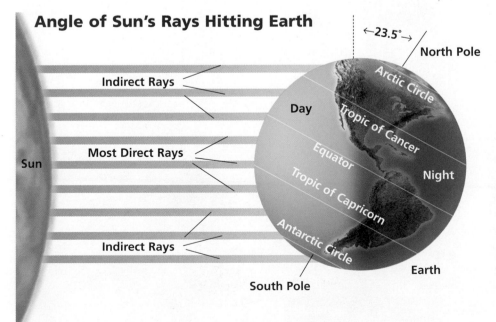

Angle of Sun's Rays Hitting Earth

← 23.5° →

North Pole

Indirect Rays

Arctic Circle

Day

Tropic of Cancer

Most Direct Rays

Equator

Sun

Tropic of Capricorn

Night

Indirect Rays

Antarctic Circle

Earth

South Pole

The tilt of Earth's axis and the position of the planet in its orbit determine where the Sun's rays will most directly strike the planet.

Interpreting the Visual Record Which areas of Earth receive only indirect rays from the Sun?

The Sun's surface is always violently churning as heat flows outward from the interior.

the Sun strike Earth shifts north and south of the equator. These vertical rays provide more energy than rays that strike at an angle.

✓ **READING CHECK:** *Physical Systems* How do rotation, revolution, and tilt affect solar energy reaching Earth?

Solar Energy and Latitude

The angle at which the Sun's rays reach Earth affects temperature. In the tropics—areas in the low latitudes near the equator—the Sun's rays are nearly vertical throughout the year. In the polar regions—the areas near the North and South Poles—the Sun's rays are always at a low angle. As a result, the poles are generally the coldest places on Earth. The **Arctic Circle** is the line of latitude located 66.5° north of the equator. It circles the North Pole. The **Antarctic Circle** is the line of latitude located 66.5° south of the equator. It circles the South Pole.

As Earth revolves around the Sun, the tilt of the poles toward and away from the Sun causes the seasons to change.

Interpreting the Visual Record At what point is the North Pole tilted toward the Sun?

The Seasons

Each year is divided into periods of time called seasons. Each season is known for a certain type of weather, based on temperature and amount of precipitation. Winter, spring, summer, and fall are examples of seasons that are described by their average temperature. "Wet" and "dry" seasons are described by their precipitation. The seasons change as Earth orbits the Sun. As this happens, the amount of solar energy received in any given location changes.

The Seasons

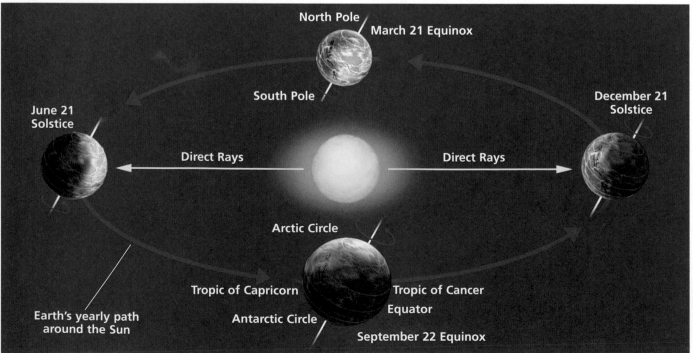

Solstice The day when the Sun's vertical rays are farthest from the equator is called a **solstice**. Solstices occur twice a year—about June 21 and about December 22. In the Northern Hemisphere the June solstice is known as the summer solstice. This is the longest day of the year and the beginning of summer. On this date the Sun's vertical rays strike Earth at the **Tropic of Cancer**. This is the line of latitude that is about 23.5° north of the equator. Six months later, about December 22, another solstice takes place. This is the winter solstice for the Northern Hemisphere. On this date the North Pole is pointed away from the Sun. The Northern Hemisphere experiences the shortest day of the year. On this date the Sun's rays strike Earth most directly at the **Tropic of Capricorn**. This line of latitude is about 23.5° south of the equator. In the Southern Hemisphere the seasons are reversed. June 21 is the winter solstice and December 22 is the summer solstice. The middle-latitude regions lie between the Tropic of Cancer and the Arctic Circle and between the Tropic of Capricorn and the Antarctic Circle.

Equinox Twice a year, halfway between summer and winter, Earth's poles are at right angles to the Sun. The Sun's rays strike the equator directly. On these days, called **equinoxes**, every place on Earth has 12 hours of day and 12 hours of night. Equinoxes mark the beginning of spring and fall. In the Northern Hemisphere the spring equinox occurs about March 21. The fall equinox occurs there about September 22. In the Southern Hemisphere the March equinox signals the beginning of fall, and the September equinox marks the beginning of spring.

Some regions on Earth, particularly in the tropics, have seasons tied to precipitation rather than temperature. Shifting wind patterns are one cause of seasonal change. For example, in January winds from the north bring dry air to India. By June the winds have shifted, coming from the southwest and bringing moisture from the Indian Ocean. These winds bring heavy rain to India. Some places in the United States also have seasons tied to moisture. East Coast states south of Virginia have a wet season in summer. These areas also have a hurricane season, lasting roughly from June to November. Some areas of the West Coast have a dry season in summer.

The seasons affect human activities. For example, in Minnesota, people shovel snow in winter to keep the walkways clear. Students waiting for a bus must wear warm clothes. The Sun rises late and sets early. As a result, people go to work and return home in darkness.

✔ **READING CHECK:** (*Physical Systems*) How do the seasons relate to the Sun's energy?

This map shows Earth's temperatures on January 28, 1997.
Interpreting the Visual Record Which hemisphere is warmer in January?

▼

▲

This temperature map for September 7, 1997, shows summer in the Northern Hemisphere.

A Atmosphere   **B** Biosphere
L Lithosphere   **H** Hydrosphere

▲

The interactions of the atmosphere, lithosphere, hydrosphere, and biosphere make up the Earth system.

Interpreting the Visual Record Which items in this image are part of the hydrosphere?

The Earth System

Geographers need to be able to explain how and why places on Earth differ from each other. One way they do this is to study the interactions of forces and materials on the planet. Together, these forces and materials are known as the Earth system.

The Earth system has four parts: the **atmosphere**, the lithosphere, the hydrosphere, and the biosphere. The atmosphere is the layer of gases—the air—that surrounds Earth. These gases include nitrogen, oxygen, and carbon dioxide. The atmosphere also contains a form of oxygen called **ozone**. A layer of this gas helps protect Earth from harmful solar radiation. Another part of the Earth system is the lithosphere. The prefix *litho* means rock. The lithosphere is the solid, rocky outer layer of Earth, including the sea floor. The hydrosphere—*hydro* means water—consists of all of Earth's water, found in lakes, oceans, and glaciers. It also includes the moisture in the atmosphere. Finally, the biosphere—*bio* means life— is the part of the Earth system that includes all plant and animal life. It extends from high in the air to deep in the oceans.

By dividing Earth into these four spheres, geographers can better understand each part and how each affects the others. The different parts of the Earth system are constantly interacting in many ways. For example, a tree is part of the biosphere. However, to grow it needs to take in water, chemicals from the soil, and gases from the air.

✓ **READING CHECK:** *The World in Spatial Terms* What are the four parts of the Earth system?

Section Review 1

Define and explain: solar system, orbit, satellite, axis, rotation, revolution, Arctic Circle, Antarctic Circle, solstice, Tropic of Cancer, Tropic of Capricorn, equinoxes, atmosphere, ozone

Reading for the Main Idea

1. *Physical Systems* What are the major objects in the solar system?

2. *The World in Spatial Terms* What are the four parts of the Earth system?

go.hrw.com
Homework Practice Online
Keyword: SG3 HP2

Critical Thinking

3. **Summarizing** Which three things determine the amount of solar energy reaching places on Earth?

4. **Drawing Inferences and Conclusions** Why are the seasons reversed in the Northern and Southern Hemispheres?

Organizing What You Know

5. **Finding the Main Idea** Use this graphic organizer to explain solstice and equinox.

Solstice	⇦⇨	Equinox

Section 2 — Water on Earth

Read to Discover

1. Which processes make up the water cycle and how are they connected?
2. How is water distributed on Earth?
3. How does water affect people's lives?

Define

water vapor
water cycle
evaporation
condensation
precipitation
tributary
groundwater
continental
shelf

WHY IT MATTERS

Scientists study other parts of our solar system to find out if water exists or might have existed elsewhere. Use **CNNfyi.com** or other **current events** sources to learn more about space agencies and their searches to detect water. Record your findings in your journal.

A limestone cavern

Characteristics of Water

Water has certain physical characteristics that influence Earth's geography. Water is the only substance on Earth that occurs naturally as a solid, a liquid, and a gas. We see water as a solid in snow and ice and as a liquid in lakes, oceans, and rivers. Water also occurs in the air as an invisible gas called **water vapor**.

Another characteristic of water is that it heats and cools slowly compared to land. Even on a very hot day, the ocean stays cool. A breeze blowing over the ocean brings cooler temperatures to shore. This keeps temperatures near the coast from getting as hot as they do farther inland. In winter the oceans cool more slowly than land. This generally keeps winters milder in coastal areas.

✓ **READING CHECK:** *Physical Systems* What are some important characteristics of water?

The Water Cycle

The circulation of water from Earth's surface to the atmosphere and back is called the **water cycle**. The total amount of water on the planet does not change. Water, however, does change its form and its location.

Water rushes through the Stewart Mountain Dam in Arizona.

The Water Cycle

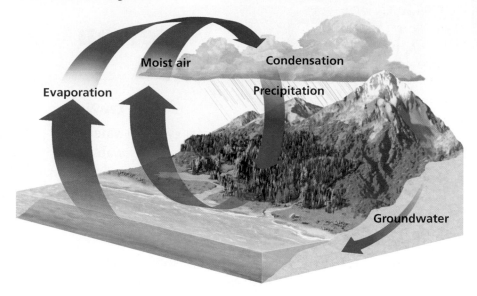

The circulation of water from one part of the hydrosphere to another depends on energy from the Sun. Water evaporates, condenses, and falls to Earth as precipitation. **Interpreting the Visual Record** How would a seasonal increase in the amount of the Sun's energy received by an area change the water cycle in that area?

The Sun's energy drives the water cycle. **Evaporation** occurs when the Sun heats water on Earth's surface. The heated water evaporates, becoming water vapor and rising into the air. Energy from the Sun also causes winds to carry the water vapor to new locations. As the water vapor rises, it cools, causing **condensation**. This is the process by which water changes from a gas into tiny liquid droplets. These droplets join together to form clouds. If the droplets become heavy enough, **precipitation** occurs—that is, the water falls back to Earth. This water can be in the form of rain, hail, sleet, or snow. The entire cycle of evaporation, condensation, and precipitation repeats itself endlessly.

✓ **READING CHECK:** *Physical Systems* What is the water cycle?

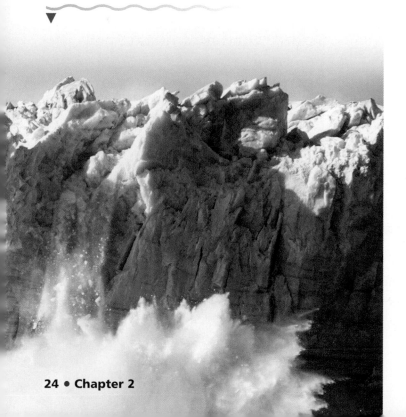

This glacier is "calving"—a mass of ice is breaking off, forming an iceberg. Most of Earth's freshwater exists as ice.

Geographic Distribution of Water

The oceans contain about 97 percent of Earth's water. About another 2 percent is found in the ice sheets of Antarctica, the Arctic, Greenland, and mountain glaciers. Approximately 1 percent is found in lakes, streams, rivers, and under the ground.

Earth's freshwater resources are not evenly distributed. There are very dry places with no signs of water. Other places have many lakes and rivers. In the United States, for example, Minnesota is dotted with more than 11,000 lakes. Dry states such as Nevada have few natural lakes. In many dry places rivers have been dammed to create artificial lakes called reservoirs.

Surface Water Water sometimes collects at high elevations, where rivers begin their flow down toward the lowlands and coasts. The first and smallest streams that form from this runoff are called headwaters. When these headwaters meet and join, they form larger streams. In turn, these streams join with other streams to form rivers. Any smaller stream or river that flows into a larger stream or river is a **tributary**. For example, the Missouri River is an important tributary of the Mississippi River, into which it flows near St. Louis, Missouri.

Lakes are usually formed when rivers flow into basins and fill them with water. Most lakes are freshwater, but some are salty. For example, the Great Salt Lake in Utah receives water from the Bear, Jordan, and Weber Rivers but has no outlet. Because the air is dry here, the rate of evaporation is very high. When the lake water evaporates, it leaves behind salts and minerals, making the lake salty.

Groundwater

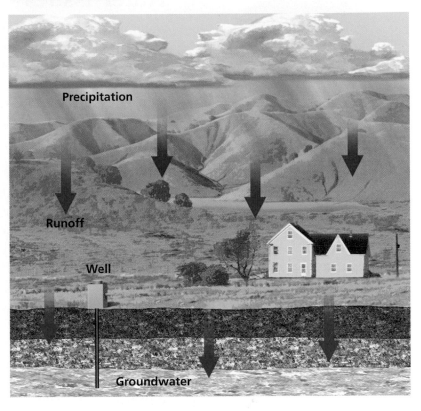

In some areas where rainfall is scarce, enough groundwater exists to support agriculture.

Interpreting the Visual Record How do people gain access to groundwater?

Groundwater Not all surface water immediately returns to the atmosphere through evaporation. Some water from rainfall, rivers, lakes, and melting snow seeps into the ground. This **groundwater** seeps down until all the spaces between soil and grains of rock are filled. In some places, groundwater bubbles out of the ground as a spring. Many towns in the United States get their water from wells—deep holes dug down to reach the groundwater. Motorized pumps allow people to draw water from very deep underground.

Oceans Most of Earth's water is found in the oceans. The Pacific, Atlantic, Indian, and Arctic Oceans connect with each other. This giant body of water covers some 71 percent of Earth's surface. These oceans also include smaller regions called seas and gulfs. The Gulf of Mexico and the Gulf of Alaska are two examples of smaller ocean areas.

Surrounding each continent is a zone of shallow ocean water. This gently sloping underwater land—called the **continental shelf**—is important to marine life. Although the oceans are huge, marine life is concentrated in these shallow areas. Deeper ocean water is home to fewer organisms. Overall, the oceans average about 12,000 feet (about 3,700 m) in depth. The deepest place is the Mariana Trench in the Pacific Ocean, at about 36,000 feet (about 11,000 m) deep.

The Continental Shelf

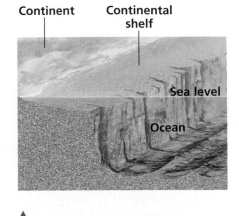

The continental shelf slopes gently away from the continents. The ocean floor drops steeply at the edge of the shelf.

✔ **READING CHECK:** *The World in Spatial Terms* How is water distributed on Earth?

This kelp forest is off the coast of southern California. The shallower parts of the oceans are home to many plants and animals.

Water Issues

Water plays an important part in our survival. As a result, water issues frequently show up in the news. Thunderstorms, particularly when accompanied by hail or tornadoes, can damage buildings and ruin crops. Droughts also can be deadly. In the mountains, heavy snowfalls sometimes cause deadly snow slides called avalanches. Heavy fog can make driving or flying dangerous. Geographers are concerned with these issues. They work on ways to better prepare for natural hazards.

Floods Water can both support and threaten life. Heavy rains can cause floods, which are the world's deadliest natural hazard. Floods kill four out of every ten people who die from natural disasters, including hurricanes, earthquakes, tornadoes, and thunderstorms.

Some floods occur in dry places when strong thunderstorms drop a large amount of rain very quickly. The water races along on the hard, dry surface instead of soaking into the ground. This water can quickly gather in low places. Creekbeds that are normally dry can suddenly surge with rushing water. People and livestock are sometimes caught in these flash floods.

Floods also happen in low-lying places next to rivers and on coastlines. Too much rain or snowmelt entering a river can cause the water to overflow the banks. Powerful storms, particularly hurricanes, can sometimes cause ocean waters to surge into coastal areas. Look at a

Davenport, Iowa, suffered severe flooding in 1993. Many cities are located along rivers even though there is a danger of floods.

Interpreting the Visual Record Why are many cities located next to rivers?

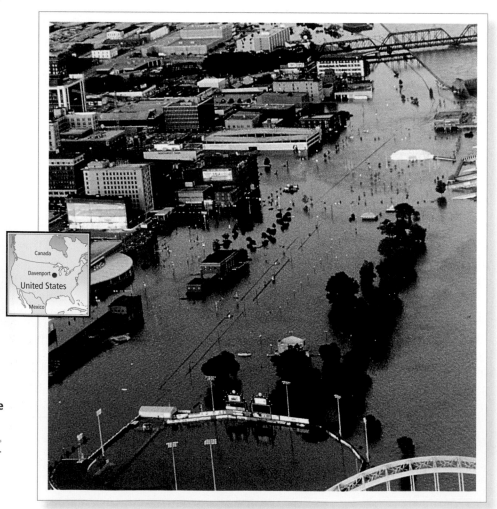

map of the United States. You will see that most major cities are located either next to a river or along a coast. For this reason, floods can be a threat to lives and property.

Flood Control Dams are a means people use to control floods. The huge Hoover Dam on the Colorado River in the United States is one example. The Aswān Dam on the Nile River in Egypt and those on the Murray River in Australia are others. Dams help protect people from floods. They also store water for use during dry periods. However, dams prevent rivers from bringing soil nutrients to areas downstream. Sometimes farming is not as productive as it was before the dams were built.

Clean Water The availability of clean water is another issue affecting the world's people. Not every country is able to provide clean water for drinking and bathing. Pollution also threatens the health of the world's oceans—particularly in the shallower seabeds where many fish live and reproduce.

Water Supply Finding enough water to meet basic needs is a concern in regions that are naturally dry. The water supply is the amount of water available for use in a region. It limits the number of living things that can survive in a place. People in some countries have to struggle each day to find enough water.

✓ **READING CHECK:** (*Environment and Society*) What are some ways in which water affects people?

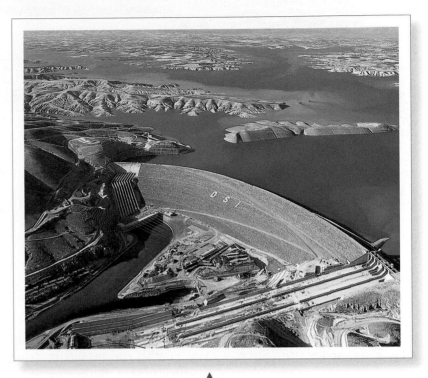

The Atatürk Dam in Turkey is 604 feet (184 m) high.

Interpreting the Visual Record How have people used dams to change their physical environment?

go.hrw.com **Homework Practice Online** Keyword: SG3 HP2

Section Review 2

Define and explain: water vapor, water cycle, evaporation, condensation, precipitation, tributary, groundwater, continental shelf

Reading for the Main Idea

1. (*Physical Systems*) What are the steps in the water cycle?

2. (*Environment and Society*) What are some major issues related to water?

Critical Thinking

3. **Analyzing Information** What are some important characteristics of water?

4. **Finding the Main Idea** Why is water supply a problem in some areas?

Organizing What You Know

5. **Sequencing** Copy the following graphic organizer. Use it to explain the water cycle.

Section 3

The Land

Read to Discover

1. What are primary landforms?
2. What are secondary landforms?
3. How do humans interact with landforms?

Define

landforms	core	subduction	alluvial fan
plain	mantle	earthquakes	floodplain
plateau	crust	fault	deltas
isthmus	magma	Pangaea	glaciers
peninsula	lava	weathering	
plate tectonics	continents	erosion	

WHY IT MATTERS

Earth's surface has been the focus of scientific research for centuries. Use CNNfyi.com logo or other **current events** sources to explore how scientists use maps to study the surface of Earth and other planets. Record your findings in your journal.

Mount Saint Helens, in southern Washington State

Landforms

Landforms are shapes on Earth's surface. One common landform is a **plain**—a nearly flat area. A **plateau** is an elevated flatland. An **isthmus** is a neck of land connecting two larger land areas. A **peninsula** is land bordered by water on three sides.

Primary Landforms

The theory of **plate tectonics** helps explain how forces raise, lower, and roughen Earth's surface. According to this theory, Earth's surface is divided into several large plates, or pieces. There are also many smaller plates. The plates slowly move. Some plates are colliding. Some are moving apart. Others are sliding by each other. Landforms created by tectonic processes are called primary landforms. These include masses of rock raised by volcanic eruptions and deep ocean trenches. The energy that moves the tectonic plates comes from inside Earth. The inner, solid **core** of the planet is surrounded by a liquid layer called the **mantle**. The outer, solid layer of Earth is called the **crust**. Currents of heat from the core travel outward through the mantle. When the currents reach the upper mantle, rocks can melt to form **magma**.

Earth's thin crust floats on top of the liquid mantle.

The Interior of Earth

Crust
(3–30 mi. or about 5–50 km)

Mantle
(1,800 mi. or about 2,900 km)

Outer core
(1,300 mi. or about 2,080 km)

Inner core
(860 mi. or about 1,390 km)

ATMOSPHERE

Plate Tectonics

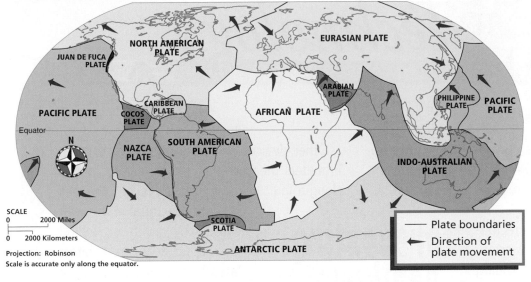

The plates that make up Earth's crust are moving, usually a few inches per year. This map shows the plates and the direction of their movement.

Magma sometimes breaks through the crust to form a volcano. After reaching Earth's surface, magma is called **lava**.

Plates cover Earth's entire surface, both the land and the ocean. In general, the plates under the oceans are made of dense rock. The plates on the **continents**—Earth's large landmasses—are made of lighter rock.

Plates Colliding When two plates collide, one plate can be pushed under another. When this occurs under the ocean, a very deep trench is sometimes created. This is happening near Japan, where the Pacific plate is slowly moving under the Eurasian and Philippine plates. Any time a heavier plate moves under a lighter one, trenches can form. This process is called **subduction**. **Earthquakes** are common in subduction zones. An earthquake is a sudden, violent movement along a fracture within Earth's crust. A series of shocks usually results from such a movement within the crust.

The borders of the Pacific plate move against neighboring plates. This causes volcanoes to erupt and earthquakes to strike in that area. The Pacific plate's edge has been called the Ring of Fire because it is rimmed by active volcanoes. Thousands of people have died and terrible destruction has resulted from the earthquakes and volcanoes there.

When a continental plate and an ocean plate collide, the lighter rocks of the continent do not sink. Instead, they crumple and form a mountain range. The Andes in South America were formed this way. When two continental plates collide, land is lifted, sometimes to great heights. The Himalayas, the world's highest mountain range, were created by the Indo-Australian plate pushing into the Eurasian plate.

Subduction and Spreading

Where Plate 2 pushes under Plate 1, a deep trench forms. This process is called subduction. Where Plates 2 and 3 move apart, lava creates a mid-ocean ridge.

Plates Colliding

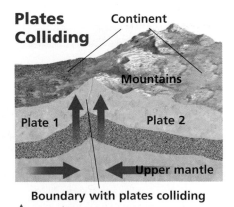

Where two continental plates collide, Earth's crust is pushed upward, forming a mountain range.

CONNECTING TO *Technology*

Since ancient times, people have tried to forecast earthquakes. A Chinese inventor even created a device to register earthquakes as early as A.D. 132.

The theory of plate tectonics gives modern-day scientists a better understanding of how and why earthquakes occur. Earthquake scientists, known as seismologists, have many tools to help them monitor movements in Earth's crust. They try to understand when and where earthquakes will occur.

The most common of these devices is the seismograph. It measures seismic waves—vibrations produced when two tectonic plates grind against each other. Scientists believe that an increase in seismic activity may signal a coming earthquake.

forecasting earthquakes

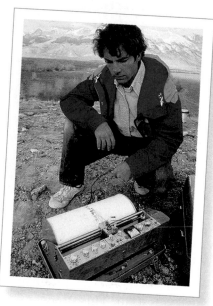

A scientist with a seismograph

Other devices show shifts in Earth's crust. Tiltmeters measure the rise of tectonic plates along a fault line. Gravimeters record changes in gravitational strength caused by rising or falling land. Laser beams can detect lateral movements along a fault line. Satellites can note the movement of entire tectonic plates.

Scientists have yet to learn how to forecast earthquakes with accuracy. Nevertheless, their ongoing work may one day provide important breakthroughs in the science of earthquake forecasting.

You Be the Geographer

1. What social and economic consequences might earthquake forecasting have?
2. What technology has helped with earthquake forecasting?

Plates Moving Apart When two plates move away from each other, hot lava emerges from the gap that has been formed. The lava builds a mid-ocean ridge—a landform that is similar to an underwater mountain range. This process is currently occurring in the Atlantic Ocean where the Eurasian plate and the North American plate are moving away from each other.

Plates Sliding Tectonic plates can also slide past each other. Earthquakes occur from sudden adjustments in Earth's crust. In California the Pacific plate is sliding northwestward along the edge of the North American plate. This has created the San Andreas Fault zone. A **fault** is a fractured surface in Earth's crust where a mass of rocks is in motion.

Tectonic plates move slowly—just inches a year. If, however, we could look back 200 million years, we would see that the continents have moved a long way. From their understanding of plate tectonics, scientists proposed the theory of continental drift. This theory states that the continents were once united in a single super-continent. They then separated and moved to the positions they are in today. Scientists call this original landmass **Pangaea** (pan-GEE-uh).

Continental Drift

About 200 million years ago it is believed there was only one continent, Pangaea, and one ocean, Panthalassa. The continental plates slowly drifted into their present-day positions.

✔ **READING CHECK:** *Physical Systems* How are primary landforms formed?

Secondary Landforms

The forces of plate tectonics build up primary landforms. At the same time, water, wind, and ice constantly break down rocks and cause rocky material to move. The landforms that result when primary landforms are broken down are called secondary landforms.

One process of breaking down and changing primary landforms into secondary landforms is called **weathering**. It is the process of breaking rocks into smaller pieces. Weathering occurs in several ways. Heat can cause rocks to crack. Water may get into cracks in rocks and freeze. This ice then expands with a force great enough to break the rock. Water can also work its way underground and slowly dissolve minerals such as limestone. This process sometimes creates caves. In

These steep peaks in Chile are part of the Andes.

Interpreting the Visual Record How do these mountains show the effects of weathering and erosion?

Elevation Profile: Guadalcanal

Elevation is the height of the land above sea level. An elevation profile is a cross-section used to show the elevation of a specific area.

Interpreting the Visual Record What is the range of elevation for Guadalcanal?

some areas small plants called lichens attach to bare rock. Chemicals in the lichens gradually break down the stone. Some places in the world experience large swings in temperature. In the Arctic the ground freezes and thaws, which tends to lift stones to the surface in unusual patterns. Regardless of which weathering process is at work, rocks eventually break down into sediment. These smaller pieces of rock are called gravel, sand, silt, or clay, depending on particle size. Once weathering has taken place, water, ice, or wind can move the material and create new landforms.

✔ **READING CHECK:** (*Physical Systems*) What is one way in which secondary landforms are created?

Erosion

Another process of changing primary landforms into secondary landforms is **erosion**. Erosion is the movement of rocky materials to another location. Moving water is the most common force that erodes and shapes the land.

Water Flowing water carries sediment. This sediment forms different kinds of landforms depending on where it is deposited. For example, a river flowing from a mountain range onto a flat area, or plain, may deposit some of its sediment there. The sediment sometimes builds up into a fan-shaped form called an **alluvial fan**. A **floodplain** is created when rivers flood their banks and deposit sediment. A **delta** is formed when rivers carry some of their sediment all the way to the ocean. The sediment settles to the bottom where the river meets the ocean. The Nile and Mississippi Rivers have two of the world's largest deltas.

Waves in the ocean and in lakes also shape the land they touch. Waves can shape beaches into great dunes, such as on the shore of Long Island. The jagged coastline of Oregon also shows the erosive power of waves.

River water, brown with sediment, enters the ocean.

Glaciers In high mountain settings and in the coldest places on Earth are **glaciers**. These large, slow-moving rivers of ice have the power to move tons of rock.

Giant sheets of thick ice called continental glaciers cover Greenland and Antarctica. Over the past 2 million years Earth has experienced several ice ages—periods of extremely cold conditions. During each ice age continental glaciers covered most of Canada and the northern United States. The Great Lakes were carved out by the movement of a continental glacier.

Wind Wind also shapes the land. Strong winds can lift soils into the air and carry them across great distances. On beaches and in deserts wind can deposit large amounts of sand to form dunes.

Blowing sand can wear down rock. The sand acts like sandpaper to polish jagged edges. An example of rocks worn down by blowing sand can be seen in Utah's Canyonlands National Park.

✓ **READING CHECK:** (*Physical Systems*) What forces cause erosion?

People and Landforms

Geographers study how people adapt their lives to different landforms. Deltas and floodplains, for example, are usually fertile places to grow food. People also change landforms. Engineers build dams to control river flooding. They drill tunnels through mountains instead of making roads over mountaintops. People have used modern technology to build structures that are better able to survive disasters like floods and earthquakes.

✓ **READING CHECK:** (*Environment and Society*) What are some examples of humans adjusting to and changing landforms?

go.hrw.com
Homework Practice Online
Keyword: SG3 HP2

Section Review 3

Define and explain: landforms, plain, plateau, isthmus, peninsula, plate tectonics, core, mantle, crust, magma, lava, continents, earthquakes, fault, Pangaea, weathering, erosion, alluvial fan, floodplain, deltas, glaciers

Reading for the Main Idea

1. (*Physical Systems*) How are primary landforms created?

2. (*Physical Systems*) What forces cause weathering and erosion?

Critical Thinking

3. Summarizing What is plate tectonics?

4. Finding the Main Idea How do people affect landforms? Give examples.

Organizing What You Know

5. Identifying Cause and Effect Copy the following graphic organizer. Use it to describe the movement of plates and the movement's effects.

movement		resulting landforms and changes
	⇨	
	⇨	
	⇨	

Building Vocabulary

On a separate sheet of paper, write sentences to define each of the following words.

1. solar system
2. orbit
3. solstice
4. equinoxes
5. atmosphere
6. water cycle
7. evaporation
8. condensation
9. precipitation
10. landforms
11. plate tectonics
12. continents
13. earthquakes
14. weathering
15. erosion

Reviewing the Main Ideas

1. *(Physical Systems)* In what ways do Earth's rotation, revolution, and tilt help determine how much of the Sun's energy reaches Earth?

2. *(Physical Systems)* Explain how the Sun's energy drives the water cycle. Be sure to include a discussion of the three elements of the cycle.

3. *(Physical Systems)* How does plate tectonics relate to the continents and their landforms?

4. *(Physical Systems)* Describe how subduction zones are created.

5. *(Physical Systems)* Describe the different ways secondary landforms are created.

Understanding Environment and Society

Water Use

The availability and purity of water are important for everyone. Research the water supply in your own city or community and prepare a presentation on it. You may want to think about the following:

- Where your city or community gets its drinking water,
- Drought or water shortages that have happened in the past,
- Actions your community takes to protect the water supply.

Thinking Critically

1. **Drawing Inferences and Conclusions** How do the four parts of the Earth system help explain why places on Earth differ?

2. **Finding the Main Idea** Describe landforms that are shaped by water and wind.

3. **Drawing Inferences and Conclusions** Why do people continue to live in areas where floods are likely to occur?

4. **Identifying Cause and Effect** Describe the landforms that result (a) when two tectonic plates collide and (b) when two plates move away from each other.

5. **Summarizing** In what ways do people interact with landforms?

6. **Analyzing Information** How might mountains be primary and secondary landforms?

Map ACTIVITY

On a separate sheet of paper, match the letters on the globe with their correct labels.

Tropic of Cancer

Tropic of Capricorn

equator

Arctic Circle

Antarctic Circle

North Pole

South Pole

Mental Mapping Skills ACTIVITY

On a separate sheet of paper, draw a freehand model of the solar system. Locate the following in relation to our Sun:

Earth

Jupiter

Mars

Mercury

Neptune

Pluto

Saturn

Uranus

Venus

WRITING ACTIVITY

Considering the vastness of the solar system, as well as the interest in exploring it, write a job description for a space explorer. What kinds of qualifications would that person need to research space? Be sure to use standard grammar, spelling, sentence structure, and punctuation in your descriptions.

Alternative Assessment

Portfolio ACTIVITY

Learning About Your Local Geography

Individual Project Compare the latitude and longitude of your state's capital city with that of the capitals of three countries. How might the seasons be similar or different in each city?

internet connect

Internet Activity: go.hrw.com
KEYWORD: SG3 GT2

Choose a topic to explore online:
- Learn more about Earth's seasons.
- Discover facts about Earth's water.
- Investigate earthquakes.

go.hrw.com

CHAPTER 3

Wind, Climate, and Natural Environments

Diver, coral, and fish, Fiji Islands

Tornado in Saskatoon, Canada

Igloo at night, Alaska Range

Read to Discover

1. How does the Sun's energy change Earth?
2. Why are wind and ocean currents important?

Define

weather
climate
greenhouse effect

air pressure
front
currents

WHY IT MATTERS

Changes in ocean temperatures create currents that affect Earth's landmasses. Use CNNfyi.com or other **current events** sources to find examples of the effects of changes in ocean temperatures, such as the La Niña weather pattern. Record your findings in your journal.

Earth from space

The Sun's Energy

All planets in our solar system receive energy from the Sun. This energy has important effects. Among the most obvious effects we see on our planet are those on **weather** and **climate**. Weather is the condition of the atmosphere at a given place and time. Climate refers to the weather conditions in an area over a long period of time. How do you think the Sun's energy affects weather and climate?

Energy Balance Although Earth keeps receiving energy from the Sun, it also loses energy. Energy that is lost goes into space. As a result, Earth—as a whole—loses as much energy as it gets. Thus, Earth's overall temperature stays about the same.

As you learned in Chapter 2, the Sun does not warm Earth evenly. The part of Earth in daylight takes in more energy than it loses. Temperatures rise. However, the rest of Earth is in darkness. That part of Earth loses more energy than it gets. Temperatures drop. In addition, when the direct rays of the Sun strike Earth at the Tropic of Cancer, it is summer in the Northern Hemisphere. Temperatures are warm. The Southern Hemisphere, on the other hand, is having winter. Temperatures are lower. The seasons reverse when the Sun's direct rays move above the Tropic of Capricorn. We can see that in any one place temperatures vary from day to day. From year to year, however, they usually stay about the same.

Stored Energy Some of the heat energy that reaches Earth is stored. One place Earth stores heat is in the air. This keeps Earth's surface warmer than if there were no air around it. The process by which

Plants—like this fossil palm found in a coal bed—store the Sun's energy. When we burn coal—the product of long-dead plants—we release the energy the plants had stored.

internet connect

GO TO: go.hrw.com
KEYWORD: SG3 CH3
FOR: Web sites about wind, climates, and environments

The Greenhouse Effect

Heat escapes

Sunlight

Heat trapped

Light from the Sun passes through the atmosphere and heats Earth's surface. Most heat energy later escapes into space.

You Be the Geographer What would happen if too much heat energy remained trapped in the atmosphere?

This snow-covered waterfront town is located on Mackinac Island, Michigan.

Earth's atmosphere traps heat is called the **greenhouse effect**. In a greenhouse the Sun's energy passes through the glass and heats everything inside. The glass traps the heat, keeping the greenhouse warm.

Water and land store heat, too. As we learned in Chapter 2, water warms and cools slowly. This explains why in fall, long after temperatures have dropped, the ocean's water is only a little cooler than in summer. Land and buildings also store heat energy. For example, a brick building that has heated up all day stays warm after the Sun sets.

✓ **READING CHECK:** *Physical Systems* How does the Sun's energy affect Earth?

Wind and Currents

Air and water both store heat. When they move from place to place, they keep different parts of the world from becoming too hot or too cold. By moving air and water, winds and ocean currents move heat energy between warmer and cooler places. Different parts of the world are kept from becoming too hot or too cold.

When the wind is blowing, air is moving from one place to another. Everyone has experienced these local winds. Global winds also exist. They move air and heat energy around Earth. Ocean currents, which are caused by wind, also move heat energy.

Canada
Mackinac
Island
United States
Mexico

Air Pressure

To understand why there are winds, we must understand **air pressure**. Air pressure is the weight of the air. Air is a mixture of gases. At sea level, a cubic foot of air weighs about 1.25 ounces (35 grams). We do not feel this weight because air pushes on us from all sides equally. The weight of air, however, changes with the weather. Cold air weighs more than warmer air. An instrument called a barometer measures air pressure.

When air warms, it gets lighter and rises. Colder air then moves in to replace the rising air. The result is wind. Wind travels from areas of high pressure to areas of low pressure. During the day land heats up faster than water. The air over the land heats up faster as well. Along the coast lower air pressure is located over land and higher air pressure is located over water. The air above land rises, and cool air flows in to shore to take its place. At night the land cools more quickly than the water. Air pressure over the land increases, and the wind changes direction.

Earth has several major areas where air pressure stays about the same throughout the year. Along the equator is an area of low air pressure. The pressure is low because the Sun is always warming this area.

Wind shapes Earth and the life that thrives here. For example, this tree has grown in the direction blown by the area's prevailing winds.

Interpreting the Visual Record How do you think wind shapes Earth's landscape?

Reading a Weather Map

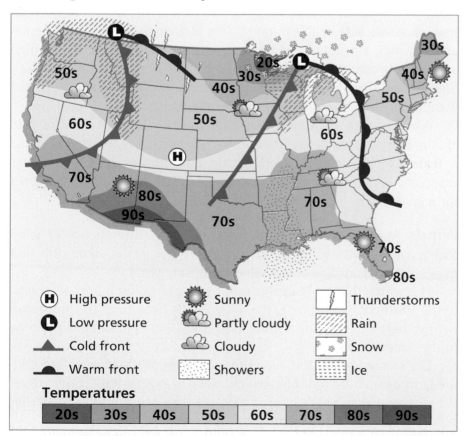

H	High pressure	☀	Sunny	⚡	Thunderstorms
L	Low pressure	⛅	Partly cloudy	▨	Rain
▲	Cold front	☁	Cloudy	❄	Snow
⬤	Warm front	⸫	Showers	▦	Ice

Temperatures

| 20s | 30s | 40s | 50s | 60s | 70s | 80s | 90s |

Weather maps show atmospheric conditions as they currently exist or as they are forecast for a particular time period. Most weather maps have legends that explain what the symbols on the map mean. This map shows a cold front sweeping through the central United States. A low-pressure system is at the center of a storm bringing rain and snow to the Midwest. Notice that temperatures behind the cold front are considerably cooler than those ahead of the front.

You Be the Geographer What is the average temperature range for the southwestern states?

Pressure and Wind Systems

Winds between Earth's high- and low-pressure zones help regulate the globe's energy balance.

You Be the Geographer What happens when warm westerlies come into contact with cold polar winds?

Polar high pressure
North Pole

Subpolar low pressure

Polar winds

60° N

Subtropical high pressure

Westerlies

30° N

Northeast trade winds

Equatorial low pressure

Doldrums

0°

Southeast trade winds

Subtropical high pressure

Westerlies

30° S

60° S

Polar Winds

Subpolar low pressure

South Pole
Polar high pressure

This ship uses wind to travel. As more wind catches the sails, the ship moves faster.

This warm air rises along the equator and moves north and south. Some of the warm air cools and sinks once it reaches about 30° latitude on either side of the equator. This change in temperature causes areas of high air pressure in the subtropics. The pressure is also high at the North and South Poles because the air is so cold. This cold air flows away from the Poles. Because the cold air is heavier, it lifts the warmer air in its path. The subpolar regions have low air pressure.

When a large amount of warm air meets a large amount of cold air, an area of unstable weather forms. This unstable weather is called a **front**. When cold air from Arctic and Antarctic regions meets warmer air, a polar front forms. When this type of front moves through an area, it can cause storms.

Winds The major areas of air pressure create the "belts" of wind that move air around Earth. Winds that blow in the same direction over large areas of Earth are called prevailing winds.

The winds that blow in the subtropics are called the trade winds. In the Northern Hemisphere, the trade winds blow from the northeast. Before ships had engines, sailors used trade winds to sail from Europe to the Americas.

The westerlies are the winds that blow from the west in the middle latitudes. These are the most common winds in the United States. When you watch a weather forecast you can see how the westerlies push storms across the country from west to east.

Few winds blow near the equator. This area is called the doldrums. Here, warm air rises rather than blowing east or west.

Ocean Currents Winds make ocean water move in the same general directions as the air above it moves. Warm ocean water from the tropics moves in giant streams, or **currents**, to colder areas. Cold water moves in streams from the polar areas to the tropics. This moves energy between different places. Warm air and warm ocean currents raise temperatures. On the other hand, cold winds and cold ocean currents lower temperatures.

The Gulf Stream is an ocean current. It moves warm water north along the east coast of the United States. The Gulf Stream then moves across the Atlantic Ocean toward western Europe. The warm air that moves with it keeps winters mild. As a result, areas such as Ireland have warmer winters than areas in Canada that are just as far north.

Ocean currents also bring heat energy into the Arctic Ocean. In the winter, warm currents create openings in the ice. These openings give arctic whales a place to breathe. They also give people a place to catch fish. Cold water also flows out of the Arctic Ocean into warmer waters of the Pacific and Atlantic Oceans. The cold water sinks below warmer water, causing mixing. This mixing brings food to sea life.

▲

Plants and animals adapt to their particular environments on Earth.

Interpreting the Visual Record How do you think the bearded seal is able to live in Norway's cold environment?

✓ READING CHECK: *Physical Systems* How do winds and currents create patterns on Earth's surface?

Section Review 1

go.hrw.com **Homework Practice Online**
Keyword: SG3 HP3

Define and explain: weather, climate, greenhouse effect, air pressure, front, currents

Reading for the Main Idea

1. *Physical Systems* How does Earth's temperature stay balanced?

2. *Physical Systems* How does the greenhouse effect allow Earth to store the Sun's energy?

Critical Thinking

3. Drawing Inferences and Conclusions How would weather in western Europe be different if there were no Gulf Stream?

4. Analyzing Information Why were the trade winds important to early sailors?

Organizing What You Know

5. Categorizing Copy the following graphic organizer. Use it to show the names, locations, and directions of wind and air pressure belts.

Name	Location	Direction

Wind, Climate, and Natural Environments • 41

CASE STUDY

HURRICANE: TRACKING A NATURAL HAZARD

Hurricanes are large circulating storms that begin in tropical oceans. Hurricanes often move over land and into populated areas. When a hurricane approaches land, it brings strong winds, heavy rains, and large ocean waves.

The map below shows the path of Hurricane Fran in 1996. Notice how Fran moved to the west and became stronger until it reached land. It began as a tropical depression and became a powerful hurricane as it passed over warm ocean waters.

Scientists who study hurricanes try to predict where these storms will travel. They want to be able to warn people in the hurricane's path. Early warnings can help people be better prepared for the deadly winds and rain. It is a difficult job because hurricanes can change course suddenly. Hurricanes are one of the most dangerous natural hazards.

One way of determining a hurricane's strength is by measuring the atmospheric pressure inside it. The lower the pressure, the stronger the storm. Hurricanes are rated on a scale of one to five. Study Table 1 to see how wind speed and air pressure are used to help determine the strength of a hurricane.

Hurricane Mitch formed in October 1998. The National Weather Service (NWS) recorded Mitch's position and strength. They learned that Mitch's pressure was one of the lowest ever recorded. The NWS estimated that Mitch's maximum sustained surface winds reached 180 miles per hour.

Table I: Saffir-Simpson Scale

HURRICANE TYPE	WIND SPEED MPH	AIR PRESSURE MB (INCHES)
Category 1	74–95	more than 980 (28.94)
Category 2	96–110	965–979 (28.50–28.91)
Category 3	111–130	945–964 (27.91–28.47)
Category 4	131–155	920–944 (27.17–27.88)
Category 5	more than 155	919 (27.16)

Source: Florida State University,
<http://www.met.fsu.edu/explores/tropical.html>

Path of Hurricane Fran, 1996

Table 2: Hurricane Mitch, 1998 Position and Strength

Date	Latitude (degrees)	Longitude (degrees)	Wind Speed (mph)	Pressure (millibars)	Storm Type
10/22	12 N	78 W	30	1002	Tropical depression
10/24	15 N	78 W	90	980	Category 2
10/26	16 N	81 W	130	923	Category 4
10/27	17 N	84 W	150	910	Category 5
10/31	15 N	88 W	40	1000	Tropical storm
11/01	15 N	90 W	30	1002	Tropical depression
11/03	20 N	91 W	40	997	Tropical storm
11/05	26 N	83 W	50	990	Tropical storm

Source: <http://www.met.fsu.edu/explores/tropical.html>

Hurricanes like Mitch cause very heavy rains in short periods of time. These heavy rains are particularly dangerous. The ground becomes saturated, and mud can flow almost like water. The flooding and mudslides caused by Mitch killed an estimated 10,000 people in four countries. Many people predicted that the region would not recover without help from other countries.

In the southeastern United States, many places have emergency preparedness units. The people assigned to these groups organize their communities. They provide food, shelter, and clothing for those who must evacuate their homes.

You Be the Geographer

1. Trace a map of the Caribbean. Be sure to include latitude and longitude lines.
2. Use the data about Hurricane Mitch in Table 2 to plot its path. Make a key with symbols to show Mitch's strength at each location.
3. What happened to Mitch when it reached land?

This satellite image shows the intensity of Hurricane Mitch. With advanced technology, hurricane tracking is helping to save lives.

Section 2 — Earth's Climate and Vegetation

Read to Discover

1. What is included in the study of weather?
2. What are the major climate types, and what types of plants live in each?

Define

rain shadow	hurricanes
monsoon	typhoons
arid	tundra climate
steppe climate	permafrost

WHY IT MATTERS

Flooding often becomes a problem during severe weather. Use CNNfyi.com or other current events sources to find examples of the effects of flooding on nations around the world. Record your findings in your journal.

A barometer

Nature has many incredible sights. Lightning is one of the most spectacular occurrences. These flashes of light are produced by a discharge of atmospheric electricity.

▼

Weather

As you have read, the condition of the atmosphere in a local area for a short period of time is called weather. Weather is a very general term. It can describe temperature, amount of sunlight, air pressure, wind, humidity, clouds, and moisture.

When warm and cool air masses come together, they form a front. Cold air lifts the warm air mass along the front. The air that is moved to higher elevations is cooled. If moisture is present in the lifted air, this cooling causes clouds to form. The moisture may fall to Earth as rain, snow, sleet, or hail. Moisture that falls in any form is called precipitation.

Another type of lifting occurs when warm, moist air is blown up against a mountain and forced to rise. The air cools as it is lifted, just as when air masses collide. Clouds form, and precipitation falls. The side of the mountain facing the wind—the windward side—often gets heavy rain. By the time the air reaches the other side of the mountain—the leeward side—it has lost most of its moisture. This can create a dry area called a **rain shadow**.

✔ READING CHECK: *Physical Systems* What is included in the study of weather?

Landforms and Precipitation

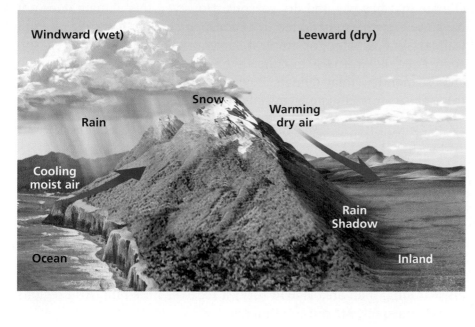

Windward (wet)   Leeward (dry)

Snow

Rain   Warming dry air

Cooling moist air

Rain Shadow

Ocean   Inland

As moist air from the ocean moves up the windward side of a mountain, it cools. The water vapor in the air condenses and falls in the form of rain or snow. Descending, the drier air then moves down the leeward side of the mountain. This drier air brings very little precipitation to areas in the rain shadow.

Low-Latitude Climates

If you charted the average weather in your community over a long period of time, you would be describing the climate for your area. Geographers have devised ways of describing climates based mainly on temperature, precipitation, and natural vegetation. In general, an area's climate is related to its latitude. In the low latitudes—the region close to the equator—there are two main types of climates: humid tropical and tropical savanna.

Humid Tropical Climate A humid tropical climate is warm and rainy all year. People living in this climate do not see a change from summer to winter. This is because the Sun heats the region throughout the year. The heat in the tropics causes a great deal of evaporation and almost daily rainstorms. One of the most complex vegetation systems in the world—the tropical rain forest—exists in this climate. The great rain forests of Brazil, Indonesia, and Central Africa are in the equatorial zone.

Some regions at higher latitudes have warm temperatures all year but have strong wet and dry seasons. Bangladesh and coastal India, for example, have an extreme wet season during the summer. Warm, moist air from the Indian Ocean reaches land. The air rises and cools, causing heavy rains. The rains continue until the wind changes direction in the fall. This seasonal shift of air flow and rainfall is known as a **monsoon**. A monsoon may be wet or dry. The monsoon system is particularly important in Asia.

The people of Tamil Nadu, India, adjust to the monsoon season.
Interpreting the Visual Record
What problems might people face during the wet monsoon?

In terms of loss of life, the worst natural disaster in U.S. history is still the hurricane that hit Galveston, Texas, on September 8, 1900. As many as 8,000 people died in Galveston.

Tropical Savanna Climate There is another type of tropical climate that has wet and dry seasons. However, this climate does not have the extreme shifts found in a monsoon climate. It is called a tropical savanna climate. The tropical savanna climate has a wet season soon after the warmest months. It has a dry season soon after the coolest months. Total rainfall, however, is fairly low. Vegetation in a tropical savanna climate is grass with scattered trees and shrubs.

✔ **READING CHECK:** (*Physical Systems*) Which climate regions are in the low latitudes?

Dry Climates

Temperature and precipitation are the most important parts of climate. Some regions, for example, experience strong hot and cold seasons. Other regions have wet and dry seasons. Some places are wet or dry all year long. If an area is **arid** (dry) it receives little rain. Arid regions usually have few streams and plants.

Desert Climate Most of the world's deserts lie near the tropics. The high air pressure and settling air keep these desert climate regions dry most of the time. Other deserts are located in the interiors of continents and in the rain shadows of mountains. Few plants can survive in the driest deserts, so there are many barren, rocky, or sandy areas. Dry air and clear skies permit hot daytime temperatures and rapid cooling at night.

Steppe Climate Another dry climate—the **steppe climate**—is found between desert and wet climate regions. A steppe receives more rainfall than a desert climate. However, the total amount of precipitation is still low. Grasses are the most common plants, but trees can grow along creeks and rivers. Farmers can grow crops but usually need to irrigate. Steppe climates occur in Africa, Australia, Central Asia, eastern Europe, in the Great Plains of the United States and Canada, and in South America.

✔ **READING CHECK:** (*The World in Spatial Terms*) What are the dry climates?

Palo Duro Canyon State Park in Texas attracts thousands of visitors each year.

Interpreting the Visual Record How can you tell that this canyon is located in a dry climate?

World Climate Regions

	Climate	Geographic Distribution	Major Weather Patterns	Vegetation
Low Latitudes	HUMID TROPICAL	along the equator	warm and rainy year-round, with rain totaling anywhere from 65 to more than 450 in. (165–1,143 cm) a year	tropical rain forest
	TROPICAL SAVANNA	between the humid tropics and the deserts	warm all year; distinct rainy and dry seasons; at least 20 in. (51 cm) of rain during the summer	tropical grassland with scattered trees
Dry	DESERT	centered along 30° latitude; some middle-latitude deserts are in the interior of large continents and along their western coasts	arid; less than 10 in. (25 cm) of rain a year; sunny and hot in the tropics and sunny with wide temperature ranges during the day in middle latitudes	a few drought-resistant plants
	STEPPE	generally bordering deserts and interiors of large continents	semiarid; about 10–20 in. (25–51 cm) of precipitation a year; hot summers and cooler winters with wide temperature ranges during a day	grassland; few trees
Middle Latitudes	MEDITERRANEAN	west coasts in middle latitudes	dry, sunny, warm summers and mild, wetter winters; rain averages 15–20 in. (38–51 cm) a year	scrub woodland and grassland
	HUMID SUBTROPICAL	east coasts in the middle latitudes	hot, humid summers and mild, humid winters; rain year-round; coastal areas are in the paths of hurricanes and typhoons	mixed forest
	MARINE WEST COAST	west coasts in the upper-middle latitudes	cloudy, mild summers and cool, rainy winters; strong ocean influence; rain averages 20–60 in. (51–152 cm) a year	temperate evergreen forest
	HUMID CONTINENTAL	east coasts and interiors of upper-middle latitude continents	four distinct seasons; long, cold winters and short, warm summers; amounts of precipitation a year vary	mixed forest
High Latitudes	SUBARCTIC	higher latitudes of the interior and east coasts of continents	extremes of temperature; long, cold winters and short, warm summers; little precipitation all year	northern evergreen forest
	TUNDRA	high-latitude coasts	cold all year; very long, cold winters and very short, cool summers; little precipitation	moss, lichens, low shrubs; permafrost marshes
	ICE CAP	polar regions	freezing cold; snow and ice year-round; little precipitation	no vegetation
	HIGHLAND	high mountain regions	temperatures and amounts of precipitation vary greatly as elevation changes	forest to tundra vegetation, depending on elevation

The Mediterranean coast of France is part of the Riviera. The Riviera is located in a Mediterranean climate region.

Interpreting the Visual Record
What features would make this area popular with tourists?

Middle-Latitude Climates

The middle latitudes are the two broad zones between Earth's polar circles (66.5° north and south latitudes) and the tropics (23.5° north and south latitudes). Most of the climates in the middle latitudes have cool or cold winters and warm or hot summers. Climates with wet and dry seasons are also found. Middle-latitude climates may include rain shadow deserts.

Mediterranean Climate Several climates have clear wet and dry seasons. One of these, the Mediterranean climate, takes its name from the Mediterranean region. This climate has hot, dry summers followed by cooler, wet winters. Much of southern Europe and coastal North Africa have a Mediterranean climate. Parts of California, Australia, South Africa, and Chile do as well. Vegetation includes scrub woodlands and grasslands.

Humid Subtropical Climate The southeastern United States is an example of the humid subtropical climate. Warm, moist air from the ocean makes this region hot and humid in the summer. Winters are mild, but snow falls occasionally. People in a humid subtropical climate experience **hurricanes** and **typhoons**. These are tropical storms that bring violent winds, heavy rain, and high seas. The humid subtropical climate supports areas of mixed forests where deciduous and coniferous forests blend. Deciduous trees lose their leaves during the fall each year. Coniferous trees have needle-shaped leaves that remain green year-round.

Marine West Coast Climate Some coastal areas of North America and much of western Europe have a marine west coast climate. Westerly winds carry moisture from the ocean across the land, causing winter rainfall. Evergreen forests can grow in these regions because of regular rain.

The Mediterranean has a variety of vegetation. This Mediterranean scrub forest is in Corfu, Greece.
Interpreting the Visual Record What kinds of vegetation do you see in this scrub forest?

Humid Continental Climate Farther inland are regions with a humid continental climate. Winters in this region bring snowfall and cold temperatures, but there are some mild periods too. Summers are warm and sometimes hot. Most of the shifting weather in this climate region is the result of cold and warm air coming together along a polar front. Humid continental climates have four distinct seasons. Much of the midwestern and northeastern United States and southeastern Canada have a humid continental climate. This climate supports mixed forest vegetation.

✓ **READING CHECK:** (*The World in Spatial Terms*) What are the middle-latitude climates?

High-Latitude Climates

Closer to the poles we find another set of climates. They are the high-latitude climates. They have cold temperatures and little precipitation.

Subarctic Climate The subarctic climate has long, cold winters, short summers, and little rain. In the inland areas of North America, Europe, and Asia, far from the moderating influence of oceans, subarctic climates experience extreme temperatures. However, summers in these regions can be warm. In the Southern Hemisphere there is no land in the subarctic climate zone. As a result, boreal (BOHR-ee-uhl) forests are found only in the Northern Hemisphere. Trees in boreal forests are coniferous and cover vast areas in North America, Europe, and northern Asia.

Tundra Climate Farther north lies the **tundra climate**. Temperatures are cold, and rainfall is low. Usually just hardy plants, including mosses, lichens, and shrubs, survive here. Tundra summers are so short and cool that a layer of soil stays frozen all year. This frozen layer is called **permafrost**. It prevents water from draining into the soil. As a result, many ponds and marshes appear in summer.

Ice Cap Climate The polar regions of Earth have an ice cap climate. This climate

Wildlife eat the summer vegetation in the Alaskan tundra.
Interpreting the Visual Record Why is there snow on the mountain peaks during summer?

The Amundsen-Scott South Pole Station is a research center in Antarctica.

Interpreting the Visual Record How does the design of this building show ways people have adapted to the ice cap climate?

is cold—the monthly average temperature is below freezing. Precipitation averages less than 10 inches (25 cm) annually. Animals adapted to the cold, like walruses, penguins, and whales, are found here. No vegetation grows in this climate.

✓ **READING CHECK:** *The World in Spatial Terms* How are tundra and ice cap climates different?

Highland Climates

Mountains usually have several different climates in a small area. These climate types are known as highland climates. If you went from the base of a high mountain to the top, you might experience changes similar to going from the tropics to the Poles! The vegetation also changes with the elevation. It varies from thick forests or desert to tundra. Lower mountain elevations tend to be similar in temperature to the surrounding area. On the windward side, however, are zones of heavier rainfall or snowfall. As you go uphill, the temperatures drop. High mountains have a tundra zone and an icy summit.

✓ **READING CHECK:** *The World in Spatial Terms* What are highland climate regions?

Homework Practice Online

Keyword: SG3 HP3

Define and explain: rain shadow, monsoon, arid, steppe climate, hurricanes, typhoons, tundra climate, permafrost

Reading for the Main Idea

1. (*Physical Systems*) How is weather different from climate?

2. (*The World in Spatial Terms*) What are the major climate regions of the world?

Critical Thinking

3. **Drawing Inferences and Conclusions** Why is it important to understand weather and climate patterns?

4. **Analyzing Information** How does latitude influence climate?

Organizing What You Know

5. **Categorizing** Copy the following graphic organizer. Use it to describe Earth's climate types.

Climate	Latitudes	Characteristics

Section 3 Natural Environments

Read to Discover

1. How do environments affect life, and how do they change?
2. What substances make up the different layers of soil?

Define

extinct
ecology
photosynthesis
food chain
nutrients

plant communities
ecosystem
plant succession
humus

WHY IT MATTERS

Plants and animals depend on their environment for survival. Use or other current events sources to find out how conservationists work to save animals whose environments are threatened. Record your findings in your journal.

Acorns, the nut of an oak tree

Environmental Change

Geographers examine the distribution of plants and animals and the environments they occupy. They also study how people change natural environments. Changes in an environment affect the plants and animals that live in that environment. If environmental changes are extreme, some types of plants and animals may become **extinct**. This means they die out completely.

Ecology and Plant Life The study of the connections among different forms of life is called **ecology**. One process connecting life forms is **photosynthesis**—the process by which plants convert sunlight into chemical energy. Roots take in minerals, water, and gases from the soil. Leaves take in sunlight and carbon dioxide from the air. Plant cells take in these elements and combine them to produce special chemical compounds. Plants use some of these chemicals to live and grow.

Plant growth is the basis for all the food that animals eat. Some animals, like deer, eat only plants. When deer eat plants, they store some of the plant food energy in their bodies. Other animals, like wolves, eat deer and indirectly get the plant food the deer ate. The plants, deer, and wolves together make up a **food chain**. A food chain is a series of organisms in which energy is passed along.

▲
Plants use a particular environment's sunlight, water, gases, and minerals to survive.

Food Web

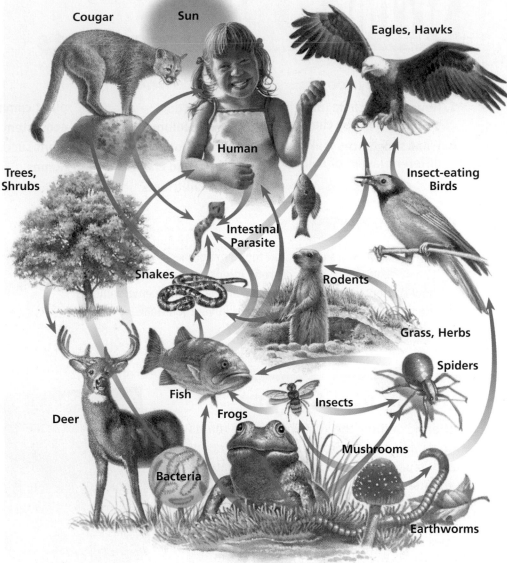

Food chains rarely occur alone in nature. More common are food webs—interlocking networks of food chains. This food web includes tiny organisms, such as parasites and bacteria, as well as human beings and other large mammals.

Not all predators are big. In Antarctica's dry areas a microscopic bacteria-eating worm that can survive years of being freeze-dried is at the top of the food chain.

Limits for Life Plants and animals cannot live everywhere. They are limited by environmental conditions. Any type of plant or animal tends to be most common in areas where it is best able to live, grow, and reproduce. A simple example shows why you do not find every kind of plant and animal in all regions on Earth. Trees do not survive in the tundra because it is too cold and there is not enough moisture. At the edge of the tundra, however, there are large boreal forests. Once in a while, wind carries tree seeds into the tundra. Some of the seeds sprout and grow. These young trees are generally small and weak. Eventually they die.

In this example life is limited by conditions of temperature and moisture. Other factors that can limit plant life include the amount of light, water, and soil **nutrients**. Nutrients are substances promoting growth. Some plant and animal life is limited by other plants and animals that compete for the same resources.

CONNECTING TO *Science*

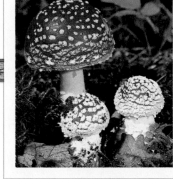

There are more than 2,000 species of harmless mushrooms.

Soil Factory

The next time you see a fallen tree in the forest, do not think of it as a dead log. Think of it as a soil factory. As the tree decays and crumbles, it adds valuable nutrients to the forest soil. These nutrients enrich the soil. They also make it possible for new trees and plants to grow.

The fallen tree does not do its work alone, however. It is aided by many different living organisms that break down the wood and turn it into humus. Humus is a rich blend of organic material that mixes with the soil. A downed tree that lies on the forest floor is buzzing with the activity of hundreds of species of insects and plants that live and work inside it.

When a tree falls, insects, bacteria and other microorganisms invade the wood and start the process of decay. Insects like weevils, bark beetles, carpenter ants, and termites, among others, bore into the wood and break it down further. These insects, in turn, attract birds, spiders, lizards, and other predators who feed on insect life. Before long, the fallen tree is brimming with life. This happens even as the tree breaks apart on the forest floor.

Fallen trees provide as much as one third of the organic matter in forest soil. As forest ecologist Chris Maser notes, "Dead wood is no wasted resource. It is nature's reinvestment in biological capital."

You Be the Geographer
1. How do fallen trees decompose?
2. How is fertile soil produced by downed trees?

Plant Communities Groups of plants that live in the same area are called **plant communities**. In harsh environments, such as tundra, plant communities tend to be simple. They may be made up of just a few different types of plants. Regions that receive more rainfall and have more moderate temperatures tend to have more complex plant communities. The greatest variety of plants and animals can be found in the rain forests of the tropics. This environment is warm and moist all year.

Each plant community has plants adapted to the environment of the region. Near the Arctic, for example, the shortage of sunlight limits plant growth. Some of the flowers that grow here turn to follow the Sun as it moves across the sky. Thus the flowers collect as much sunlight as they can. In other regions there are plants adapted to survive in poor soils or with limited moisture. Some large trees, for example, have deep roots that can reach water and soil nutrients far below the surface. Their spreading branches also collect large amounts of sunlight for photosynthesis.

Plants adapt to the sunlight, soil, and temperature of their region. They may also be suited to other plants found in their communities. For example, many ferns grow well in the shade found underneath trees. Some vines grow up tree trunks to reach sunlight.

All of the plants and animals in an area together with the nonliving parts of their environment—like climate and soil—form what is called an **ecosystem**. The size of an ecosystem varies, depending on how it is defined. A small pond, for example, can be considered an ecosystem. The entire Earth can also be considered an ecosystem.

Ecosystems can be affected by natural events like droughts, fires, floods, severe frosts, and windstorms. Human activities can also disturb ecosystems. This happens when land is cleared for development, new kinds of plants and animals are brought into an area, or pollution is released into air and water.

Forest Succession After a Fire

A Forest fire in progress

B Early plant growth

C Middle stage

D Forest recovered

▲

Difficult conditions after a forest fire mean that the first plants to grow back must be very hardy.
You Be the Geographer In this series of photos, which plants are the first to grow back?

Plant Succession When natural or human forces disturb a plant community, the community may be replaced by a different group of plants suited to the new conditions. The gradual process by which one group of plants replaces another is called **plant succession**.

To better understand plant succession, imagine an area just after a forest fire. The first plants to return to the area need plenty of sunshine. These plants hold the soil in place. They also provide shade for the seeds of other plants. Gradually, seeds from small trees and shrubs grow under the protection of the first plants. These new plants grow taller and begin to take more and more of the sunlight. Many of the smaller plants die. Later, taller trees in the area replace the shorter trees and shrubs that grew at first.

It is important to remember that plant communities are not permanent. The conditions they experience change over time. Some changes affect a whole region. For example, a region's climate may gradually become colder, drier, warmer, or wetter. Additional changes may occur if new plants are introduced to the community.

✓ **READING CHECK:** *Physical Systems* How do environments affect life, and how do they change?

Soils

In any discussion of plants, plant communities, or plant succession, it is important to know about the soils that support plant life. All soils are not the same. The type of soil in an area can contribute to the kinds of plants that can be grown there. It can also affect how well a plant grows. Plants need soil with minerals, water, and small air spaces if they are to survive and grow.

Soils contain decayed plant and animal matter, called **humus**. Soils rich in humus are fertile. This means they can support an abundance of plant life. Humus is formed by insects and bacteria that live in soil. They break down dead plants and animals and make the nutrients available to plant roots. Insects also make small air spaces as they move through soils. These air pockets contain moisture and gases that plant roots need for growth.

The processes that break down rocks to form soil take hundreds or even thousands of years. Over this long period of time soil tends to form layers. If you dig a deep hole, you can see these layers. Soils typically have three layers. The thickness of each layer depends on the conditions in a specific location. The top layer is called topsoil. It includes humus, insects, and plants. The layer beneath the surface soil is called the subsoil. Only the deep roots of some plants, mostly trees, reach the subsoil. Underneath this layer is broken rock that eventually breaks down into more soil. As the rock breaks down it adds minerals to the soil.

Soils can lose their fertility in several ways. Erosion by water or wind can sweep topsoil away. Nutrients can also be removed from soils by leaching. This occurs when rainfall dissolves nutrients in topsoil and washes them down into lower soil layers, out of reach of most plant roots.

✓ **READING CHECK:** (*Physical Systems*) What are the physical processes that produce fertile soil?

Soil Layers

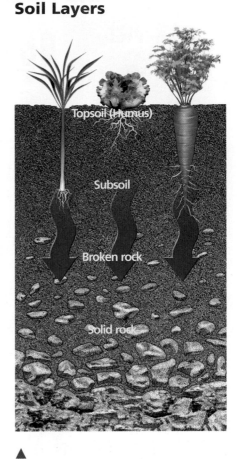

▲ The three layers of soil are the topsoil, subsoil, and broken rock. **Interpreting the Visual Record What do you think has created the cracks in the rocky layer below the broken rock?**

Section Review 3

Define and explain: extinct, ecology, photosynthesis, food chain, nutrients, plant communities, ecosystem, plant succession, humus

Reading for the Main Idea

1. (*Physical Systems*) Why cannot all plants and animals live everywhere? Provide an example to illustrate your answer.

2. (*Physical Systems*) What makes up soil, and what produces fertile soil?

Homework Practice Online Keyword: SG3 HP3

Critical Thinking

3. **Analyzing Information** What keeps tundra plant communities simple?

4. **Summarizing** How does plant succession occur?

Organizing What You Know

5. **Sequencing** Copy the following graphic organizer. Use it to describe a food chain.

Building Vocabulary

On a separate sheet of paper, write sentences to define each of the following words.

1. weather
2. climate
3. greenhouse effect
4. air pressure
5. front
6. currents
7. rain shadow
8. monsoon
9. arid
10. permafrost
11. extinct
12. ecology
13. nutrients
14. ecosystem
15. humus

Reviewing the Main Ideas

1. (*The World in Spatial Terms*) What are the major wind belts? Describe each.
2. (*Physical Systems*) How is the area around mountains affected by precipitation?
3. (*The World in Spatial Terms*) Into what main divisions can climate be grouped?
4. (*Environment and Society*) What do people do to change ecosystems?
5. (*Physical Systems*) What elements make up soil? How is fertile soil created?

Understanding Environment and Society

Tornadoes

Prepare an outline for a presentation on tornadoes. As you prepare your presentation from the outline, think about the following:

- How tornadoes are formed.
- How experts are able to forecast their occurrence more accurately.
- The safety precautions taken by people in tornado-prone areas.

Thinking Critically

1. **Finding the Main Idea** How does Earth store the Sun's energy?
2. **Analyzing Information** What effect do wind patterns have on ocean currents?
3. **Drawing Inferences and Conclusions** Why is it important to study the weather?
4. **Drawing Inferences and Conclusions** Why is it important to understand the concept of latitude when learning about Earth's many climates?
5. **Drawing Inferences and Conclusions** Why is it important for scientists to study soils?

Map ACTIVITY

On a separate sheet of paper, match the letters on the map with their correct labels.

The following natural disasters are often experienced in the United States:

- **hurricanes on the East Coast**
- **hurricanes on the Gulf Coast**
- **forest fires on the West Coast**
- **tornadoes in Texas, Oklahoma, Kansas, and Nebraska**

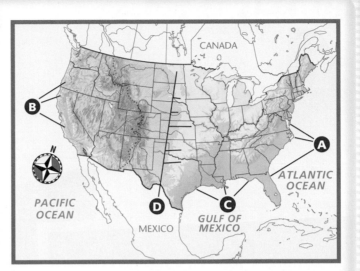

Mental Mapping Skills ACTIVITY

Draw a freehand map of the globe. Draw lines to show the equator and low, middle, and high latitudes. Draw the continents in the appropriate areas.

WRITING ACTIVITY

After studying different climate regions, decide in which of the regions you would like to live. Write a journal entry describing what your life would be like in this particular area. Be sure to use standard grammar, spelling, sentence structure, and punctuation in your story.

Alternative Assessment

Portfolio ACTIVITY

Learning About Your Local Geography

Understanding Cause and Effect

Research your local weather patterns. Create a graph that shows how recent weather conditions have affected humans, plants, and animals in your part of the state.

🖅 internet connect

Internet Activity: go.hrw.com
KEYWORD: SG3 GT3

Choose a topic to explore online:

- Learn more about using weather maps.
- Follow El Niño, an ocean phenomenon that affects weather.
- Build a food web.

CHAPTER 4

Earth's Resources

Precious gems

Wind turbines

Valley in the
Andes of Ecuador

Section 1

Soil and Forests

Read to Discover

1. What physical processes produce fertile soil?
2. What processes threaten soil fertility?
3. Why are forests valuable resources, and how are they being protected?

Define

renewable resources
crop rotation
terraces

desertification
deforestation
reforestation

WHY IT MATTERS

Many people work to balance concerns about saving the rain forests with local economic needs. Use CNN**fyi**.com or other **current events** sources to learn more about these efforts. Record your findings in your journal.

Corn, a major food crop

Soil

Soil is one of the most important **renewable resources** on Earth. Renewable resources are those that can be replaced by Earth's natural processes.

Soil types vary depending on geographic factors. As you learned in Chapter 3, soil contains rock particles and humus. It also contains water and gases. Because soil types vary, some are better able to support plant life than others.

Soil Fertility Soil conservation—protecting the soil's ability to nourish plants—is one challenge facing farmers. Plants must take up nutrients like calcium, nitrogen, phosphorus, and potassium in order to grow. These essential nutrients may become used up if fields are always planted with the same crops. Farmers can add these nutrients to soils in the form of fertilizers, sometimes called plant food. The first fertilizers used were manures. Later, chemical fertilizers were used to increase yields.

Some farmers choose not to use chemical fertilizers. Others cannot afford to use them. They rely on other ways to keep up the soil's ability to produce. One such method is **crop rotation**. This is a system of growing different crops on the same land over a period of years.

On this farm, fields are planted with corn and alfalfa. Alfalfa is a valued crop because it replaces nutrients in the soil.

▼

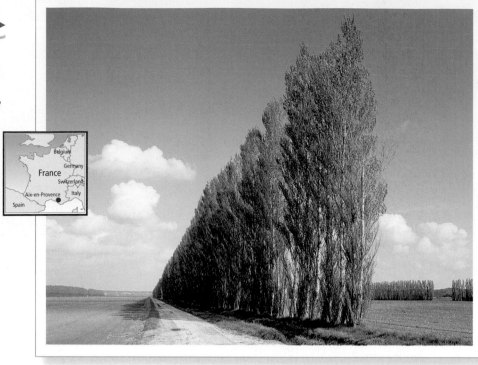

A row of poplar trees divides farmland near Aix-en-Provence, France. **Interpreting the Visual Record** What effect will these trees have on erosion?

About 47,000 aspen trees in Utah share a root system and a set of genes. These trees are actually a single organism. These aspens cover 106 acres (43 hectares) and weigh at least 13 million pounds (5.9 million kg). Together they are probably the world's heaviest living thing.

Salty Soil Salt buildup is another threat to soil fertility. In dry climates farmers must irrigate their crops. They use well water or water brought by canals and ditches. Much of this water evaporates in the dry air. When the water evaporates, it leaves behind small amounts of salt. If too much salt builds up in the soil, crops cannot grow.

Erosion The problem of soil erosion is faced by farmers all over the world. Farmers have to work to keep soil from being washed away by rainfall. Soil can also be blown away by strong winds. To prevent soil loss, some farmers plant rows of trees to block the wind. Others who farm on steep hillsides build **terraces** into the slope. Terraces are horizontal ridges like stair steps. By slowing water movement the terraces stop the soil from being washed away. They also provide more space for farming.

Loss of Farmland The loss of farmland is a serious problem in many parts of the world. In some places farming has worn out the soil, and it can no longer grow crops. Livestock may then eat what few plants remain. Without plants to hold the soil in place, it may blow away. The long-term process of losing soil fertility and plant life is called **desertification**. Once this process begins, the desert can expand as people move on to better soils. They often repeat the destructive practices, damaging ever-larger areas.

Farmland is also lost when cities and suburbs expand into rural areas. Nearby farmers sell their land. The land is then used for housing or businesses, rather than for agriculture. This is happening in many poorer countries. It also happens in richer nations like the United States.

✓ **READING CHECK:** *Environment and Society* What physical processes help soil fertility, and what threatens it?

Forests

Forests are renewable resources because new trees can be planted in a forest. If cared for properly, they will be available for future generations. Forests are important because they provide both people and wildlife with food and shelter. People depend on forests for a wide variety of products. Wood products include lumber, plywood, and shingles for building houses. Other wood-based manufactured products include cellophane, furniture, some plastics, and fibers such as rayon. Trees also supply fats, gums, medicines, nuts, oils, turpentine, waxes, and rubber. The forests are valuable not only for their products. People also use forests for recreational activities, such as camping and hiking.

Deforestation The destruction or loss of forest area is called **deforestation**. It is happening in the rain forests of Africa, Asia, and Central and South America. People clear the land and use it for farming, industry, and housing. Pollution also causes deforestation.

Protecting Forests Many countries, including the United States, are trying to balance their economic needs regarding forests with conservation efforts. Since the late 1800s Congress has passed laws to protect and manage forest and wilderness areas. In addition to protecting forests, people can also plant trees in places where forests have been cut down. This replanting is called **reforestation**. In some cases the newly planted trees can be "harvested" again in a few years.

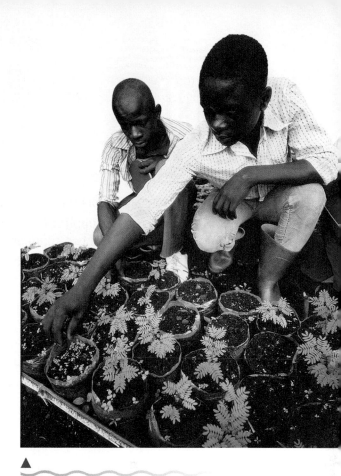

▲
Villagers work on a reforestation project in Cameroon.

✔ **READING CHECK:** (*Environment and Society*) Why is preserving forests important, and how can people contribute to it?

Section Review 1

go.hrw.com
Homework Practice Online
Keyword: SG3 HP4

Define and explain: renewable resources, crop rotation, terraces, desertification, deforestation, reforestation

Reading for the Main Idea

1. (*Environment and Society*) What physical processes produce fertile soil?

2. (*Environment and Society*) What do forests provide, and how can they be protected?

Critical Thinking

3. **Finding the Main Idea** Which two natural forces contribute to soil erosion? How can erosion be prevented?

4. **Drawing Inferences and Conclusions** Why is it important to manage forests?

Organizing What You Know

5. **Categorizing** Copy the following graphic organizer. Use it to discuss whether or not rain forests should be protected.

Reasons for . . .	Reasons against . . .

Section 2 Water and Air

Read to Discover

1. Why is water an important resource?
2. What threatens our supplies of freshwater, and how can we protect these supplies?
3. What are some problems caused by air pollution?

Define

semiarid
aqueducts
aquifers
desalinization
acid rain
global warming

WHY IT MATTERS

Countries around the world have worked together to resolve problems regarding Earth's atmosphere. Use **CNNfyi**.com or other **current events** sources to learn about these efforts. Record your findings in your journal.

A water tank

Water

Dry regions are found in many parts of the world, including the western United States. There are also **semiarid** regions—regions that receive a small amount of rain. Semiarid places are usually too dry for farming. However, these areas may be suitable for grazing animals.

Water Supply Many areas of high mountains receive heavy snowfall in the winter. When that snow melts, it forms rivers that flow from the mountains to neighboring regions. People in dry regions use various means to bring the water where it is needed for agricultural and other uses. They build canals, reservoirs, and **aqueducts**—artificial channels for carrying water.

Some places have water deep underground in **aquifers**. These are water-bearing layers of rock, sand, or gravel. Some are quite large. For example, the Ogallala Aquifer stretches across the Great Plains from Texas to South Dakota. People drill wells to reach the water in the aquifer.

People in dry coastal areas have access to plenty of salt water. However, they typically do not have enough freshwater. In Southwest Asia this situation is common. To create a supply of

As people make their homes in dry areas, they add to the demand for water. ▼

Canada
United States
San Bernardino
Mexico

freshwater, people in these places have built machines that take the salt out of seawater. This process, known as **desalinization**, is expensive and takes a lot of energy. However, in some places, it is necessary.

Water Conservation In recent decades people have developed new ways to save water. Many factories now recycle water. Farmers are able to irrigate their crops more efficiently. Cities build water treatment plants to purify water that might otherwise be wasted. Some people in dry climates are using desert plants instead of grass for landscaping. This means that they do not need to water as often.

It is important for people in all climates to conserve water. Wasting water in one location could mean that less water is available for use in other places.

Water Quality Industries and agriculture also affect the water supply. In many countries there are still places that cannot afford to build closed sewer systems. Some factories also operate without pollution controls because such controls would add a great deal of cost to operation.

Industrialized countries like the United States have water treatment plants and closed sewer systems. However, water can still be polluted when farmers use too much chemical fertilizer and pesticides. These chemicals can get into local streams. Waste from industries may also contain chemicals, metals, or oils that can pollute streams and rivers.

Rivers carry pollution to the oceans. The pollution can harm marine life such as fish and shellfish. Eating marine life from polluted waters can make people sick. So can drinking polluted water. Balancing industrial and agricultural needs with the need for clean water continues to be a challenge faced by many countries.

✓ **READING CHECK:** (*Environment and Society*) Why is water an important resource, and how does its availability affect people?

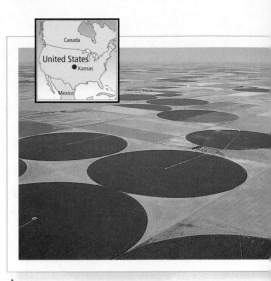

▲

Pivoting sprinklers irrigate these circular cornfields in Kansas.
Interpreting the Visual Record Why might irrigation be necessary in these fields?

Air

Air is essential to life. Plants and animals need the gases in the air to live and grow.

Human activities can pollute the air and threaten the health of life on the planet. Burning fuels for heating, for transportation, and to power factories releases chemicals into the air. Particularly in large cities, these chemicals build up in the air. The chemicals create a mixture called smog.

Some cities have special problems with air pollution. Denver, Los Angeles, and Mexico City, for example, are located in bowl-shaped valleys that can trap air pollution. This pollution sometimes builds up to levels that are dangerous to people's health.

Heavy smog clouds the Los Angeles skyline.

▼

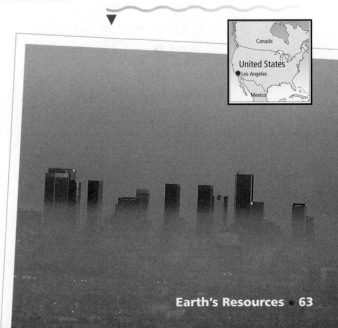

This satellite image of the Southern Hemisphere shows a thinning in the ozone layer in October 1979.

▼

▲

By October 1992 the thinning area, shown in purple, had grown much larger.

Acid Rain When air pollution combines with moisture in the air, it can form a mild acid. This can be similar in strength to vinegar. When it falls to the ground, this moisture is called **acid rain**. It can damage or kill trees. Acid rain can also kill fish.

Many countries have laws to limit pollution. However, pollution is an international problem. Winds can blow away air pollution, but the wind is only moving the pollution to another place. Pollution can pass from one country to another. It can even pass from one continent to another. Countries that limit their own pollution can still be affected by pollution from other countries.

Pollution and Climate Change Smog and acid rain are short-term effects of air pollution. Air pollution may also have long-term effects by changing conditions in Earth's atmosphere. Certain kinds of pollution damage the ozone in the upper atmosphere. This ozone layer protects living things by absorbing harmful ultraviolet light from the Sun. Damage to Earth's ozone layer may cause health problems in people. For example, it could lead to an increase in skin cancer.

Another concern is **global warming**—a slow increase in Earth's average temperature. The Sun constantly warms Earth's surface. The gases and water vapor in the atmosphere trap some of this heat. This helps keep Earth warm. Without the atmosphere, this heat would return to space. Evidence suggests that pollution causes the atmosphere to trap more heat. Over time this would make Earth warmer.

Scientists agree that Earth's climate has warmed during the last century. However, they disagree about exactly why. Some scientists say that temperatures have warmed because of air pollution caused by human activities, particularly the burning of fossil fuels. Others think warmer temperatures have resulted from natural causes. Scientists also disagree about what has caused the thinning of the ozone layer.

✓ **READING CHECK:** (*Environment and Society*) What are the different points of view about air pollution and climate change?

go.
hrw
.com
Homework Practice Online
Keyword: SG3 HP4

Section Review 2

Define and explain: semiarid, aqueducts, aquifers, desalinization, acid rain, global warming

Reading for the Main Idea

1. (*Environment and Society*) How have people changed the environment to increase the water supply in drier areas?

2. (*Environment and Society*) How do people cause water pollution?

3. (*Environment and Society*) What kinds of human activities have polluted the air?

Critical Thinking

4. Drawing Inferences and Conclusions Why is desalinization rarely practiced?

Organizing What You Know

5. Identifying Cause and Effect Use this graphic organizer to explain air pollution.

(Causes:)———(Air Pollution)———(Effects:)

Section 3

Minerals

Read to Discover

1. What are minerals?
2. What are the two types of minerals?

Define

nonrenewable resources

minerals

metallic minerals

nonmetallic minerals

Quartz crystals

Minerals

You have learned that renewable resources such as trees are always being produced. **Nonrenewable resources** are those that cannot be replaced by natural processes or are replaced very slowly.

Earth's crust is made up of substances called **minerals**. Minerals are an example of a nonrenewable resource. They provide us with many of the materials we need. More than 3,000 minerals have been identified, but fewer than 20 are common. Around 20 minerals make up most of Earth's crust. Minerals have four basic properties. First, they are inorganic. Inorganic substances are not made from living things or the remains of living things. Second, they occur naturally, rather than being manufactured like steel or brass. Third, minerals are solids in crystalline form, unlike petroleum or natural gas. Finally, minerals have a definite chemical composition or combination of elements. Although all minerals share these four properties, they can be very different from one another. Minerals are divided into two basic types: metallic and nonmetallic.

Metallic Minerals Metals, or **metallic minerals**, are shiny and can conduct heat and electricity. Metals are solids at normal room temperature. An exception is mercury, a metal that is liquid at room temperature.

Gold is one of the heaviest of all metals and is easily worked. For thousands of years people have highly valued gold. Precious metals are commonly made into jewelry and coins. Silver and platinum are other precious metals.

The Most-Common Elements in Earth's Crust

Silicon (Si) 27.7%

Aluminum (Al) 8.1%

Iron (Fe) 5.0%

Calcium (Ca) 3.6%

Sodium (Na) 2.8%

Potassium (K) 2.6%

Magnesium (Mg) 2.1%

All others 1.5%

Oxygen (O) 46.6%

Interpreting the Chart

What element makes up almost 47 percent of Earth's crust?

Art made from recycled products

Many Americans now make a habit of recycling. They put their cans, bottles, and newspapers by the curb for pickup or take them to recycling centers. However, some people do their recycling in a different way. They use their junk to create art.

Much recycled art is folk art. These objects have a practical purpose but are made with creativity and a

sense of style. The making of folk art objects from junk is common in the world's poorer countries, where resources are scarce.

Some examples of recycled folk art include dust pans made from license plates (Mexico), jugs made from old tires (Morocco), briefcases made from flattened tin cans (Senegal), and a toy helicopter made from plastic containers and film canisters (Haiti). As scientist Stephen J. Gould has written, "In our world of material wealth, where so many broken items are thrown away rather than mended . . . we forget that most of the world fixes everything and discards nothing."

Americans do have a tradition of making recycled art, however. The Amish make quilts from old scraps of cloth. Other folk artists build whimsical figures out of bottle caps and wire. Some modern artists create sculptures from "found objects" like machine parts, bicycle wheels, and old signs. Junk art can even be fashion. One movie costume designer went to the Academy Awards ceremony wearing a dress made of credit cards!

Understanding What You Read
1. How do some societies turn junk into art?
2. Where is much recycled folk art made?

Iron is the cheapest metal. Iron can be combined with certain other minerals to make steel. Aluminum is another common metal. This lightweight metal is used in such items as soft drink cans and airplanes. We handle copper every time we pick up a penny.

Nonmetallic Minerals Minerals that lack the characteristics of a metal are called **nonmetallic minerals**. These vary in their appearance. Quartz, a mineral often found in sand, looks glassy. Talc has a pearly appearance. Most nonmetallic minerals have a dull surface and are poor conductors of heat or electricity.

Diamonds are minerals made of pure carbon. They are the hardest naturally occurring substance. The brilliant look of diamonds has made them popular gems. Their hardness makes them valuable for industrial use. Other gemstones, like rubies, sapphires, and emeralds, are also nonmetallic minerals.

Gold is a metallic mineral.

Mineral and Energy Resources in the United States

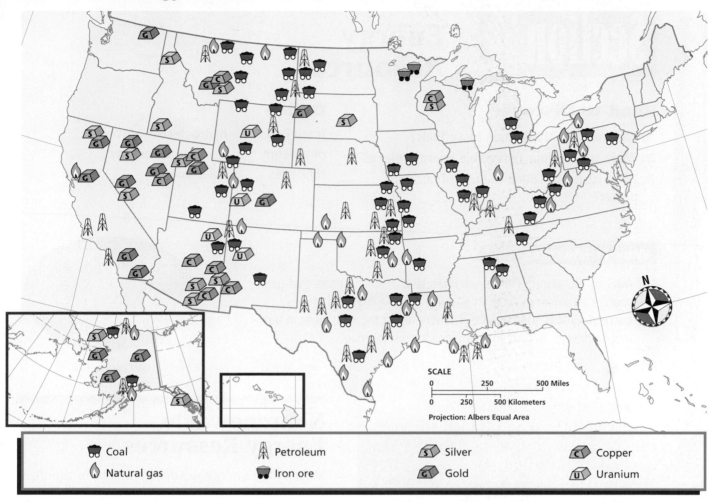

Coal	Petroleum	**S** Silver	**C** Copper
Natural gas	Iron ore	**G** Gold	**U** Uranium

SCALE
0 — 250 — 500 Miles
0 — 250 — 500 Kilometers
Projection: Albers Equal Area

Other mineral substances also have important uses. For example, people need salt to stay healthy. Sulfur is used in many ways, from making batteries to bleaching dried fruits. Graphite, another form of carbon, is used in making pencils.

✓ **READING CHECK:** *Physical Systems* What are the two types of minerals?

go.hrw.com **Homework Practice Online**
Keyword: SG3 HP4

Section Review 3

Define and explain: nonrenewable resources, minerals, metallic minerals, nonmetallic minerals

Reading for the Main Idea

1. *Physical Systems* What is a nonrenewable resource?

2. *Environment and Society* Why are minerals important? What is the difference between a metallic mineral and a nonmetallic mineral?

Critical Thinking

3. Summarizing How can minerals be used?

4. Drawing Inferences and Conclusions What makes gold such an important mineral?

Organizing What You Know

5. Contrasting Copy the following graphic organizer. Use it to contrast types of minerals.

Metallic minerals	Nonmetallic minerals

Read to Discover

1. What are the three main fossil fuels?
2. What are the four renewable energy sources?
3. What issues surround the use of nuclear power?

Define

fossil fuels
petroleum
refineries

hydroelectric power
geothermal energy
solar energy

WHY IT MATTERS

Automobile manufacturers are interested in building cars that use sources of power other than gasoline. Use CNNfyi.com or other **current events** sources to learn more about these changes in automobile design. Record your findings in your journal.

An oil tanker

▲
A miner digs coal in a narrow tunnel.

Nonrenewable Energy Resources

Most of the energy we use comes from the three main **fossil fuels**: coal, petroleum, and natural gas. Fossil fuels were formed from the remains of ancient plants and animals. These remains gradually decayed and were covered with sediment. Over long periods of time, pressure and heat changed these materials into fossil fuels. All fossil fuels are nonrenewable resources.

Coal Until the 1900s people mostly used wood and coal as sources of energy. Coal was used to make steel in giant furnaces and to run factories. However, the burning of coal polluted the air. The way coal is burned today has improved so that it releases less pollution. This new technology is more expensive, however. Some of the largest coal deposits are located in Australia, China, Russia, India, and the United States.

Petroleum Industrialized societies now use **petroleum**—an oily liquid—for a variety of purposes. When it is first pumped out of the ground, petroleum is called crude oil. It is then shipped or piped to **refineries**—factories where crude oil is processed, or refined. Petroleum is made into gasoline, diesel and jet fuels, and heating oil.

Who Has the Oil?

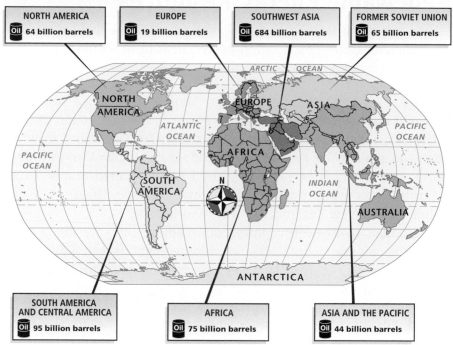

NORTH AMERICA	EUROPE	SOUTHWEST ASIA	FORMER SOVIET UNION
Oil 64 billion barrels	Oil 19 billion barrels	Oil 684 billion barrels	Oil 65 billion barrels

SOUTH AMERICA AND CENTRAL AMERICA	AFRICA	ASIA AND THE PACIFIC
Oil 95 billion barrels	Oil 75 billion barrels	Oil 44 billion barrels

Source: *BP Amoco Statistical Review of World Energy 2001*

◄ More than half of all known oil deposits are located in Southwest Asia. New deposits are still being found, but Southwest Asia will probably continue to hold the largest share.

Petroleum is not evenly distributed on Earth. Of the oil reserves that have been discovered, more than 65 percent are found in Southwest Asia. Most of that is in Saudi Arabia. North America has around 7 percent of the world's known oil, while South America has around 10 percent. Other regions have oil in small amounts.

Natural Gas The use of natural gas is growing rapidly. Natural gas is gas that comes from Earth's crust through natural openings or drilled wells. Large natural gas fields are found in Russia and Southwest Asia. Northern Canada also has large amounts of natural gas. However, the fields are located in the far north. Frozen seas and low temperatures make it difficult to pump and ship the gas safely.

Natural gas is the cleanest-burning fossil fuel. It produces much less air pollution than gasoline or diesel fuel. It is usually transported by pipeline, making it most useful for factories and electrical plants. It is also used for heating and cooking. Vehicles that run on natural gas have to carry the fuel in special, bulky containers. However, some large cities now have buses and taxis that use natural gas to help cut down on air pollution.

✓ **READING CHECK:** *Physical Systems*
What physical processes produced fossil fuels?

The Alaska pipeline carries oil from north to south across Alaska.
Interpreting the Visual Record Why do you think this pipeline is above ground?

▼

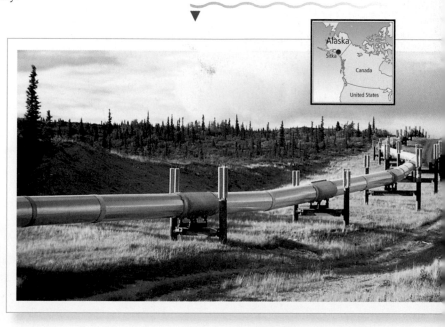

Renewable Energy Resources

People have also learned to use several renewable energy resources. They include water power, wind power, heat from within Earth, and the Sun's energy.

Water The most commonly used renewable energy source is **hydroelectric power**. Hydroelectric power is the production of electricity by waterpower. Dams harness the energy of falling water to power generators. These generators produce electricity. Dams produce about 9 percent of the electricity used in the United States. Other countries producing hydroelectric power include Brazil, Canada, China, Egypt, New Zealand, Norway, and Russia.

Although hydroelectric power does not pollute the air, it does affect the environment. Fish and wildlife habitats can be affected when reservoirs, or artificial lakes, are created by dams. Reservoirs may also cover farmland and forests.

Wind For thousands of years, wind has powered sailing ships and boats. People have also long used wind power to turn windmills. Such mills were used to pump water out of wells or to grind grain into flour. In some places windmills are still used for these purposes.

Today, wind has a new use. It can create electricity by turning a system of fan blades called a turbine. "Wind farms" with hundreds of wind turbines have been built in some windy places.

Geothermal Energy The heat of Earth's interior—**geothermal energy**—can also be used to generate electricity. This internal heat escapes through hot springs and steam vents on Earth's surface. This geothermal energy can be captured to power electric generators.

Wind turbines are just one source of electricity.

Interpreting the Visual Record How does this photo show human adaptation to the environment?

The Sun The Sun's heat and light are known as **solar energy**. This energy can be used to heat water or homes. Special solar panels also absorb solar energy to make electricity. In the past, converting solar energy into electricity was expensive. New research, however, may make solar energy cheaper in the future.

✔ **READING CHECK:** *Physical Systems* What are four renewable energy sources?

Experimental cars like this one run on solar energy.

Nuclear Energy

In the late 1930s scientists discovered nuclear energy. They learned that energy could be released by changes in the nucleus, or core, of atoms. Nuclear energy was first used to make powerful bombs. Scientists found out that nuclear energy can also be used to produce electricity. Lithuania, France, Belgium, Ukraine, and Sweden rely on nuclear energy for much of their power. This reduces their dependence on imported oil.

There are serious concerns about the use of nuclear power. Several nuclear power plants have had accidents. In 1986 an accident at a nuclear reactor in Chernobyl in Ukraine killed dozens of people. It also caused cancer in thousands more. Homes and farms in the area of the reactor had to be abandoned.

Nuclear energy produces waste that remains dangerous for thousands of years. People do not agree on how nuclear waste can be stored or transported safely. Because of this some countries are reducing their dependence on nuclear energy. Denmark and New Zealand avoid it altogether. The United States does not intend to expand its use of nuclear energy. As a result, scientists continue to search for other renewable energy sources.

✔ **READING CHECK:** *Environment and Society* What are the concerns associated with nuclear power?

Section Review 4

Homework Practice Online
Keyword: SG3 HP4

Define and explain: fossil fuels, petroleum, refineries, hydroelectric power, geothermal energy, solar energy

Reading for the Main Idea

1. *Physical Systems* What are the three main fossil fuels, and how were they formed?

2. *Physical Systems* What are the four most common renewable energy sources? Describe how each of these harnesses energy.

Critical Thinking

3. **Finding the Main Idea** How do dams affect the environment?

4. **Analyzing Information** What are some of the problems associated with nuclear energy?

Organizing What You Know

5. **Contrasting** Copy the following graphic organizer. Use it to contrast the characteristics of renewable and nonrenewable resources.

Renewable resources	↔	Nonrenewable resources

Building Vocabulary

On a separate sheet of paper, write sentences to define each of the following words.

1. renewable resources
2. desertification
3. deforestation
4. reforestation
5. aquifers
6. acid rain
7. nonrenewable resources
8. fossil fuels
9. hydroelectric power
10. solar energy

Reviewing the Main Ideas

1. *Environment and Society* Why is fertile soil important, and how is it created?
2. *Environment and Society* What actions have people taken to increase their supply of water?
3. *Environment and Society* What are minerals, and why are they important to us?
4. *Environment and Society* For what are fossil fuels used?
5. *Environment and Society* What are the four most common renewable energy sources, and how is each used?

Understanding Environment and Society

Chernobyl

On April 26, 1986, a nuclear reactor exploded in Chernobyl. Radiation caused serious problems in Ukraine and Belarus, as well as in Eastern and Western Europe. Create an outline for a presentation based on information about the following:

• Conditions of the environment then and now.
• Preventive measures taken to prevent future accidents.

Thinking Critically

1. **Drawing Inferences and Conclusions** Why does the issue of use of rain forests cause such disagreement? What is happening to Earth's rain forests?
2. **Summarizing** What are the major causes of water and air pollution, and how does pollution affect life on this planet?
3. **Drawing Inferences and Conclusions** Why are minerals valued by society?
4. **Contrasting** How are metallic minerals different from nonmetallic minerals?
5. **Drawing Inferences and Conclusions** Why does the use of nuclear energy continue to be a debated topic?

Map ACTIVITY

On a separate sheet of paper, match the letters on the map with their correct region. Then write the amount of oil known to be located in each region.

Africa

Europe

former Soviet Union

South and Central America

Southwest Asia

Mental Mapping Skills ACTIVITY

On a separate sheet of paper, draw a freehand map of the United States. Label areas that have copper. Compare this map with a physical map of the United States. What, if any, physical features are located in the same regions as copper deposits?

WRITING ACTIVITY

Write a short paper explaining which mineral is most important to you. Justify your selection with facts you have learned. Be sure to use standard grammar, spelling, sentence structure, and punctuation.

Alternative Assessment

Portfolio ACTIVITY

Learning About Your Local Geography

Environmental Issues Study your local environment. What issues of preservation and use are important to the people of your community? How does your government handle these issues?

◢ internet connect

Internet Activity: go.hrw.com
KEYWORD: SG3 GT4

Choose a topic to explore Earth's resources:
- Trek through different kinds of forests.
- Investigate global warming.
- Make a recycling plan.

CHAPTER 5

The World's People

The Colosseum, Rome, Italy

1998 Olympic opening ceremony, Nagano, Japan

Easter Island, Chile

Section 1

Culture

Read to Discover

1. What is culture?
2. Why are cultural symbols important?
3. What influences how cultures develop?
4. How did agriculture affect the development of culture?

Define

culture	acculturation
culture region	symbol
culture traits	domestication
ethnic groups	subsistence agriculture
multicultural	commercial agriculture
race	civilization

WHY IT MATTERS

Throughout history, culture has both brought people together and created conflict among groups. Use **CNNfyi.com** or other **current events** sources to learn about cultural conflicts around the globe. Record your findings in your journal.

Flags at the South Pole

Aspects of Culture

The people of the world's approximately 200 countries speak hundreds of different languages. They may dress in different ways and eat different foods. However, all societies share certain basic institutions, including a government, an educational system, an economic system, and religious institutions. These vary from society to society and are often based on that society's **culture**. Culture is a learned system of shared beliefs and ways of doing things that guides a person's daily behavior. Most people around the world have a national culture shared with people of their own country. They may also have religious practices, beliefs, and language in common with people from other countries. Sometimes a culture dominates a particular region. This is known as a **culture region**. In a culture region, people may share certain **culture traits**, or elements of culture, such as dress, food, or religious beliefs. West Africa is an example of a culture region. Culture can also be based on a person's job or age. People can belong to more than one culture and can choose which to emphasize.

Race and Ethnic Groups Cultural groups share beliefs and practices learned from parents, grandparents, and ancestors. These groups are sometimes called **ethnic groups**. An ethnic group's shared culture may include its religion, history, language, holiday traditions, and special foods.

When people from different cultures live in the same country, the country is described as **multicultural** or multiethnic. Many countries

Thousands of Czechs and Germans settled in Texas in the mid-1800s. Dancers from central Texas perform a traditional Czech dance.

▼

World Religions

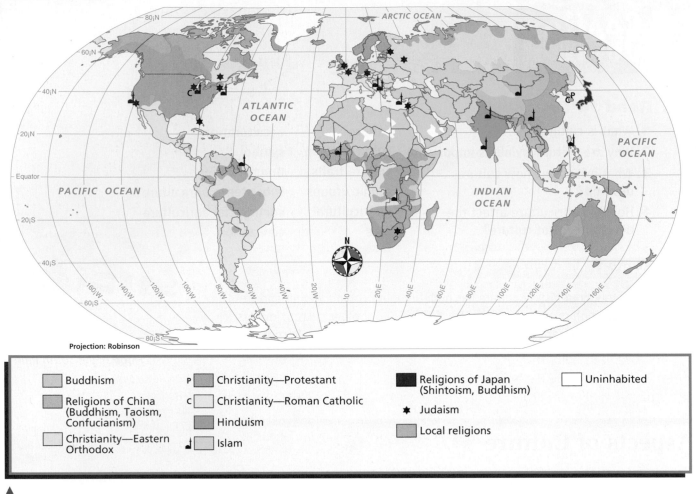

Projection: Robinson

Legend		
Buddhism	P Christianity—Protestant	Religions of Japan (Shintoism, Buddhism)
Religions of China (Buddhism, Taoism, Confucianism)	C Christianity—Roman Catholic	★ Judaism
Christianity—Eastern Orthodox	Hinduism	Local religions
	Islam	Uninhabited

Religion is one aspect of culture.

A disc jockey sits at the control board of a Miami radio station that plays Cuban music.

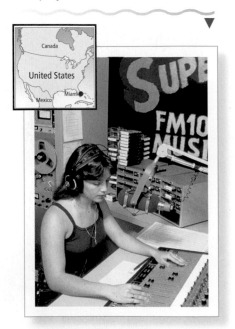

are multicultural. In some countries, such as Belgium, different ethnic groups have cooperated to form a united country. In other cases, such as in French-speaking Quebec, Canada, ethnic groups have frequently been in conflict. Sometimes, people from one ethnic group are spread over two or more countries. For example, Germans live in different European countries: Germany, Austria, and Czechoslovakia. The Kurds, who are a people with no country of their own, live mostly in Syria, Iran, Iraq, and Turkey.

Race is based on inherited physical or biological traits. It is sometimes confused with ethnic group. For example, the Hispanic ethnic group in the United States includes people who look quite different from each other. However, they share a common Spanish or Latin American heritage. As you know, people vary in physical appearance. Some of these differences have developed in response to climate factors like cold and sunlight. Because people have moved from region to region throughout history, these differences are not clear-cut. Each culture defines race in its own way, emphasizing particular biological and ethnic characteristics. An example can be seen in Rwanda, a country in East Africa. In this country, the Hutu and the Tutsi have carried on a bitter civil war. Although both are East African, each one considers itself different from the other. Their definition of race involves height and facial features. Around the world, people tend to identify races based on obvious physical traits. However, these definitions of race are based primarily on attitudes, not actual biological differences.

Cultural Change Cultures change over time. Humans invent new ways of doing things and spread these new ways to others. The spread of one culture's ways or beliefs to another culture is called diffusion. Diffusion may occur when people move from one place to another. The English language was once confined to England and parts of Scotland. It is now one of the world's most widely spoken languages. English originally spread because people from England founded colonies in other regions. More recently, as communication among cultures has increased, English has spread through English-language films and television programs. English has also become an international language of science and technology.

People sometimes may borrow aspects of another culture as the result of long-term contact with another society. This process is called **acculturation**. For example, people in one culture may adopt the religion of another. As a result, they might change other cultural practices to conform to the new religion. For example, farmers who become Muslim may quit raising pigs because Islam forbids eating pork.

✓ **READING CHECK:** (*Human Systems*) What is the definition of culture?

Cultural Differences

A **symbol** is a sign that stands for something else. A symbol can be a word, a shape, a color, or a flag. People learn symbols from their culture. The sets of sounds of a language are symbols. These symbols have meaning for the people who speak that language. The same sound may mean something different to people who speak another language. The word *bad* means "evil" in English, "cool" to teenagers, and "bath" in German.

If you traveled to another country, you might notice immediately that people behave differently. For instance, they may speak a different language or wear different clothes. They might celebrate different holidays or salute a different flag. Symbols reflect the artistic, literary, and religious expressions of a society or culture. They also reflect that society's belief systems. Language, clothing, holidays, and flags are all symbols. Symbols help people communicate with each other and create a sense of belonging to a group.

✓ **READING CHECK:** (*Human Systems*) How do symbols reflect differences among societies and cultures?

▲

Cultures mix in New York City's Chinatown.

Interpreting the Visual Record Why might immigrants to a new country settle in the same neighborhood?

GO TO: go.hrw.com
KEYWORD: SG1 CH5
FOR: Web sites about the world's people

Fans cheer for the U.S. Olympic soccer team.

Interpreting the Visual Record Why do you think symbols such as flags create strong emotions?

▼

A couple prepares for a wedding ceremony in Kazakhstan.

Interpreting the Visual Record What aspects of these people's clothing indicate that they are dressed for a special event?

The layout of Marrakech, Morocco, is typical of many North African cities.

Interpreting the Visual Record How are the streets and houses of Marrakech different from those in your community?

Development of a Culture

All people have the same basic needs for food, water, clothing, and shelter. People everywhere live in families and mark important family changes together. They usually have rituals or traditions that go with the birth of a baby, the wedding of a couple, or the death of a grandparent. All human societies need to deal with natural disasters. They must also deal with people who break the rules of behavior. However, people in different places meet these needs in unique ways. They eat different foods, build different kinds of houses, and form families in different ways. They have different rules of behavior. Two important factors that influence the way people meet basic needs are their history and environment.

History Culture is shaped by history. A region's people may have been conquered by the same outsiders. They may have adopted the same religion. They may have come from the same area and may share a common language. However, historical events may have affected some parts of a region but not others. For example, in North America French colonists brought their culture to Louisiana and Canada. However, they did not have a major influence on the Middle Atlantic region of the United States.

Cultures also shape history by influencing the way people respond to the same historical forces. Nigeria, India, and Australia were all colonized by the British. Today each nation still uses elements of the British legal system, but with important differences.

Environment The environment of a region can influence the development of culture. For example, in Egypt the Nile River is central to people's lives. The ancient Egyptians saw the fertile soils brought by the flooding of the Nile as the work of the gods. Beliefs in mountain spirits were important in many mountainous regions of the world. These areas include Tibet, Japan, and the Andes of South America.

Culture also determines how people use and shape their landscape. For example, city plans are cultural. Cities in Spain and its former colonies are organized around a central plaza, or square, with a church and a courthouse. On the other hand, Chinese cities are oriented to the four compass points. American cities often follow a rectangular grid plan. Many French city streets radiate out from a central core.

✓ **READING CHECK:** (*Human Systems*) What are some ways in which culture traits spread?

Development of Agriculture

For most of human history people ate only wild plants and animals. When the food ran out in one place, they migrated, or moved to another place. Very few people still live this way today. Thousands of years ago, humans began to help their favorite wild plant foods to grow. They probably cleared the land around their campsites and dumped seeds or fruits in piles of refuse. Plants took root and grew. People may also have dug water holes to encourage wild cattle to come and drink. People began cultivating the largest plants and breeding the tamest animals. Gradually, the wild plants and animals changed. They became dependent on people. This process is called **domestication**. A domesticated species has changed its form and behavior so much that it depends on people to survive. Domestic sheep can no longer leap from rock to rock like their wild ancestors. However, the wool of domestic sheep is more useful to humans. It can be combed and twisted into yarn.

Domestication happened in many parts of the world. In Peru llamas and potatoes were domesticated. People in ancient Mexico and Central America domesticated corn, beans, squash, tomatoes, and hot peppers. None of these foods was grown in Europe, Asia, or Africa before the time of Christopher Columbus's voyages to the Americas. Meanwhile, Africans had domesticated sorghum and a kind of rice. Cattle, sheep, and goats were probably first raised in Southwest Asia. Wheat and rye were first domesticated in Central Asia. The horse was also domesticated there. These domesticated plants and animals were unknown in the Americas before the time of Columbus.

This ancient Egyptian wall painting shows domesticated cattle.

Interpreting the Visual Record Can you name other kinds of domesticated animals?

Thousands of years ago, domesticated dogs came with humans across the Bering Strait into North America. A breed called the Carolina dog may be descended almost unchanged from those dogs. The reddish yellow, short-haired breed also appears to be closely related to Australian dingoes.

Agriculture and Environment Agriculture changed the landscape. To make room for growing food, people cut down forests. They also built fences, dug irrigation canals, and terraced hillsides. Governments were created to direct the labor needed for these large projects. Governments also defended against outsiders and helped people resolve problems. People could now grow enough food for a whole year. Therefore, they stopped migrating and built permanent settlements.

Types of Agriculture Some farmers grow just enough food to provide for themselves and their own families. This type of farming is called **subsistence agriculture**. In the wealthier countries of the world, a small number of farmers can produce food for everyone. Each farm is large and may grow only one product. This type of farming is called **commercial agriculture**. In this system companies rather than individuals or families may own the farms.

Agriculture and Civilization Agriculture enabled farmers to produce a surplus of food—more than they could eat themselves. A few people could make things like pottery jars instead of farming. They traded or sold their products for food. With more food a family could feed more children. As a result, populations began to grow. More people became involved in trading and manufacturing. Traders and craftspeople began to live in central market towns. Some towns grew into cities, where many people lived and carried out even more specialized tasks. For example, cities often supported priests and religious officials. They were responsible for organizing and carrying out religious ceremonies. When a culture becomes highly complex, we sometimes call it a **civilization**.

✓ **READING CHECK:** *Environment and Society* In what ways did agriculture affect culture?

Homework Practice Online

Keyword: SG3 HP5

Section Review 1

Define and explain: culture, culture region, culture trait, ethnic groups, multicultural, race, acculturation, symbol, domestication, subsistence agriculture, commercial agriculture, civilization

Reading for the Main Idea

1. *Human Systems* How can an individual belong to more than one cultural group?

2. *Human Systems* What institutions are basic to all societies?

Critical Thinking

3. Drawing Inferences and Conclusions In what ways do history and environment influence or shape a culture? What examples can you find in the text that explain this relationship?

4. Analyzing Information What is the relationship between the development of agriculture and culture?

Organizing What You Know

5. Summarizing Copy the following graphic organizer. Use it to describe culture by listing shared beliefs and practices.

Culture

Section 2 — Population, Economy, and Government

Read to Discover

1. Why does population density vary, and how has the world's population changed?
2. How do geographers describe and measure economies?
3. What are the different types of economic systems?
4. How do governments differ?

Define

primary industries
secondary industries
tertiary industries
quaternary industries
gross national product
gross domestic product
developed countries
developing countries
free enterprise
factors of production
entrepreneurs
market economy
command economy
traditional economy
democracy
unlimited government
limited government

WHY IT MATTERS

Human population has increased dramatically in the past 200 years. Use CNNfyi.com or other **current events** sources to find current projections for global or U.S. populations. Record your findings in your journal.

Newborn baby

Calculating Population Density

The branch of geography that studies human populations is called demography. Geographers who study it are called demographers. They look at such things as population size, density, and age trends. Some countries are very crowded. Others are only thinly populated. Demographers measure population density by dividing a country's population by its area. The area is stated in either square miles or square kilometers. For example, the United States has 74 people for every square mile (29/sq km). Australia has just 6 people per square mile (2.3/sq km). Japan has 869 people per square mile (336/sq km), and Argentina has 35 people per square mile (14/sq km).

These densities include all of the land in a country. However, people may not be able to live on some land. Rugged mountains, deserts, frozen lands, and other similar places usually have very few people. Instead, people tend to live in areas where the land can be farmed. Major cities tend to be located in these same regions of dense population.

✓ **READING CHECK:** *Human Systems* What is population density?

Shoppers crowd a street in Tokyo, Japan.
▼

Differences in Population Density

Looking at this book's maps of world population densities allows us to make generalizations. Much of eastern and southern Asia is very densely populated. There are dense populations in Western Europe and in eastern areas of North America. There are also places with very low population densities. Canada, Australia, and Siberia have large areas where few people live. The same is true for the Sahara Desert. Parts of Asia, South America, and Africa also have low population densities.

Heavily populated areas attract large numbers of people for different reasons. Some places have been densely populated for thousands of years. Examples include the Nile River valley in Egypt and the Huang River valley in China. These places have fertile soil, a steady source of water, and a good growing climate. These factors allow people to farm successfully. People are also drawn to cities. The movement of people from farms to cities is called urbanization. In many countries people move to cities when they cannot find work in rural areas. In recent years this movement has helped create huge cities. Mexico City, Mexico; São Paulo, Brazil; and Lagos, Nigeria, are among these giant cities. Some European cities experienced similar rapid growth when they industrialized in the 1800s. During that period people left farms to come to the cities to work in factories.

✓ **READING CHECK:** (*Human Systems*) Why does population density vary?

World Population Growth

Source: U.S. Census

Interpreting the Chart Approximately when did world population growth begin to increase significantly?

Population Growth

Researchers estimate that about 10,000 years ago the world's entire human population was less than 10 million. The annual number of births was roughly the same as the annual number of deaths.

After people made the shift from hunting and gathering to farming, more food was available. People began to live longer and have more children. The world's population grew. About 2,000 years ago, the world had some 200 million people. By A.D. 1650 the world's population had grown to about 500 million. By 1850 there were some 1 billion people. Better health care and food supplies helped more babies survive into adulthood and have children. By 1930 there were 2 billion people on Earth. Just 45 years later that number had doubled to 4 billion. In 1999 Earth's population reached 6 billion. By the year 2025 the world's population could grow to about 9 billion.

Births add to a country's population. Deaths subtract from it. The number of births per 1,000 people in a year is called the birthrate. Similarly, the death rate is the annual number of deaths per 1,000 people. The birthrate minus the death rate equals the rate of natural increase. This number is expressed as a percentage. A country's population changes when people enter or leave the country.

✓ **READING CHECK:** (*Human Systems*) What is the rate of natural increase?

Economic Activity

All of the activities that people do to earn a living are part of a system called the economy. This includes people going to work, making things, selling things, buying things, and trading services. Economics is the study of the production, distribution, and use of goods and services.

Types of Economic Activities Geographers divide economic activities into primary, secondary, tertiary, and quaternary industries. **Primary industries** are activities that directly involve natural resources or raw materials. These industries include farming, mining, and cutting trees.

The products of primary industries often have to go through several stages before people can use them. **Secondary industries** change the raw materials created by primary activities into finished products. For example, the sawmill that turns a tree into lumber is a secondary industry.

Tertiary industries handle goods that are ready to be sold to consumers. The stores that sell products are included in this group. The trucks and trains that move products to stores are part of this group. Banks, insurance companies, and government agencies are also considered tertiary industries.

The fourth part of the economy is known as **quaternary industries**. People in these industries have specialized skills. They work mostly with information instead of goods. Researchers, managers, and administrators fall into this category.

Economic Indicators A common means of measuring a country's economy is the **gross national product** (GNP). The GNP is the value of all goods and services that a country produces in one year. It includes goods and services made by factories owned by that country's citizens but located in foreign countries. Most geographers use **gross domestic product** (GDP) instead of GNP. GDP includes only those goods and services produced within a country. GDP divided by the country's population is called per capita GDP. This figure shows individual purchasing power and is useful for comparing levels of economic development.

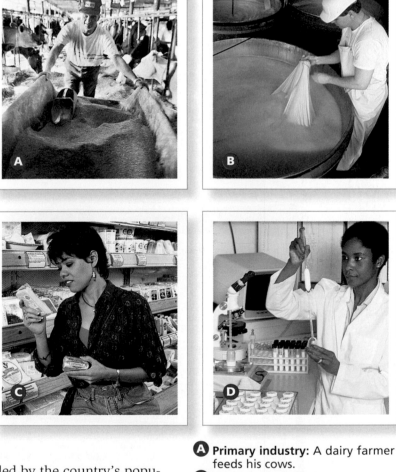

Ⓐ **Primary industry:** A dairy farmer feeds his cows.
Ⓑ **Secondary industry:** Cheese is prepared in a factory.
Ⓒ **Tertiary industry:** A grocer is selling cheese to a consumer.
Ⓓ **Quaternary industry:** A technician inspects dairy products in a lab.

✓ **READING CHECK:** *Human Systems* What are primary, secondary, tertiary, and quaternary industries?

Economic Development

Geographers use various measures including GNP, GDP, per capita GDP, life expectancy, and literacy to divide the world into two groups. Industrialized countries like the United States, Canada, Japan, and most European countries are wealthier. They are called **developed countries**. These countries have strong secondary, tertiary, and quaternary industries. They have good health care systems. Developed countries have good systems of education and a high literacy rate. The literacy rate is the percentage of people who can read and write. Most people in developed countries live in cities and have access to telecommunications systems—systems that allow long-distance communication. Geographers study the number of telephones, televisions, or computers in a country. They sometimes use these figures to estimate the country's level of technology.

Developing countries make up the second group. They are in different stages of moving toward development. About two thirds of the world's people live in developing countries. These countries are poorer. Their citizens often work in farming or other primary industries and earn low wages. Cities are often crowded with poorly educated people hoping to find work. They usually have little access to health care or telecommunications. Some developing countries have made economic progress in recent decades. South Korea and Mexico are good examples. These countries are experiencing strong growth in manufacturing and trade. However, some of the world's poorest countries are developing slowly or not at all.

✓ **READING CHECK:** (*Human Systems*) How do geographers distinguish between developed and developing countries?

Comparing Developed and Developing Countries

COUNTRY	POPULATION	RATE OF NATURAL INCREASE	PER CAPITA GDP	LIFE EXPECTANCY	LITERACY RATE	TELEPHONE LINES
United States	281.4 million	0.9%	$ 36,200	77	97%	194 million
France	59.5 million	0.4%	$ 24,400	79	99%	35 million
South Korea	47.9 million	0.9%	$ 16,100	75	98%	24 million
Mexico	101.8 million	1.5%	$ 9,100	72	90%	9.6 million
Poland	38.6 million	−0.03%	$ 8,500	73	99%	8 million
Brazil	174.4 million	0.9%	$ 6,500	63	83%	17 million
Egypt	69.5 million	1.7%	$ 3,600	64	51%	3.9 million
Myanmar	42 million	0.6%	$ 1,500	55	83%	250,000
Mali	11 million	3.0%	$ 850	47	31%	23,000

Sources: Central Intelligence Agency, *The World Factbook 2001*

Interpreting the Visual Record Which countries have the highest literacy rate?

Economic Systems

Countries organize their economies in different ways. Most developed countries organize the production and distribution of goods and services in a system called **free enterprise**. The United States operates under a free enterprise system. There are many benefits to this system. Companies are free to make whatever goods they wish. Employees can seek the highest wages for their work. People, rather than the government, control the **factors of production**. Factors of production are the things that determine what goods are produced in an economy. They include the natural resources that are available for making goods for sale. They also include the capital, or money, needed to pay for production and the labor needed to manufacture goods. The work of **entrepreneurs** (ahn-truh-pruh-NUHRS) makes up a fourth factor of production. Entrepreneurs are people who start businesses in a free enterprise system. Business owners in a free enterprise system sell their goods in a **market economy**. In such an economy, business owners and customers make decisions about what to make, sell, and buy.

In contrast, the governments of some countries control the factors of production. The government decides what, and how much, will be produced. It also sets the prices of goods to be sold. This is called a **command economy**. Some countries with a command economy are governed by an economic and political system called communism. Under communism, the government owns almost all the factors of production. Very few countries today are communist. Cuba is an example of a communist nation.

Finally, there are some societies around the world that operate within a **traditional economy**. A traditional economy is one that is based on custom and tradition. Economic activities are based on laws, rituals, religious beliefs, or habits developed by the society's ancestors. The Mbuti people of the Democratic Republic of the Congo practice a traditional economy, for example.

✔ **READING CHECK:** (*Human Systems*) What are the three types of economies?

◀

Large shopping malls, such as this one in New York City's Trump Tower, are common in countries that have market economies and a free enterprise system. Shoppers here can find a wide range of stores and goods concentrated in one area.

World Governments

Just as countries use different economic systems, they also have different ways of organizing their governments. As you have read, some countries are communist—their governments control both the political and economic systems. Other countries are controlled by one ruler, such as a monarch or a dictator. For example, Saudi Arabia is ruled by a monarch. King Fahd bin Abd al-Aziz Al Saud is both the chief of state and the head of government.

In other countries, a relatively small group of people controls the government. Many countries—including the United States, New Zealand, and Germany—have democratic governments. In a **democracy**, voters elect leaders and rule by majority. Ideas about democratic government began in ancient Greece. The American and French Revolutions established the world's first modern democratic governments in the late 1700s. Today, most developed countries are democracies with free enterprise economies. However, some countries with democratic governments, such as Russia and India, struggle with economic issues.

How a government is organized determines whether it has limited or unlimited powers. **Unlimited governments**, such as the French monarchy before the French Revolution, have total control over their citizens. They also have no legal controls placed on their actions. In a **limited government**, government leaders are held accountable by citizens through their constitutions and the democratic process. These limitations help protect citizens from abuses of power. Today, many countries around the world, including the United States, have limited governments.

✔ **READING CHECK:** (*Human Systems*) What is the difference between limited and unlimited government?

Define and explain: primary industries, secondary industries, tertiary industries, quaternary industries, gross national product, gross domestic product, developed countries, developing countries, free enterprise, factors of production, entrepreneurs, market economy, command economy, traditional economy, democracy, unlimited governments, limited government

Reading for the Main Idea

1. (*Environment and Society*) What geographic factors influence population density?

2. (*Human Systems*) What characteristics do developed countries share?

Critical Thinking

3. Finding the Main Idea What are the different economic systems? Describe each.

4. Drawing Inferences and Conclusions How did democracy develop, and why did it help create limited government?

Organizing What You Know

5. Summarizing Copy the following graphic organizer. Use it to study your local community and classify the businesses in your area.

Primary Industries	Secondary Industries	Tertiary Industries	Quaternary Industries
•	•	•	•
•	•	•	•

Section 3 Population Growth Issues

Read to Discover

1. What problems are associated with high and low population growth rates?

2. What are two different views of population growth and resources?

Define

scarcity
carrying capacity

Population sign for Anatone, Washington

Population Growth Rates

With the help of technology, humans can survive in a wide range of environments. People can build houses and wear clothing to survive in cold climates. Food can be grown in one place and shipped to another. For these reasons and others the human population has grown tremendously.

Population growth rates differ from place to place. Many developed countries have populations that are growing very slowly, holding steady, or even shrinking. However, the populations of most developing countries continue to grow rapidly.

▲
An Inuit family in northern Canada uses a snowmobile to pull a sled.

Growth Rate Issues In general, a high population growth rate will hinder a country's economic development. Countries must provide jobs, education, and medical care for their citizens. A rapidly growing population can strain a country's resources and lead to **scarcity**—when demand is greater than supply. Many of the countries with the highest growth rates today are among the world's poorest.

However, a shortage of young people entering the workforce lowers a country's ability to produce goods. Young people are needed to replace older people who retire or die. Many countries with very low growth rates or shrinking overall populations must support a growing number of older people. These people may need more health care.

Uneven Resource Distribution Natural resources such as fresh water, minerals, and fertile land are not distributed evenly. A country's resources cannot always support its population. However, the country may be able to acquire needed resources by trading with other countries. In this system of economic interdependence, two countries can exchange resources or goods so that each gets what it needs. Japan, for example, has few energy resources but is a world leader in manufacturing. Japan sells manufactured goods to others, particularly the United States. Japan then uses the money to buy oil from Saudi Arabia.

The need for scarce resources usually leads countries to trade peacefully. However, it can also lead to military conflict. One country might try to take over a resource-rich area of a neighboring country. If we hope to avoid future wars over resources, the world's people must share resources more equally.

✓ **READING CHECK:** *Human Systems* How does scarcity of resources affect international trade and economic interdependence?

World Population and Resources

Some people think Earth can easily support a much larger human population. They base this view partly on history. For example, new fertilizers and special seeds mean more food can be grown today than ever before. They also think that scientists will probably discover new energy resources. The Sun, for example, is a vast energy source. Today we can only use a fraction of its power, however. Another way to support more people would be to make better use of existing resources. For example, we can recycle materials and reduce the amount of waste we generate.

Many farmers in India still use traditional methods.

Interpreting the Visual Record What in this photo indicates a less developed agricultural society?

A buildup of salt has ruined this field in southern Iraq. This land is now useless for growing crops, thus contributing to the lack of land suitable for farming.

Other people hold the opposite opinion. They argue that the world is already showing signs of reaching its **carrying capacity**. Carrying capacity is the maximum number of a species that can be supported by an area's scarce resources. The amount of land available for farming is shrinking. Many areas are experiencing a shortage of fresh water. Oil, a nonrenewable resource, will eventually run out. Pollution is damaging the atmosphere and the oceans. The rich nations of the world are not always willing to share with poorer nations. In the future, these people think food and water supplies will run short in many countries. People without enough to eat will become ill more easily, leading to widespread disease. Such problems may lead a country to invade its neighbors to capture resources.

These are challenging issues that reach into all areas of life. They will become even more important in the future. A better understanding of geography will help you understand and deal with these issues.

✔ **READING CHECK:** *Environment and Society* What are two different views on population growth and resources?

go.hrw.com Homework Practice Online Keyword: SG3 HP5

Section Review 3

Define and explain: scarcity, carrying capacity

Reading for the Main Idea

1. *Human Systems* What problems are associated with rapid population growth?

2. *Human Systems* What are two viewpoints about future population growth?

Critical Thinking

3. **Analyzing Information** How has technology helped the worldwide human population grow?

4. **Finding the Main Idea** How do countries deal with the uneven distribution of resources?

Organizing What You Know

5. **Contrasting** Copy the following graphic organizer. Use it to discuss two arguments about population growth.

Earth's ability to support a much larger population		Earth's inability to support a much larger population
	⇦ ⇨	

Reviewing What You Know

Building Vocabulary

On a separate sheet of paper, write sentences to define each of the following words.

1. culture
2. ethnic groups
3. multicultural
4. acculturation
5. symbol
6. domestication
7. subsistence agriculture
8. civilization
9. limited government
10. entrepreneurs
11. command economy
12. market economy
13. factors of production
14. free enterprise
15. carrying capacity

Reviewing the Main Ideas

1. *(Human Systems)* What is culture, and why should people study it?
2. *(Environment and Society)* What is the difference between subsistence and commercial agriculture?
3. *(Human Systems)* What are some of the different ways countries organize governments?
4. *(Human Systems)* Why are telecommunications devices useful as economic indicators?
5. *(Environment and Society)* How do population growth rates affect resources?

Understanding Environment and Society

Domestication

Do you know how, when, and why people first domesticated dogs, cats, pigs, and hawks? What about oranges? Pick a domesticated plant or animal to research. As you prepare your presentation consider the following:

- Where the crop or animal was first domesticated.
- Differences between it and its wild ancestors.
- Humans spreading it to new areas.

Thinking Critically

1. **Drawing Inferences and Conclusions** Why are ethnic groups sometimes confused with races?
2. **Making Generalizations and Predictions** Over the past 2,000 years, how many times has world population doubled? By when is it projected to double again? What might be the effect of this increase?
3. **Finding the Main Idea** What are the four basic divisions of industry? Give examples.
4. **Summarizing** What are the three economic systems, and what are the benefits of the U.S. free-enterprise system?
5. **Making Generalizations and Predictions** Do you think Earth has a carrying capacity for its human population? Why or why not?
6. **Summarizing** Explain unlimited and limited government. Give examples of each.

Map ACTIVITY

On a separate sheet of paper, match the letters on the map with their correct labels.

Buddhism

Christianity— Eastern Orthodox

Christianity— Protestant

Christianity— Roman Catholic

Hinduism

Islam

Mental Mapping Skills ACTIVITY

Draw a map of the world and label Japan, Australia, the United Kingdom, and Argentina. Based on your knowledge of climates, population density, and resources, which of these countries probably depend on imported food? Which ones probably export food? Express this information on your map.

W R I T I N G

ACTIVITY Study the economy of your local community. Has the local economy grown or declined since 1985? Why? Predict how your local area could change economically during the next 10 years. Be sure to use standard grammar, spelling, sentence structure, and punctuation.

Alternative Assessment

Portfolio ACTIVITY

Learning About Your Local Geography

Factors of Production Recall the discussion of the factors of production. Create a model showing how these factors influence the economy of your community.

internet connect

Internet Activity: go.hrw.com
KEYWORD: SG3 GT5

Choose a topic to explore online:
- Visit famous buildings and monuments around the world.
- Compare facts about life in different countries.
- Examine world population growth.

FOCUS ON REGIONS

What is a Region?

Think about where you live, where you go to school, and where you shop. These places are all part of your neighborhood. In geographic terms, your neighborhood is a region. A region is an area that has common features that make it different from surrounding areas.

What regions do you live in? You live on a continent, in a country, and in a state. These are all regions that can be mapped.

Regions can be divided into smaller regions called subregions. For example, Africa is a major world region. Africa's subregions include North Africa, West Africa, East Africa, central Africa,

and southern Africa. Each subregion can be divided into even smaller subregions.

Regional Characteristics Regions can be based on physical, political, economic, or cultural characteristics. Physical regions are based on Earth's natural features, such as continents, landforms, and climates. Political regions are based on countries and their subregions, such as states, provinces, and cities. Economic regions are based on money-making activities such as agriculture or industries. Cultural regions are based on features such as language, religion, or ethnicity.

▲
East Africa is a subregion of Africa. It is an area of plateaus, rolling hills, and savanna grasslands.

Major World Regions

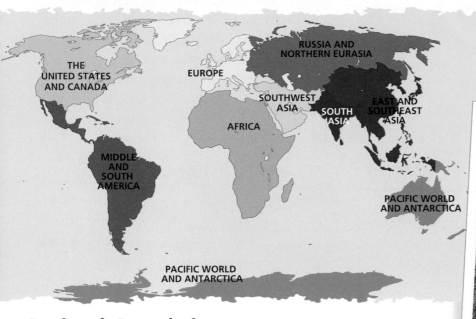

THE UNITED STATES AND CANADA

EUROPE

RUSSIA AND NORTHERN EURASIA

SOUTHWEST ASIA

AFRICA

SOUTH ASIA

EAST AND SOUTHEAST ASIA

MIDDLE AND SOUTH AMERICA

PACIFIC WORLD AND ANTARCTICA

PACIFIC WORLD AND ANTARCTICA

INTERNATIONAL BOUNDARY
DO NOT PROCEED BEYOND THIS POINT.

▲

The international border between Kenya and Tanzania is a clearly defined regional boundary.

Regional Boundaries All regions have boundaries, or borders. Boundaries are where the features of one region meet the features of a different region. Some boundaries, such as coastlines or country borders, can be shown as lines on a map. Other regional boundaries are less clear.

Transition zones are areas where the features of one region change gradually to the features of a different region. For example, when a city's suburbs expand into rural areas, a transition zone forms. In the transition zone, it may be hard to find the boundary between rural and urban areas.

Types of Regions There are three basic types of regions. The first is a formal region. Formal regions are based on one or more common features. For example, Japan is a formal region. Its people share a common government, language, and culture.

The second type of region is a functional region. Functional regions are based on movement and activities that connect different places. For example, Paris, France, is a functional region. It is based on the goods, services, and people that move throughout the city. A shopping center or an airport might also be a functional region.

The third type of region is a perceived region. Perceived regions are based on people's shared feelings and beliefs. For example, the neighborhood where you live may be a perceived region.

The three basic types of regions overlap to form complex world regions. In this textbook, the world is divided into nine major world regions (see map above). Each has general features that make it different from the other major world regions. These differences include physical, cultural, economic, historical, and political features.

Understanding What You Read

1. Regions can be based on what types of characteristics?

2. What are the three basic types of regions?

Geo SKILLS

Building Skills for Life: Drawing Mental Maps

We create maps in our heads of all kinds of places—our homes, schools, communities, country, and the world. Some of these places we know well. Others we have only heard about. These images we carry in our heads are shaped by what we see and experience. They are also influenced by what we learn from news reports or other sources. Geographers call the maps that we carry around in our heads mental maps.

We use mental maps to organize spatial information about people and places. For example, our mental maps help us move from classroom to classroom at school or get to a friend's home. A mental map of the United States helps us list the states we would pass through driving from New York City to Miami.

We use our mental maps of places when we draw sketch maps. A sketch map showing the relationship between places and the relative size of places can be drawn using very simple shapes. For example, triangles and rectangles could be used to sketch a map of the world. This quickly drawn map would show the relative size and position of the continents.

Think about some simple ways we could make our map

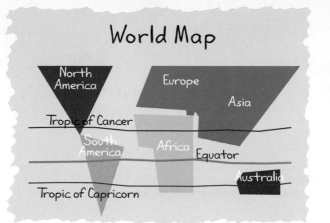

World Map

North America
Europe
Asia
Tropic of Cancer
South America
Africa
Equator
Australia
Tropic of Capricorn

of the world more detailed. Adding the equator, Tropic of Cancer, and Tropic of Capricorn would be one way. Look at a map of the world in your textbook's Atlas. Note that the bulge in the continent of Africa is north of the equator. Also note that all of Asia is north of the equator. Next note that the Indian subcontinent extends south from the Tropic of Cancer. About half of Australia is located north of the Tropic of Capricorn. As your knowledge of the world increases, your mental map will become even more detailed.

PRACTICING THE SKILL

1. Look at the maps in your textbook's Atlas. Where does the prime meridian fall in relation to the continents?

2. On a separate sheet of paper, sketch a simple map of the world from memory. First draw the equator, Tropic of Cancer, Tropic of Capricorn, and prime meridian. Then sketch in the continents. You can use circles, rectangles, and triangles.

3. Draw a second map of the world from memory. This time, draw the international date line in the center of your map. Add the equator, Tropic of Cancer, and Tropic of Capricorn. Now sketch in the continents. What do you notice?

HANDS on

Mental maps are personal. They change as we learn more about the world and the places in it. For example, they can include details about places that are of interest only to you.

What is your mental map of your neighborhood like? Sketch your mental map of your neighborhood. Include the features that you think are important and that help you find your way around. These guidelines will help you get started.

1. Decide what your map will show. Choose boundaries so that you do not sketch more than you need to.

2. Determine how much space you will need for your map. Things that are the same size in reality should be about the same size on your map.

3. Decide on and note the orientation of your map. Most maps use a directional indicator. On most maps, north is at the top.

4. Label reference points so that others who look at your map can quickly and easily figure out what they are looking at. For example, a major street or your school might be a reference point.

5. Decide how much detail your map will show. The larger the area you want to represent, the less detail you will need.

6. Use circles, rectangles, and triangles if you do not know the exact shape of an area.

7. As you think of them, fill in more details, such as names of places or major land features.

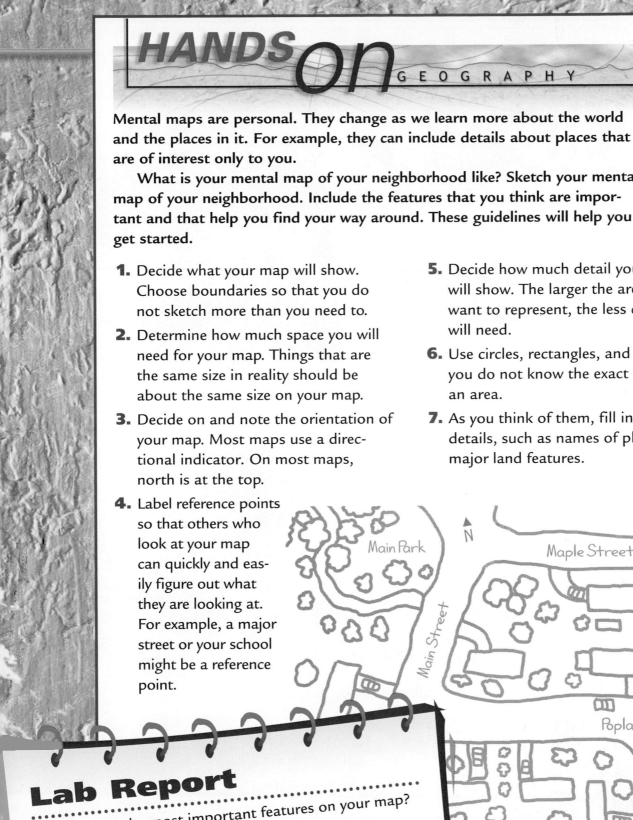

Lab Report

1. What are the most important features on your map? Why did you include them?

2. Compare your sketch map to a published map of the area. How does it differ?

3. At the bottom, list three ways that you could make your sketch map more complete.

UNIT 2

United States and Canada

CHAPTER 6
The United States

CHAPTER 7
Canada

Canadian Rocky Mountains

CN Tower and SkyDome, Toronto, Canada

An Englishman in Texas

Jon Hall grew up in the London suburbs. He studied Greek and Latin as a student in Texas. Here he contrasts what he sees as the British and Texan attitudes toward personal space and sports. **WHAT DO YOU THINK?** *How do you think people in your community feel about these topics?*

As an Englishman, the absence in Texas of fences and walls and clearly marked boundaries made me rather nervous at first. In London, with thousands of people in a small space, everyone is uptight about fencing off *their* little bit of land. In Texas, front yards and parks and parking lots sprawl casually without boundaries. And Texans really are more open and friendly than others. On the street, in a store, in a restaurant, greeting strangers is just the thing to do.

Brits and Texans support sports differently. In Britain, the spectators tend to be males between 15 and 45 years old—definitely not a family atmosphere. But at Texas football games, you'll see grandparents with their grandkids and guys and gals on dates. At the high school level too, there is much wider participation: the band, cheerleaders, parents, fans. I played soccer for my high school and most Saturdays we'd have a crowd of about seven.

◄ American teenagers

Street scene in Austin, Texas

Understanding Primary Sources

1. Why does Jon Hall think the people of London are more concerned about boundaries than Texans?

2. According to Jon Hall, what gives Texas football games a "family atmosphere?"

American buffalo

The United States and Canada

Elevation Profile

15,000 ft. — 4,572 m

Rocky Mountains

Sierra Nevada

Profile at 40°N latitude

10,000 ft. — 3,048 m

Coast Range

Interior Plains

Appalachian Mountains

Atlantic Coastal Plain

5,000 ft. — 1,524 m
4,000 ft. — 1,220 m

Pacific Ocean

Allegheny Plateau

Atlantic Ocean

3,000 ft. — 914 m
2,000 ft. — 610 m
1,000 ft. — 305 m
Sea Level — Sea Level

Approximately 2,600 miles

The United States and Canada:
Comparing Sizes

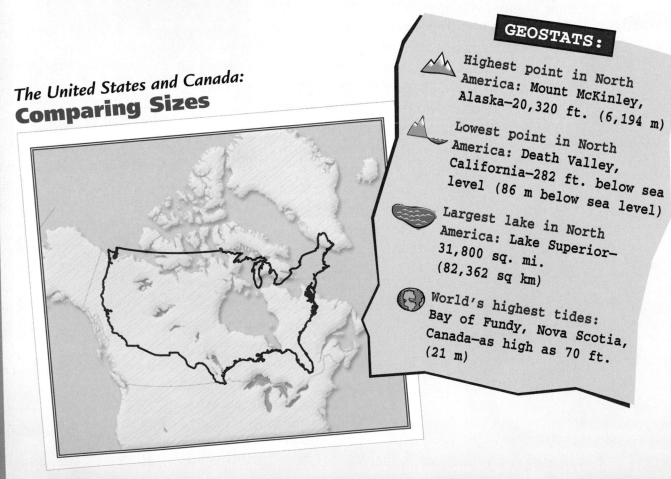

GEOSTATS:

Highest point in North America: Mount McKinley, Alaska—20,320 ft. (6,194 m)

Lowest point in North America: Death Valley, California—282 ft. below sea level (86 m below sea level)

Largest lake in North America: Lake Superior— 31,800 sq. mi. (82,362 sq km)

World's highest tides: Bay of Fundy, Nova Scotia, Canada—as high as 70 ft. (21 m)

ELEVATION

FEET	METERS
13,120	4,000
6,560	2,000
1,640	500
656	200
(Sea level) 0	0 (Sea level)
Below sea level	Below sea level
	Ice caps

HAWAII

Niihau Kauai *PACIFIC OCEAN*
Kaula
Oahu
Molokai
Lanai Maui
Kahoolawe
Hawaii

SCALE
0   100   200 Miles
0   100   200 Kilometers
Projection: Albers Equal Area

To understand the relative location of Hawaii as well as the vast distance separating it from the rest of the United States, see the Atlas map in the front of this textbook.

SCALE
0   500   1000 Miles
0   500   1000 Kilometers
Projection: Azimuthal Equal Area

1. (Places and Regions) Where is the highest point in North America? Which southwestern desert includes an area below sea level?

2. (Places and Regions) Which two large lakes are entirely within Canada?

3. (Places and Regions) What are four tributaries of the Mississippi River?

Critical Thinking

4. Drawing Inferences and Conclusions
Compare this map to the **population map** of the region. What is one physical feature that many of the largest cities have in common? What is the connection between the cities' locations and these physical features?

1. _Places and Regions_ Compare this map to the **physical map** of the region. What physical feature forms part of the border between the United States and Mexico?

Critical Thinking

2. Comparing Compare this map to the **climate** and **population maps**. Which U.S. border—the Canadian or Mexican—has a denser population? Why?

3. Comparing Which Canadian province or territory appears to be the largest? the second largest? Why is it hard to compare their sizes?

CLIMATE
- Humid tropical
- Tropical savanna
- Desert
- Steppe
- Mediterranean
- Humid subtropical
- Marine west coast
- Humid continental
- Subarctic
- Tundra
- Ice cap
- Highland

HAWAII

SCALE
0   100   200 Miles
0   100   200 Kilometers
Projection: Albers Equal Area

To understand the relative location of Hawaii as well as the vast distance separating it from the rest of the United States, see the Atlas map in the front of this textbook.

SCALE
0   500   1000 Miles
0   500   1000 Kilometers
Projection: Azimuthal Equal Area

1. *Places and Regions* Which U.S. state has the greatest diversity of climates? What are three states that have only one climate type?

2. *Places and Regions* Compare this map to the **physical** and **population maps** of the region. Which climate region contains the most big cities? Which climate regions do not have big cities?

Critical Thinking

3. Comparing Compare this map to the **physical map**. What may have limited settlement of the U.S. Great Plains?

POPULATION DENSITY

Persons per sq. mile	Persons per sq. km
520	200
260	100
130	50
25	10
3	1
0	0

● Metropolitan areas with more than 2 million inhabitants

○ Metropolitan areas with 1 million to 2 million inhabitants

HAWAII

SCALE
0   100   200 Miles
0   100   200 Kilometers
Projection: Albers Equal Area

To understand the relative location of Hawaii as well as the vast distance separating it from the rest of the United States, see the Atlas map in the front of this textbook.

SCALE
0   500   1000 Miles
0   500   1000 Kilometers
Projection: Azimuthal Equal Area

1. *Places and Regions* Which country appears to have a larger population?

2. *Places and Regions* What are Canada's two largest cities?

3. *Places and Regions* Based on the map, which area of the United States do you think was settled first? Why?

Critical Thinking

4. Analyzing Information Use the map on this page to create a chart, graph, database, or model of population centers in the United States and Canada.

LAND USE

- Livestock raising
- Commercial farming
- Forests
- Manufacturing
- Limited economic activity
- ● Major manufacturing and trade centers

RESOURCES

- 🛒 Coal
- 🜍 Natural gas
- 🜚 Oil
- ✳ Nuclear power
- ⚡ Hydroelectric power
- Ⓖ Gold
- Ⓢ Silver
- Ⓤ Uranium
- ⬡ Other minerals
- 🐟 Seafood

HAWAII

PACIFIC OCEAN

● Honolulu

SCALE — 20°N
0   100   200 Miles
0   100   200 Kilometers
Projection: Albers Equal Area

To understand the relative location of Hawaii as well as the vast distance separating it from the rest of the United States, see the Atlas map in the front of this textbook.

SCALE
0   500   1000 Miles
0   500   1000 Kilometers
Projection: Azimuthal Equal Area

---

1. *Places and Regions* Look at the **physical map**. In which area of North America are gold, silver, and uranium found?

2. *Places and Regions* Which two states on the Gulf of Mexico produce large amounts of oil and natural gas?

3. *Environment and Society* Which type of land use is most common throughout Canada?

Critical Thinking

4. Analyzing Information Create a chart, graph, database, or model of economic activities in the United States and Canada.

Fast FACTS

The United States

UNITED STATES

CAPITAL:
Washington, D.C.

AREA:
3,717,792 sq. mi.
(9,629,091 sq km)

POPULATION: 281,421,906

MONEY:
U.S. dollar (US$)

LANGUAGES:
English, Spanish (spoken by
a large minority)

 Iowa

CAPITAL: Des Moines
NICKNAME:
Hawkeye State

 Mississippi

CAPITAL: Jackson
NICKNAME:
Magnolia State

 Kansas

CAPITAL: Topeka
NICKNAME:
Sunflower State

 Missouri

CAPITAL: Jefferson City
NICKNAME:
Show Me State

Alabama

CAPITAL: Montgomery
NICKNAME:
Heart of Dixie,
Camellia State

Delaware

CAPITAL: Dover
NICKNAME:
First State,
Diamond State

Kentucky

CAPITAL: Frankfort
NICKNAME:
Bluegrass State

Montana

CAPITAL: Helena
NICKNAME:
Treasure State

Alaska

CAPITAL: Juneau
NICKNAME:
The Last Frontier
(unofficial)

Florida

CAPITAL: Tallahassee
NICKNAME:
Sunshine State

Louisiana

CAPITAL: Baton Rouge
NICKNAME:
Pelican State

Nebraska

CAPITAL: Lincoln
NICKNAME:
Cornhusker State

Arizona

CAPITAL: Phoenix
NICKNAME:
Grand Canyon State

Georgia

CAPITAL: Atlanta
NICKNAME:
Peach State, Empire
State of the South

Maine

CAPITAL: Augusta
NICKNAME:
Pine Tree State

 Nevada

CAPITAL: Carson City
NICKNAME:
Sagebrush State,
Battle Born State, Silver State

 Arkansas

CAPITAL: Little Rock
NICKNAME:
Natural State,
Razorback State

Hawaii

CAPITAL: Honolulu
NICKNAME:
Aloha State

Maryland

CAPITAL: Annapolis
NICKNAME:
Old Line State,
Free State

New Hampshire

CAPITAL: Concord
NICKNAME:
Granite State

 California

CAPITAL: Sacramento
NICKNAME:
Golden State

Idaho

CAPITAL: Boise
NICKNAME:
Gem State

Massachusetts

CAPITAL: Boston
NICKNAME:
Bay State, Old Colony

New Jersey

CAPITAL: Trenton
NICKNAME:
Garden State

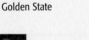 **Colorado**

CAPITAL: Denver
NICKNAME:
Centennial State

Illinois

CAPITAL: Springfield
NICKNAME:
Prairie State

Michigan

CAPITAL: Lansing
NICKNAME:
Great Lakes State,
Wolverine State

New Mexico

CAPITAL: Santa Fe
NICKNAME:
Land of Enchantment

Connecticut

CAPITAL: Hartford
NICKNAME:
Constitution State,
Nutmeg State

Indiana

CAPITAL: Indianapolis
NICKNAME:
Hoosier State

Minnesota

CAPITAL: St. Paul
NICKNAME:
Gopher State,
North Star State

New York

CAPITAL: Albany
NICKNAME:
Empire State

Countries, states, provinces, and territories not drawn to scale.

North Carolina
CAPITAL: Raleigh
NICKNAME:
Tar Heel State, Old
North State

Pennsylvania
CAPITAL: Harrisburg
NICKNAME:
Keystone State

Texas
CAPITAL: Austin
NICKNAME:
Lone Star State

North Dakota
CAPITAL: Bismarck
NICKNAME:
Peace Garden State

Rhode Island
CAPITAL: Providence
NICKNAME:
Little Rhody,
Ocean State

Utah
CAPITAL: Salt Lake City
NICKNAME:
Beehive State

West Virginia
CAPITAL: Charleston
NICKNAME:
Mountain State

Ohio
CAPITAL: Columbus
NICKNAME:
Buckeye State

South Carolina
CAPITAL: Columbia
NICKNAME:
Palmetto State

Vermont
CAPITAL: Montpelier
NICKNAME:
Green Mountain State

Wisconsin
CAPITAL: Madison
NICKNAME:
Badger State

Oklahoma
CAPITAL: Oklahoma
City
NICKNAME:
Sooner State

South Dakota
CAPITAL: Pierre
NICKNAME:
Coyote State, Mount
Rushmore State

Virginia
CAPITAL: Richmond
NICKNAME:
Old Dominion

Wyoming
CAPITAL: Cheyenne
NICKNAME:
Equality State,
Cowboy State

Oregon
CAPITAL: Salem
NICKNAME:
Beaver State

Tennessee
CAPITAL: Nashville
NICKNAME:
Volunteer State

Washington
CAPITAL: Olympia
NICKNAME:
Evergreen State

Canada

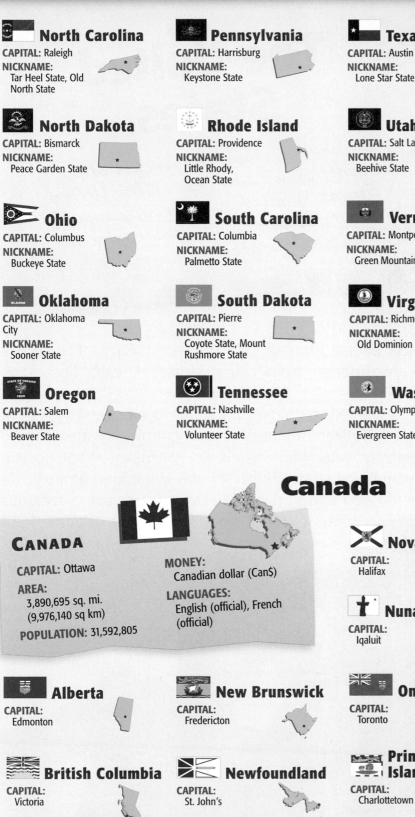

CANADA
CAPITAL: Ottawa
AREA:
3,890,695 sq. mi.
(9,976,140 sq km)
POPULATION: 31,592,805

MONEY:
Canadian dollar (Can$)
LANGUAGES:
English (official), French
(official)

Nova Scotia
CAPITAL:
Halifax

Saskatchewan
CAPITAL:
Regina

Nunavut
CAPITAL:
Iqaluit

Yukon Territory
CAPITAL:
Whitehorse

Alberta
CAPITAL:
Edmonton

New Brunswick
CAPITAL:
Fredericton

Ontario
CAPITAL:
Toronto

British Columbia
CAPITAL:
Victoria

Newfoundland
CAPITAL:
St. John's

Prince Edward Island
CAPITAL:
Charlottetown

Manitoba
CAPITAL:
Winnipeg

Northwest Territories
CAPITAL:
Yellowknife

Quebec
CAPITAL:
Quebec

⎘ internet connect

COUNTRY STATISTICS
GO TO: go.hrw.com
KEYWORD: SG3 FactsU2
FOR: more facts about the
United States and Canada

Sources: Central Intelligence Agency, *The World Factbook 2001; The World Almanac and Book of Facts 2001*

CHAPTER 6

The United States

Before we study the world's other countries, we will look at the United States. What do you already know about the people and geography of the United States?

In this book you will meet people from all over the world. Each of them has cultural traditions that are different from yours. However, each has many things in common.

What is culture? As you learned in Chapter 5, culture is a learned system of shared beliefs and behaviors. To learn about American culture, we are going to start by meeting an American: you. What beliefs do you have? What do you like to eat? How old will you be when you finish school? What kind of music do you like? What language do you speak at home? Do you practice a religious faith? Which holidays do you celebrate? All of these things reflect something about our American culture, as well as our diversity.

Section 1 Physical Geography

Read to Discover

1. What are the major physical features of the United States?
2. What climate regions are found in the United States?
3. What natural resources does the United States have?

Define

contiguous
Continental Divide
basins

Locate

Coastal Plain
Appalachian Mountains
Interior Plains
Rocky Mountains
Great Lakes
Mississippi River
Great Plains
Columbia River
Great Basin
Colorado Plateau
Sierra Nevada
Cascade Range
Aleutian Islands

WHY IT MATTERS

Some of the U.S. states are at risk for earthquakes. Use CNNfyi.com or other **current events** sources to find out about earthquakes in the United States. Record your findings in your journal.

Bald eagle

The United States: Physical-Political

Physical Features

The 48 **contiguous** American states and the District of Columbia lie between the Atlantic and Pacific Oceans. Contiguous states are those that border each other. Two states are not contiguous: Alaska, to the northwest of Canada, and Hawaii, in the Pacific Ocean. The United States also has territories in the Pacific Ocean and the Caribbean Sea. We will now look at the physical features of the 50 states. You can use the map on the next page to follow along.

The East The eastern United States rises from the Coastal Plain to the Appalachian Mountains. The Coastal Plain is a low region that lies close to sea level. It rises gradually inland. The Coastal Plain stretches from New York to Mexico along the Atlantic and Gulf of Mexico coasts.

The Appalachians include mountain ranges and river valleys from Maine to Alabama. The mountains are very old. Erosion has lowered and smoothed the peaks for more than 300 million years. The highest mountain in the Appalachians rises to just 6,684 feet (2,037 m).

At the foot of the Appalachians, between the mountains and the Coastal Plain, is the Piedmont. The Piedmont is a region of rolling plains. It begins in New Jersey and extends as far south as Alabama.

The Interior Plains Vast plains make up most of the United States west of the Appalachians. This region is called the Interior Plains. The Interior Plains stretch westward to the Rocky Mountains.

After the last ice age, glaciers shrank. They left rolling hills, lakes, and major river systems in the northern Interior Plains. The Great Lakes were created by these retreating ice sheets. From west to east, the Great Lakes are Lake Superior, Lake Michigan, Lake Huron, Lake Erie, and Lake Ontario.

The Mississippi River and its tributaries drain the Interior Plains. Along the way, they deposit rich soils that produce fertile farmlands. A tributary is a stream or river that flows into a larger stream or river. Tributaries of the Mississippi include the Missouri and Ohio Rivers.

The Great Smoky Mountains of Tennessee are a range of the Appalachian Mountains.

Interpreting the Visual Record

What clues from this photograph might tell you that these mountains are very old?

Canada

United States

Mexico

Physical Regions of the United States and Canada

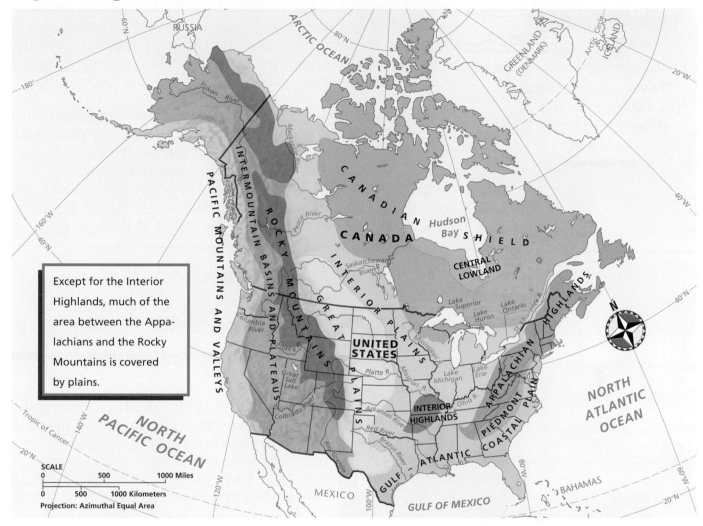

Except for the Interior Highlands, much of the area between the Appalachians and the Rocky Mountains is covered by plains.

SCALE
0   500   1000 Miles
0   500   1000 Kilometers
Projection: Azimuthal Equal Area

In some places on its way to the Gulf of Mexico, the great Mississippi River is 1.5 miles (2.4 km) wide!

The flattest part of the Interior Plains is the Great Plains region. It lies closest to the Rocky Mountains. The region has a higher elevation than the rest of the Interior Plains. The Great Plains extend from Mexico in the south into Canada in the north.

The West As we continue westward, we reach the Rocky Mountains. The Rockies include a series of mountain ranges separated by high plains and valleys. They extend from Mexico to the cold Arctic. Many Rocky Mountain peaks reach more than 14,000 feet (4,267 m).

Running along the crest of the Rockies is the **Continental Divide**. It divides the flow of North America's rivers. Rivers east of the divide, such as the Missouri, flow eastward. Rivers west of the divide, such as the Columbia, flow westward.

West of the Rockies is a region of plateaus and **basins**. A basin is a region surrounded by higher land, such as mountains. The Great Basin in Nevada and Utah, for example, is surrounded by high mountains. Southeast of the Great Basin is

The Rio Grande cuts through Big Bend National Park along the Texas-Mexico border.
Interpreting the Visual Record What landforms are found in this area?

Do you remember what you learned about tectonic activity? See Chapter 2 to review.

the Colorado Plateau. The Colorado Plateau lies in Utah, Colorado, New Mexico, and Arizona. West of the Great Basin lie the Sierra Nevada, the Coast Ranges, and many valleys. The Cascade Range in the Pacific Northwest was formed by volcanic eruptions. Volcanic eruptions and earthquakes are a danger in the Pacific states. In this area, the North American plate is colliding with the Pacific plate.

Hawaii and Alaska Farther west, Hawaii and Alaska also experience tectonic activity. The Hawaiian Islands were formed by large volcanoes that have risen from the floor of the Pacific Ocean. Alaska's Aleutian (uh-LOO-shuhn) Islands also have volcanic origins.

Southeastern and south-central Alaska are very mountainous. The highest mountain in North America is Mount McKinley, in the Alaska Range. The American Indian name for Mount McKinley is Denali. It soars to a height of 20,320 feet (6,194 m).

✓ **READING CHECK:** (*Places and Regions*) What are the major physical features of the United States?

Ⓐ Winter storm in Massachusetts
Ⓑ Spring meadow in California
Ⓒ Summer in Florida
Ⓓ Fall in Colorado

Climate

The climates of the United States are varied. The country has 11 climate types—the greatest variety of climates of any country.

The East Most of the eastern United States is divided into two climate regions. In the north is a humid continental climate with snowy winters and warm, humid summers. Southerners experience the milder winters and warm, humid summers of a humid subtropical climate. Coastal areas often experience tropical storms. Southern Florida, with a tropical savanna climate, is warm all year.

The Interior Plains Humid continental, humid subtropical, and steppe climates meet in the interior states. People there sometimes experience violent weather, such as hail and tornadoes. The steppe climate of the Great Plains supports wide grasslands. Summers are hot, and droughts can be a problem. Blinding snowstorms called blizzards sometimes occur during winters, which can be very cold.

The West Climates in the West are mostly dry. Steppe and varied highland climates dominate much of the Rocky Mountain region. Temperatures and the amount of rain and snow vary.

Much of the Southwest has a desert climate. The West Coast has two climate types. The forested north has a wet and mild marine west coast climate. A drier Mediterranean climate is found in the south.

Except in the southeast, most of Alaska has very cold subarctic and tundra climates. Hawaii is the only state within the tropics. Northeasterly trade winds bring rain to eastern sides of the islands. Hawaii's western slopes have a drier tropical savanna climate.

✓ **READING CHECK:** *The World in Spatial Terms* What climate regions are found in the United States?

Natural Resources

The United States has many resources. Some of the most productive farmlands in the world are found in the Interior Plains. Ranches and farms produce beef, wheat, corn, and soybeans. California, Florida, Texas, and other areas grow fruit, vegetables, and cotton.

Alaska, California, Texas, and other states supply oil and natural gas. Coal and other minerals are found in Appalachian and western states. Gold and silver mines also operate in some western states.

Forests, especially in the Northwest and the Southeast, are important sources of lumber. The Atlantic Ocean, Gulf of Mexico, and Pacific Ocean are rich sources of fish and other seafood. The natural beauty of the country is also a valuable resource for tourism. All these resources help support industry and other economic activities.

✓ **READING CHECK:** *Places and Regions* What natural resources does the United States have?

Our Amazing Planet

Redwoods, the tallest trees in the world, grow in California and Oregon. They can grow well over 300 feet (90 m) high with trunks 20 feet (6 m) in diameter. Some redwood trees are more than 1,500 years old!

Homework Practice Online
Keyword: SG3 HP6

Define and explain: contiguous, Continental Divide, basins

Working with Sketch Maps On a map of the United States that you draw or that your teacher provides, label the following: Coastal Plain, Appalachian Mountains, Interior Plains, Rocky Mountains, Great Lakes, Mississippi River, Great Plains, Columbia River, Great Basin, Colorado Plateau, Sierra Nevada, Cascade Range, and Aleutian Islands.

Reading for the Main Idea

1. (*Places and Regions*) What are the two major mountain regions in the United States? What major landform region lies betweeen them?

2. (*Places and Regions*) What resources are found in the country? Why are they important for the economy?

3. (*Places and Regions*) What parts of the United States have particularly rich farmlands?

Critical Thinking

4. **Drawing Inferences and Conclusions** The Rockies are higher than the Appalachians. How is this fact a clue to the relative age of the two mountain systems?

Organizing What You Know

5. **Categorizing** Copy the following graphic organizer. Use it to categorize the major physical features and climates of the East, Interior Plains, and West.

	Physical Features	Climates
East		
Interior Plains		
West (including Alaska, and Hawaii)		

Section 2 — The History and Culture of the United States

Read to Discover

1. What was the history of the United States?
2. What rights and responsibilities do U.S. citizens have?
3. How have different groups of people added to the cultural diversity of the United States?

Define

colonies
plantations
annexed
textiles
bilingual

Locate

Boston
New York

WHY IT MATTERS

In the 1800s and early 1900s, immigrants poured into the United States from various parts of Europe. Use **CNNfyi.com** or other **current events** sources to find out about current immigration to the United States. Record your findings in your journal.

American quilt from the 1800s

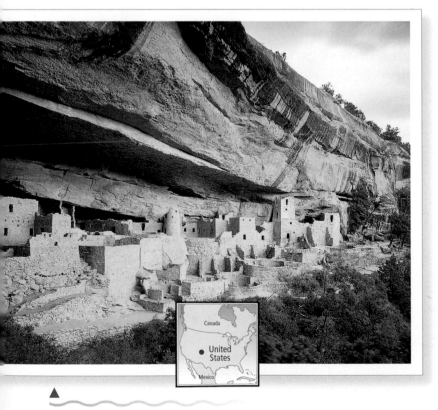

▲ Anasazi homes were built of stone and sun-dried clay bricks. They were built in openings in high cliffs.

History and Government

There are more than 2 million American Indians living in the United States today. They are the descendants of the first people in the Americas. Scientists believe people first crossed into North America from Asia at least 20,000 years ago. Over time, these peoples spread throughout the Americas. They developed many different cultures and civilizations. These cultures included the Maya, Aztec, and Inca.

A variety of cultures developed in North America. For example, after about A.D. 700, the Anasazi in the southwestern United States developed a complex irrigation system. This system made it possible for the Anasazi to grow crops in a dry region. Some people in the Mississippi River and Ohio River valleys farmed. They also built large mounds. These mounds were built for different purposes, including burials.

There also were various peoples in the Northeast, such as the Iroquois and Algonquian. These peoples hunted and gathered wild foods and grew some crops.

This painting shows a southern plantation as a small community.

Interpreting the Visual Record
How were products from this plantation sent to markets?

Colonial Era Europeans began settling in North America in the 1500s. The Spanish, French, English, Dutch, and others established **colonies**. A colony is a territory controlled by people from a foreign land. By the mid-1700s the British Empire included more than a dozen colonies along the Atlantic coast. New cities such as Boston and New York became major seaports in the British colonies. Spain and France claimed much of the land west of the British colonies.

Some settlers established **plantations**. A plantation is a large farm that grows mainly one crop to sell. Plantations were particularly common in the rich soils and mild climates of the southern British colonies. Many of the colonial plantations produced cotton or tobacco.

Beginning in the 1600s, thousands of enslaved Africans were brought to the colonies. Most were put to work on plantations. Slavery continued in the United States until after the Civil War in 1865. About 13 percent of Americans today are descended from Africans brought to this country by force.

Expansion The American colonies declared independence from the British Empire in 1776. Gradually, the United States expanded. By 1850 the United States stretched from the Atlantic Ocean to the Pacific Ocean. The United States bought Alaska from Russia in 1867. In 1898 Hawaii was **annexed**, or formally added to, the United States.

Industrial Growth The economy of the United States grew rapidly in the 1800s. By the late 1800s, important industries included steel, oil, and **textiles**, or cloth products. The steel industry grew around cities that were near coal and iron ore deposits. Most of those new industrial cities were in Appalachian and Midwest states.

The development of waterways and railroads helped industry and people move farther into the interior. The chance for a better life also attracted millions of immigrants. Immigration was particularly heavy in the late 1800s and early 1900s. The cultural diversity of the United States is a result of this historical pattern of immigration.

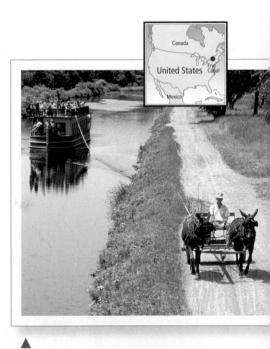

New York's Erie Canal was built in the early 1800s. It allowed barges to move goods to and from farms and factories along the route.

Interpreting the Visual Record
How did the canal influence the economic development of New York farmland?

The United States • 113

War and Peace Despite two world wars and other conflicts in the 1900s, the United States continued to prosper. Many Americans died in World Wars I and II. However, no battles were fought on the U.S. mainland. This spared the country the terrible damage seen in Europe, Asia, and the Pacific. After World War II, the United States and the Soviet Union became rivals in what was known as the Cold War. The Cold War lasted until the 1990s. U.S. troops served in several foreign wars in the last half of the 1900s. Today, the United States is a leading member of many international organizations.

Government The United States has a limited, democratic government based on the U.S. Constitution. This document spells out the powers and functions of the branches of the federal government. The national government includes an elected president and Congress. In general, the national government handles national issues. Many powers are left to the 50 state governments.

Rights and Responsibilities American citizens have many rights and responsibilities, including the right to vote. They are encouraged to play an active role in government. Without such participation, the democratic system suffers. In this regard, the United States is similar to other democratic countries, like Germany and Great Britain. It differs from countries with minority rule, like China, where the government limits political rights.

✓ **READING CHECK:** (*Human Systems*) What were some major events in the history of the United States?

The U.S. Constitution has served as a model for governments in other countries.

▼

The Granger Collection, New York

A Diverse People

The United States is home to people who speak many languages. About 17 million people in this country speak Spanish. Many of these people live in areas near Spanish-speaking countries like Mexico and Cuba.

Some people are **bilingual**. Bilingual means having the ability to speak two languages. By the 1990s more than 30 million U.S. residents spoke a language other than English. These languages include Spanish, French, Chinese, Russian, Arabic, and Navajo.

The United States is also home to many religious faiths. Most people are Protestant Christians or Roman Catholics. However, many cities have Jewish synagogues and Islamic

The faces of Presidents George Washington, Thomas Jefferson, Theodore Roosevelt, and Abraham Lincoln are carved into Mount Rushmore, South Dakota.

▼

Canada

Mount
Rushmore ●

United States

Mexico

mosques, as well as places of worship for other religions. This religious variety adds to cultural diversity by contributing distinct ideas and customs to American life.

America's food is as diverse as its people. Chinese, Mexican, and Arab dishes are now part of the American diet. They join traditional foods such as fried chicken.

Americans have varied traditions and enjoy many different forms of entertainment. They celebrate a variety of holidays, such as *Cinco de Mayo* or Saint Patrick's Day. Many Americans celebrate Independence Day on July 4 with fireworks, concerts, and picnics.

Many religious holidays are also celebrated in the United States. These include the Christian holidays of Christmas and Easter and the Jewish celebrations of Hanukkah, Yom Kippur, and Rosh Hashanah. Some African Americans also celebrate Kwanzaa. Kwanzaa is based on a traditional African festival.

The United States has been home to many noted artists and writers. You might, for example, be familiar with the art of Georgia O'Keeffe. American writers include Mark Twain, Emily Dickinson, and Langston Hughes. In addition, musical forms such as blues, jazz, and rock 'n' roll have origins in this country.

American movies, television programs, and sports also are popular elsewhere. In many ways the United States influences the rest of the world through its culture.

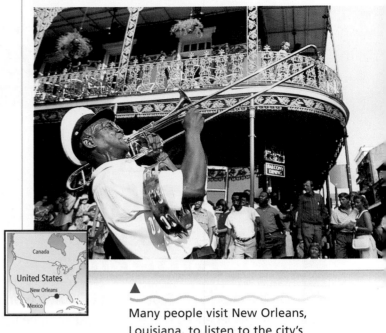

Many people visit New Orleans, Louisiana, to listen to the city's popular jazz bands.

Interpreting the Visual Record
What can you learn about the climate of New Orleans by looking at the building in this picture?

✓ **READING CHECK:** (*Human Systems*) How has cultural diversity enriched life in the United States?

Section Review 2

Define and explain: colonies, plantations, annexed, textiles, bilingual

Working with Sketch Maps On the map that you created in Section 1, label Boston and New York. In a box in the margin, identify the location of the thirteen British colonies that became the United States.

Reading for the Main Idea

1. (*Human Systems*) How long did it take for the United States to expand from the Atlantic Ocean to the Pacific Ocean?

2. (*Human Systems*) What are the roles and responsibilities of citizens of the United States?

Homework Practice Online
Keyword: SG3 HP6

Critical Thinking

3. **Drawing Inferences and Conclusions** How do you think American culture has been able to influence people and culture around the world? What affect has it had?

4. **Analyzing Information** How are the many cultural traditions of the United States reflected in its religious holidays? Give examples.

Organizing What You Know

5. **Sequencing** Copy the following time line. Use it to list important events that took place in North America during the centuries shown. The time line has been started for you.

1500s	1600s	1700s	1800s	1900s

1500s
Europeans begin to settle North America.

CONNECTING TO *History*

An ATTACK on America

On the morning of September 11, 2001, the United States experienced one of the greatest tragedies in its history. Terrorists—individuals who use violence to achieve political goals—hijacked four commercial airliners flying out of airports in Boston, Massachusetts; Newark, New Jersey; and Washington, D.C. The terrorists crashed two of the planes into the Twin Towers of New York City's World Trade Center, causing the buildings to collapse. The third plane hit the Pentagon, and the fourth crashed in rural Pennsylvania. Thousands of people were killed and injured in the attacks.

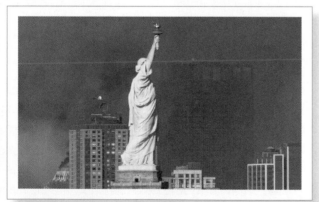

Smoke rises from the site of the World Trade Center towers.

People around the nation watched in shock and disbelief as the crisis unfolded on television. The administration of President George W. Bush and members of the U.S. Congress declared these attacks acts of war against the United States. The president tried to reassure the nation.

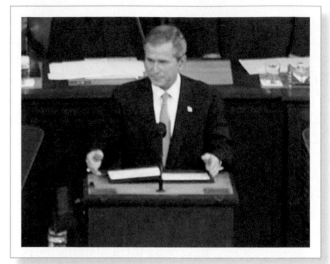

President George W. Bush, addressing Congress

❝ *Terrorist attacks can shake the foundations of our biggest buildings, but they cannot touch the foundation of America. These acts shattered steel, but they cannot dent the steel of American resolve.* **❞**
—President George W. Bush,
Speech on September 11, 2001

World leaders expressed their concern for the people of the United States. Referring to World Wars I and II, European Commission president Romano Prodi offered support. "In the darkest days of European history, America stood close by us and today we stand close by America." British prime minister Tony Blair stated that the attacks were "an attack on the free and democratic world everywhere." People around the world gathered to remember the victims of the attacks, holding candlelight services and moments of silence.

Within only a few days of the attacks, a massive federal investigation uncovered many details about the hijackers and their plans. The president and other U.S. officials worked quickly to build an international coalition, or alliance, to fight terrorism. Included in the coalition were members of the North Atlantic Treaty Organization. Russia also offered diplomatic and other support, as did Japan, Jordan, Egypt, and several other nations.

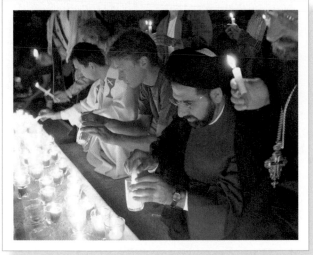

Multifaith memorial service for the victims

The investigation led to terrorist Osama bin Laden and his network, al Qaeda, based in Afghanistan. Bin Laden and his network were also suspects in previous overseas attacks against the United States. U.S. leaders demanded that the ruling government of Afghanistan, the Taliban, turn bin Laden over to U.S. authorities, but Taliban leaders refused. With international support, the United

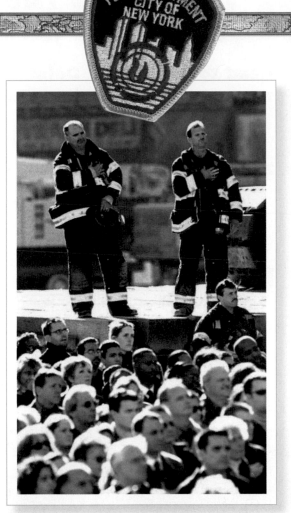

Firefighters played a key role in the search and recovery efforts at the attack sites.

States and Great Britain launched attacks on Taliban and al Qaeda targets, toppling the Taliban government. As Americans tightened security around the nation, President Bush warned them that the fight against terrorism would be a long one.

Understanding What You Read

1. What is terrorism?
2. Why is international support needed to fight terrorism?

U.S. aircraft carrier departing as part of a battlegroup launched in response to the September 11 attacks

Section 3 The Economy

Read to Discover

1. What are the major economic characteristics of the five regions of the United States?
2. What are some of the challenges the United States faces today?

Define

second-growth forests
megalopolis
diversify
Corn Belt
Dairy Belt
Wheat Belt
center-pivot irrigation
strip mining
trade deficit

Locate

Washington, D.C.
Philadelphia
Baltimore
Atlanta
Houston
New Orleans
Miami
Dallas
Chicago
Detroit
Phoenix
Las Vegas
San Diego
San Francisco
Seattle
Portland

WHY IT MATTERS

Managing pollution is a challenge for the U.S. government. Use **CNNfyi.com** or other **current events** sources to find out about pollution problems and clean-up efforts in this country. Record your findings in your journal.

Computer microchip

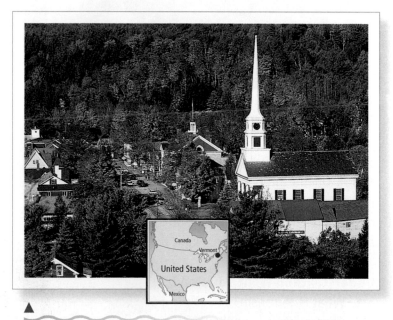

▲ Small towns and beautiful scenery can be found throughout Vermont and the rest of New England.

A Prosperous Country

The United States is the richest country in the world. The value of all American products and services exceeds that of any other country. Now we will examine how each American region contributes to this powerful economy. These five regions are the Northeast, the South, the Midwest, the Interior West, and the Pacific.

The Northeast

The Northeast includes 12 states and shares a border with Canada. First we will look at the New England states. These are Maine, New Hampshire, Vermont, Massachusetts, Rhode Island, and Connecticut. Then we will turn to the Middle Atlantic states. They are New York, Pennsylvania, New Jersey, Delaware, Maryland, and West Virginia.

New England A short growing season and rocky terrain limit farming in New England. As a result, most farms in this region are small. Some are now used as second homes or retirement retreats for people living in cities.

Cool, shallow waters off the coast are good fishing areas. Cod and shellfish are the most valuable seafood. The U.S. government has set rules to prevent overfishing in some areas.

The early shipbuilding industry in New England used wood from the region's forests. Nearly all of New England's forests today are **second-growth forests**. These are the trees that cover an area after the original forest has been cut. In the fall New England's forests burst into color. The beautiful fall scenery draws many tourists.

New England was the country's first industrial area. Textile mills and shoe factories were built along rivers and swift streams. The flowing water provided power for the mills. Today, many banks, investment houses, and insurance companies are based in the region. In addition, the area has many respected colleges and universities. These schools include Harvard, Yale, the Massachusetts Institute of Technology, and many others.

Middle Atlantic States
Soils are better for farming in the Middle Atlantic states. However, the region's expanding cities have taken over more and more farmland.

Major coal-mining areas are found in the Appalachians, particularly in West Virginia and Pennsylvania. Coal is used in the steelmaking process. The steel industry helped make Pittsburgh, in western Pennsylvania, the largest industrial city in the Appalachians.

Today nearly every kind of manufacturing and service industry can be found in the Middle Atlantic states. Major seaports allow farmers and companies to ship their products to markets around the world. In addition, tourists visit natural and historical sites. These sites include Niagara Falls between New York and Canada and Gettysburg, a major Civil War battleground in Pennsylvania.

United States

Country	Population/ Growth Rate	Life Expectancy	Literacy Rate	Per Capita GDP
United States	281,421,906 0.9%	74, male 80, female	97%	$36,200

Sources: Central Intelligence Agency, *The World Factbook 2001;* U.S. Census Bureau

Interpreting the Chart What is the U.S. per capita GDP?

New York City is an important seaport.

Interpreting the Visual Record Why do you suppose shipping helped the major cities of the Northeast grow?

Megalopolis Overlapping the two areas of the Northeast is a huge, densely populated urban area. This area is called a **megalopolis**. A megalopolis is a string of cities that have grown together. Here it stretches along the Atlantic coast from Boston to Washington, D.C. D.C. stands for District of Columbia. The three other major cities are New York City, Philadelphia, and Baltimore. At least 40 million people live in this urban area.

Except for Washington, D.C., all of these cities were founded during the colonial era. They grew because they were important seaports. Today, they are major industrial and financial centers as well. These cities are connected by roads, railroads, and airline routes. Many of the world's largest companies have home offices there. Washington, D.C., is the country's capital and the center for government offices.

✔ **READING CHECK:** (*Places and Regions*) What are some of the major economic features of the Northeast?

The South

The South includes 12 states. They are Virginia, North Carolina, South Carolina, Georgia, Florida, Alabama, Mississippi, Tennessee, Kentucky, Arkansas, Louisiana, and Texas. The region has long coastlines along the Atlantic Ocean and the Gulf of Mexico. Texas shares a long border with Mexico.

Agriculture Historically, the South was rural and agricultural. Many small towns and farming areas still stretch across the region. The South has long been a major producer of cotton, tobacco, and citrus fruit. In recent years, some farmers have decided to **diversify**. This means those farmers are producing a variety of crops instead of just one.

Many visitors to San Antonio, Texas, enjoy dining along the Riverwalk. **Interpreting the Visual Record How does architecture along the Riverwalk reflect San Antonio's cultural history?**

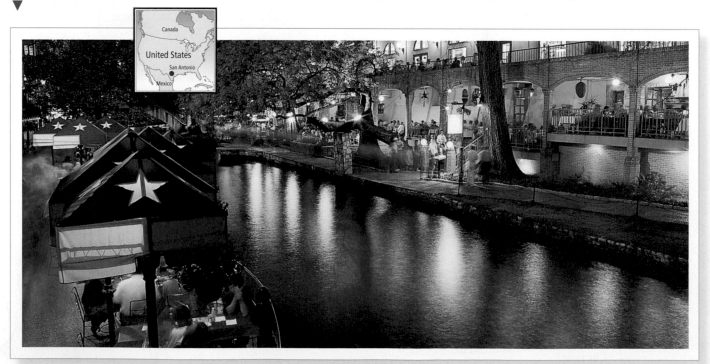

Industry The South has become more urban and industrial in recent decades. The South's cities, such as Atlanta, have grown along with the economy. More than 3.5 million people live in and around Atlanta.

Today, many textile factories operate in the Piedmont areas of Georgia, the Carolinas, and Virginia. Some cities, such as Austin, Texas, also have growing computer, software, and publishing companies. The Texas Gulf Coast and the lower Mississippi River area have huge oil refineries and petrochemical plants. Their products are shipped from Houston, New Orleans, and other major seaports.

Warm weather and beautiful beaches draw many vacationers to resorts in the South. Resort areas include eastern Virginia and Florida. Many people also vacation in the coastal islands of North and South Carolina and Texas.

Many cities in the South have important links with countries in both Central and South America. This is largely because they are located close to those countries. For example, Miami is an important travel connection with Caribbean countries, Mexico, and South America. Atlanta, Houston, and Dallas also are major transportation centers.

✓ **READING CHECK:** (*Places and Regions*) How does geography effect the economic resources of the South?

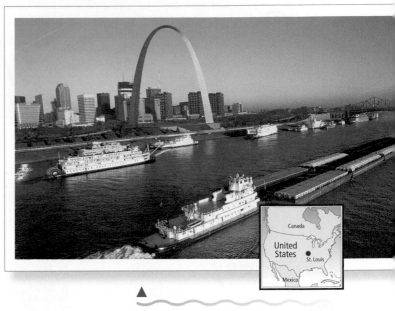
▲ The Mississippi River flows past the Gateway Arch in St. Louis, Missouri. The city was known as the "gateway to the West" in the 1800s.

The Midwest

The Midwest includes eight states: Ohio, Michigan, Indiana, Illinois, Wisconsin, Minnesota, Iowa, and Missouri. All but Iowa and Missouri have shorelines on the Great Lakes.

A Corn can be processed in a variety of ways. Some corn is cooked and then canned.
B Corn is ground and used for livestock feed.
C Corn also might be wet-milled or dry-milled. Then grain parts are used to make different products.
D Corn by-products, such as cornstarch and corn syrup, are used to make breads, breakfast cereals, and snack foods.

Corn: From Field to Consumer

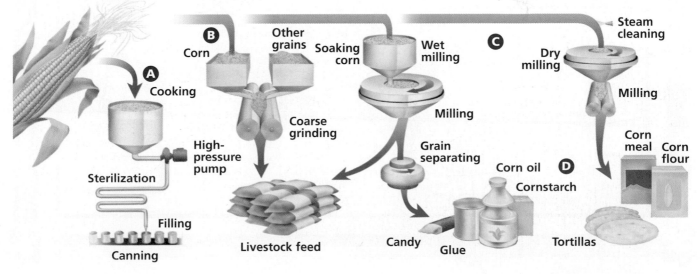

CONNECTING TO Technology

The Great Lakes and St. Lawrence Seaway

The St. Lawrence Seaway permits ships to go between the Great Lakes and the Atlantic Ocean. This waterway's canals and locks allow ships to move from one water level to another. The difference in water levels is significant. For example, Lake Erie is about 570 feet (174 m) above sea level. Farther to the east, Montreal is about 100 feet (30 m) above sea level. Ships moving from one water level to another enter a lock. The water level inside the lock is raised or lowered. It is changed to match the water level in the waterway ahead of the ship. From there, the ship can move on to the next lock.

Higher water levels

Engineers lower water to downstream level

Power station

Upstream gates closed
Lock chamber

Control station

Downstream gates open

Lower water levels

Moving through a canal lock

Understanding What You Read

1. What U.S. cities are located along the shores of the Great Lakes? Why might they have been established here?

2. Which of the Great Lakes lies at the highest elevation? Which lies at the lowest elevation?

Agriculture Good soils and flat land have helped make the Midwest one of the world's great farming regions. Farmers produce corn, dairy products, and soybeans and raise livestock.

The core of the Midwest's corn-growing region is the **Corn Belt**. It stretches from central Ohio to central Nebraska. Much of the corn is used to feed livestock, such as beef cattle and hogs. Soybean production has also become important.

States in the **Dairy Belt** are major producers of milk, cheese, and other dairy products. The Dairy Belt lies north of the Corn Belt. This area includes Wisconsin and most of Minnesota and Michigan. Much of the Dairy Belt is pasture. Farmers also grow crops to feed dairy cows.

Many of the Midwest's farm and factory products are shipped to markets by water. One route is along the Mississippi River to the Gulf of Mexico. The other is through the Great Lakes. This route continues through the St. Lawrence Seaway to the Atlantic Ocean.

Industry One of the busiest shipping ports on the Great Lakes is Chicago, Illinois. This city also has one of the world's busiest airports. Chicago is linked to the rest of the region by highways and railroads. Its industries attracted many immigrants in the late 1800s. They moved there to work in steel mills, meat-packing plants, and other businesses. Today, Chicago is the third-largest city in the United States.

Other Midwest cities were also founded on important transportation routes on the Great Lakes and major rivers. The locations of these cities gave industries access to nearby farm products, coal, and iron ore. Those resources have supported thriving industries. These industries include food processing, iron, steel, machinery, and automobile manufacturing. Detroit, Michigan, has been the nation's leading automobile producer since the early 1900s.

The Midwest's traditional industries declined in the late 1900s. In addition, industrial pollution threatened the Great Lakes and surrounding areas. In response, companies have modernized their plants and factories. The region has also attracted new industries. Many produce high-technology products. The Midwest is again a prosperous region. Also, stricter pollution laws have made many rivers and the Great Lakes much cleaner.

✓ READING CHECK: (*Places and Regions*) What are the major economic activities of the Midwest? What resources support them?

The Interior West

The Interior West includes 13 states. They stretch from Idaho, Montana, and North Dakota southward to Arizona, New Mexico, and Oklahoma. West Texas might also be considered part of this region. The Interior West includes the Great Plains and the Rocky Mountains.

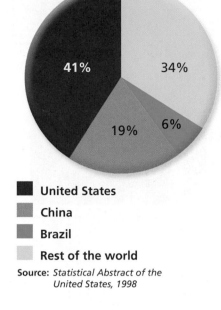

Major Producers of Corn

41%
34%
19%
6%

■ United States
■ China
■ Brazil
□ Rest of the world

Source: *Statistical Abstract of the United States, 1998*

Interpreting the Chart Which nation produces the most corn?

Natural sandstone pillars, arches, and other unusual formations draw many visitors to Monument Valley in Arizona and Utah.

Interpreting the Visual Record What natural force do you think may have created sandstone structures like this one?

▼

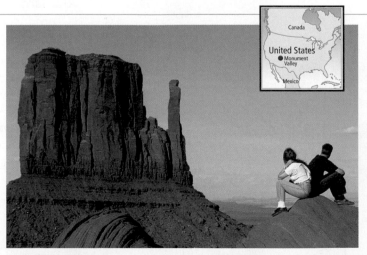

Canada

United States
● Monument
Valley

Mexico

Yellowstone's natural beauty makes it one of the most popular national parks in the United States.

Agriculture Ranching became important in the region in the 1800s. Great herds of cattle and flocks of sheep roamed the Great Plains. Today, ranching in the region is often combined with wheat farming.

The greatest wheat-growing area is known as the **Wheat Belt**. It stretches across the Dakotas, Montana, Nebraska, Oklahoma, Colorado, and Texas. Much of the farmland in the Interior West must be irrigated. One method of irrigation uses long sprinkler systems mounted on huge wheels. The wheels rotate slowly. In this way the sprinkler irrigates the area within a circle. This is called **center-pivot irrigation**. From the air, parts of the irrigated Great Plains resemble a series of green circles.

Mining and Industry The Interior West also has rich deposits of coal, oil, gold, silver, copper, and other minerals. However, mining can cause problems. For example, coal miners in parts of the Great Plains strip away soil and rock. This process is called **strip mining**. This kind of mining leads to soil erosion and other problems. Today, laws require miners to restore mined areas.

One of the Interior West's greatest resources is its natural beauty. Parks, such as Yellowstone, are scattered throughout the region. Warm, sunny cities like Phoenix and Las Vegas are growing rapidly.

✔ **READING CHECK:** *Places and Regions* How does geography affect the major resources of the Interior West?

The Pacific States

The Pacific states are California, Oregon, Washington, Alaska, and Hawaii. Alaska is separated from the 48 contiguous states by Canada and the Pacific Ocean. Hawaii is a series of islands far to the west in the Pacific.

California More than 10 percent of all Americans live in California, in large part because of its mild climate and wealth of resources. More than 90 percent of the people in California live in urban areas. The Los Angeles, San Diego, and San Francisco Bay urban areas are among the largest in the country. California is the leading agricultural producer and leading industrial state. Big companies own many farms in central and southern areas. Crops include cotton, nuts, vegetables, and fruit. Aerospace, construction, entertainment, computers, software, and tourism are important industries in the state.

Northwest States Forests and fish are two of the most important resources in Oregon and Washington. Both resources have been the focus of environmental debates, and environmentalists and industry leaders continue to work on ways to resolve their differences.

Seattle is Washington's largest city. It is home to many important industries, including a major computer software company. More than half of the people in Oregon live in and around Portland.

San Francisco, California, lies across the Bay Bridge from Oakland.

Interpreting the Visual Record **What does the fact that this bridge connects two large cities tell you about the San Francisco Bay area?**

Alaska and Hawaii Alaska's economy is largely based on oil, forests, and fish. As in Washington and Oregon, there are debates over developing these resources. For example, some people want to limit oil drilling in wild areas of Alaska. Others want to expand drilling.

Hawaii's natural beauty, mild climate, and fertile soils are its most important resources. Millions of tourists visit the islands each year.

✓ **READING CHECK:** *Places and Regions* What are the economic features of the Pacific states?

Challenges Today

The United States faces many challenges today. For example, other countries look to the United States for help in resolving international conflicts. Also, U.S. soldiers have fought in several conflicts overseas.

Another challenge is trade. The United States has a **trade deficit**. This means the value of American exports is lower than the value of its imports. People have debated the best way to help American companies sell their goods abroad. Some feel the government should play an active role in promoting exports and protecting American industries. Others think that the market should be allowed to work on its own.

The United States also faces challenges at home. These have long included fighting poverty, crime, and pollution. Many people are also concerned about urban sprawl around rapidly growing cities. These are likely to remain difficult challenges during the new century.

✓ **READING CHECK:** *Human Systems* What are some of the challenges the United States faces today?

Pacific salmon return from the sea to deposit their eggs in the same rivers or streams in which they were hatched. Some species of salmon swim against the current through rapids and even waterfalls for more than 2,000 miles (3,200 km) up Alaska's Yukon River!

go.hrw.com **Homework Practice Online** Keyword: SG3 HP6

Define and explain: second-growth forests, megalopolis, diversify, Corn Belt, Dairy Belt, Wheat Belt, center-pivot irrigation, strip mining, trade deficit

Working with Sketch Maps On the map you created for Section 2, label the 50 states and the following places: Washington, D.C., Philadelphia, Baltimore, Atlanta, Houston, New Orleans, Miami, Dallas, Chicago, Detroit, Phoenix, Las Vegas, San Diego, San Francisco, Seattle, and Portland. In a box in the margin, identify major U.S. seaports on your map.

Reading for the Main Idea

1. *Places and Regions* What five major cities make up the Northeast's megalopolis?

2. *Human Systems* How has the economy of the South changed in recent years?

3. *Human Systems* How do farm and industrial products from the Midwest get to markets elsewhere?

Critical Thinking

4. **Drawing Inferences and Conclusions** Why do you think a trade deficit can be a problem for a country?

Organizing What You Know

5. **Categorizing** Copy the following graphic organizer. Use it to list important economic characteristics and cities of the five regions of the United States.

Northeast	South	Midwest	Interior West	Pacific States

Reviewing What You Know

Building Vocabulary

On a separate sheet of paper, write sentences to define each of the following words.

1. contiguous
2. Continental Divide
3. basins
4. colonies
5. plantations
6. annexed
7. textiles
8. bilingual
9. second-growth forests
10. megalopolis
11. diversify
12. Corn Belt
13. center-pivot irrigation
14. strip mining
15. trade deficit

Reviewing the Main Ideas

1. *(Places and Regions)* What are the two major mountain regions of the United States?

2. *(Places and Regions)* Where are the Corn Belt, Dairy Belt, and Wheat Belt located?

3. *(Places and Regions)* Where did the steel industry grow in the late 1800s?

4. *(Human Systems)* What water routes are used to transport products from the Midwest to markets outside the region?

5. *(Places and Regions)* Where are the dry climate regions located in the United States?

Understanding Environment and Society

Resource Use

Timber from forests is an important natural resource in parts of the United States. The timber industry has created many jobs. As you prepare your presentation about this industry, consider the following:

- In which states timber is important.
- How timber is harvested.
- How harvesting timber affects the environment.

Thinking Critically

1. **Contrasting** How is the physical geography of the Appalachians different from that of the Rocky Mountains? Why is this true?

2. **Drawing Inferences and Conclusions** How has climate affected agriculture in the Interior West?

3. **Making Generalizations and Predictions** Explain the relationship between rights and responsibilities in the United States. How do you think this relationship might be different in other nations?

4. **Finding the Main Idea** What cities were supported in their development by nearby mineral resources? How?

5. **Drawing Inferences and Conclusions** Why do you think megalopolises form?

Map ACTIVITY

On a separate sheet of paper, match the letters on the map with their correct labels.

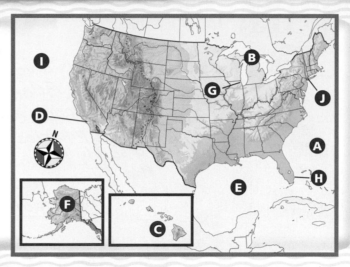

Atlantic Ocean	Great Lakes
Pacific Ocean	New York City
Alaska	Los Angeles
Hawaii	Miami
Gulf of Mexico	Chicago

Mental Mapping Skills ACTIVITY

On a separate sheet of paper, draw a freehand map of the United States. Make a key for your map and label the following:

Appalachian Mountains	Mississippi River
Coastal Plain	Rocky
Great Plains	Mountains
Interior Plains	

WRITING ACTIVITY

You might be familiar with the song "America the Beautiful." It reminds the listener of the physical beauty of the United States—"from sea to shining sea." Write a short poem, song, or rap describing the physical geography of the eastern, interior, or western United States. Be sure to use standard grammar, spelling, sentence structure, and punctuation.

Alternative Assessment

Portfolio ACTIVITY

Learning About Your Local Geography

Cultures in Your State Research the ethnic groups, cultural traditions, and physical geography of your state. On poster board, create an outline map of the state with illustrations showing examples of your state's diversity.

internet connect

Internet Activity: go.hrw.com
KEYWORD: SG3 GT6

Choose a topic to explore about the United States:
- Visit America's national parks.
- Experience life in the early colonies.
- Learn about holidays celebrated in the United States.

CHAPTER 7

Canada

Canada is a vast land that stretches from the Atlantic to the Pacific. Its landscape ranges from tall mountains to flat prairies and from dense forests to sandy beaches. You will learn that the culture of Canada is as varied as its physical features.

Hello, my name is Bella Morris. Like the boy shown here, I am an Inuit (Eskimo) in Canada. I was born and raised in the northern Arctic region of Canada.

I spent my early childhood years traveling, harvesting, fishing, and hunting on the Arctic tundra. My family spent many months following the seasonal patterns of the animals. In those early years, I traveled by dog team, lived in an igloo, and watched my father and uncles hunt whales. I also helped prepare many of our traditional foods, especially during the season for harvesting wild berries and herbs. I spent winter months listening to the legends and hunting stories of my people while learning to sew the warm fur clothing needed to survive in the Arctic.

I did well in school, but I only went as far as ninth grade. Twenty years later I went back to school and university, graduating with a bachelor's degree in education. Today, I work as a First Nations District Coordinator for my school district. I am helping to bridge the cultural differences between the First Nations children (Inuit and Canadian Indian) and children of European and Asian descent.

Haloo! Inuuyunga kanadamiutauyunga.

◀

Translation: Hello! I am an Inuit. I come from Canada.

Section 1 Physical Geography

Read to Discover

1. What are Canada's major landforms, rivers, and lakes?
2. What are the major climate types and natural resources of Canada?

Define

potash
pulp
newsprint

Locate

Rocky Mountains
Appalachian Mountains
Canadian Shield
Hudson Bay

Great Lakes
St. Lawrence River
Great Bear Lake
Great Slave Lake

WHY IT MATTERS

The United States and Canada share a 5,526-mile-long border. Use CNNfyi.com or other current events sources to find out what political and environmental issues surround this border. Record your findings in your journal.

A Canadian coin

Canada: Physical-Political

ELEVATION	
FEET	**METERS**
13,120	4,000
6,560	2,000
1,640	500
656	200
(Sea level) 0	0 (Sea level)
Below sea level	Below sea level

Ice caps
⊛ National capital
★ Provincial capitals
• Other cities

SCALE
0   250   500 Miles
0 250 500 Kilometers
Projection: Azimuthal Equal Area

Size comparison of Canada to the contiguous United States

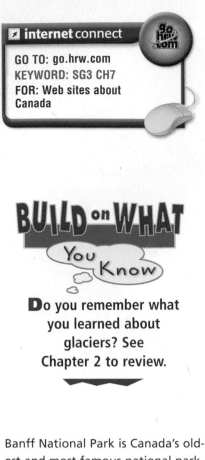

BUILD on WHAT
You Know

Do you remember what
you learned about
glaciers? See
Chapter 2 to review.

Banff National Park is Canada's oldest and most famous national park. The park's many visitors are treated to spectacular views of Canada's Rocky Mountains.

Interpreting the Visual Record What types of climate would you expect to find here?

Physical Features

The physical geography of Canada has much in common with that of the United States. Both countries share some major physical regions. For example, the Coast Mountains and the Rocky Mountains extend into western Canada. Broad plains stretch across the interiors of both countries. Also, the Appalachian Mountains extend into southeastern Canada.

The Canadian Shield, a region of rocky uplands, borders Hudson Bay. To the south are some of Canada's most fertile soils, in the St. Lawrence River Valley and the Great Lakes region. The Great Lakes are Lake Erie, Lake Huron, Lake Michigan, Lake Ontario, and Lake Superior.

Canada has thousands of lakes and rivers. Many of Canada's lakes were carved out by Ice Age glaciers. The Great Bear and Great Slave are two of Canada's larger lakes. The most important river is the St. Lawrence. The St. Lawrence River links the Great Lakes to the Atlantic Ocean.

✓ **READING CHECK:** _Places and Regions_ What are the major physical features of Canada?

Climate

The central and eastern parts of southern Canada have a humid continental climate. The mildest area of Canada is in the southwest. This region has a marine west coast climate. Here, winters are rainy and heavy snow falls in the mountains. Much of central and northern Canada has a subarctic climate. The far north has tundra and ice-cap climates. Permafrost underlies about half of Canada.

✓ **READING CHECK:** _Places and Regions_ What are Canada's climates?

Resources

Canada's Atlantic and Pacific coastal waters are among the world's richest fishing areas. Canada's many lakes and streams provide freshwater fish and attract tourists as well. Wheat farmers and cattle producers benefit from Canada's fertile soil.

Minerals are the most valuable of Canada's natural resources. The Canadian Shield contains many mineral deposits. Canada is a leading source of the world's nickel, zinc, and uranium. Lead, copper, gold, silver, and coal are also present. Saskatchewan has the world's largest deposits of **potash**, a mineral used to make fertilizer. Alberta produces most of Canada's oil and natural gas.

A belt of coniferous forests stretches across Canada from Labrador to the Pacific coast. These trees provide lumber and **pulp**. Pulp—softened wood fibers—is used to make paper. The United States, the United Kingdom, and Japan get much of their **newsprint** from Canada. Newsprint is cheap paper used mainly for newspapers.

✔ **READING CHECK:** *Environment and Society* How do Canada's major resources affect its economy?

Canada's resources can be shipped to markets through Vancouver in British Columbia.

Logs are floated down British Columbia's rivers and lakes to sawmills. Timber is an important resource in Canada.

go.hrw.com
Homework Practice Online
Keyword: SG3 HP7

Section Review 1

Define and explain: potash, pulp, newsprint

Working with Sketch Maps On a map of Canada that you draw or that your teacher provides, label the following: Rocky Mountains, Appalachian Mountains, Canadian Shield, Hudson Bay, Great Lakes, St. Lawrence River, Great Bear Lake, and Great Slave Lake.

Reading for the Main Idea

1. *Places and Regions* What are Canada's major landforms?

2. *Places and Regions* What river links the Great Lakes to the Atlantic Ocean?

Critical Thinking

3. Drawing Inferences and Conclusions Why do you think there are so many lakes in Canada?

4. Drawing Inferences and Conclusions Where would you expect to find Canada's mildest climate? Why?

Organizing What You Know

5. Finding the Main Idea Use the following graphic organizer to identify Canadian resources and their economic benefits.

Natural Resources

Section 2 · History and Culture

Read to Discover

- How did France and Britain affect Canada's history?
- How have immigrants influenced Canadian culture?

Define

provinces
dominion
Métis

Locate

Quebec
Ontario
Nova Scotia
New Brunswick
Newfoundland

Prince Edward Island
British Columbia
Manitoba
Alberta
Saskatchewan

WHY IT MATTERS

European contact forever changed Native Americans who lived in areas that are now the United States and Canada. Use CNNfyi.com or other current events sources to find out what life is like for Native Americans in Canada today.

Totem pole from British Columbia

A French artist shows an early expedition in Canada led by French explorer Jacques Cartier. Cartier explored the St. Lawrence River area up to present-day Montreal in the 1500s.

History

Cree. Déné. Inuit. Mohawk. Ojibwa. These are among the names of Canada's First Nations. Native Canadians lived in all parts of what is now Canada before Europeans arrived.

European Settlement The first Europeans to settle in Canada were probably the Vikings, or Norse. They arrived around A.D. 1000. Norse settlement of North America either failed or was abandoned. European exploration resumed at the end of the 1400s. At that time explorers and fishers from several areas of western Europe began crossing the Atlantic.

These newcomers affected the native inhabitants in many different ways. For example, European diseases such as smallpox killed many people. It is difficult to estimate how many people died. There were also other effects, including the mixing of cultures. Europeans greatly valued the furs that Native Canadians hunted and trapped. The Canadians valued European metal goods like kettles and axes. The two groups began to adopt aspects of each other's culture, including foods, clothing, and means of transportation.

The French built the Fortress of Louisbourg in Nova Scotia in the early 1700s. It was an important city and trading port in New France. The British captured the fortress in 1758.

Interpreting the Visual Record What materials were used to build the fortress? What does that tell you about Nova Scotia's resources?

New France France was the first European country to successfully settle parts of what would become Canada. Quebec City was founded in 1608. The French called their new territories in North America New France. At its height, New France included much of eastern Canada and the central United States. New France was important for several reasons. It was part of the French Empire. It was a base that could be used to spread France's religion and culture. It was also an important commercial area for France's empire.

France and Britain were rival colonial powers. Part of their competition included building and defending their empires around the world. The French built trade and diplomatic relations with American Indians. The French did this to increase their power and influence on the continent. Furs, fish, and other products were traded between New France and other parts of the French Empire. Manufactured goods from France and other countries in Europe became the main imports to New France. French missionaries tried to convert native people to Christianity. Some did become Christians, while others held to their traditional beliefs.

New France lasted a century and a half before it was conquered by the British. During that time, it shaped the geography of Canada in important ways. The descendants of French settlers form one of Canada's major ethnic groups today. Almost a quarter of present-day Canadians are of French ancestry. This has deeply affected Canada's culture and politics.

British Conquest and American Revolution The Seven Years' War (1756–63) was mainly fought in Europe. This same period of conflict in the American colonies was called the French and Indian

Canadian Ethnic Groups

- **British Isles origin** — 26%
- **French origin** — 23%
- **Other European** — 15%
- **Canadian Indian** — 28%
- **Mixed background** — 2%
- **Other, mostly Asian, African, Arab** — 6%

Source: Central Intelligence Agency, *The World Factbook 2001*

Interpreting the Chart What is the largest ethnic group in Canada?

The British flag flies alongside the provincial flag at government buildings in Victoria, British Columbia. Canada is a member of the British Commonwealth of Nations. In fact, the British monarch also is Canada's.

War. As a result of that war the British took control of New France. A small number of French went back to France. However, the great majority of the *habitants* (inhabitants) stayed. For most of them, few changes occurred in their daily activities. They farmed the same land, prayed in the same churches, and continued to speak French. Few English-speaking settlers came to what is now called Quebec.

The American Revolution pushed new groups of people into other areas of British North America. Many United Empire Loyalists—Americans who remained loyal to the king of England—fled north. Most Loyalists either could not stay in the new United States or were too afraid to remain. For some, their political views may have led them to move to British-controlled territories. For many others, it was the desire to get free land. This movement of people was part of a larger westward migration of pioneers.

After the American Revolution, the borders of British North America were redrawn. Quebec was divided into two colonies. Lower Canada was mostly French-speaking, and Upper Canada was mostly English-speaking. The boundary between Upper and Lower Canada forms part of the border between the **provinces** of Quebec and Ontario today. Provinces are administrative divisions of a country. To the east, Nova Scotia (noh-vuh SKOH-shuh) was also divided. A new province called New Brunswick was created where many of the British Loyalists lived.

Creation of Canada For two generations these colonies developed separately. The British also maintained colonies in Newfoundland, Prince Edward Island, the western plains, and the Pacific coast. The colonies viewed themselves as different from other parts of the British Empire. Therefore, the British Parliament created the Dominion of Canada in 1867. A **dominion** is a territory or area of influence. For Canadians, the creation of the Dominion was a statement of independence. They saw a future separate from that of the

United States. The motto of the new Dominion was "from sea to sea." However, it included only New Brunswick, Nova Scotia, and the southern parts of Ontario and Quebec.

How would Canadians create a nation from sea to sea? With railroads. The Canadian heartland in Ontario and Quebec was already well served by railroads. From the heartland the Intercolonial Railway would run east to the Atlantic Ocean. The Canadian Pacific Railroad would be the first of three transcontinental railroads running west to the Pacific Ocean. It was completed in 1885. Both British Columbia and Prince Edward Island were quickly added to the Dominion.

Canada also acquired vast lands between the original provinces and British Columbia. It also expanded to the north. Much of this land was bought from the Hudson's Bay Company, a British fur-trading business. Most of the people in this area were Canadian Indians and **Métis** (may-TEES). Métis, people of mixed European and native ancestry, considered themselves a separate group. With the building of the railroads and the signing of treaties with Native Canadians, the way was opened for settlement of the area. Manitoba became a province in 1870. Alberta and Saskatchewan followed in 1905.

Government Canada is a federation today. It has a central government led by a prime minister. Its 10 provincial governments are each led by a premier. Canada's central government is similar to our federal government. Its provincial governments are much like our state governments. A federal system lets people keep their feelings of loyalty to their own province. At the same time they remain part of a larger national identity.

✔ **READING CHECK:** (*Human Systems*) How is Canada's government similar to that of the United States?

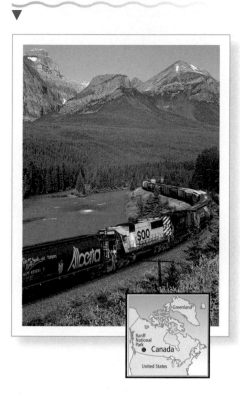

This train follows the Bow River in Banff National Park in Alberta.
Interpreting the Visual Record How did railroad technology help people change their environment?

Culture

A history of colonial rule and waves of immigration have shaped Canada today. The country is home to a variety of ethnic groups and cultures. They have combined to form a single country and Canadian identity.

Immigration During the late 1800s and early 1900s, many immigrants from Europe came to Canada. Many farmed, but others worked in mines, forests, and factories. British Columbia became the first Canadian province to have a substantial Asian minority. Many Chinese Canadians helped build the railroads.

These immigrants played an important part in the economic boom that Canada experienced in the early 1900s. Quebec, New Brunswick,

	Canada			
COUNTRY	**POPULATION/ GROWTH RATE**	**LIFE EXPECTANCY**	**LITERACY RATE**	**PER CAPITA GDP**
Canada	31,592,805 0.99%	76, male 83, female	97%	$24,800
United States	281,421,906 0.9%	74, male 80, female	97%	$36,200

Sources: Central Intelligence Agency, *The World Factbook 2001*; U.S. Census Bureau

Interpreting the Chart Which country has the greater growth rate?

Visitors enjoy the sights and sounds of a children's festival in Vancouver. Vancouver and other Canadian cities are home to large and increasingly diverse populations.

▼

and Ontario produced wheat, pulp, and paper. British Columbia and Ontario supplied minerals and hydroelectricity. By the 1940s Canadians enjoyed one of the highest standards of living in the world.

Movement to Cities In recent years Canadians have moved from farms to the cities. Some settlements in Newfoundland—which became Canada's 10th province in 1949—and rural Saskatchewan disappeared because the people left. Many Canadians have moved to Ontario to find jobs. Others moved to British Columbia for its mild climate. Resources such as oil, gas, potash, and uranium have changed the economies of the western provinces. The economic center of power remains in the cities of southern Ontario and southwestern Quebec. Toronto is now Canada's largest city. Many Canadian businesses have their main offices there.

After World War II, another wave of immigrants from Europe came to Canada. They were joined by other people from Africa, the Caribbean, Latin America, and particularly Asia. Asian businesspeople have brought a great deal of wealth to Canada's economy. Most immigrants have settled in Canada's large cities. Toronto has become one of the most culturally diverse cities in the world. Many Canadians now enjoy Thai, Vietnamese, and other Asian foods. Chinese New Year parades and other colorful festivals attract tourists.

✓ **READING CHECK:** *Human Systems* How has immigration changed Canada?

Section Review 2

Define and explain: provinces, dominion, Métis

Working with Sketch Maps On the map you created in Section 1, label Quebec, Ontario, Nova Scotia, New Brunswick, Newfoundland, Prince Edward Island, British Columbia, Manitoba, Alberta, and Saskatchewan. Which provinces seem to use lines of latitude as boundaries?

Reading for the Main Idea

1. *Human Systems* How did French and British colonization influence Canada's history?

2. *Human Systems* How did immigrants contribute to Canada?

go.hrw.com
Homework Practice Online
Keyword: SG3 HP7

Critical Thinking

3. **Identifying Cause and Effect** Why did Europeans come to Canada? What was the effect of the arrival of Europeans on the First Nations?

4. **Summarizing** How and why was the country of Canada created?

Organizing What You Know

5. **Sequencing** Copy the following graphic organizer. Use it to explain how the Dominion of Canada developed. Add boxes as needed.

Quebec	⇨	Ontario	⇨	

Section 3 — Canada Today

Read to Discover

1. How has regionalism affected Canada?
2. Into what major areas and provinces is Canada divided?

Define

regionalism
maritime
Inuit

Locate

Gulf of
  St. Lawrence
Labrador
Halifax
Windsor
Quebec City

Montreal
Toronto
Ottawa
Edmonton
Calgary
Winnipeg

Vancouver
Yukon
  Territory
Northwest
  Territories
Nunavut

WHY IT MATTERS

French- and English-speaking Canadians continue to have cultural and political differences. Use **CNNfyi.com** or other **current events** sources to find out what conflicts have taken place between these groups. Record your findings in your journal.

The maple leaf, a symbol of Canada

Regionalism

English is the main language in most of Canada. In Quebec, however, French is the dominant language. The cultural differences between English and French Canada have created problems. When Canadians from different regions discuss important issues, they are often influenced by **regionalism**. Regionalism refers to the strong connection that people feel toward their region. Sometimes, this connection is stronger than their connection to their country as a whole.

Regionalism was very important in America during the 1800s. At that time the United States split into the North and the South as its citizens fought the Civil War. The country was divided over issues such as slavery. People supported whichever group shared their beliefs. In Canada many residents of Quebec, or Quebecois (kay-buh-KWAH), believe their province should be given a special status. Quebecois argue that this status would recognize the cultural differences between their province and the rest of Canada. Some even want Quebec to become independent.

On the other hand, many English-speaking Canadians think Quebec already has too many privileges. Others, especially in western Canada, want the provinces to have more freedom from national control. Most Canadians, however, still support a united Canada. Strong feelings of regionalism will continue to be an important issue in Canada's future.

Demonstrators say *"oui"* (yes) to independence for Quebec.

✓ **READING CHECK:** (*Human Systems*) Why do some people in Quebec want independence from the rest of Canada?

The harbor at Avalon Peninsula is home to many fishing boats.

Interpreting the Visual Record Why do you think most people in the Maritime Provinces live in coastal cities?

Our Amazing Planet

Canada's Bay of Fundy has some of the highest tides in the world — up to 70 feet (21 m). The tide brings water from the North Atlantic into the narrow bay. The bore, or leading wave of the incoming water, can roar like a big truck as the tide rushes in.

The Eastern Provinces

New Brunswick, Nova Scotia, and Prince Edward Island are often called the Maritime Provinces. **Maritime** means "on or near the sea." Each of these provinces is located near the ocean. Prince Edward Island is a small island, and Nova Scotia occupies a peninsula. New Brunswick has coasts on the Gulf of St. Lawrence and on the Bay of Fundy. Newfoundland is usually not considered one of the Maritime Provinces. It includes the island of Newfoundland and a large region of the mainland called Labrador.

A short growing season and poor soils make farming difficult in the eastern provinces. Most of the region's economy is related to forestry and fishing.

Many people in the eastern provinces are descendants of families that emigrated from the British Isles. In addition, many French-speaking families have moved from Quebec to New Brunswick. Most of the region's people live in coastal cities. The cities have industrial plants and serve as fishing and shipping ports. Halifax, Nova Scotia, is the region's largest city.

✓ **READING CHECK:** *Places and Regions* Why are the eastern provinces called the Maritime Provinces?

The Heartland

Inland from the eastern provinces are Quebec and Ontario. More than half of all Canadians live in these heartland provinces. In fact, the chain of cities that extends from Windsor, Ontario, to the city of Quebec is the country's most urbanized region.

CONNECTING TO *Literature*

Anne of Green Gables
by Lucy Maud Montgomery

Canada's smallest province, Prince Edward Island, was the birthplace (in 1874) of one of the country's best-loved writers. Lucy Maud Montgomery based her Anne of Green Gables *series on the island she loved. She created characters and situations that lived in the minds of readers. Since its publication in 1908,* Anne of Green Gables *put the tiny island on the map, inspiring tours and festivals. It has even drawn tourists from as far away as Japan. They come to capture the spirit of the brave orphan. In this passage, young Anne is being driven to Green Gables by her new guardian, Matthew. He is kind but hardly imaginative!*

Anne says, "When I don't like the name of a place or a person I always imagine a new one and always think of them so. There was a girl at the asylum [orphanage] whose name was Hepzibah Jenkins, but I always imagined her as Rosalia DeVere." . . .

They had driven over the crest of a hill. Below them was a pond. . . . A bridge spanned it midway and from there to its lower end, where an amber-hued belt of sand hills shut it in from the dark-blue gulf beyond, the water was a glory of many shifting hues. . . .

"That's Barry's pond," said Matthew.

"Oh, I don't like that name, either. I shall call it—let me see—the Lake of Shining Waters. Yes, that is the right name for it. I know because of the thrill. When I hit on a name that suits exactly it gives me a thrill. Do things ever give you a thrill?"

Matthew ruminated.[1] "Well now, yes. It always kind of gives me a thrill to see them ugly white grubs[2] that spade up in the cucumber beds. I hate the look of them."

"Oh, I don't think that can be exactly the same kind of thrill. Do you think it can? There doesn't seem to be much connection between grubs and lakes of shining waters, does there? But why do other people call it Barry's pond?"

"I reckon because Mr. Barry lives up there in that house."

Analyzing Primary Sources

1. Why is *Anne of Green Gables* popular outside of Prince Edward Island?
2. How does imagination affect a person's view of the world?

Definitions ¹ruminate: to think over in the mind slowly   ²grubs: wormlike insect larvae

Day draws to a close in Toronto, Ontario. The city is located at the site of a trading post from the 1600s. Today Toronto is one of North America's major cities.

Quebec The city of Quebec is the capital of the province. The city's older section has narrow streets, stone walls, and French-style architecture. Montreal is Canada's second-largest city and one of the largest French-speaking cities in the world. About 3.3 million people live in the Montreal metropolitan area. It is the financial and industrial center of the province. Winters in Montreal are very cold. People in the city center use underground passages and overhead tunnels to move between buildings.

Ontario Ontario is Canada's leading manufacturing province. It is also Canada's most populous province. About 4.7 million people live in the metropolitan area of Toronto, Ontario's capital. Toronto is a major center for industry, finance, education, and culture. Toronto's residents have come from many different regions, including China, Europe, and India. Between Toronto and Montreal lies Ottawa, Canada's capital. In Ottawa many people speak both English and French. It has grand government buildings, parks, and several universities.

✓ **READING CHECK:** *Places and Regions* What are the major cities of Canada's heartland?

Canada's Prairie Provinces are home to productive farms like this one near Brandon, Manitoba.
Interpreting the Visual Record **What can you tell about the physical geography of this region of Canada?**

The Western Provinces

Farther to the west are the major farming regions of Manitoba, Saskatchewan, and Alberta. These three provinces are called the Prairie Provinces. Along the Pacific coast is British Columbia.

The Prairie Provinces More people live in Quebec than in all of the Prairie Provinces combined. The southern grasslands of these provinces are part of a rich wheat belt. Farms here produce far more wheat than Canadians need. The extra wheat is exported. Oil and natural gas production also are important in Alberta. Rocky Mountain resorts in western Alberta attract many tourists. The major cities of the Prairie Provinces are Edmonton, Calgary, and Winnipeg.

British Columbia British Columbia is Canada's westernmost province. This mountainous province has rich natural resources, including forests, salmon, and important minerals. Almost 4 million people live in British Columbia. Nearly half of them are in the coastal city of Vancouver. Vancouver is a multicultural city with large Chinese and Indian populations. It also is a major trade center.

✓ **READING CHECK:** *Environment and Society* How does geography affect the location of economic activities in the Prairie Provinces?

The Canadian North

Canada's vast northern lands include the Yukon Territory, the Northwest Territories, and Nunavut (NOO-nah-vuht). Nunavut is a new territory created for the **Inuit** (Eskimos) who live there. *Nunavut* means "Our Land" in the Inuit language. Nunavut is part of Canada, but the people have their own local government. The three territories cover more than one third of Canada but are home to only about 100,000 people. Boreal forests, tundra, and frozen Arctic ocean waters separate isolated towns and villages.

✓ **READING CHECK:** Who lives in Nunavut?

In the St. Elias Mountains in the Yukon Territory is the world's largest nonpolar ice field. The field covers an area of 15,822 square miles (40,570 sq km) and stretches into Alaska.

The Inuit have long hunted beluga whales for meat, blubber, and skin.

▼

Homework Practice Online
Keyword: SG3 HP7

Define and explain: regionalism, maritime, Inuit

Working with Sketch Maps On the map that you created in Section 2, locate and label the major cities of Canada's provinces and territories. Where are most of these major cities located? What may have led to their growth?

Reading for the Main Idea

1. *Places and Regions* How does regionalism affect Canada's culture?

2. *The World in Spatial Terms* Into which provincial groups is Canada divided?

Critical Thinking

3. Drawing Inferences and Conclusions What makes the heartland a good area in which to settle?

4. Finding the Main Idea Why was Nunavut created?

Organizing What You Know

5. Categorizing Use the following graphic organizer to identify Canada's regions and provinces.

Region	Provinces

Building Vocabulary

On a separate sheet of paper, write sentences to define each of the following words.

1. potash
2. pulp
3. newsprint
4. provinces
5. dominion
6. Métis
7. regionalism
8. maritime
9. Inuit

Reviewing the Main Ideas

1. *Places and Regions* How large is Canada compared to the rest of the world's countries?
2. *Places and Regions* What types of natural resources can be found in Canada? Where is Canada's major wheat-farming area?
3. *Human Systems* What groups of people have made Canada their home?
4. *Human Systems* How do the people of Quebec show their regionalism?
5. *Places and Regions* What is Ottawa's relative location? Why is the city important?

Understanding Environment and Society

Resource Use

The Canadian economy depends on industries such as fishing, lumber, mining, and fossil fuels. As you create a presentation for your class, you may want to think about:

- Actions the Canadian government might take to conserve Canada's resources.
- What might happen if nothing is done to conserve Canada's resources.

Thinking Critically

1. **Comparing** How is Canada's government similar to that of the United States?
2. **Finding the Main Idea** How has immigration changed Canada?
3. **Drawing Inferences and Conclusions** How have past events shaped current conflicts in Canada?
4. **Drawing Inferences and Conclusions** If fishing and lumber are the primary industries of the Maritime Provinces, what are some likely secondary industries? List three industries.
5. **Summarizing** What geographic factors are responsible for economic activities in the Canadian Provinces?

Map ACTIVITY

On a separate sheet of paper, match the letters on the map with their correct labels.

Great Slave Lake
Great Bear Lake
Newfoundland
Prince Edward
 Island
Manitoba

Alberta
Toronto
Calgary
Vancouver
Nunavut

Mental Mapping Skills ACTIVITY

On a separate sheet of paper, draw a map of Canada and label the following:

British Columbia
Great Lakes
Hudson Bay
Ontario

Ottawa
Quebec
Saskatchewan
Yukon Territory

WRITING ACTIVITY

Write three paragraphs explaining where in Canada you might like to live and why. Name a province and describe the geographic, climatic, political, and cultural features that make it attractive to you. Be sure to use standard grammar, sentence structure, spelling, and punctuation.

Alternative Assessment

Portfolio ACTIVITY

Learning About Your Local Geography

Individual Project Canada's cold climate helped make winter sports popular there. What sports are popular in your region? How do they compare with Canada's sports? Create a thematic map of your region that shows the location of different sporting activities.

internet connect

Internet Activity: go.hrw.com
KEYWORD: SG3 GT7

Choose a topic to explore about Canada:
- Take a trip to the Yukon Territory.
- Learn about Canada's First Nations.
- Meet the people of Quebec.

FOCUS ON ECONOMY

NAFTA

Borders and Barriers   Canada, Mexico, and the United States are the three largest countries in North America. They have very large and productive economies. Borders separate each country and create barriers between them. For example, one barrier is the use of different types of currency in each country. In Canada, people use Canadian dollars. In Mexico, they use Mexican pesos. In the United States, people use U.S. dollars. You cannot buy a cheeseburger in Canada with Mexican pesos because of this barrier. Another barrier is the different laws that each country has. This creates a barrier to law enforcement.

The NAFTA agreement was signed by the leaders of Mexico, the United States, and Canada in 1992 and took effect on January 1, 1994. NAFTA created the largest free trade area in the world.

▼

Some barriers between Canada, the United States, and Mexico are being removed. For example, barriers to trade are changing. The North American Free Trade Agreement (NAFTA) is causing these changes. With NAFTA, Canada, the United States, and Mexico have agreed to follow some common rules about trading. These new rules make it easier to trade across borders.

Beginnings of NAFTA   NAFTA began on January 1, 1994. The purpose of NAFTA is to improve nearly all aspects of trade between the three countries. It promotes free trade by lowering or removing taxes on goods traded between Canada, the United States, and Mexico. For example, NAFTA eliminates tariffs between them. A tariff is a kind of tax. Tariffs are paid on goods that are exported to other countries. For example, when apples are exported from the United States to Japan, Japan collects a tariff.

Because of NAFTA, many agricultural and industrial products are not taxed when they are imported from the other member countries. Therefore, these goods can be easily traded from one country to another. NAFTA also eases barriers for corporations. For example, a company might be based in the United States. That company is now able to set up factories in Mexico without the problem of special taxes or tariffs.

NAFTA Trade Flows

This map shows trade among the United States and its NAFTA partners in billions of U.S. dollars. Numbers in parentheses show the percentage of each country's total exports. Trade among all three countries has greatly increased since NAFTA began in 1994.

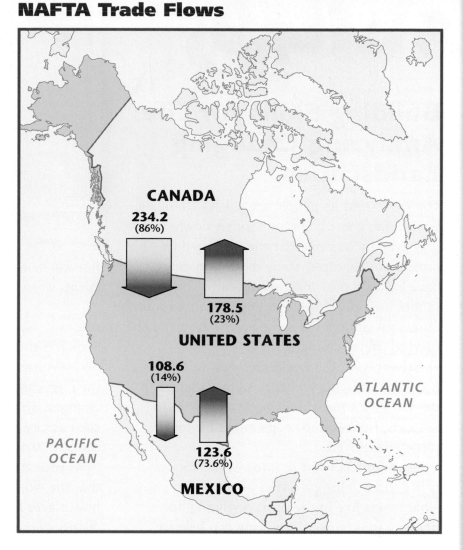

CANADA
234.2
(86%)

178.5
(23%)

UNITED STATES

108.6
(14%)

PACIFIC OCEAN

123.6
(73.6%)

MEXICO

ATLANTIC OCEAN

Removing Barriers Some people in both the United States and Canada have criticized the NAFTA agreement. They believe NAFTA has caused many Americans and Canadians to lose their jobs. Some corporations have closed factories in the United States and Canada. These corporations then opened new factories in Mexico. People are also worried that NAFTA might harm the environment. Under NAFTA, fewer environmental laws and regulations must be followed. This may cause environmental problems such as increased pollution or pesticide use.

Other people support NAFTA. They point out that trade among Canada, the United States, and Mexico has increased since NAFTA began. There are now more jobs in all three countries. For example, the United States exports more agricultural products to Mexico now. NAFTA also helps all three countries by increasing their total production of goods. For example, T-shirts are made from cotton. With NAFTA, cotton grown in Mexico, the United States, or Canada is cheaper than cotton from other countries. This helps cotton growers in all NAFTA countries.

The borders between Canada, the United States, and Mexico are slowly becoming less important. NAFTA is removing trade barriers between these countries and increasing their economic connections.

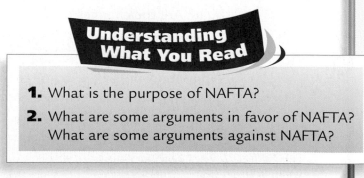

Understanding What You Read

1. What is the purpose of NAFTA?

2. What are some arguments in favor of NAFTA? What are some arguments against NAFTA?

Building Skills for Life: Analyzing Changing Landscapes

▲

This map from the mid-1600s shows Quebec when it was a French colony.

The world and its people are always changing. Sometimes these changes happen slowly. They may even be so slow that they are hard to notice. For example, some mountain ranges have built up over millions of years. These ranges are now slowly eroding. Because mountains look almost the same every day, it may be hard to notice changes.

Other times, the world changes quickly. Mudslides can bury villages so fast that people do not have time to escape. In less than 30 seconds, houses and crops might be completely destroyed.

Geographers want to know what the world is like today. However, they also need to know what it was like in the past. Analyzing how places have changed over time can help us better understand the world. For example, suppose you took a trip to Quebec. You would notice that most people there speak French. If you knew that Quebec used to be a French colony, it would help you understand why French is the main language today.

Understanding how places have changed in the past can also help us predict future changes. This is an important goal for people such as city planners, government officials, and transportation engineers.

As you study geography, try to remember that the world is always changing. Think about how places have changed and why these changes are important. Ask yourself how places might change in the future. Be aware that maps, photographs, newspapers, and other tools of geography can become outdated. After all, the world does not wait for geography!

PRACTICING THE SKILL

1. Find an area in your community that you think is changing quickly. Observe the changes. Are new businesses, houses, or roads being built? Are the changes big or small?

2. Talk to a parent, grandparent, or neighbor. Ask how your community, town, or city has changed during the last 20 to 30 years. What are some of the major changes? Does this person remember some old places that are no longer there?

3. Look for an old book, magazine, or map. Try to find one that is at least 30 years old. How is it different from a current book, magazine, or map?

HANDS on
GEOGRAPHY

You can analyze changing landscapes by comparing old photographs of a place to new ones. Important changes might be easy to see. For example, new buildings and new roads often stand out on the more recent photographs.

Look at the two photographs below. They show a small section of Las Vegas, Nevada. The photograph on the left was taken in 1963. The photograph on the right was taken 35 years later in 1998. Now compare the two photographs. What do you notice?

◄ Las Vegas, 1963

▲ Las Vegas, 1998

Lab Report

1. How do you know these two photographs show the same place? What evidence do you see?

2. How did this section of Las Vegas change between 1963 and 1998? Do you think these are big changes or small ones?

3. Find a street map of Las Vegas and try to figure out exactly what part of the city the photographs show. Then compare the map with the 1998 photograph. What information does the map give about this section of the city?

UNIT 3

Middle and South America

Congress Building, Brasília, Brazil

Dancer, Puerto Vallarta, Mexico

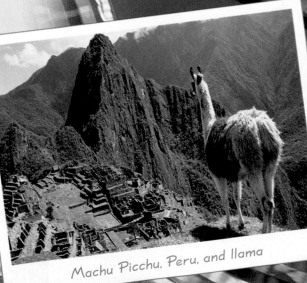
Machu Picchu, Peru, and llama

A Conservationist in Costa Rica

Sandy Wiseman works for a conservation organization in Canada. He often organizes trips to rain forests. Here Dr. Wiseman tells about a morning hike through a Costa Rican forest. **WHAT DO YOU THINK?** *Which of the animals he mentions would you like to see for yourself?*

Birds of many kinds were already active in the canopy. From high in the treetops, parrots and parakeets were squawking and feeding, not just themselves but dozens of other creatures with the fruit they dropped to the forest floor.

A tiny clear-winged butterfly floated in jerks along the path and came to rest on a leaf over the trail. Its transparent wings made it almost invisible. Later I spotted a small anteater. Only after it heard me reach for my camera did it stand up with nose held high to taste the air. The anteater spread wide its hooked forepaws as if to invite a hug, in a defensive pose. Within a minute it resumed its foraging, shuffling, and sniffing into the forest.

I now thought better of hurrying through the woods. I would sit for a while and take in my surroundings. With patient observation and quiet thought, the richness of the rain forest rekindles [renews] marvel and wonder.

Clear-winged butterfly, Costa Rica

Understanding Primary Sources

1. How do the parrots and parakeets feed other animals?

2. How does Sandy Wiseman react to seeing the creatures in the rain forest?

Blue poison dart frog

Middle and South America

Elevation Profile

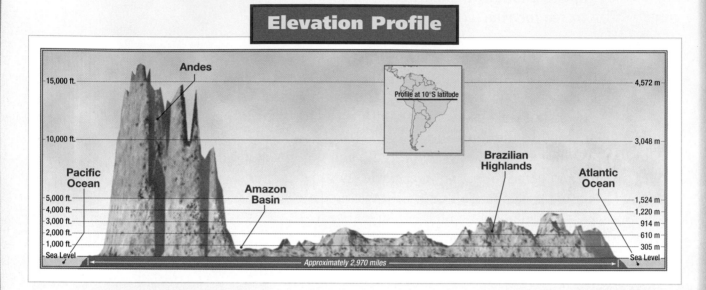

Andes

15,000 ft. — 4,572 m

Profile at 10°S latitude

10,000 ft. — 3,048 m

Pacific Ocean

Brazilian Highlands

Atlantic Ocean

Amazon Basin

5,000 ft. — 1,524 m
4,000 ft. — 1,220 m
3,000 ft. — 914 m
2,000 ft. — 610 m
1,000 ft. — 305 m
Sea Level — Sea Level

Approximately 2,970 miles

The United States and Middle and South America:
Comparing Sizes

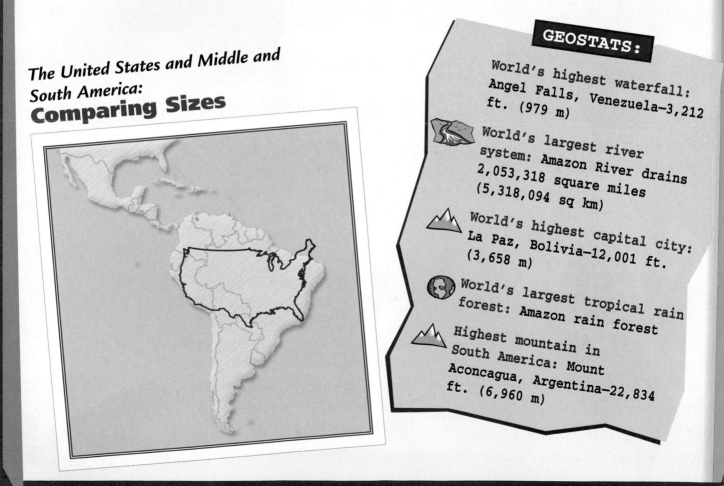

GEOSTATS:

World's highest waterfall: Angel Falls, Venezuela–3,212 ft. (979 m)

World's largest river system: Amazon River drains 2,053,318 square miles (5,318,094 sq km)

World's highest capital city: La Paz, Bolivia–12,001 ft. (3,658 m)

World's largest tropical rain forest: Amazon rain forest

Highest mountain in South America: Mount Aconcagua, Argentina–22,834 ft. (6,960 m)

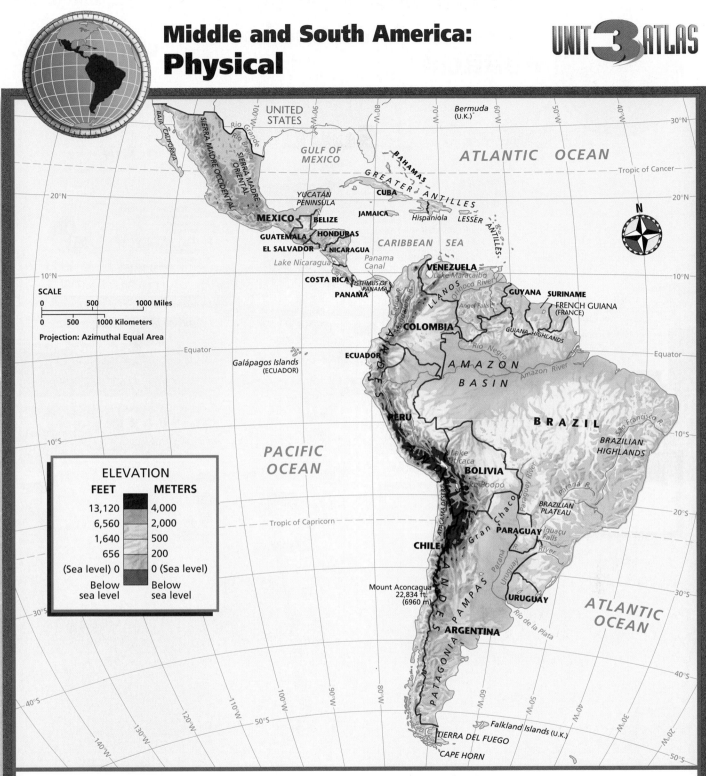

ELEVATION

FEET	METERS
13,120	4,000
6,560	2,000
1,640	500
656	200
(Sea level) 0	0 (Sea level)
Below sea level	Below sea level

SCALE

0   500   1000 Miles

0   500   1000 Kilometers

Projection: Azimuthal Equal Area

1. *Places and Regions* Which country has two highland regions and a large plateau?

2. *Places and Regions* Which country has two large peninsulas that extend into different oceans?

3. *Places and Regions* Which island groups separate the Caribbean Sea from the Gulf of Mexico and the Atlantic Ocean?

Critical Thinking

4. Drawing Inferences and Conclusions Find central Mexico on the map. Why do you think east-west travel might be difficult in this area? What physical feature do you think would make travel easier in northern Brazil?

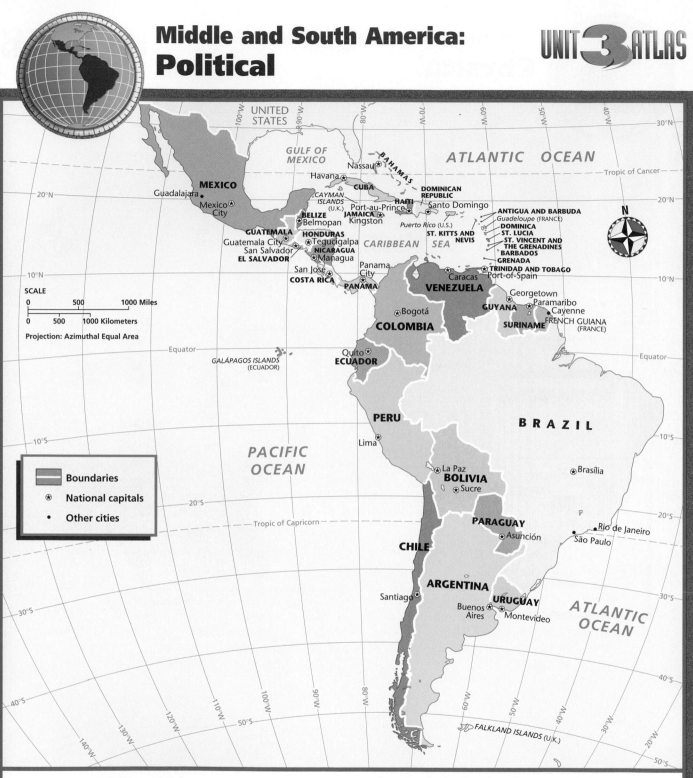

SCALE

0 — 500 — 1000 Miles

0 — 500 — 1000 Kilometers

Projection: Azimuthal Equal Area

Boundaries

⊛ National capitals

• Other cities

---

1. *Places and Regions* Which country connects Middle America and South America?

2. *Places and Regions* What is the largest country in Middle America? in South America?

Critical Thinking

3. Comparing Compare this map to the **physical map** of the region. What are some rivers

that mark the borders between different countries in South America?

4. Analyzing Information Compare this map to the **land use and resources** and **physical maps** of the region. Why would it be difficult to mark the boundaries where Colombia, Brazil, and Peru meet?

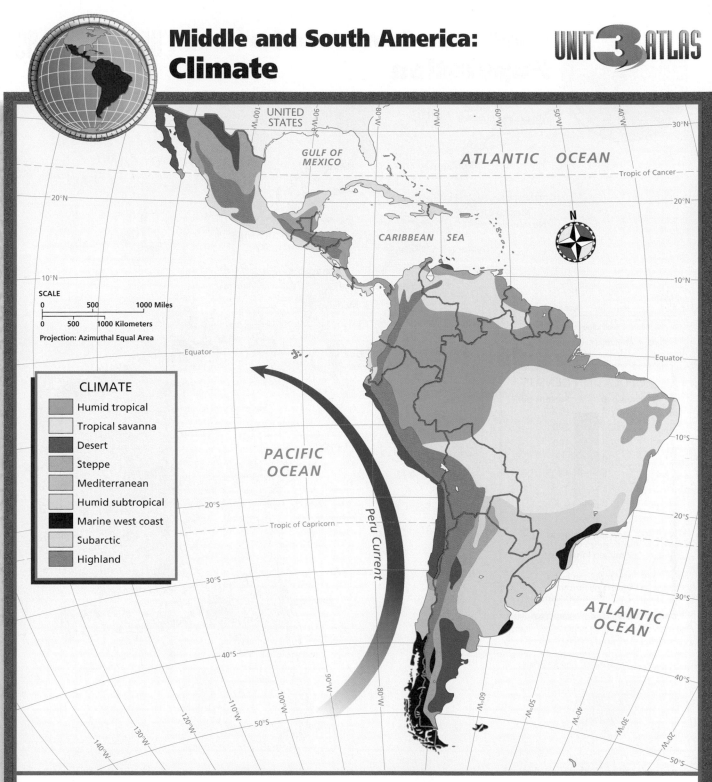

CLIMATE
- Humid tropical
- Tropical savanna
- Desert
- Steppe
- Mediterranean
- Humid subtropical
- Marine west coast
- Subarctic
- Highland

SCALE

0   500   1000 Miles

0   500   1000 Kilometers

Projection: Azimuthal Equal Area

1. *Physical Systems* Which two climate types cover the largest area?

2. *Places and Regions* Which countries have coastal areas with cool damp climates?

3. *Places and Regions* Compare this map to the **physical map** of the region. What type of climate does most of the Amazon Basin have?

Critical Thinking

4. Drawing Inferences and Conclusions
Compare this map to the **population map**. How might climate affect the distribution of Brazil's population?

POPULATION DENSITY

Persons per sq. mile	Persons per sq km
520	200
260	100
130	50
25	10
3	1
0	0

⬤ Metropolitan areas with more than 2 million inhabitants

○ Metropolitan areas with 1 million to 2 million inhabitants

SCALE

0 500 1000 Miles

0 500 1000 Kilometers

Projection: Azimuthal Equal Area

1. *Places and Regions* Which area in South America has no place with more than three people per square mile?

2. *Places and Regions* Compare this map to the **physical map** of the region. Which two islands have cities with populations of more than 2 million?

Critical Thinking

3. Analyzing Information Use the map on this page to create a chart, graph, database, or model of population centers in Middle and South America.

LAND USE

- Hunting and gathering
- Commercial farming
- Livestock raising
- Subsistence farming
- Manufacturing
- Limited economic activity
- ● Major manufacturing and trade centers

RESOURCES

- Coal
- Natural gas
- Oil
- Nuclear power
- Hydroelectric power
- G Gold
- S Silver
- Other minerals
- Timber
- Seafood

SCALE
0   500   1000 Miles
0   500   1000 Kilometers
Projection: Azimuthal Equal Area

1. *Places and Regions* What is the major natural resource in the small Caribbean islands?

2. *Places and Regions* Which two countries in Middle America have nuclear power plants? Which South American countries have them?

3. *Places and Regions* What types of agriculture are important in the Buenos Aires region?

Critical Thinking

4. Analyzing Information Use the map on this page to create a chart, graph, database, or model of economic activities in Middle and South America.

Fast FACTS
Middle and South America

ANTIGUA AND BARBUDA

CAPITAL:
Saint John's

AREA:
171 sq. mi. (442 sq km)

POPULATION:
66,970

MONEY:
East Caribbean dollar (XCD)

LANGUAGES:
English

CHILDREN BORN/WOMAN:
2.3

BELIZE

CAPITAL:
Belmopan

AREA:
8,867 sq. mi. (22,966 sq km)

POPULATION:
256,062

MONEY:
Belizean dollar (BZD)

LANGUAGES:
English (official), Spanish, Mayan, Garifuna (Carib)

CHILDREN BORN/WOMAN:
4.1

ARGENTINA

CAPITAL:
Buenos Aires

AREA:
1,068,296 sq. mi. (2,766,890 sq km)

POPULATION:
37,384,816

MONEY:
Argentine peso (ARS)

LANGUAGES:
Spanish (official), English, Italian, German, French

CHILDREN BORN/WOMAN:
2.4

BOLIVIA

CAPITAL:
La Paz, Sucre

AREA:
424,162 sq. mi. (1,098,580 sq km)

POPULATION:
8,300,463

MONEY:
boliviano (BOB)

LANGUAGES:
Spanish, Quechua, Aymara (all official)

CHILDREN BORN/WOMAN:
3.5

BAHAMAS

CAPITAL:
Nassau

AREA:
5,382 sq. mi. (13,940 sq km)

POPULATION:
297,852

MONEY:
Bahamian dollar (BSD)

LANGUAGES:
English, Creole (among Haitian immigrants)

CHILDREN BORN/WOMAN:
2.3

BRAZIL

CAPITAL:
Brasília

AREA:
3,286,470 sq. mi. (8,511,965 sq km)

POPULATION:
174,468,575

MONEY:
real (BRL)

LANGUAGES:
Portuguese (official), Spanish, English, French

CHILDREN BORN/WOMAN:
2.1

BARBADOS

CAPITAL:
Bridgetown

AREA:
166 sq. mi. (430 sq km)

POPULATION:
275,330

MONEY:
Barbadian dollar (BBD)

LANGUAGES:
English

CHILDREN BORN/WOMAN:
1.6

CHILE

CAPITAL:
Santiago

AREA:
292,258 sq. mi. (756,950 sq km)

POPULATION:
15,328,467

MONEY:
Chilean peso (CLP)

LANGUAGES:
Spanish

CHILDREN BORN/WOMAN:
2.2

Countries not drawn to scale.

COLOMBIA

CAPITAL: Bogotá
AREA:
439,733 sq. mi.
(1,138,910 sq km)
POPULATION:
40,349,388

MONEY:
Colombian peso (COP)
LANGUAGES:
Spanish
CHILDREN BORN/WOMAN:
2.7

COSTA RICA

CAPITAL: San José
AREA:
19,730 sq. mi. (51,100 sq km)
POPULATION:
3,773,057

MONEY:
Costa Rican colon (CRC)
LANGUAGES:
Spanish (official), English
CHILDREN BORN/WOMAN:
2.5

CUBA

CAPITAL: Havana
AREA:
42,803 sq. mi.
(110,860 sq km)
POPULATION:
11,184,023

MONEY:
Cuban peso (CUP)
LANGUAGES:
Spanish
CHILDREN BORN/WOMAN:
1.6

DOMINICA

CAPITAL: Roseau
AREA:
291 sq. mi. (754 sq km)
POPULATION:
70,786

MONEY:
East Caribbean dollar (XCD)
LANGUAGES:
English (official), French patois
CHILDREN BORN/WOMAN:
2.0

DOMINICAN REPUBLIC

CAPITAL:
Santo Domingo
AREA:
18,815 sq. mi. (48,730 sq km)
POPULATION:
8,581,477

MONEY:
Dominican peso (DOP)
LANGUAGES:
Spanish
CHILDREN BORN/WOMAN:
3.0

ECUADOR

CAPITAL: Quito
AREA:
109,483 sq. mi.
(283,560 sq km)
POPULATION:
13,183,978

MONEY:
U.S. dollar (USD)
LANGUAGES:
Spanish (official), ethnic languages including Quechua
CHILDREN BORN/WOMAN:
3.1

EL SALVADOR

CAPITAL:
San Salvador
AREA:
8,124 sq. mi. (21,040 sq km)
POPULATION:
6,237,662

MONEY:
Salvadoran colon (SVC)
LANGUAGES:
Spanish, Nahua
CHILDREN BORN/WOMAN:
3.3

FRENCH GUIANA (Overseas department of France)

CAPITAL:
Cayenne
AREA:
35,135 sq. mi. (91,000 sq km)
POPULATION:
177,562

MONEY:
French franc (FRF); euro (EUR)
LANGUAGES:
French
CHILDREN BORN/WOMAN:
3.2

GRENADA

CAPITAL:
St. George's
AREA:
131 sq. mi. (340 sq km)
POPULATION:
89,227

MONEY:
East Caribbean dollar (XCD)
LANGUAGES:
English (official), French patois
CHILDREN BORN/WOMAN:
2.5

Sources: Central Intelligence Agency, *The World Factbook 2001; The World Almanac and Book of Facts 2001;* pop. figures are 2001 estimates.

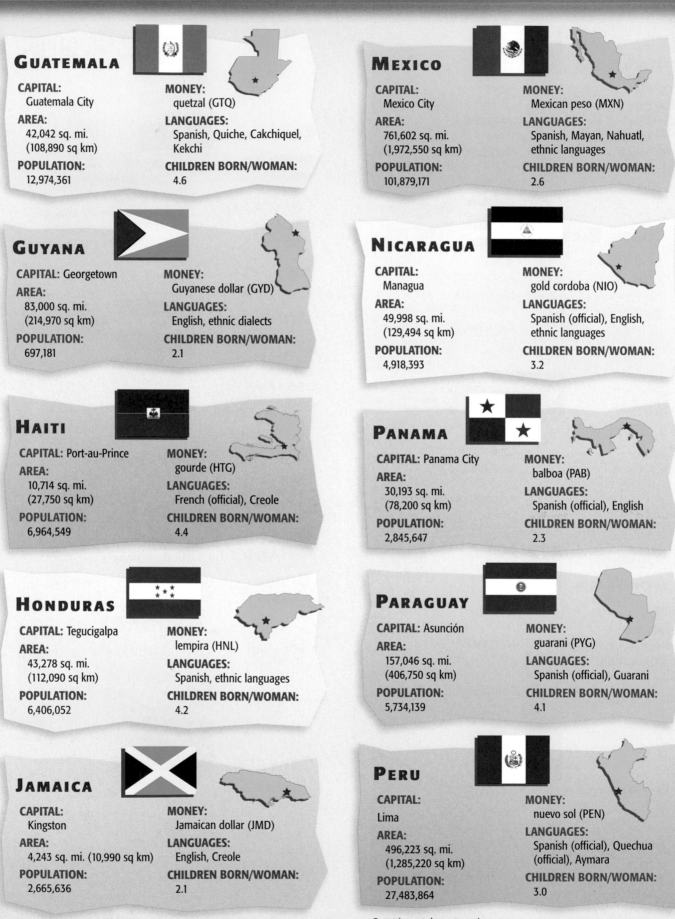

GUATEMALA

CAPITAL:
Guatemala City

AREA:
42,042 sq. mi.
(108,890 sq km)

POPULATION:
12,974,361

MONEY:
quetzal (GTQ)

LANGUAGES:
Spanish, Quiche, Cakchiquel,
Kekchi

CHILDREN BORN/WOMAN:
4.6

GUYANA

CAPITAL: Georgetown

AREA:
83,000 sq. mi.
(214,970 sq km)

POPULATION:
697,181

MONEY:
Guyanese dollar (GYD)

LANGUAGES:
English, ethnic dialects

CHILDREN BORN/WOMAN:
2.1

HAITI

CAPITAL: Port-au-Prince

AREA:
10,714 sq. mi.
(27,750 sq km)

POPULATION:
6,964,549

MONEY:
gourde (HTG)

LANGUAGES:
French (official), Creole

CHILDREN BORN/WOMAN:
4.4

HONDURAS

CAPITAL: Tegucigalpa

AREA:
43,278 sq. mi.
(112,090 sq km)

POPULATION:
6,406,052

MONEY:
lempira (HNL)

LANGUAGES:
Spanish, ethnic languages

CHILDREN BORN/WOMAN:
4.2

JAMAICA

CAPITAL:
Kingston

AREA:
4,243 sq. mi. (10,990 sq km)

POPULATION:
2,665,636

MONEY:
Jamaican dollar (JMD)

LANGUAGES:
English, Creole

CHILDREN BORN/WOMAN:
2.1

MEXICO

CAPITAL:
Mexico City

AREA:
761,602 sq. mi.
(1,972,550 sq km)

POPULATION:
101,879,171

MONEY:
Mexican peso (MXN)

LANGUAGES:
Spanish, Mayan, Nahuatl,
ethnic languages

CHILDREN BORN/WOMAN:
2.6

NICARAGUA

CAPITAL:
Managua

AREA:
49,998 sq. mi.
(129,494 sq km)

POPULATION:
4,918,393

MONEY:
gold cordoba (NIO)

LANGUAGES:
Spanish (official), English,
ethnic languages

CHILDREN BORN/WOMAN:
3.2

PANAMA

CAPITAL: Panama City

AREA:
30,193 sq. mi.
(78,200 sq km)

POPULATION:
2,845,647

MONEY:
balboa (PAB)

LANGUAGES:
Spanish (official), English

CHILDREN BORN/WOMAN:
2.3

PARAGUAY

CAPITAL: Asunción

AREA:
157,046 sq. mi.
(406,750 sq km)

POPULATION:
5,734,139

MONEY:
guarani (PYG)

LANGUAGES:
Spanish (official), Guarani

CHILDREN BORN/WOMAN:
4.1

PERU

CAPITAL:
Lima

AREA:
496,223 sq. mi.
(1,285,220 sq km)

POPULATION:
27,483,864

MONEY:
nuevo sol (PEN)

LANGUAGES:
Spanish (official), Quechua
(official), Aymara

CHILDREN BORN/WOMAN:
3.0

Countries not drawn to scale.

PUERTO RICO (U.S. Commonwealth)

CAPITAL:
San Juan

AREA:
3,515 sq. mi. (9,104 sq km)

POPULATION:
3,937,316

MONEY:
U.S. dollar (USD)

LANGUAGES:
Spanish, English

CHILDREN BORN/WOMAN:
1.9

SAINT KITTS AND NEVIS

CAPITAL:
Basseterre

AREA: 101 sq. mi. (261 sq km)

POPULATION:
38,756

MONEY:
East Caribbean dollar (XCD)

LANGUAGES: English

CHILDREN BORN/WOMAN:
2.4

SAINT LUCIA

CAPITAL:
Castries

AREA:
239 sq. mi. (620 sq km)

POPULATION:
158,178

MONEY:
East Caribbean dollar (XCD)

LANGUAGES:
English (official), French patois

CHILDREN BORN/WOMAN:
2.4

SAINT VINCENT AND THE GRENADINES

CAPITAL:
Kingstown

AREA:
150 sq. mi. (389 sq km)

POPULATION:
115,942

MONEY:
East Caribbean dollar (XCD)

LANGUAGES:
English, French patois

CHILDREN BORN/WOMAN:
2.1

SURINAME

CAPITAL:
Paramaribo

AREA:
63,039 sq. mi.
(163,270 sq km)

POPULATION:
433,998

MONEY:
Surinamese
guilder (SRG)

LANGUAGES: Dutch (official),
English, Sranang Tongo

CHILDREN BORN/WOMAN:
2.5

TRINIDAD AND TOBAGO

CAPITAL:
Port-of-Spain

AREA:
1,980 sq. mi. (5,128 sq km)

POPULATION:
1,169,682

MONEY:
Trinidad and Tobago dollar (TTD)

LANGUAGES:
English, Hindi, French, Spanish

CHILDREN BORN/WOMAN:
1.8

URUGUAY

CAPITAL: Montevideo

AREA:
68,039 sq. mi.
(176,220 sq km)

POPULATION:
3,360,105

MONEY:
Uruguayan peso (UYU)

LANGUAGES:
Spanish, Portunol

CHILDREN BORN/WOMAN:
2.4

VENEZUELA

CAPITAL:
Caracas

AREA:
352,143 sq. mi.
(912,050 sq km)

POPULATION:
23,916,810

MONEY:
bolivar (VEB)

LANGUAGES:
Spanish (official), many
ethnic languages

CHILDREN BORN/WOMAN:
2.5

---

internet connect

go.hrw.com

COUNTRY STATISTICS
GO TO: go.hrw.com
KEYWORD: SG3 FactsU3
FOR: more facts about Middle
and South America

CHAPTER 8

Mexico

Now we will study Mexico, our neighbor to the south. More than 100 million people live in Mexico. Below you will meet Ellie, a Mexican student.

*H*ola! My name is Ellie, and I am 14. If you are my friend, I will greet you with a fast kiss on the cheek. I live in a small village, San Francisco Acatepec, on the edge of the city of Puebla. Our house is made of adobe and has a big yard. Our house is surrounded by a big adobe wall. We have a vegetable garden, flowers, and a lot of trees. I live with my mom and dad, my older brother (he's in the ninth grade), my three cats, and two dogs.

I am in the eighth grade. School starts at 8:00 A.M. On Monday mornings, we salute the flag and sing the Mexican national anthem. School ends at 2:15 but on Friday I have to stay till 4:45 to take an additional drama class. I love drama since I want to be an actress someday and a marine biologist.

My favorite holiday is Dia de los Muertos (Day of the Dead). On that day, we make bread and put out offerings to honor the dead. We put out clothes, sugar cane, chocolate, sugar candy skulls, flowers, bread, pictures, incense, and candles.

¿Has estado alguna vez en México?

Translation: Have you ever been to Mexico?

Section 1

Physical Geography

Read to Discover

1. What are the main physical features of Mexico?
2. What climate types, plants, and animals are found in Mexico?
3. What are Mexico's main natural resources?

Define

sinkholes

Locate

Gulf of Mexico
Baja California
Gulf of California
Río Bravo (Rio Grande)

Mexican Plateau
Sierra Madre Oriental
Sierra Madre Occidental

Mount Orizaba
Yucatán Peninsula

Scarlet macaw

WHY IT MATTERS

The Río Bravo (Rio Grande) marks the border between the United States and Mexico. Use CNNfyi.com or other current events sources to find information on this major river. Record your findings in your journal.

Mexico: Physical-Political

Size comparison of Mexico to the contiguous United States

ELEVATION

FEET	METERS
13,120	4,000
6,560	2,000
1,640	500
656	200
(Sea level) 0	0 (Sea level)
Below sea level	Below sea level

⊛ National capital
• Other cities

UNITED STATES

Tijuana
Mexicali
Ciudad Juárez
Chihuahua
Conchos
Nuevo Laredo
Monterrey
Matamoros
Saltillo
Culiacán
Mazatlán
MEXICO
San Luis Potosí
Tampico
León
Guadalajara
Lake Chapala
Mexico City
Puebla
Veracruz
Mount Orizaba 18,700 ft. (5700 m)
Acapulco
ISTHMUS OF TEHUANTEPEC
Mérida
Cancún
Cozumel Island
Campeche
YUCATÁN PENINSULA
Bay of Campeche

BAJA CALIFORNIA
GULF OF CALIFORNIA
SIERRA MADRE OCCIDENTAL
MEXICAN PLATEAU
SIERRA MADRE ORIENTAL
SIERRA MADRE DEL SUR
PACIFIC OCEAN
GULF OF MEXICO
Tropic of Cancer
Yucatán Channel
CUBA
CARIBBEAN SEA
GULF OF TEHUANTEPEC

Río Bravo
Rio Grande
Yaqui River
Río Santiago
Balsas River
Usumacinta River
Grijalva River

SCALE

0 — 250 — 500 Miles
0 — 250 — 500 Kilometers

Projection: Albers Equal Area

Volcanic Mount Orizaba rises southeast of Mexico City.

Interpreting the Visual Record What kinds of climates do you think people living in this area might experience?

internet connect

GO TO: go.hrw.com
KEYWORD: SG3 CH8
FOR: Web sites about Mexico

Thousands of monarch butterflies migrate south to the mountains of central Mexico for the winter.

Physical Features

Mexico is a large country. It has a long coast on the Pacific Ocean. It has a shorter one on the Gulf of Mexico. In far southern Mexico, the two bodies of water are just 137 miles (220 km) apart. This part of Mexico is called the Isthmus of Tehuantepec (tay-WAHN-tah-pek). The Caribbean Sea washes the country's sunny southeastern beaches. Beautiful Caribbean and Pacific coastal areas attract many tourists.

Baja (BAH-hah) California is a long, narrow peninsula. It extends south from Mexico's northwestern border with the United States. The peninsula separates the Gulf of California from the Pacific Ocean. One of Mexico's few major rivers, the Río Bravo, forms the Mexico-Texas border. In the United States this river is called the Rio Grande.

Plateaus and Mountains Much of Mexico consists of a rugged central region called the Mexican Plateau. The plateau's wide plains range from 3,700 feet (1,128 m) to 9,000 feet (2,743 m). Isolated mountain ridges rise much higher. Two mountain ranges form the edges of the Mexican Plateau. The Sierra Madre Oriental rise to the east. The Sierra Madre Occidental lie in the west.

At the southern end of the plateau lies the Valley of Mexico. Mexico City, the capital, is located there. The mountains south of Mexico City include towering, snowcapped volcanoes. Volcanic eruptions and earthquakes are a threat in this area. The highest peak, Mount Orizaba (oh-ree-SAH-buh), rises to 18,700 feet (5,700 m).

The Yucatán The Yucatán (yoo-kah-TAHN) Peninsula is generally flat. Limestone underlies much of the area, and erosion has created numerous caves and **sinkholes**. A sinkhole is a steep-sided depression formed when the roof of a cave collapses. The climate in the northern part of the peninsula is hot and dry. Scrub forest is the main vegetation. Farther south, rainfall becomes much heavier. Tropical rain forests cover much of the southern Yucatán.

✓ **READING CHECK:** *Places and Regions* What are Mexico's major physical features?

The States of Mexico

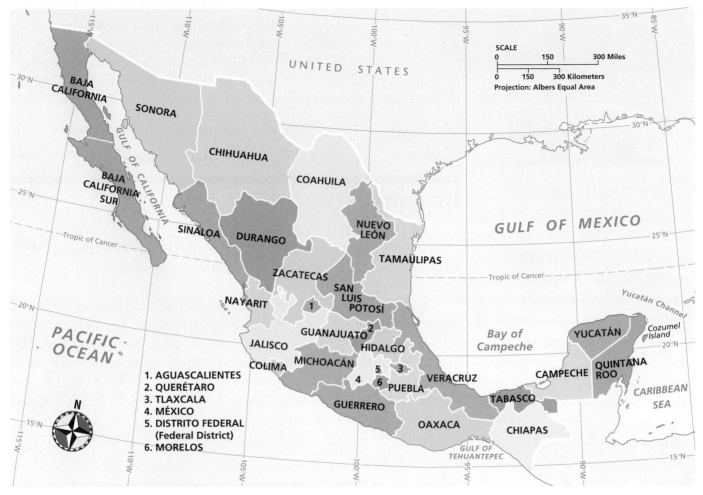

UNITED STATES

SCALE
0 — 150 — 300 Miles
0 — 150 — 300 Kilometers
Projection: Albers Equal Area

BAJA CALIFORNIA

SONORA

CHIHUAHUA

BAJA CALIFORNIA SUR

GULF OF CALIFORNIA

COAHUILA

SINALOA

DURANGO

NUEVO LEÓN

GULF OF MEXICO

ZACATECAS

TAMAULIPAS

Tropic of Cancer

NAYARIT

1

SAN LUIS POTOSÍ

Yucatán Channel

PACIFIC OCEAN

GUANAJUATO

2

HIDALGO

Bay of Campeche

YUCATÁN

Cozumel Island

JALISCO

COLIMA

MICHOACÁN

5

4 6 PUEBLA

3

VERACRUZ

CAMPECHE

QUINTANA ROO

CARIBBEAN SEA

N

GUERRERO

TABASCO

1. AGUASCALIENTES
2. QUERÉTARO
3. TLAXCALA
4. MÉXICO
5. DISTRITO FEDERAL (Federal District)
6. MORELOS

OAXACA

CHIAPAS

GULF OF TEHUANTEPEC

Climate, Vegetation, and Wildlife

Mexico's climate varies by region. Its mountains, deserts, and forests also support a variety of plants and animals.

A Tropical Area Mexico extends from the middle latitudes into the tropics. It has desert, steppe, savanna, and humid tropical climates. Most of northern Mexico is dry. There, Baja California's Sonoran Desert meets the Chihuahuan (chee-WAH-wahn) Desert of the plateau. Desert scrub vegetation and dry grasslands are common. Cougars, coyotes, and deer can be found in some areas of the north.

The forested plains along Mexico's southeastern coast are hot and humid much of the year. Summer is the rainy season. Forests cover about 20 percent of Mexico's land area. Tropical rain forests provide a home for anteaters, jaguars, monkeys, parrots, and other animals.

Many varieties of cactus thrive in the Sonoran Desert.

Interpreting the Visual Record Why do you think large trees are not found in the Sonoran Desert?

Nogales United States

Mexico

Guatemala

Climate Variations In some areas changes in elevation cause climates to vary widely within a short distance. Many people have settled in the mild environment of the mountain valleys. The valleys along Mexico's southern coastal areas also have pleasant climates.

The areas of high elevation on the Mexican Plateau experience surprisingly cool temperatures. Freezing temperatures sometimes reach as far south as Mexico City.

✓ **READING CHECK:** *Places and Regions* What are Mexico's climate zones?

Resources

Petroleum is Mexico's most important energy resource. Oil reserves lie primarily under southern and Gulf coastal plains as well as offshore in the Gulf of Mexico. In 1997 Mexico had the world's eighth-largest crude oil reserves.

Mining is also important in Mexico. Some gold and silver mines begun centuries ago are still in operation. Fresnillo has been a silver-mining center since 1569. New mines have been developed in Mexico's northern and southern mountains. Silver is the most valuable part of Mexico's mining industry. In 1997 one silver mine in the state of Zacatecas produced 706 tons (641,037 kg) of silver. Mexico also produces large amounts of copper, gold, lead, and zinc.

Water is a limited resource in parts of Mexico. Water scarcity, particularly in the dry north, is a serious issue.

✓ **READING CHECK:** *Environment and Society* What problems might water scarcity cause for Mexican citizens?

Our Amazing Planet

So much water has been pumped from under Mexico City that the ground is sinking, or subsiding. Parts of the central city have subsided about 25 feet (7.6 m) in the last 100 years. This has damaged buildings, pipes, sewers, and subway tunnels.

Section Review 1

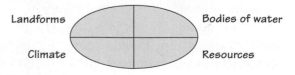
go.hrw.com **Homework Practice Online** Keyword: SG3 HP8

Define and explain: sinkholes

Working with Sketch Maps On a map of Mexico that you draw or that your teacher provides, label the following: Gulf of Mexico, Baja California, Gulf of California, Río Bravo (Rio Grande), Mexican Plateau, Sierra Madre Oriental, Sierra Madre Occidental, Mount Orizaba, and Yucatán Peninsula. In a caption, describe the Yucatán.

Reading for the Main Idea

1. *Places and Regions* What are Mexico's major physical features?

2. *Places and Regions* What are the major climate zones of Mexico?

Critical Thinking

3. **Drawing Inferences and Conclusions** Based on physical features and climate, which areas of Mexico provide the best conditions for people to live?

4. **Drawing Inferences and Conclusions** How do you think Mexico's geography affects movement and communication between different parts of the country?

Organizing What You Know

5. **Summarizing** Copy the following graphic organizer. Use it to describe Mexico's physical geography.

Landforms

Bodies of water

Climate

Resources

Section 2 — History and Culture

Read to Discover

1. What early cultures developed in Mexico?
2. What was Mexico like under Spanish rule and after independence?
3. What are some important features of Mexican culture?

Define

chinampas
conquistadores
epidemic
empire
mestizos

mulattoes
missions
ejidos
haciendas

WHY IT MATTERS

There are many aspects of Spanish influence still found in present-day Mexico. Use **CNN fyi.com** or other **current events** sources to find information about Mexican history. Record your findings in your journal.

An Aztec serpent pendant

Early Cultures

Mesoamerica (*meso* means "in the middle") is the cultural area including Mexico and much of Central America. Many scientists think the first people to live in Mesoamerica arrived from the north about 12,000 years ago. By about 5,000 years ago, people in Mesoamerica were growing beans, peppers, and squash. They also domesticated an early form of corn. It eventually developed into the corn that we see today.

By about 1500 B.C. many people throughout the region were living in small farming villages. Along the humid southern coast of the Gulf of Mexico lived the Olmec people. The Olmec built temples, pyramids, and huge statues. They traded carved jade and obsidian, a volcanic stone, throughout eastern Mexico.

By about A.D. 200, other complex cultures were developing in what is now Mexico. Many of these civilizations had large city centers. Those centers had apartments, great avenues, open plazas, and pyramid-shaped temples. Some temple areas throughout Mesoamerica had stone ball courts. Players on those courts competed in a game somewhat like basketball. However, this ball game was not simply a sport. It had deep religious importance. Players who lost might be sacrificed to the gods.

Maya ruins include stone carvings and pyramid-type structures. Figures such as this Chac Mool are thought to represent the rain god.

This copy of an original Aztec tax record shows items that were to be collected as tribute.

Interpreting the Visual Record What items besides tunics and headgear can you identify?

The Maya ruins of Tulum, an ancient Maya ceremonial and religious center, lie on the Caribbean coast.

Interpreting the Visual Record Why do you think the Maya built a large wall around this city?

The Maya Maya civilization developed in the tropical rain forest of southeastern Mexico, Guatemala, Belize, and Honduras. Maya city-states were at their peak between about A.D. 250 and 800. The Maya made accurate astronomical calculations and had a detailed calendar. Modern scholars can now read some Maya writing. This has helped us understand their civilization.

The Maya grew crops on terraced hillsides and on raised fields in swampy areas. They dug canals, piling the rich bottom mud onto the fields alongside the canals. This practice enriched the soil. Using this productive method of farming, the Maya supported an extremely dense population.

Sometime after A.D. 800, Maya civilization collapsed. The cities were abandoned. This decline may have been caused by famine, disease, warfare, or some combination of factors. However, the Maya did not die out. Millions of people of Maya descent still live in Mexico and Central America today.

The Aztec A people called the Aztec began moving into central Mexico from the north about A.D. 1200. They later established their capital on an island in a lake in the Valley of Mexico. Known as Tenochtitlán (tay-nawch-teet-LAHN), this capital grew into a splendid city. Its population in 1519 is estimated to have been at least 200,000. It was one of the largest cities in the world at that time. The Aztec conquered other Indian peoples around them. They forced these peoples to pay taxes and provide captives for sacrifice to Aztec gods.

The Aztec practiced a version of raised-field agriculture in the swampy lakes of central Mexico. The Aztec called these raised fields **chinampas** (chuh-NAM-puhs). There they grew the corn, beans, and peppers that most people ate. Only rich people in this society ate meat. On special occasions common people sometimes ate dog meat. The upper classes also drank chocolate.

✓ **READING CHECK:** What were the main features of Mexico's early civilizations?

United States

Mexico

Tulum National Park

Guatemala

CONNECTING TO History

TENOCHTITLÁN

Tenochtitlán—now Mexico City—was founded by the Aztec in the early 1300s. According to their legends, they saw an eagle sitting atop a cactus on a swampy island in Lake Texcoco. The eagle held a snake in its mouth. A prophecy had instructed them to build a city where they saw such an eagle.

Within 200 years this village had become an imperial capital and the largest city in the Americas. It was a city of pyramids, palaces, markets, and gardens. Canals and streets ran through the city. Stone causeways connected the island to the mainland.

Bernal Díaz, a Spanish soldier, described his first view of the Aztec capital in 1519.

❝ When we saw so many cities and villages built in the water and other great towns on dry land and that straight and level Causeway going towards [Tenochtitlán], we were amazed and said that it was like the enchantments they tell of in the legend of Amadis, on account of the great towers and temples and buildings rising from the water, and all built of masonry. And some of our soldiers asked whether the things that we saw were not a dream.**❞**

The Spaniards went on to conquer the Aztec and destroy Tenochtitlán. On the ruins they built Mexico City. They also drained Lake Texcoco to allow the city to expand.

Understanding What You Read

1. Where and when was Tenochtitlán first built?
2. What was the Spaniards' reaction to Tenochtitlán?

A sketch map of the Aztec capital of Tenochtitlán

Colonial Mexico and Independence

Spanish Conquest Hernán Cortés, a Spanish soldier, arrived in Mexico in 1519 with about 600 men. These **conquistadores** (kahn-kees-tuh-DAWR-ez), or conquerors, had both muskets and horses. These were unknown in the Americas at that time. However, the most important factor in the conquest was disease. The native people of the Americas had no resistance to European diseases. The first **epidemic**, or widespread outbreak, of smallpox struck central Mexico in 1520. The death toll from disease greatly weakened the power of the Aztec. In 1521 Cortés completed his conquest of the Aztec and the other American Indian peoples of southern Mexico. They named the territory New Spain.

Colonial Mexico During this period, Spain ruled an **empire**. An empire is a system in which a central power controls a number of territories. New Spain was just one of Spain's colonies in the Americas. Mainland New Spain extended north from Mexico to what is now northern California and south to Panama.

After the initial conquest, Spanish and American Indian peoples and cultures mixed. This mix formed a new Mexican identity. The Spaniards called people of mixed European and Indian ancestry **mestizos** (me-STEE-zohs). When enslaved Africans were brought to Spanish America, they added to this blend of cultures. The Spaniards called people of mixed European and African ancestry **mulattoes** (muh-LA-tohs). Africans and Indians also intermarried.

Large areas of northern Mexico were left to the Roman Catholic Church to explore and to rule. Church outposts known as **missions** were scattered throughout the area. Mission priests often learned Indian languages and tried to convert the Indians to Catholicism.

Colonial Economy At first, the Spaniards were mainly interested in mining gold and silver in Mexico. Gradually, agriculture also became an important part of the colonial economy. Indians did most of the hard physical labor on farms and in mines. Many of them died from disease and overwork. Therefore, Spaniards began to bring enslaved Africans to the Americas as another source of labor.

Before the arrival of the Spaniards, Indian communities owned and worked land in groups. The lands they worked in common are called *ejidos* (e-HEE-thohs). After the conquest, the Spanish monarch granted **haciendas** (hah-see-EN-duhs), or huge expanses of farmlands, to favored people. Peasants, usually Indians, lived and worked on these haciendas. Cattle ranching operated according to a similar system.

Independence and After In 1810 a Catholic priest named Miguel Hidalgo y Costilla began a revolt against Spanish rule. Hidalgo was killed in 1811. However, fighting continued until independence was won in 1821.

Fifteen years later, Texas broke away from Mexico. Texas became part of the United States in 1845. Shortly after, the United States and Mexico argued over the location of their common border. This conflict led to a war in which Mexico lost about half its territory. Americans know this conflict as the Mexican War. Mexicans usually refer to it as the War of the North American Invasion.

In the early 1900s many Mexicans grew unhappy with the government of military leader Porfirio Díaz. As a result, in 1910 the Mexican Revolution broke out. Fighting between various leaders and groups lasted until 1920.

One of the major results of the revolution was land reform. The new government took land from the haciendas. This land was given back to peasant villages according to the old *ejido* system. Today *ejidos* make up about half of Mexico's farmland.

✔ **READING CHECK:** *Human Systems* How did Mexico gain independence from Spain?

The Santa Prisa Cathedral rises above the rest of Taxco in southern Mexico. The Spaniards built many beautiful cathedrals in Mexico.

United States

Mexico

Taxco

Guatemala

Mexicans light candles for relatives on the Day of the Dead.

Interpreting the Visual Record What celebrations in your community reflect special customs?

Culture and Customs

About 89 percent of Mexico's people are Roman Catholic. The Day of the Dead is an example of how cultures mix in Mexico. This holiday takes place on November 1 and 2. These are the same dates the Catholic Church celebrates All Saints' Day and All Souls' Day. The Day of the Dead honors dead ancestors. Families often place different foods on the graves of dead relatives. This recalls the Indian belief that the dead need material things just as the living do.

In Mexico ethnic identity is associated more with culture than with ancestry. One major indicator of a person's ethnic identity is language. Speaking one of the American Indian languages identifies a person as Indian. People who speak only Spanish are usually not considered Indian. This may be true even if they have Indian ancestors.

✓ **READING CHECK:** (*Human Systems*) What is the significance of the Day of the Dead?

Define and explain: *chinampas*, conquistadores, epidemic, empire, mestizos, mulattoes, missions, *ejidos*, haciendas

Working with Sketch Maps On the map you created in Section 1, shade the areas once controlled by the Maya and Aztec. Which civilization occupied the Yucatán Peninsula?

Reading for the Main Idea

1. (*Human Systems*) What were some notable achievements of the Maya and Aztec civilizations?

2. (*Human Systems*) What were the effects of Spanish rule on Mexico?

Critical Thinking

3. **Analyzing Information** What advantages did Cortés have in his conquest of the Aztec?

4. **Finding the Main Idea** What is a sign of a person's ethnic identity in Mexico?

Organizing What You Know

5. **Identifying Cause and Effect** Copy the following graphic organizer. Use it to develop a cause-and-effect chart to identify events related to the Mexican War.

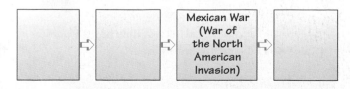

Mexican War (War of the North American Invasion)

CASE STUDY

MAQUILADORAS ALONG THE U.S.-MEXICO BORDER

Geographers are often interested in borders. Borders are more than just lines on a map. They are places where different countries, cultures, and ways of life meet. For example, the U.S.-Mexico border separates a developing country from a very rich country. This fact has had an important influence on the location of industries in the region.

On the Mexican side of the border there are many *maquiladoras* (mah-kee-lah-DOHR-ahs)— factories that can be owned by foreign companies. The first *maquiladoras* were built in the mid-1960s. Since then, their numbers have increased dramatically. There are now more than 2,000 *maquiladoras* in Mexico. They employ hundreds of thousands of workers.

Growth in *Maquiladora* Plants

Source: Instituto Nacional de Estadistica Geografia e Informatica, Mexico

▲

The U.S.-Mexico border separates Mexicali, Mexico, from Calexico, California. The large buildings on the left are *maquiladoras*.

Interpreting the Visual Record How has the border influenced land use in this area?

Many *maquiladoras* are owned by American companies. They produce goods such as vacuum cleaners, automobile parts, and electronics. These goods are usually exported to the United States. Most *maquiladoras* are located within about 20 miles (32 km) of the U.S.-Mexico border. Cities such as Tijuana, Ciudad Juárez, and Nuevo Laredo have many *maquiladoras*.

Why have so many American companies chosen to build factories across the border in Mexico? The location allows companies to take advantage of the difference in wealth between the two countries. Mexico has a much lower standard of living than the United States. Workers there get paid less. Therefore, factories in Mexico can produce goods more cheaply. The United States has a higher standard of living. People there have more money to buy goods. They buy the products that have been

U.S.-Mexico Border Region

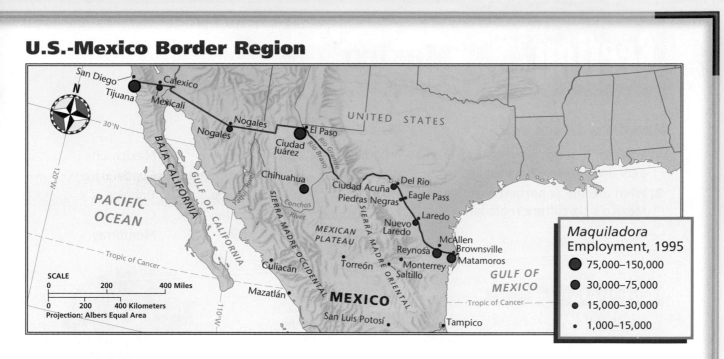

assembled in Mexico and shipped to American stores.

American companies have other reasons for building factories in Mexico. The Mexican government has given tax breaks to foreign companies that own and operate *maquiladoras*. It has encouraged the growth of *maquiladoras*. They create jobs for Mexican citizens and bring money into the country. Also, environmental laws in Mexico are not as strict as in the United States. Therefore, companies in Mexico do not have to spend as much money to control pollution.

Maquiladoras have become an important part of the border economy. They are also a good example of how borders can influence the landscape. The U.S.-Mexico border has attracted *maquiladoras* because it is more than just a line on a map. It separates two countries with different cultures, economies, and governments. Some American companies have built factories on the Mexican side of the border that export goods to the United States. These companies benefit from the different standards of living in the two countries and the border that separates them.

◀

Trucks carrying goods from Mexico to the United States are inspected by U.S. Customs officials in Laredo, Texas.

Understanding What You Read

1. Why have some American companies built factories in Mexico?

2. What are some of the goods that are produced in *maquiladoras*?

Section 3 Mexico Today

Read to Discover

1. What kind of government and economy does Mexico have today?
2. What are the important features of Mexico's six culture regions?

Define

inflation
cash crops
smog
maquiladoras
slash-and-burn
  agriculture

Locate

Tijuana
Ciudad Juárez
Acapulco
Mazatlán
Cancún

Mexico City
Guadalajara
Tampico
Campeche
Monterrey

WHY IT MATTERS

The North American Free Trade Agreement (NAFTA), signed by the United States, Mexico, and Canada, went into effect in 1994. Use CNNfyi.com or other **current events** sources to find out more about NAFTA. Record your findings in your journal.

Bean stew in a tortilla bowl

Mexico

COUNTRY	POPULATION/ GROWTH RATE	LIFE EXPECTANCY	LITERACY RATE	PER CAPITA GDP
Mexico	101,879,171 1.5%	69, male 75, female	90%	$9,100
United States	281,421,906 0.9%	74, male 80, female	97%	$36,200

Sources: Central Intelligence Agency, *The World Factbook 2001;* U.S. Census Bureau

Interpreting the Chart What does the per capita GDP in Mexico indicate about its economic development?

Government and Economy

Like that of the United States, Mexico's government includes an elected president and a congress. However, in Mexico one political party—the Partido Revolucionario Institucional (PRI)—controlled the Mexican government for 71 years. This control ended in 2000 when Vicente Fox of the National Action Party was sworn in as president.

For many years, Mexico operated more on the principles of a command economy in which the government controlled economic activity. In recent decades, however, Mexico has worked to reduce government control of the economy. Mexico's economy is growing and modernizing. However, living standards are much lower than in other nations.

Mexico began to export oil in 1911 and is a leading oil exporter today. However, problems began when the price of oil fell in the 1980s. Since then, Mexico has wrestled with debts to foreign banks, high unemployment, and **inflation**. Inflation is the rise in prices that occurs when currency loses its buying power.

The North American Free Trade Agreement (NAFTA) has helped Mexico's economy. NAFTA took effect in 1994. It made trade between Mexico, the United States, and Canada easier. Mexico's leaders hope increased trade will create more jobs in their country.

Agriculture Agriculture has long been an important part of the Mexican economy. In fact, farming is the traditional focus of life in the country. This is true even though just 12 percent of the land can grow crops. Rainfall supports agriculture in the southern part of the Mexican Plateau and in southern valleys. Plantations in coastal lowlands and on mountain slopes along the Gulf of Mexico also produce important crops. Those crops include coffee and sugarcane. Northern drylands are important for livestock ranching.

High demand in the United States has encouraged a shift to the growing of **cash crops**. A cash crop is produced primarily to sell, rather than for the farmer to eat. Trucks bring Mexican vegetables, fruits, and other cash crops to the United States.

Industry Many Mexicans work in primary and secondary industries. These include the oil industry, mining, and manufacturing. The country's fastest-growing industrial centers lie along the U.S. border. Tijuana (tee-HWAH-nah) and Ciudad Juárez (syoo-thahth HWAHR-es) are two of these major industrial centers.

Many U.S. and other foreign companies have built factories in Mexico. This is because wages are lower there. Mexican workers in these factories assemble products for export to other countries. (See the Case Study in this chapter.)

Tourism Tourism and other service industries are also important to Mexico's economy. Many tourists visit old colonial cities and Maya and Aztec monuments. Popular coastal cities and resorts include Acapulco, Mazatlán, and Cancún. Acapulco and Mazatlán are located on Mexico's Pacific coast. Cancún is on the Yucatán Peninsula.

✔ **READING CHECK:** *Environment and Society* How does geography affect the location of economic activities in Mexico?

▲
Gourds—hard-shelled ornamental fruits—are just some of Mexico's many agricultural products.

Puerto Vallarta—a popular beach resort—is on the Pacific coast.
Interpreting the Visual Record How do you think the growth of tourism has changed settlement patterns?

▼

Our Amazing Planet

Mexico City was 250 miles (400 km) away from the center of the 1985 earthquake on Mexico's Pacific coast. However, the city suffered heavy damage and thousands of deaths. The city sits on a former lake bed. The loose soil under the city made the damage worse.

Mexico's Culture Regions

Mexico's 31 states and one federal district can be grouped into six culture regions. These regions are highly diverse in their resources, climate, population, and other features.

Greater Mexico City Greater Mexico City is Mexico's most developed and crowded region. This area includes Mexico City and about 50 smaller cities. More than 20 million people live there. It is one of the most heavily populated urban areas in the world.

Mexico City is also one of the world's most polluted cities. Thousands of factories and millions of automobiles release exhaust and other pollutants into the air. Surrounding mountains trap the resulting **smog**—a mixture of smoke, chemicals, and fog. Smog can cause health problems like eye irritation and breathing difficulties.

Wealth and poverty exist side by side in Mexico City. The city has very poor slums. It also has busy highways, modern office buildings, high-rise apartments, museums, universities, and old colonial cathedrals.

Central Interior Mexico's central interior region lies north of the capital. It extends toward both coasts. Many cities here began as mining or ranching centers during the colonial period. Small towns with a central square and a colonial-style church are common.

The region has many fertile valleys and small family farms. In recent years the central interior has attracted new industries from overcrowded Mexico City. As a result, cities like Guadalajara are growing rapidly.

Oil Coast The forested coastal plains between Tampico and Campeche (kahm-PAY-chay) were once lightly settled. However, the population has grown as oil production in this region has increased. In addition, large forest areas are being cleared for farming and ranching.

Smog covers Mexico City. The city continues to work toward solutions to challenges facing it as one of the world's largest cities.

Interpreting the Visual Record What two words do you think the word *smog* comes from?

▶

Southern Mexico Many people in southern Mexico speak Indian languages. They live in the country's poorest region. It has few cities and little industry. Subsistence farming is common. Poverty and corrupt local governments have led to unrest. In the 1990s people in the state of Chiapas staged an antigovernment uprising.

Northern Mexico Northern Mexico has become one of the country's most prosperous and modern areas. NAFTA has helped the region's economy grow. Monterrey and Tijuana are important cities here. Factories called **maquiladoras** (mah-kee-lah-DORH-ahs) are located along the northern border and are often foreign-owned.

American music, television, and other forms of entertainment are popular near the border. Many Mexicans cross the border to shop, work, or live in the United States. In recent decades, the U.S. government has increased its efforts to stop illegal immigration across the border.

The Yucatán Most of the Yucatán Peninsula is sparsely populated. Mérida is this region's major city. As in other parts of Mexico, some farmers in the region practice **slash-and-burn agriculture**, in which an area of forest is burned to clear it for planting. The ashes enrich the soil. After a few years of planting crops, the soil is exhausted. The farmer then moves on to a new area of forest. Farmers can return to previously farmed areas years later.

Maya ruins and sunny beaches have made tourism a major industry in this area. The popular resort of Cancún and the island of Cozumel are located here.

✓ **READING CHECK:** ⟨ *Human Systems* ⟩ What are the six culture regions of Mexico?

▲
Celebrations, such as Danza de Los Viejitos—Dance of the Old Men—are popular throughout Mexico.

Section Review 3

Define and explain: inflation, cash crops, smog, *maquiladoras*, slash-and-burn agriculture

Working with Sketch Maps On the map you created in Section 2, label Tijuana, Ciudad Juárez, Acapulco, Mazatlán, Cancún, Mexico City, Guadalajara, Tampico, Campeche, and Monterrey. Which city is the national capital? Which cities are located at or near sea level? Which are located at higher elevations?

Reading for the Main Idea

1. ⟨ *Human Systems* ⟩ What are three economic problems faced by Mexico in recent decades?

2. ⟨ *Human Systems* ⟩ What are Mexico's six culture regions? Describe a feature of each.

Critical Thinking

3. **Analyzing Information** How have changes in the price of oil affected Mexico?

4. **Drawing Inferences and Conclusions** Why would farmers in Mexico grow only cash crops?

Organizing What You Know

5. **Categorizing** Copy the following graphic organizer. Use it to list key facts about the population and economy of each culture region in Mexico.

	Population	Economy
Greater Mexico City		
Central interior		
Oil coast		
Southern Mexico		
Northern Mexico		
Yucatán		

Building Vocabulary

On a separate sheet of paper, write sentences to define each of the following

1. conquistadores
2. epidemic
3. empire
4. mestizos
5. missions
6. haciendas
7. inflation
8. cash crops
9. smog
10. *maquiladoras*

Reviewing the Main Ideas

1. **Places and Regions** What is the Mexican Plateau?
2. **Places and Regions** Why are the coastal plains now more heavily settled?
3. **Human Systems** How did European diseases affect the Indians in Mexico?
4. **Human Systems** What were the main ethnic divisions in New Spain?
5. **Human Systems** How are agriculture and industry in Mexico and the United States related?

Understanding Environment and Society

Encouraging Tourism
Mexico's pleasant coastal climate has helped its tourist industry grow. Create a graph and presentation on the growth of tourism in Mexico. As you prepare your presentation you may want to think about the following:
- Mexico's popular tourist attractions
- Mexico's promotion of tourism
- Benefits and problems of tourism

Thinking Critically

1. **Drawing Inferences and Conclusions** Why do climates in southern Mexico vary so widely?
2. **Finding the Main Idea** How did the Maya and Aztec modify their environment to suit their needs?
3. **Analyzing Information** Why is Roman Catholicism the most common religion in Mexico?
4. **Drawing Inferences and Conclusions** Mexican workers are paid much less than U.S. workers. Why do you think this is so?
5. **Finding the Main Idea** Think about what you have learned about agriculture in Mexico. What is the major drawback of slash-and-burn agriculture?

Map ACTIVITY

On a separate sheet of paper, match the letters on the map with their correct labels.

Río Bravo   Tijuana
(Rio Grande)   Ciudad Juárez
Mexico City   Acapulco
Mount Orizaba   Cancún
Yucatán Peninsula Guadalajara

Mental Mapping Skills ACTIVITY

On a separate sheet of paper, draw a freehand map of Mexico. Make a key for your map and label the following:

Baja California
Gulf of California
Gulf of Mexico
Mexican Plateau
Sierra Madre Occidental
Sierra Madre Oriental

WRITING ACTIVITY

Imagine that you are a Spanish soldier reporting back to Spain on the situation in Mexico. Research and write a short report on the effects of disease on the Aztec. Include a map, chart, graph, model, or database illustrating the information in your report. Be sure to use standard grammar, spelling, sentence structure, and punctuation.

Alternative Assessment

Portfolio ACTIVITY

Learning About Your Local Geography

Research Project Contact your local air quality board for information on the air quality of your area. If possible, collect data going back several years. What factors account for the patterns you see over time?

internet connect

Internet Activity: go.hrw.com
KEYWORD: SG3 GT8

Choose a topic to explore about Mexico:
• Travel along Mexico's coastlines.
• See the arts and crafts of Mexico.
• Use ancient Maya hieroglyphs

Central America and the Caribbean Islands

Now we will study Central America and the islands of the Caribbean. First we will meet a student from Jamaica.

I am Aldayne and I am 11 years old. I live with my mother in Kingston, Jamaica. My house is gray—the door is green and the windows are blue. It is all on one floor, with a yard where we grow roses.

I am in the sixth grade. I am studying social studies, math, English, and history. We have three school terms a year. We go to school for three months and then have one month off. My favorite vacation month is in summer. That's when I can go to the country with my father. I catch birds, go fishing, run boats, and have cookouts.

When school is over at 2:00 P.M., I go downtown to my mother's shop. She is a dressmaker. I do my homework and sometimes do errands for her. By the time I get home, all my homework is done. While my mother makes dinner, I clean my shoes, get my clothes together, and get ready for the next day. My favorite dinners are rice and peas with spring chicken, or crispy fried chicken with chips (french fries).

Hello from Jamaica!

Section 1 · Physical Geography

Read to Discover

1. What are the physical features of Central America and the Caribbean islands?
2. What climates are found in the region?
3. What natural resources does the region have?

Define

archipelago
cloud forest
bauxite

Locate

Central America
Caribbean Sea
Cuba
Jamaica
Greater Antilles
Hispaniola

Puerto Rico
Lesser Antilles
Virgin Islands
Trinidad and
   Tobago
Bahamas

WHY IT MATTERS

Hurricanes are frequent dangers in the Caribbean region. Use CNNfyi.com or other **current events** sources to find out about recent hurricanes. Record your findings in your journal.

A conch shell

Central America and the Caribbean Islands: Physical-Political

To understand the relative location of Bermuda, as well as the distance separating it from the Caribbean countries, see the Atlas map in the front of the textbook.

Same scale as main map
32°15'N Hamilton
Bermuda (U.K.)
59°W

ELEVATION

	FEET	METERS
⊛ National capitals	13,120	4,000
	6,560	2,000
• Other cities	1,640	500
	656	200
(Sea level) 0		0 (Sea level)
Below sea level		Below sea level

GULF OF MEXICO
Tropic of Cancer
ATLANTIC OCEAN
Nassau
BAHAMAS
Straits of Florida
Havana
CUBA
Turks and Caicos Islands (U.K.)
20°N
YUCATÁN PENINSULA
Guantánamo
GREATER
DOMINICAN REPUBLIC
HAITI
Cayman Islands (U.K.)
Port-au-Prince
Hispaniola
San Juan
Puerto Rico (U.S.)
British Virgin Is. (U.K.)
20°N
MEXICO
BELIZE
Belmopan
JAMAICA
ANTILLES
Kingston
Santo Domingo
Virgin Is. (U.S.)
ANTIGUA AND BARBUDA
St. John's
GUATEMALA
Basseterre
Guadeloupe (FRANCE)
Guatemala City
HONDURAS
ST. KITTS AND NEVIS
DOMINICA
San Salvador
Tegucigalpa
N
CARIBBEAN SEA
Roseau
Martinique (FRANCE)
EL SALVADOR
Castries
ST. LUCIA
NICARAGUA
ST. VINCENT AND THE GRENADINES
BARBADOS
Managua
Lake Nicaragua
Netherlands Antilles (NETHERLANDS)
Kingstown
Bridgetown
PACIFIC OCEAN
10°N
San José
Panama Canal
LESSER ANTILLES
GRENADA
St. George's
COSTA RICA
Panama City
TRINIDAD AND TOBAGO
Port-of-Spain
10°N
PANAMA
GULF OF PANAMA

SCALE
0   200   400 Miles
0   200   400 Kilometers
Projection: Lambert Conformal Conic

Size comparison of Central America and the Caribbean to the contiguous United States

Our Amazing Planet

Dominica, in the far southeast of the region, receives up to 250 inches (835 cm) of rain per year! In contrast, Miami, Florida, receives only about 56 inches (140 cm).

Forested mountains rise above Roseau, capital of the island country of Dominica. Dominica is in the Lesser Antilles.

Interpreting the Visual Record What might the lush forest tell us about Dominica's climate?

Physical Features

Central America and the Caribbean Sea are home to 20 countries and a number of island territories. Central America includes Guatemala, Belize, Honduras, El Salvador, Nicaragua, Costa Rica, and Panama. The Caribbean islands include Cuba, Jamaica, Haiti, and the Dominican Republic. There also are nine smaller island countries.

Central America forms a bridge between North and South America. No place on this isthmus is more than 125 miles (200 km) from the sea. Mountains separate the Caribbean and Pacific coastal plains.

The Caribbean islands form an **archipelago** (ahr-kuh-PE-luh-goh), or large group of islands. The Caribbean archipelago is arranged in a long curve. It stretches from south of Florida to South America.

There are two main island groups in the Caribbean archipelago. The four large islands of the Greater Antilles (an-TI-leez) are Cuba, Jamaica, Hispaniola, and Puerto Rico. The small islands of the Lesser Antilles stretch from the Virgin Islands to Trinidad and Tobago. Another island group, the Bahamas, lies outside the Caribbean, east of Florida. It includes nearly 700 islands and thousands of reefs.

Earthquakes and volcanic eruptions are frequent in this region. Colliding plates cause this tectonic activity. The Cocos plate collides with and dives under the Caribbean plate off Central America's western coast. Another plate boundary lies to the east. The Caribbean plate borders the North American plate there. Volcanic eruptions can cause great damage.

✔ **READING CHECK:** *Places and Regions* What are the physical features of Central America and the Caribbean islands?

Climate and Vegetation

Along the Caribbean coast of Central America are humid tropical plains. The area also has dense rain forests. Inland mountains rise into mild highland climates. Most of the people live there because the temperatures are more moderate. Much of the original savanna vegetation inland has been cleared. It has been replaced by plantations and ranches. The Pacific coast has a warm and sunny tropical savanna climate.

Some of Central America's mountain areas are covered by **cloud forest**. This is a high-elevation, very wet tropical forest where low clouds are common. It is home to numerous plant and animal species.

The islands of the Caribbean have pleasant humid tropical and tropical savanna climates. Winters are usually drier than summers. The islands receive 40 to 60 inches (102 to 152 cm) of rainfall each year. On some islands the bedrock is mostly limestone. Water drains quickly. As a result, drought conditions are common.

Hurricanes are a danger in the region. Hurricanes are tropical storms that bring violent winds, heavy rain, and high seas. Most occur between June and November. They can cause great destruction and loss of life.

✓ **READING CHECK:** (*Environment and Society*) What effect do hurricanes have on people in the region?

Do you remember what you learned about tropical forests? See Chapter 3 to review.

Resources

Agriculture in the region can be profitable where volcanic ash has enriched the soil. Coffee, bananas, sugarcane, and cotton are major crops. Timber is exported from the rain forests of Belize and Honduras. Tourism is the most important industry, particularly in the Caribbean islands.

The region has few mineral resources. However, Jamaica has large reserves of **bauxite**, the most important aluminum ore. There are huge copper deposits in Panama. Energy resources are limited. This makes the region dependent on energy imports and limits economic development.

✓ **READING CHECK:** (*Environment and Society*) Why do you think tourism is the most important industry in the region?

Homework Practice Online
Keyword: SG3 HP9

Define and explain: archipelago, cloud forest, bauxite

Working with Sketch Maps On a map of the region that you draw or that your teacher provides, label the following: Central America, Caribbean Sea, Cuba, Jamaica, Greater Antilles, Puerto Rico, Hispaniola, Lesser Antilles, Virgin Islands, Trinidad and Tobago, and the Bahamas. Identify continents Central America links.

Reading for the Main Idea

1. (*Places and Regions*) What two major island groups make up the Caribbean archipelago?

2. (*Places and Regions*) In what climate region do most Central Americans live and why?

3. (*Places and Regions*) What are some of the region's crops?

Critical Thinking

4. **Making Generalizations and Predictions** What natural hazards do you think will continue to be a problem for the region? Why?

Organizing What You Know

5. **Categorizing** Copy the following graphic organizer. Use it to describe the climates, vegetation, and resources found in the region.

Climates	Vegetation	Resources

Section 2 Central America

Read to Discover

1. What was Central America's early history like?
2. How is the region's history reflected in its people today?
3. What are the countries of Central America like today?

Define

cacao
dictators
cardamom
civil war
ecotourism

Locate

Guatemala City
Lake Nicaragua
San José
Panama City
Panama Canal

WHY IT MATTERS

Civil wars caused great damage and disruption in Central America during the 1980s and early 1990s. Use **CNNfyi.com** or other **current events** sources to find out about conditions in Central American countries today. Record your findings in your journal.

Ancient jaguar pendant from Panama

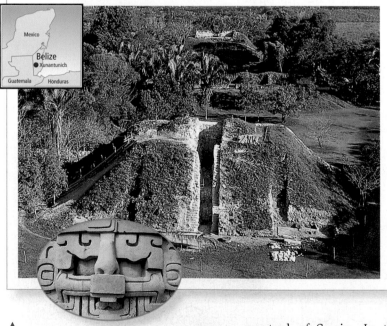

▲
Maya ruins can be found here in Belize and in other parts of Central America and Mexico.

History

More than 35 million people live in the countries of Central America. These countries have a shared history.

Early History The early peoples of Central America developed different cultures and societies. The Maya, for example, built large cities with pyramids and temples. People of Maya descent still live in Guatemala and parts of Mexico. Many of their ancient customs and traditions still influence modern life.

In the early 1500s European countries began establishing colonies in the region. Most of Central America came under the control of Spain. In the 1600s the British established the colony of British Honduras, which is now Belize. The British also occupied the Caribbean coast of Nicaragua.

European colonists established large plantations. They grew crops like tobacco and sugarcane. They forced the Central American Indians to work on the plantations. Some Indians were sent to work in gold mines elsewhere in the Americas. In addition, many Africans were brought to the region as slaves.

Independence Costa Rica, El Salvador, Guatemala, Honduras, and Nicaragua declared independence from Spain in 1821. They formed the United Provinces of Central America, but separated from each other in 1838–1839. Panama, once part of Colombia, became independent in 1903. The British left Nicaragua in the late 1800s. British Honduras gained independence as Belize in 1981.

✓ **READING CHECK:** *Human Systems* What role did Europeans play in the region's history?

Culture

Central America's colonial history is reflected in its culture today. In what ways do you think this is true?

People, Languages, and Religion The region's largest ethnic group is mestizo. Mestizos are people of mixed European and Indian ancestry. People of African ancestry make up a significant minority. Various Indian peoples also live in the region.

Spanish is the official language in most countries. However, many people speak Indian languages. In the former British colony of Belize, English is the official language.

Many Central Americans practice religions brought to the region by Europeans. Most are Roman Catholics. Spanish missionaries converted many Indians to Catholicism. However, Indian religions have influenced Catholicism in the region. Protestant Christians are a large minority in some countries, particularly Belize.

Lake Nicaragua was probably once part of an ocean bay. It is a freshwater lake, but it also has some oceanic animal life. This animal life includes the Lake Nicaragua shark. It grows to a length of about 8 to 10 feet (2.4 to 3 m).

Guatemalans celebrate the Christian holiday *Semana Santa*, or Holy Week. The street is covered with colored sand and flowers.
Interpreting the Visual Record How important do Christian holidays appear to be in the region?

CONNECTING TO Math

Stone Maya calendar

The Maya created one of the most advanced civilizations in the Americas. They built impressive cities of stone and invented a complex writing system. They also created calendars that allowed them to plan for the future.

The Maya based their calendar system on religion, mathematics, and astronomy. They believed that the days, months, and years were represented by

MAYA CALENDAR

different gods. Those gods had powers that helped determine the course of events. The Maya also understood the mathematical concepts of zero and numerical positioning. Numerical positioning is the idea that numbers can have different values depending on their position in a sequence, such as the 1 in 10 and 100. The Maya also calculated the length of the solar year. They predicted eclipses and lunar cycles.

Based on this knowledge, the Maya created two calendars. One was a religious calendar of 260 days. The other was a solar calendar of 365 days. These two calendars were used together to record historical events and to determine future actions. Using calendars, the Maya chose the best times to plant crops, hold festivals, and crown new rulers. They even believed that their calendars would help them predict the future.

Understanding What You Read
1. What were the foundations of the calendar system developed by the Maya?
2. How did the Maya's belief systems affect their use of calendars?

Food and Festivals Central America shares many traditional foods with Mexico and South America. These foods include corn and sweet potatoes. The region is also home to tomatoes, hot peppers, and **cacao** (kuh-KOW). Cacao is a small tree on which cocoa beans grow.

As in other Catholic countries, each town and country celebrates special saints' feast days. Images of the saints are paraded through the streets. A community might sponsor a fair and have dancing or plays.

Government From time to time, Central American countries have been ruled by **dictators**. A dictator is a person who rules a country with complete authority. The opponents of dictators often are arrested or even killed. Such abuses are one reason for limiting the power of government. Today the region's countries have elected governments.

✓ **READING CHECK:** *Human Systems* Why should government powers be limited?

Central America Today

Now we will take a closer look at each of the countries of Central America today.

Guatemala Guatemala is the most populous country in Central America. More than 12 million people live there. Nearly half of the country's people are Central American Indians. Many speak Maya languages. A majority of Guatemala's population are mestizos.

Most Maya live in isolated villages in the country's highlands. Fighting between rebels and government forces has killed more than 100,000 Guatemalans since the 1960s. Guatemalans hope that recent peace agreements will end this conflict.

Coffee is Guatemala's most important crop. The country also is a major producer of **cardamom**, a spice used in Asian foods.

Belize Belize is located on the Caribbean coast of the Yucatán Peninsula. It has the smallest population in Central America. Only about 236,000 people live there. The country's Maya ruins, coral reefs, and coastal resorts attract many tourists.

Honduras Honduras is a country of rugged mountains. Most people live in mountain valleys and along the northern coast. Transportation is difficult in the rugged terrain. Only 15 percent of the land is suitable for growing crops. Fruit is an important export.

El Salvador El Salvador lies on the Pacific side of Central America. Volcanic ash has made the country's soils the most fertile in the region. Important crops include coffee and sugarcane.

Most Salvadorans live in poverty. A few powerful families own much of the best land. These conditions were a major reason behind a long **civil war** in the 1980s. A civil war is a conflict between two or more groups within a country. The war killed many Salvadorans and slowed economic progress. Salvadorans have been rebuilding their country since the war ended in 1992.

Nicaragua Nicaragua is the largest Central American country. It has coasts on both the Caribbean Sea and the Pacific Ocean. Lake Nicaragua, near the Pacific coast, is the largest lake in Central America.

Nicaragua also has been rebuilding since the end of a long civil war. Its civil war ended in 1990. Free elections that year ended the rule of the Sandinistas. The Sandinistas had overthrown a dictator in 1979. They then ruled Nicaragua without elections. Today, the country is a democracy with many political voices.

A woman in the Guatemalan highlands weaves traditional fabrics.

Interpreting the Visual Record
How have available resources affected this woman's use of technology for weaving?

U.S. Banana Imports

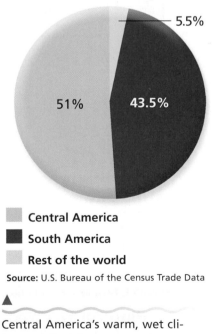

5.5%

51%   43.5%

- Central America
- South America
- Rest of the world

Source: U.S. Bureau of the Census Trade Data

Central America's warm, wet climate is ideal for growing bananas.

Interpreting the Chart From where do most of the U.S. banana imports come?

Central America

COUNTRY	POPULATION/ GROWTH RATE	LIFE EXPECTANCY	LITERACY RATE	PER CAPITA GDP
Belize	256,062 2.7%	69, male 74, female	70%	$3,200
Costa Rica	3,773,057 1.7%	74, male 79, female	95%	$6,700
El Salvador	6,237,662 1.9%	66, male 74, female	72%	$4,000
Guatemala	12,974,361 2.6%	64, male 69, female	64%	$3,700
Honduras	6,406,052 2.4%	68, male 71, female	73%	$2,700
Nicaragua	4,918,393 2.2%	67, male 71, female	66%	$2,700
Panama	2,845,647 1.3%	73, male 79, female	91%	$6,000
United States	281,421,906 0.9%	74, male 80, female	97%	$36,200

Sources: Central Intelligence Agency, *The World Factbook 2001;* U.S. Census Bureau

Interpreting the Chart **Which two Central American countries have the highest per capita GDP? Why might this be?**

Costa Rica

Costa Rica has a long history of stable, democratic government. In the last half of the 1900s, the country remained at peace. During that time, many of its neighbors were torn by civil wars. Costa Rica has also made important progress in reducing poverty.

Costa Rica's capital, San José, is located in the central highlands. Many coffee farms are also located in the highlands. Coffee and bananas are important Costa Rican crops.

Many travelers are attracted to Costa Rica's rich tropical rain forests and national parks. **Ecotourism**—the practice of using an area's natural environment to attract tourists—is an important part of Central American and Caribbean economies.

Panama

Panama lies between Costa Rica and Colombia. Most Panamanians live in areas near the Panama Canal. Canal fees and industries make the canal area the country's most prosperous region.

The Panama Canal links the Pacific Ocean to the Caribbean Sea and Atlantic Ocean. The United States finished the canal in 1914. The canal played an important role in U.S. economic and foreign policies. It also allowed the United States to control territory and extend its influence in the area. The United States controlled the canal until 1999. Then, as called for by a 1978 treaty, Panama took it over.

✔ **READING CHECK:** *The Uses of Geography* Why might Panama want control of the canal?

go. hrw .com **Homework Practice Online**
Keyword: SG3 HP9

Section Review 2

Define and explain: cacao, dictators, cardamom, civil war, ecotourism

Working with Sketch Maps On the map you created in Section 1, label the Central American countries, Guatemala City, Lake Nicaragua, San José, Panama City, and the Panama.

Reading for the Main Idea

1. *Human Systems* What two European powers had Central American colonies by the late 1600s?

2. *Human Systems* How do many Central American communities honor certain Roman Catholic saints?

Critical Thinking

3. **Finding the Main Idea** How do Central America's people, languages, and religions reflect the region's history?

4. **Contrasting** How has Costa Rica's history differed from that of its Central American neighbors?

Organizing What You Know

5. **Categorizing** Copy the following graphic organizer. Use it to write at least one important fact about each Central American country today. Add as many rows as needed to list all of the countries.

Guatemala	

Section 3 — The Caribbean Islands

Read to Discover

1. What was the Caribbean's history like?
2. How is the region's history reflected in its people today?
3. What are the countries of the Caribbean like today?

Define

Santería
calypso
reggae
merengue
guerrilla
refugees
cooperatives
plantains
commonwealth

Locate

Havana
Port-au-Prince
Santo Domingo

WHY IT MATTERS

Cuba and the United States have had a difficult relationship for many years. Use or other **current events** sources to learn about problems that trouble U.S.–Cuban relations. Record your findings in your journal.

A guiro, a musical instrument

History

The Caribbean islands include 13 independent countries. All are former European colonies.

Early History Christopher Columbus first sailed into the Caribbean Sea for Spain in 1492. He thought he had reached the Indies, or the islands near India. He called the islands the West Indies and the people who lived there Indians. Spain established colonies there. Many Caribbean Indians died from disease or war.

In the 1600s and 1700s, the English, French, Dutch, and Danish also established Caribbean colonies. They built large plantations on the islands. Crops included sugarcane, tobacco, and cotton. Europeans brought Africans to work as slaves.

Independence A slave revolt won Haiti its independence from France in 1804. By the mid-1800s the Dominican Republic had also won independence. The United States took Cuba from Spain in the Spanish-American War in 1898. Cuba gained independence in 1902. Other Caribbean countries did not gain independence until the last half of the 1900s.

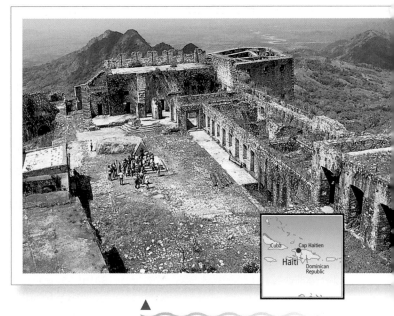

Tourists still visit Christophe's Citadel in Haiti. The fortress was built in the early 1800s after Haiti won independence from France.

✓ **READING CHECK:** *Human Systems* What was the early history of the Caribbean islands?

Caribbean Islands

Country	Population/ Growth Rate	Life Expectancy	Literacy Rate	Per Capita GDP
Antigua and Barbuda	66,970 0.7%	69, male 73, female	89%	$8,200
Bahamas	297,852 .93%	67, male 74, female	98%	$15,000
Barbados	275,330 0.5%	71, male 76, female	97%	$14,500
Cuba	11,184,023 0.4%	74, male 79, female	96%	$1,700
Dominica	70,786 -.98%	71, male 77, female	94%	$4,000
Dominican Republic	8,581,447 1.6%	71, male 76, female	82%	$5,700
Grenada	89,227 -0.06%	63, male 66, female	98%	$4,400
Haiti	6,964,549 1.4%	47, male 51, female	45%	$1,800
Jamaica	2,665,636 0.5%	74, male 78, female	85%	$3,700
St. Kitts and Nevis	38,756 -0.11%	68, male 74, female	97%	$7,000
St. Lucia	158,178 1.23%	69, male 76, female	67%	$4,500
St. Vincent and the Grenadines	115,942 0.4%	71, male 74, female	96%	$2,800
Trinidad and Tobago	1,169,682 -0.51%	66, male 71, female	98%	$9,500
United States	281,421,906 0.9%	74, male 80, female	97%	$36,200

Sources: Central Intelligence Agency, *The World Factbook 2001;* U.S. Census Bureau

Interpreting the Chart Why might life expectancy be greater in some Caribbean island countries than in others?

Culture

Today, nearly every Caribbean island shows the signs of past colonialism and slavery. These signs can be seen in the region's culture.

People, Languages, and Religion

Most islanders are of African or European descent or are a mixture of the two. Much smaller numbers of Asians also live there. Chinese and other Asians came to work on the plantations after slavery ended in the region.

English, French, and mixtures of European and African languages are spoken on many islands. For example, Haitians speak French and Creole. Creole is a Haitian dialect of French. Spanish is spoken in Cuba, the Dominican Republic, Puerto Rico, and some small islands. Dutch is the main language on several territories of the Netherlands.

Another sign of the region's past are the religions practiced there. Protestant Christians are most numerous on islands that were British territories. Former French and Spanish territories have large numbers of Roman Catholics. On all the islands, some people practice a combination of Catholicism and traditional African religions. One of these religions is **Santería**. Santería began in Cuba and spread to nearby islands and parts of the United States. It has roots in West African religions and traditions.

Food, Festivals, and Music Caribbean cooking today relies on fresh fruits, vegetables, and fish or meat. Milk or preserved foods like cheese or pickled fish are seldom used. Cooking has been influenced by foods brought from Africa, Asia, and elsewhere. For example, the samosa—a spicy, deep-fried pastry—has its origins in India. Other popular foods include mangoes, rice, yams, and okra.

People on each Caribbean island celebrate a variety of holidays. One of the biggest and most widespread is Carnival. Carnival is a time of feasts and parties before the Christian season of Lent. It is celebrated with big parades and beautiful costumes.

The islands' musical styles are popular far beyond the Caribbean. Trinidad and Tobago is the home of steel-drum and **calypso** music. Jamaica is famous as the birthplace of **reggae** music. **Merengue** is the national music and dance of the Dominican Republic.

Caribbean musical styles have many fans in the United States. However, the United States has influenced Caribbean culture as well. For example, baseball has become a popular sport in the region. It is particularly popular in the Dominican Republic and Cuba. A number of successful professional baseball players in the United States come from Caribbean countries.

✓ **READING CHECK:** (*Human Systems*) How do the cultures of the Caribbean islands reflect historical events?

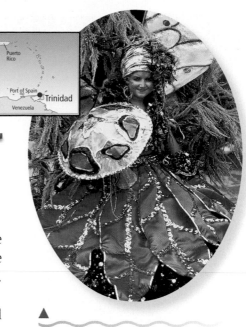

A girl joins the Carnival celebration in Trinidad and Tobago.
Interpreting the Visual Record **What does the elaborate costume imply about the popularity of Carnival?**

The Caribbean Islands Today

Now we will look at the largest island countries. We also will examine the island territory of Puerto Rico.

Cuba Cuba is the largest and the most populous country in the Caribbean. It is about the size of Tennessee but has more than twice the population. It is located just 90 miles (145 km) south of Florida. Havana, the capital, is the country's largest and most important city.

Cuba has had a Communist government since Fidel Castro seized power in 1959. Cuba has supported Communist **guerrilla** movements trying to overthrow other governments. A guerrilla takes part in irregular warfare, such as raids.

Many Cubans who oppose Castro have become **refugees** in the United States. A refugee is someone who flees to another country, usually for economic or political reasons. Many Cuban refugees and their families have become U.S. citizens. Most live in Florida.

The U.S. government has banned trade with Cuba. It also has restricted travel by U.S. citizens to the island since the 1960s. For years Cuba received economic aid and energy supplies from the Soviet Union. The collapse of the Soviet Union in the early 1990s has hurt Cuba's economy.

Today, private businesses remain limited in Cuba. Most farmland is organized into **cooperatives** and government-owned sugarcane

A worker cuts sugarcane in central Cuba. Sugarcane is Cuba's most important cash crop.

plantations. A cooperative is an organization owned by its members and operated for their mutual benefit.

Sugarcane remains Cuba's most important crop and export. Tourism has also become an important part of the economy. There has been debate in the United States over ending the ban on trade and travel to Cuba.

Haiti Haiti occupies the mountainous western third of the island of Hispaniola. It is the poorest country in the Americas. It is also one of the most densely populated. Its people have suffered under many corrupt governments during the last two centuries. Many Haitian refugees have come to the United States to escape poverty and political violence.

Port-au-Prince (pohr-toh-PRINS) is the national capital and center of industry. Coffee and sugarcane are two of the country's most important crops. Most Haitians farm small plots. Many grow **plantains**. Plantains are a type of banana used in cooking.

Dominican Republic The Dominican Republic occupies the eastern part of Hispaniola. It is a former Spanish colony. The capital is Santo Domingo. Santo Domingo was the first permanent European settlement in the Western Hemisphere.

Other Island Countries

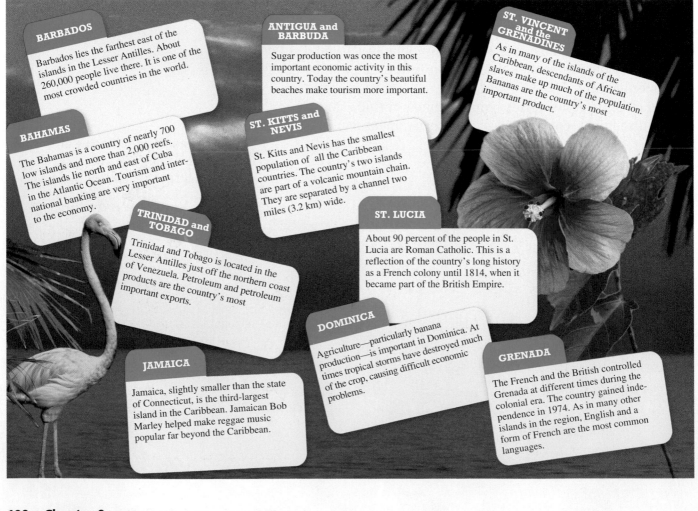

BARBADOS
Barbados lies the farthest east of the islands in the Lesser Antilles. About 260,000 people live there. It is one of the most crowded countries in the world.

BAHAMAS
The Bahamas is a country of nearly 700 low islands and more than 2,000 reefs. The islands lie north and east of Cuba in the Atlantic Ocean. Tourism and international banking are very important to the economy.

TRINIDAD and TOBAGO
Trinidad and Tobago is located in the Lesser Antilles just off the northern coast of Venezuela. Petroleum and petroleum products are the country's most important exports.

JAMAICA
Jamaica, slightly smaller than the state of Connecticut, is the third-largest island in the Caribbean. Jamaican Bob Marley helped make reggae music popular far beyond the Caribbean.

ANTIGUA and BARBUDA
Sugar production was once the most important economic activity in this country. Today the country's beautiful beaches make tourism more important.

ST. KITTS and NEVIS
St. Kitts and Nevis has the smallest population of all the Caribbean countries. The country's two islands are part of a volcanic mountain chain. They are separated by a channel two miles (3.2 km) wide.

ST. LUCIA
About 90 percent of the people in St. Lucia are Roman Catholic. This is a reflection of the country's long history as a French colony until 1814, when it became part of the British Empire.

DOMINICA
Agriculture—particularly banana production—is important in Dominica. At times tropical storms have destroyed much of the crop, causing difficult economic problems.

ST. VINCENT and the GRENADINES
As in many of the islands of the Caribbean, descendants of African slaves make up much of the population. Bananas are the country's most important product.

GRENADA
The French and the British controlled Grenada at different times during the colonial era. The country gained independence in 1974. As in many other islands in the region, English and a form of French are the most common languages.

The Dominican Republic is not a rich country. However, its economy, education, health care, and housing are more developed than Haiti's. Agriculture and tourism are important parts of the Dominican Republic's economy.

Puerto Rico Puerto Rico is the easternmost of the Greater Antilles. Once a Spanish colony, today it is a U.S. **commonwealth**. A commonwealth is a self-governing territory associated with another country. Puerto Ricans are U.S. citizens. However, they have no voting representation in the U.S. Congress.

Unemployment is higher and wages are lower in Puerto Rico than in the United States. Still, American aid and investment has helped make the economy of Puerto Rico more developed than those of other Caribbean islands. Puerto Ricans continue to debate whether their island should remain a commonwealth. Some want it to become an American state or an independent country.

Other Islands Jamaica, in the Greater Antilles, is the largest of the remaining Caribbean countries. The smallest country is St. Kitts and Nevis in the Lesser Antilles. The smallest U.S. state, Rhode Island, is nearly 12 times larger! For more about other Caribbean countries and the Bahamas, see the Other Island Countries illustration.

A number of Caribbean and nearby islands are territories of other countries. These territories include the U.S. and British Virgin Islands. The Netherlands and France also have Caribbean territories. Bermuda, an Atlantic island northwest of the Caribbean, is a British territory.

✔ **READING CHECK:** *Human Systems* How are Puerto Rican citizens' political rights different from those of other U.S. citizens?

Ocho Rios, Jamaica, and other beautiful Caribbean resorts and beaches attract many tourists.
Interpreting the Visual Record Why do you think cruise ships like the one in the photo are a popular way to travel in the Caribbean?

Section Review 3

Homework Practice Online
Keyword: SG3 HP9

Define and explain: Santería, calypso, reggae, merengue, guerrilla, refugees, cooperatives, plantains, commonwealth

Working with Sketch Maps On the map you created in Section 2, label the Caribbean countries, Havana, Port-au-Prince, and Santo Domingo.

Reading for the Main Idea

1. *Human Systems* When did European powers establish colonies in the Caribbean islands?

2. *Human Systems* What ethnic groups make up the region's population today?

3. *Human Systems* Why have Cubans and Haitians come to the United States as refugees?

Critical Thinking

4. **Comparing/Contrasting** What do the histories of Caribbean countries have in common with the history of the United States? How are they different?

Organizing What You Know

5. **Sequencing** Copy the following graphic organizer. Use it to show important events and periods in the history of the Caribbean islands since 1492.

| 1492 | 1600 | 1700 | 1804 | 1902 | 1959 |

Reviewing What You Know

Building Vocabulary

On a separate sheet of paper, write sentences to define each of the following words.

1. archipelago
2. cloud forest
3. bauxite
4. cacao
5. dictators
6. cardamom
7. civil war
8. ecotourism
9. Santería
10. calypso
11. guerrilla
12. refugees
13. cooperatives
14. plantains
15. commonwealth

Reviewing the Main Ideas

1. (*Places and Regions*) What two main island groups make up the Caribbean archipelago?
2. (*Human Systems*) When did European powers begin establishing colonies in Central America and the Caribbean islands? What were some effects on the region?
3. (*Places and Regions*) Which is the most populous country in Central America? in the Caribbean?
4. (*Human Systems*) What are some musical styles with origins in the Caribbean? What influence have they had abroad?
5. (*Human Systems*) How is the government of Cuba organized?

Understanding Environment and Society

Resource Use

Prepare a presentation and thematic map on ecotourism in the region. As you prepare your report, you may want to consider the following points:

- Which countries are among the most popular tourist destinations, and why.
- Which activities are most popular among tourists.
- How humans threaten the natural environment of the region.

Thinking Critically

1. **Drawing Inferences and Conclusions** How did slavery affect the ethnic diversity of the region?
2. **Comparing** What do the governments of all Central American countries have in common?
3. **Finding the Main Idea** Why have refugees from Cuba and Haiti come to the United States?
4. **Summarizing** What agricultural products are grown in many Central American and Caribbean countries? Why?
5. **Analyzing Information** What are some of the natural and environmental hazards in Central America and the Caribbean islands? How do you think people may have coped with these hazards?

Map ACTIVITY

On a separate sheet of paper, match the letters on the map with their correct labels.

Guatemala	Haiti
Nicaragua	Dominican Republic
Panama	Puerto Rico
Cuba	Bahamas
Jamaica	Havana

Mental Mapping Skills ACTIVITY

On a separate sheet of paper, draw a freehand map of Central America and the Caribbean. Make a key for your map and label the following:

Caribbean Sea	Lesser Antilles
Central America	Panama Canal
Greater Antilles	Santo Domingo

WRITING ACTIVITY Imagine that you have been asked to write a paragraph for a travel brochure about Central America and the Caribbean. Your paragraph should include information that tourists would want to know. This includes general information about the region's climates, vegetation, food, festivals, and other special celebrations. Be sure to use standard grammar, sentence structure, spelling, and punctuation.

Alternative Assessment

Portfolio ACTIVITY

Learning About Your Local Geography

Research Project Are Caribbean musical styles popular in your community? Design a poster advertising a festival of music that is popular where you live.

⊿ internet connect

Internet Activity: go.hrw.com
KEYWORD: SG3 GT9

Choose a topic to explore about Central America and the Caribbean islands:
- Plan an ecotour of Central America.
- Learn more about the Panama Canal.
- Hunt for hurricanes.

go.hrw.com

CHAPTER 10

Caribbean South America

Caribbean South America is a region of varied landscapes. The fertile valleys in the Andes and the rich land near the Caribbean shore were important to Spain's empire.

My name is Jorge and I live in Armenia in northwestern Colombia. Armenia is a big city about 8 hours from the capital, Bogotá. I live in a big house in the northern part of the city with my three younger brothers, my mother and father, my grandmother, and our big black dog, Rocca. Our house has two floors around a courtyard with flowers—it is pink with yellow shutters.

My father is a merchant and a farm-owner. The farm, or hacienda, is in the country about 45 minutes away by car. About 60 people work for my father there, growing coffee, plantains, yucca, and fruits like strawberries and oranges. We also raise chickens and pigs. My dad has a fleet of five trucks to carry our produce into the city for sale to groceries and restaurants. My mom has three people to help with the cooking at the farm.

¡Hola!
¿Cómo estas?

Translation: Hello! How are you?

Section 1 Physical Geography

Read to Discover

1. What are the major landforms and rivers of Caribbean South America?
2. What climate and vegetation types are found in the region?
3. What are the natural resources of this region?

Define

cordillera
tepuís
Llanos

Locate

Andes
Guiana Highlands
Orinoco River

WHY IT MATTERS

The varied physical geography of Caribbean South America has contributed to the cultural diversity of the region. Use CNNfyi.com or other **current events** sources to learn more about the geography of Caribbean South America. Record your findings in your journal.

Spectacled caiman— a crocodile

Caribbean South America: Physical-Political

SCALE
0   200   400 Miles
0   200   400 Kilometers
Projection: Modified Chamberlin Trimetric

ELEVATION

	FEET	METERS
⊛ National capitals	13,120	4,000
	6,560	2,000
• Other cities	1,640	500
	656	200
(Sea level) 0	0 (Sea level)
Below sea level	Below sea level

CARIBBEAN SEA

Pico Cristóbal Colón 19,020 ft. (5795 m)

Caracas

Lake Maracaibo

CENTRAL AMERICA

Orinoco River

ATLANTIC OCEAN

LLANOS

VENEZUELA

Angel Falls

Georgetown

Paramaribo

GUYANA

Devil's Island (FRANCE)

Kourou

Magdalena River

Bogotá

Orinoco River

GUIANA

Cayenne

SURINAME

FRENCH GUIANA (FRANCE)

Cauca River

COLOMBIA

ANDES

HIGHLANDS

PACIFIC OCEAN

Equator

AMAZON BASIN

Equator

Amazon River

SOUTH AMERICA

Size comparison of Caribbean South America to the contiguous United States

Physical Features

A rugged landscape and dense forests have often separated peoples and cultures in this region. In the west, the Andes (AN-deez) rise above 18,000 feet (5,486 m). Here the mountain range forms a three-pronged **cordillera** (kawr-duhl-YER-uh). A cordillera is a mountain system made up of parallel ranges. Many active volcanoes and earthquakes shake these mountains.

In the east the Guiana Highlands have been eroding for millions of years. However, some of the steep-sided plateaus are capped by sandstone layers that have resisted erosion. These unusual formations are called *tepuís* (tay-PWEEZ). They can reach approximately 3,000 to 6,000 feet (914 to 1,829 m) above the surrounding plains.

Between these two upland areas are the vast plains of the Orinoco (OHR-ee-NOH-koh) River basin. These plains are the **Llanos** (LAH-nohs) of eastern Colombia and western Venezuela. The northeastern edge of the Guiana Highlands slopes down to a fertile coastal plain in Guyana, Suriname, and French Guiana.

Of the region's many rivers, the Orinoco is the longest. It flows for about 1,281 miles (2,061 km) through the region on its way to the Atlantic Ocean. Large oceangoing ships can travel upriver on the Orinoco for about 225 miles (362 km).

Some remarkable animals live in and around the Orinoco. They include aggressive meat-eating fish called piranhas (puh-RAH-nuhz), 200-pound (90-kg) catfish, and crocodiles as long as 20 feet (6 m). More than 1,000 bird species live in the Orinoco River basin.

✓ **READING CHECK:** *Places and Regions* What are this region's major landforms?

Environments in the Andes change with elevation. Five different elevation zones are commonly recognized.

Interpreting the Visual Record
In which elevation zones is it possible to grow crops?

▼

Elevation Zones in the Andes

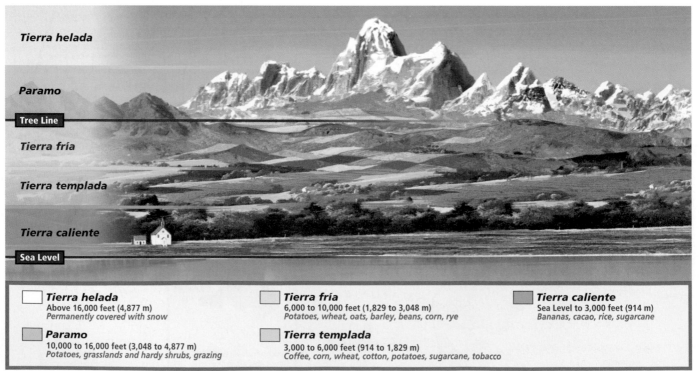

Tierra helada

Paramo

Tree Line

Tierra fría

Tierra templada

Tierra caliente

Sea Level

Tierra helada
Above 16,000 feet (4,877 m)
Permanently covered with snow

Paramo
10,000 to 16,000 feet (3,048 to 4,877 m)
Potatoes, grasslands and hardy shrubs, grazing

Tierra fría
6,000 to 10,000 feet (1,829 to 3,048 m)
Potatoes, wheat, oats, barley, beans, corn, rye

Tierra templada
3,000 to 6,000 feet (914 to 1,829 m)
Coffee, corn, wheat, cotton, potatoes, sugarcane, tobacco

Tierra caliente
Sea Level to 3,000 feet (914 m)
Bananas, cacao, rice, sugarcane

Climate and Vegetation

The climates of the Andes are divided by elevation into five zones. The *tierra caliente* (tee-E-ruh kal-ee-EN-tee), or "hot country," refers to the hot and humid lower elevations near sea level. There is little difference between summer and winter temperatures in this region. Crops such as sugarcane and bananas are grown here.

Higher up the mountains the air becomes cooler. Moist climates with mountain forests are typical here. This zone of pleasant climates is called *tierra templada* (tem-PLAH-duh), or "temperate country." Coffee is a typical crop grown in this area. The next zone is the *tierra fría* (FREE-uh), or "cold country." The *tierra fría* has forests and grasslands. Farmers can grow potatoes and wheat. Bogotá, Colombia's capital, lies in the *tierra fría*. Above the tree line is a zone called the *paramo* (PAH-rah-moh). Grasslands and hardy shrubs are the usual vegetation. Frost may occur on any night of the year in this zone. The *tierra helada* (el-AH-dah), or "frozen country," is the zone of highest elevation. It is always covered with snow.

✔ **READING CHECK:** *Places and Regions* What are the region's climate elevation zones?

South America's capybara is the world's largest rodent. Also called water hogs, capybaras live along lakes and rivers in wet tropical climates.

Resources

Good soil and moderate climates help make the region a rich agricultural area. The region has other valuable resources, including oil, iron ore, and bauxite. Lowland forests provide timber. Coastal areas yield fish and shrimp. Some rivers in the region are used to produce hydroelectric power.

✔ **READING CHECK:** *Environment and Society* How do geographic factors affect economic activities in this region?

Section Review 1

Define and explain: cordillera, *tepuís,* Llanos

Working with Sketch Maps On a map of Caribbean South America that you draw or that your teacher provides, label the following: Andes, Guiana Highlands, and Orinoco River.

Reading for the Main Idea

1. *Physical Systems* What effect do the Andes have on the region's climate?

2. *Environment and Society* Why is the Orinoco River important?

Homework Practice Online
Keyword: SG3 HP10

Critical Thinking

3. **Drawing Inferences and Conclusions** How might Colombia's location affect its trade?

4. **Analyzing Information** Which physical features make farming easier in the region? Why?

Organizing What You Know

5. **Analyzing Information** Use the graphic organizer to describe the climate and vegetation found in traveling from Bogotá to Paramaribo, Suriname.

Bogotá

Paramaribo

Colombia

Read to Discover

1. What are the main periods of Colombia's history?
2. What is Colombia like today?

Define

El Dorado
cassava

Locate

Colombia
Bogotá
Cauca River
Magdalena River

WHY IT MATTERS

Colombia remains a country troubled by violence and conflict. Use CNNfyi.com or other **current events** sources to learn more about problems in Colombia. Record your findings in your journal.

Pre-Columbian gold armor

Early History

Advanced cultures have lived in Colombia for centuries. Some giant mounds of earth, stone statues, and tombs found in Colombia are more than 1,500 years old.

The Chibcha In western Colombia, the Chibcha people had a well-developed civilization. The Chibcha practiced pottery making, weaving, and metalworking. Their gold objects were among the finest in ancient America.

The Chibcha had an interesting custom. New rulers were covered with gold dust and then taken to a lake to wash the gold off. Gold and emerald objects were thrown into the water as the new ruler washed. This custom inspired the legend of **El Dorado** (el duh-RAH-doh), or "the Golden One." The old legend of El Dorado describes a marvelous, rich land.

Spanish Conquest Spanish explorers arrived on the Caribbean coast of South America about 1500. They were helping to expand Spain's new empire. The Spanish conquered the Chibcha and seized much of their treasure. Spaniards and their descendants set up large estates. Powerful Spanish landlords forced South American Indians and enslaved Africans to work the land.

Giant stone figures near the headwaters of the Magdalena River are part of the San Agustín culture.

Interpreting the Visual Record How might the location of these figures in a remote area have helped to preserve them?

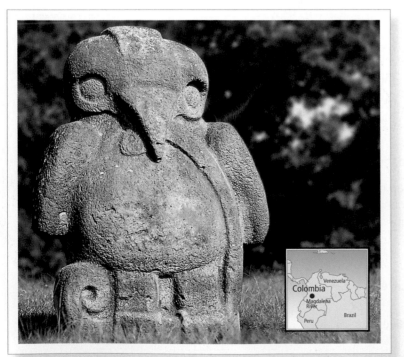

Independence In the late 1700s people in Central and South America began struggling for independence from Spain. After independence was achieved, the Republic of Gran Colombia was created. It included Colombia, Ecuador, Panama, and Venezuela. In 1830 the republic dissolved, and New Granada, now Colombia, was created. Present-day Panama was once part of New Granada.

After independence, debate raged in Colombia. People argued over how much power the central government and the Roman Catholic Church should have. Part of the problem had to do with the country's rugged geography. The different regions of Colombia had little contact with each other. They developed separate economies and identities. Uniting these different groups into one country was hard. Outbreaks of violence throughout the 1800s and 1900s killed thousands of people.

✓ **READING CHECK:** *Environment and Society* What geographic factors influenced Colombia's ability to control its territory?

Colombia				
COUNTRY	**POPULATION/ GROWTH RATE**	**LIFE EXPECTANCY**	**LITERACY RATE**	**PER CAPITA GDP**
Colombia	40,349,388 1.6%	67, male 75, female	91%	$6,200
United States	281,421,906 0.9%	74, male 80, female	97%	$36,200

Sources: Central Intelligence Agency, *The World Factbook 2001*; U.S. Census Bureau

Interpreting the Chart How much larger is the U.S. population than that of Colombia?

Colombia Today

Colombia is Caribbean South America's most populous country. The national capital is Bogotá, a city located high in the eastern Andes. Most Colombians live in the fertile valleys and basins among the mountain ranges because those areas are moderate in climate and good for farming. Rivers, such as the Cauca and Magdalena, flow down from the Andes to the Caribbean. They help connect settlements between the mountains and the coast. Cattle ranches are common in the Llanos. Few people live in the tropical rain forest regions in the south.

The guard tower of an old Spanish fort stands in contrast with the modern buildings of Cartagena, Colombia.

Interpreting the Visual Record
Why might the Spanish have chosen this location for a fort?
▼

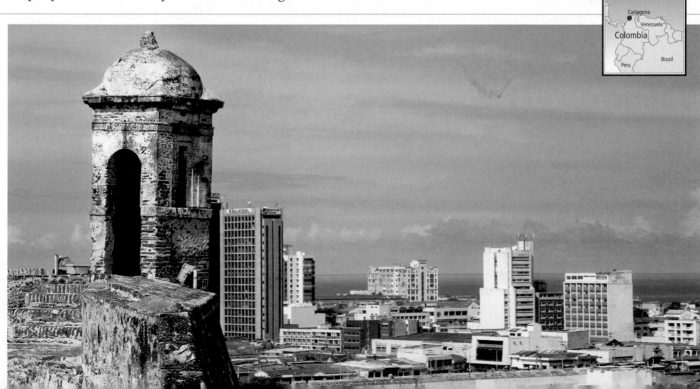

CONNECTING TO *Science*

Botanical print of
a gray cinchona

Fighting Malaria

Malaria is a disease usually transmitted by mosquitoes. It is common in the tropics. For centuries malaria was also widespread in Europe, but Europeans had no remedy. Native peoples in the South American rain forest did have a treatment, though. They used the powdered bark of the cinchona tree, which contains the drug quinine. The history of quinine and the struggle to obtain it is a story of great adventure.

The Spanish first discovered cinchona in the 1500s, when they conquered Peru. Shipments of the bark were soon arriving in Europe, where quinine was produced. Later, some countries tried to control the supply of bark. However, the Dutch smuggled cinchona seeds out of South America. They set up their own plantations in the East Indies. Before long, the Netherlands controlled most of the world's supply of quinine.

During World War II, the Axis Powers seized the Netherlands. As a result, the Allies lost their source of quinine. A crisis was prevented when some quinine was smuggled out of Germany and sold on the black market. Since then, scientists have developed synthetic drugs for the treatment of malaria. However, quinine remains an important drug. It is used to treat heart disease and is a key ingredient in tonic water.

Understanding What You Read

1. How did native peoples' use of the cinchona tree change the world?
2. How did political decisions during World War II affect the use of quinine?

Do you remember what you learned about renewable and nonrenewable resources? See Chapter 4 to review.

Economy Colombia's economy relies on several valuable resources. Rich soil produces world-famous Colombian coffee. Only Brazil produces more coffee. Other major export crops include bananas, corn, rice, and sugarcane. **Cassava** (kuh-SAH-vuh), a tropical plant with starchy roots, is an important food crop. Colombian farms also produce flowers that are exported around the world. In fact, only the Netherlands exports more cut flowers than Colombia.

In recent years oil has become Colombia's leading export. Oil is found mainly in eastern Colombia. Other natural resources include iron ore, gold, coal, and tin. Most of the world's emeralds also come from Colombia.

Even with these rich resources, many Colombians have low incomes. Colombia faces the same types of problems as other countries in Central and South America. For example, urban poverty and rapid population growth remain a challenge in Colombia.

Cultural Life The physical geography of Colombia has isolated its regions from one another. This is one reason why the people of Colombia are often known by the area in which they live. African traditions have influenced the songs and dances of the Caribbean coast. Traditional music can be heard in some remote areas. In addition to music, many Colombians enjoy soccer. They also play a Chibcha sport called *tejo*, a type of ringtoss game. Roman Catholicism is the country's main religion.

Conflict is a serious problem in Colombia today. Border conflicts with Venezuela have gone on for many years. Many different groups have waged war with each other and with Colombia's government. These groups have controlled large areas of the country. Many farmers have been forced off of their land, and the economy has been damaged. Because of this instability, the future of Colombia is uncertain.

✔ **READING CHECK:** (*Human Systems*) How have historical events affected life in Colombia today?

Homework Practice Online

Keyword: SG3 HP10

Section Review 2

Define and explain: El Dorado, cassava

Working with Sketch Maps On the map you created in Section 1, label Colombia, Bogotá, and the Cauca and Magdalena Rivers.

Reading for the Main Idea

1. (*Human Systems*) Why did Spanish explorers come to Colombia?

2. (*Human Systems*) What are some characteristics of Colombia's culture?

Critical Thinking

3. Finding the Main Idea How have Colombia's varied landscapes affected its history?

4. Summarizing How have conflicts in Colombia affected its economy?

Organizing What You Know

5. Sequencing Copy the following graphic organizer. Use it to describe Colombia's historical periods.

Early history	Spanish period	Independence	Colombia today

Venezuela

Read to Discover

1. How did the Spanish contribute to Venezuela's history?

2. What are some characteristics of Venezuela's culture?

Define

indigo
caudillos
llaneros
pardos

Locate

Venezuela
Caracas
Lake Maracaibo

Empanadas

WHY IT MATTERS

Changing oil prices can have a dramatic effect on the Venezuelan economy. Use **CNNfyi.com** or other **current events** sources to find information about current oil prices. Record your findings in your journal.

History of Venezuela

There were many small tribes of South American Indians living in Venezuela before the Spanish arrived. Most were led by chiefs and survived by a combination of hunting and farming.

Spanish Conquest Christopher Columbus landed on the Venezuelan coast in 1498. By the early 1500s the Spanish were exploring the area further. They forced South American Indians to dive for pearls and pan for gold. There was little gold, however. The settlers had to turn to agriculture. They grew **indigo** (IN-di-goh) and other crops. Indigo is a plant used to make a deep blue dye. South American Indians were forced to work the fields. When many of them died, plantation owners brought in enslaved Africans to take their place. Some slaves were able to escape. They settled in remote areas and governed themselves.

Indigo was an important crop in Venezuela during colonial times.

Margarita Island in Venezuela was the site of a Spanish fort in the 1500s.

Independence Partly because the colony was so poor, some people in Venezuela revolted against Spain. Simón Bolívar led the fight against the Spanish armies. Bolívar is considered a hero in many South American countries because he led wars of independence throughout the region. The struggle for independence finally ended in 1830, when Venezuela became an independent country.

Throughout the 1800s Venezuelans suffered from dictatorships and civil wars. The country's military leaders were called **caudillos** (kow-THEE-yohs). After oil was discovered, some caudillos kept the country's oil money for themselves. In 1958 the last dictator was forced out of power.

Oil Wealth By the 1970s Venezuela was earning huge sums of money from oil. This wealth allowed part of the population to buy luxuries. However, about 80 percent of the population still lived in poverty. Many of these people moved to the cities to find work. Some settled on the outskirts in shacks that had no running water, sewers, or electricity.

Venezuela's wealth drew many immigrants from Europe and from other South American countries. However, in the 1980s oil prices dropped sharply. Because Venezuela relied on oil for most of its income, the country suffered when prices decreased.

✔ **READING CHECK:** *Human Systems* How did the Spanish contribute to Venezuela's history?

Our Amazing Planet

Venezuela is home to the anaconda—the longest snake in the world. Adult anacondas are more than 15 feet (4.6 m) long.

Venezuela Today

Most Venezuelans live along the Caribbean coast and in the valleys of the nearby mountains. About 85 percent live in cities and towns. Caracas (kuh-RAHK-uhs), the capital, is the center of Venezuelan culture. It is a large city with a modern subway system, busy expressways, and tall office buildings. However, slums circle the city. Poverty in rural areas is also widespread. Still, Venezuela is one of South America's wealthiest countries. It is developing rapidly.

Venezuela				
COUNTRY	**POPULATION/ GROWTH RATE**	**LIFE EXPECTANCY**	**LITERACY RATE**	**PER CAPITA GDP**
Venezuela	23,916,810 1.6%	70, male 77, female	91%	$6,200
United States	281,421,906 0.9%	74, male 80, female	97%	$36,200

Sources: Central Intelligence Agency, *The World Factbook 2001;* U.S. Census Bureau

Interpreting the Chart What is the average life expectancy for someone from Venezuela?

Economy Venezuela's economy is based on oil production. Lake Maracaibo (mah-rah-KY-boh) is a bay of the Caribbean Sea. The rocks under the lake are particularly rich in oil. However, the country is trying to reduce its dependence on oil income.

The Guiana Highlands in the southeast are rich in other minerals, such as iron ore for making steel. Dams on tributaries of the Orinoco River produce hydroelectricity.

Llaneros herd cattle on the large ranches of the Llanos.

Interpreting the Visual Record How do these *llaneros* look similar to cowboys in the United States?

Agriculture Northern Venezuela has small family farms and large commercial farms. ***Llaneros*** (lah-NE-rohs)—cowboys of the Venezuelan Llanos—herd cattle on the many ranches in this region. Few people live in the Guiana Highlands. Some small communities of South American Indians practice traditional slash-and-burn agriculture there.

Cultural Life More than two thirds of Venezuela's population are ***pardos***. They are people of mixed African, European, and South American Indian ancestry. Native groups make up only about 2 percent of the population. They speak more than 25 different languages. Spanish is the official language. Most of the people are Roman Catholics. Some Venezuelan Indians follow the religious practices of their ancestors.

The *joropo*, a lively foot-stomping couples' dance, is Venezuela's national dance. *Toros coleados* is a local sport. In this rodeo event, the contestant pulls a bull down by grabbing its tail. Baseball and soccer are also popular in Venezuela.

✓ **READING CHECK:** *Human Systems* What are some aspects of Venezuela's culture?

go.hrw.com
Homework Practice Online
Keyword: SG3 HP10

Section Review 3

Define and explain: indigo, caudillos, *llaneros, pardos*

Working with Sketch Maps On the map you created in Section 2, label Venezuela, Caracas, and Lake Maracaibo. How does elevation affect the climate of Caracas?

Reading for the Main Idea

1. *Environment and Society* Why did Spanish settlers in Venezuela have to turn to agriculture?

2. *Human Systems* Who led Venezuela's revolt against Spain?

Critical Thinking

3. **Drawing Inferences and Conclusions** Why might Venezuela try to reduce its dependence on oil exports?

4. **Comparing** Compare the population densities of the Caribbean coast and the Guiana Highlands.

Organizing What You Know

5. **Analyzing Information** Copy the following graphic organizer. Use it to explain how oil is related to the history, urban poverty, and economy of Venezuela.

Oil	History	
	Urban poverty	
	Economy	

Section 4

The Guianas

Read to Discover

1. Which countries influenced the early history of the Guianas?
2. How are Guyana, Suriname, and French Guiana similar today?

Define

indentured servants
pidgin languages

Locate

Guyana
Suriname
French Guiana
Georgetown

Paramaribo
Devil's Island
Kourou
Cayenne

WHY IT MATTERS

French Guiana is the site of a modern space center. Use CNNfyi.com or other **current events** sources to find space-related sites that talk about the European Space Agency. Record your findings in your journal.

Decorated Djuka canoe paddle

Early History of the Guianas

Dense tropical rain forests cover much of the region east of Venezuela. Rugged highlands lie to the south. The physical environment of this region kept it somewhat isolated from the rest of South America. Thus, the three countries known as the Guianas (gee-AH-nuhz) have a history quite different from the rest of the continent.

European Settlement Spain was the first European country to claim the Guianas. The Spanish eventually lost the region to settlers from Great Britain, France, and the Netherlands. Sometimes a war fought in Europe determined which country held this corner of South America. The Europeans established coffee, tobacco, and cotton plantations. They brought Africans to work as slaves on these plantations. Sugarcane later became the main crop.

Asian Workers European countries made slavery illegal in the mid-1800s. Colonists in the Guianas needed a new source of labor for their plantations. They brought **indentured servants** from India, China, and Southeast Asia. Indentured servants agree to work for a certain period of time, often in exchange for travel expenses. As these people worked together, they developed **pidgin languages**. Pidgin languages are simple so that people who speak different languages can understand each other.

✓ **READING CHECK:** *Human Systems* What countries influenced the early history of the Guianas?

This Hindu temple is located in Cayenne, French Guiana.

Interpreting the Visual Record
Which architectural features resemble other buildings you have seen? Which features are different?

▼

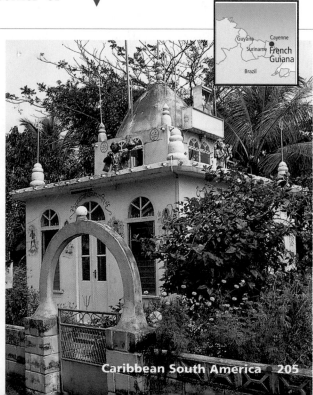

The Guianas

Country	Population/ Growth Rate	Life Expectancy	Literacy Rate	Per Capita GDP
French Guiana	177,562 2.7%	73, male 80, female	83%	$6,000
Guyana	697,181 .07%	61, male 66, female	98%	$4,800
Suriname	433,998 0.6%	69, male 74, female	93%	$3,400
United States	281,421,906 0.9%	74, male 80, female	97%	$36,200

Sources: Central Intelligence Agency, *The World Factbook 2001*; U.S. Census Bureau

Interpreting the Chart Why might the populations of Guyana and Suriname be growing slowly?

Our Amazing Planet

The goliath bird-eating spider of northeastern South America is the largest spider in the world. The record holder had a leg span more than 11 inches (28 cm) across. That is as big as a dinner plate!

The Guianas Today

The area formerly known as British Guiana gained its independence in 1966 and became Guyana. In 1975 Dutch Guiana broke away from the Netherlands to become Suriname. French Guiana remains a part of France.

Guyana *Guyana* (gy-AH-nuh) is a South American Indian word that means "land of waters." Nearly all of Guyana's agricultural lands are located along the narrow coastal plains. Guyana's most important agricultural products are rice and sugar. The country's major mineral resource is bauxite.

Guyana has a diverse population. About half of its people are of South Asian descent. Most of these people farm small plots of land or run small businesses. About one third of the population is descended from African slaves. These people control most of the large businesses and hold most of the government positions. More than one third of the country's population lives in Georgetown, the capital.

Suriname The resources and economy of Suriname (soohr-uh-NAH-muh) are similar to those of Guyana. Many farms in Suriname are found in coastal areas. Aluminum is a major export. Interior forests also supply lumber for export to other countries.

Like Guyana, Suriname has a diverse population. There are South Asians, Africans, Chinese, Indonesians, and people of mixed heritage. Muslim, Hindu, Roman Catholic, and Protestant houses of worship line the streets of the national capital, Paramaribo (pah-rah-MAH-ree-boh). Nearly half of the country's people live there.

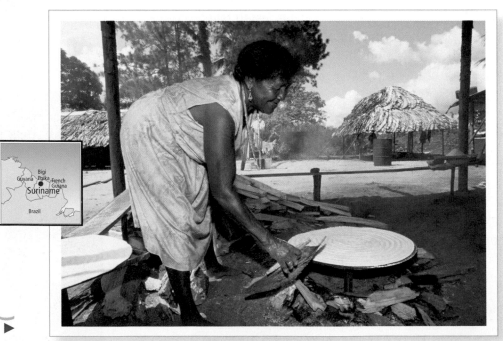

A woman cooks cassava cakes in Bigi Poika, Suriname.

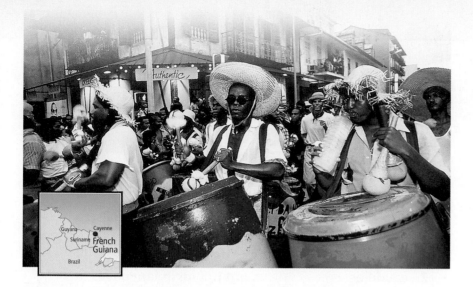

Carnival is a time for celebration in Cayenne, French Guiana.

French Guiana French Guiana (gee-A-nuh) has a status in France similar to that of a state in the United States. It sends representatives to the French Parliament in Paris. France used to send some of its criminals to Devil's Island. This island was a prison colony just off French Guiana's coast. Prisoners there suffered terribly from overwork. Devil's Island was closed in the early 1950s.

Today, forestry and shrimp fishing are the most important economic activities. Agriculture is limited to the coastal areas. The people of French Guiana depend heavily on imports for their food and energy. France developed the town of Kourou (koo-ROO) into a space center. The European Space Agency launches satellites from this town.

More than 160,000 people live in French Guiana, mostly in coastal areas. About two thirds of the people are descended from Africans. Other groups include Europeans, Asians, and South American Indians. The national capital is Cayenne (keye-EN).

✔ **READING CHECK:** (*Human Systems*) How is French Guiana different from Guyana and Suriname?

go.hrw.com
Homework Practice Online
Keyword: SG3 HP10

Section Review 4

Define and explain: indentured servants, pidgin languages

Working with Sketch Maps On the map you created in Section 3, label Guyana, Suriname, French Guiana, Georgetown, Paramaribo, Devil's Island, Kourou, and Cayenne.

Reading for the Main Idea

1. (*Environment and Society*) What crops did early settlers raise in the Guianas?

2. (*Human Systems*) Why did colonists in the Guianas bring indentured servants from Asia?

Critical Thinking

3. **Drawing Inferences and Conclusions** Why might the people of French Guiana prefer to remain a part of France?

4. **Drawing Inferences and Conclusions** Why do you think few people live in the interior of the Guianas?

Organizing What You Know

5. **Categorizing** Copy the following graphic organizer. Use it to describe the Guianas. Fill in the ovals with features of Guyana, Suriname, and French Guiana. In the center, list features they have in common.

Building Vocabulary

On a separate sheet of paper, write sentences to define each of the following

1. cordillera
2. *tepuís*
3. Llanos
4. El Dorado
5. cassava
6. indigo
7. caudillos
8. *llaneros*
9. *pardos*
10. indentured servants
11. pidgin languages

Reviewing the Main Ideas

1. (Places and Regions) What are the five common elevation zones in the Andes region?

2. (Places and Regions) What are three resources found in Caribbean South America?

3. (Environment and Society) How did geography affect political upheavals throughout the history of Colombia?

4. (Human Systems) Why did Venezuela revolt against Spanish colonial rule?

5. (Human Systems) How does the political status of French Guiana differ from that of Guyana and Suriname?

Understanding Environment and Society

Resource Use

Venezuela and Colombia both depend on income from oil exports. Create a presentation in which you use a map, graph, chart, model, or database showing the problems this could cause. You may want to think about the following:

• Why it is risky for a country to rely heavily on a single industry.
• How a country might diversify its export products.

Thinking Critically

1. **Finding the Main Idea** Why is the Orinoco River important to Caribbean South America?

2. **Finding the Main Idea** How might rapid population growth contribute to poverty in the region?

3. **Analyzing Information** Why is Roman Catholicism the main religion in Caribbean South America?

4. **Drawing Inferences and Conclusions** Why do you think most Venezuelans live along the Caribbean coast and in the valleys of the nearby mountains?

5. **Drawing Inferences and Conclusions** How are pidgin languages in the Guianas an example of cultural cooperation?

Map ACTIVITY

On a separate sheet of paper, match the letters on the map with their correct labels.

Andes
Guiana Highlands
Orinoco River
Magdalena River

Lake Maracaibo
Devil's Island
Llanos

Mental Mapping Skills ACTIVITY

On a separate sheet of paper, draw a freehand map of Caribbean South America. Make a key for your map and label:

Atlantic Ocean
Caribbean Sea
Colombia
French Guiana

Guyana
Pacific Ocean
Suriname
Venezuela

W R I T I N G ACTIVITY

Imagine that you are a teacher living in Caracas, Venezuela. Use the chapter map to write a quiz, with answers, for students in your geography class on the geography, economy, and people of Venezuela. Be sure to use standard grammar, sentence structure, spelling, and punctuation.

Alternative Assessment

Portfolio ACTIVITY

Learning About Your Local Geography

Research Project Many South American Indians build homes using local resources. Draw illustrations of some of the oldest buildings. Describe the materials used and their possible origin.

🖅 internet connect

Internet Activity: go.hrw.com
KEYWORD: SG3 GT10

Choose a topic to explore about Caribbean South America:

- Trek through the Guiana Highlands.
- Search for the treasures of El Dorado.
- Ride with the *llaneros* of Venezuela.

go. hrw .com

CHAPTER 11

Atlantic South America

Now we will look at the four countries of Atlantic South America. Below, Mercedes tells us about growing up in Buenos Aires, one of the region's biggest cities.

Hi! I am 13, and I live in Buenos Aires, the capital of Argentina. I live in an apartment with my mom, father, two brothers, and a sister.

I wake up at 6:30 A.M. to get ready for school. For breakfast I have a cup of tea and bread with butter and *dulce de leche* (a caramel spread). It is delicious!

In school I take 12 different classes in one year. They include math, Spanish, art, geography, biology, and language (English). School ends at 1:30 P.M. every day, and then I go home to eat lunch. My mother makes us a large meal that includes meat, pasta or potatoes, soup, and salad. At 2:00 P.M., I go back to school for English.

My favorite holiday is Christmas. My whole family goes to my grandparents' house. We barbecue *lechón* (pork) for dinner and have different types of salads. We eat *turrón*, a honey and almond bar, and a special sweet bread with fruit. At midnight everyone opens their presents.

¡Hola!
Me llamo Mercedes.
Soy de Argentina.

▲

Translation: Hi! My name is Mercedes. I am from Argentina.

Section 1 Physical Geography

Read to Discover

1. What landforms and rivers are found in Atlantic South America?
2. What are the region's climates, vegetation, and wildlife like?
3. What are some of the region's important resources?

Define

Pampas
estuary
soil exhaustion

Locate

Amazon River
Brazilian Highlands
Brazilian Plateau
Gran Chaco
Patagonia

Tierra del Fuego
Andes
Paraná River
Paraguay River
Río de la Plata

WHY IT MATTERS

Itaipu Dam, on the Paraná River between Brazil and Paraguay, is an important source of hydroelectric power. Use CNNfyi.com or other **current events** sources to find out more about dam projects and their consequences. Record your findings in your journal.

Amazon rain forest monkey

Atlantic South America: Physical-Political

SOUTH AMERICA

AMAZON BASIN
Solimões River (Amazon R.)
Amazon River
Manaus
Belém

BRAZIL

PACIFIC OCEAN

MATO GROSSO PLATEAU
Brasília ⊛
São Francisco River
BRAZILIAN HIGHLANDS
Salvador

ATLANTIC OCEAN

Paraguay R.
BRAZILIAN PLATEAU

A N D E S

Pilcomayo River

PARAGUAY
Asunción ⊛
Paraná River
Iguaçu R.
Rio de Janeiro
São Paulo

GRAN CHACO
Uruguay River

Mount Aconcagua 22,834 ft. (6969 m)
Córdoba
P A M P A S
Rosario
URUGUAY
Buenos Aires
Montevideo
Río de la Plata

ARGENTINA

P A T A G O N I A

TIERRA DEL FUEGO
CAPE HORN

Equator

Tropic of Capricorn

N

SCALE
0   500   1000 Miles
0   500   1000 Kilometers

Projection: Modified Chamberlin Trimetric

ELEVATION

FEET	METERS
13,120	4,000
6,560	2,000
1,640	500
656	200
(Sea level) 0	0 (Sea level)
Below sea level	Below sea level

⊛ National capitals
• Other cities

Size comparison of Atlantic South America to the contiguous United States

Physical Features

The region of Atlantic South America includes four countries: Brazil (bruh-ZIL), Argentina (ahr-juhn-TEE-nuh), Uruguay (oo-roo-GWY), and Paraguay (pah-rah-GWY). This vast region covers about two thirds of South America. Brazil alone occupies nearly half of the continent.

Plains and Plateaus This region's landforms include mainly plains and plateaus. The Amazon River basin in northern Brazil is a giant, flat flood plain. To the southeast are the Brazilian Highlands, a region of old, eroded mountains. Farther west is the Brazilian Plateau, an area of upland plains.

South of the Brazilian Plateau is a lower region known as the Gran Chaco (grahn CHAH-koh). The Gran Chaco stretches across parts of Paraguay, Bolivia, and northern Argentina. It is an area of flat, low plains covered with low trees, shrubs, and savannas.

In central Argentina are the wide, grassy plains of the **Pampas**. Patagonia, a desert region of dry plains and plateaus, is in southern Argentina. A cool, windswept island called Tierra del Fuego lies at the southern tip of the continent. Tierra del Fuego and nearby small islands are divided between Argentina and Chile.

Mountains The Andes, South America's highest mountains, extend north-south along Argentina's border with Chile. Here we find the Western Hemisphere's highest peak, Mount Aconcagua (ah-kohn-KAH-gwah). It rises to 22,834 feet (6,960 m).

River Systems The world's largest river system, the Amazon, flows eastward across northern Brazil. The Amazon River is about 4,000 miles (6,436 km) long. It extends from the Andes Mountains to the Atlantic Ocean. Hundreds of tributaries flow into it. Together they drain a vast area. This area includes parts of nearly all of the countries of northern and central South America.

Ranchers herd sheep on the Pampas of Argentina.

Interpreting the Visual Record What other economic activities are common in flat plains regions such as this?

As a result, the Amazon also carries more water than any other river. About 20 percent of the water that runs off Earth's surface flows down the Amazon. This freshwater lowers the salt level of Atlantic waters for more than 100 miles (161 km) out.

The Paraná (pah-rah-NAH) River system drains much of the central part of the region. The Paraná River is 3,030 miles (4,875 km) long. It forms part of Paraguay's borders with Brazil and Argentina. Water from the Paraná flows into the Paraguay River. It continues on to the Río de la Plata (REE-oh day lah PLAH-tah) and the Atlantic Ocean beyond. The Río de la Plata is an **estuary**. An estuary is a partially enclosed body of water where salty seawater and freshwater mix.

✓ **READING CHECK:** *Places and Regions* What are the region's major landforms and rivers?

South America's tropical rain forest blankets an area of about 2.3 million square miles (nearly 6 million sq. km). That is more than two thirds the area of the contiguous United States!

Climate, Vegetation, and Wildlife

Tropical, moist climates are found in northern and coastal areas. They give way to cooler climates in southern and highland areas.

The Rain Forest The Amazon River basin's humid tropical climate supports the world's largest tropical rain forest. Rain falls almost every day in this region. The Amazon rain forest may contain the world's greatest variety of plant and animal life. Animals there include meat-eating fish called piranhas and predators such as jaguars and giant anacondas. The sloth, a mammal related to anteaters, moves slowly through the trees. It feeds on vegetation.

Plains and Plateaus Climates in the Brazilian Highlands vary widely. In the north, the coastal region is covered mostly with tropical rain forests and savannas. Inland from the coast, the highlands become drier and are covered with grasslands. The southeastern highlands have a mostly humid subtropical climate like the southeastern United States. These moist environments are major agricultural areas.

Southwest of the highlands, the Gran Chaco has a humid tropical climate. Because the Gran Chaco is flat, water drains slowly. Summer rains can turn areas of the region into marshlands. Wildlife there includes giant armadillos, pumas, red wolves, and at least 60 snake species.

The temperate grasslands of the Pampas stretch for almost 400 miles (644 km) southwest of the Río de la Plata. The rich soils and humid subtropical climate make the Pampas a major farming region. Farther south, warm summers and cold winters cause great annual temperature ranges in the Patagonia desert. The Andes block the Pacific Ocean's rain-bearing storms from reaching the area.

✓ **READING CHECK:** *Places and Regions* What are the climates of the region?

A sloth makes its way along tree branches in the Amazon rain forest. **Interpreting the Visual Record What do its long, sharp claws allow the sloth to do?**

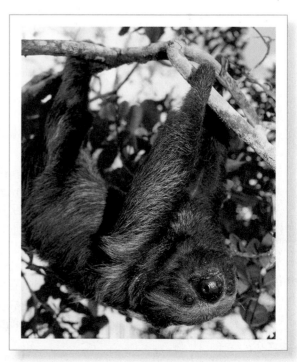

Resources

One of the region's greatest resources is the Amazon rain forest. The rain forest provides food, wood, natural rubber, medicinal plants, and many other products. However, large areas of the rain forest are being cleared for mining, ranching, and farming.

Commercial agriculture is found throughout the region. In some areas, however, planting the same crop every year has caused **soil exhaustion**. Soil exhaustion means that the soil has lost nutrients needed by plants. Overgrazing is also a problem in some places.

The region's mineral wealth includes gold, silver, copper, and iron. There are oil deposits in the region, particularly in Brazil and Patagonia. Some of the region's large rivers provide hydroelectric power. One of the world's largest hydroelectric dams is the Itaipu Dam on the Paraná River. The dam lies between Brazil and Paraguay.

✔ **READING CHECK:** *Environment and Society* How have humans modified the region's environment?

◄

People are clearing large areas of the Amazon rain forest by burning and by cutting.

Interpreting the Visual Record Why do you think someone would choose to clear rain forest areas by burning rather than by cutting?

go.hrw.com
Homework Practice Online
Keyword: SG3 HP11

Section Review 1

Define and explain: Pampas, estuary, soil exhaustion

Working with Sketch Maps On an outline map of the region that you draw or that your teacher provides, label the following: Amazon River, Brazilian Highlands, Brazilian Plateau, Gran Chaco, Patagonia, Tierra del Fuego, Andes, Paraná River, Paraguay River, and Río de la Plata.

Reading for the Main Idea

1. (*Places and Regions*) What major landforms lie between the Amazon River basin and Patagonia?

2. (*Places and Regions*) What sets the Amazon River apart from all of the world's other rivers?

3. (*Places and Regions*) Why is the Patagonia desert dry?

Critical Thinking

4. **Drawing Inferences and Conclusions** How do you think soil exhaustion in Brazil could lead to more deforestation?

Organizing What You Know

5. **Categorizing** Copy the following graphic organizer. Use it to describe Atlantic South America.

Climates	Vegetation and wildlife	Resources

Section 2

Brazil

Read to Discover

1. What is the history of Brazil?
2. What are important characteristics of Brazil's people and culture?
3. What are Brazil's four major regions like today?

Define

favelas

Locate

Rio de Janeiro
São Paulo
Manaus
Belém

Salvador
São Francisco River
Mato Grosso Plateau
Brasília

WHY IT MATTERS

The Amazon rain forest is a tremendous resource for Brazil. Use **CNNfyi.com** or other **current events** sources to find out more about the Amazon region. Record your findings in your journal.

Brazil nuts

History

Most Brazilians are descended from three groups of immigrants. The first group included peoples who probably migrated to the Americas from northern Asia long ago. The second was made up of Portuguese and other Europeans who came after 1500. Africans brought as slaves made up the third group.

First Inhabitants Brazil's first human inhabitants arrived in the region thousands of years ago. They spread throughout the tropical rain forests and savannas.

These peoples developed a way of life based on hunting, fishing, and small-scale farming. They grew crops such as sweet potatoes, beans, and cassava. The root of the cassava plant is ground up and used as an ingredient in many foods in Brazil today. It also is used to make tapioca. Tapioca is a common food in grocery stores in the United States and other countries.

Europeans and Africans After 1500, Portuguese settlers began to move into Brazil. Favorable climates and soil helped make Brazil a large sugar-growing colony. Colonists brought slaves from Africa to work alongside Brazilian Indians on large sugar plantations. Sugar plantations eventually replaced forests along the Atlantic coast.

As elsewhere in the region, Brazilian Indians fought back against early European colonists. However, the Indians could not overcome powerful European forces.

▼

Farther inland, Portuguese settlers set up cattle ranches. These ranches provided hides and dried beef for world markets. In the late 1600s and early 1700s gold and precious gems were discovered in the southeast. A mining boom drew adventurers from around the world. The coastal city of Rio de Janeiro grew during this boom. In the late 1800s southeastern Brazil became a major coffee producer. This coffee boom promoted the growth of São Paulo.

Brazil gained independence from Portugal in 1822. An emperor ruled the country until 1889. Dictators and elected governments have ruled the country at various times since then. Today, Brazil has an elected president and legislature. Like the United States, Brazil provides its citizens the opportunity to participate in the political process through voting and other political activities.

✔ **READING CHECK:** *Human Systems* How have different peoples influenced Brazilian history?

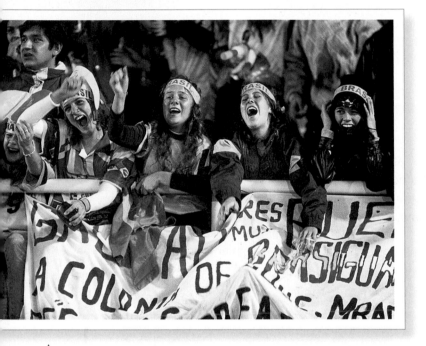

▲
Brazilian fans cheer on their country's soccer team. Soccer is very popular throughout Atlantic South America. Brazilian teams often compete in international tournaments, such as the World Cup.

Interpreting the Visual Record
Why do you think Brazilian fans are wearing the colors green and gold?

People and Culture

Nearly 40 percent of Brazil's more than 170 million people are of mixed African and European descent. More than half of Brazilians are ethnic European. They include descendants of Portuguese, Spaniards, Germans, Italians, and Poles. Portuguese is the official language. Some Brazilians also speak Spanish, English, French, Japanese, and Indian languages.

Religion Brazil has the world's largest population of Roman Catholics. About 70 percent of Brazilians are Catholic. Some Brazilians also practice Macumba (mah-KOOM-bah). Macumba combines African, Indian, and Catholic religious ideas and practices.

Carnival Other aspects of Brazilian life also reflect the country's mix of cultures. For example, Brazilians celebrate Carnival before the Christian season of Lent. However, the celebration mixes traditions from Africa, Brazil, and Europe. During Carnival, Brazilians dance the samba, which was adapted from an African dance.

Food Other examples of immigrant influences can be found in Brazilian foods. In parts of eastern Brazil, an African dish called *vatapá* (vah-tah-PAH) is popular. *Vatapá* mixes seafood, sauces, and red peppers. Many Brazilians also enjoy eating *feijoada* (fay-ZHWAH-da), a stew of black beans and meat. It is traditionally served on Saturday to large groups of people. *Feijoada* has many regional varieties.

✔ **READING CHECK:** *Human Systems* How has cultural borrowing affected Brazilian culture?

Day fades into night in Rio de Janeiro, Brazil's second-largest city. Sugarloaf Mountain stands near the entrance to Guanabara Bay. The Brazilian city is often referred to simply as Rio.

Brazil Today

Brazil is the largest and most populous country in South America. It ranks as the fifth-largest country in the world in both land area and population. Brazil also has the region's largest economy. Many Brazilians are poor, but the country has modern and prosperous areas. We will explore these and other areas by dividing the country into four regions. Those regions are the Amazon, the northeast, the southeast, and the interior. We will start in the Amazon and move southward.

The Amazon The Amazon region covers much of northern and western Brazil. Isolated Indian villages are scattered throughout the region's dense rain forest. Some Indians had little contact with outsiders until recently.

The major inland city in the region is Manaus. More than 1 million people live there. It is the Amazon's major river port and industrial city. South of the Atlantic port of Belém is a large mining district. New roads and mining projects are bringing more people and development to this region. However, development is destroying large areas of the rain forest. It also threatens the way of life of Brazilian Indians who live there. This development has created tensions among the Indians, new settlers, and miners.

The Northeast Northeastern Brazil includes many old colonial cities, such as Salvador. It is Brazil's poorest region. Many people there cannot read, and health care is poor. The region suffers from drought and has had trouble attracting industry. Cities in the region have huge slums called **favelas** (fah-VE-lahs).

Do you remember what you learned about deforestation? See Chapter 4 to review.

Brazil				
COUNTRY	POPULATION/ GROWTH RATE	LIFE EXPECTANCY	LITERACY RATE	PER CAPITA GDP
Brazil	174,468,575 0.9%	59, male 68, female	83%	$6,500
United States	281,421,906 0.9%	74, male 80, female	97%	$36,200

Sources: Central Intelligence Agency, *The World Factbook 2001;* U.S. Census Bureau

Interpreting the Chart How much greater is the U.S. per capita GDP than the Brazilian per capita GDP?

Major Producers of Coffee

- Brazil 25%
- Colombia 10%
- Rest of Middle and South America 26%
- Rest of the world 39%

Source: United Nations, Food and Agriculture Organization

Interpreting the Chart Which single South American country produces the most coffee?

The Southeast Large favelas are also found in other Brazilian cities, particularly in the southeast. Most of Brazil's people live in the southeast. However, in contrast to the northeast, the southeast is Brazil's richest region. It is rich in natural resources and has most of the country's industries and productive farms. The southeast is one of the most productive coffee-growing regions in the world.

The giant cities of São Paulo and Rio de Janeiro are located in the southeast. More than 17.7 million people live in and around São Paulo. It is the largest urban area in South America and the fourth largest in the world. The city is also Brazil's main industrial center.

Rio de Janeiro lies northeast of São Paulo. More than 10 million people live there. The city was Brazil's capital from 1822 until 1960. Today, Rio de Janeiro remains a major seaport and is popular with tourists.

The Interior The interior region is a frontier land of savannas and dry woodlands. It begins in the upper São Francisco River basin and extends to the Mato Grosso Plateau. The region's abundant land and mild climate could one day make it an important agricultural area.

Brasília, the national capital, is located in this region. Brazil's government built the city during the 1950s and 1960s. Government officials hoped the new city would help develop Brazil's interior. It has modern buildings and busy highways. Nearly 2 million people live in Brasília, although it was designed for only 500,000.

✓ **READING CHECK:** *Places and Regions* What are Brazil's four main regions?

go.hrw.com Homework Practice Online Keyword: SG3 HP11

Section Review 2

Define and explain: favelas

Working with Sketch Maps On the map you created in Section 1, label Brazil, Rio de Janeiro, São Paulo, Manaus, Belém, Salvador, São Francisco River, Mato Grosso Plateau, and Brasília. In a margin box, write a caption explaining why Brazil's government built Brasília and how the city has grown over time.

Reading for the Main Idea

1. *Human Systems* From what major immigrant groups are many Brazilians descended?

2. *Places and Regions* What is Brazil's poorest region? What is its richest and most populated region?

Critical Thinking

3. **Drawing Inferences and Conclusions** Why do you think development in the Amazon has caused conflicts among miners, settlers, and Brazilian Indians?

4. **Finding the Main Idea** How did immigration influence Brazilian culture today?

Organizing What You Know

5. **Summarizing** Copy the following graphic organizer. Use it to list how early Brazilian Indians and European settlers and their descendants have used Brazil's natural resources and natural environment. Write each example in a circle radiating from the central circle. Create as many or as few circles as you need.

Interaction with Brazil's Environment

Section 3

Argentina

Read to Discover

1. What is the history of Argentina?
2. What are important characteristics of Argentina's people and culture?
3. What is Argentina like today?

Define

encomienda
gauchos
Mercosur

Locate

Buenos Aires
Córdoba
Rosario

WHY IT MATTERS

Argentina has carried out reforms to mend its economy and promote economic growth. Use **CNNfyi.com** or other **current events** sources to find out about economic reforms in Latin America or other parts of the world. Record your findings in your journal.

Argentine gaucho's belt buckle

History

Like most of South America, what is now Argentina was originally home to groups of Indians. Groups living in the Pampas hunted wild game. Farther north, Indians farmed and built irrigation systems.

Early Argentina In the 1500s Spanish conquerors spread into southern South America. They moved into the region in search of riches they believed they would find there. They called the region Argentina, meaning "land of silver" or "silvery one."

The first Spanish settlement in Argentina was established in the early 1500s. Spanish settlements were organized under the *encomienda* system. Under that system, the Spanish monarch gave land to colonists. These landowners were granted the right to force Indians living there to work the land.

The Pampas became an increasingly important agricultural region during the colonial era. Argentine cowboys, called **gauchos** (GOW-chohz), herded cattle and horses on the open grasslands. Colonists eventually fenced off their lands into huge ranches. They hired gauchos to tend their herds of livestock. Today the gaucho, like the American cowboy, is vanishing. Still, the gaucho lives on in Argentine literature and popular culture.

In 1816 Argentina gained independence. However, a long period of instability and violence followed. Many Indians, particularly in the Pampas, were killed in wars with the Argentine

Examples of Spanish-style architecture can be seen throughout Argentina. This Roman Catholic church was built in the 1600s in Córdoba.

Argentina				
COUNTRY	POPULATION/ GROWTH RATE	LIFE EXPECTANCY	LITERACY RATE	PER CAPITA GDP
Argentina	37,384,816 1.2%	72, male 79, female	96%	$12,900
United States	281,421,906 0.9%	74, male 80, female	97%	$36,200

Sources: Central Intelligence Agency, *The World Factbook 2001;* U.S. Census Bureau

Interpreting the Chart **How does life expectancy in the United States differ from that in Argentina?**

government. As a result, Argentina has a small Indian population today. Most of these wars had ended by the late 1870s.

Modern Argentina New waves of European immigrants came to Argentina in the late 1800s. Immigrants included Italians, Germans, and Spaniards. Exports of meat and other farm products to Europe helped make the country richer.

However, throughout much of the 1900s, Argentina struggled under dictators and military governments. These unlimited governments abused human rights. Both the country's economy and its people suffered. In 1982 Argentina lost a brief war with the United Kingdom over the Falkland Islands. Shortly afterward, Argentina's last military government gave up power to an elected government.

✓ **READING CHECK:** ⟨ *Human Systems* ⟩ How was Argentina's government organized during much of the 1900s?

People and Culture

Argentina's culture has many European ties. Most of the more than 37 million Argentines are Roman Catholic. Most also are descended from Spanish, Italian, or other European settlers. Argentine Indians and mestizos make up only about 3 percent of the population. Spanish is the official language. English, Italian, German, and French are also spoken there.

Beef is an important agricultural product and a big part of the Argentine diet. A popular dish is *parrillada*. It includes sausage and steak served on a small grill. Supper generally is eaten after 9 P.M.

✓ **READING CHECK:** ⟨ *Human Systems* ⟩ Why are so many languages spoken in Argentina?

Couples practice the Argentine tango on a Buenos Aires sidewalk. Varieties of the tango are popular in some other Middle and South American countries and in parts of Spain.

Interpreting the Visual Record **How can you tell that the tango appeals to Argentines of all ages?**

CONNECTING TO *Literature*

Argentine gaucho

The Gaucho Martín Fierro

José Hernández was born in 1834. A sickly boy, he was sent to regain his health on Argentina's Pampas. The gauchos lived freely on the plains there, herding cattle. As an adult, Hernández took part in his country's political struggles. He fled to Brazil after a failed revolt. In 1872 he published his epic poem, The Gaucho Martín Fierro. *In this excerpt, Martín Fierro recalls his happier times as an Argentine cowboy.*

Ah, those times! . . . you felt proud
to see how a man could ride.
When a gaucho really knew his job,
even if the colt went over backwards,
not one of them wouldn't land on his feet
with the halter-rein in his hand. . . .

Even the poorest gaucho
had a string of matching horses;
he could always afford some amusement,
and people were ready for
   anything. . . .
Looking out across the land
you'd see nothing but cattle
   and sky.

When the branding-time came round
that was work to warm you up!
What a crowd! lassoing the running steers
and keen to hold and throw them. . . .
What a time that was! in those days surely
there were champions to be seen. . . .

And the games that would get going
when we were all of us together!
We were always ready for them,
as at times like those
a lot of neighbors would turn up
to help out the regular hands.

Analyzing Primary Sources
1. What does Martín Fierro remember about the "old days"?
2. In what ways is a gaucho's life similar to that of an American cowboy?

Argentina Today

Argentina has rich natural resources and a well-educated population. The Pampas are the most developed agricultural region. About 12 percent of Argentina's labor force works in agriculture. Large ranches and farms produce beef, wheat, and corn for export to other countries.

Much of Argentina's industry is located in and around Buenos Aires, the national capital. Buenos Aires is the second-largest urban area in South America. Its location on the coast and near the Pampas has contributed to its economic development. It is home to nearly a

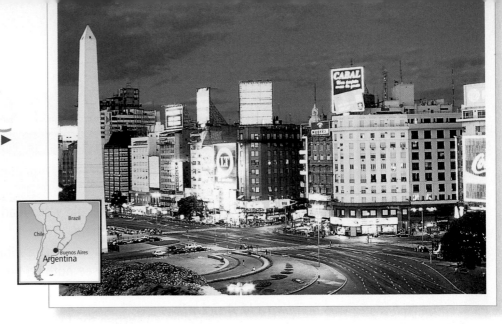

Wide European-style avenues stretch through Buenos Aires. Large advertisements compete for attention in the lively city.

third of all Argentines. Other large Argentine cities include the interior cities of Córdoba and Rosario.

Recent economic reforms in Argentina have been designed to help businesses grow. In addition, Argentina is a member of **Mercosur**. Mercosur is a trade organization that promotes economic cooperation among its members in southern and eastern South America. Brazil, Uruguay, and Paraguay also are members. Chile and Bolivia are associate members of Mercosur.

Argentina has made progress since the return of democracy in 1983. Today, Argentina has an elected president and legislature. The economy has been growing. The country still faces challenges, but Argentines now have more political freedom and economic opportunities.

✔ **READING CHECK:** *Places and Regions* What is Argentina like today?

Section Review 3

Define and explain: *encomienda,* gauchos, Mercosur

Working with Sketch Maps On the map you created in Section 2, label Argentina, Buenos Aires, Córdoba, and Rosario.

Reading for the Main Idea

1. *Human Systems* What happened to Argentine Indians in the Pampas in the 1800s? How did that affect Argentine society?

2. *Places and Regions* Where is much of Argentina's industry located? Why?

go.hrw.com
Homework Practice Online
Keyword: SG3 HP11

Critical Thinking

3. Finding the Main Idea In what ways does Argentine culture reflect European influences? What are some examples of these influences?

4. Analyzing Information How does Mercosur help Argentina's economy grow today? How does location play a part in that process?

Organizing What You Know

5. Sequencing Copy the following time line. Use it to identify important dates, events, and periods in the history of Argentina.

```
+-------+-------+-------+-------+
1500    1600    1800    1900    2000
```

Section 4 · Uruguay and Paraguay

Read to Discover

1. What are the people and economy of Uruguay like today?
2. What are the people and economy of Paraguay like today?

Define

landlocked

Locate

Montevideo
Asunción

Handcrafted Paraguayan fabric

Uruguay

Uruguay lies along the Río de la Plata. The Río de la Plata is the major estuary and waterway of southern South America. It stretches about 170 miles (274 km) inland from the Atlantic Ocean.

Uruguay's capital, Montevideo (mawn-tay-bee-THAY-oh), is located on the north shore of the Río de la Plata. The city is also the business center of the country.

Like its neighbors, Uruguay at times has been ruled by the military. However, in general the country has a strong democratic tradition of respect for political freedom.

Portugal claimed Uruguay during the colonial era. However, the Spanish took over the area by the 1770s. By that time, few Uruguayan Indians remained. Uruguay declared independence from Spain in 1825.

The People People of European descent make up about 88 percent of Uruguay's population. About 12 percent of the population is either mestizo, African, or Indian.

Roman Catholicism is the main religion in the country. Spanish is the official language, but many people also speak Portuguese.

More then 90 percent of Uruguayans live in urban areas. More than a third of the people live in and around Montevideo. The country has a high literacy

Government buildings and monuments surround Independence Square in Montevideo, the capital of Uruguay.

▼

The town of Colonia del Sacramento, Uruguay, was founded in 1680. Today it is an internationally recognized historical site.

rate. In addition, many Uruguayans have good jobs and can afford a wide range of consumer goods.

Economy Uruguay's economy is tied to the economies of Brazil and Argentina. In fact, more than half of Uruguay's foreign trade is with these two Mercosur partners. In addition, many Brazilians and Argentines vacation at beach resorts in Uruguay.

Uruguay's humid subtropical climate and rich soils have helped make agriculture an important part of the economy. As in Argentina, ranchers graze livestock on inland plains. Beef is an important export.

Uruguay has few mineral resources. An important source of energy is hydroelectric power. One big challenge is developing the poor rural areas in the interior, where resources are in short supply.

✓ **READING CHECK:** *Places and Regions* What geographic factors support agriculture in Uruguay?

Uruguay and Paraguay

COUNTRY	POPULATION/ GROWTH RATE	LIFE EXPECTANCY	LITERACY RATE	PER CAPITA GDP
Paraguay	5,734,139 2.6%	71, male 77, female	92%	$4,750
Uruguay	3,360,105 0.7%	72, male 79, female	97%	$9,300
United States	281,421,906 0.9%	74, male 80, female	97%	$36,200

Sources: Central Intelligence Agency, *The World Factbook 2001;* U.S. Census Bureau

Interpreting the Chart How does Paraguay's per capita GDP compare to that of Uruguay?

Paraguay

Paraguay shares borders with Bolivia, Brazil, and Argentina. It is a **landlocked** country. Landlocked means it is completely surrounded by land, with no direct access to the ocean.

The Paraguay River divides the country into two regions. East of the river is the country's most productive agricultural land. The region west of the river is part of the Gran Chaco. This region has low trees and thorny shrubs. Ranchers graze livestock in some parts of western Paraguay.

Spanish settlers claimed Paraguay in the early 1500s. The country won independence from Spain in 1811. Paraguay was ruled off and on by dictators until 1989. Today, the country has an elected government.

The People About 95 percent of Paraguayans are mestizos. European descendants and Paraguayan Indians make up the rest of the population. Spanish is the official language. Almost all people speak both Spanish and Guaraní (gwah-ruh-NEE), an Indian language. As in Uruguay, most people are Roman Catholic.

Asunción (ah-soon-SYOHN) is Paraguay's capital and largest city. It is located along the Paraguay River near the border with Argentina.

Economy Much of Paraguay's wealth is controlled by a few rich families and companies. These families and companies have great influence over the country's government.

Agriculture is an important part of Paraguay's economy. Much of the economy is traditional—many people are subsistence farmers. They grow just enough to feed themselves and their families. In fact, nearly half of the country's workers are farmers. They grow corn, cotton, soybeans, and sugarcane, some for profit. Paraguay also has a market economy, with thousands of small businesses but not much industry. Many Paraguayans have moved to neighboring countries to find work.

Paraguay's future may be promising as the country learns how to use its resources effectively. For example, the country has built hydroelectric dams on the Paraná River. These dams provide Paraguay with much more power than it needs. Paraguay sells the surplus electricity to Brazil and Argentina.

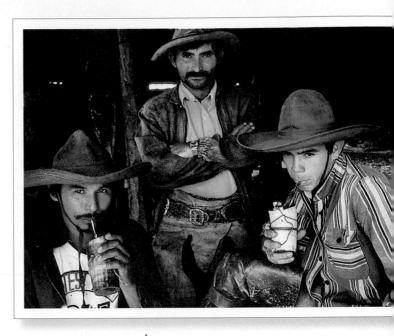

These Paraguayan cowboys are drinking yerba maté (yer-buh MAH-tay). The herbal tea is popular in the region. It is made from the leaves and shoots of a South American shrub called the maté.

✓ **READING CHECK:** (*Human Systems*) How is Paraguay's economy organized?

Section Review 4

go.hrw.com **Homework Practice Online** Keyword: SG3 HP11

Define and explain: landlocked

Working with Sketch Maps On the map you created in Section 3, label Uruguay, Paraguay, Montevideo, and Asunción. In a box in the margin, briefly explain the significance of Montevideo and Asunción.

Reading for the Main Idea

1. (*Human Systems*) When and from what country did Uruguay win independence? What about Paraguay?

2. (*Places and Regions*) Where is Paraguay's most productive agricultural land?

3. (*Environment and Society*) How has Paraguay used its natural resources for economic development?

Critical Thinking

4. **Comparing** What disadvantages do you think a landlocked country might have when compared with countries that are not landlocked?

Organizing What You Know

5. **Comparing/Contrasting** Copy the following graphic organizer. Use it to compare and contrast the populations of Uruguay and Paraguay.

Uruguay	Paraguay

Reviewing What You Know

Building Vocabulary

On a separate sheet of paper, write sentences to define each of the following words.

1. Pampas
2. estuary
3. soil exhaustion
4. favelas
5. *encomienda*
6. gauchos
7. Mercosur
8. landlocked

Reviewing the Main Ideas

1. (Human Systems) Which country in Atlantic South America was a Portuguese colony? What colonial power controlled the other countries before they became independent?

2. (Places and Regions) What major river systems drain much of northern and central Atlantic South America? What economic roles do they play?

3. (Places and Regions) Which is the richest region in Brazil? Which is the poorest?

4. (Places and Regions) What and where is the Río de la Plata?

5. (Places and Regions) What is the most important agricultural area in Argentina?

Understanding Environment and Society

Resource Use

Paraguay and Uruguay both harness energy through hydroelectric dams. Create a presentation on the use of dams for hydroelectric power. Consider the following:

- Government decisions to expand the use of hydroelectric power.
- Benefits of hydroelectric power.
- How hydroelectric power is harnessed.

Thinking Critically

1. How are European influences reflected in the religions, languages, and other cultural characteristics of the countries of Atlantic South America?

2. Why are large areas of Brazil's tropical rain forest being cleared?

3. How do the climates of northern Brazil and southern Argentina differ?

4. How might Mercosur help the economies of the region's countries?

5. How are the ethnic populations of Uruguay and Paraguay different?

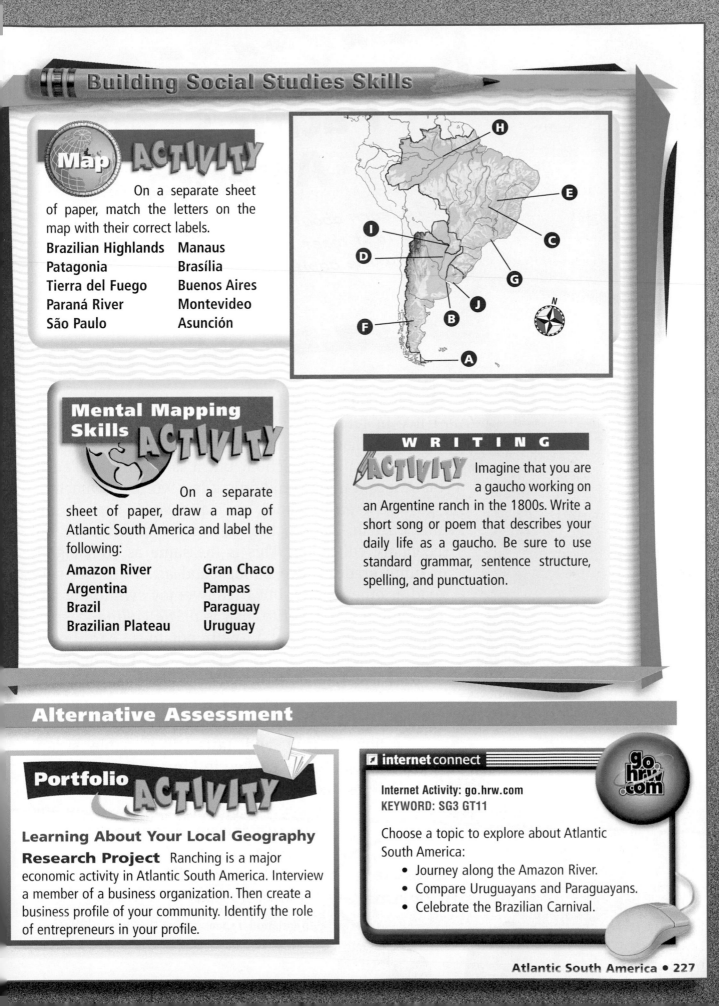

Map ACTIVITY

On a separate sheet of paper, match the letters on the map with their correct labels.

Brazilian Highlands   Manaus
Patagonia   Brasília
Tierra del Fuego   Buenos Aires
Paraná River   Montevideo
São Paulo   Asunción

Mental Mapping Skills ACTIVITY

On a separate sheet of paper, draw a map of Atlantic South America and label the following:

Amazon River   Gran Chaco
Argentina   Pampas
Brazil   Paraguay
Brazilian Plateau   Uruguay

WRITING ACTIVITY

Imagine that you are a gaucho working on an Argentine ranch in the 1800s. Write a short song or poem that describes your daily life as a gaucho. Be sure to use standard grammar, sentence structure, spelling, and punctuation.

Alternative Assessment

Portfolio ACTIVITY

Learning About Your Local Geography

Research Project Ranching is a major economic activity in Atlantic South America. Interview a member of a business organization. Then create a business profile of your community. Identify the role of entrepreneurs in your profile.

internet connect

Internet Activity: go.hrw.com
KEYWORD: SG3 GT11

Choose a topic to explore about Atlantic South America:
- Journey along the Amazon River.
- Compare Uruguayans and Paraguayans.
- Celebrate the Brazilian Carnival.

go.hrw.com

CHAPTER 12

Pacific South America

To learn about Pacific South America, we first meet Mariana. She lives in Lima, the capital of Peru.

Hi! My name is Mariana Gonzales. I am 13 years old. I live in Lima, Peru, with my parents and my twin brother, Alejo. We speak Spanish. There is a Peruvian language called Quechua, but it is mostly spoken in the Andes. I understand only a few words of Quechua. I go to a French school, so I also speak French and some English. I am in the third grade of what we call secondary education. This is the same as your eighth or ninth grade. I love biology and art. I am not very good at other sports, but I really enjoy swimming and badminton. My favorite dish is *ají de gallina*, a spicy chicken dish. We eat it with potatoes, hard-boiled eggs, black olives, and rice. There are lots of delicious exotic fruits in my country. Have you heard of cherimoya, papaya, *cocona*, or *maracuyá*? My favorite dessert is *lucuma* ice cream. It's made from a yellowish fruit and tastes like maple syrup. My favorite place to go in Lima is the Museo de Oro, or "gold museum". The incredible jewelry and other objects there really bring my country's ancient history to life.

As tumpa ta runasimita rimani.

◄

Translation: I speak a little Quechua.

Section 1 — Physical Geography

Read to Discover

1. What are the major physical features of the region?
2. What climates and vegetation exist in this region?
3. What are the region's major resources?

Define

strait
selvas
Peru Current
El Niño

Locate

Andes
Strait of Magellan
Tierra del Fuego
Cape Horn
Amazon River
Iquitos
Altiplano
Lake Titicaca
Lake Poopó
Atacama Desert

WHY IT MATTERS

The Atacama Desert offers a large variety of natural features including mountains, geysers, and the "Valley of the Moon." Use **CNNfyi.com** or other **current events** sources to discover other natural wonders of this area. Record your findings in your journal.

Peruvian hummingbird

Pacific South America: Physical-Political

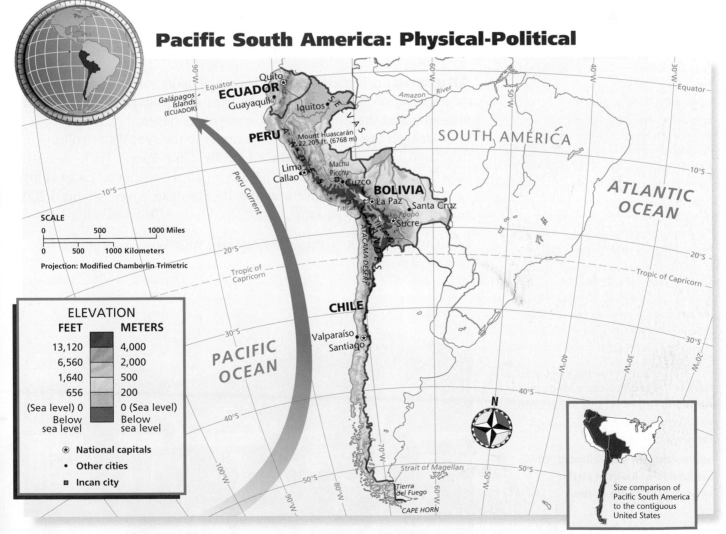

ELEVATION

FEET	METERS
13,120	4,000
6,560	2,000
1,640	500
656	200
(Sea level) 0	0 (Sea level)
Below sea level	Below sea level

⊛ National capitals
• Other cities
◼ Incan city

SCALE
0   500   1000 Miles
0   500   1000 Kilometers
Projection: Modified Chamberlin Trimetric

Size comparison of Pacific South America to the contiguous United States

Physical Features

Shaped like a shoestring, Chile (CHEE-lay) stretches about 2,650 miles (4,264 km) from north to south. However, at its broadest point Chile is just 221 miles (356 km) wide. As its name indicates, Ecuador (E-kwuh-dawr) lies on the equator. Peru (puh-ROO) forms a long curve along the Pacific Ocean. Bolivia (buh-LIV-ee-uh) is landlocked.

Mountains The snowcapped Andes run through all four of the region's countries. Some ridges and volcanic peaks rise more than 20,000 feet (6,096 m) above sea level. Because two tectonic plates meet at the region's edge, earthquakes and volcanoes are constant threats. Sometimes these earthquakes disturb Andean glaciers, sending ice and mud rushing down the mountain slopes.

In Chile's rugged south, the peaks are covered by an ice cap. This ice cap is about 220 miles (354 km) long. Mountains extend to the continent's southern tip. There, the Strait of Magellan links the Atlantic and Pacific Oceans. A **strait** is a narrow passageway that connects two large bodies of water. The large island south of the strait is Tierra del Fuego, or "land of fire." It is divided between Chile and Argentina. At the southernmost tip of the continent, storms swirl around Chile's Cape Horn. Many other islands lie along Chile's southern coast.

Tributaries of the Amazon River begin high in the Andes. In fact, ships can travel upriver about 2,300 miles (3,700 km) on the Amazon. This allows ships to sail from the Atlantic Ocean to Iquitos, Peru.

Altiplano In Ecuador, the Andes range splits into two ridges. The ridges separate further in southern Peru and Bolivia. A broad, high plateau called the Altiplano lies between the ridges.

Rivers on the Altiplano have no outlet to the sea. Water collects in two large lakes, Lake Titicaca and salty Lake Poopó (poh-oh-POH). Lake Titicaca lies at 12,500 feet (3,810 m) above sea level. Large ships carry freight and passengers across it. The lake covers about 3,200 square miles (8,288 sq km).

✔ **READING CHECK:** (*Places and Regions*) What are the major physical features of the region?

BUILD on WHAT You Know

Do you remember what you learned about earthquakes? See Chapter 2 to review.

Llamas are used to carry loads in the Altiplano region. Llamas are related to camels and can travel long distances without water.

Interpreting the Visual Record Why are llamas well suited to the environment of the Andes?

Climate and Vegetation

Climate and vegetation vary widely in Pacific South America. Some areas, such as Chile's central valley, have a mild Mediterranean climate. Other areas have dry, wet, or cold weather conditions.

Grasslands and Forests Mountain environments change with elevation. The Altiplano region between the mountain ridges is a grassland with few trees. Eastern Ecuador, eastern Peru, and northern Bolivia are part of the Amazon River basin. These areas have a humid tropical climate. South Americans call the thick tropical rain forests in this region *selvas*. In Bolivia the rain forest changes to grasslands in the southeast. Far to the south, southern Chile is covered with dense temperate rain forests. Cool, rainy weather is typical of this area of rain forests.

Deserts Northern Chile contains the Atacama Desert. This desert is about 600 miles (965 km) long. Rain is extremely rare, but fog and low clouds are common. They form when the cold **Peru Current** chills warmer air above the ocean's surface. Cloud cover keeps air near the ground from being warmed by the Sun. The area receives almost no sunshine for about six months of the year. Yet it seldom rains. As a result, coastal Chile is one of the cloudiest—and driest— places on Earth.

In Peru, rivers cut through the dry coastal region. They bring snowmelt down from the Andes. About 50 rivers cross Peru. The rivers have made settlement possible in these dry areas.

Our Amazing Planet

The Atacama Desert is one of the driest places on Earth. Some spots in the desert have not received any rain for more than 400 years. Average rainfall is less than 0.004 inches (0.01 cm) per year.

El Niño About every two to seven years, an ocean and weather pattern affects the dry Pacific coast. This weather pattern is called **El Niño**. Cool ocean water near the coast warms. As a result, fish leave what is normally a rich fishing area. Areas along the coast often suffer flooding from heavy rains. El Niño is caused by the buildup of warm water in the Pacific Ocean. Ocean and weather events around the world can be affected. Some scientists think that greenhouse gases made a long El Niño during the 1990s even worse.

✔ **READING CHECK:** *Physical Systems* How does El Niño affect Earth?

Resources

The countries of Pacific South America have many important natural resources. The coastal waters of the Pacific Ocean are rich in fish. Forests in southern Chile and east of the Andes in Peru and Ecuador provide lumber. In addition, the region has oil, natural gas, silver, gold, and other valuable mineral resources. Bolivia has large deposits of tin. It also has resources such as copper, lead, and zinc. Chile has large copper deposits. In fact, Chile is the world's leading producer and exporter of copper.

✔ **READING CHECK:** *Environment and Society* How has Chile's copper supply affected its economy?

▲
A Bolivian miner uses a jackhammer to mine for tin.

go.hrw.com
Homework Practice Online
Keyword: SG3 HP12

Section Review 1

Define strait, *selvas,* Peru Current, El Niño

Working with Sketch Maps On a map of South America that you draw or that your teacher provides, label the following: Andes, Strait of Magellan, Tierra del Fuego, Cape Horn, Amazon River, Iquitos, Altiplano, Lake Titicaca, Lake Poopó, and Atacama Desert. Where is Lake Titicaca, and what is it like?

Reading for the Main Idea

1. (*Places and Regions*) What is the main landform region of Pacific South America?

2. (*Physical Systems*) What is El Niño? What effect does El Niño have on coastal flooding in Peru?

Critical Thinking

3. **Finding the Main Idea** What would you encounter on a journey from Iquitos, Peru, to Tierra del Fuego?

4. **Making Generalizations and Predictions** What problem would people living on the dry coast of Chile experience, and how could they solve it?

Organizing What You Know

5. **Categorizing** Copy the following graphic organizer. Use it to describe the landforms, climate, vegetation, and sources of water of Pacific South America.

	Western	Central	Eastern
Landforms			
Climate			
Vegetation			
Water sources			

Section 2 History and Culture

Read to Discover

1. What were some achievements of the region's early cultures?
2. What was the Inca Empire like?
3. What role did Spain play in the region's history?
4. What governmental problems have the region's people faced?

Define

quinoa
quipus
viceroy
creoles
coup

Locate

Cuzco
Machu Picchu

An ancient gold ornament from Peru

WHY IT MATTERS

Hiram Bingham of Yale University discovered the ruins of the "lost city" of Machu Picchu in 1911. Use CNNfyi.com or other **current events** sources to learn more about famous historical sites in Pacific South America. Record your findings in your journal.

This Peruvian woman is separating seeds from the quinoa plant.

Early Cultures

Thousands of years ago, agriculture became the basis of the region's economy. To raise crops in the steep Andes, early farmers cut terraces into the mountainsides. Peoples of the region developed crops that would be important for centuries to come. They domesticated **quinoa** (KEEN-wah), a native Andean plant that yields nutritious seeds. They also grew many varieties of potatoes. Domesticated animals included the llama (LAH-muh) and alpaca (al-PA-kuh). Both have thick wool and are related to camels. Early inhabitants raised and ate guinea pigs, which are related to mice. The people wove many fabrics from cotton and wool. These fabrics had complicated, beautiful patterns.

Peru's first advanced civilization reached its height in about 900 B.C. The main town was located in an Andean valley. This town contained large stone structures decorated with carved jaguars and other designs. Later, people in coastal areas used sophisticated irrigation systems to store water and control flooding. They also built pyramids about 100 feet (30 m) high. Huge stone carvings remain near the Bolivian shores of Lake Titicaca. They were carved by the people of the Tiahuanaco (TEE-uh-wuh-NAH-koh) culture. Another people scratched outlines of animals and other shapes into the surface of the Peruvian desert. These designs are hundreds of feet long.

✓ **READING CHECK:** *Human Systems* What were some achievements of the region's early cultures?

The ruins of Machu Picchu, an Inca city, were discovered in 1911.

Interpreting the Visual Record Why might the Inca have chosen this site for a settlement?

Quipus were used by the Inca to keep records.

Interpreting the Visual Record How might quipus have made it easier for the Inca to control their empire?

The Inca

By the early 1500s, one people ruled most of the Andes region. This group, the Inca, conquered the other cultures around them. They controlled an area reaching from what is now southern Colombia to central Chile. The Inca Empire stretched from the Pacific Coast inland to the *selvas* of the Amazon rain forest. Perhaps as many as 12 million people from dozens of different ethnic groups were included. The Inca called their empire Tawantinsuyu (tah-WAHN-tin-SOO-yoo), which means "land of the four quarters." Four highways that began in the Inca capital, Cuzco (KOO-skoh), divided the kingdom into four sections.

The Inca Empire The Inca adopted many of the skills of the people they ruled. They built structures out of large stone blocks fitted tightly together without cement. Buildings in the Andean city of Machu Picchu have survived earthquakes and the passing of centuries. Inca metalworkers created gold and silver objects, some decorated with emeralds. Artists made a garden of gold plants with silver stems. They even made gold ears for the corn plants.

Perhaps the Inca's greatest achievement was the organization of their empire. Huge irrigation projects turned deserts into rich farmland that produced food for the large population. A network of thousands of miles of stone-paved roads connected the empire. Along the highways were rest houses, temples, and storerooms. The Inca used storerooms to keep supplies of food. For example, they stored potatoes that had been freeze-dried in the cold mountain air.

To cross the steep Andean valleys, the Inca built suspension bridges of rope. The Inca had no wheeled vehicles or horses. Instead, teams of runners carried messages throughout the land. An important message could be moved up to 150 miles (241 km) in one day.

The runners did not carry letters, however, because the Inca did not have a written language. Instead, they used **quipus** (KEE-pooz). Quipus were complicated systems of knots tied on strings of various colors. Numerical information about important events, populations, animals, and grain supplies was recorded on quipus. Inca officials were trained to read the knots' meaning.

Civil War Although it was rich and efficient, the Inca Empire did not last long. When the Inca emperor died in 1525, a struggle began. Two of his sons fought over who would take his place. About seven years later, his son Atahualpa (ah-tah-WAHL-pah) won the civil war.

✓ **READING CHECK:** *Human Systems* What was the Inca's greatest achievement?

Inca Roads

The road system was one of the greatest achievements of Inca civilization. The roads crossed high mountains, tropical rain forests, and deserts.

The main road, Capac-nan, or "royal road," connected the capitals of Cuzco and Quito. These cities were more than 1,500 miles (2,414 km) apart. This road crossed jungles, swamps, and mountains. It was straight for most of its length. Inca roads were built from precisely cut stones. One Spanish observer described how the builders worked.

> **"** *The Indians who worked these stones used no mortar; they had no steel for cutting and working the stones, and no machines for transporting them; yet so skilled was their work that the joints between the stones were barely noticeable.* **"**

Another longer highway paralleled the coast and joined Capac-nan, creating a highly

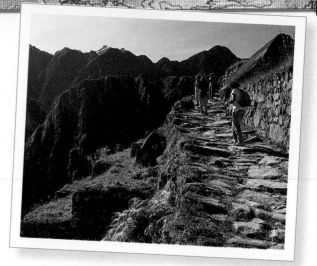

Inca roads had stairways to cross steep peaks.

efficient network. Along these roads were rest houses. The Inca also built suspension bridges to span deep ravines. They built floating bridges to cross wide rivers.

When the Spanish conquered the region in the 1530s, they destroyed the road system. Today, only fragments of the Inca roads still exist.

Understanding What You Read

1. How might the road system have allowed the Inca to control their territory?
2. What were the main features of the Inca road system?

Spain in Pacific South America

While on his way to Cuzco to be crowned, Atahualpa met Spanish explorer Francisco Pizarro. Pizarro's small group of men and horses had recently landed on the continent's shore. Pizarro wanted Inca gold and silver.

Conquest and Revolt Pizarro captured Atahualpa, who ordered his people to fill a room with gold and silver. These riches were supposed to be a ransom for his freedom. However, Pizarro ordered the Inca emperor killed. The Spaniards continued to conquer Inca lands.

The stonework of an Inca temple in Cuzco now forms the foundation of this Catholic church.
Interpreting the Visual Record What does this photo suggest about how the Spanish viewed the religious practices of the Inca?

Simón Bolívar was a soldier and political leader in the early 1800s. He fought against the Spanish and helped win independence for several South American countries.

By 1535 the Inca Empire no longer existed. The last Inca rulers fled into the mountains. A tiny independent state in the foothills of the eastern Andes survived several decades more.

The new Spanish rulers often dealt harshly with the South American Indians. Many Indians had to work in gold and silver mines and on the Spaniards' plantations. Inca temples were replaced by Spanish-style Roman Catholic churches. A **viceroy**, or governor, appointed by the king of Spain enforced Spanish laws and customs.

From time to time, the people rebelled against their Spanish rulers. In 1780 and 1781 an Indian named Tupac Amarú II (too-PAHK ahm-AHR-oo) led a revolt. This revolt spread, but was put down quickly.

Independence By the early 1800s, the desire for independence had grown in South America. The people of Pacific South America began to break away from Spain. **Creoles**, American-born descendants of Europeans, were the main leaders of the revolts. Chile became an independent country in 1818. Ecuador achieved independence in 1822, and Peru became independent two years later. Bolivia became independent in 1825. In the 1880s Bolivia lost a war with Chile. As a result, Bolivia lost its strip of seacoast and became landlocked.

✓ **READING CHECK:** *Human Systems* What was Spain's role in the region's history?

Government

Since gaining their independence, the countries of Pacific South America have had periods during which their governments were unstable. Often military leaders have taken control and limited citizens' rights. However, in recent decades the region's countries have moved toward more democratic forms of government. These governments now face the challenge of widespread poverty.

Ecuador is a democracy. Ecuador's government is working to improve housing, medical care, and literacy. Bolivia has suffered from a series of violent revolutions and military governments. It is now also a democracy. Bolivia has had one of the most stable elected governments in the region in recent years.

Peru's recent history has been particularly troubled. A terrorist group called the Sendero Luminoso, or "shining path," was active in the 1980s. The group carried out deadly guerrilla attacks. With the arrest of the group's leader in 1992, hopes for calm returned. Peru has an elected president and congress.

Chile has also recently ended a long violent period. In 1970, Chileans elected a president who had been influenced by communist ideas. A few years later he was overthrown and killed during a military **coup** (KOO). A coup is a sudden overthrow of a government by a small group of people. In the years after the coup, the military rulers tried to crush their political enemies. The military government was harsh and often violent. Thousands of people were imprisoned or killed. In the late 1980s the power of the rulers began to weaken. After more than 15 years of military rule, Chileans rejected the military dictatorship. A new, democratic government was created. Chileans now enjoy many new freedoms.

▲
Young Peruvians hold a political campaign rally.

✓ **READING CHECK:** (**Human Systems**) How has unlimited government been a problem for some of the nations in the region?

Section Review 2

Homework Practice Online
Keyword: SG3 HP12

Define and explain: quinoa, quipus, viceroy, creoles, coup

Working with Sketch Maps On the map you created in Section 1, label Cuzco and Machu Picchu. Then shade in the area ruled by the Inca. What may have limited Inca expansion eastward?

Reading for the Main Idea

1. (**Human Systems**) How did the Inca communicate across great distances?

2. (**Environment and Society**) What attracted the Spanish conquerors to Pacific South America?

Critical Thinking

3. **Analyzing Information** What governmental problems have many of the region's nations experienced?

4. **Drawing Inferences and Conclusions** Why do you think many leaders of the independence movement were creoles rather than Spaniards?

Organizing What You Know

5. **Sequencing** Copy the following graphic organizer. Use it to show important events in the history of Pacific South America.

☐ ⇨ ☐ ⇨ ☐ ⇨ ☐ ⇨ ☐

Section 3 Pacific South America Today

Read to Discover

1. What are the three regions of Ecuador?
2. How might Bolivia develop its economy?
3. What are the features of Peru's regions?
4. How is Chile different from its neighbors in Pacific South America?

Define

Quechua
junta

Locate

Guayaquil   Callao
Quito   Lima
La Paz   Santiago
Sucre   Valparaíso
Santa Cruz

WHY IT MATTERS

Spanish explorers named the Galapagos Islands in the 1500s. Use **CNNfyi**.com or other **current events** sources to learn more about the Galapagos Islands and the environmental concerns of that area. Record your findings in your journal.

A spicy Andean stew

Ecuador's Galápagos Islands are famous for animals, like these giant tortoises, found nowhere else in the world.

Ecuador Today

Many of Ecuador's people live in the coastal lowland. The country's largest city, Guayaquil (gwy-ah-KEEL), is located there. Guayaquil is Ecuador's major port and commercial center. The coastal lowland has valuable deposits of natural gas. It is also an important agricultural region. Rich fishing waters lie off the coast.

The Andean region in the heart of Ecuador is where Quito, the national capital, is located. Open-air markets and Spanish colonial buildings attract many tourists to Quito. Modern buildings surround the old city.

Large numbers of people are moving to the third region, the eastern lowlands. Here in the Amazon Basin are economically essential oil deposits.

Spanish is the official language of Ecuador. However, about 19 percent of the population speaks South American Indian languages such as **Quechua** (KE-chuh-wuh). Quechua was the language of the Inca. Ecuador's Indians are politically active and are represented in the parliament. However, many of them continue to live in terrible poverty.

✓ **READING CHECK:** *Human Systems*
How do Ecuador's Indians participate in and influence the political process?

La Paz lies in a valley in the Andes. Because of recent population growth, the city has spread up the valley walls.

Interpreting the Visual Record How might the growth of La Paz affect the region's environment?

Bolivia Today

Bolivia has two capitals. La Paz is located in a valley of the Altiplano. At 12,001 feet (3,658 m), it is the highest capital in the world. It is also Bolivia's chief industrial city. Bolivia's congress meets in La Paz but the supreme court meets in Sucre (soo-kray), farther south. The country's fastest-growing region surrounds the city of Santa Cruz, east of the Andes.

In the plains of eastern Bolivia there are few roads and little money for investment. However, the region's fertile soil, adequate rainfall, and grazing land can help in its development. The country has other valuable resources, including natural gas and various metals, such as tin. However, coups and revolutions have slowed development. Bolivia remains a poor country.

Bolivia's population has the highest percentage of Indians of any South American country. Many Bolivian Indians follow customs and lifestyles that have existed for centuries. They often dress in traditional styles. Women wear full, sweeping skirts and derby hats. Men wear striped ponchos.

Bolivian music is bright and festive. Common instruments include flutes, drums, bronze gongs, and copper bells. The charango is a string instrument that resembles a small guitar. Its sound box is made from the shell of an armadillo.

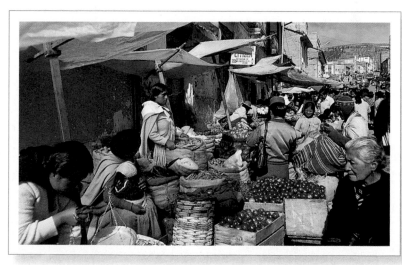

Shoppers buy food at a vegetable market in La Paz.

✔ **READING CHECK:** (*Human Systems*) What is Bolivia's music like?

Pacific South America

Country	Population/ Growth Rate	Life Expectancy	Literacy Rate	Per Capita GDP
Bolivia	8,300,463 1.8%	62, male 67, female	83%	$2,600
Chile	15,328,467 1.1%	73, male 79, female	95%	$10,100
Ecuador	13,183,978 2%	69, male 74, female	90%	$2,900
Peru	27,483,864 1.7%	68, male 73, female	89%	$4,550
United States	281,421,906 0.9%	74, male 80, female	97%	$36,200

Sources: Central Intelligence Agency, *The World Factbook 2001;* U.S. Census Bureau

Interpreting the Chart Why is Bolivia's per capita GDP lower than those of other countries in the region?

Peru Today

Peru is making progress in its struggle against poverty and political violence. However, the government has been criticized for using harsh methods to solve political problems.

Peru, like Ecuador, has three major regions. The dense rain forests in eastern Peru provide lumber. Tropical fruit trees grow there. The Amazon River flows through this region.

The Andes highlands include the Altiplano and the heartland of what was the Inca Empire. Stone structures from the Inca period draw thousands of tourists to Machu Picchu and Cuzco. Potatoes and corn are among the crops grown in this region. Many of the people in the highlands are South American Indians. Millions of Peruvians speak Quechua.

Important mineral deposits are located near the Pacific coast. This is Peru's most modern and developed region. Hydroelectric projects on coastal rivers provide energy. The seaport city of Callao (kah-YAH-oh) serves Lima (LEE-mah), the capital, a few miles inland. Nearly one third of all Peruvians live in these two cities. Callao is Peru's leading fishing and trade center. Industry and government jobs draw many people from the countryside to Lima.

✓ **READING CHECK:** *Human Systems* What draws people to Callao and Lima?

Tourists explore icy landscapes in southern Chile.

Chile Today

In the late 1980s Chile ended the rule of a **junta** (HOOHN-tuh) and became a democracy. A junta is a small group of military officers who rule a country after seizing power. Chile is now also one of the most stable countries in South America. Its economy is also one of the most advanced. Chile's prospects for the future seem bright.

Chile's economy is based on mining, fishing, forestry, and farming. Copper mining is especially important. It accounts for more than one third of the country's exports. In fact, Chile has the world's largest open-pit copper mine. It is located in the Atacama Desert near the town of Chuquicamata.

About one third of all Chileans live in Central Chile. It includes the capital, Santiago, and its nearby seaport, Valparaíso (bahl-pah-rah-EE-soh). The mild Mediterranean climate allows farmers to grow a wide range of crops. Grapes grow well there, and wine is exported around the world. Cool, mountainous southern Chile has forests, oil, and farms. Few people live there, however. Northern Chile includes the Atacama Desert. Croplands along valleys there are irrigated by streams flowing down from the Andes.

Although poverty remains a problem, Chile's economy is becoming stronger. Small businesses and factories are growing quickly. More Chileans are finding work, and wages are rising. Chile hopes that the price of its main export, copper, remains high. Chile's economy would suffer if the world price of copper fell.

Chile wants to expand its trade links with the United States. Some people have suggested that Chile join the North American Free Trade Agreement (NAFTA). This free-trade group currently includes Canada, the United States, and Mexico.

✓ **READING CHECK:** Environment and Society How does copper affect Chile's economy?

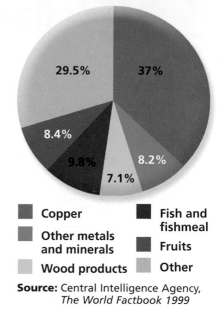

Chile's Export Products

29.5% | 37%
8.4%
9.8% | 8.2%
7.1%

■ Copper   ■ Fish and fishmeal
■ Other metals and minerals   ■ Fruits
■ Wood products   ■ Other

Source: Central Intelligence Agency, *The World Factbook 1999*

Interpreting the Chart What percentage of Chile's export products are metals and minerals?

Section Review 3

go.hrw.com
Homework Practice Online
Keyword: SG3 HP12

Define and explain: Quechua, junta

Working with Sketch Maps On the map you created in Section 2, label Guayaquil, Quito, La Paz, Sucre, Santa Cruz, Callao, Lima, Santiago, and Valparaíso. Why are there so few cities in the eastern part of the region?

Reading for the Main Idea

1. *Places and Regions* What features are drawing people to Ecuador's eastern lowlands?

2. *Human Systems* Why do many people move from the countryside to Lima, Peru?

Critical Thinking

3. Drawing Inferences and Conclusions What might be a disadvantage of Chile depending so heavily on its copper industry?

4. Analyzing Information Why have changes in Bolivia's government slowed development?

Organizing What You Know

5. Summarizing Copy the following graphic organizer. Use it to write phrases that describe each country.

Bolivia	
Chile	
Ecuador	
Peru	

Building Vocabulary

On a separate sheet of paper, write sentences to define each of the following words.

1. strait
2. *selvas*
3. El Niño
4. quinoa
5. quipus
6. viceroy
7. creoles
8. coup
9. Quechua
10. junta

Reviewing the Main Ideas

1. (*Places and Regions*) What is the Altiplano, and what kind of vegetation is found there?

2. (*Physical Systems*) What are some of the effects of El Niño?

3. (*Human Systems*) What are three types of construction projects that helped the Inca organize their empire?

4. (*Human Systems*) What happened when the Spaniards arrived in Pacific South America?

5. (*Human Systems*) What trend have the countries of this region experienced in their forms of government?

6. (*Places and Regions*) How are northern, central, and southern Chile different?

Understanding Environment and Society

Population and Industry

Potosí, Bolivia, has long been a major mining center in the Americas. Create a presentation, including a map, graph, chart, model, or database, on aspects of Potosís mining industry. Consider the following:

- Where tin is mined in the area.
- How much tin Potosí produces each year.
- How a drop in tin production might affect Potosí.

Include a five-question quiz on your presentation to challenge fellow students.

Thinking Critically

1. **Analyzing Information** Why is Spanish the most widely spoken language in Pacific South America?

2. **Drawing Inferences and Conclusions** Why do you think the region's countries have had so many unstable governments since gaining their independence?

3. **Finding the Main Idea** How might Bolivia's landlocked position affect the country's economy?

4. **Analyzing Information** What role do Ecuador's Indians play in its political system? Identify and explain the importance of this role.

Map ACTIVITY

On a separate sheet of paper, match the letters on the map with their correct labels.

Peru Current	Lake Poopó
Strait of	Atacama Desert
Magellan	Quito
Tierra del	La Paz
Fuego	Lima
Amazon River	Santiago

Mental Mapping Skills ACTIVITY

On a separate sheet of paper, draw a freehand map of Pacific South America. Make a key for your map and label the following:

Altiplano	Chile
Andes	Ecuador
Bolivia	Peru

WRITING ACTIVITY

Imagine that you are making a film about Ecuador, Bolivia, Peru, or Chile. Write a summary of the film you would like to make. List land features, industries, peoples, and customs that you want to cover. Explain why you think these topics would be interesting to audiences. Be sure to use standard grammar, spelling, sentence structure, and punctuation.

Alternative Assessment

Portfolio ACTIVITY

Learning About Your Local Geography

Languages Most people in Pacific South America speak Spanish. Research languages in your area. Make a pie chart showing the percentage of people who speak each language.

internet connect

Internet Activity: go.hrw.com
KEYWORD: SG3 GT12

Choose a topic to explore Pacific South America:
- Analyze Chile's climate.
- Hike the Inca Trail and visit Machu Picchu.
- Learn about Andean languages.

Seawater Agriculture

Water is one of the most important resources on Earth. All life needs water to survive. As the world's population grows, more and more places are facing water shortages. For example, freshwater is scarce in Sonora and Baja California, Mexico. People have used up most of the groundwater in the region for agriculture. The water table is so low that many wells can no longer be used.

About 97 percent of Earth's water is in oceans. However, seawater is too salty for people or animals to drink. Most plants will die quickly if they are exposed to seawater. Desalinization machines can make seawater more useful. These machines take the salt out of seawater. However, this process is expensive. Many countries cannot afford it.

Growing Plants in the Desert Some people want to grow salt-tolerant plants in deserts and irrigate them with seawater. Finding crops that can grow in these conditions would allow people to grow more food. Such crops would also ease pressure on freshwater supplies.

Using desert land could also help the environment. Farming in deserts might keep people from clearing forests. The demand for farmland is so great in some places that using the desert could make a difference. In the coming years, new farmland will be needed to feed the world's growing population.

Saltbush, shown here in California's Owens Valley, is one type of salt-tolerant plant that can be used to feed livestock

Many plants do grow along seacoasts and in deserts. Mangrove trees, for example, grow in shallow coastal waters. Some researchers have tried growing various salt-tolerant plants in the coastal deserts of Sonora, Mexico. They were looking for salt-tolerant plants that could be used to feed livestock or people. Three plants—glasswort (*Salicornia*), sea blite (*Suaeda*), and saltbush (*Atriplex*), proved useful for feeding livestock.

A Perfect Crop? Glasswort may be the most promising salt-tolerant plant. Fresh glasswort is a vegetable that can be eaten. Known as "sea asparagus," it is an expensive delicacy in Europe. Glasswort also produces seeds that are high in protein and oil. The oil can be used for cooking. It is similar to safflower oil and has a nutty taste. After the oil is removed, seed meal is left. Seed meal can be used as a protein supplement for livestock. Glasswort's usefulness could greatly help Mexico. For example, Mexico imports seeds used to make cooking oil. Using glasswort seeds grown in Mexico would help the economy and create jobs.

Glasswort is a productive plant. It can be as productive as soybeans or other crops. Growing glasswort does require more water than most crops grown with freshwater. However, irrigating a field with seawater in Sonora cost about one third what it would cost to use freshwater.

Glasswort requires frequent watering because it absorbs water slowly. The water that stays in the ground becomes much saltier than seawater. As a result, the plants must be watered frequently. In sandy desert soils the water quickly drains back to the sea. Therefore, salts do not build up in the root zone. Salt buildup in the soil affects some 20 percent of the world's fields irrigated with freshwater. For example, this has happened in California's Central Valley. When salt buildup occurs, drainage systems must be built. These systems are very expensive.

Growing glasswort can help the environment in another way. Glasswort fields can recycle wastewater from coastal shrimp farms. This

Glasswort grows in shallow, salty water. Research has shown that glasswort can be irrigated with seawater and used to feed both people and animals.

wastewater is high in nutrients. If it is released directly into the ocean, it can cause algae blooms or disease. However, if this water is used to irrigate glasswort fields, the plants absorb many of the nutrients. The water can then be drained back into the ocean.

Researchers hope their work in Mexico will help people in other dry regions. However, it is still too early to tell whether it will be profitable to grow glasswort on a large scale.

Understanding What You Read

1. Why do people want to grow crops with seawater?

2. What are some uses of the glasswort plant?

Building Skills for Life: Understanding Migration Patterns

Many people from Japan migrated to the area around São Paulo, Brazil in the 1900s.

People have always moved to different places. This movement is called migration. Understanding migration patterns is very important in geography. These patterns help explain why certain places are the way they are today. In South America, for example, there are people whose ancestors came from Africa, Asia, Europe, and North America. All of these people migrated to South America sometime in the past.

Why do people migrate? There are many different reasons. Sometimes, people do not want to move, but they are forced to. This is called forced migration. Other times, people migrate because they are looking for a better life. This is an example of voluntary migration.

Geographers who study migration patterns often use the words *push* and *pull*. They identify situations that push people out of places. For example, wars often push people away. They also identify situations that pull people to new places. A better job might pull someone to a

new place. Usually, people migrate for a combination of reasons. They might be pushed from a place because there is not enough farmland. They might also be pulled to a new place by good farmland.

Geographers are also interested in barriers to migration. Barriers make it harder for people to migrate. There are cultural barriers, economic barriers, physical barriers, and political barriers. For example, deserts, mountains, and oceans can make it harder for people to migrate. Unfamiliar languages and ways of life can also block migration.

Migration changes people and places. Both the places that people leave and the places where they arrive are changed. Can you think of some ways that migration has changed the world?

THE SKILL

1. List some factors that can push people out of a place or pull them to a new place.

2. Research the migration of your ancestors or a friend's ancestors. Where did they come from? When did they migrate? Why?

3. Imagine you had to migrate to a new place. Where would you go? Why would you pick this place? Do you think you would be scared, excited, or both?

HANDS on GEOGRAPHY

The following passage was written by a woman from Argentina who migrated to the United States. Read the passage and then answer the Lab Report questions.

" My nephew and I came from a faraway country called Argentina. When I mention this country to others, they say, "Oh, Argentina! It is so beautiful!" However, as beautiful as Argentina is, life there is very difficult now.

In Argentina, there are three social classes: rich, middle class, and poor. The middle class, of which I am a member, is the largest. We are the workers and the businesspeople. Because of bad economic decisions and corrupt government, the middle class has almost disappeared. Factories have closed, and people have no work. The big companies move to other countries. The small businesses depend on the big companies and often have to close. Argentina has a very high rate of unemployment. Many people are hungry.

My husband and I had some friends who worked in Argentina. They advised us to sell everything we owned and move to Houston.

They told us that life was better there and they had relatives who would help us find a house to rent. They told us a lawyer would help us put our papers in order so we could work. I had a small sewing shop with some sewing machines, which I sold so I could travel. "

▲ Poverty and unemployment are problems in some parts of Argentina.
Interpreting the Visual Record What evidence can you see of poor living conditions?

Lab Report

1. What pushed the author out of Argentina?
2. Why did she choose Houston as her destination?
3. According to the author, what do other people think Argentina is like? does she agree?

UNIT 4

Europe

Geirangerfjord, Norway

Regatta on the Grand Canal, Venice, Italy

A Professor in the Czech Republic

Meredith Walker teaches English at Clemson University. She also teaches English As a Second Language courses. Here she describes a visit to Prague, the capital of the Czech Republic. **WHAT DO YOU THINK?** *Does Prague sound like a city you would like to see?*

The castle in Prague sits on a hill high above the Vltava River. This river divides the city. A castle has stood on that hillside for 1,000 years. Rising from the inner courtyard of the castle is a huge medieval building, St. Vitus' Cathedral. Together, the castle and cathedral look almost magical, especially at night when spotlights shine on them. The castle is the most important symbol of the city. A great Czech writer, Franz Kafka, believed that the castle influenced everything and everyone in the city.

Another important landmark in Prague is Charles Bridge, one of eight bridges that cross the Vltava River. The bridge is part of the route that kings once traveled on their way to the castle to be crowned. Today, large crowds of tourists walk there. Many stop to photograph some of the 22 statues that line the bridge. No cars are allowed on the bridge today.

The first time I walked across the bridge, heading up toward the castle, it was at night. Fireworks were lighting the sky all around me. It was a colorful welcome.

Street scene in Prague, Czech Republic

Portuguese girls in native costume

Whooper swan

Understanding Primary Sources

1. How does the city's physical geography help make the castle a symbol of Prague?

2. How did the fireworks display affect Meredith Walker's feelings about Prague?

Europe

Elevation Profile

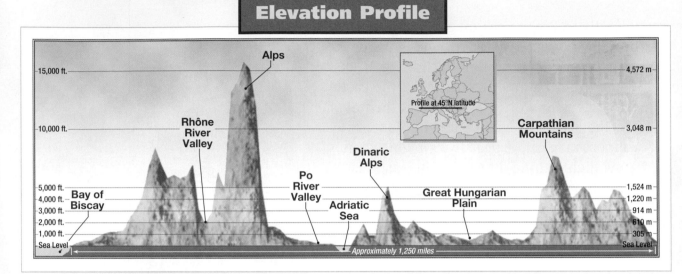

- Alps
- 15,000 ft. — 4,572 m
- Rhône River Valley
- Profile at 45°N latitude
- Carpathian Mountains
- 10,000 ft. — 3,048 m
- Dinaric Alps
- Po River Valley
- Great Hungarian Plain
- 5,000 ft. — 1,524 m
- Bay of Biscay
- 4,000 ft. — 1,220 m
- Adriatic Sea
- 3,000 ft. — 914 m
- 2,000 ft. — 610 m
- 1,000 ft. — 305 m
- Sea Level — Sea Level
- Approximately 1,250 miles

The United States and Europe:
Comparing Sizes

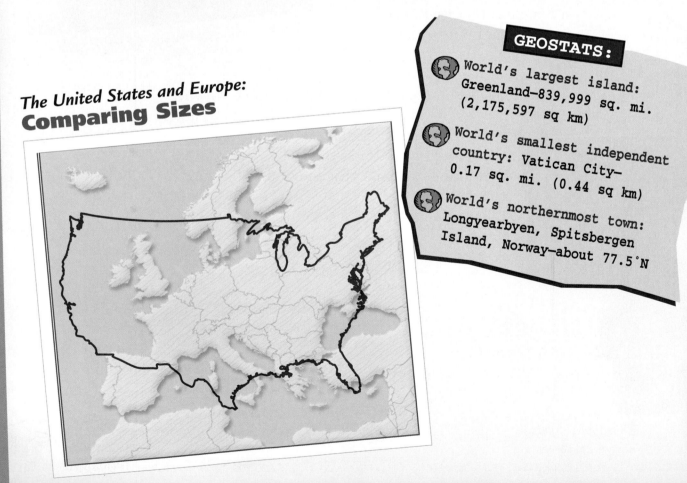

GEOSTATS:

🌍 World's largest island: Greenland–839,999 sq. mi. (2,175,597 sq km)

🌍 World's smallest independent country: Vatican City– 0.17 sq. mi. (0.44 sq km)

🌍 World's northernmost town: Longyearbyen, Spitsbergen Island, Norway–about 77.5°N

ELEVATION

FEET	METERS
13,120	4,000
6,560	2,000
1,640	500
656	200
(Sea level) 0	0 (Sea level)
Below sea level	Below sea level
	Ice caps

SCALE
0   250   500 Miles
0   250   500 Kilometers
Projection: Azimuthal Equal Area

1. (*Places and Regions*) What are two mountain ranges that occupy peninsulas?

2. (*Places and Regions*) What are the two major plains of Europe? Which is larger?

Critical Thinking

3. Analyzing Information In the days before air travel, which physical feature would have made it difficult to travel between Italy and the countries to its north?

4. Analyzing Information Which physical feature would have made travel between Greece, Italy, and Spain fairly easy?

Europe: Political map showing countries, national capitals, and other cities.

Legend:
- Boundaries
- ⊛ National capitals
- • Other cities

Greenland (DENMARK) inset map, SCALE 0 250 500 Miles / 0 250 500 Kilometers, Projection: Polyconic

SCALE 0 250 500 Miles / 0 250 500 Kilometers, Projection: Azimuthal Equal Area

1. *Places and Regions* Which countries border both the Atlantic and the Mediterranean?

2. *Places and Regions* Compare this map to the **physical map** of the region. Which physical feature helps form the boundary between Spain and France?

Critical Thinking

3. Comparing Which countries have the shortest coastlines on the Adriatic Sea?

4. Drawing Inferences and Conclusions The United Kingdom has not been invaded successfully since A.D. 1066. Why?

CLIMATE
- Steppe
- Mediterranean
- Humid subtropical
- Marine west coast
- Humid continental
- Subarctic
- Tundra
- Ice cap
- Highland

Greenland
(DENMARK)

SCALE
0   250   500 Miles
0   250 500 Kilometers
Projection: Polyconic

North Atlantic Drift

ARCTIC   OCEAN

NORWEGIAN
SEA

NORTH
SEA

BALTIC
SEA

NORTHERN
EURASIA

English Channel

ADRIATIC   SEA

AEGEAN
SEA

ATLANTIC
OCEAN

MEDITERRANEAN   SEA

Strait of
Gibraltar

AFRICA

SCALE
0   250   500 Miles
0   250   500 Kilometers
Projection: Azimuthal Equal Area

1. *Physical Systems* Which climate type takes its name from a sea in the region?

2. *Places and Regions* Which two independent countries have climate types that are not found in any other European country? Which climate types do these two countries have?

Critical Thinking

3. **Comparing** Compare this map to the **physical** and **population maps**. Which physical feature in central Europe has a highland climate and relatively few people? This physical feature is in which countries?

ARCTIC OCEAN

Arctic Circle

Denmark Strait

NORWEGIAN SEA

N

Greenland
(DENMARK)

Arctic Circle

ATLANTIC OCEAN

SCALE
0   250   500 Miles
0 250 500 Kilometers
Projection: Polyconic

Helsinki

Stockholm

NORTH SEA   Copenhagen   BALTIC SEA   NORTHERN EURASIA

Rotterdam
Amsterdam   Hamburg
Berlin   Warsaw

London   Katowice

English Channel   Prague

POPULATION DENSITY

Persons per sq. mile		Persons per sq km
520		200
260		100
130		50
25		10
3		1
0		0

Paris

Munich   Vienna

Lyons   Budapest

Milan   Belgrade   Bucharest

Marseilles   Sofia

ADRIATIC SEA

Porto

Madrid   Barcelona   Rome

Lisbon   Naples   AEGEAN SEA

● Metropolitan areas with more than 2 million inhabitants

○ Metropolitan areas with 1 million to 2 million inhabitants

Strait of Gibraltar   MEDITERRANEAN SEA

Athens

Projection: Azimuthal Equal Area

AFRICA

1. (*Places and Regions*) Examine the **climate map**. Why are northern Norway, Sweden, and Finland so thinly populated?

2. (*Places and Regions*) Compare this map to the **political map**. Which countries have between 25 and 130 persons per square mile in all areas?

Critical Thinking

3. Analyzing Information   Use the map to create a chart, graph, database, or model of population centers in Europe.

Europe: Land Use and Resources

Greenland (DENMARK)

SCALE
0 250 500 Miles
0 250 500 Kilometers
Projection: Polyconic

ATLANTIC OCEAN

ARCTIC OCEAN

NORWEGIAN SEA

NORTHERN EURASIA

LAND USE

- Nomadic herding
- Livestock raising
- Commercial farming
- Forests
- Manufacturing
- Limited economic activity
- ● Major manufacturing and trade centers

RESOURCES

- Coal
- U Uranium
- Natural gas
- Other minerals
- Oil
- Seafood
- Nuclear power
- Hydroelectric power
- Geothermal power

Narvik

Oslo
Stockholm
Helsinki

Copenhagen
Rostock
Hamburg
Bremen
Berlin
Warsaw
RUHR
Frankfurt
Prague
Munich
Vienna
Bratislava
Budapest
Bucharest
Zurich
Ljubljana
Lyon
Milan
Turin
Genoa
Marseille
Sofia
Rome
Thessaloniki
Barcelona
Naples
Athens
Palermo
Catania

Dublin
London
Rotterdam
Brussels
Paris

Oporto
Lisbon
Madrid

NORTH SEA
English Channel
BALTIC SEA
ADRIATIC SEA
BLACK SEA
AEGEAN SEA
MEDITERRANEAN SEA

AFRICA

Denmark Strait
Arctic Circle

SCALE
0 250 500 Miles
0 250 500 Kilometers
Projection: Azimuthal Equal Area

Strait of Gibraltar

---

1. (Places and Regions) What is the only country in the region that uses geothermal power?

2. (Places and Regions) Which country in the region mines uranium?

3. (Places and Regions) In which body of water is oil and gas production concentrated?

Critical Thinking

4. Analyzing Information Use the map on this page to create a chart, graph, database, or model of economic activities in Europe.

Fast FACTS
Europe

ALBANIA

CAPITAL: Tiranë

AREA:
11,100 sq. mi. (28,748 sq km)

POPULATION: 3,510,484

MONEY: lek (ALL)

LANGUAGES:
Albanian, Greek

CARS: data not available

ANDORRA

CAPITAL:
Andorra la Vella

AREA:
181 sq. mi. (468 sq km)

POPULATION: 67,627

MONEY:
euro (€), 1-01-2002

LANGUAGES:
Catalan (official), French
Castilian

CARS: 35,358

AUSTRIA

CAPITAL: Vienna

AREA:
32,378 sq. mi.
(83,858 sq km)

POPULATION: 8,150,835

MONEY:
euro (€),
1-01-2002

LANGUAGES: German

CARS: 3,780,000

BELGIUM

CAPITAL:
Brussels

AREA:
11,780 sq. mi. (30,510 sq km)

POPULATION: 10,258,762

MONEY:
euro (€), 1-01-2002

LANGUAGES:
Dutch, French, German

CARS: 4,420,000

BOSNIA AND HERZEGOVINA

CAPITAL:
Sarajevo

AREA:
19,741 sq. mi. (51,129 sq km)

POPULATION: 3,922,205

MONEY:
marka (BAM)

LANGUAGES:
Croatian, Serbian, Bosnian

CARS: data not available

BULGARIA

CAPITAL: Sofia

AREA:
42,822 sq. mi.
(110,910 sq km)

POPULATION: 7,707,495

MONEY:
lev (BGL)

LANGUAGES:
Bulgarian

CARS: 1,650,000

CROATIA

CAPITAL:
Zagreb

AREA:
21,831 sq. mi.
(56,542 sq km)

POPULATION: 4,334,142

MONEY:
Croatian kuna (HRK)

LANGUAGES:
Croatian

CARS: 698,000

CZECH REPUBLIC

CAPITAL: Prague

AREA:
30,450 sq. mi.
(78,866 sq km)

POPULATION: 10,264,212

MONEY:
Czech koruna (CZK)

LANGUAGES:
Czech

CARS: 4,410,000

DENMARK

CAPITAL:
Copenhagen

AREA:
16,639 sq. mi.
(43,094 sq km)

POPULATION: 5,352,815

MONEY:
Danish krone (DKK)

LANGUAGES:
Danish, Faroese, Greenlandic
(an Inuit dialect), German

CARS: 1,790,000

ESTONIA

CAPITAL:
Tallinn

AREA:
17,462 sq. mi.
(45,226 sq km)

POPULATION: 1,423,316

MONEY:
Estonian kroon (EEK)

LANGUAGES:
Estonian (official), Russian,
Ukrainian, English, Finnish

CARS: 338,000

Countries not drawn to scale.

FINLAND

CAPITAL: Helsinki
AREA:
130,127 sq. mi.
(337,030 sq km)
POPULATION: 5,175,783
MONEY:
euro (€), 1-01-2002
LANGUAGES: Finnish, Swedish
CARS: 1,940,000

FRANCE

CAPITAL: Paris
AREA:
211,208 sq. mi.
(547,030 sq km)
POPULATION: 59,551,227
MONEY:
euro (€), 1-01-2002
LANGUAGES: French
CARS: 25,500,000

GERMANY

CAPITAL: Berlin
AREA:
137,846 sq. mi.
(357,021 sq km)
POPULATION: 83,029,536
MONEY:
euro (€), deutsche mark (DM)
LANGUAGES: German
CARS: 41,330,000

GREECE

CAPITAL:
Athens
AREA:
50,942 sq. mi.
(131,940 sq km)
POPULATION: 10,623,835
MONEY:
euro (€), 1-01-2002
LANGUAGES:
Greek (official), English, French
CARS: 2,340,000

HUNGARY

CAPITAL: Budapest
AREA:
35,919 sq. mi.
(93,030 sq km)
POPULATION: 10,106,017
MONEY:
forint (HUF)
LANGUAGES:
Hungarian
CARS: 2,280,000

ICELAND

CAPITAL: Reykjavik
AREA:
39,768 sq. mi.
(103,000 sq km)
POPULATION: 277,906
MONEY:
Icelandic krona (ISK)
LANGUAGES:
Icelandic
CARS: 132,468

IRELAND

CAPITAL:
Dublin
AREA:
27,135 sq. mi. (70,280 sq km)
POPULATION: 3,840,838
MONEY:
euro (€), 1-01-2002
LANGUAGES:
English, Irish (Gaelic)
CARS: 1,060,000

ITALY

CAPITAL:
Rome
AREA:
116,305 sq. mi.
(301,230 sq km)
POPULATION: 57,679,825
MONEY:
euro (€), 1-01-2002
LANGUAGES:
Italian, German, French, Slovene
CARS: 31,000,000

LATVIA

CAPITAL: Riga
AREA:
24,938 sq. mi.
(64,589 sq km)
POPULATION: 2,385,231
MONEY: Latvian lat (LVL)
LANGUAGES:
Lettish (official), Lithuanian, Russian
CARS: 252,000

LIECHTENSTEIN

CAPITAL: Vaduz
AREA:
62 sq. mi. (160 sq km)
POPULATION:
32,528
MONEY:
Swiss franc (CHF)
LANGUAGES: German
CARS: data not available

Sources: Central Intelligence Agency, *The World Factbook 2001; The World Almanac and Book of Facts 2001;* population figures are 2001 estimates.

LITHUANIA

CAPITAL: Vilnius

AREA:
25,174 sq. mi.
(65,200 sq km)

POPULATION:
3,610,535

MONEY:
litas (LTL)

LANGUAGES:
Lithuanian (official), Polish,
Russian

CARS: 653,000

LUXEMBOURG

CAPITAL:
Luxembourg

AREA:
998 sq. mi. (2,586 sq km)

POPULATION:
429,080

MONEY: euro (€),
Luxembourg franc (LuxF)

LANGUAGES:
Luxembourgish, German,
French

CARS: 231,666

MACEDONIA

CAPITAL: Skopje

AREA:
9,781 sq. mi.
(25,333 sq km)

POPULATION: 2,046,209

MONEY:
Macedonian denar (MKD)

LANGUAGES:
Macedonian, Albanian,
Turkish, Serbo-Croatian

CARS: 263,000

MALTA

CAPITAL:
Valletta

AREA:
122 sq. mi. (316 sq km)

POPULATION:
394,583

MONEY:
Maltese lira (MTL)

LANGUAGES:
Maltese (official), English
(official)

CARS: 122,100

MOLDOVA

CAPITAL: Chișinău

AREA:
13,067 sq. mi.
(33,843 sq km)

POPULATION: 4,431,570

MONEY:
Moldovan leu (MDL)

LANGUAGES:
Moldovan (official), Russian,
Gagauz

CARS: 169,000

MONACO

CAPITAL:
Monaco

AREA:
0.75 sq. mi. (1.95 sq km)

POPULATION:
31,842

MONEY:
euro (€), 1-01-2002

LANGUAGES:
French (official), English,
Italian, Monegasque

CARS: 17,000

NETHERLANDS

CAPITAL: Amsterdam

AREA:
16,033 sq. mi.
(41,526 sq km)

POPULATION: 15,981,472

MONEY:
euro (€), 1-01-2002

LANGUAGES: Dutch

CARS: 5,810,000

NORWAY

CAPITAL: Oslo

AREA:
125,181 sq. mi.
(324,220 sq km)

POPULATION: 4,503,440

MONEY:
Norwegian
krone (NOK)

LANGUAGES: Norwegian

CARS: 1,760,000

POLAND

CAPITAL: Warsaw

AREA:
120,728 sq. mi.
(312,685 sq km)

POPULATION: 38,633,912

MONEY:
zloty (PLN)

LANGUAGES:
Polish

CARS: 7,520,000

PORTUGAL

CAPITAL: Lisbon

AREA:
35,672 sq. mi.
(92,391 sq km)

POPULATION: 10,066,253

MONEY:
euro (€), 1-01-2002

LANGUAGES: Portuguese

CARS: 2,950,000

Countries not drawn to scale.

ROMANIA

CAPITAL:
Bucharest

AREA:
91,699 sq. mi.
(237,500 sq km)

POPULATION: 22,364,022

MONEY:
leu (ROL)

LANGUAGES:
Romanian, Hungarian,
German

CARS: 2,390,000

SAN MARINO

CAPITAL:
San Marino

AREA:
23.6 sq. mi. (61.2 sq km)

POPULATION: 27,336

MONEY:
euro (€), 1-01-2002

LANGUAGES:
Italian

CARS: 24,825

SLOVAKIA

CAPITAL:
Bratislava

AREA:
18,859 sq. mi.
(48,845 sq km)

POPULATION: 5,414,937

MONEY:
Slovak koruna (SKK)

LANGUAGES:
Slovak (official), Hungarian

CARS: 994,000

SLOVENIA

CAPITAL:
Ljubljana

AREA:
7,820 sq. mi.
(20,253 sq km)

POPULATION: 1,930,132

MONEY:
tolar (SIT)

LANGUAGES:
Slovenian, Serbo-Croatian

CARS: 657,000

SPAIN

CAPITAL:
Madrid

AREA:
194,896 sq. mi.
(504,782 sq km)

POPULATION: 40,037,995

MONEY:
euro (€), peseta (Pta)

LANGUAGES:
Castilian Spanish, Catalan,
Galician

CARS: 15,300,000

SWEDEN

CAPITAL: Stockholm

AREA:
173,731 sq. mi.
(449,964 sq km)

POPULATION: 8,875,053

MONEY:
Swedish krona (SEK)

LANGUAGES: Swedish

CARS: 3,700,000

SWITZERLAND

CAPITAL:
Bern

AREA:
15,942 sq. mi.
(41,290 sq km)

POPULATION: 7,283,274

MONEY:
Swiss franc (CHF)

LANGUAGES:
German, French, Italian

CARS: 3,320,000

UNITED KINGDOM

CAPITAL: London

AREA:
94,525 sq. mi.
(244,820 sq km)

POPULATION: 59,647,790

MONEY: British pound (GBP)

LANGUAGES:
English, Welsh, Scottish form
of Gaelic

CARS: 25,590,000

VATICAN CITY

CAPITAL: Vatican City

AREA:
0.17 sq. mi. (0.44 sq km)

POPULATION: 890

MONEY:
euro (€), 1-01-2002

LANGUAGES: Italian, Latin

CARS: data not available

YUGOSLAVIA

CAPITAL: Belgrade

AREA: 39,517 sq. mi.
(102,350 sq km)

POPULATION: 10,677,290

MONEY: New Yugoslav
dinar (YUM)

CARS: 1,000,000

LANGUAGES:
Serbian, Albanian

☑ **internet** connect

go.hrw.com

COUNTRY STATISTICS
GO TO: go.hrw.com
KEYWORD: SG3 FactsU4
FOR: more facts about
Europe

Sources: Central Intelligence Agency, *The World Factbook 2001*; *The World Almanac and Book of Facts 2001*; population figures are 2001 estimates.

CHAPTER 13

Southern Europe

Southern Europe's peninsulas, islands, mountains, and plateaus form a beautiful region. Tourists enjoy visiting this region to see its historical and cultural treasures.

Ciao. I am Paolo. I am 11 years old. I live in an apartment with my parents and my *nonna,* which is Italian for "grandma." Nonna is teaching me how to cook while she makes dinner for the family. I have no brothers or sisters, but on Sundays my aunts and uncles and three cousins all come for a big lunch. After lunch, the cousins play outside on the playground swings.

In the mornings, I walk to school with my mother before she goes to her job as a professor. My school is not too strict. We study English, Italian, and religion. After school I practice with my team at the swim club.

My favorite holiday is Christmas. On Christmas Eve we go to my other grandmother's house for a special dinner. We have smoked salmon, then grilled trout and spaghetti with mussels. Then there are special Christmas sweets: Pandoro—a cake sprinkled with sugar, and Torrone—a candy log with chocolate and nuts.

Abito a Roma, la capitale dell'Italia.

Translation: I live in Rome, the capital of Italy.

Section 1

Physical Geography

Read to Discover

1. What are the major landforms and rivers of southern Europe?
2. What are the major climate types and resources of this region?

Define

mainland
sirocco

Locate

Mediterranean Sea
Strait of Gibraltar

Iberian Peninsula
Cantabrian Mountains
Pyrenees Mountains
Alps
Apennines
Aegean Sea
Peloponnesus

Ebro River
Douro River
Tagus River
Guadalquivir River
Po River
Tiber River

WHY IT MATTERS

Southern Europe's location on peninsulas encouraged its cultures to become great seafarers. Use CNNfyi.com or other current events sources to find examples of trade on the region's oceans today. Record your findings in your journal.

Cave painting from 12,000 B.C.

Southern Europe: Physical-Political

ELEVATION

	FEET	METERS
⊛ National capitals	13,120	4,000
• Other cities	6,560	2,000
	1,640	500
■ Historic sites	656	200
	(Sea level) 0	0 (Sea level)
	Below sea level	Below sea level

SCALE

0   100   200   300 Miles

0 100 200 300 Kilometers

Projection: Azimuthal Equal Area

Size comparison of southern Europe to the contiguous United States

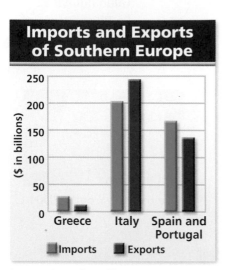
Physical Features

Southern Europe is also known as Mediterranean Europe because most of its countries are on the sea's shores. The Mediterranean Sea stretches some 2,300 miles (3,700 km) from east to west. *Mediterranean* means "middle of the land" in Latin. In ancient times, the Mediterranean was considered the center of the Western world, since it is surrounded by Europe, Africa, and Asia. The narrow Strait of Gibraltar (juh-BRAWL-tuhr) links the Mediterranean to the Atlantic Ocean.

The Land Southern Europe is made up of three peninsulas. Portugal and Spain occupy one, Italy occupies another, and Greece is located on a third peninsula. Portugal and Spain are on the Iberian (eye-BIR-ee-uhn) Peninsula. Much of the peninsula is a high, rocky plateau. The Cantabrian (kan-TAY-bree-uhn) and the Pyrenees (PIR-uh-neez) Mountains form the plateau's northern edge. Italy's peninsula includes the southern Alps. A lower mountain range, the Apennines (A-puh-nynz), runs like a spine down the country's back. Islands in the central and western Mediterranean include Italy's Sicily and Sardinia (sahr-DI-nee-uh), as well as Spain's Balearic (ba-lee-AR-ik) Islands.

Greece's **mainland**, or the country's main landmass, extends into the Aegean (ee-JEE-uhn) Sea in many jagged little peninsulas. The largest one is the Peloponnesus (pe-luh-puh-NEE-suhs). Greece is mountainous and includes more than 2,000 islands. The largest island is Crete (KREET).

On all three peninsulas, coastal lowlands and river valleys provide excellent areas for growing crops and building cities. Soils on the region's uplands are thin and stony. They are also easily eroded. In this area of young mountains, earthquakes are common. They are particularly common in Greece and Italy.

The Rivers Several east-west rivers cut through the Iberian Peninsula. The Ebro River drains into the Mediterranean. The Douro, Tagus, and Guadalquivir (gwah-thahl-kee-VEER) Rivers, however, flow to the Atlantic Ocean. The Po (POH) is Italy's largest river. It creates a fertile agricultural region in northern Italy. Farther south, along the banks of the much smaller Tiber River, is the city of Rome.

✓ **READING CHECK:** *Physical Systems* What physical processes cause problems in parts of southern Europe?

Imports and Exports of Southern Europe

Source: Central Intelligence Agency, *The World Factbook, 2001*

Interpreting the Graph Which country has the fewest imports and exports?

Greece, a land of mountains and sea, is home to the ancient city of Lindos on the island of Rhodes.

Climate and Resources

Much of southern Europe enjoys a warm, sunny climate. Most of the rain falls during the mild winter. Rainfall sometimes causes floods and mudslides due to erosion from overgrazing and deforestation. A hot, dry wind from North Africa called a **sirocco** (suh-RAH-koh) picks up some moisture over the Mediterranean Sea. It blows over Italy during spring and summer. The Po Valley is humid. Northern Italy's Alps have a highland climate. In Spain, semiarid climates are found in pockets. Northern Spain is cool and humid.

Workers prepare to separate a giant block of marble from a wall in a quarry in Carrara, Italy.

Southern Europeans have often looked to the sea for trade. Important Mediterranean ports include Barcelona, Genoa, Naples, Piraeus (py-REE-uhs)—the port of Athens—and Valencia. Lisbon, the capital of Portugal, is an important Atlantic port. The Atlantic Ocean supports Portugal's fishing industry. Although the Mediterranean suffers from pollution, it has a wealth of seafood.

The region's resources vary. Northern Spain has iron ore mines. Greece mines bauxite, chromium, lead, and zinc. Italy and Greece quarry marble. Falling water generates hydroelectricity throughout the region's uplands. Otherwise, resources are scarce.

The region's sunny climate and natural beauty have long attracted visitors. Millions of people explore castles, museums, ruins, and other cultural sites each year. Spain's beaches help make that country one of Europe's top tourist destinations.

✔ **READING CHECK:** *Places and Regions* What climate types and natural resources are found in the region?

Section Review 1

Homework Practice Online
go.hrw.com
Keyword: SG3 HP13

Define and explain: mainland, sirocco

Working with Sketch Maps On a map of southern Europe that you draw or that your teacher provides, label Greece, Italy, Spain, and Portugal. Also label the Mediterranean Sea and the Strait of Gibraltar.

Reading for the Main Idea

1. *Places and Regions* Why is southern Europe known as Mediterranean Europe?

2. *Places and Regions* What countries occupy the region's three main peninsulas?

3. *Environment and Society* Why might people settle in river valleys and in coastal Southern Europe?

Critical Thinking

4. **Drawing Inferences and Conclusions** In what ways could the region's physical geography aid the development of trade?

Organizing What You Know

5. **Summarizing** Copy the following graphic organizer. Use it to list the region's physical features, climates, and resources.

	Physical Features	Climate	Resources
Spain and Portugal			
Italy			
Greece			

Section 2

Greece

Read to Discover

1. What were some of the achievements of the ancient Greeks?
2. What are two features of Greek culture?
3. What is Greece like today?

Define
city-states
mosaics

Locate
Athens
Thessaloníki

Ancient coin of Alexander the Great

History

The Greek islands took an early lead in the development of trade and shipping between Asia, Africa, and Europe. By about 2000 B.C. large towns and a complex civilization existed on Crete.

Ancient Greece About 800 B.C. Greek civilization arose on the mainland. The mountainous landscape there favored small, independent **city-states**. Each Greek city-state, or *polis,* was made up of a city and the land around it. Each had its own gods, laws, and form of government. The government of the city-state of Athens was the first known democracy. Democracy is the form of government in which all citizens take part. Greek philosophers, artists, architects, and writers made important contributions to Western civilization. For example, the Greeks are credited with inventing theater. Students still study ancient Greek literature and plays.

Eventually, Greece was conquered by King Philip. Philip ruled Macedonia, an area north of Greece. About 330 B.C. Philip's son, Alexander the Great, conquered Asia Minor, Egypt, Persia, and part of India. His empire combined Greek culture with influences from Asia and Africa. In the 140s B.C. Greece and Macedonia were conquered by the Roman Empire.

The Greeks believed that the Temple of Delphi—shown below—was the center of the world.

Interpreting the Visual Record Why do you think remains of this temple have lasted for so many years?

The Byzantine Empire About A.D. 400 the Roman Empire was divided into two parts. The western half was ruled from Rome. It soon fell to Germanic peoples the Romans called barbarians. Barbarian means both *illiterate* and *wanderer*. The eastern half of the Roman Empire was known as the Byzantine Empire. It was ruled from Constantinople. Constantinople was located on the shore of the Bosporus in what is now Turkey. This city—today known as Istanbul—served as a gathering place for people from Europe and Asia. The Byzantine Empire carried on the traditions of the Roman Empire for another 1,000 years. Gradually, an eastern form of Christianity developed. It was influenced by Greek language and culture. It became known as Eastern Orthodox Christianity. It is the leading form of Christianity in Greece, parts of eastern Europe, and Russia.

The Acropolis in Athens was built in the 400s B.C. The word *acropolis* is Greek for "city at the top."

Interpreting the Visual Record Why would it be important to build a city on a hill?

Turkish Rule In 1453 Constantinople was conquered by the Ottoman Turks, a people from Central Asia. Greece and most of the rest of the region came under the rule of the Ottoman Empire. It remained part of this empire for nearly 400 years. In 1821 the Greeks revolted against the Turks, and in the early 1830s Greece became independent.

Government In World War II Greece was occupied by Germany. After the war Greek communists and those who wanted a king and constitution fought a civil war. When the communists lost, the military took control. Finally, in the 1970s the Greek people voted to make their country a republic. They adopted a new constitution that created a government with a president and a prime minister.

✓ **READING CHECK:** *Human Systems* What were some of the achievements of ancient Greece?

Culture

Turkish influences on Greek art, food, and music can still be seen. However, Turkey and Greece disagree over control of the islands and shipping lanes of the Aegean Sea.

Religion Some 98 percent of Greeks are Eastern Orthodox Christians, commonly known as Greek Orthodox. Easter is a major holiday and cause for much celebration. The traditional Easter meal is eaten on Sunday—roasted lamb, various vegetables, Easter bread, and many desserts. Because the Greek Orthodox Church has its own calendar, Christmas and Easter are usually celebrated one to two weeks later than in the West.

The people of Karpathos and their religious leaders are participating in an Easter celebration.

Connecting to Math

Greek postage stamp of the Pythagorean Theorem

Greek Math and Science

Greek civilization made many contributions to world culture. We still admire Greek art and literature. Greek scholars also paved the way for modern mathematics and science.

More than 2,000 years ago Thales (THAY-leez), a philosopher, began the use of deduction in mathematical proofs. Pythagoras (puh-THAG-uh-ruhs) worked out an equation to calculate the dimensions of a right triangle. The equation became known as the Pythagorean Theorem. By 300 B.C. Euclid (YOO-kluhd) had stated the basic principles of geometry in his book *Elements*. Soon after, Archimedes (ahr-kuh-MEED-eez) calculated the value of *pi*. This value is used to measure circles and spheres. He also explained how and why the lever, a basic tool, works.

Aristarchus (ar-uh-STAHR-kuhs), an astronomer, worked out a model of the solar system. His model placed the Sun at the center of the universe. Eratosthenes (er-uh-TAHS-thuh-neez) estimated the circumference of Earth with great accuracy.

Two important figures in the life sciences were Hippocrates (hip-AHK-ruh-teez) and Aristotle (AR-uh-staht-uhl). Hippocrates was a doctor who treated medicine as a science. He understood that diseases have natural causes. Aristotle gathered information on a wide variety of plants and animals. He helped establish the importance of observation and classification in the study of nature. In many ways, the Greeks began the process of separating scientific fact from superstition.

Understanding What You Read
1. How did Greeks further the study of mathematics?
2. What were some of the Greeks' scientific achievements?

This Greek vase shows a warrior holding a shield. Kleophrades is thought to have made this vase, which dates to 500 B.C.

This mosaic of a dog bears the inscription "Good Hunting."

The Arts The ancient Greeks produced beautiful buildings, sculpture, poetry, plays, pottery, and gold jewelry. They also made **mosaics** (moh-ZAY-iks)—pictures created from tiny pieces of colored stone—that were copied throughout Europe. The folk music of Greece shares many features with the music of Turkey and Southwest Asia. In 1963 the Greek writer George Seferis won the Nobel Prize in literature.

✓ **READING CHECK:** *Human Systems* Why is there a Turkish influence in Greek culture?

Greece Today

When people think of Greece now, they often recall the past. For example, many have seen pictures of the Parthenon, a temple built in the 400s B.C. in Athens. It is one of the world's most photographed buildings.

Economy Greece today lags behind other European nations in economic growth. More people work in agriculture than in any other industry. However, only about 19 percent of the land can be farmed because of the mountains. For this reason old methods of farming are used rather than modern equipment. Farmers raise cotton, tobacco, vegetables, wheat, lemons, olives, and raisins.

Service and manufacturing industries are growing in Greece. However, the lack of natural resources limits industry. Tourism and shipping are key to the Greek economy.

Cities About 20 percent of the Greek labor force works in agriculture. About 40 percent of Greeks live in rural areas. In the past few years, people have begun to move to the cities to find better jobs.

Athens, in central Greece, is the capital and by far the largest city. About one third of Greece's population lives in the area in and around Athens. Athens and its seaport, Piraeus, have attracted both people and industries. Most of the country's economic growth is centered there. However, the city suffers from air pollution, which causes health problems. Air pollution also damages historical sites, such as the Parthenon. Greece's second-largest city is Thessaloníki. It is the major seaport for northern Greece.

✓ **READING CHECK:** (*Environment and Society*) How does scarcity of natural resources affect Greece's economy?

Greece

COUNTRY	POPULATION/ GROWTH RATE	LIFE EXPECTANCY	LITERACY RATE	PER CAPITA GDP
Greece	10,623,835 0.2%	76, male 81, female	95%	$17,200
United States	281,421,906 0.9%	74, male 80, female	97%	$36,200

Sources: Central Intelligence Agency, *The World Factbook 2001*; U.S. Census Bureau

Interpreting the Chart Why might life expectancy be higher in Greece than in the United States?

Section Review 2

Define and explain: city-states, mosaics

Working with Sketch Maps On the map you created in Section 1, label Athens and Thessaloníki. What physical features do these cities have in common? What economic activities might they share?

Reading for the Main Idea

1. (*Human Systems*) What groups influenced Greek culture?

2. (*Human Systems*) For what art forms is Greece famous?

go. hrw .com **Homework Practice Online**
Keyword: SG3 HP13

Critical Thinking

3. **Drawing Inferences and Conclusions** How did the physical geography of this region influence the growth of major cities?

4. **Finding the Main Idea** On what does Greece rely to keep its economy strong?

Organizing What You Know

5. **Sequencing** Create a time line that documents the history of ancient Greece from 2000 B.C. to A.D. 1453.

2000 B.C.   A.D. 1453

Section 3 · Italy

Read to Discover

1. What was the early history of Italy like?
2. How has Italy added to world culture?
3. What is Italy like today?

Define

pope
Renaissance
coalition
   governments

Locate

Rome   Milan
Genoa   Turin
Naples   Florence

WHY IT MATTERS

Leonardo da Vinci and Galileo are just two famous Italians who have made significant contributions to science and art. Use CNNfyi.com or other current events sources to find examples of recent Italian scientists and artists. Record your findings in your journal.

Artifact from a warrior's armor, 400s B.C.

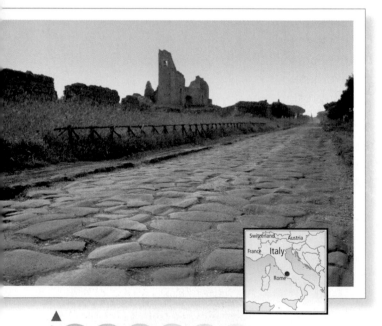

The Appian Way was a road from Rome to Brindisi. It was started in 312 B.C. by the emperor Claudius.
Interpreting the Visual Record How do you think this road has withstood more than 2,000 years of use?

History

About 750 B.C. a tribe known as the Latins established the city of Rome on the Tiber River. Over time, these Romans conquered the rest of Italy. They then began to expand their rule to lands outside Italy.

Roman Empire At its height about A.D. 100, the Roman Empire stretched westward to what is now Spain and Portugal and northward to England and Germany. The Balkans, Turkey, parts of Southwest Asia, and coastal North Africa were all part of the empire. Roman laws, roads, engineering, and the Latin language could be found throughout this huge area. The Roman army kept order, and people could travel safely throughout the empire. Trade prospered.

The Romans made advances in engineering, including roads and aqueducts—canals that transported water. They also learned how to build domes and arches. Romans also produced great works of art and literature.

About A.D. 200, however, the Roman Empire began to weaken. The western part, with its capital in Rome, fell in A.D. 476. The eastern part, the Byzantine Empire, lasted until 1453.

Roman influences in the world can still be seen today. Latin developed into the modern languages of French, Italian, Portuguese, Romanian, and Spanish. Many English words have Latin origins as well. Roman laws and political ideas have influenced the governments and legal systems of many modern countries.

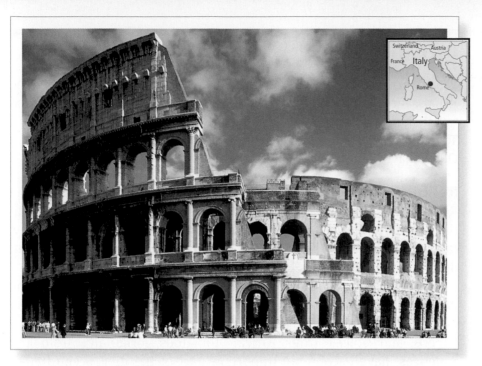

◀

The Colosseum is a giant amphitheater. It was built in Rome between A.D. 70 and 80 and could seat 50,000 people.

Interpreting the Visual Record
For what events do you think the Colosseum was used? What type of modern buildings look like this?

Christianity began in the Roman province of Judaea (modern Israel and the West Bank). It then spread through the Roman Empire. Some early Christians were persecuted for refusing to worship the traditional Roman gods. However, in the early A.D. 300s the Roman emperor, Constantine, adopted Christianity. It quickly became the main religion of the empire. The **pope**—the bishop of Rome—is the head of the Roman Catholic Church.

The Renaissance Beginning in the 1300s a new era of learning began in Italy. It was known as the **Renaissance** (re-nuh-SAHNS). In French this word means "rebirth." During the Renaissance, Italians rediscovered the work of ancient Roman and Greek writers. Scholars applied reason and experimented to advance the sciences. Artists pioneered new techniques. Leonardo da Vinci, painter of the *Mona Lisa*, was also a sculptor, engineer, architect, and scientist. Another Italian, Galileo Galilei, perfected the telescope and experimented with gravity.

Christopher Columbus opened up the Americas to European colonization. Although Spain paid for his voyages, Columbus was an Italian from the city of Genoa. The name *America* comes from another Italian explorer, Amerigo Vespucci.

Government Italy was divided into many small states until the late 1800s. Today Italy's central government is a democracy with an elected parliament. Italy has had many changes in leadership in recent years. This has happened because no political party has won a majority of votes in Italian elections. As a result, political parties must form **coalition governments**. A coalition government is one in which several parties join together to run the country. Unfortunately, these coalitions usually do not last long.

✓ **READING CHECK:** (*Human Systems*) How is the Italian government different from that of the United States?

▲

Leonardo da Vinci painted the *Mona Lisa* about 1503–06.

Interpreting the Visual Record **Why do you think Leonardo's painting became famous?**

This view of the Pantheon in Rome shows the oculus—the opening at the top. The Pantheon was built as a temple to all Roman gods.

Interpreting the Visual Record Why did the Romans need to design buildings that let in light?

▼

In Rome people attend mass in St. Peter's Square, Vatican City. Vatican City is an independent state within Rome.

Interpreting the Visual Record How does a plaza, or open area, help create a sense of community?

▼

Culture

People from other places have influenced Italian culture. During the Renaissance, many Jews who had been expelled from Spain moved to Italian cities. Jews often had to live in segregated areas called ghettoes. Today immigrants have arrived from former Italian colonies in Africa. Others have come from the eastern Mediterranean and the Balkans.

Religion and Food Some 98 percent of Italians belong to the Roman Catholic Church. The leadership of the church is still based in the Vatican in Rome. Christmas and Easter are major holidays in Italy. Italians also celebrate All Saints Day on November 1 by cleaning and decorating their relatives' graves.

Italians enjoy a range of regional foods. Recipes are influenced by the history and crops of each area. In the south, Italians eat a Mediterranean diet of olives, bread, and fish. Dishes are flavored with lemons from Greece and spices from Africa. Tomatoes, originally from the Americas, have become an important part of the diet. Some Italian foods, such as pizza, are popular in the United States. Modern pizza originated in Naples. Northern Italians eat more rice, butter, cheeses, and mushrooms than southern Italians.

The Arts The ancient Romans created beautiful glassware and jewelry as well as marble and bronze sculptures. During the Renaissance, Italy again became a center for art, particularly painting and sculpture. Italian artists discovered ways to make their paintings more lifelike. They did this by creating the illusion of three dimensions. Italian writers like Francesco Petrarch and Giovanni Boccaccio wrote some of the most important literature of the Renaissance. More recently, Italian composers have written great operas. Today, Italian designers, actors, and filmmakers are celebrated worldwide.

✓ **READING CHECK:** *Human Systems* What are some examples of Italian culture?

Italy Today

Italy is slightly smaller than Florida and Georgia combined, with a population of about 57 million. A shared language, the Roman Catholic Church, and strong family ties continue to bind Italians together.

Economy After its defeat in World War II, Italy rebuilt its industries in the north. Rich soil and plenty of water make the north Italy's "breadbasket," or wheat growing area. Italy's most valuable crop is grapes. Although grapes are grown throughout the country, northern Italy produces the best crops. These grapes help make Italy the world's largest producer of wine. Tourists are also important to Italy's economy. They visit northern and central Italy to see ancient ruins and Renaissance art. Southern Italy remains poorer with lower crop yields. Industrialization there also lags behind the north. Tourist resorts, however, are growing in the south and promise to help the economy.

Cities The northern cities of Milan, Turin, and Genoa are important industrial centers. Their location near the center of Europe helps companies sell products to foreign customers. Also in the north are two popular tourist sites. One is Venice, which is famous for its romantic canals and beautiful buildings. The other is Florence, a center of art and culture. Rome, the capital, is located in central Italy. Naples, the largest city in southern Italy, is a major manufacturing center and port.

✔ **READING CHECK:** *Environment and Society* What geographic factors influence Italy's economy?

Italy

Country	Population/ Growth Rate	Life Expectancy	Literacy Rate	Per Capita GDP
Italy	57,679,825 .07%	76, male 83, female	98%	$22,100
United States	281,421,906 0.9%	74, male 80, female	97%	$36,200

Sources: Central Intelligence Agency, *The World Factbook 2001*; U.S. Census Bureau

Interpreting the Chart What is the difference in the growth rate of Italy and the United States?

Section Review 3

Homework Practice Online
Keyword: SG3 HP13

Define and explain: pope, Renaissance, coalition governments

Working with Sketch Maps On the map you created in Section 2, label Florence, Genoa, Milan, Naples, Rome, and Turin. Why are they important?

Reading for the Main Idea

1. *Human Systems* What were some of the important contributions of the Romans?

2. *Human Systems* What are some art forms for which Italy is well known?

Critical Thinking

3. **Finding the Main Idea** Which of Italy's physical features encourage trade? Which geographical features make trading difficult?

4. **Analyzing Information** Why is the northern part of Italy known as the country's "breadbasket"?

Organizing What You Know

5. **Finding the Main Idea** Copy the following graphic organizer. Use it to describe the movement of goods and ideas to and from Italy during the early days of trade and exploration.

Section 4 Spain and Portugal

Read to Discover

1. What were some major events in the history of Spain and Portugal?
2. What are the cultures of Spain and Portugal like?
3. What are Spain and Portugal like today?

Define

Moors
dialect
cork

Locate

Lisbon
Madrid
Barcelona

WHY IT MATTERS

Some Basque separatists have used violence to try to gain their independence from Spain. Use CNNfyi.com or other **current events** sources to find examples of this problem. Record your findings in your journal.

Paella, a popular dish in Spain

History

Beautiful paintings of bison and other animals are found in caves in northern Spain. Some of the best known are at Altamira and were created as early as 16,000 B.C. Some cave paintings are much older. These paintings give us exciting clues about the early people who lived here.

Ancient Times Spain has been important to Mediterranean trade for several thousand years. First, the Greeks and then the Phoenicians, or Carthaginians, built towns on Spain's southern and eastern coasts. Then, about 200 B.C. Iberia became a part of the Roman Empire and adopted the Latin language.

These windmills in Consuegra, Spain, provided water for the people of the region.

Interpreting the Visual Record How do you think windmills pump water?

The Muslim North Africans, or **Moors**, conquered most of the Iberian Peninsula in the A.D. 700s. Graceful Moorish buildings, with their lacy patterns and archways, are still found in Spanish and Portuguese cities. This is particularly true in the old Moorish city of Granada in southern Spain.

Great Empires From the 1000s to the 1400s Christian rulers fought to take back the peninsula. In 1492 King Ferdinand and Queen Isabella conquered the kingdom of Granada, the last Moorish outpost in Spain. That same year, they sponsored the voyage of Christopher Columbus to the Americas. Spain soon established a large empire in the Americas.

The Portuguese also sent out explorers. Some of them sailed around Africa to India. Others crossed the Atlantic and claimed Brazil. In the 1490s the Roman Catholic pope drew a line to divide the world between Spain and Portugal. Western lands, except for Brazil, were given to Spain, and eastern lands to Portugal.

With gold and agricultural products from their American colonies, and spices and silks from Asia, Spain and Portugal grew rich. In 1588 Philip II, king of Spain and Portugal, sent a huge armada, or fleet, to invade England. The Spanish were defeated, and Spain's power began to decline. However, most Spanish colonies in the Americas did not win independence until the early 1800s.

Government In the 1930s the king of Spain lost power. Spain became a workers' republic. The new government tried to reduce the role of the church and to give the nobles' lands to farmers. However, conservative military leaders under General Francisco Franco resisted. A civil war was fought from 1936 to 1939 between those who supported Franco and those who wanted a democratic form of government. Franco's forces won the war and ruled Spain until 1975. Today Spain is a democracy, with a national assembly and prime minister. The king also plays a modest role as head of state.

Portugal, like Spain, was long ruled by a monarch. In the early 1900s the monarchy was overthrown. Portugal became a democracy. However, the army later overthrew the government, and a dictator took control. A revolution in the 1970s overthrew the dictatorship. For a few years disagreements between the new political parties brought violence. Portugal is now a democracy with a president and prime minister.

✔ **READING CHECK:** *Human Systems* How did Spain and Portugal move from unlimited to limited governments?

The interior of the Great Mosque in Córdoba, Spain, shows the lasting beauty of Moorish architecture. A cathedral was built within the mosque after Christians took back the city.
Interpreting the Visual Record Why do you think arches are important in certain building designs?

One of the world's most endangered wild cats is the Iberian lynx. About 50 survive in a preserve on the Atlantic coast of Spain.

Spain and Portugal

Country	Population/ Growth Rate	Life Expectancy	Literacy Rate	Per Capita GDP
Portugal	10,066,253 0.2%	72, male 80, female	87%	$15,800
Spain	40,037,995 0.1%	75, male 83, female	97%	$18,000
United States	281,421,906 0.9%	74, male 80, female	97%	$36,200

Sources: Central Intelligence Agency, *The World Factbook 2001;* U.S. Census Bureau

Interpreting the Chart How do the growth rates of these countries compare?

Culture

The most widely understood Spanish **dialect** (DY-uh-lekt), or variation of a language, is Castilian. This is the form spoken in central Spain. Spanish and Portuguese are not the only languages spoken on the Iberian Peninsula, however. Catalan is spoken in northeastern Spain (Catalonia). Basque is spoken by an ethnic group living in the Pyrenees.

Spain faces a problem of unrest among the Basque people. The government has given the Basque area limited self-rule. However, a small group of Basque separatists continue to use violence to protest Spanish control.

Food and Festivals Spanish and Portuguese foods are typical of the Mediterranean region. Many recipes use olives and olive oil, lemons, wheat, wine, and fish. Foods the explorers brought back from the Americas—such as tomatoes and peppers—are also important.

Both Spain and Portugal remain strongly Roman Catholic. The two countries celebrate major Christian holidays like Christmas and Easter. As in Italy, each village has a patron saint whose special day is the occasion for a fiesta, or festival. A bull fight, or *corrida*, may take place during the festival.

The Arts Spanish and Portuguese art reflects the many peoples who have lived in the region. The decoration of Spanish porcelain recalls Islamic art from North Africa. The sad melodies of the Portuguese fado singers and the intense beat of Spanish flamenco dancing also show African influences. In the 1900s the Spanish painter Pablo Picasso boldly experimented with shape and perspective. He became one of the most famous artists of modern times.

✔ **READING CHECK:** *Human Systems* How has the mixture of different ethnic groups created some conflict in Spanish society?

Flamenco dancers perform at a fair in Málaga, Spain.

Spain and Portugal Today

Like Greece and Italy, both Spain and Portugal belong to the European Union (EU). The EU allows free trade, travel, and exchange of workers among its members. The economies of Spain and Portugal have been growing rapidly. However, they remain poorer than the leading EU countries.

Agricultural products of Spain and Portugal include wine, fruit, olives, olive oil, and **cork**. Cork is the bark stripped from a certain type of oak tree. Spain exports oranges from the east, beef from the north, and lamb from ranches on the Meseta. Portugal also makes and exports clothing and timber products. Spain makes cars and trucks, and most of its industry is located in the north. Tourism is also an important part of the Spanish economy. This is particularly true along Spain's coasts and on the Balearic Islands.

Portugal's capital and largest city is Lisbon. It is located on the Atlantic coast at the mouth of the Tagus River. Madrid, Spain's capital and largest city, is located inland on the Meseta. Spain's second-largest city is the Mediterranean port of Barcelona.

✓ **READING CHECK:** (*Places and Regions*) What are Spain and Portugal like today?

Porto, Portugal, combines modern industry with the historical sea trade.

▲ A worker uses an ax to strip the bark from a cork oak.

Section Review 4

go.hrw.com **Homework Practice Online**
Keyword: SG3 HP13

Define and explain: Moors, dialect, cork

Working with Sketch Maps On the map that you created in Section 3, label Lisbon, Madrid, and Barcelona. How are Lisbon and Barcelona different from Madrid?

Reading for the Main Idea

1. (*Human Systems*) How do the performing arts of this region reflect different cultures?

2. (*Human Systems*) How have Spain and Portugal worked to improve their economies?

Critical Thinking

3. **Analyzing Information** Which groups influenced the culture of Spain and Portugal?

4. **Summarizing** How was the government of Spain organized during the 1900s?

Organizing What You Know

5. **Sequencing** Copy the following graphic organizer. Use it to list important events in the history of Spain and Portugal from the 700s to the 1600s.

Building Vocabulary

On a separate sheet of paper, write sentences to define each of the following words.

1. mainland
2. sirocco
3. city-states
4. mosaics
5. pope
6. Renaissance
7. coalition governments
8. Moors
9. dialect
10. cork

Reviewing the Main Ideas

1. *(Places and Regions)* What are the important physical features of southern Europe?

2. *(Environment and Society)* Why has southern Europe been a major tourist attraction for centuries?

3. *(Human Systems)* What are the major economic differences between northern and southern Italy?

4. *(Human Systems)* What is the main religion in Italy? Where is the leadership of this religion based?

5. *(Human Systems)* How did both Spain and Portugal become wealthy during the 1400s and 1500s?

Understanding Environment and Society

The Arts

Environment influences a culture's art. For example, grapes might be featured in a mosaic. Create a presentation about the influence of the environment on the arts. Write a description of each piece and explain how it might have been influenced by the artist's environment.

Thinking Critically

1. **Drawing Influences and Conclusions** In what ways do you think the geography of southern Europe made trade and exploration possible?

2. **Summarizing** What parts of Greek culture have been most strongly influenced by Turkish customs? Why is this the case?

3. **Drawing Inferences and Conclusions** Recall what you have learned about the Roman Empire. What about the Italian peninsula made it a good location for a Mediterranean empire?

4. **Drawing Inferences and Conclusions** How are agricultural products of southern Europe used in food?

5. **Finding the Main Idea** Why do many tourists continue to visit historical cities in southern Europe?

Map ACTIVITY

On a separate sheet of paper, match the letters on the map with their correct labels.

Alps	Po River
Apennines	Tiber River
Aegean Sea	Naples
Peloponnesus	Sicily
Ebro River	Meseta

Mental Mapping Skills ACTIVITY

On a separate sheet of paper, draw a freehand map of southern Europe. Make a key for your map and label the following:

Athens	Portugal
Greece	Rome
Italy	Spain
Mediterranean Sea	Strait of Gibraltar

WRITING ACTIVITY Find a recording of Portuguese fado music. Then write a review that explains what the lyrics of the songs reveal about Portuguese culture. Be sure to use standard grammar, spelling, sentence structure, and punctuation in your review.

Alternative Assessment

Portfolio ACTIVITY

Learning About Your Local Geography

Individual Project The cultures of southern European influence the United States in many ways. Investigate southern European influences in your community. List some of those influences in a chart.

internet connect

Internet Activity: go.hrw.com
KEYWORD: SG3 GT13

Choose a topic to explore southern Europe:
- Explore the islands and peninsulas on the Mediterranean coast.
- Take an online tour of ancient Greece.
- Learn the story of pizza.

CHAPTER 14

West-Central Europe

West-central Europe is an important agricultural, industrial, and manufacturing area. The countries of this region export many different products. They are some of the richest countries in the world.

Gruss dich (Hello). My name is Lizzi (LEE-zee). I live in southern Germany in the village of Deutenhausen. Lizzi is short for Felicitas—my grandmother's name—which means "happiness." I am in the eighth grade at the gymnasium, or high school. I live in a big house on a farm with my three older sisters, my parents, and my grandmother. My parents are farmers and also own a restaurant. In summer, I make sure the cows have enough water and I chase the geese home. I also help my parents chop vegetables in the restaurant. I don't want to be a farmer when I grow up! I hope to become a doctor and work in an emergency room.

At about 7:30, I take the bus to school in Weilheim, about 2 miles (3 km) away. My favorite subject is art. My school is not very strict, and we do not wear uniforms. I study German, geography, English, and Latin. Next year I will start classical Greek.

After school is over at 12:30, I go home to have lunch with my grandmother. Then, I play with my friends outdoors, even when it rains.

Willkommen in Deutschland. Wie geht es dir?

◄

Translation: Welcome to Germany! How are you?

Section 1 Physical Geography

Read to Discover

1. Where are the area's major landform regions?
2. What role do rivers, canals, and harbors play in the region?
3. What are west-central Europe's major resources?

Define

navigable
loess

Locate

Northern European Plain
Pyrenees
Alps
Seine River
Rhine River
Danube River
North Sea
Mediterranean Sea
English Channel
Bay of Biscay

WHY IT MATTERS

Nuclear power is important in West-Central Europe. However, nuclear reactors can pose problems for the environment. Use **CNNfyi.com** or other **current events** sources to find out more about alternative sources of power. Record your findings in your journal.

Neuschwanstein Castle, Germany

West-Central Europe: Physical-Political

ELEVATION

FEET	METERS
13,120	4,000
6,560	2,000
1,640	500
656	200
(Sea level) 0	0 (Sea level)
Below sea level	Below sea level

⊛ National capitals
• Other cities

SCALE
0   100   200   300 Miles
0   100   200   300 Kilometers
Projection: Azimuthal Equal Area

Size comparison of west-central Europe to the contiguous United States

The Rhine River has been an important transportation route since Roman times.

Interpreting the Visual Record How might the Rhine influence the location of German industry?

The Alps have many large glaciers, lakes, and valleys.

Physical Features

West-central Europe includes France, Germany, Belgium, the Netherlands, Luxembourg, Switzerland, and Austria. Belgium, the Netherlands, and Luxembourg are called the Benelux countries. The word Benelux is a combination of the first letters of each country's name. They are also sometimes called the Low Countries. Large areas of Switzerland and Austria lie in the Alps mountain range. For this reason, they are called the Alpine countries.

Lowlands The main landform regions of west-central Europe are arranged like a fan. The outer edge of the fan is the Northern European Plain. Brittany, a peninsula jutting from northern France, rises slightly above the plain. In Belgium and the Netherlands, the Northern European Plain dips below sea level.

Uplands Toward the middle of the fan a wide band of uplands begins at the Pyrenees (PIR-uh-neez) Mountains. Another important uplands region is the Massif Central (ma-SEEF sahn-TRAHL) in France. Most of the southern two thirds of Germany is hilly. The Schwarzwald (SHFAHRTS-vahlt), or Black Forest, occupies the southwestern corner of Germany's uplands region.

Mountains At the center of the fan are the Alps, Europe's highest mountain range. Many peaks in the Alps reach heights of more than 14,000 feet (4,267 m). The highest peak, France's Mont Blanc (mawn BLAHN), reaches to 15,771 feet (4,807 m). Because of their high elevations, the Alps have large glaciers and frequent avalanches. During the Ice Age, glaciers scooped great chunks of rock out of the mountains, carving peaks such as the Matterhorn.

✓ **READING CHECK:** *Places and Regions* What are the area's major landforms?

Climate and Waterways

West-central Europe's marine west coast climate makes the region a pleasant place to live. Winters can be cold and rainy, but summers are mild. However, areas that lie farther from the warming influence of the North Atlantic are colder. For example, central Germany receives more snow than western France. The Alps have a highland climate.

Snowmelt from the Alps feeds west-central Europe's many **navigable** rivers. Navigable rivers are deep enough and wide enough to be used by ships. France has four major rivers: the Seine (SEN), the Loire (LWAHR), the Garonne (gah-RAWN), and the

Rhone (ROHN). Germany has five major rivers: the Rhine (RYN), the Danube (DAN-yoob), the Elbe (EL-buh), the Oder (OH-duhr), and the Weser (VAY-zuhr). These rivers and the region's many canals are important for trade and travel. Many large harbor cities are located where rivers flow into the North Sea, Mediterranean Sea, English Channel, or Bay of Biscay. The region's heavily indented coastline has hundreds of excellent harbors.

✓ **READING CHECK:** *Environment and Society* What economic role do rivers, canals, and harbors play in west-central Europe?

Resources

Most of the forests that once covered west-central Europe were cut down centuries ago. The fields that remained are now some of the most productive in the world. Germany's plains are rich in **loess** (LES)—fine, wind-blown soil deposits. Germany and France produce grapes for some of the world's finest wines. Switzerland's Alpine pastures support dairy cattle.

The distribution of west-central Europe's mineral resources is uneven. Germany and France have deposits of iron ore but must import oil. Energy resources are generally in short supply in the region. However, there are deposits of coal in Germany and natural gas in the Netherlands. Nuclear power helps fill the need for energy, particularly in France and Belgium. Alpine rivers provide hydroelectric power in Switzerland and Austria. Natural beauty is perhaps the Alpine countries' most valuable natural resource, attracting millions of tourists every year.

✓ **READING CHECK:** *Environment and Society* What geographic factors contribute to the economy of the region?

▲ The Grindelwald Valley in Switzerland has excellent pastures.

Do you remember what you learned about hydroelectric power? See Chapter 4 to review.

go.hrw.com **Homework Practice Online** Keyword: SG3 HP14

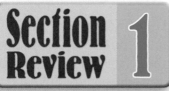

Section Review 1

Define and explain: navigable, loess

Working with Sketch Maps On a map of west-central Europe that you draw or that your teacher provides, label the following: the Northern European Plain, Alps, North Sea, Mediterranean Sea, English Channel, and Bay of Biscay.

Reading for the Main Idea

1. *Places and Regions* What are the landform regions of west-central Europe?

2. *Places and Regions* What type of climate dominates this region?

Critical Thinking

3. **Making Generalizations and Predictions** What might be the advantages of having many good harbors and navigable rivers?

4. **Drawing Inferences and Conclusions** How do you think an uneven distribution of resources has affected this region?

Organizing What You Know

5. **Categorizing** Copy the following graphic organizer. Use it to describe the major rivers of west-central Europe. Add rows as needed.

River	Country/Countries	Flows into. . .

Section 2 France

Read to Discover

1. Which foreign groups affected the historical development of France?
2. What are the main features of French culture?
3. What products does France export?

WHY IT MATTERS

France is a key member of NATO, the North Atlantic Treaty Organization. Use CNNfyi.com or other current events sources to find out more about NATO. Record your findings in your journal.

Define
medieval
NATO
impressionism

Locate
Brittany
Normandy
Paris
Marseille
Nice

French croissants

▲
In this illustration messengers inform Charlemagne of a recent military victory.

History

France has been occupied by people from many other parts of Europe. In ancient times, France was part of a region known as Gaul. Thousands of years ago, people moved from eastern Europe into Gaul. These people spoke Celtic languages related to modern Welsh and Gaelic. Breton is a Celtic language still spoken in the region of Brittany.

Early History About 600 B.C. the Greeks set up colonies on Gaul's southern coast. Several centuries later, the Romans conquered Gaul. They introduced Roman law and government to the area. The Romans also established a Latin-based language that developed into French.

Roman rule lasted until the A.D. 400s. A group of Germanic people known as the Franks then conquered much of Gaul. It is from these people that France takes its name. Charlemagne was the Franks' greatest ruler. He dreamed of building a Christian empire that would be as great as the old Roman Empire. In honor of this, the pope crowned Charlemagne Emperor of the Romans in

A.D. 800. During his rule, Charlemagne did much to strengthen government and improve education and the arts in Europe.

The Franks divided Charlemagne's empire after his death. Invading groups attacked from many directions. The Norsemen, or Normans, were one of these groups. They came from northern Europe. The area of western France where the Normans settled is known today as Normandy.

The period from the collapse of the Roman Empire to about 1500 is called the Middle Ages, or **medieval** period. The word medieval comes from the Latin words *medium,* meaning "middle," and *aevum,* meaning "age." During much of this period kings in Europe were not very powerful. They depended on cooperation from nobles, some of whom were almost as powerful as kings.

In 1066 a noble, the duke of Normandy, conquered England, becoming its king. As a result, the kings of England also ruled part of France. In the 1300s the king of England tried to claim the throne of France. This led to the Hundred Years' War, which lasted from 1337 to 1453. Eventually, French armies drove the English out of France. The French kings then slowly increased their power over the French nobles.

During the Middle Ages the Roman Catholic Church created a sense of unity among many Europeans. Many tall, impressive cathedrals were built during this time. Perhaps the most famous is the Cathedral of Notre Dame in Paris. It took almost 200 years to build.

French and English knights clash in this depiction of the Hundred Years' War.

Revolution and Napoléon's Empire From the 1500s to the 1700s France built a global empire. The French established colonies in the Americas, Asia, and Africa. During this period most French people lived in poverty and had few rights. In 1789 the French Revolution began. The French overthrew their king and established an elected government. About 10 years later a brilliant general named Napoléon Bonaparte took power. As he gained control, he took the title of emperor. Eventually, Napoléon conquered most of Europe. Napoléon built new roads throughout France, reformed the French educational system, and established the metric system of measurement. In 1815 an alliance including Austria, Great Britain, Prussia, and Russia finally defeated Napoléon. The French king regained the throne.

World Wars During World War I (1914–18) the German army controlled parts of northern and eastern France. In the early years of World War II, Germany defeated France and occupied the northern and western parts of the country. In 1944, Allied armies including U.S., British, and Canadian soldiers landed in Normandy and drove the Germans out. However, after two wars in 30 years France was devastated. Cities, factories, bridges, railroad lines, and train stations had been destroyed. The North Atlantic Treaty Organization, or **NATO**, was formed in 1949 with France as a founding member. This military alliance was created to defend Western Europe against future attacks.

Napoléon Bonaparte became the ruler of France and conquered most of Europe.

The euro replaced the currencies of most of the individual EU countries.

Interpreting the Visual Record What are the advantages of a shared currency?

Many French cheeses, such as Brie, Camembert, and Roquefort, are named after the places where they are made.

Workers harvest grapes at a vineyard in the Rhone Valley near Lyon.

Interpreting the Visual Record Has modern technology changed the grape-growing process?

Government In the 1950s and 1960s most French colonies in Asia and Africa achieved independence. However, France still controls several small territories around the world. Today, France is a republic with a parliament and an elected president. France is also a founding member of the European Union (EU). France is gradually replacing its currency, the franc, with the EU currency, the euro.

✓ **READING CHECK:** *Human Systems* Which foreign groups have affected France's historical development?

Culture

About 90 percent of French people are Roman Catholic, and 3 percent practice Islam. Almost all French citizens speak French. However, small populations of Bretons in the northwest and Basques in the southwest speak other languages. In Provence-Alpes-Côte d'Azur and Languedoc-Roussillon in the south and on the island of Corsica, some people speak regional dialects along with French. Immigrants from former colonies in Africa, the Caribbean, and Southeast Asia also influence French culture through their own styles of food, clothing, music, and art.

Customs In southern France people eat Mediterranean foods like wheat, olives and olive oil, cheeses, and garlic. In the north food is more likely to be prepared with butter, herbs, and mushrooms. Wine is produced in many French regions, and France produces more than 400 different cheeses. French people celebrate many festivals, including Bastille Day on July 14. On this date in 1789 a mob stormed the Bastille, a royal prison in Paris. The French recognize this event as the beginning of the French Revolution.

The Arts and Literature France has a respected tradition of poetry, philosophy, music, and the visual arts. In the late 1800s and early 1900s France was the center of an artistic movement called **impressionism**. Impressionist artists tried to capture the rippling of light rather than an exact, realistic image. Famous impressionists include Monet, Renoir, and Degas. French painters, like Cézanne and Matisse, influenced styles of modern painting. Today, France is a world leader in the arts and film industry.

✔ **READING CHECK:** (*Human Systems*) How did French art affect the world?

France

COUNTRY	POPULATION/ GROWTH RATE	LIFE EXPECTANCY	LITERACY RATE	PER CAPITA GDP
France	59,551,227 0.4%	75, male 83, female	99%	$24,400
United States	281,421,906 0.9%	74, male 80, female	97%	$36,200

Sources: Central Intelligence Agency, *The World Factbook 2001;* U.S. Census Bureau

Interpreting the Chart How do France's life expectancy and literacy rate compare to those of the United States?

France Today

France is a major agricultural and industrial country. Its resources, labor force, and location in the heart of Europe have helped spur economic growth. France exports wheat, olives, wine, and cheeses as well as other dairy products. French factories produce cars, airplanes, shoes, clothing, machinery, and chemicals. France's largest city is Paris, which has nearly 10 million people in its metropolitan area. Other major cities include Marseille, Nice, Lyon, and Lille. France's major cities are linked by high-speed trains and excellent highways.

✔ **READING CHECK:** (*Human Systems*) What are some products that France exports?

go.hrw.com **Homework Practice Online** Keyword: SG3 HP14

Define and explain: medieval, NATO, impressionism

Working with Sketch Maps On the map you created in Section 1, label Brittany, Normandy, Paris, Marseille, and Nice.

Reading for the Main Idea

1. (*Human Systems*) What were the main periods of French history?

2. (*Human Systems*) What are the main features of French culture?

Critical Thinking

3. **Finding the Main Idea** What were some long-lasting achievements of Charlemagne and Napoléon?

4. **Summarizing** What is the French economy like?

Organizing What You Know

5. **Identifying Cause and Effect** Copy the following graphic organizer. Use it to list the causes and effects of the Hundred Years' War.

Section 3

Germany

Read to Discover

1. What effects have wars had on Germany?
2. What are Germany's major contributions to world culture?
3. How did the division of Germany affect its economy?

Define

Reformation
Holocaust
chancellor

Locate

Berlin
Bonn
Essen
Frankfurt
Munich
Hamburg
Cologne

WHY IT MATTERS

The Berlin Wall had fallen by 1990, and East and West Germany were reunited as a single nation. What have been the effects of reunification? Use **CNNfyi**.com or other **current events** sources to find out more about Germany. Record your findings in your journal.

A VW Turbo beetle

This medieval castle overlooks a German town.

Interpreting the Visual Record What geographic features made this a good place to build a fortress?

▼

History

Many Germans are descendants of tribes that migrated from northern Europe in ancient times. The Romans conquered the western and southern fringes of the region. They called this land Germania, from the name of one of the tribes that lived there.

The Holy Roman Empire When the Roman Empire collapsed, the Franks became the most important tribe in Germany. The lands ruled by the Frankish king Charlemagne in the early 800s included most of what is now Germany. Charlemagne's empire was known as the Holy Roman Empire.

Reformation and Unification During the 1500s Germany was the center of the **Reformation**—a movement to reform Christianity. The reformers were called Protestants. Protestants rejected many practices of the Roman Catholic Church. At the time, Germany was made up of many small states. Each state was ruled by a prince who answered to the Holy Roman emperor. Many of the princes became Protestants. This angered the Holy Roman emperor, who was Catholic. He sent armies against the princes. Although the princes won the right to choose the religion of their states, conflict continued. This conflict eventually led to the Thirty Years' War (1618–48). This war was costly. Many towns were destroyed and nearly one third of the population died. Germany remained divided for more than 200 years. In the late 1800s Prussia, the strongest state, united Germany.

World Wars In 1914 national rivalries and a conflict in the Balkans led to World War I. Austria, Germany, and the Ottoman Empire, later joined by Bulgaria, fought against Britain, France, and Russia, later joined by Italy and the United States. By 1918 Germany and its allies were defeated.

During the 1920s Austrian war veteran Adolf Hitler led a new political party in Germany called the Nazis. The Nazis took power in 1933. In the late 1930s Germany invaded Austria, Czechoslovakia, and finally Poland, beginning World War II. By 1942 Germany and Italy had conquered most of Europe. The Nazis forced many people from the occupied countries into concentration camps to be enslaved or killed. About 6 million Jews and millions of other people were murdered in a mass killing called the **Holocaust**.

To defeat Germany, several countries formed an alliance. These Allies included Britain, the Soviet Union, the United States, and many others. The Allies defeated Germany in 1945. Germany and its capital, Berlin, were divided into Soviet, French, British, and U.S. occupation zones. Britain, France, and the United States later combined their zones to create a democratic West Germany with its capital at Bonn. In its zone, the Soviet Union set up the Communist country of East Germany with an unlimited totalitarian government. Its capital became East Berlin; however, West Berlin became part of West Germany. In 1961 the East German government built the Berlin Wall across the city to stop East Germans from escaping to the West.

Reunification and Modern Government West Germany's roads, cities, railroads, and industries were rebuilt after the war with U.S. financial aid. East Germany was also rebuilt, but it was not as prosperous as West Germany. Unlike the West German government, the East German government allowed people very little freedom. Also, its command economy— managed by the government—was less productive than the free enterprise, market system of West Germany. In the late 1980s East Germans and people throughout Eastern Europe demanded democratic reform. In 1989 the Berlin Wall was torn down. In 1990 East and West Germany reunited. Germany's capital again became Berlin. Today, all Germans enjoy democratic rights. A parliament elects the president and prime minister, or **chancellor**. Germany is a member of the EU and NATO.

✓ READING CHECK: (*Human Systems*) How were the economies of East and West Germany organized following World War II?

German youth salute Adolf Hitler in Nürnberg in 1938.

For nearly 30 years the Berlin Wall separated East and West Berlin. Many people in West Berlin protested by painting graffiti on the wall.

Interpreting the Visual Record Why would the government make the wall solid instead of a barrier that would allow people visual access?

Culture

About 34 percent of Germans are Roman Catholic, and 38 percent are Protestant. Most other Germans have no religious association. Many of these people are from eastern Germany, where the communist government suppressed religion from 1945 to 1990.

Diversity About 90 percent of Germany's inhabitants are ethnic Germans. However, significant numbers of Turks, Poles, and Italians have come to Germany to live and work. These "guest workers" do not have German citizenship. Germany has also taken in thousands of refugees from Eastern Europe during the last 50 years.

Customs Traditional German food emphasizes the products of the forests, farms, and seacoasts. Each region produces its own varieties of sausage, cheese, wine, and beer. German celebrations include Oktoberfest; *Sangerfast,* a singing festival; and *Fastnacht*, a religious celebration. The major German festival season is Christmas. The Germans began the custom of bringing an evergreen tree indoors at Christmas and decorating it with candles.

The Arts and Literature Germany has a great tradition of literature, music, and the arts. The first European to print books using movable metal type was a German, Johannes Gutenberg. In the 1700s and 1800s, Germany led Europe in the development of classical music. World-famous German composers include Johann Sebastian Bach and Ludwig van Beethoven. The operas of Richard Wagner revived the folktales of ancient Germany.

✓ **READING CHECK:**　*Human Systems*　What technology and other contributions have Germans made to world culture?

Crowds gather in a German town for a Christmas market. Christmas markets have been popular in Germany for more than 400 years. From the beginning of Advent until Christmas, booths are set up on the market place in most cities. Here people can buy trees, decorations, and gifts.

Interpreting the Visual Record **What does this photo suggest about the importance of Christmas in Germany?**

Germany Today

Germany has a population of 83 million, more people than any other European country. Germany also has Europe's largest economy. Nearly one fourth of all goods and services produced by the EU come from Germany.

Economy Ample resources, labor, and capital have made Germany one of the world's leading industrial countries. The nation exports a wide variety of products. You may be familiar with German automakers like Volkswagen, Mercedes-Benz, and BMW. The German government provides education, medical care, and pensions for its citizens, but Germans pay high taxes. Unemployment is high. Many immigrants work at low-wage jobs. These "guest workers" are not German citizens and cannot receive many government benefits. Since reunification, Germany has struggled to modernize the industries, housing, and other facilities of the former East Germany.

Cities Germany's capital city, Berlin, is a large city with wide boulevards and many parks. Berlin was isolated and economically restricted during the decades after World War II. However, Germans are now rebuilding their new capital to its former splendor.

Near the Rhine River and the coal fields of Western Germany is a huge cluster of cities, including Essen and Düsseldorf. They form Germany's largest industrial district, the Ruhr. Frankfurt is a city known for banking and finance. Munich is a manufacturing center. Other important cities include Hamburg, Bremen, Cologne, and Stuttgart.

✓ **READING CHECK:** (**Human Systems**) How did the division of Germany affect its economy?

Germany

COUNTRY	POPULATION/ GROWTH RATE	LIFE EXPECTANCY	LITERACY RATE	PER CAPITA GDP
Germany	83,029,536 0.3%	74, male 81, female	99%	$23,400
United States	281,421,906 0.9%	74, male 80, female	97%	$36,200

Sources: Central Intelligence Agency, *The World Factbook 2001*; U.S. Census Bureau

Interpreting the Chart **What might the literacy rate of Germany suggest about its culture?**

Section Review 3

Homework Practice Online
Keyword: SG3 HP14

Define and explain: Reformation, Holocaust, chancellor

Working with Sketch Maps On the map you created in Section 2, label Berlin, Bonn, Essen, Frankfurt, Munich, Hamburg, and Cologne.

Reading for the Main Idea

1. (**Human Systems**) How did wars affect the development of Germany in the 1900s?

2. (**Human Systems**) What are some notable features of the German economy?

Critical Thinking

3. Drawing Inferences and Conclusions   How has Germany's history influenced the religious makeup of the population?

4. Summarizing   What have been some results of the unification of Germany in 1990?

Organizing What You Know

5. Sequencing   Create a time line listing key events in the history of Germany from 1000 B.C. to 1990.

1000 B.C. ———————————————— A.D. 1990

Section 4 The Benelux Countries

Read to Discover

1. How were the Benelux countries influenced by larger countries?
2. What is this region's culture like?
3. What are the Benelux countries like today?

Define

cosmopolitan

Locate

Flanders   Antwerp
Wallonia   Brussels
Amsterdam

WHY IT MATTERS

The Benelux countries are key members of the European Union (EU). Use **CNNfyi.com** or other **current events** sources to find out more about the membership, functions, and goals of the EU. Record your findings in your journal.

Dutch wooden shoes

▲

The Dutch city of Rotterdam is one of the world's busiest ports.

Interpreting the Visual Record Why might this city be an important transportation center?

History

Celtic and Germanic tribes once lived in this region, as in most of west-central Europe. They were conquered by the Romans. After the fall of the Roman Empire and the conquests of Charlemagne, the region was ruled alternately by French rulers and by the Holy Roman emperor.

In 1555 the Holy Roman emperor presented the Low Countries to his son, King Philip II of Spain. In the 1570s the Protestants of the Netherlands won their freedom from Spanish rule. Soon after, the Netherlands became a great naval and colonial power. Belgium had been ruled at times by France and the Netherlands. However, by 1830 Belgium had broken away to become an independent kingdom.

Both world wars scarred this region. Many of the major battles of World War I were fought in Belgium. Then in World War II Germany occupied the Low Countries. In 1949 Belgium, the Netherlands, and Luxembourg were founding members of NATO. Later they joined the EU. Today, each of the three countries is ruled by a parliament and a monarch. The monarchs' duties are mostly ceremonial. The Netherlands controls several Caribbean islands. However, its former colonies in Asia and South America are now independent.

✓ **READING CHECK:**   *Human Systems* How are the governments of the Benelux countries organized?

CONNECTING TO *Technology*

Dutch Polders

Much of the Netherlands lies below sea level and was once covered with water. For at least 2,000 years, the Dutch have been holding back the sea. First they lived on raised earthen mounds. Later they built walls or dikes to keep the water out. After building dikes, the Dutch installed windmills to pump the water out of reclaimed areas, called polders.

Using this system, the Dutch have reclaimed large amounts of land. Cities like Amsterdam and Rotterdam sit on reclaimed land. The dike and polder system has become highly sophisticated. Electric pumps have largely replaced windmills, and dikes now extend along much of the country's coastline. However, this system is difficult to maintain. It requires frequent and expensive repairs. Creating polders has also produced sinking lowlands and other environmental damage. As a result, the Dutch are considering changes to the system. These changes might include restoring some of the polders to wetlands and lakes.

A polder in the Netherlands

Understanding What You Read
1. What are polders?
2. How did the Dutch use technology to live on land previously under water?

Culture

The people of Luxembourg and Belgium are mostly Roman Catholic. The Netherlands is more evenly divided among Catholic, Protestant, and those who have no religious ties.

Dutch is the language of the Netherlands. Flemish is a language related to Dutch that is spoken in Flanders, the northern part of Belgium. Belgium's coast and southern interior are called Wallonia. People in Wallonia speak mostly French and are called Walloons. In the past, cultural differences between Flemish and Walloons have produced conflict in Belgium. Today street signs and other notices are often printed in both Flemish and French. The Benelux countries are also home to immigrants from Asia and Africa.

These children in Brussels, Belgium, are wearing traditional clothing.

▼

Benelux Countries

COUNTRY	POPULATION/ GROWTH RATE	LIFE EXPECTANCY	LITERACY RATE	PER CAPITA GDP
Belgium	10,258,762 0.2%	75, male 81, female	98%	$25,300
Luxembourg	442,972 1.3%	74, male 81, female	100%	$36,400
Netherlands	15,807,641 0.5%	75, male 81, female	99%	$24,400
United States	281,421,906 0.9%	74, male 80, female	97%	$36,200

Sources: Central Intelligence Agency, *The World Factbook 2001*; U.S. Census Bureau

Interpreting the Chart Which country's per capita GDP is closest to that of the United States?

The region's foods include dairy products, fish, and sausage. The Dutch spice trade led to dishes flavored with spices from Southeast Asia. The Belgians claim they invented french fries, which they eat with mayonnaise.

The Netherlands and Belgium have been world leaders in fine art. In the 1400s and 1500s, Flemish artists painted realistic portraits and landscapes. Dutch painters like Rembrandt and Jan Vermeer experimented with different qualities of light. In the 1800s Dutch painter Vincent van Gogh portrayed southern France with bold brush strokes and bright colors.

✓ **READING CHECK:** *Human Systems* What is the relationship between cultures in Belgium?

The Benelux Countries Today

The Netherlands is famous for its flowers, particularly tulips. Belgium and the Netherlands export cheeses, chocolate, and cocoa. Amsterdam and Antwerp, Belgium, are major diamond-cutting centers. The Netherlands also imports and refines oil. Luxembourg earns much of its income from services such as banking. The region also produces steel, chemicals, and machines. Its **cosmopolitan** cities are centers of international business and government. A cosmopolitan city is one that has many foreign influences. Brussels, Belgium, is the headquarters for many international organizations such as the EU and NATO.

✓ **READING CHECK:** *Places and Regions* What are the Benelux countries like today?

go. hrw .com **Homework Practice Online** Keyword: SG3 HP14

Section Review 4

Define and explain: cosmopolitan

Working with Sketch Maps On the map you created in Section 3, label Flanders, Wallonia, Amsterdam, Antwerp, and Brussels.

Reading for the Main Idea

1. *Human Systems* What are the main cultural features of the Benelux countries?

2. *Human Systems* In what ways do the people of the Benelux countries differ?

Critical Thinking

3. **Drawing Inferences and Conclusions** Why might the economies of the Benelux countries be dependent on international trade?

4. **Analyzing Information** Why have groups in Belgium been in conflict?

Organizing What You Know

5. **Comparing** Copy the following graphic organizer. Use it to compare the Benelux countries' industries.

Belgium	Luxembourg	Netherlands

Read to Discover

1. What are some of the major events in the history of the Alpine countries?
2. What are some cultural features of this region?
3. How are the economies of Switzerland and Austria similar?

Define

cantons
nationalism

Locate

Geneva	Zurich
Salzburg	Basel
Vienna	Bern

WHY IT MATTERS

When people think of chocolate they often think of Switzerland, one of the world's leading producers of chocolate. Use CNN fyi.com or other **current events** sources to find out more about chocolate. Record your findings in your journal.

Swiss cuckoo clock

History

Austria and Switzerland share a history of Celtic occupation, Roman and Germanic invasions, and rule by the Holy Roman Empire.

Switzerland Swiss **cantons**, or districts, gradually broke away from the Holy Roman Empire, and in the 1600s Switzerland became independent. Today Switzerland is a confederation of 26 cantons. Each controls its own internal affairs, and the national government handles defense and international relations. Switzerland's location in the high Alps has allowed it to remain somewhat separate from the rest of Europe. It has remained neutral in the European wars of the last two centuries. Switzerland has not joined the United Nations, EU, or NATO. Because of this neutrality, the Swiss city of Geneva is home to many international organizations.

Austria During the Middle Ages, Austria was a border region of Germany. This region was the home of the Habsburgs, a powerful family of German nobles. From the 1400s onward the Holy Roman emperor was always a Habsburg. At the height of their power the Habsburgs ruled Spain and the Netherlands, as well as large areas of Germany, eastern Europe, and Italy. This empire included different

The International Red Cross in Geneva has offices in almost every country in the world.

Interpreting the Visual Record What symbol of the Red Cross is displayed on this building?

293

The Danube River passes through Vienna, the capital of Austria. **Interpreting the Visual Record** How does this river influence movement and trade?

Austrians wearing carved wooden masks celebrate the return of spring and milder weather.

ethnic groups, each with its own language, government, and system of laws. The empire was united only in its allegiance to the emperor and in its defense of the Roman Catholic religion.

With the conquests of Napoléon after 1800, the Holy Roman Empire was formally eliminated. It was replaced with the Austrian Empire, which was also under Habsburg control. When Napoléon was defeated, the Austrian Empire became the dominant power in central Europe.

Through the 1800s the diverse peoples of the empire began to develop **nationalism**, or a demand for self-rule. In 1867 the Austrians agreed to share political power with the Hungarians. The Austrian Empire became the Austro-Hungarian Empire. After World War I the empire was dissolved. Austria and Hungary became separate countries. Shortly before World War II the Germans took over Austria and made it part of Germany. After the war, the Allies occupied Austria. Today Austria is an independent member of the EU.

✓ **READING CHECK:** *Human Systems* What were the major events in the history of the Alpine countries?

Culture

About 46 percent of the population in Switzerland is Roman Catholic, and 40 percent is Protestant. Austria's population is mainly Roman Catholic. Only about 5 percent of its people are Protestant, while 17 percent follow Islam or other religions.

Languages and Diversity About 64 percent of Swiss speak German, 19 percent speak French, and 8 percent speak Italian. Small groups in the southeast speak a language called Romansh. Other European languages are also spoken in Switzerland. Austria is almost entirely German-speaking, but contains small minorities of Slovenes and Croatians.

Customs Christmas is a major festival in both countries. People make special cakes and cookies at this time. In rural parts of Switzerland people take cattle up to the high mountains in late spring and return in the fall. Their return is celebrated by decorating homes and cows' horns with flowers. A special feast is also prepared.

The Alpine region is particularly well known for its music. In the 1700s Mozart wrote symphonies and operas in the Austrian city of Salzburg. Every year a music festival is held there in his honor. Austria's capital, Vienna, is also known as a center of music and fine art.

✓ **READING CHECK:** (*Human Systems*) What role have the arts played in this region?

The Alpine Countries

Country	Population/ Growth Rate	Life Expectancy	Literacy Rate	Per Capita GDP
Austria	8,150,835 0.2%	75, male 81, female	98%	$25,500
Switzerland	7,283,274 0.3%	77, male 83, female	99%	$28,600
United States	281,421,906 0.9%	74, male 80, female	97%	$36,200

Sources: Central Intelligence Agency, *The World Factbook 2001;* U.S. Census Bureau

Interpreting the Chart How do the populations of the Alpine countries compare with that of the United States?

The Alpine Countries Today

Switzerland and Austria both produce dairy products, including many kinds of cheese. Switzerland is also famous for the manufacturing of watches, optical instruments, and other machinery. Swiss chemists discovered how to make chocolate bars. Switzerland is a major producer of chocolate, although it must import the cocoa beans.

Switzerland and Austria are linked to the rest of Europe by excellent highways, trains, and airports. Several long tunnels allow trains and cars to pass through mountains in the Swiss Alps. Both countries attract many tourists with their mountain scenery, lakes, and ski slopes.

Located on the Danube, Vienna is Austria's commercial and industrial center. Switzerland's two largest cities are both in the German-speaking north. Zurich is a banking center, while Basel is the starting point for travel down the Rhine to the North Sea. Switzerland's capital is Bern, and Geneva is located in the west.

✓ **READING CHECK:** (*Human Systems*) How are the economies of Switzerland and Austria similar?

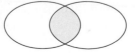
go.hrw.com **Homework Practice Online** Keyword: SG3 HP14

Section Review 5

Define and explain: cantons, nationalism

Working with Sketch Maps On the map you created in Section 4, label Geneva, Salzburg, Vienna, Zurich, Basel, and Bern.

Reading for the Main Idea

1. (*Human Systems*) What were the main events in the history of the Alpine countries?

2. (*Human Systems*) What are some notable aspects of Swiss and Austrian culture?

Critical Thinking

3. **Drawing Inferences and Conclusions** How might geography have been a factor in Switzerland's historical neutrality?

4. **Drawing Inferences and Conclusions** How have foreign invasions of Austria shaped its history?

Organizing What You Know

5. **Comparing/Contrasting** Use this graphic organizer to compare and contrast the culture, language, economies, and history of Switzerland and Austria.

Building Vocabulary

On a separate sheet of paper, write sentences to define each of the following words.

1. navigable
2. loess
3. medieval
4. impressionism
5. Reformation
6. Holocaust
7. chancellor
8. cosmopolitan
9. cantons
10. nationalism

Reviewing the Main Ideas

1. *Places and Regions* What is the climate of west-central Europe like?

2. *Human Systems* What were the effects of religious conflicts on Germany?

3. *Places and Regions* What energy resources are available to the countries of this region?

4. *Human Systems* Name five artists from west-central Europe who have made notable contributions to culture.

5. *Human Systems* What international organizations have created ties between countries of west-central Europe since World War II?

Understanding Environment and Society

Cleaning up Pollution
Create a presentation on East German industries' pollution of the environment. Include a chart, graph, database, model, or map showing patterns of pollutants, as well as the German government's clean-up effort. Consider the following:
• Pollution in the former East Germany.
• Pollution today.
• Costs of stricter environmental laws.
Write a five-question quiz, with answers about your presentation to challenge fellow students.

Thinking Critically

1. **Drawing Inferences and Conclusions** What geographic features have encouraged travel and trade in west-central Europe? What geographic features have hindered travel and trade?

2. **Finding the Main Idea** How have the people of Switzerland altered their environment?

3. **Analyzing Information** What landform regions give France natural borders? Which French borders do not coincide with physical features?

4. **Drawing Inferences and Conclusions** Why might Brussels, Belgium, be called the capital of Europe?

5. **Comparing** What demographic factors are shared by all countries of west-central Europe today? How do they reflect levels of economic development?

Map ACTIVITY

On a separate sheet of paper, match the letters on the map with their correct labels.

Northern European Plain	Danube River
Pyrenees	North Sea
Alps	Mediterranean Sea
Seine River	Paris
Rhine River	Berlin

Mental Mapping Skills ACTIVITY

On a separate sheet of paper, draw a freehand map of west-central Europe. Make a key for your map and label the following:

Austria	Luxembourg
Belgium	the Netherlands
France	North Sea
Germany	Switzerland

WRITING ACTIVITY

Imagine you are taking a boat tour down the Rhine River. You will travel from Basel, Switzerland, to Rotterdam, the Netherlands. Keep a journal describing the places you see and the stops you make. Be sure to use standard grammar, spelling, sentence structure, and punctuation.

Alternative Assessment

Portfolio ACTIVITY

Learning About Your Local Geography
Agricultural Products Some countries in west-central Europe are major exporters of agricultural products. Research the agricultural products of your state. Draw a map that shows important products and areas they are produced.

internet connect

Internet Activity: go.hrw.com
KEYWORD: SG3 GT14

Choose a topic to explore about west-central Europe:
- Tour the land and rivers of Europe.
- Travel back in time to the Middle Ages.
- Visit Belgian and Dutch schools.

go. hrw .com

CHAPTER 15

Northern Europe

Now we will study the countries of northern Europe. First we meet Lars, a student in Norway. He lives in a place where the Sun does not rise during much of the winter.

Hi! My name is Lars. I am 13, and I live in Tromsø, one of the northernmost cities in Europe. I am in my seventh year at school. In school we study Norwegian, plus English, French or German, social studies, science, music, art, and cooking. If I do well in junior high, I will go to an academic high school and prepare for a university.

Usually I walk to school, which is about 3 km (1.9 miles) away. In the winter, everyone skis to school. The Sun never shines on many winter days because we live north of the Arctic Circle. On January 20, when the Sun appears again for just a few minutes, we celebrate Sun Day.

In the summer the Sun never sets. This is my favorite time of the year. It still can be cold then. Last summer the temperature was mostly around 6° or 7°C (about 43° or 44°F).

Jeg bor i midnattssolens land.

◄

Translation: I live in the Land of the Midnight Sun.

Section 1 · Physical Geography

Read to Discover

1. What are the region's major physical features?
2. What are the region's most important natural resources?
3. What climates are found in northern Europe?

Define

fjords   lochs   North Atlantic Drift

Locate

British Isles
English Channel
North Sea
Great Britain

Ireland
Iceland
Greenland
Scandinavian
   Peninsula

Jutland Peninsula
Kjølen Mountains
Northwest Highlands
Shannon River
Baltic Sea

WHY IT MATTERS

An important physical feature of Northern Europe is the North Sea. Use CNNfyi.com or other current events sources to learn more about America's dependence on oil. Record your findings in your journal.

A Viking ship post

Northern Europe: Physical-Political

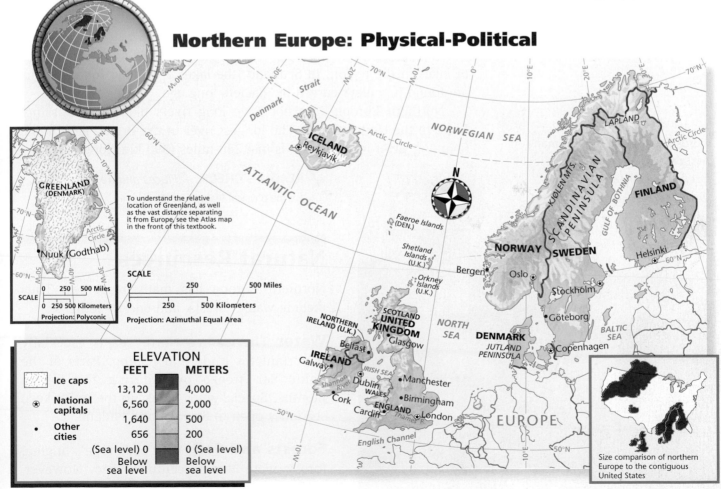

To understand the relative location of Greenland, as well as the vast distance separating it from Europe, see the Atlas map in the front of this textbook.

GREENLAND (DENMARK)
Nuuk (Godthab)

SCALE
0   250   500 Miles
0   250 500 Kilometers
Projection: Polyconic

SCALE
0   250   500 Miles
0   250   500 Kilometers
Projection: Azimuthal Equal Area

ELEVATION

	FEET	METERS
Ice caps		
	13,120	4,000
National capitals	6,560	2,000
	1,640	500
Other cities	656	200
	(Sea level) 0	0 (Sea level)
	Below sea level	Below sea level

ICELAND
Reykjavik

Denmark Strait

Arctic Circle

NORWEGIAN SEA

LAPLAND

Arctic Circle

ATLANTIC OCEAN

Faeroe Islands (DEN.)

Shetland Islands (U.K.)

Orkney Islands (U.K.)

KJØLEN MTS.

SCANDINAVIAN PENINSULA

GULF OF BOTHNIA

FINLAND

Helsinki

NORWAY   SWEDEN

Bergen   Oslo

Stockholm

Göteborg

BALTIC SEA

NORTH SEA

DENMARK
JUTLAND PENINSULA
Copenhagen

NORTHERN IRELAND (U.K.)
SCOTLAND
UNITED KINGDOM
Belfast   Glasgow
IRELAND
Galway
IRISH SEA
Shannon River   Dublin
WALES   Manchester
Cork   Birmingham
ENGLAND
Cardiff   London
Thames R.

EUROPE

English Channel

Size comparison of northern Europe to the contiguous United States

Our Amazing Planet

Scotland's Loch Ness contains more fresh water than all the lakes in England and Wales combined. It is deeper, on average, than the nearby North Sea.

Physical Features

Northern Europe includes several large islands and peninsulas. The British Isles lie across the English Channel and North Sea from the rest of Europe. They include the islands of Great Britain and Ireland and are divided between the United Kingdom and the Republic of Ireland. This region also includes the islands of Iceland and Greenland. Greenland is the world's largest island.

To the east are the Scandinavian and Jutland Peninsulas. Denmark occupies the Jutland Peninsula and nearby islands. The Scandinavian Peninsula is divided between Norway and Sweden. Finland lies farther east. These countries plus Iceland make up Scandinavia.

Landforms The rolling hills of Ireland, the highlands of Great Britain, and the Kjølen (CHUH-luhn) Mountains of Scandinavia are part of Europe's Northwest Highlands region. This is a region of very old, eroded hills and low mountains.

Southeastern Great Britain and southern Scandinavia are lowland regions. Much of Iceland is mountainous and volcanic. More than 10 percent of it is covered by glaciers. Greenland is mostly covered by a thick ice cap.

Coasts Northern Europe has long, jagged coastlines. The coastline of Norway includes many **fjords** (fee-AWRDS). Fjords are narrow, deep inlets of the sea set between high, rocky cliffs. Ice-age glaciers carved the fjords out of coastal mountains.

Lakes and Rivers Melting ice-age glaciers left behind thousands of lakes in the region. In Scotland, the lakes are called **lochs**. Lochs are found in valleys carved by glaciers long ago.

Northern Europe does not have long rivers like the Mississippi River in the United States. The longest river in the British Isles is the Shannon River in Ireland. It is just 240 miles (390 km) long.

✔ **READING CHECK:** *Places and Regions* What are the physical features of the region?

Fjords like this one shelter many harbors in Norway.
Interpreting the Visual Record
How are fjords created?

▼

Norway
Sweden Finland

Natural Resources

Northern Europe has many resources. They include water, forests, and energy sources.

Water The ice-free North Sea is especially important for trade and fishing. Parts of the Baltic Sea freeze over during the winter months. Special ships break up the ice to keep sea lanes open to Sweden and Finland.

Forests and Soil Most of Europe's original forests were cleared centuries ago. However,

Sweden and Finland still have large, coniferous forests that produce timber. The region's farmers grow many kinds of cool-climate crops.

Energy Beneath the North Sea are rich oil and natural gas reserves. Nearly all of the oil reserves are controlled by the nearby United Kingdom and Norway. However, these reserves cannot satisfy all of the region's needs. Most countries import oil and natural gas from southwest Asia, Africa, and Russia. Some, such as Iceland, use geothermal and hydroelectric power.

✔ **READING CHECK:** *Environment and Society* In what way has technology allowed people in the region to keep the North Sea open during the winter?

Climate

Despite its northern location, much of the region has a marine west coast climate. Westerly winds blow over a warm ocean current called the **North Atlantic Drift**. These winds bring mild temperatures and rain to the British Isles and coastal areas. Atlantic storms often bring even more rain. Snow and frosts may occur in winter.

Central Sweden and southern Finland have a humid continental climate. This area has four true seasons. Far to the north are subarctic and tundra climates. In the forested subarctic regions, winters are long and cold with short days. Long days fill the short summers. In the tundra region it is cold all year. Only small plants such as grass and moss grow there.

✔ **READING CHECK:** *Places and Regions* What are the region's climates?

Do you remember what you learned about ocean currents? See Chapter 3 to review.

go.
hrw
.com
Homework Practice Online
Keyword: SG3 HP15

Define and explain: fjords, lochs, North Atlantic Drift

Working with Sketch Maps On an outline map that you draw or that your teacher provides, label the following: British Isles, English Channel, North Sea, Great Britain, Ireland, Iceland, Greenland, Scandinavian Peninsula, Jutland Peninsula, Kjølen Mountains, Northwest Highlands, Shannon River, and Baltic Sea. In the margin, write a short caption explaining how the North Atlantic Drift affects the region's climates.

Reading for the Main Idea

1. *Places and Regions* Which parts of northern Europe are highland regions? Which parts are lowland regions?

2. *Places and Regions* What major climate types are found in northern Europe?

Critical Thinking

3. **Finding the Main Idea** How has ice shaped the region's physical geography?

4. **Making Generalizations and Predictions** Think about what you have learned about global warming. How might warmer temperatures affect the climates and people of northern Europe?

Organizing What You Know

5. **Summarizing** Copy the following graphic organizer. Use it to describe the region's important natural resources.

Water	Forests and soil	Energy

Section 2 The United Kingdom

Read to Discover

1. What are some important events in the history of the United Kingdom?
2. What are the people and culture of the country like?
3. What is the United Kingdom like today?

Define

textiles
constitutional monarchy
glen

Locate

England
Scotland
Wales
Northern Ireland
Irish Sea
London

Birmingham
Manchester
Glasgow
Cardiff
Belfast

WHY IT MATTERS

The United States has been heavily influenced by the British people. Use **CNNfyi.com** or other **current events** sources to find out about present-day ties between the United States and Great Britain. Record your findings in your journal.

British crown

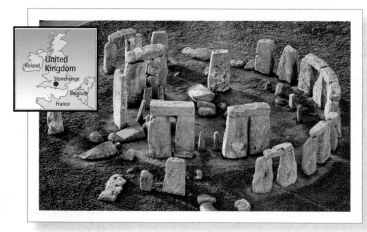

▲ Early peoples of the British Isles built Stonehenge in stages from about 3100 B.C. to about 1800 B.C.

History

Most of the British are descended from people who came to the British Isles long ago. The Celts (KELTS) are thought by some scholars to have come to the islands around 450 B.C. Mountain areas of Wales, Scotland, and Ireland have remained mostly Celtic.

Later, from the A.D. 400s to 1000s, new groups of people came. The Angles and Saxons came from northern Germany and Denmark. The Vikings came from Scandinavia. Last to arrive in Britain were the Normans from northern France. They conquered England in 1066. English as spoken today reflects these migrations. It combines elements from the Anglo-Saxon and Norman French languages.

A Global Power England became a world power in the late 1500s. Surrounded by water, the country developed a powerful navy that protected trade routes. In the 1600s the English began establishing colonies around the world. By the early 1800s they had also united England, Scotland, Wales, and Ireland into one kingdom. From London the United Kingdom built a vast British Empire. By 1900 the empire covered nearly one fourth of the world's land area.

▶ This beautiful Anglo-Saxon shoulder clasp from about A.D. 630 held together pieces of clothing.

The United Kingdom also became an economic power in the 1700s and 1800s. It was the cradle of the Industrial Revolution, which began in the last half of the 1700s. Large supplies of coal and iron and a large labor force helped industries grow. The country also developed a good transportation network of rivers, canals, and railroads. Three of the early industries were **textiles**, or cloth products, shipbuilding, iron, and later steel. Coal powered these industries. Birmingham, Manchester, and other cities grew up near Britain's coal fields.

Decline of Empire World wars and economic competition from other countries weakened the United Kingdom in the 1900s. All but parts of northern Ireland became independent in 1921. By the 1970s most British colonies also had gained independence. Most now make up the British Commonwealth of Nations. Members of the Commonwealth meet to discuss economic, scientific, and business matters.

   The United Kingdom still plays an important role in world affairs. It is a leading member of the United Nations (UN), the European Union (EU), and the North Atlantic Treaty Organization (NATO).

The Government The United Kingdom's form of government is called a **constitutional monarchy**. That is, it has a monarch—a king or queen—but a parliament makes the country's laws. The monarch is the head of state but has largely ceremonial duties. Parliament chooses a prime minister to lead the national government.

   In recent years the national government has given people in Scotland and Wales more control over local affairs. Some people think Scotland might one day seek independence.

✔ **READING CHECK:**   *Human Systems*   How are former British colonies linked today?

▲

Queen Elizabeth I (1533–1603) ruled England as it became a world power in the late 1500s.

The British government is seated in London, the capital. The Tower Bridge over the River Thames [TEMZ] is one of the city's many famous historical sites.

Interpreting the Visual Record
Why do you think London became a large city?

▼

Millions of Americans watched the Beatles, a British rock band, perform on television in 1964. The Beatles and other British bands became popular around the world.

Interpreting the Visual Record How do you think television helps shape world cultures today?

Culture

Nearly 60 million people live in the United Kingdom today. English is the official language. Some people in Wales and Scotland also speak the Celtic languages of Welsh and Gaelic [GAY-lik]. The Church of England is the country's official church. However, many Britons belong to other Protestant churches or are Roman Catholic.

Food and Festivals Living close to the sea, the British often eat fish. One popular meal is fish and chips—fried fish and potatoes. However, British food also includes different meats, oat porridge and cakes, and potatoes in many forms.

The British celebrate many religious holidays, such as Christmas. Other holidays include the Queen's official birthday celebration in June. In July many Protestants in Northern Ireland celebrate a battle in 1690 in which Protestants defeated Catholic forces. In recent years the day's parades have sometimes sparked protests and violence between Protestants and Catholics.

Art and Literature British literature, art, and music have been popular around the world. Perhaps the most famous British writer is William Shakespeare. He died in 1616, but his poetry and plays, such as *Romeo and Juliet*, remain popular. In the 1960s the Beatles helped make Britain a major center for modern popular music. More recently, British performers from Elton John to the Spice Girls have attracted many fans.

✓ **READING CHECK:** *Human Systems* What aspects of British culture have spread around the world?

The United Kingdom

COUNTRY	POPULATION/ GROWTH RATE	LIFE EXPECTANCY	LITERACY RATE	PER CAPITA GDP
United Kingdom	59,647,790 0.2%	75, male 81, female	99%	$22,800
United States	281,421,906 0.9%	74, male 80, female	97%	$36,200

Sources: Central Intelligence Agency, *The World Factbook 2001;* U.S. Census Bureau

Interpreting the Chart How does the literacy rate in the United Kingdom compare with that of the United States?

The United Kingdom Today

Nearly 90 percent of Britons today live in urban areas. London, the capital of England, is the largest city. It is located in southeastern England. London is also the capital of the whole United Kingdom.

More than 7 million people live in London. The city is a world center for trade, industry, and services, particularly banking and insurance. London also has one of the world's busiest airports. Many tourists visit London to see its famous historical sites, theaters, and shops. Other important cities include Glasgow, Scotland; Cardiff, Wales; and Belfast, Northern Ireland.

The Economy Old British industries like mining and manufacturing declined after World War II. Today, however, the economy is stronger. North Sea reserves have made the country a major producer of oil and natural gas. Birmingham, Glasgow, and other cities are attracting new industries. One area of Scotland is called Silicon Glen. This is because it has many computer and electronics businesses. **Glen** is a Scottish term for a valley. Today many British work in service industries, including banking, insurance, education, and tourism.

Agriculture Britain's modern farms produce about 60 percent of the country's food. Still, only about 1 percent of the labor force works in agriculture. Important products include grains, potatoes, vegetables, and meat.

Northern Ireland One of the toughest problems facing the country has been violence in Northern Ireland. Sometimes Northern Ireland is called Ulster. The Protestant majority and the Roman Catholic minority there have bitterly fought each other. Violence on both sides has resulted in many deaths.

Many Catholics believe they have not been treated fairly by the Protestant majority. Therefore, many want Northern Ireland to join the mostly Roman Catholic Republic of Ireland. Protestants fear becoming a minority on the island. They want to remain part of the United Kingdom. Many people hope that recent agreements made by political leaders will lead to a lasting peace. In 1999, for example, Protestant and Roman Catholic parties agreed to share power in a new government. However, there have been problems putting that agreement into effect.

READING CHECK: *Human Systems* What has been the cause of conflict in Northern Ireland?

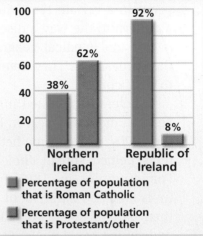

Religion: A Divided Island

Source: *The Statesman's Year Book,* 1998–99.

Interpreting the Graph How does the number of Roman Catholics in the Republic of Ireland differ from that of Northern Ireland?

Section Review 2

Homework Practice Online
Keyword: SG3 HP15

Define and explain: textiles, constitutional monarchy, glen

Working with Sketch Maps On the map you created in Section 1, label the United Kingdom, England, Scotland, Wales, Northern Ireland, Irish Sea, London, Birmingham, Manchester, Glasgow, Cardiff, and Belfast.

Reading for the Main Idea

1. *Human Systems* What peoples came to the British Isles after the Celts? When did they come?

2. *Places and Regions* What was the British Empire?

Critical Thinking

3. **Contrasting** How is the British government different from the U.S. government?

4. **Drawing Inferences and Conclusions** Why do you think Protestants in Northern Ireland want to remain part of the United Kingdom?

Organizing What You Know

5. **Sequencing** Create a timeline that lists important events in the period.

800 B.C.   A.D. 2000

MAPPING THE SPREAD OF CHOLERA

Medical geographers want to discover why a disease occurs in a particular place. Does a disease occur in a certain type of environment? Is there a pattern to the way a disease spreads? Mapping is one tool medical geographers use to answer these questions. They first used maps in this way to fight cholera.

Cholera has existed in India for hundreds of years. It did not appear in Europe, however, until the 1800s. At that time better transportation systems helped spread cholera around the world. For example, in 1817 India experienced an unusually bad outbreak of the disease. India was then part of the British Empire. British soldiers and ships carried cholera to new places. By 1832 the disease had spread to the British Isles and to North America.

No one knew what caused cholera. In fact, no one knew about bacteria or how they caused disease. What was known was that sick people suffered from diarrhea and vomiting. They often died quickly. In just 10 days in 1854, more than 500 people in one London neighborhood died from cholera. Dr. John Snow thought he knew why.

Dr. Snow believed that people got cholera from dirty water. To test his theory, he mapped the location of some of London's public water pumps. (Houses at that time did not have running water.) Then he marked the location of each cholera death on his map. He found most of the deaths were scattered around the water pump on Broad Street. He persuaded officials to remove the pump's handle. After the pump was shut down, there were few new cases of cholera. Not everyone, however, believed Dr. Snow's evidence.

This illustration shows London's Regent Street in about 1850. An outbreak of cholera in this neighborhood killed hundreds of people in 1854.

Cholera Deaths in London, 1854

Dr. Snow plotted cholera deaths for the first 10 days of September 1854 on a map of the neighborhood. Dr. Snow believed that people were getting impure water from the Broad Street pump. A check of the pump showed that a leaking sewer had contaminated the pump's water.

Interpreting the Map What does the map tell you about the relationship between deaths and the Broad Street pump?

Bacteria was discovered in the 1880s. Yet many people still believed that bad air from river mud or swamps spread diseases like cholera. It took another epidemic to convince everyone that dirty water made people sick.

In 1892 an outbreak of cholera in the German port city of Hamburg ended the debate. Once again, the locations of people who became sick were mapped. This mapping was the key to proving that water could spread cholera.

At the time, a street separated Hamburg and another town, Altona. Both towns got their water from the Elbe River. There was, however, an important difference in the two towns' water supplies. Altona had a system for cleaning its water. Hamburg did not. People living on the Hamburg side of the street got sick. Those on the Altona side of the street did not. The air on both sides of the street was the same. Therefore, no one could argue that bad air caused the outbreak. Hamburg then moved quickly to install a system to clean its water.

Understanding What You Read

1. Why did Dr. Snow make a map of a neighborhood's cholera deaths and the location of its water pumps?

2. Why was it important that people on the Hamburg side of the street got sick but people on the Altona side did not?

Dr. John Snow, 1813–1858, was one of the first medical geographers.

Section 3 The Republic of Ireland

Read to Discover

1. What are the key events in Ireland's history?
2. What are the people and culture of Ireland like?
3. What kinds of economic changes has Ireland experienced in recent years?

Define

famine
bog
peat

Locate

Dublin
Cork
Galway

WHY IT MATTERS

Millions of Americans trace their heritage to Ireland. Use CNNfyi.com or other **current events** sources to learn about Ireland and its people today. Record your findings in your journal.

An Irish harp

History

The Irish are descendants of the Celts. Irish Gaelic, a Celtic language, and English are the official languages. Most people in Ireland speak English. Gaelic is spoken mostly in rural western areas.

English Conquest England conquered Ireland in the A.D. 1100s. By the late 1600s most of the Irish had become farmers on land owned by the British. This created problems between the two peoples. Religious differences added to these problems. Most British were Protestant, while most Irish were Roman Catholic. Then, in the 1840s, millions of Irish left for the United States and other countries because of a poor economy and a potato **famine**. A famine is a great shortage of food.

Independence The Irish rebelled against British rule. In 1916, for example, Irish rebels attacked British troops in the Easter Rising.

Stone fences divide the green fields of western Ireland, the Emerald Isle.

Interpreting the Visual Record What kind of climate would you expect to find in a country with rich, green fields such as these?

At the end of 1921, most of Ireland gained independence. Some counties in northern Ireland remained part of the United Kingdom. Ties between the Republic of Ireland and the British Empire were cut in 1949.

Government Ireland has an elected president and parliament. The president has mostly ceremonial duties. Irish voters in 1990 elected a woman as president for the first time.

The parliament makes the country's laws. The Irish parliament chooses a prime minister to lead the government.

✓ **READING CHECK:** (*Human Systems*) What are some important events in Ireland's history?

Culture

Centuries of English rule have left their mark on Irish culture. For example, today nearly everyone in Ireland speaks English. Irish writers, such as George Bernard Shaw and James Joyce, have been among the world's great English-language writers.

A number of groups promote traditional Irish culture in the country today. The Gaelic League, for example, encourages the use of Irish Gaelic. Gaelic and English are taught in schools and used in official documents. Another group promotes Irish sports, such as hurling. Hurling is an outdoor game similar to field hockey and lacrosse.

Elements of Irish culture have also become popular outside the country. For example, traditional Irish folk dancing and music have attracted many fans. Music has long been important in Ireland. In fact, the Irish harp is a national symbol. Many musicians popular today are from Ireland, including members of the rock band U2.

More than 90 percent of the Irish today are Roman Catholic. St. Patrick's Day on March 17 is a national holiday. St. Patrick is believed to have brought Christianity to Ireland in the 400s.

✓ **READING CHECK:** (*Human Systems*) What is Irish culture like today?

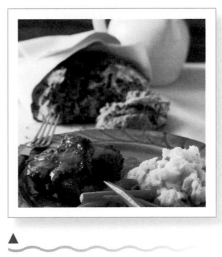

▲
Many Irish enjoy a meal of lamb chops with mustard sauce, soda bread, carrots, and mashed potatoes.

Ireland Today

Ireland used to be one of Europe's poorest countries. Today it is a modern, thriving country with a strong economy and growing cities.

Ireland

COUNTRY	POPULATION/ GROWTH RATE	LIFE EXPECTANCY	LITERACY RATE	PER CAPITA GDP
Ireland	3,840,838 1.1%	74, male 80, female	98%	$21,600
United States	281,421,906 0.9%	74, male 80, female	97%	$36,200

Sources: Central Intelligence Agency, *The World Factbook 2001;* U.S. Census Bureau

Interpreting the Chart How does life expectancy in Ireland compare with that of the United States?

Economy Until recently, Ireland was mostly an agricultural country. This was true even though much of the country is either rocky or boggy. A **bog** is soft ground that is soaked with water. For centuries, **peat** dug from bogs has been used for fuel. Peat is made up of dead plants, usually mosses.

Today Ireland is an industrial country. Irish workers produce processed foods, textiles, chemicals, machinery, crystal, and computers. Finance, tourism, and other service industries are also important.

How did this change come about? Ireland's low taxes, well-educated workers, and membership in the European Union have attracted many foreign companies. Those foreign companies include many from the United States. These companies see Ireland as a door to millions of customers throughout the EU. In fact, goods from their Irish factories are exported to markets in the rest of Europe and countries in other regions.

Cities Many factories have been built around Dublin. Dublin is Ireland's capital and largest city. It is a center for education, banking, and shipping. Nearly 1 million people live there. Housing prices rapidly increased in the 1990s as people moved there for work.

Other cities lie mainly along the coast. These cities include the seaports of Cork and Galway. They have old castles, churches, and other historical sites that are popular among tourists.

✓ **READING CHECK:** *Human Systems* What important economic changes have occurred in Ireland and why?

Section Review 3

Define and explain: famine, bog, peat

Working with Sketch Maps On the map you created in Section 2, label Ireland, Dublin, Cork, and Galway. In the margin explain the importance of Dublin to the Republic of Ireland.

Reading for the Main Idea

1. *Human Systems* What were two of the reasons many Irish moved to the United States and other countries in the 1800s?

2. *Human Systems* What are some important reasons why the economy in Ireland has grown so much in recent years?

Critical Thinking

3. **Drawing Inferences and Conclusions** Why do you think the Irish fought against British rule?

4. **Drawing Inferences and Conclusions** Why do you suppose housing prices rapidly increased in Dublin in the 1990s?

Organizing What You Know

5. **Comparing/Contrasting** Copy the following graphic organizer. Use it to compare and contrast the history, culture, and governments of the Republic of Ireland and the United Kingdom.

Ireland	United Kingdom
Conquered by England in the 1100s	Created vast world empire

go.hrw.com **Homework Practice Online** Keyword: SG3 HP15

Section 4

Scandinavia

Read to Discover

1. What are the people and culture of Scandinavia like?
2. What are some important features of each of the region's countries, plus Greenland, and Lapland?

Define

neutral
uninhabitable
geysers

Locate

Oslo
Bergen
Stockholm
Göteborg
Copenhagen
Nuuk (Godthab)

Reykjavik
Gulf of Bothnia
Gulf of Finland
Helsinki
Lapland

WHY IT MATTERS

Much of the fish Americans eat comes from the nations of Scandinavia. Use **CNNfyi.com** or other **current events** sources to learn more about the economic importance of these nations. Record your findings in your journal.

Smoked salmon, a popular food in Scandinavia

People and Culture

Scandinavia once was home to fierce, warlike Vikings. Today the countries of Norway, Sweden, Denmark, Iceland, and Finland are peaceful and prosperous.

The people of the region enjoy high standards of living. They have good health care and long life spans. Each government provides expensive social programs and services. These programs are paid for by high taxes.

The people and cultures in the countries of Scandinavia are similar in many ways. For example, the region's national languages, except for Finnish, are closely related. In addition, most people in Scandinavia are Lutheran Protestant. All of the Scandinavian countries have democratic governments.

✓ **READING CHECK:**
Human Systems How are the people and cultures of Scandinavia similar?

A Viking ship

Scandinavia

Country	Population/ Growth Rate	Life Expectancy	Literacy Rate	Per Capita GDP
Denmark	5,352,815 0.3%	74, male 80, female	100%	$25,500
Finland	5,175,783 0.2%	74, male 81, female	100%	$22,900
Iceland	277,906 0.5%	77, male 82, female	100%	$24,800
Norway	4,503,440 0.5%	76, male 82, female	100%	$27,700
Sweden	8,875,053 .02%	77, male 83, female	99%	$22,200
United States	281,421,906 0.9%	74, male 80, female	97%	$36,200

Sources: Central Intelligence Agency, *The World Factbook 2001;* U.S. Census Bureau

Interpreting the Chart What is noteworthy about life expectancy in Iceland, Norway, and Sweden?

Norway

Norway is a long, narrow, and rugged country along the western coast of the Scandinavian Peninsula. Norway once was united with Denmark and then Sweden. In 1905 Norway became independent. Today Norway is a constitutional monarchy with an elected parliament.

About 75 percent of the people live in urban areas. The largest cities are the capital, Oslo, and Bergen on the Atlantic coast. Oslo is a modern city. It lies at the end of a wide fjord on the southern coast. The city is Norway's leading seaport, as well as its industrial and cultural center.

Norway has valuable resources, especially oil and natural gas. However, Norway's North Sea oil fields are expected to run dry over the next century. A long coastline and location on the North Sea have helped make Norway a major fishing and shipping country. Fjords shelter Norway's harbors and its fishing and shipping fleets.

Sweden

Sweden is Scandinavia's largest and most populous country. It is located between Norway and Finland. Most Swedes live in cities and towns. The largest cities are Stockholm, which is Sweden's capital, and Göteborg. Stockholm is located on the Baltic Sea coast. It is a beautiful city of islands and forests. Göteborg is a major seaport.

Like Norway, Sweden is a constitutional monarchy. The country has been at peace since the early 1800s. Sweden remained **neutral** during World Wars I and II. A neutral country is one that chooses not to take sides in an international conflict.

Sweden's main sources of wealth are forestry, farming, mining, and manufacturing. Wood, iron ore, automobiles, and wireless telephones are exports. Hydroelectricity is important.

Riddarhomem—the Isle of Knights— is one of several islands on which the original city of Stockholm was built.

Interpreting the Visual Record Why might a group of islands be a good place to build a city?

CONNECTING TO Art

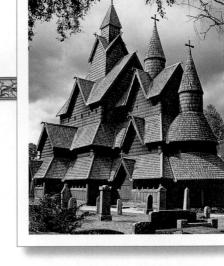

A stave church in Norway

Stave Churches

In Norway you will find some beautiful wooden churches built during the Middle Ages. They are known as stave churches because of their corner posts, or staves. The staves provide the building's basic structure. Today stave churches are a reminder of the days when Viking and Christian beliefs began to merge in Norway.

As many as 800 stave churches were built in Norway during the 1000s and 1100s. Christianity was then beginning to spread throughout the country. It was replacing the old religious beliefs of the Viking people. Still, Viking culture is clearly seen in stave buildings.

Except for a stone foundation, stave churches are made entirely of wood. Workers used methods developed by Viking boat builders. For example, wood on Viking boats was coated with tar to keep it from rotting. Church builders did the same with the wood for their churches. They also decorated the churches with carvings of dragons and other creatures. The stave church at Urnes even has a small Viking ship decorated with nine candles.

When the plague, or Black Death, arrived in Norway about 1350, many communities were abandoned. Many stave churches fell apart. Others were replaced by larger stone buildings. Today only 28 of the original buildings remain. They have been preserved for their beauty and as reminders of an earlier culture.

Understanding What You Read
1. What are staves?
2. How did stave churches reflect new belief systems in Norway?

Denmark

Denmark is the smallest and most densely populated of the region's countries. Most of Denmark lies on the Jutland Peninsula. About 500 islands make up the rest of the country.

Denmark is also a constitutional monarchy. The capital and largest city is Copenhagen. It lies on an island between the Jutland Peninsula and Sweden. Some 1.4 million people—about 25 percent of Denmark's population—live there.

About 60 percent of Denmark's land is used for farming. Farm products, especially meat and dairy products, are important exports. Denmark also has a modern industrial economy. Industries include food processing, machinery, furniture, and electronics.

Greenland's capital lies on the island's southwestern shore.

Interpreting the Visual Record
Why do most people in Greenland live along the coast?

Greenland

The huge island of Greenland is part of North America, but it is a territory of Denmark. Greenland's 56,000 people have their own government. They call their island Kalaallit Nunaat. The capital is Nuuk, also called Godthab. Most of the island's people are Inuit (Eskimo). Fishing is the main economic activity. Some Inuit still hunt seals and small whales.

The island's icy interior is **uninhabitable**. An uninhabitable area is one that cannot support human settlement. Greenland's people live mostly along the southwestern coast in the tundra climate regions.

Iceland

Between Greenland and Scandinavia is the country of Iceland. This Atlantic island belonged to Denmark until 1944. Today it is an independent country. It has an elected president and parliament.

Unlike Greenland, Iceland is populated mostly by northern Europeans. The capital and largest city is Reykjavik (RAYK-yuh-veek). Nearly 40 percent of the country's people live there.

Icelanders make good use of their country's natural resources. For example, about 70 percent of the country's exports are fish. These fish come from the rich waters around the island. In addition, hot water from Iceland's **geysers** heats homes and greenhouses. The word *geyser* is an Icelandic term for hot springs that shoot hot water and steam into the air. Volcanic activity forces heated underground water to rise from the geyser.

Finland

Finland is the easternmost of the region's countries. It lies mostly between two arms of the Baltic Sea: the Gulf of Bothnia and the Gulf of Finland. The capital and largest city is Helsinki, which is located on the southern coast.

Our Amazing Planet

The Great Geysir in southwestern Iceland can spout water nearly 200 feet (61 m) into the air. Some geysers shoot steam and boiling water to a height of more than 1,600 feet (nearly 500 m)!

The original Finnish settlers probably came from northern Asia. Finnish belongs to a language family that includes Estonian and Hungarian. About 6 percent of Finns speak Swedish. Finland was part of Sweden from the 1100s to 1809. It then became part of Russia. Finland gained independence at the end of World War I.

As in the other countries of the region, trade is important to Finland. The country is a major producer of paper and other forest products as well as wireless telephones. Metal products, shipbuilding, and electronics are also important industries. Finland imports energy and many of the raw materials needed in manufacturing.

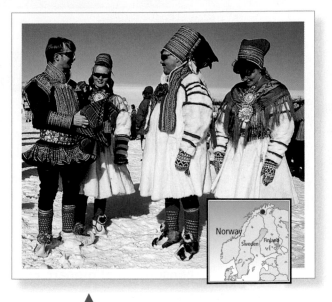

Lapland

Across northern Finland, Sweden, and Norway is a culture region known as Lapland. This region is populated by the Lapps, or Sami, as they call themselves.

The Sami are probably descended from hunters who moved to the region from northern Asia. The languages they speak are related to Finnish. The Sami have tried to keep their culture and traditions, such as reindeer herding. Many now earn a living from tourism.

▲

Young Sami couples here are dressed in traditional clothes for the Easter reindeer races in northern Norway.

Interpreting the Visual Record What climates would you find in the lands of the Sami?

✓ **READING CHECK:** (*Human Systems*) Around what activities are the economies of the countries and territories discussed in this section organized?

Section Review 4

Define and explain: neutral, uninhabitable, geysers

Working with Sketch Maps On the map you created in Section 3, label the countries of Scandinavia, Oslo, Bergen, Stockholm, Göteborg, Copenhagen, Nuuk (Godthab), Reykjavik, Gulf of Bothnia, Gulf of Finland, Helsinki, and Lapland. In the margin describe the people of the Lapland region.

Reading for the Main Idea

1. (*Human Systems*) What are two of the cultural similarities among the peoples of Scandinavia?

2. (*Environment and Society*) In what ways have Icelanders adapted to their natural environment?

3. (*Human Systems*) How have the history and culture of Finland been different from that of other countries in Scandinavia?

Critical Thinking

4. Making Generalizations and Predictions How do you think the location of Greenland and the culture of its people will affect the island's future relationship with Denmark?

Organizing What You Know

5. Summarizing Copy the following graphic organizer. Label the center of the organizer "Scandinavia." In the ovals, write one characteristic of each country and region discussed in this section. Then do the same for the other countries, as well as for Greenland and Lapland.

Scandinavia

Building Vocabulary

On a separate sheet of paper, write sentences to define each of the following words.

1. fjords
2. lochs
3. North Atlantic Drift
4. constitutional monarchy
5. famine
6. bog
7. peat
8. neutral
9. uninhabitable
10. geysers

Reviewing the Main Ideas

1. *Places and Regions* What islands make up the British Isles? What bodies of water surround the British Isles?

2. *Places and Regions* What are the three main climates in northern Europe?

3. *Places and Regions* What large North Atlantic island is a territory of Denmark?

4. *Human Systems* What happened to the British Empire?

5. *Human Systems* What are the two major religions in Northern Ireland? What do these religions have to do with violence in Northern Ireland?

Understanding Environment and Society

Resource Use

Prepare a presentation, along with a map, graph, chart, model, or database, on the distribution of oil and natural gas in the North Sea. You may want to think about the following:

• How oil and natural gas are recovered there.

• How countries divided up the North Sea's oil and natural gas.

Write a five-question quiz, with answers, about your presentation to challenge fellow students.

Thinking Critically

1. **Drawing Inferences and Conclusions** Why do you think British literature, art, and music have been popular around the world?

2. **Drawing Inferences and Conclusions** Why do you think industrial cities like Birmingham and Manchester in Great Britain grew up near coal deposits?

3. **Drawing Inferences and Conclusions** Why do you think most Irish speak English rather than Gaelic?

4. **Making Generalizations and Predictions** How do you think Scandinavians have adapted to life in these very cold environments?

5. **Finding the Main Idea** Why are climates in the British Isles milder than in much of Scandinavia?

Map ACTIVITY

On a separate sheet of paper, match the letters on the map with their correct labels.

London	Oslo
Manchester	Stockholm
Belfast	Copenhagen
Dublin	Reykjavik
Cork	Helsinki

Mental Mapping Skills ACTIVITY

On a separate sheet of paper, draw a freehand map of northern Europe. Make a key for your map and label the following:

Baltic Sea	Ireland
Denmark	Norway
Finland	Scandinavian
Great Britain	Peninsula
Iceland	Sweden

WRITING ACTIVITY

Use print resources to find out more about the Vikings and how they lived in their cold climate. Write a short story set in a Viking village or on a Viking voyage. Describe daily life in the village or on the voyage. Include a bibliography showing references you used. Be sure to use standard grammar, spelling, sentence structure, and punctuation.

Alternative Assessment

Portfolio ACTIVITY

Learning About Your Local Geography

Research Project Northern Europe's social programs are supported by taxes. Research the taxes that people in your area must pay. Interview residents, asking their feelings about taxes.

internet connect

Internet Activity: go.hrw.com
KEYWORD: SG3 GT15

Choose a topic to explore northern Europe:
- Explore the islands and fjords on the Scandinavian coast.
- Visit historic palaces in the United Kingdom.
- Investigate the history of skiing.

go.hrw.com

Eastern Europe

In this chapter you will learn about countries that share common physical features but have developed very different cultures. First, however, we meet Marta, a Hungarian student.

Hello! My name is Marta, and I am from Kecskemét (KECH-ke-mayt), Hungary. My mother is a secretary, and my father is an agricultural engineer. I am in my last year of high school.

Our apartment has no living or dining room, just a kitchen, a tiny balcony, a bathroom, a hallway, and two bedrooms. In the morning, we eat in my parents' room, where we also study and talk during the day.

Our lives changed very much in 1991 when the Soviet Union collapsed. Before this, we had to study Russian in school. Also, my family is Catholic, but we had to have church services in secret. My parents would have risked losing their jobs if anyone found out. Now everyone goes to church freely. My favorite sports in school are basketball, swimming, and fencing. On Friday night we have parties organized by the school. Sometimes we go to the movies. In the summer, I used to work picking cherries. Now I work in a factory processing chickens.

Üdvözöljük Magyarországon!

Translation: Welcome to Hungary!

Section 1 Physical Geography

Read to Discover

1. What are the major physical features of Eastern Europe?
2. What climates and natural resources does this region have?

Define

oil shale
lignite
amber

Locate

Baltic Sea
Adriatic Sea
Black Sea
Danube River
Dinaric Alps
Balkan Mountains
Carpathian Mountains

WHY IT MATTERS

The Danube and its tributaries are important transportation links in Eastern Europe. The rivers also help spread pollution. Use CNNfyi.com or other current events sources to find examples of pollution problems facing the region's rivers. Record your findings in your journal.

Amber

Eastern Europe: Physical-Political

ELEVATION

FEET	METERS
13,120	4,000
6,560	2,000
1,640	500
656	200
(Sea level) 0	0 (Sea level)
Below sea level	Below sea level

⊛ National capitals
• Other cities

Size comparison of Eastern Europe to the contiguous United States

SCALE
0   200   400 Miles
0   200   400 Kilometers
Projection: Azimuthal Equal Area

Our Amazing Planet

Amber is golden, fossilized tree sap. The beaches along the eastern coast of the Baltic Sea are the world's largest and most famous source of amber. Baltic amber is approximately 40 million years old.

Physical Features

Eastern Europe stretches southward from the often cold, stormy shores of the Baltic Sea. In the south are the warmer and sunnier beaches along the Adriatic and Black Seas. We can divide the countries of this region into three groups. Poland, the Czech Republic, Slovakia, and Hungary are in the geographical heart of Europe. The Baltic countries are Estonia, Latvia, and Lithuania. Yugoslavia, Bosnia and Herzegovina, Croatia, Slovenia, Macedonia, Romania, Moldova, Bulgaria, and Albania are the Balkan countries.

Landforms Eastern Europe is a region of mountains and plains. The plains of Poland and the Baltic countries are part of the huge Northern European Plain. The Danube River flows through the Great Hungarian Plain, also called the Great Alföld.

The Alps extend from central Europe southeastward into the Balkan Peninsula. Where they run parallel to the Adriatic coast, the mountains are called the Dinaric (duh-NAR-ik) Alps. As the range continues eastward across the peninsula its name changes to the Balkan Mountains. The Carpathian (kahr-PAY-thee-uhn) Mountains stretch from the Czech Republic across southern Poland and Slovakia and into Ukraine. There they curve south and west into Romania. In Romania they are known as the Transylvanian Alps.

Rivers Eastern Europe's most important river for trade and transportation is the Danube. The Danube stretches for 1,771 miles (2,850 km) across nine countries. It begins in Germany's Alps and flows eastward to the Black Sea. Some 300 tributaries flow into the Danube. The river carries and then drops so much silt that its Black Sea delta grows by 80 to 100 feet (24 to 30 m) every year. The river also carries a heavy load of industrial pollution.

✔ **READING CHECK:** *Places and Regions* What are the main physical features in Eastern Europe?

This aerial view of the Danube Delta shows Romania's rich farmland.

▼

Climate and Resources

The eastern half of the region has long, snowy winters and short, rainy summers. Farther south and west, winters are milder and summers become drier. A warm, sunny climate has drawn visitors to the Adriatic coast for centuries.

Eastern Europe's mineral and energy resources include coal, natural gas, oil, iron, lead, silver, sulfur, and zinc. The region's varied resources support many industries. Some areas of the Balkan region and Hungary are major producers of bauxite. Romania has oil. Estonia has deposits of **oil shale**, or layered rock that yields oil when heated. Estonia uses this oil to generate electricity, which is exported to other Baltic countries and Russia. Slovakia and Slovenia mine a soft form of coal called **lignite**. Nevertheless, many countries must import their energy because demand is greater than supply.

For thousands of years, people have traded **amber**, or fossilized tree sap. Amber is found along the Baltic seacoast. Salt mining, which began in Poland in the 1200s, continues in central Poland today.

During the years of Communist rule industrial production was considered more important than the environment. The region suffered serious environmental damage. Air, soil, and water pollution, deforestation, and the destruction of natural resources were widespread. Many Eastern European countries have begun the long and expensive task of cleaning up their environment.

✔ **READING CHECK:** (*Environment and Society*) What factors affect the location of economic activities in the region?

Do you remember what you learned about climate types? See Chapter 3 to review.

Section Review 1

go.hrw.com **Homework Practice Online** Keyword: SG3 HP16

Define and explain: oil shale, lignite, amber

Working with Sketch Maps On a map of Eastern Europe that you draw or that your teacher provides, label the following: Baltic Sea, Adriatic Sea, Black Sea, Danube River, Dinaric Alps, Balkan Mountains, and Carpathian Mountains.

Reading for the Main Idea

1. (*Places and Regions*) On which three major seas do the countries of Eastern Europe have coasts?

2. (*Environment and Society*) What types of mineral and energy resources are available in this region? How does this influence individual economies?

Critical Thinking

3. Making Generalizations and Predictions Would this region be suitable for agriculture? Why?

4. Identifying Cause and Effect How did Communist rule contribute to the pollution problems of this region?

Organizing What You Know

5. Summarizing Copy the following graphic organizer. Use it to summarize the physical features, climate, and resources of the heartland, the Baltics, and the Balkans. Then write and answer one question about the region's geography based on the chart.

Region	Physical features	Climate	Resources

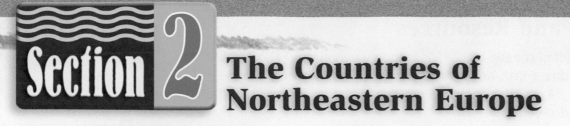

Section 2 · The Countries of Northeastern Europe

Read to Discover

1. What peoples contributed to the early history of northeastern Europe?
2. How was northeastern Europe's culture influenced by other cultures?
3. How has the political organization of this region changed since World War II?

Define

Indo-European

Locate

Estonia	Lithuania	Warsaw
Poland	Latvia	Vistula River
Czech Republic	Prague	Bratislava
Slovakia	Tallinn	Budapest
Hungary	Riga	

WHY IT MATTERS

Jerzy Giedroye, a Polish editor living in France, helped keep the free exchange of ideas alive in Eastern Europe during Communist rule. Use **CNNfyi.com** or other **current events** sources to discover the efforts of people like Giedroye. Record your findings in your journal.

Musical score by Hungarian Béla Bartók

The Teutonic knights, a German order of soldier monks, brought Christianity and feudalism to northeastern Europe. They built this castle at Malbork, Poland, in the 1200s.

History

Migrants and warring armies have swept across Eastern Europe over the centuries. Each group of people brought its own language, religion, and customs. Together these groups contributed to the mosaic of cultures we see in Eastern Europe today.

Early History Among the region's early peoples were the Balts. The Balts lived on the eastern coast of the Baltic Sea. They spoke **Indo-European** languages. The Indo-European language family includes many languages spoken in Europe. These include Germanic, Baltic, and Slavic languages. More than 3,500 years ago, hunters from the Ural Mountains moved into what is now Estonia. They spoke a very different, non-Indo-European language. The language they spoke provided the early roots of today's Estonian and Finnish languages. Beginning around A.D. 400, a warrior people called the Huns invaded the region from Asia. Later, the Slavs came to the region from the plains north of the Black Sea.

In the 800s the Magyars moved into the Great Hungarian Plain. They spoke a language related to Turkish. In the 1200s the Mongols rode out of Central Asia into Hungary. At the same time German settlers pushed eastward, colonizing Poland and Bohemia—the western region of the present-day Czech Republic.

Emerging Nations Since the Middle Ages, Austria, Russia, Sweden, and the German state of Prussia have all ruled parts of Eastern Europe. After World War I ended in 1918, a new map of Eastern Europe was drawn. The peace treaty created two new countries: Yugoslavia and Czechoslovakia. Czechoslovakia included the old regions of Bohemia, Moravia, and Slovakia. At about the same time, Poland, Lithuania, Latvia, and Estonia also became independent countries.

✔ **READING CHECK:** (*Human Systems*) What peoples contributed to the region's early history?

Culture

The culture and festivals of this region show the influence of the many peoples who contributed to its history. As in Scandinavia, Latvians celebrate a midsummer festival. The festival marks the summer solstice, the year's longest day. Poles celebrate major Roman Catholic festivals. Many of these have become symbols of the Polish nation. The annual pilgrimage, or journey, to the shrine of the Black Madonna of Częstochowa (chen-stuh-KOH-vuh) is an example.

Traditional Foods The food of the region reflects German, Russian, and Scandinavian influences. As in northern Europe, potatoes and sausages are important in the diets of Poland and the Baltic countries. Although the region has only limited access to the sea, the fish of lakes and rivers are often the center of a meal. These fish often include trout and carp. Many foods are preserved to last through the long winter. These include pickles, fruits in syrup, dried or smoked hams and sausages, and cured fish.

The Arts, Literature, and Science
Northeastern Europe has made major contributions to the arts, literature, and sciences. For example, Frédéric Chopin (1810–1849) was a famous Polish pianist and composer. Marie Curie (1867–1934), one of the first female physicists, was also born in Poland. The writer Franz Kafka (1883–1924) was born to Jewish parents in Prague (PRAHG), the

Hungarian dancers perform in traditional dress.
Interpreting the Visual Record
How does this Hungarian costume compare to those you have seen from other countries?

Northeastern Europe

COUNTRY	POPULATION/ GROWTH RATE	LIFE EXPECTANCY	LITERACY RATE	PER CAPITA GDP
Czech Republic	10,264,212 −0.1%	71, male 78, female	100%	$12,900
Estonia	1,423,316 −0.6%	64, male 76, female	100%	$10,000
Hungary	10,106,017 −0.3%	67, male 76, female	99%	$11,200
Latvia	2,385,231 −0.8%	63, male 75, female	100%	$7,200
Lithuania	3,610,535 −0.3%	63, male 76, female	98%	$7,300
Poland	38,633,912 −0.03%	69, male 78, female	99%	$8,500
Slovakia	5,414,937 0.1%	70, male 78, female	not available	$10,200
United States	281,421,906 0.9%	74, male 80, female	97%	$36,200

Sources: Central Intelligence Agency, *The World Factbook 2001;* U.S. Census Bureau

Interpreting the Chart Based on the data in the table, which two countries have the lowest levels of economic development?

This suspension bridge spans the Western Dvina River in Riga, the capital of Latvia.

present-day capital of the Czech Republic. Astronomer Nicolaus Copernicus (1473–1543) was born in Toruń (TAWR-oon), a city in north-central Poland. He set forth the theory that the Sun—not Earth—is the center of the universe.

✔ **READING CHECK:** *Human Systems* How is the region's culture a reflection of its past and location?

Northeastern Europe Today

Estonia, Latvia, and Lithuania lie on the flat plain by the eastern Baltic Sea. Once part of the Russian Empire, the Baltic countries gained their independence after World War I ended in 1918. However, they were taken over by the Soviet Union in 1940 and placed under Communist rule. The Soviet Union collapsed in 1991. Since then, the countries of northeastern Europe have been moving from communism to capitalism and democracy.

Estonia A long history of Russian control is reflected in Estonia today. Nearly 30 percent of Estonia's population is ethnic Russian. Russia remains one of Estonia's most important trading partners. However, Estonia is also building economic ties to other countries, particularly Finland. Ethnic Estonians have close cultural ties to Finland. In fact, the Estonian language is related to Finnish. Also, most people in both countries are Lutherans. Ferries link the Estonian capital of Tallinn (TA-luhn) with Helsinki, Finland's capital.

CONNECTING TO *Literature*

Toy robot

While he wrote many books, Czech writer Karel Capek is probably best known for his play R.U.R. This play added the word robot *to the English language. The Czech word* robota *means "drudgery" or forced labor. The term is given to the artificial workers that Rossum's Universal Robots factory make to free humans from drudgery. Eventually, the Robots develop feelings and revolt. The play is science fiction. Here, Harry Domin, the factory's manager, explains the origin of the Robots to visitor Helena Glory.*

ROBOT ROBOTA

Domin: "Well, any one who has looked into human anatomy will have seen at once that man is too complicated, and that a good engineer could make him more simply. So young Rossum began to overhaul anatomy and tried to see what could be left out or simplified. . . . [He] said to himself: 'A man is something that feels happy, plays the piano, likes going for a walk, and in fact, wants to do a whole lot of things that are really unnecessary. . . .

But a working machine must not play the piano, must not feel happy, must not do a whole lot of other things. A gasoline motor must not have tassels or ornaments, Miss Glory. And to manufacture artificial workers is the same thing as to manufacture gasoline motors. The process must be of the simplest, and the product of the best from a practical point of view. . . .

Young Rossum . . . rejected everything that did not contribute directly to the progress of work—everything that makes man more expensive. In fact, he rejected man and made the Robot. My dear Miss Glory, the Robots are not people. Mechanically they are more perfect than we are, they have an enormously developed intelligence, but they have no soul."

Analyzing Primary Sources

1. Why does Rossum design the Robots without human qualities?
2. How has Karel Capel's play influenced other cultures?

Latvia Latvia is the second largest of the Baltic countries. Its population has the highest percentage of ethnic minorities. Some 57 percent of the population is Latvian. About 30 percent of the people are Russian. The capital, Riga (REE-guh), has more than 1 million people. It is the largest urban area in the three Baltic countries. Like Estonia, Latvia also has experienced strong Scandinavian and Russian influences. As well as having been part of the Russian Empire, part of the country once was ruled by Sweden. Another tie between Latvia, Estonia, and the Scandinavian countries is religion. Traditionally most people in these countries are Lutheran. In addition, Sweden and Finland are important trading partners of Latvia today.

This Polish teenager wears traditional dress during a local festival.

Lithuania Lithuania is the largest and southernmost Baltic country. Its capital is Vilnius (VIL-nee-uhs). Lithuania's population has the smallest percentage of ethnic minorities. More than 80 percent of the population is Lithuanian. Nearly 9 percent is Russian, while 7 percent is Polish. Lithuania has ancient ties to Poland. For more than 200 years, until 1795, they were one country. Roman Catholicism is the main religion in both Lithuania and Poland today. As in the other Baltic countries, agriculture and production of basic consumer goods are important parts of Lithuania's economy.

Poland Poland is northeastern Europe's largest and most populous country. The total population of Poland is about the same as that of Spain. The country was divided among its neighbors in the 1700s. Poland regained its independence shortly after World War I. After World War II the Soviet Union established a Communist government to rule the country.

In 1989 the Communists finally allowed free elections. Many businesses now are owned by people in the private sector rather than by the government. The country has also strengthened its ties with Western countries. In 1999 Poland, the Czech Republic, and Hungary joined the North Atlantic Treaty Organization (NATO).

Warsaw, the capital, has long been the cultural, political, and historical center of Polish life. More than 2 million people live in the urban area. The city lies on the Vistula River in central Poland. This location has made Warsaw the center of the national transportation and communications networks as well.

The Former Czechoslovakia Czechoslovakia became an independent country after World War I. Until that time, its lands had been part of the Austro-Hungarian Empire. Then shortly before World War II, it fell under German rule. After the war the Communists, with the support of the Soviet Union, gained control of the government. As in Poland, the Communists lost power in 1989. In 1993 Czechoslovakia peacefully split into two countries. The western part became the Czech Republic. The eastern part became Slovakia. This peaceful split helped the Czechs and Slovaks avoid the ethnic problems that have troubled other countries in the region.

The Czech Republic The Czech Republic experienced economic growth in the early 1990s. Most of the country's businesses are completely or in part privately owned. However, some Czechs worry that the government remains too involved in the economy. As in Poland, a variety of political parties compete in free elections. Czech lands have coal and other important

Prague's Charles Bridge is lined with historical statues.

Interpreting the Visual Record How does this bridge compare to other bridges you have seen?

mineral resources that are used in industry. Much of the country's industry is located in and around Prague, the capital. The city is located on the Vltava River. More than 1.2 million people live there. Prague has beautiful medieval buildings. It also has one of Europe's oldest universities.

Slovakia Slovakia is more rugged and rural, with incomes lower than in the Czech Republic. The move toward a freer political system has been slow. However, progress has been made. Bratislava (BRAH-tyee-slah-vah), the capital, is located on the Danube River. The city is the country's most important industrial area and cultural center. Many rural Slovaks move to Bratislava looking for better-paying jobs. Most of the country's population is Slovak. However, ethnic Hungarians account for more than 10 percent of Slovakia's population.

Hungary Hungary separated from the Austro-Hungarian Empire at the end of World War I. Following World War II, a Communist government came to power. A revolt against the government was put down by the Soviet Union in 1956. The Communists ruled until 1989.

Today the country has close ties with the rest of Europe. In fact, most of Hungary's trade is with members of the European Union. During the Communist era, the government experimented with giving some businesses the freedom to act on their own. For example, it allowed local farm managers to make key business decisions. These managers kept farming methods modern, chose their crops, and marketed their products. Today, farm products from Hungary's fertile plains are important exports. Much of the country's manufacturing is located in and around the capital, Budapest (BOO-duh-pest). Budapest is Hungary's largest city. Nearly 20 percent of the population lives there.

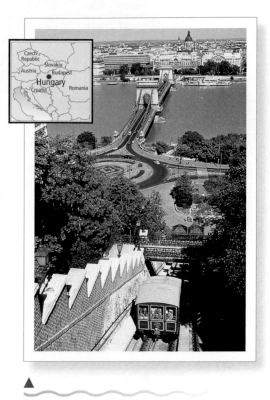

The Danube River flows through Budapest, Hungary.

Interpreting the Visual Record Why might Hungary's capital have grown up along a river?

✔ **READING CHECK:** (*Human Systems*) How have the governments and economies of the region been affected by recent history?

Section Review 2

go.hrw.com Homework Practice Online Keyword: SG3 HP16

Define and explain: Indo-European

Working with Sketch Maps On the map you drew in Section 1, label the countries of the region, Prague, Tallinn, Riga, Warsaw, Vistula River, Bratislava, and Budapest.

Reading for the Main Idea

1. (*Human Systems*) How did invasions and migrations help shape the region?

2. (*Places and Regions*) What has the region contributed to the arts?

Critical Thinking

3. **Drawing Inferences and Conclusions** How did the Soviet Union influence the region?

4. **Summarizing** What social changes have taken place here since the early 1990s?

Organizing What You Know

5. **Sequencing** Copy the following graphic organizer. Use it to show the history of the Baltics since 1900.

1900	1945	1999

Section 3 — The Countries of Southeastern Europe

Read to Discover

1. How did Southeastern Europe's early history help shape its modern societies?
2. How does culture both link and divide the region?
3. How has the region's past contributed to current conflicts?

Define

Roma

Locate

Bulgaria	Albania	Zagreb
Romania	Yugoslavia	Ljubljana
Croatia	Kosovo	Skopje
Slovenia	Montenegro	Bucharest
Serbia	Macedonia	Moldova
Bosnia and	Belgrade	Chişinău
Herzegovina	Podgorica	Sofia
	Sarajevo	Tiranë

WHY IT MATTERS

Bosnia and the other republics of the former Yugoslovia have experienced ethnic violence since independence. Use CNNfyi.com or other **current events** sources to check on current conditions in the region. Record your findings in your journal.

Dolls in traditional Croatian dress

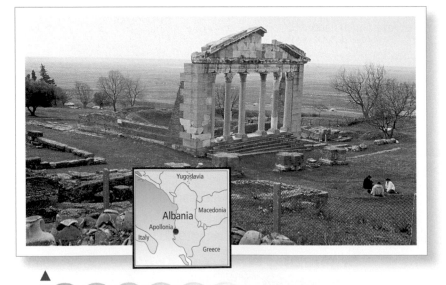

▲ These ancient ruins in southern Albania date to the 500s B.C.

Interpreting the Visual Record What cultural influence does this building show?

History

Along with neighboring Greece, this was the first region of Europe to adopt agriculture. From here farming moved up the Danube River valley into central and western Europe. Early farmers and metalworkers in the south may have spoken languages related to Albanian. Albanian is an Indo-European language.

Early History Around 750–600 B.C. the ancient Greeks founded colonies on the Black Sea coast. The area they settled is now Bulgaria and Romania. Later, the Romans conquered most of the area from the Adriatic Sea to the Danube River and across into Romania. When the Roman Empire divided into west and east, much of the Balkans and Greece became part of the Eastern Roman Empire. This eastern region eventually became known as the Byzantine Empire. Under Byzantine rule, many people of the Balkans became Orthodox Christians.

Kingdoms and Empires Many of today's southeastern European countries first appear as kingdoms between A.D. 800 and 1400. The Ottoman Turks conquered the region and ruled until the 1800s. The Ottomans, who were Muslims, tolerated other religious faiths. However, many peoples, such as the Bosnians and Albanians, converted to Islam. As the Ottoman Empire began to weaken in the late 1800s, the Austro-Hungarians took control of Croatia and Slovenia. They imposed Roman Catholicism.

Slav Nationalism The Russians, meanwhile, were fighting the Turks for control of the Black Sea. The Russians encouraged Slavs in the Balkans to revolt against the Turks. The Russians appealed to Slavic nationalism— to the Slav's sense of loyalty to their country. The Serbs did revolt in 1815 and became self-governing in 1817. By 1878 Bulgaria and Romania were also self-governing.

The Austro-Hungarians responded to Slavic nationalism by occupying additional territories. Those territories included the regions of Bosnia and Herzegovina. To stop the Serbs from expanding to the Adriatic coast, European powers made Albania an independent kingdom.

In August 1914 a Serb nationalist shot and killed the heir to the Austro-Hungarian throne. Austria declared war on Serbia. Russia came to Serbia's defense. These actions sparked World War I. All of Europe's great powers became involved. The United States entered the war in 1917.

Creation of Yugoslavia At the end of World War I Austria-Hungary was broken apart. Austria was reduced to a small territory. Hungary became a separate country but lost its eastern province to Romania. Romania also gained additional lands from Russia. Albania remained independent. The peace settlement created Yugoslavia. *Yugoslavia* means "land of the southern Slavs." Yugoslavia brought the region's Serbs, Bosnians, Croatians, Macedonians, Montenegrins, and Slovenes together into one country. Each ethnic group had its own republic within Yugoslavia. Some Bosnians and other people in Serbia were Muslims. Most Serbs were Orthodox Christians, and the Slovenes and Croats were Roman Catholics. These ethnic and religious differences created problems that eventually led to civil war in the 1990s.

✓ **READING CHECK:** (*Human Systems*) How is southeastern Europe's religious and ethnic makeup a reflection of its past?

This bridge at Mostar, Bosnia, was built during the 1600s. This photograph was taken in 1982.

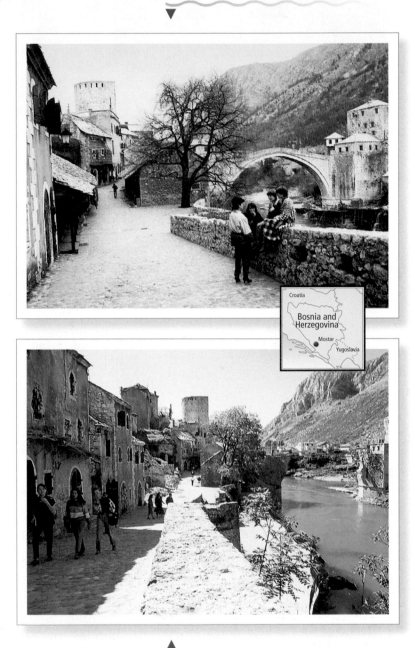

This photograph shows Mostar after civil war in the 1990s.

Interpreting the Visual Record What differences can you find in the two photos?

Ethnic Albanians worship at a mosque in Pristina, Serbia.

Culture

The Balkans are the most diverse region of Europe in terms of language, ethnicity, and religion. It is the largest European region to have once been ruled by a Muslim power. It has also been a zone of conflict between eastern and western Christianity. The three main Indo-European language branches—Romance (from Latin), Germanic, and Slavic—are all found here, as well as other branches like Albanian. Non-Indo-European languages like Hungarian and Turkish are also spoken here.

Balkan diets combine the foods of the Hungarians and the Slavs with those of the Mediterranean Greeks, Turks, and Italians. In Greek and Turkish cuisines, yogurt and soft cheeses are an important part of most meals, as are fresh fruits, nuts, and vegetables. Roast goat or lamb are the favorite meats for a celebration.

In the Balkans Bosnian and ethnic Albanian Muslims celebrate the feasts of Islam. Christian holidays—Christmas and Easter—are celebrated on one day by Catholics and on another by Orthodox Christians. Holidays in memory of ancient battles and modern liberation days are sources of conflict between ethnic groups.

✓ **READING CHECK:** *Places and Regions* Why is religion an important issue in southeastern Europe?

Our Amazing Planet

The Danube Delta, on the Romanian coast of the Black Sea, is part of a unique ecosystem. Most of the Romanian caviar-producing sturgeon are caught in these waters. Caviar is made from the salted eggs from three types of sturgeon fish. Caviar is considered a delicacy and can cost as much as $50 per ounce.

Southeastern Europe Today

Like other southeastern European countries, Yugoslavia was occupied by Germany in World War II. A Communist government under Josip Broz Tito took over after the war. Tito's strong central government prevented ethnic conflict. After Tito died in 1980, Yugoslavia's Communist government held the republics together. Then in 1991 the republics of Slovenia, Croatia, Bosnia and Herzegovina, and Macedonia began to break away. Years of bloody civil war followed. Today the region struggles with the violence and with rebuilding economies left weak by years of Communist-government control.

Yugoslavia The republics of Serbia and Montenegro remain united and have kept the name of Yugoslavia. Belgrade is the capital of both Serbia and Yugoslavia. It is located on the Danube River. The capital of Montenegro is Podgorica (PAWD-gawr-eet-sah). The Serbian government supported ethnic Serbs fighting in civil wars in Croatia and in Bosnia and Herzegovina in the early 1990s. Tensions between ethnic groups also have been a problem within Serbia. About 65 percent of the people in Serbia and Montenegro are Orthodox Christians. In the southern Serbian province of Kosovo, the majority of people are ethnic Albanian and Muslim. Many of the Albanians want independence. Conflict between Serbs and Albanians led to civil war in the late 1990s. In 1999 the United States, other Western countries, and Russia sent troops to keep the peace.

Bosnia and Herzegovina Bosnia and Herzegovina generally are referred to as Bosnia. Some 40 percent of Bosnians are Muslims, but large numbers of Roman Catholic Croats and Orthodox Christian Serbs also live there. Following independence, a bloody civil war broke out between these groups as they struggled for control of territory. During the fighting the once beautiful capital of Sarajevo (sar-uh-YAY-voh) was heavily damaged.

Croatia Croatia's capital is Zagreb (ZAH-greb). Most of the people of Croatia are Roman Catholic. In the early 1990s, Serbs made up about 12 percent of the population. In 1991 the ethnic Serbs living in Croatia claimed part of the country for Serbia. This resulted in heavy fighting. By the end of 1995 an agreement was reached and a sense of stability returned to the country. Many Serbs left the country.

Slovenia Slovenia is a former Austrian territory. It looks to Western European countries for much of its trade. Most people in Slovenia are Roman Catholic, and few ethnic minorities live there. Partly because of the small number of ethnic minorities, little fighting occurred after Slovenia declared independence from Yugoslavia. The major center of industry is Ljubljana (lee-oo-blee-AH-nuh), the country's capital.

These Muslim refugees are walking to Travnik, Bosnia, with the assistance of UN troops from Britain in the 1990s.
Interpreting the Visual Record What effect might the movement of refugees have on a region?

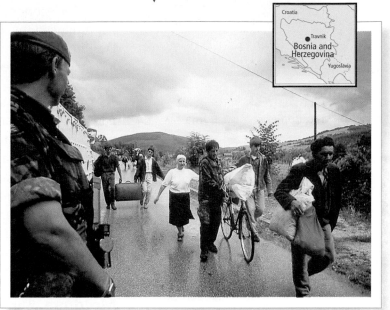

Slovenia's capital, Ljubljana, lies on the Sava River.

Ethnic Groups in Macedonia

- 67%
- 23%
- 4%
- 2%
- 2%

Macedonians
Albanians
Turks
Roma
Serbs
Other

In 2001 ethnic Albanian rebels launched months of fighting in hopes of gaining more rights for Macedonia's Albanian minority.

Interpreting the Chart What percentage of Macedonia's people are Albanian?

Macedonia When Macedonia declared its independence from Yugoslavia, Greece immediately objected to the country's new name. Macedonia is also the name of a province in northern Greece that has historical ties to the republic. Greece feared that Macedonia might try to take over the province.

Greece responded by refusing to trade with Macedonia until the mid-1990s. This slowed Macedonia's movement from the command—or government-controlled—economy it had under Communist rule to a market economy in which consumers help to determine what is to be produced by buying or not buying certain goods and services. Despite its rocky start, in recent years Macedonia has made progress in establishing free markets.

Romania A Communist government took power in Romania at the end of World War II. Then in 1989 the Communist government was overthrown during bloody fighting. Change, however, has been slow. Bucharest, the capital, is the biggest industrial center. Today more people work in agriculture than in any other part of the economy. Nearly 90 percent of the country's population is ethnic Romanian. **Roma**, or Gypsies as they were once known, make up almost 2 percent of the population. They are descended from people who may have lived in northern India and began migrating centuries ago. Most of the rest of Romania's population are ethnic Hungarian.

Moldova Throughout history control of Moldova has shifted many times. It has been dominated by Turks, Polish princes, Austria, Hungary, Russia, and Romania. Not surprisingly, the country's population reflects this diverse past. Moldova declared its independence in

Turkish Roma girls

1991 from the Soviet Union. However, the country suffers from difficult economic and political problems. About 40 percent of the country's labor force works in agriculture. Chişinău (kee-shee-NOW), the major industrial center of the country, is also Moldova's capital.

Bulgaria Mountainous Bulgaria has progressed slowly since the fall of communism. However, a market economy is growing gradually, and the people have more freedoms. Most industries are located near Sofia (SOH-fee-uh), the capital and largest city. About 9 percent of Bulgaria's people are ethnic Turks.

Albania Albania is one of Europe's poorest countries. The capital, Tiranë (ti-RAH-nuh), has a population of about 270,000. About 70 percent of Albanians are Muslim. Albania's Communist government feuded with the Communist governments in the Soviet Union and, later, in China. As a result, Albania became isolated. Since the fall of its harsh Communist government in the 1990s, the country has tried to move toward both democracy and a free market system.

✓ **READING CHECK:** (*Human Systems*) What problems does the region face, and how are they reflections of its Communist past?

Southeastern Europe

COUNTRY	POPULATION/ GROWTH RATE	LIFE EXPECTANCY	LITERACY RATE	PER CAPITA GDP
Albania	3,510,484 0.9%	69, male 75, female	93%	$3,000
Bosnia and Herzegovina	3,922,205 1.4%	69, male 74, female	not available	$1,700
Bulgaria	7,707,495 −1.1%	68, male 75, female	98%	$6,200
Croatia	4,334,142 1.5%	70, male 78, female	97%	$5,800
Macedonia	2,046,209 0.4%	72, male 76, female	not available	$4,400
Moldova	4,431,570 0.05%	60, male 69, female	96%	$2,500
Romania	22,364,022 −0.2%	66, male 74, female	97%	$5,900
Yugoslavia (Serbia and Montenegro)	10,677,290 −0.3%	70, male 76, female	93%	$2,300
United States	281,421,906 0.9%	74, male 80, female	97%	$36,200

Sources: Central Intelligence Agency, *The World Factbook 2001;* U.S. Census Bureau

Interpreting the Chart Based on the table, which southeastern European country has the highest level of economic development?

Section Review 3

go.hrw.com **Homework Practice Online**
Keyword: SG3 HP16

Define and explain: Roma

Working with Sketch Maps On the map you drew in Section 2, label the region's countries and their capitals. They are listed at the beginning of the section. In a box in the margin, identify the countries that once made up Yugoslavia.

Reading for the Main Idea

1. (*Human Systems*) How has the region's history influenced its religious and ethnic makeup?

2. (*Human Systems*) What events and factors have contributed to problems in Bosnia and other countries in the region since independence?

Critical Thinking

3. **Summarizing** How was Yugoslavia created?

4. **Analyzing Information** How are the region's governments and economies changing?

Organizing What You Know

5. **Categorizing** Copy the following graphic organizer. Use it to identify languages, foods, and celebrations in the region.

Reviewing What You Know

Building Vocabulary

On a separate sheet of paper, write sentences to define each of the following words.

1. oil shale
2. lignite
3. amber
4. Indo-European
5. Roma

Reviewing the Main Ideas

1. (*Places and Regions*) What are the major landforms of Eastern Europe?

2. (*Human Systems*) What groups influenced the culture of Eastern Europe? How can these influences be seen in modern society?

3. (*Environment and Society*) What were some environmental effects of Communist economic policies in Eastern Europe?

4. (*Human Systems*) What political and economic systems were most common in Eastern Europe before the 1990s? How and why have these systems changed?

5. (*Human Systems*) List the countries that broke away from Yugoslavia in the early 1990s. What are the greatest sources of tension in these countries?

Understanding Environment and Society

Economic Geography

During the Communist era, the Council for Economic Assistance, or COMECON, played an important role in planning the economies of countries in the region. Create a presentation comparing the practices of this organization to the practices now in place in the region. Consider the following:

- How COMECON organized the distribution of goods and services.
- How countries in the region now organize distribution.

Thinking Critically

1. **Drawing Inferences and Conclusions** How has Eastern Europe's location influenced the diets of the region's people?

2. **Analyzing Information** What is Eastern Europe's most important river for transportation and trade? How can you tell that the river is important to economic development?

3. **Identifying Cause and Effect** What geographic factors help make Warsaw the transportation and communication center of Poland? Imagine that Warsaw is located along the Baltic coast of Poland or near the German border. How might Warsaw have developed differently?

4. **Comparing/Contrasting** Compare and contrast the breakups of Yugoslavia and Czechoslovakia.

5. **Summarizing** How has political change affected the economies of Eastern European countries?

Map ACTIVITY

On a separate sheet of paper, match the letters on the map with their correct labels.

Baltic Sea
Adriatic Sea
Black Sea
Danube River
Dinaric Alps

Balkan Mountains
Carpathian Mountains

Mental Mapping Skills ACTIVITY

Using the chapter map or a globe as a guide, draw a freehand map of Eastern Europe and label the following:

Bosnia and Herzegovina
Croatia
Czech Republic
Estonia

Hungary
Macedonia
Poland
Yugoslavia

WRITING ACTIVITY

Imagine that you are a teenager living in Romania and want to write a family memoir of life in Romania. Include accounts of life for your grandparents under strict Soviet rule and life for your parents during the Soviet Union's breakup. Also describe your life in free Romania. Be sure to use standard grammar, spelling, sentence structure, and punctuation.

Alternative Assessment

Portfolio ACTIVITY

Learning About Your Local Geography

Cooperative Project Ask international agencies or search the Internet for help in contacting a boy or girl in Eastern Europe. As a group, write a letter to the teen, telling about your daily lives.

internet connect

Internet Activity: go.hrw.com
KEYWORD: SG3 GT16

Choose a topic to explore Eastern Europe:
• Investigate the conflicts in the Balkans.
• Take a virtual tour of Eastern Europe.
• Learn about Baltic amber.

FOCUS ON GOVERNMENT

The European Union

What if . . . ? Imagine you are traveling from Texas to Minnesota. You have to go through a border checkpoint in Oklahoma to prove your Texas identity. The guard charges a tax on the cookies you are bringing to a friend in Minnesota. Buying gas presents more problems. You try to pay with Texas dollars, but the attendant just looks at you. You discover that they speak "Kansonian" in Kansas and use Kansas coins. All this would make traveling from one place to another much more difficult.

The European Union Fortunately, that was just an imaginary situation. However, it is similar

The Eurostar train carries passengers from London to Paris. These two cities are only about 200 miles (322 km) apart. However, they have different cultures and ways of life.

to what might happen while traveling across Europe. European countries have different languages, currencies, laws, and cultures. For example, someone from France has different customs than someone from Ireland.

However, many Europeans also share common interests. For example, they are interested in peace in the region. They also have a common interest in Europe's economic success.

A shared belief in economic and political cooperation has resulted in the creation of the European Union (EU). The EU has 15 countries that are members. They are: Austria, Belgium, Denmark, Finland, France, Germany, Great Britain, Greece, Ireland, Italy, Luxembourg, the Netherlands, Portugal, Spain, and Sweden.

The Beginnings of a Unified Europe

Proposals for an economically integrated Europe first came about in the 1950s. After World War II, the countries of Europe had many economic problems. A plan was made to unify the coal and steel production of some countries. In 1957 France, Germany, Italy, Belgium, the Netherlands, and Luxembourg formed the European Economic Community (EEC). The name was later shortened to simply the European Community (EC). The goal of the EC was to combine each country's economy into a single market. Having one market would make trading among them easier. Eventually, more countries became interested in joining the EC. In 1973 Britain, Denmark, and Ireland joined. In the 1980s Greece, Portugal, and Spain joined.

The European Union (EU)

The 15 EU countries produce a wide range of exports and are one of the world's richest markets.

The flag of the EU features 12 gold stars on a blue background. The EU's currency, the euro, replaced the currencies of most EU countries.

In the early 1990s, a meeting was held in Maastricht, the Netherlands, to discuss the future of the EC. This resulted in the Maastricht Treaty. The treaty officially changed the EC's name from the European Community to the European Union (EU).

The Future Some people believe the EU is laying the foundation for a greater sense of European identity. A European Court of Justice has been set up to enforce EU rules. According to some experts, this is helping to build common European beliefs, responsibilities, and rights.

The introduction of a common currency, the euro, will continue in the future. Currently, each country has its own form of money. For example, France uses the Franc. Italy uses the lira. On January 1, 2002, the euro became a common form of money for most EU countries. With the exception of Denmark, Sweden, and the United Kingdom, the euro replaced the currencies of member countries.

Another goal of the EU is to extend membership to other countries.

The EU has resulted in many important changes in Europe. Cooperation between member countries has increased. Trade has also increased. EU members have adopted a common currency and common economic laws. The EU is creating a more unified Europe. Some people even believe that the EU might someday lead to a "United States of Europe."

Understanding What You Read

1. What was the first step toward European economic unity?

2. What is the euro? How will it affect the other currencies of the EU countries?

Building Skills for Life: Analyzing Settlement Patterns

There are many different kinds of human settlements. Some people live in villages where they farm and raise animals. Others live in small towns or cities and work in factories or offices. Geographers analyze these settlement patterns. They are interested in how settlements affect people's lives.

All settlements are unique. Even neighboring villages are different. One village might have better soil than its neighbors. Another village might be closer to a main road or highway. Geographers are interested in the unique qualities of human settlements.

Geographers also study different types of settlements. For example, many European settlements could be considered medieval cities. Medieval cities are about 500–1,500 years old. They usually have walls around them and buildings made of stone and wood. Medieval cities also have tall churches and narrow, winding streets.

▲

This illustration shows a German medieval city in the 1400s.

Analyzing settlement patterns is important. It helps us learn about people and environments. For example, the architecture of a city might give us clues about the culture, history, and technology of the people who live there.

You can ask questions about individual villages, towns, and cities to learn about settlement patterns. What kinds of activities are going on? How are the streets arranged? What kinds of transportation do people use? You can also ask questions about groups of settlements. How are they connected? Do they trade with each other? Are some settlements bigger or older than others? Why is this so?

PRACTICING THE SKILL

1. How do you think a city, a town, and a village are different from each other? Write down your own definition of each word on a piece of paper. Then look them up in a dictionary and write down the dictionary's definition. Were your definitions different?

2. Analyze the settlement where you live. How old is it? How many people live there? What kinds of jobs do people have? How is it connected to other settlements? How is it unique?

3. Besides medieval cities, what other types of cities can you think of? Make a list of three other possible types.

HANDS on GEOGRAPHY

One type of settlement is called a planned city. A planned city is carefully designed before it is built. Each part fits into an overall plan. For example, the size and arrangement of streets and buildings might be planned.

There are many planned cities in the world. Some examples are Brasília, Brazil; Chandigarh, India; and Washington, D.C. Many other cities have certain parts that are planned, such as individual neighborhoods. These neighborhoods are sometimes called planned communities.

Suppose you were asked to plan a city. How would you do it? On a separate sheet of paper, create your own planned city. These guidelines will help you get started.

1. First, decide what the physical environment will be like. Is the city on the coast, on a river, or somewhere else? Are there hills, lakes, or other physical features in the area?

2. Decide what to include in your city. Most cities have a downtown, different neighborhoods, and roads or highways that connect areas together. Many cities also have parks, museums, and an airport.

3. Plan the arrangement of your city. Where will the roads and highways go? Will the airport be close to downtown? Try to arrange the different parts of your city so that they fit together logically.

4. Draw a map of your planned city. Be sure to include a title, scale, and orientation.

▲

Some people think the city plan for Brasília looks like a bird, a bow and arrow, or an airplane. **Interpreting the Visual Record** What do you notice about the arrangement of Brasília's streets?

Lab Report

1. How was your plan influenced by the physical environment you chose?

2. How do you think planned cities are different from cities that are not planned?

3. What problems might people have when they try to plan an entire city?

Russia and Northern Eurasia

CHAPTER 17
Russia

CHAPTER 18
Ukraine, Belarus, and the Caucasus

CHAPTER 19
Central Asia

Dancers in Russian national dress

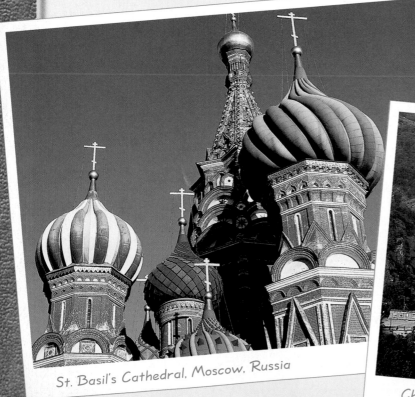

St. Basil's Cathedral, Moscow, Russia

Church overlooking the Black Sea, Ukraine

Journalists in Russia

Journalists Gary Matoso and Lisa Dickey traveled more than 5,000 miles across Russia. They wrote this account of their visit with Buyanto Tsydypov. He is a Buryat farmer who lives in the Lake Baikal area. The Buryats are one of Russia's many minority ethnic groups. **WHAT DO YOU THINK?** *If you visited a Buryat family, what would you like to see or ask?*

"You came to us like thunder out of the clear blue sky," said our host. The surprise of our visit did not, however, keep him from greeting us warmly.

Buyanto brought us to a special place of prayer. High on a hillside, a yellow wooden frame holds a row of tall, narrow sticks. On the end of each stick, Buddhist prayer cloths flutter in the biting autumn wind.

In times of trouble and thanks, Buryats come to tie their prayer cloths—called *khimorin*—to the sticks and make their offerings to the gods. Buyanto builds a small fire. He unfolds an aqua-blue *khimorin* to show the drawings.

"All around are the Buddhist gods," he says, "and at the bottom we have written our names and the names of others we are praying for."

He fans the flames slowly with the cloth, purifying it with sacred smoke. After a time he moves to the top of the hill where he ties the *khimorin* to one of the sticks.

Buryat people, Lake Baikal area, Russia

Understanding Primary Sources

1. How do you know that Buyanto Tsydypov was surprised to meet the two American journalists?

2. What is a *khimorin*?

Brown bear

Russia and Northern Eurasia

Elevation Profile

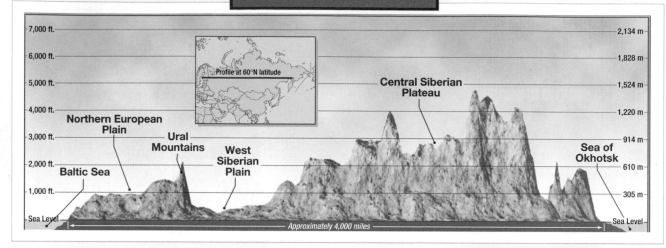

Profile at 60°N latitude

7,000 ft.	2,134 m
6,000 ft.	1,828 m
5,000 ft.	1,524 m
4,000 ft.	1,220 m
3,000 ft.	914 m
2,000 ft.	610 m
1,000 ft.	305 m
Sea Level	Sea Level

Northern European Plain

Ural Mountains

West Siberian Plain

Central Siberian Plateau

Sea of Okhotsk

Baltic Sea

Approximately 4,000 miles

Comparing Sizes

The United States and Russia and Northern Eurasia

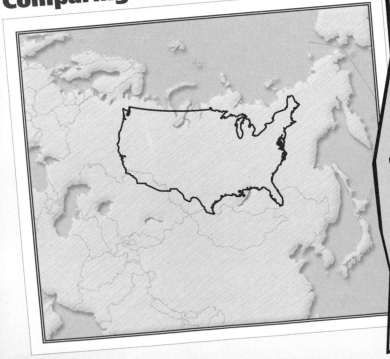

GEOSTATS:

Russia

- World's largest country in area: 6,659,328 sq. mi. (17,075,200 sq km)

- World's sixth-largest population: 145,470,197 (July 2001 estimate)

- World's largest lake: Caspian Sea—143,244 sq. mi. (371,002 sq km)

- World's deepest lake: Lake Baikal—5,715 ft. (1,742 m)

- Largest number of time zones: 11

- Highest mountain in Europe: Mount Elbrus—18,510 ft. (5,642 m)

ELEVATION

FEET	METERS
13,120	4,000
6,560	2,000
1,640	500
656	200
(Sea level) 0	0 (Sea level)
Below sea level	Below sea level

SCALE
0   500   1000 Miles
0   500   1000 Kilometers
Projection: Two-Point Equidistant

1. *Places and Regions* In what general direction do the great rivers of Siberia flow?

2. *Places and Regions* Which countries have areas that are below sea level?

Critical Thinking

3. Drawing Inferences and Conclusions Russia has often been invaded by other countries. Which part of Russia might be easy to invade? Why do you think this area would be a good invasion route?

4. Comparing Northern Russia appears to have many good harbors. Compare this map to the **climate map** of the region. Why have few harbors been developed on Russia's north coast?

1. _Places and Regions_ Compare this map to the **physical map** of the region. Do any physical features define a border between Russia and the countries of Europe?

Critical Thinking

2. Analyzing Information About how far apart are Russia and the Alaskan mainland? the Russian mainland and the North Pole?

3. Analyzing Information Which borders separating the countries south and southeast of Russia appear to follow natural features?

4. Drawing Inferences and Conclusions Compare this map to the **physical** and **climate maps** of the region. Why do you think the boundary between Kazakhstan and northwestern Uzbekistan is two straight lines?

CLIMATE

Desert	Humid continental
Steppe	Subarctic
Mediterranean	Tundra
Humid subtropical	Highland

SCALE
0   500   1000 Miles

0   500   1000 Kilometers
Projection: Two-Point Equidistant

---

1. *Places and Regions* Compare this map to the **political map**. Which is the only country that has a humid subtropical climate?

2. *Physical Systems* Which climate types stretch across Russia from Europe to the Pacific?

3. *Places and Regions* Compare this map to the **political map**. Which country has only a humid continental climate?

Critical Thinking

4. Drawing Inferences and Conclusions Compare this map to the **land use and resources map**. Why do you think nomadic herding is common east of the Caspian Sea?

5. Comparing Compare this to the **political map**. In which countries would you expect to find the highest mountains? Why?

POPULATION DENSITY

Persons per sq. mile	Persons per sq km
520	200
260	100
130	50
25	10
3	1
0	0

● Metropolitan areas with more than 2 million inhabitants

○ Metropolitan areas with 1 million to 2 million inhabitants

SCALE
0   500   1000 Miles
0   500   1000 Kilometers
Projection: Two-Point Equidistant

1. *Places and Regions* Which countries have a large area with more than 260 people per square mile and cities of more than 2 million people?

2. *Places and Regions* Which country has areas in the north where no one lives?

Critical Thinking

3. Making Generalizations and Predictions What can you assume about landforms and farming in western Russia just by looking at the **population map**? Check the **physical** and **land use and resources maps** to be sure.

4. Analyzing Information Use the map on this page to create a chart, graph, database, or model of population centers in Russia and northern Eurasia.

LAND USE

- Nomadic herding
- Livestock raising
- Commercial farming
- Subsistence farming
- Forests
- Manufacturing
- Limited economic activity
- • Major manufacturing and trade centers

RESOURCES

- Coal
- Natural gas
- Oil
- Nuclear power
- Hydroelectric power
- Gold
- Silver
- Diamonds
- Other minerals
- Seafood

SCALE
0   500   1000 Miles
0   500   1000 Kilometers
Projection: Two-Point Equidistant

1. (Places and Regions) Where are most oil reserves in the region located?

2. (Places and Regions) Where are most gold mines in the region located?

3. (Places and Regions) Which country has diamonds? Which countries in the region have silver deposits?

Critical Thinking

4. Comparing Compare this to the **physical map**. Which waterways might be used to transport mineral resources mined near Irkutsk to manufacturing and trade centers?

5. Analyzing Information Use the map on this page to create a chart, graph, database, or model of economic activities in the region.

Fast FACTS

Russia and Northern Eurasia

ARMENIA

CAPITAL:
Yerevan

AREA:
11,506 sq. mi. (29,800 sq km)

POPULATION:
3,336,100

MONEY:
dram (AMD)

LANGUAGES:
Armenian, Russian

UNEMPLOYMENT:
20 percent

BELARUS

CAPITAL:
Minsk

AREA:
80,154 sq. mi. (207,600 sq km)

POPULATION:
10,350,194

MONEY:
Belarusian rubel (BYB/BYR)

LANGUAGES:
Byelorussian, Russian

UNEMPLOYMENT:
2.1 percent (and many underemployed workers)

AZERBAIJAN

CAPITAL:
Baku

AREA:
33,436 sq. mi. (86,600 sq km)

POPULATION:
7,771,092

MONEY:
manat (AZM)

LANGUAGES:
Azeri, Russian, Armenian

UNEMPLOYMENT:
20 percent

GEORGIA

CAPITAL:
T'bilisi

AREA:
26,911 sq. mi. (69,700 sq km)

POPULATION:
4,989,285

MONEY:
lari (GEL)

LANGUAGES:
Georgian (official), Russian, Armenian, Azeri

UNEMPLOYMENT:
14.9 percent

KAZAKHSTAN

CAPITAL:
Astana

AREA:
1,049,150 sq. mi. (2,717,300 sq km)

POPULATION:
16,731,303

MONEY:
tenge (KZT)

LANGUAGES:
Kazakh, Russian

UNEMPLOYMENT:
13.7 percent

KYRGYZSTAN

CAPITAL:
Bishkek

AREA:
76,641 sq. mi. (198,500 sq km)

POPULATION:
4,753,003

MONEY:
Kyrgyzstani som (KGS)

LANGUAGES:
Kirghiz, Russian

UNEMPLOYMENT:
6 percent

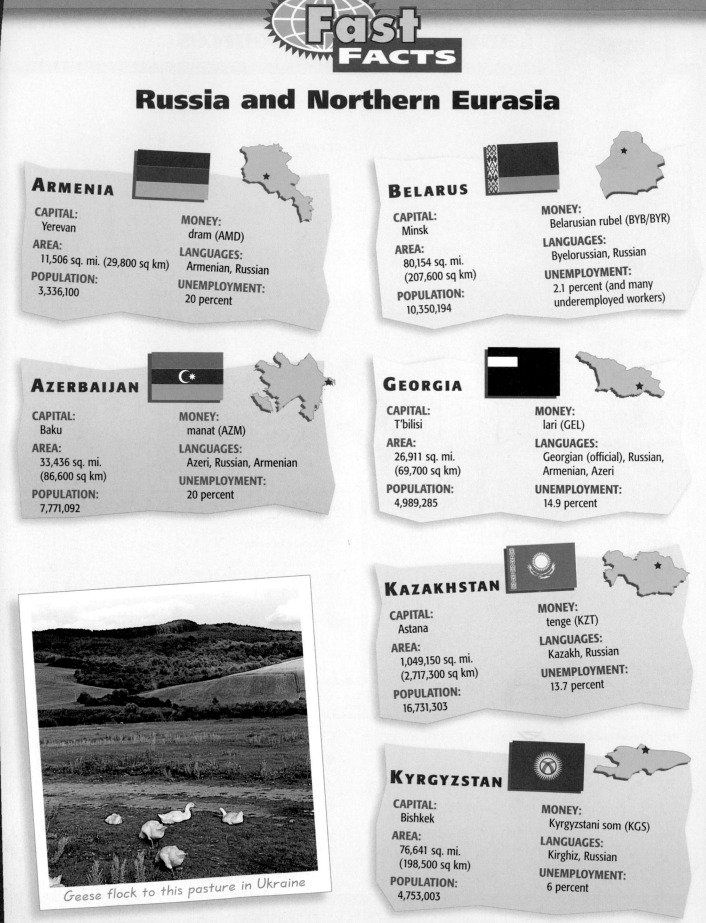

Geese flock to this pasture in Ukraine

Countries not drawn to scale.

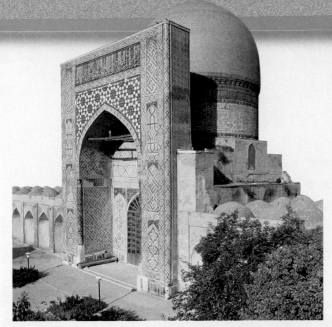

Mosque in Uzbekistan

UKRAINE

CAPITAL: Kiev

AREA: 233,089 sq. mi. (603,700 sq km)

POPULATION: 48,760,474

MONEY: hryvna

LANGUAGES: Ukranian, Russian, Romanian, Polish, Hungarian

UNEMPLOYMENT: 4.3 percent officially registered (and many unregistered or underemployed)

RUSSIA

CAPITAL: Moscow

AREA: 6,592,735 sq. mi. (17,075,200 sq km)

POPULATION: 145,470,197

MONEY: Russian ruble (RUR)

LANGUAGES: Russian

UNEMPLOYMENT: 10.5 percent (and many underemployed workers)

UZBEKISTAN

CAPITAL: Tashkent

AREA: 172,741 sq. mi. (447,400 sq km)

POPULATION: 25,155,064

MONEY: Uzbekistani sum (UZS)

LANGUAGES: Uzbek, Russian, Tajik

UNEMPLOYMENT: 10 percent (and many underemployed)

TAJIKISTAN

CAPITAL: Dushanbe

AREA: 55,251 sq. mi. (143,100 sq km)

POPULATION: 6,578,681

MONEY: somoni (SM)

LANGUAGES: Tajik (official), Russian

UNEMPLOYMENT: 5.7 percent (and many underemployed workers)

internet connect

COUNTRY STATISTICS

GO TO: go.hrw.com

KEYWORD: SG3 FACTSU5

FOR: more facts about Russia and northern Eurasia

TURKMENISTAN

CAPITAL: Ashgabat

AREA: 188,455 sq. mi. (488,100 sq km)

POPULATION: 4,603,244

MONEY: Turkmen manat (TMM)

LANGUAGES: Turkmen, Uzbek, Russian

UNEMPLOYMENT: data not available

Sources: Central Intelligence Agency, *The World Factbook 2001; The World Almanac and Book of Facts 2001;* pop. figures are 2001 estimates.

CHAPTER 17

Russia

Now we will learn about Russia. First we will meet Polina, who lives in Moscow, the capital. She is in the eleventh grade at State School 637 and will graduate in the spring.

Privyet! (Hi!) My name is Polina and I am 17. I live in an apartment in Moscow with my mother and father. Our apartment has two rooms. Every day except Sunday I wake up at 7:00 A.M., have some bread and cheese with tea, and take the subway to school. At the end of eighth grade, we had to choose whether to study science or humanities. I chose humanities. My favorite subjects are history, literature, and English—my history teacher is great!

We have about five or six classes with a 15-minute break between each one. During the breaks, I often eat a snack like *pirozhki*, a small meat pie, at the school snack bar. I go home at 2:00 P.M. for lunch (meat, potatoes, and a salad of cooked vegetables and mayonnaise) and a nap. When I wake up, I go out with my friends to a park. Sometimes my parents and I join my uncle, aunt, and grandmother for Sunday dinner. My uncle makes my favorite dishes, like meat salad with mayonnaise. I love ice cream, too!

Привет!
Я живу в Москве.

Translation: Hi! I live in Moscow.

Section 1 Physical Geography

Read to Discover

1. What are the physical features of Russia?
2. What climates and vegetation are found in Russia?
3. What natural resources does Russia have?

Define

taiga
steppe

Locate

Arctic Ocean
Caucasus Mountains
Caspian Sea
Ural Mountains
West Siberian Plain

Central Siberian
  Plateau
Kamchatka Peninsula
Kuril Islands
Volga River
Baltic Sea

WHY IT MATTERS

Like many nations, Russia is concerned about environmental issues. Use CNNfyi.com and other **current events** sources to investigate environmental concerns there. Record your findings in your journal.

A Siberian sable

Russia: Physical-Political

ARCTIC OCEAN

North Pole

BERING SEA

NORTH SEA

BARENTS SEA

Bering Strait

PACIFIC OCEAN

KAMCHATKA PENINSULA

Murmansk

Novaya Zemlya

BALTIC SEA

Kaliningrad
RUSSIA

St. Petersburg (Leningrad)

Lake Ladoga

NORTHERN EUROPEAN PLAIN

Moscow

Nizhniy Novgorod (Gorky)

Kazan'

Yekaterinburg (Sverdlovsk)

Chelyabinsk

Magnitogorsk

Volgograd (Stalingrad)

Astrakhan

Mt. Elbrus 18,510 ft. (5642 m)

CAUCASUS MTS.

BLACK SEA

CASPIAN SEA

Dnepr R. (Dnieper R.)

Don R.

Volga River

URAL MOUNTAINS

Ob River

WEST SIBERIAN PLAIN

Yenisey R.

SIBERIA

CENTRAL SIBERIAN PLATEAU

Lena River

RUSSIA

KUZNETSK BASIN

Trans-Siberian Railroad

Novosibirsk

Ob River

Yenisey R.

Lake Baikal

Baikal-Amur Mainline

Amur R.

Khabarovsk

Ussuri R.

Vladivostok

SEA OF OKHOTSK

Sakhalin Island

Kuril Islands

SEA OF JAPAN

ELEVATION

	FEET	METERS
	13,120	4,000
	6,560	2,000
	1,640	500
	656	200
	(Sea level) 0	0 (Sea level)
	Below sea level	Below sea level

★ National capital
• Other cities

SCALE
0   500   1000 Miles
0   500   1000 Kilometers
Projection: Two-Point Equidistant

Size comparison of Russia to the contiguous United States

Physical Features

Russia was by far the largest republic of what was called the Union of Soviet Socialist Republics, or the Soviet Union. Russia is the largest country in the world. It stretches 6,000 miles (9,654 km), from Eastern Europe to the Bering Sea and Pacific Ocean.

The Land Much of western, or European, Russia is part of the Northern European Plain. This is the country's heartland, where most Russians live. To the north are the Barents Sea and the Arctic Ocean. Far to the south are the Caucasus (KAW-kuh-suhs) Mountains. There Europe's highest peak, Mount Elbrus, rises to 18,510 feet (5,642 m). The Caucasus Mountains stretch from the Black Sea to the Caspian (KAS-pee-uhn) Sea. The Caspian is the largest inland body of water in the world.

East of the Northern European Plain is a long range of eroded low mountains and hills. These are called the Ural (YOOHR-uhl) Mountains. The Urals divide Europe from Asia. They stretch from the Arctic coast in the north to Kazakhstan in the south. The highest peak in the Urals rises to just 6,214 feet (1,894 m).

East of the Urals lies a vast region known as Siberia. Much of Siberia is divided between the West Siberian Plain and the Central Siberian Plateau. The West Siberian Plain is a large, flat area with many marshes. The Central Siberian Plateau lies to the east. It is a land of elevated plains and valleys.

A series of high mountain ranges runs through southern and eastern Siberia. The Kamchatka (kuhm-CHAHT-kuh) Peninsula, Sakhalin (sah-kah-LEEN) Island, and the Kuril (KYOOHR-eel) Islands surround the Sea of Okhotsk (uh-KAWTSK). These are in the Russian Far East. The rugged Kamchatka Peninsula and the Kurils have active volcanoes. Earthquakes and volcanic eruptions are common. The Kurils separate the Sea of Okhotsk from the Pacific Ocean.

Rivers Some of the world's longest rivers flow through Russia. These include the Volga (VAHL-guh) and Don Rivers in European Russia. The Ob (AWB), Yenisey (yi-ni-SAY), Lena (LEE-nuh), and Amur (ah-MOOHR) Rivers are located in Siberia and the Russian Far East. The Amur forms part of Russia's border with China.

The Volga is Europe's longest river. Its course and length make it an important transportation route. It flows southward for 2,293 miles (3,689 km) across the Northern European Plain to the Caspian Sea. Barges can travel by canal from the Volga to the Don River. The Don empties into the Black Sea. Canals also connect the Volga to rivers that drain into the Baltic Sea far to the northwest.

In Siberia, the Ob, Yenisey, and Lena Rivers all flow thousands of miles northward. Eventually, they reach Russia's Arctic coast. These and other Siberian rivers that drain into the Arctic Ocean freeze in winter. In spring, these rivers thaw first in the south. Downstream in

▲

A train chugs through the cold Siberian countryside.

Interpreting the Visual Record What does this photograph tell you about the physical features and climate of Siberia?

Our Amazing Planet

The coldest temperature ever recorded outside of Antarctica in the last 100 years was noted on February 6, 1933, in eastern Siberia: −90° F (−68°C).

the north, however, the rivers remain frozen much longer. As a result, ice jams there block water from the melting ice and snow. This causes annual floods in areas along the rivers.

✓ **READING CHECK:** (*Places and Regions*) What are the major physical features of Russia?

Climate and Vegetation

Nearly all of Russia is located at high northern latitudes. The country has tundra, subarctic, humid continental, and steppe climates. Because there are no high mountain barriers, cold Arctic winds sweep across much of the country in winter. Winters are long and cold. Ice blocks most seaports until spring. However, the winters are surprisingly dry in much of Russia. This is because the interior is far from ocean moisture.

Winters are particularly severe throughout Siberia. Temperatures often drop below –40°F (–40°C). Although they are short, Siberian summers can be hot. Temperatures can rise to 100°F (38°C).

Vegetation varies with climates from north to south. Very cold temperatures and permafrost in the far north keep trees from taking root. Mosses, wildflowers, and other tundra vegetation grow there.

The vast **taiga** (TY-guh), a forest of mostly evergreen trees, grows south of the tundra. The trees there include spruce, fir, and pine. In European Russia and in the Far East are deciduous forests. Many temperate forests in European Russia have been cleared for farms and cities.

Wide grasslands known as the **steppe** (STEP) stretch from Ukraine across southern Russia to Kazakhstan. Much of the steppe is used for growing crops and grazing livestock.

✓ **READING CHECK:** (*Physical Systems*) How does Russia's location affect its climate?

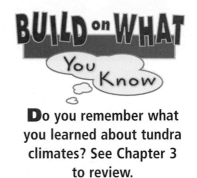

Do you remember what you learned about tundra climates? See Chapter 3 to review.

Camels graze on open land in southern Siberia near Mongolia.

A blast furnace is used to process nickel in Siberia. Nickel is just one of Russia's many natural resources.

Resources

Russia has enormous energy, mineral, and forest resources. However, those resources have been poorly managed. For example, much of the forest west of the Urals has been cut down. Now wood products must be brought long distances from Siberia. Still, the taiga provides a vast supply of trees for wood and paper pulp.

Russia has long been a major oil producer. However, many of its oil deposits are far from cities, markets, and ports. Coal is also plentiful. More than a dozen metals are available in large quantities. Russia also is a major diamond producer. Many valuable mineral deposits in remote Siberia have not yet been mined.

✓ READING CHECK: *Places and Regions* How might the location of its oil deposits prevent Russia from taking full advantage of this resource?

Homework Practice Online
Keyword: SG3 HP17

Section Review 1

Define and explain: taiga, steppe

Working with Sketch Maps On a map of Russia that you sketch or that your teacher provides, label the following: Arctic Ocean, Caucasus Mountains, Caspian Sea, Ural Mountains, West Siberian Plain, Central Siberian Plateau, Kamchatka Peninsula, Kuril Islands, Volga River, and Baltic Sea.

Reading for the Main Idea

1. (*Places and Regions*) What low mountain range in central Russia divides Europe from Asia?

2. (*Places and Regions*) How is the Volga River linked to the Baltic and Black Seas?

3. (*Environment and Society*) What are winters like in much of Russia? How might they affect people?

Critical Thinking

4. **Making Generalizations and Predictions** How might Russia's natural resources make the country more prosperous?

Organizing What You Know

5. **Categorizing** Copy the following graphic organizer. Use it to list the climates, vegetation, and resources of Russia.

Climates	Vegetation	Resources

Section 2 History and Culture

Read to Discover

1. What was Russia's early history like?
2. How did the Russian Empire grow and then fall?
3. What was the Soviet Union?
4. What is Russia like today?

Define

czar
abdicated
allies
superpowers
Cold War
consumer goods

Locate

Moscow

Russian caviar, blini (pancakes), and smoked salmon

WHY IT MATTERS

Russia is well known for its ballet companies. Use **CNNfyi.com** or other **current events** sources to discover more about Russia's culture and its international recognition in the field of dance and other arts. Record your findings in your journal.

Early Russia

The roots of the Russian nation lie deep in the grassy plains of the steppe. For thousands of years, people moved across the steppe bringing new languages, religions, and ways of life.

Early Migrations Slavic peoples have lived in Russia for thousands of years. In the A.D. 800s, Viking traders from Scandinavia helped shape the first Russian state among the Slavs. These Vikings called themselves Rus (ROOS). The word *Russia* comes from their name. The state they created was centered on Kiev. Today Kiev is the capital of Ukraine.

In the following centuries, missionaries from southeastern Europe brought Orthodox Christianity and a form of the Greek alphabet to Russia. Today the Russian language is written in this Cyrillic alphabet.

Mongols After about 200 years, Kiev's power began to decline. In the 1200s, Mongol invaders called Tatars swept out of Central Asia across the steppe. The Mongols conquered Kiev and added much of the region to their vast empire.

The Mongols demanded taxes but ruled the region through local leaders. Over time, these local leaders established various states. The strongest of these was Muscovy, north of Kiev. Its chief city was Moscow.

▲
This painting from the mid-1400s shows a battle between soldiers of two early Russian states.

✓ **READING CHECK:** *Human Systems* What was the effect of Viking traders on Russia?

History of Russian Expansion

Russia
1462–1533

Territory gained by

1689

1725

1801

1945

Maximum extension of Russian territory

Russian boundary in 1993

North Pole

ARCTIC OCEAN

Finland: Russian territory 1809–1918

Baltic republics: independent 1918–1940 and 1991

Poland: Russian territory 1815–1918

St. Petersburg

Moscow

BALTIC SEA

BLACK SEA

CASPIAN SEA

BERING SEA

SEA OF OKHOTSK

SEA OF JAPAN

Alaska, settled by Russians beginning in 1784, was sold to the United States in 1867.

Russian territory 1871–1881

PACIFIC OCEAN

SCALE
0   500   1000 Miles
0   500   1000 Kilometers
Projection: Two-Point Equidistant

The colors in this map show land taken by the Russian Empire and the Soviet Union over time.

Interpreting the Map When was the period of Russia's greatest expansion?

Ivan the Terrible became grand prince of Moscow in 1533. He was just three years old. He ruled Russia from 1547 to his death in 1584.

The Russian Empire

In the 1400s Muscovy won control over parts of Russia from the Mongols. In 1547 Muscovy's ruler, Ivan IV—known as Ivan the Terrible—crowned himself **czar** (ZAHR) of all Russia. The word *czar* comes from the Latin word *Caesar* and means "emperor."

Expansion Over more than 300 years, czars like Peter the Great (1672–1725) expanded the Russian empire. By the early 1700s the empire stretched from the Baltic to the Pacific.

Russian fur traders crossed the Bering Strait in the 1700s and 1800s. They established colonies along the North American west coast. Those colonies stretched from coastal Alaska to California. Russia sold Alaska to the United States in 1867. Around the same time, Russia expanded into Central Asia.

Decline The Russian Empire's power began to decline in the late 1800s. Industry grew slowly, so Russia remained largely agricultural. Most people were poor farmers. Far fewer were the rich, factory workers, or craftspeople. Food shortages, economic problems, and defeat in war further weakened the empire in the early 1900s.

In 1917, during World War I, the czar **abdicated**, or gave up his throne. Later in 1917 the Bolshevik Party, led by Vladimir Lenin, overthrew the government. This event is known as the Russian Revolution.

✓ **READING CHECK:** *Human Systems* What conflict brought a change of government to Russia?

The Soviet Union

The Bolsheviks, or Communists, established the Soviet Union in 1922. Most of the various territories of the Russian Empire became republics within the Soviet Union.

Under Lenin and his successor, Joseph Stalin, the Communists took over all industries and farms. Religious practices were discouraged. The Communists outlawed all other political parties. Many opponents were imprisoned, forced to leave the country, or even killed.

The Soviet leaders established a command economy, in which industries were controlled by the government. At first these industries grew dramatically. However, over time the lack of competition made them inefficient and wasteful. The quality of many products was poor. Government-run farms failed to produce enough food to feed the population. By the late 1950s the Soviet Union had to import large amounts of grain.

Cold War The Soviet Union in the 1950s was still recovering from World War II. The country had been a major battleground in the war. The United States and the Soviet Union had been **allies**, or friends, in the fight against Germany. After the war the two **superpowers**, or powerful countries, became rivals. This bitter rivalry became known as the **Cold War**. The Cold War lasted from the 1940s to the early 1990s. The Soviet Union and the United States built huge military forces, including nuclear weapons. The two countries never formally went to war with each other. However, they supported allies in small wars around the world.

Collapse of the Soviet Union The costs of the Cold War eventually became too much for the Soviet Union. The Soviet government spent more and more money on military goods. **Consumer goods** became expensive and in short supply. Consumer goods are products used at home and in everyday life. The last Soviet leader, Mikhail Gorbachev, tried to bring about changes to help the economy. He also promoted a policy allowing more open discussion of the country's problems. However, the various Soviet republics pushed for independence. Finally, in 1991 the Soviet Union collapsed. The huge country split into 15 republics.

In late 1991 Russia and most of the other former Soviet republics formed the Commonwealth of Independent States, or CIS. The CIS does not have a strong central government. Instead, it provides a way for the former Soviet republics to address shared problems.

✓ **READING CHECK:**
Human Systems What was the Cold War, and how did it eventually cause the Soviet Union's collapse?

Tourists can visit the czar's Summer Palace in St. Petersburg.
Interpreting the Visual Record How do you think the rich lifestyle of the czars helped the Bolsheviks gain support?

A man lights candles in front of portraits of the last czar, Nicholas II, and his wife. Russians are divided over what kind of government their country should have today.
Interpreting the Visual Record Why do you think some Russians might wish to have a czar again?

CONNECTING TO *Literature*

AUNT RIMMA'S TREAT

The former Soviet Union was composed of many republics, which are now independent countries. Nina Gabrielyan's The Lilac Dressing Gown *is told from the point of view of an Armenian girl living in Moscow before the Soviet breakup.*

Aunt Rimma. . . came to visit and gave me a pink caramel which I, naturally, popped straight in my mouth. "Don't swallow it," Aunt Rimma says in an odd sort of voice. "You're not supposed to swallow it, only chew it." "Why," I ask, puzzled by her solemn tone. "It's chewing gum," she says with pride in her eyes. "Chewing gum?" I don't know what she means. "American chewing gum," Aunt Rimma explains. "Mentor's sister sent it to us from America." "Oh, from America? Is that where the capitalists are? What is she doing there?" "She's living there," says Aunt Rimma, condescending to my foolishness.

But I am not as foolish as I used to be. I know that Armenians live in Armenia. Our country is very big and includes many republics: Armenia, Georgia, Azerbaijan, Tajikistan, Uzbekistan, Ukraine, Belorussia [Belarus], the Caucasus and Transcaucasia. All this together is the Soviet Union. Americans . . . live in America. Clearly, Mentor's sister cannot possibly be American. . . . Rimma goes on boasting: "Oh! the underwear they have there! . . . And the children's clothes!"

I begin to feel a bit envious. . . . Nobody in our house has anyone living in America, but Aunt Rimma does. My envy becomes unbearable. So I decide to slay our boastful neighbor on the spot: "Well we have cockroaches! This big! Lots and lots of them!'"

Analyzing Primary Sources

1. How does the Armenian girl's frame of reference affect her view of the United States?
2. What does Aunt Rimma seem to think the United States is like?

Russia Today

Russia has been making a transition from communism to democracy and a free market economy since 1991. Change has been slow, and the country faces difficult challenges.

People and Religion More than 146 million people live in Russia today. More than 80 percent are ethnic Russians. The largest of Russia's many minority groups are Ukrainians and Tatars. These Tatars are the descendants of the early Mongol invaders of Russia.

In the past, the government encouraged ethnic Russians to settle in areas of Russia far from Moscow. They were encouraged to move to places where other ethnic groups were in the majority. Today, many non-Russian peoples in those areas resent the domination of ethnic Russians. Some non-Russians want independence from Moscow. At times this has led to violence and even war, as in Chechnya in southern Russia.

Since 1991 a greater degree of religious expression has been allowed in Russia. Russian Orthodox Christianity is becoming popular again. Cathedrals have been repaired, and their onion-shaped domes have been covered in gold leaf and brilliant colors. Muslims around the Caspian Sea and the southern Urals are reviving Islamic practices.

Food and Festivals

Bread is an important part of the Russian diet. It is eaten with every meal. It may be a rich, dark bread made from rye and wheat flour or a firm white bread. As in other northern countries, the growing season is short and winter is long. Therefore, the diet includes many canned and preserved foods, such as sausages, smoked fish, cheese, and vegetable and fruit preserves.

Black caviar, one of the world's most expensive delicacies, comes from Russia. The fish eggs that make up black caviar come from sturgeon. Sturgeon are fish found in the Caspian Sea.

The anniversary of the 1917 Russian Revolution was an important holiday during the Soviet era. Today the Orthodox Christian holidays of Christmas and Easter are again becoming popular in Russia. Special holiday foods include milk puddings and cheesecakes.

The Arts and Sciences

Russia has given the world great works of art, literature, and music. For example, you might know *The Nutcracker,* a ballet danced to music composed by Peter Tchaikovsky (1840–93). It is a popular production in many countries.

Russia

Country	Population/ Growth Rate	Life Expectancy	Literacy Rate	Per Capita GDP
Russia	145,470,197 −0.4%	62, male 73, female	98%	$7,700
United States	281,421,906 0.9%	74, male 80, female	97%	$36,200

Sources: Central Intelligence Agency, *The World Factbook 2001;* U.S. Census Bureau

Interpreting the Chart How many times greater is the U.S. population than the Russian population?

Ballet dancers perform Peter Tchaikovsky's *Swan Lake* at the Mariinsky Theater in St. Petersburg.

Many Russian writers are known for how they capture the emotions of characters in their works. Some writers, such as Aleksandr Solzhenitsyn (1918–), have written about Russia under communism.

Russian scientists also have made important contributions to their professions. For example, in 1957 the Soviet Union launched *Sputnik*. It was the first artificial satellite in space. Today U.S. and Russian engineers are working together on space projects. These include building a large space station and planning for a mission to Mars.

Government Like the U.S. government, the Russian Federation is governed by an elected president and a legislature called the Federal Assembly. The Federal Assembly includes representatives of regions and republics within the Federation. Non-Russians are numerous or in the majority in many of those regions and republics.

The government faces tough challenges. One is improving the country's struggling economy. Many government-owned companies have been sold to the private sector. However, financial problems and corruption have made people cautious about investing in those companies.

Corruption is a serious problem. A few people have used their connections with powerful government officials to become rich. In addition, many Russians avoid paying taxes. This means the government has less money for salaries and services. Agreement on solutions to these problems has been hard.

READING CHECK: *Human Systems* What are the people and culture of Russia like today?

Republics of the Russian Federation

Adygea	Karachay-Cherkessia
Alania	Karelia
Bashkortostan	Khakassia
Buryatia	Komi
Chechnya	Mari El
Chuvashia	Mordvinia
Dagestan	Sakha
Gorno-Altay	Tatarstan
Ingushetia	Tuva
Kabardino-Balkaria	Udmurtia
Kalmykia	

Section Review 2

go.hrw.com
Homework Practice Online
Keyword: SG3 HP17

Define and explain: czar, abdicated, allies, superpowers, Cold War, consumer goods

Working with Sketch Maps On the map you created in Section 1, label Moscow. In the margin, explain the role Kiev played in Russia's early history.

Reading for the Main Idea

1. *Places and Regions* How did Russia get its name?

2. *Human Systems* What was the Bolshevik Party?

3. *Places and Regions* What are some of the challenges that Russia faces today?

Critical Thinking

4. **Comparing** Compare the factors that led to the decline of the Russian Empire and the Soviet Union. List the factors for each.

Organizing What You Know

5. **Summarizing** Copy the following graphic organizer. Use it to identify important features of Russia's ethnic population, religion, food, and arts and sciences.

Russian people and culture

Section 3 The Russian Heartland

Read to Discover

1. Why is European Russia considered the country's heartland?
2. What are the characteristics of the four regions of European Russia?

Define

light industry
heavy industry
smelters

Locate

St. Petersburg
Nizhniy Novgorod
Astrakhan
Yekaterinburg
Chelyabinsk
Magnitogorsk

WHY IT MATTERS

Following the fall of Communism, some Russian cities' landscapes began to change. In the larger cities like Moscow there are newer buildings and more restaurants. Use **CNNfyi.com** or other **current events** sources to find information about Moscow and other large Russian cities. Record your findings in your journal.

Jeweled box made by Peter Carl Fabergé

The Heartland

The European section of Russia is the country's heartland. The Russian nation expanded outward from there. It is home to the bulk of the Russian population. The national capital and large industrial cities are also located there.

The plains of European Russia make up the country's most productive farming region. Farmers focus mainly on growing grains and raising livestock. Small gardens near cities provide fresh fruits and vegetables for summer markets.

The Russian heartland can be divided into four major regions. These four are the Moscow region, the St. Petersburg region, the Volga region, and the Urals region.

✓ **READING CHECK:** *Places and Regions* Why is European Russia the country's heartland?

The Moscow Region

Moscow is Russia's capital and largest city. More than 9 million people live there. In addition to being Russia's political center, Moscow is the country's center for transportation and communication. Roads, railroads, and air routes link the capital to all points in Russia.

At Moscow's heart is the Kremlin. The Kremlin's red brick walls and towers were built in the late 1400s. The government offices, beautiful palaces, and gold-domed churches within its walls are popular tourist attractions.

Twenty towers, like the one in the lower left, are spaced along the Kremlin's walls.

Interpreting the Visual Record What was the advantage of locating government buildings and palaces within the walls of one central location?

Vendors sell religious art and other crafts at a sidewalk market in Moscow.

Interpreting the Visual Record What do the items in this market suggest about the status of religion in Russia since the communist era?

Moscow is part of a huge industrial area. This area also includes the city of Nizhniy Novgorod, called Gorky during the communist era. About one third of Russia's population lives in this region.

The Soviet government encouraged the development of **light industry**, rather than **heavy industry**, around Moscow. Light industry focuses on the production of lightweight goods, such as clothing. Heavy industry usually involves manufacturing based on metals. It causes more pollution than light industry. The region also has advanced-technology and electronics industries.

The St. Petersburg Region

Northwest of Moscow is St. Petersburg, Russia's second-largest city and a major Baltic seaport. More than 5 million people live there. St. Petersburg was Russia's capital and home to the czars for more than 200 years. This changed in 1918. Palaces and other grand buildings constructed under the czars are tourist attractions today. St. Petersburg was known as Leningrad during the communist era. Much of the city was heavily damaged during World War II.

The surrounding area has few natural resources. Still, St. Petersburg's harbor, canals, and rail connections make the city a major center for trade. Important universities and research institutions are located there. The region also has important industries.

✔ **READING CHECK:** *Human Systems*
Why are Moscow and St. Petersburg such large cities?

The Mariinsky Theater of Opera and Ballet is one of St. Petersburg's most beautiful buildings. It was called the Kirov during the communist era.

The Volga Region

The Volga region stretches along the middle part of the Volga River. The Volga is often more like a chain of lakes. It is a major shipping route for goods produced in the region. Hydroelectric power plants and nearby deposits of coal and oil are important sources of energy.

During World War II, many factories were moved to the Volga region. This was done to keep them safe from German invaders. Today the region is famous for its factories that produce goods such as motor vehicles, chemicals, and food products. Russian caviar comes from a fishery based at the old city of Astrakhan on the Caspian Sea.

The Urals Region

Mining has long been important in the Ural Mountains region. Nearly every important mineral except oil has been discovered there. Copper and iron **smelters** are still important. Smelters are factories that process copper, iron, and other metal ores.

Many large cities in the Urals started as commercial centers for mining districts. The Soviet government also moved factories to the region during World War II. Important cities include Yekaterinburg (yi-kah-ti-reem-BOOHRK) (formerly Sverdlovsk), Chelyabinsk (chel-YAH-buhnsk), and Magnitogorsk (muhg-nee-tuh-GAWRSK). Now these cities manufacture machinery and metal goods.

✔ **READING CHECK:** *Places and Regions* What industries are important in the Volga and Urals regions?

▲ A fisher gathers sturgeon in a small shipboard pool in the Volga region. The eggs for making caviar are taken from the female sturgeon. Then the fish is released back into the water.

Section Review 3

Define and explain: light industry, heavy industry, smelters

Working with Sketch Maps On the map you created in Section 2, label St. Petersburg, Nizhniy Novgorod, Astrakhan, Yekaterinburg, Chelyabinsk, and Magnitogorsk. In the margin of your map, write a short caption explaining the significance of Moscow and St. Petersburg.

Reading for the Main Idea

1. *Places and Regions* Why might so many people settle in Russia's heartland?

2. *Places and Regions* Where did the Soviet government move factories during World War II?

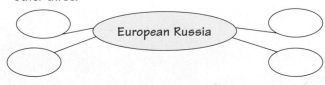

go.hrw.com **Homework Practice Online** Keyword: SG3 HP17

Critical Thinking

3. **Drawing Inferences and Conclusions** Why do you think the Soviet government encouraged the development of light industry around Moscow?

4. **Finding the Main Idea** What role has the region's physical geography played in the development of European Russia's economy?

Organizing What You Know

5. **Contrasting** Use this graphic organizer to identify European Russia's four regions. Write one feature that makes each region different from the other three.

European Russia

Section 4

Siberia

Read to Discover

1. What is the human geography of Siberia like?

2. What are the economic features of the region?

3. How has Lake Baikal been threatened by pollution?

Define

habitation fog

Locate

Siberia
Trans-Siberian Railroad
Baikal-Amur Mainline
Kuznetsk Basin
Ob River
Yenisey River
Novosibirsk
Lake Baikal

WHY IT MATTERS

It takes more than a week by train to cross Russia. The Trans-Siberian Railroad and the Baikal-Amur Mainline let travelers see more of the country. Use **CNNfyi.com** or other **current events** sources to learn more about these rail systems. Record your findings in your journal.

Russian matryoshka *nesting doll*

A Sleeping Land

East of European Russia, across the Ural Mountains, is Siberia. Siberia is enormous. It covers more than 5 million square miles (12.95 million sq. km) of northern Asia. It extends all the way to the Pacific Ocean. That is nearly 1.5 times the area of the United States! To the north of Siberia is the Arctic Ocean. To the south are the Central Asian countries, Mongolia, and China.

Many people think of Siberia as simply a vast, frozen wasteland. In fact, in the Tatar language, *Siberia* means "Sleeping Land." In many ways, this image is accurate. Siberian winters are long, dark, and severe. Often there is little snow, but the land is frozen for months. During winter, **habitation fog** hangs over cities. A habitation fog is a fog caused by fumes and smoke from cities. During the cold Siberian winter, this fog is trapped over cities.

Siberia has lured Russian adventurers for more than 400 years. It continues to do so today. This vast region has a great wealth of natural resources. Developing those resources may be a key to transforming Russia into an economic success.

Reindeer graze around a winter camp in northern Siberia.
Interpreting the Visual Record What climate does this area appear to have, tundra or subarctic?

People Siberia is sparsely populated. In fact, large areas have no human population at all. Most of the people live in cities in western and southern parts of the region.

Ethnic Russians make up most of the population. However, minority groups have lived there since long before Russians began to expand into Siberia.

Settlements Russian settlement in Siberia generally follows the route of the Trans-Siberian Railroad. Construction of this railway started in 1891. When it was completed, it linked Moscow and Vladivostok, a port on the Sea of Japan.

Russia's Trans-Siberian Railroad is the longest single rail line in the world. It is more than 5,700 miles (9,171 km) long. For many Siberian towns, the railroad provides the only transportation link to the outside world. Another important railway is the Baikal-Amur Mainline (BAM), which crosses many mountain ranges and rivers in eastern Siberia.

✔ **READING CHECK:** (*Places and Regions*) Where is Russian settlement located in Siberia, and why do you think this is the case?

▲ The Omsk (AWMSK) Cathedral in Omsk, Siberia, provides an example of Russian architecture. Omsk was founded in the early 1700s.

Siberia's Economy

The Soviet government built the Baikal-Amur Mainline so that raw materials from Siberia could be easily transported to other places. Abundant natural resources form the foundation of Siberia's economy. They are also important to the development of Russia's struggling economy. Siberia's natural resources include timber, mineral ores, diamonds, and coal, oil, and natural gas deposits.

Although Siberia has rich natural resources, it contains a small percentage of Russia's industry. The harsh climate and difficult terrain have discouraged settlement. Many people would rather live in European Russia, even though wages may be higher in Siberia.

Lumbering and mining are the most important Siberian industries. Large coal deposits are mined in the Kuznetsk Basin, or the Kuzbas. The Kuzbas is located in southwestern Siberia between the Ob and Yenisey Rivers. It is one of Siberia's most important industrial regions.

Siberia's largest city, Novosibirsk, is located near the Kuznetsk Basin. The city's name means "New Siberia." About 1.5 million people live there. It is located about halfway between Moscow and Vladivostok on the Trans-Siberian Railroad. Novosibirsk is Siberia's manufacturing and transportation center.

✔ **READING CHECK:** (*Environment and Society*) How do Siberia's natural resources influence the economies of Siberia and Russia?

▲ A worker repairs an oil rig in Siberia.

Interpreting the Visual Record How is this worker protected from the cold Siberian climate?

The scenery around Lake Baikal is breathtaking. The lake is seven times as deep as the Grand Canyon.

Interpreting the Visual Record
How would pollution affect this lake and the plants and animals that live there?

Lake Baikal covers less area than do three of the Great Lakes: Superior, Huron, and Michigan. Still, Baikal is so deep that it contains about one fifth of all the world's freshwater!

Lake Baikal

Some people have worried that economic development in Siberia threatens the region's natural environment. One focus of concern has been Lake Baikal (by-KAHL), the "Jewel of Siberia."

Baikal is located north of Mongolia. It is the world's deepest lake. In fact, it holds as much water as all of North America's Great Lakes. The scenic lake and its surrounding area are home to many kinds of plants and animals. Some, such as the world's only freshwater seal, are endangered.

For decades people have worried about pollution from a nearby paper factory and other development. They feared that pollution threatened the species that live in and around the lake. In recent years scientists and others have proposed plans that allow some economic development while protecting the environment.

✓ **READING CHECK:** *Environment and Society* How has human activity affected Lake Baikal?

go.hrw.com **Homework Practice Online** Keyword: SG3 HP17

Section Review 4

Define and explain: habitation fog

Working with Sketch Maps On the map you created in Section 3, label Siberia, Trans-Siberian Railroad, Baikal-Amur Mainline, Kuznetsk Basin, Ob River, Yenisey River, Novosibirsk, and Lake Baikal.

Reading for the Main Idea

1. *Places and Regions* What are the boundaries of Siberia?

2. *Human Systems* Where do most people in Siberia live? Why?

3. *Places and Regions* Why does this huge region with many natural resources have little industry?

Critical Thinking

4. **Making Generalizations and Predictions** Do you think Russians should be more concerned about rapid economic development or protecting the environment? Why?

Organizing What You Know

5. **Categorizing** Use this organizer to list the region's resources and industries that use them.

| Natural Resources | ⇨ | Major Industries |

Section 5 · The Russian Far East

Read to Discover

1. How does the Russian Far East's climate affect agriculture in the region?
2. What are the major resources and cities of the region?
3. What island regions are part of the Russian Far East?

Define

icebreakers

Locate

Sea of Okhotsk
Sea of Japan
Amur River
Khabarovsk
Vladivostok
Sakhalin Island

A Russian figurine

WHY IT MATTERS

Because of conflict over the Kuril Islands, Russia and Japan did not sign a peace agreement to end World War II. Use **CNNfyi.com** or other **current events** sources to find information on this controversy and other political concerns. Record your findings in your journal.

Agriculture

Off the eastern coast of Siberia are the Sea of Okhotsk and the Sea of Japan. Their coastal areas and islands make up a region known as the Russian Far East.

The Russian Far East has a less severe climate than the rest of Siberia. Summer weather is mild enough for some successful farming. Farms produce many goods, including wheat, sugar beets, sunflowers, meat, and dairy products. However, the region cannot produce enough food for itself. As a result, food must also be imported.

Fishing and hunting are important in the region. There are many kinds of animals, including deer, seals, rare Siberian tigers, and sables. Sable fur is used to make expensive clothing.

✓ **READING CHECK:** *Environment and Society* How does scarcity of food affect the Russian Far East?

◄

The Siberian tiger is endangered. The few remaining of these large cats roam parts of the Russian Far East. They are also found in northern China and on the Korean Peninsula.

Do you remember what you learned about plate tectonics? See Chapter 2 to review.

Economy

Like the rest of Siberia, the Russian Far East has a wealth of natural resources. These resources have supported the growth of industrial cities and ports in the region.

Resources Much of the Russian Far East remains forested. The region's minerals are only beginning to be developed. Lumbering, machine manufacturing, woodworking, and metalworking are the major industries there.

The region also has important energy resources, including coal and oil. Another resource is geothermal energy. This resource is available because of the region's tectonic activity. Two active volcanic mountain ranges run the length of the Kamchatka Peninsula. Russia's first geothermal electric-power station was built on this peninsula.

Cities Industry and the Trans-Siberian Railroad aided the growth of cities in the Russian Far East. Two of those cities are Khabarovsk (kuh-BAHR-uhfsk) and Vladivostok (vla-duh-vuh-STAHK).

More than 600,000 people live in Khabarovsk, which was founded in 1858. It is located where the Trans-Siberian Railroad crosses the Amur River. This location makes Khabarovsk ideal for processing forest and mineral resources from the region.

Vladivostok is slightly larger than Khabarovsk. *Vladivostok* means "Lord of the East" in Russian. The city was established in 1860 on the coast of the Sea of Japan. Today it lies at the eastern end of the Trans-Siberian Railroad.

Vladivostok is a major naval base and the home port for a large fishing fleet. **Icebreakers** must keep the city's harbor open in winter. An icebreaker is a ship that can break up the ice of frozen waterways. This allows other ships to pass through them.

Historical monuments and old architecture compete for attention in Vladivostok.

The Soviet Union considered Vladivostok very important for defense. The city was therefore closed to foreign contacts until the early 1990s. Today it is an important link with China, Japan, the United States, and the rest of the Pacific region.

✓ **READING CHECK:** *Environment and Society* How do the natural resources of the Russian Far East affect its economy?

Islands

The Russian Far East includes two island areas. Sakhalin is a large island that lies off the eastern coast of Siberia. To the south is the Japanese island of Hokkaido. The Kuril Islands are much smaller. They stretch in an arc from Hokkaido to the Kamchatka Peninsula.

Sakhalin has oil and mineral resources. The waters around the Kurils are important for commercial fishing.

Russia and Japan have argued over who owns these islands since the 1850s. At times they have been divided between Japan and Russia or the Soviet Union. The Soviet Union took control of the islands after World War II. Japan still claims rights to the southernmost islands.

Like other Pacific regions, Sakhalin and the Kurils sometimes experience earthquakes and volcanic eruptions. An earthquake in 1995 caused severe damage on Sakhalin Island, killing nearly 2,000 people.

✓ **READING CHECK:** *Environment and Society* How does the environment of the Kuril Islands and Sakhalin affect people?

▲ An old volcano created Crater Bay in the Kuril Islands. The great beauty of the islands is matched by the terrible power of earthquakes and volcanic eruptions in the area.

Interpreting the Visual Record What do you think happened to the volcano that formed Crater Bay?

Section Review 5

go.hrw.com
Homework Practice Online
Keyword: SG3 HP17

Define and explain: icebreakers

Working with Sketch Maps On the map you created in Section 4, label the Sea of Okhotsk, the Sea of Japan, the Amur River, Khabarovsk, Vladivostok, and Sakhalin Island. In the margin, explain which countries dispute possession of Sakhalin Island and the Kuril Islands.

Reading for the Main Idea

1. *Places and Regions* How does the climate of the Russian Far East compare to the climate throughout the rest of Siberia?

2. *Places and Regions* What are the region's major crops and energy resources?

Critical Thinking

3. **Drawing Inferences and Conclusions** In what ways do you think Vladivostok is "Lord of the East" in Russia today?

4. **Drawing Inferences and Conclusions** Why do you think Sakhalin and the Kuril Islands have been the subject of dispute between Russia and Japan?

Organizing What You Know

5. **Finding the Main Idea** Copy the following graphic organizer. Use it to explain how the location of each city has played a role in its development.

Khabarovsk	Vladivostok

CHAPTER 17
Reviewing What You Know

Building Vocabulary

On a separate sheet of paper, write sentences to define each of the following words.

1. taiga
2. steppe
3. czar
4. abdicated
5. allies

6. superpower
7. Cold War
8. consumer goods
9. light industry
10. heavy industry

11. smelters
12. habitation fog
13. icebreakers

Reviewing the Main Ideas

1. (Places and Regions) What are the major physical features of Russia? Where in Siberia are large coal deposits?

2. (Places and Regions) What landform separates Europe from Asia?

3. (Human Systems) How is Russia's government organized, and how does it compare with that of the United States?

4. (Places and Regions) What four major regions make up European Russia?

5. (Places and Regions) Where were Russian factories relocated during World War II and why?

Understanding Environment and Society

Resource Use
The grasslands of the steppe are one of Russia's most valuable agricultural resources. Create a presentation on farming in the steppe. You may want to consider the following:
- The crops that are grown in the Russian steppe.
- The kinds of livestock raised in the region.
- How the climate limits agriculture in the steppe.

Thinking Critically

1. **Finding the Main Idea** In what ways might Siberia be important to making Russia an economic success?

2. **Contrasting** What kind of economic system did the Soviet Union have, and how did it differ from that of the United States?

3. **Drawing Inferences and Conclusions** Why is transportation an issue for Russia? What have

Russians done to ease transportation between European Russia and the Russian Far East?

4. **Analyzing Information** How does Vladivostok's location make it an important link between Russia and the Pacific world?

5. **Identifying Cause and Effect** What problems existed in the Russian Empire and the Soviet Union in the 1900s, and what was their effect?

Map ACTIVITY

On a separate sheet of paper, match the letters on the map with their correct labels.

Arctic Ocean

Caucasus
  Mountains

Caspian Sea

West Siberian
  Plain

Central Siberian
  Plateau

Kamchatka
  Peninsula

Volga River

Moscow

St. Petersburg

Vladivostok

Mental Mapping Skills ACTIVITY

On a separate sheet of paper, draw a freehand map of Russia and label the following:

Baltic Sea

Kuril Islands

Lake Baikal

Sakhalin Island

Siberia

Ural Mountains

WRITING ACTIVITY

Imagine that you are a tour guide on a trip by train from St. Petersburg to Vladivostok. Use the chapter map or a classroom globe to write a one-page description of some of the places people would see along the train's route. How far would you travel? Be sure to use standard grammar, spelling, sentence structure, and punctuation.

Alternative Assessment

Portfolio ACTIVITY

Learning About Your Local Geography Youth Organizations The Baikal-Amur Mainline (BAM) was built partly by youth organizations. Make a list of some projects of youth organizations in your community.

internet connect

Internet Activity: go.hrw.com
KEYWORD: SG3 GT17

Choose a topic to explore about Russia:
- Take a trip on the Trans-Siberian Railroad.
- Examine the breakup of the Soviet Union.
- View the cultural treasures of Russia.

go.hrw.com

CHAPTER 18

Ukraine, Belarus, and the Caucasus

This region consists of plains in the north and mountains in the south. Both of these physical features made this area important to ancient invaders. Before you learn the history of this region, you should meet Ana.

Hi! I am a senior in high school in the city of Tbilisi, Georgia. I live with my parents and my younger sister. I go to school from 9:00 A.M. to 2:00 P.M. and study foreign languages—English and Spanish. I hope to be a journalist. In school the teachers decide which classes everyone must take.

After school I do my homework as fast as possible and then get together with my friends. I come home in the early evening and listen to music, read, or watch television.

We also have great food. My favorite dish is baked chicken with nuts. If you came to Georgia, I would take you to the mountains, to the seaside, and to some hot springs. We might also go to a festival where you could see Georgians in the country's national dress. Women wear a long red or purple robe with a white head scarf. Men wear a black suit or robe with gold embroidery.

Привіт! Я Анна.

▲ Translation: Hi! I am Ana.

Section 1 | Physical Geography

Read to Discover

1. What are the region's major physical features?
2. What climate types and natural resources are found in the region?

Define

nature reserves

Locate

Black Sea
Caucasus Mountains

Caspian Sea
Pripyat Marshes
Carpathian
 Mountains
Crimean Peninsula
Sea of Azov

Mount Elbrus
Dnieper River
Donets Basin

WHY IT MATTERS

Ukraine is trying to create a nature reserve to protect its natural environment. Use CNNfyi.com or other current events sources to find information about how other countries are trying to protect their environments. Record your findings in your journal.

A gold pig from Kiev

Ukraine, Belarus, and the Caucasus: Physical-Political

SCALE
0   200   400 Miles
0   200   400 Kilometers
Projection: Two-Point Equidistant

ELEVATION

FEET	METERS
13,120	4,000
6,560	2,000
1,640	500
656	200
(Sea level) 0	0 (Sea level)
Below sea level	Below sea level

⊛ National capitals
• Other cities

NORTHERN EUROPEAN PLAIN
EUROPE
CARPATHIAN MOUNTAINS

Vitsyebsk
Minsk
BELARUS
Pripyat (Pinsk) Marshes
Homyel'
Chernobyl
Kiev
UKRAINE
Dnieper River
Kharkiv
Donets River
Dnipropetrovs'k
Kryvyy Rih
Donets'k
DONETS BASIN
Odessa
SEA OF AZOV
CRIMEAN PENINSULA
Sevastopol'
Yalta

RUSSIA

Mount Elbrus
18,510 ft. (5642 m)
CAUCASUS MOUNTAINS
CASPIAN SEA
GEORGIA
T'bilisi
Baku
ARMENIA **AZERBAIJAN**
Yerevan
AZERBAIJAN
Naxçivan

BLACK SEA
AEGEAN SEA

Size comparison of Ukraine, Belarus, and the Caucasus to the contiguous United States

Physical Features

The countries of Ukraine (yoo-KRAYN) and Belarus (byay-luh-ROOS) border western Russia. Belarus is landlocked. Ukraine lies on the Black Sea. Georgia, Armenia (ahr-MEE-nee-uh), and Azerbaijan (a-zuhr-by-JAHN) lie in a rugged region called the Caucasus (KAW-kuh-suhs). It is named for the area's Caucasus Mountains. The Caucasus region is located between the Black Sea and the Caspian Sea.

Landforms Most of Ukraine and Belarus lie in a region of plains. The Northern European Plain sweeps across northern Belarus. The Pripyat (PRI-pyuht) Marshes, also called the Pinsk Marshes, are found in the south. The Carpathian Mountains run through part of western Ukraine. The Crimean (kry-MEE-uhn) Peninsula lies in southern Ukraine. The southern Crimean is very rugged and has high mountains. It separates the Black Sea from the Sea of Azov (uh-ZAWF).

In the north along the Caucasus's border with Russia is a wide mountain range. The region's and Europe's highest peak, Mount Elbrus (el-BROOS), is located here. As you can see on the chapter map, the land drops below sea level along the shore of the Caspian Sea. South of the Caucasus is a rugged, mountainous plateau. Earthquakes often occur in this region.

Rivers One of Europe's major rivers, the Dnieper (NEE-puhr), flows south through Belarus and Ukraine. Ships can travel much of its length. Dams and reservoirs on the Dnieper River provide hydroelectric power and water for irrigation.

Vegetation Mixed forests were once widespread in the central part of the region. Farther south, the forests opened onto the grasslands of the steppe. Today, farmland has replaced much of the original vegetation.

Ukraine is trying to preserve its natural environments and has created several **nature reserves**. These are areas the government has set aside to protect animals, plants, soil, and water.

✓ **READING CHECK:** (*Places and Regions*) What are the region's major physical features?

Snow-capped Mount Elbrus is located along the border between Georgia and Russia. The surrounding Caucasus Mountains lie along the dividing line between Europe and Asia.

Interpreting the Visual Record What physical processes do you think may have formed the mountains in this region of earthquakes?

Russia

● Mt. Elbrus

Georgia

Turkey

Climate

Like much of western Russia, the northern two thirds of Ukraine and Belarus have a humid continental climate. Winters are cold. Summers are warm but short. Southern Ukraine has a steppe climate. Unlike the rest of the country, the Crimean Peninsula has a Mediterranean climate. There are several different climates in the Caucasus. Georgia's coast has a mild climate similar to the Carolinas in the United States. Azerbaijan contains mainly a steppe climate. Because it is so mountainous, Armenia's climate changes with elevation.

✓ **READING CHECK:** *Places and Regions* What climate types are found in this area?

BUILD on WHAT You Know

Do you remember what you learned about steppe climates? See Chapter 3 to review.

Resources

Rich farmlands are Ukraine's greatest natural resource. Farming is also important in Belarus. Lowland areas of the Caucasus have rich soil and good conditions for farming.

The Donets (duh-NYETS) Basin in southeastern Ukraine is a rich coal-mining area. Kryvyy Rih (kri-VI RIK) is the site of a huge open-pit iron-ore mine. The region's most important mineral resources are Azerbaijan's large and valuable oil and gas deposits. These are found under the shallow Caspian Sea. Copper, manganese, iron, and other metals are also present in the Caucasus.

✓ **READING CHECK:** *Environment and Society* How have this region's natural resources affected economic development?

go.hrw.com **Homework Practice Online** **Keyword: SG3 HP18**

Section Review 1

Define and explain: nature reserves

Working with Sketch Maps On a map of Europe that you draw or that your teacher provides, label the following: Black Sea, Caucasus Mountains, Caspian Sea, Pripyat Marshes, Carpathian Mountains, Crimean Peninsula, Sea of Azov, Mount Elbrus, Dnieper River, and Donets Basin. Where in the region is a major coal-mining area?

Reading for the Main Idea

1. *Places and Regions* What three seas are found in this region?

2. *Places and Regions* What creates variation in Armenia's climate?

Critical Thinking

3. **Drawing Inferences and Conclusions** Why has so much farming developed in Ukraine, Belarus, and the Caucasus?

4. **Drawing Inferences and Conclusions** How do you think heavy mining in this region could create pollution?

Organizing What You Know

5. **Categorizing** Copy the following graphic organizer. Use it to describe the region's physical features, climates, and resources.

	Physical features	Climate	Resources
Belarus			
Caucasus			
Ukraine			

Section 2 Ukraine and Belarus

Read to Discover

1. Which groups have influenced the history of Ukraine and Belarus?

2. What are some important economic features and environmental concerns of Ukraine?

3. How has the economy of Belarus developed?

Define

serfs

Cossacks

soviet

Locate

Ukraine

Belarus

Kiev

Chernobyl

Minsk

WHY IT MATTERS

Energy created by nuclear power plants is important to the United States, Ukraine, and Belarus. Go to **CNNfyi.com** or other **current events** sources to find information about nuclear energy. Record your findings in your journal.

A hand-painted Ukrainian egg

These are the syllables for the Russian word for geography, written in the Cyrillic alphabet.

History and Government

About 600 B.C. the Greeks established trading colonies along the coast of the Black Sea. Much later—during the A.D. 400s—the Slavs began to move into what is now Ukraine and Belarus. Today, most people in this region speak closely related Slavic languages.

Vikings and Christians In the 800s Vikings took the city of Kiev. Located on the Dnieper River, it became the capital of the Vikings' trading empire. Today, this old city is Ukraine's capital. In the 900s the Byzantine, or Greek Orthodox, Church sent missionaries to teach the Ukrainians and Belorussians about Christianity. These missionaries introduced the Cyrillic alphabet.

St. Sophia Cathedral in Kiev was built in the 1000s. It was one of the earliest Orthodox cathedrals in this area. Religious images decorate the dome's interior.

Mongols and Cossacks A grandson of Genghis Khan led the Mongol horsemen that conquered Ukraine in the 1200s. They destroyed most of the towns and cities there, including Kiev.

Later, northern Ukraine and Belarus came under the control of Lithuanians and Poles. Under foreign rule, Ukrainian and Belorussian **serfs** suffered. Serfs were people who were bound to the land and worked for a lord. In return, the lords provided the serfs with military protection and other services. Some Russian and Ukrainian serfs left the farms and formed bands of nomadic horsemen. Known as **Cossacks**, they lived on the Ukrainian frontier.

The Russian Empire North and east of Belarus, a new state arose around Moscow. This Russian kingdom of Muscovy won independence from the Mongols in the late 1400s. The new state set out to expand its borders. By the 1800s all of modern Belarus and Ukraine were under Moscow's rule. Now the Cossacks served the armies of the Russian czar. However, conditions did not improve for the Ukrainian and Belorussian serfs and peasants.

Soviet Republics The Russian Revolution ended the rule of the czars in 1917. Ukraine and Belarus became republics of the Soviet Union in 1922. Although each had its own governing **soviet**, or council, Communist leaders in Moscow made all major decisions.

Ukraine was especially important as the Soviet Union's richest farming region. On the other hand, Belarus became a major industrial center. It produced heavy machinery for the Soviet Union. While Ukraine and Belarus were part of the Soviet Union, the Ukrainian and Belorussian languages were discouraged. Practicing a religion was also discouraged.

After World War II economic development continued in Ukraine and Belarus. Factories and power plants were built with little concern for the safety of nearby residents.

This watercolor on rice paper depicts Kublai Khan. He was the founder of the vast Mongol empire in the 1200s. The Mongols conquered large areas of Asia and Europe, including Ukraine.

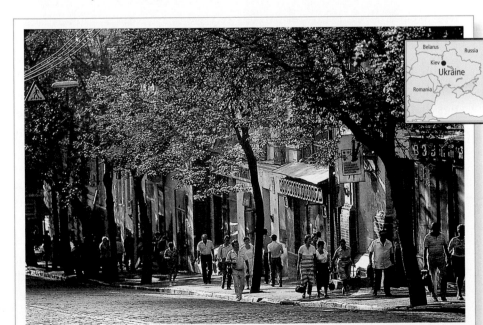

Kiev remained an important cultural and industrial center during the Soviet era. Parts of the city were destroyed during World War II and had to be rebuilt. Today tree-lined streets greet shoppers in the central city.

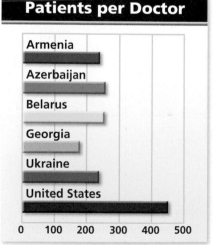

Near the end of World War II, Soviet, American, and British leaders met at Livadia Palace in Yalta, Ukraine. There they planned the defeat and occupation of Germany.

End of Soviet Rule When the Soviet Union collapsed in 1991, Belarus and Ukraine declared independence. Each now has a president and a prime minister. Both countries still have economic problems. Ukraine has also had disagreements with Russia over control of the Crimean Peninsula and the Black Sea naval fleet.

✓ **READING CHECK:** (**Human Systems**) Which groups have influenced the history of Ukraine and Belarus?

Patients per Doctor

Country	
Armenia	
Azerbaijan	
Belarus	
Georgia	
Ukraine	
United States	

0   100   200   300   400   500

Source: *The World Book Encyclopedia of People and Places*

Interpreting the Graph In what country is the number of patients per doctor greatest?

Ukraine

Ethnic Ukrainians make up about 75 percent of Ukraine's population. The largest minority group in the country is Russian. There are other ties between Ukraine and Russia. For example, the Ukrainian and Russian languages are closely related. In addition, both countries use the Cyrillic alphabet.

Economy Ukraine has a good climate for growing crops and some of the world's richest soil. As a result, agriculture is important to its economy. Ukraine is the world's largest producer of sugar beets. Ukraine's food-processing industry makes sugar from the sugar beets. Farmers also grow fruits, potatoes, vegetables, and wheat. Grain is made into flour for baked goods and pasta. Livestock is also raised. Ukraine is one of the world's top steel producers. Ukrainian factories make automobiles, railroad cars, ships, and trucks.

CONNECTING TO Science

A combine used during July harvest

Wheat: From Field to Consumer

Wheat is one of Ukraine's most important farm products. The illustration below shows how wheat is processed for use by consumers.

• The head of the wheat plant contains the wheat kernels, wrapped in husks. The kernel includes the bran or seed coat, the endosperm, and the germ from which new wheat plants grow.

• Whole wheat flour contains all the parts of the kernel. White flour is produced by grinding only the endosperm. Vitamins are added to some white flour to replace vitamins found in the bran and germ.

• People use wheat to make breads, pastas, and breakfast foods. Wheat by-products are used in many other foods.

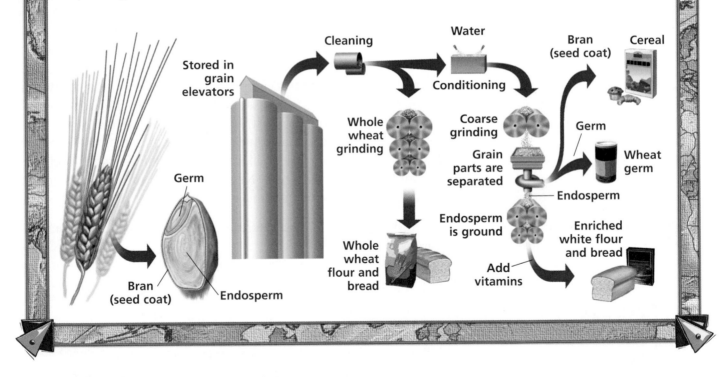

Environment During the Soviet period, Ukraine experienced rapid industrial growth. There were few pollution controls, however. In 1986 at the town of Chernobyl, the world's worst nuclear-reactor disaster occurred. Radiation spread across Ukraine and parts of northern Europe. People near the accident died. Others are still suffering from cancer. Many Ukrainians now want to reduce their country's dependence on nuclear power. This has been hard because the country has not developed enough alternative sources of power.

✓ **READING CHECK:** *Environment and Society* How has the scarcity of alternative sources of power affected Ukraine?

Belarus and Ukraine

COUNTRY	POPULATION/ GROWTH RATE	LIFE EXPECTANCY	LITERACY RATE	PER CAPITA GDP
Belarus	10,350,194 −0.2%	62, male 75, female	98%	$7,500
Ukraine	48,760,474 −0.9%	61, male 72, female	98%	$3,850
United States	281,421,906 0.9%	73, male 80, female	97%	$36,200

Sources: Central Intelligence Agency, *The World Factbook 2001;* U.S. Census Bureau

Interpreting the Chart How does life expectancy in the region compare to that of the United States? Why do you think this is the case?

Belarus

The people of Belarus are known as Belorussians, which means "white Russians." Ethnically they are closely related to Russians. Their language is also very similar to Russian.

Culture Ethnic Belorussians make up about 75 percent of the country's population. Russians are the second-largest ethnic group. Both Belorussian and Russian are official languages. Belorussian also uses the Cyrillic alphabet. Minsk, the capital of Belarus, is the administrative center of the Commonwealth of Independent States.

Economy Belarus has faced many difficulties. Fighting in World War II destroyed most of the agriculture and industry in the country. Belarus also received the worst of the radiation fallout from the Chernobyl nuclear disaster, which contaminated the country's farm products and water. Many people developed health problems as a result. Another problem has been slow economic progress since the collapse of the Soviet Union. Belarus has resisted economic changes made by other former Soviet republics.

There are various resources in Belarus, however. The country has a large reserve of potash, which is used for fertilizer. Belarus leads the world in the production of peat, a source of fuel found in the damp marshes. Mining and manufacturing are important to the economy. Flax, one of the country's main crops, is grown for fiber and seed. Cattle and pigs are also raised. Nearly one third of Belarus is covered by forests that produce wood and paper products.

✓ **READING CHECK:** *Human Systems* How has the economy of Belarus developed?

Section Review 2

Define and explain: serfs, Cossacks, soviet

Working with Sketch Maps On your map from Section 1, label Ukraine, Belarus, Kiev, Chernobyl, and Minsk.

Reading for the Main Idea

1. *Human Systems* What contributions were made by early groups that settled in this region?

2. *Human Systems* What ethnic groups and languages are found in this region today?

go. hrw .com **Homework Practice Online**
Keyword: SG3 HP18

Critical Thinking

3. **Finding the Main Idea** How did the end of Soviet rule affect Ukraine and Belarus?

4. **Summarizing** How has the nuclear disaster at Chernobyl affected the region?

Organizing What You Know

5. **Sequencing** Copy the time line below. Use it to trace the region's history from the A.D. 900s to today.

A.D. 900   Today

Section 3

The Caucasus

Read to Discover

1. What groups influenced the early history and culture of the Caucasus?
2. What is the economy of Georgia like?
3. What is Armenia like today?
4. What is Azerbaijan like today?

Define

homogeneous
agrarian

Locate

Georgia
Armenia
Azerbaijan

WHY IT MATTERS

Each of the countries in this section has been involved in a war since the collapse of the Soviet Union in 1991. Use CNNfyi.com or other **current events** sources to find information about the reasons for this unrest. Record your findings in your journal.

Cover of The Knight in Panther's Skin

History

In the 500s B.C. the Caucasus region was controlled by the Persian Empire. Later it was brought under the influence of the Byzantine Empire and was introduced to Christianity. About A.D. 650, Muslim invaders cut the region off from Christian Europe. By the late 1400s other Muslims, the Ottoman Turks, ruled a vast empire to the south and west. Much of Armenia eventually came under the rule of that empire.

Modern Era During the 1800s Russia took over eastern Armenia, much of Azerbaijan, and Georgia. The Ottoman Turks continued to rule western Armenia. Many Armenians spread throughout the Ottoman Empire. However, they were not treated well. Their desire for more independence led to the massacre of thousands of Armenians. Hundreds of thousands died while being forced to leave Turkey during World War I. Some fled to Russian Armenia.

After the war Armenia, Azerbaijan, and Georgia were briefly independent. By 1922 they had become part of the Soviet Union. They again became independent when the Soviet Union collapsed in 1991.

This wall painting is one of many at the ancient Erebuni Citadel in Yerevan, Armenia's capital. The fortress was probably built in the 800s B.C. by one of Armenia's earliest peoples, the Urartians.

▼

This Georgian family's breakfast includes local specialties such as *khachapuri*—bread made with goat cheese.

Interpreting the Visual Record
What other agricultural products do you see on the table?

Government Each country has an elected parliament, president, and prime minister. In the early 1990s there was civil war in Georgia. Armenia and Azerbaijan were also involved in a war during this time. Ethnic minorities in each country want independence. Disagreements about oil and gas rights may cause more regional conflicts in the future.

✓ **READING CHECK:** (*Human Systems*) How has conflict among cultures been a problem in this region?

Georgia

Georgia is a small country located between the high Caucasus Mountains and the Black Sea. It has a population of about 5 million. About 70 percent of the people are ethnic Georgians. The official language, Georgian, has its own alphabet. This alphabet was used as early as A.D. 400.

As in all the former Soviet republics, independence and economic reforms have been difficult. Georgia has also suffered from civil war. By the late 1990s the conflicts were fewer but not resolved.

Georgia has little good farmland. Tea and citrus fruits are the major crops. Vineyards are an important part of Georgian agriculture. Fish, livestock, and poultry contribute to the economy. Tourism on the Black Sea has also helped the economy. Because its only energy resource is hydropower, Georgia imports most of its energy supplies.

✓ **READING CHECK:** (*Human Systems*) In what way has scarcity of energy resources affected Georgia's economy?

Armenia

Armenia is a little smaller than Maryland. It lies just east of Turkey. It has fewer than 4 million people and is not as diverse as other countries

The Orthodox Christian Agartsya Monastery was built in Armenia in the 1200s.

Interpreting the Visual Record
Why do you think this building's exterior is so well preserved?

in the Caucasus. Almost all the people are Armenian, belong to the Armenian Orthodox Church, and speak Armenian.

Armenia's progress toward economic reform has not been easy. In 1988 a massive earthquake destroyed nearly one third of its industry. Armenia's industry today is varied. It includes mining and the production of carpets, clothing, and footwear.

Agriculture accounts for about 40 percent of Armenia's gross domestic product. High-quality grapes and fruits are important. Beef and dairy cattle and sheep are raised on mountain pastures.

✔ **READING CHECK:** ⬚ *Environment and Society*
How did the 1998 earthquake affect the people of Armenia?

The Caucasus

COUNTRY	POPULATION/ GROWTH RATE	LIFE EXPECTANCY	LITERACY RATE	PER CAPITA GDP
Armenia	3,336,100 −0.2%	62, male 71, female	99%	$3,000
Azerbaijan	7,771,092 0.3%	59, male 68, female	97%	$3,000
Georgia	4,989,285 −0.6%	61, male 68, female	99%	$4,600
United States	281,421,906 0.9%	74, male 80, female	97%	$36,200

Sources: Central Intelligence Agency, *The World Factbook 2001;* U.S. Census Bureau

Interpreting the Chart Which country has the lowest per capita GDP in the region? Why might this be the case?

Azerbaijan

Azerbaijan has nearly 8 million people. Its population is becoming ethnically more **homogeneous**, or the same. The Azeri, who speak a Turkic language, make up about 90 percent of the population.

Azerbaijan has few industries except for oil production. It is mostly an **agrarian** society. An agrarian society is organized around farming. The country's main resources are cotton, natural gas, and oil. Baku, the national capital, is the center of a large oil-refining industry. Oil is the most important part of Azerbaijan's economy. Fishing is also important because of the sturgeon of the Caspian Sea.

✔ **READING CHECK:** ⬚ *Human Systems* What are some cultural traits of the people of Azerbaijan?

go.hrw.com
Homework Practice Online
Keyword: SG3 HP18

Section Review 3

Define and explain: homogeneous, agrarian

Working with Sketch Maps On the map you created for Section 2, label Georgia, Armenia, and Azerbaijan. How has the location of this region helped and hindered its growth?

Reading for the Main Idea

1. ⬚ *Human Systems* Which groups influenced the early history of the Caucasus?

2. ⬚ *Human Systems* Which country controlled the Caucasus during most of the 1900s?

Critical Thinking

3. **Analyzing Information** Why has economic reform been difficult in Armenia?

4. **Finding the Main Idea** How is Azerbaijan's economy organized?

Organizing What You Know

5. **Comparing/Contrasting** Copy the following graphic organizer. Use it to show the similarities and differences among the countries of the Caucasus region.

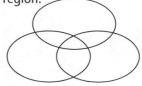

Reviewing What You Know

Building Vocabulary

On a separate sheet of paper, write sentences to define each of the following words.

1. nature reserves
2. serfs
3. Cossacks
4. soviet
5. homogeneous
6. agrarian

Reviewing the Main Ideas

1. **Human Systems** Which industries have traditionally been very important to the economies of the countries covered in this chapter?

2. **Human Systems** What is the relative location of Kiev? Which group of people founded Kiev?

3. **Human Systems** What peoples were apparently the first to settle in Belarus and Ukraine?

4. **Environment and Society** How did industrialization under Soviet rule affect these regions?

5. **Environment and Society** What effect did the earthquake in 1988 have on Armenia's economy?

Understanding Environment and Society

Resource Use

Prepare a chart and presentation on oil and natural gas production in the Caucasus. In preparing your presentation, consider the following:

• When and where oil and natural gas were discovered.

• The importance of oil and natural gas production to the former Soviet Union.

• How oil is transported from there to international markets today.

When you have finished your chart and presentation, write a five-question quiz, with answers, about your chart to challenge fellow students.

Thinking Critically

1. **Drawing Inferences and Conclusions** How might ethnic diversity affect relations among countries?

2. **Analyzing Information** How did the location of Ukraine and Belarus contribute to their devastation during World War II?

3. **Analyzing Information** Of the countries covered in this chapter, which do you think was the most important to the former Soviet Union? Why do you think this was so?

4. **Summarizing** Why did the countries of the Caucasus develop so differently from Russia, Ukraine, and Belarus?

5. **Finding the Main Idea** Why are the economies of each of the Caucasus countries so different from one another?

Map ACTIVITY

On a separate sheet of paper, match the letters on the map with their correct labels.

Caucasus Mountains

Crimean Peninsula

Pripyat Marshes

Mount Elbrus

Carpathian Mountains

Donets Basin

Chernobyl

Mental Mapping Skills ACTIVITY

On a separate sheet of paper, draw a freehand map of Ukraine, Belarus, and the Caucasus. Include Russia and Turkey for location reference. Make a map key and label the following:

Armenia

Dnieper River

Azerbaijan

Georgia

Belarus

Russia

Black Sea

Turkey

Caspian Sea

Ukraine

WRITING

ACTIVITY Choose one of the countries covered in this chapter to research. Write a report about your chosen country's struggle to establish stability since 1991. Include information about the country's government and economic reforms. Describe the social, political, and economic problems the country has faced. Be sure to use standard grammar, sentence structure, spelling, and punctuation.

Alternative Assessment

Portfolio ACTIVITY

Learning About Your Local Geography

Cooperative Project What is an important crop in your region of the United States? Work with a partner to create an illustrated flowchart that shows how this crop is made ready for consumers.

☑ **internet** connect

Internet Activity: go.hrw.com
KEYWORD: SG3 GT18

Choose a topic to explore about Ukraine, Belarus, and the Caucasus.

- Trek through the Caucasus Mountains.
- Design Ukrainian Easter eggs.
- Investigate the Chernobyl disaster.

go.hrw.com

CHAPTER 19

Central Asia

Leila is a student from Central Asia, a region of grasslands, scorching deserts, and high mountains.

S*alam!* (Hi!)—we also say "privyet," which is "hi" in Russian. My name is Leila, and I am 16. I live in Turkmenabat, the "city of Turkmen," with my parents, my three older brothers, and my younger sister. My oldest brother's wife also lives with us. My father is a professor of British studies at Turkmenabat University and my mother teaches cooking and sewing at the high school. Our house is on a canal with lots of trees. It is surrounded by a high wall, and has a balcony and an open roof where we can go if we want to be outdoors in privacy.

I am in the ninth and last year at School Number Five. The school has about 2,000 students in nine grades from kindergarten to high school. We go to school six days a week and study 18 different subjects. There is no choice of courses. I could have gone to a Russian school, but my parents chose a Turkmen one. At school, we line up by class and do 5 minutes of exercises before classes start. Each class has 25 boys and girls who stay together from kindergarten through high school. We are like a second family.

Salam!
Men Türkmenistanda
ýaşaýaryn.

Translation: Hello, I live in
Turkmenistan.

Section 1 — Physical Geography

Read to Discover

1. What are the main landforms and climates of Central Asia?
2. What resources are important to Central Asia?

Define

landlocked
oasis

Locate

Pamirs
Tian Shan
Aral Sea
Kara-Kum

Kyzyl Kum
Syr Dar'ya
Amu Dar'ya
Fergana Valley

WHY IT MATTERS

The countries of Uzbekistan, Kazakhstan, and Turkmenistan have large oil and natural gas reserves. Use CNNfyi.com or other current events sources to find examples of efforts to develop these resources. Record your findings in your journal.

A Bactrian camel and rider

Central Asia: Physical-Political

Size comparison of Central Asia to the contiguous United States

ELEVATION		
	FEET	METERS
National capitals	13,120	4,000
	6,560	2,000
Other cities	1,640	500
	656	200
	(Sea level) 0	0 (Sea level)
	Below sea level	Below sea level

SCALE
0   250   500 Miles
0   250   500 Kilometers
Projection: Two-Point Equidistant

Ismail Semani Peak
24,590 ft. (7495 m)

Mountain climbers make camp before attempting to scale a peak in the Pamirs.

Our Amazing Planet

With temperatures above 122°F (50°C), it is not surprising that the creatures that live in the Kara-Kum are a tough group. Over a thousand species live there, including cobras, scorpions, tarantulas, and monitor lizards. These lizards can grow to more than 5 feet (1.5m) long.

Lynxes can still be found in the mountains of Central Asia.

Interpreting the Visual Record How are these lynxes well suited to the environment in which they live?

Landforms and Climate

This huge, **landlocked** region is to the east of the Caspian Sea. Landlocked means the region does not border an ocean. The region lies north of the Pamirs (puh-MIRZ) and Tian Shan (TYEN SHAHN) mountain ranges.

Diverse Landforms As the name suggests, Central Asia lies in the middle of the largest continent. Plains and low plateaus cover much of this area. Around the Caspian Sea the land is as low as 95 feet (29 m) below sea level. However, the region includes high mountain ranges along the borders with China and Afghanistan.

Arid Lands Central Asia is a region of mainly steppe, desert, and highland climates. Summers are hot, with a short growing season. Winters are cold. Rainfall is sparse. However, north of the Aral (AR-uhl) Sea rainfall is heavy enough for steppe vegetation. Here farmers can grow crops using rain, rather than irrigation, as their water source. South and east of the Aral Sea lie two deserts. One is the Kara-Kum (kahr-uh-KOOM) in Turkmenistan. The other is the Kyzyl Kum (ki-ZIL KOOM) in Uzbekistan and Kazakhstan. Both deserts contain several **oasis** settlements where a spring or well provides water.

✓ **READING CHECK:** *Places and Regions* What are the landforms and climates of Central Asia?

Resources

The main water sources in southern Central Asia are the Syr Dar'ya (sir duhr-YAH) and Amu Dar'ya (uh-MOO duhr-YAH) rivers. These rivers flow down from the Pamirs and then across dry plains. Farmers have used them for irrigation for thousands of years. When it first flows down from the mountains, the Syr Dar'ya passes through the

Fergana Valley. This large valley is divided among Uzbekistan, Kyrgyzstan, and Tajikistan. As the river flows toward the Aral Sea, irrigated fields line its banks.

During the Soviet period, the region's population grew rapidly. Also, the Soviets encouraged farmers to grow cotton. This crop grows well in Central Asia's sunny climate. However, growing cotton uses a lot of water. Increased use of water has caused the Aral Sea to shrink.

A Dying Sea Today, almost no water from the Syr Dar'ya or Amu Dar'ya reaches the Aral Sea. The rivers' waters are used up by human activity. The effect on the Aral Sea has been devastating. It has lost more than 60 percent of its water since 1960. Its level has dropped 50 feet (15 m) and is still dropping. Towns that were once fishing ports are now dozens of miles from the shore. Winds sweep the dry seafloor, blowing dust, salt, and pesticides hundreds of miles.

Mineral Resources The Central Asian countries' best economic opportunity is in their fossil fuels. Uzbekistan, Kazakhstan, and Turkmenistan all have huge oil and natural gas reserves. However, transporting the oil and gas to other countries is a problem. Economic and political turmoil in some surrounding countries has made it difficult to build pipelines.

Several Central Asian countries are also rich in other minerals. They have deposits of gold, copper, uranium, zinc, and lead. Kazakhstan has vast amounts of coal. Rivers in Kyrgyzstan and Tajikistan could be used to create hydroelectric power.

This boat sits rusting on what was once part of the Aral Sea. The sea's once thriving fishing industry has been destroyed.

✓ **READING CHECK:** *Environment and Society* How has human activity affected the Aral Sea?

Section Review 1

Define and explain: landlocked, oasis

Working with Sketch Maps On a map of Central Asia that you draw or that your teacher provides, label the following: Pamirs, Tian Shan, Aral Sea, Kara-Kum, Kyzyl Kum, Syr Dar'ya, Amu Dar'ya, and Fergana Valley.

Reading for the Main Idea

1. *Environment and Society* What has caused the drying up of the Aral Sea?

2. *Places and Regions* What mineral resources does Central Asia have?

Critical Thinking

3. Analyzing Information Why did the Soviets encourage Central Asian farmers to grow cotton?

4. Finding the Main Idea What factors make it hard for the Central Asian countries to export oil and gas?

Organizing What You Know

5. Sequencing Copy the following graphic organizer. Use it to describe the courses of the Syr Dar'ya and Amu Dar'ya, including human activities that use water.

Melting snows in the Pamirs	⇨		⇨	Aral Sea

Section 2 History and Culture

Read to Discover

1. How did trade and invasions affect the history of Central Asia?

2. What are political and economic conditions like in Central Asia today?

Define

nomads

caravans

WHY IT MATTERS

Even though the Soviet Union has collapsed, traces of its influence remain in Central Asia, particularly in government. Use **CNNfyi.com** or other **current events** sources to find examples of political events in these countries. Record your findings in your journal.

An ancient Kyrgyz stone figure

History

For centuries, Central Asians have made a living by raising horses, cattle, sheep, and goats. Many of these herders lived as **nomads**, people who often move from place to place. Other people became farmers around rivers and oases.

Trade At one time, the best land route between China and the eastern Mediterranean ran through Central Asia. Merchants traveled in large groups, called **caravans**, for protection. The goods they carried included silk and spices. As a result, this route came to be called the Silk Road. Cities along the road became centers of wealth and culture.

Central Asia's situation changed after Europeans discovered they could sail to East Asia through the Indian Ocean. As a result, trade through Central Asia declined. The region became isolated and poor.

Bukhara, in Uzbekistan, was once a powerful and wealthy trading center of Central Asia.

Interpreting the Visual Record
What architectural features can you see that distinguish Bukhara as an Islamic city?

▼

CONNECTING TO History

Silk processing in modern Uzbekistan

The Silk Road

The Silk Road stretched 5,000 miles (8,000 km) across Central Asia from China to the Mediterranean Sea. Along this route passed merchants, armies, and diplomats. These people forged links between East and West.

The facts of the Silk Road are still wrapped in mystery. Chinese trade and military expeditions probably began moving into Central Asia in the 100s B.C. Chinese trade goods soon were making their way to eastern Mediterranean ports.

Over the next several centuries, trade in silk, spices, jewels, and other luxury goods increased. Great caravans of camels and oxcarts traveled the Silk Road in both directions. They crossed the harsh deserts and mountains of Central Asia. Cities like Samarqand and Bukhara grew rich from the trade. In the process, ideas and technology also moved between Europe and Asia.

Travel along the Silk Road was hazardous. Bandits often robbed the caravans. Some travelers lost their way in the desert and died. In addition, religious and political turmoil occasionally disrupted travel.

Understanding What You Read
1. What was the Silk Road?
2. Why was the Silk Road important?

Invasions and the Soviet Era About A.D. 500, Turkic-speaking nomads from northern Asia spread through Central Asia. In the 700s Arab armies took over much of the region, bringing Islam. In the 1200s the armies of Mongol leaders conquered Central Asia. Later, another Turkic people, the Uzbeks, took over parts of the region. In the 1800s the Russian Empire conquered Central Asia.

After the Russian Revolution, the Soviet government set up five republics in Central Asia. The Soviets encouraged ethnic Russians to move to this area and made the nomads settle on collective ranches or farms. Religion was discouraged. Russian became the language of government and business. The government set up schools and hospitals. Women were allowed to work outside the home.

✓ **READING CHECK:** (**Human Systems**) What type of government system did the five republics set up by the Soviet Union have?

A Kyrgyz teacher conducts class.
Interpreting the Visual Record
How is this class similar to yours?

▼

Central Asia Today

The five republics became independent countries when the Soviet Union broke up in 1991. All have strong economic ties to Russia. Ethnic Russians still live in every country in the region. However, all five countries are switching from the Cyrillic alphabet to the Latin alphabet. The Cyrillic alphabet had been imposed on them by the Soviet Union. The Latin alphabet is used in most Western European languages, including English, and in Turkey.

Government All of these new countries have declared themselves to be democracies. However, they are not very free or democratic. Each is ruled by a strong central government that limits opposition and criticism.

Economy Some of the Central Asian countries have oil and gas reserves that may someday make them rich. For now, though, all are suffering economic hardship. Causes of the hardships include outdated equipment, lack of funds, and poor transportation links.

Farming is important in the Central Asian economies. Crops include cotton, wheat, barley, fruits, vegetables, almonds, tobacco, and rice. Central Asians raise cattle, sheep, horses, goats, and camels. They also raise silkworms to make silk thread.

Industry in Central Asia includes food processing, wool textiles, mining, and oil drilling. Oil-rich Turkmenistan and Kazakhstan also process oil into other products. Kazakhstan and Uzbekistan make heavy equipment such as tractors.

✓ **READING CHECK:** (*Human Systems*) How do political freedoms in the region compare to those of the United States?

Section Review 2

Define and explain: nomads, caravans

Working with Sketch Maps On the map you created in Section 1, draw and label the five Central Asian countries.

Reading for the Main Idea

1. (*Environment and Society*) How have the people of Central Asia made a living over the centuries?

2. (*Human Systems*) What are four groups that invaded Central Asia?

3. (*Human Systems*) How did Soviet rule change Central Asia?

Critical Thinking

4. **Drawing Inferences and Conclusions** What does the switch to the Latin alphabet suggest about the Central Asian countries?

Organizing What You Know

5. **Categorizing** Copy the following graphic organizer. Use it to categorize economic activities in Central Asia. Place the following items in the chart: making cloth, growing crops, mining metals, making food products, raising livestock, making chemicals from oil, drilling for oil, and manufacturing tractors.

Primary industries	Secondary industries

Section 3 The Countries of Central Asia

Read to Discover

1. What are some important aspects of culture in Kazakhstan?
2. How does Kyrgyz culture reflect nomadic traditions?
3. Why have politics in Tajikistan in recent years been marked by violence?
4. What are two important art forms in Turkmenistan?
5. How is Uzbekistan's population significant?

Define

yurt
mosques

Locate

Tashkent
Samarqand

A warrior's armor from Kazakhstan

WHY IT MATTERS

Since the collapse of the Soviet Union, religious freedom is more common in Central Asia. Use CNNfyi.com or other **current events** sources to find examples of religious and ethnic differences in the countries of Central Asia. Record your findings in your journal.

Kazakhstan

Of the Central Asian nations, Kazakhstan was the first to be conquered by Russia. Russian influence remains strong there. About one third of Kazakhstan's people are ethnic Russians. Kazakh and Russian are both official languages. Many ethnic Kazakhs grow up speaking Russian at home and have to learn Kazakh in school.

Kazakhstanis celebrate the New Year twice—on January 1 and again on Nauruz, the start of the Persian calendar's year. Nauruz falls on the spring equinox.

Food in Central Asia combines influences from Southwest Asia and China. Rice, yogurt, and grilled meat are common ingredients. One Kazakh specialty is smoked horsemeat sausage with cold noodles.

✓ **READING CHECK:** *Human Systems* How has Kazakhstan been influenced by Russia?

A woman in Uzbekistan grills meat on skewers.
▼

Kyrgyzstan

Kyrgyzstan has many mountains, and the people live mostly in valleys. People in the southern part of the country generally share cultural ties with Uzbekistan. People in northern areas are more linked to nomadic cultures and to Kazakhstan.

Ethnic Makeup of Kazakhstan and Uzbekistan

Kazakhstan

- 53.4%
- 30%
- 14.1%
- 2.5%

Uzbekistan

- 80%
- 11.5%
- 5.5%
- 3%

Legend:
- ■ Kazakh
- ■ Russian
- ■ Uzbek
- ■ Other

Source: Central Intelligence Agency, *The World Factbook 2001*

Interpreting the Chart How does the number of Russians in Kazakhstan compare to that in Uzbekistan?

The word *kyrgyz* means "forty clans." Clan membership is still important in Krygyz social, political, and economic life. Many Kyrgyz men wear black and white felt hats that show their clan status.

Nomadic traditions are still important to many Kyrgyz. The **yurt** is a movable round house of wool felt mats over a wood frame. Today the yurt is a symbol of the nomadic heritage. Even people who live in cities may put up yurts for weddings and funerals.

✓ **READING CHECK:** *Human Systems* In what ways do the Kyrgyz continue traditions of their past?

Tajikistan

In the mid-1990s Tajikistan experienced a civil war. The Soviet-style government fought against a mixed group of reformers, some of whom demanded democracy. Others called for government by Islamic law. A peace agreement was signed in 1996, but tensions remain high.

The other major Central Asian languages are related to Turkish. However, the Tajik language is related to Persian. Tajiks consider the great literature written in Persian to be part of their cultural heritage.

✓ **READING CHECK:** *Human Systems* What has happened in politics in recent years in Tajikistan?

Turkmenistan

The major first language of Turkmenistan is Turkmen. In 1993 Turkmenistan adopted English, rather than Russian, as its second official language. However, some schools teach in Russian, Uzbek, or Kazakh.

Islam has experienced a revival in Central Asia since the breakup of the Soviet Union. Many new **mosques**, or Islamic houses of worship, are being built and old ones are being restored. Donations from other Islamic countries, such as Saudi Arabia and Iran, have helped

Turkoman women display carpets. Central Asian carpets are famous for their imaginative patterns, bright colors, and expert artistry.

Interpreting the Visual Record Why were carpets suited to the nomadic way of life?

these efforts. The government of Turkmenistan supports this revival and has ordered schools to teach Islamic principles. However, like the other states in the region, Turkmenistan's government views Islam with some caution. It does not want Islam to become a political movement.

Historically, the nomadic life required that all possessions be portable. Decorative carpets were the essential furniture of a nomad's home. They are still perhaps the most famous artistic craft of Turkmenistan. Like others in Central Asia, the people of Turkmenistan also have an ancient tradition of poetry.

✓ **READING CHECK:** (*Human Systems*) What are two forms of art in Turkmenistan, and how do they reflect its cultural traditions?

Central Asia

COUNTRY	POPULATION/ GROWTH RATE	LIFE EXPECTANCY	LITERACY RATE	PER CAPITA GDP
Kazakhstan	16,731,303 .03%	58, male 69, female	98%	$5,000
Kyrgyzstan	4,753,003 1.4%	59, male 68, female	97%	$2,700
Tajikistan	6,578,681 2.1%	61, male 67, female	98%	$1,140
Turkmenistan	4,603,244 1.9%	57, male 65, female	98%	$4,300
Uzbekistan	25,155,064 1.6%	60, male 68, female	99%	$2,400
United States	281,421,906 0.9%	74, male 80, female	97%	$36,200

Sources: Central Intelligence Agency, *The World Factbook 2001;* U.S. Census Bureau

Interpreting the Chart **Which country has the lowest per capita GDP in the region?**

Uzbekistan

Uzbekistan has the largest population of the Central Asian countries—about 24 million people. Uzbek is the official language. People are required to study Uzbek to be eligible for citizenship.

Tashkent and Samarqand are ancient Silk Road cities in Uzbekistan. They are famous for their mosques and Islamic monuments. Uzbeks are also known for their art of embroidering fabric with gold.

✓ **READING CHECK:** (*Human Systems*) What is one of an Uzbekistan citizen's responsibilities?

go. hrw .com **Homework Practice Online** Keyword: SG3 HP19

Section Review 3

Define and explain: yurt, mosques

Working with Sketch Maps On the map you created in Section 2, label Tashkent and Samarqand.

Reading for the Main Idea

1. (*Places and Regions*) In which Central Asian nation is the influence of Russia strongest? Why is this true?

2. (*Human Systems*) What were the two sides in Tajikistan's civil war fighting for?

3. (*Human Systems*) What is the role of Islam in the region today?

Critical Thinking

4. **Finding the Main Idea** What are two customs or artistic crafts of modern Central Asia that are connected to the nomadic lifestyle?

Organizing What You Know

5. **Contrasting** Copy the following graphic organizer. Use it to describe the conditions in Central Asia during the Soviet era and today.

	Soviet era	Today
Type of government		
Official language		
Alphabet		
Government attitude toward Islam		

CASE STUDY

KAZAKHS: PASTORAL NOMADS OF CENTRAL ASIA

Nomads are people who move around from place to place during the year. Nomads usually move when the seasons change so that they will have enough food to eat. Herding, hunting, gathering, and fishing are all ways that different nomadic groups get their food.

Nomads that herd animals are called pastoral nomads. Their way of life depends on the seasonal movement of their herds. Pastoral nomads may herd cattle, horses, sheep, goats, yaks, reindeer, camels, or other animals. Instead of keeping their animals inside fenced pastures, pastoral nomads let them graze on open fields. However, they must make sure the animals do not overgraze and damage the pastureland. To do this, they keep their animals moving throughout the year. Some pastoral nomads live in steppe or desert environments. These nomads often have to move their animals very long distances between winter and summer pastures.

The Kazakhs of Central Asia are an example of a pastoral nomadic group. They have herded horses, sheep, goats, and cattle for hundreds of years. Because they move so much, the Kazakhs do not have permanent homes. They bring their homes with them when they travel to new places.

A Kazakh nomad keeps a watchful eye over a herd of horses.

▼

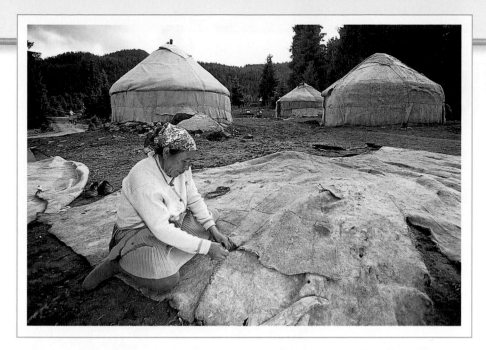

Yurts are carefully stitched together by hand. When it is time to move to new pastures, they are carried from place to place on horseback or on small wagons.

The Kazakhs live in tent-like structures called yurts. Yurts are circular structures made of bent poles covered with thick felt. Yurts can be easily taken apart and moved. They are perfect homes for the Kazakhs' nomadic lifestyle.

During the year, a Kazakh family may move its herds of sheep, horses, and cattle as far as 500 miles (805 km). For one Kazakh family, each year is divided into four different parts. The family spends the first part of the year in winter grazing areas. Then, in early spring, they move to areas with fresh grass shoots. When these spring grasses are gone, the family moves their animals to summer pastures. In the fall, the animals are kept for six weeks in autumn pastures. Finally, the herds are taken back to their winter pastures. Each year, the cycle is repeated.

The nomadic lifestyle of the Kazakhs has changed, however. In the early 1800s people from Russia and eastern Europe began to move into the region. These people were farmers. They started planting crops in areas that the Kazakhs used for pasture. This made it more difficult for the Kazakhs to move their animals during the year. Later, when Kazakhstan was part of the Soviet Union, government officials encouraged the Kazakhs to settle in villages and cities. Many Kazakhs still move their animals during the year. However, tending crops has also become an important way to get food.

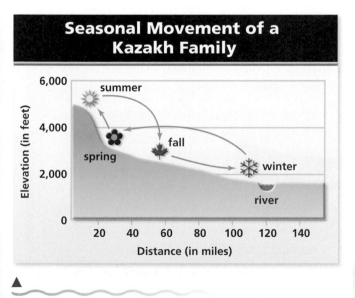

During the year, a Kazakh family may move its herds to several different pasture areas as the seasons change.

Interpreting the Graph Why do you think animals are moved to higher elevations during the summer and to lower elevations during the winter?

Understanding What You Read

1. Why do some pastoral nomads have to travel such great distances?

2. How has the nomadic lifestyle of the Kazakhs changed during the last 100 years?

Reviewing What You Know

Building Vocabulary

On a separate sheet of paper, write sentences to define each of the following words.

1. landlocked
2. oasis
3. nomads
4. caravans
5. yurt
6. mosques

Reviewing the Main Ideas

1. (Places and Regions) What types of climates are most common in Central Asia?

2. (Environment and Society) What problems have resulted from the shrinking of the Aral Sea?

3. (Human Systems) How did Soviet rule change Central Asians' way of life?

4. (Human Systems) What kinds of ties do the Central Asian countries have to Russia today?

5. (Places and Regions) What are the various languages spoken in Central Asia?

Understanding Environment and Society

Aral Sea in Danger
The rapid disappearance of the Aral Sea is a serious concern in Central Asia. Research and create a presentation on the Aral Sea. You may want to think about the following:

- Actions that could be taken to preserve the Aral Sea.
- What could be done to help slow the dropping of the sea's water level.
- Possible consequences if the level of the Aral Sea continues to drop.

Include a bibliography of the sources you used.

Thinking Critically

1. **Summarizing** How have politics influenced language and the alphabet used in Central Asia?

2. **Finding the Main Idea** How do the artistic crafts of Central Asia reflect the nomadic lifestyle?

3. **Analyzing Information** Why did the Soviets encourage cotton farming in the region? What were the environmental consequences?

4. **Finding the Main Idea** What obstacles are making it hard for the Central Asian countries to export their oil?

5. **Summarizing** What are some reasons the Central Asian countries have experienced slow economic growth since independence? How are they trying to improve the situation?

Map ACTIVITY

On a separate sheet of paper, match the letters on the map with their correct labels.

Caspian Sea	Kara-Kum
Pamirs	Kyzyl Kum
Tian Shan	Tashkent
Aral Sea	Samarqand

Mental Mapping Skills ACTIVITY

On a separate sheet of paper, draw a freehand map of Central Asia. Make a key for your map and label the following:

Amu Dar'ya	Syr Dar'ya
Aral Sea	Tajikistan
Kazakhstan	Turkmenistan
Kyrgyzstan	Uzbekistan

WRITING ACTIVITY

Imagine that you are a caravan trader traveling along the Silk Road during the 1200s. Write a journal entry describing your journey from the Mediterranean Sea through Central Asia. Be sure to use standard grammar, spelling, sentence structure, and punctuation.

Alternative Assessment

Portfolio ACTIVITY

Learning About Your Local Geography

History The Mongol conqueror Genghis Khan is a hero to many Central Asians. Use biographies or interviews with residents to find out about a person who is special to your area. Report your findings.

internet connect

Internet Activity: go.hrw.com
KEYWORD: SG3 GT9

Choose a topic to explore about Central Asia:
- Study the climate of Central Asia.
- Travel along the historic Silk Road.
- Learn about nomads and caravans.

go.hrw.com

FOCUS ON CULTURE

Facing the Past and Present

Patterns of trade and culture can change quickly in our modern world. For example, the United States used to trade primarily with Europe. Most immigrants to the United States also came from Europe. Today, the American connection to Europe has faded. The United States now trades more with Japan and other Pacific Rim countries than with Europe. New ideas, new technology, and immigrants to the United States come from all around the world.

Central Asia Since the breakup of the Soviet Union, similar changes have taken place in Central Asia. In the past, Central Asia had many ties to the Soviet Union. For example, the economies of the two regions were linked. Central Asia exported cotton and oil to Russia and to countries in Eastern Europe. In exchange, Central Asia received a variety of manufactured goods. The Soviet Union also heavily influenced the culture of Central Asia. Many Central Asians learned to speak Russian.

Looking South Today, Central Asia's links to the former Soviet Union have weakened. At the same time, its ancient ties to Southwest Asia have grown stronger. The Silk Road once linked Central Asian cities to Southwest Asian ports on the Mediterranean. Now the peoples of Central Asia are looking southward once again. New links are forming between Central Asia and Turkey. Many people in Central Asia are traditionally Turkic in culture and language. Turkey's business leaders are working to expand their industries in Central Asia. Also, regular air travel from Turkey to cities in Central Asia is now possible as well.

Religion also links both Central Asia and Southwest Asia. Islam was first introduced into Central Asia in the A.D. 700s. It eventually became the region's dominant religion. However, Islam declined during the Soviet era. Missionaries from Arab countries and Iran are now working to strengthen this connection. Iran is also spending millions of dollars to build roads and rail lines to Central Asia.

◄

These children are learning about Islam in Dushanbe, Tajikistan. Although the former Communist government discouraged the practice of religion, today Islam flourishes in the independent Central Asian republics.

Language Groups of Southwest and Central Asia

DOMINANT LANGUAGES

Turkic	Greek
Iranic	Other
Semitic	Sparsely populated

This map shows the major language groups that link peoples throughout Southwest and Central Asia. Very often, however, the links between peoples are overshadowed by differences in culture and history.

Central Asia and Southwest Asia share a similar climate, environment, and way of life. Both regions are dry, and water conservation and irrigation are important. Many people in both regions grow cotton and herd animals. In addition, both Central Asia and Southwest Asia are dealing with changes caused by the growing influence of Western culture. Some people are worried that compact discs, videotapes, and satellite television from the West threaten traditional beliefs and ways of life. Shared fears of cultural loss may bring Central Asia and Southwest Asia closer together.

Defining the Region As the world changes, geographers must reexamine this and other regions of the world. Will geographers decide to include the countries of Central Asia in the region of Southwest Asia? Will Russia regain control of Central Asia? The geographers are watching and waiting.

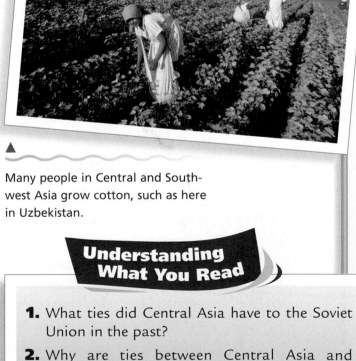

Many people in Central and Southwest Asia grow cotton, such as here in Uzbekistan.

Understanding What You Read

1. What ties did Central Asia have to the Soviet Union in the past?

2. Why are ties between Central Asia and Southwest Asia growing today?

Geo SKILLS

Building Skills for Life: Addressing Environmental Problems

The natural environment is the world around us. It includes the air, animals, land, plants, and water. Many people today are concerned about the environment. They are called environmentalists. Environmentalists are worried that human activities are damaging the environment. Environmental problems include air, land, and water pollution, global warming, deforestation, plant and animal extinction, and soil erosion.

People all over the world are working to solve these environmental problems. The governments of many countries are trying to work together to protect the environment. International organizations like the United Nations are also addressing environmental issues.

▲

An oil spill in northwestern Russia caused serious environmental damage in 1995.

Interpreting the Visual Record
Can you see how these people are cleaning up the oil spill?

THE SKILL

1. **Gather Information.** Create a plan to present to the city council for solving a local environmental problem. Select a problem and research it using databases or other reference materials. How does it affect people's lives and your community's culture or economy?

2. **List and Consider Options.** After reviewing the information, list and consider options for solving this environmental problem.

3. **Consider Advantages and Disadvantages.** Now consider the advantages and disadvantages of taking each option. Ask yourself questions like, "How will solving this environmental problem affect business in the area?" Record your answers.

4. **Choose, Implement, and Evaluate a Solution.** After considering the advantages and disadvantages, you should create your plan. Be sure to make your proposal clear. You will need to explain the reasoning behind the choices you made in your plan.

PRACTICING

HANDS on GEOGRAPHY

The countries of the former Soviet Union face some of the worst environmental problems in the world. For more than 50 years, the region's environment was polluted with nuclear waste and toxic chemicals. Today, environmental problems in this region include air, land, and water pollution.

One place that was seriously polluted was the Russian city of Chelyabinsk. Some people have called Chelyabinsk the most polluted place on Earth. The passage below describes some of the environmental problems in Chelyabinsk. Read the passage and then answer the Lab Report questions.

Chelyabinsk was one of the former Soviet Union's main military production centers. A factory near Chelyabinsk produced nuclear weapons. Over the years, nuclear waste from this factory polluted a very large area. A huge amount of nuclear waste was dumped into the Techa River. Many people in the region used this river as their main source of water. They also ate fish from the river.

In the 1950s many deaths and health problems resulted from pollution in the Techa River. Because it was so polluted, the Soviet government evacuated 22 villages along the river. In 1957 a nuclear accident in the region released twice as much radiation as the Chernobyl accident in 1986. However, the accident near Chelyabinsk was kept secret. About 10,000 people were evacuated. The severe environmental problems in the Chelyabinsk region led to dramatic increases in birth defects and cancer rates.

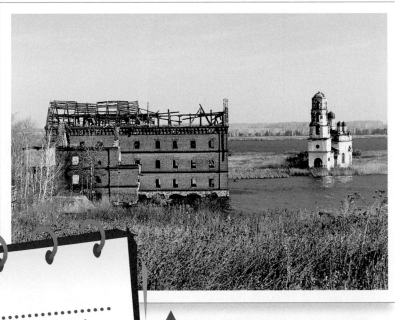

▲ The village of Mitlino was evacuated after a nuclear accident in 1957.

Lab Report

1. How did environmental problems near Chelyabinsk affect people who lived in the region?

2. What might be done to address environmental problems in the Chelyabinsk region?

3. How can a geographical perspective help to solve these problems?

UNIT 6

Southwest Asia

CHAPTER 20
The Arabian Peninsula, Iraq, Iran, and Afghanistan

CHAPTER 21
The Eastern Mediterranean

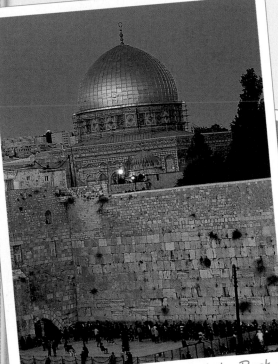

Western Wall and Dome of the Rock, Jerusalem, Israel

Bottle trees, Yemen

An Exchange Student in Turkey

Sara Lewis was an American exchange student in Turkey. Here she describes how teenagers live in Istanbul, Turkey's largest city, and the month-long fast of Ramadan. **WHAT DO YOU THINK?** *What would it be like to live in a place where you can see the remains of thousands of years of history?*

The people of Istanbul are very traditional and family-oriented, but today's Turk also has European-style tastes. Turkish teens go dancing and hang out in coffeehouses. All around them, though, are reminders of the past. There are many monuments left over from Greek, Roman, Byzantine, and Ottoman times.

Islam plays a big part in daily life. Five times every day I can hear the people being called to prayer. For more than a month, my host parents fasted during Ramadan. They didn't eat or drink anything while the sun was up. My host sister and I fasted for one day. By the time the sun went down we were starving! I'm glad we weren't expected to continue the fast. Then we shopped for new clothes. It is the custom to wear new clothes to the feast at the end of Ramadan. The fresh clothes seem to stand for the cleanliness one achieves during the month of fasting.

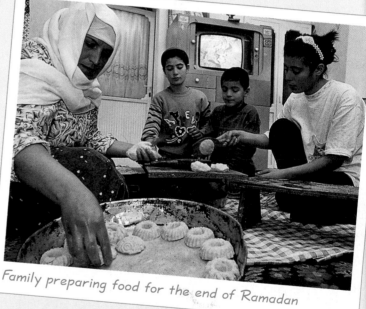

Family preparing food for the end of Ramadan

Jewish girls, Zefat, Israel

Understanding Primary Sources

1. What do modern Turkish teenagers do for fun?

2. How is Ramadan observed in Turkey?

Sooty falcon

Southwest Asia

Elevation Profile

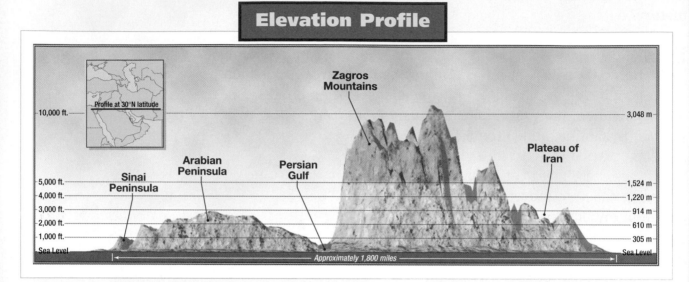

Profile at 30°N latitude

Zagros Mountains

10,000 ft. — 3,048 m

Plateau of Iran

Arabian Peninsula

Persian Gulf

Sinai Peninsula

5,000 ft. — 1,524 m
4,000 ft. — 1,220 m
3,000 ft. — 914 m
2,000 ft. — 610 m
1,000 ft. — 305 m
Sea Level — Sea Level

Approximately 1,800 miles

The United States and Southwest Asia: Comparing Sizes

GEOSTATS:

- World's lowest point on land: the Dead Sea, in Israel and Jordan—1,312 feet (400 m) below sea level

- World's leading exporter of oil: Saudi Arabia

- Approximate amount of proven oil reserves in Saudi Arabia: 261 billion barrels

- Estimated number of barrels of oil that pass through the Strait of Hormuz every day: 15.4 million

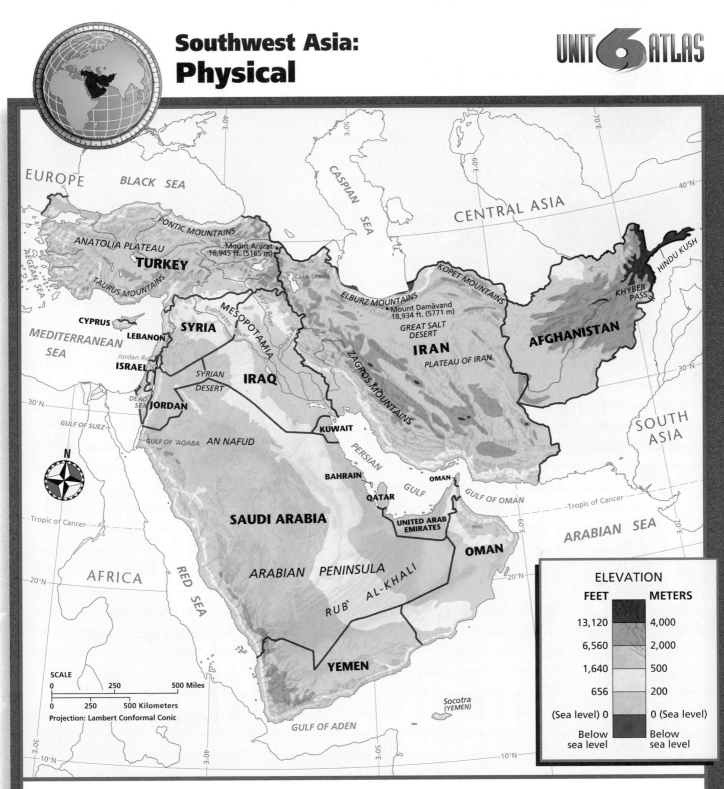

ELEVATION

FEET		METERS
13,120		4,000
6,560		2,000
1,640		500
656		200
(Sea level) 0		0 (Sea level)
Below sea level		Below sea level

SCALE
0   250   500 Miles
0   250   500 Kilometers
Projection: Lambert Conformal Conic

1. *Environment and Society* What landforms might make north-south travel difficult in Iran?

2. *Places and Regions* Where are the region's highest mountains? What are these mountains called?

3. *Places and Regions* Which country is partly in Europe and partly in Asia?

Critical Thinking

4. Analyzing Information How might one travel overland from Syria to Oman? Why?

5. Comparing Compare this map to the **population map**. What physical features contribute to Iraq's relatively high population density?

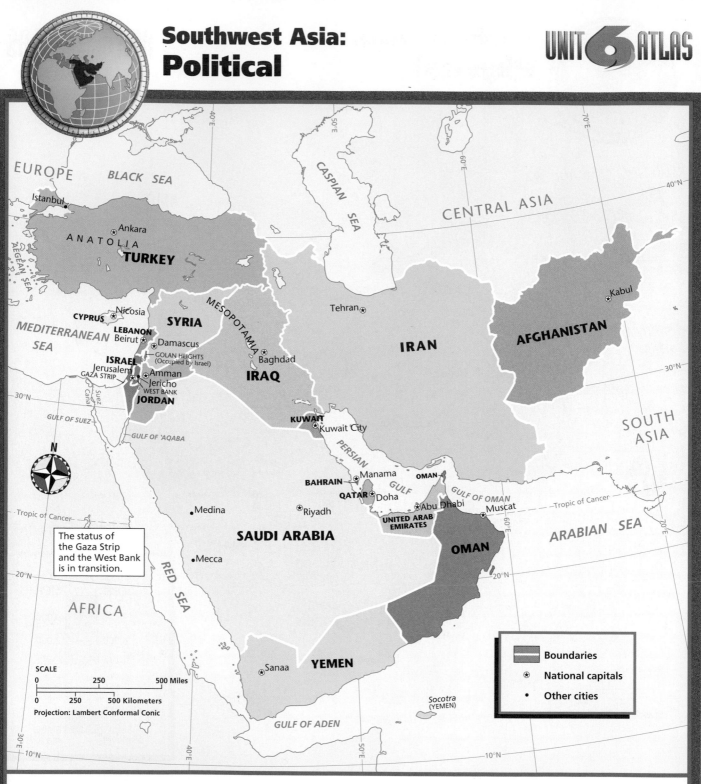

1. *Places and Regions* What are the region's two largest countries? the region's smallest?

Critical Thinking

2. Comparing Examine the **climate map**. Why do you think so many of the boundaries in this region are straight lines? Why might

some maps show Saudi Arabia's southern border as a dotted line?

3. Drawing Inferences and Conclusions Which countries lie along the Persian Gulf and the Gulf of Oman? Why might conflicts occur among these countries?

EUROPE
BLACK SEA
AEGEAN SEA
MEDITERRANEAN SEA
CASPIAN SEA
CENTRAL ASIA
SOUTH ASIA
PERSIAN GULF
GULF OF OMAN
Tropic of Cancer
ARABIAN SEA
AFRICA
RED SEA
Tropic of Cancer
GULF OF ADEN

40°E 50°E 60°E 70°E 40°N 30°N 20°N 70°E 10°N 50°E 40°E 30°N 10°N 20°N 30°N

N

SCALE
0   250   500 Miles
0   250   500 Kilometers
Projection: Lambert Conformal Conic

CLIMATE
- Desert
- Steppe
- Mediterranean
- Humid subtropical
- Highland

1. *Places and Regions* Which countries have desert climates?

2. *Places and Regions* Which two countries have only a Mediterranean climate?

Critical Thinking

3. Comparing Compare this map to the **population map**. How might climate influence the region's population patterns?

4. Analyzing Information Compare this map to the **physical** and **land use and resources maps**. Why is commercial farming possible in central Iraq?

EUROPE

BLACK SEA

Istanbul

Ankara

Izmir

AEGEAN SEA

Adana

Tabriz

CASPIAN SEA

CENTRAL ASIA

Mashhad

Kabul

Aleppo

Tehran

MEDITERRANEAN SEA

Damascus

Baghdad

Isfahan

Tel Aviv-Yafo

Shiraz

SOUTH ASIA

Riyadh

PERSIAN GULF

GULF OF OMAN

Jidda

AFRICA

RED SEA

N

Tropic of Cancer

GULF OF ADEN

SCALE

0   250   500 Miles

0   250   500 Kilometers

Projection: Lambert Conformal Conic

POPULATION DENSITY

Persons per sq. mile		Persons per sq. km
520		200
260		100
130		50
25		10
3		1
0		0

● Metropolitan areas with more than 2 million inhabitants

○ Metropolitan areas with 1 million to 2 million inhabitants

1. *Places and Regions* Which country has two cities of more than 2 million people?

2. *Places and Regions* Compare this map to the **physical map** of the region. Which desert area has almost no residents?

3. *Places and Regions* Which country has an area of high population density but no big cities?

Critical Thinking

4. Analyzing Information Use this map to create a chart, graph, database, or model of population centers in Southwest Asia.

5. Analyzing Information Look at Istanbul's location. Why is it good for a large city?

Southwest Asia:
Land Use and Resources

RESOURCES

- • Major manufacturing and trade centers
- — Oil pipelines
- — Shipping lanes

- Coal
- Natural gas
- Oil
- Hydroelectric power

- Gold
- Other minerals
- Seafood

LAND USE

- Nomadic herding
- Livestock raising
- Commercial farming
- Subsistence farming
- Forests
- Limited economic activity

SCALE
0   250   500 Miles
0   250   500 Kilometers
Projection: Lambert Conformal Conic

---

1. *Human Systems* By what route would an oil tanker travel from Abadan to Mediterranean ports?

2. *Places and Regions* What two energy resources are often found together in the region?

3. *Places and Regions* Which countries have gold? Which countries have deposits of coal?

Critical Thinking

4. Analyzing Information Use this map to create a chart, graph, database, or model of economic activities in Southwest Asia.

5. Drawing Inferences and Conclusions Why might vegetables be costly in Kuwait?

Fast FACTS

Southwest Asia

AFGHANISTAN

CAPITAL:
Kabul

AREA:
250,000 sq. mi.
(647,500 sq km)

POPULATION:
26,813,057

MONEY:
afghani (AFA)

LANGUAGES:
Pashtu, Afghan Persian (Dari), Turkic languages

TELEPHONE LINES:
29,000 (1996)

BAHRAIN

CAPITAL:
Manama

AREA:
239 sq. mi.
(620 sq km)

POPULATION:
645,361

MONEY:
Bahraini dinar (BHD)

LANGUAGES:
Arabic, English, Farsi, Urdu

TELEPHONE LINES:
152,000 (1997)

CYPRUS

CAPITAL:
Nicosia

AREA:
3,571 sq. mi. (9,250 sq km)

POPULATION:
762,887

MONEY:
Cypriot pound (£C), Turkish lira (TRL)

LANGUAGES:
Greek, Turkish, English

TELEPHONE LINES:
Greek Cypriot area: 405,000 (1998); Turkish Cypriot area: 83,162 (1998)

IRAN

CAPITAL:
Tehran

AREA:
636,293 sq. mi.
(1,648,000 sq km)

POPULATION:
66,128,965

MONEY:
Iranian rial (IRR)

LANGUAGES:
Persian, Turkic, Kurdish

TELEPHONE LINES:
6,313,000 (1997)

IRAQ

CAPITAL:
Baghdad

AREA:
168,753 sq. mi.
(437,072 sq km)

POPULATION: 23,331,985

MONEY:
Iraqi dinar (IQD)

LANGUAGES:
Arabic, Kurdish

TELEPHONE LINES:
675,000 (1997)

ISRAEL

CAPITAL:
Jerusalem

AREA:
8,019 sq. mi.
(20,770 sq km)

POPULATION:
5,938,093

MONEY:
new Israeli shekel (ILS)

LANGUAGES:
Hebrew (official), Arabic, English

TELEPHONE LINES:
2,800,000 (1999)

JORDAN

CAPITAL:
Amman

AREA:
35,637 sq. mi.
(92,300 sq km)

POPULATION:
5,153,378

MONEY:
Jordanian dinar (JOD)

LANGUAGES:
Arabic, English

TELEPHONE LINES:
403,000 (1997)

KUWAIT

CAPITAL:
Kuwait

AREA:
6,880 sq. mi.
(17,820 sq km)

POPULATION:
2,041,961

MONEY:
Kuwaiti dinar (KWD)

LANGUAGES:
Arabic, English

TELEPHONE LINES:
412,000

Countries not drawn to scale.

LEBANON

CAPITAL:
Beirut

AREA:
4,015 sq. mi.
(10,400 sq km)

POPULATION: 3,627,774

MONEY:
Lebanese pound (LBP)

LANGUAGES:
Arabic (official), French

TELEPHONE LINES:
700,000 (1999)

OMAN

CAPITAL:
Muscat

AREA:
82,031 sq. mi.
(212,460 sq km)

POPULATION: 2,662,198

MONEY:
Omani rial (OMR)

LANGUAGES:
Arabic (official), English

TELEPHONE LINES:
201,000 (1997)

QATAR

CAPITAL:
Doha

AREA:
4,416 sq. mi.
(11,437 sq km)

POPULATION:
769,152

MONEY:
Qatari rial (QAR)

LANGUAGES:
Arabic (official), English

TELEPHONE LINES:
142,000 (1997)

SAUDI ARABIA

CAPITAL:
Riyadh

AREA:
756,981 sq. mi.
(1,960,582 sq km)

POPULATION:
22,757,092

MONEY:
Saudi riyal (SAR)

LANGUAGES:
Arabic

TELEPHONE LINES:
3,100,000

SYRIA

CAPITAL:
Damascus

AREA:
71,498 sq. mi.
(185,180 sq km)

POPULATION: 16,728,808

MONEY:
Syrian pound (SYP)

LANGUAGES:
Arabic (official), Kurdish

TELEPHONE LINES:
1,313,000 (1997)

TURKEY

CAPITAL: Ankara

AREA:
301,382 sq. mi.
(780,580 sq km)

POPULATION:
66,493,970

MONEY:
Turkish lira (TRL)

LANGUAGES: Turkish (official),
Kurdish

TELEPHONE LINES:
19,500,000 (1999)

UNITED ARAB EMIRATES

CAPITAL: Abu Dhabi

AREA:
32,000 sq. mi.
(82,880 sq km)

POPULATION: 2,407,460

MONEY:
Emirati dirham (AED)

LANGUAGES:
Arabic (official), Persian

TELEPHONE LINES: 915,223
(1998)

YEMEN

CAPITAL:
Sanaa

AREA:
203,849 sq. mi.
(527,970 sq km)

POPULATION:
18,078,035

MONEY:
Yemeni rial (YRl)

LANGUAGES:
Arabic

TELEPHONE LINES:
291,359 (1999)

internet connect

COUNTRY STATISTICS
GO TO: go.hrw.com
KEYWORD: SG3 FactsU6
FOR: more facts about
Southwest Asia

go.hrw.com

Sources: Central Intelligence Agency, *The World Factbook 2001; The World Almanac and Book of Facts 2001*

CHAPTER 20

The Arabian Peninsula, Iraq, Iran, and Afghanistan

Let's meet Mitra, a girl who lives in Tehran, the capital of Iran.

I am Mitra and I am 13 years old. I live with my sister and my parents on the top floor of a house in Tehran, the capital of Iran. On the ground floor, my father has a business printing pictures on metal, and the lower two floors are rented to tenants. My dad is also the president of an architectural firm in Tehran, but he is always working at home when we are home from school. Our house has a wall all around, touching the wall of the houses on both sides. Behind the house is a huge garden with roses and fruit trees. My sister is seven years older and works with my dad making architectural drawings. She raises chickens in the garden and collects their eggs. Food is sometimes hard to get, so we are very glad to have the chickens. My dad built them a very nice house, and it is exciting to watch the baby chicks hatch. The roof of our house is flat, and in nice weather we sit up there and look out to the mountains around the city. In the summer we sleep there too.

سلام بر شما!

Translation: Greetings to you.

Section 1 · Physical Geography

Read to Discover

1. What are the major physical features of the region?
2. What climates are found in this region?
3. What are the region's important resources?

Define

exotic rivers
wadis
fossil water

Locate

Persian Gulf
Arabian Peninsula
Red Sea
Arabian Sea
Tigris River

Euphrates River
Elburz Mountains
Zagros Mountains
Hindu Kush
Rub' al-Khali

WHY IT MATTERS

This region holds about half of the world's known reserves of oil, or petroleum. Use **CNNfyi.com** or other **current events** sources to find out how and why oil is so important in the world today. Record your findings in your journal.

Golden lion from Iran

The Arabian Peninsula, Iraq, Iran, and Afghanistan: Physical-Political

SCALE
0 — 250 — 500 Miles
0 — 250 — 500 Kilometers
Projection: Lambert Conformal Conic

ELEVATION

FEET	METERS
13,120	4,000
6,560	2,000
1,640	500
656	200
(Sea level) 0	0 (Sea level)
Below sea level	Below sea level

⊛ National capitals
• Other cities

Size comparison of the Arabian Peninsula, Iraq, Iran, and Afghanistan to the contiguous United States

internet connect

GO TO: go.hrw.com
KEYWORD: SG3 CH20
FOR: Web sites about the
Arabian Peninsula, Iraq,
Iran, and Afghanistan

Physical Features

The 10 countries of this region are laid out like a semicircle, with the Persian Gulf in the center. They are Saudi Arabia, Kuwait (koo-WAYT), Bahrain (bah-RAYN), Qatar (KAH-tuhr), the United Arab Emirates (E-muh-ruhts), Oman (oh-MAHN), Yemen (YE-muhn), Iraq (i-RAHK), Iran (i-RAN), and Afghanistan (af-GA-nuh-stan).

This area can be divided into three landform regions. The Arabian Peninsula is a large rectangular area. The Red Sea, Gulf of Aden, Arabian Sea, and Persian Gulf border the peninsula. North of the Arabian Peninsula is the plain of the Tigris (TY-gruhs) and Euphrates (yooh-FRAY-teez) Rivers. In ancient times, this area was called Mesopotamia (me-suh-puh-TAY-mee-uh), or the "land between the rivers." East of this plain is a region of mountains and plateaus. It stretches through Iran and Afghanistan.

The surface of the Arabian Peninsula rises gradually as one moves westward from the Persian Gulf. The highest point is in the southwest, in the mountains of Yemen.

North of the Arabian Peninsula is a low, flat plain. It runs from the Persian Gulf into northern Iraq. The Tigris and Euphrates Rivers flow across this plain. They are what are known as **exotic rivers**. Exotic rivers begin in humid regions and then flow through dry areas.

East of this low plain the land climbs sharply. Most of Iran is a plateau bordered by mountains. The Elburz (el-BOOHRZ) Mountains and Kopet-Dag range lie in the north. The Zagros (ZA-gruhs) Mountains lie in the southwest. Afghanistan includes many mountain ranges, such as the towering Hindu Kush range.

✔ **READING CHECK:** (*Places and Regions*) What are the major physical features of this area?

Build on What You Know

Do you remember what you learned about desert climates? See Chapter 3 to review.

Cold nighttime temperatures and extremely hot days help break rock into sand in Saudi Arabia's Rub' al-Khali, or "empty quarter."

Interpreting the Visual Record How do you think wind affects these sand dunes?

Climate

Most of Southwest Asia has a desert climate. A nearly constant high-pressure system in the atmosphere causes this climate. Some areas—mostly high plateaus and the region's edges—do get winter rains or snow. These areas generally have steppe climates. Some mountain peaks receive more than 50 inches (130 cm) of rain per year.

The desert can be both very hot and very cold. In summer, afternoon temperatures can reach 129°F (54°C). During the night, however, the temperature may drop quickly. Temperatures sometimes dip below freezing during winter nights.

The Rub' al-Khali (ROOB ahl-KAH-lee), or "empty quarter," of southern Saudi Arabia is the largest sand desert in the world. In northern Saudi Arabia is the An Nafud (ahn nah-FOOD), another desert.

✓ **READING CHECK:** *Places and Regions* What are the climates of this region?

Resources

Water is an important resource everywhere, but in this region it is crucial. Many desert regions are visited only by nomads and their animal herds. In many places, springs or wells provide water. Nomads sometimes get water by digging shallow wells into dry streambeds called **wadis**. Wells built with modern technology can reach water deep underground. The groundwater in these wells is often **fossil water**. Fossil water is water that is not being replaced by rainfall. Wells that pump fossil water will eventually run dry.

Other than water, oil is the region's most important mineral resource. Most of the oilfields are located near the shores of the Persian Gulf. The countries of the region are not rich in resources other than oil. Iran is an exception, with deposits of many metals.

✓ **READING CHECK:** *Places and Regions* What are the region's important resources?

Beneath the Red Sea lie many valuable resources, such as oil, sulfur, and metal deposits.

go.hrw.com **Homework Practice Online**
Keyword: SG3 HP20

Section Review 1

Define and explain: exotic rivers, wadis, fossil water

Working with Sketch Maps On a map of the Arabian Peninsula, Iraq, Iran, and Afghanistan that you draw or that your teacher provides, label the following: Persian Gulf, Arabian Peninsula, Red Sea, Arabian Sea, Tigris River, Euphrates River, Elburz Mountains, Zagros Mountains, Hindu Kush, and Rub' al-Khali.

Reading for the Main Idea

1. *Places and Regions* Why do you think Mesopotamia was important in ancient times?

2. *Places and Regions* What is the region's climate?

Critical Thinking

3. Drawing Inferences and Conclusions Why do you think the Persian Gulf is important to international trade?

4. Drawing Inferences and Conclusions What settlement pattern might you find in this region?

Organizing What You Know

5. Summarizing Copy the following graphic organizer. Use it to list as many details of landforms, resources, and climate as you can. Place them in the correct part of the diagram.

Arabian Peninsula   Iraq   Iran and Afghanistan

Section 2 — The Arabian Peninsula

Read to Discover

1. What are Saudi Arabia's history, government, and people like?
2. What kinds of government and economy do the other countries of the Arabian Peninsula have?

Define

Muslims
caliph
Sunni
Shia
Qur'an
OPEC

Locate

Mecca
Riyadh

Spicy Arabian food

WHY IT MATTERS

Saudi Arabia has long been an important U.S. ally in this region. Use **CNNfyi.com** or other **current events** sources to learn about current relations between the United States and Saudi Arabia. Record your findings in your journal.

Saudi Arabia

Saudi Arabia is by far the largest country of the Arabian Peninsula. Although the kingdom of Saudi Arabia was not created until the 1930s, the region has long been an important cultural center.

Islam The history of the Arabian Peninsula is closely linked to Islam. This religion was founded by Muhammad, a merchant from the Arabian town of Mecca. Around A.D. 610 he had a vision that he had been named a prophet by Allah, or God. Arab armies and merchants carried Muhammad's teachings to new areas. Islam spread quickly across North Africa, much of Asia, and parts of Europe. Followers of Islam are called **Muslims**. Islam provides a set of rules to guide human behavior.

The Islamic world was originally ruled by a religious and political leader called a **caliph**. Gradually this area broke up into several empires. There are also religious divisions within Islam. Followers of the largest branch of Islam are called **Sunni**. Followers of the second-largest branch of Islam are called **Shia**. In the late 600s

Non-Muslims are not allowed to enter Mecca, Islam's holiest city.

these two groups disagreed over who should lead the Islamic world. There are many smaller groups within Islam as well.

Islamic culture helps to unite Muslims around the world. For example, all Muslims learn Arabic to read the **Qur'an**, the holy book of Islam. Muslims are also expected to visit the holy city of Mecca at least once. These practices and many others help make Muslims part of one community.

Government and Economy

In the 1920s a local ruler from the Saud family of central Arabia conquered his neighbors and in 1932 created the kingdom of Saudi Arabia. Members of the Saud family have ruled the country ever since. Riyadh, a city near the center of the country, became the capital.

Saudi Arabia is a monarchy with no written constitution or elected legislature. Most government officials are relatives of the king. The king may ask members of his family, Islamic scholars, and tribal leaders for advice on important decisions.

In recent years, Saudi Arabia and the United States have established a close relationship. Both countries have strategic military and economic interests in the region. Saudi Arabia purchases U.S. weapons, such as fighter planes. In 1990, when Iraq invaded Kuwait, the Saudi government allowed U.S. military forces to operate from Saudi Arabia.

Oil and related industries are the most important part of the Saudi economy. Saudi Arabia has the world's largest reserves of oil. It is also the world's leading exporter of oil. Saudi Arabia is a leader of the Organization of Petroleum Exporting Countries, or **OPEC**. The members of OPEC try to influence the price of oil on world markets.

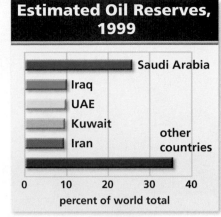

Estimated Oil Reserves, 1999

Saudi Arabia
Iraq
UAE
Kuwait
Iran
other countries

percent of world total

Source: *Encyclopaedia Britannica*

Interpreting the Graph Which nation in the region has the largest oil reserves?

Opened in 1986, this causeway links Saudi Arabia to Bahrain.

Interpreting the Visual Record How important do you think modern transportation systems are to a country's economy?

Fossil water has been used to convert desert land northwest of Riyadh into circular fields.

Interpreting the Visual Record Why do you think these fields are circular?

A *sabchat* is a thick, slushy deposit of sand, silt, mud, and salt found in coastal Saudi Arabia. A *sabchat* can trap people and animals who do not see it in time.

Oil was discovered in Saudi Arabia in the 1930s. Before this time farming and herding had been the main economic activities. Crops included barley, dates, fruits, millet, vegetables, and wheat. Nomads kept herds of sheep, goats, horses, and camels.

Like other oil-rich states in the region, Saudi Arabia has tried to increase its food production. Because freshwater is scarce, desalination plants are used to remove the salt from seawater. This water is then used in farming. Income from oil allows the Saudi government to pay for this expensive process. Even so, Saudi Arabia imports much of its food.

People and Customs Nearly all Saudis are ethnic Arabs and speak Arabic. About 85 percent are Sunni. The rest are Shia. Most Saudis now live in cities, and a sizable middle class has developed. The Saudi government provides free health care and education to its citizens.

More than 5 million foreigners live and work in Saudi Arabia. Most come from Turkey, Egypt, Jordan, Yemen, and countries in southern and eastern Asia. Many Americans and Europeans work in the country's oil industry.

Saudi laws and customs limit women's freedoms. For example, a woman rarely appears in public without her husband or a male relative. Women are also not allowed to drive cars. In 1999, women made up just 5 percent of Saudi Arabia's workforce.

Islamic practices are an important part of Saudi Arabia's culture. Muslims pray five times each day. Friday is their holy day. Because Islam encourages modesty, Saudi clothing keeps arms and legs covered. Men traditionally wear a loose, ankle-length shirt. They often wear a cotton headdress held in place with a cord. These are practical in the desert, giving protection from sun, wind, and dust. Saudi women usually wear a black cloak and veil when they are in public.

Two major celebrations mark the Islamic calendar. Each year, some 2 million Muslims travel to Mecca to worship. The journey ends with 'Id al-Adha, the Festival of Sacrifice. The year's second celebration is 'Id al-Fitr, a feast ending the month of Ramadan. During Ramadan, Muslims do not eat or drink anything between dawn and sunset.

✔ **READING CHECK:** (*Human Systems*) What is significant about Saudi Arabia's history, government, and people?

Other Countries of the Arabian Peninsula

Six small coastal countries share the Arabian Peninsula with Saudi Arabia. All are heavily dependent on oil. All but Yemen are monarchies, and each is overwhelmingly Islamic. Oil is a major part of each country's economy. However, possession of differing amounts of oil has made some countries much richer than others.

CONNECTING TO *Math*

Muslim astronomers in the 1500s

Muslim Contributions to Mathematics

During the period of Western history called the Dark Ages, European art, literature, and science declined. However, during this same period Islamic civilization, stretching from Spain to the borders of China, was flowering. Muslim scholars made important advances in art, literature, medicine, and mathematics.

The system of numerals we call Arabic, including the use of the zero, was first created in India. However, it was Muslim thinkers who introduced that system to Europe. They also developed algebra, geometry, and trigonometry. In fact, words like *algebra* and *algorithm* are translations of Arabic words.

Other Muslims advanced the study of astronomy and physics. Arab geographers calculated distances between cities, longitudes and latitudes, and the direction from one city to another. Muslims developed the first solution for cubic equations. They also defined ratios and used mathematics to explain the rainbow.

Understanding What You Read

1. Where did the Arabic system of numerals originate, and how did it get to Europe?
2. How did Muslim scholars contribute to our knowledge of geography?

Kuwait The country of Kuwait was established in the mid-1700s. Trade and fishing were once the main economic activities there. Oil, which was discovered in the 1930s, has made Kuwait very rich. The Iraqi invasion of 1990 caused massive destruction.

As in Saudi Arabia, a royal family dominates politics in Kuwait. In 1992, however, Kuwait held elections for a legislature. Less than 15 percent of Kuwait's population were given the right to vote. These people were all men from well-established families.

Bahrain and Qatar Bahrain is a group of small islands in the western Persian Gulf. It is a constitutional monarchy that is headed by a ruling royal family and a legislature. These islands have been a center of trade since ancient times. In 1986 a 15.5 mile (25 km) bridge was completed that connects Bahrain to Saudi Arabia, making movement between the two countries easier.

The Arabian Peninsula

COUNTRY	POPULATION/ GROWTH RATE	LIFE EXPECTANCY	LITERACY RATE	PER CAPITA GDP
Bahrain	645,361 (228,424 noncitizens) 1.7%	71, male 76, female	85%	$15,900
Kuwait	2,041,961 (1,519,913 noncitizens) 3.4%	75, male 77, female	79%	$15,000
Oman	2,622,198 3.4%	70, male 74, female	80%	$7,700
Qatar	769,152 3.2%	70, male 75, female	79%	$20,300
Saudi Arabia	22,757,092 (5,360,526 noncitizens) 3.3%	66, male 70, female	63%	$10,500
United Arab Emirates	2,407,460 (1,576,472 noncitizens) 1.6%	72, male 77, female	79%	$22,800
Yemen	18,078,035 3.4%	58, male 62, female	38%	$820
United States	281,421,906 0.9%	74, male 80, female	97%	$36,200

Sources: Central Intelligence Agency, *The World Factbook 2001;* U.S. Census Bureau

Interpreting the Chart Which country has the lowest standard of living?

Oil was discovered in Bahrain in the 1930s, creating wealth for the country. However, by the 1990s this oil was starting to run out, and banking and tourism are now becoming important to the economy. Bahrain also refines crude oil imported from nearby Saudi Arabia.

Qatar occupies a small peninsula in the Persian Gulf. Like Bahrain, Qatar is ruled by a powerful monarch. In the 1990s, Qatar's ruler announced a plan to make the country more democratic. He also ended censorship of Qatari newspapers and television.

Qatar has sizable oil reserves and even larger reserves of natural gas—some of the largest in the world.

The United Arab Emirates The United Arab Emirates, or UAE, consists of seven tiny kingdoms. They are ruled by emirs. This country also has great reserves of oil and natural gas. Profits from these resources have created a modern, comfortable lifestyle for the people of the UAE. The government has also worked to build up other industries.

Like Saudi Arabia and many of the small Persian Gulf countries, the UAE depends on foreign workers. In the UAE, foreign workers outnumber citizens.

Oman Oman is located just outside the mouth of the Persian Gulf. The country is slightly smaller than Kansas. In ancient times, Oman was a major center of trade for merchants traveling the Indian Ocean. Today, Oman's economy is heavily dependent on oil. However, Oman does not have the oil wealth of Kuwait or the UAE. Therefore, the government, ruled by the Al Bu Sa'id family, is attempting to create new industries.

◀

Kindergarten students in the United Arab Emirates kneel to pray.

Interpreting the Visual Record For what cultural reason do you think these girls and boys are seated in separate rows?

Yemen Yemen is located on the southern corner of the Arabian Peninsula. It borders the Red Sea and the Gulf of Aden. Yemen was formed in 1990 by the joining of North Yemen and South Yemen. The country has an elected government and several political parties. However, political corruption and internal conflicts have threatened this young democracy.

In ancient times, farmers in this area used very advanced methods of irrigation and farming. Yemen was famous for its coffee. Today, Yemen is the poorest country on the Arabian Peninsula. Oil was not discovered there until the 1980s. It now generates a major part of the national income.

✓ **READING CHECK:** (*Human Systems*) How are the governments and economies of the countries of the Arabian Peninsula organized?

An important part of Yemen's culture is its distinctive architecture, which features tall buildings and carved wooden windows.

Homework Practice Online
Keyword: SG3 HP20

Define and explain: Muslims, caliph, Sunni, Shia, Qur'an, OPEC

Working with Sketch Maps On the map you created in Section 1, label Mecca and Riyadh. Why is Riyadh's location more suitable than Mecca's to be the capital city of Saudi Arabia?

Reading for the Main Idea

1. (*Places and Regions*) What kind of government does Saudi Arabia have?

2. (*Environment and Society*) What role does oil play in the economies of small countries on the Arabian Peninsula?

Critical Thinking

3. **Drawing Inferences and Conclusions** How might trips to Mecca help create a sense of community among Muslims?

4. **Drawing Inferences and Conclusions** Why would a country like Saudi Arabia or the United Arab Emirates bring in large numbers of foreign workers?

Organizing What You Know

5. **Comparing** Copy the following graphic organizer. Use it to list these countries' locations, governments, and economies. Place them in the appropriate part of the chart.

	Location	Government	Economy
Saudi Arabia			
Kuwait			
Bahrain			
Qatar			
UAE			
Oman			
Yemen			

CASE STUDY

SAUDI ARABIA: HOW OIL HAS CHANGED A COUNTRY

At the beginning of the 1900s, Saudi Arabia was a poor country. Most people followed traditional ways of life and lived by herding animals, farming, or fishing. There were few good roads or transportation systems, and health care was poor.

Major Oil Fields in Saudi Arabia

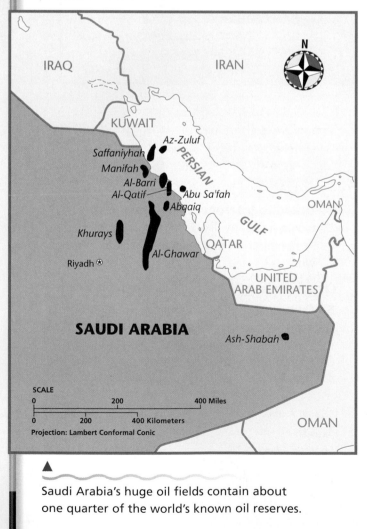

▲

Saudi Arabia's huge oil fields contain about one quarter of the world's known oil reserves.

Then, in the mid-1930s, oil was discovered in Saudi Arabia. Soon, even larger oil reserves were found. Eventually it was learned that Saudi Arabia had the largest oil reserves in the world. Most of the country's oil reserves are located in eastern Saudi Arabia along the Persian Gulf coast. The Al-Ghawar oil field, discovered in 1948, is the largest in the world. In addition to this field, Saudi Arabia has at least nine other major oil fields. The discovery of these huge oil reserves changed Saudi Arabia's economy and society.

Rising income from oil exports gave Saudi Arabia's government more and more money to invest. New airports, apartments, communications systems, oil pipelines, and roads were built. In 1960 Saudi Arabia had about 1,000 miles (1,600 km) of roads. By 1997 it had about 91,000 miles (145,600 km). Saudi Arabia's cities grew as people left small villages. These changes helped modernize Saudi Arabia's economy.

Saudi society was also affected. The standard of living rose, and people had more money to spend on goods. Foreign companies began to open stores and restaurants in Saudi Arabia. New schools were built throughout the country, and education became available to all citizens. The literacy rate increased from about 3 percent to about 63 percent. Thousands of Saudis traveled to other countries, and many new universities were opened. Health care also improved.

As Saudi Arabia's economy grew, many foreign workers came to the country to work. In the early 2000s foreign workers made up about 25 percent of Saudi Arabia's population. These workers included people from Yemen, Egypt, Palestine, Syria, Iraq, South Korea, and the Philippines. Americans and Europeans also went to Saudi Arabia to work in the oil industry.

The development of the oil industry greatly increased Saudi Arabia's importance in the world. In 1960 Saudi Arabia was a founding member of

◄
Oil is refined in eastern Saudi Arabia. Then it is pumped into ships and exported to countries around the world.

the Organization of Petroleum Exporting Countries (OPEC). Members of OPEC try to influence the price of oil on the world market. Saudi Arabia's huge oil reserves make it one of OPEC's most powerful member countries.

The Saudi government has also bought military equipment from the United States and other countries. This military strength has increased Saudi Arabia's importance in the Persian Gulf region. Since 1991, Saudi Arabia has given large sums to countries that sided with it against Iraq in the Persian Gulf War. Egypt, Turkey, and Syria have especially benefited from this aid.

Today, Saudi Arabia is a wealthy country. This wealth has come almost entirely from the sale of oil. Saudi Arabia is currently the world's leading oil exporter. Oil provides about 90 percent of the government's export earnings. Saudi Arabia exports oil to Japan, the United States, South Korea, and many other countries.

◄

Since the mid-1960s Saudi Arabia has expanded its transportation network. A modern road system now connects many parts of the country.

Understanding What You Read

1. What was Saudi Arabia like before oil was discovered there?

2. How has oil changed Saudi Arabia's economy and society?

Section 3 Iraq

Read to Discover

1. What were the key events in Iraq's history?
2. What are Iraq's government and economy like?
3. What is the makeup of Iraq's population?

Define

embargo

Locate

Baghdad

Why It Matters

The United States has used both economic and military action against Iraq in the 1990s and early 2000s. Use or other **current events** sources to learn about U.S. relations with Iraq today. Record your findings in your journal.

A Sumerian clay tablet

Murals and posters of Saddam Hussein can be found throughout Baghdad, Iraq's capital.

History

The history of Mesopotamia, an ancient region in Iraq, stretches back to some of the world's first civilizations. The Sumerian, Babylonian, and Assyrian cultures arose in this area. The Persians conquered Mesopotamia in the 500s B.C. Alexander the Great made it part of his empire in 331 B.C.

In the A.D. 600s the Arabs conquered Mesopotamia. The people of the area gradually converted to Islam. The city of Baghdad became one of the world's greatest centers of trade and culture. However, it was destroyed by the Mongols in 1258.

In the 1500s Mesopotamia became part of the Ottoman Empire. During World War I it was taken over by the British. In 1932 the British set up the kingdom of Iraq and placed a pro-British ruler in power. In the 1950s a group of Iraqi army officers overthrew this government. After several more changes in government, the Ba'ath Party took power in 1968.

A Ba'ath leader named Saddam Hussein slowly gained more power. In the late 1970s he became president of Iraq and leader of the armed forces.

In 1980 Iraq invaded Iran. Saddam Hussein hoped to take advantage of the confusion following the Iranian Revolution. The Iranians fought back, however, and the Iran-Iraq War dragged on until 1988. Hundreds of thousands of people were killed on both sides. Each side tried to attack the other's oil tankers and refineries. Both countries' economies were damaged.

In 1990, Iraq invaded the small, oil-rich country of Kuwait. Saddam Hussein used an old claim that Kuwait was part of Iraq to justify this invasion. Many Western leaders believed that Iraq should not be allowed to conquer its neighbors. They were also concerned that Iraq would control such a large share of the world's oil. Also, Iraq had missiles, poison gas, and perhaps nuclear weapons. An alliance of countries, led by the United States and Great Britain, sent troops, tanks, and planes to Saudi Arabia. In the Persian Gulf War of 1991 this alliance forced the Iraqis out of Kuwait.

✔ **READING CHECK:** (*Human Systems*) What are some key events in Iraq's history?

Iraq

COUNTRY	POPULATION/ GROWTH RATE	LIFE EXPECTANCY	LITERACY RATE	PER CAPITA GDP
Iraq	23,332,985 2.8%	66, male 68, female	58%	$2,500
United States	281,421,906 0.9%	74, male 80, female	97%	$36,200

Sources: Central Intelligence Agency, *The World Factbook 2001;* U.S. Census Bureau

Interpreting the Chart What percentage of the Iraqi population is literate?

Government and Economy

The government of Iraq is still firmly controlled by the Ba'ath Party and Saddam Hussein. The Iraqi leader has built up a large army and a secret police force. He has also placed his relatives in many important government positions.

Iraq has the world's second-largest known oil reserves, but its economy has suffered recently. Before the war with Iran, Iraq was the world's second-largest oil exporter. That war and the Persian Gulf War damaged Iraq's oil industry. Furthermore, the United Nations placed an **embargo**, or limit on trade, on Iraq. Today, Iraq exports much less oil than it did in the 1980s.

Other industries include construction, mining, and manufacturing. Many factories produce weapons for Iraq's army. More than 3 million people live in Baghdad, and most of Iraq's industries are there.

Irrigation from the Tigris and Euphrates Rivers supports Iraq's farming sector. Chief crops include barley, dates and other fruit, cotton, rice, vegetables, and wheat.

✔ **READING CHECK:** (*Human Systems*) How is Iraq's government organized, and what is its economy like?

Our Amazing Planet

Dust storms occur throughout Iraq and can rise to several thousand feet above the ground. These storms often happen during the summer. Five or six usually strike central Iraq in July, the worst month.

Many Iraqis shop for food in local markets.

▼

427

▲

The Ma'dan, sometimes called the Marsh Arabs, are a minority group in Iraq. They live in Iraq's southern marshes.

People

Nearly all Iraqis are Muslim. More than 75 percent of the population are Arabs. Some 15 to 20 percent are Kurds, and the rest belong to small minority groups. Many Kurds living in Iraq's northern mountains have resisted control by the Baghdad government. After the Gulf War, Shia Arabs living in southern Iraq also rebelled against Saddam Hussein. The Iraqi government has used military force to crush these uprisings.

✓ **READING CHECK:** *Human Systems* What is the makeup of Iraq's population?

Section Review 3

Define and explain: embargo

Working with Sketch Maps On the map you created in Section 2, label Baghdad. Where would you expect most of Iraq's population to be concentrated? Why?

Reading for the Main Idea

1. *Human Systems* What are some different groups that have controlled Mesopotamia?

2. *Human Systems* What is Iraq's government like?

go.hrw.com **Homework Practice Online** Keyword: SG3 HP20

Critical Thinking

3. **Finding the Main Idea** Why did several countries force Iraqi troops out of Kuwait?

4. **Analyzing Information** How have recent wars affected Iraq's economy?

Organizing What You Know

5. **Sequencing** Create a time line tracing the history of the area now known as Iraq. List events from the Arab conquest to 1991.

A.D. 600s   1991

Section 4 — Iran and Afghanistan

Read to Discover

1. What were some important events in Iran's history?
2. What are Iran's government and people like?
3. What problems does Afghanistan face today?

Define

shah
theocracy

Locate

Tehran
Khyber Pass
Kabul

A Persian manuscript

WHY IT MATTERS

The nation of Afghanistan has been involved in many conflicts in recent history. Use **CNNfyi.com** or other **current events** sources to learn about the situation in Afghanistan today. Record your findings in your journal.

Iran

Iran is a large country with a large population, rich history, and valuable natural resources. A revolution in 1979 made Islam the guiding force in Iran's government.

History The Persian Empire, established in the 500s B.C., was centered in what is now Iran. It was the greatest empire of its time and was an important center of learning. In the 300s B.C. Alexander the Great conquered the Persian Empire. In the A.D. 600s Arabs invaded the region and established Islam. Persian cultural and scientific contributions became elements of Islamic civilization. Later, different peoples ruled the region, including the Mongols and the Safavids.

In the dry climates of Iran and Afghanistan, some farmers still use an ancient method of irrigating crops. Runoff from mountains is moved through underground tunnels, called *qanats* (kuh-NAHTS), to fields below the mountains.

▼

Qanat Irrigation System

Mountains

Water from mountains seeps into water table

Ventilation and access shafts

Water tunnel

Surface canal

Irrigated fields

In 1921 an Iranian military officer took power and encouraged reform. He claimed the old Persian title of **shah**, or king. In 1941 the Shah's son took control. He was an ally of the United States and Britain and tried to modernize Iran. His programs were unpopular, however, and in 1979 he was overthrown.

Iran's new government set up an Islamic republic. Soon afterward, relations with the United States broke down. A mob of students attacked the U.S. Embassy in Iran's capital, Tehran, in November 1979. They took Americans hostage with the approval of Iran's government. More than 50 Americans were held by force for a year. The Iranian Revolution itself was soon followed by a long, destructive war with Iraq beginning in 1980.

Government and Economy Iran is a **theocracy**—a government ruled by religious leaders. The country has an elected president and legislature. An expert on Islamic law is the supreme leader, however.

Iran's government has supported many hard-line policies. For example, the country's government has called for the destruction of the state of Israel. Iran has also supported terrorist groups in other countries. However, in the late 1990s signs indicated that Iran was trying to make democratic reforms.

Iran has the fifth-largest oil reserves in the world. Oil is its main industry. Iran is a member of OPEC. Iran's other industries include construction, food processing, and the production of beautiful woven carpets. About one third of Iran's workforce is employed in agriculture.

During Iran's New Year celebrations grass is used to symbolize spring and life.

People and Customs Iran has a population of about 65 million—one of the largest in Southwest Asia. It is also quite diverse. Ethnic Persians make up a slight majority. Other groups include ethnic Azerbaijanis, Kurds, Arabs, and Turkmans. Persian is the official language. Almost all Iranians speak Persian, although some speak it as a second language. The region's other languages include several Kurdish dialects, some Turkic languages, and Arabic.

The Shia branch of Islam is Iran's official religion. About 90 percent of Iranians are Shia. About 10 percent of Iran's residents are Sunni Muslim. The rest are Christian, Jewish, or practice other religions.

In addition to the Islamic holy days, Iranians celebrate Nauruz—the Persian New Year. They also recognize the anniversary of the Iranian Revolution on February 11. Iranian food features rice, bread, vegetables, fruits, and lamb. Strong tea is a popular drink among many Iranians.

✔ **READING CHECK:** (*Human Systems*) What are Iran's government and people like?

Afghanistan

Afghanistan is a landlocked country of high mountains and fertile valleys. Merchants, warriors, and missionaries have long used the Khyber (KY-buhr) Pass to reach India. This narrow passage through the Hindu Kush lies between Afghanistan and Pakistan.

History and People In 1979 the Soviet Union sent troops into Afghanistan to help the communist government there in a civil war. This led to a long war between Soviet troops and Afghan rebels. The Soviets left in 1989, and an alliance of Afghan groups took power. Turmoil continued, and in the mid-1990s a radical Muslim group known as the Taliban arose. Its leaders took over most of the country, including the capital, Kabul. The Taliban ruled Afghanistan strictly. For example, they forced women to wear veils and to stop working outside the home.

In 2001 Taliban officials came into conflict with the United States. Investigation of terrorist attacks on September 11 on Washington, D.C., and New York City led to terrorist Osama bin Laden and his al Qaeda network, based in Afghanistan. U.S. and British forces then attacked Taliban and al Qaeda targets and toppled the Taliban government.

The long period of war has damaged Afghanistan's industry, trade, and transportation systems. Farming and herding are the most important economic activities now.

Afghans belong to many different ethnic groups. The most numerous are the Pashtun, Tajik, Hazara, and Uzbek. Almost all Afghans are Muslims, and about 84 percent are Sunni.

✓ **READING CHECK:** (*Human Systems*) What are some of the challenges Afghanistan faces today?

Iran and Afghanistan

Country	Population/ Growth Rate	Life Expectancy	Literacy Rate	Per Capita GDP
Afghanistan	26,813,057 3.5%	47, male 45, female	32% (1999)	$800
Iran	66,128,965 0.7%	69, male 71, female	79% (1999)	$6,300
United States	278,058,881 0.9%	74, male 80, female	97% (1994)	$36,200

Sources: Central Intelligence Agency, *The World Factbook 2001*; U.S. Census Bureau

Interpreting the Chart How many times greater is the U.S. per capita GDP than Afghanistan's?

Section Review 4

Define and explain: shah, theocracy

Working with Sketch Maps On the map you created in Section 3, label Tehran, Khyber Pass, and Kabul. What physical features do Tehran and Kabul have in common?

Reading for the Main Idea

1. (*Places and Regions*) What ethnic and religious groups live in Iran?

2. (*Human Systems*) How have Afghanistan's recent wars affected the country?

Homework Practice Online
Keyword: SG3 HP20

Critical Thinking

3. **Making Generalizations and Predictions** What challenges might the Iranian government face in the future?

4. **Drawing Inferences and Conclusions** How might Afghanistan's political problems be affected by its rugged physical geography?

Organizing What You Know

5. **Sequencing** Copy the following graphic organizer. Use it to show the main events in Iran in recent decades.

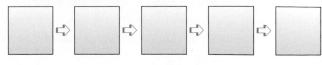

Building Vocabulary

On a separate sheet of paper, write sentences to define each of the following words.

1. exotic rivers
2. wadis
3. fossil water
4. Muslims
5. Sunni
6. Shia
7. Qur'an
8. OPEC
9. embargo
10. theocracy

Reviewing the Main Ideas

1. (*Places and Regions*) What are the three landform regions that make up this part of Southwest Asia?
2. (*Places and Regions*) What is the most important resource of this region?
3. (*Places and Regions*) Which countries in this area have large reserves of oil?
4. (*Places and Regions*) Which small country has some of the largest natural gas reserves in the world?
5. (*Places and Regions*) How have wars affected politics in this region?

Understanding Environment and Society

Resource Use

Use the graph in Section 2 and other print sources to create a presentation on the importance of the oil industry in one or more of the countries discussed in this chapter. As you prepare your presentation you may want to think about the following:

- How the oil industry affects people's daily lives in this region.
- What might happen to this region's economy if scientists discover an inexpensive alternative to oil.

Thinking Critically

1. Why might it be dangerous for these countries' economies to be almost entirely dependent on the sale of oil?
2. Some of the countries of Southwest Asia are trying to increase crop production. What environmental factors might make this difficult?
3. How might Iran's recent history have been different if the 1979 revolution had not taken place?
4. Why has the United States become involved in the politics of this region?
5. What is Islam, and what are some of its practices and holidays?

Map ACTIVITY

On a separate sheet of paper, match the letters on the map with their correct labels.

Persian Gulf	Riyadh
Tigris River	Baghdad
Euphrates River	Tehran
Hindu Kush	Khyber Pass
Mecca	Kabul

Mental Mapping Skills ACTIVITY

On a separate sheet of paper, draw a freehand map of the region. Make a key for your map and label the following:

Afghanistan	Qatar
Iran	Saudi Arabia
Iraq	United Arab
Kuwait	Emirates
Oman	Yemen

WRITING ACTIVITY Imagine that you have been asked to write a travel brochure about one of the following countries: Afghanistan, Iran, Iraq, or Saudi Arabia. Use your textbook, the library, and the Internet to research your country. Then write a few paragraphs about its climate, attractions, and cultural events.

Alternative Assessment

Portfolio ACTIVITY

Learning About Your Local Geography

Individual Project Contact your local utility company for information on where your electricity is generated and what fuel or energy source is used. Draw a diagram of your local power supply system.

internet connect

Internet Activity: go.hrw.com
KEYWORD: SG3 GT20

Choose a topic to explore about the Arabian Peninsula, Iraq, Iran, and Afghanistan:
- Visit Mesopotamia.
- Discover the importance of camels.
- See Arabian arts and crafts.

go.hrw.com

CHAPTER 21

The Eastern Mediterranean

The next student we will meet lives in Turkey, a country that lies partly in Europe, partly in Asia.

My name is Adalet, and I am in the tenth grade at Ted College, a private school in Ankara, the capital of Turkey. I live in an apartment a little outside the city with my mom and dad. We live on the twelfth floor, and have a view of the city, the distant mountains, and of course the parking lot. In the summers, my favorite time is when I can go to stay with my grandma and my grandpa in their summer house on the Aegean Sea, in Kusadasi near the ancient Greek city of Ephesus. I sleep until 11:00 A.M. or noon, then spend the day at the beach with my friends until the sun goes down.

On school days, from September to June, I get up at 8:00 A.M., put on my school uniform, and have breakfast of corn flakes or bread and cheese with milk or tea. At school we go directly to our classes. I am studying biology, physics, algebra, geometry, history, Turkish, and English. The English, science, and math classes are taught in English, the others in Turkish.

Türkiye'den selamlar!

▲
Translation: Greetings from Turkey!

Section 1 — Physical Geography

Read to Discover

1. What are the main physical features of the eastern Mediterranean?
2. What are the climate types of the region?
3. What natural resources are found in this area?

Define

phosphates
asphalt

Locate

Dardanelles
Bosporus
Sea of Marmara
Jordan River
Dead Sea
Syrian Desert
Negev

An ancient temple in Petra, Jordan

WHY IT MATTERS

The people who live in the Eastern Mediterranean region have needed irrigation and other technology to adapt to the land. Use **CNNfyi.com** or other **current events** sources to find information on ways that other people have modified their environment. Record your findings in your journal.

The Eastern Mediterranean: Physical-Political

SCALE
0   200   400 Miles
0   200   400 Kilometers
Projection: Lambert Conformal Conic

ELEVATION
	FEET	METERS
⊛ National capitals	13,120	4,000
• Other cities	6,560	2,000
	1,640	500
	656	200
	(Sea level) 0	0 (Sea level)
	Below sea level	Below sea level

Size comparison of the eastern Mediterranean to the contiguous United States

The status of the Gaza Strip and the West Bank is in transition.

Our Amazing Planet

The Dead Sea, which covers an area of just 394 square miles (1,020 sq km), contains approximately 12.7 billion tons of salt. Each year the Jordan River deposits 850,000 additional tons.

Istanbul lies on both sides of the waterway known as the Bosporus. This waterway divides Europe from Asia.

Interpreting the Visual Record Why do you think the Bosporus would be an important crossroads of trade?

Physical Features

The countries of the eastern Mediterranean are Turkey, Lebanon, Syria, Jordan, and Israel. In addition to its own territory, Israel controls areas known as the Occupied Territories. These include the West Bank, the Gaza Strip, and the Golan Heights.

On Two Continents The eastern Mediterranean region straddles two continents. A small part of Turkey lies on Europe's Balkan Peninsula. This area consists of rolling plains and hills. A narrow waterway, made up of the Dardanelles (dahrd-uhn-ELZ), the Bosporus (BAHS-puh-ruhs), and the Sea of Marmara (MAHR-muh-ruh), separates Europe from Asia. The larger, Asian part of Turkey is mostly plateaus and highlands.

Hills, Valleys, and Plains Heading south from Turkey and into Syria, we cross a narrow plain. The Euphrates River, fed by precipitation in Turkey's eastern mountains, flows southeast through this plain. Farther south are more hills and plateaus. Two main ridges run north-south. One runs from southwestern Syria through western Jordan. The other, closer to the coast, runs through Lebanon, Israel, and the West Bank. The Jordan River valley separates these two ridges. A narrow coastal plain rims the region along its seacoasts. In western Turkey the coastal plain is wider.

River and Sea The Jordan River begins in Syria and flows south. Israel and the West Bank lie on the west side of the river. The country of Jordan lies on the east side. The Jordan River flows into the Dead Sea. This unusual body of water is the lowest point on any continent—1,312 feet (400 m) below sea level. It is so salty that swimmers cannot sink in it.

✓ **READING CHECK:** *Places and Regions* What are the region's main physical features?

Climate

Dry climates are the rule in most of this region. However, there are important variations. Turkey's Black Sea coast and the Mediterranean coast all the way to Israel have a Mediterranean climate. Central Syria and lands farther south have a desert climate. A small area of north-eastern Turkey has a humid subtropical climate.

The Syrian Desert covers much of Syria and Jordan. It usually receives less than five inches (12.7 cm) of rainfall a year. Another desert, the Negev (NE-gev), lies in southern Israel.

✔ **READING CHECK:** *Places and Regions* What are the climates of the eastern Mediterranean?

Resources

Unlike nearby countries in Southwest Asia, the countries of the eastern Mediterranean do not have large oil reserves. The people of this region make their living from the land in other ways.

Limited Farming Commercial farming is possible only where rain or irrigation provides enough water. Subsistence farming and livestock herding are common in drier areas. Desert areas support a few nomadic herders.

Mineral Resources Many minerals, including sulfur, mercury, and copper, are found in the region. **Phosphates**—mineral salts containing the element phosphorus—are produced in Syria, Jordan, and Israel. Phosphates are used to make fertilizers. The area also exports **asphalt**—the dark tar-like material used to pave streets. The Dead Sea is a source of mineral salts.

✔ **READING CHECK:** *Places and Regions* What natural resources are found in this area?

A shepherd in eastern Turkey watches his sheep.

Interpreting the Visual Record Why is livestock herding common in many parts of the eastern Mediterranean region?

▼

Homework Practice Online
Keyword: SG3 HP21

Section Review 1

Define and explain: phosphates, asphalt

Working with Sketch Maps On a map of the eastern Mediterranean that you draw or that your teacher provides, label the following: Dardanelles, Bosporus, Sea of Marmara, Jordan River, Dead Sea, Syrian Desert, and the Negev.

Reading for the Main Idea

1. *Places and Regions* What country lies on two continents?

2. *Places and Regions* What are the most common climates of the region?

3. *Places and Regions* How do geographic factors affect the economic activities of the region?

Critical Thinking

4. Drawing Inferences and Conclusions How do you think the Dead Sea got its name?

Organizing What You Know

5. Categorizing Copy the following graphic organizer. Use it to list the major landforms and bodies of water of each region.

Country/ territory	Landforms and bodies of water

Section 2 Turkey

Read to Discover

1. What is the history of the area that is now Turkey?
2. What kind of government and economy does Turkey have?
3. How is Turkish society divided?

Define

secular

Locate

Ankara
Istanbul

A replica of the legendary Trojan Horse in Turkey

WHY IT MATTERS

Turkey built dams on the Tigris and Euphrates Rivers to provide electricity and water for its people. The dams created conflict with Turkey's neighbors, Syria and Iraq. Use **CNNfyi**.com or other **current events** sources to find information about water issues around the world. Record your findings in your journal.

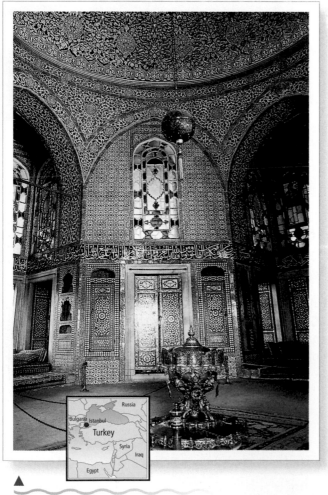

Ottoman monarchs lived in the Topkapi Palace built in 1462.

History

Turkey, except for the small part that lies in Europe, makes up a region called Asia Minor. In ancient times this area was part of the Hittite and Persian Empires. In the 330s B.C. Alexander the Great conquered Asia Minor. Later it became part of the Roman Empire. Byzantium, renamed Constantinople, was one of the most important cities of the empire. After the fall of Rome, Constantinople became the capital of the Byzantine Empire.

In the A.D. 1000s the Seljuk Turks invaded Asia Minor. The Seljuks were a nomadic people from Central Asia who had converted to Islam. In 1453 another Turkish people, the Ottoman Turks, captured the city of Constantinople. They made it the capital of their Islamic empire.

Ottoman Empire During the 1500s and 1600s the Ottoman Empire was very powerful. It controlled territory in North Africa, Southwest Asia, and southeastern Europe. In the 1700s and 1800s the empire gradually weakened.

In World War I the Ottoman Empire fought on the losing side. When the war ended, the Ottomans lost all their territory outside of what is now Turkey. Greece even invaded western Asia Minor in an attempt to take more land. However, the Turkish army pushed out the invaders. Military officers

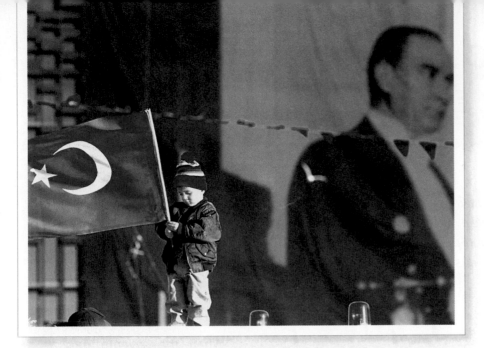

then took over the government. Their leader was a war hero, Mustafa Kemal. He later adopted the name Kemal Atatürk, which means "father of the Turks." He formally dissolved the Ottoman Empire and created the nation of Turkey. He made the new country a democracy and moved the capital to Ankara. Constantinople was renamed Istanbul in 1930.

Modern Turkey Atatürk wanted to modernize Turkey. He believed that to be strong Turkey had to westernize. He banned the fez, the traditional hat of Turkish men, and required that they wear European-style hats. The Latin alphabet replaced the Arabic one. The European calendar and metric system replaced Islamic ones. Women were encouraged to vote, work, and hold office. New laws made it illegal for women to wear veils.

✓ **READING CHECK:** *Human Systems* What is the history of what is now Turkey?

Turkish women harvest grapes.
Interpreting the Visual Record What kind of climate do Turkey's coastal plains have?

Government and Economy

Today, Turkey has a legislature called the National Assembly. A president and a prime minister share executive power. The Turkish military has taken over the government three times. However, each time it has returned power to civilian hands.

Although most of its people are Muslim, Turkey is a **secular** state. This means that religion is kept separate from government. For example, the religion of Islam allows a man to have up to four wives. However, by Turkish law a man is permitted to have just one wife. In recent years Islamic political parties have attempted to increase Islam's role in Turkish society.

CONNECTING TO *Literature*

Statue of Gilgamesh

Gilgamesh is the hero of this ancient story that was popular all over Southwest Asia. In this passage Utnapishtim (oot-nuh-peesh-tuhm), whom the gods have given everlasting life, tells Gilgamesh about surviving a great flood.

Epic of Gilgamesh

"In those days . . . the people multiplied, the world bellowed like a wild bull, and the great god was aroused by the clamor[1]. Enlil (en-LIL) heard the clamor and he said to the gods in council, 'The uproar of mankind is intolerable[2] and sleep is no longer possible by reason of the babel[3].' So the gods agreed to exterminate[4] mankind. Enlil did this, but Ea (AY-uh) because of his oath warned me in a dream. . . . 'Tear down your house, I say, and build a boat. . . . then take up into the boat the seed of all living creatures.'

Utnapishtim does as he is told. He builds a boat and fills it with supplies, his family, and animals. Then terrible rains come and flood Earth.

"When the seventh day dawned the storm from the south subsided, the sea grew calm, the flood was stilled; I looked at the face of the world and there was silence, all mankind was turned to clay. . . . I opened a hatch and the light fell on my face. Then I bowed low, I sat down and I wept, . . . for on every side was the waste of water."

Analyzing Primary Sources
1. Why did the god bring the flood?
2. Why does Utnapishtim cry?

Vocabulary   [1]clamor: noise   [2]intolerable: not bearable   [3]babel: confusing noise   [4]exterminate: kill off

---

Turkey's economy includes modern factories as well as village farming and craft making. The most important industries are clothing, chemicals, and oil processing. About 43 percent of Turkey's labor force works in agriculture. Grains, cotton, sugar beets, and hazelnuts are major crops. The Turkish economy has grown rapidly in recent years, but inflation is a problem. Large numbers of Turks have left Turkey in search of better jobs. As of 1994 an estimated 1.5 million Turks were working abroad to earn higher wages.

In the 1990s Turkey began building dams on the Tigris and Euphrates Rivers. These will provide electricity and irrigation water. However, the dams have caused concern for Syria and Iraq. They are disturbed that another country controls the sources of their water.

✓ **READING CHECK:**   *Human Systems*   What kind of government and economy does Turkey have?

People and Culture

Turkey has more than 64 million people. Ethnic Turks make up 80 percent of the population. Kurds are the largest minority. They are about 20 percent of the population. Since ancient times the Kurds have lived in what is today southeastern Turkey. Kurds also live in nearby parts of Iran, Iraq, and Syria. In the 1980s and 1990s some Kurds fought for independence from Turkey. The Turkish government has used military force against this rebellion.

Kemal Atatürk's changes created a cultural split between Turkey's urban middle class and rural villagers. The lifestyle and attitudes of middle-class Turks have much in common with those of middle-class Europeans. Most Turks, though, are more traditional. Islam influences their attitudes on matters such as the role of women. This cultural division is a factor in Turkish politics.

Turkish cooking is much like that of the rest of the Mediterranean region. It features olives, vegetables, cheese, yogurt, and bread. Shish kebab—grilled meat on a skewer—is a favorite Turkish dish.

✓ **READING CHECK:** (*Human Systems*) What are the divisions in Turkish society?

▶

Crowds pass through a square near the University of Istanbul. Different styles of dress reflect the diverse attitudes that exist in Turkey today.

Section Review 2

Define and explain: secular

Working with Sketch Maps On the map you created in Section 1, label Ankara and Istanbul. What are the advantages of Istanbul's location?

Reading for the Main Idea

1. (*Human Systems*) How did Atatürk try to modernize Turkey?

2. (*Human Systems*) What foods are popular in Turkish cooking?

Critical Thinking

3. **Finding the Main Idea** Why were some Turks unhappy with changes brought about by Atatürk?

4. **Analyzing Information** Why is the Turkish government building dams on the Tigris and Euphrates Rivers? How will this affect countries downriver?

Organizing What You Know

5. **Sequencing** Create a timeline listing major events in Turkey's history. List major people, groups, invasions, empires, and changes in government.

400 B.C.   A.D. 2000

Section 3

Israel and the Occupied Territories

Read to Discover

1. What was the early history of Israel like?
2. What is modern Israel like?
3. What is the conflict over the Occupied Territories?

Define

Diaspora
Zionism

Locate

Jerusalem
Gaza Strip
Golan Heights
West Bank
Tel Aviv

WHY IT MATTERS

For thousands of years there has been conflict surrounding present-day Israel and the Occupied Territories. Use CNNfyi.com or other **current events** sources to find information about the current state of affairs in this region. Record your findings in your journal.

A fragment of the Dead Sea Scrolls

The ancient port of Caesarea lies on the coast of Israel. It was the regional capital during the time of Roman control. Today the harbor structure is partly underwater.

▼

Ancient Israel

The Hebrews, the ancestors of the Jews, first established the kingdom of Israel about 3,000 years ago. It covered roughly the same area as the modern State of Israel. In the 60s B.C. the Roman Empire conquered the region, which they called Palestine. After a series of Jewish revolts, the Romans forced most Jews to leave the region. This scattering of the Jewish population is known as the **Diaspora**.

During the era of Roman control, a Jewish man named Jesus began preaching a new religion. He said he was the son of God. Jesus taught that faith and love for others were more important than Judaism's many laws about daily life. His teachings particularly appealed to the poor and powerless. Both Roman and Jewish rulers saw Jesus's teachings as dangerous. Jesus was tried and executed. His followers believe he was resurrected. Christianity—Jesus's teachings and the belief in his resurrection—spread through the Roman Empire. In time, Christianity became the most common religion of the Mediterranean region.

The Arabs conquered Palestine in the mid-600s. From the 1000s to the 1200s, European armies launched a series of invasions called the Crusades. The Crusaders captured Jerusalem in 1099. In time the Crusaders were pushed out of the area altogether.

Israeli soldiers stand guard on a hill overlooking the Gaza Strip.

From the 1500s to World War I, Palestine was part of the Ottoman Empire. At the end of the war, it came under British control.

✓ **READING CHECK:** (*Human Systems*) What significant events occurred in the early history of the area of Israel?

Modern Israel

In the late 1800s a movement called **Zionism** began among European Jews. Zionism called for Jews to establish a country or community in Palestine. Tens of thousands of Jews moved to the area.

After World War II, the United Nations recommended dividing Palestine into Arab and Jewish states. This plan created conflict among the peoples there. Fighting broke out between Israel and surrounding Arab countries. The Israeli forces defeated the Arabs.

Many Palestinians fled to other Arab states, particularly to Jordan and Lebanon. Some used terrorist attacks to strike at Israel. Israel and its Arab neighbors also fought wars in 1956, 1967, and 1973.

Government and Economy Israel has a prime minister and a parliament, called the Knesset. There are two major political parties and many smaller parties.

Israel has built a strong military for protection from the Arab countries around it. Terrorist attacks have also occurred. At age 18 most Israeli men and women must serve in the military.

Eastern Mediterranean

COUNTRY	POPULATION/ GROWTH RATE	LIFE EXPECTANCY	LITERACY RATE	PER CAPITA GDP
Israel*	5,938,093 1.6%	77, male 81, female	95%	$18,900
Jordan	5,153,378 3%	75, male 80, female	87%	$3,500
Lebanon	3,627,774 1.4%	69, male 74, female	86%	$5,000
Syria	16,728,808 2.5%	68, male 70, female	71%	$3,100
Turkey	66,493,970 1.2%	69, male 74, female	85%	$6,800
United States	281,421,906 0.9%	74, male 80, female	97%	$36,200

*Does not include the West Bank and Gaza Strip.
Sources: Central Intelligence Agency, *The World Factbook 2001;* U.S. Census Bureau

Interpreting the Chart Which country in the region has the largest population?

The West Bank in Transition

SCALE
0 5 10 Miles
0 5 10 Kilometers
Projection:
Transverse Cylindrical

Control of the West Bank:
- Israeli
- Palestinian civil, Israeli security
- Palestinian before 1998
- Palestinian, 1998
- City of Jerusalem

The Gaza Strip is densely populated and has few natural resources. Israel captured this territory from Egypt in 1967.

Israel has a modern, diverse economy. Items like high-technology equipment and cut diamonds are important exports. Tourism is a major industry. Israel's lack of water limits farming. However, using highly efficient irrigation, Israel has successfully increased food production. It imports grain but exports citrus fruit and eggs.

Languages and Diversity Israel's population includes Jews from all parts of the world. Both Hebrew and Arabic are official languages. When they arrive in Israel, many Jews speak English, Russian, German, Hungarian, Yiddish, or Arabic. The government provides classes to help them learn Hebrew.

About 82 percent of Israel's population is Jewish. The rest is mostly Palestinian. About three fourths of these are Muslim. The rest are Christian.

Food and Festivals Israeli food is influenced by Jewish religious laws. Jews are forbidden to eat pork and shellfish. They also cannot eat meat and milk products at the same meal. The country's food is as diverse as the population. Eastern European dishes are popular, as are Southwest Asian foods.

For Jews, Saturday is a holy day. Yom Kippur, the most important Jewish holiday, is celebrated in October. Passover, in the spring, celebrates the Hebrews' escape from captivity in Egypt. During Passover, people eat matzo (MAHT-suh), a special bread without yeast.

✔ **READING CHECK:** *Human Systems* What are modern Israel's government, economy, and culture like?

The Occupied Territories

In 1967 Israel captured the Gaza Strip, the Golan Heights, and the West Bank. These are sometimes called the Occupied Territories.

Disputed Land The Gaza Strip is a small, crowded piece of coastal land. More than a million Palestinians live there. The area has almost no resources. The Golan Heights is a hilly area on the Syrian border. In 1981 Israel formally declared the Golan Heights part of Israel. Syria still claims this territory.

The West Bank is the largest of the occupied areas, with a population of about 1.6 million. Since Israel took control of the West Bank, more than 100,000 Jews have moved into settlements there. The Palestinians consider this an invasion of their land. This has caused tension and violence between Arabs and Israelis.

Israel annexed East Jerusalem in 1980. Even before this, the Israeli government had moved the capital from Tel Aviv to Jerusalem. Most foreign countries have chosen not to recognize this transfer. The Palestinians still claim East Jerusalem as their rightful capital.

Control of Jerusalem is a difficult and often emotional question for Jews, Muslims, and Christians. The city contains sites that are holy to all three religions.

The Future of the Territories In the 1990s Israel agreed to turn over parts of the Occupied Territories to the Palestinians. In return, the Palestinian leadership—the Palestinian Authority—agreed to work for peace. Parts of the Gaza Strip and West Bank have been transferred to the Palestinian Authority. More areas of the West Bank are expected to be handed over in the future.

The future of the peace process is uncertain. Some Palestinian groups have continued to commit acts of terrorism. Some Jewish groups believe for religious reasons that Israel must not give up the West Bank. Other Israelis fear they would be open to attack if they withdrew from the territories.

✓ **READING CHECK:** *Human Systems* Why have the Occupied Territories been a source of conflict?

Muslim women gather to pray at the Dome of the Rock in Jerusalem.
▼

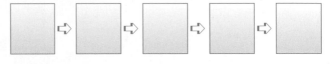

Section Review 3

Define and explain: Diaspora, Zionism

Working with Sketch Maps On the map you created in Section 2, label Jerusalem, Gaza Strip, Golan Heights, West Bank, and Tel Aviv.

Reading for the Main Idea

1. *Environment and Society* How has technology allowed Israel to increase its food production?

2. *Human Systems* What historical factors helped create a culturally diverse region in Israel?

Critical Thinking

3. **Finding the Main Idea** How do political boundaries in Israel create conflicts?

4. **Summarizing** What are some difficult issues involved in the Israeli-Palestinian peace process?

Organizing What You Know

5. **Sequencing** Copy the following graphic organizer. Use it to list the sequence of events that led to the formation of modern Israel.

☐ ⇨ ☐ ⇨ ☐ ⇨ ☐ ⇨ ☐

The Eastern Mediterranean • 445

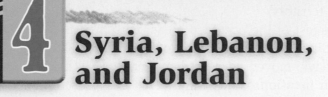

Section 4 — Syria, Lebanon, and Jordan

Read to Discover
1. What kind of government and economy does Syria have?
2. How is Lebanese society divided?
3. What events have shaped the history of Jordan?

Define
mandate

Locate
Damascus
Beirut
Amman

WHY IT MATTERS

Syria, Jordan, and Lebanon have experienced conflicts due to religious or ethnic differences of people living there. Use **CNN fyi**.com or other **current events** sources to find information about other countries struggling with such conflicts. Record your findings in your journal.

Spices in an outdoor market

Syria

The capital of Syria, Damascus, is believed to be the oldest continuously inhabited city in the world. For centuries it was a leading regional trade center. Syria became part of the Ottoman Empire in the 1500s. After World War I, France controlled Syria as a **mandate**. Mandates were former territories of the defeated nations of World War I. They were placed under the control of the winning countries after the war. Syria finally became independent in the 1940s.

Politics and Economy From 1971 to 2000, the Syrian government was led by Hafiz al-Assad. Assad increased the size of Syria's military. He wanted to match Israel's military strength and protect his rule from his enemies within Syria. Assad's son, Bashar, was elected president after his father's death in 2000.

Syria's government owns the country's oil refineries, larger electrical plants, railroads, and some factories. Syria's key manufactured goods are textiles, food products, and chemicals. Agriculture remains important.

Roman columns still stand in the ancient city of Apamea, Syria.

Syria has only small deposits of oil and natural gas. It is rich in limestone, basalt, and phosphates.

People Syria's population of more than 17 million is about 90 percent Arab. The other 10 percent includes Kurds and Armenians. About 74 percent of Syrians are Sunni Muslim. Another 16 percent are Alawites and Druze, members of small branches of Islam. About 10 percent of Syrians are Christian. There are also small Jewish communities in some cities.

✓ **READING CHECK:** *Places and Regions* How is Syria's economy organized?

Lebanon

Lebanon is a small, mountainous country on the Mediterranean coast. It is home to several different groups of people. At times these different groups have fought each other.

History and People During the Ottoman period many religious and ethnic minority groups settled in Lebanon. After World War I Lebanon, along with Syria, became a French mandate. Lebanon finally gained independence in the 1940s.

The Lebanese are overwhelmingly Arab, but they are divided by religion. Most Lebanese are either Muslim or Christian. Each of those groups is divided into several smaller groups. Muslims are divided into Sunni, Shia, and Druze. The Maronites are the largest of the Christian groups in Lebanon. At the time of independence, there were slightly more Christians than Muslims. Over time, however, Muslims became the majority.

▲
People must drill for water in dry areas of Syria.

Interpreting the Visual Record
Judging from this photo, how has technology affected the lifestyle of people in desert areas?

▲
This photograph from the early 1900s shows a tall cedar tree in the mountains of northern Lebanon. Lebanon's cedars have long been a symbol of the country.

A vendor in Beirut sells postcards of what the city looked like before it was scarred by war.

Interpreting the Visual Record What were the effects of the civil war in Lebanon?

Civil War For some decades after independence, Christian and Muslim politicians managed to share power. A complex system assigned certain government positions to different religious groups. For example, the president was always a Maronite. However, over time this cooperation broke down. The poorest group, the Shia, grew rapidly but were not given additional power. Tensions mounted. Adding to the divisions between Lebanese was the presence of hundreds of thousands of Palestinian refugees living in Lebanon. Ethnic and religious groups armed themselves, and in the 1970s fighting broke out. Warfare between Lebanese groups lasted until 1990. Tens of thousands of people died, and the capital, Beirut, was badly damaged.

During the 1990s Lebanon's economy slowly recovered from the civil war. The refining of crude oil brought in by pipeline is a leading industry. Other industries include food processing, textiles, cement, chemicals, and jewelry making. Lebanese farmers produce tobacco, fruit, grains, and vegetables.

✔ **READING CHECK:** (*Human Systems*) What is causing divisions in Lebanese society?

Jordan

Jordanian children play with a camel. At one time a majority of Jordanians were nomads. Today most of Jordan's people live in urban areas.

Jordan's short history has been full of conflict. Great Britain drew its borders, and Jordan's royal family is actually from Arabia. The country has few resources and several powerful neighbors. In addition, most of its people think of another country as their homeland. Yet Jordan has survived.

History and Government The country of Jordan (called Transjordan until 1949) was created from Ottoman territory following World War I. The British controlled the area as a mandate. They established an Arabian prince named Abdullah as the monarch of the new country. Abdullah had helped the British in World War I, but he had been driven out of Saudi Arabia. In the 1940s the country became fully independent. After the creation of Israel and the war of 1948, Jordan annexed the Arab lands of the West Bank.

At the time of its independence, Jordan's population was small. Most Jordanians lived a nomadic or seminomadic life. After each of the Arab-Israeli wars of 1948 and 1967, hundreds of thousands of Palestinian Arab refugees came to live in Jordan. These immigrants strained Jordan's resources. In addition, a cultural division arose between the Palestinians and the "original" Jordanian Arabs. After 1967 Palestinians actually made up a majority of Jordan's people.

From 1952 to 1999 Jordan was ruled by King Hussein. Most observers, both inside and outside Jordan, considered him one of the

A truck crosses the Jordan River near the Dead Sea. The river is a key source of water for agriculture and other uses.
Interpreting the Visual Record What countries and territories border the Jordan River?

best rulers in the region. Hussein's popularity allowed him to begin some democratic reforms in the 1980s and 1990s. Today, the division between Palestinian and Jordanian Arabs causes less conflict.

Economy and Resources Jordan is a poor country with limited resources. The country does produce phosphates, cement, and potash. Tourism and banking are becoming important industries. Jordan depends on economic aid from the oil-rich Arab nations and the United States. Amman, the capital, is Jordan's only large city.

Jordanian farmers raise fruits and vegetables in the Jordan River valley, using irrigation. Some highland areas receive enough winter rainfall to grow grains. Raising sheep and goats is an important source of income. However, overgrazing has caused soil erosion. A crucial resource issue for Jordan is its shortage of water.

✓ **READING CHECK:** (*Human Systems*) How did King Hussein affect Jordan's history?

Bo you remember what you learned about uneven resource distribution? See Chapter 5 to review.

go.hrw.com **Homework Practice Online**
Keyword: SG3 HP21

Section Review 4

Define and explain: mandate

Working with Sketch Maps On the map you created in Section 3, label Damascus, Beirut, and Amman.

Reading for the Main Idea

1. (*Human Systems*) How did Hafiz al-Assad affect Syria?

2. (*Human Systems*) What divisions led to conflict in Lebanon?

3. (*Places and Regions*) Which of the countries discussed in this section does not border the Mediterranean Sea?

Critical Thinking

4. **Finding the Main Idea** How have foreign countries influenced Jordan?

Organizing What You Know

5. **Categorizing** Use the graphic organizer to gather information about Syria, Lebanon, and Jordan.

	Syria	Lebanon	Jordan
Major religion(s)			
Type of government			
Major problem(s)			
Greatest strength(s)			

The Eastern Mediterranean • 449

Reviewing What You Know

Building Vocabulary

On a separate sheet of paper, write sentences to define each of the following words.

1. phosphates
2. asphalt
3. secular
4. Diaspora
5. Zionism
6. mandate

Reviewing the Main Ideas

1. (Human Systems) People and customs from what three continents have influenced the eastern Mediterranean region?

2. (Human Systems) What three major religions have holy sites in Jerusalem?

3. (Human Systems) How has westernization changed Turkey's government, economy, and culture?

4. (Human Systems) What is the conflict over the Occupied Territories?

5. (Environment and Society) How do people in this area make their living from the land?

Understanding Environment and Society

Conflicts over Water

Freshwater is a scarce resource throughout much of the eastern Mediterranean. Create a presentation and model on issues of water supply and demand. Consider the following:

- Ways people in this region obtain freshwater.
- Human activities that consume water.
- Problems between countries when water supplies are strained.

Create a five-question quiz, with answers, about your model that you can use to challenge your classmates.

Thinking Critically

1. **Drawing Inferences and Conclusions** Why do you think Atatürk moved Turkey's capital from Istanbul to Ankara?

2. **Finding the Main Idea** How has human migration to Israel affected its population?

3. **Analyzing Information** How is the Dead Sea unusual? What are its commercial uses?

4. **Analyzing Information** How did refugees from Palestine affect Jordan?

5. **Drawing Inferences and Conclusions** Why did attempts to balance religious groups' participation in Lebanon's government fail?

Map **ACTIVITY** On a separate sheet of paper, match the letters on the map with their correct labels.

Dardanelles	Negev
Bosporus	Istanbul
Sea of Marmara	Tel Aviv
Jordan River	Jerusalem
Dead Sea	Damascus

Mental Mapping Skills **ACTIVITY**

On a separate sheet of paper, draw a freehand map of the eastern Mediterranean and label the following:

Gaza Strip	Lebanon
Golan Heights	Syria
	Turkey
Israel	West Bank
Jordan	

WRITING
ACTIVITY Imagine that your family is about to travel to the eastern Mediterranean for a vacation. Your parents have asked you to help plan the trip. Write about the places you would like to visit and the reasons you would find them interesting. Be sure to use standard grammar, spelling, sentence structure, and punctuation.

Alternative Assessment

Portfolio **ACTIVITY**

Learning About Your Local Geography

Individual Project For thousands of years the eastern Mediterranean has been a crossroads between Europe, Asia, and Africa. Show how your community is linked to other towns and cities in a graphic organizer.

internet connect

Internet Activity: go.hrw.com
KEYWORD: SG3 GT21

Choose a topic to explore about the eastern Mediterranean:

- Visit the Dead Sea.
- Compare Israeli and Arab foods.
- Travel to historic Jerusalem.

FOCUS ON REGIONS

Differences and Connections

In this textbook the countries of Africa are grouped together. This has been done to emphasize the region's connections. Yet any region as large as Africa has important differences from place to place. East Africa is different from West Africa, and West Africa is different from North Africa. This is also true of other large regions. In South America, for example, Brazil is different from Argentina in many important ways.

North Africa and Southwest Asia One subregion of Africa that geographers often include in another region is North Africa. These geographers see more connections between North Africa and Southwest Asia than between North Africa and the rest of the continent. For example, in both areas Arabic is the main language. The major religion is Islam. Political issues also tie North Africa to its eastern neighbors, as does physical geography. The countries of North Africa and Southwest

The Muhammad Ali Mosque is one of many beautiful places of worship for Muslims in Cairo, Egypt. Although various religions, including Judaism and Christianity, are practiced in North Africa and Southwest Asia, most people in the two regions are Muslim.

Asia are part of a vast desert region. These countries face common issues such as water conservation and water management.

The African Continent There are also many reasons for placing North Africa in a region with the rest of Africa. People in Africa share some important historical, cultural, and economic ties. For example, ancient Egyptians had close contact with other peoples in Africa. In turn, cultures south of the Sahara contributed to the development of Egypt's great Nile Valley civilizations. Farther west, Mediterranean peoples have long traded with West African kingdoms south of the Sahara. Such contact helped spread

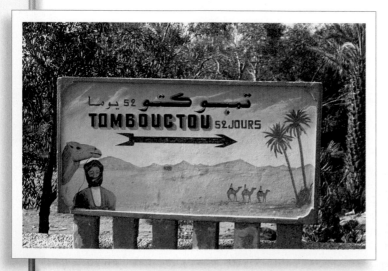

This sign in Morocco is in both Arabic and French. Arabic is spoken throughout North Africa and many parts of Southwest Asia.

Regional Links

Language, religion, and climate are some of the ties between North Africa and Southwest Asia. Arabic speakers, Muslims, and desert climates are dominant throughout much of the two regions and in parts of the surrounding transition zones.

Islam among the peoples of North Africa and the rest of the continent. Today, there are mosques as far south as Nigeria and Tanzania.

North Africa also has political connections to the rest of Africa. Many African countries face similar political and economic challenges. In part, these issues arise from their shared colonial history. To resolve some of these issues, the countries of North Africa are working with other African countries. They have formed associations such as the Organization of African Unity.

Transition Zones There are many differences and connections between North Africa and the rest of the continent. Perhaps they are most evident in a band of countries that lie just south of the Sahara. These countries stretch from Mauritania in the west to Ethiopia and Sudan in the east. They form a transition zone. In other words, they resemble both North Africa and Africa south of the

Sahara. In Chad and Sudan, for example, strong political and cultural differences separate north and south. The northern regions of these countries are tied closely to North Africa. The southern regions of these countries are tied closely to African countries to the south.

North Africa and the countries in the transition zone have important connections to two major world regions. Which region they are placed in depends on the geographer's point of view. Understanding the differences among countries and their connections to other areas of the world is important. It is more important than deciding where on a map a region begins or ends.

Understanding What You Read

1. What ties are there between North Africa and Southwest Asia?
2. What ties are there between North Africa and the rest of the African continent?

Geo SKILLS

Building Skills for Life: Interpreting the Past

Both people and places are a product of the past. Therefore, understanding the geography of past times is important. It gives us a more complete understanding of the world today.

History and geography can hardly be separated. All historical events have to happen somewhere. These events are affected by local geography. For example, wheat and barley were domesticated in an area of Southwest Asia called the Fertile Crescent. This region received enough rainfall for these crops to grow.

Geographers who specialize in studying the past are called historical geographers. Historical geographers are interested in where things used to be and how they developed. They also try to understand how people's beliefs and values influenced historical events. In other words, why did people do what they did?

All geographers must be skilled at interpreting the past. Cultural geographers might study how old buildings and houses reflect earlier times. Physical geographers may need to reconstruct past landscapes. For example,

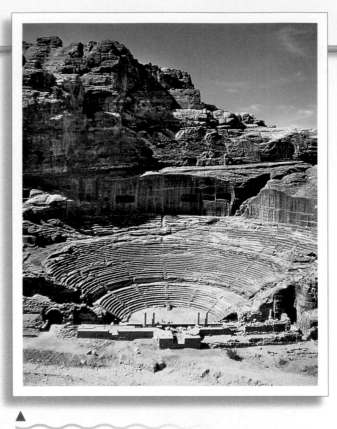

▲

Ancient ruins in Petra, Jordan, can provide clues to the region's past.

many rivers have changed their course. Understanding where a river used to flow could help explain its present course.

In your study of geography, think about how a place's history has shaped the way it is today. Look for clues that can tell you about its past. Ask yourself how people may have thought about a place in earlier times. No matter where you are, the evidence of the past is all around!

PRACTICING THE SKILL

1. Look at some of the buildings in your community. How old do you think they are? Do some look older than others? Can you describe how building styles in your community have changed over time? Why do you think styles have changed?

2. Analyze an important historical event that occurred in your state. What happened? Where did it happen? How was the event influenced by local geography?

3. Interpret the settlement history of your state or community. When was it settled? What attracted people to it? How do you think they felt about the place at the time?

HANDS on GEOGRAPHY

One way to interpret the past is by studying old travel accounts. They often have detailed information about the people, places, and daily life of past times.

One famous travel account describes the journeys of Ibn Battuta. Ibn Battuta was one of the greatest travelers in history. During the mid-1300s he traveled about 75,000 miles (120,700 km) throughout parts of Asia and Africa. Near the end of his travels, he gave a long account of the many places he visited. This account is a valuable historical document today.

The following passage is taken from Ibn Battuta's travel account. In this passage, Ibn Battuta is visiting the Sultan of Birgi, a town in what is now western Turkey. Read the passage, and then answer the Lab Report questions.

❝ In the course of this audience the sultan asked me this question: "Have you ever seen a stone that fell from the sky?" I replied, "I have never seen one, nor ever heard tell of one." "Well," he said, "a stone did fall from the sky outside this town of ours," and then called some men and told them to bring the stone. They brought in a great black stone, very hard and with a glitter in it—I reckoned its weight to amount to a hundredweight. The sultan ordered the stonebreakers to be summoned, and four of them came and on his command to strike it they beat upon it as one man four times with iron hammers, but made no impression on it. I was astonished at this phenomenon, and he ordered it to be taken back to its place. ❞

▲ This painting shows Ibn Battuta during his travels in the mid-1300s.

Lab Report

1. What did the "stone that fell from the sky" look like? What do you think it was?

2. Why do you think Ibn Battuta was "astonished" by what he saw?

3. What can this story tell us about the historical geography of this region?

Africa

Holding back the desert in Morocco

Cape Town, South Africa

A Physician in Sierra Leone

Dr. James Li went to Africa fresh out of medical school to work as a general practice physician. Here he describes what it was like to work at a hospital in Sierra Leone. **WHAT DO YOU THINK?** *What might Dr. Li's patients think about health care in the United States?*

Malaria, tuberculosis, and leprosy were widespread in our hospital population. We often saw patients who had walked over 100 miles for treatment. None of the patients in our area had access to clean water. Phone lines installed by the British had been cut down and the copper wires melted to make cooking pots. Our hospital was in the remote jungle, about six hours by dirt road from the nearest major city. It had 140 beds. In the clinic, we saw several hundred other patients each day. Food for the staff and patients was grown on the hospital grounds.

I came to love the people who were our patients, particularly the very young and the very old. In the midst of shortages, I met people who lived happily and suffered the tragedies of utter poverty with a dignity that would have failed me. These reflections fill me with a strange combination of awe, sadness, humility, and excitement.

Hospital in Butare, Rwanda

Masai dancers, Kenya

Understanding Primary Sources

1. What were conditions like at Dr. Li's hospital?

2. How does Dr. Li describe the culture of Sierra Leone?

Giraffe

Africa

Elevation Profile

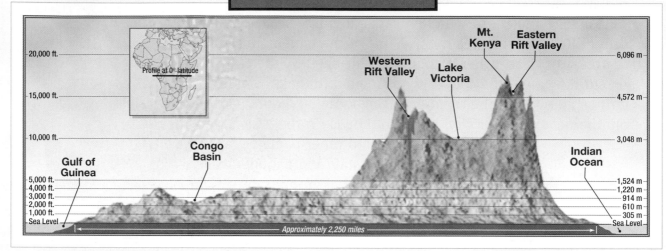

- 20,000 ft. — 6,096 m
- 15,000 ft. — 4,572 m
- 10,000 ft. — 3,048 m
- 5,000 ft. — 1,524 m
- 4,000 ft. — 1,220 m
- 3,000 ft. — 914 m
- 2,000 ft. — 610 m
- 1,000 ft. — 305 m
- Sea Level — Sea Level

Profile at 0° latitude

Mt. Kenya
Eastern Rift Valley
Western Rift Valley
Lake Victoria
Congo Basin
Gulf of Guinea
Indian Ocean

Approximately 2,250 miles

The United States and Africa: Comparing Sizes

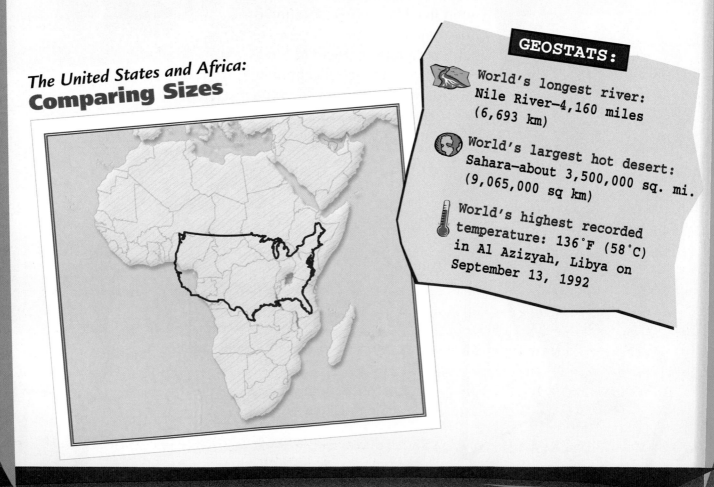

GEOSTATS:

World's longest river: Nile River—4,160 miles (6,693 km)

World's largest hot desert: Sahara—about 3,500,000 sq. mi. (9,065,000 sq km)

World's highest recorded temperature: 136°F (58°C) in Al Azizyah, Libya on September 13, 1992

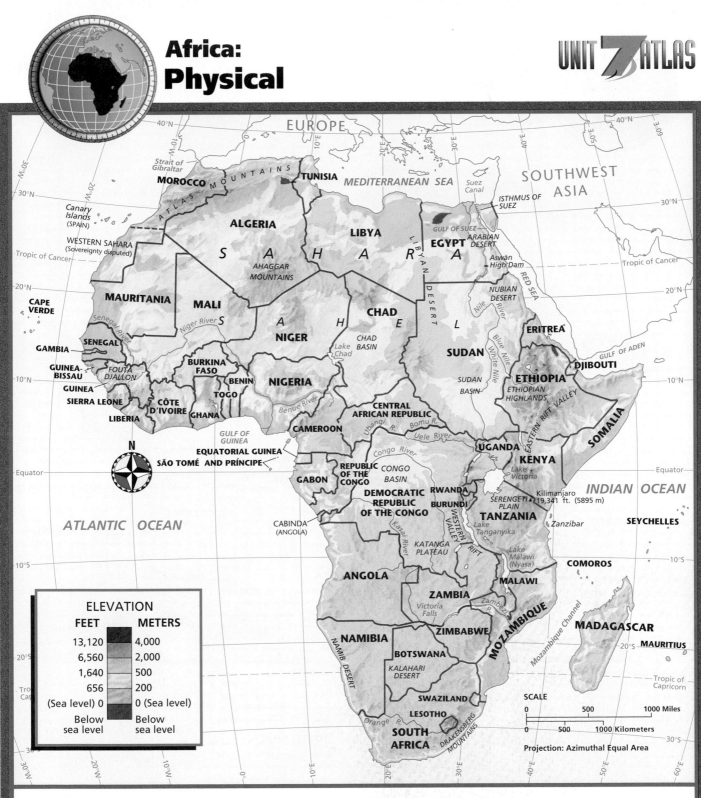

Africa: Physical map

EUROPE

MOROCCO TUNISIA MEDITERRANEAN SEA SOUTHWEST ASIA

Strait of Gibraltar
ATLAS MOUNTAINS
Suez Canal
ISTHMUS OF SUEZ

Canary Islands (SPAIN)
WESTERN SAHARA (Sovereignty disputed)
Tropic of Cancer

ALGERIA
LIBYA
EGYPT
ARABIAN DESERT
GULF OF SUEZ
Aswān High Dam
Tropic of Cancer

S A H A R A
AHAGGAR MOUNTAINS

CAPE VERDE
MAURITANIA
MALI
NIGER
CHAD
CHAD BASIN
Lake Chad
NUBIAN DESERT
RED SEA
Nile
White Nile
Blue Nile
ERITREA
GULF OF ADEN

GAMBIA
SENEGAL
Senegal River
Niger River
S A H E L
SUDAN
DJIBOUTI

GUINEA-BISSAU
FOUTA DJALLON
BURKINA FASO
BENIN
NIGERIA
TOGO
SUDAN BASIN
ETHIOPIA
ETHIOPIAN HIGHLANDS

GUINEA
SIERRA LEONE
CÔTE D'IVOIRE
GHANA
LIBERIA
Benue River
CENTRAL AFRICAN REPUBLIC
CAMEROON
Ubangi R.
Bomu R.
Uele River
SOMALIA

GULF OF GUINEA
EQUATORIAL GUINEA
SÃO TOMÉ AND PRÍNCIPE
Congo River
UGANDA
KENYA
Lake Victoria
EASTERN RIFT VALLEY

Equator
GABON
REPUBLIC OF THE CONGO
CONGO BASIN
RWANDA
BURUNDI
Kilimanjaro 19,341 ft. (5895 m)
SERENGETI PLAIN
INDIAN OCEAN
Equator

ATLANTIC OCEAN
CABINDA (ANGOLA)
DEMOCRATIC REPUBLIC OF THE CONGO
Kasai River
KATANGA PLATEAU
WESTERN RIFT VALLEY
TANZANIA
Lake Tanganyika
Zanzibar
SEYCHELLES

Lake Malawi (Nyasa)
COMOROS

ANGOLA
MALAWI
ZAMBIA
Zambezi R.
Victoria Falls
MOZAMBIQUE
Mozambique Channel
MADAGASCAR
MAURITIUS

NAMIBIA
ZIMBABWE
BOTSWANA
KALAHARI DESERT
Tropic of Capricorn

NAMIB DESERT
SWAZILAND
LESOTHO
Orange R.
SOUTH AFRICA
DRAKENSBERG MOUNTAINS

ELEVATION

FEET	METERS
13,120	4,000
6,560	2,000
1,640	500
656	200
(Sea level) 0	0 (Sea level)
Below sea level	Below sea level

N

SCALE
0   500   1000 Miles
0   500   1000 Kilometers
Projection: Azimuthal Equal Area

---

1. (*Places and Regions*) Which region of Africa has the highest mountains? Which country appears to have the largest number of high mountains?

2. (*Places and Regions*) Which countries have areas that lie below sea level? Where is the highest point in Africa?

Critical Thinking

3. Analyzing Information   Which North African mountains might create a rain-shadow effect?

4. Comparing   Compare this map to the **climate map** of the region. Which areas might have tropical rain forests?

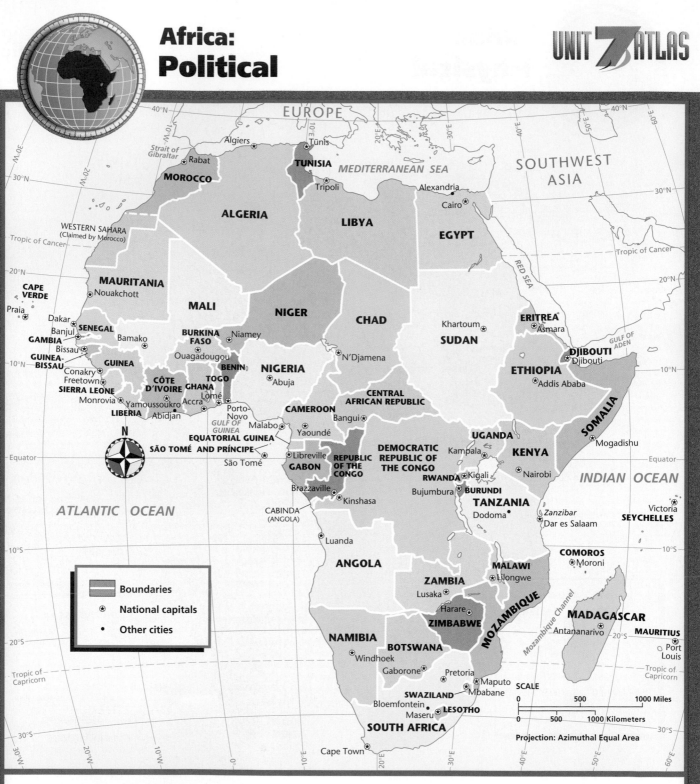

EUROPE

MEDITERRANEAN SEA

SOUTHWEST ASIA

Strait of Gibraltar
Algiers ✴
Tûnis ✴
TUNISIA
Rabat ✴
MOROCCO
Tripoli ✴
ALGERIA
LIBYA
Alexandria •
Cairo ✴
EGYPT
WESTERN SAHARA (Claimed by Morocco)
Tropic of Cancer
Tropic of Cancer

CAPE VERDE
Nouakchott ✴
MAURITANIA
MALI
NIGER
CHAD
Khartoum ✴
SUDAN
ERITREA
Asmara ✴
DJIBOUTI
Djibouti ✴
GULF OF ADEN
Praia ✴
Dakar •
SENEGAL
Banjul ✴
GAMBIA
Bamako ✴
BURKINA FASO
Niamey ✴
N'Djamena ✴
ETHIOPIA
Addis Ababa •
Bissau ✴
GUINEA-BISSAU
Ouagadougou ✴
NIGERIA
Conakry ✴
GUINEA
BENIN
Abuja ✴
Freetown ✴
CÔTE D'IVOIRE
TOGO
GHANA
CENTRAL AFRICAN REPUBLIC
SOMALIA
Mogadishu •
SIERRA LEONE
Monrovia ✴
Yamoussoukro •
Accra ✴
Lomé ✴
CAMEROON
Bangui ✴
LIBERIA
Abidjan •
Porto-Novo ✴
UGANDA
Malabo ✴
EQUATORIAL GUINEA
Yaoundé ✴
Kampala ✴
KENYA
GULF OF GUINEA
SÃO TOMÉ AND PRÍNCIPE
São Tomé ✴
Libreville ✴
DEMOCRATIC REPUBLIC OF THE CONGO
Nairobi •
INDIAN OCEAN
Equator
GABON
REPUBLIC OF THE CONGO
RWANDA
Kigali ✴
Equator
Brazzaville ✴
Kinshasa ✴
Bujumbura ✴
BURUNDI
TANZANIA
Dodoma •
Zanzibar •
Dar es Salaam •
Victoria ✴
SEYCHELLES
CABINDA (ANGOLA)
Luanda ✴
COMOROS
Moroni ✴
ATLANTIC OCEAN
ANGOLA
MALAWI
Lilongwe ✴
ZAMBIA
Lusaka ✴
Harare ✴
MADAGASCAR
Antananarivo ✴
MAURITIUS
MOZAMBIQUE
Mozambique Channel
Port Louis •
NAMIBIA
ZIMBABWE
BOTSWANA
Windhoek ✴
Gaborone ✴
Pretoria ✴
Maputo ✴
SCALE
Mbabane ✴
SWAZILAND
Bloemfontein •
Maseru ✴
LESOTHO
SOUTH AFRICA
Cape Town •

N

Boundaries
✴ **National capitals**
• **Other cities**

SCALE
0   500   1000 Miles
0   500   1000 Kilometers
Projection: Azimuthal Equal Area

---

1. (Places and Regions) Which country is completely surrounded by another country?

2. (Places and Regions) Which country lies mostly on the mainland but has its capital on an island?

3. (Places and Regions) What is the largest African island country? What are the other island countries?

Critical Thinking

4. Comparing Compare this map to the **climate map** of the region. Why do you think the capitals of Algeria, Tunisia, and Libya all lie on the Mediterranean Sea?

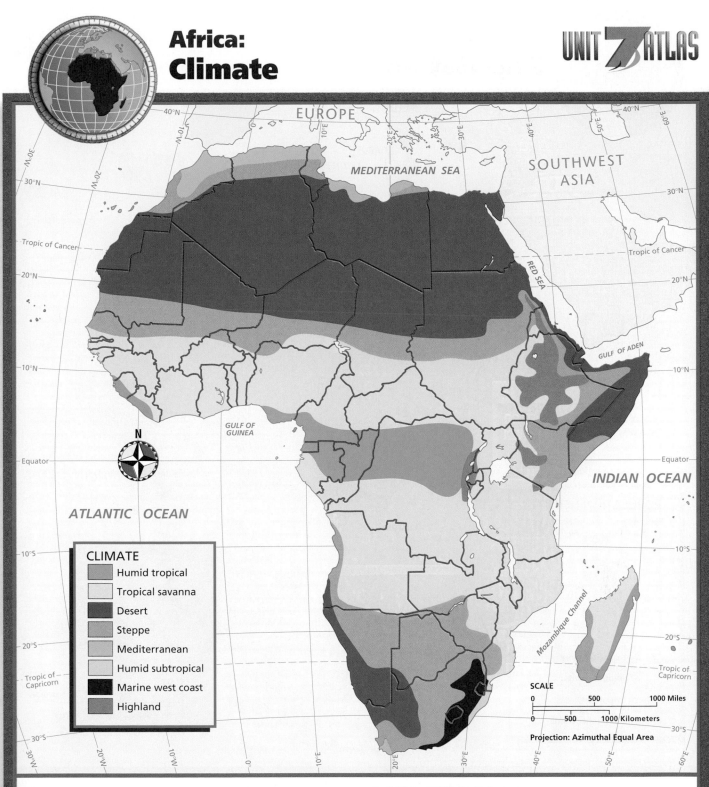

CLIMATE
- Humid tropical
- Tropical savanna
- Desert
- Steppe
- Mediterranean
- Humid subtropical
- Marine west coast
- Highland

SCALE

0   500   1000 Miles

0   500   1000 Kilometers

Projection: Azimuthal Equal Area

1. *Physical Systems* Where are humid tropical climates found in Africa?

2. *Places and Regions* Compare this map to the **land use and resources map** of the region. Which climate region in North Africa has limited economic activity?

Critical Thinking

3. Comparing Compare this map to the **land use and resources** and **population maps** of the region. Why might the eastern part of South Africa be more densely populated than the western part?

Africa: Population

POPULATION DENSITY

Persons per sq. mile	Persons per sq km
520	200
260	100
130	50
25	10
3	1
0	0

● Metropolitan areas with more than 2 million inhabitants

○ Metropolitan areas with 1 million to 2 million inhabitants

SCALE

0 ——— 500 ——— 1000 Miles

0 ——— 500 ——— 1000 Kilometers

Projection: Azimuthal Equal Area

---

1. *Places and Regions* Which country has the most cities with more than 2 million people? Compare this map to the **physical map** of the region. Which river flows through or near these cities?

2. *Places and Regions* What are the two largest African cities shown south of the equator?

Critical Thinking

3. Analyzing Information Use the map on this page to create a chart, graph, database, or model of population centers in Africa.

Africa: Land Use and Resources

EUROPE

MEDITERRANEAN SEA

Tangier
Constantine
Algiers
Oran
Tunis
Rabat
Casablanca
Tripoli
Benghazi
Alexandria
Cairo

SOUTHWEST ASIA

Suez Canal

RED SEA

Tropic of Cancer

Dakar

Khartoum

Massawa

GULF OF ADEN

Conakry

Addis Ababa

Abidjan
Lagos

ATLANTIC OCEAN

GULF OF GUINEA

Equator

Kisangani
Kampala
Kisumu
Nairobi

INDIAN OCEAN

Pointe-Noire
Kinshasa

Mombasa
Dar es Salaam

N

Likasi
Lubumbashi

Harare

Mozambique Channel

Pretoria

Tropic of Capricorn

Johannesburg
Durban

SCALE
0   500   1000 Miles
0   500   1000 Kilometers

Projection: Azimuthal Equal Area

Cape Town
Port Elizabeth

LAND USE

- Nomadic herding
- Livestock raising
- Commercial farming
- Subsistence farming
- Limited economic activity
- Manufacturing
- ● Major manufacturing and trade centers

RESOURCES

- Coal
- Natural gas
- Oil
- Hydroelectric power
- Gold
- Silver
- Platinum
- Diamonds
- Uranium
- Other minerals
- Seafood

1. *Places and Regions* Which region of Africa seems to have the most mineral resources?

2. *Environment and Society* What type of farming is the most common in Africa?

3. *Environment and Society* Compare this map to the **physical map** of the region. Which rivers support commercial farming in dry areas?

Which river in southeastern Africa provides hydroelectric power to the region?

Critical Thinking

4. **Analyzing Information** Use the map on this page to create a chart, graph, database, or model of economic activities in Africa.

Africa

ALGERIA

CAPITAL:
Algiers

AREA:
919,590 sq. mi.
(2,381,740 sq km)

POPULATION:
31,736,053

MONEY:
Algerian dinar (DZD)

LANGUAGES:
Arabic (official), French,
Berber

PEOPLE PER DOCTOR:
1,066

ANGOLA

CAPITAL:
Luanda

AREA:
481,351 sq. mi.
(1,246,700 sq km)

POPULATION:
10,366,031

MONEY:
kwanza (AOA)

LANGUAGES:
Portuguese (official), Bantu
languages

PEOPLE PER DOCTOR:
data not available

BENIN

CAPITAL:
Porto-Novo

AREA:
43,483 sq. mi.
(112,620 sq km)

POPULATION:
6,590,782

MONEY:
CFAF*

LANGUAGES:
French (official), Fon, Yoruba,
other ethnic languages

PEOPLE PER DOCTOR:
14,216

BOTSWANA

CAPITAL:
Gaborone

AREA:
231,803 sq. mi.
(600,370 sq km)

POPULATION:
1,586,119

MONEY:
pula (BWP)

LANGUAGES:
English (official), Setswana

PEOPLE PER DOCTOR:
4,395

BURKINA FASO

CAPITAL:
Ouagadougou

AREA:
105,869 sq. mi.
(274,200 sq km)

POPULATION:
12,272,289

MONEY:
CFAF*

LANGUAGES:
French (official), ethnic
languages

PEOPLE PER DOCTOR:
27,158

BURUNDI

CAPITAL:
Bujumbura

AREA:
10,745 sq. mi.
(27,830 sq km)

POPULATION:
6,223,897

MONEY:
Burundi franc (BIF)

LANGUAGES:
Kirundi (official), French
(official), Swahili

PEOPLE PER DOCTOR:
16,667

CAMEROON

CAPITAL:
Yaoundé

AREA:
183,567 sq. mi.
(475,440 sq km)

POPULATION:
15,803,220

MONEY:
CFAF*

LANGUAGES:
English (official), French (official), 24 ethnic language
groups

PEOPLE PER DOCTOR:
14,286

CAPE VERDE

CAPITAL:
Praia

AREA:
1,557 sq. mi. (4,033 sq km)

POPULATION:
405,163

MONEY:
Cape Verdean escudo (CVE)

LANGUAGES:
Portuguese, Crioulo

PEOPLE PER DOCTOR:
3,448

*Communaute Financiere Africaine franc

Countries not drawn to scale.

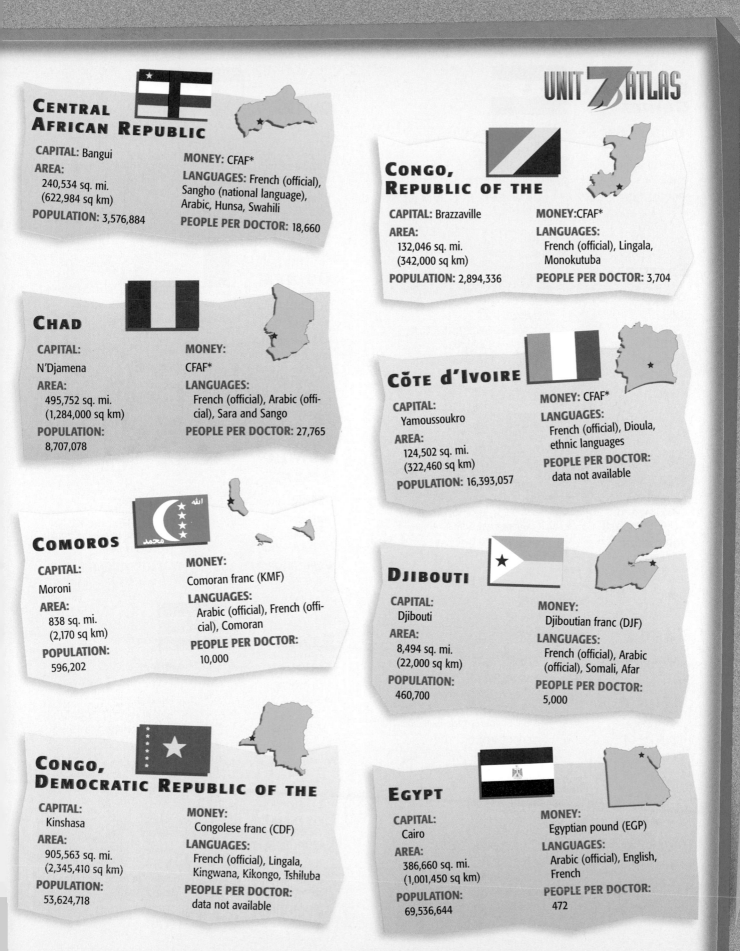

CENTRAL AFRICAN REPUBLIC

CAPITAL: Bangui
AREA:
240,534 sq. mi.
(622,984 sq km)
POPULATION: 3,576,884

MONEY: CFAF*
LANGUAGES: French (official),
Sangho (national language),
Arabic, Hunsa, Swahili
PEOPLE PER DOCTOR: 18,660

CHAD

CAPITAL:
N'Djamena
AREA:
495,752 sq. mi.
(1,284,000 sq km)
POPULATION:
8,707,078

MONEY:
CFAF*
LANGUAGES:
French (official), Arabic (offi-
cial), Sara and Sango
PEOPLE PER DOCTOR: 27,765

COMOROS

CAPITAL:
Moroni
AREA:
838 sq. mi.
(2,170 sq km)
POPULATION:
596,202

MONEY:
Comoran franc (KMF)
LANGUAGES:
Arabic (official), French (offi-
cial), Comoran
PEOPLE PER DOCTOR:
10,000

CONGO, DEMOCRATIC REPUBLIC OF THE

CAPITAL:
Kinshasa
AREA:
905,563 sq. mi.
(2,345,410 sq km)
POPULATION:
53,624,718

MONEY:
Congolese franc (CDF)
LANGUAGES:
French (official), Lingala,
Kingwana, Kikongo, Tshiluba
PEOPLE PER DOCTOR:
data not available

CONGO, REPUBLIC OF THE

CAPITAL: Brazzaville
AREA:
132,046 sq. mi.
(342,000 sq km)
POPULATION: 2,894,336

MONEY: CFAF*
LANGUAGES:
French (official), Lingala,
Monokutuba
PEOPLE PER DOCTOR: 3,704

CÔTE d'IVOIRE

CAPITAL:
Yamoussoukro
AREA:
124,502 sq. mi.
(322,460 sq km)
POPULATION: 16,393,057

MONEY: CFAF*
LANGUAGES:
French (official), Dioula,
ethnic languages
PEOPLE PER DOCTOR:
data not available

DJIBOUTI

CAPITAL:
Djibouti
AREA:
8,494 sq. mi.
(22,000 sq km)
POPULATION:
460,700

MONEY:
Djiboutian franc (DJF)
LANGUAGES:
French (official), Arabic
(official), Somali, Afar
PEOPLE PER DOCTOR:
5,000

EGYPT

CAPITAL:
Cairo
AREA:
386,660 sq. mi.
(1,001,450 sq km)
POPULATION:
69,536,644

MONEY:
Egyptian pound (EGP)
LANGUAGES:
Arabic (official), English,
French
PEOPLE PER DOCTOR:
472

Sources: Central Intelligence Agency, *The World Factbook 2001; The World Almanac and Book of Facts 2001; United Nations Development Programme: Health Profile,* pop. figures are 2001 estimates.

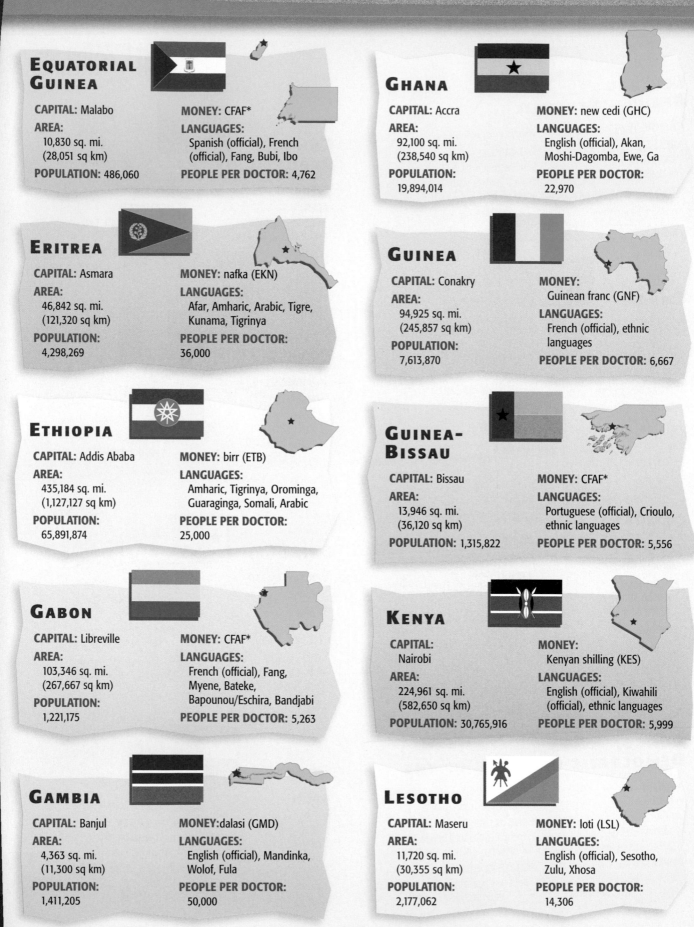

EQUATORIAL GUINEA

CAPITAL: Malabo

AREA:
10,830 sq. mi.
(28,051 sq km)

POPULATION: 486,060

MONEY: CFAF*

LANGUAGES:
Spanish (official), French (official), Fang, Bubi, Ibo

PEOPLE PER DOCTOR: 4,762

ERITREA

CAPITAL: Asmara

AREA:
46,842 sq. mi.
(121,320 sq km)

POPULATION:
4,298,269

MONEY: nafka (EKN)

LANGUAGES:
Afar, Amharic, Arabic, Tigre, Kunama, Tigrinya

PEOPLE PER DOCTOR:
36,000

ETHIOPIA

CAPITAL: Addis Ababa

AREA:
435,184 sq. mi.
(1,127,127 sq km)

POPULATION:
65,891,874

MONEY: birr (ETB)

LANGUAGES:
Amharic, Tigrinya, Orominga, Guaraginga, Somali, Arabic

PEOPLE PER DOCTOR:
25,000

GABON

CAPITAL: Libreville

AREA:
103,346 sq. mi.
(267,667 sq km)

POPULATION:
1,221,175

MONEY: CFAF*

LANGUAGES:
French (official), Fang, Myene, Bateke, Bapounou/Eschira, Bandjabi

PEOPLE PER DOCTOR: 5,263

GAMBIA

CAPITAL: Banjul

AREA:
4,363 sq. mi.
(11,300 sq km)

POPULATION:
1,411,205

MONEY: dalasi (GMD)

LANGUAGES:
English (official), Mandinka, Wolof, Fula

PEOPLE PER DOCTOR:
50,000

GHANA

CAPITAL: Accra

AREA:
92,100 sq. mi.
(238,540 sq km)

POPULATION:
19,894,014

MONEY: new cedi (GHC)

LANGUAGES:
English (official), Akan, Moshi-Dagomba, Ewe, Ga

PEOPLE PER DOCTOR:
22,970

GUINEA

CAPITAL: Conakry

AREA:
94,925 sq. mi.
(245,857 sq km)

POPULATION:
7,613,870

MONEY:
Guinean franc (GNF)

LANGUAGES:
French (official), ethnic languages

PEOPLE PER DOCTOR: 6,667

GUINEA-BISSAU

CAPITAL: Bissau

AREA:
13,946 sq. mi.
(36,120 sq km)

POPULATION: 1,315,822

MONEY: CFAF*

LANGUAGES:
Portuguese (official), Crioulo, ethnic languages

PEOPLE PER DOCTOR: 5,556

KENYA

CAPITAL:
Nairobi

AREA:
224,961 sq. mi.
(582,650 sq km)

POPULATION: 30,765,916

MONEY:
Kenyan shilling (KES)

LANGUAGES:
English (official), Kiwahili (official), ethnic languages

PEOPLE PER DOCTOR: 5,999

LESOTHO

CAPITAL: Maseru

AREA:
11,720 sq. mi.
(30,355 sq km)

POPULATION:
2,177,062

MONEY: loti (LSL)

LANGUAGES:
English (official), Sesotho, Zulu, Xhosa

PEOPLE PER DOCTOR:
14,306

*Communaute Financiere Africaine franc

Countries not drawn to scale.

LIBERIA

CAPITAL: Monrovia
AREA:
43,000 sq. mi.
(111,370 sq km)
POPULATION:
3,225,837

MONEY:
Liberian dollar (LRD)
LANGUAGES:
English (official), many ethnic languages
PEOPLE PER DOCTOR: 8,333

LIBYA

CAPITAL: Tripoli
AREA:
679,358 sq. mi.
(1,759,540 sq km)
POPULATION:
5,240,599

MONEY: Libyan dinar (LYD)
LANGUAGES:
Arabic, Italian, English
PEOPLE PER DOCTOR:
data not available

MADAGASCAR

CAPITAL: Antananarivo
AREA:
226,656 sq. mi.
(587,040 sq km)
POPULATION:
15,982,563

MONEY:
Malagasy franc (MGF)
LANGUAGES:
French (official), Malagasy (official)
PEOPLE PER DOCTOR: 4,167

MALAWI

CAPITAL: Lilongwe
AREA:
45,745 sq. mi.
(118,480 sq km)
POPULATION:
10,548,250

MONEY:
Malawian kwacha (MWK)
LANGUAGES: English (official), Chichewa (official), many ethnic languages
PEOPLE PER DOCTOR: 50,000

MALI

CAPITAL: Bamako
AREA:
478,764 sq. mi.
(1,240,000 sq km)
POPULATION: 11,008,518

MONEY: CFAF*
LANGUAGES:
French (official), Bambara, many ethnic languages
PEOPLE PER DOCTOR: 25,000

MAURITANIA

CAPITAL:
Nouakchott
AREA:
397,953 sq. mi.
(1,030,700 sq km)
POPULATION:
2,747,312

MONEY:
ouguiya (MOR)
LANGUAGES:
Hasaniya Arabic (official), Wolof (official), Pular, Soninke, French
PEOPLE PER DOCTOR: 11,085

MAURITIUS

CAPITAL:
Port Louis
AREA:
718 sq. mi.
(1,860 sq km)
POPULATION:
1,189,825

MONEY:
Mauritian rupee (MUR)
LANGUAGES:
English (official), Creole, French, Hindi, Urdu, Hakka, Bojpoori
PEOPLE PER DOCTOR: 1,182

MOROCCO

CAPITAL:
Rabat
AREA:
172,413 sq. mi.
(446,550 sq km)
POPULATION:
30,645,305

MONEY:
Moroccan dirham (MAD)
LANGUAGES:
Arabic (official), Berber, French
PEOPLE PER DOCTOR: 2,923

MOZAMBIQUE

CAPITAL:
Maputo
AREA:
304,494 sq. mi.
(801,590 sq km)
POPULATION:
19,371,057

MONEY:
metical (MZM)
LANGUAGES:
Portuguese (official), ethnic languages
PEOPLE PER DOCTOR:
131,991

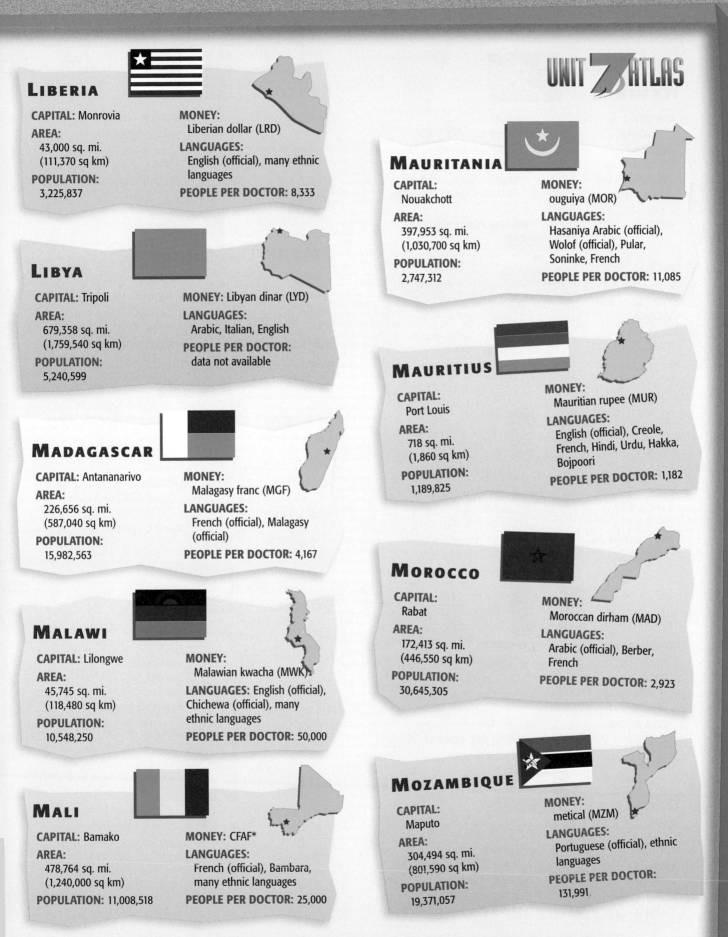

Sources: Central Intelligence Agency, *The World Factbook 2001*; *The World Almanac and Book of Facts 2001*; *United Nations Development Programme: Health Profile*; pop. figures are 2001 estimates.

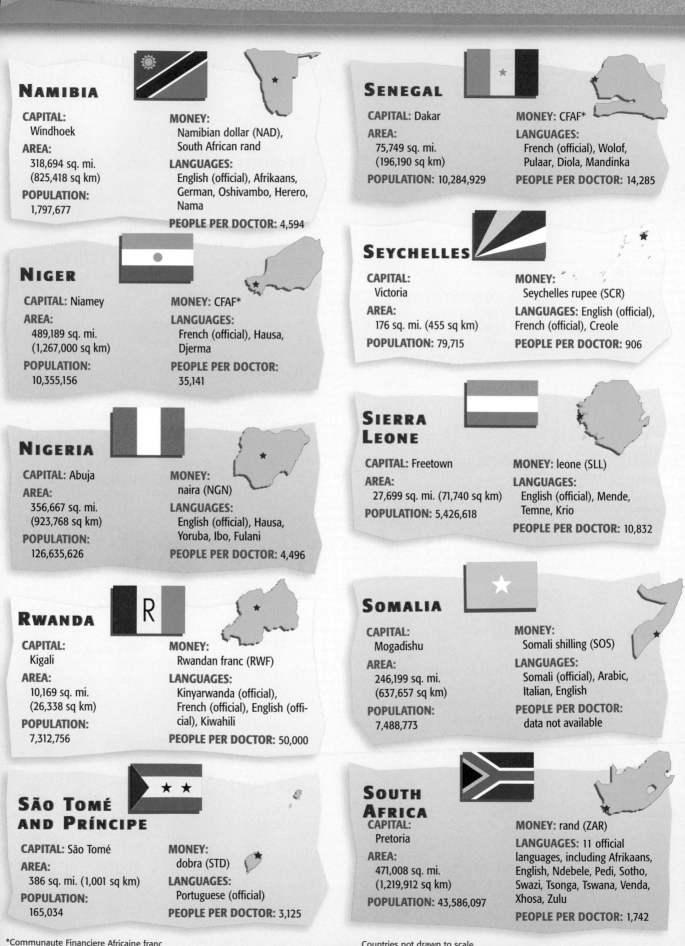

NAMIBIA

CAPITAL:
Windhoek

AREA:
318,694 sq. mi.
(825,418 sq km)

POPULATION:
1,797,677

MONEY:
Namibian dollar (NAD),
South African rand

LANGUAGES:
English (official), Afrikaans,
German, Oshivambo, Herero,
Nama

PEOPLE PER DOCTOR: 4,594

NIGER

CAPITAL: Niamey

AREA:
489,189 sq. mi.
(1,267,000 sq km)

POPULATION:
10,355,156

MONEY: CFAF*

LANGUAGES:
French (official), Hausa,
Djerma

PEOPLE PER DOCTOR:
35,141

NIGERIA

CAPITAL: Abuja

AREA:
356,667 sq. mi.
(923,768 sq km)

POPULATION:
126,635,626

MONEY:
naira (NGN)

LANGUAGES:
English (official), Hausa,
Yoruba, Ibo, Fulani

PEOPLE PER DOCTOR: 4,496

RWANDA

CAPITAL:
Kigali

AREA:
10,169 sq. mi.
(26,338 sq km)

POPULATION:
7,312,756

MONEY:
Rwandan franc (RWF)

LANGUAGES:
Kinyarwanda (official),
French (official), English (offi-
cial), Kiwahili

PEOPLE PER DOCTOR: 50,000

SÃO TOMÉ AND PRÍNCIPE

CAPITAL: São Tomé

AREA:
386 sq. mi. (1,001 sq km)

POPULATION:
165,034

MONEY:
dobra (STD)

LANGUAGES:
Portuguese (official)

PEOPLE PER DOCTOR: 3,125

SENEGAL

CAPITAL: Dakar

AREA:
75,749 sq. mi.
(196,190 sq km)

POPULATION: 10,284,929

MONEY: CFAF*

LANGUAGES:
French (official), Wolof,
Pulaar, Diola, Mandinka

PEOPLE PER DOCTOR: 14,285

SEYCHELLES

CAPITAL:
Victoria

AREA:
176 sq. mi. (455 sq km)

POPULATION: 79,715

MONEY:
Seychelles rupee (SCR)

LANGUAGES: English (official),
French (official), Creole

PEOPLE PER DOCTOR: 906

SIERRA LEONE

CAPITAL: Freetown

AREA:
27,699 sq. mi. (71,740 sq km)

POPULATION: 5,426,618

MONEY: leone (SLL)

LANGUAGES:
English (official), Mende,
Temne, Krio

PEOPLE PER DOCTOR: 10,832

SOMALIA

CAPITAL:
Mogadishu

AREA:
246,199 sq. mi.
(637,657 sq km)

POPULATION:
7,488,773

MONEY:
Somali shilling (SOS)

LANGUAGES:
Somali (official), Arabic,
Italian, English

PEOPLE PER DOCTOR:
data not available

SOUTH AFRICA

CAPITAL:
Pretoria

AREA:
471,008 sq. mi.
(1,219,912 sq km)

POPULATION: 43,586,097

MONEY: rand (ZAR)

LANGUAGES: 11 official
languages, including Afrikaans,
English, Ndebele, Pedi, Sotho,
Swazi, Tsonga, Tswana, Venda,
Xhosa, Zulu

PEOPLE PER DOCTOR: 1,742

*Communaute Financiere Africaine franc

Countries not drawn to scale.

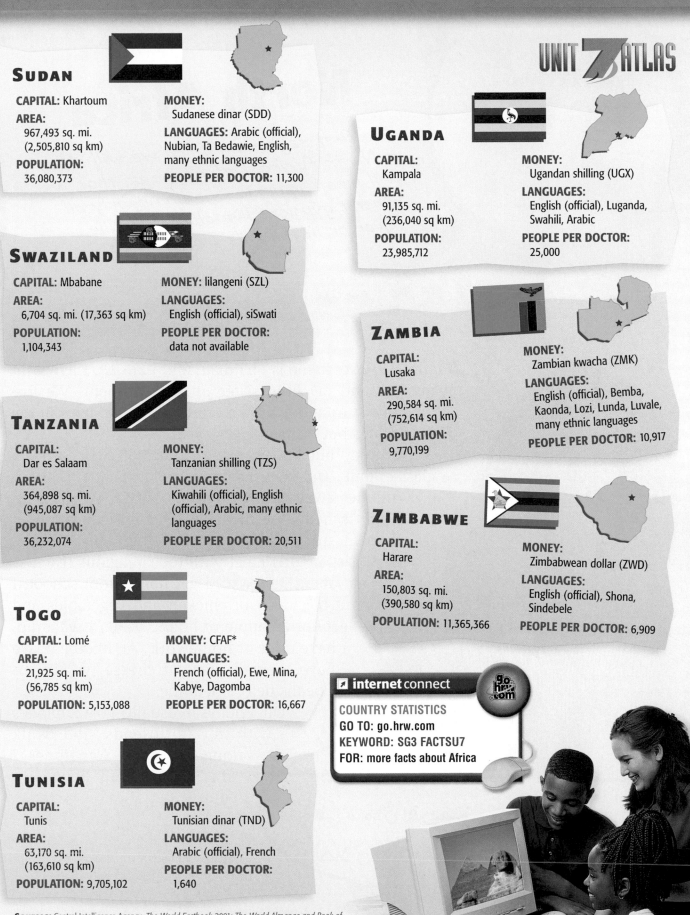

SUDAN

CAPITAL: Khartoum

AREA:
967,493 sq. mi.
(2,505,810 sq km)

POPULATION:
36,080,373

MONEY:
Sudanese dinar (SDD)

LANGUAGES: Arabic (official),
Nubian, Ta Bedawie, English,
many ethnic languages

PEOPLE PER DOCTOR: 11,300

SWAZILAND

CAPITAL: Mbabane

AREA:
6,704 sq. mi. (17,363 sq km)

POPULATION:
1,104,343

MONEY: lilangeni (SZL)

LANGUAGES:
English (official), siSwati

PEOPLE PER DOCTOR:
data not available

TANZANIA

CAPITAL:
Dar es Salaam

AREA:
364,898 sq. mi.
(945,087 sq km)

POPULATION:
36,232,074

MONEY:
Tanzanian shilling (TZS)

LANGUAGES:
Kiwahili (official), English
(official), Arabic, many ethnic
languages

PEOPLE PER DOCTOR: 20,511

TOGO

CAPITAL: Lomé

AREA:
21,925 sq. mi.
(56,785 sq km)

POPULATION: 5,153,088

MONEY: CFAF*

LANGUAGES:
French (official), Ewe, Mina,
Kabye, Dagomba

PEOPLE PER DOCTOR: 16,667

TUNISIA

CAPITAL:
Tunis

AREA:
63,170 sq. mi.
(163,610 sq km)

POPULATION: 9,705,102

MONEY:
Tunisian dinar (TND)

LANGUAGES:
Arabic (official), French

PEOPLE PER DOCTOR:
1,640

UGANDA

CAPITAL:
Kampala

AREA:
91,135 sq. mi.
(236,040 sq km)

POPULATION:
23,985,712

MONEY:
Ugandan shilling (UGX)

LANGUAGES:
English (official), Luganda,
Swahili, Arabic

PEOPLE PER DOCTOR:
25,000

ZAMBIA

CAPITAL:
Lusaka

AREA:
290,584 sq. mi.
(752,614 sq km)

POPULATION:
9,770,199

MONEY:
Zambian kwacha (ZMK)

LANGUAGES:
English (official), Bemba,
Kaonda, Lozi, Lunda, Luvale,
many ethnic languages

PEOPLE PER DOCTOR: 10,917

ZIMBABWE

CAPITAL:
Harare

AREA:
150,803 sq. mi.
(390,580 sq km)

POPULATION: 11,365,366

MONEY:
Zimbabwean dollar (ZWD)

LANGUAGES:
English (official), Shona,
Sindebele

PEOPLE PER DOCTOR: 6,909

internet connect

go.hrw.com

COUNTRY STATISTICS
GO TO: go.hrw.com
KEYWORD: SG3 FACTSU7
FOR: more facts about Africa

Sources: Central Intelligence Agency, *The World Factbook 2001; The World Almanac and Book of Facts 2001; United Nations Development Programme: Health Profile;* pop. figures are 2001 estimates.

North Africa

The first region in Africa we will study is North Africa. Before we do that, we will meet Shaimaa. She and nearly all other Egyptians live along the Nile River or in the Nile Delta.

Ahlan! (Hi!) My name is Shaimaa, and I am 18. I live with my mother and my little sister in an apartment. We live about an hour from downtown Cairo. My father lives in the United States but visits us every year.

Every day but Friday, I get up at 7:00 A.M., drink a glass of milk, and then meet my friends. School is about 15 minutes away on the metro (subway). We go to an all-girls school. We all have religious education in school. I study Islam with the other Muslim girls. The Christian girls meet with their religious teacher.

At about 3:00 P.M., I get home from school. I eat a big lunch of chicken and vegetables and sleep for a couple of hours. When I wake up, I have a lot of homework. At 10:00 P.M. we have a small meal of cheese, yogurt, or beans before bedtime.

On Fridays I usually go to movies with my girlfriends and walk along the Nile. Sometimes I stay home and listen to music.

أنا طالبة في القاهرة,
في شمال افريقيا.
أهلاً وسهلاً بكم

◄

Translation: I am a student in Cairo, in North Africa. Welcome to all of you.

Section 1 Physical Geography

Read to Discover

1. What are the major physical features of North Africa?
2. What climates, plants, and wildlife are found in North Africa?
3. What are North Africa's major resources?

Define

ergs
regs
depressions
silt

Locate

Red Sea
Mediterranean Sea
Sahara
Nile River
Sinai Peninsula
Ahaggar
   Mountains

Atlas Mountains
Qattara
   Depression
Nile Delta
Lake Nasser
Suez Canal

WHY IT MATTERS

Most Egyptians live along the banks of the Nile River. The river's flooding is both beneficial and destructive. Use CNNfyi.com or other **current events** sources to find out how Egyptians are affected by the river. Record your findings in your journal.

A tomb painting from ancient Egypt

North Africa: Physical-Political

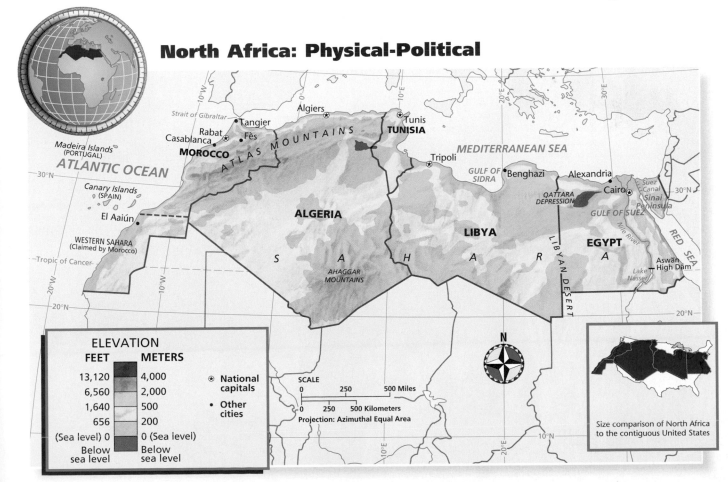

internet connect

GO TO: go.hrw.com
KEYWORD: SG3 CH22
FOR: Web sites about North Africa

Physical Features

North Africa includes Morocco, Algeria, Tunisia, Libya, and Egypt. The region stretches from the Atlantic Ocean to the Red Sea. Off the northern coast is the Mediterranean Sea. In the south is the Sahara (suh-HAR-uh), a vast desert. The region also has mountains, the northern Nile River valley, and the Sinai (SY-ny) Peninsula.

The Sahara The huge Sahara covers most of North Africa and stretches southward. The name *Sahara* comes from the Arabic word for "desert." The Sahara is the largest desert in the world. It is so big that nearly all of the United States would fit into it.

Large areas of this very dry region have few people or none at all. Great "seas" of sand dunes called **ergs** cover about a quarter of the desert. Much of the rest of the Sahara is made up of broad, windswept gravel plains. These gravel plains are called **regs**.

Mountains Do you think of deserts as flat regions? Well, the Sahara is not flat. Some sand dunes and ridges rise as high as 1,000 feet (305 m). The Sahara also has mountain ranges. For example, the Ahaggar (uh-HAH-guhr) Mountains are located in the central Sahara. Their highest peak is 9,842 feet (3,000 m). The Atlas Mountains on the northwestern side of the Sahara are higher. Mountains there rise to 13,671 feet (4,167 m).

There also are very low areas in the Sahara. These low areas are called **depressions**. The Qattara (kuh-TAHR-uh) Depression in western Egypt is 440 feet (134 m) below sea level. Other low areas often have large, dry lake beds. Water from rare rain storms collects there.

Oases like this one in Algeria are scattered throughout the vast Sahara.

Interpreting the Visual Record How do these trees survive in the desert's harsh, dry climate?

The Nile
The world's longest river, the Nile, flows northward through the eastern Sahara. The Nile empties into the Mediterranean Sea. It is formed by the union of two rivers, the Blue Nile and the White Nile. They meet in Sudan, south of Egypt.

The Nile River valley is like a long oasis in the desert. Water from the Nile irrigates surrounding farmland. The Nile fans out near the Mediterranean Sea, forming a large river delta. About 99 percent of Egypt's population lives in the Nile River valley and the Nile Delta.

For centuries rain far to the south caused annual floods along the northern Nile that left rich **silt** in surrounding fields. Silt is finely ground soil good for growing crops. The Aswān High Dam, which was completed in 1971, was built to control flooding. Water trapped by the dam formed Lake Nasser in southern Egypt. However, the dam also traps silt, preventing it from being carried downriver. Today Egypt's farmers must use fertilizers to enrich the soil.

The Sinai and Suez Canal
East of the Nile is the triangular Sinai Peninsula. Barren, rocky mountains and desert cover the Sinai. Between the Sinai and the rest of Egypt is the Suez Canal. The canal was built by the French in the 1860s. See the Case Study about the Suez Canal in this chapter.

✓ **READING CHECK:** *Places and Regions* What are the major physical features of North Africa?

Water from the Nile River irrigates rich farmlands along the river and in its delta. You can clearly see the Nile Delta in the satellite photograph. The irrigated farmlands of the delta are shown in red.

Interpreting the Visual Record
Why do you think most Egyptians live near the Nile River?

The Arabian camel has long been used for transportation in the Sahara. It can store water in the fat of its hump. Camels have survived for more than two weeks without drinking.

Climate, Vegetation, and Animals

There are three main climates in North Africa. A desert climate covers most of the region. Temperatures range from mild to very hot. How hot can it get? Temperatures as high as 136°F (58°C) have been recorded in Libya! However, the humidity is very low. As a result, temperatures can drop quickly after sunset.

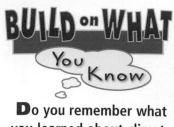

Do you remember what you learned about climate regions? See Chapter 3 to review.

Olives like these in Morocco are an important agricultural product in North Africa. Olives and olive oil are common ingredients in many foods around the Mediterranean.

▼

In some areas there has been no rain for many years. However, rare storms can cause flash floods. In places these floods as well as high winds have carved bare rock surfaces out of the land. Storms of sand and dust can also be severe.

Hardy plants and animals live in the desert. Grasses, small shrubs, and even trees grow where there is enough water. Usually this is in oases. Gazelles, hyenas, baboons, foxes, and weasels are among the region's mammals.

Much of the northern coast west of Egypt has a Mediterranean climate. Winters there are mild and moist. Summers are hot and dry. Plant life includes grasses, shrubs, and even a few forests in the Atlas Mountains. Areas between the Mediterranean climate and the Sahara have a steppe climate. Shrubs and grasses grow there.

✓ **READING CHECK:** (*Physical Systems*) How does climate affect the plants and wildlife of North Africa?

Resources

Good soils and rain or river water aid farming in coastal areas and the Nile River valley. Common crops are wheat, barley, olives, grapes, citrus fruits, and cotton. The region also has good fishing waters.

Oil and gas are important resources, particularly for Libya, Algeria, and Egypt. Morocco mines iron ore and minerals used to make fertilizers. The Sahara has minerals such as copper, gold, and silver.

✓ **READING CHECK:** (*Places and Regions*) What are North Africa's major resources?

Homework Practice Online
Keyword: SG3 HP22

Define and explain: ergs, regs, depressions, silt

Working with Sketch Maps On a map of North Africa that you draw or that your teacher provides, label the following: Red Sea, Mediterranean Sea, Sahara, Nile River, Sinai Peninsula, Ahaggar Mountains, Atlas Mountains, Qattara Depression, Nile Delta, Lake Nasser, and the Suez Canal. In a box in the margin, identify the dam that created Lake Nasser.

Reading for the Main Idea

1. (*Places and Regions*) What two mountain ranges are found in North Africa?

2. (*Places and Regions*) What part of Egypt is east of the Suez Canal?

3. (*Environment and Society*) How did the Nile affect farming in the river valley?

Critical Thinking

4. **Drawing Inferences and Conclusions** Where would you expect to find most of North Africa's major cities?

Organizing What You Know

5. **Summarizing** Use this graphic organizer to describe the physical features of North Africa.

Climates	Plants and Animals	Resources

Section 2 · History and Culture

Read to Discover

1. What are the major events in the history of North Africa?
2. What are some important facts about the people and culture of North Africa?

Define

pharaohs

hieroglyphs

Bedouins

Locate

Alexandria

Cairo

Fès

Western Sahara

WHY IT MATTERS

Egypt was home to one of the world's earliest and most complex civilizations. Use **CNNfyi.com** or other **current events** sources to find examples of new archaeological finds from Egypt. Record your findings in your journal.

Woven carpet from Morocco

History

The Nile River valley was home to some of the world's oldest civilizations. Sometime after 3200 B.C. lands along the northern Nile were united into one Egyptian kingdom.

The early Egyptians used water from the Nile to grow wheat, barley, and other crops. They also built great stone pyramids and other monuments. Egyptian **pharaohs**, or kings, were buried in the pyramids. How did the Egyptians build these huge monuments? See Connecting to Technology on the next page.

The Egyptians also traded with people from other places. To identify themselves and their goods, the Egyptians used **hieroglyphs** (HY-ruh-glifs). Hieroglyphs are pictures and symbols that stand for ideas or words. They were the basis for Egypt's first writing system.

West of Egypt were people who spoke what are called Berber languages. These people herded sheep and other livestock. They also grew wheat and barley in the Atlas Mountains and along the coast.

Invaders Because of North Africa's long coastline, the region was open to invaders over the centuries. Those invaders included people from the eastern Mediterranean, Greeks, and Romans. For example, one invader was the Macedonian king Alexander the Great. He founded the city of Alexandria in Egypt in 332 B.C. This city became an important seaport and trading center on the Mediterranean coast.

Beginning in the A.D. 600s, Arab armies from Southwest Asia swept across North Africa. They brought the Arabic language and Islam to the

The tombs of early Egyptian pharoahs were decorated with paintings, crafts, and treasures. You can see hieroglyphs across the top of this wall painting.

The monuments of ancient Egypt are among the great wonders of the world. They are thousands of years old. These pyramids, temples, and other structures reflect the power of Egyptian rulers. They also show the skills of Egyptian engineers.

The most famous of Egypt's monuments are the huge stone pyramids at Giza. Giza is near Cairo. The pyramids there were built more than 4,000 years ago as tombs for Egyptian rulers. The largest structure is the Great Pyramid. At its base the pyramid's sides are each about 755 feet (230 m) long. The pyramid rises nearly 500 feet (152 m) above the desert floor.

Another famous set of monuments is found farther south at the Valley of the Kings. The Valley of the Kings lies along the Nile River. Between 1500 B.C. and 1000 B.C., the Egyptians built tombs into the sides of cliffs there. They also carved huge sculptures and columns on the cliff faces. Near the tombs they built giant stone temples.

How did the Egyptians build these giant monuments? Workers had to cut large blocks of stone far away and roll them on logs to the Nile. From there the blocks could be moved on barges. At the building site, the Egyptians finished carving the blocks with special tools. Then they built dirt and brick ramps on the sides of the structures. They hauled the blocks up the ramps.

Egyptian Monuments

The average weight of each of the 2.3 million blocks in the Great Pyramid is 2.5 tons (2.25 metric tons). It is estimated that many thousands of workers were needed to move the heavy blocks into place. Together, these workers and Egyptian engineers built amazing monuments that have stood for thousands of years.

Understanding What You Read

1. What kinds of monuments did the Egyptians build and why?
2. How did the Egyptians' belief systems affect their use of technology in building monuments?

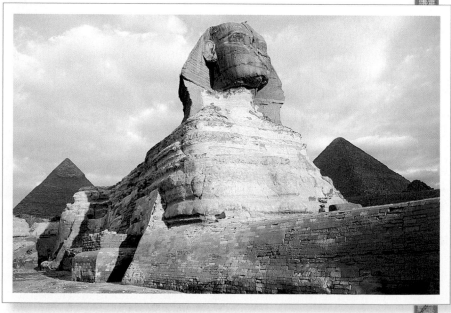

The Sphinx and pyramids at Giza, Egypt

region. Today most North Africans are Muslim and speak Arabic. Under Muslim rule, North African cities became major centers of learning, trade, and craft making. These cities included Cairo in Egypt and Fès in Morocco.

European Control In the 1800s European countries began to take over the region. By 1912 they controlled all of North Africa. In that year Italy captured Libya from the Ottoman Empire. Spain already controlled northern Morocco. France ruled the rest of Morocco as well as Tunisia and Algeria. Egypt was under British control.

Egypt gained limited independence in 1922. The British kept military bases there and maintained control of the Suez Canal until 1956. During World War II the region was a major battleground. After the war, North Africans pushed for independence. Libya, Morocco, and Tunisia each won independence in the 1950s.

Algeria was the last North African country to win independence. Many French citizens had moved to the country. They considered Algeria part of France. Algeria finally won independence in 1962, after a long, bitter war. Most French residents of Algeria then moved to France.

Modern North Africa Since independence, the countries of North Africa have tried to build stronger ties with other Arab countries. For example, Egypt led other Arab countries in several wars against Israel. However, in 1979 Egypt signed a peace treaty with Israel.

In 1976 Morocco took over the former Spanish colony of Western Sahara. Western Saharan rebels have been trying to win independence from Morocco since then.

✓ **READING CHECK:** *Places and Regions* What were some major events in the history of North Africa?

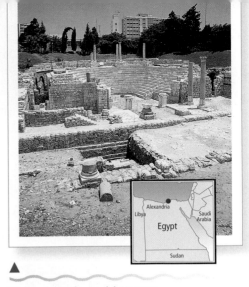

▲
The ruins of an old Roman amphitheater remain in Alexandria, Egypt.

The inset photograph shows the beautiful doors of the royal palace in Fès, Morocco.

Interpreting the Visual Record **What interesting architectural features do you see in the photograph?**

▼

The floor of the beautiful Muhammad Ali mosque in Cairo is covered with carpet. Muslim men kneel and bow with their faces to the ground to pray.

Interpreting the Visual Record Why do you think there are no chairs in this picture?

A variety of vegetables and meat surround a large serving of couscous.

Interpreting the Visual Record What does this food tell you about agricultural products of the region?

Culture

As you have read, the histories of the North African countries have much in common. You will also find many cultural similarities among those countries.

Language and Religion Egyptians, Berbers, and **Bedouins** make up nearly all of Egypt's population. Bedouins are nomadic herders who travel throughout deserts of Egypt and Southwest Asia. Most people in the countries to the west are of mixed Arab and Berber ancestry. Arabic is the major language. Some people speak Berber languages.

Most ethnic Europeans left North Africa after the region's countries became independent. However, French, Italian, and English still are spoken in many areas.

Most North Africans are Muslims. Of the region's countries, Egypt has the largest number of non-Muslims. About 6 percent of Egyptians are Christians or practice other religions.

Food and Festivals What kind of food would you eat on a trip to North Africa? Grains, vegetables, fruits, and nuts are common there. Many meals include couscous (KOOS-koos). Couscous is made from wheat and looks like small pellets of pasta. It is steamed over boiling water or soup. Often it is served with vegetables or meat, butter, and olive oil. Some people mix their couscous with a fiery hot sauce called *harissa*.

A popular dish in Egypt is *fuul*. It is made from fava beans mashed with olive oil, salt, pepper, garlic, and lemons. The combination is then served with hard-boiled eggs and bread.

Important holidays in North Africa include the birthday of the prophet of Islam, Muhammad. The birthday is marked with lights, parades, and special sweets of honey, nuts, and sugar. During the holy month of Ramadan, Muslims abstain from food and drink during the day.

Art and Literature North Africa has long been known for its beautiful architecture, wood carving, and other crafts. Women weave a variety of textiles. Among these are beautiful carpets that feature geometric designs and bright colors.

The region has also produced important writers and artists. For example, Egyptian poetry and other writing date back thousands of years. One of Egypt's most famous writers is Naguib Mahfouz. In 1988 he became the first Arab writer to win the Nobel Prize in literature. Egypt also has a growing movie industry. Egyptian films in Arabic have become popular throughout Southwest Asia and North Africa.

Many North Africans also enjoy popular music based on singing and poetry. The musical scale there has many more notes than are common in Western music. As a result, North African tunes seem to wail or waver. Musicians often use instruments such as the three-stringed *sintir* of Morocco.

This Algerian woman and her daughter are using a loom to weave a rug. The loom allows a rug maker to weave horizontal and vertical threads together.

✓ **READING CHECK:** (*Human Systems*) What are some important facts about the people and culture of North Africa?

Homework Practice Online
Keyword: SG3 HP22

Define and explain: pharaohs, hieroglyphs, Bedouins

Working with Sketch Maps On the map you drew in Section 1, label Alexandria, Cairo, Fès, and Western Sahara. In a box in the margin, identify the country that claims Western Sahara.

Reading for the Main Idea

1. (**Places and Regions**) What early civilization thrived along the northern Nile River about 3200 B.C.?

2. (**Human Systems**) How did Islam and the Arabic language come to North Africa?

3. (**Human Systems**) Which European countries controlled countries in North Africa by 1912?

Critical Thinking

4. **Drawing Inferences and Conclusions** Look at the world map in the textbook's Atlas. Why do you think the Suez Canal is an important waterway for world shipping?

Organizing What You Know

5. **Summarizing** Copy the following graphic organizer. Use it to identify at least six important facts about the languages, religions, food, festivals, art, and literature of North Africa.

Culture in North Africa

North Africa • 479

CASE STUDY

THE SUEZ CANAL: A STRATEGIC WATERWAY

The movement of goods and people around the world has increased dramatically during the past 100 years. In the world's oceans, more ships are sailing from port to port through busy shipping lanes. Just as highways can get crowded with cars, shipping lanes can get crowded with ships. These crowded areas are called choke points. Choke points are narrow routes that ships must pass through to get to other areas. The Suez Canal, Panama Canal, Strait of Malacca, Strait of Hormuz, and Strait of Gibraltar are all examples of important choke points around the world.

Choke points often have great strategic importance. In times of war, they can be important for moving ships and troops to other parts of the world. During peacetime, ships must pass through them to transport goods to world markets.

The Suez Canal in Egypt is an important choke point in the world's shipping lanes. It is also a very strategic waterway. Opened in 1869, the Suez Canal connects the Mediterranean Sea with the Red Sea. This shortens the journey for ships sailing between Europe and Asia by about 6,000 miles (9,654 km).

The history of the Suez Canal is closely tied to the growth of world trade and ocean shipping. Before World War II, the canal linked Great Britain to its colonies in East Africa, Asia, and the Pacific. Beginning in the 1930s, the development of the oil industry in the Persian Gulf made the canal even more important. It became a major shipping route for tankers carrying oil to Europe and North America.

The Suez Canal was built mainly to serve international trade. However, it has also been used by military ships. In 1905 Russian navy ships used the canal during the Russo-Japanese War. In the 1930s Italy moved troops through the canal to eastern Africa before invading Ethiopia.

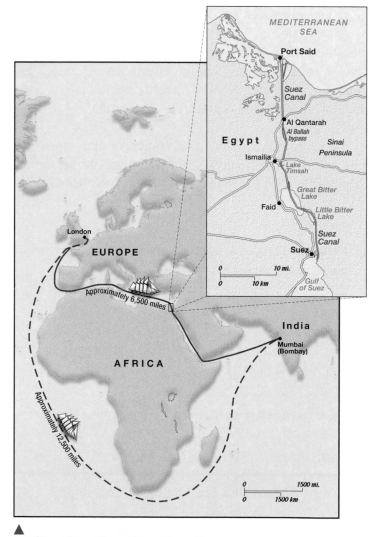

▲ A ship traveling from London to Mumbai has a much shorter journey if it travels through the Suez Canal.

Interpreting the Map **How do you think the Suez Canal affected trade between Great Britain and India?**

An important test for the Suez Canal involved relations between Egypt and Israel. In the 1950s Egypt refused to allow ships from Israel to use the canal. Even ships from countries that traded with Israel were prevented from using it. In 1956–57 the Suez Canal was closed after Israeli and Egyptian forces began fighting. It was closed again during 1967–75 after more fighting between the two countries. For several years the canal was the front line between the Israeli and Egyptian armies. While it was closed, ships were forced to make the much longer journey around Africa. This created a demand for larger ships that could carry more cargo.

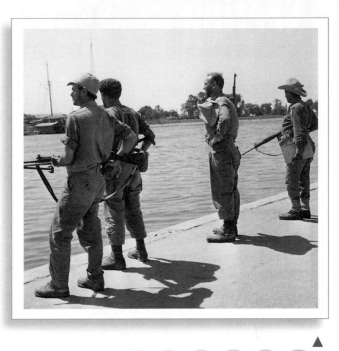

Israeli troops look across the Suez Canal in 1967.

A French newspaper shows a warship crossing the Suez Canal in 1904 (left). Today, the canal is an important shipping lane (below).

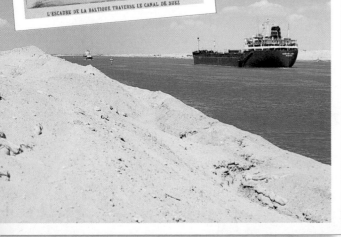

Today, the Suez Canal is one of the busiest shipping lanes in the world. Each day, about 55 ships make the 15-hour journey through the canal. Ships heading north carry oil, coal, metals, and other goods to Europe and North America. Ships heading south carry wheat, corn, barley, manufactured goods, and other products to Asia.

Many modern ocean ships are now too big to use the Suez Canal. As a result, the canal's economic importance has declined in recent years. However, the Suez Canal is still an important waterway to many countries.

Understanding What You Read

1. What are choke points? Why are they important?

2. How has the strategic importance of the Suez Canal changed since the 1930s?

Section 3 — Egypt Today

Read to Discover

1. What are the people and cities of Egypt like today?

2. What are Egypt's important economic activities?

3. What challenges does Egypt face today?

WHY IT MATTERS

An ongoing debate in Egypt is the place of Islam in society and the government. Use **CNN fyi.com** or other **current events** sources to find out how Egyptians view this debate. Record your findings in your journal.

Define

fellahin

Locate

Egypt

A gold mask from the tomb of King Tutankhamen

People and Cities

Egypt is North Africa's most populous country. More than 67 million people live there.

Rural Egypt More than half of all Egyptians live in small villages and other rural areas. Most rural Egyptians are farmers called **fellahin** (fel-uh-HEEN). They own very small plots of land. Most fellahin also work large farms owned by powerful families. Many also depend on money sent home by family members working abroad. Many Egyptians work in Europe or oil-rich countries in Southwest Asia.

Cities Egypt's capital and largest city is Cairo. More than 10 million people live there. Millions more live in surrounding cities.

A muezzin (moo-E-zuhn) calls Muslims to prayer in Cairo. A muezzin often makes his calls from the door or the minaret, or tower, of a mosque. His calls—or recordings played through speakers— can be heard throughout Islamic communities five times daily.

Tourist ships sit on the Nile River in Luxor. Tourists visit the ruins of a beautiful temple built there more than 2,300 years ago. These and other historical sites make tourism an important part of Egypt's economy.

Cairo was founded more than 1,000 years ago along the Nile. Its location at the southern end of the delta helped it grow. The city lies along old trading routes between Asia and Europe. Later it was connected by railroad to Mediterranean ports and the Suez Canal.

Today Cairo is a mixture of modern buildings and small, mud-brick houses. People continue to move there from rural areas. Many live in makeshift housing. Traffic and pollution are serious problems.

Alexandria has more than 4 million people. It is located in the Nile Delta along the Mediterranean coast. The city is a major seaport and home to many industries.

✔ **READING CHECK:** *Places and Regions* What are Egypt's people and cities like today?

Our Amazing Planet

Fish is an important food for people living along the Nile. One fish, the giant Nile perch, can grow to a weight of 300 pounds (136 kg).

Economy

To provide for its growing population, Egypt is working to expand its industries. Textiles, tourism, and oil are three of the most important industries. The Suez Canal is another source of income. Ships pay tolls to pass through it. Ships use the canal to avoid long trips around southern Africa. This makes the canal one of the world's busiest waterways.

About 40 percent of Egyptian workers are farmers. A warm, sunny climate and water for irrigation make the Nile Delta ideal for growing cotton. Farmlands along the Nile River are used for growing vegetables, grain, and fruit.

✔ **READING CHECK:** *Places and Regions* How does the Suez Canal affect Egypt's economy?

Egypt

Country	Population/ Growth Rate	Life Expectancy	Literacy Rate	Per Capita GDP
Egypt	69,536,644 1.7%	62, male 66, female	51%	$3,600
United States	281,421,906 0.9%	74, male 80, female	97%	$36,200

Sources: Central Intelligence Agency, *The World Factbook 2001;* U.S. Census Bureau

Interpreting the Chart How does the growth rate of Egypt compare to that of the United States?

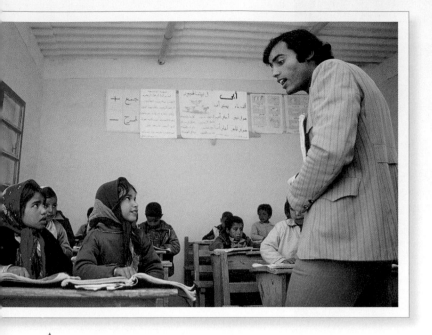

These Bedouin students attend a modern school in the Sinai. Improving education for all Egyptians is an important challenge facing the country. Among North African countries, only Morocco has a lower literacy rate than Egypt.

Challenges

Egypt faces important challenges today. For example, the country's farmland is limited to the Nile River valley and delta. To keep the land productive, farmers must use more and more fertilizer. This can be expensive. In addition, overwatering has been a problem. It has brought to the surface salts that are harmful to crops. These problems and a rapidly growing population have forced Egypt to import much of its food.

In addition, Egyptians are divided over their country's role in the world. Many want their country to remain a leader among Arab countries. However, others want their government to focus more on improving life for Egyptians at home.

Many Egyptians live in severe poverty. Many do not have clean water for cooking or washing. The spread of disease in crowded cities is also a problem. In addition, about half of Egyptians cannot read and write. Still, Egypt's government has made progress. Today Egyptians live longer and are much healthier than 50 years ago.

Another challenge facing Egyptians is the debate over the role of Islam in the country. Some Muslims want to shape the country's government and society along Islamic principles. However, some Egyptians worry that such a change would mean fewer personal freedoms. Some supporters of an Islamic government have turned to violence to advance their cause. Attacks on tourists in the 1990s were particularly worrisome. A loss of tourism would hurt Egypt's economy.

✓ **READING CHECK:** (*Places and Regions*) What are some of the challenges Egypt faces today?

go.hrw.com **Homework Practice Online**
Keyword: SG3 HP22

Section Review 3

Define and explain: fellahin

Working with Sketch Maps On the map you drew in Section 2, label Egypt. In a box in the margin, identify the capital of Egypt.

Reading for the Main Idea

1. (*Human Systems*) What is the relationship between religion and culture in Egypt today?

2. (*Places and Regions*) What industries and crops are important to Egypt's economy?

Critical Thinking

3. Analyzing Information Why do so many Egyptians live along the Nile and in the Nile Delta?

4. Finding the Main Idea How has Cairo's location shaped its development?

Organizing What You Know

5. Summarizing Copy the following graphic organizer. Use it to describe some of the challenges facing Egypt today.

Challenges

Read to Discover

1. What are the region's people and cities like today?
2. What are the countries' important economic activities?
3. What challenges do the countries face today?

Define

Casbah
souks
free port
dictator

Locate

Libya
Tunisia
Algeria
Morocco
Tripoli
Benghazi

Algiers
Casablanca
Rabat
Tunis
Strait of Gibraltar

WHY IT MATTERS

Libya has been ruled by a dictator. Use **CNNfyi.com** or other **current events** sources to find out more about Libya's dictatorship. Record your findings in your journal.

Moroccan pottery

People and Cities

Western Libya, Tunisia, Algeria, and Morocco are often called the Maghreb (MUH-gruhb). This Arabic word means "west" or "the direction of the setting sun." Most of the Maghreb is covered by the Sahara. There you will find sandy plains and rocky uplands. Cities and farmland are located in narrow coastal strips of land. These strips lie between the Atlantic and Mediterranean coasts in the north and the Sahara and Atlas Mountains farther inland.

Libya is almost completely desert. Fertile land is limited to small areas along the coast. Cities and most of the population are found in those coastal areas. Libya is the most urbanized country in the region. More than 85 percent of Libya's more than 5 million people live in cities. The largest cities are Benghazi and the capital, Tripoli.

Algiers is a large city and is Algeria's capital. The central part of Algiers is a maze of winding alleys and tall walls. This old district is called the **Casbah**. The Casbah is basically an old fortress. **Souks**, or marketplaces, are found there today. The centers of other North African cities also have Casbahs.

Other large cities include Casablanca and Rabat in Morocco and Tunis in Tunisia. Another Moroccan city, Tangier, overlooks the Strait of Gibraltar. This beautiful city was once a Spanish territory. Today tourists can take a quick ferry ride from Spain across the strait to Tangier, a **free port**. A free port is a city in which almost no taxes are placed on goods sold there.

✔ **READING CHECK:** *Places and Regions* What geographic factors explain the region's population patterns?

Urbanization in North Africa

- Algeria 56%
- Morocco 45%
- Libya 86%
- Egypt 53%
- Tunisia 63%
- United States 76%

Source: *The World Almanac and Book of Facts 2001*
Percentages of population living in urban areas

Interpreting the Chart Which country is the most urbanized?

Libya, Tunisia, Algeria, and Morocco

Country	Population/ Growth Rate	Life Expectancy	Literacy Rate	Per Capita GDP
Algeria	31,736,053 1.7%	69, male 71, female	62%	$5,500
Libya	5,240,599 2.4%	74, male 78, female	76%	$8,900
Morocco	30,645,305 1.7%	67, male 72, female	44%	$3,500
Tunisia	9,705,102 1.7%	72, male 76, female	67%	$6,500
United States	281,421,906 0.9%	74, male 80, female	97%	$36,200

Sources: Central Intelligence Agency, *The World Factbook 2001;* U.S. Census Bureau

Interpreting the Chart According to the data in the chart, which country is the least economically developed?

Marrakech (muh-RAH-kish) is a popular tourist resort in central Morocco. It sits in the foothills of the Atlas Mountains.

Economy

Oil, mining, and tourism are important industries in these countries. Oil is the most important resource, particularly in Libya and Algeria. Money from oil pays for schools, health care, other social programs, and military equipment. The region's countries also have large deposits of natural gas, iron ore, and lead.

Morocco is the only North African country with little oil. However, the country is an important producer and exporter of fertilizer.

About 20 percent of the workers in Libya, Tunisia, and Algeria are farmers. In Morocco farmers make up about half of the labor force. North Africa's farmers grow and export wheat, other grains, olives, fruits, and nuts. However, the region's desert climate and poor soils limit farming, particularly in Libya. Libya imports most of its food.

The Maghreb countries have close economic relationships with European countries. This is partly because of old colonial ties between North Africa and Europe. In addition, European countries are located nearby, lying just across the Mediterranean Sea. Formal agreements between North African countries and the European Union (EU) also have helped trade. Today about 80 percent of Tunisia's trade is with EU countries. The largest trade partners of Algeria, Libya, and Morocco are also EU members. Many European tourists visit North Africa.

✓ **READING CHECK:** *Places and Regions* How does the oil industry affect Libya's and Algeria's schools, health care, and other social programs?

Challenges

The countries of the Maghreb have made much progress in health and education. However, important challenges remain. Among these challenges is the need for more economic freedom. Each of these countries has had elements of a command economy, in which government owns and operates industry. However, in recent years the region's governments have moved to loosen that control. They have sold some government-owned businesses. They have also taken other steps to help private industry grow.

Political freedoms are limited for many North Africans. Many have little say in their governments. For example, since 1969 Libya has been ruled by a **dictator**, Mu'ammar al-Gadhafi. A dictator is someone who rules a country with complete power. Gadhafi has supported bombing, kidnapping, and other acts of violence against Israel and Israel's supporters. As a result, countries have limited their economic relationships with Libya.

As in Egypt, another challenge is conflict over the role of Islam in society. For example, in Algeria some groups want a government based on Islamic principles and laws. In 1992 the government canceled elections that many believed would be won by Islamic groups. Violence between Algeria's government and some Islamic groups has claimed thousands of lives since then.

These Islamic students at a religious school in Libya are reciting verses from the Qur'an. Religious education is important in this mostly Islamic region.

✔ **READING CHECK:** (*Places and Regions*) What are some of the challenges the region's countries face today?

Section Review 4

Define and explain: Casbah, souks, free port, dictator

Working with Sketch Maps On the map you created in Section 3, label Libya, Tunisia, Algeria, Morocco, Tripoli, Benghazi, Algiers, Casablanca, Rabat, Tunis, and the Strait of Gibraltar. In a box in the margin, identify the national capitals of the region's countries.

Reading for the Main Idea

1. (*Places and Regions*) What are the old, central districts of many North African cities like?

2. (*Places and Regions*) What type of economy have these nations had, and how is this changing?

go.hrw.com **Homework Practice Online**
Keyword: SG3 HP22

Critical Thinking

3. **Finding the Main Idea** Where are the region's farms and most of its people found today? Why?

4. **Analyzing Information** How are the political rights of North Africans different from those of people in the United States?

Organizing What You Know

5. **Summarizing** Copy the following graphic organizer. Use it to list industries, resources, farm products, and trade partners of the Maghreb countries.

Industries	
Resources	
Farm products	
Trade partners	

CHAPTER 22 Reviewing What You Know

Building Vocabulary

On a separate sheet of paper, write sentences to define each of the following words.

1. ergs
2. regs
3. depressions
4. silt
5. pharaohs
6. hieroglyphs
7. Bedouins
8. fellahin
9. Casbah
10. souks
11. free port
12. dictator

Reviewing the Main Ideas

1. (Places and Regions) How does geography affect settlement patterns in North Africa?
2. (Places and Regions) What are North Africa's main climates?
3. (Places and Regions) What are some important challenges facing Egypt today?
4. (Places and Regions) What are the most important industries in North Africa?
5. (Places and Regions) Which is the most urbanized country in North Africa?

Understanding Environment and Society

Farming and Fertilizer
Egyptian farmers must use large amounts of fertilizer. Create a presentation about the use of fertilizer. Consider the following:
- The kinds of chemicals, minerals, and other materials most commonly used as fertilizers.
- How fertilizers work.
- The positive and negative effects of using fertilizer.

Thinking Critically

1. **Finding the Main Idea** How do you think the Sahara has influenced settlement in the region?
2. **Finding the Main Idea** Why are most of North Africa's cities and population located in coastal areas?
3. **Analyzing Information** Why is the Suez Canal important to world trade?
4. **Finding the Main Idea** In what way has Islam influenced politics in North Africa?
5. **Making Generalizations and Predictions** Based on what you have read, what kinds of challenges do you think North Africans will face in coming decades? Explain your answer.

Map ACTIVITY

On a separate sheet of paper, match the letters on the map with their correct labels.

Sinai Peninsula	Western Sahara
Ahaggar	Tripoli
Mountains	Algiers
Atlas Mountains	Casablanca
Nile Delta	Strait of
Cairo	Gibraltar

Mental Mapping Skills ACTIVITY

On a separate sheet of paper, draw a freehand map of North Africa. Make a key for your map and label the following:

Algeria	Red Sea
Egypt	Sahara
Libya	Tunisia
Morocco	

WRITING ACTIVITY

Imagine that you are a Bedouin teenager in the Sahara. Write a one-paragraph journal entry about a typical day in your life. How do you cope with the desert heat? What is it like living without a permanent home? What religion do you practice? What do you eat? Use the library and other resources to help you. Be sure to use standard grammar, spelling, sentence structure, and punctuation.

Alternative Assessment

Portfolio ACTIVITY

Learning About Your Local Geography

Research Project Use an almanac to identify your state's largest cities. Sketch a map of your state. Mark the three largest cities and major physical features such as rivers, mountains, and coastlines.

internet connect

Internet Activity: go.hrw.com
KEYWORD: SG3 GT22

Choose a topic to explore about North Africa:
- Journey through the Sahara.
- Examine the rich history of North Africa.
- Practice using Arabic calligraphy.

CHAPTER 23

West Africa

We move south now to West Africa. The land becomes much wetter as we move southward. Before we continue, we meet Ousseina from Niger.

Ina kwanna! (Good morning!) My name is Ousseina, and I am 11. I have an identical twin sister whose name is Hassana. I live in Niamey, the capital of Niger, with my sister, our grandmother, our parents, and many aunts and uncles. We have a large compound of many one- or two-room houses around a common courtyard. After breakfast, my sister and I go from door to door, greeting all the elders in our compound.

We have to walk many miles to school, but we meet all our friends along the way. Some of our friends speak Hausa like us. Others speak a different language of Niger. In the afternoon, we go home to sleep because it is so hot—more than 110°F (43°C)! Late in the afternoon we return to school for more classes.

After school, we help grandma pound spices for dinner, sweep the room, and wash the dishes. At bedtime, grandma tells us stories and sings.

Ni Ousseina ce. Gidana yana Nijar.

Translation: I am Ousseina. My home is in Niger.

Section 1 · Physical Geography

Read to Discover

1. What landforms and climates are found in West Africa?
2. Why is the Niger River important to the region?
3. What resources does West Africa have?

Define

zonal
Sahel
harmattan
tsetse fly
bauxite

Locate

Sahara
Niger River

Gulf of Guinea

Colorful Nigerian tapestry

WHY IT MATTERS

West African countries have often faced problems in managing their natural resources. Use CNNfyi.com or other **current events** sources to find problems faced by countries in the region regarding resources and the environment. Record your findings in your journal.

West Africa: Physical-Political

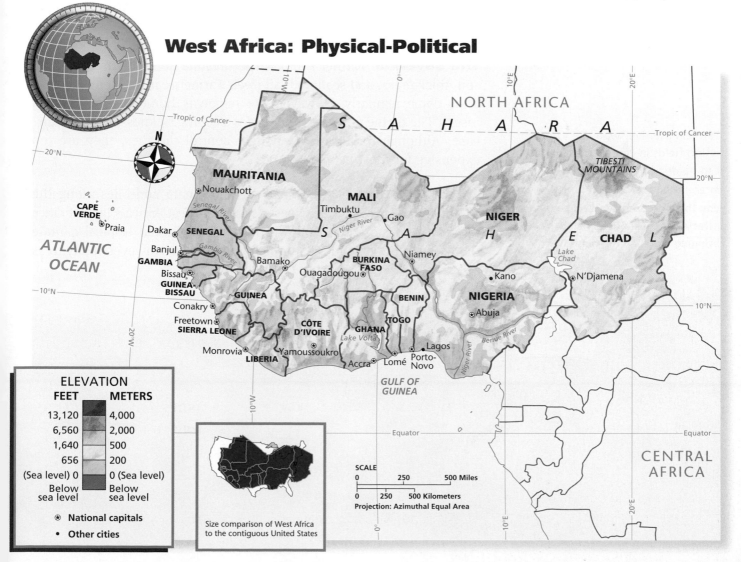

ELEVATION

FEET	METERS
13,120	4,000
6,560	2,000
1,640	500
656	200
(Sea level) 0	0 (Sea level)
Below sea level	Below sea level

⊛ National capitals
• Other cities

SCALE
0   250   500 Miles
0   250   500 Kilometers
Projection: Azimuthal Equal Area

Size comparison of West Africa to the contiguous United States

West Africa • 491

internet connect

GO TO: go.hrw.com
KEYWORD: SG3 CH23
FOR: Web sites about
West Africa

BUILD on WHAT You Know

Do you remember what you learned about desertification? See Chapter 4 to review.

Farmers use river water to irrigate onion fields in central Mali. Farming can be difficult in the dry Sahel.
Interpreting the Visual Record How do you think economic factors have affected the use of technology in bringing water to the fields?

Landforms and Climate

West Africa is largely a region of plains. There are low mountains in the southwest and high mountains in the northeast. Four major climate types stretch from east to west in bands or zones. Therefore, geographers say the region's climates are **zonal**.

The Sahara The northernmost parts of the region lie within the Sahara, the first climate zone. The Sahara is the world's largest desert. It stretches across northern Africa from the Atlantic Ocean to the Red Sea. Large areas of this dry climate zone have few or no people.

The Sahel South of the Sahara is a region of dry grasslands called the **Sahel** (sah-HEL). This second climate zone has a steppe climate. Rainfall varies greatly from year to year. In some years it never rains. During winter a dry, dusty wind called the **harmattan** (hahr-muh-TAN) blows south from the Sahara.

During the late 1960s a drought began in the Sahel. Crops failed for several years, and there was not enough grass for the herds. Animals overgrazed the land, and people cut the few large trees for firewood. Wind blew away fertile soil, and the Sahara expanded southward. Without plants for food, many animals and people died. Recent years have been rainier, and life has improved.

The Savanna Farther south is the savanna zone. It contains good soil, thick grass, and scattered tall trees. Farmers can do well when the rains come regularly. However, the region is home to a dangerous insect. The **tsetse** (TSET-see) **fly** carries sleeping sickness, a deadly disease. Although insecticides can help control the flies, they are too expensive for most people to buy.

The Coast and Forest The fourth climate zone lies along the Atlantic and Gulf of Guinea coasts. Many of West Africa's largest cities lie in this coastal zone. You will find a wet, humid tropical climate there. Plentiful rain supports tropical rain forests. However, many trees

Algeria
Mauritania
Mali
Niger
Guinea
Burkina Faso
Côte d'Ivoire

have been cut to make room for growing populations. As a result, environmental damage is a serious problem.

✓ **READING CHECK:** ⟨ *Places and Regions* ⟩ What are the region's landforms and climate zones?

The Niger River

The most important river in West Africa is the Niger (NY-juhr). The Niger River starts in low mountains just 150 miles (241 km) from the Atlantic Ocean. It flows eastward and southward for 2,600 miles (4,183 km) and empties into the Gulf of Guinea.

The Niger brings life-giving water to West Africa. In the Sahel it divides into a network of channels, swamps, and lakes. This network is known as the inland delta. The Niger's true delta on the Gulf of Guinea is very wide. Half of Nigeria's coastline consists of the delta.

✓ **READING CHECK:** ⟨ *Environment and Society* ⟩ Why is the Niger River important to West Africa?

▲

The hippopotamus is just one of the many animal species living in the Niger region. Hippopotamuses are good swimmers and can stay underwater for as long as six minutes.

Resources

West Africa's mineral riches include diamonds, gold, iron ore, manganese, and **bauxite**. Bauxite is the main source of aluminum. Nigeria is a major exporter of oil. In fact, oil and related products make up about 95 percent of that country's exports.

✓ **READING CHECK:** ⟨ *Places and Regions* ⟩ What are some of the region's resources?

go.
hrw
.com **Homework Practice Online**
Keyword: SG3 HP23

Section Review 1

Define and explain: zonal, Sahel, harmattan, tsetse fly, bauxite

Working with Sketch Maps On a map of West Africa, label the following: Sahara, Sahel, Niger River, and Gulf of Guinea.

Reading for the Main Idea

1. ⟨ *Physical Systems* ⟩ What effect has drought had on West Africa's vegetation?

2. ⟨ *Places and Regions* ⟩ What natural resources are found in West Africa?

3. ⟨ *Places and Regions* ⟩ What is West Africa's most important river? Describe its two delta regions.

Critical Thinking

4. Making Generalizations and Predictions Where in the region would you expect to find the densest populations? Why?

Organizing What You Know

5. Summarizing Copy the following graphic organizer. Use it to list and describe the region's climate zones.

Zones	Characteristics

Section 2

History and Culture

Read to Discover

1. What great African kingdoms once ruled the region?
2. How did contact with Europeans affect West Africa?
3. What challenges do the region's governments face?
4. What are some features of West African culture?

Define

archaeology
oral history
animism

Locate

Timbuktu

Bronze figure of a hunter, lower Niger area

WHY IT MATTERS

Many West African countries struggled to win their independence from colonial powers and are still struggling to maintain stable governments. Use **CNNfyi.com** or other **current events** sources to find examples of political events in these countries. Record your findings in your journal.

West Africa's History

Much of what we know about West Africa's early history is based on **archaeology**. Archaeology is the study of the remains and ruins of past cultures. **Oral history**—spoken information passed down from person to person through generations—offers other clues.

Great Kingdoms Ancient artifacts suggest that the earliest trading towns developed in the Niger's inland delta. Traders brought dates and salt from the desert. People from the Sahel sold animals and hides. Other trade goods were grains, fish, kola and other tropical nuts, and metals, such as gold. (Much later, kola nuts provided the flavor for cola drinks.) This trade helped African kingdoms grow. One of the earliest West African kingdoms, Ghana (GAH-nuh), had become rich and powerful by about A.D. 800.

These early West African cliff paintings illustrate features from a ceremonial ritual for young people.

Interpreting the Visual Record What kinds of images do you see on this cliff wall?

Some 200 years later, North African merchants began crossing the Sahara to trade in Ghana. These merchants introduced Islam to West Africa. In time, Islam became the main religion practiced in the Sahel.

Later Ghana fell to Muslim warriors from Morocco. The Muslim empire of Mali (MAH-lee) replaced the kingdom of Ghana. Mali stretched from the Niger's inland delta to the Atlantic coast. Mansa Mūsā was king of Mali during the early 1300s. Famous for his wealth and wise rule, Mansa Mūsā supported artists, poets, and scholars.

The kingdom of Songhay (SAWNG-hy) came to power as Mali declined. With a university, mosques, and more than 100 schools, the Songhay city of Timbuktu was a cultural center. By about 1600, however, Moroccan invasions had weakened the kingdom.

Forested areas south of the Sahel were also home to great civilizations. In what is now Nigeria, wealthy kings were buried with brass sculptures and other treasures.

✓ **READING CHECK:** (*Human Systems*) What are some of the great African kingdoms that once ruled the region?

The Slave Trade During the 1440s Portuguese explorers began sailing along the west coast of Africa. The Europeans called it the Gold Coast for the gold they bought there. Once they could buy gold where it was mined, the Europeans stopped buying it from Arab traders. As a result, the trans-Sahara trade and the great trade cities faded.

For a while, both Europeans and Africans profited from trade with each other. However, by the 1600s the demand for labor in Europe's American colonies changed everything. European traders met this demand by selling enslaved Africans to colonists. The slave trade was very profitable for these traders.

The slave trade had devastating effects on West African communities. Families were broken up when members were kidnapped and enslaved. Many Africans died on the voyage to the Americas. Most who survived were sent to the West Indies or Brazil. The slave trade finally ended in the 1800s. By then millions of Africans had been forced from their homes.

Colonial Era and Independence In the late 1800s, many European countries competed for colonies in West Africa. France claimed most of the region's northwest. Britain, Germany, and Portugal seized the rest.

In all of West Africa only tiny Liberia remained independent. Americans had founded it in the 1820s as a home for freed slaves. Sierra Leone, a British colony, also became a home for freed slaves.

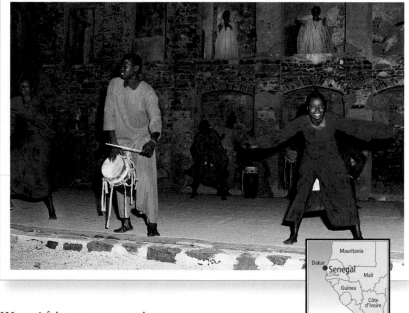

▲ There are many reminders of the slave trade and its effects on West Africans. Performers here reenact the treatment of enslaved Africans in an old slave house in Dakar, Senegal.

Interpreting the Visual Record How does this photograph show slavery's effect on creative expression?

Some Europeans moved to West Africa to run the colonies. They built roads, bridges, and railroads. Teachers and missionaries set up Christian churches and schools. After World War II, Africans increasingly worked for independence. Most of the colonies gained independence during the 1950s and 1960s. Portugal, the last European country to give up its West African colonies, did so in 1974.

✓ **READING CHECK:** *Human Systems* What impact did contact with Europeans have on West Africa?

Challenges

Independence brought a new set of challenges to the region. The borders that the Europeans had drawn ignored human geography. Sometimes borders separated members of one ethnic group. Other borders grouped together peoples that did not get along. As a result, many West Africans were more loyal to their ethnic groups than to their new countries. In addition, too few people had been trained to run the new governments. Dictators took control in many countries. Civil wars and military rulers still trouble the region. Some countries have made progress, however. For example, in 1996 Chad created its first democratic constitution.

The governments of West African countries have several difficult problems in common. Birthrates are high. As a result, more and more people must make a living from the small amount of fertile land. In addition, many people are moving to already crowded cities even though urban jobs are few. These countries must also find ways to educate more of their people. Many families cannot afford to send their children to school.

✓ **READING CHECK:** *Places and Regions* What are three challenges the region faces?

A roadside market provides a glimpse of crowded Lagos, Nigeria's largest city. More than 10 million people live in and around Lagos. Overcrowded cities are a problem throughout much of the region.

CONNECTING TO Literature

Marriage Is a Private Affair
by Chinua Achebe

Chinua Achebe was born in an Ibo village in Nigeria in 1930. Many of his writings explore the changes colonialism brought to Africa. They also look at the conflict between old and new ways. In this story, Achebe looks at different views a father and son have about marriage.

A Nigerian church carving

"Father," began Nnaemeka suddenly, "I have come to ask for forgiveness."

"Forgiveness? For what, my son?" he asked in amazement.

"It's about this marriage question."

"Which marriage question?"

"I can't—we must—I mean it is impossible for me to marry Nweke's daughter."

"Impossible? Why?" asked his father.

"I don't love her."

"Nobody said you did. Why should you?" he asked.

"Marriage today is different . . ."

"Look here, my son," interrupted his father, "nothing is different. What one looks for in a wife are a good character and a Christian background."

Nnaemeka saw there was no hope along the present line of argument.

"Moreover," he said. "I am engaged to marry another girl who has all of Ugoye's good qualities, and who . . ."

His father did not believe his ears. "What did you say?" he asked slowly and disconcertingly[1]. . . .

"Whose daughter is she, anyway?"

"She is Nene Atang."

"What!" All the mildness was gone again. "Did you say Neneataga, what does that mean?"

"Nene Atang from Calabar. She is the only girl I can marry." This was a very rash reply and Nnaemeka expected the storm to burst.

Analyzing Primary Sources

1. What universal theme does the passage illustrate?
2. Why do you think the father and son disagree about marriage?

Vocabulary [1]disconcertingly: disturbingly

These homes in Burkina Faso are made of a mixture of mud, water, and cow dung. Trees are scarce in the Sahel and savanna zones. As a result, there is little wood for construction. Women are responsible for painting and decorating the walls of the homes.

Interpreting the Visual Record
For what purpose are the roofs apparently used?

Culture

Hundreds of ethnic groups exist in West Africa today. Hundreds of languages are spoken in the region. In some areas, using the colonial languages of French or English helps people from different groups communicate. West African languages that many people share, such as Fula and Hausa, also aid communication.

Religion The traditional religions of West Africa have often been forms of **animism**. Animism is the belief that bodies of water, animals, trees, and other natural objects have spirits. Animists also honor the memories of ancestors. In some isolated areas animism still forms the basis of most religious practices. Today most people of the Sahel practice Islam. Farther south live many Christians.

Clothing and Homes Some West Africans, particularly in cities, wear Western-style clothing. Others wear traditional robes, pants, blouses, and skirts. These are often made from colorful patterned cotton fabric. Because of the warm climate, most clothing is loose and flowing. Many women wear beautiful folded and wrapped headdresses. In the desert men often wear turbans. Both men and women may use veils to protect their faces from blowing sand.

Rural homes are small and simple. Many homes in the Sahel and savanna zones are circular. Straw or tin roofs sit atop mud, mud-brick, or straw huts. However, in cities you will find some modern buildings.

✔ **READING CHECK:** (*Human Systems*) What are some features of West African culture?

Section Review 2

Define and explain: archaeology, oral history, animism

Working with Sketch Maps On the map you created in Section 1, label Timbuktu. What made Timbuktu an important Songhay city?

Reading for the Main Idea

1. (*Human Systems*) How did European contact affect West Africa's people?

2. (*Human Systems*) Where in West Africa are Islam and Christianity practiced?

Homework Practice Online
Keyword: SG3 HP23

Critical Thinking

3. **Drawing Inferences and Conclusions** How might shared histories and challenges lead to more cooperation among the region's countries?

4. **Drawing Inferences and Conclusions** Why do you think mud bricks are used in West Africa?

Organizing What You Know

5. **Summarizing** Use the following graphic organizer to summarize challenges facing West Africa.

West Africa

Section 3 The Sahel Countries

Read to Discover

1. What are Mauritania, Mali, and Niger like today?
2. What challenges do Chad and Burkina Faso face?

Define

millet
sorghum
malaria
staple

Locate

Nouakchott
Senegal River
Gao
Tibesti Mountains
Lake Chad
Ouagadougou

WHY IT MATTERS

The shrinking of Lake Chad over the last several decades has been a major concern for the people of Chad. Many blame a changing environment and poor managing of the lake's resources. Use CNNfyi.com or other **current events** sources to find information about Lake Chad. Record the findings in your journal.

Carved mask from Mauritania

Mauritania, Mali, and Niger

Most of the people in these three large countries are Muslim. Mauritania, in fact, has laws based on Islam. These countries are also former French colonies, and French influence remains. In Mali and Niger, the official language is French. However, the people there speak more than 60 different local languages.

Today, drought and the expanding desert make feeding the people in these countries difficult. In the Sahel nomads depend on their herds of cattle, goats, and camels. In the savanna regions farmers grow **millet** and **sorghum**. These grain crops can usually survive drought.

Mauritania Many Mauritanians are Moors, people of mixed Arab and Berber origin. They speak Arabic. In the past, Moors enslaved some of the black Africans. Today, tension between the two groups continues.

▶

Women carry goods for sale in a market in central Mali. Much of Mali's economic activity takes place in the Niger River's inland delta.
Interpreting the Visual Record Why is Mali's economic activity centered around the inland delta?

Mud and other local materials were used to build many mosques in the Sahel. This mosque is located in Djenné [je-NAY], Mali. The majority of people living in the Sahel are Muslims.

The Tuareg (TWAH-reg) people of the Sahara and Sahel pound powdered blue dye into their flowing robes. They do this rather than dip the fabric in precious water. The blue powder wears off onto the skin, where it may help hold in moisture.

The Sahel Countries

COUNTRY	POPULATION/ GROWTH RATE	LIFE EXPECTANCY	LITERACY RATE	PER CAPITA GDP
Burkina Faso	12,272,289 2.7%	46, male 47, female	19%	$1,000
Chad	8,707,078 3.3%	49, male 53, female	48%	$1,000
Mali	11,008,518 3%	46, male 48, female	31%	$850
Mauritania	2,747,312 2.9%	49, male 53, female	47%	$2,000
Niger	10,355,156 2.7%	42, male 41, female	14%	$1,000
United States	281,421,906 0.9%	74, male 80, female	97%	$36,200

Sources: Central Intelligence Agency, *The World Factbook 2001;* U.S. Census Bureau

Interpreting the Chart Based on the numbers in the chart, which two countries in the region are the least economically developed?

Most Mauritanians were once nomadic herders. Today, the expanding Sahara has crowded more than half of the nomads into the cities. Just 40 years ago, Nouakchott (nooh-AHK-shaht), Mauritania's capital, was a small village. More than 700,000 people live there now. About half of the population lives in shacks at the city's edges.

Throughout the country, people are very poor. Only in the far south, near the Senegal River, can farmers raise crops. Fishing in the Atlantic Ocean is another source of income.

Mali To the east of Mauritania lies landlocked Mali. The Sahara covers much of northern Mali. In the south lies a wetter farming region. About 80 percent of Mali's people fish or farm along the Niger River. Cotton is the country's main export. Timbuktu and Gao (GOW), ancient trading cities, continue to attract tourists.

Health conditions in Mali are poor. **Malaria**, a disease spread by mosquitoes, is a major cause of death among children.

Niger The Niger River flows through just the southwestern corner of landlocked Niger. Only about 3 percent of Niger's land is good for farming. All of the country's farmland lies along the Niger River and near the Nigerian border. Much of the rest of Niger lies within the Sahara. Farmers raise cotton, peanuts, beans, peas, and rice. Millet and sorghum are two of the region's **staple**, or main, food crops. The grains are cooked like oatmeal. Nomads in the desert region depend on the dairy products they get from their herds for food.

✔ **READING CHECK:** *Places and Regions* What is it like to live in Mauritania, Mali, and Niger?

Chad and Burkina Faso

Drought has also affected the former French colonies of Chad and Burkina Faso (boohr-KEE-nuh FAH-soh). These countries are among the world's poorest and least developed. Most people farm or raise cattle.

Chad Chad is located in the center of Africa. The Tibesti Mountains in northern Chad rise above the Sahara. Lake Chad is in the south. Not long ago, the lake had a healthy fishing industry. It even supplied water to several other countries. However, drought has evaporated much of the lake's water. At one time, Lake Chad had shrunk to just one third its size in 1950.

The future may be better for Chad. A civil war ended in the 1990s. Also, oil reserves now being explored may help the economy.

Burkina Faso This country's name means "land of the honest people." Most of its people follow traditional religions. The country has thin soil and few mineral resources. Few trees remain in or near the capital, Ouagadougou (wah-gah-DOO-goo). They have been cut for firewood and building material. Jobs in the city are also scarce. To support their families many young men work in other countries. However, foreign aid and investment are starting to help the economy.

✓ **READING CHECK:** *Places and Regions* What are the challenges facing Chad and Burkina Faso?

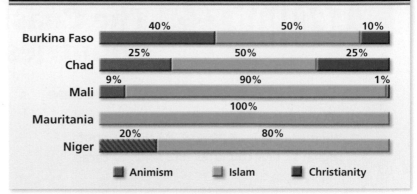

Major Religions of the Sahel Countries

Burkina Faso	40%	50%	10%
Chad	25%	50%	25%
Mali	9%	90%	1%
Mauritania		100%	
Niger	20%	80%	

■ Animism   ■ Islam   ■ Christianity

Source: Central Intelligence Agency, *World Factbook 2001*

▲

Although most people in the Sahel are Muslim, some practice forms of animism and Christianity.

Interpreting the Graph Which country's population is entirely Muslim? Which countries have significant numbers of Christians?

Section Review 3

Define and explain: millet, sorghum, malaria, staple

Working with Sketch Maps On the map you created in Section 2, draw the boundaries of Mauritania, Mali, Niger, Chad, and Burkina Faso. Then label Nouakchott, Senegal River, Gao, Tibesti Mountains, Lake Chad, and Ouagadougou. In a box in the margin, describe what has happened to Lake Chad in recent decades.

Reading for the Main Idea

1. *Places and Regions* Why has Nouakchott grown so rapidly?

2. *Places and Regions* Which European language is most common in the Sahel countries? Why?

go.hrw.com
Homework Practice Online
Keyword: SG3 HP23

Critical Thinking

3. Drawing Inferences and Conclusions How do the typical foods of Niger relate to the country's water resources?

4. Comparing What do Chad and Burkina Faso have in common with the other Sahel countries?

Organizing What You Know

5. Comparing Copy the following graphic organizer. Label each of the star's points with one of the Section 3 countries. In the center, list characteristics the countries share.

Section 4 The Coastal Countries

Read to Discover

1. What is life in Nigeria like today?
2. What economic challenges do the region's other countries face?

Define

secede
griots
cacao

Locate

Abuja   Monrovia
Lagos   Lake Volta
Dakar

WHY IT MATTERS

Nigeria has made a great deal of economic progress but there are problems that still hurt the nation's economy. Use CNN fyi.com or other **current events** sources to find examples of Nigerian social, economic, and political affairs. Record your findings in your journal.

A gold ornament from Ghana

▲

The faces of Nigeria are very young. About 45 percent of all Nigerians are younger than 15 years old. Only about 22 percent of all Americans are that young.

Interpreting the Visual Record
How is the clothing shown here similar to clothing worn by students in your school?

Nigeria

The largest country along West Africa's coast is Nigeria. With more than 113 million people, it has Africa's largest population.

Nigeria's People Nigeria was once an important British colony. Like many other colonies, Nigeria's borders included many ethnic groups. Today, a great variety of ethnic groups live in Nigeria. The Yoruba, Fula, Hausa, and Ibo are four of the largest ethnic groups. More than 200 languages are spoken there.

Nigeria's ethnic groups have not always gotten along. In the 1960s the Ibo tried to **secede**. That is, they tried to break away from Nigeria and form their own country. They called it Biafra (bee-AF-ruh). However, the Ibo lost the bloody war that followed.

Avoiding ethnic conflicts has continued to be an issue in Nigeria. It was important in choosing a site for a new Nigerian capital in the late 1970s. Leaders chose Abuja (ah-BOO-jah) because it was centrally located in an area of low population density.

Nigeria's Economy Nigeria has some of the continent's richest natural resources. Oil is the country's most important resource. Major oil fields are located in the Niger River delta and just off the coast. Oil accounts for 95 percent of the country's export earnings. Nigeria also

Oil drilling rigs like this one are common in areas of southern Nigeria. Oil accounts for about 20 percent of Nigeria's GDP. Oil revenues pay for about 65 percent of the government's budget.

The headdresses and patterned clothing worn by these women in Dakar are common in Senegal.

has good roads and railroads. Lagos (LAY-gahs), the former capital, is the country's largest city. The city is a busy seaport and trade center.

Although the country has rich resources, many Nigerians are poor. A major cause of the poverty there is a high birthrate. Nigeria can no longer feed its growing population without importing food. Another cause is the economy's dependence on oil. When prices are low, the whole country suffers. A third cause of Nigeria's poverty is a history of bad government. Corrupt government officials have used their positions to enrich themselves.

✓ **READING CHECK:** *Places and Regions* What are Nigeria's people and economy like today?

Other Coastal Countries

Several small West African countries lie along the Atlantic Ocean and the Gulf of Guinea. They are struggling to develop their economies.

Senegal and Gambia Senegal (se-ni-GAWL) wraps around Gambia (GAM-bee-uh). The odd border was created by French and British diplomats. Senegal, a former French colony, is larger and richer than Gambia, a former British colony. Dakar (dah-KAHR) is Senegal's capital and an important seaport and manufacturing center. Senegal and Gambia have many similarities. Peanuts are their most important crop. Common foods include chicken stew and fish with a peanut sauce. Tourism is growing slowly.

The Coastal Countries

COUNTRY	POPULATION/ GROWTH RATE	LIFE EXPECTANCY	LITERACY RATE	PER CAPITA GDP
Benin	6,590,782 / 3%	49, male 51, female	38%	$1,030
Cape Verde	405,163 / 0.9%	66, male 73, female	72%	$1,700
Côte d'Ivoire	16,393,221 / 2.5%	44, male 46, female	49%	$1,600
Gambia	1,411,205 / 3%	52, male 56, female	48%	$1,100
Ghana	19,894,014 / 1.8%	56, male 59, female	65%	$1,900
Guinea	7,613,870 / 2%	44, male 48, female	36%	$1,300
Guinea-Bissau	1,315,822 / 2.2%	47, male 52, female	54%	$850
Liberia	3,225,837 / 1.9%	50, male 53, female	38%	$1,100
Nigeria	126,635,626 / 2.6%	51, male 51, female	57%	$950
Senegal	10,284,929 / 2.9%	61, male 64, female	33%	$1,600
Sierra Leone	5,426,618 / 3.6%	43, male 49, female	31%	$510
Togo	5,153,088 / 2.6%	52, male 56, female	52%	$1,500
United States	281,421,906 / 0.9%	74, male 80, female	97%	$36,200

Sources: Central Intelligence Agency, *The World Factbook 2001;* U.S. Census Bureau

Interpreting the Chart Which country in the region has the highest life expectancy?

Many of the people speak a language called Wolof (WOH-lawf). **Griots** (GREE-ohz) are important to the Wolof-speakers and other West Africans. Griots are storytellers who pass on the oral histories of their tribes or peoples. Sometimes the griots combine music with their stories, which may take hours or days to tell. Wolof women wear complex hairstyles and gold jewelry.

Guinea, Guinea-Bissau, and Cape Verde

Guinea's main natural resource is a huge supply of bauxite. Its small neighbor to the east, Guinea-Bissau (GI-nee bi-SOW), has undeveloped mineral resources. Cape Verde (KAYP VUHRD) is a group of volcanic islands in the Atlantic. It is West Africa's only island country. Farming and fishing bring in the most money there.

Liberia and Sierra Leone

Liberia is Africa's oldest republic. Monrovia, Liberia's capital, was named for U.S. president James Monroe. The freed American slaves who settled Liberia and their descendants lived in coastal towns. They often clashed with the Africans already living there. Those Africans and their descendants were usually poorer and lived in rural areas. In the 1980s conflicts led to a bitter civil war. Sierra Leone (lee-OHN) has also experienced violent civil war. The fighting has wrecked the country's economy. Now, both Liberia and Sierra Leone must rebuild. They do have natural resources on which to build stronger economies. Liberia produces rubber and iron ore. Sierra Leone exports diamonds.

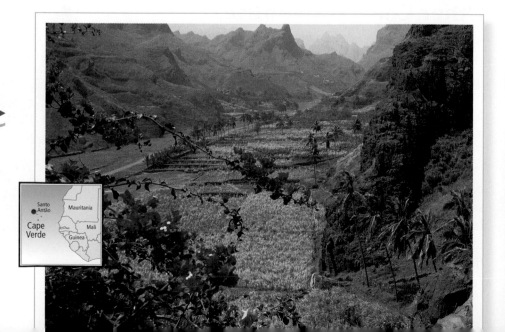

Flowers color the countryside on Santa Antão island in Cape Verde. However, farming can be difficult because droughts are common in the island country.

Interpreting the Visual Record What kinds of vegetation do you see on the island?

Ghana and Côte d'Ivoire The countries of Ghana and Côte d'Ivoire (koht-dee-VWAHR) have rich natural resources. Those resources may help them build strong economies. Ghana is named for the ancient kingdom, although the kingdom was northwest of the modern country. Ghana has one of the largest human-made lakes in the world—Lake Volta. Gold, timber, and **cacao** (kuh-KOW) are major products. Cocoa and chocolate are made from the seeds of the cacao tree. The tree came originally from Mexico and Central America.

Côte d'Ivoire is a former French colony whose name means "Ivory Coast" in English. It is a world leader in cacao and coffee exports. Côte d'Ivoire also boasts Africa's largest Christian church building.

Togo and Benin Unstable governments have troubled both Togo and Benin (buh-NEEN) since independence. Both have experienced periods of military rule. Their fragile economies have contributed to their unstable and sometimes violent politics. These long, narrow countries are poor. The people depend on farming and herding for income. Palm tree products, cacao, and coffee are the main crops in Togo and Benin.

✔ **READING CHECK:** *Places and Regions* What are characteristics of the economies of the coastal countries?

▲

A storyteller passes on a legend to children in Côte d'Ivoire. Oral storytellers use facial expressions, gestures, and even music and dance. Those techniques help draw listeners into a story.

Interpreting the Visual Record What role might oral storytellers like the one shown here play in a place where many people cannot read?

Section Review 4

Define and explain: secede, griots, cacao

Working with Sketch Maps On the map that you drew in Section 3, draw the boundaries for the coastal countries. Label Abuja, Lagos, Dakar, Monrovia, and Lake Volta. In a box in the margin, identify the largest and most populous country on West Africa's coast.

Reading for the Main Idea

1. *Places and Regions* How is Cape Verde different from the other countries in the region?

2. *Places and Regions* What is Nigeria's most important natural resource? Why?

Homework Practice Online
Keyword: SG3 HP23

Critical Thinking

3. Finding the Main Idea Why must Liberia and Sierra Leone rebuild their economies?

4. Analyzing Information Why was choosing a new capital important to Nigeria's future?

Organizing What You Know

5. Summarizing Copy the following graphic organizer. Use it to list three main causes of poverty in Nigeria today.

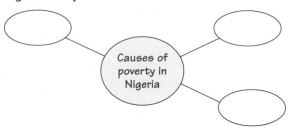

Causes of poverty in Nigeria

Building Vocabulary

On a separate sheet of paper, write sentences to define each of the following words.

1. zonal
2. Sahel
3. harmattan
4. tsetse fly
5. bauxite

6. archaeology
7. oral history
8. animism
9. millet
10. sorghum

11. malaria
12. staple
13. secede
14. griots
15. cacao

Reviewing the Main Ideas

1. *(Places and Regions)* What are the four climate zones of West Africa?

2. *(Places and Regions)* How do the Niger River's two delta regions differ?

3. *(Human Systems)* How did Islam come to West Africa?

4. *(Environment and Society)* How has drought affected the countries of the Sahel?

5. *(Environment and Society)* On what natural resource does Nigeria's economy depend?

Understanding Environment and Society

Health

Prepare a presentation, including a chart, graph, database, or model, about disease in West Africa. Consider the following:

- The parts of West Africa in which the tsetse fly, mosquitoes, and other dangerous insects are common.
- What diseases the insects spread.
- How these insects have affected human settlement and activities.

Then create a five-question quiz, with answers, about your presentation to challenge fellow students.

Thinking Critically

1. **Drawing Inferences and Conclusions** Why are many of West Africa's largest cities located in the coastal and forest zone?

2. **Finding the Main Idea** What role did trade play in the early West African kingdoms and later European colonies in the region?

3. **Analyzing Information** What are three cultural features of West Africa influenced by Europeans?

4. **Drawing Inferences and Conclusions** How have borders set by European colonial powers led to conflicts such as Nigeria's war in Biafra in the late 1960s?

5. **Contrasting** How is Liberia's history different from that of other West African countries?

Map ACTIVITY

On a separate sheet of paper, match the letters on the map with their correct labels.

Niger River	Tibesti
Gulf of Guinea	Mountains
Timbuktu	Lake Chad
Nouakchott	Abuja
Senegal River	Lagos
	Lake Volta

Mental Mapping Skills ACTIVITY

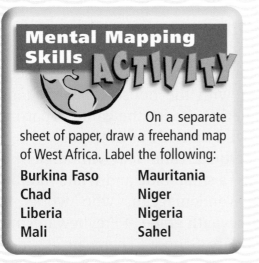

On a separate sheet of paper, draw a freehand map of West Africa. Label the following:

Burkina Faso	Mauritania
Chad	Niger
Liberia	Nigeria
Mali	Sahel

WRITING ACTIVITY

Imagine that you are an economic adviser to a West African country of your choice. Use print resources to prepare a short economic report for your country's leader. Identify the country's important natural resources and what can be done with them. In addition, describe economic advantages or disadvantages of the country's climate, location, and physical features. Be sure to use standard grammar, spelling, sentence structure, and punctuation.

Alternative Assessment

Portfolio ACTIVITY

Learning About Your Local Geography

Group Project The borders of today's African countries were largely drawn by Europeans. With your group, research how the borders of your state were decided.

◪ internet connect

Internet Activity: go.hrw.com
KEYWORD: SG3 GT23

Choose a topic to explore about West Africa:
- Find out about giant baobab trees.
- Meet the people of West Africa.
- Learn about the history of the slave trade.

CHAPTER 24

East Africa

East Africa has been identified by historians as the cradle of the human race. It has made great contributions to the development of world civilization.

My name is Tsiyon. I am 13, and I live in Addis Ababa, the capital of Ethiopia. My house is very far from the city center. I live with my parents and my brothers. We have a servant who helps my mother with the housework. My mother stays at home. My father works for the game department, doing research on the wild animals of Ethiopia.

After a breakfast of bread and tea with milk, I ride to school in a city taxi—a small blue and white minibus—with my brother, Wondemagegn, who works in a garage. I am in the seventh grade at Freyhewat Number Two Junior Secondary School. There are 82 kids in my class! I am in school from 8:00 A.M. to 3:00 P.M. I am studying Amharic—an Ethiopian language— English, math, science, and sports. When I grow up, I want to be a doctor.

At noon, I eat a lunch I brought from home. When I get home, I help my mother sweep the house. Then I watch television. In the evenings, I do my homework.

Indemin adderu?

Translation: How did you pass the night?

Section 1 Physical Geography

Read to Discover

1. What are the major landforms of East Africa?
2. Which rivers and lakes are important in this region?
3. What are East Africa's climate types and natural resources?

Define

rifts

Locate

Great Rift Valley
Mount Kilimanjaro
Lake Victoria
White Nile
Blue Nile

A bat-eared fox from Tanzania

WHY IT MATTERS

Many scientists believe that the first humans on Earth lived on the land that we now call East Africa. Use CNNfyi.com or other **current events** sources to learn about recent discoveries related to the beginnings of humankind. Record your findings in your journal.

East Africa: Physical-Political

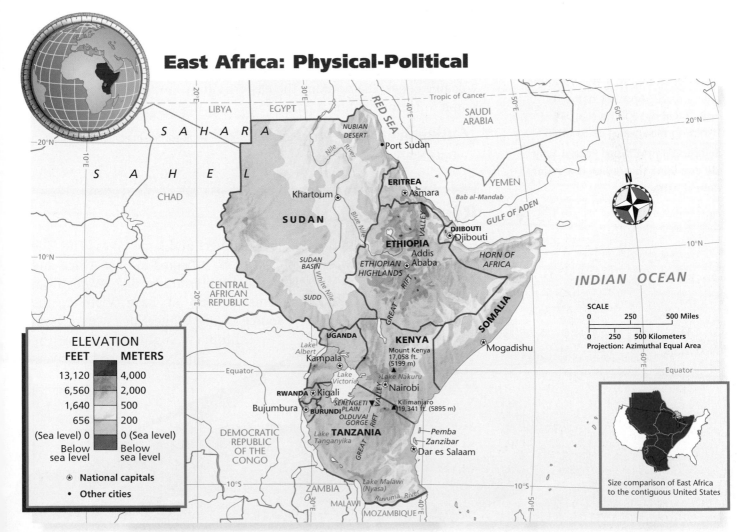

ELEVATION
FEET	METERS
13,120	4,000
6,560	2,000
1,640	500
656	200
(Sea level) 0	0 (Sea level)
Below sea level	Below sea level

⊛ National capitals
• Other cities

SCALE
0   250   500 Miles
0   250   500 Kilometers
Projection: Azimuthal Equal Area

Size comparison of East Africa to the contiguous United States

Our Amazing Planet

Baobab (BOW-bab) trees are one of the few kinds of trees on the African savanna. It is also one of the largest trees in the world. It can grow as large as 30 feet (9 m) in diameter and to a height of 60 feet (18 m). The trunks are often used to store water or as temporary shelters.

This is a crater rim view of Mount Kilimanjaro. Another name for this volcano is Kilima Njaro— "shining mountain" in Swahili.
Interpreting the Visual Record Why do you think this region is a major tourist attraction?

The Land

East Africa is a land of high plains and plateaus. In the north, deserts and dry grasslands define the landscape. In the southwest, large lakes dot the plateaus. In the east, sandy beaches and beautiful coral reefs run along the coast. East Africa's most striking features are its great **rifts**. They cut from north to south across the region. Rifts are long, deep valleys with mountains or plateaus on either side. Rifts form when Earth's tectonic plates move away from each other.

The Rift Valleys Deep beneath East Africa's surface, Earth's mantle is churning. This movement causes the land to arch and split along the rift valleys. If you look at the Great Rift Valley from the air, it looks like a giant scar. The Great Rift Valley is made up of two rifts—the eastern rift and the western rift. The rift walls are usually a series of steep cliffs. These cliffs drop an average of about 9,000 feet (2,743 m) to the valley floor. The eastern rift begins north of the Red Sea. The rift continues south through Eritrea (er-uh-TREE-uh) and Ethiopia (ee-thee-OH-pee-uh) into southern Tanzania (tan-zuh-NEE-uh). The western rift extends from Lake Albert in the north to Lake Malawi (mah-LAH-wee), also known as Lake Nyasa, in the south.

Mountains and Plains East Africa also has many volcanic mountains. Mount Kilimanjaro (ki-luh-muhn-JAHR-oh), at 19,341 feet (5,895 m), is Africa's tallest mountain. Although this part of Africa is along the equator, the mountain is so high that snow covers its two volcanic cones. Plains along the eastern rift in Tanzania and Kenya are home to famous national parks.

✓ **READING CHECK:** *Places and Regions* What are the major landforms of East Africa?

Rivers and Lakes

East Africa is the site of a number of rivers and large lakes. The Nile is the world's longest river. It begins in East Africa and flows north to the Mediterranean Sea. Water from small streams collects in Lake Victoria, the source of the White Nile. Waters from Ethiopia's highlands form the Blue Nile. These two rivers meet at Khartoum, Sudan, to create the mighty Nile. The Nile provides a narrow, fertile lifeline through Sudan by providing irrigation in the desert.

Lake Victoria is Africa's largest lake in area, but it is shallow. Along the western rift is a chain of great lakes. Many of the lakes along the drier eastern rift are quite different. Heat from Earth's interior makes some of these eastern lakes so hot that no human can swim in them. Others, like Lake Nakuru, are too salty for most fish. However, algae in Lake Nakuru provides food for more than a million flamingos.

✔ **READING CHECK:** (*Places and Regions*) Which rivers and lakes are most important in this region?

▲ Lake Nakuru is known in part for the many flamingos that gather there.

Climate and Resources

Northern Sudan and the northeast coast have desert and steppe climates. The climate changes to tropical savanna as you travel south. However, the greatest climate changes occur along the sides of the rift valleys. The rift floors are dry, with grasslands and thorn shrubs. In contrast, the surrounding plateaus and mountains have a humid highland climate and dense forests. Rain falls at the high elevations, but the valleys are in rain shadows.

Most East Africans are farmers or herders. However, the region does have mineral resources such as coal, copper, diamonds, gold, iron ore, and lead.

✔ **READING CHECK:** (*Places and Regions*) What are East Africa's climate types and natural resources?

BUILD on WHAT You Know

Do you remember what you learned about rain shadows? See Chapter 3 to review.

go.hrw.com **Homework Practice Online**
Keyword: SG3 HP24

Section Review 1

Define and explain: rifts

Working with Sketch Maps On a map of East Africa that you draw or that your teacher provides, label the following: Great Rift Valley, Mount Kilimanjaro, Lake Victoria, White Nile, and Blue Nile. How do the mountains help support the river systems?

Reading for the Main Idea

1. (*Places and Regions*) What are the major landforms of East Africa?

2. (*Places and Regions*) Which rivers and lakes are located in this part of Africa?

3. (*Physical Systems*) Why are volcanic mountains found in parts of East Africa?

Critical Thinking

4. **Drawing Inferences and Conclusions** How do you think the climate types found in East Africa influence what grows there?

Organizing What You Know

5. **Summarizing** Copy the following graphic organizer. Use it to describe what you know about East Africa's physical geography.

	Vegetation	Climates
Coasts		
Rift Valleys		
Plateaus/mountains		

East Africa • 511

Section 2 · East Africa's History and Culture

Read to Discover

1. What important events and developments influenced the history of East Africa?

2. What is the culture of East Africa like?

Define

Swahili

WHY IT MATTERS

Recent conflicts in East Africa have taken millions of lives. Many of these conflicts are the result of the region's history. Use CNN**fyi**.com or other **current events** sources to learn more about conflicts in East Africa today. Record your findings in your journal.

A Turkana woman

History

Several early civilizations developed at the site known as Meroë, near where the branches of the Nile come together. These civilizations had their own forms of writing. Each controlled a major trade route. East Africans traded ivory and gold, among other things.

This statue depicts a prince from the early Nubian civilization of northern Sudan.

Christianity and Islam Like Egypt, Ethiopia was an early center of Christianity. In the A.D. 500s Christianity spread into neighboring Nubia, which is now part of Egypt and Sudan. In Nubia, Christian kingdoms lasted until about 1500. Ethiopia still has a large Christian population today.

Arab armies conquered Egypt and North Africa by about A.D. 700. However, these armies were not able to keep control of East Africa. Gradually, Arabic-speaking nomads spread into northern Sudan from Egypt. They brought their Islamic faith with them. At the same time, Islam spread to the coastal region of what is now Somalia. Christianity is believed to have been introduced in Ethiopia as early as the A.D. 300s. Christian kingdoms, particularly in Ethiopia, have fought wars with Muslim leaders. Religion continues to be a source of conflict in this East African region.

The Slave Trade The east coast slave trade dates back more than 1,000 years. Most slaves went to Islamic countries in Africa and Asia. The Portuguese had begun setting up forts and settlements on the East African coast by the early 1500s. At first, the Europeans made little

This sketch shows a slave market in Zanzibar. Arab traders took advantage of local rivalries and encouraged powerful African leaders to capture their enemies and sell them into slavery.

Interpreting the Visual Record
What does this piece of art tell us about the historical culture of this region?

effort to move into the interior. However, in the late 1700s the East African island of Zanzibar became an international slave-trading center. Later, plantations like those of the Americas were set up with slave labor to grow cloves and sugarcane.

Africa Divided In the mid-1800s European adventurers traveled into the African interior searching for the source of the Nile. Here they found rich lands well suited for agriculture. In the 1880s the European powers divided up most of the continent. Most of Africa's modern borders resulted from this process. Control over much of East Africa went to the British. Germany colonized Tanzania, Rwanda, and Burundi. After World War I, with the defeat of Germany, the British took over Tanzania. Belgium gained control of Rwanda and Burundi.

Conflict Within East Africa, just Kenya was settled by large numbers of Europeans. The colonial rulers usually controlled their countries through African deputies. Many of these deputies were traditional chiefs, who often favored their own peoples. This tended to strengthen ethnic rivalries. These ethnic divisions have made it hard for governments to create feelings of national identity.

Independence Ethiopia was never colonized. Its mountains provided natural protection, and its peoples and emperors resisted colonization. It was, however, annexed by Italy from 1936 to 1941. Most East African countries were granted independence by European colonizers in the early 1960s. More recently, East Africa has become headquarters for some international companies and organizations.

✔ **READING CHECK:** (*Human Systems*) Which European countries influenced the history of East Africa?

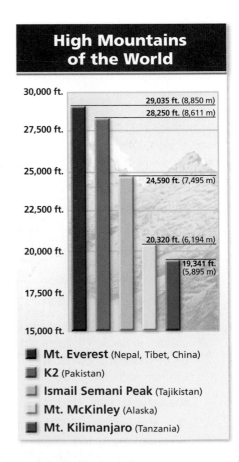

High Mountains of the World

- 30,000 ft.
- 29,035 ft. (8,850 m)
- 28,250 ft. (8,611 m)
- 27,500 ft.
- 25,000 ft.
- 24,590 ft. (7,495 m)
- 22,500 ft.
- 20,320 ft. (6,194 m)
- 20,000 ft.
- 19,341 ft. (5,895 m)
- 17,500 ft.
- 15,000 ft.

- ■ **Mt. Everest** (Nepal, Tibet, China)
- ■ **K2** (Pakistan)
- ■ **Ismail Semani Peak** (Tajikistan)
- ■ **Mt. McKinley** (Alaska)
- ■ **Mt. Kilimanjaro** (Tanzania)

Interpreting the Graph **How much taller is Mt. Everest than K2?**

▲
Afar nomads stop for rest in a desert region of northern Ethiopia.

Culture

East Africa has the world's longest history of human settlement. Gradually, the region developed the continent's greatest diversity of people and ways of life. The **Swahili** language is widely spoken in East Africa. This Bantu language has been greatly influenced by Arabic. In fact, the word Swahili comes from the Arabic word meaning "on the coast."

East Africa shares many challenges with other African regions. One challenge is that populations are growing faster than the economies that support them. Many jobless people have crowded into the cities. Another challenge is religious and ethnic conflict. Such conflict and other political problems have slowed economic progress. Often a country's wealth is spent on weapons rather than helping people.

The ethnic conflicts have roots in the region's history. Colonial borders drawn by Europeans often lumped different ethnic groups into one country. Differences between groups have led to conflict in some countries since independence.

The worst ethnic conflict has been in Rwanda and Burundi. Thousands of Tutsi were killed by the Hutu in Rwanda in the 1990s. There also has been fighting between Muslims and Christians in the northern part of the region.

✓ **READING CHECK:** (*Human Systems*) What conflicts have occurred between groups in East Africa?

go.hrw.com **Homework Practice Online**
Keyword: SG3 HP24

Section Review 2

Define and explain: Swahili

Working with Sketch Maps On the map you created in Section 1, highlight the location of the bodies of water you labeled. Why do you think early civilizations settled near these bodies of water?

Reading for the Main Idea

1. (*Human Systems*) Which European countries influenced the history of this area?

2. (*Human Systems*) What are the main religions practiced in East Africa?

Critical Thinking

3. **Finding the Main Idea** What conflicts have occurred because of political boundary lines?

4. **Drawing Inferences and Conclusions** Why might Swahili be a particularly important language in East Africa?

Organizing What You Know

5. **Sequencing** Create a time line listing historical events in East Africa from the A.D. 400s to the 1990s. Be sure to include the adoption of Christianity, the slave trade, exploration, colonial rule, independence, and ethnic conflict.

A.D. 400   1990s

Section 3 The Countries of East Africa

Read to Discover

1. Why did settlers come to Kenya?
2. How was Tanzania created?
3. What are Rwanda and Burundi like?
4. What is Uganda like?
5. What are the physical features of Sudan?

Define

gorge

Locate

Kenya
Tanzania
Rwanda
Burundi
Uganda
Sudan

Sudanese jar from the A.D. 100s

WHY IT MATTERS

Thousands of tourists enjoy the beautiful wildlife preserves and national parks of Kenya, Uganda, and Tanzania each year. Use CNNfyi.com or other **current events** sources to find out about travel and sightseeing opportunities in these countries. Record your findings in your journal.

Kenya

Kenya's first cities were founded along the coast of the Indian Ocean by Arab traders. Beginning in the 1500s Portugal controlled this coast for about 200 years. Arabs then recaptured it.

During the 1800s British merchants began trading on the coast. They built a railway from Mombasa to Lake Victoria. British settlers then came to take advantage of the fertile highlands. People from India and Pakistan also came to work on the Europeans' farms. Many of the local people, particularly the Kikuyu, moved out of their traditional areas. They became farmworkers or took jobs in the cities. After World War II many Africans protested British colonial rule. There were peaceful demonstrations as well as violent ones.

One conflict was over land. The British and the Kikuyu viewed land differently. The British considered land a sign of personal wealth, power, and property. The Kikuyu saw land as a source of food rather than something to be bought or sold. This caused conflict because the British wanted the land. Kenya gained independence from Britain in the 1960s, and its government has been quite stable ever since.

Kenya is a popular tourist destination. Tourism is a major source of income for the country. Kenya's greatest challenge is its rapidly increasing population. There is no empty farmland left in most areas. Much of Kenya has been set aside as national parkland.

As in the rest of Africa, Europeans once ruled colonies in East Africa. Fort Jesus, founded in 1593 by the Portuguese, is a national monument in Kenya.

East Africa

COUNTRY	POPULATION/ GROWTH RATE	LIFE EXPECTANCY	LITERACY RATE	PER CAPITA GDP
Burundi	6,223,897 2.4%	45, male 47, female	35%	$720
Kenya	30,765,916 1.3%	47, male 48, female	78%	$1,500
Rwanda	7,312,756 1.2%	38, male 40, female	48%	$900
Sudan	36,080,373 2.8%	56, male 58, female	46%	$1,000
Tanzania	36,232,074 2.6%	51, male 53, female	68%	$710
Uganda	23,985,712 2.9%	43, male 44, female	62%	$1,100
United States	281,421,906 0.9%	74, male 80, female	97%	$36,200

Sources: Central Intelligence Agency, *The World Factbook 2001;* U.S. Census Bureau

Interpreting the Chart Which country has the lowest literacy rate?

These giraffe feed on the tree-studded grasslands of the Serengeti. This reserve was opened in 1974 and is Kenya's most famous and popular animal reserve.

Many people would like to farm these lands. If the national parks are converted to farmland, however, African wildlife would be endangered. In addition, the tourism industry would likely suffer.

✔ **READING CHECK:** *Human Systems* Why did settlers come to Kenya?

Tanzania

South of Kenya is the large country of Tanzania. It was created in the 1960s when Tanganyika and the island of Zanzibar united. Today many tourists come to explore numerous national parks and Mount Kilimanjaro. The mountain's southern slopes are a rich agricultural region that provides coffee and tea for exports. Also in Tanzania is the Serengeti Plain. On this plain, herds of antelope and zebras still migrate freely, following the rains. Nearby is a famous archaeological site, Olduvai Gorge. A **gorge** is a narrow, steep-walled canyon. Evidence of some of the earliest humanlike fossils have been found in Olduvai Gorge.

Tanzania is a country of mainly poor subsistence farmers. Poor soils and limited technology have restricted productivity. This country has minerals, particularly gold and diamonds. Although the Tanzanian government has tried to make the country more self-sufficient, it has not yet succeeded.

✔ **READING CHECK:** *Places and Regions* How was the country of Tanzania created?

CONNECTING TO *Science*

Olduvai Gorge, Tanzania

Many scientists believe the human species has its origins in Africa. Archaeologists there have discovered fossil remains of humans and humanlike animals several million years old. Some of the most important finds have occurred at a site known as Olduvai Gorge.

Located in Tanzania, Olduvai is a steep-sided canyon some 30 miles (48 km) long. It is up to 300 feet (90 m) deep. The exposed sides of this gorge contain fossil deposits estimated to be more than 4 million years old. Along with the fossils, scientists found stone tools and the remains of numerous humanlike animals.

OLDUVAI GORGE

Archaeologists Louis and Mary Leakey played a key role in uncovering Olduvai's secrets. In 1931 Louis Leakey found remains of ancient tools and bones in the gorge. Then in 1959 Mary Leakey found the skeleton of an *Australopithecus*, the first humanlike creature to walk upright. Several years later, the Leakeys found the remains of a more advanced species. The new find was known as *Homo habilis*. The species could make stone tools.

These discoveries helped provide some of the missing links between humans and their ancestors. Today archaeological work at Olduvai Gorge continues to add to our understanding of human origins.

Understanding What You Read
1. What is Olduvai Gorge?
2. What part has Olduvai played in the search for human origins?

Rwanda and Burundi

These two countries in fertile highlands were once German colonies. After World War I the Belgians ruled them. In the 1960s, after they gained independence, they were divided into two countries. Both countries are mostly populated by two ethnic groups—the Tutsi and the Hutu. Violence between the groups has killed thousands. Rwanda and Burundi have the densest rural settlement in Africa. Foreign aid has helped improve farming and health care.

✓ **READING CHECK:** (*Human Systems*) Why did the creation of Rwanda and Burundi create conflict?

Our Amazing Planet

Red colobus monkeys of Zanzibar eat charcoal, which absorbs poisons in the fruit-tree leaves the monkeys sometimes eat.

Uganda

Uganda, another site of an ancient empire, is found on the plateau north and west of Lake Victoria. Economic progress has been slow. Foreign investment stopped as a result of a violent dictatorship. In the 1970s the country's economy collapsed. Limited peace and democracy were achieved in the late 1980s.

✔ **READING CHECK:** (*Human Systems*) What is Uganda like today?

▲ Alfred Louis Sargent created this engraving of Khartoum, Sudan, in the 1800s.

Sudan

Sudan is Africa's largest country. It has three physical regions. The Sahara makes up the northern half of the country. Dry savannas extend across the country's center. Much of southern Sudan is taken up by a swamp called the Sudd. Sudan is mainly an agricultural country, but it is also developing some of its mineral resources. Oil reserves have not yet been developed.

Modern Sudanese culture shows influences of Arab and traditionally African cultures. Arab Muslims make up about 40 percent of the population and have political power. They dominate northern Sudan. Khartoum, the capital, is located in this area. During the last several decades there has been a civil war between northern Muslims and southerners who practice Christianity or traditional African religions.

✔ **READING CHECK:** (*Human Systems*) What conflict has been occurring in Sudan?

go.hrw.com

Homework Practice Online
Keyword: SG3 HP24

Section Review 3

Define and explain: gorge

Working with Sketch Maps On the map you created in Section 2, label Kenya, Tanzania, Rwanda, Burundi, Uganda, and Sudan. Why are some of the countries of this region agriculturally fertile while others are not?

Reading for the Main Idea

1. (*Places and Regions*) What makes the highlands of Kenya important?

2. (*Places and Regions*) Which areas of East Africa are tourist attractions?

Critical Thinking

3. **Making Generalizations and Predictions** How might irrigation help a region's economic development?

4. **Finding the Main Idea** How has unrest hurt Rwanda and some other East African countries?

Organizing What You Know

5. **Summarizing** Copy the following graphic organizer. Use it to list each country in this section. In one column list resources important to its development, and in the next column list obstacles that could prevent the country's economic success.

Country	Resources	Obstacles

Section 4 The Horn of Africa

Read to Discover
1. What are the main physical features of Ethiopia?
2. What is Eritrea like?
3. What is Somalia like?
4. What are the physical and cultural characteristics of Djibouti?

Define
droughts

Locate
Ethiopia
Eritrea
Somalia
Djibouti
Bab al-Mandab

WHY IT MATTERS

The United States sent food aid and 15,000 troops to Somalia in the 1990s to try to bring peace to the war-torn nation. Use or other **current events** sources to investigate current conditions in Somalia. Record your findings in your journal.

A classic Swahili sailing dhow

Ethiopia

Ethiopia is one of the world's poorest countries. The rugged mountain slopes and upland plateaus have rich volcanic soil. Agriculture is Ethiopia's chief economic activity. It exports coffee, livestock, and oilseeds. However, during the last 30 years the region has experienced serious **droughts**. Droughts are periods when little rain falls and crops are damaged. Aid has been sent from around the world. Nevertheless, several million people starved during the 1980s.

Except for a time when Ethiopia was at war with Italy, the Ethiopian highlands have never been under foreign rule. The mountains protected the interior of the country from invasion. Most of the highland people are Christian, while most of the lowland people are Muslim.

✓ **READING CHECK:** *Places and Regions* What physical features are found in Ethiopia?

As Afar nomads in Ethiopia move their encampment, they are continually challenged by the environment. **Interpreting the Visual Record How important are these camels for the Afar? What purpose do they serve?**

▼

The Horn of Africa

COUNTRY	POPULATION/ GROWTH RATE	LIFE EXPECTANCY	LITERACY RATE	PER CAPITA GDP
Djibouti	460,700 2.6%	49, male 53, female	46%	$1,300
Eritrea	4,298,269 3.8%	54, male 59, female	25%	$710
Ethiopia	65,891,874 2.7%	44, male 46, female	36%	$600
Somalia	7,448,773 3.5%	45, male 48, female	24%	$600
United States	281,421,906 0.9%	74, male 80, female	97%	$36,200

Sources: Central Intelligence Agency, *The World Factbook 2001;* U.S. Census Bureau

Interpreting the Chart Which country in the region has the highest level of economic development, and why?

The main mosque, Khulafa el Rashidin, was built in 1937 with Italian Carrara marble in Asmara, Eritrea.

Interpreting the Visual Record What architectural elements of this building have you seen in other regions you have studied?

Eritrea

Eritrea, located on the Red Sea, was once part of Ethiopia. In the late 1800s the Italians made this area a colony. In the 1960s it became an Ethiopian province. After years of war, Eritrea broke away from Ethiopia in 1993. The economy has slowly improved since then. The population is made up of Muslims and Christians.

✓ **READING CHECK:** *Places and Regions* What is Eritrea like today?

Somalia

Somalia is a land of deserts and dry savannas. Most Somalis are nomadic herders. Livestock and bananas are the main exports. Somalia is less diverse than most other African countries. Most residents of Somalia are members of the Somali people. Most Somali share the same culture, religion (Islam), language (Somali), and way of life (herding). Somalia has been troubled by civil war. In the 1990s widespread starvation caused by the war and a severe drought attracted international attention. The United Nations sent aid and troops to the country. U.S. troops were sent to Somalia to assist with this operation.

✓ **READING CHECK:** *Environment and Society* How have drought and conflict affected Somalia?

Djibouti

Djibouti is a small desert country. It lies on the Bab al-Mandab. This the narrow strait that connects the Red Sea and the Indian Ocean. The strait lies along a major shipping route. This has helped Djibouti's economy. In the 1860s Djibouti came under French control. It gained independence in 1977. The French government still contributes economic and military support to the country. Its port, which serves landlocked Ethiopia, is a major source of income. Djibouti is heavily dependent on food imports.

The people of Djibouti include the Issa and the Afar. The Issa are closely tied to the people of Somalia. The Afar are related to the people of Ethiopia. Members of both groups are Muslim. Somalia and Ethiopia have both wanted to control Djibouti. So far the country has maintained its independence.

✓ **READING CHECK:** **Places and Regions** What are Djibouti's physical and cultural features?

Djibouti's Lake Assal has one of the lowest surface levels on the planet. It lies 515 feet (157 m) below sea level. The only way to reach this area is by use of a four-wheel drive vehicle.

Interpreting the Visual Record **What about the surrounding physical geography would appear to limit access to this lake?**

Section Review 4

Define and explain: droughts

Working with Sketch Maps On the map you created in Section 3, label Ethiopia, Eritrea, Somalia, Djibouti, and Bab al-Mandab. What physical features help the economies of the region?

Reading for the Main Idea

1. **Places and Regions** What physical features have helped protect Ethiopia from foreign invasion?

2. **Places and Regions** What country was part of Ethiopia until it broke away in 1993?

Critical Thinking

3. **Drawing Inferences and Conclusions** Why do you think France remains interested in Djibouti?

4. **Finding the Main Idea** Why have foreign aid agencies been involved in East Africa?

Organizing What You Know

5. **Analyzing Information** Copy the following graphic organizer. Use it to show the major religions of these countries. Add boxes as needed.

Country	Religion

East Africa • 521

CHAPTER 24

Reviewing What You Know

Building Vocabulary

On a separate sheet of paper, write sentences to define each of the following words.

1. rifts
2. Swahili
3. gorge
4. droughts

Reviewing the Main Ideas

1. (*Places and Regions*) What are East Africa's main natural resources?

2. (*Physical Systems*) What caused the formation of the Great Rift Valley of East Africa?

3. (*Human Systems*) How have Arabs, Portuguese, the British, and the Kikuyu affected Kenya?

4. (*Environment and Society*) What factors have slowed Tanzania's economic growth?

5. (*Environment and Society*) How have droughts in the Horn of Africa affected its people and their relationship with the rest of the world?

Understanding Environment and Society

Environmental Issues

Many East African countries have endured ethnic, religious, and political conflicts. Sometimes environmental issues can cause conflict. Prepare a presentation, including a graph, database, or model, comparing conflicts in East Africa over environmental issues. You may want to think about the following:

- Specific conflicts about environmental issues.
- Steps East Africans might take to eliminate these conflicts.

You may want to compare your data to facts you have learned about other regions in Africa for more ideas.

Thinking Critically

1. **Finding the Main Idea** What is the significance of the Nile River in this region's human history?

2. **Analyzing Information** Why are foreign investors hesitant to invest in many countries of this region?

3. **Summarizing** Why do most East Africans make their living by farming and herding?

4. **Making Generalizations and Predictions** What problems have resulted in part from the boundary lines drawn by European powers, and how might the countries of East Africa overcome these problems?

5. **Analyzing Information** How has Ethiopia avoided falling under foreign rule for most of its history?

Map ACTIVITY

On a separate sheet of paper, match the letters on the map with their correct labels.

Great Rift Valley   White Nile
Mount   Blue Nile
 Kilimanjaro   Bab
Lake Victoria   al-Mandab

Mental Mapping Skills ACTIVITY

On a separate sheet of paper, draw a freehand map of East Africa. Make a key for your map and label the following:

Burundi   Rwanda
Djibouti   Somalia
Eritrea   Sudan
Ethiopia   Tanzania
Kenya   Uganda

WRITING ACTIVITY

Imagine that you have been awarded an all-expenses-paid vacation to East Africa. Write a letter to your travel agent explaining what you want to do on your trip. List and describe physical features you want to see and African wildlife and historical sites you would like to explore. Be sure to use standard grammar, spelling, sentence structure, and punctuation.

Alternative Assessment

Portfolio ACTIVITY

Learning About Your Local Geography

Cooperative Project Much of Africa's precolonial history was memorized by elders, rather than written down. Prepare an oral history of how older people in your community recall a certain historical event.

🔗 **internet** connect

**Internet Activity: go.hrw.com
KEYWORD: SG3 GT24**

Choose a topic to explore about East Africa:
- Hike Mount Kilimanjaro.
- Learn about cultural groups in East Africa.
- Travel back to ancient Nubian kingdoms.

Central Africa

The fourth region in Africa we will study includes the 10 countries of central Africa. Before we begin, meet Akalemwa Ngenda, a student living in Zambia.

Lumela, ni muituti mwa naha Zambia.

*B*wanji? (How are you?) This is how you say *hi* in Nyanja, a common language spoken by most people in my country, Zambia. At home, I would say "Mucwañi?" to my father in Lozi, my own language. My name is Akalemwa, and I am 18. *Akalemwa* means "the one you cannot outrun." I am in the twelfth grade at Choma Secondary School in Zambia's southern province. Choma is a small town. My family's house is near the hospital, about 2.5 kilometers (1.6 mi.) from town. My father is a medical assistant in charge of village health clinics for our region. My mother is a nurse. I have an older half sister, two older brothers, two younger sisters, and five younger brothers. Our house has three bedrooms and a vegetable garden.

I attend a Protestant missionary school. We sleep in a dormitory at school. Our school year has three three-month terms, starting in January. We have a month vacation after each one. I want to be a doctor, so I am studying math, physics, chemistry, biology, English, and geography.

▲
Translation: Hi, I am a student in Zambia.

Section 1 Physical Geography

Read to Discover

1. What are the major physical features of central Africa?
2. What climates, plants, and animals are found in the region?
3. What major natural resources does central Africa have?

Define

basin
canopy
copper belt
periodic markets

Locate

Congo Basin
Western Rift Valley
Lake Tanganyika
Lake Malawi
Congo River
Zambezi River

WHY IT MATTERS

The rain forests of Central Africa are home to many plant and animal species. Use CNNfyi.com or other **current events** sources to find information about rain forests around the world. Record your findings in your journal.

A copper and wood religious artifact from Gabon

Central Africa: Physical-Political

Our Amazing Planet

One of the Congo River's most common animals is the crocodile. This sharp-toothed reptile can grow to about 20 feet (6 m) in length. It swims by sweeping its long tail from side to side.

Local people call Victoria Falls *Mosi-oa-Tunya*, which means "the smoke that thunders." The Zambezi River plunges 355 feet (108 m) over a cliff between Zambia and Zimbabwe.

Physical Features

Central Africa stretches southward from Cameroon and the Central African Republic to Angola and Zambia. The Atlantic Ocean lies off the western coast.

Think of the region as a big soup bowl with a wide rim. Near the middle of the bowl is the Congo Basin. A **basin** is a generally flat region surrounded by higher land such as mountains and plateaus.

In northwestern Cameroon are volcanic mountains. The highest is 13,353 feet (4,070 m). Central Africa's highest mountains lie along the Western Rift Valley. Some of these snow-capped mountains rise to more than 16,700 feet (5,090 m). The Western Rift Valley stretches southeastward from the Democratic Republic of the Congo. Lake Tanganyika (tan-guhn-YEE-kuh) and Lake Malawi are found there.

Two major river systems drain the region. In the north the Congo River flows westward to the Atlantic Ocean. Hundreds of smaller rivers flow into the Congo. In the south the Zambezi (zam-BEE-zee) River flows eastward to the Indian Ocean. The Zambezi is famous for its great falls, hydroelectric dams, and lakes.

✔ **READING CHECK:** (*Places and Regions*) What are the major physical features of central Africa?

Climates, Plants, and Animals

Central Africa lies along the equator and in the low latitudes. The Congo Basin and much of the Atlantic coast have a humid tropical climate. It is wet and warm all year. This climate supports a large, dense tropical rain forest.

The many different kinds of trees in the tropical rain forest form a complete **canopy**. This is the uppermost layer of the trees where the limbs spread out. Leaves block sunlight to the ground below.

Small antelopes, hyenas, elephants, and okapis live in the rain forest region. The okapi is a short-legged relative of the giraffe. Many insects also live in the forest. However, few other plants or creatures live on the forest floor. This is because little sunlight shines through the canopy. Many animals live in the trees. They include birds, monkeys, bats, and snakes. Large areas of the tropical rain forest are being cleared rapidly for farming and timber. This threatens the plants, animals, and people who live there.

North and south of the Congo Basin are large areas with a tropical savanna climate. Those areas are warm all year, but they have distinct dry and wet seasons. There are grasslands, scattered trees, and shrubs. Only in the high eastern mountains is there a highland climate. Dry steppe and even desert climates are found in the far south.

✓ **READING CHECK:** (*Places and Regions*) What are the region's climates, plants, and animals?

Resources

Central Africa's rivers are among the region's most important natural resources. They are used for travel, trade, and producing hydro-electricity. Other energy resources are oil, natural gas, and coal.

Central Africa has many minerals, including copper, uranium, tin, zinc, diamonds, gold, and cobalt. Most of Africa's copper is found in an area called the **copper belt**, which includes northern Zambia and the southern Democratic Republic of the Congo.

Central African countries have mostly traditional economies. Most people in central Africa are subsistence farmers. However, an increasing number of farmers are growing crops for sale. Common crops include coffee, bananas, and corn. In rural areas, people trade their products in **periodic markets**. A periodic market is an open-air trading market. It is set up regularly at a crossroads or in a town.

✓ **READING CHECK:** (*Places and Regions*) What is central Africa's most important natural resource, and why?

▲

Elephants have created a network of trails and clearings throughout the tropical rain forest. Many animals will gather at forest clearings.

go.hrw.com **Homework Practice Online**
Keyword: SG3 HP25

Section Review 1

Define and explain: basin, canopy, copper belt, periodic markets

Working with Sketch Maps On a map of central Africa that you draw or that your teacher provides, label the following: Congo Basin, Western Rift Valley, Lake Tanganyika, Lake Malawi, Congo River, and Zambezi River. In a box in the margin, describe the location of the highest mountains.

Reading for the Main Idea

1. (*Places and Regions*) What major landforms and rivers are found in the region?

2. (*Physical Systems*) Why do few plants and animals live on the floor of the tropical rain forest?

3. (*Places and Regions*) For the most part, what type of economy do Central African countries have?

Critical Thinking

4. **Making Generalizations and Predictions** How might central Africa become a rich region?

Organizing What You Know

5. **Summarizing** Copy the following graphic organizer. Use it to describe the region's climates, plants and animals, and major resources.

Climates	Plants and Animals	Resources

Section 2 — History and Culture

Read to Discover

1. What is the history of central Africa, and what challenges do the people there face today?
2. What are the people and cultures of central Africa like?

Why It Matters

One of the major challenges for central Africa is dealing with malaria. Use CNNfyi.com or other **current events** sources to find information about the disease and how to prevent it. Record your findings in your journal.

Define

ivory
dialects

Locate

Brazzaville
Kinshasa

Bag made from raffia palm fibers, Cameroon

History

This carved mask was created by a Bantu-speaking people called the Fang. Most live in Cameroon, Equatorial Guinea, and Gabon. Their ancestors moved there in the 1800s.

▼

Early humans lived in central Africa many thousands of years ago. They had different languages and cultures. About 2,000 years ago new peoples began to move into the region from western Africa. Those new peoples spoke what are called Bantu languages. Today, Bantu languages are common in most of the region.

Early History Several early Bantu-speaking kingdoms formed in central Africa. Among the most important was the Kongo Kingdom. It was located around the mouth of the Congo River. The Kongo and other central Africans traded with peoples in western and eastern Africa.

Some of the early kingdoms used slaves. In the late 1400s, Europeans came to the region. They began to trade with some African kingdoms for slaves. The Europeans took many enslaved Africans to the Americas. Europeans also wanted the region's forest products and other resources, such as **ivory**. Ivory is a cream-colored material that comes from elephant tusks. It is used in making fine furniture, jewelry, and crafts.

Some African kingdoms became richer by trading with Europeans. However, all were gradually weakened or destroyed by the Europeans. European countries divided all of central Africa into colonies in the late 1800s. The colonial powers were France, the United Kingdom, Belgium, Germany, Spain, and Portugal.

The Europeans drew colonial borders that ignored the homelands of central Africa's ethnic groups. Many groups were lumped together in colonies. These groups spoke different languages and had different ways of life. These differences resulted in conflicts, particularly after the colonies won independence.

Modern Central Africa African colonies did not gain independence until after World War II. The largest central African colony was the Belgian Congo. It is now the Democratic Republic of the Congo. That country won independence in 1960. Angola won independence from Portugal in 1975. It was the last European colony in central Africa.

Independence for some African countries came after bloody wars. After independence, fighting between some ethnic groups continued within the new countries. The region also became a battleground in the Cold War. The United States and the Soviet Union supported their allies in small wars throughout Africa. The region's wars killed many people and caused great damage. Some fighting continues off and on in the region.

Challenges Today Ending these wars is one of central Africa's many challenges today. The region's countries must also develop their natural resources more effectively. This would help the many poor people who live there. Another great challenge is stopping the spread of diseases such as malaria and AIDS. These diseases are killing millions of people and leaving many orphans.

✔ **READING CHECK:** *Human Systems* What role did Europeans play in central Africa's history?

Culture

Today, about 100 million people live in central Africa. They belong to many different ethnic groups with varying customs.

Zambian women are grinding wheat to prepare it for cooking. They are using rods called pestles. The container is called a mortar. This technique is used for grinding many ingredients.

Interpreting the Visual Record How and why is the technology used to grind wheat different from what people in other places might use?

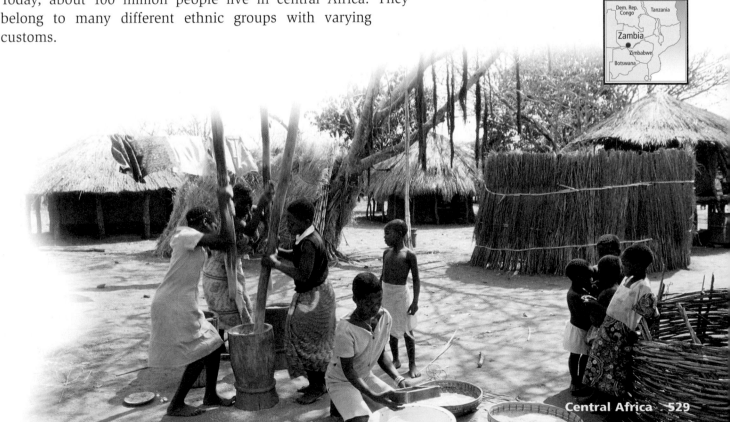

CONNECTING TO *History*

A headrest from early Luanda, a Bantu kingdom

BANTU LANGUAGES

About 2,000 years ago, the movement of groups of people began to change Africa. Traders, farmers, and other people moved across the southern third of Africa. Experts believe these people came from areas that are now part of Nigeria and Cameroon. Their movement across Africa lasted many centuries. During this period new languages developed. We call them Bantu languages. The grammar and root sounds of the different Bantu languages remain similar.

Some Bantu speakers moved southward along the Atlantic coast. Others moved eastward to Kenya and then turned southward. Over time they reached the tip of southern Africa. The Bantu speakers mixed with peoples who already lived in these lands.

The migration of Bantu speakers had important effects on African life. They brought new ways for growing food. They used tools made of iron, which others also began to use. The Bantu-speakers of course brought their languages. Today, many Africans speak Swahili, Zulu, and other Bantu languages.

Understanding What You Read

1. From where did the Bantu peoples come?
2. How did their movement shape Africa?

BUILD on WHAT You Know

Do you remember what you learned about world religions? See Chapter 5 to review.

Peoples and Languages As you have read, many central Africans speak Bantu languages. However, those languages can be very different from each other. In fact, hundreds of different languages and **dialects** are spoken in the region. A dialect is a variation of a language.

Many people in the region speak African languages in everyday life. However, the official languages of the central African countries are European. French is the official language of the former French colonies in the north. It is also the official language of the Democratic Republic of the Congo. English is the official language in Zambia and Malawi. Portuguese is spoken in Angola and the island country of São Tomé and Príncipe. Spanish and French are the official languages of tiny Equatorial Guinea.

Religion Many people in the former French, Spanish, and Portuguese colonies are Roman Catholic. Protestant Christianity is most common in former British colonies. Many people practice traditional African religions. In some cases Christian and African practices have been combined.

These Cameroon juju dancers are calling attention to the destruction of the tropical rain forest. Note the headpieces that represent some of the forest's animals.

Many Muslims live near the mostly Muslim countries of the Sahel in the north. Zambia also has many Muslims as well as Hindus. The Hindus are the descendants of immigrants from southern Asia.

Food In most central African countries, corn, rice, grains, and fish are common foods. In the tropical rain forest, plantains, cassava, and various roots are important foods. For example, in Cameroon you might eat a dish called *fufu*. *Fufu*, a thick, pasty ball of mashed cassava, yams, or plantains, is served with chicken, fish, or a beef gravy.

The Arts *Makossa* dance music from Cameroon has become popular throughout Africa. It can be played with various instruments, including guitars and electric keyboards. The cities of Brazzaville and Kinshasa on the Congo River are the home of *soukous* music.

The region is also famous for carved masks, sculpture, and beautiful cotton gowns. The gowns are dyed in bright colors. They often show pictures that represent things important to the wearer.

The *likembe*, or thumb piano, was invented in the lower Congo region. Today its music is heard in many African countries.

Interpreting the Visual Record
How is the *likembe* played?

✓ **READING CHECK:** (*Human Systems*) What are some characteristics of the people and culture of central Africa?

go.hrw.com **Homework Practice Online**
Keyword: SG3 HP25

Define and explain: ivory, dialects

Working with Sketch Maps On the map you created in Section 1, label Brazzaville and Kinshasa.

Reading for the Main Idea

1. (*Human Systems*) Why are many languages that are spoken today in central Africa related?

2. (*Human Systems*) What have been some of the causes of wars in central Africa?

3. (*Human Systems*) What arts are popular in the region?

Critical Thinking

4. **Finding the Main Idea** How did Europeans influence the culture of the region?

Organizing What You Know

5. **Summarizing** Copy the following graphic organizer. Use it to identify central Africa's challenges.

Challenges

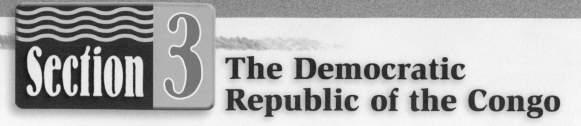

Section 3

The Democratic Republic of the Congo

Read to Discover

1. What is the history of the Democratic Republic of the Congo?
2. What are the people and culture of the country like?
3. What is the economy of the country like?

Define

civil war

Locate

Lubumbashi

WHY IT MATTERS

The Democratic Republic of the Congo faces many challenges. Use CNNfyi.com or other **current events** sources to find out more about some of the challenges facing the nation today. Record your findings in your journal.

A wooden cup of the Congo region

History

Portuguese sailors made contact with the Kongo Kingdom in 1482. Over time the slave trade and other problems weakened the Kongo and other African kingdoms.

A Belgian Colony In the 1870s King Leopold II of Belgium took control of the Congo Basin. The king ruled the Congo Free State as his personal colony until 1908. His soldiers treated the Africans harshly. They forced people to work in mines and on plantations. These policies brought international criticism.

The Belgian government took control of the colony from the king in 1908. Many Belgian businesses and people moved there. They mined copper and other resources. The giant colony won independence from tiny Belgium in 1960.

A New Country Many Belgians fled the country after 1960. There were few teachers, doctors, and other professionals left in the former colony. In addition, people from different areas and ethnic groups fought each other. These problems were partly to blame for keeping the country poor.

A dictator, who later changed his name to Mobutu Sese Seko, came to power in 1965. He was an ally of the United States during the Cold War. Mobutu changed the country's name to Zaire in 1971. During his rule, the country suffered from economic problems and government corruption.

A dancer performs in a coming-of-age ceremony for young people. Many such African traditions have survived the period of colonial rule by Europeans.

A new government took over in 1997 after a **civil war**. A civil war is a war between two or more groups within a country. The new government changed the country's name to the Democratic Republic of the Congo. However, fighting between ethnic groups has continued.

✓ **READING CHECK:** *Human Systems* What has the history of the Democratic Republic of the Congo been like?

The People

More than 50 million people live in the Democratic Republic of the Congo today. The population is very diverse. It is divided among more than 200 ethnic groups. The Kongo people are among the largest groups. These groups speak many different languages, but the official language is French. About half of the country's people are Roman Catholic. Protestant Christians, Muslims, and people who practice traditional African religions also live in the country.

More than 4 million people live in Kinshasa, the capital and largest city. Kinshasa is a river port located along the Congo River near the Atlantic coast. The crowded city has some modern buildings. However, most of the city consists of poor slums.

✓ **READING CHECK:** *Human Systems* What are the people and culture of the Democratic Republic of the Congo like?

The Democratic Republic of the Congo

COUNTRY	POPULATION/ GROWTH RATE	LIFE EXPECTANCY	LITERACY RATE	PER CAPITA GDP
Democratic Republic of the Congo	53,624,718 3.1%	47, male 51, female	77%	$600
United States	281,421,906 0.9%	74, male 80, female	97%	$36,200

Sources: Central Intelligence Agency, *The World Factbook 2001;* U.S. Census Bureau

Interpreting the Chart How does the literacy rate of the Democratic Republic of the Congo compare to that of the United States?

A family sells charcoal along a road in the northern Democratic Republic of the Congo. Charcoal is a major fuel source. In many rural areas there is no electricity.

▼

The Congo River lies in the distance in this photograph of Kinshasa.

Major World Copper Producers

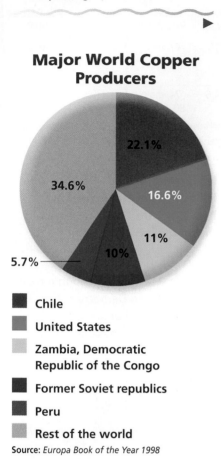

22.1%

34.6%

16.6%

11%

10%

5.7%

- ■ Chile
- ■ United States
- ☐ Zambia, Democratic Republic of the Congo
- ■ Former Soviet republics
- ■ Peru
- ☐ Rest of the world

Source: *Europa Book of the Year 1998*

Interpreting the Chart How much of the world's copper do Zambia and the Democratic Republic of the Congo produce?

The Economy

The Democratic Republic of the Congo is a treasure chest of minerals and tropical resources. For example, the south is part of central Africa's rich copper belt. Much of the copper from the area is shipped through the city of Lubumbashi (loo-boom-BAH-shee). The country also has gold, diamonds, and cobalt. The country's tropical rain forest also supplies wood, food, rubber, and other products.

However, the country's people are very poor. Most people live in rural areas. They must farm and trade for food. Civil war, bad government, and crime have scared many foreign businesses away. As a result, the country's rich resources have helped few of its people.

For the economy to improve, the country needs peace and a stable government. Schools must be improved and better health care provided. The country also must repair and expand roads and railways. If its challenges are met, the country's resources can make the future brighter.

✓ **READING CHECK:** *Environment and Society* How might the economy of the country improve?

go.hrw.com **Homework Practice Online**
Keyword: SG3 HP25

Section Review 3

Define and explain: civil war

Working with Sketch Maps On the map you created in Section 2, label the Democratic Republic of the Congo and Lubumbashi. Why is Lubumbashi economically important?

Reading for the Main Idea

1. *Places and Regions* What European country ruled what is now the Democratic Republic of the Congo as a colony until 1960?

2. *Places and Regions* What were some problems the country faced after independence?

Critical Thinking

3. **Finding the Main Idea** In what ways is the Democractic Republic of the Congo a culturally diverse country? What ethnic group is among the largest?

4. **Drawing Inferences and Conclusions** How might better schools and transportation help the country's economy?

Organizing What You Know

5. **Sequencing** Copy the following time line. Use it to identify important groups and individuals in the history of the present-day Democratic Republic of the Congo.

1482 —————————————————— 2000

Section 4 · The Other Central African Countries

Read to Discover

1. What are the people and economies of the northern central African countries like?
2. What are the people and economies of the southern central African countries like?

Define

exclave

Locate

Douala
Yaoundé
Luanda

WHY IT MATTERS

Poverty is a serious problem for the people of northern central Africa. Use CNNfyi.com or other **current events** sources to find information about poverty and other challenges in the region. Record your findings in your journal.

Fruit and nuts from the tropical rain forest

Northern Central Africa

Six countries make up northern central Africa. Four are Cameroon, the Central African Republic, Gabon, and the Republic of the Congo. They gained independence from France in 1960. Cameroon had been a German colony until after World War I. Tiny Equatorial Guinea gained independence from Spain in 1968. The island country of São Tomé and Príncipe won independence from Portugal in 1975.

The People Cameroon is by far the most populous country in this region. About 15.8 million people live there. The Central African Republic has the second-largest population, with 3.5 million. Tiny São Tomé and Príncipe has only about 165,000 people.

A large variety of ethnic groups are found in northern central Africa. Many people are moving from rural areas to cities to search for jobs. Governments are struggling to provide basic services in those crowded cities.

Douala (doo-AH-lah) and Yaoundé (yown-DAY) in Cameroon are the largest cities. Each has more than 1 million people. Douala is an important seaport on the Atlantic coast. Yaoundé is Cameroon's capital. Brazzaville, the capital of the Republic of the Congo, also has 1 million people. The city is a major Congo River port.

The Economy Most of the area's countries are very poor. Most people are farmers. Gabon has the strongest economy

Although the region's cities are growing rapidly, most people still live in rural areas. This small village is located in northern Cameroon. As in much of rural Africa, several buildings make up a family's home. **Interpreting the Visual Record** What is similar about the construction of these houses?

Northern Central Africa

Country	Population/ Growth Rate	Life Expectancy	Literacy Rate	Per Capita GDP
Cameroon	15,803,220 2.4%	54, male 55, female	63%	$1,700
Central African Republic	3,576,884 1.9%	42, male 46, female	60%	$1,700
Congo, Republic of the	2,894,336 2.2%	44, male 51, female	75%	$1,100
Equatorial Guinea	486,060 2.5%	52, male 56, female	78%	$2,000
Gabon	1,221,175 1.0%	49, male 51, female	63%	$6,300
São Tomé and Príncipe	165,034 3.2%	64, male 67, female	73%	$1,100
United States	281,421,906 0.9%	74, male 80, female	97%	$36,200

Sources: Central Intelligence Agency, *The World Factbook 2001;* U.S. Census Bureau

Interpreting the Chart Which country in the region has the smallest population? the largest?

in central Africa. More than half of the value of its economy comes from the oil industry. Oil is important in Cameroon as well as in the Republic of the Congo.

The mighty Congo River is also a vital trade and transportation route. As a result, it plays a major role in the region's economy. Many of the region's goods and farm products are shipped down river to Brazzaville. Brazzaville lies across the Congo River from Kinshasa. From Brazzaville, goods are shipped by railroad to a port on the Atlantic coast.

✔ **READING CHECK:** (*Human Systems*) What are the people and economies of northern central Africa like?

Southern Central Africa

Zambia, Malawi, and Angola make up the southern part of central Africa. The British gave Zambia and Malawi independence in 1964. Angola won independence from Portugal in 1975.

The People The populations of the three southern countries are nearly the same size. They range from about 9.7 million in Zambia to more than 11 million in Angola. Angola and Zambia are much larger in area than Malawi. Large parts of Angola and Zambia have few people. Most people in the region live in rural areas. They grow crops and herd cattle and goats.

Riverboats carry the king of Zambia's Lozi people to a dryland home during the flooding season. This event is an annual ritual for the Lozi, who live in western Zambia. As in other central African countries, many different ethnic groups live in Zambia.

Interpreting the Visual Record How can you tell these people are taking part in a formal tradition?

Angola's capital, Luanda, is the southern region's largest city. More than 2 million people live there. Seen from the sea, Luanda looks like a modern city. The city has many high-rise buildings and factories. Unfortunately, Luanda and its people have suffered from poverty and years of war. Rebels fought the Portuguese in the 1960s and early 1970s. After independence, the country plunged into civil war. Fighting has continued off and on since then. Many people have been killed or injured by land mines.

The Economy In peacetime, the future of Angola could be bright. There are many places with fertile soils. The country has large deposits of diamonds and oil. The oil is found offshore north of Luanda and in the **exclave** of Cabinda. An exclave is part of a country that is separated by territory of other countries. Cabinda is separated from the rest of Angola by the Democratic Republic of the Congo.

Much of Zambia's income comes from rich copper mines. However, 85 percent of Zambia's workers are farmers. Most of the country's energy comes from hydroelectric dams and power plants along rivers.

Almost 90 percent of Malawi's people live in rural areas. Nearly all of them are farmers. The building of factories and industries has been slow. Aid from other countries and religious missionaries has been important to the economy.

Southern Central Africa

Country	Population/ Growth Rate	Life Expectancy	Literacy Rate	Per Capita GDP
Angola	10,366,031 2.2%	37, male 40, female	42%	$1,000
Malawi	10,548,250 1.5%	37, male 38, female	56%	$900
Zambia	9,770,199 1.9%	37, male 38, female	78%	$880
United States	281,421,906 0.9%	74, male 80, female	97%	$36,200

Sources: Central Intelligence Agency, *The World Factbook 2001;* U.S. Census Bureau

Interpreting the Chart Which country in the region has the highest literacy rate?

✓ READING CHECK: *Human Systems* What are the people and economies of the southern central African countries like?

Define and explain: exclave

Working with Sketch Maps On the map you created in Section 3, label the countries of northern and southern central Africa, and Douala, Yaoundé, and Luanda. In a box in the margin, describe Luanda.

Reading for the Main Idea

1. *Places and Regions* Which country has the strongest economy in central Africa?

2. *Environment and Society* What significance does oil have in the economies of many countries in the region?

3. *Human Systems* What has happened in Angola since that country won its independence?

go. hrw .com **Homework Practice Online** Keyword: SG3 HP25

Critical Thinking

4. Analyzing Information Why is Brazzaville important to the region's economy?

Organizing What You Know

5. Summarizing Copy the following graphic organizer. Divide it into nine rows below the headings. Use it to list the countries discussed in this section. Then identify the European country that colonized each central African country. Finally, list the date each country won independence.

Country	European colonial ruler	Year of independence

CHAPTER 25

Reviewing What You Know

Building Vocabulary

On a separate sheet of paper, write sentences to define each of the following words.

1. basin
2. canopy
3. copper belt
4. periodic markets
5. ivory
6. dialects
7. civil war
8. exclave

Reviewing the Main Ideas

1. (Places and Regions) What two river systems are most important in central Africa? Where are the region's highest mountains found?

2. (Human Systems) How were the Bantu languages introduced to central Africa?

3. (Human Systems) What religions are practiced by people in the Democratic Republic of the Congo?

4. (Human Systems) What European countries once colonized central Africa?

5. (Environment and Society) How important has oil been to Gabon's economy?

Understanding Environment and Society

Health

Malaria has been a problem for thousands of years. Create a presentation about malaria. In preparing your presentation, consider the following:
- What malaria is and how it is spread.
- Where malaria is most common.
- What health experts have done to fight malaria.

Thinking Critically

1. **Drawing Inferences and Conclusions** Why do few large animals live on the floor of central Africa's tropical rain forests?

2. **Finding the Main Idea** How have borders drawn by European colonial powers contributed to ethnic conflicts in central Africa?

3. **Analyzing Information** How have their locations on major rivers or near important natural resources aided the growth of cities such as Brazzaville and Lubumbashi?

4. **Drawing Inferences and Conclusions** Why do you think European languages are still the official languages in the countries of central Africa?

5. **Finding the Main Idea** How did the Cold War contribute to problems in central Africa?

Map ACTIVITY

On a separate sheet of paper, match the letters on the map with their correct labels.

Congo Basin

Western Rift Valley

Lake Tanganyika

Lake Malawi

Congo River

Zambezi River

Kinshasa

Lubumbashi

Douala

Luanda

Mental Mapping Skills ACTIVITY

On a separate sheet of paper, draw a freehand map of central Africa. Make a key for your map and label the following:

Angola

Democratic Republic of the Congo

Malawi

Republic of the Congo

Zambia

WRITING ACTIVITY

Imagine that you have been hired to write a magazine article describing challenges facing central Africans. Write a descriptive headline and a brief summary for your proposed article. The article should cover the region's economic, political, and health challenges. Be sure to use standard grammar, spelling, sentence structure, and punctuation.

Alternative Assessment

Portfolio ACTIVITY

Learning About Your Local Geography

Group Project Plan a periodic market. List items grown or produced locally. Then design an advertisement to persuade farmers or craft makers to sell at the market.

internet connect

Internet Activity: go.hrw.com
KEYWORD: SG3 GT25

Choose a topic to explore about central Africa:
- Identify threats to the Congo Basin.
- Visit the people of central Africa.
- Learn the importance of African cloth.

go.hrw.com

Southern Africa

Southern Africa is a region going through many changes. Some people in the area have a comfortable lifestyle, but others live in severe poverty.

*A*batsu! (Good morning!) My name is Kha//'an[1] and I am a San person from Namibia. I am in ninth grade at the Tsumkwe[2] Secondary School. We do not have a house, only a small shelter to store our things. We live near the gate in the fence at M'Kata. If you turn east when you arrive there, you will see our blankets under the tree. When we are seeking shade or shelter, we go and sit under the tree.

My mother and father passed away when I was five years old, and my elder brother took care of me. I live with my brother, and the government helps us survive by giving us food rations.

At school I live in a hostel. We wake up at five in the morning and have breakfast at six. Breakfast is only bread. We have maize meal, tea, and milk at noon. My favorite subjects are English, history, physical science, and mathematics. When I grow up, I want to be a doctor.

=Xai-o![3] Mi o Kha//'an.

◄

Translation: Greetings! I am Kha//'an.

[1] The "//" is a click made by clucking the tongue at the sides of the mouth.
[2] The "k" in Tsumkwe is another kind of click. It is made by placing the tongue on the roof of the mouth and bringing it down with a "pop."
[3] The = is a click made by placing the tip of the tongue on the ridge behind the upper front teeth and bringing it down with a "pop."

Section 1 Physical Geography

Read to Discover

1. What are the major physical features and climates of southern Africa?
2. What resources are found in the region?

Define

enclaves
the veld
pans

Locate

Drakensberg
Inyanga Mountains
Cape of Good Hope
Kalahari Desert
Namib Desert
Orange River
Aughrabies Falls
Limpopo River

WHY IT MATTERS

The rich mineral resources of southern Africa, such as gold, diamonds, and platinum, are important to international economic stability. Use **CNNfyi.com** or other **current events** sources to find examples of how this region is using its resources. Record your findings in your journal.

Pygmy mouse lemur

Southern Africa: Physical-Political

Size comparison of southern Africa to the contiguous United States

The Drakensberg range rises sharply in eastern South Africa.
Interpreting the Visual Record Why do you think tourists are attracted to this region?

Our Amazing Planet

Drakensberg means "dragon mountain" in the Afrikaans language. The Zulu, one of the peoples of the region, call it Kwathlamba, meaning "barrier of pointed spears" or "piled-up rocks."

Countries of the Region

Lining southern Africa's coasts are Namibia (nuh-MI-bee-uh), South Africa, and Mozambique (moh-zahm-BEEK). Botswana (bawt-SWAH-nah), Zimbabwe (zim-BAH-bway), and the two tiny countries of Lesotho (luh-SOH-toh) and Swaziland (SWAH-zee-land) are all land-locked. Lesotho and Swaziland are **enclaves**—countries surrounded or almost surrounded by another country. Madagascar (ma-duh-GAS-kuhr), off the east coast, is the world's fourth-largest island.

Physical Features and Climate

The surface of southern Africa is dominated by a large plateau. The southeastern edge of this plateau is a mountain range called the Drakensberg (DRAH-kuhnz-buhrk). The steep peaks rise as high as 11,425 feet (3,482 m) from the plains along the coast. Farther north, another mountain range, the Inyanga (in-YANG-guh) Mountains, forms the plateau's eastern edge.

The open grassland areas of South Africa are known as **the veld** (VELT). Kruger National Park covers 7,523 square miles (19,485 sq km) of the veld. The park contains lions, leopards, elephants, rhinoceroses, hippos, baboons, and antelope.

Climate The region's climates range from desert to cool uplands. Winds carry moisture from the Indian Ocean. These winds are forced upward by the Drakensberg and Inyanga Mountains. The eastern slopes are rainy, but climates are drier farther inland and westward. Most of the interior of southern Africa is semiarid and has steppe and savanna vegetation.

Near the Cape of Good Hope, winter rains and summer drought create a Mediterranean climate. Off the Cape, storms and rough seas are common.

Deserts and Rivers In the central and western parts of the region, savanna and steppe give way to two major deserts. The Kalahari (ka-luh-hahr-ee) occupies most of Botswana. Here ancient streams have drained into low, flat areas, or **pans**. Minerals left behind when the water evaporated form a glittering white layer.

The Namib (NAH-mib) Desert lies along the Atlantic coast. Inland, the Namib blends into the Kalahari and steppe. Almost no rain falls, but at night fog rolls in from the ocean. Some plants and animals survive by using the fog as a source of water.

Southern Africa has some of the world's most spectacular rivers and waterfalls. The Orange River passes through the Aughrabies (oh-KRAH-bees) Falls as it flows to the Atlantic. When the water is highest, the Aughrabies Falls are several miles wide. The water tumbles down 19 separate waterfalls. The Limpopo (lim-POH-poh) River is the region's other major river. It flows into the Indian Ocean.

✓ **READING CHECK:** ⟨ *Places and Regions* ⟩ What are southern Africa's physical features and climate?

▧ **internet** connect
GO TO: go.hrw.com
KEYWORD: SG3 CH26
FOR: Web sites about southern Africa

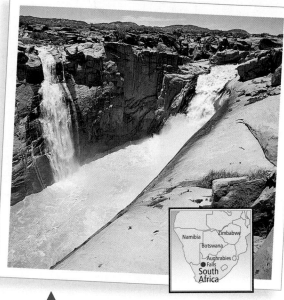

The Orange River flows down the spectacular Aughrabies Falls. The falls are near the Namibian border in northwestern South Africa.

Resources

Southern Africa is very rich in mineral resources. Gold, diamonds, platinum, copper, uranium, coal, and iron ore are all found in the region. Where rain is plentiful or irrigation is possible, farmers can grow a wide range of crops. Ranchers raise livestock on the high plains. Some nomadic herders still live in desert areas.

✓ **READING CHECK:** ⟨ *Places and Regions* ⟩ What are the main resources of southern Africa?

Homework Practice Online
Keyword: SG3 HP26

Section Review 1

Define and explain: enclaves, the veld, pans

Working with Sketch Maps On a map of southern Africa that you draw or that your teacher provides, label the following: Drakensberg, Inyanga Mountains, Cape of Good Hope, Kalahari Desert, Namib Desert, Orange River, Aughrabies Falls, and Limpopo River. The Orange River forms part of the border between what two countries?

Reading for the Main Idea

1. ⟨ *Places and Regions* ⟩ What are the major landforms of southern Africa?

2. ⟨ *Places and Regions* ⟩ What are the main natural resources of the region?

3. ⟨ *Physical Systems* ⟩ How do physical processes affect southern Africa's climate?

Critical Thinking

4. Drawing Inferences and Conclusions How do you think the climate off the Cape of Good Hope has affected shipping in the area?

Organizing What You Know

5. Summarizing Copy the following graphic organizer. Use it to list the landforms, climates, and resources of southern Africa.

Section 2 Southern Africa's History and Culture

Read to Discover

1. What was the early history of southern Africa like?

2. How did Europeans gain control of southern Africa, and what changes did this cause?

Define
Boers

Locate
Cape Town

WHY IT MATTERS

Among the many problems facing southern Africa are frequent natural disasters. Use CNNfyi.com or other **current events** sources to find examples of these disasters and how officials work to deal with them. Record your findings in your journal.

Modern sculpture from Zimbabwe

▲

Ancient rock art of southern Africa often includes hunters and animals.

Interpreting the Visual Record What do these images suggest about the people who made them?

Early History

Southern Africa's landscape and climate have influenced the region's history. For example, monsoon winds blow from the Indian Ocean to southern Africa from November to February. From May to September the wind blows the other way, from Africa to Asia. Ancient ships used these winds to make regular trading voyages between the two continents.

The Khoisan Some of the oldest human fossils have been found in southern Africa. By about 18,000 B.C., groups of hunter-gatherers were living throughout the mainland region. They left distinctive paintings of people and animals on rock surfaces. Some descendants of these people still live in certain desert regions. They speak languages of the Khoisan language family, which share unusual "click" sounds. However, most Khoisan people were absorbed into groups that moved into the region later.

Bantu Migrations Some 1,500–2,000 years ago a different group of people spread from central Africa into southern Africa. They spoke another family of languages known as Bantu. Today, most southern Africans speak one of the more than 200 Bantu languages. Scholars believe the early Bantu people introduced the use of iron to make tools. The Bantu are also thought to have introduced cattle herding to the region.

Shona and Swahili By about A.D. 1000 one Bantu group, the Shona, had built an empire. It included much of what is now Zimbabwe and Mozambique. They farmed, raised cattle, and traded gold with other groups on the coast. They also constructed stone-walled towns called *zimbabwe*. The largest town, now called Great Zimbabwe, may have had 10,000 to 20,000 residents. Great Zimbabwe was abandoned in the 1400s.

People fish with nets in the Indian Ocean. Fishing is an important industry in Mozambique and Madagascar.

Among Great Zimbabwe's trading partners were the Swahili-speaking people of the east coast. These were Africans who had adopted Islam and many Arab customs by the A.D. 1100s. The Swahili-speakers were sailors and traders. Archaeologists have found Chinese porcelain at Great Zimbabwe. This suggests that Africa and East Asia were connected by an Indian Ocean trade network.

Madagascar Madagascar's early history is quite different from the rest of southern Africa. Madagascar's first settlers came from Asia, rather than Africa, about A.D. 700. The island's culture shows the influence of both Africa and Asia. Malagasy, Madagascar's official language, is related to languages spoken in Indonesia. Malagasy also includes many words from the Bantu language family.

Mozambique In the early 1500s the Portuguese set up forts in Mozambique. They hoped to take over the region's gold trade from the Swahili-speakers and Arabs. The Portuguese also established large estates along the Zambezi River that used slave labor. In the 1700s and 1800s Mozambique became an important part of the slave trade. Africans were captured there and sent as slaves to Brazil and other parts of the world.

The Portuguese built this prison in Mozambique in the 1800s.

Interpreting the Visual Record How might this architecture reflect European influences?

✓ **READING CHECK:** (*Human Systems*) What were some key events in the early history of southern Africa?

In this painting, British ships sail past the Cape of Good Hope. The distinctively shaped Table Mountain is visible in the distance.

Interpreting the Visual Record How are these ships propelled?

Our Amazing Planet

Much of southern Africa was a malaria zone. Quinine, a medicine made from a South American tree, could combat malaria. Using this medicine, Europeans were able to move into lowland areas where malaria was common.

In this 1935 photograph, elephant tusks and rhino horns are inspected in a London warehouse.

The Dutch, British, and Portuguese in South Africa

The land around the Cape of Good Hope lacked the gold and copper of the Zambezi Valley. However, it had a Mediterranean climate. It also was free of the mosquitoes and tsetse flies that spread tropical diseases. In 1652 the Dutch set up a trade station at a natural harbor near the Cape. This small colony would eventually become known as Cape Town. It provided supplies to Dutch ships sailing between the Dutch East Indies and Europe. The Dutch brought in slaves to work in the colony. Some were Malays from Southeast Asia. Others were Africans bought at slave markets in other parts of Africa.

Afrikaners and Afrikaans The main language spoken in the colony was Dutch. Over time, Khoisan, Bantu, and Malay words were added, creating a new language called Afrikaans. White descendants of the original colonists are called Afrikaners. Some European men married Khoisan or Malay women. People descended from Malays, Khoisan, or a mixture of these with Europeans are called Coloureds.

A British Colony Afrikaner frontier farmers called **Boers** gradually spread out from the original colony. Then, in the early 1800s, Great Britain took over the area of the Cape. The Boers resisted the British colonial government. Many Boers packed all their belongings into wagons and moved farther east and north. This movement was called the Great Trek.

At about the same time, a Bantu-speaking group, the Zulu, became a powerful fighting force. They conquered the surrounding African peoples, creating their own empire. When the Boers moved into the northern plains, they entered Zulu territory. The two sides clashed over control of the land. Eventually the Zulu were challenged by the British and defeated after a series of battles.

Trade in Slaves and Ivory The British banned slavery in their empire in 1833. The Portuguese colonies of Angola and Mozambique remained as Africa's main slave markets. The slave trade eventually ended in the late 1800s. African trade began to focus on ivory—the tusks of elephants. Hunters wiped out the entire elephant population in some parts of southern Africa.

Diamonds, Gold, and Colonies In the 1860s diamonds were discovered in the northern part of the Cape Colony. In 1886 gold was discovered in the Transvaal, an area controlled by the Boers. Thousands of British and others came to South Africa. Railroads were built to connect the interior with the coast.

As the British moved north from the Cape Colony, some Boers moved into what is now Botswana. Afraid that the Boers would take over his country, Botswana's ruler asked for British protection. In 1885 Botswana (then known as Bechuanaland) came under British control. What is now Namibia became German South-west Africa—a German colony. In 1889 what is now Zimbabwe came under control of the British South Africa Company as part of Rhodesia. It became a self-governing British colony in 1923.

South Africa In 1899 tensions over land and mineral wealth led to war between the Boers and the British. The Boers were greatly outnumbered, but held off the British army for three years. In the end the Boers were defeated. Their territory was added to the British colony of South Africa. In 1920, following Germany's defeat in World War I, Namibia was placed under South Africa's control.

This old steam train still operates in South Africa. The British built this and other railroads during the colonial period.
Interpreting the Visual Record
Why did the Europeans connect the interior with the coast?

✓ **READING CHECK:** (**Human Systems**) How did Europeans gain control of southern Africa, and what changes did this cause?

Section Review 2

go.hrw.com
Homework Practice Online
Keyword: SG3 HP26

Define and explain: Boers

Working with Sketch Maps On the map you created in Section 1, label Cape Town. What were the advantages of Cape Town's location?

Reading for the Main Idea

1. (**Human Systems**) How did the Bantu affect the history of southern Africa?

2. (**Human Systems**) How do archaeologists believe Chinese porcelain came to Great Zimbabwe?

Critical Thinking

3. **Finding the Main Idea** How did the slave trade affect southern Africa?

4. **Analyzing Information** What European groups settled in southern Africa? How did these groups interact with each other?

Organizing What You Know

5. **Sequencing** Copy the following time line. Use it to mark important events in the history of southern Africa from 18,000 B.C. to 1920.

18,000 B.C. ———————————————— 1920

Section 3 South Africa Today

Read to Discover

1. What was South Africa's policy of apartheid?
2. What factors led to the end of apartheid?
3. What is South Africa's economy like?
4. What are South Africa's prospects for the future?

Why It Matters

South Africa is working to make sure all citizens are treated fairly today. Use CNNfyi.com to find examples of recent events in South Africa that reflect these efforts. Record your findings in your journal.

Define

apartheid
townships
sanctions

Locate

Witwatersrand
Johannesburg
Durban
Port Elizabeth

Zulu in traditional warrior's clothing

Nelson Mandela was sentenced to life imprisonment in 1964 but was released in 1990. In 1994 he was elected president of South Africa.

Racial Divisions

In the early 1900s South Africa's government, which was dominated by Afrikaners, became increasingly racist. Some black South Africans opposed the government. They formed the African National Congress (ANC) in 1912 to defend their rights. However, the trend toward racial division and inequality continued.

After World War II South Africa became an independent country. The South African government set up a policy of separation for its different peoples. This policy was called **apartheid**, meaning "apartness." The government divided people into three groups: whites, coloureds and Asians, and blacks—the overwhelming majority. Coloureds and Asians were only allowed to live in certain areas. Each African tribe or group was given its own rural "homeland."

The whites owned most of the good farmland. They also owned the mines and other natural resources. Black Africans had no rights in white areas. Blacks' land, housing, and health care were poor compared to those for whites. Education for blacks was limited, and classes were often taught in Afrikaans. Coloureds' facilities were poor but slightly better than those for blacks. People who protested these rules were sent to prison. One of those imprisoned was a lawyer named Nelson Mandela, a leader of the ANC.

Many blacks found work in white-owned industries, mines, shops, and farms. They had to live in separate areas called **townships**. These were often crowded clusters of tiny homes. They were far from the jobs in the cities and mines.

✓ **READING CHECK:** Human Systems What was apartheid?

In townships like Kayalitsha, black workers lived in crude shacks.

Interpreting the Visual Record How did the apartheid system affect the roles and responsibilities of South Africans?

Pressure against South Africa

Many people around the world objected to South Africa's apartheid laws. Some countries banned trade with South Africa. Some companies in the United States and Europe refused to invest their money in South Africa. Many international scientific and sports organizations refused to include South Africans in their meetings and competitions. These penalties, called **sanctions**, were intended to force South Africa to end apartheid.

South Africa and Its Neighbors During the 1960s, 1970s, and 1980s other countries in southern Africa gained their independence from colonial rule. British colonists in Rhodesia protested Britain's decision to grant independence. They declared their own white-dominated republic in 1970. This break resulted in years of violence and civil war. Finally the white government agreed to hold elections. They turned the country over to the black majority. The new government renamed the country Zimbabwe.

Mozambique was granted independence in 1975 after 10 years of war against Portuguese rule. However, rebels backed by Rhodesia and South Africa plunged Mozambique into another long war. Despite violent resistance, Namibia continued to be ruled by South Africa until independence in 1990.

The End of Apartheid As other countries in southern Africa gained independence, South Africa became more and more isolated. Protest within the country increased. The government outlawed the ANC. Many ANC members were jailed or forced to leave the country. Antiapartheid protesters turned increasingly to violence. South African

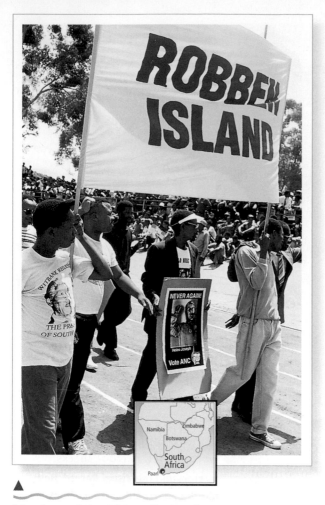

Members of the African National Congress lead a rally celebrating Nelson Mandela's release from prison.

These are uncut, or rough, diamonds. Diamonds are the hardest mineral. This makes them useful for certain types of cutting and drilling.

Interpreting the Visual Record
Why do you think some diamonds are more suitable for industrial uses than for jewelry?

forces attacked suspected rebel bases in neighboring countries like Botswana and Zimbabwe.

Finally, in the late 1980s South Africa began to move away from the apartheid system. In 1990 the government released Nelson Mandela from prison. Mandela was elected president in 1994 after all South Africans were given the right to vote.

Today all races have equal rights in South Africa. Public schools and universities are open to all, as are hospitals and transportation. However, economic equality has been slow in coming. White South Africans are still wealthier than the vast majority of black South Africans. Also, divisions between different black ethnic groups have caused new tensions. Still, South Africans now hope for a better future.

✓ **READING CHECK:** (*Human Systems*) Why and how did South Africa do away with apartheid?

South Africa's Economy

South Africa's government is trying to create jobs and better conditions for black workers and farmers. However, South Africa's mineral wealth and industries are still mostly owned by white people. Even officials who favor reform are afraid that too-rapid change will weaken the economy. They fear it will drive educated and wealthy whites to leave the country. The government has avoided taking white-owned farmland to divide among black farmers.

South Africa's energy resources include coal and hydroelectric power. Rich uranium mines provide fuel for nuclear power plants. In addition to gold and diamonds, mineral resources include copper, platinum, iron ore, and chromium.

The Witwatersrand region around Johannesburg is the continent's largest industrial area. South African and foreign companies build computers, cars, televisions, and many other products needed for modern life. The major port is Durban on the Indian Ocean coast. Cape Town and Port Elizabeth are other important ports.

✓ **READING CHECK:** (*Human Systems*) How has apartheid continued to affect South Africa's economy today?

South Africa's Future

South Africa has more resources and industry than most African countries but faces severe problems. It must begin to deliver equal education and economic opportunities to the entire population.

Cape Town has grown into a large industrial city. In this photograph, the harbor is visible beyond the tall buildings of the business district.

New problems have arisen since the end of apartheid. Crime has increased in the large cities. Also, South Africa, like the rest of the region, is facing a terrible AIDS epidemic.

There are 11 official languages in South Africa, although English is used in most areas. South Africa produces fine wines from the region around Cape Town. It has a unique cooking style combining Dutch, Malay, and African foods. The country also has a lively tradition of literature and the arts. Today, traditional ethnic designs are used in clothing, lamps, linens, and other products. These are sold to tourists and locals alike.

South Africa

Country	Population/ Growth Rate	Life Expectancy	Literacy Rate	Per Capita GDP
South Africa	43,586,097 0.3%	48, male 49, female	82%	$8,500
United States	281,421,906 0.9%	74, male 80, female	97%	$36,200

Sources: Central Intelligence Agency, *The World Factbook 2001*; U.S. Census Bureau

✓ **READING CHECK:** *Places and Regions* What are the challenges faced by South Africa?

Interpreting the Visual Record What is South Africa's per capita GDP?

go. hrw .com **Homework Practice Online**

Keyword: SG3 HP26

Section Review 3

Define and explain: apartheid, townships, sanctions

Working with Sketch Maps On the map you created in Section 2, label Witwatersrand, Johannesburg, Durban, and Port Elizabeth.

Reading for the Main Idea

1. *Human Systems* What was the system of apartheid, and how did it affect the roles and responsibilities of South Africans?

2. *Human Systems* How did people around the world protest apartheid?

3. *Places and Regions* What challenges remain for South Africa?

Critical Thinking

4. **Analyzing Information** Why is South Africa the continent's most economically developed country?

Organizing What You Know

5. **Summarizing** Use this graphic organizer to list information about life in South Africa during apartheid and since the system ended.

During apartheid	Since apartheid ended

Section 4 The Other Southern African Countries

Read to Discover

1. What groups have influenced Namibia's culture?
2. What factors have helped Botswana's economy?
3. What is Zimbabwe's economy like?
4. Why has Mozambique remained so poor?
5. What events have marked Madagascar's recent history?

Define

Organization of African Unity (OAU)

Locate

Windhoek
Gaborone
Harare
Maputo

WHY IT MATTERS

Like many African countries, Madagascar has suffered in recent years from environmental problems. Use CNNfyi.com or other **current events** sources to find examples of how Madagascar is coping with its environmental problems. Record your findings in your journal.

Grilled shrimp from Mozambique

Namibia

Most Namibians live in the savannas of the north or in the cooler central highlands. Windhoek, the capital, is located in these highlands. About 7 percent of the population is white, mainly of German descent. The rest of the population is divided among several different ethnic groups. Most Namibians are Christian. English is the official language. However, schooling was in Afrikaans until recently.

At independence in 1990, white farmers held most of the productive land. Most of Namibia's income comes from the mining of diamonds, copper, lead, zinc, and uranium. Fishing in the Atlantic Ocean and sheep ranching are also important sources of income.

Namibian culture shows many different influences. In many rocky areas, ancient rock engravings and paintings of the Khoisan are preserved. Beer and pastries reflect the period of German colonization.

✓ **READING CHECK:** *Human Systems* What are Namibia's cultural influences?

A San grandmother and child drink water from an ostrich egg. The San people traditionally lived by hunting and gathering. However, just a few live this way today.

Interpreting the Visual Record What factors do you think might lead many San people to give up their traditional way of life?

Botswana

Botswana is a large, landlocked, semiarid country. Thanks to mineral resources and stable political conditions, Botswana is one of Africa's success stories. Cattle ranching and mining of copper and diamonds are the principal economic activities. Recently, international companies have set up factories here. A new capital,

Gaborone, was built after independence. Like the other countries of the region, Botswana belongs to the **Organization of African Unity (OAU)**. The OAU, founded in 1963, tries to promote cooperation between African countries.

Botswana's population is less than 1.6 million. About 79 percent belong to a single ethnic group, the Tswana. Most of the population live in the savanna and steppe areas of the east and south. The San and other minority groups mostly live in the northern swamps and the Kalahari Desert. About half of Botswana's people are Christian. The rest follow traditional African religions.

Botswana's major river, the Okavango, flows from Angola into a huge basin. The swamps of this basin are home to elephants, crocodiles, antelope, lions, hyenas, and other animals. Many tourists travel to Botswana to see these wild animals in their habitat.

Traditional crafts of Botswana include ostrich-eggshell beadwork and woven baskets with complex designs. People there also produce colorful wool tapestries and rugs.

✓ **READING CHECK:** (*Places and Regions*) Why might Botswana be considered a success story?

▲
The Okavango River spreads out to form a large swampy area. Dense vegetation allows only small boats to move through the narrow channels.

Zimbabwe

Zimbabwe's capital is Harare. Zimbabwe gained independence in 1980. Since then, the country has struggled to create a more equal distribution of land and wealth. White residents make up less than 1 percent of the population. However, they still own most of the large farms and ranches.

Zimbabwe exports tobacco, corn, sugar, and beef. It now manufactures many everyday items, including shoes, batteries, and radios. Exports of gold, copper, chrome, nickel, and tin are also important to Zimbabwe's economy.

The AIDS epidemic threatens to kill hundreds of thousands of Zimbabwe's people, leaving many orphans behind. These effects will make economic growth harder. Other diseases such as malaria and tuberculosis are often deadly. There are also tensions between the majority Shona people and the minority Ndebele.

Artists in Zimbabwe have revived the tradition of stone sculpture found at Great Zimbabwe. Some of the larger pieces are among the most striking examples of modern art in the world.

✓ **READING CHECK:** (*Places and Regions*) What is Zimbabwe's economy like?

Other Southern African Countries

COUNTRY	POPULATION/ GROWTH RATE	LIFE EXPECTANCY	LITERACY RATE	PER CAPITA GDP
Botswana	1,586,119 0.5%	37, male 38, female	70%	$6,600
Madagascar	15,982,563 3%	53, male 58, female	80%	$800
Mozambique	19,371,057 1.3%	37, male 36, female	42%	$1,000
Namibia	1,797,677 1.4%	42, male 39, female	38%	$4,300
Zimbabwe	11,365,366 0.2%	39, male 36, female	85%	$2,500
United States	281,421,906 0.9%	74, male 80, female	97%	$36,200

Sources: Central Intelligence Agency, *The World Factbook 2001;* U.S. Census Bureau

Interpreting the Chart Which countries are the least economically developed in the region, according to the chart?

CONNECTING TO History

The Granger Collection, New York

In 1884–85, representatives of Europe's colonial countries met in Berlin. These countries included Belgium, France, Germany, Great Britain, Italy, Portugal, and Spain. Each was conquering areas in Africa. Their claims to territory were beginning to overlap. Leaders began to worry that a rivalry in Africa might trigger a war in Europe.

AFRICA'S BORDERS

Cartoon of France and Britain dividing Africa

The Berlin conference was called to agree to boundaries for these African colonies. No Africans were invited to the conference. The European representatives divided up Africa among themselves. The new borders sometimes followed physical features, such as lakes and mountains. Many simply followed straight lines of latitude or longitude. Often people from the same ethnic group were separated by the new borders. In other places, ethnic groups hostile to each other were grouped together.

Most of the European colonies in Africa became independent after 1960. However, the leaders of the new African countries have mostly avoided drawing new boundary lines. So these countries still struggle with the borders they inherited from the Berlin Conference. These borders have made it hard for many African countries to build national loyalty among their citizens.

Understanding What You Read
1. How were Africa's borders established?
2. What consequences have these borders had for modern Africa?

Do you remember what you learned about uneven resource distribution? See Chapter 5 to review.

Mozambique

Mozambique is one of the world's poorest countries. Its economy was badly damaged by civil war after independence from Portugal. Today, Mozambique's ports of Maputo—the capital—and Beira once again ship many products from interior Africa. The taxes collected on these shipments are an important source of revenue. Energy sources include coal and new hydroelectric dams on the Zambezi River. Plantations grow cotton, cashews, sugar, and tea.

Most of Mozambique's people belong to various Bantu ethnic groups. Each group has its own language. However, the country's official language is Portuguese. About 30 percent of the people are Christian, and 20 percent are Muslim.

Mozambique is famous for its fiery pepper or *peri-peri* sauces. They are often served on shrimp and rice.

✓ **READING CHECK:** (*Places and Regions*) What factor limited Mozambique's economic development?

Madagascar

Madagascar is a former French colony. It was ruled by a socialist dictator until the early 1990s. At that point the people demanded a new political system. The optimism that came with democracy faded as the new leaders struggled with poverty. Surprisingly, in 1996 the people voted the former dictator back into power.

Nearly all of Madagascar's people are still very poor. There is little industry. Most of the country's income comes from exports of coffee, sugar, vanilla, and cloves. Most of the people depend on subsistence farming.

Madagascar has many animals found nowhere else. This is because the island has been separated from the African mainland for millions of years. Some 40 species of lemurs, relatives of apes, live only on this island. However, destruction of the rain forests threatens many of Madagascar's animals with extinction.

Malagasy and French are spoken throughout Madagascar. About 55 percent of the people follow traditional African religions. Some 40 percent are Christian, and about 5 percent are Muslim.

✓ **READING CHECK:** (*Places and Regions*) What has Madagascar's recent history been like?

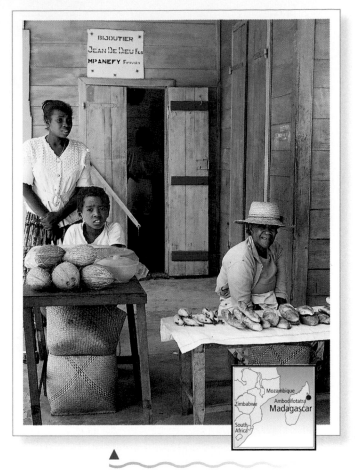

▲

Remnants of French culture can still be seen in Madagascar.
Interpreting the Visual Record **Which of these vendors' foods suggests a connection to French culture?**

Section Review 4

go.hrw.com
Homework Practice Online
Keyword: SG3 HP26

Define and explain: Organization of African Unity (OAU)

Working with Sketch Maps On the map you created in Section 3, label Windhoek, Gaborone, Harare, and Maputo. Which cities are located on the plateau of the southern African interior?

Reading for the Main Idea

1. (*Human Systems*) How have diseases affected Zimbabwe's people and economy?

2. (*Human Systems*) How did civil war affect Mozambique?

3. (*Environment and Society*) What minerals does Namibia have, and how do they affect its economy?

Critical Thinking

4. **Drawing Inferences and Conclusions** How do you think the fact that Botswana's population is almost entirely of a single ethnic group has affected its politics?

Organizing What You Know

5. **Summarizing** Copy the following graphic organizer. Use it to list information about southern African cultures.

Country	Culture
Namibia	
Botswana	
Zimbabwe	
Mozambique	
Madagascar	

Reviewing What You Know

Building Vocabulary

On a separate sheet of paper, write sentences to define each of the following words.

1. enclaves
2. the veld
3. pans
4. Boers
5. apartheid
6. townships
7. sanctions
8. Organization of African Unity (OAU)

Reviewing the Main Ideas

1. **(Places and Regions)** What are southern Africa's two deserts like?

2. **(Environment and Society)** What made it possible for early southern Africans to trade with Asians?

3. **(Human Systems)** What did the original Bantu migrants bring to southern Africa?

4. **(Environment and Society)** How have mineral resources affected South Africa?

5. **(Human Systems)** What three racial groups were defined and separated by apartheid? Which group made up the majority of the population?

Understanding Environment and Society

City Location

Johannesburg grew because of gold deposits nearby. Cape Town's location is excellent for a port. Create a presentation on why cities are located where they are. As you prepare your presentation you may want to think about the following:

- What physical features seem to contribute to the growth of cities around the world?
- Which major cities of southern Africa owe their locations to deposits of minerals?

Thinking Critically

1. **Drawing Inferences and Conclusions** In what parts of southern Africa do you think most farming takes place? Why?

2. **Analyzing Information** What finally motivated the South African government to end the apartheid system?

3. **Summarizing** Who were the Afrikaners, and what role did they play in the history of southern Africa?

4. **Summarizing** What factors have slowed the economic development of the countries in this region?

5. **Finding the Main Idea** How did the discovery of diamonds and gold affect the settlement of Europeans in southern Africa?

Map ACTIVITY

On a separate sheet of paper, match the letters on the map with their correct labels.

Drakensberg   Kalahari Desert
Inyanga   Namib Desert
   Mountains   Orange River
Cape of Good   Limpopo River
   Hope   Harare

Mental Mapping Skills ACTIVITY

On a separate sheet of paper, draw a freehand map of southern Africa. Make a key for your map and label the following:

Botswana   Namibia
Madagascar   South Africa
Mozambique   Zimbabwe

WRITING ACTIVITY

Write a brief essay in which you compare and contrast Botswana and Mozambique. How are the physical features of these two countries similar or different? How do these features affect the economies of Botswana and Mozambique? What are the major industries? Be sure to use standard grammar, spelling, sentence structure, and punctuation.

Alternative Assessment

Portfolio ACTIVITY

Learning About Your Local Geography
Mineral Resources Southern Africa is rich in minerals. Working in a group, list mineral resources found in your area. Then create a display about local mineral resources.

🗗 **internet** connect

Internet Activity: go.hrw.com
KEYWORD: SG3 GT26

Choose a topic to explore about southern Africa:
- Explore the Namib Desert.
- Go on a South African safari.
- Investigate apartheid.

Kenya's Tree Planters

Ten million young trees scattered throughout Kenya offer new hope to farmers and families. The trees were planted by women who farm these lands. "We are planting trees to ensure our own survival," says Wangari Maathai. She is the founder of Kenya's Green Belt Movement.

Deforestation

Like many other developing countries, Kenya is a country of farmers and herders. The most productive farmlands are in the highlands. This area was once green with trees and plants. Over the past century, however, much of this land has been cleared. Today, less than 10 percent of the original forests remain. Many trees were cut for firewood, which people use for cooking.

Without tree roots to hold the soil in place, the land eroded. The land was losing its fertility.

Farmers moved to the savannas in search of better land.

Wangari Maathai recognized what was happening. "When I would visit the village where I was born," she says, "I saw whole forests had been cleared for cultivation and timber. People were moving onto hilly slopes and riverbeds and marginal areas that were only bush when I was a child." Maathai was shocked to find children suffering from malnutrition. People were no longer eating foods such as beans and corn. Instead, they were eating refined foods such as rice. They were doing this because these foods need less cooking—and thus less firewood.

The Green Belt Movement

On June 5, 1977, in honor of World Environment Day, Maathai and a few supporters planted seven trees in Nairobi, Kenya's capital. Thus began the Green Belt Movement. This movement then spread through the Kenyan highlands and captured people's attention around the world.

From the beginning, Maathai knew that the success of her efforts depended mainly on women. In Kenya, men tend cash crops such as coffee and cotton. Women collect firewood and grow corn, beans, and other food crops. It is the women who grow the food their families eat. The women were the first to see the connection between poor soil and famine.

◀
Many of the trees in Kenya's highlands have been cleared for crops.

The movement's workers encouraged women in Kenya to plant trees. They pointed out that women would not have to walk miles to collect firewood. They would have wood available nearby for fires, fences, and buildings. If the tree seedlings survived, the women would also be paid a small sum of money.

First, a few small nurseries were started to give out free seedlings. The nurseries are staffed by local women who are paid for their work. Nurseries also train and pay local people known as Green Belt Rangers. The Rangers visit farms, check on seedlings, and offer advice.

Before long, nurseries were appearing in communities throughout the highlands. Kenyan women talked to friends and neighbors about the benefits of planting trees. Neighbors encouraged Esther Wairimu to plant seedlings. Five years later, her fields were surrounded by mango, blue gum, and other trees. "I have learned that a tree… is life," she says.

Today, the advantages of planting trees are clear. Farmers now have fuel and shade. Even

Workers from the Green Belt Movement teach school-children in Kenya how to care for tree seedlings.

more important, the soil is being protected from erosion. The number of Green Belt nurseries has grown to 3,000. Most are run by women.

Expanding the Movement

Maathai believes that local people must work together to protect the environment. She stresses that the Green Belt Movement relies on farmers. The movement receives little government support. Most of the money comes from small personal donations.

Now Maathai dreams of spreading her movement to other African countries. "We must never lose hope…," she says. "One person *can* make a difference."

Wangari Maathai (right) has encouraged Kenyan women to plant millions of trees. Women are paid for the seedlings they plant that survive.

Your Turn

Working in small groups, think of an environmental issue facing your community or state.

1. Develop a plan that demonstrates how "one person can make a difference."

2. Present your group's plan to the rest of the class.

Building Skills for Life: Understanding Ecosystems

The plants and animals in an area, together with the nonliving parts of their environment, form an ecosystem. An important thing to remember about ecosystems is that each part is interconnected.

Life on Earth depends on the energy and nutrients flowing through ecosystems. Energy and nutrients move between plants, animals, and soils through food chains and food webs.

Most ecosystems involve three groups of organisms: producers, consumers, and decomposers. Producers make their own food. Plants are producers. They make food by combining carbon dioxide, nutrients from the soil, sunlight, and water. Consumers are unable to make food. They have to get food from producers or from other consumers. Humans are consumers. We eat plants (producers) and animals (consumers). Decomposers get food from dead organisms and wastes. Bacteria and fungi are decomposers.

Elephants have adapted to the ecosystem of Africa's Namib Desert.

▼

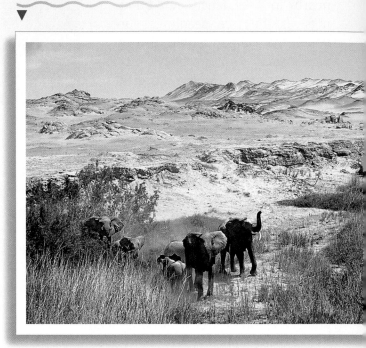

Like all forms of life, humans depend on ecosystems for survival. Knowing how ecosystems work helps us understand how we are connected to both living and nonliving things. It can also help us manage, protect, and use our environments wisely.

PRACTICING THE SKILL

1. Describe an ecosystem in the region where you live. What plants and animals live there? How are they connected?

2. Make a table showing some of the producers, consumers, and decomposers in an ecosystem. What do you think would happen if one of these groups suddenly disappeared?

3. Try to identify some ways that human activities have changed ecosystems in your community. Have some plants or animals disappeared?

HANDS on GEOGRAPHY

Like all organisms, lions are part of an ecosystem. Lions survive by killing and eating other animals, such as zebras and gazelles. After lions have killed an animal, they eat their fill. Then other animals such as vultures and hyenas eat what is left.

The lion itself is food for other organisms. Small animals like ticks, fleas, and mosquitoes drink the lion's blood. The lion's waste serves as food for organisms that live in the soil. When the lion dies, it will be eaten by other animals.

How does the lion fit into its ecosystem? You can answer this question by drawing a connections web. These guidelines will help you get started.

1. Draw a picture of a lion.

2. Think of interactions that lions have with other parts of their environment.

3. Include these interactions in your drawing. For example, lions eat zebras, so you could add a zebra to your drawing.

4. Draw lines connecting the lion to other parts of its environment. For example, you could draw a line connecting the lion and the zebra.

5. Be sure to extend the connections to include nonliving parts of the environment as well. For example, lions eat zebras, zebras eat grass, and grass depends on sunlight.

6. Continue making connections on your diagram. When you are done, answer the Lab Report questions.

Lab Report

1. Label the producers, consumers, and decomposers on your connections web. To which group do lions belong?

2. How are lions dependent on nonliving parts of their environment?

3. Imagine there are no more lions. How do you think the ecosystem shown in your connections web would be affected?

UNIT 8

East and Southeast Asia

CHAPTER 27
China, Mongolia, and Taiwan

CHAPTER 28
Japan and the Koreas

CHAPTER 29
Southeast Asia

Shwedagon Pagoda, Yangon, Myanmar

Rice paddies near Guilin, China

A Peace Corps Volunteer in Mongolia

Matt Heller served as a Peace Corps volunteer in Mongolia. He worked as an English teacher and coordinated a greenhouse reconstruction project. **WHAT DO YOU THINK?** *What kinds of changes would you have to make in your life to live in Mongolia?*

I've been a Peace Corps volunteer in Mongolia for eighteen months. I live in a *ger*, a tent with a small wood stove in the center. It is strong and practical, perfect for a nomadic herder. I, however, am an English teacher in a small school in rural Mongolia. *Ger* life is hard. It makes twenty-year-olds look thirty-five. It makes your soul hard.

Mongolians are very proud of their history. Once, while sitting on the train going from Ulaanbaatar to my own town, Bor-Undur, a Mongolian pointed to his arm and said, "In here is the blood of Genghis Khan. Beware." There is no argument to that statement. I responded, "Yes, older brother (a respectful title addressed to elders), your country is beautiful. Mongolians are lucky."

Along with many other things, I'm learning how Mongolians live. In the steppe there is very little snow, only biting wind and dust. It gets as cold as −50 degrees, not counting the wind chill factor. If I leave tea in a mug, it will freeze by morning. I've broken three mugs that way.

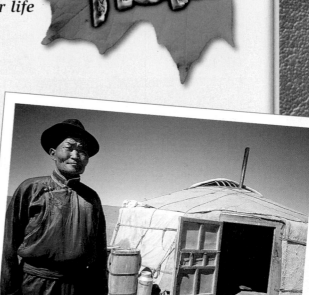

A Mongolian outside his home

Festival of Ages parade, Kyoto, Japan

Understanding Primary Sources

1. What conclusion does Matt Heller make about Mongolians and their past?

2. How does Matt Heller describe the climate in Mongolia?

Giant panda

East and Southeast Asia

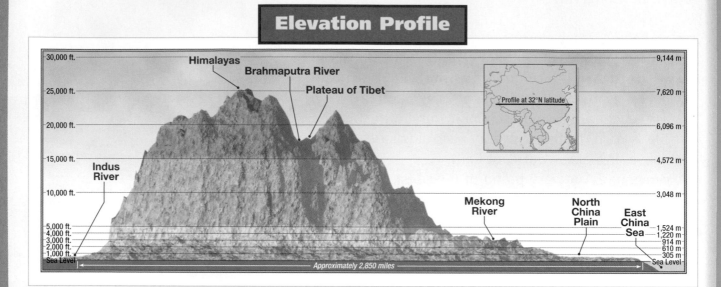

Elevation Profile

30,000 ft. — 9,144 m

Himalayas

25,000 ft. — 7,620 m

Brahmaputra River

Plateau of Tibet

Profile at 32°N latitude

20,000 ft. — 6,096 m

15,000 ft. — 4,572 m

Indus River

10,000 ft. — 3,048 m

Mekong River

North China Plain

East China Sea

5,000 ft. — 1,524 m
4,000 ft. — 1,220 m
3,000 ft. — 914 m
2,000 ft. — 610 m
1,000 ft. — 305 m
Sea Level — Sea Level

Approximately 2,850 miles

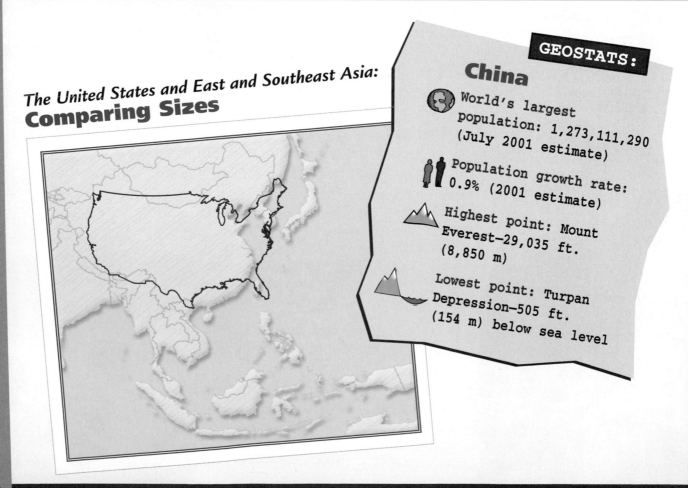

The United States and East and Southeast Asia:
Comparing Sizes

GEOSTATS:

China

🌐 World's largest population: 1,273,111,290 (July 2001 estimate)

👥 Population growth rate: 0.9% (2001 estimate)

⛰ Highest point: Mount Everest—29,035 ft. (8,850 m)

🏔 Lowest point: Turpan Depression—505 ft. (154 m) below sea level

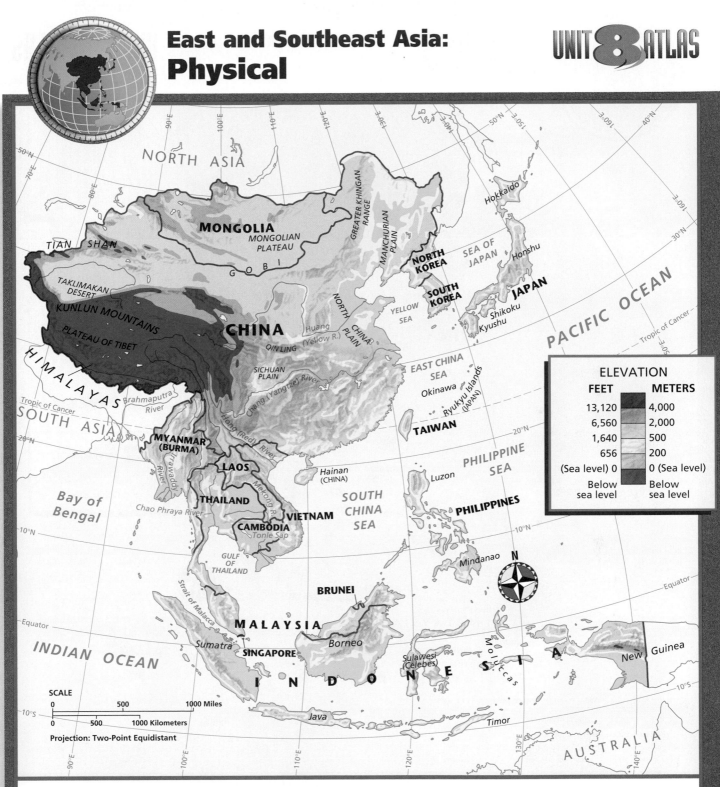

ELEVATION

FEET		METERS
13,120		4,000
6,560		2,000
1,640		500
656		200
(Sea level) 0		0 (Sea level)
Below sea level		Below sea level

SCALE

0   500   1000 Miles

0   500   1000 Kilometers

Projection: Two-Point Equidistant

---

1. *Places and Regions* Which of the region's physical features could make travel and trade difficult?

2. *Places and Regions* What are the region's three largest island countries?

3. *Places and Regions* Which countries have territory on the mainland and on islands?

Critical Thinking

4. Comparing Compare this map to the **population map**. What physical features might prevent western China from becoming densely populated? Why might eastern China be so densely populated?

East and Southeast Asia:
Political

NORTH ASIA

MONGOLIA
⊛Ulaanbaatar

Great Wall of China
⊛Beijing

CHINA

NORTH KOREA
P'yongyang⊛ ⊛Seoul
SOUTH KOREA

SEA OF JAPAN

Hokkaido

Honshu
Tokyo⊛ JAPAN

YELLOW SEA

Shikoku
Kyushu

PACIFIC OCEAN

Tropic of Cancer

SOUTH ASIA
Tropic of Cancer

EAST CHINA SEA

Okinawa
Taipei⊛
Ryukyu Islands (JAPAN)

TAIWAN

MYANMAR (BURMA)
Hanoi⊛
LAOS
⊛Vientiane

Yangon (Rangoon)⊛

Bay of Bengal

THAILAND
Bangkok⊛
CAMBODIA
VIETNAM

Phnom Penh⊛
GULF OF THAILAND

Strait of Malacca

Macao ● ●Hong Kong

Hainan (CHINA)

SOUTH CHINA SEA

PHILIPPINE SEA

Luzon

Manila⊛ PHILIPPINES

Mindanao

N

BRUNEI
⊛Bandar Seri Begawan

Kuala Lumpur⊛
MALAYSIA
⊛Singapore
SINGAPORE

Sumatra

Borneo

Equator

INDONESIA

Sulawesi

Moluccas

New Guinea

INDIAN OCEAN

Jakarta⊛

Java

Timor

AUSTRALIA

Equator

Boundaries
⊛ **National capitals**
● **Other cities**

SCALE
0   500   1000 Miles
0   500   1000 Kilometers
Projection: Two-Point Equidistant

1. (*Places and Regions*) Which country entirely on the mainland shares a border with just one of the region's other countries?

2. (*Places and Regions*) What is the only landlocked country in Southeast Asia? Which country in East Asia is landlocked?

Critical Thinking

3. **Comparing** Compare this map to the **physical map** of the region. Which physical feature forms the border of southwestern China? Which other physical features form natural borders in the region?

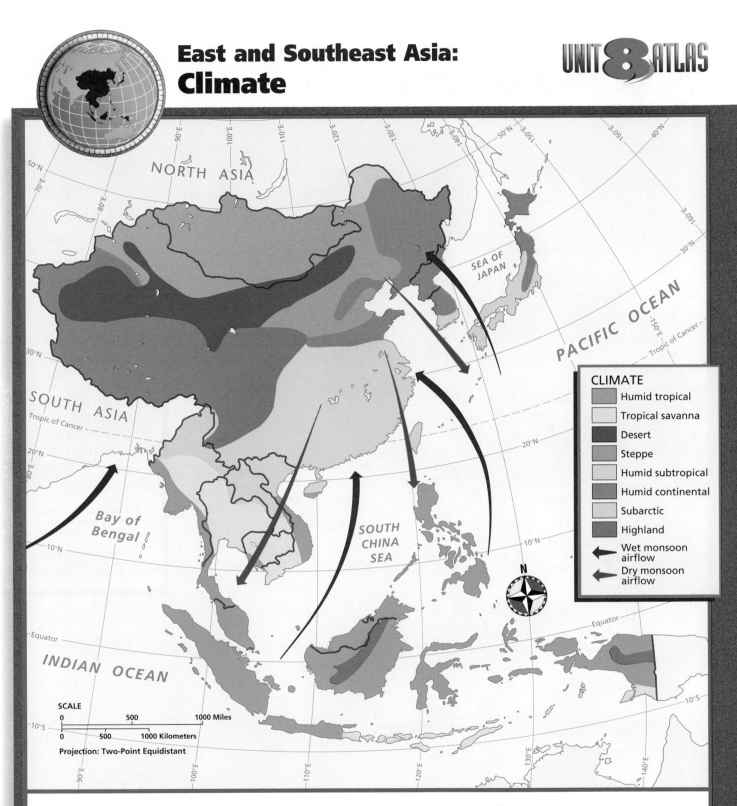

CLIMATE
- Humid tropical
- Tropical savanna
- Desert
- Steppe
- Humid subtropical
- Humid continental
- Subarctic
- Highland
- ← Wet monsoon airflow
- ← Dry monsoon airflow

SCALE
0 — 500 — 1000 Miles
0 — 500 — 1000 Kilometers
Projection: Two-Point Equidistant

1. **Places and Regions** Compare this map to the **political map** of the region. What kind of climate does most of Mongolia have?

2. **Physical Systems** Study the monsoon airflow patterns shown on this map. In which directions do the wet and dry monsoons flow?

Critical Thinking

3. **Drawing Inferences and Conclusions** Why might this region have such a variety of climate types?

4. **Drawing Inferences and Conclusions** Why might the South China Sea be stormy?

POPULATION DENSITY

Persons per sq. mile	Persons per sq km
520	200
260	100
130	50
25	10
3	1
0	0

● Metropolitan areas with more than 2 million inhabitants

○ Metropolitan areas with 1 million to 2 million inhabitants

SCALE
0   500   1000 Miles
0   500   1000 Kilometers
Projection: Two-Point Equidistant

1. (*Places and Regions*) What is the population density in the area between Shanghai and Beijing?

2. (*Environment and Society*) Compare this map to the **physical map** of the region. Which physical features help explain the low population density in western China?

Critical Thinking

3. Analyzing Information Use the map on this page to create a chart, graph, database, or model of population centers in East and Southeast Asia.

RESOURCES

- Coal
- Natural gas
- Oil
- Nuclear power
- Hydroelectric power
- Gold
- Silver
- Other minerals
- Seafood

LAND USE

- Commercial farming
- Subsistence farming
- Forest
- Nomadic herding
- Limited economic activity
- Manufacturing
- Major manufacturing and trade centers

SCALE

0   500   1000 Miles

0   500   1000 Kilometers

Projection: Two-Point Equidistant

---

1. *Places and Regions* Which two countries have large areas where nomadic herding is common?

2. *Places and Regions* Where in China is most commercial farming found? In which countries is subsistence farming common?

Critical Thinking

3. Analyzing Information Use the map on this page to create a chart, graph, database, or model of economic activities in East and Southeast Asia.

Fast FACTS

East and Southeast Asia

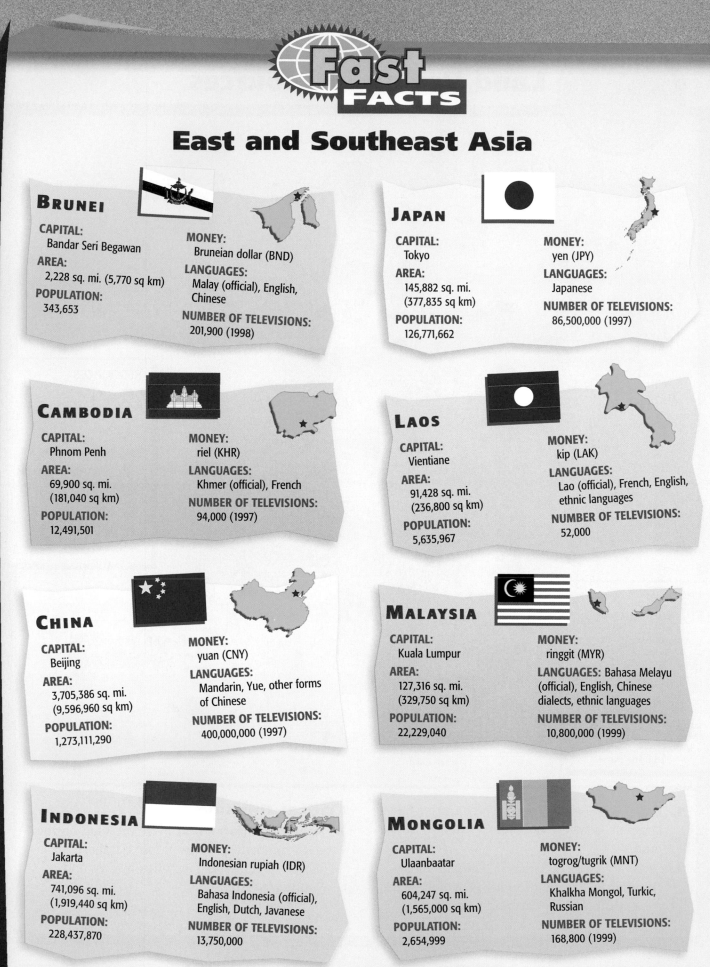

BRUNEI

CAPITAL:
Bandar Seri Begawan

AREA:
2,228 sq. mi. (5,770 sq km)

POPULATION:
343,653

MONEY:
Bruneian dollar (BND)

LANGUAGES:
Malay (official), English, Chinese

NUMBER OF TELEVISIONS:
201,900 (1998)

JAPAN

CAPITAL:
Tokyo

AREA:
145,882 sq. mi. (377,835 sq km)

POPULATION:
126,771,662

MONEY:
yen (JPY)

LANGUAGES:
Japanese

NUMBER OF TELEVISIONS:
86,500,000 (1997)

CAMBODIA

CAPITAL:
Phnom Penh

AREA:
69,900 sq. mi. (181,040 sq km)

POPULATION:
12,491,501

MONEY:
riel (KHR)

LANGUAGES:
Khmer (official), French

NUMBER OF TELEVISIONS:
94,000 (1997)

LAOS

CAPITAL:
Vientiane

AREA:
91,428 sq. mi. (236,800 sq km)

POPULATION:
5,635,967

MONEY:
kip (LAK)

LANGUAGES:
Lao (official), French, English, ethnic languages

NUMBER OF TELEVISIONS:
52,000

CHINA

CAPITAL:
Beijing

AREA:
3,705,386 sq. mi. (9,596,960 sq km)

POPULATION:
1,273,111,290

MONEY:
yuan (CNY)

LANGUAGES:
Mandarin, Yue, other forms of Chinese

NUMBER OF TELEVISIONS:
400,000,000 (1997)

MALAYSIA

CAPITAL:
Kuala Lumpur

AREA:
127,316 sq. mi. (329,750 sq km)

POPULATION:
22,229,040

MONEY:
ringgit (MYR)

LANGUAGES: Bahasa Melayu (official), English, Chinese dialects, ethnic languages

NUMBER OF TELEVISIONS:
10,800,000 (1999)

INDONESIA

CAPITAL:
Jakarta

AREA:
741,096 sq. mi. (1,919,440 sq km)

POPULATION:
228,437,870

MONEY:
Indonesian rupiah (IDR)

LANGUAGES:
Bahasa Indonesia (official), English, Dutch, Javanese

NUMBER OF TELEVISIONS:
13,750,000

MONGOLIA

CAPITAL:
Ulaanbaatar

AREA:
604,247 sq. mi. (1,565,000 sq km)

POPULATION:
2,654,999

MONEY:
togrog/tugrik (MNT)

LANGUAGES:
Khalkha Mongol, Turkic, Russian

NUMBER OF TELEVISIONS:
168,800 (1999)

Countries not drawn to scale.

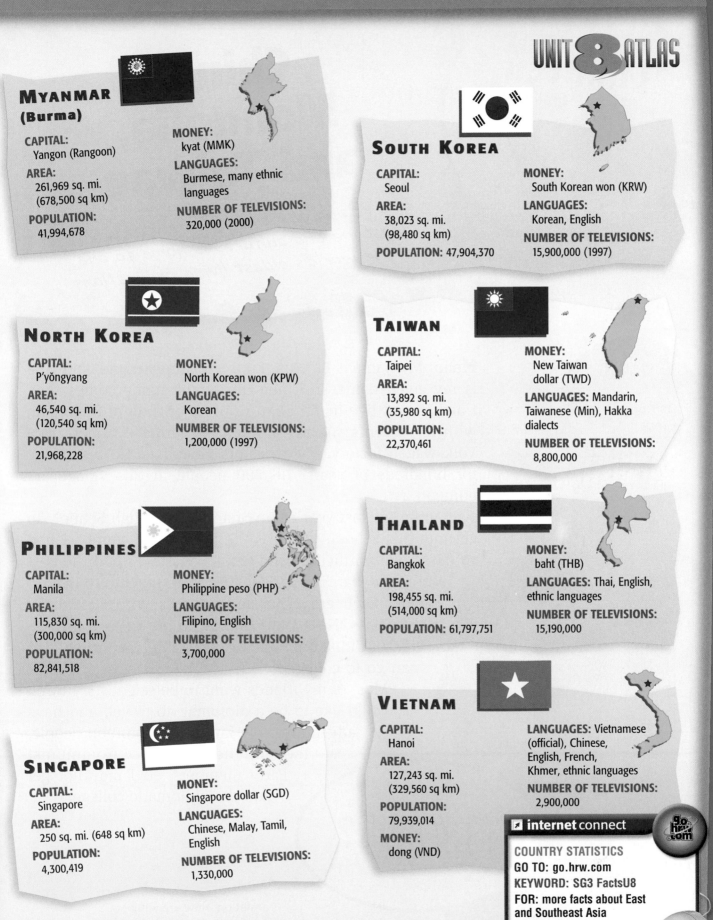

MYANMAR (Burma)

CAPITAL:
Yangon (Rangoon)

AREA:
261,969 sq. mi.
(678,500 sq km)

POPULATION:
41,994,678

MONEY:
kyat (MMK)

LANGUAGES:
Burmese, many ethnic languages

NUMBER OF TELEVISIONS:
320,000 (2000)

NORTH KOREA

CAPITAL:
P'yŏngyang

AREA:
46,540 sq. mi.
(120,540 sq km)

POPULATION:
21,968,228

MONEY:
North Korean won (KPW)

LANGUAGES:
Korean

NUMBER OF TELEVISIONS:
1,200,000 (1997)

PHILIPPINES

CAPITAL:
Manila

AREA:
115,830 sq. mi.
(300,000 sq km)

POPULATION:
82,841,518

MONEY:
Philippine peso (PHP)

LANGUAGES:
Filipino, English

NUMBER OF TELEVISIONS:
3,700,000

SINGAPORE

CAPITAL:
Singapore

AREA:
250 sq. mi. (648 sq km)

POPULATION:
4,300,419

MONEY:
Singapore dollar (SGD)

LANGUAGES:
Chinese, Malay, Tamil, English

NUMBER OF TELEVISIONS:
1,330,000

SOUTH KOREA

CAPITAL:
Seoul

AREA:
38,023 sq. mi.
(98,480 sq km)

POPULATION: 47,904,370

MONEY:
South Korean won (KRW)

LANGUAGES:
Korean, English

NUMBER OF TELEVISIONS:
15,900,000 (1997)

TAIWAN

CAPITAL:
Taipei

AREA:
13,892 sq. mi.
(35,980 sq km)

POPULATION:
22,370,461

MONEY:
New Taiwan dollar (TWD)

LANGUAGES: Mandarin, Taiwanese (Min), Hakka dialects

NUMBER OF TELEVISIONS:
8,800,000

THAILAND

CAPITAL:
Bangkok

AREA:
198,455 sq. mi.
(514,000 sq km)

POPULATION: 61,797,751

MONEY:
baht (THB)

LANGUAGES: Thai, English, ethnic languages

NUMBER OF TELEVISIONS:
15,190,000

VIETNAM

CAPITAL:
Hanoi

AREA:
127,243 sq. mi.
(329,560 sq km)

POPULATION:
79,939,014

MONEY:
dong (VND)

LANGUAGES: Vietnamese (official), Chinese, English, French, Khmer, ethnic languages

NUMBER OF TELEVISIONS:
2,900,000

🔲 internet connect

COUNTRY STATISTICS
GO TO: go.hrw.com
KEYWORD: SG3 FactsU8
FOR: more facts about East and Southeast Asia

Sources: Central Intelligence Agency, *The World Factbook 2001; The World Almanac and Book of Facts 2001;* pop. figures are 2001 estimates.

China, Mongolia, and Taiwan

This region of Asia with its varied landscape and cultures is home to one of the world's oldest living civilizations.

Hello! My name is Lu Hua. Lu is my family name, and Hua is my given name. In China the family name comes first. I am 16 and live in Jin Shan County, outside of Shanghai, with my parents and my brother. My father is a clerk in a Volkswagen factory. My ancestors have lived in this village for hundreds of years. All 200 people in this village are named Lu.

I am in my last year at Jin Shan County High School. To get into this school, which is the best in the county, I had to pass a very difficult exam when I was 11. I had the best score that year. The school goes from seventh to twelfth grade. Each grade has four classes with 50 kids in each class. Now I am hoping to go on to a university. In China only one or two out of a hundred kids can go to college.

Most of my friends want to be scientists. I think I would like to be a diplomat, to travel, and have adventures. My family are common people, though, not Chinese Communist Party members, so I may not get into the diplomatic college.

你好嗎?

◀ Translation: How are you?

Section 1 — Physical Geography

Read to Discover

1. What are the physical features of China, Mongolia, and Taiwan?
2. What types of climate are found in China, Mongolia, and Taiwan?
3. What natural resources do China, Mongolia, and Taiwan have?

Define

dikes
arable

Locate

Himalayas
Mount Everest
Kunlun Mountains
Tian Shan
Plateau of Tibet
Taklimakan Desert
Tarim Basin

Gobi
North China Plain
Huang He
Chang River
Sichuan (Red) Basin
Xi River

WHY IT MATTERS

China was once one of the most isolated countries in the world. Today, however, it plays a major role in the world community. Use CNNfyi.com or other current events sources to find out more about China's role in world affairs. Record your findings in your journal.

Mask made of gold

China, Mongolia, and Taiwan: Physical-Political

Size comparison of China, Mongolia, and Taiwan to the contiguous United States

ELEVATION

FEET	METERS
13,120	4,000
6,560	2,000
1,640	500
656	200
(Sea level) 0	0 (Sea level)
Below sea level	Below sea level

⊛ National capitals
• Other cities

These snow-covered mountains are in the Wolong Nature Reserve in central China.

Interpreting the Visual Record What climate types would you expect to find in this area of the reserve?

internet connect

GO TO: go.hrw.com
KEYWORD: SG3 CH27
FOR: Web sites about China, Mongolia, and Taiwan

BUILD on WHAT You Know

Do you remember what you learned about plateaus? See Chapter 2 to review.

Physical Features

China has some of the world's tallest mountains, driest deserts, and longest rivers. Mongolia (mahn-GOHL-yuh) is China's neighbor to the north. It is a large, rugged, landlocked country. Burning hot summers and bitter cold winters are common there. In contrast, Taiwan (TY-WAHN) is a green tropical island just off the coast of mainland China.

Mountains The towering Himalayas (hi-muh-LAY-uhz), the world's tallest mountain range, run along China's southwestern border. Mount Everest lies in the Himalayas on China's border with Nepal. At 29,035 feet (8,850 m), it is the world's tallest mountain. If you move north from the Himalayas, you will find several other mountain ranges. These are the Kunlun Mountains (KOON-LOON), the Tian Shan (TYEN SHAHN), and the Altay Mountains (al-TY). To the east, on Mongolia's eastern border with China, you will see the Greater Khingan (KING-AHN) Range.

Mountains stretch the length of Taiwan and cover the eastern half of the island. In some places, the mountains end in steep cliffs at the edge of the Pacific Ocean. To the west of the mountains is a fertile coastal plain.

Plateaus, Basins, and Deserts Isolated plateaus and basins separate the region's mountain ranges. The huge Plateau of Tibet lies between the Himalayas and the Kunlun Mountains. With an average elevation of 16,000 feet (4,877 m), it is the world's highest plateau. The Taklimakan (tah-kluh-muh-KAHN) Desert is a huge expanse of sand. It occupies the central part of the Tarim (DAH-REEM) Basin in western China. In the northeastern corner of the basin, the Turpan (toohr-PAHN) Depression drops about 505 feet (154 m) below sea level.

The Mongolian Plateau covers most of the country of Mongolia. The Gobi (GOH-bee) takes up much of the central and southeastern sections of the plateau. The Gobi is the coldest desert in the world and covers more than 500,000 square miles (1,295,000 sq km). Much of the Gobi is gravel and bare rock.

Plains China and Mongolia have few areas of lowlands made up of coastal and river floodplains. However, these fertile plains support the major population centers. Millions of people live in the North China Plain. It is the largest plain in China and is crossed by major rivers.

Rivers The river known as the Huang (HWAHNG) rises on the eastern edge of the Plateau of Tibet. It flows eastward through the North China Plain and empties into the Yellow Sea. It takes its name, which means "yellow river," from the yellowish mud it carries. Winds carry loess, a yellowish-brown soil, from the Gobi to northern China. The Huang picks up the loess as the river flows through the region. On its way to the sea the river dumps the loess, raising the river bottom. This can lead to flooding. Floodwaters deposit a layer of rich silt that is good for farming but also cause great damage and loss of life. As a result, the Huang has long been known as China's Sorrow. The Chinese have tried to control the Huang by building **dikes**. These high banks of earth or concrete help reduce flooding.

The Chang (CHAHNG), or Yangtze (YAHNG-TSE), River also rises in the Plateau of Tibet. It flows eastward for 3,434 miles (5,525 km) across central China through the fertile Sichuan (SEE-CHWAHN), or Red, Basin. The Chang is China's—and Asia's—longest river. In fact, its name means "long river." The Chang is one of China's most important transportation routes. It is connected to the Huang by the world's oldest and longest canal system, the Grand Canal. The Xi (SHEE) River is southern China's most important river and transportation route.

✓ **READING CHECK:** *Places and Regions* What are the major physical features of this region?

C hina has greater potential for hydroelectric power than any other country in the world. When completed in 2009, the Three Gorges Dam on the Chang River will be the world's largest dam.

Climate

China, Mongolia, and Taiwan are part of a huge region with several different climates. China's precipitation varies. The southeastern coastal region is the country's most humid area. As you move northwestward the climate becomes steadily drier. The extreme northwest has a true desert climate.

Seasonal monsoon winds greatly affect the climate of the region's southern and eastern parts. In winter, winds from Central Asia bring dry, cool-to-cold weather to eastern

The Gobi is the world's third-largest desert. Herders ride Bactrian camels. **Interpreting the Visual Record What characteristics of a desert environment can be seen in this photo?**

China, Mongolia, and Taiwan

Country	Population/ Growth Rate	Life Expectancy	Literacy Rate	Per Capita GDP
China	1,273,111,290 0.9%	70, male 74, female	82%	$3,600
Mongolia	2,654,999 1.5%	62, male 67, female	83%	$1,780
Taiwan	22,370,461 0.8%	74, male 80, female	94%	$17,400
United States	281,421,906 0.9%	74, male 80, female	97%	$36,200

Sources: Central Intelligence Agency, *The World Factbook 2001;* U.S. Census Bureau

Interpreting the Chart **Which country has the fastest rate of population growth?**

This bronze vessel dates to the A.D. 1000s. Found in a tomb, it is just over a foot long (30 cm) and is covered with detailed animal designs.

Interpreting the Visual Record **What features of this object suggest animal characteristics?**

Asia. In summer, winds from the Pacific bring warm, wet air. This creates hot, rainy summers. Typhoons sometimes hit the coastal areas during the summer and fall. Typhoons are violent storms with high winds and heavy rains similar to hurricanes. They often bring flooding and cause a great deal of damage.

✓ **READING CHECK:** *Places and Regions* What are the climates of China, Mongolia, and Taiwan like?

Resources

China has a wide range of mineral resources. These include gold, iron ore, lead, salt, uranium, and zinc, as well as energy resources such as coal and oil. China has greater coal reserves than any other country. At the present rate of use, these reserves will last another 1,000 years. China also produces enough oil to meet most of its own needs.

Mongolia has deposits of coal, copper, gold, iron ore, and oil. Taiwan's most important natural resource is its arable land, or land that is suitable for growing crops.

✓ **READING CHECK:** *Places and Regions* What are the region's resources?

go.hrw.com Homework Practice Online
Keyword: SG3 HP27

Section Review 1

Define and explain: dikes, arable

Working with Sketch Maps On a map of China, Mongolia, and Taiwan that you draw or that your teacher provides, label the following: the Himalayas, Mount Everest, Kunlun Mountains, Tian Shan, Plateau of Tibet, Taklimakan Desert, Tarim Basin, Gobi, North China Plain, Huang He, Chang River, Sichuan Basin, and Xi River. Where do you think the most fertile areas of the region are located?

Reading for the Main Idea

1. *Places and Regions* What and where is the world's largest plateau? What is the world's tallest mountain? Where is it located?

2. *Environment and Society* What are three major rivers in eastern and southern China? How does the Huang affect China's people?

3. *Places and Regions* What is the region's driest area?

Critical Thinking

4. Drawing Inferences and Conclusions What do you think might be the major factors that influence this region's climate?

Organizing What You Know

5. Summarizing Summarize the natural environments of China, Mongolia, and Taiwan.

Country	Physical Features	Climates	Resources

Read to Discover

1. What are some of the major events in the history of China?
2. What are some features of China's culture?

Define

emperor
dynasty
porcelain
martial law
pagodas

Locate

China
Great Wall

A bronze flying horse from the Han dynasty

History

Farmers have cultivated rice in southern China for some 7,000 years. Warm, wet weather made the region ideal for growing rice. Rice remains one of the region's main sources of food. Farmers in drier northern China grew a grain called millet and other crops. The early Chinese also grew hemp for fiber for clothing and spun silk from the cocoons of silkworms. Various cultures developed, particularly along the region's rivers.

The Qin Dynasty and the Great Wall Beginning about 2000 B.C. northern Chinese living in the Huang valley formed kingdoms. As Chinese civilization began to develop, peoples from various regions organized into large states. Each state was governed by an **emperor—** a ruler of a large empire. An emperor is often a member of a **dynasty**. A dynasty is a ruling family that passes power from one generation to the next. Beginning in about 500 B.C., the Chinese began building earthen

The Great Wall of China, including its branches and curves, stretches more than 2,000 miles (3,218 km).

▼

Archaeologists have discovered 6,000 of these uniquely crafted soldiers near Xi'an. Each of these figures from the Qin dynasty has different facial features.

This vase from the Ming dynasty is an example of early Chinese art.

Interpreting the Visual Record How does this vase compare to artifacts left by other early cultures you have studied?

walls hundreds of miles long. These walls separated the kingdoms from the northern nomads and from each other. Records show that the first emperor of the Qin, also spelled Ch'in (CHIN), dynasty ordered the building of the Great Wall along China's northern border. People began to connect the sections of walls about 200 B.C.

The Qin dynasty is well known for its contributions to China's culture. It left behind many historical artifacts. For example, when the first emperor died, he was buried with thousands of life-sized warriors and horses made of clay. You might wonder why someone would want their tomb filled with clay figures. It was an ancient Chinese funeral tradition to bury masters with clay soldiers for protection. Since the Qin emperor had made many enemies during his life, he wanted protection after his death.

During the Qin dynasty the Chinese used a writing system to record their history. This system was similar to the one used in China today. China's name also dates from this time period. In Chinese, China means "Qin kingdom" or "middle kingdom." This name may refer to the Chinese belief that China was the center, or middle, of the world.

The Han Dynasty The Han dynasty came after the Qin dynasty. From the 200s B.C. to the A.D. 200s, the Han dynasty expanded its kingdom southward. The Han also extended the Great Wall westward to protect the Silk Road. This road was originally used by trading caravans taking silk and other Chinese goods to regions west of China. During the Han dynasty the Chinese invented the compass, which aided travel.

The dynasties that followed the Han made China even more powerful. The Chinese continued to make important contributions to society. Later contributions include paper and **porcelain** (POHR-suh-luhn), a type of very fine pottery.

Mongols, Ming Dynasty, and the Manchu In the 1200s Mongol armies led by Genghis Khan conquered China. *Khan* is a title that means "ruler." The Mongols were feared and known for spreading terror throughout the region. Their use of horses added to their military advantage.

Within 100 years the Ming dynasty seized control of China. After several battles with the Mongols, the Ming emperors closed China to outsiders. These emperors strengthened the Great Wall and focused on the development of their own culture.

In the 1600s a group called the Manchu began expanding from their home in Manchuria. Manchuria is located in far northeastern China. The Manchus conquered Inner Mongolia, Korea, and all of northern China. Led by the Qing (CHING) dynasty, the Manchu controlled China for more than 260 years. The dynasty's strong government slowly weakened, however, and was overthrown in the early 1900s.

Outside Influences Marco Polo was one of the few Europeans to visit China before the 1500s. Europeans reached China by following the Silk Road. None came by sea before the 1500s. In the 1500s Portuguese sailors established a trade colony at Macao (muh-KOW) in south China. French and British sailors and traders followed. The Chinese believed that foreigners had little to offer other than silver in return for Chinese porcelain, silk, and tea. Even so, Europeans introduced crops like corn, hot chili peppers, peanuts, potatoes, sweet potatoes, and tobacco. By the 1800s the European countries wanted to control China's trade. A series of conflicts caused China to lose some of its independence. For example, during this period the British acquired Hong Kong. The British, Germans, and French also forced China to open additional ports. China did not regain total independence until the mid-1900s.

The Republics of China In 1912 a revolutionary group led by Sun Yat-sen (SOOHN YAHT-SUHN) forced the last emperor to abdicate, or give up power. This group formed the first Republic of China. Mongolia and Tibet each declared their independence.

After Sun Yat-sen's death the revolutionaries split into two groups, the Nationalists and the Communists. A military leader named Chiang Kai-shek (chang ky-SHEK) united China under a Nationalist government. The Communists opposed him, and a civil war began. During

The Catalan Atlas from the 1300s shows Marco Polo's family traveling by camel caravan.
Interpreting the Visual Record What kind of information might this atlas provide?

▼

This time line reviews major events in China's rich history. The last Chinese dynasty was overthrown in 1912.
Interpreting the Time Line
What events have shaped China's government in the 1900s?

▼

Historical China: A Time Line

Event	Date
Qin becomes China's first dynasty	200s B.C.
Rise of Ming dynasty	1368
People's Republic of China is formed under Mao Zedong	1949
The Cultural Revolution	1966–1976

5000 B.C. — A.D. 1 — 1000 — 1200 — 1400 — 1600 — 1800 — 2000

Event	Date
First rice farmers cultivate the area near the Chang River	5000 B.C.
Han dynasty dominates China	206 B.C. – A.D. 220
Mongols invade China	1200s
Republic is established with the overthrow of the Manchu dynasty	1912
Japanese invade China	1937
Government troops crush protesters in Tiananmen Square	1989

World War II both groups fought the Japanese. The Communists finally defeated the Nationalists in 1949. Led by Mao Zedong (MOW ZUH-DOOHNG), the Communists set up the People's Republic of China. Mao's version of communism is known as Maoism. Only one political party—the Communist Party—was allowed.

Chiang Kai-shek and his Nationalists retreated to Taiwan. There they created a government for what they called the Republic of China. This government maintained its control through **martial law**, or military rule, for many years.

Mao's China Under Mao the government took over the country's economy. His government seized private land and organized it into large, government-run farms. Factories were also put under state control. The central government decided the amount and type of food grown on a farm. It also regulated the production of factory goods, owned all housing, and decided where people should live. Sometimes families were separated or forced to relocate. Women were given equal status and assigned equal work duties. To control China's huge population, the government tried to restrict couples to one child per family. Religious worship was prohibited. Despite the efforts to organize the economy, there were planning errors. In the 1960s a famine killed about 30 million people.

The Cultural Revolution In 1966 Mao began a movement called the Cultural Revolution. The Revolution was an attempt to make everyone live a peasant way of life. Followers of Mao were known as Red Guards. They closed schools and universities. Millions of people were sent to the countryside to work in the fields. Opponents were imprisoned or executed.

This image of Mao Zedong is a recognizable symbol of the Cultural Revolution.

The Potala Palace in Tibet was built in the A.D. 600s. Today, it has more than 1,000 rooms and is used for religious and political events.

After Mao's death in 1976, the new Chinese communist leadership admitted some past mistakes. It tried to modernize the government. Today, farmers can grow and market their own crops on a portion of their rented land. Almost every inch of productive land is used. China is able to meet most of its food needs. The Chinese enjoy a more varied diet of chicken, fish, fruits, meat, and vegetables. Many of China's large, inefficient state-run factories are being closed or turned over to private industries. Millions of Chinese have started small businesses.

A few Chinese have become wealthy. Some business owners can afford to build private homes and to buy cars, computers, and televisions. However, most Chinese are poor. State employees are paid low wages, live in tiny apartments, and cannot afford cars.

Although the government has allowed individuals some economic freedom, it restricts freedom of speech and religion. In 1989 the Chinese army was called in to attack pro-democracy student demonstrators in Tiananmen Square in Beijing (BAY-JING). Many students were injured or killed. Other rebellions among China's ethnic minorities, particularly in Tibet, have been crushed.

✔ **READING CHECK:** *Human Systems* What are some major events in China's history?

▲

The Chinese New Year is also called the Lunar New Year. This is because the cycles of the moon are the basis for the Chinese calendar. The New Year is sometimes called the Spring Festival.

Interpreting the Visual Record What object are parade participants carrying? What does it resemble?

Culture

About 92 percent of China's population consider themselves Han Chinese. Almost everyone can speak one of the seven major Chinese dialects. Mandarin Chinese is the official language and the most common.

Values and Beliefs Several philosophies and religions began in China. Taoism (TOW-i-zuhm), or Daoism (DOW-i-zuhm), is an ancient Chinese religion. Taoists believe that humans should try to follow a path that agrees with nature and avoids everyday concerns. The word *dào* means "the path." Each object or natural feature is thought to have its own god or spirit that may reward good deeds or bring bad luck.

The teachings of Confucius also have been important to Chinese culture. Confucius was a philosopher who lived from 551 to 479 B.C. His teachings stressed the importance of family. Confucius believed that children should

CONNECTING TO *Literature*

Confucius, a Chinese philosopher

This Chinese tale comes from the Hsiao Ching, *or* Book of Filial Piety—*which means "devotion to parents." A student of a follower of Confucius is believed to have written it about 400* B.C. *This story encourages children to protect their parents.*

A Loving Son

Wu Meng was eight years old and very dutiful to his parents. His family was so poor that they could not afford to furnish their beds with mosquito-curtains. Every summer night thousands of mosquitoes attacked them, feasting upon their flesh and blood.

Wu Meng looked at his tired parents asleep on their bed as thousands of mosquitoes fiercely attacked them. Wu saw them sucking his parents' blood, which caused his heart to grieve.

To protect his parents, Wu decided that he would not drive the mosquitoes away from himself. Lying on the bed, he threw off his clothes, and soon feeling the pain of the mosquito attacks, he cried: "I have no fear of you, nor have you any reason to fear me. Although I have a fan, I will not use it, nor will I strike you with my hand. I will lie very quietly and let you gorge to the full." Such was his love for his parents!

Analyzing Primary Sources

1. How does this tale reflect traditional Chinese philosophical beliefs?
2. Why do you think the author of the *Hsiao Ching* wrote this story?

respect their parents and subjects should respect their ruler. He believed people should treat those under their control justly and argued that state power should be used to improve people's lives.

The religion called Buddhism also has been important in China. It was founded by an Indian prince, Siddhartha Gautama. Gautama was born in Nepal about 563 B.C. He decided to search for truth and knowledge. Enlightenment—peace and a sense of being one with the universe—came to him while he was sitting under a Bo or Bodhi tree. As a result, he was given the name Buddha, which means "awakened or enlightened one." Buddhism reached China from India about A.D. 100. It became the country's main religion between the 300s and 500s. Indian architecture also became popular in China. Chinese **pagodas**, or Buddhist temples, are based on Indian designs. Pagodas have an upward-curving roof. Some pagodas are 15 stories tall.

Lifestyle Chinese culture highly values education. Chinese children are required to attend nine years of school. However, just 1 to 2 percent of students pass the difficult entrance exams to get into a university.

The Chinese government tries to control many aspects of everyday life. For example, parents are allowed to have just one child. This is because the government is trying to slow population growth.

The government also controls the newspapers and telephone system. This allows it to limit the flow of information and ideas. Satellite TV, the Internet, and e-mail are becoming more widespread, however. This makes it more difficult for the government to control communication between individuals.

Chinese food varies widely from region to region. Food in Beijing is heavily salted and flavored with garlic and cilantro. Sichuan-style cooking features hot pepper sauces. Cantonese cooking was introduced to the United States by immigrants from Guangzhou (GWAHNG-JOH).

Traditional Chinese medicine stresses herbal products and harmony with the universe. People around the world have used acupuncture. This therapy involves inserting fine needles into specific parts of the body for pain relief. Many Chinese herbal remedies have been used by American drug companies as the basis for modern medicines.

China has rich literary traditions. Painting, porcelain, sculpture, and carving of ivory, stone, and wood are also popular. Performing arts emphasize traditional folktales and stories shown in dances or operas with elaborate costumes.

✔ **READING CHECK:** (*Human Systems*) What is China's culture like?

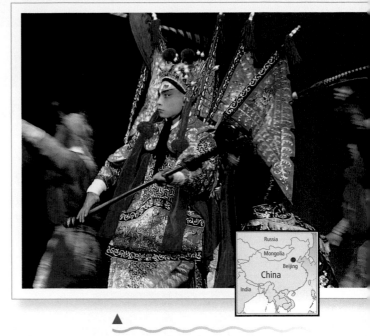

For more than 200 years the Beijing Opera, or Peking Opera, has been recognized worldwide for its artistic contributions. Originally performed for the royal family, it is now viewed by the public and is aired on Chinese television and radio stations.

Homework Practice Online
Keyword: SG3 HP27

Define and explain: emperor, dynasty, porcelain, martial law, pagodas

Working with Sketch Maps On the map you created in Section 1, label China and the Great Wall. Why do you think the Chinese chose to build the Great Wall where they did?

Reading for the Main Idea

1. (*Human Systems*) What contributions did the Qin and Han dynasties make to Chinese history?

2. (*Human Systems*) How did Mao's rule change China?

3. (*Human Systems*) How has China changed since Mao's death in 1976?

Critical Thinking

4. **Summarizing** What are three philosophies or religions that have been important in China? Describe them.

Organizing What You Know

5. **Summarizing** Copy the following graphic organizer. Use it to describe the Ming and the Manchu.

Ming Dynasty	Manchu

Read to Discover

1. Where do most of China's people live?
2. What are the major cities in China, and what are they like?
3. What is China's economy like?
4. What challenges does China face?

Define

command economy
multiple cropping
most-favored-
   nation status

Locate

Beijing   Chongqing
Shanghai   Hong Kong
Nanjing   Macao
Wuhan

WHY IT MATTERS

In 1997 Hong Kong was returned to China after nearly 100 years of British rule. Use **CNNfyi.com** or other **current events** sources to find out more about developments in Hong Kong's free market economy since its return to Chinese rule. Record your findings in your journal.

The Bei Si pagoda

China's Population

China has the largest population in the world—some 1.25 billion people. That number is equal to about 20 percent of the world's population. More people live in China than in all of Europe, Russia, and the United States combined. China's population is growing rapidly—by about 11 million each year. Some years ago, China's leaders took steps to bring the growth rate under control. They encouraged people to delay getting married and starting families. As you have read, they also have limited the size of families.

China's population is not evenly distributed across the land. The western half of the country, which is mostly desert and mountain ranges, is almost empty. Just 10 percent of China's people live there. The rest are crowded into the country's eastern half. In fact, more people live in the North China Plain than in the entire United States. However, this region is only about the size of Texas. Most Chinese live in the countryside. Even so, China has 40 cities with populations greater than 1 million.

✔ **READING CHECK:** (*Human Systems*) Where do most of China's people live?

COMPARING POPULATIONS

China and the United States

China

United States

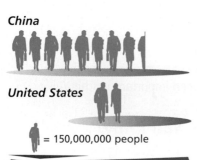

👤 = 150,000,000 people

Source: Central Intelligence Agency, *The World Factbook 2001*

Interpreting the Chart How many people does one figure on the chart represent?

China's Cities

Studying China's physical features helps explain why its residents live where they do. By locating rivers and river valleys, we can see where millions of people could best survive.

Several of China's most important cities are located on the Chang River. Shanghai, the country's largest city, lies on the Chang Delta. It serves as China's leading industrial center and is the major seaport. Shanghai's skyline is constantly changing. New hotels and office buildings seem to rise from the city center almost daily.

Using the map in Section 1, follow the course of the Chang River inland. Locate the cities of Nanjing and Wuhan (WOO-HAHN). These two industrial centers were built around iron-ore and coal mines. If you continue to follow the river upstream, you will reach Chongqing (CHOOHNG-CHING), located in the Sichuan Basin. It is one of the few large cities in China's interior. Guangzhou, located at the mouth of the Xi River, is southern China's largest city. Long famous as a trading center, it was known in the West as Canton. Today Guangzhou is one of China's major industrial cities.

Beijing, also known as Peking, is China's capital. It was established more than 3,000 years ago as a trading center. Beijing is the largest city in northern China and is well known for its cultural heritage. Beijing has famous tourist sites like the "Forbidden City," the great palace of the last emperor.

About 90 miles (145 km) southeast of Guangzhou is Hong Kong, a former British colony. With a population of 6.5 million, Hong Kong is one of the world's most densely populated places. It is only half as large as Rhode Island, but has more than seven times as many residents. Hong Kong is China's major southern seaport and is a center for banking and international trade. It is also a major tourist destination.

Hong Kong's dragon-boat races have changed over the past 2,000 years from a cultural festival to an international sport.

Towering skyscrapers mark Shanghai's skyline.
Interpreting the Visual Record How can you tell this city is growing rapidly?

The British occupied the island of Hong Kong in the 1830s. In the late 1800s Hong Kong was leased to the British for 99 years. The lease ran out in 1997, and Hong Kong then became a special administrative region of China. The British left. Hong Kong has some political independence and is allowed to maintain its free-market economy. Macao, a nearby port city, was once a Portuguese colony. At the end of 1999, it was returned to China. It was the last foreign territory in China.

✔ READING CHECK: *Places and Regions* What are the major cities of China?

In 1997 Hong Kong was returned to China. The return put an end to more than 150 years of British control.

China's Economy

When the Chinese Communists took power in 1949 they set up a **command economy**. In this type of economy, the government owns most industries and makes most economic decisions. It set almost all production goals, prices, and wages. In the late 1970s, however, the government began to introduce some elements of free enterprise.

Agriculture Only about 10 percent of China's land is good for farming. Nevertheless, China is a world leader in the production of many crops. China's huge workforce makes this possible. More than 50 percent of Chinese workers earn a living from farming. Having many farmers means the land can be worked intensively to produce high yields. China's farmers have also increased production by cutting terraces into hillsides to create new farmland.

China is divided between rice-growing and wheat-growing regions. The divide lies midway between the Huang and the Chang River. To the south, rice is the main crop. Here **multiple cropping** is common because the weather is warm and wet. Multiple cropping means that two or three crops are raised each year on the same land. This practice makes southern China more prosperous than northern China.

Models of rice fields like these have been found in Han dynasty tombs.

Interpreting the Visual Record What resources appear to be necessary for growing rice in this region?

Industry When the Communists came to power, the Chinese economy was based almost entirely on farming. The Communist government introduced programs to build industry. Today, China is an industrial giant. It produces everything from satellites and rockets to toys and bicycles. Mining is also important. For example, China is a leading producer of iron ore.

✔ **READING CHECK:** *Human Systems* What kind of economy does China have?

Future Challenges

China has enjoyed remarkable economic success in recent years. As a result, the standard of living has improved in most of China. Most Chinese are much better off than they were just a few years ago. However, by global standards China remains a relatively poor country. In addition, China's drive to industrialize has caused major problems. The smoke and waste pumped out by industries have badly polluted the air and water.

Another challenge involves the government's unwillingness to match the new economic freedoms with political reforms. China's human rights record has affected its economic relations with other countries. The U.S. government has considered canceling China's **most-favored-nation status** several times. Countries with this status get special trade advantages from the United States. China's future economic health might depend on its government's willingness to accept political reforms and join the world economic community.

✔ **READING CHECK:** *Human Systems* What challenges does China face?

By the mid-1990s clothing, electrical equipment, footwear, textiles, and other consumer goods were among China's leading exports. Employees of the Bei Bei Shoe Factory glue soles on by hand on an assembly line in Shanghai.

Interpreting the Visual Record Why might companies choose to use people rather than machines on this type of assembly line?

Section Review 3

go.hrw.com
Homework Practice Online
Keyword: SG3 HP27

Define and explain: command economy, multiple cropping, most-favored-nation status

Working with Sketch Maps On the map you created in Section 2, label Beijing, Shanghai, Nanjing, Wuhan, Chongqing, Hong Kong, and Macao. In the margin of your map, draw a box for each city. List the characteristics of each city in its box.

Reading for the Main Idea

1. (*Places and Regions*) Where do most people in China live? Why?

2. (*Places and Regions*) Along which rivers are several of China's most important cities located? Why?

3. (*Environment and Society*) What farming practices have allowed the Chinese to increase production?

Critical Thinking

4. **Finding the Main Idea** How has the Chinese government changed its economic policies since the late 1970s? What has been the impact of these changes?

Organizing What You Know

5. **Summarizing** Copy the following graphic organizer. Use it to describe the kinds of challenges facing China today. Identify specific environmental, political, and economic challenges.

Challenges

Section 4 Mongolia and Taiwan

Read to Discover

1. How has Mongolia's culture developed?
2. What is Taiwan's culture like?

Define

gers

Locate

Mongolia
Ulaanbaatar
Taiwan
Kao-hsiung
Taipei

WHY IT MATTERS

Tensions between China and Taiwan have remained high since 1949. These tensions affect not only China and Taiwan but also their neighbors in the region. Use CNNfyi.com or other **current events** sources to find the latest information about relations between China and Taiwan. Record your findings in your journal.

Mythical animal statue at Taroka Gorge, Taiwan

Mongolia

Mongolia is home to the Mongol people and has a fascinating history. You will learn of invaders and conquests and a culture that prizes horses.

Mongolia's History Today when people discuss the world's leading countries, they do not mention Mongolia. However, 700 years ago Mongolia was perhaps the greatest power in the world. Led by Genghis Khan, the Mongols conquered much of Asia, including China. Later leaders continued the conquests, building the greatest empire the world had seen. The Mongol Empire reached its height in the late 1200s.

It stretched from Europe's Danube River in the west to the Pacific Ocean in the east. Over time, however, the empire declined. In the late 1600s Mongolia fell under the rule of China.

In 1911, with Russian support, Mongolia declared its independence from China. Communists took control of the country 13 years later and established the Mongolian People's Republic. The country then came under the influence of the Soviet Union. Mongolia became particularly dependent on the Soviet Union for economic aid. This aid ended when the Soviet Union collapsed

This engraving shows early Mongolian soldiers.

▼

Nomads of Mongolia live in *gers* like those shown here.

Interpreting the Visual Record What in this photo suggests this would not be a permanent settlement?

in the early 1990s. Since then, Mongolians have struggled to build a democratic government and a free-market economy.

Mongolia's Culture Despite years of Communist rule and recent Western influence, the Mongolian way of life remains quite traditional. Many people still follow a nomadic lifestyle. They live as herders, driving their animals across Mongolia's vast grasslands. They make their homes in **gers** (GUHRZ). These are large, circular felt tents that are easy to raise, dismantle, and move.

Since most people live as herders, horses play an important role in Mongolian life. Mongolian children learn to ride when they are very young—often before they are even five years old. In Mongolia, the most powerful piece in the game of chess is the horse, not the queen.

Mongolia Today Mongolia is a large country—slightly larger than Alaska. Its population numbers just over 2.5 million. Some 25 percent of Mongolians live in Ulaanbaatar (oo-lahn-BAH-tawr), the capital city. Ulaanbaatar is also Mongolia's main industrial and commercial center. Mongolia's other cities are quite small. Not one has a population greater than 100,000.

✔ **READING CHECK:** (*Human Systems*) What are some elements of Mongolian culture?

Our Amazing Planet

In the Gobi, temperatures can range from -40°F (-40°C) in January to 113°F (45°C) in July. Some areas of this desert receive little more than 2 inches (5 cm) of rain each year.

Taiwan

For many years the island of Taiwan was known in the West as Formosa. This name came from Portuguese sailors who visited the island in the late 1500s. They thought the island was so lovely that they called it *Ilha Formosa*, or "beautiful island."

Chiang Kai-shek served in the Japanese army before returning to China to help overthrow the Manchu dynasty. He was head of the Nationalist government in China for 20 years, then moved with his followers to Taiwan.

Taiwan has good farmlands, but the island's eastern half is mountainous.

Interpreting the Visual Record How do the trees shown here compare to trees common where you live?

Taiwan's History The Chinese began settling Taiwan in the A.D. 600s. Some 600 years later the Japanese took control of eastern Taiwan. The search for spices brought European traders to Taiwan. The Dutch, Portuguese, and Spanish all tried to set up bases there. However, raiders from mainland China drove out these Europeans in the mid-1600s.

The struggle among the Chinese, Japanese, and Europeans for control of Taiwan continued until the late 1800s. In 1895 a treaty between the Chinese and the Japanese gave Taiwan to Japan. The Japanese then tried to force their way of life on the people of Taiwan. The Taiwanese rebelled against these efforts, but their revolts were crushed by the Japanese military.

After Japan's surrender at the end of World War II in 1945, China once again took command of Taiwan. In 1949 Mao Zedong established the People's Republic of China in mainland China. Chiang Kai-shek and the Nationalist Chinese government fled to Taiwan. The Nationalist government controlled Taiwan through martial law for decades. In recent years, however, the government has expanded democratic rights. China still claims that Taiwan is a province of China—not an independent country.

Taiwan's Culture Taiwan's history is reflected in its culture. Its population is about 85 percent native Taiwanese. They are descendants of people who migrated from China to Taiwan over hundreds of years. Chinese ways dominate Taiwan's culture. However, some building styles and certain foods reflect Japanese influences. European and American practices and customs have strongly influenced Taiwan's way of life in recent years. This is particularly true in the cities.

Taiwan Today Taiwan has a modern, industrial economy and a population of nearly 22 million. These people live on an island the size of Delaware and Maryland combined. Most people live on the western coastal plain of Taiwan. Population densities there can reach higher than 2,700 per square mile (1,042 per sq km). Taiwan's two largest cities, Kao-hsiung (KOW-SHYOOHNG) and Taipei (TY-PAY), are located on the coastal plain. Taipei is the capital city. It faces serious overcrowding and environmental problems. The thousands of cars, motorcycles, and trucks that clog Taipei's streets each day cause severe air pollution.

In the early 1950s Taiwan's economy was still largely based on agriculture. Today, however, only about 10 percent of workers make a living as farmers. Even so, Taiwan still produces enough rice—the country's chief food crop—to feed all of its people. Taiwan's farmers also grow fruits, sugarcane, tea, and vegetables.

Taiwan now has one of Asia's most successful economies. It is a world leader in the production and export of computers and sports equipment.

▲

Taipei, Taiwan, was founded in the 1700s and has developed into an important city for overseas trade.

Interpreting the Visual Record What characteristics of Taipei shown here resemble other cities?

✓ **READING CHECK:** (*Human Systems*) What are some elements of the culture of Taiwan?

go.hrw.com **Homework Practice Online**
Keyword: SG3 HP27

Define and explain: *gers*

Working with Sketch Maps On the map you created in Section 3, label Mongolia, Ulaanbaatar, Taiwan, Kao-hsiung, and Taipei. In the border of your map, draw a box for each city. Describe each city in its box. How has the history of each city played a part in its growth?

Reading for the Main Idea

1. (*Human Systems*) How do most people earn a living in Mongolia?

2. (*Human Systems*) Write a brief outline of the significant individuals or groups that have influenced Taiwan's history.

3. (*Human Systems*) How has Taiwan's economy changed since the early 1950s?

Critical Thinking

4. Analyzing Information What are some problems Taiwan faces today?

Organizing What You Know

5. Summarizing Copy the following graphic organizer. Use it to design and write two postcards to a friend describing life in Mongolia. In your postcards, note how life follows traditional patterns yet is also undergoing changes.

Reviewing What You Know

Building Vocabulary

On a separate sheet of paper, write sentences to define each of the following words.

1. dikes
2. arable
3. emperor
4. dynasty
5. porcelain
6. martial law
7. pagodas
8. command economy
9. multiple cropping
10. most-favored-nation status
11. *gers*

Reviewing the Main Ideas

1. (Places and Regions) What physical features separate this region's mountain ranges?

2. (Places and Regions) Why is the Huang called the Yellow River?

3. (Environment and Society) What idea did the first emperor of the Qin dynasty have that greatly affected the landscape of China?

4. (Human Systems) What country discussed in this chapter once ruled a vast empire that stretched into Europe?

5. (Environment and Society) What are Taiwan's leading exports?

Understanding Environment and Society

Resource Use

Growing industries and cities are taking over farmland in China. Create a presentation about potential problems caused by this situation. Consider the following:

- Actions China's government has already taken to try to solve the problem of its growing population.
- Problem in balancing population and food supply.

Thinking Critically

1. **Drawing Inferences and Conclusions** Why do you think so few Europeans reached China before the 1500s?

2. **Drawing Inferences and Conclusions** How might Chinese history have been different if Europeans had not forced trade upon the Chinese?

3. **Finding the Main Idea** What was the Cultural Revolution and how did it affect life in China?

4. **Making Generalizations and Predictions** In what ways does modern technology threaten the Chinese government's ability to control the flow of information in the country? What changes might the free flow of information bring to China?

5. **Analyzing Information** How is Taiwan's history reflected in the island's culture today?

Map ACTIVITY

On a separate sheet of paper, match the letters on the map with their correct labels.

Mount Everest   Chang River
Plateau of Tibet   Great Wall
North China   Shanghai
 Plain   Hong Kong
Huang   Ulaanbaatar

Mental Mapping Skills ACTIVITY

On a separate sheet of paper, draw a freehand map of China, Mongolia, and Taiwan. Make a key for your map and label the following:

China   Mongolia
Gobi   Pacific Ocean
Himalayas   Taiwan

WRITING ACTIVITY

Imagine that you are a Chinese university professor. Using the time line in section 2, the text, and other sources, write a brief lesson plan on China's history. You may want to include some visuals, such as photographs of artifacts, in your lesson plan. Be sure to use standard grammar, spelling, sentence structure, and punctuation.

Alternative Assessment

Portfolio ACTIVITY

Learning About Your Local Geography

Cooperative Project Fishing is an important source of food in China. Is fishing important in your community? Draw and label three types of fish available in your community.

internet connect

Internet Activity: go.hrw.com
KEYWORD: SG3 GT27

Choose a topic to explore about China, Mongolia, and Taiwan:
- Follow the Great Wall of China.
- Visit the land of Genghis Khan.
- See the artistic treasures of China.

CHAPTER 28

Japan and the Koreas

Now we continue east to North and South Korea and the island nation of Japan. First we meet Akiko, a Japanese student whose school day may be very different from yours.

*K*onichiwa! (Good afternoon!) I'm Akiko, and I'm in the seventh grade at Yamate school. Every morning except Sunday I put on my school uniform and eat rice soup and pickles before I leave for school. The train I take is so crowded I can't move. At school, I study reading, math, English, science, and writing. I know 1,800 Japanese characters, but I need to know about 3,000 to pass the ninth grade exams. For lunch, I eat rice and cold fish my mom packed for me. Before we can go home, we clean the school floors, desks, and windows. My dad usually isn't home until after 11:00 P.M., so my mom helps me with my homework in the "big" (8 feet by 8 feet) room of our three-room apartment. In the evenings, I go to a *juku* school to study for the ninth grade exams. If I do not do well, I will not go to a good high school, and my whole family will be ashamed. On Sundays, I sometimes go with my parents to visit my grandparents, who are rice farmers. I like rock music a lot, especially U2.

こんにちは.
私は東京に
住んでいます.

Translation: Good afternoon. I live in Tokyo.

Section 1 Physical Geography

Read to Discover

1. What are the physical features of Japan and the Koreas?
2. What natural resources does the region have?
3. Which climate types are found in the region?

Define

tsunamis
Oyashio Current
Japan Current

Locate

Korean Peninsula
Sea of Japan
Hokkaido
Honshu
Shikoku
Kyushu

WHY IT MATTERS

Weather plays an important role in Japanese life. Use CNNfyi.com or other current events sources to find examples of how weather has affected Japanese history and society. Record the findings in your journal.

Japanese bonsai

Japan and the Koreas: Physical-Political

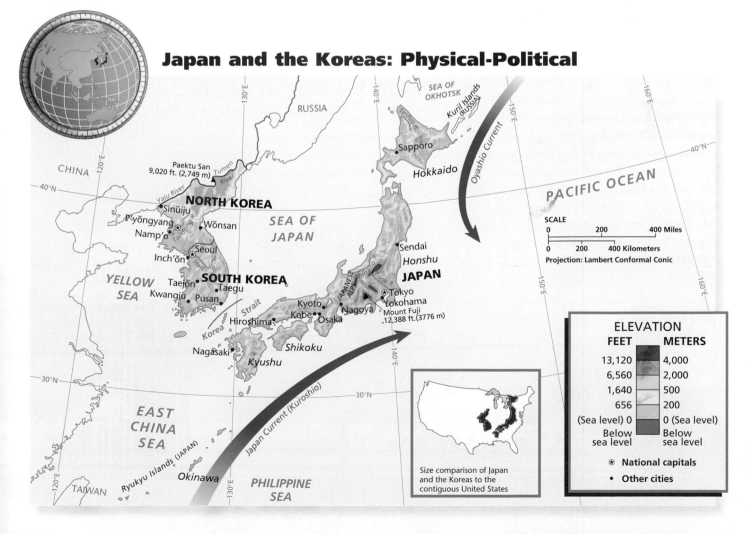

SEA OF OKHOTSK

Kuril Islands (RUSSIA)

RUSSIA

Oyashio Current

Sapporo

Hokkaido

PACIFIC OCEAN

40°N

CHINA

Paektu San 9,020 ft. (2,749 m)

Tumen River

Yalu River

NORTH KOREA

Sinŭiju

P'yŏngyang • Wŏnsan

Namp'o

Taedong R.

Seoul

Inch'ŏn

Han R.

SEA OF JAPAN

Sendai

Honshu

JAPAN

JAPANESE ALPS

Shinano R.

Tone R.

Tokyo

Yokohama

Mount Fuji 12,388 ft.(3776 m)

SCALE

0   200   400 Miles
0   200   400 Kilometers
Projection: Lambert Conformal Conic

40°N

YELLOW SEA

Taejŏn

SOUTH KOREA

Taegu

Kwangju • Pusan

Hiroshima

Korea Strait

Kyoto

Kobe • Osaka

Nagoya

Shikoku

Kyushu

Nagasaki

30°N

EAST CHINA SEA

Japan Current (Kuroshio)

Ryukyu Islands (JAPAN)

Okinawa

TAIWAN

PHILIPPINE SEA

30°N

Size comparison of Japan and the Koreas to the contiguous United States

ELEVATION

FEET		METERS
13,120		4,000
6,560		2,000
1,640		500
656		200
(Sea level) 0		0 (Sea level)
Below sea level		Below sea level

⊛ National capitals
• Other cities

Our Amazing Planet

The world's largest crab lives off the southeastern coast of Japan. The giant spider crab can grow larger than 12 feet (3.6 m) across (from claw to claw). It can also weigh more than 40 pounds (18 kg)!

A *shinkansen*, or bullet train, speeds past Mount Fuji. This Hiroshima-to-Kokura train travels at an average 162.3 mph (261.8 kmh) but has a maximum speed of 186 mph (300 kmh).

Interpreting the Visual Record What physical features might make building railroads in this region of Japan difficult?

Physical Features

The Korean Peninsula extends southward about 600 miles (965 km) from mainland Asia. The peninsula is relatively close to southern Japan.

The Korean Peninsula is about the same size as Utah. It contains two countries, North Korea and South Korea. The Yalu and Tumen Rivers separate North Korea from China. The Tumen River also forms a short border with Russia. Off the coast of the Korean Peninsula lie more than 3,500 islands.

The Sea of Japan separates Japan from the Eurasian mainland. The narrow Korea Strait lies between South Korea and the island country of Japan. No place in Japan is more than 90 miles (145 km) from the sea. Japan is about the size of California. It is made up of four large islands called the home islands. The country also includes more than 3,000 smaller islands. The home islands from north to south are Hokkaido (hoh-KY-doh), Honshu (HAWN-shoo), Shikoku (shee-KOH-koo), and Kyushu (KYOO-shoo). South of the home islands are Japan's Ryukyu (ree-YOO-kyoo) Islands. Okinawa is the largest of these islands. Fewer than half of the Ryukyus are inhabited.

Mountains Rugged and heavily forested mountains are a common sight in the landscape of this region. Mountains cover about 75 percent of Japan. Many of Japan's mountains were formed by volcanic activity. The country's longest mountain range, the Japanese Alps, forms a volcanic spine through Honshu. The small amount of plains in these countries is found along the coasts and river valleys.

The Ring of Fire Japan lies along the Pacific Ring of Fire—a region of volcanic activity and earthquakes. Under Japan the dense

Pacific plate dives beneath the lighter Eurasian and Philippine plates. This subduction zone borders the Pacific side of the Japanese islands, forming the Japan Trench. This is one of the deepest places on the ocean floor. The movement of one tectonic plate below another builds up tension in Earth's crust. The Eurasian plate buckles and pushes up, creating mountains and fractures in the crust. Magma flows up through these fractures. Where magma rises to the surface, it forms volcanoes. Today, Japan has about 40 active volcanoes. Mount Fuji (FOO-jee), Japan's highest peak, is an inactive volcano.

Because Japan lies along a subduction zone, earthquakes are also common. As many as 1,500 occur every year. Most are minor quakes. In 1995, however, an earthquake killed more than 5,000 people in Kobe.

Underwater earthquakes sometimes create huge waves called **tsunamis** (tsooh-NAH-mees). These dangerous waves can travel hundreds of miles per hour. They can also be as tall as a 10-story building when they reach shore. In 1993 a tsunami caused terrible destruction when it struck the coast of Hokkaido.

Unlike Japan, the Korean Peninsula is not located in a subduction zone. As a result, it has no active volcanoes and is dominated by eroded mountains. Earthquakes are quite rare.

✓ **READING CHECK:** (*Places and Regions*) What are the physical features of Japan and the Koreas?

BUILD on WHAT You Know

Do you remember what you learned about plateaus? See Chapter 2 to review.

Natural Resources

Except for North Korea, the region is not rich in natural resources. It has no oil or natural gas. The Korean Peninsula's mountainous terrain and rivers, however, are good for producing hydroelectric power. North Korea also has iron ore, copper, zinc, lead, and coal.

Japan lies near one of the world's best fisheries. East of Japan the cool **Oyashio** (oh-YAH-shee-oh) **Current** dives beneath the warm, less dense **Japan Current**. The cool water scours the bottom, bringing nutrients to the surface. Fish can find plentiful food to eat in this rich marine environment.

✓ **READING CHECK:**
(*Places and Regions*) What are the region's natural resources?

▲ Every hour an artificial volcano erupts at Ocean Dome, the world's largest indoor beach, at Miyazaki, Japan.

Climate

The Koreas and Japan each have two climate regions. Hokkaido, northern Honshu, and the northern part of the Korean Peninsula have a humid continental climate. The Oyashio Current keeps areas near the coast of northern Japan cool in summer. Winters are long and cold, and the growing season is short. The rest of the Korean Peninsula and Japan have a humid subtropical climate. Winters are mild. Summers are hot and humid. The Japan Current, which flows northward from the tropical North Pacific, warms southern Japan. This part of the region experiences heavy rains and typhoons during the summer. Some areas receive up to 80 inches (203 cm) of rain each year.

✓ **READING CHECK:**

Places and Regions What is the region's climate?

◄

Terracing creates more arable land for some South Korean farmers. These fields overlook the Sea of Japan.

Interpreting the Visual Record How do the terraces here hold water?

go.hrw.com **Homework Practice Online** Keyword: SG3 HP28

Section Review 1

Define and explain: tsunamis, Oyashio Current, Japan Current

Working with Sketch Maps On a map of Japan and the Koreas that you draw or that your teacher provides, label the following: the Korean Peninsula, Sea of Japan, Hokkaido, Honshu, Shikoku, and Kyushu. On what physical features might Japan and the Koreas depend for their economies?

Reading for the Main Idea

1. (*Physical Systems*) How has Japan's location in a subduction zone made it different from the Koreas?

2. (*Physical Systems*) How do ocean currents affect the climates of Japan?

Critical Thinking

3. **Drawing Inferences and Conclusions** How do you think residents are affected by this region's mountainous terrain and the nearness of the sea?

4. **Making Generalizations and Predictions** What can you predict about South Korea's and Japan's economies?

Organizing What You Know

5. **Summarizing** List the landforms, natural resources, and climates of Japan, North Korea, and South Korea.

	Landforms	Resources	Climate
Japan			
South Korea			
North Korea			

Section 2 The History and Culture of Japan

Read to Discover

1. What was Japan's early history and culture like?
2. How did the modernization of Japan take place?

Define

Shintoism
shamans
samurai
shogun
Diet

WHY IT MATTERS

Japanese cultural traditions are important not only in Japan but also in other societies. Use **CNNfyi.com** or other **current events** sources to find information on Japanese cultural traditions. Record the findings in your journal.

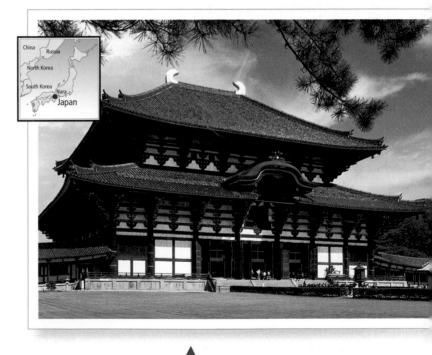

A ukiyo-e, a Japanese woodblock print

Early Japan

Japan's first inhabitants came from central Asia thousands of years ago. Rice farming was introduced to Japan from China and Korea about 300 B.C. As the population increased, farmers irrigated new land for growing rice. They also built dikes and canals to channel water into the rice paddies. Local chieftains organized the workers and controlled the flow of water. This control allowed the chieftains to extend their political power over larger areas.

Religion The earliest known religion of Japan, **Shintoism**, centers around the *kami*. *Kami* are spirits of natural places, sacred animals, and ancestors. Many of Japan's mountains and rivers are sacred in Shintoism. **Shamans**, or priests who communicated with the spirits, made the *kami*'s wishes known.

Buddhism and Confucianism were later introduced from China. Buddhist shrines were often located next to older *kami* shrines. Today, as in the past, most Japanese practice Shintoism and Buddhism. As you learned in Chapter 27, the principles of Confucianism include respect for elders, parents, and rulers.

Todaiji Temple in Nara, Japan, contains the largest wooden hall in the world and a statue of Buddha that is more than 48 feet (15 m) tall.

Interpreting the Visual Record What interesting features do you see in this building's architecture?

CONNECTING TO *Literature*

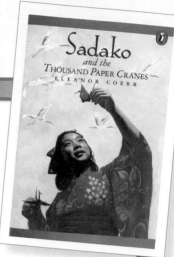

Sadako and the Thousand Paper Cranes
by Eleanor Coerr

On August 6, 1945, the United States dropped an atomic bomb on Hiroshima, Japan, trying to bring an end to World War II. Sadako and the Thousand Paper Cranes *is based on the story of a real little girl who lived in Hiroshima at the time of the bombing. Ten years later, she died as a result of the radiation from the bomb.*

Sadako and the Thousand Paper Cranes

That afternoon Chizuko was Sadako's first visitor. She smiled mysteriously as she held something behind her back. "Shut your eyes," she said. . . . Chizuko put some pieces of paper and scissors on the bed. "Now you can look," she said.

"What is it?" Sadako asked, staring at the paper.

Chizuko was pleased with herself. "I've figured out a way for you to get well," she said proudly. "Watch!" She cut a piece of gold paper into a large square. In a short time she had folded it over and over into a beautiful crane.

Sadako was puzzled. "But how can that paper bird make me well?"

"Don't you remember that old story about the crane?" Chizuko asked. "It's supposed to live for a thousand years. If a sick person folds one thousand paper cranes, the gods will grant her wish and make her healthy again." She handed the crane to Sadako. "Here's your first one."

Analyzing Primary Sources

1. How do the cranes reflect traditional Japanese culture?
2. How does Chizuko's visit to Sadako reflect her feelings about her friend?

The Shoguns In the A.D. 700s Japan began to develop a political system of its own. Many small feudal domains were each ruled by a lord. **Samurai** (SA-muh-ry) were warriors who served the lords. Rivalries were put aside when a foreign threat appeared. For example, the feudal domains united against the Mongols in the 1200s. After a victory, the emperor sometimes named the warriors **shogun**. Shogun means "great general" and is the highest rank for a warrior.

In the mid-1500s, Portuguese traders arrived in Japan. Spanish missionaries followed, introducing Christianity to Japan. Later, Europeans were forced to leave. Japanese leaders feared that foreign ideas might undermine Japanese society. Japan remained cut off from the Western world until the mid-1850s.

✓ **READING CHECK:** (*Human Systems*) What was early Japan like?

Modern Japan

In 1853 U.S. commodore Matthew Perry's warships sailed into Tokyo Bay. Perry displayed U.S. naval power and brought gifts that showed the wonders of American technology. Perry's arrival convinced the Japanese that they needed to become as politically strong as the Americans and Europeans. In the 1860s Japan began to industrialize and modernize its educational, legal, and governmental systems.

An Imperial Power Japan needed resources in order to industrialize. As a result, it began to expand its empire around 1900. Japan annexed, or took control of, Korea in 1910. Japan also took over northeastern China and its supply of coal and iron ore. Japan continued to expand in Asia during the late 1930s.

World War II During World War II Japan was an ally of Germany and Italy. Japan brought the United States into the war in 1941 by attacking the U.S. naval base at Pearl Harbor, Hawaii. Japan conquered much of Southeast Asia and many Pacific islands before being defeated by U.S. and Allied forces in 1945. With the end of World War II Japan lost its empire.

Government After World War II the United States occupied Japan until 1952. With U.S. aid, Japan began to rebuild into a major world industrial power. Japan also established a democratic government. Today, Japan is a constitutional monarchy with several political parties. The government is made up of the **Diet** (DY-uht)—an elected legislature—and a prime minister. Japan's emperor remains a symbol of the nation, but he has no political power.

▲
Commodore Matthew Perry arrives in Japan in 1853.

✓ **READING CHECK:** (*Places and Regions*) How did Japan modernize?

Define and explain: Shintoism, shamans, samurai, shogun, Diet

Working with Sketch Maps On the map you created in Section 1, label China and Korea. In a box in the margin, identify the body of water that separates Korea from Japan. Why do you think China and Korea had a strong influence on Japan's culture and history?

Reading for the Main Idea

1. (*Human Systems*) What religions have been practiced in Japan, and from where did they come?

2. (*Places and Regions*) Why did Japan decide to trade with the United States and Europe?

Critical Thinking

3. Finding the Main Idea How and why did rice farming develop in Japan?

4. Analyzing Information What influences do the principles of Confucianism have on the Japanese?

Organizing What You Know

5. Sequencing Copy the following graphic organizer. Use it to show important developments in modern Japanese history from the 1850s to today.

□ ⇨ □ ⇨ □ ⇨ □ ⇨ □

Japan and the Koreas • 601

Section 3

Japan Today

Read to Discover

1. Where do most Japanese live?
2. What are the major Japanese cities like?
3. What is life in Japan like?
4. How has the Japanese economy developed?

Define

megalopolis
kimonos
futon
intensive
  cultivation
work ethic
protectionism
trade surplus

Locate

Inland Sea
Osaka
Tokyo
Kobe
Kyoto

Small child in a traditional kimono

WHY IT MATTERS

The Japanese economy has struggled for the last several years due to a number of factors. The health of the Japanese economy is not only important to Japan but to much of the world. Use **CNN.fyi.com** or other **current events** sources to find information on the Japanese economy. Record the findings in your journal.

▲
Beyond Tokyo's Nijubashi Bridge is the Imperial Palace, the home of the emperor.

Where People Live

Japan is one of the world's most densely populated countries. It is slightly smaller than California but has nearly four times as many people! There are an average of 863 people per square mile (333/sq km). However, Japan is very mountainous. Within its area of livable land, population density averages 7,680 people per square mile (2,964/sq km).

Most people live on the small coastal plains, particularly along the Pacific and the Inland Sea. Japan's major cities and farms compete for space on these narrow coastal plains. Only about 11 percent of Japan's land is arable, or fit for growing crops.

The Japanese have reclaimed land from the sea and rivers. In some places, they have built dikes to block off the water. They have drained the land behind the dikes so it could be used for farming or housing. They have even built artificial islands. The airport near Osaka, for example, was built on an artificial island in the early 1990s.

✔ **READING CHECK:** (*Human Systems*) Where do most people in Japan live?

Japan's Cities

Japan's cities, like major cities everywhere, are busy, noisy, and very crowded. Almost 30 million people live within 20 miles of the Imperial Palace in Tokyo. This densely populated area forms a **megalopolis**. A megalopolis is a giant urban area that often includes more than one city as well as the surrounding suburban areas. Yokohama is Japan's major seaport.

Most of Tokyo was built recently. An earthquake in 1923 and bombings during World War II destroyed most of the old buildings.

Tokyo is the capital and the center of government. Japan's banking, communications, and education are also centered here. Tokyo is densely populated, and land is scarce. As a result, Tokyo's real estate prices are among the world's highest.

Tokyo's Ginza shopping district is the largest in the world. Some department stores sell houses and cars and provide dental care. They also offer classes on how to properly wear **kimonos**—traditional robes—and to arrange flowers.

High rents in Ginza and elsewhere in Tokyo encourage the creative use of space. Tall buildings line the streets. However, shops are also found below the streets in the subway stations. Another way the Japanese have found to maximize space is the "capsule hotel." The guests in these hotels sleep in compartments too small to stand in upright. Businesspeople often stay in these hotels rather than commuting the long distances to their homes.

So many people commute to and from Tokyo that space on the trains must also be maximized. During peak travel periods, commuters are crammed into cars. They are helped by workers hired to push as many people into the trains as possible.

Another megalopolis in Japan is located in the Kansai region. It has three major cities: Osaka (oh-SAH-kah), Kobe (KOH-bay), and Kyoto (KYOH-toh). Industrial Osaka has been a trading center for centuries. Kobe is an important seaport. Kyoto was Japan's capital for more than 1,000 years.

✔ **READING CHECK:**

Places and Regions What is life like in Japan's major cities?

Japan

COUNTRY	POPULATION/ GROWTH RATE	LIFE EXPECTANCY	LITERACY RATE	PER CAPITA GDP
Japan	126,771,662 0.2%	78, male 84, female	99%	$24,900
United States	281,421,906 0.9%	74, male 80, female	97%	$36,200

Sources: Central Intelligence Agency, *The World Factbook 2001;* U.S. Census Bureau

Interpreting the Chart How does life expectancy in Japan compare to that of the United States?

Japanese workers stay focused on their responsibilities on an electronics production line.

▼

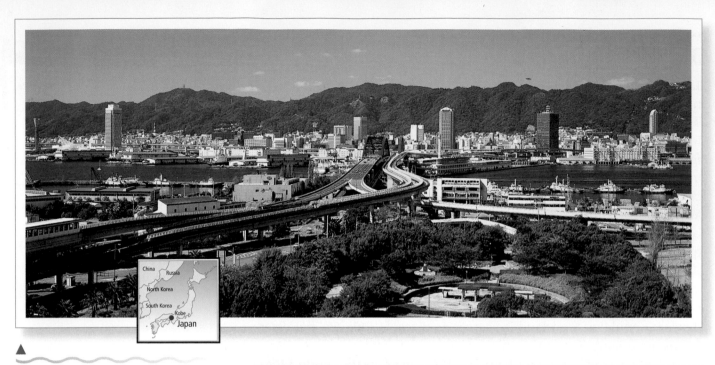

▲

The port of Kobe is located in the central part of the Japanese islands.

▲

Japanese and American all-star baseball teams compete in Yokohama.

Interpreting the Visual Record How is this scoreboard different from one in the United States?

Life in Japan

Japan is a very homogeneous nation. In other words, almost everyone—more than 99 percent of the population—is ethnically Japanese and shares a common language and culture. Japanese society has traditionally been dominated by men, but this is changing. More Japanese women have jobs today than in the past, but most women are still expected to be dutiful wives and mothers. Many quit their jobs when they marry.

Many Japanese families live in suburbs, where housing is cheaper. As a result, many Japanese spend as much as three hours commuting to and from work.

Because land is so scarce, most Japanese homes do not have large yards. Most homes are also smaller than typical American homes. Rooms are usually used for more than one purpose. For example, a living room may also serve as a bedroom. During the day, people sit on cushions at low tables. At night, they sleep on the floor on a **futon** (FOO-tahn)—a lightweight cotton mattress. In the morning they put the mattress away, and the bedroom becomes a living room again.

For most occasions, people wear Western-style clothing. Many Japanese wear kimonos at festivals and weddings. Listening to music and playing video games are popular leisure activities. Baseball, golf, and skiing are also popular. On festival days, families may gather to enjoy the cherry blossoms or visit a local shrine or temple. They might also watch the ancient sport of sumo wrestling or traditional dramas on television. Many Japanese enjoy traditional arts such as the tea ceremony, flower arranging, growing dwarf potted trees called bonsai, and kite flying.

✓ **READING CHECK:** *Human Systems* What is life like in Japan?

Japan's Economy

Japan has few natural resources. It therefore imports many of the raw materials it uses to run its industries. Oil is one key material that Japan must import. The country produces about one third of its energy through nuclear power.

The sea is an important source of food. Japan has the world's largest fishing industry. It also imports fish from all over the world. Fish is a major part of the Japanese diet. In fact, Tokyo's largest fish market sells about 5 million pounds of seafood each day. The average Japanese eats more than 100 pounds of fish each year. In contrast, the average American eats less than 5 pounds each year.

Agriculture Most Japanese farms are located on Honshu. Many farmers own their land and live in small villages. Farms in Japan are much smaller than those in the United States. The average Japanese farm is about 2.5 acres (1 hectare). Most American farms are about 150 times larger. Japan's shortage of land means that there is little pastureland for livestock. Meat is a luxury. The Japanese get most of their protein from fish and soybeans.

Farmers make the most of their land by terracing the hillsides. This means cutting the hillside into a series of small flat fields. The terraces look like broad stair steps. The terraces give farmers more room to grow crops. Japanese farmers use **intensive cultivation**—the practice of growing food on every bit of available land. Even so, Japan must import about two thirds of its food.

Farmers are encouraged to stay on the land and to grow as much rice as possible. However, many farms are too small to be profitable. To solve this problem, the Japanese government buys the rice crop. The price is set high enough to allow farmers to support their families. The government then resells it at the same price. Because this price is much higher than the world market price, the government restricts rice imports.

Seeds of the tea plant were first brought to Japan about A.D. 800. Tea is now an important product of southern Japan. Top-quality teas are harvested by hand only. Workers pick just the tender young leaves at the plant's tip.

Interpreting the Visual Record
How might using machines for harvesting leaves affect the quality of the tea?

▼

Industry Japan imports most of its raw resources. These resources are then used to make goods to sell in other countries. For example, Japan is known for its high-quality automobiles. Japan also makes televisions, cameras, and compact disc players.

There are many reasons for Japan's economic success. Most Japanese have a strong **work ethic**. This is the belief that work in itself is worthwhile. Most Japanese work for large companies and respect their leaders. In return, employers look after workers' needs. They offer job security, exercise classes, and other benefits.

The Japanese have also benefited from investments in other countries. For example, some Japanese companies have built automobile factories in the United States. Other Japanese companies have invested in the American entertainment and real estate industries.

Japan and the Global Market Japan's economy depends on trade. In the past the government set up trade barriers to protect Japan's industries from foreign competition. This practice is called **protectionism**. This has helped Japan build up a huge **trade surplus**. A trade surplus means that a nation exports more than it imports. Other countries have objected to Japan's trade practices. Some countries have even set up barriers against Japanese goods. As a result, Japan has eased some trade barriers.

Japan has other economic problems, too. Some Asian countries that pay lower wages are able to produce goods more cheaply than Japan. The most important problem Japan—and Asia—faced in the 1990s was an economic slowdown. It threatened the country's prosperity. Japan is now in a recovery and slow-growth period.

✓ **READING CHECK:** (*Human Systems*) How have Japan's leaders tried to protect the nation's economy?

▲
A worker in this Japanese automobile factory does his job with the help of a robot.

Section Review 3

go.hrw.com
Homework Practice Online
Keyword: SG3 HP28

Define and explain: megalopolis, kimonos, futon, intensive cultivation, work ethic, protectionism, trade surplus

Working with Sketch Maps On the map you created in Section 2, label Inland Sea, Osaka, Tokyo, Kobe, and Kyoto. Draw a box in the margin of your map. What do the cities have in common? Write your answer in the margin box.

Reading for the Main Idea

1. (*Environment and Society*) How does Japan's physical geography affect farming?

2. (*Human Systems*) How has Japan developed its industries without plentiful raw materials?

Critical Thinking

3. Drawing Inferences and Conclusions In what ways do the daily lives of Japanese reflect influences of Western culture?

4. Drawing Inferences and Conclusions Why do you suppose other countries might be concerned about Japan's surplus?

Organizing What You Know

5. Summarizing Copy the following graphic organizer. Use it to list the activities and services available in Tokyo.

Tokyo

The History and Culture of the Koreas

Read to Discover

1. What was Korea's ancient history like?
2. What were the major events of Korea's early modern period?
3. Why was Korea divided after World War II, and what were the effects of the division?

Define

demilitarized zone

Locate

North Korea
South Korea

WHY IT MATTERS

The Korean War left many lingering problems for Koreans and Americans alike. Use CNNfyi.com or other **current events** sources to find examples of current relations between the United States and North and South Korea. Record the findings in your journal.

A tray decorated with mother-of-pearl inlay

Ancient Korea

Korea's earliest inhabitants were nomadic hunters from north and central Asia. About 1500 B.C. they adopted rice farming, which had been introduced from China. Then, in 108 B.C., the Chinese invaded Korea. This invasion marked the beginning of a long period of Chinese influence on Korean culture. The Chinese introduced their system of writing and their system of examinations for government jobs. They also introduced Buddhism and Confucianism to Korea.

Korea's original religion—shamanism—continued to be practiced, along with the newer traditions introduced from China. According to shamanism, natural places and ancestors have spirits. Many mountains are particularly sacred to Koreans. Shamanism is still practiced in South Korea.

Over the centuries, Korean tribes eventually recaptured most of the peninsula. In the A.D. 600s the kingdom of Silla (SI-luh) united the peninsula. Korea's golden age began. Korea became known in Asia for its architecture, painting, ceramics, and fine jewelry.

A weaver demonstrates his craft near Seoul.

This celadon vase is from the A.D. 1000s.

Heavy fencing and explosives have kept people out of the demilitarized zone for decades. As a result, this land has provided a safe home for rare animal and plant species. Some scientists hope that in the future the DMZ can be set aside as a nature preserve, which would attract tourists while protecting the wildlife.

During the Silla period Korea began using the results of examinations to award government jobs. Generally only boys who were sons of noblemen could take the examinations. People from the lower classes could not rise to important positions by studying and passing the examinations, as they could in China.

By the early 900s a new kingdom had taken power. The modern name of Korea comes from this kingdom's name, Koryo. During the Koryo dynasty, Korean artisans invented the first movable metal type. During the following dynasty, scholars developed the Hangul (HAHN-gool) alphabet, which was officially adopted in 1446. Hangul was much easier to use with the Korean language than Chinese characters had been. Because Hangul had only 24 symbols, it was easier to learn. It had previously been necessary to memorize about 20,000 Chinese characters to read the Buddhist scriptures.

✓ **READING CHECK:** (*Human Systems*) How did the Chinese influence Korea's ancient history?

Early Modern Korea

By the early 1600s China again controlled Korea. For 300 years Korea remained under Chinese control. Closed off to most other outsiders, Korea became known as the Hermit Kingdom. During this period, Catholicism was introduced into Korea through missionaries in China. Korea's Christian community was sometimes persecuted and remained small until the mid-1900s.

In the mid-1890s Japan defeated China in the Sino-Japanese War. This cleared the way for Japan to annex Korea in 1910. The Japanese ruled harshly. They took over the Korean government and many businesses and farms. Koreans were forced to take Japanese names, and

Japanese was taught in the schools. Japan ruled Korea until the end of World War II.

✔ **READING CHECK:** (*Places and Regions*) What were some major events in Korea's early modern period?

A Divided Korea

At the end of World War II, U.S. and Soviet troops oversaw the Japanese departure from Korea. The Soviets helped Communist leaders take power in the north. The United States backed a democratic government in the south. The United Nations hoped that the Koreas would reunite. However, the United States and the Soviet Union could not agree on a plan. In 1948 South Korea officially became the Republic of Korea. North Korea became the Democratic People's Republic of Korea led by Korean Communist dictator Kim Il Sung.

In 1950 North Korea tried to unify the country by invading South Korea, resulting in the Korean War. The United Nations sent troops—mostly U.S.—to defend South Korea. Communist China sent forces to North Korea. A truce was declared in 1953, but Korea remains divided. The border between North Korea and South Korea is a strip of land roughly 2.4 miles (4 km) wide called the **demilitarized zone** (DMZ). This buffer zone separates the two countries. A total of about 1 million U.S., South Korean, and North Korean soldiers patrol the DMZ. It is the world's most heavily guarded border.

In the early 1970s and early 1990s North and South Korea tried to reach an agreement for reunification. The negotiations failed. Still, Koreans remain hopeful that their country will one day be reunited.

✔ **READING CHECK:** (*Places and Regions*) What were some events in Korea's history after World War II?

Casting bronze bells is an ancient Korean craft. The largest bell in South Korea, completed in A.D. 771, is more than 12 feet (3.6 m) tall and weighs about 25 tons (110,000 kg). When struck, it is said that the bell's tone can be heard 40 miles (64 km) away.

go.hrw.com
Homework Practice Online
Keyword: SG3 HP28

Section Review 4

Define and explain: demilitarized zone

Working with Sketch Maps On the map you created in Section 3, label North Korea and South Korea. In the margin, draw a box and include in it information that explains the significance of the DMZ. When was it established?

Reading for the Main Idea

1. (*Human Systems*) What were some of the accomplishments of the early Koreans before about 1600? What dynasty gave Korea its name?

2. (*Human Systems*) What long-lasting effect did the Korean War have on the Korean Peninsula?

Critical Thinking

3. **Analyzing Information** How has the Korean Peninsula been influenced by other countries?

4. **Making Generalizations and Predictions** What might be preventing North Korea and South Korea from reuniting?

Organizing What You Know

5. **Sequencing** Copy the following time line. Use it to list the important events of Korean history from 1500 B.C. through the 1500s.

```
+--------------------------------+
1500 B.C.                    1500s
```

Section 5

South and North Korea Today

Read to Discover

1. What are South Korea's government and society like?
2. What is South Korea's economy like?
3. What is North Korea like?
4. How has North Korea's government affected the country's development?

Define

entrepreneurs
chaebol
kimchi
famine

Locate

Seoul
Pusan
P'yŏngyang

Korean-style vegetables

WHY IT MATTERS

North and South Korea are still struggling to reach an understanding after some 50 years since the end of the Korean War. Use **CNNfyi.com** or other **current events** sources to find examples of the political, economic, and diplomatic relations between the two countries. Record the findings in your journal.

North Korea and South Korea

COUNTRY	POPULATION/ GROWTH RATE	LIFE EXPECTANCY	LITERACY RATE	PER CAPITA GDP
North Korea	21,968,228 1.2%	68, male 74, female	99%	$1,000
South Korea	47,904,370 0.9%	71, male 79, female	98%	$16,100
United States	281,421,906 0.9%	74, male 80, female	97%	$36,200

Sources: Central Intelligence Agency, *The World Factbook 2001;* U.S. Census Bureau

Interpreting the Chart How does North Korea's per capita GDP compare to that of South Korea?

South Korea's People and Government

South Korea is densely populated. There are 1,197 people per square mile (462/sq km). Most people live in the narrow, fertile plain along the western coast of the Korean Peninsula. Travel in the peninsula's mountainous interior is difficult, so few people live there. South Korea's population is growing slowly, at about the same rate as in most industrialized countries.

South Korea's Cities Because South Korea is densely populated, space is a luxury—just as it is in Japan. Most South Koreans live in small apartments in crowded cities. Seoul (SOHL) is the country's capital and largest city. The government, the economy, and the educational system are centered there. After the Korean War, the population exploded because refugees flocked to Seoul seeking work and housing. By 1994 the city had nearly 11 million residents. Today, Seoul is one of the world's most densely populated cities. It has some 7,000 people per square mile (2,703/sq km).

South Korea's second-largest city is Pusan (POO-sahn). This major seaport and industrial center lies on the southern coast. Pusan also has an important fishing industry.

The rapid growth of South Korea's cities has brought problems. Housing is expensive. The many factories, cars, and coal-fired heating systems sometimes cause dangerous levels of air pollution. Industrial waste has also polluted the water.

Postwar Government South Korea is technically a democracy, but it was run by military dictators until the late 1980s. More recently, South Korea introduced a multiparty democratic government. The government controls economic development but does not own businesses and property.

✓ **READING CHECK:** (*Human Systems*) What kind of government does South Korea have?

South Korean Society

Like Japan's, South Korea's population is homogeneous. Most Koreans complete high school. About half go on to some form of higher education. Women are beginning to hold important jobs.

Traditional Families Most Koreans marry someone they meet through their parents. Most families still value sons. This is because only a son can take over the family name. Only a son can lead the ceremonies to honor the family's ancestors. Some couples who do not have a son adopt a boy with the same family name. This is not too difficult because there are few family names in Korea.

Religion Today, Christianity is the most common religion, followed closely by Buddhism. Whatever their religion, most Koreans take part in ceremonies to honor their ancestors. Most also follow Confucian values. Many Koreans still ask shamans for personal advice.

✓ **READING CHECK:** (*Human Systems*) What is South Korea's society like?

This view looks out over the busy harbor of Pusan. Travelers can take a ferry from Pusan across the Korean Strait to Japan.
Interpreting the Visual Record How does this photo show the importance of shipping to this region's economy?

This is one of many statues of Kim Il Sung in P'yŏngyang. He led North Korea from the end of World War II until his death in 1994. Although dead, Kim Il Sung was declared the "Eternal President" of North Korea in 1998.

Interpreting the Visual Record How does this statue compare to monuments honoring important people in the history of the United States?

South Korea's Economy

After the war, South Korea industrialized quickly, and its market economy grew. By the 1990s it had become one of the strongest economies in Asia.

Industry Koreans' strong sense of family often carries over into work. Large groups of relatives may become **entrepreneurs**. This means they use their money and talents to start and manage a business. Businesses are sometimes linked through family and personal ties into huge industrial groups called *chaebol*.

The government has encouraged the use of nuclear power. It also has encouraged the growth of high-technology industries. These industries make electronic goods for export. Other important industries are steel, shipbuilding, automobiles, and textiles. In the late 1990s South Korea, like many other Asian countries, experienced an economic slowdown. It is now making a rapid recovery.

Agriculture South Korea has the peninsula's richest agricultural land. However, less than 20 percent of the land can be farmed. The shortage of land means that South Korea must import about half of its food.

Most South Korean farms are small and lie along the western and southern coasts. The rugged terrain makes using heavy machinery difficult. As a result, farmers must do much of their work by hand and with small tractors. Since the late 1980s there has been a shortage of farmworkers.

Farmers grow rice on about half their land. Other important crops are Chinese cabbage and soybeans. Soybeans are used to make soy sauce and tofu, or bean curd. Chinese cabbage that has been spiced and pickled is called **kimchi**. This is Korea's national dish.

✓ **READING CHECK:** (*Places and Regions*) What is South Korea's economy like?

North Korea's People and Government

North Korea's Communist Party controls the government. For many years, North Korea had ties and traded mostly with other Communist countries. Since the Soviet Union's breakup in 1991, North Korea has been largely isolated from the rest of the world. In the late 1990s North Korea angered many countries by trying to develop nuclear weapons and missiles.

Population Like South Korea and Japan, North Korea has a homogeneous population. North Korea is not as densely populated as South Korea. In North Korea, there are 513 people per square mile (198/sq km).

North Korea's Capital The capital of North Korea is P'yŏngyang (pyuhng-YANG). About 2.6 million people live there. North Korea's only university is in P'yŏngyang. Few private cars can be seen on the city streets. Most residents use buses or the subway system to get around. At night, many streets are dark because the city frequently experiences shortages of electricity.

✓ **READING CHECK:** (*Places and Regions*) What is North Korea like?

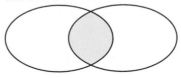

North Korea's Economy

North Korea has a command economy. This means that the central government plans the economy and controls what is produced. The government also owns all the land and housing and controls access to jobs.

North Korea's best farmland is along the west coast. Only 14 percent of North Korea's land can be farmed. Most of this land is owned by the state. It is farmed by cooperatives—groups of farmers who work the land together. Some people have small gardens to grow food for themselves or to sell at local markets.

North Korea does not produce enough food to feed its people. It lost its main source of food and fertilizer when the Soviet Union collapsed. Poor harvests in the mid-1990s made the situation worse. **Famine**, or severe food shortages, resulted. The government's hostility toward the West made getting aid difficult. Thousands starved.

North Korea is rich in mineral resources. It has also developed a nuclear power industry. North Korea makes machinery, iron, and steel. However, its factories use outdated technology.

✓ **READING CHECK:** (*Human Systems*) How has North Korea's government affected the country's economic development?

▲

Rice farming requires large amounts of human energy for transplanting, weeding, and harvesting. These farmers are planting seedlings.

Interpreting the Visual Record Why do you think it would be difficult to use machinery for transplanting here?

go.hrw.com **Homework Practice Online**
Keyword: SG3 HP28

Section Review 5

Define and explain: entrepreneurs, *chaebol*, kimchi, famine

Working with Sketch Maps On the map you created in Section 4, label Seoul, Pusan, and P'yŏngyang. Why do you think these cities remain important? Write your answer in a box in the margin.

Reading for the Main Idea

1. (*Places and Regions*) How did South Korea's cities change after the Korean War?

2. (*Environment and Society*) How does North Korea's physical geography affect its farmers?

3. (*Places and Regions*) What kind of economies do North and South Korea have, and how are they different?

Critical Thinking

4. Finding the Main Idea How have entrepreneurs affected South Korea's economy?

Organizing What You Know

5. Categorizing List characteristics of the government, industry, and agriculture of North and South Korea since World War II. Where the circles overlap, list things the countries share.

Reviewing What You Know

Building Vocabulary

On a separate sheet of paper, write sentences to define each of the following words.

1. tsunamis
2. shamans
3. samurai
4. shogun
5. Diet
6. kimonos
7. futon
8. intensive cultivation
9. work ethic
10. protectionism
11. trade surplus
12. demilitarized zone
13. entrepreneurs
14. kimchi
15. famine

Reviewing the Main Ideas

1. *Places and Regions* What are the geographic features of Japan? of Korea?

2. *Human Systems* Which other Asian countries have influenced the culture of Japan? What contributions did they make?

3. *Places and Regions* What factors have contributed to Japan's economic success?

4. *Human Systems* Why were there foreign troops on the Korean Peninsula in the 1950s?

5. *Places and Regions* Why has Seoul grown rapidly since the Korean War? What is life in the city like?

Understanding Environment and Society

Resource Use

Japan's cultured-pearl industry is an example of how the Japanese have adapted to their limited amount of land by making creative use of the sea. Create a presentation about the pearl industry. As you create your presentation, consider the following:

- The kinds of pearls that are found there.
- Where and how pearls are produced.
- Things that could hurt Japan's role in the pearl industry.

Thinking Critically

1. **Analyzing Information** How have geographic features affected where people live in Japan and the Korean Peninsula?

2. **Contrasting** What physical features make Japan different from the Koreas? Create a chart to organize your answer.

3. **Finding the Main Idea** How have the Japanese changed the physical landscape to meet their needs?

4. **Analyzing Information** How has Tokyo developed into a megalopolis?

5. **Contrasting** How do the economies of North and South Korea differ?

Map ACTIVITY

On a separate sheet of paper, match the letters on the map with their correct labels.

Hokkaido   Tokyo
Honshu   Seoul
Shikoku   P'yŏngyang
Kyushu

Mental Mapping Skills ACTIVITY

On a separate sheet of paper, draw a freehand map of Japan and the Koreas. Make a key for your map and label the following:

China   North Korea
Inland Sea   Sea of Japan
Japan   South Korea

WRITING ACTIVITY

Imagine that you are traveling in Japan, North Korea, or South Korea. Write a one-page letter to a friend describing the places you have visited and an adventure you have had during your stay. Be sure to use standard grammar, spelling, sentence structure, and punctuation.

Alternative Assessment

Portfolio ACTIVITY

Learning About Your Local Geography

Cooperative Project Japan and South Korea are very densely populated. How densely populated is your state? With your group, research the population densities of counties within your state. Create a population density map of the area you have researched.

internet connect

Internet Activity: go.hrw.com
KEYWORD: SG3 GT28

Choose a topic to explore Japan and the Koreas:
- Investigate volcanoes.
- Visit Japan and the Koreas.
- Compare your school to a Japanese school.

CHAPTER 29

Southeast Asia

Our study of the world now takes us to Southeast Asia. This vast region stretches from Myanmar eastward to New Guinea in the Pacific Ocean.

***S**awaddee!* (May you have good fortune!) I am Chosita, and I am 14 years old. I live in Bangkok with my parents and my older sister. We get up early for school because traffic in Bangkok is very heavy. By 6:00 A.M. we are on the road. My school has an eatery where street vendors sell all kinds of food—noodles in broth with beef, stir-fried noodles with meat and greens, dessert cakes of taro, pumpkin, and sticky rice, and fruits like rambutan, mangosteen, durian, and mango.

We go to school from June to September and from November to February. Our big vacation is March through May.

Our school has 38 students and two teachers in each class. I will not learn to use the computer until next year because we are the last class under the old school policy. The new policy has all students begin learning the computer in fourth grade.

สวัสดีค่ะ ดิฉันชื่อ โชสิตา ดิฉันอยู่ที่กรุงเทพฯ ซึ่งเป็นเมืองหลวงของประเทศไทยค่ะ

Translation: Hi! My name is Chosita. I live in Bangkok, the capital of Thailand.

Section 1 Physical Geography

Read to Discover

1. What are the major physical features of Southeast Asia?
2. What climates, vegetation, and wildlife are found in the region?
3. What resources does Southeast Asia have?

Define

mainland
archipelagos

Locate

Indochina Peninsula
Malay Peninsula
New Guinea
Malay Archipelago
Philippines

Irian Jaya
Borneo
Java
Sumatra
Mekong River

WHY IT MATTERS

Indonesia is made up of thousands of islands. Many have their own culture. There are ongoing conflicts between these groups. Use **CNNfyi.com** or other **current events** sources to find examples of this problem. Record your findings in your journal.

Golden statue from Thailand

Southeast Asia: Physical-Political

ELEVATION

FEET	METERS
13,120	4,000
6,560	2,000
1,640	500
656	200
(Sea level) 0	0 (Sea level)
Below sea level	Below sea level

⊛ National capitals
• Other cities
■ Historic sites

Size comparison of Southeast Asia to the contiguous United States

internet connect

GO TO: go.hrw.com
KEYWORD: SG3 CH29
FOR: Web sites about
Southeast Asia

BUILD on WHAT You Know

Do you remember what you learned about the Pacific Ring of Fire? See Chapter 2 to review.

Physical Features

Southeast Asia is made up of two peninsulas and two large island groups. The Indochina and Malay (muh-LAY) Peninsulas lie on the Asian **mainland**. A mainland is a region's main landmass. The two large groups of islands, or **archipelagos** (ahr-kuh-PE-luh-gohs), lie between the mainland and New Guinea. They are the Malay Archipelago—made up mostly of Indonesia—and the Philippines. The Philippines are sometimes considered part of the Malay Archipelago. Western New Guinea is called Irian Jaya. It is part of Indonesia.

Landforms Southeast Asia's highest mountains are on the mainland in northern Myanmar (MYAHN-mahr). Mountain ranges fan out southward into Thailand (TY-land), Laos (LOWS), and Vietnam (vee-ET-NAHM). Between the mountains are low plateaus and river floodplains. The floodplains are rich farmlands.

Some of the large islands also have high mountains. Those islands include Borneo, Java, Sumatra, New Guinea, and some in the Philippines. They are part of the Pacific Ring of Fire. Earthquakes and volcanic eruptions often shake this part of the world.

Rivers Five major river systems drain the mainland. Many people and the largest cities are found near these rivers. The greatest river is the Mekong (MAY-KAWNG). The Mekong River flows southeast from China to southern Vietnam. You will read about the other rivers later in this chapter.

✓ **READING CHECK:** (*Places and Regions*) What are Southeast Asia's major physical features?

The Mekong River flows through a floodplain along the border between Thailand and Laos.

Interpreting the Visual Record What might happen to low islands and surrounding areas during the wet monsoon?

Climate, Vegetation, and Wildlife

The warm temperatures of this tropical region generally do not change much during the year. However, northern and mountain areas tend to be cooler.

Much of the rainfall on the mainland is seasonal. Wet monsoon winds from nearby warm oceans bring heavy rains in the summer. Dry monsoons from the northeast bring drier weather in winter. Most of the islands are wet all year. Typhoons bring heavy rains and powerful winds to the island countries.

The region's tropical rain forests are home to many kinds of plants and animals. About 40,000 kinds of flowering plants grow in Indonesia alone. Rhinoceroses, orangutans, tigers, and elephants also live in the region. However, many of these plants and animals are endangered. Southeast Asia's rain forests are being cleared for farmland, tropical wood, and mining.

✓ **READING CHECK:** (*Places and Regions*) What are the region's climates, vegetation, and wildlife like?

◄ *Orangutan* is a Malaysian word for "man of the forest." These apes once lived in jungles throughout much of Southeast Asia. Hunting by humans has thinned the orangutan population in much of the region. Most orangutans today live on Borneo and Sumatra.

Resources

Southeast Asia's rain forests produce valuable wood and other products. Thailand, Indonesia, and Malaysia (muh-LAY-zhuh) are the world's largest producers of natural rubber. The rubber tree is native to South America. However, it grows well in Southeast Asia's tropical climates.

Rich volcanic soils, floodplains, and tropical climates are good for farming. Abundant water and good soils in river deltas are ideal for growing rice. Coconuts, palm oil, sugarcane, coffee, and spices are also key products. Countries here also mine tin, iron ore, oil, and gas.

✓ **READING CHECK:** (*Places and Regions*) What are the region's important resources?

Our Amazing Planet

A plant in Indonesia produces the world's largest flower —about 3 feet (1 m) across!

Homework Practice Online
Keyword: SG3 HP29

Section Review 1

Define and explain: mainland, archipelagos

Working with Sketch Maps On a map of Southeast Asia that your teacher provides or that you draw, label the following: Indochina Peninsula, Malay Peninsula, New Guinea, Malay Archipelago, Philippines, Irian Jaya, Borneo, Java, Sumatra, and the Mekong River. In a box in the margin, describe the Mekong River.

Reading for the Main Idea

1. (*Places and Regions*) Where are the region's highest mountains?

2. (*Places and Regions*) Where are large cities found?

3. (*Places and Regions*) Which countries are the world's largest producers of natural rubber?

Critical Thinking

4. Making Generalizations and Predictions What do you think might happen to the region's wildlife if much of the tropical rain forests continue to be destroyed?

Organizing What You Know

5. Summarizing Copy the following graphic organizer. Use it to describe the region's climates, vegetation and wildlife, and resources.

Climates	Vegetation and wildlife	Resources

Section 2 History and Culture

Read to Discover

1. What are some important events in the history of Southeast Asia?

2. What are the people and culture of Southeast Asia like today?

Define

refugees

Locate

Angkor
Cambodia
Thailand
Vietnam
Laos

Indonesia
Malaysia
Timor
Myanmar
Singapore

WHY IT MATTERS

Sea trade routes have always been important in this region but have also created a piracy problem. Use **CNNfyi.com** or other **current events** sources to find examples of piracy in this region. Record your findings in your journal.

Assorted peppers from Myanmar

The Khmer built the beautiful Angkor Wat in the A.D. 1100s in Angkor. This vast temple in present-day Cambodia was dedicated to Vishnu, a Hindu god.

Interpreting the Visual Record How does this temple's architecture compare to other religious buildings you have seen?

History

Southeast Asia was home to some of the world's earliest human settlements. Over time many peoples moved there from China and India. The Khmer (kuh-MER) developed the most advanced of the region's early societies. The Khmer Empire was based in Angkor in what is now Cambodia (kam-BOH-dee-uh). It controlled a large area from the early A.D. 800s to the mid-1200s.

Colonial Era Europeans began to establish colonies in Southeast Asia in the 1500s. By the end of the 1800s, the Portuguese, British, Dutch, French, and Spanish controlled most of the region. The United States won control of the Philippines from Spain after the Spanish-American War in 1898. Just Siam (sy-AM), now called Thailand, remained independent.

Japan invaded and occupied most of Southeast Asia during World War II. After Japan was defeated in 1945, the United States granted the Philippines independence a year later. European countries tried to regain control of their colonies in the region. Some Southeast Asians decided to fight for independence. One of the bloodiest wars was in French Indochina. The French finally left in 1954. Their former colonies of Vietnam, Laos, and Cambodia became independent. By the mid-1960s, European rule had ended in most of the region.

Modern Era Unfortunately, fighting did not end in some countries when the Europeans left. Vietnam split into two countries. In the 1960s the United States sent troops to defend South Vietnam against communist North Vietnam. Civil wars also raged in Laos and Cambodia. Communist forces took power in all the countries in 1975. North and South Vietnam were then united into one country.

The region's wars caused terrible destruction. Millions died, including more than 50,000 Americans. About 1 million Vietnamese **refugees** tried to escape the communist takeover in South Vietnam. Refugees are people who flee their own country, usually for economic or political reasons. Many refugees from the region came to the United States.

In Cambodia more than 1 million people died under a cruel communist government. That government ruled from 1975 to 1978. Then Vietnam invaded Cambodia in 1978, sparking another conflict. That war continued off and on until the mid-1990s. Many Cambodian refugees fled to Thailand.

Communists and other groups also fought against governments in the Philippines, Indonesia, and Malaysia. In 1975 Indonesia invaded the former Portuguese

Hanoi's Ho Chi Minh Mausoleum honors the communist leader who fought for Vietnam's independence. He led North Vietnam from 1954 to his death in 1969. Many U.S. soldiers and Vietnamese died during the war he led against South Vietnam.

CHU TỊCH
HO-CHI-MINH

colony of East Timor. The East Timorese demanded independence. However, the Indonesian military kept a tight grip on the region. The people of East Timor voted for independence in 1999. East Timor then plunged again into violence. The United Nations sent troops to restore peace and manage the area before independence was achieved.

Governments The region's countries have had different kinds of governments. Many have been ruled by dictators. Some countries, such as the Philippines and Indonesia, now have governments elected by the people.

In other countries, the people still have little say in their government. For example, Myanmar is ruled by a military government. That government has jailed and even killed its opponents. Vietnam and Laos are still ruled by Communist governments. Only recently have Indonesians been allowed to vote in free elections. In some countries, such as Singapore, the same party always wins elections.

✓ **READING CHECK:** *Places and Regions* What were some key events in Southeast Asian history?

Culture

The populations of most countries in Southeast Asia are very diverse. This is because many different peoples have moved to the area over time. Today, for example, nearly 70 percent of the people in Myanmar are Burmese. However, Chinese, Asian Indians, and many other ethnic groups also live there.

The Shwedagon Pagoda is a beautiful Buddhist shrine in Yangon, Myanmar. Pagodas are important parts of a Buddhist temple complex. **Interpreting the Visual Record What architectural features do you see in the photograph?**

▼

Many ethnic Chinese live in the largest cities of most Southeast Asian countries. In Singapore they are a majority of the population—more than 75 percent. Singapore is a tiny country at the tip of the Malay Peninsula.

Languages and Religions The peoples of Southeast Asia speak many different languages. For example, in the former Dutch colony of Indonesia, most people speak Bahasa Indonesia. However, Javanese, other local dialects, English, and Dutch are also spoken there. European and Chinese languages are spoken in many other countries.

In addition, Indians, Chinese, Arab traders, and Europeans brought different religions to the region. For example, Hinduism is practiced in the region's Indian communities. However, Buddhism is the most common religion in the mainland countries today. Islam is the major religion in Malaysia, Brunei, and Indonesia. In fact, Indonesia has the largest Islamic population in the world. Nearly 90 percent of its more than 228 million people are Muslim.

Christians are a minority in most of the former European colonies. However, more than 80 percent of people in the Philippines, a former Spanish colony, are Roman Catholic.

Food Southeast Asian foods have been influenced by Chinese, South Asian, and European cooking styles. There are many spicy, mild, and sweet varieties. Rice is the most important food in nearly all of the countries. It is served with many other foods and spices, such as curries and chili peppers. Coconut is also important. It is served as a separate dish or used as an ingredient in other foods.

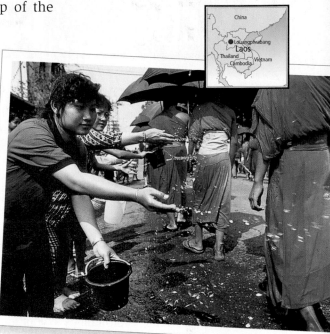

Women in Laos sprinkle water on passing Buddhist monks during a New Year festival. This custom symbolizes the washing away of the old year. It is said to bring good luck to people in the year ahead.

Interpreting the Visual Record
What kinds of clothes are the monks wearing?

✓ **READING CHECK:** (*Human Systems*) How have migration and cultural borrowing influenced the region's culture?

Section Review 2

Define and explain: refugees

Working with Sketch Maps On the map you created in Section 1, label the region's countries, Angkor, and Timor. In a box in the margin, describe the recent history of East Timor.

Reading for the Main Idea

1. (*Places and Regions*) What was the Khmer Empire?

2. (*Human Systems*) How did Europeans influence the region's history and culture?

go.hrw.com **Homework Practice Online** Keyword: SG3 HP29

Critical Thinking

3. **Drawing Inferences and Conclusions** Why do you think European countries wanted to regain their Southeast Asian colonies following World War II?

4. **Finding the Main Idea** What religion is most common in the mainland countries? in the island countries?

Organizing What You Know

5. **Sequencing** Copy the following time line. Use it to identify important people, years, periods, and events in Southeast Asia's history.

A.D. 800   2000

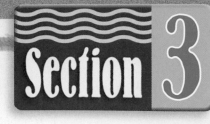

Section 3 Mainland Southeast Asia Today

Read to Discover

1. Where do people in the mainland countries live today?
2. What are the economies of the mainland countries like?

Define

klongs

Locate

Bangkok
Yangon
Hanoi
Ho Chi Minh City
Chao Phraya River

Irrawaddy River
Hong (Red) River
Vientiane
Phnom Penh

WHY IT MATTERS

The region's cities are growing rapidly. This can create problems with the city's everyday functioning. Use **CNNfyi.com** or other **current events** sources to find examples of urbanization problems in the region. Record your findings in your journal.

Golden door of a Buddhist temple

People and Cities

Most mainland Southeast Asians today live in rural areas. Many are farmers in fertile river valleys and deltas. Fewer people live in remote hill and mountain villages.

However, the region's cities have been growing rapidly. People are moving to urban areas to look for work. The cities have many businesses, services, and opportunities that are not found in rural areas. Many of the cities today are crowded, smoggy, and noisy.

Look at the chapter map. You will find that the largest cities are located along major rivers. Location near rivers places these cities near important rice-growing areas. Access to rivers also makes them key

A Vietnamese man sells incense sticks in Ho Chi Minh City.

Interpreting the Visual Record Why might people in warm, sunny climates wear hats like the one in this photo?

shipping centers for farm and factory products. The largest cities are Bangkok, Yangon, Hanoi, and Ho Chi Minh City.

Bangkok The mainland's largest city is Bangkok, Thailand's capital. Bangkok lies near the mouth of the Chao Phraya (chow PRY-uh) River. More than 7 million people live there. Much of Bangkok is connected by **klongs**, or canals. The *klongs* are used for transportation and for selling and shipping goods. They also drain water from the city.

Other Cities The region's second-largest city is Yangon, formerly known as Rangoon. It is Myanmar's capital and major seaport. The city is located in the Irrawaddy River delta on the coast of the Andaman Sea. To the east, Vietnam's largest cities are also located in major river deltas. The capital, Hanoi (ha-NOY), is located in the Hong (Red) River delta in the north. Ho Chi Minh City is located in the Mekong River delta in the south. Ho Chi Minh City was once known as Saigon and was South Vietnam's capital. Today it is an important seaport and business center with more than 4.6 million people.

✓ **READING CHECK:** (*Places and Regions*) Where do most people in mainland Southeast Asia live today and why?

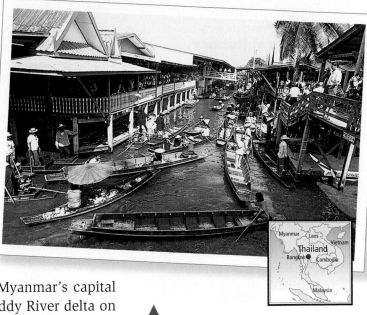

▲ Boat traffic can be heavy along Bangkok's *klongs*. These canals have been part of the city's original transportation system for centuries.

Economy

War, bad governments, and other problems have slowed progress in most of the mainland countries. However, rich resources could make the future brighter for the people there.

Vietnam Vietnam's economy has been slowly recovering since the end of the war in 1975. In recent years, the Communist government has begun moving from a command economy to a more market-oriented one. Some people are now allowed to own private businesses. Most Vietnamese remain farmers.

Most of Vietnam's factories, coal, oil, and other resources are in the north. The Hong and Mekong River deltas are major farming areas. Rice is the most important crop and food. In many places it is planted twice each year.

Laos This mountainous, landlocked country has few good roads, no railroads, and few telephones and televisions. Only some cities have

Mainland Southeast Asia

COUNTRY	POPULATION/ GROWTH RATE	LIFE EXPECTANCY	LITERACY RATE	PER CAPITA GDP
Cambodia	12,491,501 2.3%	55, male 59, female	35%	$1,300
Laos	5,635,967 2.5%	52, male 55, female	57%	$1,700
Myanmar	41,994,678 0.6%	54, male 57, female	83%	$1,500
Thailand	61,797,751 0.9%	66, male 72, female	94%	$6,700
Vietnam	79,939,014 1.5%	67, male 72, female	94%	$1,950
United States	281,421,906 0.9%	74, male 80, female	97%	$36,200

Sources: Central Intelligence Agency, *The World Factbook 2001;* U.S. Census Bureau

Interpreting the Chart According to the data in the chart, which country in the region is the most economically developed?

Major Producers of Natural Rubber

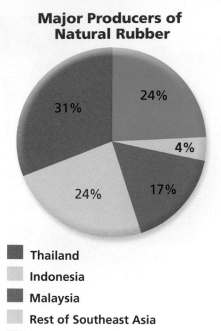

- ■ Thailand
- ■ Indonesia
- ■ Malaysia
- ■ Rest of Southeast Asia
- ■ Rest of the world

Source: United Nations, *Monthly Bulletin of Statistics,* July 1999

Interpreting the Chart Which country is the largest producer of natural rubber?

▶

Trees like these in Thailand make the region the world's largest producer of natural rubber.

electricity. The economy is mostly traditional—most people are subsistence farmers. They produce just enough food for themselves and their families. The Communist government in Vientiane (vyen-TYAHN), the capital, has also recently begun allowing more economic freedom.

Cambodia Economic progress in Cambodia has been particularly slow because of war and political problems. Agriculture is the most important part of the economy. The capital and largest city, Phnom Penh (puh-NAWM PEN), is located along the Mekong River. It lies in Cambodia's southern rice-growing area.

Thailand Thailand's economy has had problems but is the strongest of the mainland countries. This is partly because Thailand has rich resources. These resources include timber, natural rubber, seafood, rice, many minerals, and gems. Factories produce computers and electronics. Many Thai operate small businesses. Tourism is also important.

Myanmar This former British colony is also called Burma. It gained independence in 1948 and was officially renamed Myanmar in 1989. It has rich resources, including copper, tin, iron ore, timber, rubber, and oil. However, a harsh military government has limited political freedom. This has slowed economic progress.

✓ **READING CHECK:** *Places and Regions*
What are the mainland economies like?

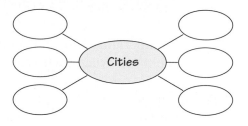
Homework Practice Online
Keyword: SG3 HP29

Section Review 3

Define and explain: *klongs*

Working with Sketch Maps On the map you created in Section 2, label Bangkok, Yangon, Hanoi, Ho Chi Minh City, Chao Phraya River, Irrawaddy River, Hong (Red) River, Vientiane, and Phnom Penh. Describe the mainland's largest city.

Reading for the Main Idea

1. *Places and Regions* Where do most mainland Southeast Asians live and why?

2. *Human Systems* Why are many people moving to cities?

3. *Places and Regions* Which country has the strongest economy and why?

Critical Thinking

4. **Finding the Main Idea** What kinds of problems appear to have slowed economic progress in the region?

Organizing What You Know

5. **Summarizing** Copy the following graphic organizer. Use it to describe the mainland's major cities. In each of its six circles, write the name of a city. In the circles, write important facts about the cities.

Cities

Section 4 Island Southeast Asia Today

Read to Discover

1. What are the major cities of the island countries?
2. What are the economies of the island countries like?

Define

kampongs
sultan

Locate

Jakarta
Manila
Kuala Lumpur
Luzon
Bali

A decorative Indonesian fabric called a batik (buh-TEEK)

WHY IT MATTERS

Some countries in this region have higher per capita GDPs as a result of their growing economies. Use CNNfyi.com or other current events sources to check economic growth in this region. Record your findings in your journal.

People and Cities

Indonesia is the largest of the island countries and the world's fourth-most-populous country. The country's more than 17,000 islands were known as the Dutch East Indies until 1949. Malaysia, Singapore, and Brunei were British colonies. The British granted independence to Malaysia in 1963. Singapore split from Malaysia in 1965. In 1984 Brunei became the region's last European colony to gain independence. As you have read, the Philippines gained independence from the United States in 1946. More than 7,000 islands make up that country.

Many people live in rural areas in the island countries. However, the island countries are more urbanized than the mainland countries. As on the mainland, many people are moving to cities in search of jobs. One country, Singapore, is simply a large city on a small island.

Modern skyscrapers tower over colonial-era buildings in Singapore. The city has one of the world's busiest ports.

Interpreting the Visual Record What does Singapore's architecture tell you about its economy and culture?

Wayang *puppets*

Puppetry is an art form with roots in ancient civilizations, including Greece, Rome, China, and India. On the Indonesian island of Java, one of the world's great puppet traditions is known as *wayang*. This shadow puppet theater still entertains audiences.

Wayang puppets are beautiful works of art. The puppets are made from thin sheets of painted leather. They are pierced with holes so that light can shine through them. Then they are mounted on sticks. The performance takes place behind a screen. A light source is placed behind the puppets. The puppet's shadows fall on the screen and are visible to the audience on the other side.

Wayang performances tell stories from the *Ramayana* and the *Mahabharata*. These are two long poems of the Hindu religion. Hinduism came to Java from India hundreds of

Shadow Puppets

years ago. The puppets play the parts of gods, heroes, and villains. A performance usually lasts all night and includes the traditional music of Java. The music is played by an orchestra that includes gongs and other traditional instruments.

Over the years, *wayang* artists have developed other types of puppets. Some puppets are wooden forms. A new generation of artists is even creating computerized stories for *wayang* theater.

Understanding What You Read

1. Where did puppetry originate?
2. What is a *wayang* performance like?

In 1883 a huge volcanic eruption on the Indonesian island of Krakatau killed thousands. Ash in the atmosphere colored sunsets around the world for months.

Jakarta The region's largest city is Jakarta, Indonesia's capital. More than 11 million people live there. It is located on Java, which is by far Indonesia's most populous island. Many Indonesians live in **kampongs** around Jakarta. A kampong is a traditional village. It has also become the term for the crowded slums around large cities.

Singapore If you traveled from Jakarta to Singapore, you would find two very different cities. Singapore is one of the most modern and cleanest cities in the world. Crime rates also are very low. How has Singapore accomplished this?

Its government is very strict. For example, fines for littering are stiff. People caught transporting illegal drugs can be executed. The government even bans chewing gum and certain movies and music.

Is the lack of some individual freedoms a good trade-off for less crime, a clean city, and a strong economy? Some people in Singapore say yes. Others believe Singapore can be just as successful with less government control.

Other Cities The region's other large cities include Manila and Kuala Lumpur. More than 10 million people live in Manila, the capital of the Philippines. The city is a major seaport and industrial center on Luzon. Luzon is the country's largest and most populated island.

Kuala Lumpur is Malaysia's capital as well as its cultural, business, and transportation center. It is a modern city with two of the world's tallest buildings, the twin Petronas Towers.

✓ **READING CHECK:** *Places and Regions* What are some of the major cities of the island countries?

Economy

The economies of the island countries grew rapidly until the mid-1990s. Then economic and political problems slowed growth for a while. However, rich resources are helping the economies there to recover. In addition, wages and labor costs are low in many of the countries. This means that companies there can manufacture many products more cheaply for export.

Indonesia Europeans once called Indonesia the Spice Islands because of its cinnamon, pepper, and nutmeg. Today, its rich resources include natural rubber, oil, natural gas, and timber. Indonesia also has good farmlands for rice and other crops. Busy factories turn out clothing, electronics, and furniture. Some islands, such as Bali, are popular with tourists.

Island Southeast Asia

COUNTRY	POPULATION/ GROWTH RATE	LIFE EXPECTANCY	LITERACY RATE	PER CAPITA GDP
Brunei	343,653 2.1%	71, male 76, female	88%	$17,600
Indonesia	228,437,870 1.6%	66, male 71, female	84%	$2,930
Malaysia	22,229,040 2.4%	68, male 74, female	84%	$7,900
Philippines	82,841,518 1.7%	65, male 71, female	95%	$3,600
Singapore	4,300,419 1.7%	77, male 83, female	94%	$26,500
United States	281,421,906 0.9%	74, male 80, female	97%	$36,200

Sources: Central Intelligence Agency, *The World Factbook 2001;* U.S. Census Bureau

Interpreting the Chart According to the chart, which country's economic development is closest to that of the United States?

Farming is an important economic activity in the Philippines. In mountain areas, farmers plant rice and other crops in terraced fields. These flat terraces hold water and slow erosion along mountainsides.

▼

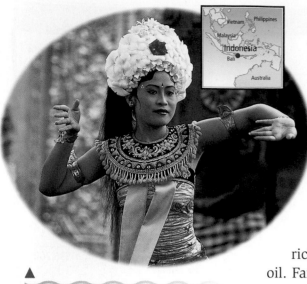

Bali dancers are popular tourist attractions in Indonesia, a country with many different dance styles. This *Barong* dancer uses her hands, arms, and eyes to help tell a traditional story.

Large areas of Indonesia's tropical rain forests are often burned for farming. Smoke from the fires can spread for hundreds of miles. The smoke sometimes blots out sunlight, smothering cities in haze.

The Philippines The Philippines is mostly an agricultural country today. A big problem is the gap between rich and poor Filipinos. A few very rich Filipinos control most of the land and industries. Most farmers are poor and own no land.

The economy has improved in recent years. Companies sell many electronics and clothing products to overseas customers, particularly in the United States. The country also has rich resources, including tropical forests, copper, gold, silver, and oil. Farmers grow sugarcane, rice, corn, coconuts, and tropical fruits.

Singapore Singapore is by far the most economically developed country in all of Southeast Asia. The British founded the city at the tip of the Malay Peninsula in 1819. This location along major shipping routes helped make Singapore rich. Goods are stored there before they are shipped to their final stop. In addition, many foreign companies have opened banks, offices, and high-technology industries there.

Malaysia Malaysia is made up of two parts. The largest part lies on the southern Malay Peninsula. The second part lies on the northern portion of Borneo. Well-educated workers and rich resources make Malaysia's future look bright. The country produces natural rubber, electronics, automobiles, oil, and timber. The government is trying to attract more high-technology companies to the country. Malaysia is also the world's leading producer of palm oil.

Electronics and technology products are increasingly important to the region's economies. This Filipino is working at a semiconductor manufacturing plant.

Interpreting the Visual Record Why do you think the person in the photograph is dressed this way?

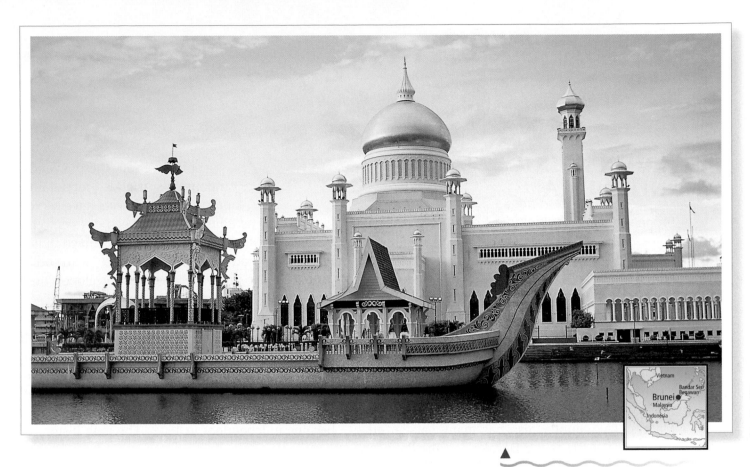

This beautiful mosque in Brunei's capital reflects the country's oil wealth. Money from oil and natural gas production pays for many social services there.

Brunei Large deposits of oil have made Brunei rich. This small country on the island of Borneo is ruled by a **sultan**. A sultan is the supreme ruler of a Muslim country. Brunei shares the island of Borneo with Indonesia and Malaysia.

✓ **READING CHECK:** *Places and Regions* How do rich resources affect the economies of the island countries?

Section Review 4

Define and explain: kampongs, sultan

Working with Sketch Maps On the map you created in Section 3, label Jakarta, Manila, Kuala Lumpur, Luzon, and Bali. In a box in the margin, identify the most heavily populated islands in Indonesia and the Philippines.

Reading for the Main Idea

1. *Places and Regions* What is the region's largest city? What is the importance of Manila and Kuala Lumpur to their countries?

2. *Places and Regions* Why was Indonesia once called the Spice Islands? What European country once controlled nearly all of Indonesia?

Critical Thinking

3. **Analyzing Information** Some Singaporeans say that limiting some individual freedoms is a good trade-off for less crime and a better economy. Do you agree? Why or why not?

4. **Comparing/Contrasting** How have Singapore and Brunei become rich countries?

Organizing What You Know

5. **Summarizing** Copy the following graphic organizer. Use it to list the nine Southeast Asian countries that are former European colonies. Next to each country's name, write the name of the European country that once controlled it.

Southeast Asian country	European colonial power

CASE STUDY

MULTIETHNIC INDONESIA

Indonesia is a multiethnic country—a country with many different ethnic groups. The national motto of Indonesia is *Bhinneka Tunggal Ika*, which means "the many are one." This motto comes from the many different ethnic groups that live there.

More than 300 different ethnic groups live in Indonesia. Most of these groups speak their own language and have their own way of life. No single ethnic group holds a majority. The largest are the Javanese, Sundanese, Madurese, and Coastal Malays. The country also has many smaller ethnic groups, such as the Dayaks and the Balinese. Why does Indonesia have so many different ethnic groups? Part of the answer lies in the country's diverse physical geography.

Indonesia is a very large country. It is made up of more than 17,000 islands. About 228 million people live on these islands. Indonesia's islands, mountains, and dense rain forests have served as boundaries between different ethnic groups. Many small ethnic groups lived in isolation and had very little contact with other peoples. Over time, these groups developed their own cultures, languages, and ways of life.

The modern country of Indonesia has its roots in the early 1600s. About this time, Dutch traders built forts in the area. They wanted to protect the trade routes used by Dutch ships to transport spices and other goods. The Dutch remained an important force in the region until Indonesia became independent in 1949. The long history of

Most Indonesians are related to the peoples of East Asia. However, in the eastern islands, most people are of Melanesian origin. Over the centuries, many Arabs, Indians, and Europeans have added to the country's ethnic diversity.

▼

Ethnic Groups in Indonesia

- Acehnese
- Balinese
- Batak
- Bonfia
- Coastal Malays
- Javanese
- Kupangese
- Land Dayak group
- Larantuka
- Loinang group
- Madurese
- Mori Laki group
- Redjang Lampong group
- Sundanese

◄ The Balinese are one of Indonesia's many ethnic groups. Unlike most other Indonesians, Hinduism is their main religion.

Dutch control helped unify the islands into the modern country of Indonesia.

In addition to this shared past, several other factors have helped unify Indonesia. For example, Indonesia's government has promoted the country's official language, Bahasa Indonesia. Although most Indonesians speak more than one language, Bahasa Indonesia is used in schools and government. The use of this language has been an important force in uniting the country. The government has also tried to develop a common Indonesian culture. It has promoted national holiday celebrations, education, popular art, and television and radio programs.

A shared history, a common education system, and an official language help give isolated ethnic groups an Indonesian identity. However, the country's multiethnic society still faces some important challenges. In certain parts of Indonesia, people want independence. For example, in 1999 people in East Timor voted for independence from Indonesia. This caused a great deal of unrest. Most people there supported the vote, but others did not. When some groups rioted, many Timorese left the area for their own safety. The Acehnese, an ethnic group on the island of Sumatra, have also been seeking independence.

Ethnic Groups in Indonesia

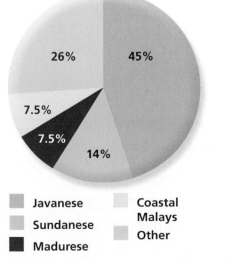

- 45%
- 26%
- 7.5%
- 7.5%
- 14%

Javanese	Coastal Malays
Sundanese	Other
Madurese	

Source: Central Intelligence Agency, *The World Factbook 2001*

Understanding What You Read

1. How diverse is Indonesia's society? What has helped to promote cooperation among the different ethnic groups that live in the country?

2. What are some important challenges facing Indonesia today?

Reviewing What You Know

Building Vocabulary

On a separate sheet of paper, write sentences to define each of the following words.

1. mainland
2. archipelagos
3. refugees
4. *klongs*
5. kampongs
6. sultan

Reviewing the Main Ideas

1. (Places and Regions) What peninsulas and archipelagos make up Southeast Asia?
2. (Places and Regions) Where will you find the highest mountains in Southeast Asia?
3. (Places and Regions) What factors have slowed economic progress in mainland Southeast Asia?
4. (Places and Regions) What resources are important to the economies of the region?
5. (Human Systems) How did European countries influence Southeast Asia?

Understanding Environment and Society

Rice Farming

Rice is the main crop and most common food in Southeast Asia. Develop a presentation about rice farming. In developing your presentation, consider the following:

- How rice is grown.
- What growing conditions are needed.
- Where rice is grown in Southeast Asia.

Thinking Critically

1. **Drawing Inferences and Conclusions** Why are some cities located near river deltas so large?
2. **Finding the Main Idea** What outside cultures have strongly influenced the development of Southeast Asian culture?
3. **Analyzing Information** How did the Philippines and Vietnam gain independence?
4. **Finding the Main Idea** How do the climates of mainland countries differ from those in the island countries? What natural disasters are a danger in the region?
5. **Analyzing Information** How do labor costs affect the island countries' economies?

Map ACTIVITY

On a separate sheet of paper, match the letters on the map with their correct labels.

Indochina Peninsula

Malay Peninsula

Malay Archipelago and the Philippines

Irian Jaya

Borneo

Mekong River

Timor

Bangkok

Jakarta

Manila

Mental Mapping Skills ACTIVITY

On a separate sheet of paper, draw a freehand map of Southeast Asia. Make a key for your map and label the following:

Andaman Sea

Hanoi

Java

Kuala Lumpur

Philippines

Singapore

Sumatra

Yangon

WRITING ACTIVITY

Imagine that you are an economic adviser for a poor Southeast Asian country. Write a one-paragraph summary explaining how some countries in the region built stronger economies. Use the report to suggest policies your chosen country might adopt to build its economy. Be sure to use standard grammar, spelling, sentence structure, and punctuation.

Alternative Assessment

Portfolio ACTIVITY

Learning About Your Local Geography

Individual Project Find out how your local community was affected by the Vietnam War. Interview community members, locate and read old newspapers or firsthand accounts, and present an oral report.

internet connect

Internet Activity: go.hrw.com
KEYWORD: SG3 GT29

Choose a topic to explore about Southeast Asia:

- Explore an Indonesian rain forest.
- Learn about shadow puppets.
- See buildings of Southeast Asia.

ENVIRONMENT

Indonesia's Threatened Rain Forests

Why Are Rain Forests Important?

Do you know where bananas, pineapples, and oranges originally came from? Each of these plants first grew in a tropical rain forest.

Tropical rain forests are considered by many to be the most important forests in the world. It is estimated that about half of all species of plants, animals, and insects on Earth live in tropical rain forests. Rain forest trees and plants help maintain global temperatures. They also help hold rain-drenched soil in place. This prevents it from washing away and clogging rivers. About one fourth of all medicines currently found in drugstores come from tropical rain forests.

Tropical rain forests can be found in many countries along the equator and between about 20° north and south latitude. One of the largest rain forests is in Brazil's Amazon Basin. In Africa, rain forests are found in many countries, such as Gabon and the Democratic Republic of the Congo. In Southeast Asia, rain forests are found in countries such as Thailand, Vietnam, and Indonesia.

Deforestation in Indonesia

Indonesia has large areas of tropical rain forest in Borneo, Sumatra, and Irian Jaya. These areas are home to many unusual species of plants and animals. For example, the largest flower in the world, the *Rafflesia arnoldii*, is found there.

Indonesia's tropical rain forests are being rapidly cut down. About 4,700 square miles (12,170 sq km) of rain forest are lost each year. This rate of deforestation is second only to Brazil's. Some people have predicted that much of Indonesia's

▲

Found in the rain forests of Sumatra, the *Rafflesia arnoldii* is the largest known flower in the world. It can weigh up to 24 pounds (11 kg) and can measure about 3 feet (1 meter) across.

rain forests will be gone in just 10 years. When the rain forests are cleared, animals such as the endangered orangutan do not have a home.

There are many reasons that Indonesia's tropical rain forests are being cleared. Trees from tropical rain forests produce beautiful woods. They are used to make furniture, boats, and houses. The demand for special trees and wood has made logging a profitable business. Much of the logging is done by large corporations that do not replant the areas that are cut.

Deforestation in Indonesia also occurs because people need land to farm and raise animals. They also need wood for fuel. People clear the land using a method called slash-and-burn. Large trees are cut, or slashed, and left on the ground. Then the land is burned during the dry season. This clears the land of vegetation and prepares it for farming. In 1997 large areas of land in Indonesia were cleared. Huge fires burned out of control. The fires burned an area roughly the size of Denmark. Smoke filled the sky and caused some airplanes and ships to crash.

Protecting Indonesia's Rain Forests

Some people in Indonesia are trying to protect the rain forests. Parks and nature reserves have been set up that are off-limits to logging companies. Some groups are finding ways to earn money without cutting down trees. Selling fruits and nuts from the rain forest is one way. Also, international organizations such as the Rainforest Action Network are helping to protect the forests. Some environmental groups are even pressuring countries to stop buying trees that come from tropical rain forests.

Much of the timber cut in Indonesia and other Southeast Asian countries is exported to Japan. Indonesia exports about 2 million tons of plywood and 145,000 tons of lumber to Japan each year.

Orangutans live in the tropical rain forests of Borneo and Sumatra. Deforestation has seriously reduced their habitat. The word *orangutan* means "man of the forest."

Understanding What You Read

1. Why are Indonesia's tropical rain forests being cut down?

2. What is being done to protect Indonesia's tropical rain forests?

Building Skills for Life: Interpreting Cultural Landscapes

Cultural landscapes are the forms put on the land by people. For example, buildings, field patterns, and roads are all a part of cultural landscapes. Cultural landscapes show a people's way of life.

Different cultures create distinctive cultural landscapes. For example, a village in China looks very different from a village in France. By comparing how the two villages look, we can begin to see how their cultures are different.

Geographers interpret cultural landscapes. They observe a landscape, describe what they see, and try to explain how it reflects the culture of the place. This is called reading the cultural landscape.

You can read cultural landscapes too. To read a cultural landscape, start by describing

what you see. What kinds of buildings are there? What are they used for? What kinds of clothing are people wearing? Then, think about how what you see relates to the place's culture. What would it be like to live there? What do people there do for fun?

Cultural landscapes tell a story. By reading and interpreting these stories, you can learn a lot about people and geography.

Architecture is an important part of the cultural landscape at the Black Dragon Pool in southern China.

THE SKILL

1. Try to read the cultural landscapes of your community. What forms have people put on the land? What do they tell you about the daily life of the people who live there?

2. Watch a television show or movie and interpret the cultural landscapes you see. What is distinctive about them? How are they different from the cultural landscapes you are used to? Can you guess where the program was filmed?

3. Look carefully at the pictures in a newspaper or magazine without reading the captions. Do the pictures tell a story? Is culture a part of this story?

HANDS on GEOGRAPHY

The photographs below show two very different cultural landscapes. What can these photographs tell us about each place's culture and way of life? Look closely at each photograph and then answer the Lab Report questions.

◀

A cultural landscape in East Asia

▲

A cultural landscape in Southeast Asia

Lab Report

1. What do these two photographs show? On a separate sheet of paper, write a short description of each photograph.

2. Do these two photographs tell you something about each place's culture and way of life? On a separate sheet of paper, describe what you think the culture of these two places is like.

3. Are there some things about a place's culture that you cannot learn from just looking at a photograph? What are they? If you took a trip to these two places, what else could you learn about their cultures?

UNIT 9

South Asia

CHAPTER 30
India

CHAPTER 31
The Indian Perimeter

Swayambhunath Stupa, Kathmandu, Nepal

Karakoram Range, Pakistan

A Scholar in India

Emily K. Bloch coordinates educational programs at the South Asia Outreach center at the University of Chicago. Her special area of interest is South Asian children's literature. Here she describes the many types of transportation she has used in India. **WHAT DO YOU THINK?** *Which type of transportation would you enjoy the most?*

I n my travels throughout India, I've had the good fortune to ride on a variety of vehicles. I've ridden in buses and cycle-rickshaws, taxis and three-wheeled scooters, on a motorcycle through Calcutta and on the crossbar of a bicycle. I rode in a howdah [seat] on the back of an elephant in a wildlife sanctuary. I even had an uncomfortable, but very welcome, lift in a bullock cart.

But my favorite mode of travel is also one of the most popular in India—riding the great trains. The railway, with more than 1.5 million employees, is the largest employer in the world. It has nearly 40,000 miles of track. Eleven thousand trains, connecting more than 7,000 stations, carry about 12 million people daily. Though the luxury of the princely rail lines beckons, and the first-class cars provide food and bed-linens, I love the crowded, second-class, wooden-benches experience and look forward to my next journey side by side with my fellow Indian and foreign travelers.

Women in festival dress, Rajasthan, India

Polo players at elephant festival, Jaipur, India

Understanding Primary Sources

1. What do Emily Bloch's transportation experiences illustrate about the use of technology in India?

2. Which method of travel does Emily Bloch prefer? Why?

White Bengal tiger

South Asia

Elevation Profile

Profile at 25°N latitude

10,000 ft.   3,048 m

Indus River
Aravalli Range
Indo-Gangetic Plain
Ganges River

5,000 ft.   1,524 m
4,000 ft.   1,220 m
3,000 ft.   914 m
2,000 ft.   610 m
1,000 ft.   305 m
Sea Level   Sea Level

Approximately 1,600 miles

The United States and South Asia: Comparing Sizes

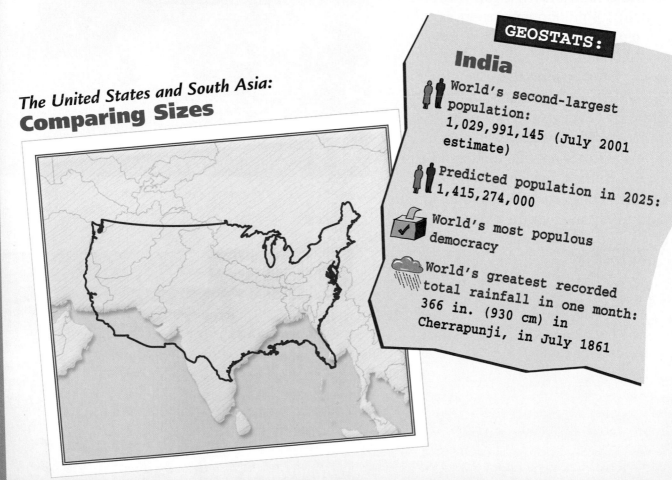

GEOSTATS:

India

World's second-largest population: 1,029,991,145 (July 2001 estimate)

Predicted population in 2025: 1,415,274,000

World's most populous democracy

World's greatest recorded total rainfall in one month: 366 in. (930 cm) in Cherrapunji, in July 1861

ELEVATION

FEET	METERS
13,120	4,000
6,560	2,000
1,640	500
656	200
(Sea level) 0	0 (Sea level)
Below sea level	Below sea level

SCALE
0   300   600 Miles
0   300   600 Kilometers
Projection: Two-Point Equidistant

1. *Places and Regions* Which country has the lowest overall elevation? Which countries have mountains that stretch from their western to eastern borders?

2. *Places and Regions* Which two rivers that drain the Deccan Plateau flow directly into the Bay of Bengal?

Critical Thinking

3. Drawing Inferences and Conclusions Based on the map, do you think it would be easier for travelers or invaders to come to northern India by land or by sea? Why might this be the case?

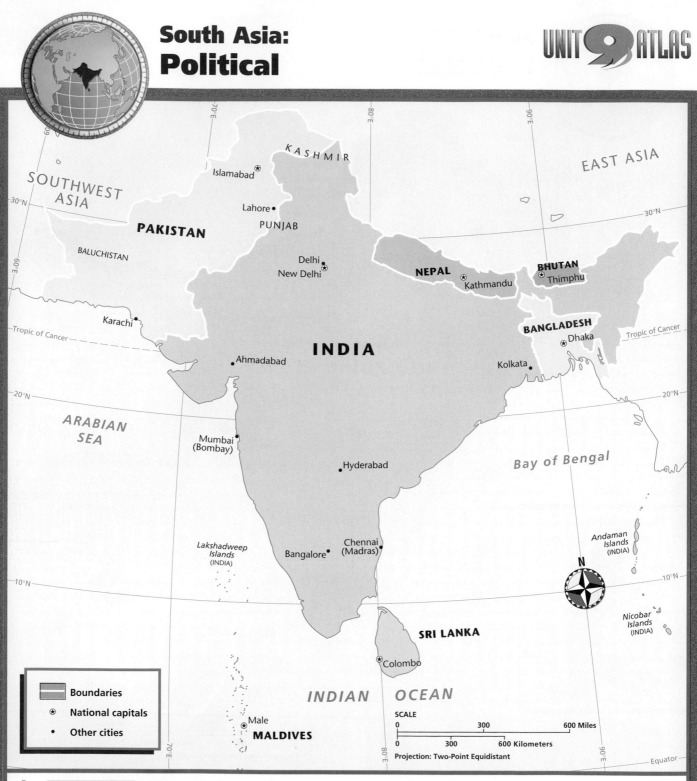

Map of South Asia showing political boundaries, national capitals, and other cities, including Pakistan, India, Nepal, Bhutan, Bangladesh, Sri Lanka, and Maldives.

SOUTHWEST
ASIA

KASHMIR

EAST ASIA

Islamabad ⊛

Lahore •

PAKISTAN

PUNJAB

BALUCHISTAN

Delhi •
New Delhi ⊛

NEPAL
⊛ Kathmandu

BHUTAN
⊛ Thimphu

Karachi •

BANGLADESH
⊛ Dhaka

Tropic of Cancer

Tropic of Cancer

Ahmadabad •

INDIA

Kolkata •

ARABIAN
SEA

Mumbai •
(Bombay)

Hyderabad •

Bay of Bengal

Lakshadweep
Islands
(INDIA)

Bangalore •

Chennai •
(Madras)

Andaman
Islands
(INDIA)

N

Nicobar
Islands
(INDIA)

SRI LANKA

Colombo •

INDIAN   OCEAN

Male •
MALDIVES

| Boundaries |
| ⊛ National capitals |
| • Other cities |

SCALE
0 ———— 300 ———— 600 Miles
0 ———— 300 ———— 600 Kilometers
Projection: Two-Point Equidistant

Equator

1. *Places and Regions* What are the region's two island countries? Which is larger?

2. *Places and Regions* Which country is almost completely surrounded by India?

3. *Places and Regions* Compare this map to the **physical map**. Which small countries might be called the "Mountain Kingdoms?"

Critical Thinking

4. Drawing Inferences and Conclusions
Bangladesh was once part of Pakistan. What role do you think Bangladesh's location may have played in its drive for independence?

SOUTHWEST ASIA

EAST ASIA

30°N

Tropic of Cancer

ARABIAN SEA

20°N

Bay of Bengal

INDIAN OCEAN

CLIMATE

- Humid tropical
- Tropical savanna
- Desert
- Steppe
- Humid subtropical
- Highland
- ← Wet monsoon air flow
- ← Dry monsoon air flow

N

10°N

SCALE

0   300   600 Miles

0   300   600 Kilometers

Projection: Two-Point Equidistant

Tropic of Cancer

Equator

1. **Places and Regions** Compare this map to the **physical map.** Which landform in south central India has a steppe climate?

2. **Places and Regions** Compare this map to the **land use and resources map** of the region. Which climate regions have the least economic activity?

Critical Thinking

3. **Analyzing Information** Compare this map to the **political map** of the region. Other than those with mainly highland climates, which country appears to be least affected by monsoons?

South Asia: Population

POPULATION DENSITY

Persons per sq. mile	Persons per sq km
520	200
260	100
130	50
25	10
3	1
0	0

● Metropolitan areas with more than 2 million inhabitants

○ Metropolitan areas with 1 million to 2 million inhabitants

SCALE
0 — 300 — 600 Miles
0 — 300 — 600 Kilometers
Projection: Two-Point Equidistant

1. (Places and Regions) Compare this map to the **physical map**. Which large Indian city is located on the Ganges Delta?

2. (Places and Regions) Compare this map to the **physical map** of the region. What is the name of the large densely populated area in the northeastern part of the region?

Critical Thinking

3. Analyzing Information Use the map on this page to create a chart, graph, database, or model of population centers in South Asia.

South Asia:
Land Use and Resources

LAND USE

- Nomadic herding
- Livestock raising
- Commercial farming
- Subsistence farming
- Manufacturing
- Forests
- Limited economic activity
- ● Major manufacturing and trade centers

RESOURCES

- 🪨 Coal
- 🔥 Natural gas
- ⛏ Oil
- ⚡ Hydroelectric power
- ✳ Nuclear power
- Ⓖ Gold
- Ⓢ Silver
- Ⓤ Uranium
- ◈ Other minerals
- 🌲 Timber
- 🐟 Seafood

SCALE
0 — 300 — 600 Miles
0 — 300 — 600 Kilometers
Projection: Two-Point Equidistant

1. (*Places and Regions*) Which country has the largest area used for nomadic herding?

2. (*Places and Regions*) Which country has the largest area used for manufacturing?

3. (*Places and Regions*) Which city is near the region's gold, silver, and uranium mines?

4. (*Places and Regions*) Which country does not produce hydroelectric power?

Critical Thinking

5. Analyzing Information Use this map to create a chart, graph, database, or model of economic activities in South Asia.

Fast FACTS

South Asia

BANGLADESH

CAPITAL:
Dhaka

AREA:
55,598 sq. mi.
(144,000 sq km)

POPULATION:
131,269,860

MONEY:
taka (BDT)

LANGUAGES:
Bangla (official), English

ARABLE LAND:
73 percent

BHUTAN

CAPITAL:
Thimphu

AREA:
18,147 sq. mi.
(47,000 sq km)

POPULATION:
2,049,412

MONEY:
ngultrum (BTN),
Indian rupee (INR)

LANGUAGES:
Dzongkha

ARABLE LAND:
2 percent

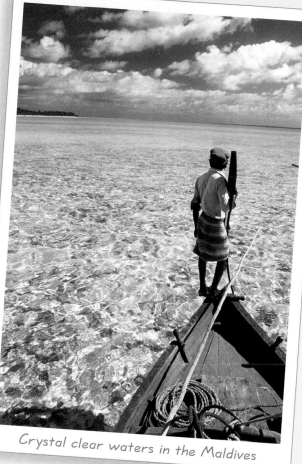

Crystal clear waters in the Maldives

INDIA

CAPITAL:
New Delhi

AREA:
1,269,338 sq. mi.
(3,287,590 sq km)

POPULATION:
1,029,991,145

MONEY: Indian rupee (INR)

LANGUAGES:
Hindi (official), English (associate official), 14 other official languages, many ethnic languages

ARABLE LAND: 56 percent

MALDIVES

CAPITAL:
Male

AREA:
116 sq. mi.
(300 sq km)

POPULATION:
310,764

MONEY:
rufiyaa (MVR)

LANGUAGES:
Maldivian Divehi, English

ARABLE LAND:
10 percent

Countries not drawn to scale.

Buddhist monks in Kandy, Sri Lanka

NEPAL

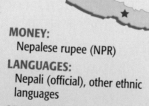

CAPITAL:
Kathmandu

AREA:
54,363 sq. mi.
(140,800 sq km)

POPULATION:
25,284,463

MONEY:
Nepalese rupee (NPR)

LANGUAGES:
Nepali (official), other ethnic languages

ARABLE LAND:
17 percent

PAKISTAN

CAPITAL:
Islamabad

AREA:
310,401 sq. mi.
(803,940 sq km)

POPULATION:
144,616,639

MONEY:
Pakistani rupee (PKR)

LANGUAGES:
Punjabi, Sindhi, Siraiki, Pashtu, Urdu (official), Balochi, Hindko, Brahui, English, many ethnic languages

ARABLE LAND:
27 percent

SRI LANKA

CAPITAL: Colombo

AREA:
25,332 sq. mi.
(65,610 sq km)

POPULATION:
19,408,635

MONEY:
Sri Lankan rupee (LKR)

LANGUAGES:
Sinhalese, Tamil, English

ARABLE LAND:
14 percent

internet connect

COUNTRY STATISTICS
GO TO: go.hrw.com
KEYWORD: SG3 FactsU9
FOR: more facts about South Asia

Sources: Central Intelligence Agency, *The World Factbook 2001*; *The World Almanac and Book of Facts 2001*; pop. figures are 2001 estimates.

India

India is a huge country with an ancient culture and a population of a billion people. However, you might find you have quite a bit in common with a student from India.

Hi! My name is Rojo, and I am 16. I live with my mother, father, and dog, Jacki. I live in Vaduthala, a small town outside the city of Cochin on the southern tip of India. I live in a one-floor house, with three bedrooms, two bathrooms, living area, dining area, kitchen, cooking terrace, front yard with lots of plants, and a road down to the lake. To cook, my mom usually goes outside to the cooking terrace and makes fish curry. That way, the whole house does not smell like the food.

I am a senior at the State Bank Officers Association High School. This term I am studying math, physics, chemistry, and computer science. My favorite subject is math, because I can use it in so many different ways. The computer language I am studying is based on math. We speak in English in school. At home or with friends, we speak Malayalam, the most common language of the state of Kerala.

Entha vishaisham?

◄ 〜〜〜〜〜〜〜

Translation: What's new?

Section 1 — Physical Geography

Read to Discover

1. What are the three main landform regions of India?
2. What are the major rivers in India?
3. What climate types does India have?
4. What natural resources does India have?

Define

teak

Locate

Gangetic Plain
Deccan
Eastern Ghats
Western Ghats

Ganges River
Bay of Bengal
Brahmaputra River
Thar Desert

An Indian black cobra

India: Physical-Political

internet connect

GO TO: go.hrw.com
KEYWORD: SG3 CH30
FOR: Web sites about India

Do you remember what you learned about plate tectonics? See Chapter 2 to review.

A farmer plows rice fields in northern India. The Himalayas rise in the distance.
Interpreting the Visual Record
Why do so many of India's people live on the Gangetic Plain?

Landforms

India has three main landform regions: the Himalayas, the Gangetic (gan-JE-tik) Plain, and the Deccan (DE-kuhn). The Himalayas run along the country's northern border and were created when two tectonic plates collided and pushed Earth's crust up.

The vast Gangetic Plain lies to the south of the Himalayas. It stretches about 1,500 miles (2,415 km) across northern India. About half of India's population lives there.

South of the Gangetic Plain is the triangular peninsula known as the Deccan. Most of its area is a plateau, which is divided by many hills and valleys. The plateau's edges are defined by the Eastern Ghats (GAWTS) and Western Ghats. These low mountain ranges separate the plateau's eastern and western edges from narrow coastal plains.

✓ **READING CHECK:** *Places and Regions* What are the three main landform regions of India?

Rivers

India's most important river, the Ganges (GAN-jeez), begins on the southern slopes of the Himalayas. It then flows southeastward across northern India. It spreads into a huge delta before flowing into the Bay of Bengal. Hindus call the Ganges the "Mother River" and consider it sacred. Rich silt left by the Ganges has made the Gangetic Plain India's farming heartland.

The Brahmaputra (brahm-uh-POO-truh) River starts in the Plateau of Tibet. It flows through the far northeastern corner of India. From there the Brahmaputra flows southward through Bangladesh, where it empties into the Ganges Delta. The Narmada (nuhr-MUH-duh), Godavari (go-DAH-vuh-ree), and Krishna (KRISH-nuh) Rivers drain the Deccan. A large irrigation project along the Narmada River is under construction. It will include more than 40 branch canals.

✓ **READING CHECK:** *Places and Regions* What are India's most important rivers?

Climate

India has a variety of climate types. Areas in the Himalayas have highland climates with snow and glaciers. The Thar Desert near the border with Pakistan is hot and dry year-round. The Gangetic Plain has a humid tropical climate. Farther south in the Deccan there are tropical savanna and steppe climates.

Seasonal winds—monsoons—bring moist air from the Indian Ocean in summer. In winter the wind brings dry air from the Asian interior. The timing of the monsoons is very important to farmers in India. If the summer rains come too soon or too late, food production suffers.

✓ **READING CHECK:** *Places and Regions* What are India's climates?

Resources

India's fertile farmlands are important to its economy. Most of India's people work in agriculture. The country also produces cash crops for export. These include cashew nuts, cotton, jute, spices, sugarcane, tea, and tobacco.

Large deposits of iron ore, bauxite, uranium, and coal are among India's mineral resources. There are some oil reserves, but not enough to meet the country's needs. Gemstones are a valuable export.

India's forests are an important resource, as well as home to wildlife. **Teak**, one of the most valuable types of wood, grows in India and Southeast Asia. Teak is very strong and durable and is used to make ships and furniture.

✓ **READING CHECK:** *Places and Regions* What are India's natural resources?

Section Review 1

Define and explain: teak

Working with Sketch Maps On a map of India that you draw or that your teacher provides, label the following: Gangetic Plain, Deccan, Eastern Ghats, Western Ghats, Ganges River, Bay of Bengal, Brahmaputra River, and Thar Desert. How would you describe the relative location of India?

Reading for the Main Idea

1. *Places and Regions* What is the main mountain range of India?

2. *Places and Regions* What are some of India's most important cash crops? What type of wood is a valuable forest product?

Critical Thinking

3. Making Generalizations and Predictions What do you think happens to India's crops if the monsoon rains come too soon? too late?

4. Summarizing How does the Ganges affect economic activities in India?

Organizing What You Know

5. Summarizing Copy the following graphic organizer. Use it to list the landforms, climates, and resources of India.

Section 2 — India's History

Read to Discover

1. What outside groups affected India's history?
2. What was the Mughal Empire like?
3. How did Great Britain gain control of India?
4. Why was India divided when it became independent?

Define

Sanskrit
sepoys
boycott

Locate

Delhi
Kolkata
Mumbai

WHY IT MATTERS

India's history has been shaped by invasions, conquests, and colonization. Use CNNfyi.com or other current events sources to find information about how daily life in India has been shaped by its history. Record your findings in your journal.

Coat of arms of the East India Company

Early Indian Civilizations

The first urban civilization on the Indian Subcontinent was centered around the Indus River valley. Its territory was mainly in present-day Pakistan but also extended into India. Scholars call this the Harappan civilization after one of its cities, Harappa. By about 2500 B.C. the people of this civilization were living in large, well-planned cities. Scholars believe the Harappans traded by sea with the peoples of Mesopotamia. The Harappans had a system of writing, but scholars have not been able to read it. As a result, very little is known about Harappan religion and customs.

Mohenjo Daro was one of the largest cities of the Harappan civilization.

Interpreting the Visual Record How might you tell from this photo that Harappan cities were well planned?

▼

The Indo-Aryans By about 1500 B.C. a new group of people had come into northern India. Scholars call these people Indo-Aryans. Their language was an early form of **Sanskrit**. Sanskrit is still used in India in religious ceremonies.

The Indo-Aryans took control of northern India. These new arrivals mixed with Indian groups that were already living there. Their religious beliefs and customs mixed as well, forming the beginnings of the Hindu religion.

Hills and mountains prevented the Indo-Aryans from conquering southern India. However, Sanskrit and other Indo-Aryan cultural traits spread to the south.

The Coming of Islam About A.D. 1000, Muslim armies began raiding northwestern India. In the early 1200s a Muslim kingdom was established at Delhi. Because the monarch was known as a sultan, this kingdom was called the Delhi sultanate. The Delhi sultanate eventually gained control over most of northern India. It also became a leading center of Islamic art, culture, and science. Most Indians, however, kept their own religions and did not convert to Islam.

Over the next two centuries the Delhi sultanate expanded into the Deccan. However, in the early 1500s a new invasion from Central Asia swept into India. This new conquest marked the beginning of the Mughal (MOO-guhl) Empire.

✓ **READING CHECK:** *Human Systems* How did outside groups affect early Indian history?

This carved-lion pillar comes from Sarnath, an ancient city in northern India. The pillar was created in the 200s B.C. and is now the state emblem of India.

This illustration is from a book of the life of Babur, the first Mughal emperor. It shows Babur surrounded by servants and nobles.

The Mughal Empire

The founder of the Mughal Empire was Babur, whose name meant "the Tiger." Babur was descended from Mongol emperor Genghis Khan. He was not only a brilliant general, but also a gifted poet. Babur defeated the last sultan of Delhi and took over most of northern India. After his death, however, Babur's lands were divided among his sons. They fought each other for years.

Babur's grandson, Akbar, finally emerged to reunite the Mughal Empire. He recaptured northern India and then expanded his empire into central India. Akbar was a good ruler as well as a successful conqueror. He reorganized the government and the tax system to make them more efficient. The fertile farmland and large population of the Gangetic Plain made the Mughal Empire rich. It quickly became one of the most powerful states in the world. The reign of Akbar and his successors was a golden age of architecture, painting, and poetry.

CONNECTING TO *Literature*

Indian writer R.K. Narayan's My Days: A Memoir *describes the author's childhood in the early 1900s. In the following passage Narayan recalls traveling from boarding school to his parents' new home. At that time, travel was complicated and sometimes dangerous.*

My Days: A Memoir

At the proper time, I was awakened and put into a huge mat-covered wagon drawn by a pair of bullocks; I sat on a bed of straw covered over with a carpet; a stalwart[1] peon[2] from Hassan high school was seated beside the driver. Manja was his name . . . Part of the way as we traveled along, Manja got off and walked ahead of the caravan, carrying a staff menacingly. Some spots in that jungle and mountain country were well-known retreats of highway robbers; one form of protection was to travel in a closely moving caravan with Manja waving a staff at the head of the column, uttering blood-curdling challenges. That was enough to keep off robbers in those days.

We passed along miles and miles of tree-shaded highway, gigantic mango and blueberry trees and lantana[3] shrubs in multicolored bloom stretching away endlessly. A couple of times the bullocks were rested beside a pond or a well. The road wound up and down steep slopes—the sort of country I had never known before. . . . The overpowering smell of straw in the wagon and the slow pace of the bullocks with their bells jingling made me drowsy . . . After hours of tossing on straw, we came to a bungalow[4] set in a ten-acre field. [It was my parents' new home.] . . . The moment I was received into the fold at the trellised ivy-covered porch, I totally ignored Manja, and never looked in his direction, while he carried my baggage in.

A bullock cart and a double-decker bus in India

Analyzing Primary Sources

1. What are some of the words the author uses to describe the countryside?
2. How do you think Manja's description of this journey might be different from the author's?

Vocabulary ¹stalwart: strong and reliable ²peon: a menial laborer ³lantana: shrub with colorful flowers
⁴bungalow: one-story house with low roof that originated in Bengal, India

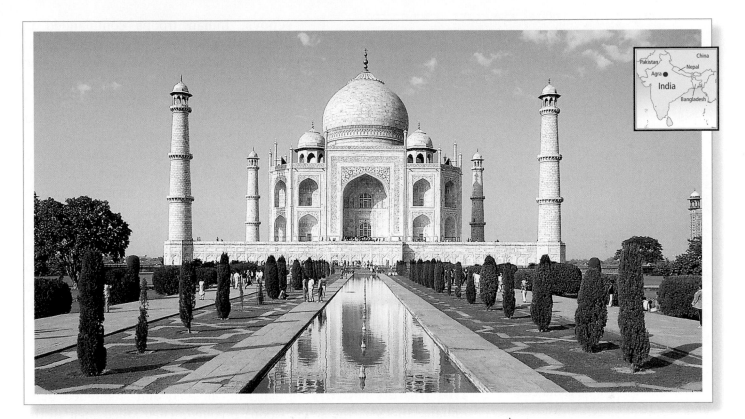

The Taj Mahal is one of the most famous buildings in the world.

The ruling Mughals were Muslim, but Islam remained a minority religion in India. Most people continued to practice Hinduism. Akbar himself was tolerant and curious about other religions. He invited religious scholars and priests—including Christians, Hindus, Jains, and Muslims—to his court. He even watched them debate.

Akbar's grandson, Shah Jahan, is remembered for the impressive buildings and monuments he had built. These include the famous Taj Mahal. This grand building contains the tomb of Shah Jahan's beloved wife, Mumtaz Mahal.

In the 1600s and 1700s the Mughal Empire slowly grew weaker. Wars in the Deccan and revolts in many parts of the empire drained Mughal resources. At about this time, Europeans became an important force in Indian history.

✔ **READING CHECK:** *Human Systems* What was the Mughal Empire like?

Construction of the Taj Mahal began in 1631 and was not completed until 1653. Almost 20,000 people worked on the building.

The British

During the 1700s and 1800s the British slowly took control of India. At first this was done by the English East India Company. This company won rights to trade in the Mughal Empire in the 1600s. The East India Company first took control of small trading posts. Later the British gained more Indian territory.

Company Rule As the Mughal Empire grew weaker, the British East India Company expanded its political power. The company also built up its own military force. This army was made up mostly of

In September 1857, British and loyal Sikh troops stormed the gate of Delhi, defended by rebel sepoys. Bloody fighting continued until late 1858.

Interpreting the Visual Record
How did the Indian Mutiny lead to a change in the way India was governed?

sepoys, Indian troops commanded by British officers. The British used the strategy of backing one Indian ruler against another in exchange for cooperation. By the mid-1800s the company controlled more than half of India. The rest was divided into small states ruled by local princes.

The British changed the Indian economy to benefit British industry. India produced raw materials, including cotton, indigo—a natural dye—and jute. These materials were then shipped to Britain for use in British factories. Spices, sugar, tea, and wheat were also grown in India for export. Railroads were built to ship the raw materials to Calcutta (now Kolkata), Bombay (now Mumbai), and other port cities. India also became a market for British manufactured goods. Indians, who had woven cotton cloth for centuries, were now forced to buy British cloth.

The Indian Mutiny British rule angered and frightened many Indians. In 1857, the sepoy troops revolted. They killed their British officers and other British residents. The violence spread across northern India. Large numbers of British troops were rushed to India. In the end the British crushed the rebellion.

The Indian Mutiny convinced the British government to abolish the British East India Company. The British government began to rule India directly, and India became a British colony.

Anti-British Protest During the late 1800s Indian nationalism took a different form. Educated, middle-class Indians led this movement. In 1885 these Indian nationalists created the Indian National Congress to organize their protests. At first they did not demand independence. Instead, they asked only for fairer treatment, such as a greater share of government jobs. The British refused even these moderate demands.

After World War I more and more Indians began demanding the end of British rule. A lawyer named Mohandas K. Gandhi became the most important leader of this Indian independence movement.

Gandhi and Nonviolence Gandhi reached out to the millions of Indian peasants. He used a strategy of nonviolent mass protest. He called for Indians to peacefully refuse to cooperate with the British. Gandhi led protest marches and urged Indians to **boycott**, or refuse to buy, British goods. Many times the police used violence against marchers. When the British jailed Gandhi, he went on hunger strikes. Gandhi's determination and self-sacrifice attracted many followers. Pressure grew on Britain to leave India.

Mohandas Gandhi was known to his followers as the Mahatma, or the "great soul."

✓ **READING CHECK:** (*Human Systems*) What role did the British play in India?

Independence and Division

After World War II the British government decided to give India independence. The British government and the Indian National Congress wanted India to become one country. However, India's Muslims demanded a separate Muslim state. Anger and fear grew between Hindus and Muslims. India seemed on the verge of civil war.

Finally, in 1947 the British divided their Indian colony into two independent countries, India and Pakistan. India was mostly Hindu. Pakistan, which then included what is today Bangladesh, was mostly Muslim. However, the new boundary left millions of Hindus in Pakistan and millions of Muslims in India. Masses of people rushed to cross the border. Hundreds of thousands were killed in rioting and panic.

In the chaotic days of August 1947, millions of people left their homes to cross the new border between India and Pakistan. These Muslims are preparing to leave New Delhi by train.

✔ **READING CHECK:** *Places and Regions* Why was India divided when it became independent?

Homework Practice Online
Keyword: SG3 HP30

Define and explain: Sanskrit, sepoys, boycott

Working with Sketch Maps On the map you created in Section 1, label Delhi, Kolkata, and Mumbai. What bodies of water are important to each of these cities?

Reading for the Main Idea

1. *Human Systems* What made the Mughal Empire one of the most powerful states in the world?

2. *Human Systems* How did the British East India Company gain control of most of India?

3. *Human Systems* Who was the most important leader of the Indian independence movement, and what was his strategy?

Critical Thinking

4. **Finding the Main Idea** Why was the British colony of India divided into two countries?

Organizing What You Know

5. **Sequencing** Copy the following time line. Use it to mark important events in Indian history from 2500 B.C. to A.D. 1947.

|---|---|
| 2500 B.C. | A.D. 1947 |

Section 3 India Today

Read to Discover

1. What four major religions originated in India?
2. What is the caste system?
3. What languages are important in India?
4. What kind of government does India have, and what is India's economy like?

Define

reincarnation
karma
nirvana
caste system
Dalits
green revolution

Locate

Kashmir

Masala dosa, *a rice and lentil dish from India*

This bronze statue depicts the Hindu god Siva.

Cows mingle with pedestrians and bicyclists in the street of an Indian town.

WHY IT MATTERS

Religion has played a tremendous role in both the past and present culture of India. Use CNNfyi.com or other **current events** sources to find information about religion in India. Record your findings in your journal.

Religions of India

Religion is an important part of Indian culture. Four major religions—Hinduism, Buddhism, Jainism, and Sikhism—originated in India. Christianity and Islam, both of which originated elsewhere, also have millions of followers in India. About 81 percent of India's people are Hindu. About 12 percent of Indians are Muslim, and 2.3 percent are Christian. Around 2 percent are Sikh, and 2.5 percent are Buddhist, Jain, Parsi, or followers of another religion. Remember that 1 percent of India's population is about 10 million people!

Hinduism Hinduism is one of the oldest religions in the world. Hindus worship many gods. These include Brahma the Creator, Vishnu the Preserver, and Siva the Destroyer. Hinduism teaches that all gods and all living beings are part of a single spirit.

Two beliefs central to the Hindu religion are **reincarnation** and **karma**. Reincarnation is the belief that the soul is reborn again and again in different forms. Karma is the positive or negative force caused by a person's actions. Hindus believe that a person with good karma may be reborn as a person of higher status. A person with bad karma may be reborn with lower status, or as an animal or insect.

Hinduism also teaches a special respect for cows. Hindus do not eat beef. Even today, cows can be seen roaming cities and villages.

Buddhism Buddhism was founded in northern India in the 500s B.C. by a man named Siddhartha Gautama. Gautama became known as the Buddha, or "Enlightened One."

The Buddha taught his followers they could avoid sorrow if they followed certain rules. For example, he told them not to lie, steal, or be greedy. By following these rules, Buddhists believe they can escape from the suffering of life. This escape from suffering is known as **nirvana**.

Buddhism spread from India to other parts of Asia. Buddhism is no longer widely practiced in India. However, the religion is very important in Sri Lanka, China, Japan, and Southeast Asia.

Jainism Jainism was founded at about the same time as Buddhism. It teaches that all things in nature—animals, plants, and stones—have souls. Jains reject all forms of violence against any living thing. They are strict vegetarians. Some even cover their noses with cloth to avoid breathing in insects and thus killing them.

Jains make up only a small minority. However, they have made many contributions to Indian art, mathematics, and literature.

Sikhism Sikhism was founded in the late 1400s. It combines elements of Hinduism and Islam. Members of this religion are called Sikhs. Traditionally, many Sikh men have become soldiers. They continue to play an important role in India's army.

The Buddha is often depicted in poses of meditation.

Interpreting the Visual Record

What elements of this statue could show examples of meditation?

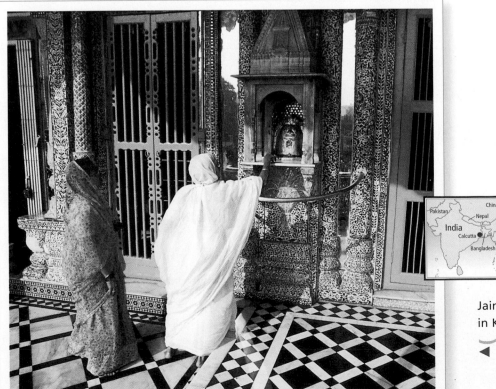

Jain women worship at a temple in Kolkata.

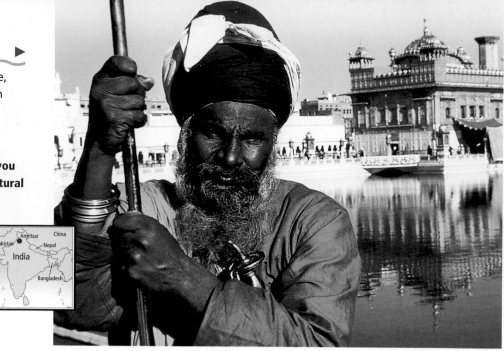

A Sikh guards the Golden Temple, the center of the Sikh religion, in Amritsar, India. Sikh men can be recognized by their beards and special turbans.

Interpreting the Visual Record Do you know of any other religious or cultural groups whose members have a distinctive way of dressing?

Most Sikhs live in the state of Punjab in northern India. Some Sikhs want to break away from India and form an independent country. The Indian government has refused to allow this, and violent clashes have resulted.

✓ **READING CHECK:** (*Human Systems*) What four religions originated in India?

Castes

Another key feature of Indian society is the **caste system**. Castes are groups of people whose birth determines their position in society. The castes are ranked in status, from highest to lowest. People from a higher caste cannot marry or even touch people of lower castes.

Many Dalits, like this woman in Goa, still perform jobs that Indians consider dirty or impure. Despite government efforts, most Dalits still live in poverty.

Interpreting the Visual Record What factors might keep most Dalits from getting better jobs?

The people at the bottom, called **Dalits**, do work that higher castes consider unclean. They wash and cremate dead bodies, process cow hides into leather goods, and sweep up trash.

Gandhi tried to improve people's attitudes toward the Dalits. He called them "Children of God." After independence, the Indian government officially ended the caste system. However, it is still a strong force in Indian society. The government also tried to improve economic conditions for the Dalits. Today some Dalits are educated and have good jobs. The majority, though, are still poor.

✓ **READING CHECK:** *Human Systems* How does the caste system create conflict in Indian society?

India				
COUNTRY	POPULATION/ GROWTH RATE	LIFE EXPECTANCY	LITERACY RATE	PER CAPITA GDP
India	1,029,991,145 1.7%	62, male 64, female	52%	$2,200
United States	281,421,906 0.9%	74, male 80, female	97%	$36,200

Sources: Central Intelligence Agency, *The World Factbook 2001;* U.S. Census Bureau

Interpreting the Chart How does India's economic development compare with that of the United States?

Languages

India's people speak an amazing number of different languages. There are 24 languages with a million or more speakers, plus hundreds of other languages. Hindi is the main language of about 30 percent of the people, mostly in northern India. In 1965 it became the official national language. However, the states of southern India have resisted the push to adopt Hindi. English is still commonly used in government, business, and higher education throughout India.

✓ **READING CHECK:** *Human Systems* What languages are important in India?

Government and Economy

India has made a great deal of economic progress since gaining independence, but the country remains poor. Rapid population growth strains the country's resources, and the divisions among India's people make it difficult to govern.

Government India is ruled by a democratic government. With more than 1 billion people, the country is the world's largest democracy. The structure of the government is based on Britain's parliamentary system. However, as in the United States, India's central government shares power with state governments.

Indian politics have sometimes been marked by violence and assassinations. The government used force to defeat Sikh rebels in 1984. There have also been outbreaks of

Parliament House, New Delhi, is the home of India's legislative branch.

Interpreting the Visual Record What form of government does India have? What is one feature that India's government shares with the U.S. government?

▼

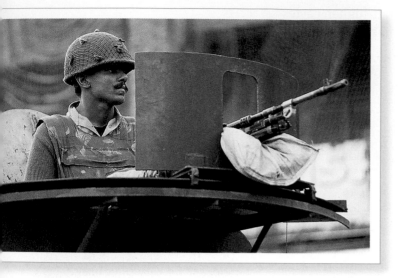

India has stationed large numbers of troops in Kashmir.

Peppers are harvested in northern India.

Interpreting the Visual Record What is one way agricultural products are transported in India?

violence between Hindus and Muslims. In 1992 a mob of Hindus tore down a mosque that stood on a Hindu holy site. Riots broke out in many parts of India as a result.

India's border with Pakistan has been in dispute since 1947. Both countries claim a mountainous region called Kashmir. Before India gained independence, Kashmir was ruled by a Hindu prince. Most of its people were Muslim, however. India and Pakistan have fought over Kashmir several times. Today, both countries have nuclear weapons, making the prospect of a future war even more frightening.

Economy India's economy is a mixture of the traditional and the modern. In thousands of villages, farmers work the fields just as they have for centuries. At the same time, modern factories and high-tech service industries demonstrate India's potential for wealth. However, the country still does not have enough good roads and telecommunications systems.

Close to 60 percent of India's workforce are farmers. Farming makes up 25 percent of India's GDP. Most farmers work on small farms less than 2.5 acres (1 hectare) in size. Many grow barely enough to feed themselves and their families. In recent years, the government has worked to promote commercial farming.

India's leading crops include rice, wheat, cotton, tea, sugarcane, and jute. Cattle and water buffalo are raised to pull plows and to provide milk.

Beginning in the 1960s, the Indian government started agricultural programs known as the **green revolution**. This effort encouraged farmers to adopt more modern methods. It promoted greater use of fertilizers, pesticides, and new varieties of wheat and rice. Crop yields increased. In years with good weather, India is self-sufficient in food and can export farm products.

India is considered a developing country. However, its economy is large enough to rank among the world's top 10 industrial countries. India's industries include textiles, jewelry, cars, bicycles, oil products, chemicals, food processing, and electronics.

India's moviemaking industry is one of the world's largest. Mumbai is a major moviemaking center. Movies are an incredibly popular form of entertainment, as millions of Indians cannot read. Many Indian movie stars have gone into politics. Indian movies have a distinctive style. They usually feature music and dancing and often draw on themes from Indian myths. Indian movies are popular in many other countries as well.

India now has a large, well-educated middle class. These people have enough money for luxuries like cable television and personal computers. Some Indians are very rich. Yet the majority of Indians are still poor.

▲

Red-hot steel is poured into molds in a foundry near Kolkata.

Interpreting the Visual Record
Which of India's industries might use the steel produced here?

✓ **READING CHECK:** (*Places and Regions*) What are India's government and economy like?

Section Review 3

Define and explain: reincarnation, karma, nirvana, caste system, Dalits, green revolution

Working with Sketch Maps On the map that you created in Section 2, label the Kashmir region of India. What other country claims Kashmir?

Reading for the Main Idea

1. (*Human Systems*) What are the main religions practiced in India? Which religion has the largest number of followers?

2. (*Environment and Society*) How did India's government increase agricultural output in the 1960s?

Critical Thinking

3. **Drawing Inferences and Conclusions** Why might India's government find it difficult to improve the economic situation of the Dalits?

4. **Finding the Main Idea** Why are movies such a popular form of entertainment in India?

Organizing What You Know

5. **Categorizing** Copy the following graphic organizer. Use it to list the leading crops and industries of India.

Leading crops	Leading industries

Reviewing What You Know

Building Vocabulary

On a separate sheet of paper, write sentences to define each of the following words.

1. teak
2. Sanskrit
3. sepoys
4. boycott
5. reincarnation
6. karma
7. nirvana
8. caste system
9. Dalits
10. green revolution

Reviewing the Main Ideas

1. *(Places and Regions)* How were the Himalayas formed?
2. *(Human Systems)* What was the first urban civilization on the Indian Subcontinent?
3. *(Human Systems)* Who brought Sanskrit to India?
4. *(Human Systems)* What are the Hindu ideas of reincarnation and karma?
5. *(Human Systems)* What factors divide Indian society?

Understanding Environment and Society

Cows in India

The Hindu respect for cows has influenced the way Indians interact with their environment. Create a presentation about cows in India. As you prepare your presentation, consider the following:

- How Hindus' respect for cows has affected cattle populations in India.
- What cows eat, and whether humans ever have to compete with cows for food in India.
- How Hindu ideas of reincarnation and karma affect Indians' treatment of cows.

Thinking Critically

1. **Drawing Inferences and Conclusions** Why do you think Hindi has not become the language of all of India?

2. **Summarizing** How do India's natural resources affect its economy?

3. **Finding the Main Idea** How did the Indian government's promotion of new farming technology affect India's farming culture?

4. **Drawing Inferences and Conclusions** Why do you think the Mughal Empire under Akbar and his successors was considered a "golden age"?

5. **Drawing Inferences and Conclusions** How might the growth of a well-educated, high-tech workforce affect India's economy?

Map ACTIVITY

On a separate sheet of paper, match the letters on the map with their correct labels.

Himalayas	Ganges River
Gangetic Plain	Brahmaputra
Deccan	River
Eastern Ghats	Thar Desert
Western Ghats	

Mental Mapping Skills ACTIVITY

On a separate sheet of paper, draw a freehand map of the Indian Subcontinent. Make a key for your map and label the following:

Bangladesh	Kashmir
Bay of Bengal	Nepal
India	Pakistan
Indian Ocean	

WRITING ACTIVITY

Write a one- to two-page report about how religion influences life in India. List and describe India's major religions, then write about how they relate to politics, border disputes, social classes, daily life, languages, the economy, and so on. Be sure to use standard grammar, spelling, sentence structure, and punctuation.

Alternative Assessment

Portfolio ACTIVITY

Learning About Your Local Geography

The Seasons The change of the seasons is important to daily life in India. Create a poster on how temperature and precipitation of all four seasons affect daily life in your area.

internet connect

Internet Activity: go.hrw.com
KEYWORD: SG3 GT30

Choose a topic to explore about India:
- Tour the regions of India.
- Travel to ancient India.
- Learn about Mohandas Gandhi.

go.hrw.com

CHAPTER 31

The Indian Perimeter

The countries of this region, along with the Himalayas, help create India's border. After you meet Rehan you will learn that this land is one of majestic beauty with a rich heritage.

I am Rehan, and I am 14. I am an only child and live with my parents in Karachi, a big sprawling city like Los Angeles. On one side is the sea, on the other is the desert.

If you came to visit me in Pakistan, I would take you to the beach to watch the beautiful sunsets and ride on a camel. My parents used to take me there for camel rides when I was very little. Next I would take you to see the old colonial architecture in the city center. Then we would go and have a meal in a roadside cafe—grilled beef or lamb kabobs on a stick. I usually get up very early for school. By 7:10 A.M. I have breakfast—cereal and toast—and leave for school with my father. He is a doctor with an office near my school. I am in the second year (equivalent to grade 10) of a boys' private school styled after the British public school system.

Next year, I am going to America with my mother. My parents want me to have a chance to go to a world-class university.

السلام عليكم!

Translation: God's peace be upon you!

Section 1 Physical Geography

Read to Discover

1. What major physical features are located in the Indian Perimeter?
2. What climates and natural resources are found in this region?
3. What are the physical features of the island countries?

Define

cyclones
storm surges

Locate

Brahmaputra River
Ganges River
Himalayas
Mount Everest
Tarai
Karakoram Range

Hindu Kush
Khyber Pass
Indus River
Thar Desert

WHY IT MATTERS

In 2001 Pakistan played an important role in world events when the United States asked to use its airspace to conduct military actions against terrorist leader Osama bin Laden. Use **CNNfyi.com** or other **current events** sources to find the latest information on Pakistan's role in world affairs. Record your findings in your journal.

A relief sculpture of a Bodhi tree

The Indian Perimeter: Physical-Political

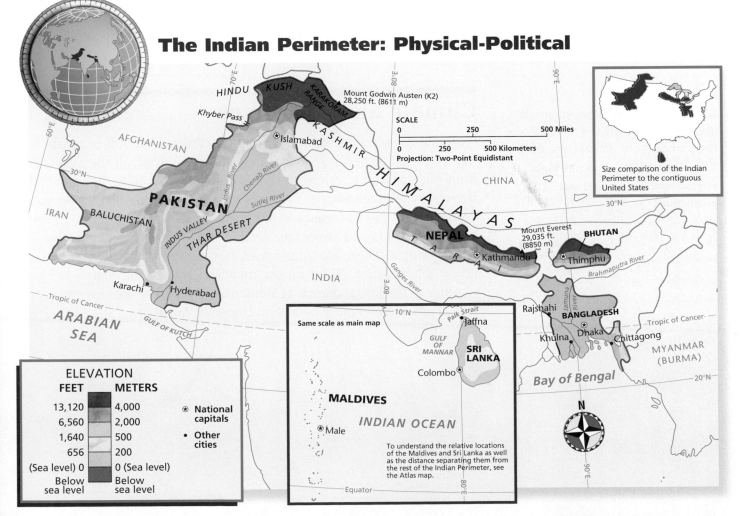

Mount Godwin Austen (K2)
28,250 ft. (8611 m)

SCALE
0   250   500 Miles
0   250   500 Kilometers
Projection: Two-Point Equidistant

Size comparison of the Indian Perimeter to the contiguous United States

HINDU KUSH
KARAKORAM RANGE
Khyber Pass
AFGHANISTAN
Islamabad
KASHMIR
CHINA
PAKISTAN
Indus River
Chenab River
Sutlej River
HIMALAYAS
IRAN
BALUCHISTAN
INDUS VALLEY
THAR DESERT
Mount Everest
29,035 ft. (8850 m)
NEPAL
BHUTAN
Kathmandu
Thimphu
TARAI
Brahmaputra River
Karachi
Hyderabad
INDIA
Ganges River
Jamuna River
Rajshahi
BANGLADESH
Tropic of Cancer
ARABIAN SEA
GULF OF KUTCH
Khulna
Dhaka
Chittagong
MYANMAR (BURMA)
Palk Strait
Jaffna
GULF OF MANNAR
SRI LANKA
Colombo
Bay of Bengal
MALDIVES
INDIAN OCEAN
Male
Equator

Same scale as main map

To understand the relative locations of the Maldives and Sri Lanka as well as the distance separating them from the rest of the Indian Perimeter, see the Atlas map.

ELEVATION

FEET	METERS
13,120	4,000
6,560	2,000
1,640	500
656	200
(Sea level) 0	0 (Sea level)
Below sea level	Below sea level

⊛ National capitals
• Other cities

BUILD on WHAT You Know

Do you remember what you learned about deltas? See Chapter 2 to review.

internet connect

GO TO: go.hrw.com
KEYWORD: SG3 CH31
FOR: Web sites about the Indian Perimeter

Terraced fields in the mountains of Nepal allow farmers to increase their production of millet and corn.
Interpreting the Visual Record How can terracing lead to increased crop production?

Physical Features

The broad delta formed by the Brahmaputra (brahm-uh-POO-truh) and Ganges (GAN-jeez) Rivers covers most of Bangladesh. Some 200 rivers and streams crisscross this eastern part of the Indian Subcontinent. These numerous waterways, the low elevation of the land, and heavy monsoon rains combine to bring frequent floods to Bangladesh. Although these floods cause great damage, they leave behind a layer of fertile soil.

North of Bangladesh is Bhutan. This tiny country lies high in the mountain range known as the Himalayas (hi-muh-LAY-uhz). To the west is Nepal. The Himalayas occupy some 75 percent of Nepal's land area. Mount Everest, Earth's highest mountain, is located on Nepal's border with China. The Tarai (tuh-RY) is a low plain along Nepal's southern border. It is the country's main farming area. West of the Himalayas is the Karakoram (kah-rah-KOHR-oohm) Range. To the west the Karakorams merge into another mountain range, the Hindu Kush.

On Pakistan's western border is the Khyber (KY-buhr) Pass. For centuries, invaders and traders have traveled through this high mountain pass to India. East of the Khyber Pass is the Indus River. The Indus Valley lies mostly to the east of the river. This valley is Pakistan's main farming region and its most heavily populated area. East of these fertile lands is the Thar (TAHR) Desert, or the Great Indian Desert. A barren, hilly, and dry plateau in western Pakistan joins the plateaus of Iran.

✔ **READING CHECK:** *Places and Regions* What are the major physical features of this region?

Climate and Resources

Bangladesh has one of the world's wettest climates. Rainfall is generally more than 60 inches (127 to 152 cm) each year. Most of the rain falls from June to October, during the wet summer monsoon. In the early and late weeks of the monsoon, **cyclones** sweep in from the Bay of Bengal. These violent storms resemble the hurricanes of the Caribbean. They bring high winds and heavy rain. Cyclones are often accompanied by **storm surges**. These are huge waves of water that are whipped up by fierce winds. The summer monsoon brings hot, wet weather to the lowland areas of Bhutan and Nepal. In the mountains climates are generally much cooler. Much of

Pakistan has a desert climate, receiving less than 10 inches (25 cm) of rain each year. Summer temperatures can reach as high as 120°F (49°C).

Bangladesh's most important resource is its fertile farmland. About 15 percent of Bangladesh is forested, so it has some timber supplies. However, severe deforestation and soil erosion have plagued the region, particularly in Nepal. Bhutan and Nepal have farmland in lowland areas. Both countries have some minerals, but few are mined. Pakistan has large natural gas reserves but limited oil supplies. It has to import oil to meet its energy needs. Pakistan's other natural resources include coal, limestone, and salt.

✔ **READING CHECK:** *Places and Regions* What are the natural resources of the region?

The Island Countries

The Indian Perimeter region also includes Sri Lanka and the Maldives. Sri Lanka is a large island located just off the southeastern tip of India. Plains cover most of the island's northern half and coastal areas. Mountains and hills rise in the south-central part of the island.

About 1,200 tiny tropical islands in the Indian Ocean make up the Maldives. The island group stretches from south of India to the equator. Only about 200 of the islands are inhabited. None rises more than 6 feet (1.8 m) above sea level.

✔ **READING CHECK:** *Places and Regions* What are the physical features of the island countries?

In May 1997 a cyclone and storm surges devastated Bangladesh. More than 1.5 million people were left homeless.

go.hrw.com **Homework Practice Online** Keyword: SG3 HP31

Define and explain: cyclones, storm surges

Working with Sketch Maps On a map of India and the Indian Perimeter that you draw or that your teacher provides, label the following: Brahmaputra River, Ganges River, Himalayas, Mount Everest, Tarai, Karakoram Range, Hindu Kush, Khyber Pass, Indus River, and Thar Desert. Where is Earth's highest mountain located? What plains area is Nepal's main farming region?

Reading for the Main Idea

1. *Places and Regions* Why has the Khyber Pass been important in the history of Pakistan and India?

2. *Places and Regions* How have erosion and deforestation affected the region? Which country has been most affected by these problems?

3. *Places and Regions* What island countries are found in the region? How are they different from each other?

Critical Thinking

4. **Drawing Inferences and Conclusions** How do you think climate affects life in Pakistan and Bangladesh?

Organizing What You Know

5. **Summarizing** Copy the following graphic organizer. Use it to describe the landforms, climates, and resources of the region.

	Major Landforms	Climates	Resources
Pakistan			
Bangladesh			
Bhutan			
Nepal			

Section 2 Pakistan and Bangladesh

Read to Discover

1. What is the history of Pakistan?
2. What are some features of Pakistan's culture?
3. What is the history of Bangladesh?
4. What challenges face Bangladesh today?

Define

cholera

Locate

Pakistan | Lahore
Bangladesh | Islamabad
Karachi | Dhaka

WHY IT MATTERS

Since 1947, when Great Britain granted both nations independence, Pakistan and India have fought three wars. In recent years the countries have clashed over a revolt in the Indian state of Kashmir. Use **CNNfyi.com** or other **current events** sources to find out more about Pakistan's relations with India. Record your findings in your journal.

A floral-patterned container from Pakistan

These tombs in Pakistan were built in the 1500s–1700s. Women's graves had floral carvings. Horses and swords decorated men's tombs.

Interpreting the Visual Record How do these tombs differ from modern-day grave sites in your community?

Pakistan's History

An ancient civilization developed in the Indus River valley about 2500 B.C. Ruins of cities show that this was a large and well-organized society. The cause of the disappearance of this civilization about 1500 B.C. remains a mystery.

Over time the fertile Indus River valley was inhabited and conquered by many different groups. It has been part of the empires of Persia, Alexander the Great, and the Mughals. About A.D. 1000 Turkish invaders established Islam in the area. Islam has been the main religion there ever since.

In the early 1600s merchants from England formed the English East India Company to increase the spice trade. It later became known as the British East India Company. Although trade was only moderately successful, the company established England's power in India. It was not until 1947 that India gained independence.

Upon independence, India became two countries. The division into two countries was based on religion. India was mostly Hindu. East and West Pakistan were inhabited mainly by Muslims. Although East Pakistan and West Pakistan were mostly Muslim, they had other cultural differences. These differences led East Pakistan to break away in 1971. It became known as Bangladesh.

✓ **READING CHECK:** *Human Systems* What was Pakistan's early history like?

Pakistan Today

Pakistan's population is 97 percent Muslim. The country has many different languages and ethnic groups. A small number of Christians, Buddhists, and Hindus also live in Pakistan. Urdu is Pakistan's official language. However, less than 10 percent of the population speak it as their primary language. Many upper-class Pakistanis speak English.

Population Pakistan has the world's seventh largest population. The cities contain about a third of that population. The largest are the port city of Karachi (kuh-RAH-chee), Lahore (luh-HOHR), and the capital, Islamabad. Like the rest of the region, Pakistan is experiencing rapid population growth. In fact, the Indian Subcontinent accounted for about 30 percent of the world's population growth in the late 1990s. How does Pakistan support so many people? The Indus River valley has one of the world's largest irrigation systems. It allows the country to grow enough food for the large population. However, overall economic progress has been slow.

Culture In Pakistan a woman joins her husband's family at marriage. Marriages are usually arranged by parents. The young woman's parents often pay a large amount of money to the young man's family.

Pakistan celebrates many of the same Islamic festivals as other Southwest Asian countries. Festival meals are similar to those of Iran in their emphasis on rice, the region's staple food. Meals also include the grilled meat of chickens, goats, and sheep, as well as delicious breads. Pakistani foods feature strong spices and flavors.

✓ **READING CHECK:** (*Human Systems*) What is the culture of Pakistan like?

Pakistan and Bangladesh

COUNTRY	POPULATION/ GROWTH RATE	LIFE EXPECTANCY	LITERACY RATE	PER CAPITA GDP
Bangladesh	131,269,860 1.6%	61, male 60, female	56%	$1,570
Pakistan	144,616,639 2.1%	61, male 62, female	43%	$2,000
United States	281,421,906 0.9%	74, male 80, female	97%	$36,200

Sources: Central Intelligence Agency, *The World Factbook 2001;* U.S. Census Bureau

Interpreting the Chart **Which country in the region has a larger population?**

Pakistan's flag symbolizes the country's commitment to Islam and the Islamic world. The crescent and star are symbols of Islam. The vertical white stripe represents religious minorities.

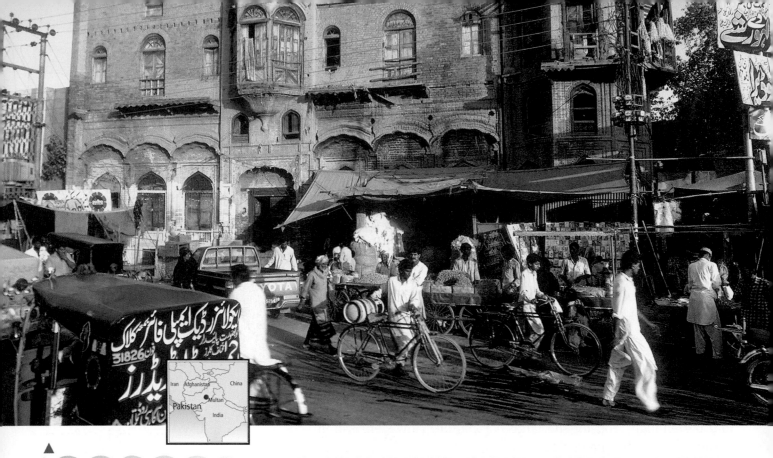

Multan is a commercial and industrial center with several colleges and a university. The city came under Muslim control in the A.D. 700s.

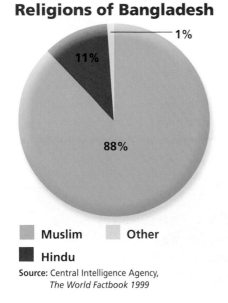

Religions of Bangladesh

- 1%
- 11%
- 88%

▇ Muslim   ▇ Other
▇ Hindu

Source: Central Intelligence Agency, *The World Factbook 1999*

Interpreting the Chart What percentage of the population of Bangladesh is Muslim?

Bangladesh's History

Bangladesh is part of a region known as Bengal. Bengal's many rivers are used for transporting goods. This is one reason why the area was important to Europeans in the 1500s. From the 1500s through the 1700s, the Mughal Empire combined Islam and regional Indian traditions to create a distinctive culture in this region. Eventually, the Mughal Empire weakened. The British East India Company then expanded its control over the area.

Because the British East India Company was so powerful, it could control what was traded. Therefore, British goods came into the region, but few goods other than rice and jute were exported. With a decline in trade, industry suffered. As a result, the region's economy became more agricultural in the 1800s. As you learned earlier, East Pakistan became the independent country of Bangladesh in 1971.

✓ **READING CHECK:** *Places and Regions* What has Bangladesh's history been like?

Bangladesh Today

Unlike other South Asian countries, Bangladesh has only one main ethnic group—the Bengalis. They make up 98 percent of the population. Social standing is based mostly on wealth and influence rather than on heredity or caste. Muslims may move up or down in status. Even among the country's Hindus, caste has much less importance than it does in India.

Population Bangladesh is about the same size as Wisconsin. However, it has a population nearly half the size of the entire U.S. population. Only 24 percent of Bangladesh's population lives in cities. The country's capital and largest city is Dhaka (DA-kuh). Cities and rural areas are densely populated. On average in Bangladesh there are 3,324 people per square mile (885/sq km).

Flooding and disease are two of the country's biggest challenges. Occasional violent tropical cyclones bring huge storm surges on shore. In addition, runoff from heavy rains in the distant Himalayas causes extensive flooding. When the land is flooded, sewage often washes into the water. As a result, Bangladesh has often suffered from epidemics of diseases like **cholera**. Cholera is a severe intestinal infection.

Culture Family life in Bangladesh is different from that in Pakistan. For example, many Bangladeshi women keep close ties to their own families after marriage. However, as in other South Asian countries, marriages are arranged by parents. Most couples typically do not know each other prior to their wedding.

More girls are going to secondary schools and universities than ever. Even so, the literacy rate for women remains just about half that of men. Bangladesh's official language, Bengali (Bangla), is the language spoken in schools. The country celebrates Islam's main festivals with feasts that feature fish and rice.

Pedicabs crowd a Dhaka street. A pedicab is a ricksha pulled by a bicycle. It is a common form of transportation in parts of Asia.

✓ **READING CHECK:** *Places and Regions* What are some challenges that Bangladesh faces today?

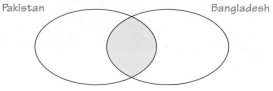
Section Review 2

Define and explain: cholera

Working with Sketch Maps On the map you created in Section 1, label Pakistan, Bangladesh, Karachi, Lahore, Islamabad, and Dhaka. What does the name of Pakistan's capital indicate about the country's dominant religion?

Reading for the Main Idea

1. *Places and Regions* Why were East and West Pakistan separated from India in 1947? When did East and West Pakistan split into two independent countries?

2. *Environment and Society* What technology allows Pakistan to grow enough food for its large population?

3. *Environment and Society* What climatic condition contributes to the high disease rate in Bangladesh? How?

Critical Thinking

4. Contrasting/Comparing How are marriage and married life in Pakistan different from marriage and married life in Bangladesh? How are they similar?

Organizing What You Know

5. Comparing/Contrasting Copy the following graphic organizer. Use it to compare and contrast Pakistan and Bangladesh.

Pakistan   Bangladesh

The Indian Perimeter • 675

TOURISM IN NEPAL

Tourism is one of the largest industries in the world. It generates about $450 billion each year! In many developing countries, tourism has become an important source of income. By creating new and better-paying jobs, tourism helps raise the standard of living. For some developing countries, income from tourism might be the difference between poverty and having basic education or health care. However, tourism can also have negative effects. It can disrupt local cultures, change people's traditional way of life, and damage the environment.

Nepal has experienced both the advantages and disadvantages that tourism can have for developing countries. Nepal is a mountainous, landlocked country with a very low standard of living. Most people in Nepal are farmers who live in small, isolated villages. However, tourism is bringing an end to Nepal's isolation. Tourism is creating new economic opportunities for some of Nepal's residents.

One group in Nepal that is being affected by tourism is the Sherpa. The Sherpa are a group of people that live near Mount Everest. They are very skilled mountain climbers. As tourism to Nepal grows, people are traveling to this region to hike and climb. These adventure tourists hire Sherpa to help them climb Himalayan peaks like Mount Everest. As a result, some Sherpa communities have become much wealthier than their neighbors.

The growth of tourism has changed the Sherpa's way of life in several ways. With more men working for tourists as mountain guides, Sherpa women have become more involved in farming. Income from tourism has also created a gap between the people with money and people without money. At some local religious festivals, tourists now outnumber the local Sherpa. These changes and others are affecting the Sherpa's culture and daily life.

◀ Aluminum cans are crushed at Everest Base Camp and then taken to Nepal's capital to be recycled. A government ban on glass bottles has forced hikers and local residents to switch to aluminum cans.

Photographer Alison Wright stands next to a Sherpa guide near Solu Khumbu, Nepal. The Sherpa are famous for their mountain-climbing skills.

Many Sherpa work as porters for mountain-climbing expeditions.

Tourism has brought more money into Nepal. Each tourist has to pay for a permit to climb Nepal's mountains. For example, it costs about $50,000 for a permit to climb Mount Everest. Some 50 teams of climbers attempted to reach the summit of Everest in 2000. Tourism has become an important and growing source of income for Nepal's government.

However, tourism has also damaged the country's environment. Hikers in Nepal leave behind an estimated 110,000 pounds (50,000 kg) of garbage each year! Garbage has become a serious concern in the Mount Everest region. In fact, some people have called Everest Base Camp the "world's highest garbage dump." Large garbage dumps have also appeared in other mountain-climbing areas of Nepal. Chopping down trees for firewood is another concern. Tourist lodges use large amounts of wood for cooking and for heating. In some areas, this demand for wood has caused deforestation and soil erosion.

Understanding What You Read

1. How has tourism changed the daily life of the Sherpa?

2. What are some of the advantages of tourism for Nepal? What are some disadvantages?

Section 3 The Himalayan and Island Countries

Read to Discover

1. What are some important features of Nepal?
2. How has Bhutan developed over time?
3. What is Sri Lanka like?
4. What are some economic activities of the Maldives?

Define

stupas
graphite
atolls

Locate

Nepal   Kathmandu
Bhutan   Thimphu
Sri Lanka   Colombo
Maldives   Male

WHY IT MATTERS

Nepal is the home of Mount Everest, the highest mountain in the world. Climbing Mount Everest has become increasingly popular in recent years. Use **CNNfyi.com** or other **current events** sources to find information on the environmental impact of climbing on Mount Everest. Record your findings in your journal.

A sculpture from Sri Lanka's Temple of the Tooth

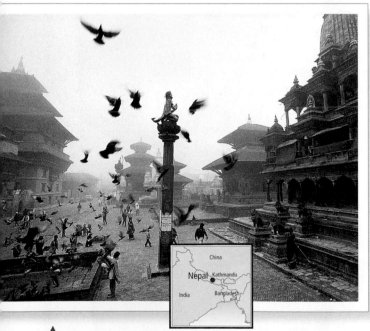

▲

A temple to the Hindu god Krishna can be seen from Durban Square in Patan, near Kathmandu, Nepal. The pillar in the square honors Krishna's companion, Garuda.

Interpreting the Visual Record **What architectural style is evident in these buildings?**

Nepal

Nepal's history is linked to the early civilizations of northern India. Nepal shared its languages, culture, and economic base with peoples to the south. It was probably in Nepal that Gautama, the Buddha, was born about 563 B.C. Some of the oldest monuments to the Buddha are **stupas** in Nepal. They date back to before 300 B.C. Stupas are mounds of earth or stones covering the ashes of the Buddha or relics of Buddhist saints. Like India, Nepal adopted Buddhism at first but was mostly Hindu by A.D. 1200. About 90 percent of Nepal's people are now Hindus.

The British never formally ruled Nepal. Their army did defeat the Nepalese army in the early 1800s. As a result, the British took away the territories claimed by Nepal and sent an official to maintain indirect control. The British later recognized Nepal's independence. Nepal now is a constitutional monarchy with a king and elected parliament.

One of Nepal's ethnic groups is the Sherpa. The Sherpa guide and serve as porters for Himalayan expeditions. Norkey Tenzing, a Sherpa, and Sir Edmund Hillary, an explorer from New Zealand, climbed Mount Everest in 1953. They were the first to reach the summit.

✔ **READING CHECK:** *Places and Regions* What has the history of Nepal been like?

Connecting to Technology

CLIMBING MOUNT EVEREST

The world's highest peak, Mount Everest, sits on the border between China and Nepal. At 29,035 feet (8,850 m), it is one of the world's greatest mountaineering challenges.

After many failed attempts, two climbers—Edmund Hillary and Norkey Tenzing—finally reached the summit in 1953. One factor in their success was the use of advanced equipment. This equipment included special boots, oxygen bottles, and radio gear. Since then, technology has continued to play a key role in efforts to scale the Himalayas.

Today's climbers use a wide range of sophisticated gear. This gear includes everything from space-age mountaineering clothes to remote sensors and satellite-tracking devices. Even so, climbing Everest remains very dangerous. In the 1990s more than 50 climbers lost their lives trying to scale the peak. Now scientists are testing new medical technologies on Mount Everest in hopes of preventing such tragedies in the future.

A joint project of the National Aeronautics and Space Administration (NASA) and Yale University has been analyzing the effects of high-altitude climbing on the human body. In 1998 this project sent a team of climbers up Mount Everest wearing "bio-packs." These packs included high-tech devices to monitor heart rate, blood oxygen, and other vital signs.

This data was transmitted instantly to a base camp on Everest. There doctors could analyze the results. Scientists believe that this kind of "telemedicine" will help save lives in other extreme environments, including outer space.

Understanding What You Read

1. How do climbers use technology on Mount Everest?
2. How might climbers benefit from the use of new medical technology?

Sir Edmund Hillary (left) and Norkey Tenzing (right)

Nepal Today

Like the other countries of the Indian Perimeter, Nepal's economy is based on agriculture. More than 80 percent of the people make a living from farming. Most are subsistence farmers. The best farmland is found on the Tarai—Nepal's "breadbasket." Farmers there grow such crops as rice, other grains, and sugarcane. In the hills north of the Tarai, farmers grow fruits, grains, and vegetables. Kathmandu (kat-man-DOO), Nepal's capital and largest city, is located in this central region. For the most part, the Himalayan region is not good for

Nepalese women are experts at winnowing grain. Winnowing is the process of separating chaff from grain by fanning.

farming. Farmers graze cattle, goats, sheep, and yaks on the lower slopes. Yaks are large, longhaired oxen. In addition, some farmers grow grain and fruit trees on terraces cut into mountainsides.

With few resources and limited access to world trade routes, Nepal has developed few industries. Most of its industries are based on farm products, such as jute. Jute is a plant fiber that is used in making twine. Tourism is one of the fastest-growing and most important industries in Nepal. Tourists like to hike and climb in the mountains.

Tourism brings in much-needed income to Nepal. However, the constant stream of hikers and climbers threatens the country's environment. How? Many visitors leave behind trash. Also, their need for firewood contributes to deforestation and soil erosion. This problem is worsened as Nepalese clear woodland for farming and for wood for fuel. In response, Nepal's government has restricted access by visitors to some of the most affected areas.

✓ **READING CHECK:**   *Places and Regions*   What is Nepal like?

Folk dancers in traditional dress perform near Thimphu, Bhutan.

Bhutan

Little is known about the early history of Bhutan. Buddhism was practiced there as early as the A.D. 600s. Most of the people are of Tibetan origin and are Buddhist. In the 1600s a Tibetan monk helped organize Bhutan as a unified state. Then in the late 1700s the East India Company's business dealings increased British influence.

Bhutan, although very isolated, was under Indian control during British rule over that country.

Bhutan's ruler, or maharaja, declared a constitutional monarchy in 1969.

✓ **READING CHECK:** *Places and Regions* What has the history of Bhutan been like?

Bhutan Today

Until the mid-1970s, the government of Bhutan followed a policy of near total isolation. Even today, the country's international ties are somewhat limited.

Much of Bhutan's economy is traditional. More than 90 percent of the people make a living as subsistence farmers. Most grow rice, wheat, corn, and potatoes in fertile valleys and on mountainside terraces. A few grow fruits and spices for export. On mountain pastures, farmers raise cattle, goats, sheep, and yaks. Thimphu (thim-POO) is Bhutan's capital.

Timber and hydroelectricity are among Bhutan's most important resources. The country sells both to India, its main trading partner. Tourism is also a source of income for Bhutan. However, the government limits the number of visitors to just 7,000 a year. By restricting tourism, the government hopes to protect Bhutan's way of life from outside influences and environmental damage.

✓ **READING CHECK:** *Places and Regions* What is Bhutan like today?

Sri Lanka

When Buddhism swept over India between the 400s and 200s B.C., Buddhist missionaries came to Sri Lanka. From Sri Lanka, traders spread Buddhism eastward to what are now Thailand and Indonesia. About 74 percent of Sri Lankans today belong to the Sinhalese ethnic group, and most are Buddhists. Sri Lanka has many dome-shaped stupas honoring the Buddha. Many are shaded by trees said to have been grown from cuttings of the original bo tree. It is believed the Buddha achieved enlightenment under this tree.

Throughout its history, Sri Lanka has been largely independent from India. In the 1500s the Portuguese established a trading post on the island. They were overthrown by the Dutch. The Dutch turned over Sri Lanka, then known as Ceylon, to the British in the late 1700s. The British granted independence in 1948. The new government made Sinhalese the official language and promoted Buddhism. An Indian and Hindu minority group, the Tamils, protested. Fighting between Tamils and the government has killed many people.

✓ **READING CHECK:** *Places and Regions* How have Europeans played a role in Sri Lanka's history?

Himalayan and Island Countries

COUNTRY	POPULATION/ GROWTH RATE	LIFE EXPECTANCY	LITERACY RATE	PER CAPITA GDP
Bhutan	2,049,412 2.1%	53, male 52, female	42%	$1,100
Maldives	310,764 3.0%	61, male 64, female	93%	$2,000
Nepal	25,284,463 2.3%	59, male 58, female	28%	$1,360
Sri Lanka	19,408,635 0.9%	70, male 75, female	90%	$3,250
United States	281,421,906 0.9%	74, male 80, female	97%	$36,200

Sources: Central Intelligence Agency, *The World Factbook 2001;* U.S. Census Bureau

Interpreting the Chart Which country has the lowest literacy rate?

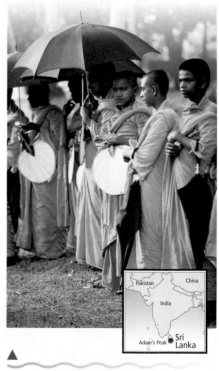

▲ Buddhist monks prepare to pray at the top of Adam's Peak. The "yellow" robe is a symbol of Buddhism. The color of the robe varies according to the dye used. Some are bright orange, or saffron.

The Dalada Maligawa (Temple of the Tooth) houses the sacred tooth of Buddha. Pilgrims come to pay respect to the Tooth Relic during daily ceremonies.

Interpreting the Visual Record What architectural features of this temple have you seen in other world regions?

Semiprecious stones such as the sapphire, ruby, cat's eye, topaz, and garnet are mined in Sri Lanka.

Sri Lanka Today

Caste determines how Sri Lankans behave toward one another. As in India, many Sri Lankans believe associating with a member of a lower caste brings bad karma. Bad karma forces a person to undergo endless reincarnations, or rebirths. It also prevents him or her from finding nirvana, or spiritual release.

Sri Lanka has several features in common with the countries of the mainland Indian Perimeter. First, it is a mainly rural country. Less than 25 percent of Sri Lankans live in cities. Second, about 38 percent of Sri Lankans make a living from farming. They grow rice, fruits, and vegetables. Sri Lankan farmers also grow coconuts, rubber, and tea for export. Sri Lanka has a number of industries. They include food processing, textiles and apparel, telecommunications, insurance, and banking.

Mining is another important economic activity in Sri Lanka. The main resources mined are graphite and precious gems. Sri Lanka leads the world in **graphite** exports. Graphite is a form of carbon used in pencils and many other products. Recently, manufacturing—particularly of textiles and clothing—has grown in importance. Many textile and clothing factories are found in Colombo, the capital of Sri Lanka. Located on the west coast, Colombo is the country's largest city. It is also its most important commercial center and seaport. Sri Lanka's economy has grown in recent years. However, continuing ethnic conflicts between the Sinhalese majority and the Tamil minority threaten the country's progress.

READING CHECK: *Places and Regions* What is Sri Lanka like today?

The Maldives

The Maldives were originally settled by Buddhists from Sri Lanka. Today the main religion is Islam. Education includes traditional teachings of the Qur'an. However, there are no colleges or universities.

The Maldives consists of 19 **atolls**. An atoll is a ring of coral surrounding a body of water called a lagoon. These atolls sit atop an ancient submerged volcanic plateau. Altogether, the islands cover about 115 square miles (298 sq km). The largest island, Male (MAH-lay), is home to about one fourth of the population. A city by the same name serves as the country's capital. Only about 25 percent of the people live in cities.

Tourism is the Maldives largest industry. Fishing, particularly of tuna, is another of the country's chief economic activities. Exports of fresh, dried, frozen, and canned fish account for about half the country's income. Breadfruit—a fruit that resembles bread when baked—and coconuts are the Maldives' main food crops. Most other food must be imported. A small clothing industry and boat-building and repair are other sources of income for this island country.

These fishers are working together to corral fish in large nets.
Interpreting the Visual Record Why must so many people be involved in catching fish in this way?

Coconuts are the fruit of the coconut palm. The inside of the fruit contains edible meat and juice. Fiber from the outer husk can be used to make brushes, matting, and fishnets.

✓ **READING CHECK:** (*Environment and Society*) What geographic factors affect the economic activities of the Maldives?

Section Review 3

Define and explain: stupas, graphite, atolls

Working with Sketch Maps On the map you created in Section 2, label Nepal, Bhutan, Sri Lanka, Maldives, Kathmandu, Thimphu, Colombo, and Male.

Reading for the Main Idea

1. (*Environment and Society*) How have the people of Nepal used the lower slopes of the Himalayas?

2. (*Human Systems*) How does the caste system affect social interaction in Sri Lanka?

3. (*Places and Regions*) What are the major economic activities of the Maldives?

 go.hrw.com **Homework Practice Online** Keyword: SG3 HP31

Critical Thinking

4. Comparing In what ways have the cultures, people, and histories of India and the countries in this section been linked?

Organizing What You Know

5. Categorizing Copy the following graphic organizer. Use it to list the benefits and drawbacks of tourism in Nepal and Bhutan.

Tourism in Nepal and Bhutan

Benefits	Drawbacks

Reviewing What You Know

Building Vocabulary

On a separate sheet of paper, write sentences to define each of the following words.

1. cyclones
2. storm surges
3. cholera
4. stupas
5. graphite
6. atolls

Reviewing the Main Ideas

1. *(Places and Regions)* What is Pakistan's most important river? What two rivers are important to Bangladesh?

2. *(Human Systems)* What are some peoples who have conquered and ruled parts of the region over time?

3. *(Human Systems)* Which three countries of the Indian Perimeter are dominated by Islam? Which two are primarily Buddhist? Which one is populated mostly by Hindus?

4. *(Places and Regions)* What are some important resources of the Indian Perimeter?

5. *(Places and Regions)* What kinds of islands make up the Maldives?

Understanding Environment and Society

Deforestation

Nepal and other countries of the world are having problems with deforestation. How might the Nepalese government and others work to solve this problem? As you prepare your presentation, you may want to think about the following:

- The causes of deforestation in Nepal and other parts of the world.
- Examples of what other countries did in their efforts to slow deforestation.

Thinking Critically

1. **Drawing Inferences and Conclusions** What role do you think the Khyber Pass might have played in the history of this region?

2. **Finding the Main Idea** How has tourism benefited countries in the region? What problems has it caused?

3. **Analyzing Information** How did the British East India Company affect the history of this region?

4. **Analyzing Information** Is the population of the Indian Perimeter countries mostly rural or mostly urban? Explain your answer.

5. **Drawing Inferences and Conclusions** How has religion played a role in shaping the region's borders?

Map ACTIVITY

On a separate sheet of paper, match the letters on the map with their correct labels.

Brahmaputra River

Ganges River

Himalayas

Tarai

Hindu Kush

Khyber Pass

Indus River

Thar Desert

Mental Mapping Skills ACTIVITY

On a separate sheet of paper, draw a freehand map of India and the Indian Perimeter. Make a key for your map and label the following:

Bangladesh

Bhutan

India

Maldives

Mount Everest

Nepal

Pakistan

Sri Lanka

W R I T I N G ACTIVITY

Imagine that you are moving to one of the countries of the Indian Perimeter. In which country would you choose to live? State your choice and explain your reasons in two or three paragraphs. Explain how landforms, climate, culture, and economy influenced your decision. Be sure to use standard grammar, spelling, sentence structure, and punctuation.

Alternative Assessment

Portfolio ACTIVITY

Learning About Your Local Geography

Individual Project Floods often devastate Bangladesh. Present a newscast on your state's most recent flood or other natural disaster. What body of water flooded? What caused the flood?

internet connect

Internet Activity: go.hrw.com
KEYWORD: SG3 GT31

Choose a topic to explore about the Indian Perimeter.
- Climb the Himalayas.
- Learn about Sri Lanka's history.
- Visit the regions of Pakistan.

ENVIRONMENT

Saving Tigers

The Tiger

In the early 1800s India's tiger population was very large. By 1900, hunters had reduced the tiger population to about 40,000. To protect these tigers, India's British rulers placed strict limits on hunting them. Laws against illegal hunting were strictly enforced. After India won its independence in 1947, the hunting laws were often ignored, however. As a result, fewer than 2,000 tigers remained in India by 1972.

Why Are Tigers Endangered?

Unfortunately, laws have not kept people from hunting tigers. Tiger bones are used in traditional Chinese medicines. The bones are in high demand. International treaties now make it illegal to sell any part of an endangered species. However, the international trade in tiger bones continues.

Loss of habitat also threatens tiger survival. India's population has about doubled in the last 50 years. More land is now farmed to feed these additional people. As a result, many forests where tigers lived have been cleared for farming. As tiger habitat has decreased, so has the number of tigers.

International Efforts to Save the Tiger

Many people realized that tigers would not survive in the wild without protection. As a result, several international organizations and governments are working to ensure the tiger's future.

India's Project Tiger

In 1973 the Indian government took steps to try to save its remaining tigers. With support from the World Wildlife Fund, nine tiger reserves were created as part of Project Tiger. By 1997, 23 reserves had been set up throughout India.

Each reserve has a core area. No one can enter this area without a park ranger. The core area is surrounded by a buffer zone. People can use land in these zones in ways that do not harm the environment.

Once on the verge of extinction, tigers have rebounded in India due largely to Project Tiger.

▼

Realm of the Tiger

REALM OF THE TIGER
- Project Tiger reserves
- Tiger roaming areas

SCALE
0 — 2000 Miles
0 — 3500 Kilometers
Projection: Miller Cylindrical

ASIA

CHINA

Tropic of Cancer

AFRICA

ARABIAN SEA

INDIA

BAY OF BENGAL

SOUTH CHINA SEA

INDIAN OCEAN

Some rare Bengal tigers, such as this cub, are white. In the last 100 years, only about a dozen white tigers have been seen in the wild.

Some conservationists are reaching out to nearby villagers. Villagers have often felt that tigers are being protected at their expense. The conservationists want to show that tiger reserves can also help villagers. One organization has introduced new types of water buffalo that need very little grazing land. To boost the local economy, it has helped women sell their handicrafts in urban areas. The Global Environment Facility and the World Bank also want to help. They plan to spend about $10 million to aid villages around India's Ranthambhore National Park.

China's Year of the Tiger Despite these efforts, the number of tigers remains low. In 1998, the Chinese Year of the Tiger, conservationists in Hong Kong tried a new approach. They started an advertising campaign to remind people how important tigers are in traditional Chinese culture. The advertisements showed children dressed in clothes with popular tiger designs. The advertise-

ments read, "They protect your children; who will protect them?" Chinese conservationists hope their campaign will encourage people to stop using medicines made with tiger bones. They also hope it will encourage people to join the fight to save the world's tigers.

Your Turn

Imagine you are planning a worldwide campaign to save tigers in the wild. Write a short report that explains your plan and answers the following questions:

1. How would the Project Tiger reserves and the Chinese advertising campaign fit into your plan?

2. Do you think it is more important to save tiger habitat or to keep people from hunting them? why?

Geo SKILLS

Building Skills for Life: Drawing Diagrams

Diagrams are drawings that explain how things work or fit together. They can be helpful in many different situations. For example, suppose you bought a bicycle and had to put it together. How would you do it? The easiest way would be to follow a diagram.

The goal of a diagram is to explain something. Diagrams are not intended to show exactly how something looks in real life. Diagrams should be easy to understand, neat, and simple.

In geography, diagrams are often used to show how different things are related. Physical geographers use diagrams to explain how sea and land breezes develop or how volcanoes form. Cultural geographers use diagrams to show settlement patterns and housing styles.

You can draw diagrams too. To draw a diagram, first decide exactly what you want it to show. Choose a short, descriptive title. Plan your diagram by making a quick sketch. How many drawings will you need? How will you arrange them? Then carefully draw your diagram. Label the important features. Use colors, patterns, and symbols if you need to. Use a ruler for straight lines and write the title at the top. Then add a short caption at the bottom that explains your diagram.

Sea and Land Breezes

As warm air rises, it creates an area of low pressure over the land.

The cool air moves toward the land, producing a sea breeze.

Air over the water is cooler and creates an area of high pressure.

Air over land is cooler and creates an area of high pressure.

The cool air moves toward the water, producing a land breeze.

Air over the water is warmer and creates an area of low pressure.

Breezes from the ocean cool the warmer land surface during the day. At night, cooler land surface breezes blow toward the ocean.

PRACTICING THE SKILL

1. Choose a diagram from a book, magazine, or newspaper. Write a short paragraph about the diagram. What does it show? Is it clear and easy to understand? why or why not?

2. Draw a diagram that shows how wind moves a sailboat through water.

3. Draw a diagram that shows how rocks can break off a mountain and cause a landslide.

HANDS on GEOGRAPHY

The Himalayas are the highest mountains on Earth. Nine of the ten highest peaks in the world are located there. The Himalayas have 110 peaks that rise above 24,000 feet (7,315 m).

How did the Himalayas get to be so high? When were they formed? Drawing a diagram is one way to show how the Himalayas became the world's highest mountains.

Read the paragraph below. It describes how and when the Himalayas formed. Use this information to draw a diagram showing how the Himalayas became the world's highest mountains.

The Himalayas were formed long ago by the movement of Earth's tectonic plates. About 180 million years ago, the Indo-Australian plate broke off from the ancient supercontinent Gondwana and began moving north. This plate included what is now the Indian Subcontinent. About 50 million years ago, the Indo-Australian plate collided with the Eurasian plate and was forced under it. As the Indo-Australian plate was pulled under the Eurasian plate, the Himalayas began to rise. They grew slowly at first. Then, about 30 million years ago, the Himalayas began rising faster. However, they did not become the highest mountains in the world until about 500,000 years ago. The Himalayas are still rising today.

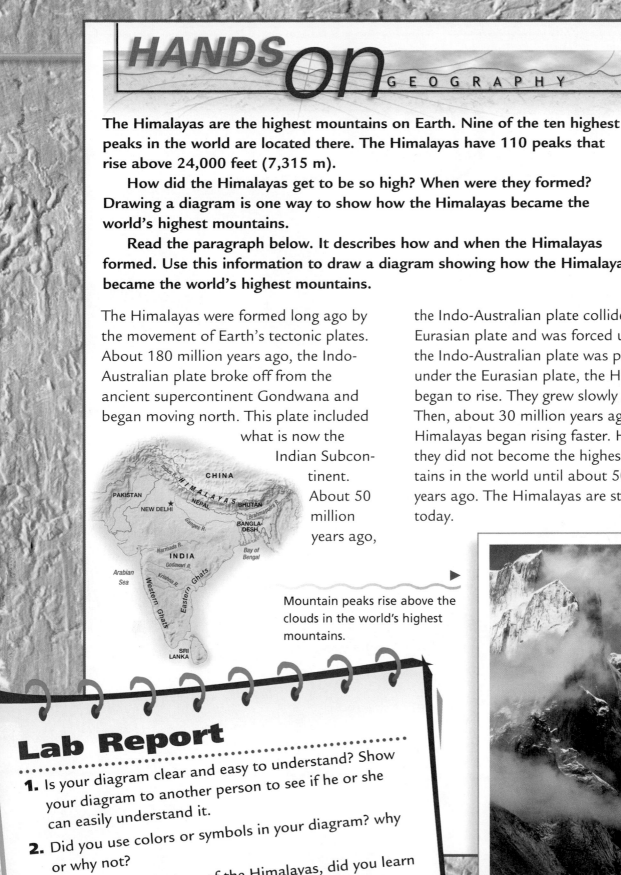

Mountain peaks rise above the clouds in the world's highest mountains.

Lab Report

1. Is your diagram clear and easy to understand? Show your diagram to another person to see if he or she can easily understand it.

2. Did you use colors or symbols in your diagram? why or why not?

3. By drawing a diagram of the Himalayas, did you learn something about diagrams in general? What did you learn?

UNIT 10

The Pacific World and Antarctica

CHAPTER 32
Australia and New Zealand

CHAPTER 33
The Pacific Islands and Antarctica

King penguins watching photographer, Antarctica

House in Sepik River area, Papua New Guinea

Teenagers of Melbourne, Australia

A Film Critic in New Zealand

David Gerstner is a film critic and lecturer from New York City. In 1999 he moved to New Zealand. He found the country was very different than he thought it would be. **WHAT DO YOU THINK?** *What do you know about New Zealand?*

Notes FROM THE field

First I was surprised that New Zealand has such lively cities. I had thought it was all mountains and bush. I was also surprised by the laid-back New Zealand approach to personal interaction. Celebrities, politicians, and the "common folk" have an easier time getting together. For example, I have become friends with some of New Zealand's well-known filmmakers, writers, and fashion designers—all within a year. The social playing field is more level than in the United States.

In fact, a friend and I literally ran into Jenny Shipley, who was then New Zealand's Prime Minister, on a busy street in the capital, Wellington. She was with her daughter. There were no secret service guards with them—like there would be with the U.S. president. We even had our picture taken with her! The easy-going Kiwi style of security is refreshing. However, for a New Yorker it is sometimes unsettling.

Wellington, New Zealand

Understanding Primary Sources

1. Why was David Gerstner surprised by New Zealand's cities?

2. What does this passage illustrate about New Zealand's culture?

Koalas

The Pacific World and Antarctica

Elevation Profile

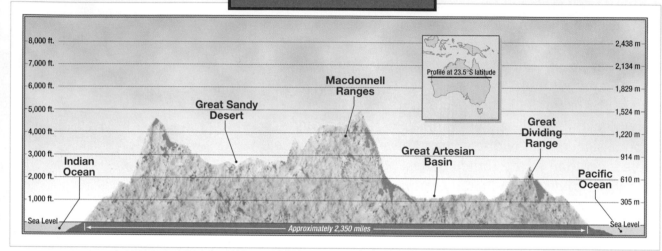

8,000 ft. — 2,438 m
7,000 ft. — 2,134 m
6,000 ft. — 1,829 m
5,000 ft. — 1,524 m
4,000 ft. — 1,220 m
3,000 ft. — 914 m
2,000 ft. — 610 m
1,000 ft. — 305 m
Sea Level — Sea Level

Profile at 23.5°S latitude

Indian Ocean
Great Sandy Desert
Macdonnell Ranges
Great Artesian Basin
Great Dividing Range
Pacific Ocean

Approximately 2,350 miles

The United States and the Pacific World and Antarctica: Comparing Sizes

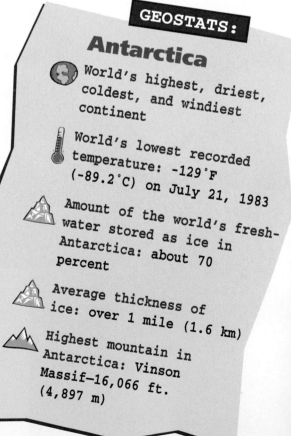

GEOSTATS:
Antarctica

- World's highest, driest, coldest, and windiest continent

- World's lowest recorded temperature: -129°F (-89.2°C) on July 21, 1983

- Amount of the world's fresh-water stored as ice in Antarctica: about 70 percent

- Average thickness of ice: over 1 mile (1.6 km)

- Highest mountain in Antarctica: Vinson Massif—16,066 ft. (4,897 m)

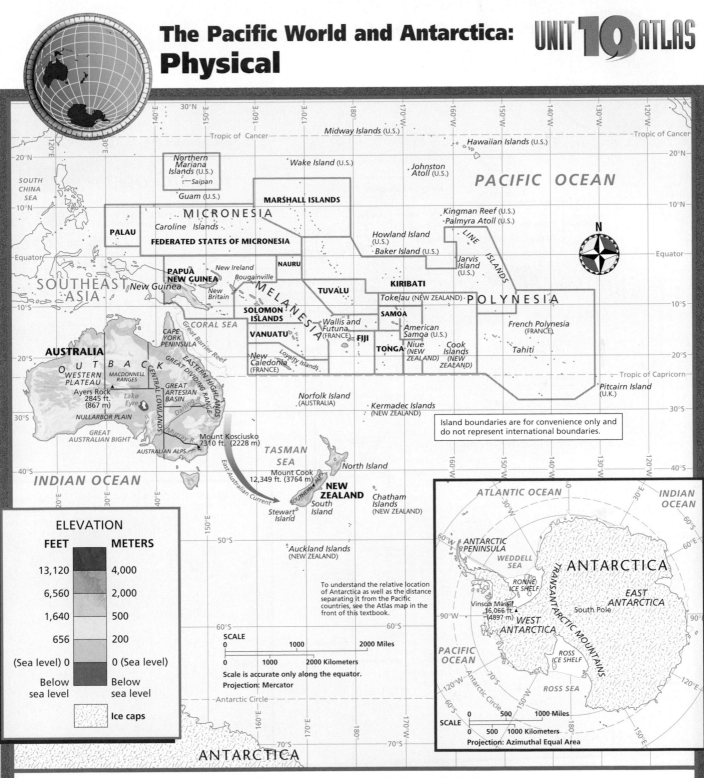

ELEVATION

FEET	METERS
13,120	4,000
6,560	2,000
1,640	500
656	200
(Sea level) 0	0 (Sea level)
Below sea level	Below sea level

Ice caps

To understand the relative location of Antarctica as well as the distance separating it from the Pacific countries, see the Atlas map in the front of this textbook.

SCALE
0 ____ 1000 ____ 2000 Miles
0 ____ 1000 ____ 2000 Kilometers
Scale is accurate only along the equator.
Projection: Mercator

Island boundaries are for convenience only and do not represent international boundaries.

SCALE
0 ____ 500 ____ 1000 Miles
0 ____ 500 ____ 1000 Kilometers
Projection: Azimuthal Equal Area

1. *Places and Regions* What is the highest point in Australia? in the region?

2. *Places and Regions* About how far apart are Guam and Tahiti? New Zealand and Australia?

3. *Places and Regions* What physical features cover most of Australia?

Critical Thinking

4. **Comparing** Which country is more mountainous, Australia or New Zealand?

5. **Analyzing Information** Compare this map to the **climate map** of the region. Which Australian mountain range seems to cause a rain-shadow effect?

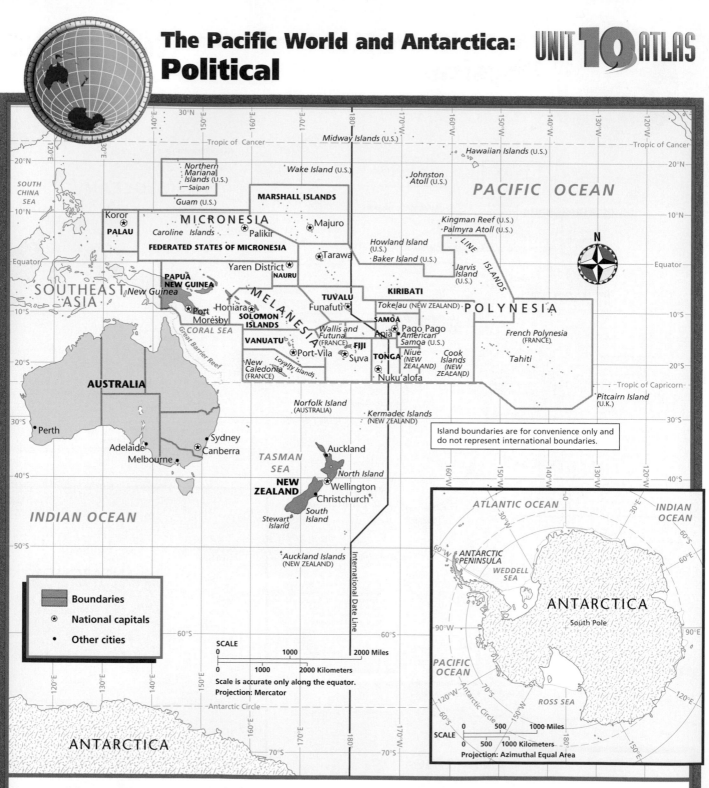

Island boundaries are for convenience only and do not represent international boundaries.

Boundaries

⊛ **National capitals**

• **Other cities**

SCALE
0   1000   2000 Miles

0   1000   2000 Kilometers

Scale is accurate only along the equator.
Projection: Mercator

SCALE
0   500   1000 Miles

0   500   1000 Kilometers
Projection: Azimuthal Equal Area

1. (Places and Regions) Which country occupies half of a large island? Which country occupies two large islands?

2. (Places and Regions) What is the only country in the region that has a land boundary with another country?

Critical Thinking

3. Analyzing Information What is one thing you can tell about governments in the region just by looking at the map?

4. Drawing Inferences and Conclusions Why do you think the international date line is not a straight line?

CLIMATE

- Humid tropical
- Tropical savanna
- Desert
- Steppe
- Humid subtropical
- Highland
- ← Wet monsoon air flow
- ← Dry monsoon air flow

SCALE
0   1000   2000 Miles
0   1000   2000 Kilometers
Scale is accurate only along the equator.
Projection: Mercator

Island boundaries are for convenience only and do not represent international boundaries.

SCALE
0   500   1000 Miles
0   500   1000 Kilometers
Projection: Azimuthal Equal Area

PACIFIC OCEAN

SOUTH CHINA SEA

SOUTHEAST ASIA

Great Barrier Reef

CORAL SEA

TASMAN SEA

INDIAN OCEAN

ANTARCTICA

ATLANTIC OCEAN

WEDDELL SEA

INDIAN OCEAN

South Pole

PACIFIC OCEAN

ROSS SEA

Antarctic Circle

Hawaiian Islands (U.S.)

1. **Places and Regions** What type of climate does New Zealand have?

2. **Places and Regions** Which country has the greatest variety of climate types?

3. **Places and Regions** Compare this map to the **population map** of the region. What type of climate does Perth have?

Critical Thinking

4. **Making Generalizations and Predictions** Compare this map to the **physical map**. How might the East Australian Current affect New Zealand's weather?

5. **Comparing** How might climate affect Papua New Guinea's population patterns?

The Pacific World and Antarctica: Population

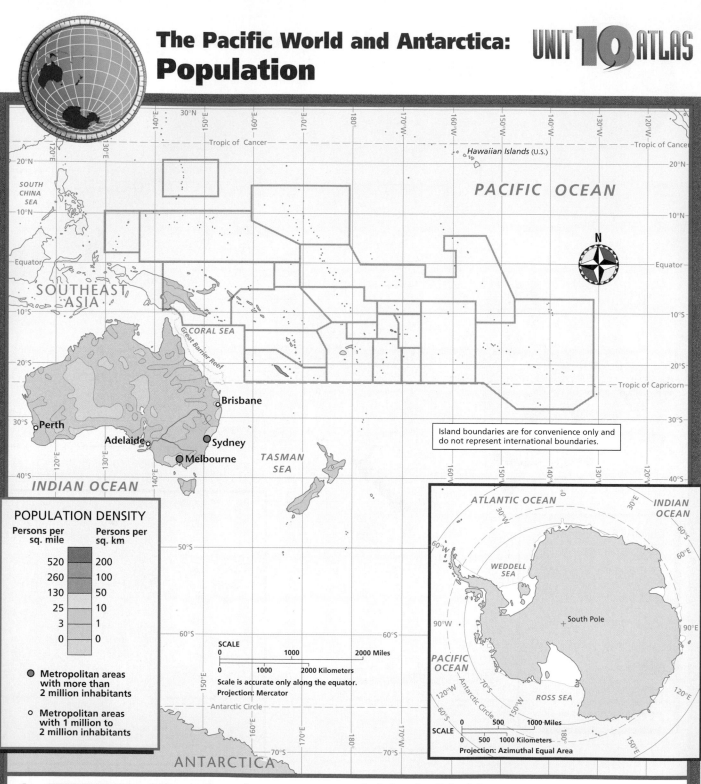

POPULATION DENSITY

Persons per sq. mile	Persons per sq. km
520	200
260	100
130	50
25	10
3	1
0	0

● Metropolitan areas with more than 2 million inhabitants

○ Metropolitan areas with 1 million to 2 million inhabitants

SCALE
0   1000   2000 Miles
0   1000   2000 Kilometers
Scale is accurate only along the equator.
Projection: Mercator

Island boundaries are for convenience only and do not represent international boundaries.

Hawaiian Islands (U.S.)

PACIFIC OCEAN

SOUTH CHINA SEA

SOUTHEAST ASIA

CORAL SEA

Great Barrier Reef

Brisbane

Perth

Adelaide

Sydney

Melbourne

TASMAN SEA

INDIAN OCEAN

ANTARCTICA

Antarctic Circle

ATLANTIC OCEAN

INDIAN OCEAN

WEDDELL SEA

South Pole

PACIFIC OCEAN

ROSS SEA

Antarctic Circle

SCALE
0   500   1000 Miles
0   500   1000 Kilometers
Projection: Azimuthal Equal Area

1. *Places and Regions* What is the only country with cities of over 2 million people?

2. *Places and Regions* What region of Australia has the highest population density?

3. *Places and Regions* Compare this map to the **physical map**. What is the densely populated island northwest of New Zealand?

Critical Thinking

4. Analyzing Information What large landmass has no permanent population? Why?

5. Analyzing Information Use the map on this page to create a chart, graph, database, or model of population centers in the Pacific world and Australia.

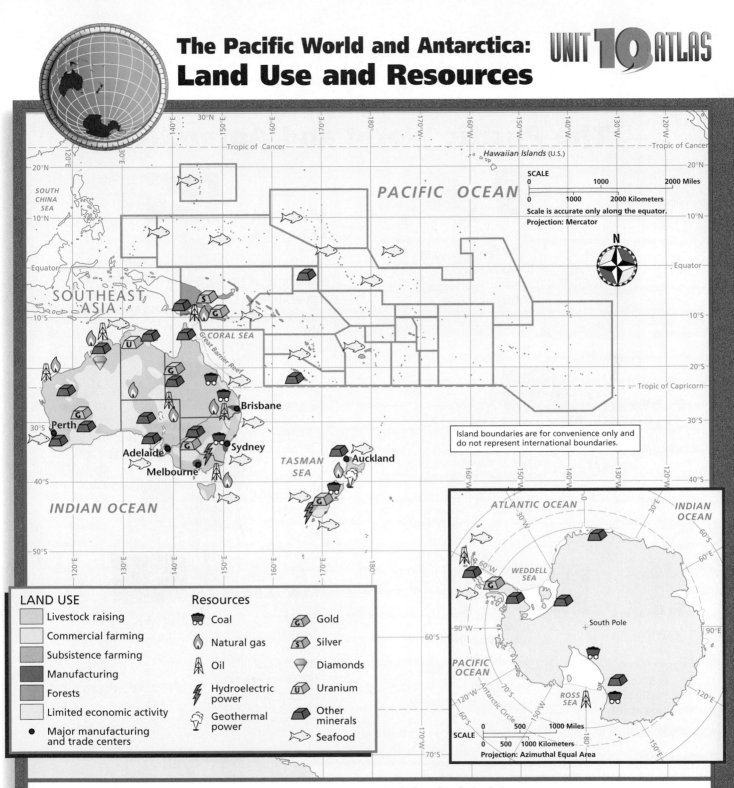

LAND USE
- Livestock raising
- Commercial farming
- Subsistence farming
- Manufacturing
- Forests
- Limited economic activity
- ● Major manufacturing and trade centers

Resources
- Coal
- Natural gas
- Oil
- Hydroelectric power
- Geothermal power
- G Gold
- S Silver
- Diamonds
- U Uranium
- Other minerals
- Seafood

Island boundaries are for convenience only and do not represent international boundaries.

1. *Places and Regions* What cities are part of Australia's major manufacturing and trade centers?

2. *Places and Regions* What resources are available in Papua New Guinea but not in Australia?

3. *Places and Regions* What is the main resource of most of the small Pacific islands?

Critical Thinking

4. Analyzing Information Use the map on this page to create a chart, graph, database, or model of economic activities in the Pacific world and Australia.

Fast FACTS

The Pacific World and Antarctica

AUSTRALIA

CAPITAL:
Canberra

AREA:
2,967,893 sq. mi.
(7,686,850 sq km)

POPULATION:
19,357,594

MONEY:
Australian dollar (AUD)

LANGUAGES:
English, ethnic languages

POPULATION AGED 0-14 YEARS:
21 percent

MARSHALL ISLANDS

CAPITAL: Majuro

AREA: 70 sq. mi. (181.3 sq km)

POPULATION: 70,822

MONEY: United States dollar (USD)

LANGUAGES:
English (official), Marshallese dialects, Japanese

POPULATION AGED 0-14 YEARS: 49 percent

FEDERATED STATES OF MICRONESIA

CAPITAL: Palikir

AREA: 271 sq. mi. (702 sq km)

POPULATION: 134,597

MONEY:
United States dollar (USD)

LANGUAGES:
English (official), Trukese, Pohnpeian, Yapese, Kosrean

POPULATION AGED 0-14 YEARS: data not available

NAURU

CAPITAL:
no official capital

AREA:
8 sq. mi. (21 sq km)

POPULATION:
12,088

MONEY:
Australian dollar (AUD)

LANGUAGES:
Nauruan (official), English

POPULATION AGED 0-14 YEARS:
40 percent

FIJI

CAPITAL:
Suva

AREA:
7,054 sq. mi.
(18,270 sq km)

POPULATION:
844,330

MONEY:
Fijian dollar (FJD)

LANGUAGES:
English (official), Fijian, Hindustani

POPULATION AGED 0-14 YEARS:
33 percent

NEW ZEALAND

CAPITAL:
Wellington

AREA:
103,737 sq. mi.
(268,680 sq km)

POPULATION:
3,864,129

MONEY:
New Zealand dollar (NZD)

LANGUAGES:
English (official), Maori

POPULATION AGED 0-14 YEARS:
22 percent

KIRIBATI

CAPITAL:
Tarawa

AREA:
277 sq. mi. (717 sq km)

POPULATION:
94,149

MONEY:
Australian dollar (AUD)

LANGUAGES:
English (official), I-Kiribati

POPULATION AGED 0-14 YEARS:
41 percent

PALAU

CAPITAL:
Koror

AREA:
177 sq. mi. (458 sq km)

POPULATION:
19,092

MONEY:
United States dollar (USD)

LANGUAGES:
English (official), Sonsorolese, Angaur, Japanese, Tobi, Palauan

POPULATION AGED 0-14 YEARS:
27 percent

Countries not drawn to scale.

PAPUA NEW GUINEA

CAPITAL:
Port Moresby

AREA:
178,703 sq. mi.
(462,840 sq km)

POPULATION: 5,049,055

MONEY: kina (PGK)

LANGUAGES:
715 ethnic languages, pidgin English, English

POPULATION AGED 0-14 YEARS: 39 percent

SAMOA

CAPITAL:
Apia

AREA:
1,104 sq. mi. (2,860 sq km)

POPULATION:
179,058

MONEY:
tala (WST)

LANGUAGES:
Samoan (Polynesian), English

POPULATION AGED 0-14 YEARS:
32 percent

SOLOMON ISLANDS

CAPITAL:
Honiara

AREA:
10,985 sq. mi.
(28,450 sq km)

POPULATION:
480,442

MONEY:
Solomon Islands dollar (SBD)

LANGUAGES:
Melanesian pidgin, 120 ethnic languages, English

POPULATION AGED 0-14 YEARS: 44 percent

TONGA

CAPITAL:
Nuku'alofa

AREA:
289 sq. mi.
(748 sq km)

POPULATION:
104,227

MONEY:
pa'anga (TOP)

LANGUAGES:
Tongan, English

POPULATION AGED 0-14 YEARS:
41 percent

TUVALU

CAPITAL:
Funafuti

AREA:
10 sq. mi. (26 sq km)

POPULATION:
10,991

MONEY:
Tuvaluan dollar or Australian dollar (AUD)

LANGUAGES:
Tuvaluan, English

POPULATION AGED 0-14 YEARS: 33 percent

VANUATU

CAPITAL:
Port-Vila

AREA:
4,710 sq. mi. (12,200 sq km)

POPULATION:
192,910

MONEY:
vatu (VUV)

LANGUAGES:
English (official), French (official), pidgin (known as Bislama or Bichelama)

POPULATION AGED 0-14 YEARS: 36 percent

internet connect
go.hrw.com

COUNTRY STATISTICS
GO TO: go.hrw.com
KEYWORD: SG3 FactsU10
FOR: more facts about the Pacific World and Antarctica

Sources: Central Intelligence Agency, *The World Factbook 2001; The World Almanac and Book of Facts 2001*, pop. figures are 2001 estimates.

CHAPTER 32

Australia and New Zealand

In this chapter we will study Australia and nearby New Zealand. First we meet Jared and Ashleigh. Their ancestors lived in Australia long before Europeans arrived.

Hi! My name is Jared. I have a twin sister, Ashleigh. We are 14 years old and live in Cooroy, Australia, which is about two hours north of Brisbane. We live with our mother in a three-bedroom house on a hill. Our land has a big creek with a dam on it. The dam forms a big pond, or a billabong. We can jump into it from the trees along the edge. Our father lives up north in the traditional lands of our people, the Djabugayndgi.

We used to speak our native language, but we've forgotten lots of it since we've been going to school. My totem, or special animal protector, is the *Ngumba*, or platypus. My sister's is the *Badgigal*, or freshwater turtle.

Since we were three years old, we have been singing and dancing in an Aboriginal dance group called *Bibayungen*. At Christmas, the whole family gathers with about 1,000 people in our traditional lands for a big dance and music festival (*warrima* in our language).

Nyurramba garran, bulmba nganydjin ngunda!

▲
Translation: Come and see our country!

Section 1

Australia

Read to Discover

1. What are Australia's natural features and resources?
2. What is the history of Australia?
3. What is Australia like today?

Define

artesian wells
coral reef
endemic species
marsupials
outback
rugby
bush

Locate

Eastern Highlands
Central Lowlands
Western Plateau
Great Dividing Range
Tasmania
Murray-Darling Rivers

Great Artesian Basin
Great Barrier Reef
Sydney
Melbourne
Brisbane
Perth

WHY IT MATTERS

Use CNNfyi.com or other **current events** sources to find out about Aborigine culture in Australia. Record your findings in your journal.

Australian opal

Australia and New Zealand: Physical-Political

Size comparison of Australia and New Zealand to the contiguous United States

Our Amazing Planet

Ayers Rock in central Australia is composed of sandstone with bits of reflective minerals. The sandstone changes color as the Sun moves across the sky. At sunset Ayers Rock turns a fiery orange-red.

Ayers Rock, called Uluru by Aborigines, rises more than 1,100 feet (335 m) above the surrounding Western Plateau. It is all that is left after erosion wore away an ancient mountain.

Interpreting the Visual Record How has erosion affected Ayers Rock?

Australia

Ayers Rock

Natural Features

Australia is the world's smallest, flattest, and lowest continent. In addition, it is the only country that is also a continent. The country sometimes is called the Land Down Under because it lies south of the equator. Seasons there are reversed from those north of the equator. For example, when it is winter in the United States, it is summer in Australia.

Land Australia has three main landform regions. These are the Eastern Highlands, the Central Lowlands, and the Western Plateau.

The Eastern Highlands are a system of ridges, plateaus, and valleys in the eastern part of Australia. They include the Great Dividing Range. This range stretches along the eastern coast and includes the island of Tasmania. It divides Australia's rivers into those that flow eastward and those that flow westward. Australia's one major river system, the Murray-Darling, flows westward from the range.

Australia's highest mountain is in the Great Dividing Range. It rises to just 7,310 feet (2,228 m). This tells us that Australia is very old. Erosion from wind and water has lowered the continent's mountains over millions of years.

The Central Lowlands are flatter and lower than the Eastern Highlands. The Central Lowlands include the Great Artesian Basin, Australia's largest source of underground water. **Artesian wells** dot this area. Artesian wells are those in which water rises toward the surface without being pumped. The groundwater comes from rain falling on nearby mountains. As the amount of groundwater increases, some is pushed to the surface. Much of the well water here is of poor quality, so it is used mostly for watering sheep.

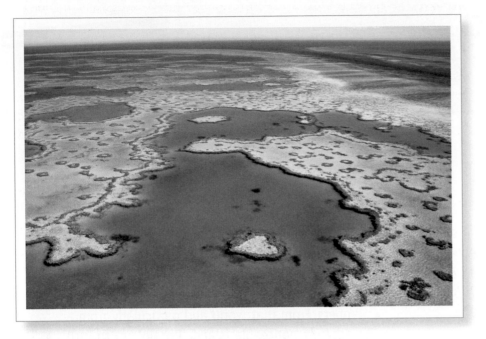

The Great Barrier Reef is really thousands of small reefs and tiny islands. Some rise barely above water level when the tide is low.

Farther west is the Western Plateau, which covers more than half of the continent. The treeless Nullarbor Plain stretches along the southern edge of the plateau. This plain is the flattest large area on any continent.

The Great Barrier Reef Off the northeastern coast of Australia is the Great Barrier Reef. It is the world's largest **coral reef**, stretching more than 1,250 miles (2,000 km). A coral reef is a ridge found close to shore in warm, tropical waters. It is made of rocky limestone material formed by the skeletons of tiny sea animals. You will read more about coral reefs in the next chapter.

The Great Barrier Reef and its shallow waters are home to many kinds of marine animals. They include fish, shellfish, and sea birds. Australia's government has made most of the reef a national park.

Climate Australia has been described as a desert with green edges. Dry desert and steppe climates cover most of the country. The eastern and southeastern edges and Tasmania have humid climates. Two coastal areas in the south and southwest have a Mediterranean climate. Summers there are long, dry, and sunny. Winters are mild and wet. The north has a tropical savanna climate. There monsoons bring strong wet and dry seasons.

Plants and Animals Australia has many **endemic species**. Endemic species are plants and animals that developed in one particular region of the world. Why does Australia have many endemic species? Australia has been separated from other continents for millions of years. However, over time many nonnative plants and animals have been brought to Australia. See the Case Study in this chapter.

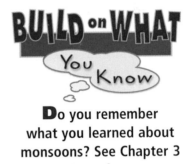

Do you remember what you learned about monsoons? See Chapter 3 to review.

The shallow ocean waters along Australia's northern coast are home to the deadly sea wasp jellyfish. Each jellyfish has as many as 60 tentacles that hang down six and a half feet (2 m). The venom from its sting can kill a human in less than five minutes.

CONNECTING TO Literature

Christmas on an Australian beach

THE LAND DOWN UNDER

Europeans began settling in Australia in the late 1700s. The following selection describes what settlers found in the Land Down Under. The selection comes from Christina Stead's For Love Alone, *published in 1944.*

In the part of the world Teresa came from, winter is in July, spring brides marry in September, and Christmas is consummated[1] with roast beef [and] suckling[2] pig . . . at 100 degrees in the shade, near the tall pine tree loaded with gifts and tinsel as in the old country, and old carols have rung out all through the night.

This island continent lies in the water hemisphere. On the eastern coast, the neighboring nation is Chile, though it is far, far east, Valparaiso being more than six thousand miles away in a straight line; her northern neighbors are those of the Timor Sea, the Yellow Sea; to the south is that cold, stormy sea full of earth-wide rollers, which stretches from there without land, south to the Pole.

The other world—the old world, the land [Northern] hemisphere—is far above her as it is shown on maps drawn upside-down by old-world cartographers. From that world and particularly from a scarcely noticeable island [Britain] up toward the North Pole the people came, all by steam; or their parents, all by sail. . . . Inside, over the Blue Mountains, are the plains heavy with wheat, then the endless dust, and after outcrops of silver, opal, and gold, Sahara, the salt-crusted bed of a prehistoric sea, and leafless mountain ranges. There is nothing in the interior; so people look toward the water, and above to the fixed stars and constellations which first guided men there.

Analyzing Primary Sources

1. How does life differ from that in the "old world" in Teresa's land?
2. How does the writer give the reader a sense of Australia's isolation?

[1]consummated: completed, marked, or celebrated; [2]suckling: a young mammal that is still nursing

---

Two of Australia's most famous native animals are the kangaroo and the koala. Both animals are **marsupials** (mahr-SOO-pee-uhls). Marsupials are animals that carry their young in pouches. Eucalyptus (yoo-kuh-LIP-tuhs) is Australia's most common tree.

Minerals Australia's **outback**, or inland region, has many mineral resources such as gold, iron ore, and bauxite. Australia also has coal, natural gas, oil, and gemstones such as opals and diamonds.

✓ **READING CHECK:** *Places and Regions* What are the natural features of Australia?

History

The first humans to live in Australia were the Aborigines (a-buh-RIJ-uh-nees). They came from Southeast Asia at least 40,000 years ago. Early Aborigines hunted animals and gathered food from wild plants. They had many different languages, traditions, and customs. The arrival of Europeans changed life for the Aborigines.

European Settlers The British began settling colonies in Australia in 1788. Many of the first settlers were British prisoners, but other British settlers came, too. As the settlers built farms and ranches, they took over the Aborigines' lands. In addition, many Aborigines died of diseases brought unintentionally by the Europeans.

Independence The British granted independence to the Australian colonies in 1901. The colonies were united into one country within the British Commonwealth of Nations. Australia fought on the side of the British and other Allied forces in World Wars I and II.

Today Australia has six states and one large territory. The national capital is Canberra. Because Australia is part of the Commonwealth, the British monarch also is Australia's monarch. However, a prime minister and parliament make Australia's laws. Some Australians want their country to leave the Commonwealth and replace the monarch with an Australian president or other official.

✓ **READING CHECK:** (*Human Systems*) How has migration affected Australia's history?

States and Territories of Australia

State	Capital
New South Wales	Sydney
Victoria	Melbourne
Queensland	Brisbane
Western Australia	Perth
South Australia	Adelaide
Tasmania	Hobart

Territory	Capital
Northern Territory	Darwin
Australian Capital Territory	Canberra

Interpreting the Chart What is the capital of Tasmania?

Culture

More than 90 percent of Australians today are of British or other European ancestry. Since the 1970s Asians have been moving to

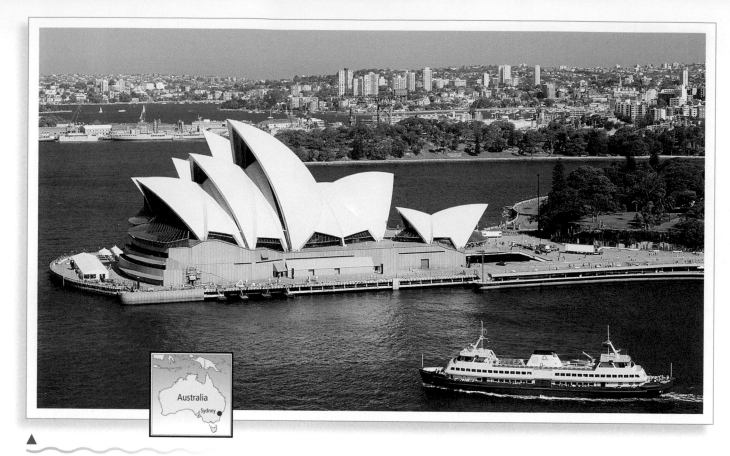

The Sydney Opera House opened on the city's harbor front in 1973. It is one of Australia's most well-known buildings.

Australia in growing numbers. As a result, about 7 percent of Australia's population today is ethnic Asian. Only about 1 percent of the country's people are Aborigines. Nearly all Australians speak English, but some Aborigines also speak native languages.

Religion and Holidays Most Australians are Christians. They celebrate many of the same holidays as people in the United States. However, their traditions may be different. For example, December falls during summer in Australia. Christmas there is time for a beach party, picnic, or some other outdoor activity.

Outdoor activities are popular in sunny Australia. Many people enjoy picnics, swimming, and sports. Popular sports include the British game of cricket, sailing, horse racing, surfing, and Australian Rules football. Many Australians also enjoy **rugby**. Rugby is a British game similar to football and soccer.

Australia

COUNTRY	POPULATION/ GROWTH RATE	LIFE EXPECTANCY	LITERACY RATE	PER CAPITA GDP
Australia	19,357,594 1.0%	77, male 83, female	100%	$23,200
United States	281,421,906 0.9%	74, male 80, female	97%	$36,200

Sources: Central Intelligence Agency, *The World Factbook 2001;* U.S. Census Bureau

Interpreting the Chart How does Australia's literacy rate compare to that of the United States?

The Arts Music and other arts are also popular in Australia. In fact, art by Aborigines has become popular around the world. The Australian government is an important source of money for the arts. For example, the government has built many public performance halls. One of the most famous is the Opera House in Australia's largest city, Sydney.

✓ **READING CHECK:** *Human Systems* What are some characteristics of Australia's people?

Australia Today

About 85 percent of Australians live in and around cities. The rest live in the **bush**, or lightly populated wilderness areas. The largest cities are Sydney and Melbourne in the southeast. Brisbane, on the eastern coast, enjoys a warm, tropical climate that attracts tourists. Towns have grown around mining and ranching areas in parts of the dry, rugged outback. Large parts of the interior have few people. The seaport of Perth is the largest city in the west.

Economy Australia is a rich, economically developed country. It is a leading producer of agricultural goods such as wool, meat, and wheat. Australia supplies nearly half of the world's wool used in clothing. One of the country's most important industries is mining, particularly in the outback. Other industries include steel, heavy machines, and computers.

Challenges Australia faces important challenges. Among these is improving the economic and political status of the Aborigines. They have only recently gained back some of the rights they lost after Europeans colonized Australia. The country also must continue to build ties with Asian and Pacific countries. At one time Australia's strongest ties were with Britain. Today, its most important trading partners are much closer Asian countries and the United States. In addition, Australia must deal with the rapid growth of its cities. It also must protect native animals and the environment.

✓ **READING CHECK:** (*Places and Regions*) What is Australia's economy like?

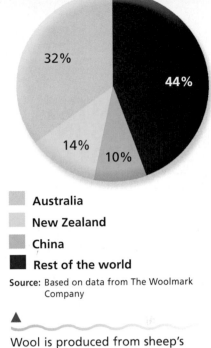

Major Producers of Wool

- Australia
- New Zealand
- China
- Rest of the world

Source: Based on data from The Woolmark Company

Wool is produced from sheep's hair. Australia has one of the world's largest flocks of sheep.

Interpreting the Chart What nearby country is the world's second-largest wool producer?

Section Review 1

go.hrw.com Homework Practice Online
Keyword: SG3 HP32

Define and explain: artesian wells, coral reef, endemic species, marsupials, outback, rugby, bush

Working with Sketch Maps On a map of Australia and New Zealand that you draw or that your teacher provides, label the following: Eastern Highlands, Central Lowlands, Western Plateau, Great Dividing Range, Tasmania, Murray River, Darling River, Great Artesian Basin, Great Barrier Reef, Sydney, Melbourne, Brisbane, and Perth. In a box in the margin, describe why the Great Artesian Basin is important to a dry country like Australia.

Reading for the Main Idea

1. (*Human Systems*) How has migration affected Australia's population? Which ethnic group is the largest?

2. (*Places and Regions*) What are two of Australia's most famous native marsupials?

3. (*Human Systems*) Who were the first humans to live in Australia? When did Europeans start settling there?

Critical Thinking

4. **Drawing Inferences and Conclusions** Why is building ties with Asian countries important for Australia today?

Organizing What You Know

5. **Categorizing** Copy the following graphic organizer. Use it to list Australia's climates, plants and animals, and mineral resources.

Climates	Plants and Animals	Resources

CASE STUDY

NONNATIVE SPECIES IN AUSTRALIA

For about the last 35 million years, Australia has been separated from the other continents by oceans. During this time Australia's plants and animals developed in isolation from the rest of the world. Eventually, a unique Australian ecosystem developed. Many interesting species of plants and animals existed only in Australia. For example, kangaroos, koalas, and eucalyptus trees were all native to Australia. They were not found anywhere else in the world.

Europeans arrived in Australia in the late 1700s. They dramatically changed the natural balance that had developed over millions of years.

Europeans brought with them many new species of plants and animals. These nonnative species have had a major impact on the environment in Australia.

European settlers turned large areas of grasslands into fields for agriculture. They set up huge wheat farms in the south and southwest. They planted sugarcane fields in the northeast. These crops had never been grown in Australia. Farmers also brought nonnative animals, such as sheep, cows, and goats, into Australia. In less than 100 years, Australia had more than 100 million sheep and 8 million cows.

Cattle are herded on the island of Tasmania in Australia.

Interpreting the Visual Record Can you see how these animals are changing the environment?

Introduced into Australia from Southeast Asia, water buffalo now eat food that Australia's native animals need to survive.

When Europeans settled in Australia they brought with them many new plants and animals. Some of these plants and animals have become pests because they damage the environment.

Many of the nonnative species that were brought into Australia spread across the continent. Some are now considered pests. These plants and animals are seriously damaging Australia's environment. For example, camels were introduced into Australia as pack animals. Now they run wild in the desert interior. Water buffalo were introduced from Southeast Asia. They trample riverbanks, killing grasses and eroding the soil. The prickly pear cactus was introduced into Australia from the United States as a garden plant. It spread across much of the country and has been very hard to control. Cane toads were introduced in the 1930s to protect Australia's sugarcane fields from cane beetles. However, they release toxic chemicals when attacked and are now threatening native species and household pets.

Of the nonnative animals introduced into Australia, rabbits have probably been the most destructive. Brought in by hunters in the 1800s, rabbits multiplied and spread quickly. With no natural predators and lots of food, their numbers increased to about 500 million. Rabbits overgrazed Australia's grasslands and caused major soil erosion.

The introduction of nonnative species into Australia has damaged the environment in several ways. Some native species have become extinct because they could not compete with nonnative species. About 13 species of mammals and one species of bird have become extinct in Australia since the late 1700s. Many more are endangered. Nonnative species such as cows, sheep, and rabbits have caused soil erosion. These animals also consume food and water that Australia's native plants and animals need to survive. As the case of Australia shows, the introduction of nonnative species into a new environment can cause serious environmental problems.

Understanding What You Read

1. How did isolation affect Australia's ecosystem?

2. What are some of the species that Europeans brought with them to Australia? How does Australia's environment now reflect their influence?

Section 2

New Zealand

Read to Discover

1. What are the natural features of New Zealand?
2. What are the history and culture of New Zealand?
3. What are New Zealand's cities and economy like today?

Define
kiwi

Locate
Tasman Sea
South Island
North Island
Southern Alps

Wellington
Auckland
Christchurch

A Maori pendant

WHY IT MATTERS

Tourism is an important part of New Zealand's economy. Use **CNNfyi**.com or other **current events** sources to find out what attracts tourists to New Zealand. Record your findings in your journal.

Natural Features

New Zealand lies southeast of Australia across the Tasman Sea. It includes two large islands—South Island and North Island. Put together, the islands are about the size of the U.S. state of Colorado.

Land The highest mountains are the Southern Alps on South Island. These rugged, glacier-capped mountains cover the western half of the island. The highest peak reaches 12,349 feet (3,764 m). A narrow coastal plain stretches along South Island's eastern side.

North Island has three major volcanic peaks separated by a volcanic plateau. Volcanic eruptions are common. Most of the rest of North Island is covered by hills and coastal plains.

The Southern Alps stretch across much of New Zealand's South Island. New Zealand's government has established large national parks throughout the mountains.

Autumn turns South Island's countryside golden near the city of Christchurch. New Zealand has four distinct seasons.

Climate, Wildlife, and Resources Unlike mostly dry Australia, New Zealand is humid. It has a mild marine west coast climate. Rain falls throughout the year. Winds from the west bring very heavy rain or snow to South Island's western side. The grassy plains of the drier eastern side are in a rain shadow. The north of North Island, in the lower latitudes, has a warmer, more tropical climate.

Much of New Zealand was once forested. Today, more than half is covered by pastures and farms. Sheep and other livestock graze in New Zealand's pastures. Sheep and their wool have long been important to the country's economy.

As in Australia, many animals in New Zealand are endemic species. The country's endemic species include different kinds of bats and flightless birds such as the **kiwi** (KEE-wee). The kiwi has hairlike feathers and sharp senses of smell and hearing. This bird is so linked with the country that New Zealanders are sometimes called Kiwis.

Many other species have been brought to New Zealand over time. For example, deer and trout have been introduced to provide sport for hunters and fishers.

New Zealand has fewer mineral resources than Australia. Its natural resources include gold, iron ore, natural gas, and coal.

✔ **READING CHECK:** *Places and Regions* What are the natural features of New Zealand?

History and Culture

New Zealand's first settlers came from other Pacific islands more than 1,000 years ago. Their descendants, the Maori (MOWR-ee), still live in New Zealand. The early settlers' main source of food was the moa—a giant, flightless bird. However, overhunting by New Zealand's early peoples wiped out the moa. The bird was extinct by the time Europeans arrived in New Zealand.

BUILD on WHAT You Know

Do you remember what you learned about the rain-shadow effect of mountains? See Chapter 3 to review.

Maori traditional art, like this carved entrance arch, survived New Zealand's colonial period.
Interpreting the Visual Record **What role does art play in Maori culture?**

New Zealand's All Black Rugby Union team performs a version of the Haka (HAH-kah) before international games. The Haka is a traditional Maori dance.

Interpreting the Visual Record
How has cultural borrowing affected this performance of the Haka?

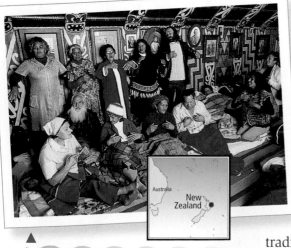

Mourners attend a funeral in a Maori carved meeting house.

European Settlers A Dutch explorer in 1642 was the first European to sight New Zealand. British explorer Captain James Cook visited New Zealand in 1769. Many British settlers started to arrive after the British signed a treaty with the Maori in 1840. However, fighting broke out as British settlers took over Maori lands.

Independence The British granted New Zealand independence in 1907. Like Australia, New Zealand became a member of the British Commonwealth of Nations. New Zealanders fought alongside the British in World Wars I and II.

The government of New Zealand is led by a prime minister. An elected parliament makes the country's laws. The capital, Wellington, is located at the southern tip of North Island.

Culture Like Australia, most of New Zealand's 3.8 million people are of European ancestry. A growing number of ethnic Asians also live in the country. The Maori make up nearly 10 percent of the population. People from other Pacific islands have also come to New Zealand.

Most New Zealanders speak English. Some Maori also speak the Maori language. Most New Zealanders also are Christian. Sports, particularly rugby, are popular.

Maori culture has not disappeared. Traditional art, music, and dance remain important in Maori culture. Many Maori weddings, funerals, and other special events still are held in traditional carved houses. The Maori call these meetinghouses *whare whakairo*. Many meetinghouses are beautifully carved and decorated.

✓ **READING CHECK:** *Human Systems* How have conflict and cooperation affected the history of New Zealand?

New Zealand Today

Today about 75 percent of New Zealanders, including most Maori, live on North Island. Most of the country's industries and agriculture are also located there.

Cities About 80 percent of New Zealanders live in urban areas. The country's largest city and seaport, Auckland, is located in the northern part of North Island. Christchurch is South Island's largest city.

Economy New Zealand is a rich, modern country with a market economy. Its mild, moist climate helped make agriculture an important part of the economy. The country is a major producer of wool, meat, dairy products, wheat, kiwifruit, and apples.

New Zealand has become more industrialized in recent years. Factories turn out processed food, wood, paper products, clothing, and machinery. Banking, insurance, and tourism are also important industries. Australia, the United States, Japan, and the United Kingdom are the country's main trade partners.

✓ **READING CHECK:** *Places and Regions* What are some of New Zealand's cities, and what is its economy like?

Cable cars provide transportation for residents and visitors in Wellington.

New Zealand

COUNTRY	POPULATION/ GROWTH RATE	LIFE EXPECTANCY	LITERACY RATE	PER CAPITA GDP
New Zealand	3,864,129 1.1%	75, male 81, female	99%	$17,700
United States	281,421,906 0.9%	74, male 80, female	97%	$36,200

Sources: Central Intelligence Agency, *The World Factbook 2001;* U.S. Census Bureau

Interpreting the Chart How does New Zealand's life expectancy compare to that of the United States?

Section Review 2

Define and explain: kiwi

Working with Sketch Maps On the map you created in Section 1, label the Tasman Sea, South Island, North Island, Southern Alps, Wellington, Auckland, and Christchurch. In a box in the margin, identify New Zealand's capital and the country's largest city.

Reading for the Main Idea

1. *Human Systems* From where did the ancestors of the Maori come?

2. *Human Systems* Describe New Zealand's economy. How has it changed in recent years?

go. hrw .com **Homework Practice Online** Keyword: SG3 HP32

Critical Thinking

3. **Contrasting** How is the physical geography of North Island different from that of South Island? Describe the physical geography of each island.

4. **Drawing Inferences and Conclusions** Why do you think most New Zealanders live on North Island?

Organizing What You Know

5. **Summarizing** Copy the following graphic organizer. Use it to list the climates, plants and animals, and resources of New Zealand.

Climates	Plants and Animals	Resources

Reviewing What You Know

Building Vocabulary

On a separate sheet of paper, write sentences to define each of the following words.

1. artesian wells
2. coral reef
3. endemic species
4. marsupials
5. outback
6. rugby
7. bush
8. kiwi

Reviewing the Main Ideas

1. (Places and Regions) What are the three main land-form regions of Australia?

2. (Places and Regions) What are the climates of the interior and the "edges" of Australia like?

3. (Human Systems) When did Europeans begin to settle in Australia and New Zealand?

4. (Places and Regions) What native peoples lived in Australia and New Zealand before the arrival of Europeans?

5. (Places and Regions) Australia and New Zealand are the world's two top producers of what agricultural product?

Understanding Environment and Society

Ranching

Create a presentation on ranching in Australia and New Zealand. In preparing your presentation, you may want to consider the following:

• How ranching contributes to the economies of the two countries.

• The geographic factors that have helped make ranching productive there.

• How ranching has affected the environment and culture of the two countries.

Thinking Critically

1. **Drawing Inferences and Conclusions** Why do you think the Great Barrier Reef would interest tourists?

2. **Drawing Inferences and Conclusions** Why do you think Australia's interior is lightly populated?

3. **Finding the Main Idea** How have humans changed the natural environments of Australia and New Zealand since the arrival of Europeans?

4. **Contrasting** How is New Zealand's climate different from Australia's? Identify the main climates in each country.

5. **Analyzing Information** What role have the arts played in Australian society?

Map ACTIVITY

On a separate sheet of paper, match the letters on the map with their correct labels.

Central Lowlands

Western Plateau

Tasmania

Great Barrier Reef

Sydney

Melbourne

Perth

Auckland

Mental Mapping Skills ACTIVITY

On a separate sheet of paper, draw a map of Australia and New Zealand. Make a key for your map and label the following:

Darling River

Eastern Highlands

Great Dividing Range

Murray River

North Island

Southern Alps

South Island

Tasman Sea

WRITING ACTIVITY

Imagine that you are a European journalist in the late 1700s writing about the peoples and unique plants and animals in Australia and New Zealand. Write two paragraphs describing those peoples and endemic species. Include details that might surprise your European readers. Be sure to use standard grammar, spelling, sentence structure, and punctuation.

Alternative Assessment

Portfolio ACTIVITY

Learning About Your Local Geography

Individual Project Make a poster about plants and animals that are common in your area, including those that are endemic species and those that have been brought to the area from elsewhere.

🖻 **internet** connect

Internet Activity: go.hrw.com
KEYWORD: SG3 GT31

Choose a topic to explore about Australia and New Zealand:

• Explore the Great Barrier Reef.
• Learn about the Aborigines of Australia.
• Tour New Zealand.

CHAPTER 33

The Pacific Islands and Antarctica

In this chapter we will study the Pacific islands and Antarctica, two very different regions.

My name is Jean Vanessa, and I am 13 years old. I live in Vabukori, a village in Port Moresby, the capital of Papua New Guinea. My mother is a journalist. My grandmother bakes our bread in a drum oven. Sometimes we sell the bread.

My house is built on stilts. It is near the village square where we have meetings and play sports. After breakfast, I take a bus to Port Moresby Grammar School. I make my own sandwiches to take for lunch.

In my society, when you are an eldest child and a girl, and if you have younger brothers and sisters, you are your mother's helper. You have to learn to cook, clean, and take care of younger children.

My favorite holidays are Christmas and New Year's. We celebrate with feasting and singing. The villagers are divided into two groups. On Christmas Day one group cooks for the other group. They sing prophet songs about Bible stories from dawn to dusk. On New Year's Day the groups exchange roles.

Daba namona!

◀ Translation: Good morning.

Section 1 Physical Geography

Read to Discover

1. What are the physical features and resources of the Pacific Islands?
2. What are the physical features and resources of Antarctica?

Define

ice shelf
icebergs
polar desert
krill

Locate

Melanesia
Micronesia
Polynesia
Tahiti
New Guinea
Papua New Guinea
Marshall Islands

New Caledonia
Transantarctic Mountains
Vinson Massif
Antarctic Peninsula

WHY IT MATTERS

Many Pacific Islands are formed by coral atolls—rings of small islands on a coral reef. Use **CNN fyi.com** or other **current events** sources to find out what environmental problems threaten coral atolls. Record your findings in your journal.

A tropical fish from near Fiji

The Formation of an Atoll

A A coral reef forms along the edges of a volcanic island.

B As the island sinks into the ocean, the reef continues to grow upward. It forms a barrier reef.

C When the island is completely underwater, the reef forms an atoll. In the middle of the ring of islands is a lagoon.

D A coral polyp builds a limestone skeleton that bonds it to a reef. When the coral polyp dies, it leaves behind its skeleton. The reef is made up of the skeletons of many dead coral polyps.

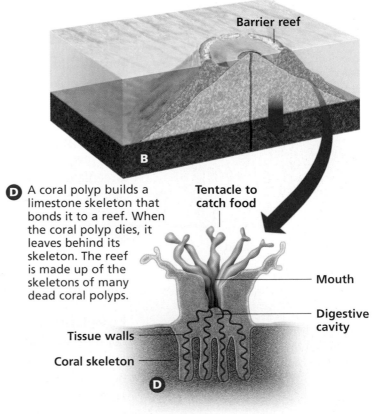

Tentacle to catch food
Mouth
Digestive cavity
Tissue walls
Coral skeleton

The airport on the left supports a healthy tourism industry in Bora-Bora, French Polynesia.

The Pacific Islands

The Pacific Ocean covers more than one third of Earth's surface. East of Indonesia and the Philippines are thousands of large and small islands. These islands are divided into three regions: Melanesia, Micronesia, and Polynesia. These regions have high and low islands. Now we will look at these islands, their climates, and their resources.

High Islands There are two kinds of high islands: oceanic and continental. Oceanic high islands were formed by volcanoes rising from the sea floor. The Polynesian islands of Tahiti and Hawaii are examples of oceanic high islands. Many continental high islands also have volcanoes. However, these large islands were formed from continental rock. They lie on Australia's continental shelf. New Guinea, which is in Melanesia, is a continental high island.

New Guinea is the world's second-largest island. Only Greenland is larger. A long mountain chain stretches across the central part of New Guinea. The range's highest mountain lies in the western half of the island. It reaches an elevation of 16,535 feet (5,040 m). The western part of New Guinea is called Irian Jaya and is part of Indonesia. Papua New Guinea occupies the eastern half of the island.

Low Islands Most of the low islands are made of coral. They barely rise above sea level. Many are atolls. For example, the Marshall Islands include two parallel chains of coral atolls. The two chains are about 800 miles (1,287 km) long. The highest point

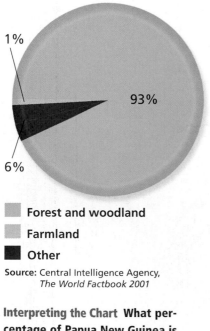

A Forested Country:
Land Use in Papua New Guinea

1%

93%

6%

- Forest and woodland
- Farmland
- Other

Source: Central Intelligence Agency, *The World Factbook 2001*

Interpreting the Chart What percentage of Papua New Guinea is farmland?

is just 33 feet (10 m) above sea level. Measured from the ground to their roofs, many buildings in your town are probably higher!

Climates and Plants Most of the Pacific Islands lie in the tropics and have a humid tropical climate. The temperatures are warm, and rain is common all year. New Guinea's central highland regions are cooler. Rainfall there is heavy, particularly on the southern slopes of the highlands. In some years more than 300 inches (762 cm) of rain fall there. Some islands, such as New Caledonia, have a tropical savanna climate. Rain there falls mostly in the summer.

The low islands have thin soils. These islands support few trees other than the coconut palm. However, the high islands have dense tropical rain forests. In fact, Papua New Guinea is one of the world's most densely forested countries. (See the pie graph on the previous page.) Many peoples living in the forests and rugged mountains of the central highlands were isolated for centuries.

Resources The islands' natural beauty and pleasant climates attract many tourists. In addition, the high islands have freshwater, good soils, and forest resources. Continental high islands also have many minerals. For example, New Guinea has copper, gold, silver, and oil. However, mining these resources is difficult in the rugged highlands and dense tropical forests.

Low islands have few resources. There is little freshwater, and thin soils limit farming. Partly because of this, low islands have smaller populations than high islands. Coconut palms and the sea are important sources of food.

✓ **READING CHECK:** *Places and Regions* What are the physical features and resources of the Pacific Islands?

Miners search for gold along a river in Papua New Guinea. They gently wash river water over pans to separate gold particles from less dense sand.

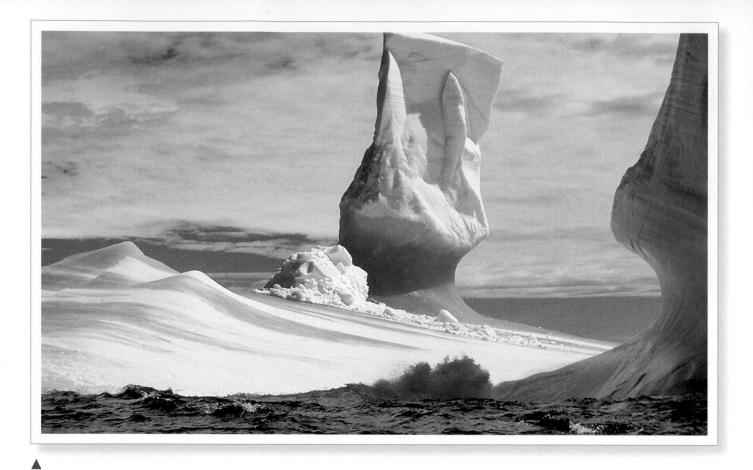

Huge icebergs like this one are found in the ocean waters around Antarctica. Icebergs are most numerous in the spring and summer. The warmer weather causes more ice to break away from ice sheets and glaciers.

Interpreting the Visual Record What forces do you think shaped this iceberg?

Antarctica

In the southernmost part of the world is the continent of Antarctica. This frozen land is very different from the tropical Pacific Islands.

The Land Antarctica is larger than the United States and Mexico combined. Ice covers about 98 percent of Antarctica's 5.4 million square miles (14 mil sq km). This ice sheet contains more than 90 percent of the world's ice. On average the ice sheet is more than one mile (1.6 km) thick.

The Transantarctic Mountains divide the continent into East Antarctica and West Antarctica. Antarctica's highest mountain peak is Vinson Massif. It rises to 16,864 feet (5,140 m). The continent also includes a few dry coastal valleys and the Antarctic Peninsula. (See the map of Antarctica in Focus On Environment at the end of this chapter.)

The weight of Antarctica's ice sheet causes the ice to flow slowly off the continent. When the ice reaches the coast, it forms a ledge over the water. This ledge is called an **ice shelf**. Sometimes huge chunks of ice, called **icebergs**, break away and drift into the ocean. Some of these icebergs are larger than the state of Rhode Island.

Climate and Wildlife Antarctica is the planet's coldest, driest, highest, and windiest continent. During the Southern Hemisphere's winter, the continent is hidden from the Sun. It remains in total darkness. During Antarctica's short summer, the Sun never sets.

Antarctica's temperatures can drop below -120°F (-84°C). Less precipitation falls in this **polar desert** than in the Sahara in Africa. A polar desert is a high-latitude region that receives little precipitation. However, there is almost no evaporation or melting of ice. As a result, Antarctica's ice has built up over thousands of years.

The continent's warmest temperatures are found on the Antarctic Peninsula, which has a tundra climate. In January, during Antarctica's summer, temperatures on the coast average just below freezing.

Only tundra plant life survives in the rare ice-free areas. A few insects are the frozen land's only land animals. Antarctica has never had a permanent human population. Marine animals live in the icy waters around the continent. These animals include penguins, seals, and whales. They depend on tiny shrimplike creatures called **krill** for food.

Resources Antarctica has many mineral resources, including iron ore, gold, copper, and coal. However, there is debate over whether these resources should be mined. Some people worry that mining would harm the continent's environment. Others question whether mining in Antarctica would even be worthwhile for businesses.

✓ **READING CHECK:** *Places and Regions* What are the physical features and resources of Antarctica?

The emperor penguin is one of the most common marine animals found in Antarctica. Penguins are flightless birds and are awkward on land. However, they are very good swimmers and are able to live in the icy climate.

◄

▲
Krill can be found in huge swarms in the waters around Antarctica.

Section Review 1

go.hrw.com
Homework Practice Online
Keyword: SG3 HP33

Define and explain: ice shelf, icebergs, polar desert, krill

Working with Sketch Maps On maps of the Pacific Islands and Antarctica that you draw or that your teacher provides, label the following: Melanesia, Micronesia, Polynesia, Tahiti, New Guinea, Papua New Guinea, Marshall Islands, New Caledonia, Transantarctic Mountains, Vinson Massif, and Antarctic Peninsula.

Reading for the Main Idea

1. *Places and Regions* What kinds of islands are found in the Pacific? How were they formed?

2. *Places and Regions* What animal life is found in Antarctica?

3. *Places and Regions* Which of the Pacific Islands is the second-largest island in the world?

Critical Thinking

4. **Making Generalizations and Predictions** What might happen if people were to begin mining Antarctica's mineral deposits on a large scale?

Organizing What You Know

5. **Summarizing** Copy the following graphic organizer. Use it to list physical features, climates, and resources of the Pacific Islands and Antarctica.

	Pacific Islands	Antarctica
Physical features		
Climates		
Resources		

Section 2 The Pacific Islands

Read to Discover

1. What is the history of the Pacific Islands?
2. What are the people and culture of the Pacific Islands like?
3. What are some challenges that Pacific Islanders face today?

Define

trust territories
Exclusive Economic Zones

Locate

Guam
Northern Mariana Islands
Wake Island
French Polynesia

A tiki, a religious object from Polynesia

WHY IT MATTERS

The physical beauty of the Pacific Islands has made many into popular vacation destinations. However, many still struggle economically. Use CNNfyi.com or other current events sources to learn about the economic challenges facing Pacific Island countries. Record your findings in your journal.

This map of the South Pacific was made by a European cartographer in 1798.

Interpreting the Visual Record
Compare this map to the unit map. How accurate was this 1798 map?

History

Scholars believe that people began settling the Pacific Islands at least 40,000 years ago. Most early settlers came from Southeast Asia. The large islands of Melanesia were the first islands in the region settled. Over time, people moved to the islands of Micronesia and Polynesia.

Europeans in the Pacific In the early 1500s Ferdinand Magellan became the first European to explore the Pacific. In the late 1700s British captain James Cook explored the region. He visited all the main island regions of the Pacific. By the late 1800s European countries controlled most of the Pacific Islands. These European countries included France, Germany, the Netherlands, Spain, and the United Kingdom.

Modern History The Pacific Islands were battlegrounds during several wars in the colonial era. For example, the Spanish-American War of 1898 cost Spain the Philippines and Guam. They became U.S. territories after the war. Spain then sold other island territories to Germany. After World War I ended in 1918, Japan took over Germany's territories in the Pacific.

Japan conquered many other islands in World War II. The United States and its allies eventually won them back and defeated Japan. The United Nations then made some islands **trust territories**. Trust territories are areas placed under the temporary control of another country. When the territory later sets up its own government, it gains independence. U.S. trust territories included much of Micronesia.

Most of the island countries won independence in the last half of the 1900s. Australia, France, New Zealand, the United Kingdom, and the United States still have Pacific territories. U.S. territories include the Northern Mariana Islands, Guam, and Wake Island.

✓ **READING CHECK:** *Places and Regions* What are some events in the history of the Pacific Islands?

Culture

About 7 million people live in Melanesia, Micronesia, and Polynesia today. Check the unit map as we look more closely at each region and its people.

Melanesia Melanesia stretches from New Guinea to Fiji. It is the most populous of the three Pacific Island regions. Papua New Guinea and Fiji have the largest populations. Nearly two thirds of all Pacific Islanders live in Papua New Guinea.

Most Melanesians live in rural areas. Many homes in Melanesia and the other regions are made of timber and thatch, or straw. Papua New Guinea's capital, Port Moresby, is Melanesia's largest city. Nearly 200,000 people live there.

Melanesia's population includes ethnic Europeans and Asians, particularly Indians and Chinese. Many ethnic Asians are descended from people brought to the islands to work on colonial plantations. In Fiji, Indians make up nearly half of the population.

Either English or French is the official language on nearly all of the islands. This is a reflection of the region's colonial history. However, hundreds of local languages also are spoken there. In fact, about 700 languages are spoken in New Guinea alone. Many Papua New Guineans live in rugged, forested areas. They have had little contact with people from other areas. These isolated peoples developed their own languages.

Europeans brought Christianity to Melanesia and the other island regions. Today, most Pacific Islanders are Christian. However, some Melanesians still practice traditional local religions.

Micronesia and Polynesia Micronesia includes more than 2,000 tiny islands north of Melanesia. It stretches from Palau in the west to Kiribati in the east. Polynesia is the largest Pacific region. Its

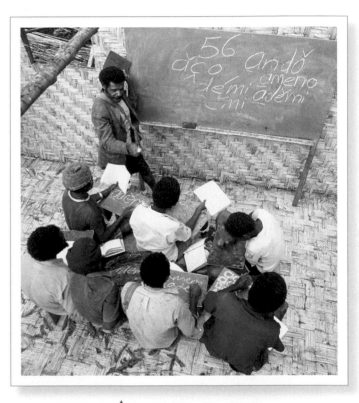

▲
Students learn the day's lessons at a school in Papua New Guinea. Papua New Guinea's government has struggled to make education available for all students. Many countries in Micronesia and Polynesia offer schooling for students through high school.

CONNECTING TO *Technology*

Pacific Boatbuilders

Long before Europeans sailed into the region, Pacific Islanders were sailing over the open sea. Pacific peoples—particularly Polynesians—regularly sailed hundreds of miles from one island to the other. This seafaring tradition depended not just on sailing skills. It also depended on the craft of boatbuilding.

The best boats were built on the Fijian island of Kabara. This island has the finest forests of *vesi* trees in the South Pacific. The *vesi* tree grows tall and straight. Its trunk is heavy and tough enough to hold up to the stresses of sea travel.

Looking out to sea from Bora-Bora

The people of Kabara built different types of boats. Some were simple canoes. Some were large boats with two hulls, or frames. The largest were as long as 100 feet (30 m). These boats were fast and could carry as many as 300 people. They were highly prized for both trading and warfare.

In recent decades the ancient craft of boatbuilding has slowly disappeared from the region. A few older people remember the traditional skills—cutting and joining the wood and weaving the sails. Many islanders worry that unless more people learn the craft, traditional boatbuilding may be forgotten.

Understanding What You Read

1. Why were good boats needed by the Pacific Islanders?
2. What has happened to the craft of boatbuilding in recent years?

corners at New Zealand, Hawaii, and Easter Island form a huge triangle.

The populations of most Micronesian and Polynesian islands are much smaller than those of Melanesia. However, towns on these small islands can be very crowded. Micronesia is the most urban of the Pacific Island regions. Most Polynesians live in rural areas.

As in Melanesia, ethnic Europeans and Asians live in Micronesia and Polynesia. Most people in these regions are Christian and speak either English or French. Some speak local languages or Japanese.

✓ **READING CHECK:** **Human Systems** What are some characteristics of the people and cultures of Melanesia, Micronesia, and Polynesia?

The Pacific Islands Today

Many people imagine sunny beaches and tourists when they think of the Pacific Islands today. The islands do attract many tourists. For example, Tahiti, in French Polynesia, is a popular vacation spot. Many vacationers from South Korea and Japan enjoy visiting Guam, in Micronesia. Despite the region's healthy tourism industry, however, the Pacific countries face important challenges.

Economy The Pacific Islands are trying to build stronger economies. Tourism, agriculture, and fishing are already important there. Some countries, particularly Papua New Guinea, export valuable minerals and forest products.

Each Pacific country claims control of the fishing and seabed minerals around its islands. The 200-nautical-mile (370 km) zones they claim are called **Exclusive Economic Zones** (EEZs). Most of the world's countries also claim EEZs. A country must pay fees to fish or mine in another country's EEZ.

Natural resources should help the island economies grow. However, many Pacific countries import more products from abroad than they export. Many countries rely on the United Nations, the European Union, Great Britain, Australia, and Japan for economic aid.

Environment Many Pacific islanders are concerned about their region's environment. Many have been angered by nuclear weapons tests conducted in the region by other countries. The United States held such tests in the islands from the 1940s to the 1960s. Radiation left some islands unsafe for people for many years. France held nuclear tests in the region until the mid-1990s.

A fisher casts his net along the coast of New Caledonia.

Pacific Islands

Country	Population/ Growth Rate	Life Expectancy	Literacy Rate	Per Capita GDP
Fiji	844,330 1.4%	66, male 71, female	92%	$7,300
Kiribati	94,149 2.3%	57, male 63, female	Not available	$850
Marshall Islands	70,822 3.9%	64, male 68, female	93%	$1,670
Micronesia, Federated States of	134,597 Not available	Not available	89%	$2,000
Nauru	12,088 2.0%	58, male 65, female	Not available	$5,000
Palau	19,092 1.7%	66, male 72, female	92%	$7,100
Papua New Guinea	5,049,055 2.4%	61, male 66, female	72%	$2,500
Samoa	179,058 −0.2%	67, male 72, female	97%	$3,200
Solomon Islands	480,442 3.0%	69, male 74, female	Not available	$2,000
Tonga	104,227 1.8%	66, male 71, female	99%	$2,200
Tuvalu	10,991 1.4%	65, male 69, female	Not available	$1,100
Vanuatu	192,910 1.7%	60, male 62, female	53%	$1,300
United States	281,421,906 0.9%	74, male 80, female	97%	$36,200

Sources: Central Intelligence Agency, *The World Factbook 2001*; U.S. Census Bureau

Interpreting the Chart What is the literacy rate like in most of the Pacific Islands?

This Fijian chief's home has many traditional handicrafts. Fiji's Great Council of Chiefs has influence in the country's political system and culture.

Interpreting the Visual Record What elements of this photograph show influences of outside cultures?

Some people who live on islands still controlled by foreign countries want independence, which has led to outbreaks of violence. This happened in the 1980s in the French territory of New Caledonia. France has agreed to give New Caledonians more control over their local government.

Culture Many Pacific Islanders are also concerned about the loss of traditional customs and beliefs. Modern travel and communications have introduced influences from other regions. Islanders worry about the cultural effects of tourism, television, processed food, and alcohol.

✔ **READING CHECK:** (*Human Systems*) What are some challenges Pacific Islanders face today?

Section Review 2

go.hrw.com
Homework Practice Online
Keyword: SG3 HP33

Define and explain: trust territories, Exclusive Economic Zones

Working with Sketch Maps On the map of the Pacific islands that you created in Section 1, label the region's countries. Then label the territories of Guam, Northern Mariana Islands, Wake Island, and French Polynesia.

Reading for the Main Idea

1. (*Human Systems*) From where did the Pacific Islands' first settlers come? Which Pacific Island region was settled first?

2. (*Human Systems*) What colonial powers once controlled most of the Pacific islands?

Critical Thinking

3. **Finding the Main Idea** In what ways did Europeans influence the islands' cultures?

4. **Finding the Main Idea** What are some of the challenges facing Pacific Islanders today?

Organizing What You Know

5. **Sequencing** Use this time line to explain important people and events in the region's history.

1500   2000

Section 3

Antarctica

Read to Discover

1. How was Antarctica explored?
2. What can research in Antarctica tell us about our planet?
3. What problems threaten Antarctica's environment?

Define

antifreeze

Locate

South Pole
Ross Ice Shelf

WHY IT MATTERS

Antarctica offers many opportunities for scientific research. Use **CNNfyi.com** or other **current events** sources to find out what current scientific investigations are taking place in Antarctica. Record your findings in your journal.

A sign near Scott Base in Antarctica

Early Explorers

Can you imagine a time when a large continent like Antarctica was a complete mystery? Today, orbiting satellites give us views of all of Earth's surface. Jet airliners and modern ships take people to all points on the globe. However, all of this has become possible only in the last century. For a long time, stormy ocean waters hid Antarctica from explorers. In the 1770s British explorer James Cook sighted icebergs in the waters around Antarctica. These icebergs suggested the existence of the vast, icy continent.

Other explorers followed. Some died in Antarctica's dangerous conditions while attempting to reach the South Pole and return. The huts of famous Antarctic explorers are still scattered across the continent. The first human expedition reached the South Pole in 1911.

Some countries have claimed parts of Antarctica. These countries and others agreed in 1959 to preserve the continent "for science and peace." The Antarctic Treaty of 1959 prevented more claims to the continent. It banned military activity there and set aside the whole continent for research.

✓ **READING CHECK:**

Environment and Society How did the physical environment affect early efforts to explore Antarctica?

British explorer Robert Scott and his team reached the South Pole in January 1912. Norwegian Roald Amundsen's team had beaten them to the spot one month earlier. Scott and the rest of his team died trying to return from the Pole.

▼

The Pacific Islands and Antarctica • 727

Do you remember what you learned about ozone? See Chapter 2 to review.

Researchers are conducting experiments in icy waters off the coast of Antarctica.

Interpreting the Visual Record **What might these underwater researchers be trying to learn?**

Research in Antarctica

Today, researchers are the only people who live in Antarctica. They live in a number of bases or stations. U.S. stations include Palmer, on the Antarctic Peninsula, and McMurdo, on the Ross Ice Shelf. The United States also maintains a base at the South Pole. Researchers at these bases are looking for clues to Earth's past and future.

Air Pollution The researchers have made important discoveries. For example, some have studied gases trapped in old Antarctic ice. They have compared these gases with gases in Earth's atmosphere today. Their studies have shown that carbon dioxide levels in the air have risen over time. Some scientists believe high levels of carbon dioxide are responsible for global warming.

Scientists are also looking for evidence that air pollution is damaging Earth's ozone layer. The ozone layer protects living things from the harmful effects of the Sun's ultraviolet rays. Scientists have found a thinning in the ozone layer above Antarctica.

Life Other research helps us understand mysteries of life on Earth. For example, researchers have studied a kind of fish that produces a natural **antifreeze**. Antifreeze is a substance added to liquid to keep the liquid from turning to ice. Natural antifreeze in their blood protects the fish in the icy waters around Antarctica. These fish may help us understand how some animals adapt to harsh environments.

✓ **READING CHECK:**   *Environment and Society*   What can research in Antarctica tell us about our planet?

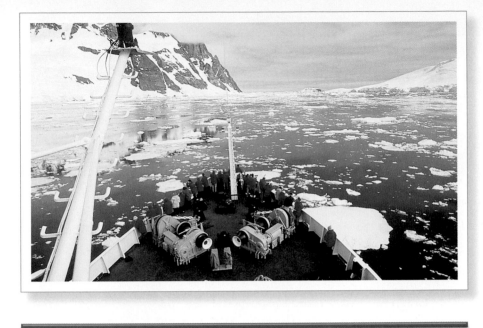

Cruise ships allow tourists to witness the icy beauty of Antarctica. About 10,000 tourists visited Antarctica annually during summer months in the late 1990s. A typical tourist trip lasts about two weeks. The only other economic activity in the region involves offshore fishing. **Interpreting the Visual Record What potential hazards do you see for ships?**

Environmental Threats

Antarctica's environment is an excellent place for research. This is because humans have disturbed little of the continent. That is changing, however. As you have read, there is already debate about whether to allow mining in Antarctica. In addition, tourists and even researchers have left behind trash, polluting the local environment. Oil spills have also caused problems.

Some people fear that mining Antarctica's resources will result in other spills and problems. To prevent this, a new international agreement was reached in 1991. This agreement forbids most activities in Antarctica that do not have a scientific purpose. It bans mining and drilling and limits tourism.

✓ **READING CHECK:** *Environment and Society* What are some of the problems threatening Antarctica's environment?

Some of Antarctica's rocks contain bacteria and other tiny forms of life. They live in small spaces that can only be seen with a microscope. These tough survivors may be thousands of years old!

 Section Review 3

Homework Practice Online
Keyword: SG3 HP33

Define and explain: antifreeze

Working with Sketch Maps On the map of Antarctica you created in Section 1, label the South Pole and Ross Ice Shelf.

Reading for the Main Idea

1. *Human Systems* Who were the first Antarctic explorers to reach the South Pole, and when did they do so?

2. *Environment and Society* What did the 1959 Antarctic Treaty do? Why do you think this kind of agreement has not been made about other places on Earth?

Critical Thinking

3. **Making Generalizations and Predictions** How might future scientific discoveries in Antarctica affect the world?

4. **Finding the Main Idea** Why did many countries in 1991 agree to ban mining and to limit tourism in Antarctica?

Organizing What You Know

5. **Summarizing** Copy the following graphic organizer. Use it to describe research in Antarctica.

Research	Purpose

The Pacific Islands and Antarctica • 729

Building Vocabulary

On a separate sheet of paper, write sentences to define each of the following words.

1. ice shelf
2. icebergs
3. polar desert
4. krill
5. trust territories
6. Exclusive Economic Zones
7. antifreeze

Reviewing the Main Ideas

1. *(Places and Regions)* What are the three Pacific Island regions? How was the United States linked to these regions after World War II?

2. *(Environment and Society)* What agreements have been made to protect Antarctica's environment?

3. *(Physical Systems)* Why is Antarctica covered in ice and snow even though it receives little precipitation?

4. *(Places and Regions)* Where are dense tropical forests found in the Pacific Islands? What trees grow on low islands?

5. *(Human Systems)* When did the first European explore the Pacific? Who was he?

Understanding Environment and Society

Resources

Create a presentation about natural resources in Antarctica. Include a thematic map showing Antarctica's resources. In preparing your presentation consider the following:

- Why some countries might want to mine them.
- What threats mining might create for the continent's environment.

Thinking Critically

1. **Drawing Inferences and Conclusions** Why do you think the Pacific Island countries want to keep their 200-nautical-mile Exclusive Economic Zones?

2. **Finding the Main Idea** How have Europeans influenced the languages and religions of the Pacific Islands?

3. **Making Generalizations and Predictions** How might Pacific Islanders work to preserve their traditional cultures?

4. **Drawing Inferences and Conclusions** Look at the map of Antarctica in the Focus On Environment feature. Why do you think researchers chose the specific locations of the U.S. stations?

5. **Making Generalizations and Predictions** Why do you think protecting Antarctica's environment is important for the research done there?

Map ACTIVITY

On a separate sheet of paper, match the letters on the map with their correct labels.

Papua New Guinea

Fiji

Marshall Islands

New Caledonia

Guam

French Polynesia

Palau

Solomon Islands

Mental Mapping Skills ACTIVITY

On two separate sheets of paper, draw freehand maps of the Pacific Islands and of Antarctica. Make keys for your maps and label the following:

Antarctica

Antarctic Peninsula

Melanesia

Micronesia

Polynesia

Transantarctic Mountains

WRITING ACTIVITY

Imagine that you are one of the first explorers trying to reach the South Pole. Write journal entries in which you describe what you have seen. Describe the conditions you have endured and the strategies you have used to survive. Use your textbook, the library, and the Internet to help you write your journal entries. Be sure to use standard grammar, spelling, sentence structure, and punctuation.

Alternative Assessment

Portfolio ACTIVITY

Learning About Your Local Geography

Cooperative Project Tourism is important to many Pacific islands. What is a tourist attraction in your community or region? Working with a group, create a brochure to attract visitors to your area.

internet connect

Internet Activity: go.hrw.com
KEYWORD: SG3 GT33

Choose a topic to explore about the Pacific Islands and Antarctica.
- Tour the Pacific Islands.
- Explore Antarctica.
- Learn about native traditions.

Preserving Antarctica

In 1912 a search party in Antarctica found the body of explorer Robert Falcon Scott. Scott had written in his diary, "Great God, what an awful place this is." He had dreamed of being the first person to reach the South Pole. However, when Scott's party arrived they found the tent and flag of Norwegian explorer Roald Amundsen. Amundsen had arrived five weeks earlier.

Almost a century later, Antarctica's modern-day explorers are research scientists. Antarctica has provided a location for international scientific research and cooperation.

A Scientific Laboratory

A wasteland to many, Antarctica is a scientific laboratory to some. Studying the continent helps scientists understand our planet. For example, the icy waters around Antarctica move north, cooling warmer waters. This movement affects ocean currents, clouds, and weather patterns. The world's climate is also affected by Antarctic sea ice. The ice acts as a shield. It keeps Earth cool by reflecting the Sun's heat energy.

Antarctic ice also provides information about the past. Buried deep within the ice are gas bubbles that are a record of Earth's air. Scientists have compared atmospheric gases trapped in Antarctic ice with atmospheric gases of today. They learned that the use of fossil fuels has raised the amount of carbon dioxide in the air. Carbon dioxide levels are now the highest in human history.

Eyes on Antarctica

Antarctica is not owned by any single country. Some countries claim parts of Antarctica, but these claims are not recognized. In 1959 the Antarctic Treaty established Antarctica as a continent for

How Antarctic Ice Affects Climate

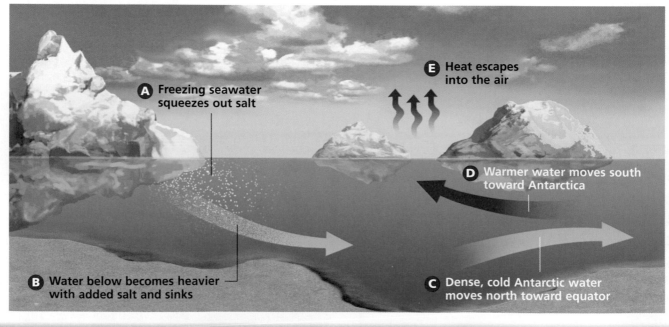

A Freezing seawater squeezes out salt

E Heat escapes into the air

D Warmer water moves south toward Antarctica

B Water below becomes heavier with added salt and sinks

C Dense, cold Antarctic water moves north toward equator science and peace. The treaty was originally signed by 12 countries and was later agreed to by more than a dozen others. The Antarctic Treaty banned military activity in the region. It also made Antarctica a nuclear-free zone and encouraged scientific research.

However, the Antarctic Treaty did not cover mining rights on the continent. When Antarctica's mineral riches were discovered, some countries wanted rights to this new source of wealth. Geographers, scientists, and environmentalists also took notice. They feared that if mining took place, Antarctica's environment would suffer. In particular, they feared that a practical method of obtaining the offshore oil would be found. Antarctica's coastline and marine life could then be threatened by oil spills.

At the same time, evidence of environmental neglect at some of Antarctica's research stations appeared. Environmentalists voiced concern about scientists' careless disposal of trash and sewage. A U.S. Coast Guard captain who worked on icebreakers described pollution at McMurdo, a U.S. research station. "Trash was just rolled down the hill. . . . One of the jobs of the icebreakers was to break up the ice where the

trash was and push it out to sea." In 1989, an Argentine ship ran aground in Antarctica, spilling thousands of gallons of oil. As a result, environmental concerns for the region increased.

Protecting Antarctica

In 1991, the countries that had signed the original Antarctic Treaty signed a new agreement called the Madrid Protocol. It forbids most activities on Antarctica that do not have a scientific purpose. It also bans mining and drilling and sets limits on tourism. Pollution concerns are addressed specifically.

In 50 years the agreement can be changed if enough of the signing countries agree. Then it becomes the responsibility of another generation to preserve Antarctica.

Antarctica

Map of Antarctica showing research stations, ice cap, and ice shelf

LEGEND
- ■ Research stations
- Ice cap
- Ice shelf

To understand the relative location of Antarctica as well as the distance separating it from the Pacific countries, see the Atlas map in the front of this textbook.

▲ Many countries have set up research stations and bases in Antarctica, such as Argentina's Camara Base on Half Moon Island.

Your Turn

Imagine you are helping to develop the Madrid Protocol.

1. Write a short description of the provisions you want included in the treaty.

2. Be sure to explain why you think these provisions are important.

Geo SKILLS

Building Skills for Life: Making Decisions About the Future

What do you think your community will be like 10 years from now? Will there be new movie theaters, neighborhoods, and shops? Will some old ones be gone? Will there be enough schools? What will traffic be like? These are the kinds of questions to ask if you are planning for the future. People need to plan ahead. Often, this requires the collection and analysis of geographic information, such as population patterns, growth rates, income levels, and other data.

▲ Map used to plan for the 2000 Olympics in Australia

THE SKILL

PRACTICING

1. **Identify a situation that requires a decision.** Suppose you were asked by your local planning commission to select the best route for a new highway. What information would you need?

2. **Gather information.** Use several resources to find information that might influence the building of a highway.

3. **Identify options.** Consider the many options you might give to a planning commission regarding a proposed highway. Be sure to record your possible options.

4. **Predict consequences.** Now take each option you came up with and consider what might be the outcome of each course of action. Ask yourself questions like, "How is this highway going to affect surrounding neighborhoods?"

5. **Take action to implement your decision.** Create a proposal for the planning commission. Explain why you chose your option and rejected others. Include maps, graphs, charts, models, or databases showing the information you collected.

HANDS on GEOGRAPHY

With nearly 4 million residents, Sydney is the biggest city in Australia. Like other large cities, Sydney is dealing with some environmental problems. The number of people and cars in Sydney is growing. As a result, the city's air pollution and traffic problems are getting worse. To protect Sydney's environment and quality of life, some residents are planning for the future.

One environmental group in Sydney has suggested building a network of trails and parks called greenways. These greenways could help relieve the city's traffic problems and reduce air pollution. Can you think of another way people in Sydney might plan for the future? These guidelines will help you get started.

1. Think of one way that residents of Sydney could plan for the future. For example, they could build an underground subway system. This plan might help reduce air pollution.

2. Create a short proposal for your plan. In your proposal, list some of the benefits that your plan would offer.

3. Create a map or drawing for your proposal. Maps and drawings help people imagine what your plan would look like.

4. Include a timetable with your proposal. How long would it take for your plan to become reality?

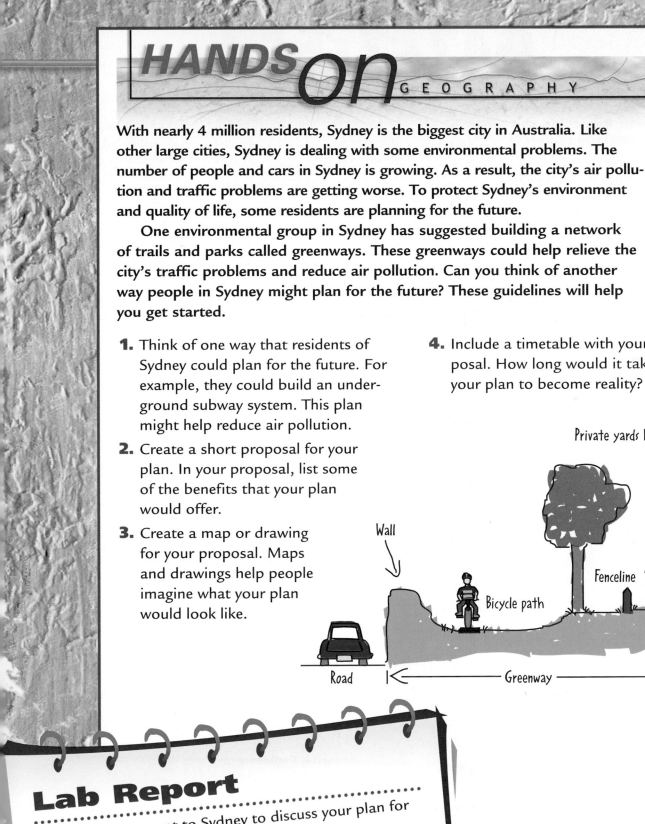

Private yards beyond

Wall

Bicycle path

Fenceline

Road

Greenway

Lab Report

1. Imagine you went to Sydney to discuss your plan for the future. Who might be interested in it?

2. How important do you think it would be for your plan to have public support?

3. Do you think your proposal would be a good idea for other cities too? why or why not?

GAZETTEER

A

Abu Dhabi (24°N 54°E) capital of the United Arab Emirates, 415

Abuja (ah-BOO-jah) (9°N 7°E) capital of Nigeria, 491

Acapulco (17°N 100°W) city on the southwestern coast of Mexico, 161

Accra (6°N 0°W) capital of Ghana, 491

Addis Ababa (9°N 39°E) capital of Ethiopia, 509

Adriatic Sea sea between Italy and the Balkan Peninsula, 319

Aegean (ee-JEE-uhn) **Sea** sea between Greece and Turkey, 261

Afghanistan landlocked country in central Asia, 415

Africa second-largest continent; surrounded by the Atlantic Ocean, Indian Ocean, and Mediterranean Sea, A2–A3

Ahaggar Mountains mountain range in southern Algeria, 471

Albania country in Eastern Europe on the Adriatic Sea, 319

Alberta province in Canada, 129

Aleutian Islands volcanic islands extending from Alaska into the Pacific Ocean, 107

Alexandria (31°N 30°E) city in northern Egypt, 471

Algeria country in North Africa located between Morocco and Libya, 471

Algiers (37°N 3°E) capital of Algeria, 471

Alps major mountain system in south-central Europe, 261

Altiplano broad, high plateau in Peru and Bolivia, 229

Amazon River major river in South America, 211

Amman (32°N 36°E) capital of Jordan, 435

Amsterdam (52°N 5°E) capital of the Netherlands, 279

Amu Dar'ya (uh-MOO duhr-YAH) river in Central Asia that drains into the Aral Sea, 387

Amur (ah-MOOHR) **River** river in northeast Asia forming part of the border between Russia and China, 351

Andes (AN-deez) great mountain range in South America, 211

Andorra European microstate in the Pyrenees mountains, A15

Andorra la Vella (43°N 2°E) capital of Andorra, A15

Angkor ancient capital of the Khmer Empire in Cambodia, 617

Angola country in central Africa, 525

Ankara (40°N 33°E) capital of Turkey, 435

Antananarivo (19°S 48°E) capital of Madagascar, 541

Antarctica continent around the South Pole, A22

Antarctic Circle line of latitude located at 66.5° south of the equator; parallel beyond which no sunlight shines on the June solstice (first day of winter in the Southern Hemisphere), A4–A5

Antarctic Peninsula peninsula stretching toward South America from Antarctica, 720

Antigua and Barbuda island country in the Caribbean, 179

Antwerp (51°N 4°E) major port city in Belgium 279

Apennines (A-puh-nynz) mountain range in Italy, 261

Apia (14°S 172°W) capital of Western Samoa, 694

Appalachian Mountains mountain system in eastern North America, 107

Arabian Peninsula peninsula in Southwest Asia between the Red Sea and Persian Gulf, 415

Arabian Sea sea between India and the Arabian Peninsula, 415

Aral (AR-uhl) **Sea** inland sea between Kazakhstan and Uzbekistan, 387

Arctic Circle line of latitude located at 66.5° north of the equator; the parallel beyond which no sunlight shines on the December solstice (first day of winter in the Northern Hemisphere), A4–A5

Arctic Ocean ocean north of the Arctic Circle; world's fourth-largest ocean, A2–A3

Argentina second-largest country in South America, 211

Armenia country in the Caucasus region of Asia; former Soviet republic, 373

Ashgabat (formerly Ashkhabad) (40°N 58°E) capital of Turkmenistan, 387

Asia world's largest continent; located between Europe and the Pacific Ocean, A3

Asmara (15°N 39°E) capital of Eritrea, 509

Astana (51°N 71°E) capital of Kazakhstan, 387

Astrakhan (46°N 48°E) old port city on the Volga River in Russia, 351

Asunción (25°S 58°W) capital of Paraguay, 211

Atacama Desert desert in northern Chile, 229

Athens (38°N 24°E) capital and largest city in Greece, 261

Atlanta (34°N 84°W) capital and largest city in the U.S. state of Georgia, 107

Atlantic Ocean ocean between the continents of North and South America and the continents of Europe and Africa; world's second-largest ocean, A2

Atlas Mountains African mountain range north of the Sahara, 471

Auckland (37°S 175°E) New Zealand's largest city and main seaport, 701

Aughrabies (oh-KRAH-bees) **Falls** waterfalls on the Orange River in South Africa, 541

Australia only country occupying an entire continent (also called Australia); located between the Indian Ocean and the Pacific Ocean, A3

Austria country in west-central Europe south of Germany, 279

Azerbaijan country in the Caucasus region of Asia; former Soviet republic, 373

Bab al-Mandab narrow strait that connects the Red Sea with the Indian Ocean, 509

Baghdad (33°N 44°E) capital of Iraq, 415

Bahamas island country in the Atlantic Ocean southeast of Florida, 179

Bahrain country on the Persian Gulf in Southwest Asia, 415

Baja California peninsula in northwestern Mexico, 161

Baku (40°N 50°E) capital of Azerbaijan, 373

Bali island in Indonesia east of Java, 617

Balkan Mountains mountain range that rises in Bulgaria, 319

Baltic Sea body of water east of the North Sea and Scandinavia, 299

Baltimore (39°N 77°W) city in Maryland on the western shore of Chesapeake Bay, 107

Bamako (13°N 8°W) capital of Mali, 491

Bandar Seri Begawan (5°N 115°E) capital of Brunei, 617

Bangkok (14°N 100°E) capital and largest city of Thailand, 617

Bangladesh country in South Asia, 669

Bangui (4°N 19°E) capital of the Central African Republic, 525

Banjul (13°N 17°W) capital of Gambia, 491

Barbados island country in the Caribbean, 179

Barcelona (41°N 2°E) Mediterranean port city and Spain's second-largest city, 261

Basel (48°N 8°E) city in northern Switzerland on the Rhine River, 279

Basseterre (17°N 63°W) capital of St. Kitts and Nevis, 179

Bay of Bengal body of water between India and the western coasts of Myanmar (Burma) and the Malay Peninsula, 651

Bay of Biscay body of water off the western coast of France and the northern coast of Spain, 279

Beijing (40°N 116°E) capital of China, 573

Beirut (34°N 36°E) capital of Lebanon, 435

Belarus country located north of Ukraine; former Soviet republic, 373

Belém (1°S 48°W) port city in northern Brazil, 211

Belfast (55°N 6°W) capital and largest city of Northern Ireland, 299

Belgium country between France and Germany in west-central Europe, 279

Belgrade (45°N 21°E) capital of Serbia and Yugoslavia on the Danube River, 319

Belize country in Central America bordering Mexico and Guatemala, 179

Belmopan (17°N 89°W) capital of Belize, 179

Benghazi (32°N 20°E) major coastal city in Libya, 471

Benin (buh-NEEN) country in West Africa between Togo and Nigeria, 491

Bergen (60°N 5°E) seaport city in southwestern Norway, 299

Berlin (53°N 13°E) capital of Germany, 279

Bern (47°N 7°E) capital of Switzerland, 279

Bhutan South Asian country in the Himalayas located north of India and Bangladesh, 669

Birmingham (52°N 2°W) major manufacturing center of south-central Great Britain, 299

Bishkek (43°N 75°E) capital of Kyrgyzstan, 387

Bissau (12°N 16°W) capital of Guinea-Bissau, 491

Black Sea sea between Europe and Asia, A14

Blue Nile East African river that flows into the Nile River in Sudan, 509

Bogotá (5°N 74°W) capital and largest city of Colombia, 195

Bolivia landlocked South American country, 229

Bombay See Mumbai.

Bonn (51°N 7°E) city in western Germany; replaced by Berlin as the capital of reunified Germany, 279

Borneo island in the Malay Archipelago in Southeast Asia, 617

Bosnia and Herzegovina country in Eastern Europe between Serbia and Croatia, 319

Bosporus a narrow strait separating European and Asian Turkey, 435

Boston (42°N 71°W) capital and largest city of Massachusetts, 107

Botswana country in southern Africa, 541

Brahmaputra River major river of South Asia that begins in the Himalayas of Tibet and merges with the Ganges River in Bangladesh, 651

Brasília (16°S 48°W) capital of Brazil, 211

Bratislava (48°N 17°E) capital of Slovakia, 319

Brazil largest country in South America, 211

Brazilian Highlands region of old, eroded mountains in southeastern Brazil, 211

Brazilian Plateau area of upland plains in southern Brazil, 211

Brazzaville (4°S 15°E) capital of the Republic of the Congo, 525

Bridgetown (13°N 60°W) capital of Barbados, 179

Brisbane (28°S 153°E) seaport and capital of Queensland, Australia, 701

British Columbia province on the Pacific coast of Canada, 129

British Isles island group consisting of Great Britain and Ireland, A15

Brittany region in northwestern France, 279

Brunei (brooh-NY) country on the northern coast of Borneo in Southeast Asia, 617

Brussels (51°N 4°E) capital of Belgium, 279

Bucharest (44°N 26°E) capital of Romania, 319

Budapest (48°N 19°E) capital of Hungary, 319

Buenos Aires (34°S 59°W) capital of Argentina, 211

Bujumbura (3°S 29°E) capital of Burundi, 509

Bulgaria country on the Balkan Peninsula in Eastern Europe, 319

Burkina Faso (boor-KEE-nuh FAH-soh) landlocked country in West Africa, 491

Burma See Myanmar.

Burundi landlocked country in East Africa, 509

Cairo (30°N 31°E) capital of Egypt, 471

Calcutta See Kolkata.

Calgary (51°N 114°W) city in the western Canadian province of Alberta, 129

Callao (kah-YAH-oh) (12°S 77°W) port city in Peru, 229

Cambodia country in Southeast Asia west of Vietnam, 617

Cameroon country in central Africa, 525

Campeche (20°N 91°W) city in Mexico on the west coast of the Yucatán Peninsula, 161

Canada country occupying most of northern North America, 129

Canadian Shield major landform region in central Canada along Hudson Bay, 129

Canberra (35°S 149°E) capital of Australia, 701

Cancún (21°N 87°W) resort city in Mexico on the Yucatán Peninsula, 161

Cantabrian (kan-TAY-bree-uhn) **Mountains** mountains in northwestern Spain, 261

Cape Horn (56°S 67°W) cape in southern Chile; southernmost point of South America, 229

Cape of Good Hope cape of the southwest coast of South Africa, 541

Cape Town (34°S 18°E) major seaport city and legislative capital of South Africa, 541

Cape Verde island country in the Atlantic Ocean off the coast of West Africa, 491

Caracas (kuh-RAHK-uhs) (11°N 67°W) capital of Venezuela, 195

Cardiff (52°N 3°W) capital and largest city of Wales, 299

Caribbean Sea arm of the Atlantic Ocean between North America and South America, A10

Carpathian Mountains mountain system in Eastern Europe, 319

Casablanca (34°N 8°W) seaport city on the western coast of Morocco, 471

Cascade Range mountain range in the northwestern United States, 107

Caspian Sea large inland salt lake between Europe and Asia, A16

Castries (14°N 61°W) capital of St. Lucia, 179

Cauca River river in western Colombia, 195

Caucasus Mountains mountain range between the Black Sea and the Caspian Sea, 351

Cayenne (5°N 52°W) capital of French Guiana, 195

Central African Republic landlocked country in central Africa located south of Chad, 525

Central America narrow southern portion of the North American continent, 179

Central Lowlands area of Australia between the Western Plateau and the Great Dividing Range, 701

Central Siberian Plateau upland plains and valleys between the Yenisey and Lena Rivers in Russia, 351

Chad landlocked country in northern Africa, 491

Chang River major river in central China, 573

Chao Phraya (chow PRY-uh) **River** major river in Thailand, 617

Chelyabinsk (chel-YAH-buhnsk) (55°N 61°E) manufacturing city in the Urals region of Russia, 351

Chernobyl (51°N 30°E) city in north-central Ukraine; site of a major nuclear accident in 1986, 373

Chicago (42°N 88°W) major city on Lake Michigan in northern Illinois, 107

Chile country in South America, 229

China country in East Asia; most populous country in the world, 573

Chişinău (formerly Kishinev) (47°N 29°E) capital of Moldova, 319

Chongqing (30°N 108°E) city in southern China along the Chang River, 573

Christchurch (44°S 173°E) city on the eastern coast of South Island, New Zealand, 701

Ciudad Juárez (syoo-thahth HWAHR-es) (32°N 106°W) city in northern Mexico near El Paso, 161

Coastal Plain North American landform region stretching along the Atlantic Ocean and Gulf of Mexico, 107

Cologne (51°N 7°E) manufacturing and commercial city along the Rhine River in Germany, 279

Colombia country in northern South America, 195

Colombo (7°N 80°E) capital city and important seaport of Sri Lanka, 669

Colorado Plateau uplifted area of horizontal rock layers in the western United States, 107

Columbia River river that drains the Columbia Basin in the northwestern United States, 107

Comoros island country in the Indian Ocean off the coast of Africa, 541

Conakry (10°N 14°W) capital of Guinea, 491

Congo Basin region in central Africa, 525

Congo, Democratic Republic of the largest and most populous country in central Africa, 525

Congo, Republic of the central African country located along the Congo River, 525

Congo River major navigable river in central Africa that flows into the Atlantic Ocean, 525

Copenhagen (56°N 12°E) seaport and capital of Denmark, 299

Córdoba (30°S 64°W) large city in Argentina northwest of Buenos Aires, 211

Cork (52°N 8°W) seaport city in southern Ireland, 299

Costa Rica country in Central America, 179

Côte d'Ivoire (KOHT-dee-VWAHR) (Ivory Coast) country in West Africa, 491

Crimean Peninsula peninsula in Ukraine that juts southward into the Black Sea, 373

Croatia Eastern European country and former Yugoslav republic, 319

Cuba country and largest island in the Caribbean, 179

Cuzco (14°S 72°W) city southeast of Lima, Peru; former capital of the Inca Empire, 229

Cyprus island republic in the eastern Mediterranean Sea, 435

Czech Republic Eastern European country and the western part of the former country of Czechoslovakia, 319

Dakar (15°N 17°W) capital of Senegal, 491
Dallas (33°N 97°W) city in northern Texas, 107
Damascus (34°N 36°E) capital of Syria and one of the world's oldest cities, 435
Danube River major river in Europe that flows into the Black Sea in Romania, 279
Dardanelles narrow strait separating European and Asian Turkey, 435
Dar es Salaam (7°S 39°E) capital and major seaport of Tanzania, 509
Dead Sea salt lake on the boundary between Israel and Jordan in southwestern Asia, 435
Deccan the southern part of the Indian subcontinent, 651
Delhi (29°N 77°E) city in India, 651
Denmark country in northern Europe, 299
Detroit (42°N 83°W) major industrial city in Michigan, 107
Devil's Island (5°N 53°W) French island off the coast of French Guiana in South America, 195
Dhaka (24°N 90°E) capital and largest city of Bangladesh, 669
Dinaric Alps mountains extending inland from the Adriatic coast to the Balkan Peninsula, 319
Djibouti country located in the Horn of Africa, 509
Djibouti (12°N 43°E) capital of Djibouti, 509
Dnieper River major river in Ukraine, 373
Doha (25°N 51°E) capital of Qatar, 415
Dominica Caribbean island country, 179
Dominican Republic country occupying the eastern part of Hispaniola in the Caribbean, 179
Donets Basin industrial region in eastern Ukraine, 373
Douro River river on the Iberian Peninsula that flows into the Atlantic Ocean in Portugal, 261
Drakensberg mountain range in southern Africa, 541
Dublin (53°N 6°W) capital of the republic of Ireland, 299
Durban (30°S 31°E) port city in South Africa, 541
Dushanbe (39°N 69°E) capital of Tajikistan, 387

Eastern Ghats mountains on the eastern side of the Deccan Plateau in southern India, 651
Eastern Highlands mountain ranges in eastern Australia, 701
East Timor eastern section of Timor administered by the United Nations until formal independence, 617
Ebro River river in Spain that flows into the Mediterranean Sea, 261
Ecuador country in western South America, 229
Edmonton (54°N 113°W) provincial capital of Alberta, Canada, 129
Egypt country in North Africa located east of Libya, 471
Elburz Mountains mountain range in northern Iran, 415
El Salvador country on the Pacific side of Central America, 179
England southern part of Great Britain and part of the United Kingdom in northern Europe, 299
English Channel channel separating Great Britain from the European continent, 279
equator the imaginary line of latitude that lies halfway between the North and South Poles and circles the globe, A4–A5
Equatorial Guinea central African country, 525
Eritrea (er-uh-TREE-uh) East African country located north of Ethiopia, 509
Essen (51°N 7°E) industrial city in western Germany, 279

Estonia country located on the Baltic Sea; former Soviet republic, 319
Ethiopia East African country in the Horn of Africa, 509
Euphrates River major river in Iraq in southwestern Asia, 415
Europe continent between the Ural Mountains and the Atlantic Ocean, A3

Fergana Valley fertile valley in Uzbekistan, Kyrgyzstan, and Tajikistan, 387
Fès (34°N 5°W) city in north-central Morocco, 471
Fiji South Pacific island country of Melanesia, 694
Finland country in northern Europe located between Sweden, Norway, and Russia, 299
Flanders northern coastal part of Belgium where Flemish is the dominant language, 279
Florence (44°N 11°E) city on the Arno River in central Italy, 261
France country in west-central Europe, 279
Frankfurt (50°N 9°E) main city of Germany's Rhineland region, 279
Freetown (9°N 13°W) capital of Sierra Leone, 491
French Guiana French territory in northern South America, 195
Funafuti (9°S 179°E) capital of Tuvalu, 694

Gabon country in central Africa located between Cameroon and the Republic of the Congo, 525
Gaborone (24°S 26°E) capital of Botswana, 541
Galway (53°N 9°W) city in western Ireland, 299
Gambia country along the Gambia River in West Africa, 491
Ganges River major river in India flowing from the Himalayas southeastward to the Bay of Bengal, 651
Gangetic (gan-JE-tik) **Plain** vast plain in northern India, 651
Gao (GOW) (16°N 0°) city in Mali on the Niger River, 491
Gaza Strip area occupied by Israel from 1967 to 1994; under Palestinian self-rule since 1994, 435
Geneva (46°N 6°E) city in southwestern Switzerland, 279
Genoa (44°N 10°E) seaport city in northwestern Italy, 261
Georgetown (8°N 58°W) capital of Guyana, 195
Georgia (Eurasia) country in the Caucasus region; former Soviet republic, 373
Germany country in west-central Europe located between Poland and the Benelux countries, 279
Ghana country in West Africa, 491
Glasgow (56°N 4°W) city in Scotland, United Kingdom, 299
Gobi desert that makes up part of the Mongolian plateau in East Asia, 573
Golan Heights hilly region in southwestern Syria occupied by Israel, 435
Göteborg (58°N 12°E) seaport city in southwestern Sweden, 299
Gran Chaco (grahn CHAH-koh) dry plains region in Paraguay, Bolivia, and northern Argentina, 211
Great Artesian Basin Australia's largest source of underground well water; located in interior Queensland, 701
Great Barrier Reef world's largest coral reef; located off the northeastern coast of Australia, 701

Great Basin dry region in the western United States, 107

Great Bear Lake lake in the Northwest Territories of Canada, 129

Great Britain major island of the United Kingdom, 299

Great Dividing Range mountain range of the Eastern Highlands in Australia, 701

Greater Antilles larger islands of the West Indies in the Caribbean Sea, 179

Great Lakes largest freshwater lake system in the world; located in North America, 107

Great Plains plains region in the central United States, 107

Great Rift Valley valley system extending from eastern Africa to Southwest Asia, 509

Great Slave Lake lake in the Northwest Territories of Canada, 129

Greece country in southern Europe located at the southern end of the Balkan Peninsula, 261

Greenland self-governing province of Denmark between the North Atlantic and Arctic Oceans, 299

Grenada Caribbean island country, 179

Guadalajara (21°N 103°W) industrial city in west-central Mexico, 161

Guadalquivir (gwah-thahl-kee-VEER) **River** important river in southern Spain, 261

Guam (14°N 143°E) South Pacific island and U.S. territory in Micronesia, 722

Guatemala most populous country in Central America, 179

Guatemala City (15°N 91°W) capital of Guatemala, 179

Guayaquil (gwy-ah-KEEL) (2°S 80°W) port city in Ecuador, 229

Guiana Highlands elevated region in northeastern South America, 195

Guinea country in West Africa, 491

Guinea-Bissau (GI-nee bi-SOW) country in West Africa, 491

Gulf of Bothnia part of the Baltic Sea west of Finland, 299

Gulf of California part of the Pacific Ocean east of Baja California, Mexico, 161

Gulf of Finland part of the Baltic Sea south of Finland, 314

Gulf of Guinea (GI-nee) gulf of the Atlantic Ocean south of western Africa, 491

Gulf of Mexico gulf of the Atlantic Ocean between Florida, Texas, and Mexico, 161

Gulf of St. Lawrence gulf between New Brunswick and Newfoundland Island in North America, 129

Guyana (gy-AH-nuh) country in South America, 195

Haiti country occupying the western third of the Caribbean island of Hispaniola, 179

Halifax (45°N 64°W) provincial capital of Nova Scotia, Canada, 129

Hamburg (54°N 10°E) seaport on the Elbe River in northwestern Germany, 279

Hanoi (ha-NOY) (21°N 106°E) capital of Vietnam, 617

Harare (18°S 31°E) capital of Zimbabwe, 541

Havana (23°N 82°W) capital of Cuba, 179

Helsinki (60°N 25°E) capital of Finland, 299

Himalayas mountain system in Asia; world's highest mountains, 573

Hindu Kush high mountain range in northern Afghanistan, 415

Hispaniola large Caribbean island divided into the countries of Haiti and the Dominican Republic, 179

Ho Chi Minh City (formerly Saigon) (11°N 107°E) major city in southern Vietnam; former capital of South Vietnam, 617

Hokkaido (hoh-KY-doh) major island in northern Japan, 595

Honduras country in Central America, 179

Hong Kong (22°N 115°E) former British colony in East Asia; now part of China, 573

Hong (Red) River major river that flows into the Gulf of Tonkin in Vietnam, 617

Honiara (9°S 160°E) capital of the Solomon Islands, 694

Honshu (HAWN-shoo) largest of the four major islands of Japan, 595

Houston (30°N 95°W) major port and largest city in Texas, 107

Huang River (Yellow River) one of the world's longest rivers; located in northern China, 573

Hudson Bay large bay in Canada, 129

Hungary country in Eastern Europe between Romania and Austria, 319

Iberian Peninsula peninsula in southwestern Europe occupied by Spain and Portugal, 261

Iceland island country between the North Atlantic and Arctic oceans, 299

India country in South Asia, 651

Indian Ocean world's third-largest ocean; located east of Africa, south of Asia, west of Australia, and north of Antarctica, A3

Indochina Peninsula peninsula in southeastern Asia that includes the region from Myanmar (Burma) to Vietnam, 617

Indonesia largest country in Southeast Asia; made up of more than 17,000 islands, 617

Indus River major river in Pakistan, 669

Inland Sea body of water in southern Japan between Honshu, Shikoku, and Kyushu, 595

Interior Plains vast area between the Appalachians and the Rocky Mountains in North America, 107

Inyanga Mountains mountain region of Zimbabwe and Mozambique, 541

Iquitos (4°S 73°W) city in northeastern Peru on the Amazon River, 229

Iran country in southwestern Asia; formerly called Persia, 415

Iraq (i-RAHK) country located between Iran and Saudi Arabia, 415

Ireland country west of Great Britain in the British Isles, 299

Irian Jaya western part of the island of New Guinea and part of Indonesia, 617

Irish Sea sea between Great Britain and Ireland, 299

Irrawaddy River important river in Myanmar (Burma), 617

Islamabad (34°N 73°E) capital of Pakistan, 669

Israel country in southwestern Asia, 435

Istanbul (formerly Constantinople) (41°N 29°E) largest city and leading seaport in Turkey, 435

Italy country in southern Europe, 261

Jakarta (6°S 107°E) capital of Indonesia, 617

Jamaica island country in the Caribbean Sea, 179

Japan country in East Asia consisting of four major islands and more than 3,000 smaller islands, 595

Java major island in Indonesia, 617

Jerusalem (32°N 35°E) capital of Israel, 435

Johannesburg (26°S 28°E) city in South Africa, 541

Jordan Southwest Asian country stretching east from the Dead Sea and Jordan River into the Arabian Desert, 435

Jordan River river in southwestern Asia that separates Israel from Syria and Jordan, 435

Jutland Peninsula peninsula in northern Europe made up of Denmark and part of northern Germany, 299

Kabul (35°N 69°E) capital and largest city of Afghanistan, 415

Kalahari Desert dry plateau region in southern Africa, 541

Kamchatka Peninsula peninsula along Russia's northeastern coast, 351

Kampala (0° 32°E) capital of Uganda, 509

Kaohsiung (23°N 120°E) Taiwan's second-largest city and major seaport, 573

Karachi (25°N 69°E) Pakistan's largest city and major seaport, 669

Karakoram Range high mountain range in northern India and Pakistan, 669

Kara-kum (kahr-uh-KOOM) desert region in Turkmenistan, 387

Kashmir mountainous region in northern India and Pakistan, 651

Kathmandu (kat-man-DOO) (28°N 85°E) capital of Nepal, 669

Kazakhstan country in Central Asia; former Soviet republic, 387

Kenya country in East Africa south of Ethiopia, 509

Khabarovsk (kuh-BAHR-uhfsk) (49°N 135°E) city in southeastern Russia on the Amur River, 351

Khartoum (16°N 33°E) capital of Sudan, 509

Khyber Pass major mountain pass between Afghanistan and Pakistan, 415

Kiev (50°N 31°E) capital of Ukraine, 373

Kigali (2°S 30°E) capital of Rwanda, 509

Kingston (18°N 77°W) capital of Jamaica, 179

Kingstown (13°N 61°W) capital of St. Vincent and the Grenadines, 179

Kinshasa (4°S 15°E) capital of the Democratic Republic of the Congo, 525

Kiribati South Pacific country in Micronesia and Polynesia, 694

Kjølen (CHUHL-uhn) **Mountains** mountain range in the Scandinavian Peninsula, 299

Kobe (KOH-bay) (35°N 135°E) major port city in Japan, 595

Kolkata (Calcutta) (23°N 88°E) giant industrial and seaport city in eastern India, 651

Korea peninsula on the east coast of Asia, 595

Koror capital of Palau, 694

Kosovo province in southern Serbia, 319

Kourou (5°N 53°W) city in French Guiana, 195

Kuala Lumpur (3°N 102°E) capital of Malaysia, 617

Kuril (KYOOHR-eel) **Islands** Russian islands northeast of the island of Hokkaido, Japan, 351

Kuwait country on the Persian Gulf in southwestern Asia, 415

Kuwait City (29°N 48°E) capital of Kuwait, 415

Kuznetsk Basin (Kuzbas) industrial region in central Russia, 351

Kyoto (KYOH-toh) (35°N 136°E) city on the island of Honshu and the ancient capital of Japan, 595

Kyrgyzstan (kir-gi-STAN) country in Central Asia; former Soviet republic, 387

Kyushu (KYOO-shoo) southernmost of Japan's main islands, 595

Kyzyl Kum (ki-zil KOOM) desert region in Uzbekistan and Kazakhstan, 387

Labrador region in the territory of Newfoundland, Canada, 129

Lagos (LAY-gahs) (6°N 3°E) former capital of Nigeria and the country's largest city, 491

Lahore (32°N 74°E) industrial city in northeastern Pakistan, 644

Lake Baikal (by-KAHL) world's deepest freshwater lake; located north of the Gobi in Russia, 351

Lake Chad shallow lake between Nigeria and Chad in western Africa, 491

Lake Malawi (also called Lake Nyasa) lake in southeastern Africa, 525

Lake Maracaibo (mah-rah-KY-buh) extension of the Gulf of Venezuela in South America, 195

Lake Nasser artificial lake in southern Egypt created in the 1960s by the construction of the Aswan High Dam, 471

Lake Nicaragua lake in southwestern Nicaragua, 179

Lake Poopó (poh-oh-POH) lake in western Bolivia, 229

Lake Tanganyika deep lake in the Western Rift Valley in Africa, 525

Lake Titicaca lake between Bolivia and Peru at an elevation of 12,500 feet (3,810 m), 229

Lake Victoria large lake in East Africa surrounded by Uganda, Kenya, and Tanzania, 509

Lake Volta large artificial lake in Ghana, 491

Laos landlocked country in Southeast Asia, 617

La Paz (17°S 68°W) administrative capital and principal industrial city of Bolivia with an elevation of 12,001 feet (3,658 m); highest capital in the world, 229

Lapland region extending across northern Finland, Sweden, and Norway, 299

Las Vegas (36°N 115°W) city in southern Nevada, 107

Latvia country on the Baltic Sea; former Soviet republic, 319

Lebanon country in Southwest Asia, 435

Lesotho country completely surrounded by South Africa, 541

Lesser Antilles chain of volcanic islands in the eastern Caribbean Sea, 179

Liberia country in West Africa, 491

Libreville (0° 9°E) capital of Gabon, 525

Libya country in North Africa located between Egypt and Algeria, 471

Liechtenstein microstate in west-central Europe located between Switzerland and Austria, 279

Lilongwe (14°S 34°E) capital of Malawi, 525

Lima (12°S 77°W) capital of Peru, 229

Limpopo River river in southern Africa forming the border between South Africa and Zimbabwe, 541

Lisbon (39°N 9°W) capital and largest city of Portugal, 261

Lithuania European country on the Baltic Sea; former Soviet republic, 319

Ljubljana (lee-oo-blee-AH-nuh) (46°N 14°E) capital of Slovenia, 319

Lomé (6°N 1°E) capital of Togo, 491

London (52°N 0°) capital of the United Kingdom, 299

Luanda (9°S 13°E) capital of Angola, 525

Lubumbashi (loo-boom-BAH-shee) (12°S 27°E) industrial city in the Democratic Republic of the Congo, 525

Luxembourg small European country bordered by France, Germany, and Belgium, 279

Luxembourg (50°N 7°E) capital of Luxembourg, 279
Luzon chief island of the Philippines, 617

Macao (22°N 113°E) former Portuguese territory in East Asia; now part of China, 573
Macedonia Balkan country; former Yugoslav republic, 319
Machu Picchu (13°S 73°W) ancient Inca city in the Andes of Peru, 229
Madagascar largest of the island countries off the eastern coast of Africa, 541
Madrid (40°N 4°W) capital of Spain, 261
Magdalena River river in Colombia that flows into the Caribbean Sea, 195
Magnitogorsk (53°N 59°E) manufacturing city of the Urals region of Russia, 351
Majuro (7°N 171°E) capital of the Marshall Islands, 694
Malabo (4°N 9°E) capital of Equatorial Guinea, 525
Malawi (muh-LAH-wee) landlocked country in central Africa, 525
Malay Archipelago (ahr-kuh-PE-luh-goh) large island group off the southeastern coast of Asia including New Guinea and the islands of Malaysia, Indonesia, and the Philippines, 617
Malay Peninsula peninsula in Southeast Asia, 617
Malaysia country in Southeast Asia, 617
Maldives island country in the Indian Ocean south of India, 669
Male (5°N 72°E) capital of the Maldives, 669
Mali country in West Africa along the Niger River, 491
Malta island country in southern Europe located in the Mediterranean Sea between Sicily and North Africa, 252
Managua (12°N 86°W) capital of Nicaragua, 179
Manama (26°N 51°E) capital of Bahrain, 415
Manaus (3°S 60°W) city in Brazil on the Amazon River, 211
Manchester (53°N 2°W) major commercial city in west-central Great Britain, 299
Manila (15°N 121°E) capital of the Philippines, 617
Manitoba prairie province in central Canada, 129
Maputo (27°S 33°E) capital of Mozambique, 541
Marseille (43°N 5°E) seaport in France on the Mediterranean Sea, 279
Marshall Islands Pacific island country in Micronesia, 694
Maseru (29°S 27°E) capital of Lesotho, 541
Masqat (Muscat) (23°N 59°E) capital of Oman, 415
Mato Grosso Plateau highland region in southwestern Brazil, 211
Mauritania African country stretching east from the Atlantic coast into the Sahara, 491
Mauritius island country located off the coast of Africa in the Indian Ocean, 541
Mazatlán (23°N 106°W) seaport city in western Mexico, 161
Mbabane (26°S 31°E) capital of Swaziland, 541
Mecca (21°N 40°E) important Islamic city in western Saudi Arabia, 415
Mediterranean Sea sea surrounded by Europe, Asia, and Africa, A14
Mekong River important river in Southeast Asia, 617
Melanesia island region in the South Pacific that stretches from New Guinea to Fiji, 715
Melbourne (38°S 145°E) capital of Victoria, Australia, 701
Mexican Plateau large, high plateau in central Mexico, 161

Mexico country in North America, 161
Mexico City (19°N 99°W) capital of Mexico, 161
Miami (26°N 80°W) city in southern Florida, 107
Micronesia island region in the South Pacific that includes the Mariana, Caroline, Marshall, and Gilbert island groups, 717
Micronesia, Federated States of island country in the western Pacific, 694
Milan (45°N 9°E) city in northern Italy, 261
Minsk (54°N 28°E) capital of Belarus, 373
Mississippi River major river in the central United States, 107
Mogadishu (2°N 45°E) capital and port city of Somalia, 509
Moldova Eastern European country located between Romania and Ukraine; former Soviet republic, 319
Monaco (44°N 8°E) European microstate bordered by France, 279
Mongolia landlocked country in East Asia, 573
Monrovia (6°N 11°W) capital of Liberia, 491
Montenegro See Yugoslavia.
Monterrey (26°N 100°W) major industrial center in northeastern Mexico, 161
Montevideo (mawn-tay-bee-THAY-oh) (35°S 56°W) capital of Uruguay, 211
Montreal (46°N 74°W) financial and industrial city in Quebec, Canada, 129
Morocco country in North Africa south of Spain, 471
Moroni (12°S 43°E) capital of Comoros, 541
Moscow (56°N 38°E) capital of Russia, 351
Mount Elbrus (43°N 42°E) highest European peak (18,510 ft.; 5,642 m); located in the Caucasus Mountains, 373
Mount Everest (28°N 87°E) world's highest peak (29,035 ft.; 8,850 m); located in the Himalayas, 573
Mount Kilimanjaro (3°S 37°E) (ki-luh-muhn-JAHR-oh) highest point in Africa (19,341 ft.; 5,895 m); located in northeast Tanzania, near Kenya border, 509
Mount Orizaba (19°N 97°W) volcanic mountain (18,700 ft.; 5,700 m) southeast of Mexico City; highest point in Mexico, 161
Mozambique (moh-zahm-BEEK) country in southern Africa, 541
Mumbai (Bombay) (19°N 73°E) India's largest city, 651
Munich (MYOO-nik) (48°N 12°E) major city and manufacturing center in southern Germany, 279
Murray-Darling Rivers major river system in southeastern Australia, 701
Muscat See Masqat.
Myanmar (MYAHN-mahr) (Burma) country in Southeast Asia between India, China, and Thailand, 617

Nairobi (1°S 37°E) capital of Kenya, 509
Namib Desert Atlantic coast desert in southern Africa, 541
Namibia (nuh-MI-bee-uh) country on the Atlantic coast in southern Africa, 541
Nanjing (32°N 119°E) city along the upper Chang River in China, 573
Naples (41°N 14°E) major seaport in southern Italy, 261
Nassau (25°N 77°W) capital of the Bahamas, 179
Nauru South Pacific island country in Micronesia, 694
N'Djamena (12°N 15°E) capital of Chad, 491
Negev desert region in southern Israel, 435
Nepal South Asian country located in the Himalayas, 669
Netherlands country in west-central Europe, 279
New Brunswick province in eastern Canada, 129

New Caledonia French territory of Melanesia in the South Pacific Ocean east of Queensland, Australia, 694

New Delhi (29°N 77°E) capital of India, 651

Newfoundland eastern province in Canada including Labrador and the island of Newfoundland, 129

New Guinea large island in the South Pacific Ocean north of Australia, 717

New Orleans (30°N 90°W) major Gulf port city in Louisiana located on the Mississippi River, 107

New York Middle Atlantic state in the northeastern United States, 107

New Zealand island country located southeast of Australia, 701

Niamey (14°N 2°E) capital of Niger, 491

Nicaragua country in Central America, 179

Nice (44°N 7°E) city on the southeastern coast in France, 279

Nicosia (35°N 33°E) capital of Cyprus, 435

Niger (NY-juhr) country in West Africa, 491

Nigeria country in West Africa, 491

Niger River river in West Africa, 491

Nile Delta region in northern Egypt where the Nile River flows into the Mediterranean Sea, 471

Nile River world's longest river (4,187 miles; 6,737 km); flows into the Mediterranean Sea in Egypt, 471

Nizhniy Novgorod (Gorky), Russia (56°N 44°E) city on the Volga River east of Moscow, 351

Normandy (France) region of northwestern France, 282–83

North America continent including Canada, the United States, Mexico, Central America, and the Caribbean islands, A2

North China Plain region of northeastern China, 573

Northern European Plain broad coastal plain from the Atlantic coast of France into Russia, 279

Northern Ireland the six northern counties of Ireland that remain part of the United Kingdom; also called Ulster, 299

Northern Mariana Islands U.S. commonwealth in the South Pacific, 694

North Island northernmost of two large continental islands of New Zealand, 701

North Korea country on the northern part of the Korean Peninsula in East Asia, 595

North Pole the northern point of Earth's axis, A22

North Sea major sea between Great Britain, Denmark, and the Scandinavian Peninsula, 279

Northwest Highlands region of rugged hills and low mountains in Europe, including parts of the British Isles, northwestern France, the Iberian Peninsula, and the Scandinavian Peninsula, 251

Northwest Territories division of a northern region of Canada, 129

Norway European country located on the Scandinavian Peninsula, 299

Nouakchott (nooh-AHK-shaht) (18°N 16°W) capital of Mauritania, 491

Nova Scotia province in eastern Canada, 129

Novosibirsk (55°N 83°E) industrial center in Siberia, Russia, 351

Nuku'alofa capital of Tonga, 694

Nunavut Native American territory of northern Canada, 129

Nuuk (Godthab) (64°N 52°W) capital of Greenland, 299

Ob River large river system that drains Russia and Siberia, 351

Oman country in the Arabian Peninsula; formerly known as Muscat, 415

Ontario province in central Canada, 129

Orange River river in southern Africa, 541

Orinoco River major river system in South America, 195

Osaka (oh-SAH-kuh) (35°N 135°E) major industrial center on Japan's southwestern Honshu island, 595

Oslo (60°N 11°E) capital of Norway, 299

Ottawa (45°N 76°W) capital of Canada; located in Ontario, 129

Ouagadougou (wah-gah-DOO-GOO) (12°N 2°W) capital of Burkina Faso, 491

Pacific Ocean Earth's largest ocean; located between North and South America and Asia and Australia, A2–A3

Pakistan South Asian country located northwest of India, 669

Palau South Pacific island country in Micronesia, 694

Palikir capital of the Federated States of Micronesia, 694

Pamirs mountain area mainly in Tajikistan in Central Asia, 387

Panama country in Central America, 179

Panama Canal canal allowing shipping between the Pacific Ocean and the Caribbean Sea; located in central Panama, 179

Panama City (9°N 80°W) capital of Panama, 179

Papua New Guinea country on the eastern half of the island of New Guinea, 694

Paraguay country in South America, 211

Paraguay River river that divides Paraguay into two separate regions, 211

Paramaribo (6°N 55°W) capital of Suriname in South America, 195

Paraná River major river system in southeastern South America, 211

Paris (49°N 2°E) capital of France, 279

Patagonia arid region of dry plains and windswept plateaus in southern Argentina, 211

Peloponnesus (pe-luh-puh-NEE-suhs) peninsula forming the southern part of the mainland of Greece, 261

Persian Gulf body of water between Iran and the Arabian Peninsula, 415

Perth (32°S 116°E) capital of Western Australia, 701

Peru country in South America, 229

Philadelphia (40°N 75°W) important port and industrial center in Pennsylvania in the northeastern United States, 107

Philippines Southeast Asian island country located north of Indonesia, 617

Phnom Penh (12°N 105°E) capital of Cambodia, 617

Phoenix (34°N 112°W) capital of Arizona, 107

Plateau of Tibet high, barren plateau of western China, 573

Podgorica (PAWD-gawr-ett-sah) capital of Montenegro, 330

Poland country in Eastern Europe located east of Germany, 319

Polynesia island region of the South Pacific Ocean that includes the Hawaiian and Line island groups, Samoa, French Polynesia, and Easter Island, 694

Po River river in northern Italy, 261

Port-au-Prince (pohr-toh-PRINS) (19°N 72°W) capital of Haiti, 179

Port Elizabeth (34°S 26°E) seaport city in South Africa, 541

Portland (46°N 123°W) seaport and largest city in Oregon, 107

Port Louis (20°S 58°E) capital of Mauritius, 541

Port Moresby (10°S 147°E) seaport and capital of Papua New Guinea, 694

Port-of-Spain (11°N 61°W) capital of Trinidad and Tobago, 179

Porto-Novo (6°N 3°E) capital of Benin, 491

Portugal country in southern Europe located on the Iberian Peninsula, 261

Port-Vila (18°S 169°E) capital of Vanuatu, 694

Prague (50°N 14°E) capital of the Czech Republic, 319

Praia (PRIE-uh) (15°N 24°W) capital of Cape Verde, 491

Pretoria (26°S 28°E) administrative capital of South Africa, 541

Prince Edward Island province in eastern Canada, 129

Pripyat Marshes (PRI-pyuht) marshlands in southern Belarus and northwest Ukraine, 373

Puerto Rico U.S. commonwealth in the Greater Antilles in the Caribbean Sea, 179

Pusan (35°N 129°E) major seaport city in southeastern South Korea, 595

P´yŏngyang (pyuhng-YANG) (39°N 126°E) capital of North Korea, 595

Pyrenees (PIR-uh-neez) mountain range along the border of France and Spain, 279

Qatar Persian Gulf country located on the Arabian Peninsula, 415

Qattara Depression lowland region (436 feet below sea level; 133 m) in western Egypt, 471

Quebec province in eastern Canada, 129

Quebec (47°N 71°W) provincial capital of Quebec, Canada, 129

Quito (0° 79°W) capital of Ecuador, 229

Rabat (34°N 7°W) capital of Morocco, 471

Rangoon See Yangon.

Red Sea sea between the Arabian Peninsula and north-eastern Africa, 415

Reykjavik (RAYK-yuh-veek) (64°N 22°W) capital of Iceland, 299

Rhine River major river in Western Europe, 279

Riga (57°N 24°E) capital of Latvia, 319

Río Bravo Mexican name for the river between Texas and Mexico, 161

Rio de Janeiro (23°S 43°W) major port in southeastern Brazil, 211

Río de la Plata estuary between Argentina and Uruguay in South America, 211

Riyadh (25°N 47°E) capital of Saudi Arabia, 415

Rocky Mountains major mountain range in western North America, 107

Romania country in Eastern Europe, 319

Rome (42°N 13°E) capital of Italy, 261

Rosario (roh-SAHR-ee-oh) (33°S 61°W) city in eastern Argentina, 211

Roseau (15°N 61°W) capital of Dominica in the Caribbean, 179

Ross Ice Shelf ice shelf of Antarctica, 693

Rub' al-Khali uninhabited desert area in southeastern Saudi Arabia, 415

Russia world's largest country, stretching from Europe and the Baltic Sea to eastern Asia and the coast of the Bering Sea, 351

Rwanda country in East Africa, 509

Sahara desert region in northern Africa, 471

St. George's (12°N 62°W) capital of Grenada in the Caribbean Sea, 179

St. John's (17°N 62°W) capital of Antigua and Barbuda in the Caribbean Sea, 179

St. Kitts and Nevis Caribbean country in the Lesser Antilles, 179

St. Lawrence River major river linking the Great Lakes with the Gulf of St. Lawrence and the Atlantic Ocean in southeastern Canada, 129

St. Lucia Caribbean country in the Lesser Antilles, 179

St. Petersburg (formerly Leningrad; called Petrograd 1914 to 1924) (60°N 30°E) Russia's second largest city and former capital, 351

St. Vincent and the Grenadines Caribbean country in the Lesser Antilles, 179

Sakhalin Island Russian island north of Japan, 351

Salvador (13°S 38°W) seaport city of eastern Brazil, 211

Salzburg state of central Austria, 279

Samarqand (40°N 67°E) city in southeastern Uzbekistan, 387

Samoa South Pacific island country in Polynesia, 694

Sanaa (15°N 44°E) capital of Yemen, 415

San Diego (33°N 117°W) California's third largest urban area, 107

San Francisco (38°N 122°W) California's second largest urban area, 107

San José (10°N 84°W) capital of Costa Rica, 179

San Juan (19°N 66°W) capital of Puerto Rico, 179

San Marino microstate in southern Europe surrounded by Italy, 261

San Salvador (14°N 89°W) capital of El Salvador, 179

Santa Cruz (18°S 63°W) city in south central Bolivia, 229

Santiago (33°S 71°W) capital of Chile, 229

Santo Domingo (19°N 70°W) capital of the Dominican Republic, 179

São Francisco River river in eastern Brazil, 211

São Paulo (24°S 47°W) Brazil's largest city, 211

São Tomé (1°N 6°E) capital of São Tomé and Príncipe, 525

São Tomé and Príncipe island country located off the Atlantic coast of central Africa, 525

Sarajevo (sar-uh-YAY-voh) (44°N 18°E) capital of Bosnia and Herzegovina, 319

Saskatchewan province in central Canada, 129

Saudi Arabia country occupying much of the Arabian Peninsula in southwestern Asia, 415

Scandinavian Peninsula peninsula of northern Europe occupied by Norway and Sweden, 299

Scotland northern part of the island of Great Britain, 299

Sea of Azov sea in Ukraine connected to and north of the Black Sea, 373

Sea of Japan body of water separating Japan from mainland Asia, 351

Sea of Marmara sea between European Turkey and the Asian peninsula of Anatolia, 435

Sea of Okhotsk inlet of the Pacific Ocean on the eastern coast of Russia, 351

Seattle (48°N 122°W) largest city in the U.S. Pacific Northwest located in Washington, 107

Seine River river that flows through Paris in northern France, 279

Senegal country in West Africa, 491

Senegal River river in west Africa, 491
Seoul (38°N 127°E) capital of South Korea, 595
Serbia See Yugoslavia.
Seychelles island country located east of Africa in the Indian Ocean, 541
Shanghai (31°N 121°E) major seaport city in eastern China, 573
Shannon River river in Ireland; longest river in the British Isles, 299
Shikoku (shee-KOH-koo) smallest of the four main islands of Japan, 595
Siberia vast region of Russia extending from the Ural Mountains to the Pacific Ocean, 351
Sichuan Basin rich agricultural and mining area along the Chang (Yangtze) River in central China, 573
Sierra Madre Occidental mountain range in western Mexico, 161
Sierra Madre Oriental mountain range in eastern Mexico, 161
Sierra Nevada located in eastern California; one of the longest and highest mountain ranges in the United States, 107
Sinai (SY-ny) **Peninsula** peninsula in northeastern Egypt, 471
Singapore island country located at the tip of the Malay Peninsula in Southeast Asia, 617
Skopje (SKAW-pye) (42°N 21°E) capital of Macedonia, 319
Slovakia country in Eastern Europe; formerly the eastern part of Czechoslovakia, 319
Slovenia country in Eastern Europe; former Yugoslav republic, 319
Sofia (43°N 23°E) capital of Bulgaria, 319
Solomon Islands South Pacific island country in Melanesia, 694
Somalia East African country located in the Horn of Africa, 509
South Africa country in southern Africa, 541
Southern Alps mountain range in South Island, New Zealand, 701
South Island the southern island of two main islands of New Zealand, 701
South Korea country occupying the southern half of the Korean Peninsula, 595
South Pole the southern point of Earth's axis, A22
Spain country in southern Europe occupying most of the Iberian Peninsula, 261
Sri Lanka island country located south of India; formerly known as Ceylon, 669
Stockholm (59°N 18°E) capital of Sweden, 299
Strait of Gibraltar (juh-BRAWL-tuhr) strait between the Iberian Peninsula and North Africa that links the Mediterranean Sea to the Atlantic Ocean, 261
Strait of Magellan strait in South America connecting the South Atlantic with the South Pacific, 229
Sucre (19°S 65°W) constitutional capital of Bolivia, 229
Sudan East African country; largest country in Africa, 509
Suez Canal canal linking the Red Sea to the Mediterranean Sea in northeastern Egypt, 471
Sumatra large island of Indonesia, 617
Suriname (soohr-uh-NAH-muh) country in northern South America, 195
Suva (19°S 178°E) capital of Fiji, 694
Swaziland country in southern Africa, 541
Sweden country in northern Europe, 299
Switzerland country in west-central Europe located between Germany, France, Austria, and Italy, 279
Sydney (34°S 151°E) largest urban area and leading seaport in Australia, 701

Syr Dar'ya (sir duhr-YAH) river draining the Pamirs in Central Asia, 387
Syria Southwest Asian country located between the Mediterranean Sea and Iraq, 435
Syrian Desert desert region covering parts of Syria, Jordan, Iraq, and northern Saudi Arabia, 435

Tagus River longest river on the Iberian Peninsula in southern Europe, 261
Tahiti French South Pacific island in Polynesia, 694
Taipei (25°N 122°E) capital of Taiwan, 573
Taiwan (TY-WAHN) island country located off the southeastern coast of China, 573
Tajikistan (tah-ji-ki-STAN) country in Central Asia; former Soviet republic, 387
Taklimakan Desert desert region in western China, 573
Tallinn (59°N 25°E) capital of Estonia, 319
Tampico (22°N 98°W) Gulf of Mexico seaport in central-eastern Mexico, 161
Tanzania East African country located south of Kenya, 509
Tarai (tuh-RY) region in Nepal along the border with India, 669
Tarawa capital of Kiribati, 694
Tarim Basin arid region in western China, 573
Tashkent (41°N 69°E) capital of Uzbekistan, 387
Tasmania island state of Australia, 701
Tasman Sea part of South Pacific Ocean between Australia and New Zealand, 701
T'bilisi (42°N 45°E) capital of Georgia in the Caucasus region, 373
Tegucigalpa (14°N 87°W) capital of Honduras, 179
Tehran (36°N 52°E) capital of Iran, 415
Tel Aviv (tehl uh-VEEV) (32°N 35°E) largest city in Israel, 435
Thailand (TY-land) country in Southeast Asia, 617
Thar (TAHR) **Desert** sandy desert of northwestern India and eastern Pakistan; also called the Great Indian Desert, 651
Thessaloníki (41°N 23°E) city in Greece, 261
Thimphu (28°N 90°E) capital of Bhutan, 669
Tian Shan (TIEN SHAHN) high mountain range separating northwestern China from Russia and some Central Asian republics, 387
Tiber River river that flows through Rome in central Italy, 261
Tibesti Mountains mountain group in northwest Chad, 491
Tierra del Fuego group of islands at the southern tip of South America, 211
Tigris River major river in southwestern Asia, 415
Tijuana (33°N 117°W) city in northwestern Mexico, 161
Timbuktu (17°N 3°W) city in Mali and an ancient trading center in West Africa, 491
Tiranë (ti-RAH-nuh) (42°N 20°E) capital of Albania, 319
Togo West African country located between Ghana and Benin, 491
Tokyo (36°N 140°E) capital of Japan, 595
Tonga South Pacific island country in Polynesia, 694
Toronto (44°N 79°W) capital of the province of Ontario, Canada, 129
Transantarctic Mountains major mountain range that divides Antarctica into East and West, 693
Trinidad and Tobago Caribbean country in the Lesser Antilles, 179
Tripoli (33°N 13°E) capital of Libya, 471
Tropic of Cancer parallel 23.5° north of the equator; parallel on the globe at which the Sun's most direct rays strike the earth during the June solstice (first day of summer in the Northern Hemisphere), A4–A5

Tropic of Capricorn parallel 23.5° south of the equator; parallel on the globe at which the Sun's most direct rays strike the earth during the December solstice (first day of summer in the Southern Hemisphere), A4–A5

Tunis (37°N 10°E) capital of Tunisia, 471

Tunisia country in North Africa located on the Mediterranean coast between Algeria and Libya, 471

Turin (45°N 8°E) city in northern Italy, 261

Turkey country of the eastern Mediterranean occupying Anatolia and a corner of southeastern Europe, 435

Turkmenistan country in Central Asia; former Soviet republic, 387

Tuvalu South Pacific island country of Polynesia, 694

Uganda country in East Africa, 509

Ukraine country located between Russia and Eastern European; former Soviet republic, 373

Ulaanbaatar (oo-lahn-BAH-tawr) (48°N 107°E) capital of Mongolia, 573

United Arab Emirates country located on the Arabian Peninsula, 415

United Kingdom country in northern Europe occupying most of the British Isles; Great Britain and Northern Ireland, 299

United States North American country located between Canada and Mexico, 107

Ural Mountains mountain range in west central Russia that divides Asia from Europe, 351

Uruguay country on the northern side of the Río de la Plata between Brazil and Argentina in South America, 211

Uzbekistan country in Central Asia; former Soviet republic, 387

Vaduz (47°N 10°E) capital of Liechtenstein, A15

Valletta (36°N 14°E) capital of Malta, 252

Valparaíso (33°S 72°W) Pacific port for the national capital of Santiago, Chile, 229

Vancouver (49°N 123°W) Pacific port in Canada, 129

Vanuatu South Pacific island country in Melanesia, 694

Vatican City (42°N 12°E) European microstate surrounded by Rome, Italy, 261

Venezuela country in northern South America, 195

Victoria (1°S 33°E) capital of the Seychelles, 541

Vienna (48°N 16°E) capital of Austria, 279

Vientiane (18°N 103°E) capital of Laos, 617

Vietnam country in Southeast Asia, 617

Vilnius (55°N 25°E) capital of Lithuania, 319

Vinson Massif (78°S 87°W) highest mountain (16,066 ft.; 4,897 m) in Antarctica, 693

Virgin Islands island chain lying just east of Puerto Rico in the Caribbean Sea, 179

Vistula River river flowing through Warsaw, Poland, to the Baltic Sea, 319

Vladivostok (43°N 132°E) chief seaport of the Russian Far East, 351

Volga River Europe's longest river; located in west central Russia, 351

Wake Island (19°N 167°E) U.S. South Pacific island territory north of the Marshall Islands, 694

Wales part of the United Kingdom occupying a western portion of Great Britain, 299

Wallonia region in southern Belgium, 279

Warsaw (52°N 21°E) capital of Poland, 319

Washington, D.C. (39°N 77°W) U.S. capital; located between Virginia and Maryland on the Potomac River, 107

Wellington (41°S 175°E) capital of New Zealand, 701

West Bank area of Palestine west of the Jordan River; occupied by Israel in 1967; political status is in transition, 435

Western Ghats (GAWTS) hills facing the Arabian Sea on the western side of the Deccan Plateau, India, 651

Western Plateau large, flat plain covering more than half of Australia, 701

Western Rift Valley westernmost of two deep troughs beginning near Lake Malawi (Lake Nyasa) in eastern Africa and continuing north into the Red Sea and then into Syria, 525

Western Sahara disputed territory in northwestern Africa; claimed by Morocco, 471

West Siberian Plain region with many marshes east of the Urals in Russia, 351

White Nile part of the Nile River system in eastern Africa, 509

Windhoek (22°S 17°E) capital of Namibia, 541

Windsor (42°N 83°W) industrial city across from Detroit, Michigan, in the Canadian province of Ontario, 129

Winnipeg (50°N 97°W) provincial capital of Manitoba in central Canada, 129

Witwatersand (WIT-wawt-uhrz-rahnd) a range of low hills in north central South Africa, 541

Wuhan (31°N 114°E) city in south central China, 573

Xi River river in southeastern China, 573

Yamoussoukro (7°N 5°W) capital of Côte d'Ivoire, 491

Yangon (Rangoon) (17°N 96°E) capital of Myanmar (Burma), 617

Yaoundé (4°N 12°E) capital of Cameroon, 525

Yekaterinburg (formerly Sverdlovsk) (57°N 61°E) city in the Urals region in Russia, 351

Yemen country located in the southwestern corner of the Arabian Peninsula, 415

Yenisey (yi-ni-SAY) major river in central Russia, 351

Yerevan (40°N 45°E) capital of Armenia, 373

Yucatán Peninsula peninsula in southeastern Mexico, 161

Yugoslavia former Eastern European country of six republics; now including only the republics of Serbia and Montenegro, 319

Yukon Territory Canadian territory bordering Alaska, 129

Zagreb (46°N 16°E) capital of Croatia, 319

Zagros Mountains mountain range of southwestern Iran, 415

Zambezi (zam-BEE-zee) **River** major river in central and southern Africa, 525

Zambia country in central Africa, 525

Zimbabwe (zim-BAH-bway) country in southern Africa, 541

Zurich (47°N 9°E) Switzerland's largest city, 279

GLOSSARY

abdicated Gave up the throne, **356**

absolute location The exact spot on Earth where something is found, often stated in latitude and longitude, **7**

acculturation The process of cultural changes that result from long-term contact with another society, **77**

acid rain A type of polluted rain, produced when pollution from smokestacks combines with water vapor, **64**

agrarian A society organized around farming, **383**

air pressure The weight of the air, measured by a barometer, **39**

allies Friendly countries that support one another against enemies, **357**

alluvial fan A fan-shaped landform created by deposits of sediment at the base of a mountain, **32**

amber Fossilized tree sap, **321**

animism A religious belief that bodies of water, animals, trees, and other natural objects have spirits, **498**

annexed Formally added, **113**

Antarctic Circle The line of latitude located at 66.5° south of the equator, **20**

antifreeze A substance added to liquid to keep the liquid from turning to ice, **728**

apartheid The South African government policy of separation of races, which began to disappear in the 1980s, **548**

aqueducts Artificial channels for carrying water, **62**

aquifers Underground, water-bearing layers of rock, sand, or gravel, **62**

arable Suitable for growing crops, **576**

archaeology The study of the remains and ruins of past cultures, **494**

archipelago (ahr-kuh-PE-luh-goh) A large group of islands, **180, 618**

Arctic Circle The line of latitude located at 66.5° north of the equator, **20**

arid Dry with little rainfall, **46**

artesian wells Wells in which water rises toward the surface without being pumped, **702**

asphalt The tar-like material used to pave streets, **437**

atmosphere The layer of gases that surrounds Earth, **22**

atolls Rings of coral surrounding lagoons, **683**

axis An imaginary line that runs from the North Pole through Earth's center to the South Pole, **19**

basins Regions surrounded by mountains or other higher land, **109, 526**

bauxite The most important aluminum ore, **181, 493**

Bedouins Nomadic herders in the deserts of Egypt and Southwest Asia, **478**

bilingual Having the ability to speak two languages, **114**

Boers Afrikaner frontier farmers, white descendants of South Africa's original European colonists, **546**

bog Soft ground that is soaked with water, **310**
boycott Refuse to buy, **658**
bush Lightly populated wilderness areas, such as parts of Australia, **707**

cacao (kuh-KOW) A small tree on which cocoa beans grow, **184, 505**
caliph A religious and political ruler in the Muslim world, **418**
calypso A type of music with origins in Trinidad and Tobago, **188**
canopy The uppermost layer of a forest's trees where limbs spread out and block out sunlight, **526**
cantons Political and administrative districts in Switzerland, **293**
caravans Groups of people who travel together for protection, **390**
cardamom A spice used in Asian foods, **185**
carrying capacity The maximum number of a species that can be supported by an area, **89**
cartography The art and science of mapmaking, **13**
Casbah The old fortress and central part of some North African cities, **485**
cash crops Crops produced primarily to sell rather than for the farmer to eat, **173**
cassava (kuh-SAH-vuh) A tropical plant with starchy roots, **200**
caste system A system in which people's position in society is determined by their birth into a particular caste or group, **662**
caudillos (kow-THEE-yohs) Military leaders who ruled Venezuela in the 1800s and 1900s, **203**
center-pivot irrigation A type of irrigation that uses sprinkler systems mounted on huge rotating wheels, **124**
chaebol Huge industrial groups of South Korean companies, banks, and other businesses, **612**
chancellor Germany's head of government, or prime minister, **287**
chinampas (chuh-NAM-puhs) The name the Aztecs gave to raised fields on which they grew crops, **166**
cholera A life-threatening intestinal infection, **675**
city-states Self-governing cities, such as those of ancient Greece, **264**
civilization A highly complex culture with growing cities and economic activity, **80**
civil war A conflict between two or more groups within a country, **185, 533**
climate The weather conditions in an area over a long period of time, **37**
climatology The field of tracking Earth's larger atmospheric systems, **13**
cloud forest A high-elevation, very wet tropical forest where low clouds are common, **181**
coalition governments Governments in which several political parties join together to run a country, **269**
Cold War The rivalry between the United States and the Soviet Union that lasted from the 1940s to the early 1990s, **357**

colonies Territories controlled by people from a foreign land, **113**
command economy An economy in which the government owns most of the industries and makes most of the economic decisions, **85**
commercial agriculture A type of farming in which farmers produce food for sale, **80**
commonwealth A self-governing territory associated with another country, **191**
condensation The process by which water changes from a gas into tiny liquid droplets, **24**
conquistadores (kahn-kees-tuh-DAWR-ez) Spanish conquerors during the era of colonization in the Americas, **167**
constitutional monarchy A government with a monarch as head of state and a parliament or other legislature that makes the laws, **303**
consumer goods Products used at home and in everyday life, **357**
contiguous Units, such as states, that connect to or border each other, **108**
Continental Divide The crest of the Rocky Mountains that divides North America's rivers into those that flow eastward and those that flow westward, **109**
continental shelf The gently sloping underwater land surrounding each continent, **25**
continents Earth's large landmasses, **29**
cooperatives Organizations owned by their members and operated for their mutual benefit, **189**
copper belt A major copper-mining region of central Africa, **527**
coral reef A ridge made up of the skeletal remains of tiny sea animals and found close to shore in warm, tropical waters, **703**
cordillera (kawr-duhl-YER-uh) A mountain system made up of parallel ranges, **196**
core The inner, solid part of Earth, **28**
cork The bark stripped from a certain type of oak tree and often used as stoppers and insulation, **275**
Corn Belt The area of the Midwestern United States from Ohio to Iowa where raising corn is a major economic activity, **123**
cosmopolitan Having many foreign influences, **292**
Cossacks Nomadic horsemen who once lived on the Ukrainian frontier, **377**
coup (KOO) A sudden overthrow of a government by a small group of people, **237**
creoles American-born descendants of Europeans in Spanish South America, **236**
crop rotation A system of growing different crops on the same land over a period of years, **59**
crust The outer, solid layer of Earth, **28**
culture A learned system of shared beliefs and ways of doing things that guide a person's daily behavior, **75**
culture region Area of the world in which people share certain culture traits, **75**
culture traits Elements of culture, **75**
currents Giant streams of ocean water that move from warm to cold or from cold to warm areas, **41**
cyclones Violent storms with high winds and heavy rain in South Asia, similar to hurricanes in the Caribbean, **670**

czar (ZAHR) Emperor of the Russian Empire, **356**

Dairy Belt The area of the Midwestern United States north of the Corn Belt in which dairy farming is a major economic activity, **123**

Dalits People at the bottom of the Indian caste system who do the work that is considered unclean, **663**

deforestation The destruction or loss of forest area, **61**

deltas Landforms created by the deposits of sediment at the mouths of rivers, **32**

demilitarized zone A buffer zone that serves as a barrier separating two countries, such as North and South Korea, **609**

democracy A political system in which a country's people elect their leaders and rule by majority, **86**

depressions Low areas, **472**

desalinization The process in which the salt is taken out of seawater, **63**

desertification The long-term process of losing soil fertility and plant life, **60**

developed countries Industrialized countries that have strong secondary, tertiary, and quaternary industries, **84**

developing countries Countries in different stages of moving toward development, **84**

dialect A variation of a language, **274, 530**

Diaspora The scattering of the Jewish population from Palestine under Roman rule, **442**

dictators People who rule a country with complete authority, **184, 487**

Diet (DY-uht) Japan's elected legislature, **601**

diffusion The movement of ideas or behaviors from one cultural region to another, **9**

dikes High banks of earth or concrete built along waterfronts to help reduce flooding, **575**

diversify For farmers, producing a variety of crops instead of just one, **120**

domestication The growing of a plant or taming of an animal by a people for their own use, **79**

dominion A territory or area of influence, **134**

droughts Periods when little rain falls and crops are damaged, **519**

dynasty A ruling family that passes power from one generation to the next, **577**

E

earthquakes Sudden, violent movement along a fracture within Earth's crust, **29**

ecology The study of the connections among different forms of life, **51**

ecosystem All of the plants and animals in an area together with the nonliving parts of their environment, **54**

ecotourism The practice of using an area's natural environment to attract tourists, **186**

ejidos (e-HEE-thohs) Lands owned and worked by groups of Mexican Indians, **168**

El Dorado (el duh-RAH-doh) "The Golden One," a legend of the early Chibcha people of Colombia, **198**

El Niño An ocean and weather pattern in the Pacific Ocean in which ocean waters become warmer, **232**

embargo A limit on trade, **427**

emperor A ruler of a large empire, **577**

empire A system in which a central power controls a number of territories, **167**

enclaves Countries surrounded or almost surrounded by another country, **542**

encomienda A system in which Spanish monarchs gave land to Spanish colonists in the Americas; landowners could force Indians living there to work the land, **219**

endemic species Plants and animals that developed in one particular region of the world, **703**

entrepreneurs People who use their money and talents to start a business, **85**

epidemic Widespread outbreak, often referring to disease, **167**

equinoxes The two days of the year when the Sun's rays strike the equator directly, **21**

ergs Great "seas" of sand dunes in the Sahara, **472**

erosion The movement by water, ice, or wind of rocky materials to another location, **32**

estuary A partially enclosed body of water where salty seawater and freshwater mix, **213**

ethnic groups Cultural groups of people who share learned beliefs and practices, **75**

evaporation The process by which heated water becomes water vapor and rises into the air, **24**

exclave A part of a country that is separated by territory of other countries, **537**

Exclusive Economic Zones Areas off a country's coast within which the country claims and controls all resources, **725**

exotic rivers Rivers that begin in humid regions and then flow through dry areas, **416**

extinct Something that dies out completely; is no longer present, **51**

F

factors of production The natural resources, money, labor, and entrepreneurs needed for business operation, **85**

famine A great shortage of food, **308, 613**

fault A fractured surface in Earth's crust where a mass of rock is in motion, **31**

favelas (fah-VE-lahs) Huge slums that surround some Brazilian cities, **217**

fellahin (fel-uh-HEEN) Egyptian farmers who own very small plots of land, **482**

fjords (fee-AWRDS) Narrow, deep inlets of the sea set between high, rocky cliffs, **300**

floodplain A landform of level ground built by sediment deposited by a river or stream, **32**

food chain A series of organisms in which energy is passed along, **51**

fossil fuels Nonrenewable resources formed from the remains of ancient plants and animals, **68**

fossil water Water that is not being replaced by rainfall, **417**

free enterprise An economic system in which people, not government, decide what to make, sell, or buy, **85**

free port A city in which almost no taxes are placed on goods sold there, **485**

front The unstable weather where a large amount of warm air meets a large amount of cold air, **40**

futon (FOO-tahn) A lightweight cotton mattress, often used in Japan, **604**

gauchos (GOW-chohz) Argentine cowboys, **219**

geography The study of Earth's physical and cultural features, **3**

geothermal energy A renewable energy resource produced from the heat of Earth's interior, **70**

gers (GUHRZ) Large, circular tents that are easy to raise, dismantle, and move; used by nomadic herders in Mongolia, **589**

geysers Hot springs that shoot hot water and steam into the air, **314**

glaciers Large, slow-moving sheets or rivers of ice, **33**

glen A Scottish term for a valley, **305**

global warming A slow increase in Earth's average temperature, **64**

gorge A narrow, steep-walled canyon, **516**

graphite A form of carbon used in pencils and many other products, **682**

greenhouse effect The process by which Earth's atmosphere traps heat, **38**

green revolution A program, begun by the Indian government in the 1960s, that encouraged farmers to modernize their methods to produce more food, **665**

griots (GREE-ohz) West African storytellers who pass on the oral histories of their tribes or people, **504**

gross domestic product The value of all goods and services produced within a country, **84**

gross national product The value of all goods and services that a country produces in one year within or outside the country, **84**

groundwater The water from rainfall, rivers, lakes, and melting snow that seeps into the ground, **25**

guerrilla An armed person who takes part in irregular warfare, such as raids, **189**

habitation fog A fog caused by fumes and smoke trapped over Siberian cities by very cold weather, **364**

haciendas (hah-see-EN-duhs) Huge farmlands granted by the Spanish monarch to favored people in Spain's colonies, **168**

harmattan (HAR-muh-TAN) A dry, dusty wind that blows south from the Sahara during winter, **492**

heavy industry Industry that usually involves manufacturing based on metals, **362**

hieroglyphs (HY-ruh-glifs) Pictures and symbols used to record information in ancient Egypt, **475**

Holocaust The mass murder of millions of Jews and other people by the Nazis in World War II, **287**

homogeneous Sharing the same characteristics, such as ethnicity, **383**

human geography The study of people, past or present, **11**

humus Decayed plant and animal matter, **55**

hurricanes Tropical storms that bring violent winds, heavy rain, and high seas, **48**

hydroelectric power A renewable energy resource produced from dams that harness the energy of falling water to power generators, **70**

icebergs Large chunks of ice that break away from glaciers and ice shelves and drift into the ocean, **720**

icebreakers Ships that can break up the ice of frozen waterways, allowing other ships to pass through them, **368**

ice shelf A ledge of ice over coastal water, **720**

impressionism A form of art that developed in France in the late 1800s and early 1900s, **285**

indentured servants People who agree to work for a certain period of time, often in exchange for travel expenses, **205**

indigo (IN-di-goh) A plant used to make a deep blue dye, **202**

Indo-European A language family that includes many languages of Europe, such as Germanic, Baltic, and Slavic languages, **322**

inflation The rise in prices that occurs when currency loses its buying power, **172**

intensive cultivation The practice of growing crops on every bit of available land, **605**

Inuit North American Eskimos, **141**

isthmus A neck of land connecting two larger land areas, **28**

ivory A cream-colored material that comes from elephant tusks and is used in making fine jewelry and handicrafts, **528**

Japan Current A warm ocean current east of Japan, **597**

junta (HOOHN-tuh) A small group of military officers who rule a country after seizing power, **241**

kampongs A traditional village in Indonesia; also the term for crowded slums around Indonesia's large cities, **628**

karma Among Hindus and Buddhists, the positive or negative force caused by a person's actions, **660**

kimchi Chinese cabbage that has been spiced and pickled; Korea's national dish, **612**

kimonos Traditional Japanese robes, **603**

kiwi (KEE-wee) A flightless bird in New Zealand; a name sometimes applied to New Zealanders, **711**

klongs Canals throughout Bangkok, Thailand, **625**

krill Tiny shrimp-like marine animals that are an important food for larger Antarctic marine life, **721**

landforms The shapes on Earth's surface, **28**

landlocked Completely surrounded by land, with no direct access to the ocean, **224, 387**

lava Magma that has broken through the crust to Earth's surface, **29**

levees Large walls, usually made of dirt, built along rivers to prevent flooding, **10**

light industry Industry that focuses on the production of lightweight goods, such as clothing, **362**

lignite A soft form of coal **321**

limited government Government in which government leaders are held accountable by citizens through their constitutions and democratic processes, **86**

Llaneros (lah-NE-rohs) Cowboys of the Venezuelan Llanos, **204**

Llanos (LAH-nohs) A plains region in eastern Columbia and western Venezuela, **196**

lochs Scottish lakes located in valleys carved by glaciers, **300**

loess (LES) Fine, windblown soil that is good for farming, **281**

magma Melted rock in the upper mantle of Earth, **28**

mainland A region or country's main landmass, **262, 618**

malaria A deadly disease spread by mosquitoes, **500**

mandate Former territories of defeated World War I countries that were placed under the control of winning countries after the war, **446**

mantle The liquid layer that surrounds Earth's core, **28**

maquiladoras (mah-kee-lah-DORH-ahs) Foreign-owned factories located along Mexico's northern border with the United States, **175**

maritime On or near the sea, such as Canada's Maritime Provinces, **138**

market economy An economy in which consumers help determine what is to be produced by buying or not buying certain goods and services, **85**

marsupials (mahr-SOO-pee-uhls) Animals that carry their young in pouches, **704**

martial law Military rule, **580**

medieval Refers to the period from the collapse of the Roman Empire to about 1500, **283**

megalopolis A giant urban area that includes a string of cities that have grown together, **120, 603**

Mercosur A trade organization that includes Argentina, Brazil, Paraguay, Uruguay, and two associate members (Bolivia and Chile), **222**

merengue The national music and dance of the Dominican Republic, **188**

mestizos (me-STEE-zohs) People of mixed European and American Indian ancestry, **168**

metallic minerals Shiny minerals, like gold and iron, that can conduct heat and electricity, **65**

meteorology The field of forecasting and reporting rainfall, temperatures, and other atmospheric conditions, **13**

Métis (may-TEES) People of mixed European and Canadian Indian ancestry in Canada, **135**

millet A grain crop that can survive drought, **499**

minerals Inorganic substances that make up Earth's crust, occur naturally, are solids in crystalline form, and have a definite chemical composition, **65**

missions Spanish church outposts established during the colonial era, particularly in the Americas, **168**

monsoon The seasonal shift of air flow and rainfall, which brings alternating wet and dry seasons, **45**

Moors Muslim North Africans, **273**

mosaics (moh-ZAY-iks) Pictures created from tiny pieces of colored stone, **266**

mosques Islamic houses of worship, **394**

most-favored-nation status A status that grants special trade advantages from the United States, **587**

mulattoes (muh-LA-tohs) People of mixed European and African ancestry, **168**

multicultural A mixture of different cultures within the same country or community, **75**

multiple cropping A type of agriculture in which two or three crops are raised each year on the same land, **586**

Muslims Followers of Islam, **418**

nationalism The demand for self-rule and a strong feeling of loyalty to one's nation, **294**

NATO North Atlantic Treaty Organization, a military alliance of various European countries, the United States, and Canada, **283**

nature reserves Areas a government has set aside to protect animals, plants, soil, and water, **374**

navigable Water routes that are deep enough and wide enough to be used by ships, **280**

neutral Not taking a side in a dispute or conflict, **312**

newsprint Cheap paper used mainly for newspapers, **131**

nirvana Among Buddhists, the escape from the suffering of life, **661**

nomads People who often move from place to place, **390**

nonmetallic minerals Minerals that lack the characteristics of metal, **66**

nonrenewable resources Resources, such as coal and oil, that cannot be replaced by Earth's natural processes or that are replaced slowly, **65**

North Atlantic Drift A warm ocean current that brings mild temperatures and rain to parts of northern Europe, **301**

nutrients Substances promoting growth, **52**

oasis A place in the desert where a spring or well provides water, **388**

oil shale Layered rock that yields oil when heated, **321**

OPEC Organization of Petroleum Exporting Countries, which tries to influence the price of oil on world markets, **419**

oral history Spoken information passed down from person to person through generations, **494**

orbit The path an object makes around a central object, such as a planet around the Sun, **17**

Organization of African Unity (OAU) An organization, founded in 1963, that tries to promote cooperation among African countries, **553**

outback Australia's inland region, **704**

Oyashio (oh-YAH-shee-oh) **Current** A cool ocean current east of Japan, **597**

ozone A form of oxygen in the atmosphere that helps protect Earth from harmful solar radiation, **22**

pagodas Buddhist temples, **582**

Pampas A wide, grassy plains region in central Argentina, **212**

Pangaea (pan-GEE-uh) Earth's single, original super-continent from which today's continents were separated, **31**

pans Low, flat, desert areas of southern Africa into which ancient streams drained, **543**

pardos Venezuelans of mixed African, European, and South American Indian ancestry, **204**

peat Matter made from dead plants, usually mosses, **310**

peninsula Land bordered by water on three sides, **28**

periodic markets Open-air trading markets in central Africa, **527**

permafrost The layer of soil that stays frozen all year in tundra climate regions, **49**

perspective Point of view based on a person's experience and personal understanding, **3**

Peru Current A cold ocean current off the coast of western South America, **231**

petroleum An oily liquid that can be refined into gasoline and other fuels and oils, **68**

pharaohs Ancient Egyptian kings, **475**

phosphates Mineral salts containing the element phosphorus; used to make fertilizers, **437**

photosynthesis The process by which plants convert sunlight into chemical energy, **51**

physical geography The study of Earth's natural landscape and physical systems, including the atmosphere, **11**

pidgin languages Simple languages that help people who speak different languages understand each other, **205**

plain A nearly flat area on Earth's surface, **28**

plantains A type of banana used in cooking, **190**

plantations Large farms that grow mainly one crop to sell, **113**

plant communities Groups of plants that live in the same area, **53**

plant succession The gradual process by which one group of plants replaces another, **54**

plateau An elevated flatland on Earth's surface, **28**

plate tectonics The theory that Earth's surface is divided into several major, slowly moving plates or pieces, **28**

polar desert A high-latitude region that receives little precipitation, **721**

pope The bishop of Rome and the head of the Roman Catholic Church, **269**

population density The average number of people living within a square mile or square kilometer, **81**

porcelain A type of very fine pottery, **578**

potash A mineral used to make fertilizer, **131**

precipitation The process by which water falls back to Earth, **24**

primary industries Economic activities that directly involve natural resources or raw materials, such as farming and mining, **83**

protectionism The practice of setting up trade barriers to shield industries at home from foreign competition, **606**

provinces Administrative divisions of a country, **134**

pulp softened wood fibers used to make paper, **131**

quaternary industries Economic activities that include specialized skills or knowledge and work mostly with information, **84**

Quechua (KE-chuh-wuh) The language of South America's Inca; still spoken in the region, **238**

quinoa (KEEN-wah) A native plant of South America's Andean region that yields nutritious seeds, **233**

quipus (KEE-pooz) Complicated systems of knots tied on strings of various colors, used by the Inca of South America to record information, **234**

Qur'an The holy book of Islam, **419**

race A group of people who share inherited physical or biological traits, **76**

rain shadow The dry area on the leeward side of a mountain or mountain range, **44**

refineries Factories where crude oil is processed, **68**

reforestation The planting of trees in places where forests have been cut down, **61**

Reformation A movement in Europe to reform Christianity in the 1500s, **286**

refugees People who flee to another country, usually for economic or political reasons, **189, 621**

reggae A type of music with origins in Jamaica, **188**

regionalism The stronger connection to one's region than to one's country, **137**

regs Broad, windswept gravel plains in the Sahara, **472**

reincarnation The belief that the human soul is reborn again and again in different bodies, **660**

relative location The position of a place in relation to another place, **7**

Renaissance (re-nuh-SAHNS) French word meaning "rebirth" and referring to a new era of learning that began in Europe in the 1300s, **269**

renewable resources Resources, such as soils and forests, that can be replaced by Earth's natural processes, **59**

revolution One complete orbit around the Sun, **19**

rifts Long, deep valleys with mountains or plateaus on either side, **510**

Roma An ethnic group also known as Gypsies who are descended from people who may have migrated from India to Europe long ago, **332**

rotation One complete spin of Earth on its axis, **19**

rugby A game with British origins; similar to football and soccer, **706**

rural An area of open land that is often used for farming, **4**

Sahel (sah-HEL) A dry grasslands region with a steppe climate south of the Sahara, **492**

samurai (SA-muh-ry) Warriors who served Japanese lords, **600**

sanctions An economic or political penalty, such as an embargo, used by one or more countries to force another country to cease an illegal or immoral act, **549**

Sanskrit An early language form in South Asia; used as a sacred language in India today, **655**

Santería A religion, with origins in Cuba, that mixes West African religions and traditions with those of Roman Catholicism, **188**

satellite A body that orbits a larger body, **18**

scarcity Situation that occurs when demand is greater than supply, **87**

secede To break away from a country to form another, **502**

secondary industries Economic activities that change raw materials created by primary industries into finished products, **83**

second-growth forests The trees that cover an area after the original forest has been cut, **119**

secular Kept separate from religion, as in a secular government or state, **439**

selvas The thick tropical rain forests of eastern Ecuador, eastern Peru, and northern Bolivia, **231**

semiarid Relatively dry with small amounts of rain, **62**

sepoys Indian troops commanded by British officers during the colonial era in India, **658**

serfs People in Russia who were bound to the land and worked for a lord, **377**

shah A king of Iran, **430**

shamans Shinto priests, **599**

Shia The second-largest branch of Islam, **418**

Shintoism The earliest known religion of Japan, **599**

shogun "Great general," the highest Japanese warrior rank, **600**

silt Finely ground soil, **473**

sinkholes A steep-sided depression formed when the roof of a cave collapses, **162**

sirocco (suh-RAH-koh) A hot, dry wind from North Africa that blows across the Mediterranean to Europe, **263**

slash-and-burn agriculture A type of agriculture in which forests are cut and burned to clear land for planting, **175**

smelters Factories that process metal ores, **363**

smog A mixture of smoke, chemicals, and fog, **174**

soil exhaustion The loss of soil nutrients needed by plants, **214**

solar energy A renewable energy resource produced from the Sun's heat and light, **71**

solar system The Sun and the objects that move about it, including planets, moons, and asteroids, **17**

solstice The days when the Sun's vertical rays are farthest from the equator, **21**

sorghum A grain crop that can survive drought, **499**

souks Marketplaces in North Africa, **485**

soviet A council of Communists who governed republics and other places in the Soviet Union, **377**

spatial perspective Point of view based on looking at where something is and why it is there, **3**

staple A region or country's main food crop, **500**

steppe (STEP) A wide, flat grasslands region that stretches from Ukraine across southern Russia to Kazakhstan, **353**

steppe climate A dry climate type generally found between desert and wet climate regions, **46**

storm surges Huge waves of water that are whipped up by fierce winds, particularly from cyclones, hurricanes, and other tropical storms, **670**

strait A narrow passageway that connects two large bodies of water, **230**

strip mining The type of mining in which soil and rock are stripped away so that miners can get to coal or other resources buried just beneath the surface, **124**

stupas Mounds of earth or stones covering the ashes of the Buddha or relics of Buddhist saints, **678**

subduction The movement of one of Earth's heavier tectonic plates underneath a lighter tectonic plate, **29**

subregions Small areas of a region, **8**

subsistence agriculture A type of farming in which farmers grow just enough food to provide for themselves and their own families, **80**

sultan The supreme ruler of a Muslim country, **631**

Sunni The largest branch of Islam, **418**

superpowers Powerful countries, **357**

Swahili A Bantu language that is widely spoken in areas of Africa, **514**

symbol A word, shape, color, flag, or other sign that stands for something else, **77**

taiga (TY-guh) A forest of evergreen trees growing south of the tundra in Russia, **353**

teak A valuable type of wood; grown in India and Southeast Asia, **653**

tepuís (tay-PWEEZ) Layers of sandstone that have resisted erosion atop plateaus in the Guiana Highlands, **196**

terraces Horizontal ridges built into the slopes of steep hillsides to prevent soil loss and aid farming, **60**

tertiary industries Economic activities that handle goods that are ready to be sold to consumers, **84**

textiles Cloth products, **113, 303**

theocracy A government ruled by religious leaders, **430**

the veld (VELT) Open grasslands areas of South Africa, **542**

townships Special areas of crowded clusters of tiny homes for black South Africans living outside cities, **548**

trade deficit The value of exports is lower than the value of imports, **125**

trade surplus The value of exports is greater than the value of imports, **606**

traditional economy Economy based on custom and tradition, **85**

tributary Any smaller stream or river that flows into a larger stream or river, **25**

Tropic of Cancer The line of latitude that is 23.5° north of the equator, **21**

Tropic of Capricorn The line of latitude that is 23.5° south of the equator, **21**

trust territories Areas placed under the temporary control of another country until they set up their own government, **723**

tsetse (TSET-see) **fly** A fly in Africa south of the Sahara that spreads sleeping sickness, a deadly disease, **492**

tsunamis (tsooh-NAH-mees) Huge waves created by undersea tectonic activity, such as earthquakes, **597**

tundra climate A cold region with low rainfall, lying generally between subarctic and polar climate regions, **49**

typhoons Tropical storms that bring violent winds, heavy rain, and high seas, **48**

uninhabitable Not capable of supporting human settlement, **314**

unlimited governments Governments that have total control over their citizens, **86**

urban An area that contains a city, **4**

viceroy The governor of a colony, **236**

wadis Dry streambeds in Southwest Asia, **417**

water cycle The circulation of water from Earth's surface to the atmosphere and back, **23**

water vapor The gaseous form of water, **23**

weather The condition of the atmosphere at a given place and time, **37**

weathering The process of breaking rocks into smaller pieces through heat, water, or other means, **31**

Wheat Belt The area of the U. S. Great Plains region in which wheat farming is a major economic activity, **124**

work ethic The belief that work in itself is worthwhile, **606**

yurt A movable round house of wool felt mats over a wood frame, **394**

Zionism The movement to establish a Jewish country or community in Palestine, **443**

zonal The climates of West Africa, which stretch east to west in bands, **492**

SPANISH GLOSSARY

Phonetic Respelling and Pronunciation Guide

Many of the key terms in this textbook have been respelled to help you pronounce them. The letter combinations used in the respelling throughout the narrative are explained in this phonetic respelling and pronunciation guide. The guide is adapted from *Webster's Tenth New College Dictionary*, *Merriam-Webster's New Geographical Dictionary*, and *Merriam-Webster's New Biographical Dictionary*.

MARK	AS IN	RESPELLING	EXAMPLE
a	alphabet	a	*AL-fuh-bet
ā	Asia	ay	AY-zhuh
ä	cart, top	ah	KAHRT, TAHP
e	let, ten	e	LET, TEN
ē	even, leaf	ee	EE-vuhn, LEEF
i	it, tip, British	i	IT, TIP, BRIT-ish
ī	site, buy, Ohio	y	SYT, BY, oh-HY-oh
	iris	eye	EYE-ris
k	card	k	KAHRD
ō	over, rainbow	oh	OH-vuhr, RAYN-boh
u̇	book, wood	ooh	BOOHK, WOOHD
ȯ	all, orchid	aw	AWL, AWR-kid
ȯi	foil, coin	oy	FOYL, KOYN
au̇	out	ow	OWT
ə	cup, butter	uh	KUHP, BUHT-uhr
ü	rule, food	oo	ROOL, FOOD
yü	few	yoo	FYOO
zh	vision	zh	VIZH-uhn

*A syllable printed in small capital letters receives heavier emphasis than the other syllable(s) in a word.

A

abdicated/abdicar Renunciar al trono, **356**

absolute location/posición exacta Lugar exacto de la tierra donde se localiza un punto, por lo general definido en términos de latitud y longitud, **6**

acculturation/aculturación Proceso de asimilación de una cultura a largo plazo por el contacto con otra sociedad, **77**

acid rain/lluvia ácida Tipo de lluvia contaminada que se produce cuando partículas de contaminación del aire se combinan con el vapor de agua de la atmósfera, **64**

agrarian/agrario Sociedad basada en la agricultura, **383**

air pressure/presión atmosférica Peso del aire, se mide con un barómetro, **39**

allies/aliados Países que se apoyan entre sí para defenderse de sus enemigos, **357**

alluvial fan/abanico aluvial Accidente geográfico en forma de abanico que se origina por la acumulación de sedimentos en la base de una montaña, **32**

amber/ámbar Savia de árbol fosilizada, **321**

animism/animismo Creencia religiosa que explica que los cuerpos de agua, los animales, los árboles y otros objetos de la naturaleza tienen un espíritu, **498**

annexed/anexado Adición formal, **113**

Antarctic Circle/círculo antártico Meridiano localizado a 66.5° al sur del ecuador, **20**

antifreeze/anticongelante Sustancia que se agrega a un líquido para evitar que se congele, **728**

apartheid/apartheid Política de separación de razas aplicada por el gobierno sudafricano. Empezó a desaparecer en la década de 1980, **548**

aqueducts/acueductos Canales artificiales usados para transportar agua, **62**

aquifers/acuíferos Capas subterráneas de roca, arena y grava en las que se almacena el agua, **62**

arable/cultivable Tierra con características que favorecen el cultivo, **576**

archaeology/arqueología Estudio de los restos de culturas pasadas, **494**

archipelago/archipiélago Grupo grande de islas, **180, 618**

Arctic Circle/círculo ártico Meridiano localizado a 66.5° al norte del ecuador, **20**

arid/árido Territorio donde la lluvia es muy escasa, **46**

artesian wells/pozos artesianos Pozos en los que el agua sube a la superficie de la tierra sin ser impulsada por medios artificiales, **702**

asphalt/asfalto Material oscuro usado para pavimentar calles, **437**

atmosphere/atmósfera Capa de gases que rodea a la tierra, **22**

atolls/atolones Anillos de coral que se forman alrededor de las lagunas, **683**

axis/eje Línea imaginaria que corre del polo norte al polo sur, pasando por el centro de la Tierra, **19**

B

basins/cuencas Regiones rodeadas por montañas u otras tierras altas, **109, 526**

bauxite/bauxita El mineral con contenido de aluminio más importante, **181, 493**

Bedouins/beduinos Ganaderos nómadas del desierto de Egipto y el sudoeste de Asia, **478**

bilingual/bilingüe Persona que habla dos idiomas, **114**

Boers/boers Agricultores africanos de raza blanca, descendientes de los primeros colonizadores europeos de Sudáfrica, **546**

bog/ciénaga Tierra suave, humedecida por el agua, **310**

boycott/boicot Rechazo de compra, **658**

bush Zonas salvajes de escasa población, como ciertas regiones de Australia, **707**

cacao/cacas Árbol pequeño que produce los granos de cacao, **184, 505**

caliph/califa Líder político y religioso del mundo musulmán, **418**

calypso/calipso Tipo de música originado en Trinidad y Tobago, **188**

canopy/dosel Capa superior de un bosque espeso en el que las ramas se entrelazan, bloqueando el paso de la luz solar, **526**

cantons/cantones Distritos políticos y administrativos de Suiza, **293**

caravans/caravanas Grupos de personas que viajan juntas por razones de seguridad, **390**

cardamom/cardamomo Especia que se usa en Asia para condimentar alimentos, **185**

carrying capacity/capacidad de carga Número máximo de especies que puede haber en una zona determinada, **89**

cartography/cartografía Arte y ciencia de la elaboración de mapas, **13**

Casbah/casbah Antigua fortaleza y centro de las ciudades del norte de África, **485**

cash crops/cultivos para la venta Cultivos producidos para su venta y no para consumo del agricultor, **173**

cassava/mandioca Planta tropical de raíces almidonadas, **200**

caste system/sistema de castas Sistema en el que la posición de una persona en la sociedad es determinada por el nivel social del grupo en el que nace, **662**

caudillos/caudillos Líderes militares que gobernaron Venezuela en los siglos XIX y XX, **203**

center pivot irrigation/irrigación de pivote central Tipo de riego que usa aspersores montados en grandes ruedas giratorias, **124**

chaebol/chaebol Enormes grupos industriales formados por compañías, bancos y otros negocios en Corea del Sur, **612**

chancellor/canciller Jefe de gobierno o primer ministro alemán, **287**

chinampas/chinampas Nombre dado por los aztecas a los campos elevados que usaban como tierras de cultivo, **166**

cholera/cólera Infección intestinal seria que puede provocar a muerte, **675**

city-states/ciudades estado Ciudades con un sistema de autogobierno, como en la antigua Grecia, **264**

civilization/civilización Cultura altamente compleja con grandes ciudades y abundante actividad económica, **80**

civil war/guerra civil conflicto entre dos o más grupos dentro de un país, **185, 533**

climate/clima condiciones meteorológicas registradas en un periodo largo, **37**

climatology/climatología Registro de los sistemas atmosféricos de la Tierra, **13**

cloud forest/bosque nuboso Bosque tropical de gran elevación y humedad donde los bancos de nubes son muy comunes, **181**

coalition governments/gobiernos de coalición Gobiernos en los que la administración del país es regida por varios partidos políticos a la vez, **269**

Cold War/guerra fría Rivalidad entre Estados Unidos y la Unión Soviética que se extendió de la década de 1940 a la década de 1990, **357**

colonies/colonias Territorios controlados por personas de otro país, **113**

command economy/economía autoritaria Economía en la que el gobierno es propietario de la mayor parte de las industrias y toma la mayoría de las decisiones en materia de economía, **586**

commercial agriculture/agricultura comercial Tipo de agricultura cuya producción es exclusiva para la venta, **80**

commonwealth/mancomunidad Territorio autogobernado que mantiene una sociedad con otro país, **191**

condensation/condensación Proceso mediante el cual el agua cambia de estado gaseoso y forma pequeñas gotas, **24**

conquistadores/conquistadores Españoles que participaron en la colonización de América, **167**

constitutional monarchy/monarquía constitucional Gobierno que cuenta con un monarca como jefe de estado y un parlamento o grupo legislador similar para la aprobación de leyes, **303**

consumer goods/bienes de consumo Productos usados en la vida cotidiana, **357**

contiguous/contiguo Unidades de territorio (como los estados) que colindan entre sí, **108**

Continental Divide/divisoria continental Cordillera que divide los ríos de Estados Unidos en dos partes: los que fluyen al este y los que fluyen al oeste, **109**

continental shelf/plataforma continental zona costera de pendiente suave que bordea a todos los continentes, **25**

continents/continentes Grandes masas de territorio sobre la Tierra, **29**

cooperatives/cooperativas Organizaciones creadas por los propietarios de una empresa y operadas para beneficio propio, **189**

Copper Belt/Región del cobre Importante región minera de producción de cobre localizada en la parte central de África, **527**

coral reef/arrecife coralino Formaciones creadas por la acumulación de los restos de animales marinos diminutos cerca de las costas en las aguas templadas de las regiones tropicales, **703**

cordillera/cordillera Sistema montañoso de cordilleras paralelas, **196**

core/núcleo Parte sólida del interior de la Tierra, **28**

cork/corcho Corteza extraída de cierto tipo de roble, usada principalmente como material de bloqueo y aislante, **275**

Corn Belt/región maicera Región del medio oeste de Estados Unidos, de Ohio a Iowa, cuya actividad agrícola se basa en el cultivo del maíz, **123**

cosmopolitan/cosmopolita Que tiene influencia de muchas culturas, **292**

Cossacks/Cosacos Arrieros nómadas que habitaban en la región fronteriza de Ucrania, **377**

coup/golpe de estado Ataque repentino de un grupo reducido de personas para derrocar a un gobierno, **237**

creoles/criollos Personas de descendencia europea nacidas en la América colonial, **236**

crop rotation/rotación de cultivos Sistema agrícola en el que se siembran productos diferentes en periodos específicos, **59**

crust/corteza Capa sólida de la superficie de la Tierra, **28**

culture/cultura Sistema de creencias y costumbres comunes que guía la conducta cotidiana de las personas, **75**

culture region/región cultural Región del mundo en la que se comparten ciertos rasgos culturales, **75**

culture traits/rasgos culturales Características de una cultura, **75**

currents/corrientes Enormes corrientes del océano que transportan agua tibia a las regiones frías y viceversa, **41**

cyclones/ciclones Tormentas violentas con fuertes lluvias, parecidas a los huracanes del Caribe, comunes en el sur de Asia, **670**

czar/zar Emperador ruso, **356**

Dairy Belt/región lechera Región del medio oeste de Estados Unidos, al norte de la franja del maíz, donde la elaboración de productos lácteos es una importante actividad económica, **123**

Dalits/dalits Personas de la clase social más baja de la India, cuyas actividades son consideradas poco salubres, **663**

deforestation/deforestación Destrucción o pérdida de un área boscosa, **61**

deltas/deltas Formaciones creadas por la acumulación de sedimentos en las desembocadura de los ríos, **32**

demilitarized zone/zona desmilitarizada Zona de protección que sirve como barrera entre dos países en conflicto, como Corea del Norte y Corea del Sur, **609**

democracy/democracia Sistema político en el que la población elige a sus líderes mediante el voto de mayoría, **86**

depressions/cavidads Zonas de elevación muy baja, **472**

desalinization/desalinización Proceso mediante el cual se extrae la sal del agua de mar, **63**

desertification/desertificación Proceso a largo plazo en el que el suelo pierde su fertilidad y vegetación, **60**

developed countries/países desarrollados Países industrializados que cuentan con industrias primarias, secundarias, terciarias y cuaternarias, **84**

developing countries/países en vías de desarrollo países que se encuentran en alguna etapa de su proceso de desarrollo, **84**

dialect/dialecto Variación de un idioma, **274, 530**

Diaspora/Diáspora Dispersión de la población judía que emigró de territorio palestino durante el imperio romano, **442**

dictators/dictadores Personas que ejercen total autoridad sobre un gobierno, **184, 487**

Diet/Dieta Legislatura electa de Japón, **601**

diffusion/difusión Extensión de ideas o conducta de una región cultural a otra, **9**

dikes/diques Grandes muros de tierra o concreto construidos para contener a un cuerpo de agua y evitar inundaciones, **575**

diversify/diversificar En la agricultura, se refiere a la siembra de varios productos y uno solo, **120**

domestication/domesticación Cuidado de una planta o animal para uso personal, **79**

dominion/dominio Territorio en el que se ejerce una influencia, **134**

droughts/sequías Periodos en los que los cultivos sufren daños debido a la escasez de lluvia, **519**

dynasty/dinastía Familia que gobierna y hereda el poder de generación en generación, **577**

earthquakes/terremotos Movimientos repentinos y fuertes que se producen en las fisuras de la superficie de la tierra, **29**

ecology/ecología Estudio de las relaciones entre las diversas formas de vida del planeta, **51**

ecosystem/ecosistema Conjunto de plantas y animales que habitan una región, junto con los elementos no vivos de ese entorno, **54**

ecotourism/ecoturismo Uso de regiones naturales para atraer visitantes, **186**

ejidos/ejidos Territorios de cultivo propiedad de los indígenas de México, **168**

El Dorado/El Dorado leyenda que habla de los chibchas, antiguos habitantes de Colombia, **198**

El Niño/El Niño Patrón oceánico y climatológico del océano Pacífico que elevó la temperatura del agua en dicho océano, **232**

embargo/embargo Límite impuesto a las relaciones comerciales, **427**

emperor/emperador Gobernante supremo de vastos territorios, **577**

empire/imperio Sistema cuyo gobierno central controla diversos territorios, **167**

enclaves/enclaves Países rodeados en su mayor parte o en su totalidad por otro país, **542**

encomienda/encomienda Sistema mediante el cual los monarcas españoles cedían territorios de América a los colonizadores de su país, quienes obligaban a los indígenas de esas dichas tierras a trabajar para ganarse el sustento, **219**

endemic species/especies endémicas Plantas y animales que se desarrollan en una región particular del planeta, **703**

entrepreneurs/empresarios Personas que usan su dinero y su talento para iniciar un negocio, **85**

epidemic/epidemia Expansión vasta, por general de una enfermedad, **167**

equinoxes/equinoccios Los dos días del año en que los rayos de sol caen directamente sobre el ecuador, **21**

ergs/ergs Grandes "mares" de arena formados por las dunas del desierto del Sahara, **472**

erosion/erosión Desplazamiento de agua, hielo, viento o minerales a otro lugar, **32**

estuary/estuario Cuerpo de agua parcialmente cerrado en el que el agua de mar se combina con agua dulce, **213**

ethnic groups/grupos étnicos Grupos culturales que comparten creencias y prácticas comunes, **75**

evaporation/evaporación Proceso mediante el cual el agua se convierte en vapor y se eleva en el aire, **24**

exclave/exclave Parte de un país separada por el territorio de uno o más países, **537**

Exclusive Economic Zones/zonas de exclusividad económica Zonas costeras de un país en las que éste tiene derecho a extraer y controlar los recursos existentes, **725**

exotic rivers/ríos exóticos Ríos originados en regiones húmedas que fluyen a zonas más secas, **416**

extinct/extinto Que deja de existir por completo, **51**

factors of production/factores de producción Los recursos naturales, el dinero, el trabajo y los empresarios que se necesitan para las operaciones de negocios, **85**

famine/hambruna Gran escasez de alimento, **308, 613**

fault/falla Fractura de la superficie de la tierra que causa el movimiento de grandes masas de rocas, **31**

favelas/favelas Grandes poblaciones localizadas en los alrededores de algunas ciudades brasileñas, **217**

fellahin/fellahin agricultores egipcios dueños de pequeñas porciones de terreno, **482**

fjords/fiordos Grietas estrechas y profundas localizadas entre altos acantilados donde se acumula el agua de mar, **300**

floodplain/llanura aluvial Especie de plataforma a nivel de la tierra, formada por la acumulación de los sedimentos de una corriente de agua, **32**

food chain/cadena alimenticia Serie de organismos que proveen alimento y energía unos a otros, **51**

fossil fuels/combustibles fósiles Recursos no renovables formados por restos muy antiguos de plantas y animales, **68**

fossil water/aguas fósiles Agua que no es reemplazada por el agua de lluvia, **417**

free enterprise/libre empresa Sistema económico en el que las personas, y no el gobierno, deciden qué productos fabrican, venden y compran, **85**

free port/puerto libre Ciudad en la que casi no se aplican impuestos a los productos que allí se adquieren, **485**

front/frente Inestabilidad climatológica en la que una gran masa de aire tibio choca con una gran masa de aire frío, **40**

futon/futón Especie de sofá ligero, también usado como cama, muy común en Japón, **604**

gauchos/gauchos Arrieros argentinos, **219**

geography/geografía Estudio de las características físicas y culturales de la Tierra, **3**

geothermal energy/energía geotérmica Fuente energética no renovable producida por el calor del interior de la tierra, **70**

gers/gers Grandes tiendas circulares que son fáciles de armar, desarmar y transportar; usadas por los ganaderos nómadas de Mongolia, **589**

geysers/géiseres Manantiales que lanzan chorros de agua caliente y vapor a gran altura, **314**

glaciers/glaciares Grandes bloques de hielo que se desplazan con lentitud sobre el agua, **33**

glen/glen Término de origen escocés que es sinónimo de valle, **305**

global warming/calentamiento global Aumento lento y constante de la temperatura de la Tierra, **64**

gorge/garganta Cañón estrecho y muy profundo, **516**

graphite/grafito Tipo de carbón usado para fabricar puntas de lápices y muchos otros productos, **682**

greenhouse effect/efecto invernadero Proceso mediante el cual la atmósfera terrestre atrapa el calor de su superficie, **38**

green revolution/revolución verde Programa iniciado por el gobierno de la India en la década de 1960 para modernizar los métodos y producir mayor cantidad de alimento, **665**

griots/griots Narradores de historias de África Occidental que pasan sus tradiciones tribales de manera oral, **504**

gross domestic product/producto interno bruto Valor de todos los bienes y servicios producidos en un país, **84**

gross national product/producto nacional bruto valor de todos los bienes y servicios producidos en un año por un país, dentro o fuera de sus límites, **84**

groundwater/agua subterránea Agua de lluvia, ríos, lagos y nieve derretida que se filtra al subsuelo, **25**

guerrilla/guerrillero Persona armada que participa en una lucha armada irregular (los ataques sorpresa, por ejemplo), **189**

habitation fog/humo residente Especie de niebla producida por el humo atrapado en la atmósfera de las ciudades siberianas debido al intenso frío, **364**

haciendas/haciendas Granjas de gran tamaño cedidas por los monarcas españoles a los colonizadores de América, **168**

harmattan/harmattan Viento seco y polvoso que sopla con fuerza hacia el sur durante el invierno en el desierto del Sahara, **492**

heavy industry/industria pesada Industria basada en la manufactura de metales, **362**

hieroglyphs/jeroglíficos imágenes y símbolos usados para registrar información en el antiguo Egipto, **475**

Holocaust/holocausto Asesinato masivo de millones de judíos y personas de otros grupos a manos de los nazis durante la Segunda Guerra Mundial, **287**

homogeneous/homogéneo Agrupamiento que comparte ciertas características, como el origen étnico, **383**

human geography/geografía humana estudio del pasado y presente de la humanidad, **11**

humus/humus Materia vegetal o animal en descomposición, **55**

hurricanes/huracanes Tormentas tropicales con intensos vientos, fuertes lluvias y altas mareas, **48**

hydroelectric power/energía hidroeléctrica Fuente energética renovable producida en generadores impulsados por caídas de agua, **70**

icebergs/icebergs Grandes bloques de hielo que se separan de los glaciales y flotan a la deriva en el océano, **720**

icebreakers/rompehielos Barcos que rompen la capa de hielo que se forma en la superficie de algunos cuerpos de agua para permitir el paso de otras embarcaciones, **368**

ice shelf/capa de hielo Cubierta de hielo que se forma en aguas costeras, **720**

impressionism/impresionismo Forma de arte desarrollada en Francia a finales del siglo XIX y principios del siglo XX, **285**

indentured servants/trabajadores por contrato Personas que trabajan por un tiempo determinado, en la mayoría de los casos a cambio de gastos de viaje, **205**

indigo/índigo Planta que se usa para fabricar un tinte de color azul oscuro, **202**

Indo-European/Indoeuropeo Familia que incluye muchos idiomas europeos como el germánico, el báltico y los dialectos eslavos, **322**

inflation/inflación Aumento de los precios que ocurre cuando la moneda de un país pierde poder adquisitivo, **172**

intensive cultivation/cultivo intenso Cultivo de productos en cualquier terreno disponible, **605**

Inuit/inuit Tribu esquimal de América del norte, **141**

isthmus/istmo Franja de tierra que conecta dos áreas de mayor tamaño, **28**

ivory/marfil Material de color crema extraído de los colmillos de los elefantes que se usa para fabricar joyería y artículos decorativos, **528**

Japan Current/Corriente de Japón corriente oceánica de aguas tibias que fluye al este de Japón, **597**

junta/junta Grupo de oficiales militares que asumen el control de un país al derrocar al poder anterior, **241**

kampongs/kampongs Aldea tradicional de Indonesia; el término también se usa para referirse a las grandes poblaciones humanas establecidas en los alrededores de las ciudades de Indonesia, **628**

karma/karma Para los hinduistas y budistas, es la fuerza positiva o negativa generada por las acciones de una persona, **660**

kimchi/kimchi Especie de col china aderezada y avinagrada que se sirve como plato tradicional en Corea, **612**

kimonos/kimonos vestidos tradicionales japoneses, **603**

kiwi/kiwi Ave que no vuela, originaria de Nueva Zelanda; a veces, este término se usa para referirse a los neozelandeses, **711**

klongs/klongs Canales de Bangkok, una ciudad de Tailandia, **625**

krill/krill Animales marinos diminutos que son una importante fuente alimenticia para otras especies marinas del Océano Atlántico, **721**

landforms/accidentes geográficos Forma de la tierra en diferentes partes de la superficie, **28**

landlocked/sin salida al mar Zona rodeada de agua por completo y sin acceso directo al océano, **224, 387**

lava/lava Magma que emerge del interior de la tierra por un orificio de la corteza, **29**

levees/diques Paredes altas, por lo general de tierra, que se construyen a la orilla de un río para prevenir inundaciones, **8**

light industry/industria ligera Industria que se enfoca en la manufactura de objetos ligeros como la ropa, **362**

lignite/lignita Tipo de carbón suave, **321**

limited government/gobierno limitado Gobierno en el que los ciudadanos hacen responsables a los dirigentes por medio de la constitución y los procesos democráticos, **86**

Llaneros/llaneros Vaqueros de los llanos de Venezuela, **204**

Llanos/llanos Planicies localizadas al este de Colombia y al oeste de Venezuela, **196**

lochs/lagos Lagos escoceses enclavados en valles labrados por los glaciales, **300**

loess/limo Suelo fino de arenisca, excelente para la agricultura, **281**

magma/magma Roca fundida que se localiza en el manto superior de la tierra, **28**

mainland/región continental Región donde se localiza la mayor porción de terreno de un país, **262, 618**

malaria/malaria Enfermedad mortal que se difunde por medio de los mosquitos, **500**

mandate/mandato Territorios que formaban parte de los países derrotados en la Primera Guerra Mundial, y que pasaron a control de los países vencedores, **446**

mantle/manto Capa líquida que rodea al centro de la Tierra, **28**

maquiladoras/maquiladoras Fábricas extranjeras establecidas en la frontera de México con Estados Unidos, **175**

maritime/marítimo En o cerca del mar, como las provincias marítimas de Canadá, **138**

market economy/economía de mercado Tipo de economía en la que los consumidores ayudan a determinar qué productos se fabrican al comprar o rechazar ciertos bienes y servicios, **333**

marsupials/marsupiales Animales que transportan a sus crías en un saco, **704**

martial law/ley marcial Ley militar, **580**

medieval/medieval Periodo de colapso del imperio romano, aproximadamente en el año 1,500 de nuestra era, **283**

megalopolis/megalópolis Enorme zona urbana que abarca una serie de ciudades que se han desarrollado juntas, **120, 603**

Mercosur/Mercosur Organización comercial en la que participan Argentina, Brasil, Paraguay, Uruguay y dos países asociados (Bolivia y Chile), **222**

merengue/merengue Tipo de música y baile nacional en la República Dominicana, **188**

mestizos/mestizos Personas cuyo origen combina las razas europeas y las razas indígenas de América, **168**

metallic minerals/minerales metálicos Minerales brillantes, como el oro y el hierro, que conducen el calor y la electricidad, **65**

meteorology/meteorología Predicción y registro de lluvias, temperaturas y otras condiciones atmosféricas, **13**

Métis/Métis Personas cuyo origen combina las razas europeas y las razas indígenas de Canadá, **135**

millet/mijo Tipo de cultivo resistente a las sequías, **499**

minerals/minerales Sustancias inorgánicas que conforman la corteza de la tierra; en su medio natural, aparecen en forma cristalina y tienen una composición química definida, **65**

missions/misiones Puestos españoles de evangelización establecidos en la época colonial, especialmente en América, **168**

monsoon/monzón Cambio de corrientes aire y lluvias que produce temporadas alternadas de humedad y sequía, **45**

Moors/moros Musulmanes del norte de África, **273**

mosaics/mosaicos Imágenes creadas con pequeños fragmentos de piedras coloreadas, **266**

mosques/mezquitas Casas de adoración islámica, **394**

most-favored-nation status/estatus de nación favorecida Estatus que otorga privilegios de intercambio comercial entre Estados Unidos y otros países, **587**

mulattoes/mulatos Personas cuyo origen combina las razas europeas y las razas indígenas de África, **168**

multicultural Mezcla de culturas en un mismo país o comunidad, **75**

multiple cropping/cultivo múltiple Tipo de agricultura en la que se producen dos o tres cultivos cada año en las mismas tierras, **586**

Muslims/Mulsulmanes Seguidores del Islam, **418**

nationalism/nacionalismo Demanda de autogo-bierno y fuerte sentimiento de lealtad hacia una nación, **294**

NATO/OTAN (Organización del Tratado del Atlántico Norte); alianza militar formada por varios países europeos, Estados Unidos y Canadá, **283**

nature reserves/reservas naturales Zonas asignadas por el gobierno para la protección de animales, plantas, suelo y agua, **374**

navigable/navegable Rutas acuáticas de profundidad suficiente para la navegación de barcos, **280**

neutral/neutral Que no toma ningún partido en una disputa o conflicto, **312**

newsprint/papel periódico Papel económico usado para imprimir publicaciones periódicas, **131**

nirvana/nirvana Para los budistas, es el escape de los sufrimientos de la vida, **661**

rain shadow/barrera montañosa Área seca en el sotavento de una montaña o de una cordillera, **44**

refineries/refinerías Fábricas donde se procesa el petróleo crudo, **68**

reforestation/reforestación Plantación de árboles donde los bosques han sido talados, **61**

Reformation/Reforma Movimiento europeo del siglo XVI para reformar el cristianismo, **286**

refugees/refugiados Personas que han escapado a otro país, generalmente por razones económicas o políticas, **189, 621**

reggae/reggae Tipo de música que tiene sus orígenes en Jamaica, **188**

regionalism/regionalismo Conexión más fuerte con la región a la que se pertenece que con el propio país, **137**

regs/regs Extensas planicies de grava azotadas por el viento, en el Sahara, **472**

reincarnation/reencarnación Creencia de que el alma humana vuelva a nacer una y otra vez en diferentes cuerpos, **660**

relative location/ubicación relativa Posición de un lugar en relación con otro, **6**

Renaissance/Renaissance Palabra francesa que significa "renacimiento" y se refiere a una nueva era de conocimiento que empieza en Europa en el siglo XIV, **269**

renewable resources/ recursos renovables Recursos, como el suelo y los bosques, que pueden reemplazarse por medio de procesos naturales de la Tierra, **59**

revolution/revolución Una vuelta completa alrededor del Sol, **19**

rifts/hendeduras Valles largos y profundos con montañas o mesetas a cada lado, **510**

Roma/Roma Grupo étnico, también conocido como gitanos, que pudo haber migrado de la India a Europa hace mucho tiempo, **332**

rotation/rotación Una vuelta completa de la Tierra sobre su propio eje, **19**

rugby/rugby Juego de origen británico similar al fútbol, **706**

rural/rural Área de terreno abierto que se usa para la agricultura, **4**

Sahel/sahel Región de pastizales secos con clima estepario del sur del Sahara, **492**

samurai/samurai Guerreros al servicio de señores japoneses, **600**

sanctions/sanciones Penalidad económica o política, como un embargo, que uno o más países usan para obligar a otro país a dejar de cometer un acto ilegal o inmoral, **549**

Sanskrit/sánscrito Idioma antiguo del sur de Asia; en la actualidad se usa en la India como lengua sagrada en la, **655**

Santería/santería Religión originaria de Cuba que mezcla religiones del oeste de África y otras tradiciones, entre otras del catolicismo romano, **188**

satellite/satélite cuerpo que da vueltas al rededor de un cuerpo grande, **18**

scarcity/escasez Situación que resulta cuando la demanda es mayor que la oferta, **87**

secede/separar Dividir un país para formar otro, **502**

secondary industries/industrias secundarias Actividades económicas que convierten en productos terminados la materia prima que producen las industrias primarias, **83**

second-growth forests/bosques reforestados Árboles que cubren una región después de que el bosque original ha sido talado, **119**

secular/seglar Que está separado de la religión, como un gobierno o estado secular, **439**

selvas/selvas Bosques tropicales exuberantes del oeste de Ecuador y Perú, y del norte de Bolivia, **231**

semiarid/semiárido Terreno relativamente seco, con lluvias escasas, **62**

sepoys/cipayos Tropas indias dirigidas por oficiales británicos durante el periodo colonial de la India, **658**

serfs/siervos Personas que, en Rusia, estaban atados a una tierra y trabajaban para un señor, **377**

shah/sha Rey de Irán, **430**

shamans/shaman Monje sintoísta, **599**

Shia/Shia La segunda más grande rama del Islam, **418**

Shintoism/shintoismo Religión más antigua conocida de Japón, **599**

shogun/shogún "Gran general" el más alto rango entre los guerreros japoneses, **600**

silt/cieno Tierra de granos muy finos, **437**

sinkholes/sumideros agujero profundo de pendiente empinada que se forma cuando el techo de una cueva se hunde, **162**

sirocco/siroco Viento seco y caliente del norte de África que viaja por el mar Mediterráneo hacia Europa, **263**

slash- and- burn agriculture/agricultura de corte y quema Tipo de agricultura en que los bosques se talan y se queman para limpiar el terreno y plantarlo, **175**

smelters/fundidoras Fábricas que procesan menas de metal, **363**

smog/smog Mezcla de humo, sustancias químicas y niebla, **174**

soil exhaustion/agotamiento del suelo Pérdida de los nutrientes del suelo que necesitan las plantas, **214**

solar energy/energía solar Recurso de energía renovable que produce la luz y el calor del Sol, **71**

solar system/sistema solar El Sol y los cuerpos celestes que se mueven en torno a él, entre otros los planetas, las lunas y los asteroides, **17**

solstice/solsticio Días en que los rayos verticales del Sol están más lejos del ecuador, **21**

sorghum/sorgo Grano de cultivo que puede sobrevivir a las sequías, **499**

souks/souks Mercados del norte de África, **485**

soviet/soviet supremo Consejo comunista que gobernó la república y otras regiones de la Unión Soviética, **377**

spatial perspective/perspectiva espacial Punto de vista basado o visto en relación con el lugar en que se encuentra un objeto, así como la razón por la que está ahí, **3**

staple/producto básico Cultivo principal de una región o un país, **500**

steppe/estepa Gran llanura de pastos altos que se extiende desde Ucrania, pasa por el sur de Rusia y llega hasta Kazajistán, **353**

steppe climate/clima estepario Tipo de clima, generalmente seco, que se encuentra entre las regiones de climas desértico y húmedo, **46**

storm surges/mareas de tormenta Grandes ondas de agua que se elevan por la fuerza del viento, en particular de los ciclones, huracanes y otras tormentas tropicales, **670**

strait/estrecho Paso angosto que une dos grandes cuerpos de agua, **230**

strip mining/minería a cielo abierto Tipo de minería en que se retiran la tierra y las rocas para extraer carbón y otros recursos que están bajo la superficie terrestre, **124**

stupas/stupas Montículos de tierra o piedras que cubren las cenizas del Buda o las reliquias de los santos budistas, **678**

subduction/subducción Movimiento en el que una placa tectónica terrestre más gruesa se sumerge debajo de una más delgada, **29**

subregions/subregiones Áreas pequeñas de una región, **10**

subsistence agriculture/agricultura de subsistencia Tipo de agricultura en que los campesinos siembran sólo lo necesario para mantenerse a ellos mismos y a sus familias, **80**

sultan/sultán Gobernante supremo de un país musulmán, **631**

Sunni/sunita La rama más grande del Islam, **418**

superpowers/superpotencias Países poderosos, **357**

Swahili/suahili Idioma bantú que se habla extensamente en África, **514**

symbol/símbolo Palabra, forma, color, estandarte o cualquier otra cosa que se use en representación de algo, **77**

taiga/taiga Bosque de árboles siempre verdes que existen en el sur de la tundra en Rusia, **353**

teak/teca Tipo de madera preciosa que crece en la India y al sudeste de Asia, **653**

tepuís/tepuís Capas de roca arenisca resistentes a la erosión en las mesetas de los altiplanos de las Guyanas, **196**

terraces/terrazas Crestas horizontales que se construyen sobre las laderas de las colinas para prevenir la pérdida de suelo y favorecer la agricultura, **60**

tertiary industries/industrias terciarias Actividades económicas que trabajan con productos listos para vender a los consumidores, **84**

textiles/textiles Productos para fabricar ropa, **113, 303**

theocracy/teocracia Gobierno regido por líderes religiosos, **430**

the veld/el veld regiones de pastos altos en el sur de África, **542**

townships/municipios Regiones de multitudes de pequeñas casas apiñadas que habitan los sudafricanos de raza negra en las afueras de las ciudades, **548**

trade deficit/déficit comercial Ocurre cuando el valor de las exportaciones es menor que el de las importaciones, **125**

trade surplus/excedente comercial Ocurre cuando el valor de las importaciones es mayor que el de las importaciones, **606**

traditional economy/economía tradicional Economía basada en las costumbres y las tradiciones, **85**

tributary/tributario Cualquier corriente pequeña o río que fluye hacia un río o una corriente más grande, **25**

Tropic of Cancer/Trópico de Cáncer Línea de latitud que está a 23.5 grados al norte del ecuador, **21**

Tropic of Capricorn/Trópico de Capricornio Línea de latitud que está a 23.5 grados al sur del ecuador, **21**

trust territories/territorios bajo administración fiduciaria Regiones que están bajo el control temporal de otro país hasta que establezca su propio gobierno, **723**

tsetse fly/mosca tse tse Mosca africana del sur del Sahara que transmite el mal del sueño, una enfermedad mortal, **492**

tsunamis/tsunamis Olas muy grandes que se forman por la actividad submarina de las placas tectónicas, tales como los terremotos, **597**

tundra climate/clima de la tundra Región fría de lluvias escasas, que por lo genera se encuentra entre los climas de las regiones subártica y polar, **49**

typhoons/tifones Tormentas tropicales de vientos violentos, fuertes lluvias y altas marejadas, **48**

uninhabitable/inhabitable Que no es propicio para el establecimiento de seres humanos, **314**

unlimited governments/gobiernos ilimitados Gobiernos que tienen un control total sobre sus ciudadanos, **86**

urban/urbano Área en que se encuentra una ciudad, **4**

viceroy/virrey Gobernador de una colonia, **236**

wadis/wadis Lechos secos de corrientes en el sudoeste de Asia, **417**

water cycle/ciclo del agua Circulación del agua del la superficie de la Tierra a la atmósfera y su regreso, **23**

water vapor/vapor de agua Estado gaseoso del agua, **23**

weather/tiempo Condiciones de la atmósfera en un tiempo y un lugar determinados, **37**

weathering/desgaste Proceso de desintegración de las rocas en pedazos pequeños por la acción del calor, el agua y otros medios, **31**

Wheat Belt/región triguera Zona de la región de las Grandes Planicies en Estados Unidos en la que la actividad principal es el cultivo del trigo, **124**

work ethic/ética laboral Creencia de que el trabajo es un mérito en sí mismo, **606**

yurt/yurta Tienda redonda y portátil de lana tejida que se coloca sobre una armazón de madera, **394**

Z

Zionism/sionismo Movimiento que trata de establecer un país o comunidad judía en Palestina, **443**

zonal/zonal Clima del este de África que se extiende en franjas de este a oeste, **49**

INDEX

D

ACKNOWLEDGMENTS

For permission to reprint copyrighted material, grateful acknowledgment is made to the following sources:

Casa Juan Diego: Adapted from *Immigrants Risk All: Cry for Argentina* by Ana Maria from *Houston Catholic Worker*, July/August 1997, accessed February 2, 2000, at http://www.cjd.org/stories/risk.html.

Doubleday, a division of Random House, Inc.: From "Marriage Is a Private Affair" from *Girls at War and Other Stories* by Chinua Achebe. Copyright © 1972, 1973 by Chinua Achebe.

FocalPoint f/8: From "October 5—Galtai" from "Daily Chronicles" and from "Buddhist Prayer Ceremony" from "Road Stories" by Gary Matoso and Lisa Dickey from *The Russian Chronicles* from *FocalPoint f/8*, accessed October 14, 1999, at http://www.f8.com/FP/Russia.

Glas Publishers (Russia): From "The Lilac Dressing Gown" by Nina Gabrielyan, translated by Joanne Turnbull from *A Will and a Way: New Russian Writing*, edited by Natasha Perova and Arch Tait. Copyright © 1996 by Glas: New Russian Writing.

HarperCollins Publishers, Inc.: From *My Days* by R. K. Narayan. Copyright © 1973, 1974 by R. K. Narayan.

James Li, M.D.: From "Africa" by James Li, M.D from *eMedicine*, accessed October 11, 1999, at http://www.emedicine.com/emerg/topic726.htm. Copyright © 1999 by James Li.

Ms. Magazine: From "Foresters Without Diplomas" by Wangari Maathai from *Ms.*, vol. 1, no. 5, March/April 1991. Copyright © 1991 by *Ms.* Magazine.

Penguin Books Ltd.: From *The Epic of Gilgamesh*, translated by N. K. Sandars (Penguin Classics 1960, Third Edition, 1972). Copyright © 1960, 1964, 1972 by N. K. Sandars.

Puffin Books, a division of Penguin Putnam Inc.: From *Sadako and the Thousand Paper Cranes* by Eleanor Coerr. Copyright © 1977 by Elizabeth Coerr.

Sandy Wiseman: From "Photo-Journey Through a Costa Rican Rainforest" by Sandy Wiseman from *EcoFuture™ PlanetKeepers*, accessed October 14, 1999, at http://www.ecofuture.org/ecofuture/pk/pkar9512.html. Copyright © 1999 by Sandy Wiseman.

Writer's House, Inc. c/o The Permissions Company: From *For Love Alone* by Christina Stead. Copyright © 1944 by Harcourt, Inc.; copyright renewed © 1972 by Christina Stead.

SOURCES CITED:
From "The Aztecs in 1519" from *The Discovery and Conquest of Mexico* by Bernal Díaz. Published by Routledge and Kegan Paul, London, 1938.

ART CREDITS

Abbreviated as follows: (t) top, (b) bottom, (l) left, (r) right, (c) center.

Unit flags of United States created by One Mile Up, Inc. Unit flags of Canadian provinces created by EyeWire, Inc. Other flags, country silhouettes, feature maps and atlas maps created by MapQuest.com., Inc. All other illustrations, unless otherwise noted, contributed by Holt, Rinehart and Winston.

Study Skills: Page S2, MapQuest.com, Inc.; S3, MapQuest.com, Inc.; S4 (cl, bl), MapQuest.com, Inc.; S5, MapQuest.com, Inc.; S6 (tr), MapQuest.com, Inc.; S7, MapQuest.com, Inc.; S8 (tr), MapQuest.com, Inc.; S9, MapQuest.com, Inc.; S10 (tc, br), Leslie Kell; S11 (cr), Leslie Kell; S11 (b), Ortelius Design; S12 (b), Leslie Kell; S12 (tr), Rosa + Wesley; S13, Uhl Studios, Inc.; S14 (br), MapQuest.com, Inc.; S15 (bl), MapQuest.com, Inc.

Chapter 1: Page 5 (cl), MapQuest.com, Inc.; 6 (bl), MapQuest.com, Inc.; 7 (tl, tr), MapQuest.com, Inc.; 8 (l, bc), MapQuest.com, Inc.; 9 (tr), MapQuest.com, Inc.; 10 (tc), MapQuest.com, Inc.; 11 (bc), MapQuest.com, Inc.; 15 (tr), MapQuest.com, Inc.

Chapter 2: Page 17 (b), Uhl Studios, Inc.; 18 (b), Uhl Studios, Inc.; 19 (bl), Uhl Studios, Inc.; 20 (b), Uhl Studios, Inc.; 22 (tl), Robert Hynes; 23 (cr), MapQuest.com, Inc.; 24 (tr), Uhl Studios, Inc.; 25 (tr, br), Uhl Studios, Inc.; 26 (b), MapQuest.com, Inc.; 28 (b), Uhl Studios, Inc.; 29 (tl), MapQuest.com, Inc.; 29 (c, br), Uhl Studios, Inc.; 31 (tr), MapQuest.com, Inc.; 32 (tr), Ortelius Design; 35 (tr), MapQuest.com, Inc.

Chapter 3: Page 38 (tl), Uhl Studios, Inc.; 38 (cl), MapQuest.com, Inc.; 39 (bl), MapQuest.com, Inc.; 40 (tr), Uhl Studios, Inc.; 42 (cr), Rosa + Wesley; 42 (b), MapQuest.com, Inc.; 43 (t), Rosa + Wesley; 45 (tl), Uhl Studios, Inc.; 46 (br), MapQuest.com, Inc.; 47 (all), MapQuest.com, Inc.; 48 (tl, bc), MapQuest.com, Inc.; 49 (tr), MapQuest.com, Inc.; 50 (tl), MapQuest.com, Inc.; 52 (tr), Robert Hynes; 55 (tr), Uhl Studios, Inc.; 57 (tr), MapQuest.com, Inc.

Chapter 4: Page 60 (tc), MapQuest.com, Inc.; 62 (bl), MapQuest.com, Inc.; 63 (tr, br), MapQuest.com, Inc.; 65 (br), Leslie Kell; 67 (t), MapQuest.com, Inc.; 69 (tl, br), MapQuest.com, Inc.; 70 (br), MapQuest.com, Inc.; 73 (tr), MapQuest.com, Inc.

Chapter 5: Page 76 (t, bl), MapQuest.com, Inc.; 77 (tr), MapQuest.com, Inc.; 78 (tl), MapQuest.com, Inc.; 81 (cr), MapQuest.com, Inc.; 83 (br), MapQuest.com, Inc.; 86 (c), Rosa + Wesley; 88 (cl), MapQuest.com, Inc.; 89 (tc), MapQuest.com, Inc.; 91 (bl), MapQuest.com, Inc.; 93 (tl), MapQuest.com, Inc.; 98 (t, bl), Ortelius Design.

Chapter 6: Page 107 (b), MapQuest.com, Inc.; 108 (bl), MapQuest.com; 109 (t, br), MapQuest.com, Inc.; 112 (bl), MapQuest.com,

Inc.; 114 (bl), MapQuest.com, Inc.; 115 (tr), MapQuest.com, Inc.; 118 (bl), MapQuest.com, Inc.; 119 (tr), Rosa + Wesley; 119 (br), MapQuest.com, Inc.; 120 (bl) MapQuest.com, Inc.; 121 (tr), MapQuest.com, Inc.; 121 (br), Uhl Studios, Inc.; 122 (tr), The John Edwards Group; 122 (b), MapQuest.com, Inc.; 123 (tr), Leslie Kell; 123 (br), MapQuest.com, Inc.; 124 (tl, bl), MapQuest.com, Inc.; 127 (tr), MapQuest.com, Inc.

Chapter 7: Page 129 (b), MapQuest.com, Inc.; 130 (cl), MapQuest.com, Inc.; 131 (tr), MapQuest.com, Inc.; 133 (tr), MapQuest.com, Inc.; 134 (tl), Leslie Kell; 134 (bl), MapQuest.com, Inc.; 135 (tr), MapQuest.com, Inc.; 135 (br), Rosa + Wesley; 136 (cl), MapQuest.com, Inc.; 138 (tl), MapQuest.com, Inc.; 140 (tl), MapQuest.com, Inc.; 143 (tr), MapQuest.com, Inc.; 145 (tr), MapQuest.com, Inc.; 150 (t, bl), Ortelius Design.

Chapter 8: Page 161 (b), MapQuest.com, Inc.; 162 (tc), MapQuest.com, Inc.; 163 (t,br), MapQuest.com, Inc.; 166 (br), MapQuest.com, Inc.; 168 (bl), MapQuest.com; 170 (tr), Leslie Kell; 171 (t), MapQuest.com, Inc.; 172 (cl), Rosa + Wesley; 173 (bl), MapQuest.com; 174 (bl), MapQuest.com, Inc.; 177 (tr), MapQuest.com, Inc.

Chapter 9: Page 179 (b), MapQuest.com, Inc.; 180 (bl), MapQuest.com, Inc.; 182 (cl), MapQuest.com, Inc.; 183 (cr), MapQuest.com, Inc.; 185 (br), Leslie Kell; 186 (tl), Rosa + Wesley; 187 (br), MapQuest.com, Inc.; 188 (tl), Rosa + Wesley; 189 (tr, bl), MapQuest.com, Inc.; 191 (tr), MapQuest.com, Inc.; 193 (tr), MapQuest.com, Inc.

Chapter 10: Page 195 (b), MapQuest.com, Inc.; 196 (b), Uhl Studios, Inc.; 198 (bc), MapQuest.com, Inc.; 199 (tr), Rosa + Wesley; 199 (cr), MapQuest.com, Inc.; 201 (tc), MapQuest.com, Inc.; 201 (cr), Leslie Kell; 202 (bl), MapQuest.com, Inc.; 203 (br), MapQuest.com, Inc.; 204 (cl), Rosa + Wesley; 205 (cr), MapQuest.com, Inc.; 206 (tl), Rosa + Wesley; 206 (bc), MapQuest.com, Inc.; 207 (tl), MapQuest.com, Inc.; 209 (tr), MapQuest.com, Inc.

Chapter 11: Page 211 (b), MapQuest.com, Inc.; 212 (bl), MapQuest.com, Inc.; 217 (tr), MapQuest.com, Inc.; 217 (br), Rosa + Wesley; 218 (tl), Leslie Kell; 220 (tl,br), MapQuest.com, Inc.; 222 (tc), MapQuest.com, Inc.; 222 (cl), Rosa + Wesley; 223 (c), MapQuest.com, Inc.; 224 (tc), MapQuest.com, Inc.; 224 (bl), Rosa + Wesley; 227 (tr), MapQuest.com, Inc.

Chapter 12: Page 229 (b), MapQuest.com, Inc.; 231 (cr), MapQuest.com, Inc.; 234 (tl), MapQuest.com, Inc.; 236 (tl), MapQuest.com, Inc.; 238 (bl), MapQuest.com, Inc.; 239 (tr), MapQuest.com, Inc.; 240 (tl), Rosa + Wesley; 241 (tr), Leslie Kell; 243 (tr), MapQuest.com, Inc.; 250 (t, bl), Ortelius Design.

Chapter 13: Page 261 (b), MapQuest.com, Inc.; 262 (bl), MapQuest.com, Inc.; 263 (tr), MapQuest.com,

Inc.; 263 (cr), Leslie Kell; 264 (br), MapQuest.com, Inc.; 265 (tc), MapQuest.com, Inc.; 267 (tr), Rosa + Wesley; 268 (cl), MapQuest.com, Inc.; 269 (tc), MapQuest.com, Inc.; 270 (bl), MapQuest.com, Inc.; 271 (tr), Rosa + Wesley; 272 (br), MapQuest.com, Inc.; 273 (c), MapQuest.com, Inc.; 274 (tl), Rosa + Wesley; 275 (tl), MapQuest.com, Inc.; 277 (tr), MapQuest.com, Inc.

Chapter 14: Page 279 (b), MapQuest.com, Inc.; 280 (tl, bc), MapQuest.com, Inc.; 281 (tr), MapQuest.com, Inc.; 284 (cr), MapQuest.com, Inc.; 285 (cl), Rosa + Wesley; 286 (bl), MapQuest.com, Inc.; 287 (cr), MapQuest.com, Inc.; 288 (tl), Leslie Kell; 288 (c), MapQuest.com, Inc.; 289 (cr), Rosa + Wesley; 290 (cl), MapQuest.com, Inc.; 292 (cl), Rosa + Wesley; 294 (tl), MapQuest.com, Inc.; 295 (cr), Rosa + Wesley; 297 (tr), MapQuest.com, Inc.

Chapter 15: Page 299 (b), MapQuest.com, Inc.; 300 (bl), MapQuest.com, Inc.; 302 (cl), MapQuest.com, Inc.; 303 (c), MapQuest.com, Inc.; 304 (bl), Rosa + Wesley; 307, Nenad Jakesevic; 305 (cr), Leslie Kell; 308 (bl), MapQuest.com, Inc.; 310 (tl), Rosa + Wesley; 310 (cl), MapQuest.com, Inc.; 311 (br), Rosa + Wesley; 312 (tl, bc), MapQuest.com, Inc.; 314 (tl), MapQuest.com, Inc.; 315 (cr), MapQuest.com, Inc.; 317 (tr), MapQuest.com, Inc.

Chapter 16: Page 319 (b), MapQuest.com, Inc.; 320 (bl), MapQuest.com, Inc.; 321 (tr), MapQuest.com, Inc.; 324 (tl), Rosa + Wesley; 324 (cl), MapQuest.com, Inc.; 326 (bc), MapQuest.com, Inc.; 327 (tr), MapQuest.com, Inc.; 328 (bl), MapQuest.com, Inc.; 329 (cr), MapQuest.com, Inc.; 330 (tc), MapQuest.com, Inc.; 331 (tr, cr), MapQuest.com, Inc.; 332 (tl), Leslie Kell; 332 (bl), MapQuest.com, Inc.; 333 (tr), Rosa + Wesley; 335 (tr), MapQuest.com, Inc.; 337 (tl), MapQuest.com, Inc.; 342 (t, bl), Ortelius Design.

Chapter 17: Page 351 (b), MapQuest.com, Inc.; 353 (br), MapQuest.com, Inc.; 356 (t), MapQuest.com, Inc.; 357 (tr, bc), MapQuest.com, Inc.; 359 (tr, cr), Rosa + Wesley; 359 (br), MapQuest.com, Inc.; 361 (br), MapQuest.com, Inc.; 362 (tl, bl), MapQuest.com, Inc.; 363 (tr), MapQuest.com, Inc.; 364 (bl), MapQuest.com, Inc.; 365 (tl), MapQuest.com, Inc.; 366 (tl), MapQuest.com, Inc.; 368 (bl), MapQuest.com, Inc.; 369 (tr), MapQuest.com, Inc.; 371 (tr), MapQuest.com, Inc.

Chapter 18: Page 373 (b), MapQuest.com, Inc.; 374 (bl), MapQuest.com, Inc.; 377 (bl), MapQuest.com, Inc.; 378 (tl), MapQuest.com, Inc.; 379 (c), Uhl Studios, Inc.; 380 (tl), Leslie Kell; 380 (cl), Rosa + Wesley; 382 (bc), MapQuest.com, Inc.; 383 (tr), Rosa + Wesley; 385 (tr), MapQuest.com, Inc.

Chapter 19: Page 387 (b), MapQuest.com, Inc.; 389 (cr), MapQuest.com, Inc.; 390 (cl), MapQuest.com, Inc.; 391 (cr), MapQuest.com, Inc.; 394 (l), Leslie

Kell; 394 (bc), MapQuest.com, Inc.; 395 (tr), Rosa + Wesley; 397 (cr), Leslie Kell; 399 (tr), MapQuest.com, Inc.; 401 (t), MapQuest.com, Inc.; 406 (t, bl), Ortelius Design.

Chapter 20: Page 415 (b), MapQuest.com, Inc.; 416 (bl), MapQuest.com, Inc.; 418 (cl), MapQuest.com, Inc.; 419 (tr), Leslie Kell; 419 (cl), MapQuest.com, Inc.; 420 (tl), MapQuest.com, Inc.; 422 (tl), Rosa + Wesley; 423 (tr), MapQuest.com, Inc.; 424, MapQuest.com, Inc.; 426 (bl), MapQuest.com, Inc.; 427 (tr), Rosa + Wesley; 427 (br), MapQuest.com, Inc.; 429 (b), Uhl Studios, Inc.; 420 (tl), Rosa + Wesley; 430 (bl), MapQuest.com, Inc.; 433 (tr), MapQuest.com, Inc.

Chapter 21: Page 435 (b), MapQuest.com, Inc.; 436 (bl), MapQuest.com, Inc.; 437 (cr), MapQuest.com, Inc.; 438 (bl), MapQuest.com, Inc.; 441 (r), MapQuest.com, Inc.; 442 (bl), MapQuest.com, Inc.; 443 (tc), MapQuest.com, Inc.; 443 (br), Rosa + Wesley; 444 (tl), MapQuest.com, Inc.; 446 (bc), MapQuest.com, Inc.; 449 (tc), MapQuest.com, Inc.; 451 (tr), MapQuest.com, Inc.; 453 (t), MapQuest.com, Inc.; 455, MapQuest.com, Inc.; 458 (t,bl), Ortelius Design.

Chapter 22: Page 471 (b), MapQuest.com, Inc.; 472 (cl), MapQuest.com, Inc.; 473 (tl), MapQuest.com, Inc.; 477 (cl,tr), MapQuest.com, Inc.; 478 (tl), MapQuest.com, Inc.; 479 (tr), MapQuest.com, Inc.; 480, Ortelius Design; 482 (bl), MapQuest.com, Inc.; 483 (cl), MapQuest.com, Inc.; 483 (br), Rosa + Wesley; 485 (br), Leslie Kell; 486 (tl), Rosa + Wesley; 486 (bl), MapQuest.com, Inc.; 489 (tr), MapQuest.com, Inc.

Chapter 23: Page 491 (b), MapQuest.com, Inc.; 492 (bl), MapQuest.com, Inc.; 494 (bl), MapQuest.com, Inc.; 495 (br), MapQuest.com, Inc.; 496 (cl), MapQuest.com, Inc.; 498 (tl), MapQuest.com, Inc.; 499 (bc), MapQuest.com, Inc.; 500 (tl), MapQuest.com, Inc.; 500 (bl), Rosa + Wesley; 501 (cr), Leslie Kell; 502 (cl), MapQuest.com, Inc.; 503 (tr), MapQuest.com, Inc.; 504 (tc), Rosa + Wesley; 504 (bc), MapQuest.com, Inc.; 507 (tr),

MapQuest.com, Inc.

Chapter 24: Page 509 (b), MapQuest.com, Inc.; 510 (cr), MapQuest.com, Inc.; 511 (tr), MapQuest.com, Inc.; 513 (br), MapQuest.com, Inc.; 515 (tr), MapQuest.com, Inc.; 516 (cl), MapQuest.com, Inc.; 516 (tl), Rosa + Wesley; 520 (tl), Rosa + Wesley; 520 (cr), MapQuest.com, Inc.; 521 (tr), MapQuest.com, Inc.; 523 (tr), MapQuest.com, Inc.

Chapter 25: Page 525 (b), MapQuest.com, Inc.; 526 (bl), MapQuest.com, Inc.; 529 (cr), MapQuest.com, Inc.; 531 (tc), MapQuest.com, Inc.; 533 (tr), Rosa + Wesley; 534 (tr), MapQuest.com, Inc.; 534 (cl), Leslie Kell; 535 (br), MapQuest.com, Inc.; 536 (tl), Rosa + Wesley; 537 (tr), Rosa + Wesley; 539 (tr), MapQuest.com, Inc.

Chapter 26: Page 541 (b), MapQuest.com, Inc.; 542 (tl), MapQuest.com, Inc.; 543 (cr), MapQuest.com, Inc.; 546 (cl), MapQuest.com, Inc.; 549 (br), Leslie Kell; 550 (bl), MapQuest.com, Inc.; 551 (cr), Rosa + Wesley; 552 (cl), MapQuest.com, Inc.; 553 (br), Rosa + Wesley; 555 (cr), MapQuest.com, Inc.; 557 (tr), MapQuest.com, Inc.; 564 (t,bl), Ortelius Design.

Chapter 27: Page 573 (b), MapQuest.com, Inc.; 574 (cl), MapQuest.com, Inc.; 575 (bc), MapQuest.com, Inc.; 576 (tl), Rosa + Wesley; 578 (tr), MapQuest.com, Inc.; 579 (b), Leslie Kell; 581 (tr, br), MapQuest.com, Inc.; 583 (cr), MapQuest.com, Inc.; 584 (bl), Rosa + Wesley; 585 (tr, cr), MapQuest.com, Inc.; 586 (tl, bl), MapQuest.com, Inc.; 587 (cr), MapQuest.com, Inc.; 589 (tl), MapQuest.com, Inc.; 590 (cl), MapQuest.com, Inc.; 593 (tr), MapQuest.com, Inc.

Chapter 28: Page 595 (b), MapQuest.com, Inc.; 596 (bl), MapQuest.com, Inc.; 597 (br), MapQuest.com, Inc.; 599 (bc), MapQuest.com, Inc.; 601 (cr), MapQuest.com, Inc.; 603 (tr, cr), Rosa + Wesley; 604 (tl, cl), MapQuest.com, Inc.; 607 (br), MapQuest.com, Inc.; 608 (tl), MapQuest.com, Inc.; 610 (cl), Rosa + Wesley; 611 (cr), MapQuest.com, Inc.; 612 (bc), MapQuest.com, Inc.; 615 (cr), MapQuest.com, Inc.

Chapter 29: Page 617 (b), MapQuest.com, Inc.; 618 (bl), MapQuest.com, Inc.; 620 (bl), MapQuest.com, Inc.; 621 (tc, br), MapQuest.com, Inc.; 623 (tr),

MapQuest.com, Inc.; 624 (bl), MapQuest.com, Inc.; 625 (tr), MapQuest.com, Inc.; 625 (br), Rosa + Wesley; 626 (tl), Leslie Kell; 627 (bl), MapQuest.com, Inc.; 629 (tr), Rosa + Wesley; 629 (br), MapQuest.com, Inc.; 630 (tl), MapQuest.com, Inc.; 631 (tr), MapQuest.com, Inc.; 632 (b), MapQuest.com, Inc.; 633 (cl), Leslie Kell; 635 (tr), MapQuest.com, Inc.; 642 (t, bl), Ortelius Design.

Chapter 30: Page 651 (b), MapQuest.com, Inc.; 652 (bl), MapQuest.com, Inc.; 654 (bl), MapQuest.com, Inc.; 657 (tr), MapQuest.com, Inc.; 660 (bl), MapQuest.com, Inc.; 661 (br), MapQuest.com, Inc.; 662 (tl, bl), MapQuest.com, Inc.; 663 (tr), Rosa + Wesley; 663 (c), MapQuest.com, Inc.; 667 (tr), MapQuest.com, Inc.

Chapter 31: Page 669 (b), MapQuest.com, Inc.; 672 (bl), MapQuest.com, Inc.; 673 (tr), Rosa + Wesley; 673 (br), MapQuest.com, Inc.; 674 (tl), MapQuest.com, Inc.; 674 (bl), Leslie Kell; 675 (tr), MapQuest.com, Inc.; 678 (bl), MapQuest.com, Inc.; 680 (bl), MapQuest.com, Inc.; 681 (tr), Rosa + Wesley; 681 (br), MapQuest.com, Inc.; 682 (tl), MapQuest.com, Inc.; 683 (tr), MapQuest.com, Inc.; 685 (tr), MapQuest.com, Inc.; 687, MapQuest.com, Inc.; 688 (cr), Stephen Durke/Washington Artists; 689 (cl), Ortelius Design; 692 (t, bl), Ortelius Design.

Chapter 32: Page 701 (b), MapQuest.com, Inc.; 702 (bl), MapQuest.com, Inc.; 706 (cl), MapQuest.com, Inc.; 706 (bl), Rosa + Wesley; 707 (tr), Leslie Kell; 709 (t), Nenad Jakesevic; 710 (bl), MapQuest.com, Inc.; 711 (tr), MapQuest.com, Inc.; 712 (bl), MapQuest.com, Inc.; 713 (tr), Rosa + Wesley; 713 (cr), MapQuest.com, Inc.; 715 (tr), MapQuest.com, Inc.

Chapter 33: Page 717 Uhl Studios, Inc.; 718 (tl), MapQuest.com, Inc.; 719 (tr), Leslie Kell; 719 (cl), MapQuest.com, Inc.; 725 (tr), Rosa + Wesley; 725 (br), MapQuest.com, Inc.; 726 (tl), MapQuest.com, Inc.; 731 (tr), MapQuest.com, Inc.; 732 (b), Uhl Studio, Inc.; 733 (tr), MapQuest.com, Inc.; 735 (cr), Leslie Kell.

PHOTO CREDITS

Cover and Title Page: Nawrocki Stock Photo

Table of Contents: iv, © SuperStock; v(t), S. Sherbell/SABA Press Photos, Inc.; v(b), © Richard Pasley/Viesti Collection; vi(t), © Stone/Robert Frerck; vii(t), © Stone/William J. Hebert; vi(b), © Robert Frerck/Odyssey/Chicago; vii(t), © Stone/William J. Hebert; vii(b), © Rosenback/ZEFA; viii(t), © Travelpix/FPG International LLC; viii(b), © The State Russian Museum/CORBIS; ix(t), Steve Raymer /NGS Image Collection; ix(b), © Marc Riboud / Magnum; x(t), © Ed Kashi; x(b), © Alex Wasinski/FPG International LLC; xi (b), Daniel J. Cox/Liaison Agency; xi (t), Giraudon/Art Resource, NY; xii (b), © C. Rennie/Art Directors & TRIP Photo Library; xii (t), Richard Bickel/CORBIS; xiii (b), Ric Ergenbright; xiii (c), CORBIS; xiv (b), Digital Stock Corp./HRW; xiv (c), © Frans Lanting/Minden Pictures; xx, Sam Dudgeon/HRW Photo; xxiii (r), CORBIS Images/HRW; xxiv (t), David Young-Wolf/PNI; xxiv (b), Klaus Lahnstein/Getty Images; Student photos S1-S35, Sam Dudgeon/HRW Photo; S4, Andy Christiansen/HRW Photo; S20, © Nik Wheeler/CORBIS; S21 (cl), Jeffrey Aaronson/Network Aspen; S21 (c), Index Stock Imagery, Inc.; S21 (tr), Amit Bhargava/Newsmakers/Getty Images; S22 (l), Norman Owen Tomalin/Bruce Coleman, Inc.; S22 (cl), Fritz Polking/Peter Arnold, Inc.; S22 (tl), Larry Kolvoord Photography; S22 (r), Runk/Schoenberger/Grant Heilman Photography; S22 (br), Wolfgang Kaehler Photography; S27 (b), Rosenback/ZEFA/Index Stock Imagery, Inc.; **Unit 1:** 1 (b), Photo © Transdia/Panoramic Images, Chicago 1998; 1 (cl), Joe Viesti/The Viesti Collection; 1 (tr), Francois Gohier/Photo Researchers, Inc.; 1 (t), © Norbert Wu/www.norbertwu.com; 1 (br), Steven David Miller/Animals Animals/Earth Scenes; **Chapter 1:** 2 (cl), © Stone/Philip & Karen Smith; 2 (bl), Sam Dudgeon/HRW Photo; 2 (t), © Joseph Sohm; ChromoSohm Inc./CORBIS; 3 (bl), © Stone/Ken McVey; 3 (tr), British Library, London, Great Britain/

Art Resource, NY; 4, Luca Turi/AP/Wide World Photos; 5 (cl), The Stock Market/Jose Fuste Raga; 5 (cr), NASA; 6 (cl), Robert Caputo/Aurora; 6 (tr), © Stone/Robert Frerck; 7-8 © Bob Daemmrich; 8 (b), K.D. Frankel/Bilderberg/Aurora; 9 (t,br), © Wolfgang Kaehler; 10, © Nik Wheeler/CORBIS; 11 (cr), © Ilene Perlman/Stock, Boston; 11 (t), © Archivo Iconografico S.A./CORBIS; 13 (cr), © Chris Rainier/CORBIS; **Chapter 2:** 16 (c), © Roger Ressmeyer/CORBIS; 16 (tl), Digital Stock Corp./HRW; 16 (t), Steve Winter/Black Star; 16 (c), T.A. Wiewandt/DRK Photo; 16 (bl), Scala/Art Resource, NY; 17, Monticello. Photo: Edward Owen; 19, © Stone/Earth Imaging; 20 (tl), courtesy of NASA, Marshall Space Flight Center; 21 (t,b), Global Hydrology and Climate Center, NASA Marshall Space Flight Center.; 23 (t), Image copyright ©2002 PhotoDisc, Inc.; 23 (b), © Gerald French/FPG International LLC; 24, © Tom Bean/CORBIS; 26 (t), © Norbert Wu/www.norbertwu.com; 26 (b), Boll/Liaison Agency; 27, © Ed Kashi; 28, © Gary Braasch/CORBIS; 30, © Stone/Andrew Rafkind; 31, © Galen Rowell/CORBIS; 32, © Yann Arhtus-Bertrand/CORBIS; **Chapter 3:** 36 (c), © Stone/Glenn Christianson; 36 (tr), © Stone/A. Witte/C. Mahaney; 36 (br), © Stone/Brian Stablyk; 36 (b), © 1999 Michael DeYoung/AlaskaStock.com; 36 (tl), Corbis Images; 37, Thomas A. Wiewandt, Ph.D., Wild Horizons; 38, © Layne Kennedy/CORBIS; 39, © Chinch Gryniewicz; Ecoscene/CORBIS; 40, © SuperStock; 41, © Flip Nicklin/Minden Pictures; 43 (cr), NASA; 44 (bl), Image copyright ©2002 PhotoDisc, Inc./HRW; 44 (t), Paul Seheult; Eye Ubiquitous/CORBIS; 45 (br), © Stone/Martin Puddy; 46 © Laurence Parent; 48 (tl), © Gail Mooney/CORBIS; 48 (b), © DiMaggio/Kalish; Peter Arnold, Inc.; 49, © Darrell Gulin/CORBIS; 50, © Galen Rowell/CORBIS; 51 (b), © Darrell Gulin/CORBIS; 51 (t), Image Copyright ©2002 PhotoDisc, Inc.; 53 (t), Robert Maier; 54 (tl), © E & P Bauer/Bruce Coleman, Inc.; 54 (tr), © Scott T. Smith/CORBIS; 54 (bl), © F. Krahmer/Bruce Coleman, Inc.; 54 (br), ©

Gary Braasch/CORBIS; 55, Photo by William E. Ferguson © William E. Ferguson; **Chapter 4:** 58 (cl), © Philip James Corwin/CORBIS; 58 (bl), Aaron Chang/The Stock Market; 58 (cr), © Morton Beebe/Corbis; 58 (t), Mike Huser/DRK Photo; 59 (b), Larry Lefever/Grant Heilman Photography; 59 (t), Coronado Rodney Jones/HRW Photo; 60, © Michael Busselle/CORBIS; 61, © Kevin Schafer; 62 (bl), © Tom Carroll/FPG International LLC; 62 (t), © Mark Reinstein/FPG International LLC; 63 (tr), Grant Heilman/Grant Heilman Photography; 63 (b), Steven Burr Williams/Liaison International; 64 (all), NASA, Goddard Space Flight Center; 65, Image Copyright ©2002 PhotoDisc, Inc./HRW; 66 (t), Sam Dudgeon/HRW Photo; 66 (b), Dr. Bode; 68 (b), © Stone/Mike Abrahams; 68 (t), © Stone/Vince Streano; 69, © Ernest Manewal/FPG International LLC; 70 (b), © Telegraph Colour Library/FPG International LLC; 71, Mark Burnett/Photo Researchers, Inc.; **Chapter 5:** 74 (t), © Gerald Brimacombe/International Stock Photography; 74 (cr), © Bob Firth/International Stock Photography; 74 (b), © Ahu Tongariki/Bruce Coleman, Inc.; 74 (c), © Wally McNamee/CORBIS; 75 (b), © Bob Daemmrich/Stock, Boston; 75 (t), © Galen Rowell/CORBIS; 76, © Bohdan Hrynewch/Stock, Boston/PNI; 77 (b), © Ron Sherman; 77 (t), © Stone/Rich La Salle; 78 (b), Bruno Barbey/Magnum Photos; 78 (t), S. Sherbell/SABA Press Photos; 79, © Werner Forman/CORBIS; 80, © Eric and David Hosking/CORBIS; 81 (b), © Rich Iwasaki/AllStock/PNI; 81 (t), © Stone/Bob Thomas; 83 (t), © Digital Vision; 84 (tl), © Michelle Gabel/The Image Works, Woodstock, NY; 84 (tr), © Richard Hamilton Smith/CORBIS; 84 (bl), Henry Friedman; 84 br), © Stephen Frisch/Stock, Boston/PNI; 85, Carolyn Schaefer/SCHAE/Bruce Coleman, Inc.; 87 (b), © Joanna B. Pinneo/Aurora; 87 (t), © Joel W. Rogers/CORBIS; 88, © Pramod Mistry/The Image Works, Woodstock, NY; 89 (t), © Ed Kashi; **Unit 2:** 96-97 (bc), Lawrence Migdale; 96 (bl), © Walter Bibikow/FPG International LLC; 96 (t), © SuperStock; 97 (cr), ©